The Florida HANDBOOK

1995–1996

25th Biennial Edition

Compiled by

ALLEN MORRIS

AND

JOAN PERRY MORRIS

THE PENINSULAR PUBLISHING COMPANY

Tallahassee   Florida

THE
Florida
HANDBOOK

1995–1996

25th Biennial Edition

Compiled by
ALLEN MORRIS
AND
JOAN PERRY MORRIS

Copyright 1995 by Allen Morris

No part of this publication may be reproduced or transmitted in any form or by any means, electronic or mechanical, including photocopying, recording, or any information storage or retrieval system, without permission in writing from the copyright holder, except for the inclusion of brief quotations in a review.

The Florida Handbook is registered by Allen Morris as a Trade Mark at the Copyright Office, Library of Congress, Washington, D.C., and by Allen Morris at the Trade Mark Office of the Commercial Recording Bureau, Department of State, Tallahassee, FL.

The Florida Handbook. 1947–
  Tallahassee, Peninsular Pub. Co.
    v. illus. (part col.) 24 cm.
  "Compiled by Allen Morris."
1. Florida. I. Morris, Allen Covington Comp.,
  1909– II. Morris, Joan Perry, 1935–
  F306.F597   917.59   49—53676*

THE PENINSULAR PUBLISHING COMPANY

P.O. BOX 5078

Tallahassee   Florida 32301

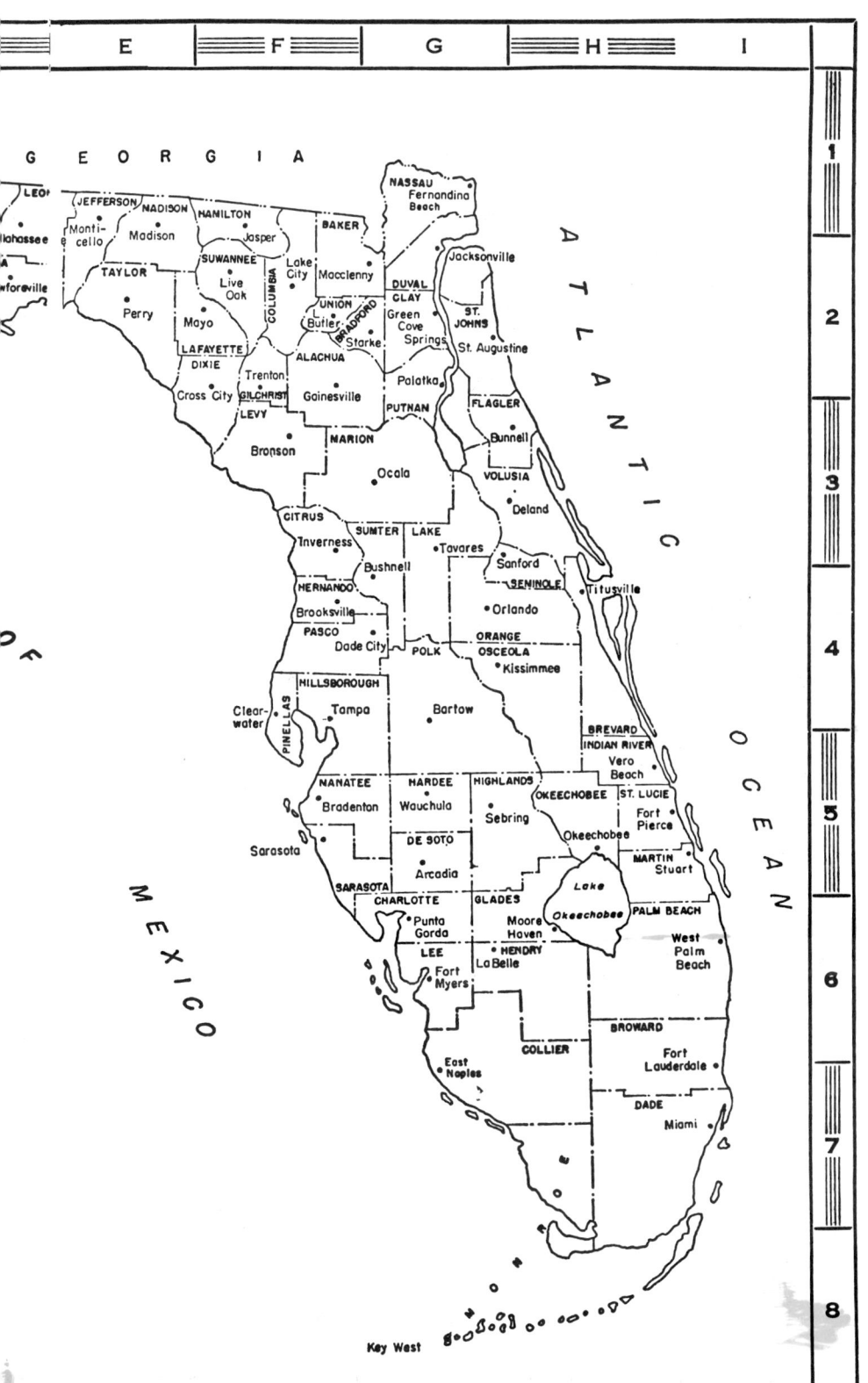

THE
Florida
HANDBOOK
1995–1996

Also by Allen Morris

AUTHOR OF/
Florida Place Names
Alachua to Zolfo Springs; Some of the Place Names of Florida
Our Florida Government
The Language of Lawmaking in Florida II
Practical Protocol for Floridians
Reconsiderations: Second Glances at Florida Legislative Events
The Speakers
Women In the Florida Legislature
"The Emergence of a Party"

COMPILER OF/
The Florida Handbook
(Biennial series started in 1947)

Florida Business Profiles
(in biennial editions, under different titles, 1952–1966)

Official Proceedings of the 1960 Democratic National Convention

Across the Threshold: The Administration of Governor LeRoy Collins

CO-AUTHOR OF/
500 Questions and Answers About Your Florida Government
(with Ann Waldron)

Florida Under Five Flags
(with Rembert W. Patrick)

Legal Background to the Government of Florida
(with Justice James B. Whitfield)

How to Win in Politics
(with Fuller Warren)

ARTICLES BY/
"Beginnings of Popular Government in Florida"
(with Amelia Rea Maguire)
Florida Historical Quarterly, July 1978

"The Unicameral Legislature in Florida"
(with Amelia Rea Maguire)
Florida Historical Quarterly, January 1980

"Florida Legislative Committees: Their Growth Since 1822"
Florida Historical Quarterly, October, 1982

"Florida's First Women Voters and the Legislature"
Florida Historical Quarterly, 1985

"Of Shipwrecks, Duels and Filibusters"
Floridian, April 5, 1970

"It's a New Kind of Ball Game in Tallahassee"
Florida Times-Union and Journal, March 29, 1970

Cover
Photography by Donn Dughi
Design by Robert Bell

For John Phelps, the Clerk of the House of Representatives, and his staff, especially Carol Jo Beaty, Gloria Skinner, Terrie Corbett, Becky Brown, Heide Brock and Diane Bell

Contents

Note: This is only a guide to major subjects. Please use the index for specific listings.

The Executive Department 1
   Organizational Chart 12
   Office of the Governor 13
   Governor, Lieutenant Governor and Cabinet 30
   Major State Departments 71
   Other State Agencies 89
Legislature 100
   Resign to Run 137
   How an Idea Becomes a Law 139
   The Legislator 144
   The Legislative Budget 177
Reapportionment 188
The Apportionment of 1992 198
The Judicial System 200
Local Government 227
Floridians in Federal Office 228
Presidents in Florida 230
Women in Government 249
Seat of Government 256
Inaugurations 274
Florida Becomes a State 280
Symbols of the State 283
Religion in Florida 314
Florida at War 318
American Governors 322
The Governor's Mansion 361
Through Some Eventful Years 369
Discovery and Exploration 401
A Toehold on the Florida Wilderness 407
The Indian People of Florida 413
Florida in the Confederacy 418
The Counties 428

Florida Literature 446
Names to Remember 455
The Everglades 466
Florida's River in the Ocean 471
Climate 472
Sports 487
Forests 490
Birds in Florida 495
State Parks 496
Citrus 501
Minerals 506
Wildlife, Fish 513
Marine Resources 523
Farming 528
Livestock 532
Education 536
Highways 545
Size and Structure 547
A Sense of Rootlessness 565
People and Statistics 572
Employment 603
Electric Power 611
Telephone 614
Licences 617
Bonds 618
Taxes 620
Elections 622
Registered Voters 628
Amendments 632
Political Party Officers 635
Election Results 636
The State Constitutions 674
Constitution 681
Index 741

Space shuttle Discovery pirouetted over the Capitol on December 18, 1992, making a detour on its route from Texas to the Kennedy Space Center. The Discovery, ridding piggyback on a 747, did a low flyover to circle the Capitol twice.
Tallahassee Democrat photo by Mike Ewen

Executive Department / 1

The Executive Department: An Introduction

"The powers of the State government shall be divided into Legislative, Executive, and Judicial branches. No person belonging to one branch shall exercise any powers appertaining to either of the other branches unless expressly provided herein."

Florida Constitution, Article II, Section 3

The State Constitution vests the "supreme executive power" in the Governor. But the Governor shares his executive responsibility with other officers, elective and appointive.

Of these, first are the members of what the Constitution designates as the "Cabinet."

The Governor and the Cabinet: left to right: Commissioner of Education Frank T. Brogan, Secretary of State Sandra B. Mortham, Commissioner of Agriculture Robert B. Crawford, Comptroller Robert F. Milligan, Governor Lawton M. Chiles, Treasurer C. William Nelson, Attorney General Robert Butterworth

Robert M. Overton

2 / Executive Department

The Cabinet consists of six officers elected statewide for terms of four years. Unlike the Governor, who may be elected once to a successive term, the Cabinet members are eligible for election term after term.

The Cabinet officers are, in the order listed in the Constitution: the Secretary of State, the Attorney General, the Comptroller, the Treasurer, the Commissioner of Agriculture, and the Commissioner of Education.

Each of the Cabinet officers heads a department of the State government. Additionally, each serves with the Governor on a number of boards which administer other departments. On all but one of these boards, a Cabinet officer's vote is equal to that of the Governor.

Prior to the ratification of the Constitution of 1968, the Cabinet officers were mandated in general terms to assist the Governor. Cabinet officers occasionally told Governor LeRoy Collins[1] (1955–1961) they would support his position on some matter before a Cabinet board even though they had differing views. The revision of the Constitution in 1968, however, deleted the mandate that "The Governor shall be assisted by" the Cabinet.[2]

The Cabinet members are now given the independent responsibility to manage the offices intrusted to them as divisions of the state's executive functions, and the Legislature can give additional responsibility as well.

This means that the Governor may not always administer these jointly shared laws as he would like to do. Sometimes in Florida this spreading of responsibility can lead to friction. Several Governors have unsuccessfully advocated the abolition of the Cabinet. But since 1885 Florida's Constitutions have reflected the people's fear that one person may exercise too much authority.

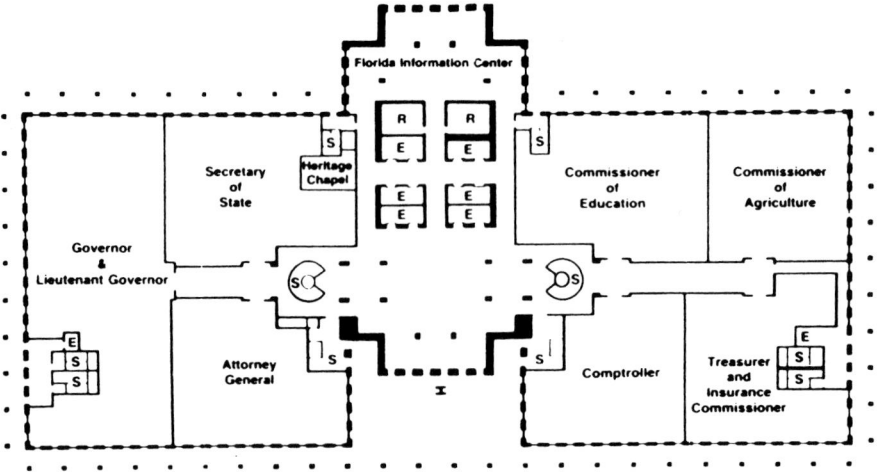

The Executive Offices are on the Plaza, or ground, level of the Capitol. "H" indicates main entrance, "E" indicates elevators, "S" indicates stairways, and "R" indicates restrooms.

Reynolds, Smith and Hills

Collegial Form

This collegial form of State government, in which the Governor shares responsibility with the Cabinet for administration through boards, is believed to be unique to Florida among the fifty states.

In the State's institutional programs prior to the 1950s each institution was responsible directly to the Governor, Cabinet and Legislature. Needs of an institution often were met in proportion to the influence of its legislators. But since then they have been consolidated and administered as groups meeting the broad needs in areas such as corrections, education and mental health. This trend was required to meet rapidly growing needs and efficiency of administration.

Once, as recently as the 1930s, the Governor and Cabinet spent an hour or more arguing over whether to authorize the purchase of a mule for the farm at the State mental hospital. An incident of that nature may not occur anymore because the growth of the State and its institutions requires most decisions to be made by administrators subject to department approval.

Changing Management

Four factors have changed the management of Florida's government since the days of the mule purchase.

First, the phenomenal growth of the State means the Governor and Cabinet cannot concern themselves as closely with the day-to-day management.

Second, the burgeoning of the government means the Governor will be involved with an increasing number of citizen groups all over the state, forcing the delegation by him of responsibilities to subordinates.

Third, the Legislature through its oversight and standing committees devotes more attention than once was the case to the execution of its laws.

Fourth, while the career service and employees unions mean the quadrennial "suitcase parade" no longer occurs with the changes of elective officers, these protections also mean greater independence of employees from supervisors and management policies of the Governor and Cabinet.

Old Chain of Command No Longer Exists

In the opinion of Governor Collins, whose residence in Tallahassee and public service, including two terms as chief executive gave him an unparalleled opportunity to observe Florida's changing state government, the old chain of command no longer exists.

"In earlier years," said Governor Collins, "rank-and-file State employees looked to their department and agency heads for leadership and direction, and these heads had a continuing direct relationship with the Governor in developing policy and in its execution.

"The Governor himself could initiate programs and actions and those helping him could coalesce into a clear-cut chain of responsibility. Now all governments are so much larger and more complex, with employees organized as they are, the earlier pattern is distorted. Decision-making seems to be greatly diffused, at times incoherent, and obfuscated."[3]

The State, at recent count, had 154,117 persons on its payroll.[4] Of these, 24,773 were employed in the field of education. The Department of Health and Rehabilitative Services had 34,220, a number so large and the fields of concern so diversified that the Department has been called unmanageable.

Based on Governor Chiles' support, the 1994 Legislature took action to reduce the scope of authority of the Department of Health and Rehabilitative Services. The Child Support Enforcement Program was transferred to the Department of Revenue and a new Department of Juvenile Justice was created to handle delinquency programs. These changes were in addition to the 1992 restructuring initiatives which established the Agency for Health Care Administration as an administrative attachment to the Department of Business and Professional Regulation. Health care regulatory activities and the Medicaid Program were transferred to this new entity, thus reducing the size and diversity of the Department of Health and Rehabilitative Services.

When mention is made of the Executive Department, the first image likely will be that of the Governor and Cabinet. Actually, there are 151 advisory bodies, as disparate as the Committee on Lay Midwifery to the Barrio Latino Commission, all with a piece of government in their hands.[5]

The Governor makes appointments to approximately 970 boards. The boards include professional and occupational boards which may be said to have statewide responsibilities, but the Governor also must concern himself with the local and regional appointment of hospital boards, housing authorities, judicial nominating committees, fire control districts, and boards of trustees for community colleges.[6]

Also he shares the sovereignty of the State through his power of appointment for, by way of example, special officers of Brink's, Family Lines Rail System and other public carriers; the Thoroughbred Racing Advisory Commission, and the Water and Sewer District of Immokalee, together with others which cause the Governor to make some 4,000 appointments over the chief executive's four-year term.

Measuring the Governor's dominion another way, there are 667 State employees paid more than the Governor.[7] The Governor must, in truth, derive his reward from the opportunity to leave the State a better place when he turns over the government to his successor than when he took the oath of faithful performance either four or eight years earlier.

Stated another way, the diffusion of responsibility means that perhaps the chief contribution to life in Florida by its Governors is the values and standards they reflect, and their moral suasion: of showing by example rather than by edict. The people have shown, by their votes and otherwise, that they appreciate a Governor with

Florida's unique form of collegial State government was depicted as a balancing act by Tampa Tribune cartoonist George White.
Cartoon collection, Museum of Florida History

whom they may not always agree but nevertheless believe he is doing what he thinks is right. They are willing to give him the benefit of the doubt.

Legislative Independence

Ratification of constitutional changes in the 1960s has strengthened the independence of the Legislature. This balancing of power was at the expense of the executive. Where the Legislature until then had met in session once every two years for 60 days, without year-round staff, today's lawmakers maintain a continuing review of the Executive Department through continuing committees. From no year-round staff in the 1950s, the Legislature in 1994 had 1,978.

There is one important power the Governor need not share with the Cabinet, and that is the making of the budget. The Governor annually draws up a budgetary plan which details all proposed expenditures for all State agencies.

Governor as Budget-Maker

As submitted to the 1994 Legislature, the Governor's spending recommendations covered some 500 printed pages. This was accompanied by an illustrated message which showed how the Governor proposed to spend 38 billion dollars during the fiscal year beginning July 1, even to the listing of the proposed State improvements county by county. This budget was subject to line by line review by the Legislature's committees on appropriations, with representatives from the executive departments being heard. These not only defended the Governor's budget and, in some instances, appealed from the judgments of the Governor's budget technicians by seeking to justify larger amounts.

The Governor's constitutional power to veto items in appropriation bills, within limit, gives him the last word to some extent. The chief limitation is that the Governor must veto an entire item, not only the descriptive language expressing the Legislature's wishes. The Governor is subject to the future limitation of not being able to put in the budget items the Legislature has omitted nor can he increase the money provided for an item.

A Limited Partnership

Thus, while it is commonly stated that the State government is made up of three independent branches—the Executive, Legislative, and Judicial—the separation between the Governor and the Legislature is not so sharp as that statement of independence might convey. Actually, it is a limited partnership.

Because newsmen, by way of headline shorthand, often speak of the Cabinet having taken some action, there has been a tendency to regard the Governor as being among the members of the Cabinet. He is not, except that he serves as Chairman of the various boards on which he sits with members of the Cabinet.

Not Governor's Cabinet

Nor is it the Governor's Cabinet. This must be stressed because so many Floridians have come here from other states where the Governor, as does the

President of the United States, has a group of personal appointees to advise him and this group often is known as the Cabinet.

As late in his administration as six months, Governor Reubin O'D. Askew (1971–1979) still was coping with the problem of the public and fellow officers of identifying the Governor with the Cabinet.

"I'd like to address the Cabinet on this," began Attorney General Robert L. Shevin at a meeting.

"Would you like to address me too?" interrupted Governor Askew.

"I was including you in the Cabinet, Governor," replied the Attorney General.

"But I'm not a member of the Cabinet," said Askew.[8]

Since the Governor shares so much of the traditional executive responsibility with members of an independent Cabinet, it is not surprising that political scientists regard Florida's system of State government as different from virtually all other states.

Despite the revision of the Constitution in 1968 and the Executive Reorganization Act which followed in 1969, which lodged far more responsibility in the Governor than he previously had possessed, the State's Executive branch retains its designation as a Cabinet government.

A longtime observer, Dr. Daisy Parker Flory, Professor Emeritus of Government of Florida State University, found the vital characteristics of the Cabinet system endure:[9]

"The six Cabinet officers are directly elected and thus directly responsible to the people. Each Cabinet official heads an important administrative division. Each Cabinet official also participates with the Governor in administering certain major departments . . .

"The 1968 Revision of the Constitution not only gives the Cabinet constitutional recognition and designation but it also directs the Legislature to place each of the executive departments of state government, unless specifically provided for otherwise in the charter, under the direct supervision of the Governor, the Lieutenant Governor, the *Governor and Cabinet*, a *Cabinet* member, or an officer or board appointed by the Governor.

"The Constitution further provides that the Legislature may require confirmation by the Senate or *the approval of three members of the Cabinet* for appointment to or removal from any designated statutory office. The Cabinet is constitutionally accorded a role in the determination of the incapacity of the Governor: four Cabinet officers may send to the Supreme Court 'a written suggestion' that the Governor is incapable to serve, the Supreme Court making the determination. Restoration of capacity, in such case, is to be similarly determined 'after docketing a written suggestion thereof by the Governor, the Legislature, or four *Cabinet* members.'"

"Spreading the Heat"

Governor Fuller Warren (1949–53) once stated the phrase "spreading the heat" was not the "most elegant, exalted language that might be used to express the idea, but it was and still is my belief that Florida's Cabinet system serves such a purpose."[10]

By that, Governor Warren meant the Cabinet system diffuses accountability. Another view is that many of the important decisions of Florida's government must be sifted through a screen of seven officials (and their staffs) so that the final product represents a collective judgment. It has been contended that this collegial responsibility is one of the reasons for the stability of Florida's State Government.

Proponents of Florida's Cabinet system have argued that decision-making by seven, as opposed to one (the Governor), spreads the responsibility and lends an additional deliberative character to actions of the Executive branch.

Opponents reply that this contention was more persuasive in the years when the Legislature met only once every two years and specifically delegated interim authority to the Governor and Cabinet to shift funds and personnel to cope with unforeseen situations.

Now, with annual legislative sessions and professionally-staffed committees functioning year-round, lawmakers contend the Legislature is performing its Constitutional role as the deliberative, policy-making branch. This, they claim, leaves to the Executive department its function of executing the laws.

One Governor's View: A Waste of Some Time

Governor Reubin O'D. Askew (1971–1979) once said the Cabinet system wasted a lot of his time.[11]

Such things as having "to learn about how big the shell of a green turtle should be before you are allowed to take them in the Atlantic and Gulf" raise questions about best use of top elected officials' time, Askew said at a meeting with student-body presidents.

"To the green turtle, it's important because it's an animal we do not want to become extinct . . . but it took several hours for the Cabinet to decide," he added.

The Departments

The 1969 Executive Reorganization vested all or conditional responsibility in the Governor for the Departments of Business and Professional Regulation, Commerce, Community Affairs, Health and Rehabilitative Services, Transportation, Environmental Protection, Offender Rehabilitation (renamed Corrections in 1978), Citrus, Lottery, and Elder Affairs. The responsibilities of Commerce were split in 1978 with creation of a Department of Labor and Employment Security. Community Affairs was renamed Veteran and Community Affairs in 1980, but Veterans' Affairs was transferred in 1982 to the Department of Administration. The Department of Administration and The Department of General Services were joined to become Management Services in 1992. In 1988, by Constitutional Amendment, Veterans' Affairs became an independent department. (Information about these departments will be found in a subsequent chapter.) The 1994 Legislature created a Department of Juvenile Justice. The Department of Elder Affairs was authorized by constitutional amendment but was not created until 1991 by an act of the Florida Legislature.

But the Governor continues to share with the six members of the Cabinet the management of the Departments of Law Enforcement, Highway Safety and Motor Vehicles, Veterans' Affairs, Internal Improvement Trust Fund, and Revenue. (Information about each of these Departments also will be found later.) The Governor, with the approval of three members of the Cabinet may grant full or conditional pardons.

Each of the Cabinet officers heads up a Department. The Secretary of State is solely responsible for the Department of State. The Attorney General for the Department of Legal Affairs. The Comptroller for the Department of Banking and Finance. The Treasurer for the Department of Insurance. The Commissioner of Agriculture for the Department of Agriculture and Consumer Services. And the Commissioner of Education for the Department of Education.

Ex Officio Boards

Many of the major administrative functions of the State government still are exercised through ex officio boards. An ex officio board is a board whose members serve by virtue of other offices they hold.

Prior to Executive Reorganization, there had accumulated forty-eight ex officio boards, ranging alphabetically in name from the Board of Administration (composed of the Governor, Comptroller, and Treasurer) to the Board for Vocational Education (composed of the Governor and Secretary of State, Attorney General, Treasurer, and Commissioner of Agriculture). Some of these seldom if ever met because of the infrequency of business to transact: for example, the Board for Confederate Pensions.

Executive Reorganization reduced the number of ex officio boards to eight with each board managing a department. Composition of the ex officio boards also was changed to provide that all members of the Cabinet should serve with the Governor on these. The exception was the Board of Administration, whose membership of Governor, Comptroller, and Treasurer was provided for in the Constitution, and thus could not be changed by the reorganization law.

Reorganization and the Independent Commissions

Reorganization also affected a large number of boards and commissions which previously had functioned with a considerable degree of independence. Many of these regulated professions and occupations. Others managed some segment of state government. A legislative architect of Executive Reorganization wrote:

"There was a great deal of overlapping responsibility and authority; there was no logical organization and there was very little communication among agencies having responsibility for the same kinds of functions. The duplication of services was costly. Worse, the quality of service which State government could offer was not adequate to meet the needs of the people.

"Much of the governing structure was haphazard and confused and there were few, if any, who really understood the division of authority and responsibility which existed. No one was identifiably responsible for the functions of State government and no one could clearly be held accountable for the actions or, in some cases, the inactions of State government."[12]

Cabinet Independence of Governor

Until the revision of the Constitution in 1968, a Florida governor could not run for reelection to a successive four-year term. The revision gave him the opportunity to run for one successive term. Members of the Cabinet have been eligible to run for reelection, term after term, and they usually have run so long as they were so minded and usually successfully.

For example, Nathan Mayo served as Commissioner of Agriculture from November 1, 1923, until his death on April 14, 1960, and R. A. Gray was Secretary of State from April 12, 1930 until his retirement on January 3, 1961.

In this century, through 1994, only six elective Cabinet incumbents have been defeated when seeking reelection.

William N. Sheats was defeated as Superintendent of Public Instruction in 1904 (but reclaimed the office in 1912); Ernest Amos was defeated as Comptroller in 1932; W. S. Cawthon was defeated as Superintendent of Public Instruction in 1936; Broward Williams was defeated as Treasurer in 1970, Fred O. Dickinson was defeated as Comptroller in 1974, and Gerald Lewis defeated as Comptroller in 1994. James W. Kynes, who had been appointed Attorney General on January 17, 1964, was edged out by Earl Faircloth in the Democratic primaries a few months later. Faircloth won by 599 votes out of 938,677 cast.

Cabinet members generally have conducted their party primary election campaigns separate from each other and from the Governor. There would be some independent campaigning even in the general elections although the emphasis then would be on unified efforts in support of slates of party nominees.

Thus, the Cabinet officers have sought to develop their own independent constituencies for political support. There is, for example, a natural affinity between the Commissioner of Agriculture and the many elements which make up the industry known as agri-business. Similarly, the office of the Comptroller is a matter of concern to banks, savings and loan associations, and other financial institutions.

Cabinet Day

Cabinet day—usually a Tuesday—has come to serve as Florida's "town meeting" with the public's business transacted with a greater degree of openness than may be found in any other state's government.

A meeting on Cabinet day affords the public an opportunity to watch State government in operation. Because the Governor and the six Cabinet officers are peers, each responsible basically to the electorate, differences of opinion usually go unconcealed.

The public largely is represented by the Capitol's newsmen. Florida has the second largest state press corps in the nation after California. Yet the audience will include others. Advance notice being required of many of the items of business, interested citizens will be in attendance. Controversial matters well can mean standing room only. Rank-and-file citizens will drop in just to see what may be happening.

Cabinet days represent the incidental opportunity of a forum for purposes other than the transacting of the business of the ex officio boards.

The presence of the Governor and Cabinet officers affords a ceremonial setting for the recognition of beauty queens, outstanding athletes, retiring state employees and others deserving of introduction. Certificates of appreciation and other awards are presented.

The Number of Departments

The Constitution of 1968 (Article IV, Section 6) declared all functions of the Executive Department "shall be allotted among not more than twenty-five departments, exclusive of those specifically provided for or authorized by this Constitution."

10 / Executive Department

Attorney General Robert A. Butterworth formally stated in 1987 that his count of the departments existing then totaled twenty-five.[13]

The constitutional status given the proposed departments of Veterans' Affairs and Elder Affairs did not crack the 25 limitation since these would be created within the constitutional exemption.

The Cabinet System

In short, while the Governor's responsibilities have been expanded, Florida's Cabinet system "appears firmly rooted."[14]

---

[1]Letter from LeRoy Collins, March 2, 1984.
[2]1885 Constitution, Article IV, Section 20; 1968 *Constitution* Article IV, Section 4.
[3]Letter from LeRoy Collins, March 2, 1984.
[4]Office of the State Comptroller, October, 1986.
[5]Committee on Regulatory Reform, Florida House of Representatives, February, 1984.
[6]Office of the Governor, February, 1984.
[7]Includes all sources of State income. Office of the State Comptroller. Bureau of State Payroll, April 1995.
[8]Tom Raum, "Governor Askew Insists He's Not a Cabinet Member," *Tallahassee Democrat,* July 8, 1971
[9]Dr. Daisy Parker Flory, "The Executive Department," *The Florida Handbook, 1971–1972,* p. 72.
[10]Letter from Fuller Warren, July 15, 1971.
[11]Remarks by Governor Reubin O'D. Askew at meeting with Florida college student-body presidents, reported by the Associated Press February 10, 1976.
[12]Richard A. Pettigrew, "Executive Reorganization: Uniformity with Flexibility," *The Florida Handbook 1971–1972,* pp. 167–168.
[13]Attorney General Robert A. Butterworth, letter to Representative Dick Locke, September 30, 1987.
[14]Dr. Daisy Parker Flory, "The Executive Department," *The Florida Handbook, 1971–1972,* p. 72.

Senate President Charley E. Johns (left) here takes the oath of office as Acting Governor from Supreme Court Justice John E. Mathews while the Chief Executive's son, Charley Jerome, holds the Bible. This photograph captures the solemnity of the ceremony in the Senate chamber at Tallahassee on the evening of September 29, 1953, after the death of Governor Dan McCarty.

Florida State Archives

Precedence for Cabinet and Supreme Court

While the revision of the Constitution in 1968 and reorganization of the Executive Branch in 1969 centralized greater responsibility in the Governor than previously had been the case, Florida still functions as "a Cabinet system of government."[1]

The revised Constitution provides for a Governor and a Lieutenant Governor, and for "a Cabinet composed of a Secretary of State, an Attorney General, a Comptroller, a Treasurer, a Commissioner of Agriculture, and a Commissioner of Education."[2]

By stating "there shall be a Cabinet," the revised Constitution recognized the name which only had been given popularly to a group of officials described by the 1885 Constitution as "administrative officers" assisting the Governor.

Members of the Cabinet are listed on the following pages in the order in which they are given in the revised Constitution. First, the Secretary of State, then the Attorney General, Comptroller, Treasurer, Commissioner of Agriculture and Commissioner of Education.[3]

Order for Seating

This same order is followed in many official ceremonies, both business and social. For many years, the Constitutional order dictated the seating when the Governor and Cabinet came together as members of the State's various management boards. In 1971 through 1974, seating was rearranged according to seniority of the individual Cabinet officers rather than that of the office. The traditional seating was resumed in 1975. The Governor always sits at the center of the boardroom table as the group faces the audience.

This protocol, or ranking, is used so that Cabinet members always will be placed or seated in the same order. It does not mean that one office is more important than another. If the question of who comes first and who comes next were left to chance, it often might be awkward. The Justices of the Supreme Court use much the same plan in the courtroom and at official and social functions. The Justices seat themselves on either side of the Chief Justice in the order of the date of their original appointment or election to the court.

Order for Receiving Lines

It is the same in the receiving line at an official function. The Governor, Lieutenant Governor, and Cabinet officers will stand in the order of listing in the Constitution. The Supreme Court Justices will be in the order of seniority after the Chief Justice. The order for other public officers depends on the geographic area served by the office. The officer who serves the whole State is placed ahead of one who serves only a few counties. The officer who serves several counties comes ahead of an officer serving only one county.

---

[1] Dr. Daisy Parker Flory, "The Executive Department," *The Florida Handbook ,1971–1972* (Tallahassee, Fla.: Peninsular Publishing Company 1971), pp. 71–72.
[2] *Florida Constitution*, Article IV, Section 4 (a).
[3] *Practical Protocol for Floridians,* Allen Morris, Florida House of Representatives, 1984.

12 / Executive Department

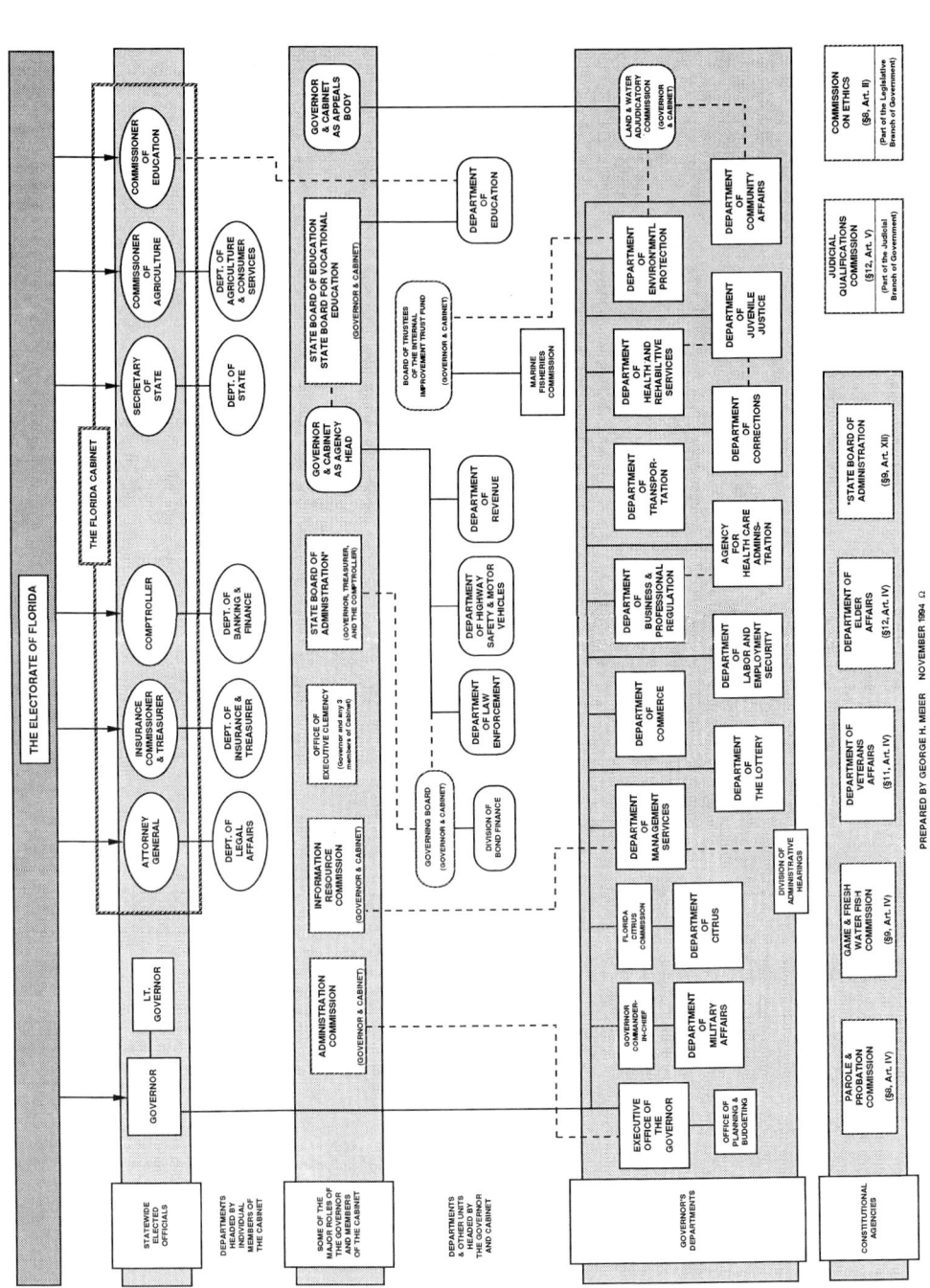

The Office of the Governor

"The Supreme Executive power shall be vested in a Governor."
Florida Constitution, Article IV, Section 1

This forcible language—"Supreme Executive power"—should be read against what already has been said of how the Governor shares authority.

Governor Farris Bryant (1961–1965) said, after leaving office, that a Governor of Florida could be either stronger or weaker than a reading of the Constitution and laws pertaining to the office would indicate. Governor Bryant explained:

"That strength or weakness will be a product of his public popularity, and his ability to provide personal leadership to the Legislature, his ability to influence the Cabinet, and his capacity to grasp the whole broad spectrum of problems and through his Little Cabinet give it necessary direction. I believe the public generally understands that."[1]

That Constitution, in Article IV, Section 1; spells out its drafters' concept of the powers and responsibilities of the Governor in these words:

"(a) The Supreme Executive power shall be vested in a Governor. He shall be commander-in-chief of all military forces of the state not in active service of the United States. He shall take care that the laws be faithfully executed, commission all officers of the state and counties, and transact all necessary business with the officers of government. He may require information in writing from all executive or administrative state, county or municipal officers upon any subject relating to the duties of their respective offices.

"(b) The Governor may initiate judicial proceedings in the name of the state against any executive or administrative state, county or municipal officer to enforce compliance with any duty or restrain any unauthorized act.

"(c) The Governor may request in writing the opinion of the Justices of the Supreme Court as to the interpretation of any portion of this constitution upon any question affecting his executive powers and duties. The Justices shall, subject to their rules of procedure, permit interested persons to be heard on the questions presented and shall render their written opinion not earlier than ten days from the filing and docketing of the request, unless in their judgment the delay would cause public injury.

"(d) The Governor shall have power to call out the militia to preserve the public peace, execute the laws of the state, suppress insurrection, or repel invasion.

"(e) The Governor shall by message at least once in each regular session inform the Legislature concerning the condition of the state, propose such reorganization of the executive department as will promote efficiency and economy, and recommend measures in the public interest.

"(f) When not otherwise provided for in this Constitution, the Governor shall fill by appointment any vacancy in state or county office for the remainder of the term of an appointive office, and for the remainder of the term of an elective office if less than twenty-eight months, otherwise until the first Tuesday after the first Monday following the next general election."

Qualifications for Election

To be elected Governor, a person must meet certain requirements primarily of age and residence. He (or she) must be, at the time of election, not less than thirty years of age and a resident of Florida for the preceding seven years.

(The same requirements of age and residence apply to the Lieutenant Governor and members of the Cabinet. Additionally, the Attorney General must have been a member of the Bar of Florida for the preceding five years.

(All of these officers also must be electors. That means they must possess the further qualification of being citizens of the United States and registered to vote.

(Upon registering, an eligible citizen must take an oath to protect and defend the Constitution of the United States and the State of Florida. If elected, an officer must take the same oath.

(Finally, no person convicted of a felony, or adjudicated in Florida or any other state to be mentally incompetent, is eligible either to vote or hold office unless the civil rights have been restored by the Office of Executive Clemency or the disability removed by a court possessing the authority to do this.)

Measuring a Governor

Beyond the Constitutional qualifications, the Governor should possess standards which Governor LeRoy Collins (1955–1961) set forth in these words:

"1. His integrity (this embraces more than his honesty it means the wholeness of his dedication to serve well the public interest);

"2. His ability to make decisions promptly and decisively (this is very important because pressures tend to encourage procrastination and equivocation to avoid offending people and interests);

"3. His administrative competence to see that his decisions are acted upon and his goals achieved; and

"4. His 'style' or 'charisma' or 'magnetic' qualities in his personality that add to his effectiveness as a leader.

"Now a Governor can do a good job and fall short on one or more of these attributes, but to be superior he needs to rate well on all four standards, I think."[2]

Training for a Governor

Governor Reubin O'D. Askew (1971–1979) once said: "They don't have schools for a Governor, so I'm learning the hard way as I go along ."[3]

Governor Askew was, however, a graduate of an institution—the Legislature—which has come to be regarded as a training school for Governors and other officials.

Of Florida's twenty-one elected Governors inaugurated in this century through 1990, seventeen had served in either the State Senate or House of Representatives or both. Five had been Speaker of the House and two had been President of the Senate. Of those without legislative experience, three had been multi-term Mayors of Jacksonville and Tampa. Only two Governors possessed no prior public service.

Service in the Legislature, and especially membership on committees responsible for drafting the appropriations bills, opens a window which hardly can be equalled as an educational opportunity to learn about the ramifications of the State government.

[See section entitled "Prior Public Service of Governors" later in this chapter.]

Term

The regular term of office of a Governor is four years. The term begins on the first Tuesday after the first Monday in January following the general election in November.

The revised Constitution of 1968 gave a Governor the opportunity to seek reelection to a successive four-year term, a right denied prior Governors. This was regarded as increasing the political and administrative potential of the Governor although the first to seek a successive term (Governor Claude R. Kirk, Jr., 1967–1971) was defeated.

Frederick B. Karl, a knowledgeable legislator with service in both the House of Representatives and the Senate, expressed this opinion of the old limitation:

"The Governor's ineligibility to succeed himself tended to undermine both the political muscle and the administrative effectiveness of the office. It tilted the balance of power in favor of the Cabinet and the Legislature, despite the Constitutional grant of 'Supreme Executive power' to the Governor."[4]

Removal from Office

The Governor can be removed from office only by the Legislature although the Supreme Court, upon the written suggestion of four members of the Cabinet, may declare the Governor physically or mentally incapable of performing his duties.

To remove the Governor, two-thirds of the Senators present must vote to convict him of the impeachment charge of misdemeanor in office. This charge—usually called an *article* of impeachment—must have been brought against the Governor by two-thirds of the members of the House of Representatives present.

Impeachment

Along with the Governor, the Lieutenant Governor, members of the Cabinet, Justices of the Supreme Court, Judges of District Courts of Appeal, and Judges of Circuit and County Courts are liable to impeachment.

An article of impeachment is an accusation lodged against an official by the House of Representatives just as an indictment returned by a grand jury or an information filed by a State Attorney or County Solicitor represents a charge against an individual. Impeachment should not be confused with conviction. [See the legislative chapter for a history of impeachments in Florida.]

An officer impeached by the House of Representatives is disqualified from performing any official duties until acquitted by the Senate, and unless the impeached official is the Governor, the Governor may fill the office by appointment until completion of the trial.

The Chief Justice of the Supreme Court, or a Justice designated by him, presides at impeachment trials. (If the Chief Justice were the officer impeached, the Governor would preside.)

The Speaker of the House of Representatives has the power at any time to appoint a committee to investigate charges against any officer subject to impeachment. The Senate may sit as a court of impeachment whether the House be in session or not, so long as the time fixed for the trial be within six months of the voting of the charge, or charges, by the House.

Conviction means removal of the offender from office and, in the discretion of the Senate, the judgment may include disqualification from holding any future office of honor, trust or profit.

Neither conviction nor acquittal by the Senate would prevent the officer being sued or prosecuted.

Incapacity of the Governor

Upon the suggestion in writing by four members of the Cabinet, the Supreme Court may determine whether the Governor is physically or mentally able to perform his duties.

The Governor may remove himself for physical disability by filing a certificate with the Secretary of State stating that fact.

Restoration of the Governor to office may be achieved in the same manner as removal. The Supreme Court may review the question of the Governor's physical or mental ability at the request in writing of the Governor, four members of the Cabinet, or the Legislature. The Governor may declare himself again physically fit to serve by filing another certificate with the Secretary of State.

Succession to Office

The Lieutenant Governor succeeds in the event of a vacancy in the office of Governor, serving either for the remainder of the term or during the period of an impeachment trial or physical or mental incapacity.

The Legislature has provided for a further gubernatorial succession in the event of catastrophe. Upon vacancy in the offices of Governor and Lieutenant Governor, the Secretary of State shall become Governor; next, the Attorney General, Comptroller, Treasurer, Commissioner of Education and Commissioner of Agriculture.

In the event this order of succession still did not provide for filling a vacancy in the office of Governor, the President of the Senate and Speaker of the House of Representatives are required to convene the Legislature in joint session within fifteen days for the purpose of choosing by majority vote a person to serve as Governor for the remainder of the term.

The same succession would prevail if the Lieutenant Governor serving as Acting Governor should be unable to perform the duties.

The Governor's Office as an Extension of the Person

The *Office of the Governor* can, in many respects, be made to mean what the person serving as Governor at the time wants it to mean. An observer has truly stated it is necessary to see the office and the man who occupies it as an entity. The Constitution, the laws, and custom impose so broad a range of duties that he may be selective as to where he will place his personal emphasis.

He may wish to use the respect which people generally feel for the office to give leadership to endeavors of many kinds. He might, for example, seek by television, radio and newspaper appeals to focus attention upon the need for safe driving. He might help in the mediation of a labor dispute. He might lead efforts to protect the environment and wildlife. He might fight for reforms in tax, ethics and election laws. People expect moral as well as legal leadership from the Office of the Governor.

The Governor travels many miles. He makes many speeches. He meets with many groups of people—Floridians and non-Floridians—interested in problems of one kind or another. All these duties and many others depend upon the aptitudes, the attitudes, and even the physical stamina of the Governor then in office.

Governor Farris Bryant (1961–1965) has written of still another facet:

"One of the unfortunate necessities about a position of political leadership, such as that of the Governor, is that at least as much time must be given to communicating with your constituency in numerous ways and in a thousand forms, as is spent resolving the problems which are your principal function.

"Especially is it necessary for a Governor to establish understanding of what he proposes to do, constantly reinterpret it to the media and the public, and to a smaller interest among the public directly affected, and finally to explain and defend what has been done so that his leadership on future items will not be adversely affected."[5]

In practice, much of the Governor's program is put into effect on a day-to-day basis by agencies under his direct supervision. By law, the heads of most of these agencies serve terms which begin and end with that of the Governor.

Because of this, an in-coming Governor has a legally free hand to select people to head agencies which can carry out certain of the planks of the platform on which he, as a candidate, stood for election.

Among these agencies are the Departments of Transportation, Business and Professional Regulation, Commerce, Health and Rehabilitative Services, Environmental Protection, Community Affairs, Citrus, Labor and Employment Security, Corrections, Lottery, Elder Affairs, Juvenile Justice and Management Services.

The Little Cabinet

The Governor appoints the heads of these agencies. All, together with the Governor's Chief of Staff, belong to what has come to be known as the *Little Cabinet,* even though that name has no formal standing.

Depending upon the Governor for the frequency of meeting, the Little Cabinet will gather to discuss some subject of the Governor's policy which would affect all of them. In recent times, governors or their chiefs of staff have convened regular weekly or monthly meetings of their Little Cabinets to discuss a wide range of administrative and policy issues.

It is through these Little Cabinet agencies that a Governor most effectively can make his administration felt. Usually a number of the planks of his campaign platform can be carried out by them without further legislation.

There are laws stating what the work of each agency should cover. But in most cases, an administrator still can place emphasis on a certain part of the agency's work. Perhaps the Governor has promised in his campaign that a certain highway would be improved. The Secretary of Transportation he appoints will try very hard to carry out that promise. Or, the Governor may have determined during his campaign that Florida needed more tourists at a certain season of the year. The Secretary of Commerce can stress the state's advantages for visitors in advertising placed at the desired time and paid for out of the money earmarked by the Legislature for tourist promotion.

The Cabinet Aides

In the performance of their duties as members of the various boards, the Governor and Cabinet officers are assisted by a group known as *Cabinet Aides*. Each officer has a chief aide and as many as three assistants. The Cabinet aides meet some days in advance of the Cabinet meeting and collectively question department heads and others with business at the Cabinet meeting. This questioning serves to give the Governor and Cabinet a preview of the business through briefings by their Cabinet aides. It also saves the time of all participants. In prior years, aides to the Governor and Cabinet members individually reviewed the departmental agendaes. The meetings are open to the press and public. In the beginning, this group was known as the *Mini Cabinet*, but as the number of aides grew the name failed to stick.

Theoretically the Cabinet aides are only fact-gatherers. However, perhaps depending upon the background of the aides, some degree of subjectivity may enter into the briefing or report an aide will give to his superior.

Some of the aides report in writing, others orally at a Cabinet agenda review session usually held on the Friday before the Tuesday Cabinet meeting. Governor Chiles' aides provide an update of controversial issues immediately after the Cabinet Aides meeting and a regular update the day before the Cabinet meeting. This provides adequate time for research and analysis.

The Cabinet aides' meetings also help those persons having business before the Cabinet in that questions arise at the aides' meeting which indicate the need for additional information.

The Governor's Power of Appointment

The Constitution vests the Governor with the power to fill vacancies in State and county offices. This is a far-reaching power.

Generally the Governor may appoint a successor who will complete the term of any *elective* officer if the remainder of that term is less than twenty - eight months. Otherwise, his appointee would serve until the first Tuesday after the first Monday following the next general election. The successor to an *appointive* officer usually serves out the unfinished term.

The Governor makes about a thousand appointments a year. Some are to fill vacancies in elective offices caused by death, resignation, retirement, or the creation of a new office. These would be temporary appointments pending the election of a successor. They would include the United States Senate, the State Cabinet, the courts, and the county offices such as sheriff, tax assessor, tax collector, and court clerk.

Most by far, however, are to appointive offices and come about through the expiration of terms. The variety of these is broad, and the Governor will depend upon the leaders in his campaign organization—his post-election patronage committees—for recommendations in the appointments to local offices.

Appointments by an outgoing Governor subject to confirmation by the Senate may be withdrawn by the incoming Governor. When Reubin O'D. Askew became Governor, he withdrew more than 100 unconfirmed appointments made by his predecessor Claude R. Kirk, Jr. Similarly, Governor Bob Martinez withdrew 277 appointments to 90 agencies by Governors Bob Graham and Wayne Mixson. Some later won office as Martinez appointees.

Governor Martinez explained: "The people of Florida sent me to Tallahassee to do a job, and I believe that the men and women who will work with me in these positions should share the philosophy and goals of my administration."

Acting Governor Charley E. Johns withdrew appointments made by his predecessor, Dan McCarty, and, in turn, Governor LeRoy Collins withdrew unconfirmed appointments made by Johns.

The Governor puts men and women on State commissions for the licensing and regulation of certain professions and occupations. Among these are: physicians, dentists, nurses, architects, building contractors, cosmetologists, sanitarians, and watchmakers.

He also selects the members of boards for such local public services as hospitals, libraries, seaports and airports, sewers, fire protection, drainage, zoning, housing, tax adjustment, and mosquito control.

Often appointees of a Governor to major State offices are from among his closest friends. This, observed Governor LeRoy Collins (1955–61), "gives rise to complaints of 'cronyism'."

"If the friendship bonds represent the sole or predominant reason for the appointment, then the charge has substance. But there are other reasons a Governor may appoint a friend other than favoritism.

"In the first place he should know well a friend's real qualifications. Also the friends know well the goals of the Governor and will most likely place the achievement of those goals uppermost in his own ambitions and work. No one more than a friend wants the Governor to succeed or know better what success requires.

"An ideal appointment is a person eminently qualified by objective standards who will give his total efforts in his job. If a friend fits this pattern his appointment will measure out very high in the public interest."[6]

By this appointive power, the Governor leaves an imprint on government which lasts beyond his own term. This is particularly true of the courts. The voters tend to keep judges in office, and many judges—if not most—were put in office first by the Governor.

The Governor's Power of Removal

The Governor can suspend any State or county officer not subject to impeachment for malfeasance, misfeasance, neglect of duty, drunkenness, incompetence, permanent inability to perform his official duties, or commission of a felony. Suspensions are subject to review by the Senate. The President of the Senate, or a majority of its membership, is empowered by the Constitution to convene a special session to consider the Governor's suspension charges and may remove or reinstate the accused official.

Among the grounds for suspension are three which may require definition. The Supreme Court has defined them. The court said *malfeasance* is the "performance of an act by an officer in his official capacity that is wholly illegal and wrongful." *Misfeasance* was described as the "performance by an officer in his official capacity of a legal act in an improper or illegal manner." *Incompetency* as a ground for suspension and removal has reference "to any physical, moral, or intellectual quality, the lack of which incapacitates one to perform the duties of his office."

Senator Frederick B. Karl of Daytona Beach served as Chairman of the Senate's committee on Executive Suspensions and, in collaboration with his law partner, William M. Barr, wrote authoritatively on the subject of such ousters. Karl and Barr expressed the opinion that the cohesion of the State as a political and governmental entity depends to a significant degree on the constitutional powers vested in the Governor to oversee the performance and functioning of public offices.

"The greatest of these powers is the Governor's prerogative to issue an executive order suspending public officials from office without prior hearing," wrote Karl and Barr. "The long shadow that this executive power casts over sixty-seven courthouses tends to establish Florida as a State instead of a loose confederation of counties.

"And the felt presence of the power in State offices makes the Governor's 'Supreme Executive power' a reality in the Executive branch and limits the extent to which an ossified, autonomous bureaucracy, impervious and indifferent to public needs and forces outside itself, can develop in Tallahassee."[7]

A majority of the Senators present determines whether the Senate shall remove or reinstate the suspended officer. If the Senate decides to reinstate the officer, he very likely will receive any pay he lost while he was kept out of office.

As indicated above the governor does not have the power to suspend officers subject to impeachment. These are the Lieutenant Governor, the six Cabinet members, Justices of the Supreme Court, the Judges of the District Court of Appeal, the Circuit and County Courts, and the Governor himself.

The Governor and Removal of Municipal Officials

In a separate category is the Governor's power to suspend and remove municipal officers. This is a power first given the Governor in the revised Constitution of 1968. He is expressly empowered to suspend any elected municipal officer indicted for crime until the officer is acquitted. In addition, the Governor is authorized by law to suspend any elected or appointed municipal officer when any grand jury indicts him for official misconduct. If found guilty, the official then may be removed by the Governor. If the accused municipal officer either is acquitted or the charge quashed, the suspension is terminated. The difference between the suspensions of State and county officials and the suspensions and removals of municipal officials is that the Senate does not act upon suspensions and removals of municipal officials.

The Governor and the Judiciary

Certain parts of the Constitution have to do with the Governor's powers and duties. The Governor has the right to ask Justices of the Supreme Court for their interpretation of such parts. These interpretations in writing are known as advisory opinions.

The Governor, in some cases, uses a power like that of a judge. He does this in the case of a person in Florida who is wanted by another state, either for trial or completion of a prison sentence there. The Governor then decides whether or not he will let that person be *extradited* or taken from Florida to that state. There are about 300 extradition requests a year from other states.

The Governor can also have a great deal to do with the quality of the judiciary. This is because of his power to fill vacancies in office. And, as has been pointed out, a judge already in office is likely to be kept in office by the voters.

The Governor and Custom

Aside from the official duties imposed by the Constitution and laws, the Governor is asked to do many things just because of custom. As the First Citizen, he will be asked to represent the state at far more functions than he can attend.

The Governor is almost always invited to fairs, parades, fiestas, and other community celebrations. Conventions of state and national groups held in Florida will often invite the Governor to speak. Bids also will come from industrial, business, trade, professional, and vocational associations: from civic clubs, fraternal orders, and church groups.

Most Governors accept all the invitations they conveniently can. They do so not only as a courtesy to their hosts, but because it gives the Governor a chance to state his views on different subjects. He may wish to gather public support for his viewpoint, and a speech or series of speeches will be helpful. When the Governor, for instance, dedicates a new building at one of the state universities, he can tell people what he thinks should be done in years to come about higher education in Florida. What he says is almost always reported through the newspapers, television, and radio. This helps shape public opinion in the direction of his own convictions.

Sometimes the Governor addresses the convention in Florida of some national association. This gives him a chance to serve the future of the state. In most cases, the audience will be made up largely of out-of-state people. He will have much to tell them about what the state has to offer them. Those people may come back to Florida as tourists, as investors, or as year-round residents.

The Governor and the Airplane

The airplane has been both a blessing and a burden to Florida's Governors. By reducing travel time, the airplane has made it possible for the Governor to accept more of the invitations the chief executive receives: some 6,000 in a typical year. On the other hand, however, the Governor finds it more difficult to plead, in declining invitations, that he cannot take the time from other duties.

Governor LeRoy Collins (1955–1961), last of the chief executives to mainly use the automobile, was said in a review of his administration to have worn out "three limousines (and several aides!) as he traveled almost incessantly within Florida. Altogether, inside Florida and out, he accepted some 860 of 8,495 speaking invitations received in his office."[8]

His successor, Governor Farris Bryant (1961–1965), said the airplane increased the demands on the Governor's time geometrically, greatly expanding the "opportunity of a Governor to reach and be reached."[9]

Mrs. Lorna Allen, secretary to Governor Reubin O'D. Askew (1971–1979) reviewed Governor Askew's schedule for 1977, and apportioned his time in these percentages:

Managing State government, 30%; working with the Legislature, 13%; meeting general public, including ceremonial functions, 12%; working with the federal government, 9%; working with local governments, 5%; political activities, 2%; recruiting and appointments, 6%; and miscellaneous activities (staff, reading, telephoning, etc.), 15%.[10]

The Governor and Correspondence

"I'll write the Governor" is a common reaction to people with a governmental question or problem. Governor Chiles receives, on average, approximately 100,000 letters annually. Fifty five percent of the Governor's mail is from individuals expressing opinions on state policies and legislative proposals. The remaining 45 percent of the mail arrives from people who have a problem with a state agency. The Governor's Office of Citizens' Services coordinates replies to everyone who writes the Governor, but draws on the expertise of staff within the Executive Office of the Governor and state agencies.

The Governor Is Seldom Off Duty

It is well to remember, too, that the Governor seldom can be regarded as off duty. He may, for example, attend a football game. But, more than likely, he will be there mostly to show officially that the game is an important one for the state university. He will go as much out of courtesy to the university as he will because the game gives him pleasure. Or the Governor may go fishing with a friend. The hours afloat well may serve more for thinking aloud about some state problem than for angling.

The Governor's Legislative Program

In the years of this century prior to 1960, when Florida could be regarded as a one-party state, there was little if any agitation ever for a party platform since this need was served by the primary election campaign planks of the candidate winning the Democratic nomination.

As Governor Millard F. Caldwell (1945–1949) stated the matter:

"The dominant party in Florida prepares no gubernatorial platform and the determination of the objectives to be followed during the succeeding four years is largely left to the candidate. The Legislature, by long-standing custom, has adopted the practice of treating the successful candidate's platform as the public mandate."[11]

The healthy condition of the State's treasury when Caldwell came into office—a condition caused by the inability of the State government to spend to the usual extent during the years of World War II—plus the nature of his requests to the lawmakers, may have colored his appraisal of the Legislature's acceptance of a gubernatorial platform as a public mandate.

In any event, at least two of his successors in office felt differently about the extent of the mandate.

Governor Farris Bryant (1961–1965), after his service, commented:

"Whether or not the program of the Governor is considered as a mandate I would now believe it to be a consequence of the Governor's political strength."[12]

And Governor Fuller Warren (1949–1953), also after his tenure wrote:

"My own experience as Governor indicates that the Legislature did not regard the platform or program on which I was elected as a mandate. Perhaps the two planks, in the platform on which I was elected Governor, that were most widely approved by the people of Florida were (1) outlawing livestock from public highways and (2) stopping the shipping of unripe citrus from Florida.

"Despite the apparent popular approval of these two planks, it was necessary to work very hard to get them enacted into law by the 1949 Legislature. Some of the other planks on which I was nominated and elected Governor in 1948 were rejected by the Legislature despite the efforts of our administration to get them enacted into law."[13]

As *Tampa Tribune* cartoonist George White viewed Governor Fuller Warren's difficulties with the 1949 Legislature.
Cartoon collection, Museum of Florida History

If ever it were true that the Legislature was inclined to accept the gubernatorial platform as a mandate, this surely has been lessened since 1969 when the Legislature turned to the philosophy of year-round committees with staffing independent of the Executive Branch. Gains in Republican voter registration in recent years have added another element to the picture. Today, the strength, or weakness, of a governor's "mandate" partly depends on whether the governor and a majority of each legislative chamber are all of the same political party.

While times have changed, however, the bully pulpit remains an effective vehicle for achieving a gubernatorial objective.

Governor Reubin O'D. Askew (1971–1979) won both legislative and voter approval of his tax reform agenda by effectively utilizing the daily visibility and speaking opportunities available to the state's chief executive. He subsequently circumvented a balky legislature to win direct voter approval of his proposed "Sunshine Amendment" setting new financial disclosure and other ethics standards for candidates and officeholders.

Similarly Governor Lawton Chiles translated the reform themes of his 1990 gubernatorial campaign into quick enactment of one of the nation's strongest election laws during the 1991 legislative session.

The Mechanics of Presenting the Governor's Program to the Legislature

The Constitution states:

"The Governor shall by message at least once in each Regular Session inform the Legislature concerning the condition of the State, propose such reorganization of the Executive Department as will promote efficiency and economy, and recommend measures in the public interest."

It has been customary for the Governor to deliver this message in person at a joint session of the Senate and House of Representatives although in years prior to 1921 this was done in writing. (During the incapacity of Governor Dan McCarty in 1953, the message was read to the Legislature at his request by Secretary of State R. A. Gray; an ailing Governor Fred P. Cone in 1939 had his message delivered to the joint session by Attorney General George Cooper Gibbs.)

The Governor's message is printed in full in the Journals of the Senate and House. Newspapers, television and radio usually devote considerable space and time to what the Governor has asked of the Legislature. Newsmen will condense the message's contents and report the comments of legislative leaders. Editorial writers will analyze the Governor's offering.

The Governor does not content himself with delivering the message. In all likelihood, his staff already will have prepared many or all of the bills necessary to implement the recommendations and these will be delivered to sympathetic members of the Senate and House for introduction in their own names or the names of committees. Only a member of the Legislature may introduce a bill, and some bills drafted in the offices of Governors have become orphans because no lawmaker was willing even to introduce them.

In the years prior to the 1970s, the Governor probably had a legislative secretary, someone brought onto the staff solely for the purpose of overseeing the movement of the Governor's program through the Legislature. Nowadays, however, because the year-round staff has grown sufficiently, one or more of the regular aides will attend to this task.

The Governor also will draw upon the resources afforded him by the Chairmen, Executive Secretaries, Directors, and other top-echelon men and women who serve in the departments directly responsible to the Governor. They will be assigned the responsibility for bills affecting their own departments but they may be asked to help also with other phases of the Governor's program. At the same time they will be seeking to fend off legislation regarded as offensive to the administration's purposes.

The Governor also will be personally involved on behalf of his program. The Governor will invite legislators in small groups to the Mansion for meals and talk. He will ask lawmakers to come to his office individually to discuss problems. Depending upon the importance of a matter, the Governor and aides will be on the telephone to campaign supporters and other individuals who may be inclined to intercede with the hometown Senator or Representative who represents them.

Opponents of the Governor's pending proposal will describe his activities as "arm-twisting."

The Governor also will take advantage of the goodwill to be gained by inviting lawmakers to his office to be photographed with him as he signs legislation of special interest to them. Copies of these photographs will be sent to them. Also as a gesture of friendly relations, the Governor and his wife will entertain all members of the Legislature at the Mansion on an evening early in the Regular Session.

The Governor faces a dilemma in dealing with the Legislature. If he presses the Legislature for enactment of his program, he well may be charged with seeking to be a dictator. If he does not, he may be accused of failing to provide leadership.

Governor Askew faced up to that problem in 1971 when the Legislature, after sixty days of Regular Session and ten days of Special Session, still was deadlocked on measures to operate the State government and to provide revenues for those operations. Governor Askew had served previously as a Representative and Senator, so he knew the legislative temper.

In an unusual address to a Joint Session of the Senate and House of Representatives in which he spoke without a prepared text, Governor Askew said, in part:

"I've been told by some that I have not pushed you hard enough, but I've been with you for twelve years and I can recall the last four years in which, as a Legislature, we were prodded many times, and I must confess that even prior to that we were prodded, and the time to prod and not to prod, if such be the case and a necessity, is not an easy one.

"I've been told that maybe I should have told you sooner than now my feelings, but I also know that that's a two-edged sword, and attempting to assert yourself prematurely can also have very grave complications. . . . I'm not a king—the people elected me only as a Governor, and so I have some respect for your authority and your power to decide."[14]

Governor Graham also had legislative experience. Governor Chiles had served in both state legislative bodies, but was unique in that he served as United States Senator before becoming governor.

The Governor and Special Sessions

The Governor also has the authority to call the Legislature into special session. This gives him a chance to center attention upon a government problem of extraordinary importance. The call for the special session states the purpose of the meeting. No other business may be carried on at such a meeting except by a two-thirds vote of each legislative house.

The Governor's Veto Power

The ultimate weapon in the Governor's arsenal is the veto. He may nullify, subject to legislative override, bills he considers offensive or contrary to the public's interest.

The Governor's veto can be overridden, or cancelled, by a two-thirds vote of each house of the Legislature. The Governor will, in a message to the Legislature, state his reasons for vetoing a measure. This gives him a chance to get public and legislative support for his position.

The time the Governor has to exercise his veto power depends upon whether the Legislature is in session. During a session, the Governor has seven consecutive days to act. If, at the end of the seven days, he has neither signed nor vetoed the proposal, it then becomes law without his signature.

Should the Legislature adjourn before the end of the seven-day period, the Governor has fifteen consecutive days after the legislative officers present the enrolled Acts to him. (See the chapter on the Legislature.) This gives him more time to study the flood of measures generally passed in the last days of that legislative session.

A Governor's veto during those fifteen days carries greater force. This is because the Legislature will not have a chance to consider overriding the veto until the next regular or special session. Very likely this will be nearly a year away.

There is another important aspect of the Governor's veto power. This is his right to strike single items out of some proposed laws having to do with the spending of State money. In most cases the Governor must review legislative enactments as a whole. Perhaps the good features in a certain bill will be more important to have than those he may not like. But he always has the right, under the Constitution, to strike out items, or separate grants of funds, in any legislative act covering more than one appropriation. This applies mostly to the *General Appropriations Act.* The General Appropriations Act makes provision for hundreds of separate grants of money for state agencies. For practical reasons, the Governor can single out any part of the General Appropriations Act. He may veto one or more items, and approve those that remain.

The Governor's Vetoes

Of the four-year Governors, Fred P. Cone (1937–1941) vetoed the greatest number of legislative Acts, 146. Runner-up was Governor Claude R. Kirk, Jr. (1967–1971), who vetoed 108 Acts. In his eight years, Governor Reubin O'D. Askew (1971–1979) vetoed 157. D. Robert (Bob) Graham vetoed 105 in his eight years, and Bob Martinez, in one term of four years, vetoed 72. Governor Chiles vetoed 74 during his first 4-year term.

The Governor as Commander in Chief

The Governor is Commander in Chief of the military forces of the state. He alone may call out the Florida National Guard and the state militia to deal with emergencies. He cannot do this, however, if the National Guard has been called into the federal service. The militia, or home guard, organized in its absence, then takes the place of the National Guard. One important use of the National Guard is in disasters, such as hurricanes and floods.

The Governor's Orders and Proclamations

The Governor can, by an *Executive Order,* exercise certain authority. When he suspends an officer, he does so by Executive Order.

He can issue *Proclamations* which are mostly of a ceremonial nature. These are for such things as Poppy Day, American Education Week, and Cancer Control Month.

The Governor and the Press

The Governor (along with other State officers) labors under the scrutiny of what has been described as "one of the largest, most aggressive press corps outside of Washington, D.C.," and second only, if that, "in size, influence and ability" to the group of statehouse reporters at Sacramento, California.[15]

Most of the Capitol press is housed in a nearby building known as the Florida Press Center. Located at 336 East College Avenue, Tallahassee, the building was erected in 1988 by some of Florida's newspapers to house their Tallahassee Capitol correspondents, in part because the papers wished to be free from any conflict of interest from the prior occupancy of rented space in the subbasement of the old Capitol. The Florida Public Television, a State-supported service, remains in the new Capitol.

As the State's First Citizen, the Governor usually has first claim on the attention of the press although there have been occasions when "hard" news diverted some or all of the newsmen elsewhere. Once when that happened a Governor complained to the Federal Communications Commission.

For better or for worse, the Florida public forms its image of the Governor and other top officials from what the Tallahassee press corps reports of what the officials say and do.

As a member of the group wrote, the Tallahassee press corps is different from those of most statehouses because:

"They are the representatives of the fractured baronies of the Florida newspaper scene, each from a jealousy guarded bit of newspaper turf in Palm Beach, or Jacksonville, or Miami, or St. Petersburg, or Gainesville . . . the list is almost endless.

"Unlike Georgia, where the Atlanta papers alone speak to the state—unlike most states with one or two predominant cities—Florida has many baronies. No newspaper speaks for all of Florida—or to all of Florida."[16]

Television has played an increasing important role in the Capitol news scene. It well may be that a vast number of Floridians form their impression of the worthiness of a Governor or other State official from how he comes across during one-minute exposures on the six o'clock news. Three statewide broadcast news-gathering networks with bureaus in Tallahassee provide viewers throughout Florida a daily highlight of significant government news.

The tie between the Governor and the Capitol press corps, and by telephone and fax machines with the news media outside Tallahassee in Florida and the nation, is his press secretaries.

Usually a press secretary is a former newsman because of the need for an awareness of the requirements of the press for information and for knowledge of deadlines. Sometimes a press secretary serves as the Governor's speech writer, although the talents required for the two functions are quite different.

The press secretary has much to do with shaping the Governor's public image although no secretarial cosmetics can disguise the chief executive's true appearance for long.

Governor Farris Bryant (1961–1965), discussing an aspect of this matter of public image, wrote:

"It is certainly true that Governors are less accessible, in a personal sense, to people as individuals because of the growth of our State; it is also true that the media have made it possible for people to 'know' their Governor in a way that was not so even fifteen years ago. Communication with the public has necessarily become mass on the one hand, or symbolic on the other."[17]

Prior Public Service of Governors

Service in public office was in the background of nineteen of the 22 Governors elected in this century through 1990. Legislative service was the dominant characteristic, with seventeen of the nineteen having served either in the House of Representatives or Senate or both.

Only two Governors, Sidney J. Catts and Claude R. Kirk, Jr., had not served in elective office before becoming Governor although both had been candidates, Catts for the U.S. Congress in Alabama and Kirk for the U.S. Senate.

Interestingly, Catts, Kirk and Martinez were the only successful gubernatorial nominees of parties other than the Democratic Party. Catts, while still a member of the Democratic Party, ran in the 1916 general election as the nominee of the Prohibition Party. Kirk, a former Democrat, was a Republican when he ran for the U.S. Senate and for Governor. Martinez had switched from the Democratic Party to Republican before running for Governor.

Occupations of the Governors

Sixteen of the 22 Governors elected in this century through 1990 were lawyers by profession or had law degrees. The exceptions were: Napoleon B. Broward, tugboat owner; Albert W. Gilchrist, civil engineer, land developer and citrus grower; Sidney J. Catts, Baptist minister; Dan McCarty, citrus grower and cattleman; Haydon Burns, business consultant; Bob Martinez, full-time mayor and former restaurateur; and Wayne Mixson, farmer-cattleman. Claude R. Kirk, Jr., insurance company and investment executive, and Bob Graham, land developer, Lawton Chiles, United States Senator, had law degrees. The count of elected Governors does not include Charley E. Johns and Wayne Mixson since they came to the office to complete the term of an elected chief executive.

The Age of Governors

Of the Governors elected in this century (through 1994), the youngest at the time of inauguration was Park Trammell at thirty-seven while the oldest was Fred P. Cone, who was sixty-six.

The median age of Governors at the time of inauguration was forty-five.

---

[1] Letter from Farris Bryant, July 8, 1971.
[2] Letter from LeRoy Collins, July 27, 1971.
[3] Askew, *Tallahassee Democrat*, July 1, 1972.
[4] William M. Barr and Frederick B. Karl, "Executive Suspension and Removal of Public Officers under the 1968 Florida Constitution," *University of Florida Law Review*, Vol. XXIII, No. 4.
[5] Letter from Farris Bryant, July 8, 1971.

⁶Letter from LeRoy Collins, July 27, 1971.
⁷William M. Barr and Frederick B. Karl, "Executive Suspension and Removal of Public Officers under the 1968 Florida Constitution, " *University of Florida Law Review*, Vol. XXIII (Summer, 1971), 635.
⁸*Florida: Across the Threshold,* The Administration of Governor LeRoy Collins (Tallahassee: 1961), p. 392.
⁹Letter from Farris Bryant, July 8, 1971.
¹⁰Memorandum from Jill Chamberlain, Assistant Press Secretary to Governor Graham, February 1, 1984.
¹¹Millard F. Caldwell, "The Governor's Duties and Responsibilities," an address before the 31st Annual Meeting of the Florida State Chamber of Commerce at St. Petersburg, December 2, 1947.
¹²Letter from Farris Bryant, July 8, 1971.
¹³Letter from Fuller Warren, July 8, 1971.
¹⁴Reubin O'D. Askew (Remarks to Legislature), *Journal,* House of Representatives, June 18, 1971, p. 43.
¹⁵James H. Minter, "The State's Ace Sleuths and Scribblers," *St. Petersburg Times* (Floridian Magazine Section), March 22, 1970.
¹⁶James H. Minter, "The State's Ace Sleuths and Scribblers," *St. Petersburg Times* (Floridian Magazine Section), March 22, 1970.
¹⁷Letter from Farris Bryant, July 8, 1971.

President Clinton was the second U.S. President to spend the night at the Governor's Mansion when he was the guest of Governor and Mrs. Chiles on March 29, 1995.   Eric F. Tournay

The Governor

Lawton M. Chiles, Democrat

"The supreme executive power shall be vested in a governor."
Florida Constitution, Article IV, Section 1

When Lawton Mainor Chiles, Jr., swore the oath of faithful performance as 41st Governor of the State of Florida, he had already established these two historic political mileposts:

1. As "Walkin' Lawton," he had hiked 1,033 miles in 91 days from Pensacola to Dade County in 1970 creating an identity which enabled him to emerge from the relative obscurity of the State Senate to election as a United States Senator.

His four Democratic opponents included a recent Governor, a then Speaker of the state House of Representatives, a former House member, and a well-known Afro-American. The three Republicans included a senior member of the United States House of Representatives and a member of the United States Court of Appeals.

2. As a candidate for governor in 1990, Chiles, to the consternation/amazement of friends, foes and national political observers, set a $100 limit on contributions. As another counterbalance for Governor Martinez's $1,500-a-plate fund-raising dinners, Chiles offered $1.50-a-guest hot-dog feasts.

His energies renewed after a 15-month hiatus from politics and Washington's federal government gridlock. Chiles mounted what *Time* magazine described as a "corny but believable populist bid." The centerpiece of Chiles' offensive was an assault on big money in politics.

Chiles' sense of timing was amazing. The pundits said he pulled even with Martinez in the week before the general election and passed him during the final weekend.

The Tallahassee Democrat's headline on the morning after election day 1994 read: "Undefeated Chiles scrapes out win of his political life." Chiles pulled off a razor thin win, over real-estate developer Jeb Bush, son of former President George Bush, with support from South Florida.

A self styled "he-coon" of political strategy, Chiles entered his second four-year term prepared for a new fight for his unfinished agenda on healthcare and tax reform.

Lawton Mainor Chiles, Jr., was born in Lakeland on April 3, 1930. He attended Lakeland public schools; graduated, University of Florida, 1952, and from the university's law school in 1955. He was chosen for Florida Blue Key, the Hall of Fame, and Alpha Tau Omega. Chiles served in the United States army as an artillery officer during the Korean conflict, 1953–1954. He was admitted to the Florida Bar in 1955 and commenced practice in Lakeland. His affiliations included Kiwanis, National Society of Sons of the American Revolution, and Polk County Association for Retarded Children. He was a legislative counselor for Florida Boys' State and the first Boys' State participant to return to Boys' State as a legislator. He served in the Florida House of Representatives in 1958–1966, and in the State Senate, 1966–1970. He was Chairman of the Florida Law Revision Commission, 1968–1970. He was elected as a Democrat to the United States Senate in 1970, reelected in 1976 and again in 1982. He retired from the Senate on January 3, 1989.

Mrs. Chiles is the former Rhea Grafton of Coral Gables. The Chiles have four adult children: Tandy Chiles Barrett, Lawton (Bud) Chiles III, Ed Chiles, and Rhea Gay Chiles-McKinnon.

The Governor and Mrs. Chiles may be regarded as interlocking parts of a team. In his inaugural address, the Governor said of Rhea Chiles: "On this platform today, I'm blessed to have my closest confidant—my best friend—my *key* political advisor—the Love of my life—my wife and the mother of my children. Rhea fills all these roles and she now is also your First Lady of Florida."

Legal basis for the office of Governor: Article IV, Section 1, Constitution, and Chap. 14, Florida Statutes. *Methods of selection:* Elected by the qualified voters. *Qualifications:* When elected, shall be an elector, not less than 30 years old, and a resident of the state for the preceding seven years. *Term:* Four years. Term ends January 5, 1999. May be elected to one successive term. *Method of Removal:* Through conviction in the Senate on impeachment charges brought by the House of Representatives. *Compensation:* $101,764 a year, and perquisites, including the use of the Executive Mansion at Tallahassee.

The Governor and Mrs. Chiles
Mickey Adair, Available Light Photography

Executive Office of the Governor

[NOTE: Unless otherwise stated, address is The Capitol, Tallahassee 32399-0001]

Executive
Lawton M. Chiles
Governor
(904) 488-2272

Lieutenant Governor
Kenneth H. "Buddy" MacKay
Lieutenant Governor
(904) 488-4711

Legislative Affairs
Lillie Bogan
Jon Moyle, Jr.
(904) 488-5000

Chief Inspector General
Janet Ferris
(904) 922-4637

Operations
Linda Loomis Shelley
Chief of Staff
(904) 488-5603

Legal
Dexter Douglass
General Counsel
(904) 488-3494

Budget Director
Robert Bradley
(904) 488-9041

Press Office
Ron Sachs, Communications Director
Jo Miglino, Press Secretary
(904) 488-5394

State departments responsible to the Governor:

Business and Professional Regulation
Commerce
Community Affairs
Health & Rehabilitative Services
Transportation
Corrections

Environmental Protection
Labor & Employment Security
Citrus
Elder Affairs
Management Services
Lottery
Juvenile Justice

State departments responsible to Governor and Cabinet:

Revenue
Highway Safety & Motor Vehicles

Law Enforcement
Veterans Affairs

(See chart of *Executive Department Organization* on page 12)

Governors of the Territory

The unified Territory of Florida was established March 30, 1822, with President Monroe signing into law a Congressional act providing for a government headed by a Governor and a Legislative Council. The Legislative Council was to be composed of 13 of the "most fit and discreet persons of the Territory," appointed annually by the President, with the advice and consent of the Senate.

William P. DuVal of Kentucky was commissioned April 17, 1822, as Governor "in and over the Territory of Florida." He arrived in Pensacola and assumed his duties as Governor on June 20, 1822.

1822–1834 William P. DuVal
1834–1835 John H. Eaton
1835–1840 Richard Keith Call
1840–1841 Robert Raymond Reid
1841–1844 Richard Keith Call
1844–1845 John Branch

Governors of the State

1845–1849 William D. Moseley—Democrat
1849–1853 Thomas Brown—Whig
A. K. Allison[1]—Democrat
1853–1857 James E. Broome—Democrat
1857–1861 Madison S. Perry—Democrat
1861–1865 John Milton—Democrat
1865 A. K. Allison[1]—Democrat
1865 William Marvin[2]
1865–1868 David S. Walker—Conservative
1868–1872 Harrison Reed—Republican
William H. Gleason[3]—Republican
Samuel T. Day[3]—Republican
1873–1874 Ossian B. Hart—Republican
1874–1877 M. L. Stearns[4]—Republican
1877–1881 George F. Drew—Democrat
1881–1885 William D. Bloxham—Democrat
1885–1889 Edward A. Perry—Democrat
1889–1893 Francis P. Fleming—Democrat
1893–1897 Henry L. Mitchell—Democrat
1897–1901 William D. Bloxham—Democrat
1901–1905 William S. Jennings—Democrat
1905–1909 Napoleon B. Broward—Democrat
1909–1913 Albert W. Gilchrist—Democrat
1913–1917 Park Trammell—Democrat
1917–1921 Sidney J. Catts—Democrat (elected as candidate of Prohibition Party)
1921–1925 Cary A. Hardee—Democrat
1925–1929 John W. Martin—Democrat
1929–1933 Doyle E. Carlton—Democrat
1933–1937 David Sholtz—Democrat
1937–1941 Fred P. Cone—Democrat
1941–1945 Spessard L. Holland—Democrat
1945–1949 Millard F. Caldwell—Democrat
1949–1953 Fuller Warren—Democrat
1953 Daniel T. McCarty—Democrat
1953–1955 Charley E. Johns[5]—Democrat
1955–1957 LeRoy Collins[6]—Democrat
1957–1961 LeRoy Collins—Democrat
1961–1965 Farris Bryant—Democrat
1965–1967 Haydon Burns[7]—Democrat
1967–1971 Claude R. Kirk, Jr.—Republican
1971–1975 Reubin O'D. Askew—Democrat
1975–1979 Reubin O'D. Askew[8]—Democrat
1979–1983 D. Robert Graham—Democrat
1983–1987 D. Robert Graham—Democrat
1987 J. Wayne Mixson[9]—Democrat

1987–1991 Robert (Bob) Martinez—
Republican

1991–1999 Lawton M. Chiles—
Democrat

---

[1]Served twice as Acting Governor: From September 16 to October 3, 1853, as Speaker of the House of Representatives during the absence from the state of Governor Brown and Senate President R. J. Floyd, and again as Senate President after the death of Governor Milton on April 1, 1865, and until ousted by Federal authorities in the latter part of May, 1865, his last official act recorded in the letter book of the Governor's office having been dated May 19.
[2]Provisional Governor by Presidential proclamation, July 13, 1865.
[3]Authority of both Gleason and Day disputed and neither usually counted in listing governors.
[4]Lieutenant Governor, became Governor upon death of O. B. Hart, March 18, 1874.
[5]President of the Senate, became Acting Governor upon death of Dan T. McCarty, September 28, 1953.
[6]Elected to complete term of Governor McCarty, inaugurated January 4, 1955.
[7]Two-year term, to change election cycle.
[8]Constitution amended in 1968 to allow Governor to seek election to successive four-year term.
[9]Served three days because of resignation of Governor Graham to take oath as United States Senator.
Constitution amended in 1968 to allow Governor to seek election to successive four-year term.

First Ladies of Florida

Territorial:
March 10–October 6, 1821 Rachel Donelson Jackson (Mrs. Andrew)
1822–1834 Nancy Hynes DuVal (Mrs. William Pope)
1834–1835 Peggy O'Neale Timberlake Eaton (Mrs. John Henry)
1835–1840 Mary Letitia Kirkman Call (Mrs. Richard Keith)
1840–1841 Mary Martha Smith Reid (Mrs. Robert Raymond)
1844–1845 Elizabeth Foort Branch (Mrs. John)

Statehood:
1845–1849 William Dunn Moseley (Widower)
1849–1853 Elizabeth Simpson Brown (Mrs. Thomas)
1853–1857 Martha Macon Hawkins Broome (Mrs. James Emilius)
1857–1861 Martha Starke Peay Perry (Mrs. Madison Starke)
1861–1865 Caroline Howze Milton (Mrs. John)
April 1–May 19, 1865 Elizabeth S. Coleman Allison (Mrs. Abraham Kurkindolle)
July 13–December 20, 1865 Harriett Newell Marvin (Mrs. William)
1865–1868 Philoclea Alson Walker (Mrs. David Shelby)
1868–1873 Chloe Merrick Reed (Mrs. Harrison)
1873–1874 Catherine Smith Campbell Hart (Mrs. Ossian Bingley)
1874–1877 Marcellus Lovejoy Stearns (Bachelor)
1877–1871 Amelia Dickens Drew (Mrs. George Franklin)
1881–1885, 1897–1901 Mary C. Davis Bloxham (Mrs. William Dunnington)
1885–1889 Wathen Herbert Taylor Perry (Mrs. Edward Alysworth)
1889–1893 Floride Lydia Pearson Fleming (Mrs. Francis Philip)
1893–1897 Mary Eugenia Spencer Mitchell (Mrs. Henry Laurens)
1901–1905 May Austin Mann Jennings (Mrs. William Sherman)
1905–1909 Annie Isabell Douglass Broward (Mrs. Napoleon Bonaparte)
1909–1913 Albert Waller Gilchrist (Bachelor)
1913–1917 Virginia Darby Trammell (Mrs. Park)
1917–1921 Alice May Campbell Catts (Mrs. Sidney Johnston)

1921–1925 Maude Randell Hardee (Mrs. Cary Augustus)
1925–1929 Lottie Wilt Pepper Martin (Mrs. John Wellborn)
1929–1933 Nell Ray Carlton (Mrs. Doyle Elam)
1933–1937 Alice May Agee Sholtz (Mrs. David)
1937–1941 Mildred Victoria Thompson Cone (Mrs. Frederick Preston)
1941–1945 Mary Agnes Groover Holland (Mrs. Spessard Lindsey)
1945–1949 Mary Rebecca Harwood Caldwell (Mrs. Millard Fillmore)
1949–1953 Barbara Manning Warren (Mrs. Fuller)
January 6–September 28, 1953 Olie Brown McCarty (Mrs. Daniel Thomas)
1953–1955 Thelma Brinson Johns (Mrs. Charley Eugene)
1955–1961 Mary Call Darby Collins (Mrs. Thomas LeRoy)
1961–1965 Julia Burnett Bryant (Mrs. Cecil Farris)
1965–1967 Mildred Carlyon Burns (Mrs. William Haydon)
1967–1971 Erika Mattfeld Kirk (Mrs. Claude Roy, Jr.)
1971–1979 Donna Lou Harper Askew (Mrs. Reuben O'Donovan)
1979–1987 Adele Khoury Graham (Mrs. D. Robert)
January 3–6, 1987 Margie Grace Mixson (Mrs. John Wayne)
1987–1991 Mary Jane Marino Martinez (Mrs. Robert)
1991–1999 Rhea Grafton Chiles (Mrs. Lawton Mainor, Jr.)

Mrs. Lawton Chiles in the kitchen of the preinaugural residence on Sixth Avenue in Tallahassee.
Mark Wallheiser, Tallahassee Democrat

The Lieutenant Governor

Kenneth H. "Buddy" MacKay,
Democrat

"There shall be a lieutenant governor. He shall perform such duties pertaining to the office of governor as shall be assigned to him by the governor, except when otherwise provided by law, and such other duties as may be prescribed by law."

Florida Constitution, Article IV, Section 2

Kenneth Hood MacKay, Jr., 14th Lieutenant Governor of the State of Florida, was elected in tandem with Governor Chiles.

"Buddy" MacKay had served in the Florida House of Representatives 1968–1974 from Marion and Alachua counties. He then went to the State Senate and served 1974–1980 from the Sixth District, Marion and Alachua counties.

He was an unsuccessful candidate for the United States Senate in 1980 but was elected as a Democrat to the United States House of Representatives, serving three terms commencing in 1983. He was elected the Democratic nominee for the United States Senate in 1988 but lost a tightly contested general election to the Republican nominee, Connie Mack. MacKay received 49.6 percent of the vote.

"Buddy" was born March 22, 1933 in Ocala. He received a B.S. and B.A. from the University of Florida in 1954, and an LL.B from the University's Law School in 1961. He was elected to Florida Blue Key and installed in the University's Hall of Fame. Mrs. MacKay is the former Anne Selph of Ocala. They have four sons, John, Ken, Ben and Andy. The Lieutenant Governor is Presbyterian. He served in the United States Air Force 1955–1958 attaining the rank of Captain. He was a lawyer in Ocala and Miami and a citrus grower.

Assigned Service of Lieutenant Governors

Tom Adams served in Governor Askew's first term as Secretary of Commerce. J.H. (Jim) Williams was Governor Askew's Secretary of Administration in his second term. J. Wayne Mixson served as Governor Graham's Secretary of Commerce during Graham's second term. Governor Martinez designated Bobby Brantley first as his legislative liaison and later as his Secretary of Commerce. Kenneth H. "Buddy" MacKay has played a broader role in the Chiles administration, helping to shape major policy initiatives and working with state agencies and the Legislature to implement them.

The Lieutenant Governor is the first in the line of succession in the event of a vacancy in the office of Governor. The Constitution also provided that in the party primaries and general elections "all candidates for the offices of Governor and Lieutenant Governor shall form joint candidacies in a manner prescribed by law so that each voter shall cast a single vote for a candidate for Governor and a candidate for Lieutenant Governor running together."

Legal basis for the Office of Lieutenant Governor: Article IV, Sections 2 and 3, Constitution, and Sections 14.056 and 20.04, Florida Statutes. *Method of selection:* Chosen by candidate for Governor to run in tandem. Elected by qualified electors. *Qualifications:* An elector, not less than 30 years of age, and resident of Florida for preceding seven years. *Term:* Four years. Present term ends January 5, 1999. *Method of removal:* By conviction in Senate on impeachment articles brought by House of Representatives. *Compensation:* $97,479 a year. *Duties:* Shall perform such duties as may be assigned by Governor.

Lieutenant Governors

Under the Constitutions of 1865 and 1868, Florida had an elected Lieutenant Governor who served as presiding officer of the Senate. This place was abolished with the adoption of the Constitution of 1885. The office was reestablished on January 7, 1969, but not as a Senate presiding officer.

These served as Lieutenant Governors: William W.J. Kelly, 1865–1868; William H. Gleason, 1868–1870; E.C. Weeks, 1870; Samuel T. Day, 1871–1873; M.L. Stearns, 1873–1874; Noble A. Hull, 1877–1879; L.W. Bethel, 1881–1885, and Milton H. Mabry, 1885–1889. (Mabry served out his term although the office was abolished by the 1885 Constitution.)

Stearns became chief executive when Governor Ossian B. Hart died on March 18, 1874.

With restoration of the office in the revision of the Constitution in 1968, Ray C. Osborne of St. Petersburg, a member of the Florida House of Representatives, was appointed by Governor Claude R. Kirk, Jr., on January 5, 1971, when he was succeeded by Tom Adams, the first Lieutenant Governor elected in tandem with a Governor. Adams served with Governor Reubin O'D. Askew in the Askew first term but was replaced by J. H. Williams for the Askew second term. Governor Bob Graham chose Wayne Mixson as his Lieutenant Governor for both of his terms.

With the resignation of Governor Bob Graham to take the oath as United States Senator on January 3, 1987, Mixson became Governor for three days as Florida's 39th Governor. Graham's resignation was occasioned by the overlappage of his terms as Governor and Senator.

Florida's first Lieutenant Governor, William W. J. Kelly served from 1865 to 1868. Escambia Lodge #15 F&A.M.

Secretary of State

Sandra B. Mortham, Republican

"The Secretary of State shall keep the records of the official acts of the Legislative and Executive Departments."
Florida Constitution, Article IV, Section 4(b)

Sandra B. Mortham, Florida's 22nd Secretary of State, was born in Erie, Pennsylvania, and came to Florida at the age of two in 1953. She attended St. Petersburg Junior College and received a bachelor of arts degree in Business and Public Administration from Eckerd College.

Secretary Mortham's rise to statewide office caps a long career of service and activism in her local community and successful races for public office. She is the first Republican woman to be elected to the Florida Cabinet, (only the second woman so elected).

She was elected Republican Leader of the Florida House of Representatives in November 1992. Upon her election, Representative Mortham became the first woman of either political party to be nominated for Speaker of the Florida House.

Elected to the House of Representatives in 1986, Mortham represented District 49 (Largo, Dunedin and Clearwater, Florida). Mortham served as Republican Leader Pro Tempore from 1990–1992. She also served as Chairman of the Pinellas County legislative delegation from 1990–1991.

Secretary Mortham is a former Largo City Commissioner and Vice Mayor. She has served on many civic and professional organizations, and served as President of the Greater Largo Chamber of Commerce.

Secretary Mortham has been a recipient of numerous awards from the education community in Florida. Mortham was recognized as an Outstanding Republican Leader in the nation and Statesman of the year of 1993.

Mortham served as Treasurer of the National Republican Legislators' Association and as Chairman of one of four standing committees at the 1992 Republican National Convention. The Atlanta Journal/Constitution called her a "political star of the future" and part of a "wave of women rising to power in the South."

She is married to Allen Mortham, who served as Assistant Principal at

Largo High School. They have two children, Allen Jr., who attends Florida State University, and Jeffrey, who attends St. Petersburg Junior College. The Morthams are members of Christ Presbyterian Church in Largo, Florida.

Legal basis for the office of Secretary of State: Article IV, Section 4, Constitution, and Chapter 15, Florida Statutes. *Method of selection:* Elected by qualified voters. *Qualifications:* An elector, not less than 30 years old, and a resident of the state for the preceding seven years. *Term:* Four years. May be reelected. Present term ends January 5, 1999. *Method of removal:* Impeachment. *Compensation:* $100,735.

HISTORY: Office of Secretary of State created by 1838 Constitution, effective with Statehood 1845. Secretary elected by joint vote of houses of Legislature. 1861 Constitution again provided for joint vote of Legislature. 1865 Constitution, elected by people. 1868 Constitution, appointed by Governor, confirmed by Senate. 1885 Constitution, elected by people. 1968 Constitution, elected by people.

The Secretaries of State

James T. Archer, *July 23, 1845-x*
A. E. Maxwell, *April 11, 1848*
C. W. Downing, *July 23, 1849*
Fred L. Villepigue, *July 1, 1853*
Benjamin F. Allen, *January 13, 1863*
George J. Alden, *August 7, 1868*
Jonathan C. Gibbs, *November 6, 1868*
S. B. McLin, *January 17, 1873*
W. D. Bloxham, *January 3, 1877*
F. W. A. Rankin, Jr., *October 1, 1880*
Jno. L. Crawford, *January 21, 1881*
H. Clay Crawford, *January 28, 1902*
W. M. Igou, *September 23, 1929*
R. A. Gray, *April 12, 1930*
Tom Adams, *January 3, 1961*
Richard B. Stone, *January 5, 1971*
Dorothy W. Glisson (Mrs. W. E.), *July 8, 1974, ad interim*
Bruce A. Smathers, *January 7, 1975*
Jesse J. McCrary, Jr., *July 19, 1978, ad interim*
George Firestone, *January 2, 1979*
Jim Smith, *August 5, 1987*
Sandra B. Mortham, *January 3, 1995*

Department of State

Head The Secretary of State, Sandra B. Mortham, The Capitol
(904) 488-3680
Assistant Secretary of State Rich Heffley
(904) 488-3680
General Counsel Don Bell
(904) 488-7690
Cabinet Aides Paul Mitchell, Kathy Miserick
(904) 488-3684
Press Secretary Stan Smith
(904) 488-3680

Legal basis: Article IV, Section 4(b), Constitution, and Chapter 15, F.S., for Secretary of State; Section 20.10 for Department of State. *Created:* 1845, for office of Secretary of State; 1969, for Department of State.

x—Date of first commission.

Note: Biographies of Secretaries Gibbs and McCrary, the only black members of the Cabinet, may be found on pages 131–132 of *The Florida Handbook 1981-1982*. Information about Secretary Glisson, the first woman Cabinet officer, also appears on page 132 of the same edition of the *Handbook*.

The Secretary of State runs the state's public records office, receiving for safekeeping documents ranging from acts of the Legislature to local ordinances and the returns of city elections involving charter changes.

The Secretary of State has a constitutional duty to safeguard the originals of legislative acts, for these are the laws binding upon citizens of Florida and persons from other states who become subject to the laws of this state.

Head of Department of State

The Secretary of State is head of the Department of State and the duties assigned in that statutory capacity are numerous. The Secretary of State oversees the operation of the department's seven divisions.

Division of Elections

The Division of Elections consists of 67 full-time employees and has an annual budget of $3.9 million for its four bureaus: Election Records, Administrative Code, Notaries Public and Information Management and Voting Systems.

During 1992, a Presidential election year and a year of legislative reapportionment, the division monitored contributions and expenditures reported by a record 1,037 state and federal candidates and 1,386 political committees. It also maintained more than 16,000 files for federal political action committees.

Due to an increase in filing fees, the number of candidates qualifying by petition rose from an average of three or four to 243 during 1992, requiring distribution of three million petition cards by the division.

The division also received an average of 7,200 telephone calls a month in 1992 seeking information and advice on election matters in addition to hundreds of walk-in and mail requests. The division filed more than 21,275 financial disclosures in 1993 and issued more than 90,720 notaries public commissions. It also investigated campaign finance law violations, certified voting systems, recorded local ordinances and codes and published the Florida Administrative Weekly for more than 2,700 subscribers.

The Division of Elections uses a computer network to collect vote totals from local offices on Election Day.

Division Director—David Rancourt (904) 488-7690
   Bureau of Elections Records (904) 488-7690
   Bureau of Administrative Code and Laws (904) 488-8427
   Bureau of Notaries (904) 488-7521

Division of Library and Information Services

This division administers the State Library, State Archives, the Florida Records Management Service and the library development and interlibrary cooperation programs. With a staff of 123, it has an operating budget of $8 million and administers state and federal grants totaling $31.3 million.

The 825,000-item library in the R.A. Gray Building in Tallahassee is the principal library for state government. It regularly processes more interlibrary loan requests than the Library of Congress.

The archives maintains more than 50 million documents and over 880,000 photographs, including records of the legislative, judicial and executive branches of Florida government. These records have great educational and legal value. Together, the library and archives research more than 54,000 inquiries each year.

The Division of Library and Information Services saves state and local government over $50 million annually through efficient records management. Florida's new State Records Storage Center includes environmentally-controlled storage for specialized media, including microfilm and magnetic tapes.

Division Director—Barratt Wilkins (904) 487-2651
   Bureau of Library Development (904) 487-2651
   Bureau of Library and Network Services (904) 487-2651
   Bureau of Archives and Records Management (904) 487-2073

Division of Corporations

The Division of Corporations is the state's central statewide repository for business filings, financing statements, fictitious name registrations, federal tax lien filings, and trademark/service mark registration.

With a staff of 195 and an annual budget of $9.2 million, this is the nation's most active state corporate division. It maintains files on 1.5 million business entities and responds to an average of 40,000 telephone, computer and written inquiries daily.

It is also one of the few agencies that makes money for the state. The division now brings in more than $105 million a year in filing fees, twelve times its budget.

The division's electronic access to public records was the first in Florida government giving direct dial-in access to the data base. It also has the first electronic certification and filing service in the nation. A telephone voice response system directs about half a million calls to 40 operators each month. These facilities have enabled the division to better serve the public and saved taxpayers over a million dollars.

Some 200,000 new corporations and fictitious business names register with the Division of Corporations each year.

Division Director—David E. Mann (904) 487-6000
   Bureau of Commercial Recording (904) 487-6900
   Bureau of Commercial Information Services (904) 487-6890
   Bureau of Data Systems and Records Management (904) 487-6802

Division of Historical Resources

With a staff of 153 and an annual operating budget of $23.3 million, this division has four major program areas: historic preservation, archaeological research, the Museum of Florida History and folklife.

The bureaus of Historic Preservation and Archaeological Research work to protect and document Florida's historic buildings and archaeological sites, including underwater sites. The Bureau of Historic Preservation administers a historical grants program that totaled $12.8 million for 1994–95.

The bureau also administers the Florida Main Street program—a downtown revitalization effort that emphasizes preservation and rehabilitation of the traditional commercial areas of our smaller cities. Since 1985, less than $2 million in state funds have been invested in this program in 32 designated Main Street cities.

The Main Street program to revitalize historic districts in smaller cities has generated $174 million in reinvestment from less than $2 million in state funds.

The Bureau of Archaeological Research maintains a computerized inventory of some 84,000 archaeological and historical sites; conserves artifacts and historical objects in its Research and Conservation Laboratory and curates archaeological collections.

The Bureau of Historical Museums manages four Tallahassee historical sites that draw more than 200,000 visitors each year: the Museum of Florida History, the Old Capitol, the Union Bank and the San Luis Archaeological and Historic Site. The bureau conducts a museum grants program totaling $500,000 annually.

The Bureau of Florida Folklife, based at the Stephen Foster Folk Cultural Center in White Springs, coordinates Rural Folklife Days in mid-November and the famous Florida Folk Festival every Memorial Day weekend. These programs present more than 500 demonstrators and performers to more than 35,000 people annually. The bureau's Folklife in Education Program reaches over 15,000 children throughout the state.

The division also oversees historic preservation boards in St. Augustine, Tallahassee, Pensacola, Tampa (Tampa-Hillsborough County), Boca Raton (Palm Beach County), and Key West (Florida Keys). The boards assist the state in the promotion and protection of its historical and archaeological sites and properties through the management of 63 properties, including museums. Collectively, the boards have 53 employees and operating budgets totaling $2.6 million.

Division Director—George Percy (904)488-1480
  Bureau of Historic Preservation (904) 487-2333
  Museum of Florida History (904) 488-1484
  Bureau of Archaeological Research (904) 487-2299
  Florida Folklife Program (904) 397-2192

Division of Licensing

The Division of Licensing protects the health, safety and welfare of the public through licensing and regulation of the private security, private investigative and recovery industries; registration of sweepstakes offered in the state of Florida and licensure of concealed weapons.

This division conducts approximately 2,150 investigations per year, many resulting in revocation of licenses or fines for violation of the various statutes.

The division has 140 employees in Tallahassee and seven regional offices operating on an annual budget of $12.3 million totally funded by licensing fees and assessments from the approximately 121,000 licenses or registrations issued annually.

The Division of Licensing issues approximately 121,000 licenses annually, many of them to people wanting to carry a concealed weapon.

Division Director—John Russi (904) 488-6982
   Bureau of License Issuance (904) 488-5381
   Concealed Weapons/Firearms (904) 488-0039
   Bureau of Regulation and Enforcement (904) 487-0482
   Bureau of Licensing Support Services (904) 488-6948

Division of Cultural Affairs

The Division of Cultural Affairs, with a full-time staff of 21, administers the third largest arts budget in the nation. The division's budget for 1994–95 totals almost $21 million in state funds and over half a million dollars in federal grants.

The division administers more than 20 grant programs benefiting artists and arts projects. Over 1,200 applications are reviewed by 16 grant panels each year. An estimated 500 grants are awarded annually to support cultural activity and programming, as well as programs for construction and renovation of cultural facilities. In addition to grants programs, the division administers promotional programs that recognize notable contributions to Florida arts, such as the Florida Artists Hall of Fame, which has honored 18 Florida artists, among them Ray Charles, Ernest Hemingway and Zora Neale Hurston. The division also produces a newsletter which is distributed to artists, cultural organizations, and other interested parties to provide them with state, regional and national arts-related information.

The Florida Arts Council, a 15-member advisory board appointed by the Secretary of State, meets quarterly to recommend grant funding and encourage cultural development statewide. The John and Mable Ringling Museum of Art is also under the Department of State. It is the official state art museum and is considered to be one of the premier museums in the Southeast.

Among the many programs administered by the division are Art in State Buildings, The ACE Project (Arts for a Complete Education), Cultural Facilities and Cultural Institutions, Florida Individual Artist Fellowships, Science Museums and Youth and Children's Museums.

Division Director—Peyton Fearington (904) 487-2980
   Bureau of Grants Services (904) 487-2980
   Bureau of State Programs (904) 487-2980

Division of Administrative Services

With staff of 52 and a budget of $2.2 million, this vital division provides all support services for the department: purchasing, personnel services and benefits, planning and budgeting, financial management and graphics

Division Director—Hal Lench (904) 488-3963
   Bureau of Personnel Services (904) 488-0100
   Bureau of Planning and Budget Services (904) 488-0204
   Bureau of Financial Management (904) 488-0100
   Bureau of General Services (904) 488-1802

"Celebrate Florida"

150 Years
of
Florida Statehood

FLORIDA SESQUICENTENNIAL COMMISSION   SANDRA B. MORTHAM, SECRETARY OF STATE

Poster designed for the Department of State in celebration of 150 years of statehood.

Attorney General

Robert A. (Bob) Butterworth, Democrat

"The Attorney General shall be the chief State legal officer."
Florida Constitution, Article IV, Section 4(c)

Bob [Robert A.] Butterworth, the 33rd Attorney General of the State of Florida was born August 20, 1942, at Passaic, New Jersey, the son of Robert and Katherine Muller Butterworth.

Mr. Butterworth had a 17-year career in law, law enforcement, and public administration when he became a candidate for Attorney General in 1986. He had been called upon by Governors Reubin O'D. Askew and Bob Graham as a troubleshooter. He was reelected without opposition in 1990, and defeated Republican Henry Ferro in 1994.

The General earned a degree of Bachelor in Business Administration with a major in accounting from the University of Florida in 1965. He received a Juris Doctorate from the University of Miami Law School in 1969 followed by advanced studies in international law. He served as an adjunct professor for Nova University's Graduate School of Criminal Law from June, 1976, until December, 1978.

Among his public responsibilities: Interim Mayor of Sunrise, from December 10, 1984, until election to fill vacancy on September 10, 1985; Executive Director of the State Department of Highway Safety and Motor Vehicles, appointed by Governor Graham and Cabinet on November 2, 1982; Sheriff of Broward County, appointed by Governor Reubin O'D. Askew on December 21, 1978, elected November, 1980; Circuit Judge, appointed by Governor Askew, and subsequently elected without opposition; County Court Judge, December 1, 1974, until January 23, 1978; and Assistant State Attorney and prosecutor in Broward and Dade counties.

He was associated in 1969-1970 with the national accounting firm of Price Waterhouse.

A resident of Broward County since 1950, at the time of election as Attorney General he and his wife, Marta Prado, a business woman, resided in Hollywood. The couple have a son, Brandon, and a daughter, BreAnne.

Legal basis for the office of Attorney General: Article IV, Section 4, Constitution, and Chapter 16, Florida Statutes. *Method of selection:* Elected by the qualified voters. *Qualifications:* An elector, not less than 30 years old, a resident of the state for the preceding seven years, and a member of The Florida Bar for the preceding five years. *Term:* Four years. May be reelected. Present term ends January 5, 1999. *Method of removal:* Impeachment. *Compensation:* $100,735

HISTORY: Office of Attorney General created by 1838 Constitution, effective with Statehood 1845, as office of Judicial Department. Attorney General elected by joint vote of houses of Legislature. 1861 Constitution again provided for joint vote of Legislature. 1865 Constitution, elected by people. 1868 Constitution, appointed by Governor, confirmed by Senate, for first time as member of Executive Department. 1885 Constitution, elected by people. 1968 Constitution, elected by people.

The Attorneys General

Joseph Branch, *July 26, 1845-x*
Augustus E. Maxwell, *July 14, 1846*
James T. Archer, *April 11, 1848*
David P. Hogue, *October 14, 1848*
Mariano D. Papy, *April 19, 1853*
John B. Galbraith, *March 2, 1861*
James D. Westcott, Jr., *1868–1868-A*
A. R. Meek, *1868–1870-A*
Sherman Conant, *1870–1871-A*
J. B. C. Drew *1871–1872-A*
H. Bisbee, Jr., *1872–1872-A*
J. P. C. Emmons, *1872–1873-A*
William A. Cocke, *January 16, 1873*
George P. Raney, *January 3, 1877*
C. M. Cooper, *January 20, 1885*
William B. Lamar, *January 8, 1889*

James B. Whitfield, *February 28, 1903*
W. H. Ellis, *February 15, 1904*
Park Trammell, *January 5, 1909*
Thomas F. West, *January 7, 1913*
Van C. Swearingen, *September 1, 1917*
Rivers Buford, *January 4, 1921*
J. B. Johnson, *December 4, 1925*
Fred H. Davis, *June 4, 1927*
Cary D. Landis, *March 9, 1931*
George Couper Gibbs, *May 16, 1938*
J. Tom Watson, *January 7, 1941*
Richard W. Ervin, *January 4, 1949*
James W. Kynes, *January 17, 1964*
Earl Faircloth, *January 5, 1965*
Robert L. Shevin, *January 5, 1971*
Jim Smith, *January 2, 1979*
Bob Butterworth, *January 6, 1987*

A—Official records of the period 1866–1872 not in possession of Secretary of State. Whereabouts unknown.

x—Date of first commission. In most instances, term of predecessor ended at noon of the same day.

Department of Legal Affairs

Head Attorney General Bob Butterworth, The Capitol, Tallahassee 32399
(904) 487-1963
Deputy Attorney General Peter Antonacci
Statewide Prosecutor Melanie Ann Hines

Legal basis: Article IV, Section 4(c), Constitution, and Chapter 16, F.S., for Attorney General, and Section 20.11, F.S., for Department of Legal Affairs. *Created:* 1845 for Attorney General; 1969, for Department of Legal Affairs.

The powers and duties of the Attorney General come from three primary sources. They come from the common law. They come also from the State Constitution. And they come from laws enacted by the Legislature.

The common law of England, as it was on July 4, 1776, still is in effect in Florida except where the common law has been replaced by the provisions of the United States and Florida Constitutions or by enactments of the Legislature.

Represents State in Courts of Appeal

At common law, it is the duty of the Attorney General to appear on behalf of the state in all suits in the courts of appeal—the District Courts of Appeal and the Supreme Court—in which the state either may be a party or is in any manner interested.

The criminal division of the Office of the Attorney General defends the state on appeals from criminal convictions through state and federal courts. It is involved in opposing writs of habeas corpus and certiorari filed by persons seeking release from custody. Additionally, the Attorney General serves as legal adviser to the Office of the Governor in extradition proceedings, those in which another state requests the return of a person in Florida charged with a criminal offense elsewhere. If the sought-after person requests a hearing, an Assistant Attorney General usually presides at the hearing and reports to the Governor.

Head of Department of Legal Affairs

As the state's chief legal officer, the Attorney General is the head of the Department of Legal Affairs.

The Department of Legal Affairs has responsibility for "providing all legal services required by any department, unless otherwise provided by law. However, the Attorney General may authorize other counsel where emergency circumstances exist and shall authorize other counsel when professional conflict of interest is present. Each board, however designated, of which the Attorney General is a member may retain legal services in lieu of those provided by the Attorney General and the Department of Legal Affairs." *Divisions:* Administration, Opinions, Criminal Law and Civil Law. The divisions maintain operations centers, regional facilities and resident offices throughout the state and are supported by advisory councils reflective of the criminal justice agencies served by the Department.

Most public agencies—state, county, district, city—inquire of the Attorney General when they have a question of law. Some hundreds of opinions will be given by the Attorney General and his staff during the course of a year. These opinions are not binding, but are often used as a basis for official action.

The Attorney General does not answer questions of law from private persons.

As a member of the Cabinet, the Attorney General serves on management boards of the Executive Branch. This places him in a policymaking position where he may vote in opposition to colleagues who could be calling on him for legal advice in the same matters.

Duality of Role

This duality of role has produced awkward moments and resulted in outside legal counsel being retained. For example, as Attorney General from January, 1941, to January, 1949, J. Tom Watson took to the courts his disagreements with the Governor and Cabinet members on board business.

It is this duality, in part, that also has likely resulted in the unwillingness of the Legislature to require state agencies to use the Attorney General's services exclusively. Too, a number of state agencies—the Department of Transportation, for example—have sufficient volume of a specialized nature as to justify the full-time employment of staff attorneys.

Law Enforcement Assistance. In 1981, Chapter 406, F.S., created a Medical Examiners Commission within the Department, with authority to oversee the distribution of state funds for medical examiner districts. Further, the Commission has the power to conduct investigations of medical examiners and remove or suspend them, if necessary.

Division Directors:
 Kent Perez, Cabinet Affairs, (904) 487-1963
 Richard Doran, Assistant Deputy for Legal Affairs, (904) 488-8253
 Les Garringer, Assistant Deputy for Economic Crimes, (904) 488-9105
 Jerry Currington, General Civil, (904) 488-9853
 Joslyn Wilson, Opinions, (904) 488-9853
 Carlos McDonald, Legislative Affairs, (904) 487-1963

The Office of Statewide Prosecutor

In 1986, the voters of Florida approved a constitutional amendment creating the position of Statewide Prosecutor. Under the amendment, the statewide prosecutor is selected by and serves at the pleasure of the Attorney General for a term of up to four years with the selection process renewed at the end of the term. The Statewide Prosecutor has the authority to investigate and prosecute organized crime and certain major felonies that cross the boundaries of Florida's 20 judicial circuits. In addition, the Statewide Prosecutor's office works closely with sheriffs, police departments and other criminal justice agencies on both the state and federal levels.

Governor and Cabinet / 49

The business of Florida's state government largely is transacted at this table by the Governor and members of the Cabinet. It is here that the public has its opportunity to address the State government.

Department of Commerce, Division of Tourism

Comptroller

Robert Milligan, Republican

"The Comptroller shall serve as the chief fiscal officer of the State, and shall settle and approve accounts against the State."
Florida Constitution, Article IV, Section 4(d)

Bob (Robert F.) Milligan, the 27th Comptroller of the State of Florida was born on December 12, 1932. He was one of seven children reared on a small farm near Teaneck, New Jersey.

He was the sixth member of his family to serve in the military, a 1956 engineering graduate of the U.S. Naval Academy at Annapolis. He earned his M.S. in Business Administration (Defense Systems Analysis-Economics) at the University of Rochester, and completed Doctoral studies in Economics at the University of Maryland.

Milligan was G-3 of a Marine Amphibious Brigade for three years. Responsible for the conduct of four to six joint/combined (NATO) exercises and contingency operations annually. He was a reconnaissance captain in Vietnam 1965–66 and returned to the war as a major three years later, responsible for training for, planning, and executing combat operations.

As a brigadier general, he was Director of Research and Development for the Marine Corps. For three years he led the modernization efforts of the Marine Corps and annually supervised the execution of a 400-million-dollar budget. He also was the Commanding General of the 6th Marine Amphibious Brigade, the first brigade tasked to implement the maritime prepositioning strategic deployment concept. Maritime prepositioning was the cornerstone of the Marine Corps' capability to rapidly provide combat ready forces in the critical early stages of Desert Shield/Storm.

As a major general, he was Commander, U.S. Forces Caribbean, a sub-unified command tasked with regional security responsibility for the Caribbean basin including Cuba. He was responsible for 11 million dollars annual training, security assistance, and military education program for 12 independent Caribbean nations.

As a lieutenant general he was Commanding General of Fleet Marine Forces, Pacific, and Marine Corps Bases, Pacific. He was a Component Commander, of the operating forces of the Marine Corp, consisting of 92,000 Marines and sailors. He was responsible for training and equipping Marine forces for joint, combined, or fleet operations, and directed the deployment, sustained logistical support, and return of 62,000 Marines committed to Desert Storm. General Milligan was accountable for development and execution of a 450 million dollar annual training and operating budget.

At the zenith of his military career, he was nominated by the Commandant of the Marine Corps and interviewed by Secretary of the Navy, Secretary of Defense, and Chairman, Joint Chiefs of Staff to become Commandant of the Marine Corps. He finished second.

General Milligan and his wife June, who have four grown children, retired to Panama City's Bay Point area in 1991 with 39 years of Navy and Marine Corps service.

He met Tom Slade, Florida Republican Party Chairman at a party breakfast and was impressed with Slade's ambition to see Republicans take over state government. Later Slade remembered the General in Panama City and recruited Milligan for the Republican slate. A self proclaimed "nonpolitician" Milligan toppled one of Florida's premier politicians in an unconventional, under-financed campaign that depended heavily on fellow ex-Marines who called friends and asked them to call their friends for Milligan.

General Milligan's stated goal is to reform the office of comptroller, and revitalize the function of the chief fiscal officer of the state.

Legal basis for the office of Comptroller: Article IV, Section 4, Constitution, and Chap. 17, Florida Statutes. *Method of selection:* Elected by qualified voters. *Qualifications:* An elector, not less than 30 years old, and a resident of the state for the preceding seven years. *Term:* Four years. May be reelected. Present term ends January 5, 1999. *Method of removal:* Impeachment. *Compensation:* $100,735

HISTORY: Office of Comptroller created by 1838 Constitution, effective with Statehood 1845. Comptroller elected by joint vote of houses of Legislature. 1861 Constitution again provided for joint vote of Legislature. 1865 Constitution, elected by people. 1868 Constitution, appointed by Governor, confirmed by Senate. 1885 Constitution, elected by people. 1968 Constitution, elected by people.

The Comptrollers

Nathaniel P. Bemis, *July 23, 1845-x*
Hugh Archer, *Aug. 26, 1845*
Nathaniel P. Bemis, *Jan. 2, 1847*
Hugh Archer, *July 24, 1847*
Simon Towle, *Dec. 28, 1847*
John Beard, *Jan. 25, 1851*
Theodore W. Brevard, *April 3, 1854*
James T. Archer, *Nov. 27, 1854*
Theodore W. Brevard, *Jan. 24, 1855*
Robert C. Williams, *Dec. 14, 1860*
Walter Gwynn, *May 26, 1863*
John Beard, *Jan. 17, 1866*
Robert H. Gamble, *Aug. 29, 1868*

Clayton A. Cowgill, *Jan. 15, 1873*
Columbus Drew, *Jan. 12, 1877*
W.D. Barnes, *Jan. 13, 1881*
W.D. Bloxham, *May 1, 1890*
W.H. Reynolds, *Jan. 3, 1897*
A.C. Croom, *July 29, 1901*
W.V. Knott, *Feb. 17, 1912*
Ernest Amos, *Jan. 2, 1917*
J.M. Lee, *Jan. 3, 1933*
C.M. Gay, *Oct. 9, 1946*
Ray E. Green, *April 11, 1955*
Fred O. Dickinson, Jr., *Sept. 1, 1965*
Gerald Lewis, *Jan. 7, 1975*
Robert F. Milligan, *Jan. 3, 1995*

x—Date of first commission. In most instances, term of predecessor ended at noon of same day.

Department of Banking and Finance

Head The Comptroller, Robert F. Milligan, The Capitol
(904) 488-0370

Legal basis: Article IV, Section 4(d), Constitution, and Section 20.12, F.S. *Created:* 1845 (as Comptroller), 1969 (as Department). Under Reorganization Act of 1969, duties, powers, and functions of the Comptroller, Office of the Comptroller, Banking Commissioner, and Securities Commission were transferred to the new Department of Banking and Finance.

The Comptroller (pronounced kon-trol-er, with the accent on the second syllable) has been thought of, first of all, as the "watchdog of the public treasury." This role is emphasized in the official seal of the office. It shows a large safe guarded by a dog, with the word "Defendo" beneath. "Defendo" means "I defend."

Head of Department of Banking and Finance

In addition to his Constitutional responsibilities, the Comptroller has been designated head of the Department of Banking and Finance by the Legislature. In the performance of these statutory duties, the Comptroller serves as Commissioner of Banking.

The Comptroller's Constitutional duties embrace the writing of millions of warrants (State checks) each year. These pay the State's debts, including the salaries of officers and employees, the benefits for welfare and unemployment, and the operating expenses of the government.

A State warrant bears the signature of the Comptroller, printed by the check-writing machine.

Duties as Chief Fiscal Officer

As chief fiscal officer, the Comptroller makes sure all money paid into the State Treasury has been correctly deposited. He also must determine whether payments sought to be made by State agencies are being charged against the proper fund. It is his duty, too, to be certain these agency expenditures are kept within the money appropriated to the individual agencies by the Legislature and released by the Department of Administration.

Supervises Financial Institutions

Among the functions of the Comptroller as head of the Department of Banking and Finance is the chartering of State banks and their supervision thereafter.

The Comptroller also supervises State savings and loans, trust companies, mortgage brokerage businesses, credit unions, and small loan companies. Teams of examiners visit all these State-supervised financial institutions from time to time to determine compliance with State laws and regulations.

The Comptroller regulates all privately-owned cemeteries and administers the disposition of money and other valuables abandoned in depositories either through locating owners or converting the proceeds for the State's school fund.

Registration of Securities

The Comptroller acts upon applications for the sale of securities within Florida.

The Division of Securities
Director Donald Saxon
Executive Center   488-9805

The Comptroller administers the Florida Securities Act through the Division of Securities. The Act, which is designed to protect investors, requires the registration of securities (with some exceptions) before they can be offered for sale to the public. Securities dealers, salespeople and investment advisors are licensed and regulated by the Comptroller.

The Division of Accounting and Auditing
Asst. Director William Monroe
1301 Capitol Tallahassee 32399-0350   (904) 488-3066

Through the Division of Accounting and Auditing, the Comptroller is responsible for the spending of $38 billion in state money each year. While the Florida Legislature determines the state's budget, the Comptroller pays all the bills. This includes all money spent by the state, from employee salaries to workers' compensation.

The Comptroller has the responsibility to ensure that all tax money is spent as the law intends. He must also determine that the state has sufficient funds to pay all bills.

The Division of Banking
Director Art Simon
1301 Capitol   488-1111

Through the Division of Banking, the Comptroller regulates all state-chartered banks, savings and loan associations and credit unions. (Federally chartered financial institutions, most of which have the words "federal" or "national" in their titles, are regulated by the federal government.)

As Banking Commissioner, the Comptroller is responsible to Floridians for ensuring that state-chartered financial institutions are operated in a sound and businesslike manner. On a regular basis, bank examiners check the records and procedures of all the financial institutions regulated by the Comptroller.

The Division of Finance
Director Linda Dilworth
Fuller Warren Building   487-2583

The Comptroller regulates finance companies doing business in Florida through the Division of Finance. The Division is responsible for the licensing and regulation of mortgage brokers, consumer finance companies, sales finance companies, retail installment sales companies, trading stamp companies and companies which issue money orders and travelers' checks. The Division also licenses and inspects private cemeteries in Florida.

The disposition of unclaimed money, property and deposits left in financial institutions (called abandoned property), is also handled through the Division of Finance.

The Treasurer and Insurance Commissioner

C. William (Bill) Nelson, Democrat

"The Treasurer shall keep all State funds and securities. He shall disburse State funds only upon the order of the Comptroller."
Florida Constitution, Article IV, Section 4(e)

C. William Nelson, a fifth-generation Floridian, was born at Victoria Hospital, Miami on September 29, 1942, the son of Nannie Merle Nelson of Chipley and Clarence W. Nelson of Melbourne, who was a high school principal, a real estate developer and a member of the first law class at the University of Miami.

While attending Melbourne High School, Mr. Nelson was President of Key Club International, 1959–1960; President of 4-H Club of Florida, 1961; and President of the Student Body 1959–1960. He was President of his Freshman Class at the University of Florida 1960–1961, but graduated with a B.A. and was Class Orator at Yale University in 1965. He earned his J.D. at the University of Virginia in 1968.

Mr. Nelson rose to the rank of Captain during his service in the United States Army 1968–1970.

While a member of the law firm Nelson, Normile and Dettmer, 1970–1979 he was elected and served in the Florida House of Representatives 1972–1978. He was elected to the United States House of Representatives from the 11th Congressional District and served from 1979–1991. During that service he was Chairman of the Space Subcommittee, Chairman of the Congressional Travel and Tourism Caucus, 1987–1991. He served on Congressional committees for Science, Space and Technology, 1979–1991; Budget, 1979–1985; and Banking Finance and Urban Affairs, 1985–1991.

Mr. Nelson trained and flew with the crew of STS-61 C, Columbia, the 24th flight of the Space Shuttle. The shuttle launched January 12, 1986 from Kennedy Space Center (not far from where his paternal grandfather, Charles Hart Nelson, homesteaded a patch of sandy soil in 1915). The landing was January 18, 1986 at Edwards Air Force Base, California. He conducted 12 experiments for cancer research and performed the first American stress test in space. The article "Preliminary Investigations of Protein Crystal Growth Using the Space Shuttle" with coauthors Dr. Charles Bugg and Dr. Lawrence DeLucas, in *Journal of Crystal Growth*, Vol. 76, p. 681, 1986 was a result of that flight.

Mr. Nelson, with Tom Gustafson as a running mate, was defeated in the 1990 Democratic primary for Governor/Lieutenant Governor of the state by the Lawton Chiles/Kenneth H. (Buddy) MacKay ticket.

In 1991 Mr. Nelson joined the law firm of Maguire, Voorhis and Wells, P.A.

Mr. Nelson is married to the former Grace H. Cavert of Jacksonville and the father of two children, a son Bill and a daughter Nan Ellen.

Mr. Nelson favors increasing the number of investigators and accountants to combat insurance fraud, and wants to impound vehicles of uninsured drivers who drive without licenses.

Legal Basis for the office of State Treasurer: Article IV, Section 4(e), Constitution, and Chap. 18, Florida Statutes. Member of State Cabinet: Article IV, Section 4(a), Constitution and Chapter 20.03(1), Florida Statutes. Head of Department of Insurance: Chapter 20.13, Florida Statutes. State Fire Marshal: Chapter 633.01, Florida Statutes. *Created:* 1845 for Treasurer; 1915 for Insurance Commissioner; 1941 for State Fire Marshal; 1969 for Department of Insurance. *Method or selection:* Elected by qualified voters. *Qualifications:* An elector, not less than 30 years old, and a resident of the state for the preceding seven years. *Term:* Four years. May be reelected. Present term ends January 5, 1999. *Method of removal:* Impeachment. *Compensation:* $100,735.

HISTORY: Office of Treasurer created by 1838 Constitution, effective with statehood 1845. Treasurer elected by joint vote of houses of Legislature. 1861 Constitution again provided for joint vote of Legislature. 1865 Constitution, elected by people. 1868 Constitution, appointed by Governor, confirmed by Senate. 1885 Constitution, elected by people. 1968 Constitution, elected by people.

The Treasurers

Benjamin Byrd, *Aug. 5, 1845-x*
William R. Hayward, *Jan. 8, 1848*
Charles H. Austin, *Jan. 24, 1853*
Simon B. Conover, *Aug. 19, 1868*
Charles H. Foster, *Jan. 16, 1873*
Walter H. Gwynn, *Jan. 9, 1877*
Henry A. L'Engle, *Feb. 1, 1881*
E.S. Crill, *Feb. 19, 1885*
F.J. Pons, *Jan. 8, 1889*
E.J. Triay, *Dec. 31, 1891*
C.B. Collins, *Jan. 3, 1893*

J.B. Whitfield, *June 19, 1897*
W.V. Knott, *March 1, 1903*
J.C. Luning, *Feb. 19, 1912*
W.V. Knott, *Sept. 28, 1928*
J. Edwin Larson, *Jan. 3, 1941*
Broward Williams, *Jan. 28, 1965*
Thomas D. O'Malley, *Jan. 5, 1971*
Philip F. Ashler, *June 3, 1975*
William D. (Bill) Gunter, Jr.,
  Nov. 9, 1976
Tom Gallagher, *Jan. 3, 1989*
C. William "Bill" Nelson, *Jan. 3, 1995*

x—Date of Commission. In most circumstances, term of predecessor ended at noon of same day.

Note: Mrs. Eudora W. Whiddon of Tallahassee has determined that three of the Treasurers, Hayward, Conover and Crill, were physicians.

The legislature, speaking through the Executive Reorganization Act of 1969, said the Treasurer "shall hereafter be named the 'Insurance Commissioner and Treasurer.'"

The same law created the Department of Insurance, with the Treasurer as its head.

The legislative action recognized the fact that, however important the duties of the Treasurer as the State's paymaster and banker, his responsibilities as Insurance Commissioner had earned him the dual title.

Additionally, the Treasurer is the State Fire Marshal.

Department of Treasury

In his Constitutional role as treasurer, he is the State's biggest banker, receiving and disbursing approximately 36 billion dollars a year.

The Treasurer pays all warrants (checks) drawn on the treasury by the Comptroller and keeps detailed records of all transactions involving the State's money.

He is also a substantial source of State revenue through short-term investments from the Treasury pool of operating money. Interest earnings for the current fiscal year exceeded $338 million. Return of treasury investments has increased every year for the last five years when compared to the return on 90-day Treasury bills.

The Treasurer provides case management services to all of State government. This function provides consulting services to state agencies and institutions and operates a state wide deposit concentration account.

The Treasurer has custody of more than $3.8 billion of securities and other assets. This includes collateral held as guaranty for public deposits of the State and its political subdivisions which are maintained by numerous regulated entities (insurance companies, warranty companies, contractors, etc.) pursuant to various Florida Statutes which are held for the protection of the depositing entities' customers and/or creditors.

The Treasurer also administers the Government Employees Deferred Compensation Program. Under Florida Statute 112.215 the State or any county or municipality may contract with its employees to defer a portion of their salary into tax sheltered insurance, annuity savings, or investment products. The Treasurer has developed and implemented such a plan covering all State employees.

Department of Insurance

It is as Insurance Commissioner that the Treasurer's duties most directly touch the daily lives of the greatest number of Floridians. He regulates fire, casualty, liability and windstorm insurance rates and approves all policy forms.

He is required to determine that insurance companies seeking to do business in Florida are financially sound.

The Insurance Commissioner tests and licenses insurance agents, soliciters, adjusters, and bail bondsmen. More than 27,810 are tested each year.

He administers laws relating to pre-need burial contracts, life care contracts, ambulance service contracts, automobile and home warranty associations, automobile clubs, premium finance companies, scholarship plans, nonprofit hospital and medical service plans, nonprofit optometric service corporations, nonprofit pharmaceutical corporations, mortgage guaranty insurance, title insurance, fraternal benefit societies, donor annuities, health maintenance organizations, pre-need dental care plans and the State's self-insurance programs for certain property and casualty coverages.

He is charged with investigating fraud in all lines of insurance, plus violations of the Insurance Code.

He administers the funds for retirement of police officers and firefighters. These funds are derived from certain premium taxes on insurance written in cities meeting requirements to use these State funds.

State Fire Marshal

The Insurance Commissioner, as Fire Marshal, has the responsibility for investigating fires and suppressing arson. As the State's chief officer for fire prevention and control, he surveys state-owned property, service stations, prisons and other buildings to determine compliance with fire safety codes. He enforces laws governing explosives, liquefied petroleum, fire extinguishers and sprinkler systems. In addition, he establishes rules and regulations for the safe operation and maintenance of these products.

The Fire Marshal administers a State certification and training program for firefighters and operates the State Fire College in Ocala. He conducts workshops and seminars across the State for law enforcement and fire service personnel.

Assistant Treasurer-Insurance Commissioner	904-922-3104
Deputy of Legal Affairs-General Counsel	904-922-3103
Deputy Insurance Commissioner	904-922-3101
Deputy Treasurer-Fire Marshal	904-922-3102
Office of Cabinet Affairs	904-922-3106
Division of Administration	904-488-5269
Division of Insurance Fraud	904-922-3115
Division of Risk Management	904-922-3120
Division of Rehabilitation and Liquidation	904-488-7973
Division of Insurance Consumer Services	904-922-3130
Division of Agent and Agency Services	904-922-3135
Division of Insurer Services	904-922-3140
Division of State Fire Marshal	904-922-3170
Division of Liquefied Petroleum Gas	904-922-3175
Division of Treasury	904-922-3165

Commissioner of Agriculture and Consumer Services

Robert B. (Bob) Crawford, Democrat

"The Commissioner of Agriculture shall have supervision of matters pertaining to agriculture except as otherwise provided by law."
Florida Constitution, Article IV, Section 4(f)

Robert Bruce (Bob) Crawford, III, Eighth Commissioner of Agriculture (and, since 1969, Consumer Affairs), of the State of Florida, was born January 26, 1948, at Bartow, in the heart of the citrus country.

He is a graduate of the University of Miami, where he was a member of the debate team and of Delta Sigma Rho, a national forensic honorary.

He was wed to Nancy Caswall of Bartow, the 1969 Future Farmers of America Sweetheart from Bartow Senior High School. At the time of his election as Commissioner, the Crawfords lived in Winter Haven with their children, Bobby and Kristin.

Commissioner Crawford was elected to the Florida House of Representatives in 1976. He served in the House as Chairman of the Committee on Criminal Justice and as Chairman of the Committee on Tourism and Economic Development. In 1982 he was elected to the Senate, where he served as Chairman of the Committee on Natural Resources and the Committee on Finance, Taxation and Claims before being elected President in 1988.

Among his legislative accomplishments as Senate President, Commissioner Crawford brought "Sunshine" to the Legislature by opening up all Senate meetings to the public.

As a legislator, he received these awards (among others): Legislator of the Year 1986, Florida Farm Bureau; Legislator of the Year 1986, Florida Retail Grocers Association; Legislator of the Year 1981, Florida Association of Realtors; Outstanding Legislator 1987, Florida Fruit and Vegetable Association; Allen Morris Awards, Most Effective Senator, 1988, and Outstanding Legislator, 1984.

Growing up in Polk County, Bob Crawford has an appreciation and understanding of agriculture that spans four decades. As a youth, he worked to "fire" orange groves to keep them warm during freezes. At the time of election, he oversaw the management of a 3,200 acre cattle ranch and citrus operation in Polk County.

As Agriculture Commissioner, he oversees the largest and most diverse Agriculture Department in the nation. Among other duties, his department manages more than one million acres of state land.

Since becoming Agriculture Commissioner, he has worked to consolidate and improve the Department's food safety programs, improve the nutritional quality of Florida's school lunch program, create a public-private partnership to recover food that was going to waste and redirect it feed the hungry, protect Florida agriculture from unfair trade policies and open up new foreign markets for Florida agricultural products.

On the consumer front, he pushed for and passed legislation giving the Department authority to regulate auto repair shops and to crack down on mechanics who defraud the public. He also tightened safety regulations for the state's fair ride industry.

He is a Baptist. Other affiliations include: Kiwanis, Jaycees past State Director; Young Democrats of Polk County past Vice President, and American Heart Association, Division 10 Campaign Chairman for Polk, Hardee and Highlands counties, 1983.

Legal Basis for the office of Commissioner of Agriculture: Article IV, Section 4, Constitution of Florida, and Chapter 570, Florida Statutes. *Method of Selection:* Election. *Qualifications:* An elector, not less than 30 years old, and a resident of the state for the preceding seven years. *Term:* Four years. May be reelected to successive terms. Present term ends January 5, 1999. *Method of removal:* Impeachment. *Compensation:* $100,735 a year.

HISTORY: 1868 Constitution created offices of Surveyor-General and Commissioner of Immigration. Surveyor-General and Commissioner appointed by Governor, confirmed by Senate. Constitution amended in 1871 to consolidate offices under name of Commissioner of Lands and Immigration. 1885 Constitution created office of Commissioner of Agriculture, absorbing duties of Commissioner of Lands and Immigration. Commissioner elected by people. 1968 Constitution, elected by people.

The Commissioners of Agriculture

L. B. Wombwell	Dec. 31, 1888 Dec. 27, 1900	Nathan Mayo	November 1, 1923 April 14, 1960
B. E. McLin	January 9, 1901 January 31, 1912	Lee Thompson ad interim	April 18, 1960
J. C. Luning	February 5, 1912 February 19, 1912	Doyle Conner	January 3, 1961
W. A. McRae	March 1, 1912 October 31, 1923	Robert B. Crawford	January 8, 1991

Department of Agriculture and Consumer Services

Head The Commissioner of Agriculture, Bob Crawford,
The Capitol, Tallahassee 32399-0810
(904) 488-3022 for Commissioner
(904) 488-6971 for Department information
Assistant Commissioner of Agriculture
Ann Wainwright
The Capitol, Tallahassee 32399-0810
(904) 488-3022

Legal Basis: Article IV, Section 4(f), Constitution, and Chapter 19, F.S., for Commissioner; Section 20.14 F.S., for Department of Agriculture and Consumer Services. *Created:* 1885, for Commissioner of Agriculture (in succession to Commissioner of Immigration, established by Constitution of 1868); 1969, as Department of Agriculture and Consumer Services.

The Office of the Commissioner of Agriculture is another of the Cabinet offices whose purposes have changed through the years.

In recognition of its new direction, the Commissioner's department was renamed the Department of Agriculture and Consumer Services by the Legislature in the Executive Reorganization of 1969.

Other evidence of change can be seen in the dropping from the Constitution in 1968 of the Commissioner's former responsibilities for keeping a Bureau of Immigration, supervising the State Prison, and managing public land matters.

The diversity of the Department's tasks may be inferred from the names of its eleven Divisions: Standards, Marketing and Development, Dairy Industry, Fruit and Vegetables, Animal Industry, Agricultural Environmental Services, Forestry, Food Safety, Plant Industry, Consumer Services, and Administration.

Food Products

Specialists of the Department check on red meat and poultry from slaughter to retail sales, on dairy products and eggs from farm to market, on fruits and vegetables from fields to retail stores, and on all packaged foods at groceries. They make certain that labels and ingredients match.

Gasoline and Oil

Chemists in the Department's laboratories test gasoline, kerosene, and diesel fuels to see if these meet State standards. Inspectors periodically inspect for accuracy the pumps at Florida's thirteen thousand service stations. Fuels for heating are similarly tested, as are the tank trucks for hauling fuels.

Consumer Support Services

Chemists analyze samples of feeds, seeds, fertilizers, and pesticides to determine that these have been properly formulated. Foods are tested to insure they contain no harmful residues. Inspectors test all weighing and measuring devices for accuracy.

Other Services

The Department works for control and eradication of livestock and poultry diseases, crop, and plant pests. Professional foresters provide tree care, reforestation, and conservation advice. The Department performs numerous marketing services and enforces the Citrus Code. The Department receives and refers consumer complaints to appropriate offices and relays consumer information to the public by press, television, radio, magazines, and other media.

Advisory and Technical Committees

Because Florida's agricultural interests are so large and varied, the Commissioner has the help of an overall Agricultural Advisory Council. Most of the members of the Council represent specific areas of agricultural and related trade interest. These members are appointed by the Commissioner after they have been nominated by industry groups.

Since the Department's responsibilities are complex, a number of its Divisions also have technical advisory committees. Again, the members of these are appointed by the Commissioner upon the recommendation of the industry organizations directly affected by the activities of a division.

Assistant Commissioner of Agriculture
The Capitol, Tallahassee 32399-0810
(904) 488-3022

Division of Administration
Director Mike Gresham, Mayo Building
Tallahassee, 32399-0800 (904) 488-5321

Division of Standards
Director Don Farmer, Laboratory Complex, 3125 Conner Boulevard,
Tallahassee 32399-1650 (904) 488-0645

Division of Marketing
Director Nelson Pugh, Mayo Building, Tallahassee 32399-0800
(904) 488-4031

Division of Dairy Industry
Director Jay B. Boosinger, 3125 Conner Boulevard, Tallahassee 32399-1650
(904) 487-1450

Division of Fruit and Vegetable Inspection
Director C. Fred Jones, P.O. Box 1072, Winter Haven 33880
(813) 294-3511

Division of Inspection
Director Steve Rutz, Mayo Building, Tallahassee 32399-0800
(904) 488-3731

Division of Animal Industry
Director Dr. William E. Pace, Mayo Building, Tallahassee 32399-0800
(904) 488-7747

Division of Chemistry
Director Dr. Don Smyly, 3125 Conner Boulevard
Tallahassee 32399-1650 (904) 488-0295

Division of Plant Industry
Director Richard Gaskalla, P.O. Box 1269, Gainesville 32602
(904) 372-3505

Division of Consumer Services
Director Karen MacFarland, Mayo Building, Tallahassee 32399-0800
(904) 488-2221, Toll Free 1-800-342-2176

Division of Forestry
Director Earl Peterson, 3125 Conner Boulevard, Tallahassee 32399-1650
(904) 488-4274

Advisory Councils

The Commissioner of Agriculture has a number of statutorily authorized advisory councils which makes recommendations and advises him on issues and policies involving the particular segment of agriculture they represent.

The councils include the Florida Consumers' Council, Agricultural Advisory Council, Agricultural and Livestock Fair Council, Plant Industry Technical Council, Fertilizer Technical Council, Pesticide Review Council, Soil and Water Conservation Council, Dairy Industry Technical Council, Animal Industry Technical Council, Florida Forestry Council, Commercial Feed Technical Council, Aquaculture Review Council, Viticulture Advisory Council, Honey Bee Technical Council, Flue-Cured Tobacco Advisory Council, Appaloosa Advisory Council, Arabian Horse Council, Quarter Horse Advisory Council, Peanut Advisory Council, Soybean Advisory Council and the Endangered Plant Advisory Council.

Citrus groves stretching as far as the eye can see represent both agricultural wealth and tourist appeal.
Florida State Archives

Longest serving cabinet member was Commissioner of Agriculture Nathan Mayo. Mayo served 36 years and five months, from November 1, 1923, until his death on April 14, 1960.
Florida State Archives

Commissioner of Education

Frank T. Brogan, Republican

"The Commissioner of Education shall supervise the public education system in the manner prescribed by law."
    Florida Constitution, Article IV, Section 4(g)

Frank T. Brogan, 5th Commissioner of Education and the 19th person to serve as Chief School Officer of the State of Florida, and his twin brother John were born in Indiana on September 6, 1953, the youngest of six children. The family moved to Cincinnati, Ohio when the twins were three. Their insurance salesman father died a few years later and they were raised by their mother who worked in restaurants to support the family.

Although Commissioner Brogan worked in a metal foundry and stocking store shelves to put himself through college he graduated Magna cum laude, with a B.S. in Education, from the University of Cincinnati in 1976. He earned a Master of Education in Administration/Supervision, with a 4.0 grade point average at Florida Atlantic University in 1981, and has been working toward a Doctorate in Educational Leadership.

After a short stint in Ft. Lauderdale as a corporate insurance agent for L.M. Reid, Inc. Commissioner Brogan began his educational career in 1978 as a teacher at Port Salerno Elementary School in Martin County. He continued in the Martin County School system as Dean of Students at Indiantown Middle School, 1983–1984, Assistant Principal and Principal of Murray Middle School 1984–1988. He was elected Superintendent of Schools in Martin County in 1988 and was re-elected (unopposed) in 1992. Under Mr. Brogan's leadership, the Martin County School District was not only streamlined for efficiency and cost effectiveness but also sought and gained total accreditation, implemented a series of dramatic new programs, and still continued to maintain high student achievement and a reduction in juvenile crime.

Mr. Brogan served on national and statewide committees in the interests of children and their education including Chairman of the Florida Classrooms First Task Force, commissioned by the Florida Legislature. Some of his other educational service has been as a member of the Education Practices Commission, the Committee of Practitioners for Vocational Educators, the

64 / Commissioner of Education

Superintendent's Mentoring Program and the South Florida Consortium of School Boards.

Mr. Brogan's civic service has included chairmanships of the Martin County Children's Services Council and the Martin County Task Force on Drug and Alcohol Abuse, as well as membership in the Martin County Juvenile Justice Association, the District XV Juvenile Justice Board and the HRS District XV Children's Committee.

"Brogan's Handy Hints for School Improvement", "How to Build an Educational Summit Conference" and the Martin County School Improvement Program on Shared Decision Making and Accountability are a few of the programs and presentations Mr. Brogan developed.

Mr. Brogan served on the Board of Directors of the Florida Association of District School Superintendents, was Vice President of the Martin County Administrators' Association, and a member of both the Florida and American Association of School Administrators.

In 1993 Mr. Brogan was the recipient of the Florida Association of Student Services Personnel Educator of the Year award, National Tech Prep Awards from both the United States Department of Education and the American Association of Community Colleges, and the Florida School Volunteer Program Superintendent Award.

Commissioner Brogan's wife Mary J. is also a lifetime educator whose most recent position was Assistant Principal at Port Salerno Elementary School.

Stated goals of Commissioner Brogan's administration include chopping the education bureaucracy in half and asking lawmakers to set up a pilot program in a local school district testing vouchers that let parents get taxpayer dollars for private-school tuition. He also wants to expand Florida's Blueprint 2000 program to give greater power to local communities to run schools.

Legal Basis for the office of Commissioner of Education: Article IV, Section 4, and Article XII, Section 2, Constitution, and Chapter 229.09, Florida Statutes. *Method of selection*: Elected by qualified voters. *Qualifications*: An elector, not less than 30 years old, and a resident of the state for the preceding seven years. *Term*: Four years. May be reelected. Present term ends January 5, 1999. *Method of removal*: Impeachment. *Compensation*: $100,735.

HISTORY: Office of Superintendent of Public Instruction created by 1868 Constitution. Superintendent appointed by governor, confirmed by Senate. 1885 Constitution, elected by people. 1968 Constitution, name of office changed to Commissioner of Education. Commissioner elected by people.

Superintendents of Public Instruction

C. Thurston Chase, *Aug. 13, 1868-x*
Henry Quarles, *Sept. 23, 1870*
Rev. Charles Beecher, *March 18, 1871*

Jonathan C. Gibbs,* *Jan. 23, 1873*
Samuel B. McLin,** *Aug. 17, 1874*
Rev. William W. Hicks, *March 1, 1875*

x—Date of first commission. In most instances, term of predecessor ended at noon of same day.
*—Black. For more information see pages 131–132 of *The Florida Handbook* 1981–1982.
**—Acting, while serving as Secretary of State.

William P. Haisley, *Jan. 6, 1877*
Eleazer K. Foster, *Jan. 31, 1881*
Albert J. Russell, *Feb. 21, 1884*
William N. Sheats, *Jan. 3, 1893*
William M. Holloway, *Jan. 3, 1905*

William N. Sheats, *Jan. 7, 1913*
W. S. Cawthon, *July 24, 1922*
Colin English, *Jan. 5, 1937*
Thomas D. Bailey, *Jan. 4, 1949*
Floyd T. Christian, *Oct. 1, 1965*

Commissioners of Education

(title of office changed in Constitutional Revision of 1968)
Floyd T. Christian, *Jan. 7, 1969*
Ralph D. Turlington, *April 25, 1974*
Betty Castor, *Dec. 31, 1986*
Douglas L. Jamerson, * *Jan. 3, 1994*
Frank T. Brogan, *Jan. 3, 1995*
* Appointed to complete Castor's unexpired term.

Department of Education

Commissioner of Education Frank T. Brogan, The Capitol
(904) 487-1785
Deputy Commissioner for Planning, Budget and Management
Frank Darden, (904) 488-6539

Head: Board of Education (Governor and Cabinet). Governor serves as chairman, Commissioner of Education as secretary and executive officer. In absence of Governor, Commissioner of Education serves as chairman.

Legal basis: Article IX, Section 2, Constitution, and Section 20.15(1), F.S. For specific powers and duties, also see Chapter 229, F.S. *Created:* 1885 (effective January 1, 1887). Established present form, 1969. *Powers and Duties:* (Constitutional) To issue bonds or motor vehicle tax anticipation certificates on behalf of counties for capital outlay. To issue bonds or refunding certificates, against revenue derived from utilities gross receipts tax, for capital outlay at universities, colleges and vocational technical schools. (Statutory) To adopt comprehensive education objectives for public education. To exercise general supervision over the divisions of the Department of Education.

The office of the Commissioner of Education was created with the ratification by the voters in 1968 of the revised Constitution. It replaced the office of Superintendent of Public Instruction.

That this was more than simply a change of title was made clear when the Legislature a few months later passed the Executive Reorganization Act. This gave the Commissioner general supervision of Florida's entire system of public education, from kindergarten through graduate school. The law said the Commissioner is the State's "chief educational officer." The Commissioner is executive director of the Department of Education, which consists of six divisions: Public Schools, Applied Technology and Adult Education, Human Resource Development, Community Colleges, Universities, and Blind Services.

Each division has a director, except that the Board of Regents serves as Director for the Division of Universities. Members of the Board of Regents are appointed by the Governor with the approval of three members of the Cabinet and consent of the Senate. The directors of the remaining four divisions are employed by the Board of Education upon the recommendation of the Commissioner of Education.

Divisions of Department of Education

Section 20.15(2), F.S., established the following divisions of the Department of Education, and additionally authorized the Commissioner of Education to establish a Division of Administration, all but the Division of Universities and the Division of Community Colleges having a Director appointed by the Commissioner of Education subject to approval by the State Board of Education. The Board of Regents serves as Director of the Division of Universities, and the State Board of Community Colleges serves as Director of the Division of Community Colleges.

Division of Public Schools
Deputy Commissioner for Education Programs Robert L. Bedford
514 Florida Education Center
(904) 488-2601

Duties: The Board and Commissioner shall, under Section 20.15(4)(a), F.S., assign to the Division of Public Schools "such powers, duties, responsibilities, and functions as shall be necessary to insure the greatest possible coordination, efficiency, and effectiveness of kindergarten through twelfth grade education."

Division of Applied Technology and Adult Education
1113 Florida Education Center
(904) 488-8961

Duties: The Board and Commissioner shall, under Section 20.15(4)(b), F.S., assign to the Division of Vocational, Adult, and Community Education "such powers, duties, responsibilities, and functions as shall be necessary to insure the greatest possible coordination, efficiency, and effectiveness of vocational education."

Division of Blind Services
Director Whit Springfield
Douglas Building, 2540 Executive Center Circle, West
(904) 488-1330

Duties: Under Section 20.15(7), F.S., the Division of Blind Services is "designed for the purpose of insuring the greatest possible efficiency and effectiveness of services to the blind."

Division of Human Resource Development
Director Wayne Pierson
(904) 922-9649

Legal basis: Section 20.15(2)(a), F.S.

Division of Community Colleges
Executive Director Clark Maxwell, Jr., 1314 Florida Education Center
(904) 488-1721

Legal basis: Chapter 240, Part III, F.S. State Board of Community Colleges is comprised of Commissioner of Education, one student, and 11 lay citizens appointed by the Governor, approved by four members of the State Board of Education, and confirmed by the Senate. *Term:* five years; student member one year. *Duties:* Under Section 20.15(4)(c), F.S., the Board and Commissioner have assigned to the State Board of Community Colleges "such powers, duties, responsibilities, and functions as shall be necessary to insure the greatest possible coordination, efficiency, and effectiveness of community colleges" except those duties specifically assigned to the Commissioner of Education in ss. 229.512, 229.551, F.S., and the duties concerning physical facilities in Chapter 235, F.S. The State Board of Community Colleges was established with the necessary powers to exercise responsibility for statewide leadership in overseeing and coordinating the individually governed public community colleges, and for the establishment and development of rules and policy which will ensure the operation and maintenance of a state community college system in a coordinated, efficient and effective manner.

Postsecondary Education Planning Commission
Executive Director Dr. William B. Proctor
210 Collins Building, Tallahassee 32399
(904) 488-7894

Legal basis: Governor's Executive Order #80-67. Section 1202 of the 1972 Amendments to U.S. Higher Education Act of 1965 (Public Law 89-318). *Created:* July 30, 1980. Eleven members of the public appointed by Governor and approved by three other members of the State Board of Education. *Duties:* To prepare and submit master plan for postsecondary education. To recommend contracts with independent institutions to conduct programs consistent with master plan. To advise Board of Education regarding need for and location of new institutions and campuses. To assist Board in such capacities as Board deems appropriate.

Education Practices Commission
Executive Director Dr. Karen Wilde
301 Florida Education Center, Tallahassee 32399
(904) 488-0547

Legal basis: Section 231.555, F.S. *Created:* October 1, 1980. Thirteen members appointed by State Board of Education from nominations by Commissioner of Education and subject to Senate confirmation. *Duties:* Interpret and apply standards of professional practice as established by State Board of Education. Revoke, suspend, or take other appropriate action against teachers accused of professional offenses.

Commission on Education Reform and Accountability
Executive Director Dr. Michael C. Biance
Collins Building, 107 West Gaines, Tallahassee 32399-0400
(904) 922-7173

Legal basis: Section 229.593 F.S. *Created* 1990. Membership: The Commissioner of Education, the Lieutenant Governor, four members appointed by the Governor, six members appointed by the President of the Senate, six members appointed by the Speaker of the House, and five members appointed by the Commissioner of Education. *Term:* Four years. *Duties:* Review and recommend procedures for a new system of school improvement and education accountability and recommend the repeal or modification of statutes, fiscal policies, and rules that stand in the way of school improvement.

Education Standards Commission
Executive Director Dr. Charlotte S. Minnick
301 Florida Education Center, Tallahassee 32399
(904) 488-1523

Legal basis: Section 231.545, F.S. *Created:* October 1, 1980. Twenty-four members appointed by State Board of Education from nominations by Commissioner of Education and subject to Senate confirmation. *Duties:* Recommend to State Board standards for approval of preservice teacher education programs. Recommend objective, independently verifiable standards of measurement of competence. Recommend guidelines for expenditure of funds for teacher education centers and recommend most feasible locations for such centers. Develop standards of professional practice for teachers.

State Board of Independent Colleges and Universities
Administrator Dr. C. Wayne Freeburg
209 Collins Building, Tallahassee 32301
(904) 488-8695

Legal basis: Chapter 246, F.S. *Created:* 1971. Nine members appointed by the Governor, confirmed by the Senate. *Duties:* The Board shall hold such meetings as are necessary; adopt and use an official seal in the authentication of its acts; make rules and regulations for its own governance; prescribe and recommend to the State Board of Education minimum standards and rules and regulations as are required or may be necessary to aid in carrying out the objectives and purposes of the law and to create the means whereby all nonpublic and out-of-state colleges shall satisfactorily meet minimum educational standards.

Board of Independent Post-Secondary Vocational, Technical, Trade and Business Schools
Administrator Sam L. Ferguson
209 Collins Building, Tallahassee 32308
(904) 488-9504

Legal basis: Chapter 74-360, Laws of Florida. *Created:* 1974. Nine members appointed by the Governor. *Duties:* Prescribe and recommend to the State Board of Education minimum standards and rules and regulations as required or as it may find necessary to aid in carrying out the objectives and purposes and to execute such standards and rules and regulations as shall be adopted by the State Board of Education on the operation and establishment of independent schools.

Board of Trustees for School for Deaf and Blind
Legal basis: Sections 242.331 and 242.3305, F.S. *Created:* 1963. *Duties:* Under the supervision and general policies adopted by State Board of Education, to manage the Florida school for the Deaf and Blind at St. Augustine. To appoint and remove the president, faculty and staff.

Division of Universities
Chancellor Dr. Charles B. Reed
Florida Education Center, 325 West Gaines Street, Tallahassee 32399-1950
(904) 488-4234   Fax (904) 487-4568
Vice Chancellor, Office of Budgets Dr. Carl W. Blackwell
Vice Chancellor, Health Affairs Dr. Patricia Haynie
Executive Vice Chancellor, Academic Programs Dr. David S. Spense
Acting Vice Chancellor, Office of Public Affairs Nancy Stepina
General Counsel, Gregg A. Gleason

Legal basis: Chapter 240 F.S. With the exception of the Commissioner of Education, all twelve members are appointed by Governor, approved by three members of the Cabinet and confirmed by the Senate as the Board of Regents. *Term:* Six years. The Commissioner of Education serves as a Regent for the duration of the term of office. A Student Regent serves a one-year term.

Duties: Primarily responsible for planning systemwide rules and policies; planning for the future needs of the State University System; planning the programmatic, financial and physical development of the system; reviewing and evaluating the instructional, research, and service programs of the universities; coordinating program development among the universities; and monitoring the fiscal performance of the universities.

The State University System operates as a Division in the Department of Education. The Board of Regents has the authority to appoint and remove the Chancellor and the presidents of the universities and to set their compensation and other conditions for employment. The Board of Regents is a body corporate established by law, and has all powers of a body corporate for the purposes created by or that may exist under provisions of the law. The Board performs the functions formerly exercised by the Anatomical Board.

There are nine active State universities. A tenth, near Fort Myers, is scheduled to open in 1997.

The institutions which make up the university system are the University of Florida in Gainesville, founded in 1853; Florida State University, founded in 1857, and Florida A&M University, founded in 1887, both in Tallahassee;

the University of South Florida serving the Tampa Bay area, founded in 1956; Florida Atlantic University in Boca Raton and Fort Lauderdale, founded in 1961; the University of West Florida in Pensacola, founded in 1963; the University of Central Florida in Orlando, founded in 1963; Florida International University in Miami, founded in 1965; and the University of North Florida, founded in 1972.

Created by Section 240.209 F.S., the Board of Regents reviews, evaluates, approves and terminates degree programs; plans for the development of the university system; determines the annual Legislative budget request; allocates funds among the nine universities; and sets tuition and enrollment policy in cooperation with the Governor and the Florida Legislature.

The university system provides teaching, research and public service to its 200,000 students and the people of Florida. The Board's Master Plan establishes goals for the system:

1. Improving the quality of undergraduate education, through such programs as raising academic standards in core subjects, improving student advising, and enhancing libraries.

2. Providing adequate access to undergraduate education while maintaining quality.

3. Establishing a stable, reliable source of state funding.

4. Developing creative and innovative cost-effective programs.

5. Increase efficiency without sacrificing quality.

6. Resolving critical problems in a rapidly growing state, including increasing minority participation in legal education.

7. Forging public-private partnerships, especially in high-technology areas, to strengthen Florida's economic performance and ability to compete in the world economy.

The universities range in size from large graduate research institutions such as the University of Florida (38,420 students), Florida State University (29,301) and the University of South Florida (36,000), to New College of the University of South Florida, the honors campus of the System, with less than 500.

The University of Florida in 1985 was admitted to the Association of American Universities, a group of 56 institutions recognized as having the best graduate and professional programs in the U.S. and Canada.

University Press of Florida
Director, Kenneth Scott
15 N.W. 15th Street, Gainesville, Florida 32603
(904) 622-1351

The University Press of Florida, which is governed by the state-wide Council of Presidents, is the official scholarly publishing arm of the State University System.

Established in 1945, the press publishes books of intellectual distinction and significance and books of general and regional interest and usefulness to the people of Florida, reflecting their rich historical, cultural, intellectual heritage and resources.

An editorial board, made up of a faculty member from each of the nine state universities, determines whether manuscripts submitted to it meet the academic, scholarly, and programmatic standards of the press. The director of the press has the responsibility to decide which of the manuscripts, which have received the approval of the faculty editorial committee, will be published.

70 / Commissioner of Education

This is the Florida Education Center (FEC) in the Capitol Complex at Tallahassee. First occupied in 1989, the building houses DOE employees formerly located in 14 sites in the capital city. The Department of Education leases the FEC from the Dept. of Management Services. It is estimated that the building will save Florida $53 million over 50 years since renting space from the state is less expensive than from the private sector.

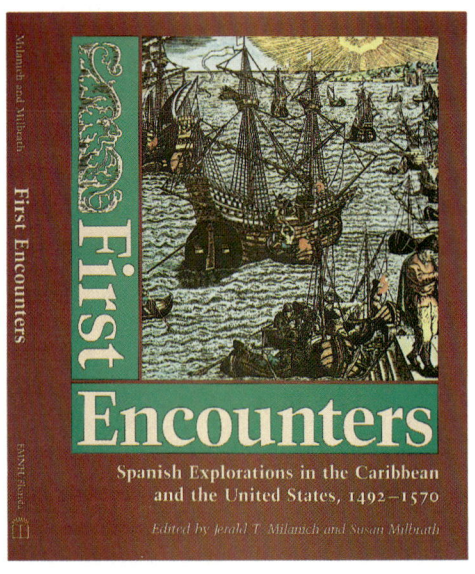

This is a sample of the attractive jackets for books published by the University Presses of Florida, an adjunct of the Board of Regents which services publications of the state's public universities.

Some recent books of special interest to Floridians are *Florida: A Short History, Atlas of Florida, The Seminoles of Florida, Florida Quilts, Idella: Marjorie Rawlings' "Perfect Maid," The Creek, Florida Nature Photography,* and the annual edition of *Florida Statistical Abstract.*

Four longtime staples of the press's list are *First Encounters, Florida Lighthouses, Florida Stories,* and *Nine Florida Stories by Marjorie Stoneman Douglas.*

Major State Departments

Board of Administration

1230 Blountstown Highway—Park 20 West—Building H
Post Office Drawer 5318—Tallahassee 32314-0063
(904) 488-4406
Executive Director—Ash Williams, Jr.

The Board of Administration is the state's chief "investment broker" and financial advisor. The Board oversees the investment of some $23 billion in state pension funds and various trust accounts. The members of the Board are the Governor, State Treasurer and State Comptroller. The Board appoints an Executive Director to manage the day-to-day affairs of the agency. It also appoints a six-member Investment Advisory Council composed of private citizens familiar with investment strategy and financial markets.

The Board must invest the billions of dollars in state pension and trust funds in order to get the highest possible risk adjusted yield. The Board functions very much like a large equity management firm and money market fund. It makes investments in stocks, bonds, real estate and cash instruments. To safeguard investments from the ups and downs of the financial markets, the Board is constrained by law as to the percentage of its funds that can go into stocks, bonds and real estate. For example, no more than 60% of the state pension fund may be invested in stocks. About three-quarters of the Board's investments are managed by some 20 outside firms. These firms include investment counselors such as Lazard Freres Asset Management and Prudential Asset Management.

The most important single responsibility of the Board is its handling of investments for the Florida Retirement System Trust Fund, which pays the retirement checks for retired state employees. In 1994, this fund totaled nearly $33 billion. The net "profit" from the Board's investment program varies from year to year, depending largely on the interest rates and the performance of the stock market. For example, in Fiscal Year 1993–94, the state's retirement portfolio grew by .1% or $3.9 billion. Duties of the Board include: (1) administer bond debt service, ranging from gas tax receipts and local road and bridge bonds to the Outdoor Recreation Fund; (2) approve legal and fiscal sufficiency of all state bond issues; (3) approve, when necessary, interest rates in excess of legal limitations; and (4) designate bank depositories for clearing accounts and revolving funds. The Board was created in 1929. Its legal basis is Article XII and Article IX of the Florida Constitution.

Department of Business and Professional Regulation

Northwood Centre
1940 N. Monroe St.
Tallahassee, FL 32399-0750
(904) 487-2252
Secretary—Rick Farrell

(The 1993 Legislature approved the merger of the Department of Business Regulation with the Department of Professional Regulation effective July 1, 1993.)

The merged Department of Business and Professional Regulation is headed by a Secretary appointed by the Governor. The Secretary serves at the pleasure of the Governor and is subject to Senate confirmation.

DBPR is composed of ten divisions and one commission—the Division of Accountancy, the Division of Administration, the Division of Alcoholic Beverages and Tobacco, the Division of Hotels and Restaurants, the Division of Land Sales, Condominiums and Mobile Homes, the Division of Pari-Mutuel Wagering, the Division of Professions, the Division of Real Estate, the Division of Regulation, the Division of Technology, Licensure and Testing and the State Athletic Commission.

The Division of Accountancy is charged with examining, licensing and regulating certified public accountants in Florida.

The Division of Administration is responsible for: all facilities occupied by the department; building leases; mail services; records administration; the child care center; and various other functions necessary to the operation of the department.

The Division of Alcoholic Beverages and Tobacco is responsible for licensing and regulating alcoholic beverage manufacturers, retailers and wholesalers as well as tobacco manufacturers, retailers and wholesalers.

The Division of Hotels and Restaurants is responsible for: licensing and regulating all public food service and lodging establishments; licensing elevators, escalators and moving walkways; and conducting certification and training programs when needed.

The Division of Land Sales, Condominiums and Mobile Homes is responsible for: regulating the sale of subdivided land; regulating the creation, sale and operation of residential condominiums, cooperative apartments, and real estate time share programs; regulating the landlord-tenant relationship at mobile home parks; licensing yacht and ship brokers and health care nursing pools; and providing licensure and certification of community association managers.

The Division of Pari-Mutuel Wagering is responsible for: regulating and licensing all pari-mutuel events; collecting revenues and monitoring financial reporting of all pari-mutuel activities; issuing occupational licenses for individuals who work at pari-mutuel facilities; and overseeing the day-to-day operations of races or games.

The Division of Professions is responsible for licensing and regulating the many different professions under the jurisdiction of DBPR.

The Division of Real Estate is responsible for licensing and regulating all real estate professionals operating in Florida.

The Division of Regulation is responsible for investigating and prosecuting complaints against professionals licensed by the department.

The Division of Technology, Licensure and Testing is responsible for all computer-related and telecommunication activities within the department.

DBPR is funded by revenue generated from application and licensure fees and the collection of tax revenues from the sale of alcoholic beverages and tobacco products and those taxes collected at pari-mutuel events.

Department of Citrus

P.O. Box 148—Lakeland 33802-0148
(813) 499-2500   Fax (813) 499-2374   S/C 595-2500
Executive Director—Daniel L. Santangelo

The Florida Citrus Commission/Department of Citrus is an executive agency of state government established in 1935 by an act of the Florida Legislature as the result of an industry request. The act, called the Florida Citrus Code, 601 F.S., states that the Department's purpose is to protect and enhance the quality and reputation of Florida citrus fruit and processed citrus products in both domestic and foreign markets. It also acts to "protect the health and welfare and stabilize and protect the citrus industry of the state," which in turn helps to promote the general welfare and social and political economy of the state.

The Department of Citrus is a trust fund agency financed by an excise tax placed on each box of citrus moved through commercial channels. The Florida Citrus Code stipulates the maximum tax and how funds generated are allocated. A portion of that tax is deposited in the state's general revenue fund to offset administrative costs.

The Florida Citrus Commission is the agency head and serves in the capacity of a board of directors for the Department of Citrus. The Commission consists of 12 members appointed by the Governor of Florida and confirmed by the Senate for three-year terms. The members of the Commission must be citrus growers, packers or processors. Seven members of the Commission must be growers; three members must represent the processing industry; and two of the Commissioners must be fresh fruit shippers.

The Commission oversees and guides the activities of the Department of Citrus. It is responsible for setting the annual amount of the excise tax as well as quality standards for all citrus grown, packed or processed in Florida. In addition, the Commission adopts rules regulating packaging and labeling of Florida citrus products and licensing requirements for packers, shippers and processors.

The Department of Citrus carries out Commission policy by conducting a wide variety of programs involving industry regulation, scientific, market and economic research, advertising, merchandising, public and industry relations, and consumer promotions. Over 80 percent of the Department's annual budget is spent on advertising and promotional activities for Florida citrus in the United States, Canada, Europe and Asia. The balance of its funds, derived from the excise tax, is spent for administration, scientific, economic and market research, and regulatory activities.

Department of Commerce

536 Collins Building—Tallahassee 32399-2000
(904) 488-3104   Fax (904) 487-1612
Secretary—Charles Dusseau

The Florida Department of Commerce was created in 1969 by Section 20.17, Florida Statutes. The administrative head of the Department is a Secretary appointed by the Governor. The Department consists of three operational divisions: Economic Development, International Trade and Development, and Tourism.

The Division of Economic Development is responsible for encouraging the development of the state economy by marketing Florida as an ideal location for business investment. The Division is organized into three bureaus: Bureau of Economic Analysis, Bureau of Industry Development and the Bureau of Business Assistance.

The Division of International Trade & Development is responsible for increasing exports of Florida products and increasing the number and quality of foreign investment projects in Florida. The Division promotes and assists Florida companies through its eight foreign offices and six Florida field offices.

The Division of Tourism is responsible for promoting and developing tourism. The Division coordinates national promotional campaigns and assists municipalities, chambers of commerce and other tourist-oriented entities in developing cooperative promotional programs. The Division is organized into three bureaus: Bureau of International Tourism, Bureau of Domestic Tourism and Bureau of Visitors Services.

The Department of Commerce works with several commissions and boards through-out the state. These include: Enterprise Florida, the Black Business Investment Board, Spaceport Florida Authority, the Florida Sports Foundation, the Florida International Affairs Commission, the Florida Entertainment Commission, the Florida First Capital Corporation, and the Tourism Advisory Council.

Department of Community Affairs

2740 Centerview Drive—Tallahassee 32399-2100
(904) 488-8466   Fax (904) 921-0781
Secretary—James F. Murley

The Department of Community Affairs was created by Section 20.18, Florida Statutes. The head of the Department is a Secretary who is appointed by the Governor and confirmed by the Senate. The Secretary serves at the pleasure of the Governor.

The Department consists of the Division of Resource Planning and Management, the Division of Emergency Management, the Division of Housing and Community Development and the Office of the Secretary. The Florida Housing Finance Agency, which is governed by a board of trustees, is attached to the Department for administrative purposes.

The Department is the state's land planning agency. It administers the state's growth management laws, including local government comprehensive planning, Areas of Critical State Concern and Developments of Regional Impact. In conjunction with the Florida Housing Finance Agency, the Department serves as the state's housing agency. It administers more than 20 programs affecting Florida's cities and counties in housing, community and economic development, criminal justice, highway safety and building codes and standards.

Finally, the Department is the state's emergency management agency. It directs and coordinates state, federal and local efforts to deal with natural and manmade emergencies, such as hurricanes and accidents at nuclear power plants.

Department of Corrections

2601 BlairStone Road—Tallahassee 32399-2500
(904) 488-7480   Fax (904) 922-2848
Secretary—Harry K. Singletary, Jr.
Information Services Administrator—Eugene Morris—(904) 488-0420

The Department of Corrections is authorized by Chapter 20.315, Florida Statutes. The head of the Department is a Secretary who is appointed by the Governor. The Secretary serves at the pleasure of the Governor and is subject to Senate confirmation.

The Department is divided into five regions that form a decentralized correctional system to administer institutional and probation and parole services. The five Regional Directors are appointed by the Secretary, and report to his Assistant Secretary for Operations. The Correctional Education School Authority and the Corrections Medical Authority are independent entities attached to the Department for administrative reasons.

The Department provides for the supervision, incarceration and rehabilitation of adult offenders. Persons tried as adults for felony offenses and sentenced to one or more years are committed to the custody of the Department. The Department currently provides incarceration for more than 56,000 inmates at 46 major prisons, six work camps and 62 smaller correctional facilities. Offenders placed on parole or sentenced to probation or community control are supervised by the Department's probation and parole officers. Currently, more than 130,000 offenders are supervised from the Department's 155 probation and parole offices.

Decisions concerning the release of adult offenders on parole are made by the Parole and Probation Commission, an autonomous agency. The Correctional Education School Authority is responsible for correctional education programs; the majority of its members are appointed by the Governor. The Corrections Medical Authority (CMA) provides expert review and recommendations on health care for the Department. While serving primarily in an advisory capacity, CMA does have rulemaking authority and is responsible for developing health care budget proposals, establishing medical education programs and resolving medical treatment disputes. CMA's members are appointed by the Governor and subject to Senate approval. The Department provides specialized field services and administrative support through its offices of Health Services, Community Services, Adult Services and Youthful Offender Programs. In addition, the office of the Inspector General is responsible for inspection of state, county and municipal correctional and detention facilities.

Department of Elder Affairs

1317 Winewood Boulevard, Bldg. E, Rm. 317
Tallahassee 32399-0700
(904) 922-5297   Fax (904) 922-6216
Secretary—E. Bentley Lipscomb

The mission of the Department of Elder Affairs is to maximize opportunities for self-sufficiency and personal independence of Florida's elders and to plan, advocate, coordinate with other agencies and administer programs and policies that assure accessible, responsive and comprehensive services and long-term care.

Department of Environmental Protection

3900 Commonwealth Blvd.
Tallahassee 32399-3900
(904) 488-1554   Fax (904) 922-5380
Secretary—Virginia B. Wetherell
Rm. 1009-C

Assistant Secretaries
Kirby Green, 488-7131. Dan Thompson, 488-9717
Executive Coordinator of Ecosystem Management
Pam McVety, 488-7454

The Department comprises the Divisions of: Administrative and Technical Services, Air Resources Management, Law Enforcement, Marine Resources, Recreation and Parks, State Lands, Waste Management, Environmental Resource Permitting, and Water Facilities. Division directors serve at the pleasure of the Secretary, except for the Director of the Division of State Lands, whose selection by the secretary is subject to confirmation by the Governor and Cabinet, sitting as the Board of Trustees of the Internal Improvement Trust Fund.

Six District Offices—Northwest in Pensacola, Northeast in Jacksonville, Central in Orlando, Southwest in Tampa, Southeast in West Palm Beach, and

South in Fort Myers—conduct the department's regulatory activities throughout the state.

The department is responsible for carrying out most of the environmental and natural resources laws of the state. Rules adopted by the department cover a wide range of subjects: air quality, surface and ground water quality and quantity, solid and hazardous waste, environmental cleanup, marine endangered species, salt water sport and commercial fisheries, oil spill prevention and cleanup, state land management, oil and gas conservation, boating safety, and management of recreation areas and parks.

The Florida Marine Patrol enforces boating safety, marine, and environmental laws throughout the state. The department—through the Board of Trustees of the Internal Improvement Trust Fund—is depository for all lands owned by the state and administers one of the nation's largest environmental land-purchasing programs.

The department's regulatory program governs activities conducted in or on waters of the state, including beaches and wetlands, requires permits for discharges to air or to water, and governs the collecting, storing, transport and disposal of solid and hazardous wastes. A new program—Ecosystem Management—is aimed at bringing the department's regulatory and natural resources programs together into a more holistic approach to protecting Florida's resources. Through an Office of Ecosystem Coordination in the Secretary's Office, the department's Ecosystem Management programs make use of all the department's administrative tools: planning, land acquisition, land and resource management, environmental education, and regulatory—to develop new and innovative approaches to environmental and resource management.

Game and Fresh Water Fish Commission

102 Farris Bryant Building—620 South Meridian Street
Tallahassee 32399-1600
(904) 488-2975   Fax (904) 488-6988
Executive Director—Dr. Allan Egbert
Assistant Executive Director—William C. Sumner—(904) 488-3084

The Florida Game and Fresh Water Fish Commission is governed by a board of five members, appointed by the Governor and confirmed by the Senate, who serve five-year terms on a staggered basis. The Executive Director is selected by Commissioners and serves at their pleasure.

The organizational structure of the Commission includes the Office of the Executive Director, the Division of Law Enforcement, the Division of Wildlife, the Division of Fisheries, the Division of Administrative Services, the Office of Environmental Services and the Office of Informational Services. The Executive Director is aided in administration through five regional offices in Panama City, Lake City, Ocala, Lakeland and West Palm Beach.

The Office of the Executive Director is responsible for informing the five-member Commission of the current status and problems of the agency and carrying out the directives of the Commission. The office coordinates Commission programs in each of the five regions, and conducts internal audits, provides agency legal counsel and coordinates agency planning and management.

The Division of Law Enforcement is charged with protecting the wildlife and freshwater aquatic life of the state. The division also assists other public agencies directly or indirectly concerning conservation and enforcement of Florida's laws.

The Division of Wildlife is charged with developing and implementing management practices to ensure perpetuation of Florida's diverse wildlife.

The Division of Fisheries maintains and enhances the aquatic life of Florida's fresh waters.

The Division of Administrative Services provides support services to all program functions of the Commission. These services include planning and budgeting, finance and accounting, personnel, property, maintenance and inventory, purchasing, and general office operations such as printing, data processing, central files, mailroom and storeroom.

The basic function of the Office of Environmental Services is to assist in the maintenance and enhancement of fish and wildlife habitat.

The Office of Informational Services informs the public of matters relating to the Commission's management such as rules and regulations and the proper use of Florida's fish and wildlife resources. It also seeks to increase public awareness of fish and wildlife values, their needs, and the role of fish and wildlife in Florida's environment.

Department of Health and Rehabilitative Services

Building 2, Room 429
1317 Winewood Boulevard—Tallahassee 32399-0700
(904) 488-7721   Fax (904) 922-2993
Acting Secretary—Edward Feaver

The Department of Health and Rehabilitative Services (HRS) was created by Section 20.19, Florida Statutes. The head of the department is the Secretary who is appointed by the Governor. The Secretary serves at the pleasure of the Governor and is subject to Senate confirmation.

Legislatively mandated responsibilities of the department include:
- integrate delivery of all health, social, and rehabilitative services offered by the state to citizens in need;
- provide assistance so that eligible clients can achieve or maintain economic self-support and self-sufficiency;
- prevent or remedy the neglect, abuse or exploitation of children and adults unable to protect their own interests;
- aid in the preservation, rehabilitation and reuniting of families;
- prevent or reduce inappropriate institutional care by providing community-based care, home-based care, or other forms of less intensive care;
- prevent the occurrence and spread of communicable diseases and other physical and mental diseases and disabilities;
- disseminate information to the public with efforts aimed at disease

prevention and maintenance and improvement of the physical and mental health of all citizens;
 • plan and develop health resources to assure effective and efficient delivery of high quality health services fully accessible to all citizens.

HRS licenses, regulates or certifies 125 functions. These fall under the categories of: Aging and Adult Services; Alcohol, Drug Abuse and Mental Health; Children, Youth and Families; Developmental Services; Health, Emergency Medical Services; Health, Entomology Services; Health, Environmental Health; Health, Laboratory Services; Health, Maternal, Child and Special Health Services; Health, Pharmacy Services; Health, Radiation Control.

Department of Highway Safety and Motor Vehicles

Executive Director—Fred O. Dickinson III
B-443 Neil Kirkman Building
Tallahassee 32399-0500
(904) 487-3132   Fax (904) 922-6274

The Department of Highway Safety and Motor Vehicles was established under Section 20.24, Florida Statutes. The head of the department is the Executive Director, who is appointed by, and serves at the pleasure of, the Governor and Cabinet.

The department is comprised of four divisions: Motor Vehicles, Administrative Services, Driver Licenses and Florida Highway Patrol. The agency's major responsibilities are vehicle registration and titling, driver testing and licensing, highway safety and traffic enforcement.

The Division of Motor Vehicles licenses importers, distributors, factory branches and all persons selling motor vehicles, mobile homes and recreational vehicles. The division's Bureau of Titles and Registrations issues millions of tag decals and new license plates annually, processes motor vehicle title applications, records liens and issues titles. The Bureau of Motor Carrier Services is responsible for registering commercial vehicles and collecting highway user taxes under the International Registration Plan and the International Fuel Tax Agreement.

The Division of Administrative Services is responsible for the agency's budget, personnel, accounting and supply functions. The Information Systems Administration houses the computer that holds the department's massive data base of vehicle and driver records.

The Division of Driver Licenses tests drivers and issues licenses at more than 170 locations around the state. It enforces license suspensions and revocations and administers the state's financial responsibility law. The division is responsible for printing all traffic citations issued in the state and maintaining individual computerized driver records.

The Division of Florida Highway Patrol is Florida's law enforcement arm on the open road. It enforces traffic and safety laws, investigates vehicular homicides, maintains a visible presence to prevent highway violence and educates the public on safe driving.

Department of Juvenile Justice

1344 Cross Creek Circle—Tallahassee 32301-3677
(904) 488-1850   Fax (904) 921-4159
Secretary—Calvin Ross
Deputy Secretary—Woodie Harper

The Department of Juvenile Justice was established by Chapter 20.316, Florida Statutes, in 1994. The head of the Department is the Secretary who is appointed by and serves at the pleasure of the Governor. The Deputy Secretary assists the Secretary in his role as agency head.

The Department is divided into four major divisions. Operations supervises and supports all of the Department's district operations, programs and facilities. Programming and Planning is responsible for strategic and long-term planning functions for detention and commitment programs as well as prevention and intervention programs. Management and Budget supports all administrative functions and services. The last division is the Executive Staff Office which includes Legislative Affairs, Public Information and Juvenile Justice Boards and Councils coordination. In the first year of operation, the Department will be assisted by an Assistant Secretary for Reorganization who will oversee the reorganization of the Juvenile Justice Program Office of the Department of Health and Rehabilitative Services into the Department.

Legislatively mandated responsibilities of the Department include; operating and managing all the state's juvenile justice detention, non-residential and residential commitment programs, aftercare programs and all other juvenile facilities and institutions. The Department is also mandated to administrator all juvenile diversion, intervention, delinquency prevention, and Children-In-Need of Services and Families-In-Need of Services programs.

The department was created with a mission to increase public safety and reduce juvenile crime. The goal of the department is to work in partnership with communities, schools and families to meet this challenge.

Department of Labor and Employment Security

303 Hartman Building—Tallahassee 32399-2152
(904) 922-7021   Fax (904) 488-8930
Secretary—Douglas L. Jamerson

The Department of Labor and Employment Security, established October 1, 1978, is the state counterpart of the U.S. Department of Labor. The Secretary of the Department is appointed by the Governor and establishes the overall policy that directs the daily administration of the agency's five program divisions—Labor, Employment and Training, Unemployment Compensation, Workers' Compensation, Safety, and Vocational Rehabilitation—and a support division, Administrative Services, as well as the office of the Chief Commissioner and the State Job Training Coordinating Council.

Staff to the secretary includes an Assistant Secretary, the Office of Legal Services, the Office of Civil Rights, the Office of Communications; and an Inspector General and an Internal Auditor.

The Division of Labor, Employment and Training administers the state Job Service programs, promotes and develops apprenticeship and pre-apprenticeship training programs, coordinates enforcement of labor laws, administers Project Independence, monitors programs under the Job Training Partnership Act and provides comprehensive labor market information.

The Division of Unemployment Compensation administers the Florida Unemployment Compensation Program through claims, tax collection and disputed claims hearings.

The Division of Workers' Compensation administers the state workers' compensation program, designed to return injured workers to productive employment.

The Division of Safety oversees the state's industrial safety program.

The Division of Administrative Services is responsible for agency support functions, including financial management, personnel and computer data systems.

The Division of Vocational Rehabilitation oversees programs designed to rehabilitate people with mental or physical disabilities which prevent them from working.

The Civil Rights administrator and staff monitor department activities for compliance with Equal Employment Opportunity requirements and Affirmative Action programs, and assist in recruiting minorities and women for department positions.

Department of Law Enforcement

Post Office Box 1489—Tallahassee 32302
(904) 488-8771   Fax (904) 488-2189
Executive Director—James T. Moore
Publication Information Administrator—Michael McHargue 488-1497

The Florida Department of Law Enforcement (FDLE) was created by Section 20.201, Florida Statutes. The head of FDLE is the Governor and Cabinet. The Executive Director of the Department is appointed by the Governor with the approval of at least three members of the Cabinet and is subject to confirmation by the Florida Senate.

FDLE is comprised of the Office of Executive Director, Division of Criminal Investigation, Division of Local Law Enforcement Assistance, Division of Criminal Justice Information Systems, Division of Criminal Justice Standards and Training and Division of Local Law Enforcement Assistance and Division of Staff Services. The Department also provides staff to the Florida Medical Examiners Commission. FDLE maintains a dual role of direct investigative and enforcement responsibilities along with the support and assistance it provides to local law enforcement and other criminal justice agencies.

Through its statewide operations bureaus, FDLE serves Florida as the primary investigative agency concerning organized, complex, and multi-jurisdictional crimes. One major tool coordinated by FDLE in its fight against complex criminal enterprises is the Integrated Approach to Combat Organized Crime. This program brings together the total responsibilities and authorities of numerous agencies, both enforcement and regulatory, necessary to effectively dismantle criminal enterprises.

FDLE also provides a myriad of support services and assistance to other criminal justice agencies through all of its organizational divisions. FDLE provides the Florida Criminal Justice community a comprehensive information system of investigative, intelligence, operational and management data through the Florida Intelligence Center (FIC) and the Florida Crime Information Center (FCIC). The FCIC provides a telecommunications network linking all criminal justice agencies statewide and is interfaced with the National Crime Information Center.

Department of the Lottery

250 Marriott Drive—Tallahassee 32399-4002
(904) 487-7728   Fax (904) 487-7709
Secretary—Dr. Marcia Mann

The Florida Lottery was created in 1987 by the Florida Public Education Lottery Act. The Act implemented Art. X, see. 15 of the State Constitution, which was adopted by the people of Florida in the 1986 general election.

The purpose of the Act is to implement the constitutional provision "in a manner that enables the people of the state to benefit from significant additional moneys for education and also enables the people of the state to play the best lottery games available."

The Act states that the legislative intent is that the net proceeds of the lottery games be used to support improvements in public education and not as a substitute for existing resources for public education; that the games be operated by a department that runs as much as possible in the manner of an entrepreneurial business enterprise; that the department be self-supporting and revenue-producing; and that the department be accountable to the Legislature and the people of the state.

The head of the department is the Secretary of the Lottery, who is appointed by the Governor, subject to confirmation by the Senate.

The Florida Lottery began ticket sales on January 12, 1988, with the "Millionaire" Instant Lottery game. The Lottery introduced computerized, on-line Lottery games in April, 1988.

Department of Management Services

307 Knight Building—Tallahassee 32399—0950
(904) 488-2786   Fax (904) 922-6149
Secretary—William H. Lindner

Special Session F, the sixth of the 1990–1992 Legislature, was called by Governor Lawton M. Chiles for the sole purpose of enacting legislation to abolish the Department of Administration, transferring its powers and duties to the Department of General Services and rename that Department the Department of Management Services.

The Department of Management Services is headed by a Secretary appointed by the Governor and confirmed by the Senate. The Department is organized into 12 divisions:

1. Division of Administration
2. Division of Building Construction
3. Division of Capital Police
4. Division of Communications
5. Division of Facilities Management
6. Division of Information Services
7. Division of Motor Pool
8. Division of Personnel Management Services
9. Division of Purchasing
10. Division of State Employees' Insurance
11. Division of Retirement
12. Division of Administrative Hearings

Chapter 94-333, Law of Florida, established the Division of Retirement as a separate entity within, but independent of, the Department of Management Services. The Bureau of Minority Business Assistance was transferred to the Department of Commerce.

Department of Military Affairs

82 Marine Street, P.O. Box 1008—St. Augustine 32085-1008
(904) 823-0100   Fax (904) 823-0152
The Adjutant General—Major General Ronald O. Harrison

The Department of Military Affairs was established by Chapter 250.05, Florida Statutes. The head of the Department is The Adjutant General who is appointed by the Governor. The appointment by the Governor is subject to Senate confirmation. The Adjutant General may serve until he is no longer a federally recognized officer of the Florida National Guard.

The Department is comprised of the Directorate of Administration; the Directorate of Military Personnel; the Directorate of Supply and Services; the Directorate of Plans, Operations, Training and Military Support; the Directorate of Maintenance; the Support Personnel Management Office; Facility Management Office; Staff Office—Florida Air National Guard; State Aviation Office; Management Information Systems Office; and the State Quartermaster.

The Department has a dual mission:

a. As a State Militia, to provide Military Units and individuals trained and equipped to function when necessary in the protection of life and property, and the preservation of peace, order and public safety as directed by competent state authority. (S.250.28, Florida Statutes.)

b. As reserve components of the Army and Air Force of the United States, to provide trained units available for Federal service in time of war or National emergency, or at such other times as the National Security may require augmentation of the Armed Forces of the United States. (Title 32, U.S. Code.)

The Adjutant General and his headquarters have an additional Federal mission to direct and coordinate the pre-attack planning and post-attack operations of all military forces made available within the state and a State mission to support civil authorities engaged in providing for the survival of the state's people and continuity of government in a nuclear environment. The Florida Air National Guard has an air sovereignty mission for the eastern seaboard of the United States to maintain aircraft armed and ready for immediate commitment, on a twenty-four hour alert status, and to intercept unidentified aircraft in or approaching the airspace of the United States.

Department of Revenue

Carlton Building—Tallahassee 32399-0100
(904) 488-5050   Fax (904) 488-0024
Executive Director—Larry Fuchs
General Tax Information—1-800-872-9909 or (904) 488-6800

The Department of Revenue is responsible for collecting more than $16 billion a year in sales and use tax, fuel tax, corporate income tax, documentary stamp tax, intangible property tax, estate tax, pollutant tax, insurance premium tax, oil and gas production tax, and solid minerals severance tax. It also is responsible for assuring that property valuations are at full market value for local government ad valorem taxes, and may process receipts for other state agencies. The Department also administers the Child Support Enforcement Program, which generated more than $386 million in payments in FY 1993–94. Created by Section 20. 21, the Department is headed by the Governor and Cabinet. The department is undergoing an organizational transition as the first agency to be budgeted according to programs as well as traditional divisions. They are:

General Tax Administration, which is responsible for tax processing, audits, taxpayer assistance, and collection and enforcement.

Property Tax, which is responsible for ad valorem administration, assessment standards, and review and central property valuations.

Child Support Enforcement, which is responsible for establishing and enforcing the collection of court-ordered support payments to children.

Division of Administration, which is responsible for planning, organizing and controlling the administrative support services for the Department.

Division of Information Systems and Services, which is responsible for development, maintenance and management of information systems and data processing.

The Department also includes Offices of the Inspector General, General Counsel, Research and Analysis, Legislative and Cabinet Services, and the Intergovernmental Relations and Taxpayer Rights Advocate.

Department of Transportation

605 Suwannee Street—Haydon Burns Building—Tallahassee
32399-0450
(904) 488-6721   Fax (904) 488-5526
Secretary—Ben G. Watts

Assistant Secretaries—
V.G. Marcoux, Assistant Secretary for District Operations
Frank Carlile, Assistant Secretary for Transportation Policy
Tom Barry, Assistant Secretary for Finance & Administration

The Florida Department of Transportation was created by the Governmental Reorganization Act of 1969, which merged the powers and responsibilities of eight state agencies into a single transportation department.

The mission of the Department of Transportation is to provide a safe interconnected statewide transportation system for Florida's citizens and visitors that ensures the mobility of people and goods, while enhancing economic prosperity and sustaining the quality of our environment.

The largest and best-known of DOT's predecessors was the State Road Department, established in 1915 with a first-year budget of $10,193. Today, the Florida Department of Transportation has an annual budget exceeding $3.0 billion, with its more than 11,000 employees providing modern transportation facilities for more than 13 million citizens.

The department is headed by a Secretary of Transportation nominated by the Florida Transportation Commission and appointed by the Governor subject to confirmation by the Florida Senate. Florida law requires that the Secretary be a "proven, effective administrator who by a combination of education and experience shall clearly possess a broad knowledge of the administrative, financial and technical aspects of the development, operation and regulation of transportation or comparable systems and facilities." The Secretary serves at the pleasure of the Governor.

The Secretary appoints three assistant secretaries, each of whom serve at the pleasure of the Secretary. The Secretary may delegate to any assistant secretary the authority to act in the Secretary's absence.

The Assistant Secretary for District Operations is responsible for the administration of the eight DOT districts, including Florida's Turnpike, and implementation of the decentralization of the department.

Eight district secretaries report through the Assistant Secretary for District Operations to the Secretary and have direct responsibility for implementing all transportation programs in the districts they oversee. They are responsible for the administration of all offices and functions within the district.

The Assistant Secretary for Transportation Policy is responsible for policy planning including the Florida Transportation Plan and the agency functional plan. Other responsibilities include statewide intermodal systems planning, design, construction and maintenance of transportation facilities, acquisition and management of transportation rights of way and administration of motor carrier compliance and safety programs.

The Assistant Secretary for Finance and Administration is responsible

86 / Major State Departments

for financial planning and management, information systems, accounting systems, administrative functions and administration of toll operations.

The department's Executive Committee is the policy-making "board of directors." It is comprised of the Secretary, the three assistant secretaries, the eight district secretaries, the State Highway Engineer, State Transportation Planner, and State Public Transportation Administrator. Non-voting members of the Executive Committee include the General Counsel, Chief Internal Auditor, Comptroller, Director of Management and Budget, Director of Administration, Director of Information Systems, Quality Management Coordinator, Director of Communications and Governmental Affairs, and Legislative Programs Administrator.

The department employs about 11,000 people throughout the state. DOT is responsible for maintaining about 11,900 centerline miles of interstate highways, toll roads, Florida's Turnpike, other US and State highways and about 5,929 bridges. The department is also responsible for inspecting and licensing 20 commercial airline service airports, 23 "reliever" airports and 87 public general aviation airports. Numerous public transit systems operate in metropolitan areas and rail lines operate over several thousand miles of track inspected by DOT.

The Florida Department of Transportation is pursuing the development of an intercity high speed rail system. It would move people at speeds ranging from 90 mph to 200 mph and provide citizens and visitors with a viable alternative to automobile and air travel.

A federal law is helping to pave the way for high speed rail. The Intermodal Surface Transportation Efficiency Act (ISTEA) of 1991 provided Florida and the nation with a new emphasis on alternative forms of transportation. New programs have been authorized with an emphasis on investment in high speed transportation systems. In addition, ISTEA created flexibility for states to use funding sources traditionally reserved for highway investment on systems like high speed rail.

Assisting the development of high speed rail is the Florida High Speed Rail Transportation Act. It was amended in 1992 to define a more workable structure for the formation of public-private partnerships to develop and implement high speed rail. Once it is completed, the high speed rail network will be the backbone of a statewide public transportation system designed to make alternative forms of travel both viable and attractive.

From highways to railways and airports to seaports, Florida's transportation system is all about moving people and goods quickly and safely. A high quality, highly efficient transportation network is needed in order to remain competitive in an increasingly global economy. The Florida Department of Transportation is committed to maintaining an interconnected, statewide transportation system that balances mobility, cost, economic prosperity, and the environment.

The Florida Turnpike

605 Suwannee Street—Tallahassee 32399-0450
5101 W. Sunrise Blvd.—Fort Lauderdale 33313
(904) 488-4671
(305) 583-3111
Jim Ely, District Secretary

• Area: The Turnpike's Mainline covers 356 miles from Wildwood to Homestead with eight service plazas. The Sawgrass Expressway and the Beeline West are also part of the Mainline.
• Facts: In 1990 the Legislature authorized the expansion of the Turnpike System. Eleven candidate expansion projects were authorized. The current plan is to open over 100 miles of new expansion projects by the year 2000.

Florida Transportation Commission

605 Suwannee Street—Tallahassee 32399-0450
(904) 488-8995
SC 278-8995
Malcolm Kirschenbaum, Chairman
Jane Mathis, Executive Director

The Florida Transportation Commission, a nine-member "citizen board", was created by the Legislature in 1987.

The Commission's primary functions are:
• to recommend major transportation policies for the Governor's approval, and assure that approved policies are properly executed;
• to assess the Department's performance and productivity quarterly and annually and report findings to the Governor and Legislature;
• to evaluate the Department of Transportation's annual budget request, Florida Transportation Plan, and Tentative 5-Year Work Program;
• to serve as a nominating commission in selecting the Secretary of Transportation.

Seven Commissioners represent all geographic areas of the state, and the two "at-large" Commissioners are appointed with **rail** expertise and **seaport/airport** expertise respectively. The nine commissioners are appointed by the Governor and confirmed by the Senate.

Department of Veterans' Affairs

PO Box 31003, St Petersburg 33731
S/C 594-2440   S/C Fax 594-2497   (813) 893-2440   Fax (813)893-2497
Executive Director—Earl G. Peck, Major General, USAF (Ret.)

The Florida Department of Veterans' Affairs (FDVA) was created by the Legislature in 1988, and it became "official" on January 3, 1989, after the electorate ratified a Constitutional amendment authorizing the Department's establishment.

History was made in Dade County on May 20, 1984, when the first scheduled Metrorail train rolled out of the Dadeland South Station. Shown here is a subsequent run on the $1.1 billion rapid transit system. Metropolitan-Dade County

Florida's veteran population exceeded 1.7 million, as reflected in the 1990 census. In 1993, the FDVA handled almost 400,000 cases assisting veterans and their dependents in obtaining benefits to which they were entitled.

The Veterans' Home of Florida, a 150-bed domiciliary home located in Lake City, opened in 1990, and provides shelter, sustenance, and incidental medical care on an ambulatory, self-care basis to assist eligible veterans who are disabled by age, disease, or circumstances not requiring hospitalization or nursing home care. Major emphasis is placed on rehabilitation.

The Florida Veterans' Nursing Home, a 120-bed facility located in Daytona Beach, officially opened its doors to its first resident in December 1993.

Other FDVA responsibilities include approving institutions for veterans' training, issuance of identification cards to 100% disabled veterans, ensuring compliance with veterans' preference in hiring, promotion of sales of the "Florida Salutes Veterans" license tag, outreach to veterans to ensure that they are aware of entitlements, and interaction with state and federal leaders and politicians to stimulate action to generate a fair-share of dollars and resources to Florida's veterans.

Other Departments, Agencies of the Executive Department

Note: The multiplicity of minor licensing boards, from Acupuncture to Veterinary Medicine, are listed under the prior entry for the Department of Professional Licensing. Exceptions are those boards which have their headquarters away from Tallahassee or are responsible to departments other than the Department of Professional Licensing.

Board of Accountancy
Executive Director Martha Willis
4001 NW 43rd Street, Gainesville 32306   (904) 336-2165

Legal basis: Chapter 473, F.S. *Created:* 1931, revised 1979 and placed within the Department of Business and Professional Regulation. *Duties:* The Board is mandated to act in the public interest by promulgating rules further defining the profession's practice act, qualifying candidates for licensure examinations, determining penalties in disciplinary cases prosecuted by the Department, monitoring probationary and suspension cases, and providing professional expertise to the Department in exams, investigations and other areas of departmental involvement.

African-American Affairs Commission
Administrator Nina Martinez
315 Carlton Building, Tallahassee 32301
(904) 922-0305

Legal basis: Section 14.27 F.S. *Created:* 1993. *Membership:* Fifteen members appointed by the Governor. *Qualifications:* African-American origin; professionally, socially and economically diverse; and representative of the geographic regions of the state. *Term:* Four years, except for staggered terms of the first members. *Chairman:* Appointed by the Governor. *Compensation:* None. *Duties:* Develop specific strategies and plans to address the economic, social, educational, health, and welfare needs of African-Americans in the state.

Armory Board
Chairman The Governor
Vice Chairman Major General Ronald O. Harrison, The Adjutant General
State Arsenal, St. Augustine   (904) 823-0364

Ex officio Members: Governor, Adjutant General, State Quartermaster (Recorder), General Officers of the Line, Regimental Commanders, Group Commanders and Senior Air Commander in the Active National Guard of the State.

Legal basis: Chapter 250.40, F.S. *Created:* 1921. *Duties:* To supervise and control all military buildings and real property devoted to military use by the State. To consider and approve plans for all armories and other buildings before they are rented, constructed or acquired for military use by the State. To receive from counties, municipalities, and other sources donations of land and money to aid in providing and maintaining arsenals, armories, camp sites, etc. To exercise eminent domain to provide necessary land for camp grounds, rifle ranges, or armories.

Athletic Commission
Executive Director Don Hazelton
319 West Madison, Rm 13, Tallahassee 32399-1610
(904) 488-8500

Legal basis: Chapter 84-246, Laws of Florida. *Created:* 1984. Three members appointed by Governor and confirmed by Senate. Commission has jurisdiction over boxing matches involving a professional. Law does not apply to amateur boxers or matches conducted or sponsored by any nationally chartered veterans' organization or any company or detachment of the Florida National Guard. Commission created within the Department of Business and Professional Regulation.

Capital Collateral Representative
Representative Michael Minerva
1533-C South Monroe Street, Tallahassee 32301   (904) 487-4376

Legal basis: Chapter 85-332, Laws of Florida. *Created:* 1985, within Judicial Branch. *Qualifications:* Member in good standing of Florida Bar for preceding five years, appointed by Governor, subject Senate confirmation, for term of four years. Any and all elected Public Defenders shall submit list of three or more nominations to Governor. Representative prohibited from election or appointment to any state office for two years after leaving office. *Duties:* To represent, without additional compensation, any person sentenced to death who shall be without counsel after termination of all direct appellate proceedings in either the Florida or United States Supreme Courts.

Citizen's Assistance Office
Director John Currie
311 Carlton Bldg., Tallahassee 32399-0001   (904) 488-7146

Legal basis: Section 1426 FS *Created* 1979. Lodged in Executive Office of the Governor. Director appointed by Governor and serves at Governor's pleasure. OCA investigates complaints relating to agencies under Governor. Also, identifies problems and needs of citizens in relation to State government. Staff serves as the Governor's liaison for Hispanic Affairs, Minority Affairs and Women's Affairs.

Correction Privatization Commission
C. Mark Hodges
Knight Building, Suite 312, 2737 Centerview Drive, Tallahassee 32399-0950
(904) 921-4034

Legal basis: Section 957 F.S. *Created:* 1993. *Membership:* Five members appointed by the Governor. *Qualifications:* None may be an employee of the Division of Corrections, and one must be a minority. *Term:* Four years. *Duties:* To enter into contracts with contractors for designing, financing, acquiring, leasing, constructing, and operating private correctional facilities.

Corrections Commission
Housed in the Dept. of Corrections

Legal basis: Section 20.315 F.S. *Created:* 1994. *Membership:* Nine members appointed by the Governor and confirmed by the Senate. *Term:* Four years. *Duties:* To oversee, in an advisory capacity, the correctional system in Florida. Recommend major correctional policies to the Governor, recommend improvements of the correctional system to the Governor and the legislature, perform an in-depth review of any need for changes in the Guidelines, evaluating the Department's budget and master plan.

Criminal Justice Standards and Training Commission
Department of Law Enforcement, P.O. Box 1489
Tallahassee 32302   (904) 487-0491

Legal basis: Section 943.11 F.S. *Membership:* Nineteen members, consisting of the Secretary of the Department of Corrections; the Attorney General; the Commissioner of Education; the Director of the Division of the Florida Highway Patrol; and 15 members to be appointed by the Governor. *Term:* 4 years. *Duties:* Certify and revoke the certification of, officers, instructors, and criminal justice training schools. Establish uniform minimum employment and training standards for the various criminal justice disciplines. Consult with municipalities or the state or any political subdivision of the state concerning the development of criminal justice training schools and programs of instruction. Authorize the issuance of certificates for criminal justice training schools and instructors. Establish minimum curricular requirements for criminal justice training schools. Promulgate rules for the certification and discipline of officers who engage in areas of high risk of harm which would in turn increase the potential liability of an employing agency.

Implement, administer, maintain and revise a job-related officer certification examination for each criminal justice discipline.

Defense Conversion and Transition Commission
Chairman Representative Alzo Reddick
Defense Conversion Commission, Univeristy of Central Florida
12443 Research Road, Suite 402, Orlando, 32826 (407) 249-4781

Legal basis: Section 288.9733 F.S. *Created:* 1993. *Membership:* A Senator appointed by the President of the Senate. A Representative appointed by the Speaker of the House. Two members of the Florida Congressional Delegation, one from the House of Representatives and one from the Senate. The Secretary of Commerce, Secretary of Labor and Employment Security, Adjutant General, executive director of the Department of Veterans' Affairs, Commissioner of Education, Chancellor of the Board of Regents, executive director of the State Board of Community Colleges, Secretary of Community Affairs, Secretary of Environmental Protection, director of the State Job Training Coordinating Council the director of the Florida Office of State-Federal Relations, the vice chair of Enterprise Florida and the chairs of officially recognized community base closure committees. *Term:* 8 years. *Duties:* Oversee implementation of major recommendations of the Florida Defense Reinvestment Task Force. Coordinate with and provide information and advice to Enterprise Florida. Act in the interest of communities, industries and workers on defense conversion and transition issues. Establish a clearinghouse to serve as a central point of contact to provide conversion and transition information, services and research to the Commission, affected communities, companies and workers. Coordinates with existing state and local programs. Identify potential sources of funding. Direct the provision of community outreach and technical assistance. Act as an umbrella organization housing and overseeing statewide defense-related initiatives.

Elections Canvassing Commission
Ex officio Members Governor and Cabinet

Legal basis: Sections 20.10 and 102.111, F.S. *Created:* 1895. Handled in the office of the Secretary of State. *Duties:* To canvass the returns of the primary and general election for all State offices and determine and declare who shall have been nominated or elected for such office. To canvass the returns for Presidential electors and Representatives to the Congress of the United States separately and distinct from those for the State offices. To make and sign certificates of election for State and National officers.

Elections Commission
Division of Elections, Department of State
The Capitol, Tallahassee (904) 488-7690

Legal basis: Section 106.24, F.S. *Created:* 1973. Seven persons appointed by Governor from lists submitted by Democratic and Republican parties. *Duties:* To inquire into alleged violations of election laws in closed session and report evidence of violations to Department of State and appropriate State Attorney.

Energy Office
2740 Centerview Dr. Tallahassee 32399-2100
Michael D. Ashworth-State Energy Conservation Program (904) 488-6764
Alexander Mack-Institutional Conservation Program (904) 488-7400

As the state's action arm for energy policy planning and implementation, the Florida Energy Office advises the Governor and Department of Community Affairs Secretary on energy issues affecting Floridians and assists the public and private sector in implementing those strategies.

The Energy Office is charged with helping Florida build an energy-efficient economy through programs to encourage energy conservation and promote the use of alternative energy sources. It also compiles statistical data on energy supplies and forecasts Florida's energy use.

The office is funded with federally-administered funds for state energy conservation programs and conservation in schools and hospitals.

Developmental Disabilities Council

Director Joe Krieger
820 East Park Avenue, Suite I100
Tallahassee 32301-2600
(904) 488-4180

Legal basis: Chapter 84-226, Laws of Florida. *Created:* 1984. Within Department of Health and Rehabilitative Services, council of 27 members, an interdepartmental and interagency body advisory for programs and services affecting persons with developmental disabilities.

Environmental Equity and Justice Commission

Chairman Dr. Charles Kidd
204 Perry Page Building, Tallahassee 32307

Legal basis: Section 760.85 F.S. *Created:* 1994. *Membership:* Seventeen members appointed by the Governor: One Florida Representative and one Florida Senator. Two members representing the civil rights community. Two representatives of the environmental community. Two members representing the business community. One member from the Department of Environmental Protection and one from the Department of Health and Rehabilitative Services. Two members representing major facilities regulated by the Department of Environmental Protection. Two members representing local government. Two members representing the universities. One environmental risk assessment professional. *Term:* 2 years. *Purpose:* To examine and determine the possible disproportionate and cumulative concentration of environmental hazards in people of color and low-income communities, to assess how Florida can best address these inequities, if any, with emphasis on future prevention, and to ensure that the public benefits resulting from the work of Florida's agencies will be fully and equitably realized by communities of color and low income, taking into account the greater degree of risk to which such communities may be exposed.

Office of Executive Clemency

Coordinator Ms. Janet H. Keels
2601 Blair Stone Rd., Tallahassee 32399-2450 (904) 488-2952
Ex officio Members Governor, Secretary of State, Attorney General, Comptroller, Treasurer, Commissioner of Agriculture, and Commissioner of Education

Legal basis: Constitutional, Article IV, Section 8, and Rules of Executive Clemency adopted by Governor and requisite members of Cabinet. *Created:* 1885 and revised 1968. *Duties:* To act upon recommendations for clemency from the Parole and Probation Commission, the investigative agency for the Board. To report to the Legislature at the beginning of each session a record of all clemency granted. Except in cases of treason or impeachment the Governor may suspend collection of fines and forfeitures and grant reprieves not exceeding 60 days. The Governor, with the approval of three members of the Cabinet, may grant full or conditional pardons, restore civil rights, commute punishment, and remit fines and forfeitures. In cases of treason, the Governor may grant reprieves until adjournment of the regular session of the Legislature next after the conviction, at which session the Legislature may grant a pardon or further reprieve; otherwise the sentence shall be executed.

Florida Inland Navigation District

Executive Director Art Wilde
1314 Marcinski Rd., Jupiter 33477 (407) 627-3386

Legal basis: Chapters 12026, Acts of 1927; 14723, Acts of 1931; 19122, Acts of 1939; 20430, Acts of 1941, and 27275, Acts of 1951. *Membership:* Appointed by Governor, not more than one from each county in District. *Duties:* To acquire and transfer free of cost to the U.S. the privately owned waterway known as Florida East Coast Canal, additional right-of-way and suitable areas for the deposit of material dredged in connection with the work and its subsequent maintenance, and to arrange for the relocations of bridges, pipelines, cables and other structure found to be obstructions to navigation.

Commission on Government Accountability to the People
Executive Director Karen Sanford
154 Holland Building, Tallahassee 32301
(904) 922-6907

Legal basis: Section 14.30 F.S. *Created:* 1994. *Membership:* Fifteen members appointed by the Governor, subject to confirmation by the Senate, with 9 members from the private sector and 6 members from the public sector. *Term:* Four years, except for staggered terms of the first members. *Chairman:* First appointed by the Governor, subsequently elected by majority vote. *Compensation:* None, but may be reimbursed for per diem and travel expenses. *Duties:* Track the impact of state agency actions upon the well-being of Florida citizens.

Gulf of Mexico Regional Fishery Management Council
Executive Director Wayne Swingle
Suite 331, Lincoln Center, 5401 West Kennedy Boulevard, Tampa 33609-2486 (813) 228-2815

Florida members: Robert P. Jones of Tallahassee, as Executive Director of Southeastern Fisheries Association; Billy Putnam of Panama City, marina operator, and Virginia B. Wetherell, as Secretary of the Department of Environmental Protection. Appointed by U.S. Secretary of Commerce. *Duties:* To develop management plans for all species of marine life in implementation of law extending United States territorial waters 200 miles offshore.

Gulf States Marine Fisheries Commission
Executive Director Larry B. Simpson
P.O. Box 726, Ocean Springs, Mississippi 39566-0726 (601) 875-5912

Legal basis: Section 370.20, F.S. *Duties:* To join with representatives of other states bordering the Gulf of Mexico in formulating recommendations for the betterment of the salt water fishing industry.

South Atlantic Regional Fishery Management Council
Executive Director Robert Mahood
Suite 306, 1 Southpart Circle, Charleston, South Carolina 29407 (803) 571-4366

Florida members: John Brownlee, North Palm Beach, Sport fishing writer, Ben Hartig, Hobe Sound, Fisherman, and Virginia Wetherell as Secretary of the Department of Environmental Protection. Appointed by the U.S. Secretary of Commerce. *Duties:* To develop management plans for all species of marine life in implementation of law extending United States territorial waters 200 miles offshore.

Governor's Mansion Commission
Chairperson Mrs. Cathy Reed
The Governor's Mansion, 700 North Adams Street, Tallahassee 32303
(904) 488-4661

Legal basis: Section 272.18 F.S. *Created:* 1957. *Membership:* Eight members, five of whom shall be private citizens appointed by the Governor, subject to confirmation by the Senate. Other members shall be the Director of the Division of Facilities Management of the Department of Management Services; one member shall be the Director of the Division of Recreation and Parks of the Department of Environmental Protection; and one employee of the Department of State with curatorial and museum expertise, designated by the Secretary of State. The spouse of the Governor or a designated representative shall be an ex officio member. *Term:* Four years. *Duties:* The commission shall keep the structure, style and character of the Governor's Mansion, its grounds, and all structures thereon consistent with its original plan of construction; recommend any major changes; catalog and maintain an inventory of the Mansion's contents; employ or utilize the services of a full-time curator; receive gifts and bequests and adopt rules governing the use of the state rooms of the Mansion.

Southeastern Interstate Forest Fire Protection Compact, Advisory Committee

Coordinator State Forester Earl Peterson
3125 Conner Blvd. Tallahassee 32399-1650
(904) 488-4274

Legal basis: Section 590.31, F.S. *Purposes:* To represent Florida on Southeastern Interstate Forest Fire Protection Compact Commission, provided by Congress so the states may legally request and lend assistance to each other in the combating of forest fires.

Health Cost Care Containment Board

Executive Director Douglas Cook
Atrium Bldg, Suite 301, 325 John Knox Road, Tallahassee 32303 (904) 488-1295

Legal basis: Section 395.501, F.S. *Created:* 1979. Nine members appointed by the Governor. *Duties:* To compile, analyze, and publish the rates, charges, costs, and revenues of the state's hospitals; to publish and disseminate an in-depth study comparing these rates, charges, and other data; to establish a uniform reporting system; to advise on the integration of state health care cost containment efforts with other state health regulations, and with the recommendations of health systems agencies and those of the designated state health planning agency; to study the extent of cross-subsidization and the success of the Voluntary Effort program for reducing the rate of increase of hospital rates. *Powers:* To review the budget of any hospital at a public hearing if that hospital's rates and charges are in the upper 20 percent of such indicators for all hospitals in its class or group; to require the submission by hospitals of data; to conduct studies for the Department of Health and Rehabilitative Services with respect to Certificates of Need; to hold public hearings, conduct investigations, and subpoena witnesses, papers, records, and documents; to inspect hospital books, audits, and records; to extract a penalty of up to $1,000 a day from any hospital refusing to file reports or other information required under the Health Care Cost Containment Act of 1979; to ask for a removal of a hospital's license for knowing and willful falsification of a report.

Commission on Hispanic Affairs

Executive Director Mariela Fraser
Chairman Victor Alvarado
RM LL06, The Capitol, 32399-0001 (904) 488-8146
FAX (904) 488-9578

Legal basis: Section 14.25, F.S. *Created:* 1977 as a commission to "provide a means by which the State may obtain a comprehensive and ongoing study relating to those citizens of Florida who are of Hispanic origin." Commission of 15 members appointed by Governor.

Northwest Florida Regional Housing Authority

Executive Director Marilyn Phillips
P.O. Box 218, Graceville 32440 (904) 263-4442

Legal basis: Section 421.30, F.S. *Created:* 1941. *Method of Selection:* Appointed by Governor. One qualified elector from each county in area of regional housing authority. *Duties:* To provide safe and sanitary housing for low income families and elderly including the handicapped and disabled.

Housing Finance Agency

Director Susan J. Leigh
227 North Bronough Street, Suite 5000, Tallahassee 32301
(904) 488-4197

Legal basis: Article VII, Section 16, State Constitution, and Part IV, Chapter 420, F.S. *Created:* October 7, 1980, as division of Department of Community Affairs. *Membership:* Secretary of Department of Community Affairs, as voting member, and eight members appointed by Governor and confirmed by Senate. *Purpose:* To encourage the investment of private capital in residential housing through the use of public financing. Bonds shall be legal investments without limitation for all public bodies, banks, trust companies, savings and loan associations, insurance companies, but shall not be a debt of the state or of any local government. The agency shall not have the power to pledge the credit, revenues, or taxing power of the state or local governments.

Commission on Human Relations
Executive Director Ronald M. McElrath
325 John Knox Road, Building F, Suite 240, Tallahassee 32303-4149
(904) 488-7082

Legal basis: Section 760.03 F.S. *Created:* 1969. *Membership:* Twelve members who are broadly representative of various racial, religious, ethnic, social, economic, political, and professional groups, with one member 60 years of age or older, appointed by the Governor, subject to confirmation by the Senate. *Term:* Four years. *Functions:* Promote and encourage fair treatment and equal opportunity for all persons regardless of race, color, religion, sex, national origin, age, handicap, or marital status and mutual understanding and respect among all members of all economic, social racial, religious, and ethnic groups; and shall endeavor to eliminate discrimination against, and antagonism between religious, racial and ethnic groups and their members.

Human Resource Development Commission
Housed within the Executive Office of the Governor

Legal basis: Section 446.31 F.S. *Created:* 1994. *Membership:* The Governor, Speaker of the House of Representatives, President of the Senate, Commissioner of Education, Secretary of Labor and Employment Security, Secretary of Health and Rehabilitative Services, and the Secretary of Commerce and five other members appointed by the Governor including: One member of the Florida Chamber of Commerce. One member of Associated Industries of Florida. Two members of the American Federation of Labor and Congress of Industrial Organizations and the chairman of the board of directors of Enterprize Florida. *Term:* 4 years. *Purpose:* To serve in an advisory capacity to the Cabinet and Legislature on all matters related to human resource development in Florida. The commission shall oversee policy and practice related to the provision of social service, education, rehabilitation, and economic development programs to develop policies that foster program coordination and cooperation while eliminating unwarranted program duplication.

Statewide Human Rights Advocacy Committee
Director William Marvin
1317 Winewood Blvd., Bldg E, Rm 21, Tallahassee 32399-0700 (904) 488-7082

Legal basis: Chapter 84.266, Laws of Florida. *Created:* 1984. Within Department of Health and Rehabilitative Services, council of eight members appointed by Governor. *Duties:* To serve as third-party mechanism for protecting the constitutional and human rights of any HRS client within a program or facility operated, funded, regulated, or licensed by the Department. To receive, investigate, and resolve reports of abuse or deprivation of human rights referred to the Committee by a district human rights committee.

Advisory Council on Intergovernmental Relations
Executive Director Dr. Mary K. Falconer
Room 4, Holland Building, Tallahassee 32301 (904) 488-9627

Legal basis: Part IV of Chapter 163, F. S. *Created:* 1977. 17 members as follows: four members of the Senate, appointed by the President; four members of the House of Representatives, appointed by the Speaker, and nine members appointed by the Governor. *Duties:* To serve as a forum. To evaluate on a continuing basis the interrelationships among local, regional, state, interstate, and federal agencies in the providing of public services. To analyze the structure and fiscal policies of the State and its political subdivisions. To conduct studies of tax and revenue matters. To examine proposed and existing Federal and State programs for their impact. To encourage and, where appropriate, coordinate studies relating to intergovernmental relations. To review recommendations of national commissions studying intergovernmental relationships. To issue annual reports of its findings and recommendations. To apply for, contract for, receive and expend for its purposes any appropriations or grants from the federal government or any other source, public or private.

International Affairs Commission
Executive Director Nat M. Turnbull, Jr.
342 Collins Building, Tallahassee 32301
(904) 922-0355

Legal basis: Section 288.803 F.S. *Created:* 1990. *Membership:* Governor, Secretary of State, Commissioner of Education, Comptroller, Commissioner of Agriculture, Secretary of Commerce, Chancellor of the State University System, executive director of the State Community College System, a member of the House of Representatives, a member of the Senate and 15 members to be appointed by the Governor. *Qualifications;* Two members actively engaged in the promotion of international trade and commerce in Florida. A member experienced in the international trade and tourism aspects of the state's deepwater ports. A member experienced in the operation of international airports in Florida. A member from the Florida International Trade and Investment Council. A member of a statewide business promotion organization. A member with extensive experience in foreign language instruction or international education. A member experienced in international law or international governmental relations. A member experienced in international banking and financial services from a major Florida banking institution. A member of a Florida company that is actively engaged in the manufacture of products for sale in foreign markets. A member of a major Florida company actively engaged in the promotion of international tourism. A member of the Florida Citrus Commission. A member of a major multinational company with offices in Florida. Two members with competence in matters of particular international concern. A member of the Small and Minority Business Advisory Council. *Term:* Four years, except for the staggered terms of the first members. *Compensation:* None, except for per diem and travel expenses. *Duties:* To serve as the primary state entity responsible for the oversight and coordination of policies and activities relating to international affairs for the state.

Land and Water Adjudicatory Commission
Executive Director Robert Bradley
2105 The Capitol, Tallahassee 32399-0001 (904) 488-7793
Ex officio Members Governor, Comptroller and Treasurer

Legal basis: Section 380.07, F.S. *Duties:* To review appeals from orders of development in areas of critical state concern. To review orders of the High Speed Rail Transportation Commission relating to land use.

State Lottery Commission
Chairman James Michael Hattaway
162 East Highway 434, Longwood 32750

Legal basis: Section 24.106 F.S. *Created:* 1987. *Membership:* Five members, all residents of the state, appointed by the Governor. *Term:* 4 years. *Purpose:* to serve as a resource for the department and to provide the secretary with private sector perspectives on the operation of a large marketing enterprise. *Duties:* to review the performance of the department. Advise the secretary and make recommendations regarding operations of the department. Identify potential improvements in this act, the rules of the department and the management of the department.

Marine Fisheries Commission
Executive Director Dr. Russell S. Nelson
2540 Executive Center, Circle West, Tallahassee 32301 (904) 447-0554

Legal basis: Section 370.026, F.S. *Created:* 1983, within Department of Environmental Protection. Seven members, appointed by Governor and confirmed by Senate. *Duties:* To exercise rulemaking authority over marine life, with exception of endangered species, subject to approval by Governor and Cabinet sitting as the head of the Department of Environmental Protection.

Medical Examiners Commission
Chairman Dr. Joan Wood
10850 Ulmerton Road, Largo, 34648 (813) 585-5671

Legal basis: Section 406.02 F.S. *Created:* 1970. *Membership:* Appointed by the Governor: Two physicians who are active medical examiners. One member who is a licensed funeral director, one State Attorney, one Public Defender, one Sheriff, one County Commissioner, the Attorney General, and the Deputy Assistant Secretary for Health. *Term:* 4 years. *Duties:* Remove or suspend district medical examiners and investigate violations. Oversee distribution of state funds for medical examiner districts.

Mental Health Institute
Director Max Derteke, M.D.
13301 North Bruce B. Downs Blvd., Tampa 33612 (813) 974-4533

Legal basis: Section 240.514, F.S. The Florida Mental Health Institute opened in 1974 as part of the Department of Health and Rehabilitative Services and was transferred to the University of South Florida in 1982. It is a 150-bed mental health "Treatment Facility" serving members of all age groups. Its mission is to carry out training, education and research in support of the state's mental health service and related systems. A wide variety of inservice and continuing education courses for employees of the Departments of Corrections, and Health and Rehabilitative Services and for employees of local mental health agencies are offered both at the FMHI campus and at locations throughout the state. Research on the needs and the functioning of mental health services is emphasized. Undergraduate and graduate students from several colleges of the University of South Florida as well as from other academic institutions take field placements, clinical internships, research assistantships and other practical assignments for academic credit. The clinical service units at the Institute all serve as demonstration units for training programs and as testing units for new clinical approaches. There are approximately 370 persons on the staff, of whom approximately 30 are faculty members. A school for 80 severely emotionally disturbed children and adolescents operates in collaboration with the Hillsborough County Public Schools. A 16-bed unit for disturbed juvenile delinquents operates in collaboration with the Department of Health and Rehabilitative Services.

National Conference of Commissioners on Uniform State Laws
Ex Officio Secretary Linda Jessen
111 West Madison Rm 612, Tallahassee 32399-1400 (904) 488-8403

Legal basis: Section 13.10, F.S. *Created:* 1985. Three members appointed by the Governor with the consent of the Senate. *Duties:* To identify areas of the law in which interstate uniformity is desirable and then to cooperate with like commissions from other states to draft and enact uniform state laws.

Parole Commission
Chairman Judith Wolson
1309 Winewood Blvd, Bldg B, Third Floor, Tallahassee 32399-2450
(904) 488-1653 Fax (904) 488-7199

Legal basis: (Article IV, Section 8(c) of the Constitution gives the Legislature power to create a Parole and Probation Commission.) Chapter 947, F.S. *Created:* 1941. *Method of selection:* Eight Commissioners, seven selected by the Governor and Cabinet on basis of investigations and comprehensive evaluation, by a special qualifications committee, and confirmed by the Senate. The Secretary of the Department of Corrections shall be a member of the Commission and participate only in policy-making decisions. *Duties:* To determine what persons shall be released from prison on parole, and to fix the time and conditions of such parole; to determine what action shall be taken in case of violation of parole, to make all necessary investigations of paroles; to report to the Office of Executive Clemency (formerly the Board of Pardons) the facts, record, histories, and conditions of persons under consideration by the Office of Executive Clemency for pardon, restoration of civil rights, commutation of sentence, remission of fine or penalty of forfeiture.

Council on Physical Fitness and Amateur Sports

Executive Director Jimmy Carnes
1330 NW 6th Street, Gainesville 32601
(904) 336-2120

Legal basis: Section 14.22 F.S. *Created:* 1974. *Membership:* Twenty five members appointed by the Governor. *Qualifications:* Appropriate interests and representing the various geographical areas of the state. *Term:* Four years, with staggered terms. *Compensation:* None, but shall receive per diem and travel expenses. *Duties:* Promote physical fitness and sports. Promote the development of a program of statewide amateur athletic competition to be known as the "Sunshine State Games." Promote the development of Olympic training centers within the state. Promote national and international amateur athletic competitions.

PRIDE

Chairman Cecelia Bryant
President Pamela Davis
2849-C Apalachee Parkway, Tallahassee 32301   (904) 487-3774

Legal basis: Section 946.502 F.S. (authority for non-profit organizations generally.)
("Pride" is the acronym for "Prison Rehabilitative Industries and Diversified Enterprises.")
Pride was created by the Legislature in 1981 as a non-profit partnership between the Legislature, the Executive Branch of State Government, the Department of Corrections, and the private sector. Pride operates a free enterprise program within prison walls.

Pride moves inmates through work stations in 42 diversified industries at 22 correctional institutions, producing products ranging from false teeth to furniture, which must meet or exceed the quality, service and price standards of Pride's customers.

Board of Real Estate Commission

Executive Director Darlene Keller
400 West Robinson Street, Orlando 32801   (407) 423-6071

Legal basis: Chapter 475, F.S. *Created:* 1927, revised 1978 and placed within the Department of Business and Professional Regulation. Seven members appointed by the Governor, confirmed by the Senate. *Duties:* The Board is mandated to act in the public interest by promulgating rules further defining the profession's practice act, qualifying candidates for licensure examinations, determining penalties in disciplinary cases prosecuted by the Department, monitoring probationary and suspension cases, and providing professional expertise to the Department in exams, investigations and other areas of departmental involvement.

State Retirement Commission

Chair Arlene S. Feuerberg
Knight Building, Suite 312, 2737 Centerview Drive,
Tallahassee 32399-0950   (904) 487-2410

Legal basis: Section 121.22 F.S. *Membership:* Seven members appointed by the Governor: One member who is retired under a state-supported system administered by the Division of Retirement; two members from different occupational backgrounds who are active members in a state-supported retirement system which is administered by the Division of Retirement; and four members who are not retirees, beneficiaries, or members of a state-supported retirement system administered by the Division of Retirement. *Term:* 4 years.

Sentencing Commission
Director John Hogenmueller
Office of State Courts Administrator, Supreme Court Building, Tallahassee 32399-1900
(904) 922-5085

Legal basis: Section 921.001 F.S. *Created:* 1982. *Membership:* Seventeen members consisting of: Two members of the Senate appointed by the President; two members of the House of Representatives appointed by the Speaker; The Chief Justice of the Supreme Court; three circuit court judges, one county court judge, and one representative of the victim advocacy profession, appointed by the Chief Justice; the Attorney General, the Secretary of the Department of Corrections. Other members appointed by the Governor: one state attorney, one public defender, one private attorney, and two members of the Governor's choice. *Term:* Members of the commission appointed by the Governor and the members from the Senate and House serve 2 year terms. The members appointed by the Chief Justice serve at his pleasure. *Purpose:* review sentencing practices and recommend modifications to the guidelines to establish a uniform set of standards to guide the sentencing judge. Conduct ongoing research on the impact of the sentencing guidelines.

Spaceport Florida Authority

Legal basis: Chapter 331, F.S., Part II. *Created:* 1989. *Purpose:* To provide a unified direction for space-related economic growth. *Spaceport Territory:* Property along Atlantic ocean in Brevard County and defined area along Gulf of Mexico in Gulf County. Administered by nine supervisors, seven appointed by Governor and two ex-officio, nonvoting members, a State Senator selected by Senate President and a State Representative selected by Speaker.

Transportation Disadvantaged Commission
Executive Director Jo Ann Hutchinson
605 Suwannee Street, M.S. 49, Tallahassee 32399-0450
(904) 488-6036

Legal basis: Section 427.012 F.S. *Created:* 1979. *Membership:* Secretary of the Department of Transportation, Secretary of the Department of Health and Rehabilitative Services, Commissioner of Education, Secretary of the Department of Labor and Employment Security, Director of Department of Veterans' Affairs, Secretary of the Department of Elderly Affairs, President of the Florida Association for Community Action. A person over 60 who is member of a recognized statewide organization representing elderly Floridians. A handicapped person who is a member of a recognized statewide organization representing handicapped Floridians. Two citizens advocate representatives. A representative of the community transportation coordinators. One member of the Early Childhood Council. Two representatives of current private for-profit or private not-for-profit transportation operators. *Term:* Office holders for their term of office. Others 4 years. *Purpose:* To accomplish the coordination of transportation services provided to the transportation disadvantaged. The goal shall to be to assure the cost-effective provision of transportation by disadvantaged without any bias or presumption in favor of multioperator systems or not-for-profit transportation operators over single operator systems or for-profit transportation operators.

Unemployment Appeals Commission
Chairman Carson Dyal
300 Webster Building, Tallahassee 32399-0681
(904) 487-2685

Legal basis: Section 20.171 F.S. *Membership:* Three members appointed by the Governor, subject to confirmation by the Senate. The chairman shall devote his entire time to his commission duties. *Compensation:* $100 for each day they are engaged in the work of the commission, not including travel expenses. *Term:* Four Years. *Duties:* The commission is vested with all authority, powers, duties, and responsibilities relating to unemployment compensation appeal proceedings under chapter 443.

The Legislature

"The legislative power of the State shall be vested in a Legislature..."
Florida Constitution, Article III, Section 1

The legislature has been described generally as the lawmaking branch of a state government. In Florida, the Legislature defined its function more precisely in these words from the Executive Reorganization Act of 1969:

"The legislative branch has the broad purpose of determining policies and programs and reviewing program performance."

Although the physical setting is much the same and rituals remain, the Legislature of today bears little resemblance in its internal workings and its philosophy to the Legislature of a few years ago. Beginning in 1966, the House of Representatives and the Senate underwent changes which gave the Legislature equality with the executive branch.

The first year-round staff for members and committees was recruited beginning in 1969. By 1994, the vitalized Legislature had 1,978 employees.

Now, the First Word

The big difference is that the Legislature now has the *first* word in lawmaking along with the *last* word.

The Florida House of Representatives in Chamber session.

The old pattern of biennial sessions meant the lawmakers were forced to delegate much of their sovereignty to executive agencies and others outside the legislative branch.

As in other states, the Governor came to be regarded as the chief legislator, presenting the Legislature not only with his message but a sheaf of bills already prepared for introduction. The Governor's legislative program became the checklist by which some judged legislative performance.

Thus, while the Legislature always possessed the last word—voting on legislation—the preparation of bills often was in other hands.

To process the grist produced by agencies of the Executive branch, the Legislature was forced to borrow many of its specialists from the same source. Other employees were recruited from among persons willing and able to work a maximum of sixty days every two years.

Governor Bob Graham, in off-the-cuff remarks to Democratic nominees of the House of Representatives on October 7, 1982, in part said:

"I appreciate the fact that our form of government is not like a parliamentary system where the Legislature and the Executive are essentially one. We have a system that's built around a division of governmental powers. Those of you who have not served in the Legislature before will find out that what the textbook said about the balance of powers in the three branches: that *ain't* just for the textbook any more. That really works."

A Turn-Around

Today's Legislature represents a turn-around, with the legislative branch able to coexist on equal terms with the Executive and Judicial branches. This has been made possible by a number of steps including these:

1. A constitutional amendment requiring a special session on the second Tuesday following regular November general elections. These sessions are for the exclusive purpose of reorganizing the Legislature, so that the new Senate President and new House Speaker may at once appoint committees to serve the two years coincident with the terms of the presiding officers. (Previously, the standing committees were appointed after the convening of a regular session and served only for the duration of that session.)

2. Revision of the Constitution in 1968 changed the regular sessions of the Legislature from a biennial to an annual basis.

3. The presiding officers have been given the joint authority to convene the Legislature in special session. (Previously, only the Governor possessed this power. Florida had a self-starter provision but its cumbersome nature meant no special session ever was convened under this method.)

4. Transfer of the state's auditing department from the Executive branch to the Legislature materially strengthened its effectiveness. No longer an appointee of the Governor, with a four-year term, the Auditor General has what amounts to life tenure and possesses independence of the executive agencies being audited. The Auditor General also provides the Legislature with a window on the performance by those Executive agencies of the tasks assigned them by the lawmakers.

5. The legislative committees have been staffed with analysts, researchers, attorneys, and other year-round personnel capable of enabling the committees to function effectively.

6. Florida retains its tradition of part-time legislators but has recognized the new demands upon their days by reason of annual session and continuing committee activity through an increase in pay plus an annual percentage increase equal to that received by state employees generally. An allowance has been made so legislators may maintain offices in their districts for the transacting of the public's business. (*See* The Legislator.)

Separation of Powers

The result of these and other changes has been the attainment of true separation of powers. This has cost money. Whether there has been a dollar-and-cents return in a more effective executive system hardly can be proven or disproven because the yardsticks—the value of money, the growth of population among these—change daily. However, the Supreme Court of Florida (through Justice John E. Mathews) stated the significance in these words (*Pepper vs. Pepper*, 66 So.2d 280):

"The separation of governmental power was considered essential in the very beginning of our Government, and the importance of the preservation of the three departments, each separate from and independent of the other becomes more important and more manifest with the passing years. Experience has shown the wisdom of this separation. If the Judicial Department of the Government can take over the Legislative powers, there is no reason why it cannot also take over the Executive powers; and in the end, all powers of the Government would be vested in one body. Recorded history shows that such encroachments ultimately result in tyranny, in despotism, and in destruction of constitutional processes."

Equality of the Houses

The Senate and the House of Representatives of our Florida government share equally the power of lawmaking. Neither can bring about the passage of a law by its independent action. Neither possesses any right in the legislative process not enjoyed by the other. Either house may originate any type of legislation.

The Legislature exercises quasi-judicial functions separate from lawmaking. The House possesses the exclusive right to impeach officers and only the Senate may try officers so accused. Only the Senate may pass judgment upon officers appointed by the Governor subject to confirmation by the Senate, and only the Senate may remove officers suspended by the Governor.

The Power of the Legislature

The Florida Supreme Court has defined the lawmaking jurisdiction of the Florida Legislature in these words:

"The legislative power to enact statutes is subject only to the limitations provided by the State and Federal Constitutions." (*City of Jacksonville vs. Bowden*, 67 Fla. 181.)

Under our overall system of state and federal government, the power to make laws is divided between the government of the United States and that of the individual states. The United States Constitution is a grant of power from the states to the federal government. It specifies in general terms the main powers of the national (federal) government. The *delegated* and *implied* powers as listed in the United States Constitution provide the basis on which the national government operates. All powers not expressly given to the national government are retained in and belong to the states. Hence, the powers of the states are not listed in the United States Constitution.

The state constitutions do not attempt to list all their *reserved* and *inherent* powers. These powers constitute the basis for all actions of a state government. This is because the state legislatures may take any action and enact any law they wish as long as those actions and laws do not violate the state constitution or the United States Constitution.

The reserved powers of state governments are many. Among them are the defining of crimes and providing the punishment for violation; also the levying and collection of taxes for state purposes. The state can authorize counties, cities, and other local governmental agencies to levy and collect taxes for their purposes. It can pass laws relating to health and safety. It can build highways. It can enact marriage and divorce laws. The state can also authorize the establishment of cities.

Laws

A law is the final product of the legislative process. It is the end result of the introduction of a bill, its passage by both houses into an act, and its approval by the Governor (or the overriding by the Legislature of his veto), and its recording by the Secretary of State. A statute is a law after it has been organized, by topic, into the compiled body of laws. HB 1 may become Chapter 75-102 of the 1975 Laws of Florida (Session Laws) and then Section 153.55 of the Florida Statutes.

General Laws

Of general laws, James Lowe, director of the House Bill Drafting Service, has written:

"Theoretically, a 'general law' is a law which is intended to have statewide application. But there are many laws which relate to less than the whole state and which are still legally 'general laws.' The Supreme Court of Florida, in an early case, declared that 'every law is general which included in its provisions all persons or things of the same genus.' A law does not have to be universal in application to be a general law. Laws relating to the location of the state capitol, a state university, the state prison or hospital are local in character but affect directly or indirectly every citizen of the state, and are regarded as general laws."

Special Laws

Of special laws, Director Lowe has written:

"As a general statement, a special act is any legislative act which meets *both* of the following criteria: 1. It applies to an area or group which is less than the total area or population of the state, and 2. Its subject matter is such that those to whom it is applicable are entitled to the publication or referendum required by Section 10 of Article III of the Florida Constitution. Having said this, it should be noted that it is often difficult to determine whether or not a particular legislative proposal comes within the scope of these two criteria. Section 11 of Article III of the Florida Constitution provides that 'there shall be no special law or general law of local application pertaining to' a specified list of topics."

Frederick H. Schultz, Jacksonville investor, served as Speaker of the House in 1969 and 1970 when he seized the opportunity for a major change in legislative direction, from committees largely passing upon proposals of the Executive Department and others to being creative in their own right. Subsequently, he served as Vice Chairman of the Board of Governors of the Federal Reserve System.

Population Laws

Of population laws, Director Lowe has written:

"A population act is the most commonly encountered type of 'general law of local application.' It is worded in such a way as to be applicable only to counties of a certain specified size. Although a population act may apply to only a few counties (or perhaps only one) it is not considered to be a special act and does not have to be advertised or made subject to a referendum.

Are population acts constitutional? They can be. Subsection (b) of Section 11 of Article III of the Florida Constitution provides in part that: 'In the enactment of general laws . . . political subdivisions or other governmental entities may be classified only on a basis reasonably related to the subject of the law.' Therefore, if the grouping of counties of a certain size can be justified on the basis of being 'reasonably related to the subject' of the bill, it is perfectly all right to enact a law which relates only to those counties."

The Legislature formerly passed in substantial volume another type of population act, which was very limited in application. These were enacted as general laws, without advertising or provision for ratification by referendum as required for local special legislation. But the population acts had a limited, "special" or "local" application because their effectiveness was limited to counties falling within prescribed minimum and maximum population brackets. For example, a law might be framed as to apply only to "the members of the county board of public instruction in all counties having a population of not less than 3,000 nor more than 3,100." Such a population act at least until the taking of the next federal census, likely would apply to only one county. Virtually all such acts likely were unconstitutional but few ever were challenged. Use of these laws largely has passed out of existence because of the granting in the 1970s of home rule powers to counties. When this was done, some 2,100 population acts were repealed.

Oldest Laws

A computer search of the Florida Statutes by Dr. Ernest E. Means, then director of Statutory Revision for the Legislature, revealed two ordinances proclaimed by Andrew Jackson on July 21, 1821, were still in force. These laws relate to the boundaries of Escambia and St. Johns counties. Nine other sections of the Florida Statutes date from 1823 and 20 from 1832.

Legislative Sessions

Regular Sessions: The 1885 Constitution called for regular sessions of the legisature to be held biennially, commencing on the first Tuesday after the first Monday in April 1887. The 1968 revision of the Constitution instituted annual regular sessions commencing on the first Tuesday after the first Monday in April.

In 1990 the Constitution was amended. In 1991 a regular session began on the first Tuesday after the first Monday in March. In 1992 and thereafter a regular session would convene on the first Tuesday after the first Monday in February of each odd numbered year, and on the first Tuesday after the first Monday in February, or such other date as may be fixed by law, of each even numbered year. (Sessions were convened in February in 1992, 1993 and 1994.)

In 1994 the Constitution was again amended to begin annual 60 day sessions on the first Tuesday after the first Monday in March. Regular sessions have a maximum life of sixty consecutive days, including Sundays, but may be extended by a three-fifths vote of each house. Thus, the first of the four regular sessions of a Governor's term is convened months after his inauguration. This first session is usually concerned in large measure with the new Governor's recommendations. These are based generally upon the platform he presented to the people as an inducement for their votes.

There are seven types of legislative session other than regular. These are:

1. *Special Session.*—The Governor may call the Legislature into special session. This kind of special session may last no longer than twenty consecutive days but may be extended by a three-fifths vote of each house.

In his proclamation convening the Legislature, the Governor states the matters which in his opinion require the extraordinary session. The Governor may later add other subjects to his original call. At such special sessions no other matters can be considered by the Legislature unless by a two-thirds vote of the members elected. This exception, however, applies only to the question of whether a bill concerning some matter not in the Governor's call may be introduced. After its introduction has been permitted, only the usual number of votes is required for passage. Ordinarily, consent is given for exclusively local measures.

2. *Apportionment Session.*—The Governor is required by the constitution to convene the Legislature in special session if the legislators have, in his opinion, failed to properly reapportion the representation in the Senate and House of Representatives. This reapportioning must be according to the specifications of Article III, Section 16(a), of the Florida Constitution. Such a session shall not exceed thirty consecutive days. The constitution says it "shall be the mandatory duty of the Legislature to adopt a joint resolution of apportionment." No business other than apportionment can be considered at this type of special session.

3. *Extended Session.*—The Legislature may extend its regular sixty-day session and any special session. This requires a three-fifths vote of the mem-

bership of both houses. There is no limit to the length of such extensions. The purpose of an extended session is to complete action on legislation already introduced. New measures may, however, be received with the consent of two-thirds of the membership of each house. That would be 80 "yea" votes in the House, 27 in the Senate.

4. *Self-Starter Session.*—The 1885 Constitution permitted the Legislature to convene itself in extraordinary session for a period not to exceed thirty days when "conditions warrant" and this provision has been carried forward as a law. Such a session can be convened only upon the affirmative votes of three-fifths of all the members of the Legislature. These votes are cast in a mail poll taken by the Secretary of State at the written request of not less than 20 percent of the membership of the Legislature.

Three unsuccessful efforts have been made by legislators to call the Legislature into session. In each instance, 20 percent of the members of the Legislature had requested the Secretary of State to poll the membership but the poll failed to produce the required affirmances of three-fifths of the members of each house.

In August, 1960, the Legislature was polled for a session to declare Florida's presidential electors uninstructed. In January, 1963, the poll concerned legislative apportionment. In August, 1972, the session would have considered the reinstatement of capital punishment and the restoration of filing fees for candidates, both having been stricken by the U.S. Supreme Court.

5. *Session Called by Presiding Officers.*—The President of the Senate and the Speaker of the House of Representatives, by joint proclamation filed with the Secretary of State, may convene the Legislature in special session. During such a special session, only such legislative business may be transacted as is within the purview of the proclamation or in a communication from the Governor or is introduced by consent of two-thirds of the membership of each house. The first such session was called for December 13, 1977, so the Senate could consider charges of misuse of office against Senator Ralph R. Poston, Jr., of Miami. Poston was reprimanded and fined $500. It was necessary that both houses be called. The House was in session 27 minutes, receiving veto messages and transacting other in-house business since the meeting had been called for the "sole and exclusive" purpose of the Poston matter which did not involve the House.

6. *Organization Session.*—A regular session of a special nature is that commanded by the constitution to be held on the fourteenth day after each general election. This session is for the exclusive purpose of organizing the houses. By selecting officers and adopting rules, the Legislature puts itself in business four months earlier than was the case prior to 1966. The significance of this has been discussed. There is no time limit on an organization session but usually the limited business can be transacted within two hours.

7. *Suspension Session of Senate.*—The President of the Senate, or a majority of its membership, may convene the Senate in special session for the purpose of considering the suspension by the Governor of a state or county officer, or the impeachment by the House of a state officer.

Up to January 1, 1978, the Senate had been called into special session four times to consider executive suspensions. Those sessions were February 17, 1969, July 8, 1970, November 16, 1970, and February 26, 1974.

Number of Special Sessions

The Legislature was called into special session 86 times between June 8, 1869, and December 1994. Of these special sessions, 10 were called by Governor Claude R. Kirk, Jr., 12 by Governor Reubin O'D. Askew, 12 by Governor Bob Graham, nine by Governor Bob Martinez, and 10 by Governor Lawton Chiles. Nine were called by the Senate President and House Speaker.

Number of Extended Sessions

The first extended session was held in 1957. Between 1957 and 1995 sixteen regular sessions were continued.

Shortest Session

The shortest session of the Legislature occurred on November 17, 1970, when the Senate and House, already in Tallahassee to reorganize after a general election, was called into special session by Governor Claude R. Kirk, Jr., to pay official expenses of Governor-elect Reubin O'D. Askew including those of his inaugural. The House was in session 21 minutes; the Senate, 15.

Longest Session

The longest session of the Legislature occurred in 1955. Called into legislative reapportionment session by Governor LeRoy Collins, the Legislature met 74 fruitless days. Then, unable to adjourn sine die without complying with the constitutional mandate to reapportion, the Legislature recessed until the next general election when the terms expired of all House members and half the Senate. Thus, the Legislature technically was in session 520 days, from June 6, 1955, until November 6, 1956.

It seemed to legislators and observers that the 1983 Legislature never would end, for there were five regular and special sessions. Cartoonist Gamble of the Florida Times-Union *captured the scene.*
Cartoon colleciion, Museum of Florida History

How Laws are Made

Each bill is prefaced by the words, "A Bill to be Entitled an Act to . . .", followed by a title summarizing its contents. Each bill also contains the phrase, "Be it Enacted by the Legislature of the State of Florida." Should this phrase be omitted, the measure is not valid. In the House of Representatives, an amendment to strike out the enacting clause is often used as a means of bringing a controversial measure to a decisive vote quickly.

An *act* passed by the Legislature becomes a *law* only after the Governor has had the opportunity to express himself on its merits. He may give his approval by signing his name to the act. Or he may allow it to become a law without his signature. Or he may disapprove the act by vetoing it. The Governor will return the act with a *message* expressing why he disapproves. It still can become law by the Legislature passing it over the veto. This overriding of a gubernatorial veto requires the agreeing votes of two-thirds of the members *present* in each house.

Introduction of Bills

Bills, then, are the raw material of the legislative process. Only a member of the Legislature or a committee can introduce a bill. Each member of the Senate and the House of Representatives may introduce as many bills as he desires, except that Speaker Ralph H. Haben, Jr., in 1981 pressured members to limit their general bills to eight. No limitation was imposed on committees. It was Speaker Haben's belief no member could shepherd more than eight bills. In 1991, Speaker T.K. Wetherell told members to limit their filings to eight bills.

The actual writing of a bill is done either by the legislator introducing it or by someone else at his direction. He can, at his request, be assisted by persons with special training employed for this purpose in the separate bill drafting offices of the House and Senate. The legislator outlines what he has in mind. These drafters are then called on to put his ideas into such language and form as can be fitted into the body of existing statute or constitutional law. These draftsmen are not called on to volunteer their opinion of the wisdom, merit, or constitutionality of the proposal.

The evolution of year-round committees means many bills are written by their staffs.

Bills dealing with local governments are most often prepared by attorneys for cities, counties, and special districts. Others are prepared at the request of the Governor to carry out phases of his legislative program. A great many of the bills introduced are prepared for the persons particularly interested in their enactment into law. In the House all bills must be approved for form before introduction.

The Governor's Message

The Constitution directs the Governor "shall by message at least once in each regular session inform the Legislature concerning the condition of the State, propose such reorganization of the Executive Department as will promote efficiency and economy, and recommend measures in the public interest." Nevertheless, the Governor, in this case, is on the same footing as any other non-legislator insofar as the introduction of bills to carry out his recommendations.

Passage of Bills

Virtually all bills are passed in each house by a majority vote (half plus one) of the members answering to roll call. The exceptions are bills for a special general election, which require the approval of three-fourths of the membership of each house, and the adoption of joint resolutions for amendments to the state Constitution, which require the approval of three-fifths of the membership of each house. A quorum for the purpose of transacting business is fixed by the Constitution at a majority of the members elected to a legislative house.

Before being brought to roll call on the question of its passage, a bill usually will have traveled to and from a committee in each house. "Usually" is the word that applies to nearly all of the legislative process, for the Legislature freely uses its very extensive discretionary power over procedure. The

Constitution and the rules of each house provide brakes and speed limits but, when so minded, the Legislature can move with a headlong swiftness bewildering to onlookers.

For example, a bill is required to be read by title in each house on three separate days (the first reading usually is accomplished by publication in the Journal), but the Constitution permits this spacing to be waived with the approval of two-thirds of the members present.

Judy Doyle of the *Tallahassee Democrat* had this personal encounter which illustrates the uncertainty of legislative life:

It was late Friday, the last day of the 1988 Regular Session, when House Speaker Jon Mills walked by. I grabbed his arm and asked if the House was going to take up the garbage bill before it recessed.

"Probably," the House honcho answered.

I rudely grabbed his arm again, demanding "Does 'probably' mean 'certainly?' "

Mills paused, glared icily and replied, "If you want certainly, you shouldn't be covering the Legislature."

Rules of Procedure

As was pointed out at the beginning of this chapter, the Legislature is limited in its power only by the Florida Constitution and the United States Constitution. How the Legislature goes about the exercise of this power—the mechanics of lawmaking—is governed to a considerable extent by rules. The Senate and the House of Representatives adopt their individual rules. It is important to keep in mind that the rules are the product of the lawmaking body itself. These rules may be changed at any time. Actually, a good deal of the business in each house is transacted by a waiver of some rule.

Much of the explanation for the Legislature's ability to move quickly, yet with ever increasing sureness of decision, can be found in the tools and services which have been furnished in recent years. Each legislator nowadays has before him a printed copy of general bills and a printed calendar of today's business. If a bill on the calendar pertains to the appropriation of public money or to taxation, it will be accompanied by a *fiscal note,* a copy of which will be in each member's file. It also may be accompanied by a staff report analyzing its contents. The user of a printed bill often can tell at a glance what changes are proposed in existing law for deletions are shown in struck-through type while additions are highlighted by italic type. He also has a Journal of yesterday's business. He has a book containing the rules of procedure, and in the House of Representatives, a continuing compilation of parliamentary precedents. This shows how these rules have been interpreted in past sessions.

The standing committees furnish year-round research and fact-finding services, which have relieved the lawmakers of their former dependence on outside sources of information.

All these services have tended to put the studious first-term legislator on a more equal footing with the experienced parliamentarian. He has a copy of the bill before him, together with the analysis of its meaning from an unbiased source. The legislator need not strain to hear and try to grasp the meaning of what is being read from the Clerk's desk or discussed from the floor.

The Veto

As previously stated, an act becomes a law only after the Governor has had his opportunity to deal with it. He may directly approve it by affixing his signature. Or he can merely imply that he approves it. He does this by allowing a certain number of days to elapse, after the act has been delivered to him by the Legislature, without exercising his right to veto. The Governor has seven consecutive days if the Legislature is in session. If the session ends before the seven days pass, the number of days is fifteen, counted from the day of the presentation of the act to him by the legislative officers. This may be a week or more after sine die adjournment because of the crush of business in the last days of a session. In a typical year, some 60 per cent of all bills passed are presented to the Governor after sine die adjournment. These bills include the General Appropriations Bill. The Governor's need for time to review the legislative product is most pronounced after the legislative adjournment.

The Legislature can override the Governor's veto, and cause the act to become law despite his disapproval. It can do this by repassing the act by a two-thirds vote of the members *present* in each house. An act vetoed after adjournment of the Legislature is returned to the house of origin at its next regular or special session.

The Florida Constitution specifically limits the contents of a bill to a single subject. Thus, Florida Governors never are faced with the problem of presidents of the United States. A President occasionally receives from Congress a measure which he regards generally as being greatly in the public interest. But the act includes a *rider* (a provision on an unrelated subject) that he finds objectionable. The President must take both or reject both. The Gov-

These are the "Babes in the Woods," members of the 1891 Senate who crossed into Georgia to escape a roundup by the Sergeant at Arms to assemble a quorum for the election of a United States Senator. Prior to 1913, legislatures elected the United States Senators. This photograph was taken on the grounds of the Florida Capitol.   Florida State Archives

ernor of Florida, moreover, may veto (take action to strike out) individual items in bills making appropriations of money for two or more functions. In practice, this power to veto appropriation items is exercised mostly in connection with the extensive *General Appropriations Bill.* In this bill the Legislature provides, on an item-by-item basis, for the financing of the departments and agencies of the state government during the state's fiscal year beginning each July 1.

As with any other veto, the Legislature possesses the power to review and override these appropriation item vetoes. But the passage of time often makes it ineffectual for the Legislature to exercise that power. Generally, the Governor's vetoes come after the Legislature has adjourned. Thus legislative review might be possible only at the next regular or special session of the Legislature, whichever comes first. A veto not considered at the next session is dead.

Effective Date

The Constitution (Article III, Section 18) says "Each law shall take effect on the sixtieth day after adjournment sine die of the session of the legislature in which enacted or as otherwise provided therein. If the law is passed over the veto of the Governor it shall take effect on the sixtieth day after adjournment sine die of the session in which the veto is overriden, on a later date fixed in the law, or on a date fixed by resolution passed by both houses of the legislature."

This sixty-day period was intended to give the public an opportunity to learn of new laws. The offices of the Attorney General and of the Secretary of State have tried to encourage the use of this or October 1 as uniform dates, so there would be time for the printing and distribution of new laws. But many laws become operative in shorter time. A clause often found in bills reads: "This law shall become effective upon becoming a law"—in other words, at once. If the Governor vetoes an act after the effective date, a new date of sixty days from sine die adjournment automatically becomes operative if the Legislature repasses the bill.

Other Legislation

The business of the Legislature is devoted mainly to the consideration of the bills that are introduced proposing new laws or modification of existing laws. There are, however, other types of legislative business. This includes the consideration of measures as *joint resolutions, concurrent resolutions, simple resolutions,* and *memorials.*

1. A *joint resolution* most commonly is used to propose an amendment to the State Constitution. The Governor cannot veto a joint resolution proposing an amendment because joint resolutions do not have the force of law until ratified by the electorate. When so used, the joint resolution can be adopted only by the YEA votes of three-fifths of the Senators (24) and three-fifths of the Representatives (72). Voting separately in each house, they must approve submission of the proposed amendment to the electorate. With the question before the voters, they can approve or reject the amendment at the next regular general election or at a special election, if one is called for that

purpose through passage of a law approved by three-fourths of the membership of the Senate (34) and the House (90).

Joint resolutions also are used to re-set the effective date of an act which has been vetoed by the Governor and repassed by the Legislature after the original date has become stale. The Constitution gives the Legislature the opportunity to provide a new effective date.

Still another use of joint resolutions is to reapportion the membership of the Legislature after each decennial federal census. Again, the Governor cannot veto the work product of the Legislature since the Constitution provides for the State Supreme Court to review the new apportionment plan.

Where a joint resolution is used for a purpose other than proposing a constitutional amendment, only a majority is needed for adoption.

2. A *concurrent resolution* deals with some matter, other than those requiring a joint resolution, involving both houses of the Legislature. A concurrent resolution does not have the force of law and needs only a voice vote to pass. A concurrent resolution may create a joint committee, express regret or praise. Or it may fix the time for the houses to meet in joint session to hear a distinguished speaker.

Ironically, one of the most important responsibilities performed by the Legislature, the ratifying of amendments to the Constitution of the United States, is accomplished through adoption of a concurrent resolution.

3. A final general type of *simple resolution* is one expressing the will only of the legislative house in which it is adopted. It is identified by the term "House Resolution" or by the term "Senate Resolution," as the case may be. More often than not, this type of resolution will deal with procedure, for example, with the daily schedule of either house. Such a procedural subject would be the hours for convening and recessing daily sessions of that body. These resolutions are often used to create committees whose membership will be drawn only from the adopting house or to express its regrets or praise.

4. A *memorial* is addressed to Congress. It expresses the sentiment of the Florida Legislature on subjects within the jurisdiction of the federal government or in which there is common interest. The Governor has nothing to do officially with memorials. The Secretary of State transmits them.

A type of bill known as a *claim bill*, or relief bill, deserves separate mention. A claim bill is one which authorizes payment by the state of a claim for compensation or damages. This applies only in situations where a lawsuit on the claim is not legally permissible. The number of claim bills likely has been fewer because the Legislature limited its sovereign immunity, or freedom from suit, in liability situations generally. This waiver applied to the state and its agencies, including counties.

A builder could, for example, ask for more money than the amount of his contract. Perhaps unforeseeable or unusual circumstances increased his cost in the construction of a state building. Or, a bystander could claim damages because he was wounded by state agents pursuing convicts.

Passage of a claim bill was necessary in these and similar cases because the state could not be sued for damages without its consent. Besides, the Constitution forbade the payment of state money without a law making an appropriation for the specific purpose. Thus, claim bills are retroactive in nature in that they make an appropriation for something already done. A jury may return a verdict for a larger amount but the state or agency being sued is limited to paying $100,000 for an individual or $200,000 for an incident. For damages beyond those amounts, the claimant must look to the Legislature to pass a claim bill.

In passing upon bills of this nature, the Legislature functions in a quasi-judicial capacity. Its committees hear testimony and review records, much as though it were being done in court. Until 1968, a claim bill could be passed only by a vote of two-thirds of the members elected to each house. Since 1968, only a majority of those voting is required.

Companion Bills

There is general use of so-called *companion bills* as a timesaving device. These are identical bills introduced in both houses, and thereby allowing committee study in each body during the same period.

If favorably reported by the committees, the companion bills can advance at the same time on the calendars of the Senate and House. When, for example, a Senate-passed companion bill reaches the House, it can be substituted for the House's own bill when this is ready for floor action.

Volume of Legislation

Those who properly regard a law with awe as the product of our system of government often are likely to be shocked by the legislative volume. More than two thousand measures affecting the people of Florida generally will be introduced at a typical session. About a fifth of these measures will be passed or adopted. In considering the total number of bills introduced, it should be kept in mind that the use of companion bills means considerable duplication.

Local Bills

Because of the granting of home rule powers in the 1970's the number of local bills has fallen off materially. In 1965, for example, there were 2,107 local bills introduced of which 1,832 passed. In 1994 the House and Senate introduced 244 local bills of which 134 passed.

Voting

The Constitution safeguards the public's interest by being quite explicit on the permanent recording of how legislators voted. This is particularly important on matters having the force of law. The Journals (record of proceedings in the nature of minutes of the meeting) must show by name how each participating member voted on roll calls for the final passage of every bill or joint resolution (proposed constitutional amendment). Other types of resolutions and memorials are not binding on the public and are usually adopted by a voice vote.

In taking the yeas and nays, the "yes" and the "no" votes, the presiding officer uses this set formula. "The question is on (designating the matter to be voted upon). All in favor of such question shall vote 'yea,' and all opposed shall vote 'nay.' "

In both the House and the Senate, an electronic roll-call machine records how members have pressed the "yea" or "nay" buttons on their desks. Their votes show up as red or green lights opposite the names of members on two large panels. The machine also displays the totals of the votes for and against the measure.

Generally, every legislator present is required to vote. However, a member whose private interest would be affected should abstain from voting. (His private interest should be distinguished from the interest which he would share with every other citizen in, say, a new tax.) This abstention will be recorded in the Journal.

The name of the presiding officer is placed at the end of the roll call. He is excused from voting on procedural questions unless his vote is necessary to break a tie; otherwise, he is required to vote on bills and other legislation just as any member.

Pairing

A legislator can be excused from attending a day's session. But perhaps some measure is to be considered in his absence and he wants his position on that measure recorded in the Journal. Usually, the member will advise the Clerk who will show the member's position in the Journal, or he may pair with another member. For example, if he wishes to be shown as favoring a bill, he will find and pair with a member on the "nay" side of the matter. Then neither actually will vote, and their pair is recorded as a footnote to the roll call. A pair has no force other than being the statement of a position. Usually, since one vote is withdrawn from each side, the arithmetic of passage or defeat will not be affected by a pair.

But if the roll call was on the passage of a joint resolution, which requires the "yeas" of three-fifths of all members elected, the absent "yea" could be important.

Proxy Voting

A legislator must be present to vote on matters pending in either house. Use of *proxy* votes, or those cast by absent members, has been outlawed. A proxy had to be in writing. It took several forms. It might by its language authorize another Senator to vote on a matter in a specific manner, either for or against a particular bill. It might authorize the holder of the proxy to act generally on behalf of the absent member, to vote as he sees fit on whatever may come before the committee. The practice of voting by proxy was an outgrowth of the multiplicity of committees, with the same members belonging to more than one. When several committees are in session at the same hour, a legislator might want to be represented at each of which he is a member. He could accomplish this by giving his proxy to another member going to the meeting he was unable to attend.

The argument against proxies was that they permitted absent legislators to vote on measures which they had not heard explained. Often the proxies of absent members controlled a bill.

The need for proxies was reduced very materially when the presiding officers began scheduling committee meetings for regular days and hours and then appointing members to committees whose meetings did not conflict. The remaining problem is that of a committee member who has a bill to be heard before a House or Senate committee meeting at the same time.

Votes Required in House and Senate

Apportionment, Legislative
   Joint Resolution..Majority of Members voting
      (Article III, s.16)
Apportionment, Congressional—Bill..................Majority of Members voting
City or county mandates:
   To pass a general law requiring the expenditure
      of funds by a city or county..2/3's of Membership
      (Article VII, s.18(a))
   To alter general law to reduce the authority
      of cities or counties to raise revenues.....................2/3's of Membership
      (Article VII, s.18(b))
   To alter general law to reduce the percentage
      of a state tax shared with cities or counties............2/3's of Membership
      (Article VII, s.18(c))
Expel Member...2/3's of Membership
      (Article III, s. 4(d))
Impeach Officer ....2/3's of Members voting
      (Article III, s. 17(a))
Income Tax
   (Corporate) over 5% ....3/5's of Membership
      (Article VII, s.5(b))
Judiciary:
   Create Judicial offices other than certified
      or when Court fails to certify ....2/3's of Membership
      (Article V, s.9)
   Repeal Rules of Practice..2/3's of Membership
      (Article V, s.2(a))
Local laws
   (add prohibited subject)..3/5's of Membership
      (Article III, s.11(a)(21))
Sessions:
   Extend Session ....3/5's of Members voting
      (Article III, s.3(d))
   Extended Session, new business.................................2/3's of Membership
      (Article III, s.3(d))
   Special Session, legislation outside call ....2/3's of Membership
      (Article III, s.3(c)(1))
State Securities (School and Higher Education Capital Outlay):
   Interest over 5% ....3/5's of Members voting
      (Article XII, s.9(d)(5))
Trust Funds (creation)...3/5's of Membership
      (Article III, s.19(f)(1))

The Legislators

A legislator is the delegate from his community to a state-wide assembly, the Legislature. He is elected by a majority of the voters in the district which he represents. The legislator should be responsive to the will of his constituents in representing them. He cannot, however, possibly determine

Legislative Scoreboard
House and Senate Bills (General and Local)

Regular and Special Sessions
Calendar
Years   1983 1984 1985 1986 1987 1988 1989 1990 1991 1992 1993 1994

Total bills introduced in
legislature (includes
companion bills)
  General   2233 1994 2309 2299 2496 2746 3001 3012 2091 2073 2281 2768
  Local   238   221   201   188   182   149   199   203   165   146   152   260
  Total   2471 2215 2510 2487 2678 2895 3200 3215 2256 2219 2433 3028

Acts passed
  General   371   400   387   331   436   451   428   399   328   244   322   380
  Local   175   157   130   142   117   127   133   120   102   50   91   128
  Total   546   557   517   473   553   578   561   519   430   294   413   508

Acts vetoed by governor
  General   4   15   11   3   11   15   21   18   16   19   15   11
  Local   7   1   1   0   2   6   —   —   2   1   1   5
  Total   11   16   12   3   13   21   21   18   18   20   16   16

Acts becoming law
  General   367   399   376   328   425   446   428   399   312   225   307   369
  Local   168   156   129   142   115   121   133   120   100   49   90   123
  Total   535   555   505   470   540   567   561   519   412   274   397   492

their collective wishes on each of the hundreds of matters presented for his vote. It is obviously necessary that voters elect men and women whose judgment can be trusted. Too, he may be in a position to collect facts not known to his constituents generally.

But in addition to passing laws the legislators have much more to do with the conduct of the state government. Members of the Legislature often, for example, receive complaints from their constituents about agen-

Legislators in conference in the chamber during a daily session, trying to work out some detail of a bill.

Legislators Captured

The 1864 Legislature had an unusual problem: "Enemy (Union troops) [has] captured, taken off and hold as prisoners" two State Senators, one Representative and a number of other state and county officials. "Under existing statutes, no provisions of law exist to remedy the evils to the public interests caused by the absence of these officers."

-Legislative Journal

The Legislature / 117

Dear Legislator:

I am a candidate for House Page for the April Session of the Legislature and will greatly appreciate your support.

GUY H. SMITH.

Tallahassee, Fla., Feb. 1st, 1911.

Guy Smith's campaign card in the 1911 race for House Page.　　Florida State Library—Florida Collection

VOTE FOR
KATHERINE B. TIPPETTS
FOR LEGISLATURE

Mrs. Katherine Bell Tippetts of St. Petersburg was one of the first two women ever to be a candidate for a seat in the Florida House of Representatives. She finished second in a field of four. Shown here is a tattered memento of Mrs. Tippetts' 1922 candidacy.

cies of the Executive branch. Resultant legislative inquiries may produce an explanation and possibly legislation to correct the problem that caused the complaint. Legislators may inquire privately, through a telephone call or letter. Or they may inquire publicly, perhaps by appearing before the governing board of the agency.

A legislative investigating committee can focus public attention on practices, which, however lawful, a government agency or even a private business might find difficult to explain or justify. Such committees often possess the right to compel the attendance of witnesses and the producing of records.

While we speak of the Legislature as the lawmaking branch of our state government, its members function in the realm known as public opinion. Laws result from someone saying, "There ought to be a law." The legislators will be held responsible, more or less, for the passage of laws. So legislators generally encourage public discussion of those matters which will come before them for consideration.

Studies of various aspects of the state government are underway continuously nowadays. The very fact that these are being made serves a salutary purpose. Also, there are the meetings of the hundreds of service clubs and other organizations in Florida. These give the legislators opportunities to discuss governmental issues and stimulate interest and reaction at the source or, as is sometimes said, "at the grassroots."

These then, are some of the ways in which members of the Legislature influence and are influenced in the administration of government, other than by the passage of laws.

Members of the Legislature

All legislators are elected by the voters. The Governor has no power to fill vacancies in the Legislature caused by death or resignation. The man or woman running as a candidate for election to the Legislature need possess no legal qualifications beyond those required of any voter except that he shall be at least twenty-one years of age, a resident of Florida for two years prior to election, and an elector and resident of the district from which elected.

Members of the Senate are referred to as *senators*. Members of the House of Representatives are referred to as *representatives*. They are also referred to as *members*. During the course of proceedings in the House of Representatives, a member will be addressed by name. In the Senate, the formal address is "The Senator from . . . (the numbered Senatorial district which he represents)." The term *legislator* applies to both senators and representatives, and is customarily used when reference is being made to members of both legislative houses.

Senators serve for a regular term of four years. This means they will represent their *districts* in four regular sessions of the Legislature. The Senate has overlapping membership in that half of its members are regularly elected every two years. Representatives serve for a regular term of two years. Thus, they represent their district in two regular sessions of the Legislature.

Representation

Seats in the Senate and House of Representatives are apportioned on the basis of population, with the Constitution requiring a redistribution by the

Legislature at its regular session in the year following proclamation of the decennial federal census. Approval of any plan of reapportionment by the State Supreme Court is required, and the court is directed to produce a plan if the Legislature cannot.

In 1972, the Legislature apportioned itself. The Senate, by constitutional requirement, reduced its size from 48 to 40. The House increased its membership from 119 to 120, the maximum permitted by the Constitution.

Single-Member Districts

The Florida Supreme Court on May 12, 1982, approved the Legislature's plan for representation of people in the Senate and House of Representatives for the ten years beginning with the general election of November, 1982.

While immediate reaction largely was centered upon the court's finding that all Senate seats were open for election in 1982, the long-range, historic significance was in the scrapping of multi-member districts.

The shift to single-member districts, each balanced in population, was achieved within the Legislature itself without meaningful resistance.

Wiped out by the Legislature was 1972's plan of apportionment which in the House included five six-member districts, six five-member districts, five four-member districts, and 21 single-member districts, and in the Senate, seven three-member districts, seven two-member districts, and five single-member districts. Proponents of the single-member district plan argued persons residing in multi-member legislative districts could not be sure who represented them. It also was contended that single-member districts would improve the opportunity for members of minority groups to win seats. Too, it was asserted that people who ordinarily would not seek office could do so because it would be easier and cheaper to mount an election campaign in the smaller districts.

The court's opinion was written by Justice Ben F. Overton. Concurring were Justices Joseph A. Boyd, Jr., James F. Alderman, Parker Lee McDonald and Raymond Ehrlich. Chief Justice Alan C. Sundberg and Justice James C. Adkins, Jr., concurred with the Legislature's drawing of the district boundaries but dissented from the majority's holding that all Senators would be required to run for new terms.

Senate Boundaries Altered

The majority held that where the boundaries of the district from which a senator had been elected were altered by the apportionment, the Senator must run even though two years might remain of his term. Because all district boundaries had been changed, all Senators were required to run. To restore staggering, those who sought office from odd-numbered districts were given terms of two years; those from even-numbered districts, terms of four years. After the initial staggering, all Senate terms would be four years.

The Legislature had adopted the reapportionment joint resolution on April 7, 1982, during a special apportionment session called by Governor Bob Graham pursuant to Article III, Section 16(a) of the Florida Constitution.

Justice Overton described the plan as "a substantial achievement in voting equality. The districts established by the plan are extremely close to exact population equality."

Ideal Senate, House Districts

The population of Florida, as established by the 1980 Federal Census, was 9,746,324. The ideal Senate district contained 243,658 people, which was the state population of 1980 divided by 40 Senate districts. The total deviation from the ideal was 2,566 people or 1.05 percent between the smallest and largest Senate districts.

The ideal House district contained 81,219 people, which was the population of the state divided by 120 districts. The total deviation between the largest and smallest House districts was 378 people, or a .46 percent deviation.

Hispanic, Black Needs Recognized

The special needs of minority voters was recognized, the Supreme Court found, seven House districts with a Hispanic population of 58 percent or higher; seven House districts with a black population of 52 percent or higher; one Senate district with a black population of 65 percent, and two Senate districts with a Hispanic population of 55 percent or higher.

The plan for Senate districts maintained the integrity of 44 counties, and House districts did so with 26 counties. In most instances, county lines were split principally because population was greater than the ideal number of people per district.

See: Reapportionment in Florida, *The Florida Handbook*, 1985-86, and The Apportionment of 1992, p. 198.

Seniority

In the United States Congress, *seniority* determines the progress of a senator or congressman in the committee system. But in the Florida Legislature, a member's length of service means little in itself.

The value of seniority, or length of service, lies in each individual. It depends on such human aspects as the familiarity with the legislative process that experience-plus-understanding gives, and in the friendships acquired with other members. Some members gain experience and friends very quickly. Lawmaking is an intuitive skill, to an extent, and involves the art of sensing how people will react.

Term of Legislators

The term of a legislator begins with the general election in the November in which he is elected. He takes office at midnight of the election day. In instances of a close vote, the actual declaration of election may be delayed until after the canvass. (Terms of other elective state officials, except county commission, school board members, and county school superintendents, commence on the first Tuesday after the first Monday in January following the general election.) County commissioners, school board members and county school superintendents regularly take office on the second Tuesday following the general election.

Presiding Officers

See Mr. Speaker & Ms. President in following chapter.

Staff

The character of employment in the Legislature has changed radically within a relatively short time. More and more legislative workers, once

Only vote in 1956 House against a "last resort" bill to close a county's public schools to avoid racial integration, was cast by Representative John B. (Jack) Orr Jr., of Miami. Orr's constituents ousted him at next election. Years later, Orr was elected Mayor of Metropolitan-Dade County. A public housing development and a city plaza have been named for Orr. He died in 1974.   Miami Herald

Donald L. Tucker of Tallahassee was one of two Florida House Speakers in this century to serve consecutive two-year terms and one of three to be elected for two terms. Tucker's achievement was all the more remarkable for the fact that he presided over four regular sessions. The others, Cary A. Hardee of Live Oak and Thomas D. Beasley of De-Funiak Springs, were Speakers when Florida had biennial sessions of the legislature. Tucker ended the error-fraught custom of giving bills their second and third readings on the same day by waiver of the Constitutional requirement for readings on separate days.

known as *attachés*, are required to possess secretarial and other skills which fit them to do the work and use the machines now employed in a modern business office.

Each house elects its recording officer, known as the Secretary in the Senate and the Clerk in the House. The President and Secretary of the Senate and the Speaker and Clerk of the House are constitutional officers. The Senate elects its Sergeant-at-Arms; the Speaker designates the House Sergeant with the consent of the members. Numerous other employees once chosen by election, from doorkeeper to pages, are now put to work by less formal means.

The first act of a member of the Legislature is the ceremonial one of taking the oath of office. In the House, the members come forward in groups of five, raise their right hands, and repeat after the judge administering the oath: "I (name) do solemnly swear that I will support, protect, and defend the Constitution and Government of the United States and of the State of Florida; that I am duly qualified to hold office under the Constitution of the State, and that I will well and faithfully perform the duties of Member of the House of Representatives on which I am now about to enter. So help me God."

Incidentally, the same oath, with the appropriate title substituted is taken by every officer of the State and county, from Governor to the Sergeants-at-Arms of the House and Senate.

The Journals

The printed records of the daily proceedings in the Senate and in the House of Representatives are known as the Journals. These are prepared by the Secretary of the Senate and the Clerk of the House. Almost without exception, the Journal of one day's proceedings is available on the desks of legislators at the convening of the next day's session.

The Journals of the Florida Legislature record primarily the formal actions, and not the words spoken by members in debate. A notable exception is the inclusion in the Journal of the text of the address of the Governor which the Constitution says he shall make to the Legislature on affairs of the state.

The Journals must be accurate, for the courts make their determination of the legality of challenged legislation from these records. The day-by-day Journals are carefully checked and, as corrected, drawn together to form the history of a session. It is this postsession version which stands as the official journal. Because of the closeness of the examination for accuracy, it usually does not become available for some months after a regular session ends.

Committees

The committee is the heart of the legislative process. The committee does what the Senate and the House of Representatives could not do so well for themselves by functioning as a whole. The committee can and should do the fact-finding spadework. This enables the lawmaking body to act with greater assurance of its exercising good judgment.

The formation of committees breaks down the membership into numerous small groups. Opportunity is thus afforded the Senate and the House for closer study of a bill than would be possible in debate on the floor. In this preliminary screening, the committee will hear from the legislator who introduced the bill. It will hear, too, from other legislators who either favor or oppose the bill.

But the committee may go outside the Legislature to learn the opinion of interested persons who may be well informed on the subject of the bill. The committee can send out for witnesses and for records. It can also use the research facilities of the Legislature to analyze the situation here and in other states.

Technically, both the Senate and the House, sitting as a committee, could do all these things. But their smaller committees can and do perform the work more efficiently and thoroughly. The volume of business in today's Florida Legislature is considerable. It certainly could not be completed if the entire body attempted to study every bill upon its introduction.

Basically, there are *standing, standing subcommittee, select,* and *conference* committees.

Sunset and Sundown

Sunset and Sundown are similar processes in that both involve the automatic repeal of various provisions of the Florida Statutes establishing state agencies unless legislative scrutiny demonstrates a continued need.

The most significant use of Sunset occurred in 1980 when laws relating to the Public Service Commission's regulation of trucks and buses were allowed to lapse.

The guillotine nature of Sunset caused practitioners of a number of professions and occupations to accept revision of their laws rather than allow their regulatory laws to expire.

Sunset review is focused on the need for and the effectiveness of a *regulatory* function which is carried out by a state agency, while Sundown reviews the continued need for *advisory* bodies, boards and commissions which are adjunct to executive agencies.

The systematic, periodic repeal of designated statutes began in Florida with the Regulatory Reform Act of 1976, ch. 76-168, Laws of Florida. The concept, however, was not new. During President Franklin Roosevelt's administration, William O. Douglas, chairman of the Securities and Exchange Commission, proposed to the President that every Federal agency be abolished in 10 years. Although the President is said to have been delighted at the idea, it was never implemented.

In 1975 the Colorado chapter of Common Cause proposed that regulatory agencies come up, on a rotating basis, for periodic review by the Legislature. If their existence could not be justified, "the sun would set on them." Colorado's idea became the nation's first Sunset law in 1976. The following year, Sunset reviews were conducted on 13 of Colorado's regulatory agencies.

Florida became the second state to enact a Sunset law with the passage of the Regulatory Reform Act of 1976, which scheduled 37 prospective repeals July 1, 1978 and continued extensive repeals July 1, 1980 and July 1, 1982. No reviews were ever conducted under this law as enacted. Subsequent laws extended the six-year cycle of review to 10 years.

The reopening of regulatory laws through Sunset has afforded foes of the status quo to strive for advantage. In 1986, contention between optometrists and ophthalmologists necessitated a special session of the Legislature.

Sunset concerns the periodic review of statutes controlling departments and agencies which exercise the state's power for regulation. *Sundown* involves the systematic review of the need for boards, committees, commissions, and councils created by statute as adjuncts to executive agencies. Agencies under either sunset or sundown automatically are terminated by specified dates unless their life has been extended by legislative action.

Identification

Bills and other legislation are numbered in the order of introduction. Senate bills are prefixed "SB" and House bills are designated "HB." An amendment to the State Constitution can be identified by the initials HJR, for House joint resolution, or SJR. Other identifying letters are HCR or SCR, for concurrent resolutions; HM or SM, for memorials, and HR or SR, for resolutions.

Standing Committees

Standing committees are those established by the Senate and the House of Representatives for the management of their business. They are established by authority of rules separately adopted by the Senate and by the House. The appointment of committee members, and the designation of the committee chairman and vice-chairman, are made in the Senate by its President and in the House by its Speaker. Proposed legislation will be referred to a standing committee. Usually, the committee then has the responsibility of first passing judgment on that legislation. Each committee may originate legislation within the field assigned to it (and indicated by the committee's name).

The committee often reports unfavorably on a measure. Under the rules usually adopted, it takes the votes of two-thirds of the members present to revive that measure for further consideration. This shows how significant the committee is in the legislative process.

There is something else that makes it even more difficult to revive a bill than the arithmetic of the two-thirds rule would indicate. It is that the committee system is so embedded in the legislative thought that members are reluctant to vote against a committee's judgment even when the facts appear to justify doing so. Many claim, perhaps rightly, that if the judgment of one committee is to be reversed, none will be safe. The Legislature would then spend much of its time in reviewing adverse committee reports.

With the evolution of the year-round Legislature, drastic changes have occurred in the structuring and purpose of committees.

The number of committees has been reduced. This has resulted in committees having more members but with those members serving on fewer committees. Thus, a member has an opportunity to achieve considerable expertise in the fields of government within the sphere of his committee responsibilities.

The reduction in the number of standing committees, coupled with the volume of business, has brought about the establishment in the House of standing subcommittees which have the power to recommend to the parent committee whether a bill should be reported favorably, favorably with amendment, or unfavorably.

(The reduction in the number of committees may be judged from these statistics: In 1933, the House of 95 representatives had 71 committees and the Senate of 38 senators had 40 committees. In 1965, the House of 112 representatives had 49 committees and the Senate of 43 had 44 committees. In 1995, the House of 120 Representatives had 28 committees and the Senate of 40 had 15 committees.)

Coupled with the recruitment and training of a cadre of analysts, researchers and other personnel possessing specialized skills, the committees have a capability for independent action which formerly did not exist. In short, committees no longer are essentially limited to stamping "favorable" or "unfavorable" upon bills submitted to them from sources outside the committee.

Upon introduction, every bill or joint resolution (except those originating in a committee of jurisdiction) will be assigned by the presiding officer to a committee. This is called *reference*. The introducer, or some other interested legislator, occasionally will suggest a committee he considers more appropriate. Or, perhaps, he suggests a committee more likely to be sympathetic to the measure. Or some opponent may urge reference to a committee he regards as potentially hostile. But the President or Speaker may persist in his original choice. The body could override him, however, and assign the bill to another committee. This has not happened in recent years. The sharp reduction in the number of committees has narrowed the choice.

Bills relating to the spending or raising of money must be referred to the

Committee on Appropriations or the Committee on Finance and Taxation. But when bills involve more than one purpose they are often jointly referred to one or more additional committees. A typical example would be a bill levying a special tax on fishing boats. This would raise a question which properly should be studied by the Committee on Natural Resources as well as the Committee on Finance and Taxation. This reference to more than one committee is known as *joint reference.*

In disposing of a bill introduced by a member, the committee will do one of four things. It can recommend the bill "favorably, " "favorably with amendments" (which are attached), or "unfavorably. " Or it can recommend a *substitute bill* of the committee's own preparation. The committee's recommendation will usually follow public consideration of the bill. This public hearing is afforded the introducer and such other persons as desire to talk either for or against the proposal.

The heart of the legislative process, a committee in session.

With the greater emphasis on independent research, a committee nowadays often will produce its own bill, the result of a study by individual members of the committee and of the committee staff. A *commitiee bill* will, if originated by a committee having jurisdiction of the subject, go to the calendar unless it has appropriation or taxation aspects. In the event of either of those, the committee bill then will go upon introduction to the appropriate revenue committee.

It also should be kept in mind that nearly every bill must travel the same long road in each house. A Senate-passed bill will be referred to one or more committees when it reaches the House of Representatives. And the same is true in the Senate of a House-passed measure.

The number of members of a committee is determined by the rules adopted by each legislative body at its biennial organization. Generally, the presiding officer is given considerable leeway.

Standing Subcommittees

The reduction in the number of standing committees caused some committees to be overwhelmed by the number of referred bills. This resulted in creation in the House in 1975 of standing subcommittees which could report bills unfavorably. Subcommittees mean a bill may be killed by as few as three votes, while at least sixty-one votes are required to pass a bill which has reached the House floor.

Select Committees

Select committees are those which have been appointed, or selected, to perform a specific task. The life of a select committee may last for a few minutes—for example, the time required for one house to notify another of its readiness to transact business on the opening day of the legislative session. Or a select committee might last for years. Any select committee which remains in existence between legislative sessions is known as an *interim* committee.

Membership of select committees is usually chosen by the presiding officers. The motion, resolution, or law authorizing the establishment of the committee may, however, restrict their power. With year-round standing committees, fewer interim committees are needed.

The legislator who introduced the measure establishing a committee is usually designated its chairman by the presiding officer. This is a matter of custom.

The powers of each select committee are set forth in the action creating it. Some are given the authority to subpoena witnesses and open records. Some are empowered to employ counsel and clerical assistance.

Committee of Conference

For a bill to become an act it must be passed by both houses in precisely the same words and figures. Because of pride, jealousy, differences of opinion, or better grasp of the substance, the second house frequently amends and returns the bill to the house of origin.

Four courses then may be taken. The originating house may concur in the amendments, thereby completing the legislative process. Or, it may reject the amendments and ask the other house to recede. Or, it may concur in some of the amendments and ask the other house to recede from those remaining. Bills may travel back and forth until, depending upon the importance of the legislation and the tenacity of the persons involved, one house surrenders, or the re-worked bill satisfies both houses.

In the case of significant bills, with substantial differences, the shortcut of a committee of conference likely will be taken almost immediately.

Conference committees are among the oldest of lawmaking procedures, dating back to early days of the British Parliament. In America, colonial legislatures used conference committees. In Congress, a conference committee was appointed on its second day, in 1789. Yet few legislators are knowledgeable about conference committees.

A conference committee in reality is composed of separate committees from the Senate and the House of Representatives. As separate committees, they vote separately, not only on the final product but on any subsidiary questions put to a vote. A majority of each committee prevails.

Conference committees are intended to reconcile differences. This suggests a give-and-take process because if a majority of the conferees from either house refused to budge, the conference would be stalemated and the bill could fail. However, this happens rarely.

Until 1967, conference committees in Florida often met in secret. While the House long had a rule requiring all committee meetings to be open and announced as to time and place, the Senate did not. Since the conference committees were composed of separate Senate-House committees, the Senate was able to close the meetings to the press and public.

The General Appropriations Bill, for the financing of the state government, more than once was hammered out at various hideaways, among these: a Senate President's cottage at St. Teresa, a Leon senator's lodge on Lake Iamonia, and the President's dining room at Florida State University. These private sessions lent themselves to cries of protest, particularly from legislators whose pet items were diminished or dropped. A conference committee possesses the power to change the Senate and House versions as it will. The committee, by striking everything after the enacting clause of the bill before it, can write a new bill, without regard even for the items or language not in controversy. It may include substance or items not in either the Senate or House versions.

The Senate and House have the conference committee report presented on a take-it-or-leave-it basis. No amendments can be offered. Occasionally, a report will be rejected and the bill sent back to conference. Usually, however, conference reports are submitted in the waning hours of a session when the shortness of time might mean the bill would be lost or the Legislature recalled in an extended or special session. Thus, the committee has the pressure of time on its side.

The Senate President and House Speaker agree upon the number of conferees, usually three to five from each house. (The General Appropriations Bill, by its magnitude, requires a conference committee of sixteen members with four alternates.) The conferees are known as managers. They generally are appointed from the committee which handled the bill but sometimes the President or Speaker will go outside the committee to select one or more conferees. Usually this occurs when the House/Senate has so amended the bill during floor consideration that the bill no longer may resemble the bill reported from the committee. Then, those who shaped the bill during floor consideration may more easily speak for the House/Senate in the conference committee.

Special Order Calendar

The House and Senate standing committees on Rules and Calendar are the final sieve through which legislation must pass to achieve chamber consideration. The regular Calendars have become a shelf list for the Rules committees of bills which have been reported favorably by all committees of reference.

Debate and the Previous Question

The question of whether debate changes votes on a significant bill is a question itself for debate. Perhaps there can be no conclusive generalization.

This is a frequent legislative scene, as one group or another throngs the rotunda between the House and Senate chambers seeking to persuade the lawmakers.

Basically, the House limits a member to fifteen minutes (ten minutes after the first thirty days of a regular session), and the Senate to ten minutes at all times. A member proposing the matter before the body has an additional five minutes to close.

Each house provides a method for limiting debate. The House by majority vote may limit debate to twenty minutes to a side or, by two-thirds vote, to a shorter time. The Senate, by a two-thirds vote, may limit debate to the amount of time stated in the motion. In each house, the introducer has the right to close.

The House has an additional means of restricting debate: a motion for the previous question. This motion requires only a majority vote for adoption. If adopted, it has a guillotine result, cutting off all further debate (except for six minutes, divided among proponents and opponents) and the offering of any further amendments or motions on second reading. The previous question itself cannot be debated.

The motion for the previous question requires the exercise of judgment by its maker and by the presiding officer, for the House occasionally is offended by its application. The Speaker attempts to judge the mood of the House before accepting the motion, for the abrupt cessation of debate or the opportunity to offer further amendments may irritate members who feel they are being deprived of a right. Complaints over the previous question usually come early in the first of the regular sessions of a term and mainly from freshmen who do not realize the meaning of the motion.

An anomaly of floor consideration, particularly in the leisurely early days of a session, is that the shorter the bill the longer the debate. Gene Ready, a Polk County Representative, said he learned this when he sought to pass a bill naming a Polk community "the blue grass capital" of Florida. A floor amendment struck "blue" which would have caused the community to be designated the marijuana center. The debate went on until the embarassed Ready finally withdrew the legislation. Years afterward Ready said, "I learned that day never to introduce a one-page bill." The same session he sponsored a plant siting bill, of some 300 pages, and not a question was raised beyond a colleague or two privately seeking his assurance the bill was sound.

Reconsideration

After the final passage of a bill, any member who voted with the prevailing side may move for reconsideration of the vote on that or the succeeding legislative day.

This has the effect of holding the bill in suspense until the vote has been reconsidered. Generally speaking, no question may be twice reconsidered.

In practice, this motion is used both by proponents and opponents of a measure.

Proponents will move for immediate reconsideration of a vote just taken, as a means of disposing of the last parliamentary means of delaying the bill. Opponents will move for reconsideration overnight so they may have additional time to collect strength.

Along with final passage, the motion to reconsider may be used to test again any vote during the progress of a bill, except that the vote on an amendment may not be reconsidered after the house has passed to another bill.

Filibusters

Practically speaking, therefore, it no longer is possible for one or two legislators to filibuster for longer than an hour or so. If members wish debate to cease, they possess the means presently to bring that about in a reasonably short time. The longest filibuster of record in Florida occurred in the House in 1931 when Representative John E. Mathews of Jacksonville held the floor for a cumulative total of approximately 19 hours over three days on May 27–29. His longest day was the 28th, when he was on his feet for some seven and three-quarter hours. This filibuster, over allocation of gasoline tax revenue to counties, resulted in a stalemate which was in the nature of a victory for Mathews. The filibuster also ended in a flurry of swinging fists.

(For other memorable filibusters, *see* "Legislative Highlights" in the 1967–68 edition of *The Florida Handbook*.)

Lobbying

"The people shall have the right peaceably to assemble, to instruct their representatives, and to petition for redress of grievances."
Florida Constitution, Declaration of Rights

The right to communicate with their lawmakers is a right guaranteed the people both by the Constitution of the United States and of the State of Florida.

Florida law defines a lobbyist in this language:

"All persons, except members of the Florida Legislature, or duly authorized staff of the Legislature designated in writing by such members, who seek to encourage the passage, defeat or modification of any legislation in the Senate or the House of Representatives, or any committee thereof, shall, before engaging in such lobbying activity in Tallahassee, register with the respective House of the Legislature."

A limited number of persons are excused by law from registering as lobbyists. These are persons who appear before legislative committees on their own behalf "without compensation or reimbursement." They are required to state the "individual capacity" of their representation when discussing legislation with senators and representatives.

The role of a lobbyist is described in these words of the Senate and House rules:

> A lobbyist shall supply facts, information, and opinions of principals to legislators from the point of view which he openly declares. A lobbyist shall not offer or propose anything which may reasonably be construed to improperly influence the official act, decision, or vote of a legislator.
>
> A lobbyist by personal example and admonition to colleagues shall maintain the honor of the legislative process by the integrity of his relationship with legislators as well as with the principals whom he represents.
>
> A lobbyist shall not knowingly and willfully falsify, conceal or cover up by any trick, scheme or device, a material fact or make or use any writing or document knowing the same to contain any false, fictitious or fraudulent statements or entry.

The names and addresses of lobbyists, together with the names and addresses of those they represent, are published. The size of lobbying activities may be judged from the fact that 2,292 persons representing 2,392 entities registered with the Legislature for 1994. Prior to 1979, separate registrations with the Senate and House were required, and until the 1993 legislative session changed the requirements, anyone who lobbied had to register. Now lobbyists must register if they are employed and receive payment for lobbying or contract for economic consideration for the purpose of lobbying, or if the person is principally employed for governmental affairs by another person or governmental entity to lobby on behalf of that other person or governmental entity. Lobbyists pay a registration fee of $30 per house for the first principal and $10 per house more for each additional principal.

Lobbyists are required to report periodically their expenses, other than personal expenditure for lodging, meals and travel.

A person deemed to have lobbied without registering may be excluded from appearing before committees or otherwise involving himself with legislation. A false lobbying report is punishable as a misdemeanor.

The House Chamber

The House chamber of the Capitol is an octagon shape. It contains 6,400 square feet, measuring 82 feet × 82 feet at its longest and widest points. The domed ceiling is 44 feet high at the center and is formed of triangular sections of acoustical panels and plaster edges. The member level is on the fourth floor and the gallery is on the fifth floor.

The walls, rostrum, and desks are all from the same flitch (tree) of teak, matched for continuity of wood grain and coloration. All metal components are of bronze. The carpet is blue and the chairs are upholstered in blue.

There was a reason for the difference between the sparkle of the House's brilliant blue carpet and teak paneling and the Senate's warm, subdued gold carpet and ebony paneling. Thomas A. Woodruff, whose firm did the interior design, was quoted by the *Jacksonville Journal* as explaining: "The House thinks of itself as being more contemporary, a body made up of younger men, and they chose colors which would reflect this. The Senate, on the other hand, has the image of being more conservative and deliberate."

Lighting is designed for even distribution of indirect light up into the dome and direct light from specific ceiling locations. The sound system causes sound to be distributed uniformly from a speaker at each member's desk. Telephones link members to their offices. The voting system is totally electronic.

Writing press and television filming areas are provided at the gallery level. Each public gallery area on both sides of the chamber is enclosed by glass to control sound and provide safety.

The Senate Chamber

The Senate chamber is a 62-foot square at the fourth floor level and a circle at the fifth floor gallery level. The ceiling is a circular dome formed with trapezoidal shaped acoustic panels in decreasing size for each ring as these approach the top of the dome, 45 feet above the chamber floor.

The walls, rostrum and desks are all from the same flitch (tree) of ebony, matched for continuity of wood grain and coloration. Chairs are upholstered

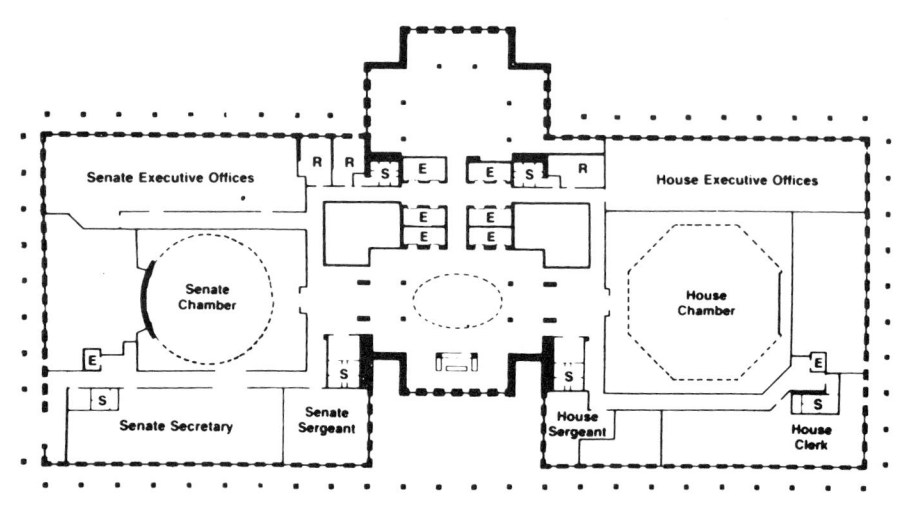

The Legislative floor of the Capitol, the fourth. Most committee and individual offices are in separate, connecting Senate and House office buildings.   Reynolds, Smith and Hills

in gold. The carpet is gold. Metal components are of bronze. Telephones link the senators with their offices. The voting system is totally electronic.

There is a video system by which amendments and short messages, keyed from the Secretary's desk, may be displayed on a screen above the President's rostrum.

Lighting is designed for even distribution of indirect light up into the dome and direct light from specific ceiling locations. Sound is distributed from speakers at each senator's desk so the volume is uniform over the chamber.

Accommodations on the gallery level are provided for writing and television press. Each public gallery is open on the chamber.

Open Doors

The Constitution (Article III, Section 4(b)) says "Sessions of each house shall be public; except sessions of the Senate when considering appointment to or removal from public office may be closed."

Generally, this means the public may be admitted during sessions to the galleries overlooking chambers of the Senate and the House. The public has, on occasion, been excluded from the galleries when the chambers were being used for non-legislative business, including party caucuses of legislators.

The Senate began in 1967 the open consideration of gubernatorial appointments or suspensions. The reversal of custom followed an incident on January 26, 1967, when four newsmen refused to leave the Senate chamber because they suspected the secret session was for a purpose other than the consideration of appointments or suspensions, the *only* constitutional justification for closing the door to non-senators. Secrecy was enforced by a Senate rule for expulsion of a senator who told what was discussed in an executive session.

The four newsmaking newsmen were Don Pride of the *St. Petersburg*

Times; Rex Newman of the John H. Perry newspapers; and John McDermott and William C. Mansfield of the *Miami Herald.* "It was a snap decision," wrote Pride at the time. After much furor, the newsmen were physically ejected by deputies of the Senate Sergeant-at-Arms.

Impeachment

The Governor, Lieutenant Governor, administrative officers of the Executive department (referred to generally as the "Cabinet"), Justices of the Supreme Court, and Judges of the Courts of Appeal, Circuit Courts and County Courts, are removable from office by impeachment. (In the case of judges, an additional method of removal has been provided through a judicial qualifications commission. See Article V, Section 12, of the Constitution.)

The House of Representatives possesses the exclusive power to vote articles (or charges) of impeachment, and the Senate to try. The Constitution was amended in 1962 to allow the Speaker to appoint a committee to investigate alleged grounds for impeachment at any time, either during or between legislative sessions. This was an outgrowth of the Holt impeachment of 1957 when considerable time of some members was diverted from their regular legislative duties by the preliminary investigation of the charges. It was felt then that means should be provided for making such inquiries when the Legislature was not in session. The Senate already possessed the right to meet as a special court of impeachment at any time within six months after the House brought its formal charges.

A vote of two-thirds of all members present of the House of Representatives is required to impeach any officer, and no accused person may be convicted by the Senate without the concurrence of two-thirds of the Senators present.

The Chief Justice presides at trials by impeachment except in the trial of himself, when the Governor presides.

Judgment of impeachment extends only to removal from office and disqualification to hold any office of "honor, trust or profit" under the state, but the accused officer, whether convicted or acquitted, is liable to criminal trial and punishment.

Articles Voted

Articles of impeachment have been voted five times by the House of Representatives and two cases carried to a vote in the Senate.

The first completed case was the trial of Circuit Judge George E. Holt of Miami in 1957. Judge Holt had been accused by the House of bringing his court into disrepute, mainly through the awarding of fees which were claimed to be excessive. The Senate returned to the capitol on July 8 and sat as a court for 23 working days before voting on August 15. The vote was 20 to 14 against Judge Holt but since the concurrence of two-thirds of the Senators voting was necessary to convict, Judge Holt was acquitted by three votes.

The second court of impeachment saw the Senate, sitting for twelve working days in September, 1963, dismiss eight articles brought against Circuit Judge Richard Kelly of Dade City. The House had, in sum, accused Judge Kelly of pursuing a "continuous course of conduct calculated to intimidate and embarrass" lawyers, officials and others, mainly in Pasco County. The Senate voted 23 to 20 to terminate the trial after hearing witnesses and the arguments of prosecution and defense.

First Impeachments

The first impeachment proceeding involved Circuit Judge James T. Magbee of Tampa, a Confederate soldier turned scalawag. He was charged with a variety of offenses which Chief Justice Glenn Terrell, who presided at the Holt trial, characterized as "a little bit frivolous" in retrospection. The House voted the articles two days before the adjournment of the 1870 regular session and the Senate did not get around to acting until a special session the same year. By that time, the House moved to discontinue the prosecution and the Senate, meeting again in January 1871, agreed to do so.

The House voted 16 articles of impeachment against Governor Harrison Reed in February, 1872, charging him with misapplication of public funds and with receiving unlawful compensation. The Senate organized as a court but adjourned without a trial during the regular session of the Legislature. At a special session in May, counsel for the Republican Governor asked the Senate to acquit him on the grounds that the Senate had adjourned its regular session without proceeding to try him, that the special session lacked jurisdiction, and that the Governor's term would expire before the next regular legislative session. The Governor's motion to discharge was granted by the Senate.

The third attempt to oust a state officer through impeachment was made against State Treasurer C. B. Collins in 1897. The House voted nine articles accusing him of mishandling public funds. The Senate organized as a court on May 28 and adjourned ultimately to June 4 when the Senators disbanded after the House withdrew the articles upon being advised by the Governor that Treasurer Collins had resigned.

Articles of impeachment were introduced by an individual House member against Governor Fuller Warren in the 1951 House, but were rejected as legally insufficient by a special committee whose finding was sustained by the House.

Adams Censure

After three quarters of a century without blemish, the "roof fell in, " as one observer phrased the situation, on the Cabinet and Supreme Court in the 1970s.

Articles of impeachment were brought against Lieutenant Governor Tom Adams, with a House committee accusing him of "misconduct and misdemeanor" through the improper use of state employees under his jurisdiction. On May 17, 1973, the House voted 61 to 55 on the articles, the resolution of impeachment failing of the constitutional two-thirds vote of the members present. A resolution of censure, based upon the same articles, then was adopted by a vote of 88 to 26. Nine of the negative votes were cast by Representatives who recorded their belief the House lacked the constitutional authority to censure an officer of the Executive department.

Christian, O'Malley Resignations

After an investigation by a House committee and a grand jury, Commissioner of Education Floyd T. Christian resigned April 25, 1974. His resignation came as the committee prepared impeachment articles. Christian had been indicted on nineteen counts of bribery, conspiracy, and perjury after the grand jury's inquiry into the commissioner's handling of state contracts. Christian pleaded no contest to the state charges and was sentenced to seven years probation and fined $11,000. On federal income tax evasion charge, Christian served six months at the Eglin prison.

State Treasurer Thomas D. O'Malley resigned July 29, 1975, after having been impeached by the House on June 2. The House voted nine articles charging Treasurer O'Malley with constitutional misdemeanors in office.

In summary, the problems at the highest level of state government ended with:

Governor Reubin O'D. Askew removing Lieutenant Governor Adams as secretary of commerce and dropping him from his reelection ticket. Adams subsequently lost bids for election as governor and as state senator.

Comptroller Fred O. "Bud" Dickinson, Jr., accused of misuse of political contributions, being voted out of office. In addition, Dickinson was fined $9,382 on an income tax evasion misdemeanor charge and the Federal government dropped two more serious charges. Dickinson agreed to pay nearly $50,000 in back taxes and penalties.

Treasurer Thomas O'Malley surrendering to federal authorities to serve a three-year prison term after being convicted of extortion and mail fraud. A four-year delay between conviction and imprisonment resulted in part from the temporary inability to locate the court reporter who recorded O'Malley's trial.

Consequences of the scandals were creation of the Ethics Commission to monitor behavior of public officials and Governor Askew's winning approval from the voters of the constitutional Sunshine Amendment, which prescribed rules of conduct.

Justices Resign

During the same session of 1975, two Justices of the Florida Supreme Court, Hal P. Dekle and David L. McCain, resigned while a House committee was investigating separate charges against them. Subsequently, on June 15, 1978, McCain was disbarred by the Supreme Court for "undermining the entire judicial process" by trying while a justice to influence lower-court judges for his friends. McCain was the first former member of the Supreme Court to lose his license to practice law. As a fugitive from federal indictments, McCain died from cancer in Jacksonville on November 12, 1986.

Conviction of Judge Smith

The first House impeachment successfully carried through to Senate conviction was that of Circuit Judge Samuel S. Smith of Lake City on September 15, 1978. The Senate convicted Smith on four articles of impeachment, denying him the right ever to hold a public office of honor and trust.

Smith sought to resign after the first of two convictions in federal court on charges of conspiracy to sell 1,500 pounds of marijuana seized by sheriff's deputies in Suwannee County. Governor Reubin O'D. Askew refused to accept the resignation. Askew pressed for removal of Smith by the Senate to prevent the judge from claiming a state pension of approximately $22,000 a year.

The first article taken up by the Senate accused Smith of debasing and degrading the office, bringing the court into "disrespect, scandal, disgrace, discredit, disrepute, and reproach." This was adopted unanimously. Three other articles, specific in nature, then were approved by votes of 32-3, 33-2, and 33-2. In May, the House had voted 115-0 to impeach Smith. Smith, suffering from a heart condition, did not attend his Senate trial on the advice of his physicians.

The most damaging evidence against Smith were tapes of conversations between Smith and Sheriff Robert Leonard of Suwannee County. The Federal Bureau of Investigation (FBI) arranged the tapings after Sheriff Leonard reported he had been approached by Judge Smith. Smith's attorney claimed the judge had been entrapped by Sheriff Leonard and the FBI. These tapes were played in the House chambers for the Smith hearing.

(For impeachment of federal judges in Florida, *see* section on the U.S. courts.)

United States Senators

The 17th Amendment to the United States Constitution deprived state legislatures on May 31, 1913, of their former right to elect United States senators. However, the Florida Legislature had recognized the voters' choice since statewide primaries commenced in 1902. (*See* index for elections of U.S. senators.)

Prefiling

To speed up committee consideration of legislation, the Legislature has authorized the Clerk and the Secretary to accept bills in advance of sessions. This is known as "prefiling ." A prefiled bill may be referred by the Speaker or President to a standing committee, after these have been appointed in November for the biennium, with the first regular session in April, although they cannot be introduced in the legislative sense for the Constitution seems to require all bills to be read or published in session, before they are formally before the body.

The Court and the Legislature

The independence of the Legislature was reinforced in the 1980s by a series of landmark decisions by the State Supreme Court.

The Justices decided:

1. Legislative audio and video tapes could not be used in court to impeach the Journals of the House of Representatives and Senate since those tapes never had been recognized by the Houses as official documents. Impeach journal, read title: *State v. Kaufman,* 430 So.2d 904 (Fla. 1983).

2. Only the House or Senate can determine the eligibility of any person claiming a legislative seat. Eligibility, election of legislators: *McPherson v. Flynn*, 397 So.2d 665 (Fla. 1981), and *Harden v. Garrett*, 483 So.2d 409 (Fla. 1985).

3. Only the House or Senate may make, interpret and enforce its own procedural rules in considering whether a rule or law requiring open meetings of committees was violated. Open meetings: *Moffitt v. Willis*, 459 So.2d 1018 (Fla. 1984).

4. When the Constitution speaks of "reading" the title of a bill, it can mean only sufficient for identification, which may be simply the bill number such as SB 1234 or HB 1234. Impeach journal, read title: *State v. Kaufman*, 430 So.2d 904 (Fla. 1983).

5. The Governor's selective veto may extend beyond the general appropriations bill to any bill with two or more appropriations, so that provision for an appropriation may be stricken without nullifying the remainder of the bill. Appropriations, veto: *Thompson v. Graham*, 481 So.2d 1212 (Fla. 1985), and *Brown v. Firestone*, 382 So.2d 654 (Fla. 1980). See also: *Florida Defenders of the Environment v. Graham*, 462 So.2d 59 (Fla. 1st DCA 1984), and *Department of Education v. Lewis*, 416 So.2d 455 (Fla. 1982).

6. Constitutional ambiguities, if any aside, the Governor has fifteen

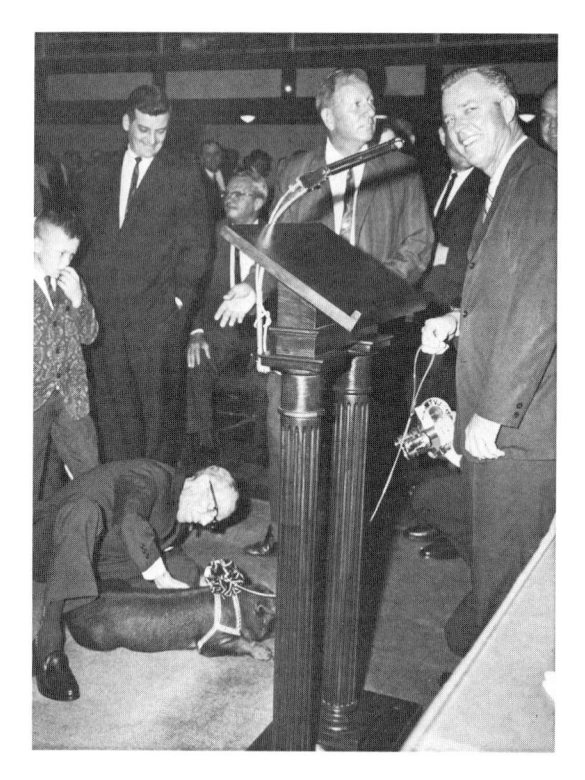

This picture likely cost a legislator his House seat. On the last day of the 1963 session, a young pig was led into the House Chamber for presentation to Representative David C. Eldredge of Miami (at far right, holding leash). A Dade colleague was the donor of the pig. He had no malice but thought of the presentation only as a joke. In Dade County at the time, however, "Porkchopper" was to many a term of opprobrium and the pig as a symbol. In the next primary campaign, thousands of copies of this photograph were distributed, the implication being that Eldredge had allied himself with the Pork Chop forces in the legislature. There was agreement among political observers that the picture caused Eldredge's defeat.

days for the veto process if a bill is presented by the Legislature either after sine die adjournment or during the last seven days of a session. Court took notice of the fact that Legislature presented sixty percent of a session's bills, including the omnibus general appropriations bill after adjournment. Presentation after adjournment: *Florida Society of Ophthalmology v. Florida Optometric Association*, 489 So.2d 1118 (Fla. 1986). Miscellaneous matters: Special sessions:*Florida Senate v. Graham*, 412 So.2d 360 (Fla. 1982). Reapportionment, elections: *In re Apportionment Law*, 414 So.2d 1040 (Fla. 1982).

Resign to Run Law

Source: Phyllis Slater

Florida's Resign to Run Law (Section 99.012, Florida Statutes) serves two purposes: it prevents an officer from using his present office to seek another, and it also spares the taxpayers the expense of having to finance special elections when an incumbent officer is elected to another office.

The law applies only to elected or appointed officers and not employees. Almost all elected officials are officers who share some of the sovereign responsibilities. The difficult question is determining whether an appointed person is an officer. A deputy to an officer, which deputy has the majority of the powers that the officer has, is an officer for the purposes of the Resign to Run Law. However, an employee working in an officer's office, and who works at the officer's direction but makes no major decisions, is an employee and not an officer.

Basically the Resign to Run Law provides that a candidate may not qualify for more than one office at a time, but this does not apply to people qualifying for political party office. A candidate may not qualify for another office if the terms of office are concurrent or overlap unless the candidate resigns from the office that he presently holds. The resignation, except for people qualifying for Federal office, must be submitted no later than ten days prior to the first day of qualifying. An office holder qualifying for Federal office must resign no later than when he qualifies for Federal office.

The resignation must be effective the earlier of one of two dates: when the office holder assumes office, if elected; or, when his successor takes office.

Any resignation submitted pursuant to the Resign to Run Law must be irrevocable. There is an exception in the law for an officer serving as a member of an appointee board of authority and who serves without salary. Such a person does not need to resign to run for another office.

An officer who is a subordinate personnel, deputy sheriff, or police officer does not need to resign unless running against his "boss." However, such a person must take a leave of absence without pay during the period he is seeking election to public office.

In addition, an officer who is a subordinate personnel, deputy sheriff, or police officer may choose between submitting an irrevocable letter of resignation or taking a leave of absence without pay from his employment during the period he is seeking election.

Claude R. Kirk campaign workers in bumper sticker dresses during his 1966 run for the Governor's office.

Forest Granger

How An Idea Becomes A Law

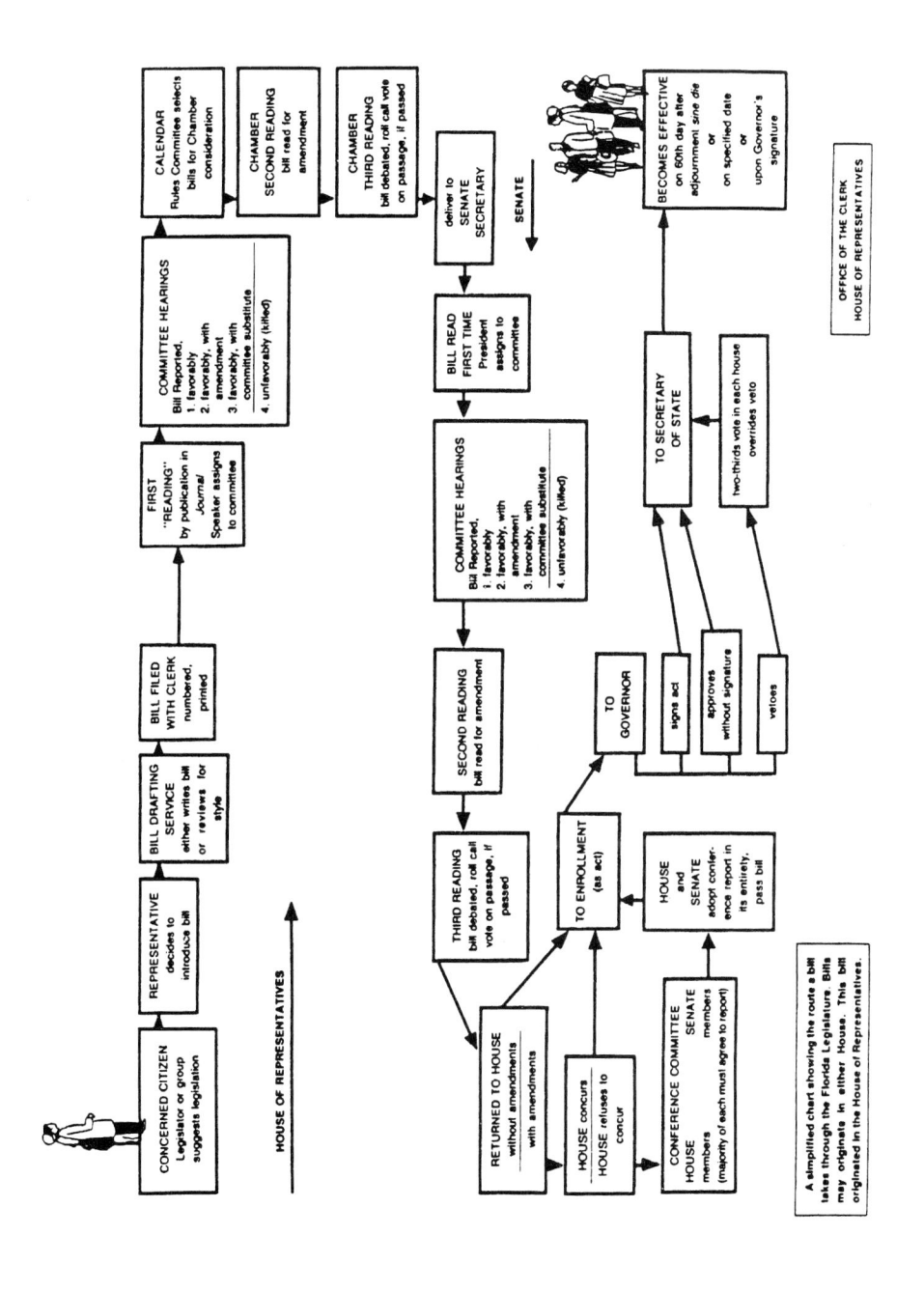

How an Idea Becomes a Law

During each two-year term of the Florida Legislature, Representatives and Senators cause to be introduced a total of two to three thousand bills. (Many of these are "companion" bills, or bills of the same text which are introduced in both houses so they will move along the legislative process until each clears all committees of reference and the bills may be merged for floor consideration.)

The idea for a bill may originate anywhere. The Governor and the Executive Department, the Judiciary, interest groups, corporations, unions, and individuals: all these provide the ideas but only a Senator or a Representative may introduce a bill. The original bill likely will be drafted for the legislator by the Senate or House drafting services. In any event, a bill must be cleared by the drafting service for legal form.

Thus, the first hurdle for a bill is finding a sponsor.

Every bill begins its legislative course by filing with the Clerk of the House or the Secretary of the Senate. If the Legislature is in session, the bill will be given first "reading" generally by publication of its title in the Journal of the house of introduction. Out of session, this action is known as "prefiling." It will bear the signature of the sponsor and those of other legislators who have joined as cosponsors. (Other members may join as cosponsors as the bill moves along.)

The Clerk or the Secretary will give the bill the number which will identify it forever. The Speaker or President will be given a copy for the purpose of referring the bill to one or more committees. Hundreds more copies are printed for members and the public. Whether a bill ultimately will become law may depend upon these references for a third to a fourth of all bills die in committee.

Thus, the second hurdle is committee reference.

Committee action is the vital stage in lawmaking. In 1994 there were nineteen standing and two other committees of the Senate and twenty-two standing and one select committee of the House. Bills are routinely referred to a committee whose bailiwick may be inferred from its name although, unlike Congress, no formal description of its area of jurisdiction exists.

The number of committees may change from the administration of one presiding officer to the next. In the House almost every bill will go to a standing subcommittee, which possesses the power to report a bill unfavorably. The Senate has standing subcommittees only of the Committee on Appropriations although select subcommittees may be created from time to time to meet special situations.

Thus, the subcommittee is the third hurdle.

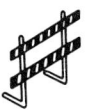

Should the bill be reported favorably by the subcommittee and parent committee, perhaps with committee amendments or a total rewrite known as a "Committee Substitute," the bill either goes to another committee of reference, if any, or to the House Calendar.

Thus, consideration by the parent committee is the fourth hurdle.

The Calendar is but a shelf list of bills available for inclusion in the Special Order Calendar. This calendar is assembled by the Committee on Rules and Calendar, and, as a generalization, only bills on the Special Order Calendar (except local bills) will be considered by the Senate or House.

Thus, the Rules committee is the fifth hurdle.

The bill finally reaches the floor for consideration. This is the stage the public usually thinks of as decisive in the life of a piece of legislation yet virtually every bill passes that reaches the floor although it may be drastically modified there by amendments. The killer amendment would, if adopted, strike the enacting clause. To be constitutionally sound, each bill must contain this language: "Be It Enacted by the Legislature of the State of Florida." In the case of joint resolutions (proposed amendments to the State Constitution), the clause commences: "Be It Resolved etc."

Floor action has two parts known as "readings." First reading occurred when the bill was introduced. "Reading" is a misleading term for the bill's title usually will not be read at all on first reading but simply published in the Journal. While the Constitution requires the title to be read on second and third readings, the Florida Supreme Court has held that modern means of informing the members of the bill before them means the title to be read need be only the bill number or sufficient of the language to identify the subject.

Second reading is basically for the purpose of considering amendments to the bill while third reading is for the purpose of debating the merits of the bill in its final amended form in that house. Amendments may be offered on third reading but can be adopted only by a two-thirds vote. These third-reading amendments generally correct errors of a technical nature which occurred on second reading. A record roll call is required by the Constitution for the passage of a bill.

Thus, floor consideration is the sixth hurdle.

Assuming this bill originated in the House, the bill now goes to the Senate, where the same course is followed, from introduction, referral, committee consideration, and floor action. If it passes, it almost certainly will be with Senate amendments. That means the bill must be returned to the House for concurrence, rejection, or modification of the Senate amendments. Sometimes a conference committee may be appointed to attempt to resolve the differences between the two houses.

Thus, the Senate course may be regarded as presenting the seventh, eighth, ninth, tenth, eleventh and twelfth hurdles.

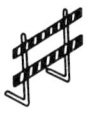

If the House and Senate finally agree upon the wording of the bill, it will be certified to the Governor by the Speaker and Clerk of the House and the President and Secretary of the Senate. The Governor has seven days to veto the bill (actually, now an "act") after its presentation to him during a session except for the final seven days. If during that period or on the seventh day the Legislature adjourns sine die or takes a recess of more than thirty days, the Governor has fifteen consecutive days from the date of presentation. If the Governor fails to act, the act becomes law. In the case of local bills, the Governor most likely will allow these to become law without signature.

By providing specifically how the Governor shall proceed, the Constitution prevented the exercise by the Governor of the "pocket veto" available to some Governors of other states and to the President of the United States.

Thus, the veto is the thirteenth hurdle.

Assuming the Governor has vetoed the act, it will be returned to the house of origin by the Secretary of State. If the Legislature is still in session, the bill may be acted upon but this is not mandatory. It can simply be abandoned. If taken up, it requires two-thirds of the members present in each house to override the veto. Should the Legislature not be in session, the veto will be laid over to the next regular or special session. If not considered then, the veto stands and the Legislature has lost its opportunity for review.

Thus, the overriding of the veto could be regarded as the fourteenth and fifteenth hurdles.

Fernando Figueredo, who represented Monroe county in the 1885 House, likely was the first Cuban exile to serve. From 1887 until 1892, he served as Superintendent of Schools for Monroe county, and from 1895 to 1899 he was first Mayor of West Tampa, a city later merged with Tampa. After Cubans claimed the island from Spain, Figueredo was, from 1902 to 1908 Secretary of Interior for the Republic and from 1909 until 1919 he was Secretary of the Treasury. In 1897 Jose Marti asked Figueredo to remain in Tampa to coordinate military expeditions into Cuba. In 1991, Representative Carlos L. Valdes of Miami Springs told the House of Figueredo's governmental career in Florida and Cuba and introduced Figueredo's namesake great-grandson.
　　　　　　　　　Leland Hawes, Tampa Tribune

The Legislator

On the day of first election to the Florida Legislature the typical representative-elect in 1994 was 41 and the typical Senator was 43.[1] Why did the fledgling lawmaker seek election?

The authority on American legislatures and legislators is Alan Rosenthal, director of the Eagleton Institute of Politics at Rutgers University. In his book *Legislative Life* he explored at length the question of motivation. This was his summation:

> For many people politics is interesting and the job of being a legislator strikes them as worthwhile. For many the prestige of being elected, or of holding office, and of being one of a relative few is appealing. For many the chance to serve the public, to accomplish something in the public interest, to do good is of major importance. A number believe they can do a better job than those already in office. For some, there is an overriding issue, a particular philosophy, or a special interest that has to be promoted. For many the prospect of exercising power, of being in command or control, has great appeal. For nearly all, in some way or another, politics is an "ego trip", a means of receiving approval, support, and attention. For most of them, there is no single reason, but rather a combination that impels them toward legislative office,[2]

or, as Stimson Bullitt wrote in *To Be A Politician:*

> "Men and women are drawn into politics by a combination of motives: power, glory, zeal for contention or success, duty, oblivion, hate, hero worship, curiosity, and enjoyment of the work."

This urge to seek elective office has been put on thumbnail by Rosenthal in these words:

> "Until you've been in politics you've never really been alive ... it's the only sport for grownups—all other games are for kids."[3]

Significance: The Key Word

A perceptive Florida witness to the phenomenon of politics was Fuller Warren. Warren served in the Florida House of Representatives from two different counties—one rural and one urban—and had been defeated as a candidate for governor before being elected in 1948. As governor-elect, he stated his view of politics:[4]

> I believe I know why people get more intensely interested in politics than they do in any other hobby or recreation such as bridge, baseball, horse racing, stamp collecting or even fishing.
>
> I think the key word is *significance.*

Yesterday's bridge game is forgotten today, or tomorrow at the latest. Yesterday's baseball game is only a topic of conversation today and the same thing holds true of a horse race or a golf match.

None of these events affect those who do not actually participate in them, except to give the non-participants something to talk about. The baseball fan is disappointed if his favorite team loses but this feeling passes quickly when the same team wins. Even if he has wagered and lost, the effect is transitory and soon forgotten.

But government is a different matter. A single election may have a great effect on the personal lives of every one of us.

Attorneys in the Florida Legislature
House of Representatives

Session	Number of Attorneys	Total Members	Percentage
1929	33	95	35%
1939	45	95	47%
1949	35	95	37%
1959	43	95	45%
1969/70	44	119	37%
1979/80	29	120	24%
1989/90	29	120	24%
1991/92	34	120	28%
1993/94	31	120	26%
1995/96	26	120	21%

Senate

Session	Number of Attorneys	Total Members	Percentage
1929	13	38	34%
1939	16	38	42%
1949	23	38	60%
1959	17	38	45%
1969/70	21	48	44%
1979/80	13	40	32%
1989/90	10	40	25%
1991/92	14	40	35%
1993/94	14	40	35%
1995/96	12	40	30%

Lawyers in Legislature

Contrary to general belief, the typical member of the Florida House of Representatives is not a lawyer. Actually, lawyers are a minority whose numbers have been decreasing and reached an all-time low of 21% in 1995–1996. Attorney is the most frequently named profession (26), but 14 were in the category of education, 14 business, 10 medical and 9 in real estate. Seven reported investing as their primary employment and seven regarded themselves as legislators. Of the other diverse professions, consultant was the most frequently named.

Thumbnail Statistics

Those married outnumbered the single by 96 to 24. Of those with children, 72 had more than one. Thirteen had only one child and 35 had none. Fifty Seven were born in Florida, fourteen in New York, and the remainder in scattered places of birth.

Only four had not attended college. Thirteen attended but left without a degree; 103 received degrees. One hundred eight reported a church affiliation, only 12 did not.

Tenure

Once elected, the typical House member may look forward to spending three to four two-year terms. This may be shortened by a member seeking election to the senate or other office.

Of the 40 members of the 1995–1996 Senate, 29 were incumbents. The Lieutenant governor and three of the six cabinet officers had served in the Legislature. Thirteen of the 25 members of the congressional delegation likewise had served: one senator and 12 of the 23 members of the United States House.

The number of legislators who move from the House to the Senate accounts in part for the higher average age of first-term senators.

Value of Incumbency

An interesting fact is how few House members are defeated for reelection. Between 1968 and 1994, the percentage of incumbents running for reelection who were successful ranged from 82 to 95 percent (twice) with over 90% in 9 of the 14 elections.[6]

Political Parties

Some generalizations can be made about political parties in the Florida legislature. The majority party elects the presiding officers, the House Speaker and the Senate president. These officers appoint the members of committees, including the chairmen. The minority has representation on committees but not in direct proportion to their membership, a few have served as chairmen.

Pay and Perquisites

Annual pay for members in 1994 was $23,244. The Senate President and House Speaker were paid a base of $32,280. Perquisites for members include:
- Up to $1,500 a month for district office expenses.
- Two year-round employees for Representatives, three or four at the President's discretion for Senators.
- Subsistence of $79 a day during the session to a maximum of $3,000 and $79 per diem for authorized travel on official business outside their district.
- Reimbursement of 25¢ a mile if travel is by automobile or tourist fare if by airplane.

- One weekly round trip home during the legislative session for members, two round trips during regular session for staff.
- Postage allowance of $450 per regular sessions plus $4000 a year for such mailings as newsletters
- Senators' additional budget allotment: $7,500 to be used for telephone toll charges, printing and postage, Senator's and district staff travel, periodicals and data processing hardware and software.
- The Speaker and President each have a $10,000 contingency fund.

Legislators may enroll in approved group insurance programs. The Legislature pays the premiums for state-sponsored health and life insurance programs. Legislators may also participate in the Florida Retirement System for elected state officials.

Characteristics of Members of Florida Legislature 1995–1996

	House—120 House No.	(%)	Senate—40 Senate No.	(%)
Sex:				
Male	95	(79.2)	34	(85.0%)
Female	25	(20.8)	6	(15.0%)
TOTAL	120		40	
Ethnic Classification:				
Anglo	92	(76.7%)	32	(80.0%)
Black	15	(12.5%)	5	(12.5%)
Hispanic	9	(7.5%)	3	(7.5%)
Not Reported	4	(3.3%)	0	(0.0%)
TOTAL	120		40	
Party Affiliation:				
Democrat	63	(52.5%)	18	(45%)
Republican	57	(47.5%)	22	(55%)
TOTAL	120		40	
Percentage of Florida and Non-Florida Natives:				
Florida Natives	57	(47.5%)	17	(42.5%)
Non-Florida Natives	63	(52.5%)	23	(57.5%)
TOTAL	120		40	
Service:				
Incumbents	93	(77.5%)	29	(72.5%)
Freshman	27	(22.5%)	11	(27.5%)
TOTAL	120		40	

Political Party Representation in Legislature

House

Year (November)	Democrats	Republicans	Total
1976	(92) 76.7%	(28) 23.3%	120
1978	(89) 74.2%	(31) 25.8%	120

Political Party Representation in Legislature (*continued*)

House

Year (November)	Democrats	Republicans	Total
1980	(81) 67.5%	(39) 32.5%	120
1982	(84) 70.0%	(36) 30.0%	120
1984	(77) 64.0%	(43) 36.0%	120
1985	(76) 63.0%	(44) 37.0%	120
1986	(76) 63.0%	(44) 37.0%	120
1988	(75) 62.5%	(45) 37.5%	120
1989	(73) 60.8%	(47) 39.2%	120
1990	(74) 61.6%	(46) 38.3%	120
*1991	(73) 60.8%	(47) 39.2%	120
*1991	(74) 61.7%	(46) 38.3%	120
1992	(74) 61.7%	(46) 38.3%	120
1993	(71) 59.2%	(49) 40.8%	120
1995	(63) 52.5%	(57) 47.5%	120

*[Member changed party affiliation]

Senate

Year (November)	Democrats	Independent	Republicans	Total
1976	(30) 75.0%	(1) 2.5%	(9) 22.5%	40
1978	(29) 72.5%	-0-	(11) 27.5%	40
1980	(27) 67.5%	-0-	(13) 32.5%	40
1982	(32) 80.0%	-0-	(8) 20.0%	40
1984	(32) 80.0%	-0-	(8) 20.0%	40
1985	(31) 78.0%	-0-	(9) 22.0%	40
1986	(30) 75.0%	-0-	(10) 25.0%	40
1988	(25) 63.5%	-0-	(15) 32.5%	40
1989	(23) 57.5%	-0-	(17) 42.5%	40
1990	(23) 57.5%	-0-	(17) 42.5%	40
1991	(20) 50.0%	-0-	(20) 50.0%	40
1992	(20) 50.0%	-0-	(20) 50.0%	40
1993	(20) 50.0%	-0-	(20) 50.0%	40
1995	(18) 45%	-0-	(22) 55%	40

Single-Member Districts

Beginning with the elections of 1982, candidates for the Legislature ran in single-member districts. (*See* separate articles on apportionment.) Because incumbents will have greater opportunity to be known than in those places which had multi-member districts, incumbents are expected now to have even more of an edge in seeking reelection.

A World Unto Itself

The Legislature in session takes on the parochial nature of a small town. When the Orange County commission voted some years ago to publish an advertisement critical of the sponsor of a local claims bill, even opponents of the bill came to his defense. A Broward County Representative, Tom Bush, told the House "this is a sovereign body that circles the wagons when a local

Ralph H. Haben, Jr., says without embarrassment that he loves the House of Representatives. As a member from the 71st House District (Hardee and parts of Manatee and Sarasota counties), he served as Speaker in 1980–1982.

Mallory E. Horne of Tallahassee, was the first Florida legislator in more than a century to serve as Speaker of the House and President of the Senate. He was Speaker for the two years commencing in November, 1962, and President in November, 1972.

body begins accusing its members." An Orange County member, an opponent of the bill, Representative Richard Crotty, said the House's spirit of camaraderie was violated when an outside force "starts tampering." The House passed the bill which otherwise it likely would have killed.

At the political capital of Florida, legislators spend most of their out-of daily-session in Tallahassee talking to colleagues. As a political scientist observed after serving as a legislator, a legislature, once convened, is inclined to become a miniature world unto itself. This, wrote Frank Smallwood, despite the fact that "any legislative body is a partial reflection of the larger society it is elected to represent."

Stepping-Stones

Aides to individual legislators and to delegations have used this experience to advantage in seeking election to the legislature. Two recent Speakers, Ralph H. Haben, Jr., and H. Lee Moffitt and Senate President Jim Scott, came to the legislature as delegation aides. Other former aides have stepped up to membership.

As Alan Rosenthal observes: "Having spent several years helping to organize a district politically and doing favors for people, they are formidable candidates when a seat becomes vacant."[7]

Qualifying Fee

A candidate for the legislature pays a qualifying fee of $1,743.30, which is seven and one half percent of the legislative salary of $23,244 a year. The qualifying fee increases with the salary.

Of the seven and one half percent fee two percent is the filing fee, of the next three percent eighty percent goes to the party and fifteen percent to General Revenue. One percent helps defray the expense of the Election Commission and one and one half percent goes into the Election Campaign Financing Trust Fund.

Ethics

A legislator is bound to an ethical course of conduct by rule and statute. The Senate admonitions are contained in Rule One; the House in Rule Five. The statute is part III of chapter 112.

Female Members

Orange county elected the first women to serve in both the House of Representatives and the Senate.

Mrs. Edna Giles Fuller of Orlando spoke for Orange in the five regular and special sessions of the 1929 and 1931 House of Representatives.

Mrs. Beth (George W.) Johnson of Orlando was elected to the Senate in 1962, after having served Orange County in the House. She first was elected in 1957 to fill a vacancy, and then was reelected in 1958 and 1960.

Interestingly, for five months, there were two Beth Johnsons in the Senate. Mrs. Elizabeth J. (Beth) Johnson of Cocoa Beach, a Republican, was elected in 1966. The Orlando Senator Johnson, a Democrat, had been reelected in 1964. The two served together until the federal court-ordered special general election of March, 1967, when Senator Johnson of Orlando was defeated and Senator Johnson of Cocoa Beach was reelected.

Fuller   Johnson

Women Presiding

Representative Mary Lou Baker (Mrs. Seale H. Matthews) of Pinellas County presided over the House for the passage of one bill on May 17, 1945, the first woman to do so. Speaker Evans Crary suggested the members address Miss Baker as "Miss Speaker."

Senator Beth (Mrs. George W.) Johnson of Orlando, representing the 19th District, was on November 15, 1966, the first woman to preside over the Senate or House by election of the membership. Senator Johnson was elected as temporary presiding officer at the Organization Session of the new Senate. She already had served on May 26, 1965, as presiding officer by invitation of the President. Miss Baker had served similarly by invitation of the Speaker.

In November, 1990, the Senate elected the first Legislative woman presiding officer in the state's history, Gwen Margolis of North Miami, a Democrat.

Political Parties

The membership of the Legislature has been predominantly Democratic but adherents of other political parties—Republican, Socialist, Populist and Whig—have won election over the years since Florida achieved statehood.

The sweep of 1928, when Republican Herbert Hoover defeated Democrat Alfred E. Smith both nationally and in Florida, carried two Republicans into the legislature from Pinellas County. They were Senator Albert R. Welsh of St. Petersburg and Representative Kenneth W. Kerr of Dunedin. Senator Welsh died after serving one session, and a Democrat was elected to complete his term. Representative Kerr also served in one regular session.

Three other Republicans had served in the House early in this century: A. D. Whitman of Wauchula represented Hardee County in the 1931 legislature, Dr. Henry C. Hood of Palm Beach, from Palm Beach County, in the 1917 legislature, and Lambert M. Ware, from Washington County in the 1903 House. A. J. Pettigrew, of Manatee in Manatee County, served as a Socialist in the 1907 House.

Republican members ceased to be novelties after Pinellas County sent up an entirely GOP House delegation to the 1951 session, Representatives William C. Cramer and Donald C. McLaren of St. Petersburg and B. E. Shaffer of Clearwater. The Republican nature of the Pinellas delegation was rounded out two years later when J. Frank Houghton of St. Petersburg came to the Senate.

The Republicans gained sufficient legislative muscle in 1967 to become an effective opposition, with 20 Senators and 39 Representatives. This was sufficient senators to uphold vetoes by GOP Governor Claude R. Kirk, Jr.

With minority strength came a greater need for party apparatus: a Minority Leader (corresponding with the majority party's President or Speaker), a Minority Leader pro tempore (matching the majority's President or Speaker pro tempore), and Whip (the majority's floor leader).

Hon. Lambert M. Ware, the Only Republican in the Florida Legislature.

When Republican Lambert M. Ware of Washington County turned up for the 1903 session, it occasioned this cartoon in the Florida Times-Union.
Cartoon collection, Museum of Florida History

Status of Men

Senator Pat Frank appeared on May 8, 1980, before the Senate Committee on Governmental Operations in its consideration of abolition of the Commission on the Status of Women.

An amused committeeman suggested, if there must be a committee on the status of women, there should be one on the status of men.

"Gentlemen," said Senator Frank, "there is a committee on the status of men" . . . pausing for emphasis . . . "it's called the Florida Senate."

The abashed committee voted to continue the Commission.

The First Republican Woman

A court-ordered reapportionment gave Pinellas County three additional seats in the House of Representatives, to be filled at special elections just before the convening of the 1963 regular session. Mary R. (Mrs. Charles H. Pearson) Grizzle of Indian Rocks Beach defeated three other Republicans in the primary and a Democratic opponent in the general election. She thus became the first Republican woman to serve in either the Florida House or Senate. She rarely had opposition after those first elections, and those opponents never were successful. In 1992, however, she was defeated.

Wilson   Grizzle

She was recognized by her Republican colleagues in the House through election in 1974 as Minority Leader pro tempore, and by Democratic Speakers through appointment to significant committees. In 1976, for example, she was a member of the committees of Appropriations, Education, and Rules and Calendar. She retired from the House in 1978 to seek election to the state Senate and was elected. Had she remained in the House, Mrs. Grizzle would have become for the 1979 session, by seniority, the first woman to be "Dean of the House."

A No-Party Legislator

Lori Wilson of Cocoa Beach first was elected to the Senate in 1972 as a no party Legislator, an independent spelled with a small "i". There had been Independents (with a capital "I") in prior Florida Legislatures, for example, one each in the Senate and Assembly in 1879, but apparently few, if any, who came to the Legislature in modern times with the same no-party determination of freedom. She did not seek reelection in 1978 but did unsuccessfully as a Republican in 1988.

Kershaw    Cherry    Meek    Girardeau

First Blacks

Joe Lang Kershaw, a Democrat and, when elected a 57-year-old civics teacher at a Coral Gables junior high school, became in 1968 the first black since 1889 to serve in the Legislature. Dade County voters sent Kershaw to the House of Representatives, where, some 30 years earlier as a student at Florida A&M University and parttime capitol janitor, he had stood on the Speaker's podium and pretended he was addressing the House. He was defeated for renomination in 1982. Available records indicate the last blacks to serve in the House before Kershaw were George A. Lewis and John R. Scott, Jr., who represented Duval County in the 1889 House.

The first black woman ever to serve in the Florida legislature, Mrs. Gwen Sawyer Cherry, was elected to the House from Dade County in 1970. She was born in Miami in 1923. A lawyer, teacher and author, she received her law degree, *cum laude,* from Florida A&M University in 1965. Representative Cherry was killed in a one-car automobile accident in Tallahassee on February 7, 1979.

One of the first two blacks to serve in the Florida Senate since 1887, and the first black woman ever to serve, was Mrs. Carrie P. Meek of Miami, who first came to the legislature in 1979, having been chosen in a special election to succeed Mrs. Cherry. She was nominated without opposition to serve in the Senate after the 1982 reapportionment. A native of Tallahassee, and an educational administrator, Mrs. Meek earned her bachelor's degree from Florida A&M University, her master's from the University of Michigan, and a doctorate in education from Florida Atlantic University was pending when she came to the Legislature. She earned letters in track and field from Florida A&M. Available records indicate the last blacks to serve in the Senate were D. C. Martin from Alachua County and Henry W. Chandler from Marion County, each in the 1887 session.

The other black elected to the Senate in 1982 was Dr. Arnette E. Girardeau, a Jacksonville dentist. Dr. Girardeau first had been elected to the House of Representatives in 1976. Unlike Mrs. Meek, Representative Girardeau had to struggle for election to the Senate, having to overcome three white opponents and one black opponent, so that he had to campaign in the first and second primaries and the general election. A native of Jacksonville, Dr. Girardeau earned his bachelor's degree and doctorate from Howard University and did postgraduate studies at Wayne State and Fisk Universities.

Party Affiliation of Blacks: Reconstruction Era

Of the blacks elected to the legislature since the 1880s all have been Democrats with one exception, that of John Plummer of Miami, a Republican. Plummer served one term, in the 1980-82 House. Plummer's election may be regarded as something of a fluke. He avoided photographs and interviews. Also, there was voter confusion with another Plummer, a white Democrat member of the House.

While "since Reconstruction" served as media shorthand to distinguish the election of blacks to the legislature beginning with Joe Lang Kershaw in 1968, Reconstruction formally ended in 1876. The "Reconstruction era" lasted some years longer.

Black pro tempore

James C. Burke, Miami Democrat, was designated by Speaker Jon L. Mills to serve as Speaker pro tempore for the sessions of 1987 and 1988. Burke was the first black to occupy the Chair.

Black Caucus

The first elections in 1982 from the new single-member legislative districts resulted in the seating of two black senators and 10 black House members.

On November 30, 1982, meeting at the Tallahassee Hilton Hotel, eleven of the twelve black legislators organized Florida's first black caucus. Senator Carrie Meek of Miami was chosen chairperson and Representative John Thomas of Jacksonville was elected vice chairperson.

Blacks in Tallahassee During Reconstruction

Dr. Joe Martin Richardson, professor of history at Florida State University, has written that blacks were of considerable importance in the Legislature during Reconstruction, though they never were in the majority.[8]

"In the first Legislature (during Reconstruction), there were nineteen freedmen present, which was the largest number of Negroes ever sent as Representatives to the Florida lawmaking body. The Negroes combined with white Northerners were always outnumbered. In 1868 of seventy-six legislators nineteen were freedmen, thirteen were from the North, twenty-three were white Democrats and twenty-one were white Southern Loyalists. Southern born whites were always in a majority in the Florida Reconstruction legislatures. In 1868 the composition according to party was fifty-two Republicans to twenty-four Democrats. Although it has been maintained that Negroes held the balance of power in the state, it would be as logical, and perhaps more so to say that it was held by the Southern white Loyalists, who generally outnumbered Negro legislators.

"The Negroes probably exerted more power in the Senate than they did in the House. Of the twenty-four Senators freedmen claimed three in 1868, five in 1869–1870, three in 1871–1872, five in 1873–1874, and six in 1875–1876. The number of freedmen in the House ranged from sixteen in 1868 to eight in 1876. There never were more than thirteen in the House after 1868. Only about thirty different freedmen served in the lower house of the legislature during the entire Reconstruction era."

Youngest State Senator

Dennis J. Patrick O'Grady of Inverness, a Republican who represented the 19th District in 1967–68, appears from available records to have been the youngest member of the state Senate.

O'Grady, born December 9, 1943, in Brooklyn, New York, was elected on March 28, 1967, in a special court-ordered statewide apportionment general election. O'Grady was a building contractor and nurseryman. When elected, he was 23 years and 3 months old.

Johnnie Wright of DeFuniak Springs, a Democrat who represented the 3rd District in 1948–51, was born April 5, 1925. He was elected on November 2, 1948, and then was 23 years and 7 months old.

Youngest House Member

A number of members of the Florida House of Representatives were elected when 21, the lawful minimum. Actually, some were chosen when 20 since Democratic nominations prior to the 1960s usually were the equivalent of election as there were relatively few Republican nominees.

O'Grady Warren

Former Governor Fuller Warren of Blountstown was among those nominated while 20. He served Calhoun County in the 1927 House. Walter Warren was nominated at 20 in 1934 to serve Putnam County in the 1935 House.

Doyle E. Conner, afterwards Commissioner of Agriculture, was elected at 21 while a student at the University of Florida to serve Bradford County in the 1950 House. At 28, Conner was the youngest Speaker of the House.

First Hispanic Members

Research indicates that Fernando Figueredo of Key West, a refugee, was the first Cuban-American to serve in the Legislature, representing Monroe County in the 1885 session of the House. After Cuba became a republic, Figueredo returned to Havana and became Treasurer of the national government. See photograph on page 136.

The first Hispanic-American to serve in the House since 1925 (when J. F. Busto represented Monroe County) was Maurice A. Ferre, a native of Puerto Rico, who was elected to the House from the 91st district for the 1967–68 sessions. He returned to Miami, where he was elected Mayor.

Miss Ileana Ros of Miami, elected in November, 1982, was the first Hispanic woman to serve in the Legislature, representing the 110th District, Dade County. She also made legislative history by wedding one of her Dade County colleagues, Representative Dexter Lehtinen of Perrine, the first marriage of two members of the Florida Legislature. They were wed on June 9, 1984. She then was known as Ileana Ros-Lehtinen. Subsequently they made more legislative history by being elected to the Senate in 1986. In 1989 she was elected to the United States House of Representatives.

Cuban-American Caucus

The Cuban-American Caucus of the House of Representatives (CACHR) was organized on May 18, 1988 as a non-profit corporation. Its purpose: to inform and educate the public of the "political, cultural, patriotic and civic aspirations of the Cuban-American and Hispanic communities of Florida." The seven Latins then members of the House of Representatives were the incorporators and first directors of the corporation.

Privileges and Penalties

Each house, under the Constitution, is the sole judge of the qualifications of its members. Each may choose its own officers, and determine its rules of procedure.

Each house may punish its own members for disorderly conduct, and each house may, with the concurrence of two-thirds of the members present, expel a member.

Representative E. Bert Riddle of Walton County was expelled from the 1961 House on an unspecified charge upon the recommendation of a special committee appointed "for the purpose of investigating a matter pertaining to the dignity of the House."[9]

The Senate on April 29, 1872, directed its secretary "to omit from the roll call the name of the late senator from the 8th Senatorial District."[10] By vacating his seat, the Senate reacted to the judgment that day of the Supreme Court upholding the bribery conviction of Senator Charles H. Pearce of Leon County.

The same Justices, on the same day, joined with the Lieutenant Governor and the Attorney General in granting Pearce a full pardon, thereby suggesting the appeals court had some question about the sufficiency of the evidence if not the procedure. Pearce, a Negro, had been recruited by the African Methodist Episcopal Church to move to Florida from Canada as a missionary in February, 1866. He served Leon County concurrently in the Senate and as Superintendent of Public Instruction. Known as the "Bishop" Pearce although he never attained higher rank than elder, Pearce subsequently served in the Legislatures of 1873 and 1874 and, as a Republican elector, cast his ballot for Rutherford B. Hayes in the contested presidential election of 1876.

Each house may, by law, compel the attendance of witnesses at an investigation held by the house or any of its committees.

Each house may, during a session, punish by fine or imprisonment any person not a member who is guilty of disorderly or contemptuous conduct in its presence, or refuses to obey a summons. Such imprisonment cannot go beyond final adjournment of the legislature.

Reprimand Proceeding

Senator Ralph R. Poston, Sr., of Miami, was reprimanded and fined $500 by the Senate at a special session on December 13, 1977, called for the purpose of considering charges he had violated laws and rules relating to standards of conduct. Specifically, Senator Poston was accused of using his public office to seek business, through the State Department of Health and Rehabilitative Service, for an Orlando-based wheelchair-ambulance service owned by him. The Senate resolved that Poston not be seated until he had tendered the fine to the comptroller, which he promptly did.

Each house may do business with a quorum of its members, a quorum having been defined by the Supreme Court as not less than a majority of all members. Vacancies from death, resignation, or failure to elect cannot be deducted in determining a quorum.

A Governor as a Legislator

Two governors served in the Florida House of Representatives subsequent to being chief executive. William Dunn Moseley, the first governor under statehood, was elected in 1855 to complete the term of a resigned representative from Putnam County. Governor Harrison Reed, a Republican, was governor between July 9, 1868, and January 7, 1873. He was elected from Duval County to the 1879 Assembly.

As Senate President, Charley E. Johns of Starke, served as acting governor upon the death of Governor Dan McCarty in 1953 and returned to the Senate after a successor had been inaugurated. Lieutenant Governor William H. Gleason, who unsuccessfully claimed the office of governor in 1868, later served in the House from Dade County.

An Outsider's View

Unquestionably, Alan S. Rosenthal knows more about the Florida Legislature than any outsider. Rosenthal is Director of Eagleton Institute of Politics at New Jersey's Rutgers University.

He was given the unique opportunity to watch and record the unfolding of the 1986 session of the Florida Legislature. He sat quietly in corners as Senate and House leaders dealt with their daily problems. He observed committees and chambers in session. He spent days and evenings at the elbow of the movers and shakers, privy to their confidential conversations. He was present at the Mansion when the legislative leaders negotiated with the Governor. Newsmen were excluded.

Single-member Districting

These are Rosenthal's post-session opinions on significant aspects of Florida lawmaking:

"In my opinion, single-member districts are beginning to make a difference in the House. Although the quality of the membership is still very high, legislators are becoming more preoccupied with their districts. This shows up, more than anywhere else, in the increasing importance of turkeys for just about everyone.

"It is the responsibility of the leadership to overcome the parochialism that results from single-member districts, and leadership carries out its responsibility quite well."[11]

Party Discipline

"I was surprised that, even with the upsurge of the Republican Party, the House and Senate are still not at all partisan bodies. Partisanship is channeled into fund raising and campaigning rather than into taking opposite sides on major issues. On only a few matters do Republicans vote as a bloc, and on even fewer does partisanship become intense."[11]

---

[1] *The Clerk's Office*, 1995, Florida House of Representatives.
[2] *Legislative Life*, Alan Rosenthal, New York: Harper & Row, 1981, page 19.
[3] *Legislative Life*, Alan Rosenthal, New York: Harper & Row, 1981, page 20.
[4] *How to Win in Politics*, Fuller Warren, Tallahassee: Peninsular, 1948.
[5] *The Clerk's Manual*, Florida House of Representatives.
[6] *The Value of Incumbency in the Florida House of Representatives*, Office of the Clerk, Tallahassee. Revised biennially.
[7] *Legislative Life*, Alan Rosenthal, New York: Harper and Row, page 21.
[8] Joe Martin Richardson, *The Negro in the Reconstruction of Florida 1865–1877*, Florida State University Studies, No. 46 pp. 187–188.
[9] Journal, 1961 House of Representatives.
[10] Journal, 1872 Senate.
[11] Letter, Alan Rosenthal to Allen Morris.

158 / The Legislator

A teddy bear in Ileana Ros-Lehtinen's seat celebrates the birth of the first child born to two sitting Representatives in the Florida House.

Why One Man Ran

Florida Representative Frank Williams had no doubt why he ran for the House. He appeared before the House Governmental Organization and Efficiency committee at the 1972 session as director of civil defense for Bradford County, seeking greater legislative recognition of that program. He had waited three days to read a prepared statement running about three minutes. Unhappily, it was Commissioner of Agriculture Doyle Conner's legislative appreciation day at the Fairgrounds and since the clock was pushing 5 o'clock and the members were anxious to leave, the committee granted Williams one minute, interrupted with questions, and then cut him off as he exceeded the minute.

In exasperation, Williams asked: "What does an average citizen have to do to get heard by this committee?" A member, Colonel William L. Gibson, responded: "Son, I suggest you be a member of the Legislature." Williams instantly decided he would do just that and exited with this parting remark to the committee, "Well, fellows, I'll see you in November", which he did at the organization session in November of that year. He was appointed to the renamed Governmental Operations Committee.

Mr. Speaker: Ms. President

The Speaker is the presiding officer of the House of Representatives. The President is the presiding officer of the Senate.

But presiding, or managing the in-chamber proceedings of a legislative house, is the least of the responsibilities which cause the Speaker and the President to be regarded as possessing unrivaled power and influence. Every Speaker or President has asked some Representative or Senator to take the gavel and preside for hours and days.

The real powers of the President and Speaker are these:

1. The exclusive right to appoint the members of all committees and to remove committee members.
2. The exclusive right to choose the chairmen of all committees.
3. The exclusive right for the initial reference of bills to committees.
4. The ability to influence, through the Chairman of the Committee on Rules and Calendar, the placing of bills on the Special Order Calendar.
5. In presiding, the President or Speaker may influence the consideration of legislation by accepting or refusing motions to limit debate and determining the mood of the body either to continue in session or adjourn.

In weighing the stages of lawmaking, it may be safely said the committee is more important than the chamber and the leadership meetings in the private offices of the President and Speaker are most important of all.

Majority Leadership

In the House, the majority office has grown, perhaps in some measure as a counter to the evolution of the minority party. During the 1985/1986 House the majority office consisted of the majority leader, the majority whip, and three deputy majority leaders, with a staff of nine. Each deputy whip has assigned members whom they advise as to the party line. This apparatus kept the Speaker informed as to the mood of the House on issues.

The legislative members of the majority office met before each legislative day to review the business before the House. Out of session, the group met once a month.

The majority office spawned a number of publications, designed to keep the majority members of the House informed. Sample speeches and newsletters were included. The Speaker also kept in touch with the issues through periodic meetings with committee chairmen.

In the Senate, because of its smaller size (40) than the House (120), the President dealt with majority Senators through leaders not demarcated by title. On issues, the President met with the individual Senators most concerned with these. There were periodic meetings with the committee chairmen.

Through those networks, the presiding officers maintained channels to the members and their activities.

Reference to Committee

The reference of bills to committees is regarded as one of the powers possessed by the Senate President or House Speaker. That is because committees, and their subcommittees, have life-or-death domination.

The presiding officers no longer have the same choice as once they did. For example, the 1947 House had 55 committees, with four judiciary committees. Today, the Speaker has 28 committees and only one judiciary committee. Thus, his choice for reference of any bill relating to the courts has been narrowed to one judiciary committee.

Also, today's Speaker is limited to referring a bill to a single committee unless, as many bills do, there are appropriation or finance and taxation implications. In such instances, the Speaker may additionally refer the bill to one or both of those committees.

The situation in the Senate differs. There is no limitation on the President. One President, vexed by a bill, referred the offensive bill to "every committee now existing or may be hereafter created." Another President said he favored staff reference of bills since the number of committees had been reduced to 16 with fairly non-conflicting jurisdictions. The Senate included three past Presidents and each of them warned him against his intention to allow references to be made by staff. Time proved the wisdom of the counsel, he said, for while 98 per cent of the bills could be referred almost automatically, the remaining two per cent demanded presidential judgment.

Successionship

Campaigns for President of the Senate and Speaker of the House commence well in advance of the term of service. In 1985, for example, the Speaker for the 1986–1988 term already had been selected although two selections were ahead: one for party designation followed by the formal election after the general election in 1986. At the same time there were Representatives who had served notice of their candidacy for terms beginning in 1988, 1990 and 1992.

There often is a tendency among editors and others to scoff at the early campaigning for the Speakership. It is true there is a disruptive period until the choice has been informally determined. But there is a factor of continuity. The Speakership of J. Hyatt Brown, for example, spawned four successive administrations with each of these Speakers having gained experience through serving in the Brown leadership.

The pursuit of the Presidency in the Senate is far more chancy. Discarded pledges and coalition with Republicans, either threatened or actual, may figure in the selection of a President just prior to the election at the Organization Session.

When the roll was called on the election of a President at the Senate Organizational Session of November 17, 1992, a 20–20 tie resulted.

Twenty Republicans had voted for Senator Ander Crenshaw of Jacksonville to be President and twenty Democrats had voted for Senator Pat Thomas of Quincy to be President.

On the third day thereafter and five formal roll calls, the Senate agreed to elect Senator Crenshaw to serve as President and Senator Thomas as President Pro Tempore until October 11, 1993. At that time, the roles were reversed, with Senator Thomas becoming President and Senator Crenshaw becoming President Pro Tempore, both to serve until November 8, 1994.

Each member of the Senate signed the resolution agreeing to the breaking of the deadlock, "backed by the trust placed in me by, and my sacred honor as a member of the Florida Senate."

Relations with Minority Party

Relations by the President and Speaker with the minority party may be described as a truce. The minority tends to be more cohesive than the majority. The minority usually avoids being obstructive and the majority tends, more or less, to give the minority consideration in the awarding of committee appointments. Politics enters into these. Some Speakers have denied the minority any committee or subcommittee chairmanships, believing to do so would be helpful to the minority in the next elections. Other Speakers have felt it prudent to share these.

The President and the Speaker exercise the right to determine the size of the staff of the minority office. One Speaker virtually wiped out the minority staff which had grown measurably through the goodwill of the Speaker's predecessor.

The President/Speaker Pro Tempore

The role of a pro tempore depends upon the President or Speaker. Until recently, the mid-1970s, the pro tempores occupied at best a ceremonial position. Then elected separately, the Speaker and his Speaker pro tempore might possess vastly different philosophies. Some pro tempores never were given the opportunity of presiding.

The President/Speaker pro tempore presides in the absence of the regular presiding officer only if some other member has not been chosen by the President/Speaker. Senate rules state the Senate may designate a presiding officer should the Chair be vacated permanently. In other words, the President pro tempore would not automatically succeed. Should the President resign, he may, prior to his resignation, designate "a member of the Majority Party to assume the duties of the Chair until a permanent successor is elected."

A change occurred in the House when Donald L. Tucker and John L. Ryals ran as a team. Ryals' position was enhanced by his concurrent service as Chairman of the Committee on House Administration, the committee which controls the money. This pattern was not followed in subsequent administrations.

The First Woman President

In November, 1990, the Senate elected the first Legislative woman presiding officer in the state's history, Gwen Margolis of North Miami, a Democrat.

The First Woman Pro Tempores

The 1985–1986 Legislature had the distinction of having the first women legislators to serve as President pro tempore and Speaker pro tempore. Senator Betty Castor of Tampa served in the Senate and Representative Elaine Gordon of Miami in the House.

Selection, Term and Perquisites of President and Speaker

The House Speaker and Senate President are elected by the majority members of each body after having been nominated by the members of their party in caucus.

The Constitution (Article III, Section 2) provides for the biennial selection of "permanent" presiding officers. Senate and House Rules define the term as two years, from one Organization Session (held on third Tuesday in even-numbered years) to the next Organization Session.

The Senate President and House Speaker have office staff in such number as they find necessary. Since the President and Speaker also are the representatives of their home districts, they receive the same per diem, subsistence and district office staff and expenses as other members.

Appeal from Rulings

The "Chair" is the symbol of parliamentary government. Hundreds of years of Parliaments, Congresses and Legislatures protect the Chair. This sanctity clothes the occupant of the Chair.

Rarely, some member has become so absorbed in seeking to pass or defeat a measure that the member will appeal from a ruling of the Chair. He will regret doing so almost immediately because the focus shifts from the parliamentary point at issue to a vote on the confidence of the body in the presiding officer. Speakers make many rulings in the course of an annual session, and some of these may be questionable because they are given during the heat of debate.

Yet the moment a member appeals from a ruling, rather than suggest the Chair reconsider, the presiding officer steps down from the rostrum and another takes his place. It is a moment of high drama, with the result being the upholding of the Chair. The ruling may be "revisited" overnight by the Chair and, if thought necessary, the ruling may be withdrawn and a new finding made.

No appeal has been successful in this century.

Minority Leadership

Minority leaders have been designated since 1951 when the Republicans first had three members of the House but formal recognition was given in 1969 when the Legislature passed a law which designated as "permanent offices of the Legislature" those, among others, of the Senate and House minority leaders. This designation enabled the budgeting of funds and the allocation of personnel for these offices.

Each party officer has an opposite number. In the House, for example, the Speaker, as the top majority leader, is matched by the Minority Leader and the Speaker pro tempore by the Minority leader pro tempore. The Republican leadership includes the minority pro tempore, the minority caucus chairman, and two minority whips. In 1992 Sandra Barringer Mortham of Largo became the first woman minority leader.

Party decisions are reached in *caucuses*. Since a caucus is a private gathering, it may or may not be open to the public. Generally, however, a caucus will be open, particularly if it is held in the House or Senate chamber.

Dual Roles of President, Speaker

The President and the Speaker serve dual roles. Each is the presiding officer of his house. Each also is the leader of a group, nowadays predominantly a political party but previously, in the one-party years, a personal faction.

The role of the presiding officers has been complicated by evolution of the two-party system. This means there is an identifiable opposition, most of whose members are inclined to vote as a group on legislation where a party position has been determined.

As a leader of a political party with a program to enact, the presiding officer occasionally finds himself in awkward positions when he must rule on questions raised in opposition to segments of that program.

There always have been factions in the Senate and House. For example, the Pork Choppers, the predominantly rural senators of the long struggle to delay legislative apportionment on a basis which more realistically recognized population in distributing legislative seats. In each contest for the Presidency or Speakership, there obviously are winners to reward and losers to ignore.

The Phantom Government

The "Phantom Government" is the title applied to the unauthorized expansion of laws enacted by the Legislature through rules adopted by State agencies.

To control the "phantom government," the Legislature in 1974 created the Joint Administrative Procedures Committee. This committee reviews the 5,000 rules promulgated each year to determine whether each proposed rule has been authorized by law.

The incident prompting the creation of the Joint Administrative Procedures Committee was the administration by the Department of Environmental Regulation of this exemption from an environmental law:

"A private, non-commercial boat dock, provided it is not more than 500 square feet in size."

That's all the law said. The Department, however, on its own, said this exemption applied only (1) if two boats of less than 25 feet or one boat of less than 50 feet were docked, (2) no boxes could be placed for storage of fishing gear, (3) no roof could cover the dock, (4) the dock could not be screened, and (5) the existence of a dock could not be used as grounds for widening the channel to the dock.

J. Hyatt Brown, D-Volusia County, served as Speaker of the 1979 and 1980 regular sessions. By his leadership, Brown came to be known as the dean of the four Speakers regarded as the Brown dynasty. Lynn Ivory

There being no basis in the law for these prohibitions, the Legislature at its next session said the rule-maker had become a law-maker. The Joint Administrative Procedures Committee was created in answer to public complaints about administration of the dock law and similar situations.

Presidents of the State Senate

NOTE: Presidents are shown only for the regular sessions at which they presided unless they were elected for a special session. Beginning in 1966, the Senate reorganized in November after the general election. Also, beginning in 1970, the Legislature resumed regular annual sessions after a hiatus of nearly a century.

Session	Senator	District	Residence or P.O. Address
1845	James A. Berthelot	7th	Tallahassee, Leon County
1846	D. H. Mays	11th	Madison, Madison County
1847	Daniel G. McLean	3rd	Euchee Anna, Walton County
1848	Erasmus Darwin Tracy	16th	(Trader's Hill, Ga.) Nassau County
1850	Robert J. Floyd	6th	Apalachicola, Franklin County
1854	Hamlin Valentine Snell	18th	Manatee, Hillsborough County
1856	Philip Dell	14th	Newnansville, Alachua County
1858	John Finlayson	10th	Monticello, Jefferson County
1860	Thomas Jefferson Eppes	5th	Apalachicola, Franklin County
1861	Thomas Jefferson Eppes	5th	Apalachicola, Franklin County
1862	Enoch J. Vann	11th	Madison, Madison County
1863	Enoch J. Vann	11th	Madison, Madison County
1864	Abraham K. Allison	7th	Quincy, Gadsden County
1889, Extra Sess.	Patrick Houston	8th	Tallahassee, Leon County
1889	Joseph B. Wall	11th	Tampa, Hillsborough County
1891	Jefferson B. Browne	24th	Key West, Monroe County
1893	William H. Reynolds	7th	Lakeland, Polk County
1895	Frederick T. Myers	8th	Tallahassee, Leon County
1897	Charles J. Perrenot	1st	Milton, Santa Rosa County
1899	Frank Adams	30th	Jasper, Hamilton County
1901	Thomas Palmer	11th	Tampa, Hillsborough County
1903	Frank Adams	30th	Jasper, Hamilton County
1905	Park M. Trammell	7th	Lakeland, Polk County
1907	W. Hunt Harris	24th	Key West, Monroe County
1909	Frederick M. Hudson	13th	Miami, Dade County
1911	Frederick P. Cone	14th	Lake City Columbia County
1913	Herbert J. Drane	7th	Lakeland, Polk County
1915	Charles E. Davis	10th	Madison, Madison County
1917	John B. Johnson	17th	Live Oak, Suwannee County
1919	James E. Calkins	16th	Fernandina, Nassau County
1921	William A. MacWIlliams	31st	St. Augustine, St. Johns County

From 1865 through 1887 the Lieutenant Governor served as President of the Senate.

Mr. Speaker: Ms. President / 165

Session	Senator	District	Residence or P.O. Address
1923	Theo. T. Turnbull	22nd	Monticello, Jefferson County
1925	John Stansel Taylor	11th	Largo, Pinellas County
1927	Samuel W. Anderson	6th	Greensboro, Gadsden County
1929	Jesse J. Parrish	37th	Titusville, Brevard County
1931	Patrick C. Whitaker	34th	Tampa, Hillsborough County
1933	Truman G. Futch	23rd	Leesburg, Lake County
1935	William C. Hodges	8th	Tallahassee, Leon County
1937	D. Stuart Gillis	3rd	DeFuniak Springs, Walton County
1939	J. Turner Butler	18th	Jacksonville, Duval County
1941	John R. Beacham	35th	West Palm Beach, Palm Beach County
1943	Philip D. Beall	2nd	Pensacola, Escambia County
1945	Walter W. Rose	19th	Orlando, Orange County
1947	Scott Dilworth Clarke	22nd	Monticello, Jefferson County
1949–1950	Newman C. Brackin	1st	Crestview, Okaloosa County
1951	Wallace E. Sturgis	20th	Ocala, Marion County
1953	Charley E. Johns	15th	Starke, Bradford County
1955	W. Turner Davis	10th	Madison, Madison County
1957	William A. Shands	32nd	Gainesville, Alachua County
1959	Dewey M. Johnson	6th	Quincy, Gadsden County
1961	W. Randolph Hodges	21st	Cedar Key, Levy County
1962–1963	F. Wilson Carraway	8th	Tallahassee, Leon County
1965	James E. Connor	9th	Brooksville, Hernando County
1967	Verle A. Pope	12th	St. Augustine, St. Johns County
Annual Sessions Commence			
1969–1970	John E. Mathews, Jr.	8th	Jacksonville, Duval County
1971–1972	Jerry Thomas	35th	Riviera Beach, Palm Beach County
1973–1974	Mallory E. Horne	4th	Tallahassee, Leon County
1974	Louis A. de la Parte, Jr.	22nd	Tampa, Hillsborough County
[President pro tempore serving as Acting President July 1–November 6, 1974]			
1975–1976	Dempsey J. Barron	3rd	Panama City, Bay County
1977–1978	Lew Brantley	8th	Jacksonville, Duval County
1979–1980	Philip D. Lewis	27th	West Palm Beach, Palm Beach County
1981–1982	Wyon D. Childers	1st	Pensacola, Escambia County
1983–1984	N. Curtis Peterson, Jr.	12th	Lakeland, Polk County
1985–1986	Harry A. Johnston, II	26th	Parts of Broward, Palm Beach
1987–1988	John W. Vogt	17th	Cocoa Beach, Brevard County
1989–1990	Robert B. Crawford	13th	Winter Haven, Polk County
1991–1992	Gwen Margolis	37th	North Miami, Dade County
1992–1993	Ander Crenshaw	38th	Jacksonville, Duval County
1993–1994	Pat Thomas	39th	Quincy, Gadsden County
1995–1996	James A. Scott	31st	Ft. Lauderdale, Broward County

Speakers of the State House of Representatives

NOTE: Speakers are shown only for the regular sessions at which they presided unless they were elected for a special session. Beginning in 1966, the House of Representatives reorganized in November after the general election. Also, beginning in 1970, the Legislature resumed annual sessions after a hiatus of nearly a century.

Session	Representative	County	Residence or Post Office
1845	Hugh Archer	Leon	Tallahassee
1845, Adj. Sess.	Isaac Ferguson, Jr.	Gadsden	Quincy
1846	Robert Brown	Columbia	
1847	Joseph B. Lancaster	Duval	Jacksonville

[Lancaster vacated Speakership December 23, 1847 to become Circuit Judge]

Session	Representative	County	Residence or Post Office
1847	John Chain	Santa Rosa	Milton
1848	Benjamin A. Putnam	St. Johns	St. Augustine
1850	Hugh Archer	Leon	Tallahassee
1852	Abraham K. Allison	Gadsden	Quincy
1854	W. F. Russell	St. Lucie	Fort Pierce
1855, Adj. Sess.	Philip Dell	Alachua	Newnansville
1856	Hamlin Valentine Snell	Manatee	Manatee
1858	John B. Galbraith	Leon	Tallahassee
1861	S. B. Love	Gadsden	Quincy
1862	Thomas Jefferson Eppes	Franklin	Apalachicola
1864	Philip Dell	Alachua	Newnansville
1865	Joseph John Williams	Leon	Tallahassee
1868	William W. Moore	Columbia	Welburn
1869	Marcellus L. Stearns	Gadsden	Quincy
1870	Marcellus L. Stearns	Gadsden	Quincy
1871	Marcellus L. Stearns	Gadsden	Quincy
1872	Marcellus L. Stearns	Gadsden	Quincy
1873	Simon B. Conover	Leon	Tallahassee
1874	Malachi Martin	Gadsden	Chattahoochee
1875	Thomas Hannah	Washington	Vernon
1877	G. G. McWhorter	Santa Rosa	Milton
1879	Charles Dougherty	Volusia	Port Orange
1881	J. J. Harris	Orange	Tuskawilla
1883	Charles Dougherty	Volusia	Port Orange
1885	Robert W. Davis	Clay	Green Cove Springs
1887	Samuel Pasco	Jefferson	Monticello

[Pasco vacated Speakership May 23, 1887, upon being elected U.S. Senator]

Session	Representative	County	Residence or Post Office
1887	George H. Browne	Orange	Oviedo
1889, Extra Sess.	John L. Gaskins	Bradford	Starke
1889	John L. Gaskins	Bradford	Starke
1891	John L. Gaskins	Bradford	Starke
1893	John B. Johnston	Pasco	Dade City
1895	William Sherman Jennings	Hernando	Brooksville
1897	Dannitte Hill Mays	Jefferson	Monticello
1899	Robert McNamee	Lake	Leesburg
1901	John W. Watson	Osceola	Kissimmee
1903	Cromwell Gibbons	Duval	Jacksonville
1905	Albert W. Gilchrist	DeSoto	Punta Gorda
1907	E. S. Matthews	Bradford	Starke
1909	Ion L. Farris	Duval	Jacksonville

Session	Representative	County	Residence or Post Office
1911	T. A. Jennings	Escambia	Pensacola
1913	Ion L. Farris	Duval	Jacksonville
1915	Cary A. Hardee	Suwannee	Live Oak
1917	Cary A. Hardee	Suwannee	Live Oak
1918, Extra Sess.	George H. Wilder	Hillsborough	Plant City
1921	Frank E. Jennings	Duval	Jacksonville
1923	L. D. Edge	Lake	Groveland
1925	A. Y. Milam	Duval	Jacksonville
1927	Fred H. Davis	Leon	Tallahassee
1929	Samuel W. Getzen	Sumter	Bushnell
1931	E. Clay Lewis, Jr.	Gulf	Port St. Joe
1933	Peter Tomasello, Jr.	Okeechobee	Okeechobee
1935	W. B. Bishop	Jefferson	Nash
1937	W. McL. Christie	Duval	Jacksonville
1939	G. Pierce Wood	Liberty	Vilas
1941	Dan McCarty	St.Lucie	Ft.Pierce
1943	Richard H. Simpson	Jefferson	Monticello
1945	Evans Crary	Martin	Stuart
1947	Thomas D. Beasley	Walton	DeFuniak Springs
1949	Perry E. Murray	Polk	Frostproof
1951	B. Elliott	Palm Beach	Pahokee
1953	C. Farris Bryant	Marion	Ocala
1955	Thomas E. (Ted) David	Broward	Hollywood
1957	Doyle E. Conner	Bradford	Starke
1959	Thomas D. Beasley	Walton	DeFuniak Springs
1961	William Chappell, Jr.	Marion	Ocala
1962–1963	Mallory E. Horne	Leon	Tallahassee
1965	E. C. Rowell	Sumter	Wildwood
1967	Ralph D. Turlington	Alachua	Gainesville

Annual
Sessions
Commenced

1969–1970	Frederick H. Schultz	Duval	Jacksonville
1971–1972	Richard A. Pettigrew	Dade	Miami
1973–1974	T. Terrell Sessums	Hillsborough	Tampa
1975–1977	Donald L. Tucker	Leon	Tallahassee

NOTE: John L. Ryals of Brandon, Hillsborough County, was elected Speaker by the 1977 House in anticipation of the resignation of Speaker Tucker, who had been appointed by President Jimmy Carter as a member of the Civil Aeronautics Board (CAB). The resignation did not materialize as Tucker withdrew his name from consideration by the U.S. Senate.

1978	Donald L. Tucker	Leon	Tallahassee
1979–1980	J. Hyatt Brown	Volusia	Daytona Beach
1981–1982	Ralph H. Haben, Jr.	Manatee	Palmetto
1983–1984	H. Lee Moffitt	Hillsborough	Tampa
1985–1986	James Harold Thompson	Gadsden	Quincy
1987–1988	Jon L. Mills	Alachua	Gainesville
1989–1990	Tom Gustafson	Broward	Fort Lauderdale
1991–1992	T. K. Wetherell	Volusia	Daytona Beach
1993–1994	Bolley L. Johnson	Santa Rosa	Milton
1995–1996	Peter Rudy Wallace	Pinellas	St. Petersburg

Florida Senate
1995–1996

James A. (Jim) Scott
President
Republican, District 11
Ft. Lauderdale

Scott

Attorney. **Born** January 14, 1942, Pikeville, Kentucky. **Moved to Florida** in 1965. **Education** University of Kentucky, B.A., 1963, J.D. 1965; Sigma Nu; Phi Alpha Delta Law Fraternity. **Married** Janice Ann Suskey of Miami, **Children**: Frank and Stacy Ann. **Affiliations** Florida, Kentucky and American Bar Associations; Broward County and South Palm Beach County Bar Associations; Fort Lauderdale Chamber of Commerce; Boca Raton Chamber of Commerce; University of Kentucky Law Alumni Association. **Legislative Service** Elected to the Senate 1976, reelected subsequently; Minority Floor Leader, 1978–80; Minority Leader 1980–82; Appropriations Committee Chairman, 1986–88 and 1992–93; Chairman of Rules and Calendar, 1989–90; Vice Chairman of Rules and Calendar 1993–94. Senate President-Designate, 1989. **Other Public Service** Associate Municipal Judge in Deerfield Beach, 1972; Broward Legislative Delegation attorney, 1972–74; Legal Aid Service of Broward County Board of Directors and Treasurer, 1974–76; **Highlights** Most Effective First Term Member, 1978; Most Effective in Debate, runner up, 1980–82 (Allen Morris Awards); Community Service Council's Distinguished Service Award, 1984; Anti-Defamation League's Torch of Liberty Award, 1985; ARC Legislator of the Year, 1987; Most Effective Member of the Senate, 1990 (Allen Morris Awards); National Republican Legislator of the Year Award, 1990, Florida Audubon Society Legislative Excellence Award, 1990, 1992 and 1993; Nature Conservancy Preservation 2000 Future Generations Award, 1993. **Military Service** U.S. Coast Guard, 1965–1968. **Religious Affiliation** Presbyterian. **Recreation** Golf and horseback riding.

The President Appoints the Committees

The President presides over the Senate and is in charge of all Senate operations. He appoints all committees and committee chairs and references all bills to committees of his choice.

—*The Senate Handbook*

Senators regularly serve four-year terms. In the 1989–1990 Senate, those elected from odd-numbered districts had four years to serve while those from even-numbered districts had two years remaining of their term. Senators from odd-numbered districts are seated on the west side of the Chamber: those from even-numbered districts, on the east side. Exceptions are made for the Rules Chairman and the President Pro Tempore. Because of legislative reapportionment, some of the Senators actually will serve only two years of the four-year term.

Joe Brown
Secretary of the Senate

Born July 15, 1932, Columbus, Georgia **Moved to Florida** 1932 **Education** University of Florida, B.S.J., 1958; Student publications and student government, Sigma Delta Chi, Alpha Gamma Rho. Florida State University, 1972–1973; graduate studies **Married** Rebecca Etheridge of Waycross, Georgia **Children** Joe, Charles, Julie, Andi, and Ivy **Legislative Service** Senate Governmental Operations Committee Staff Director 1971–1972. Senate Director of Management and Staff 1973–1974. Senate Secretary April 2, 1974–present.

Brown

Counties in District and Senator

Democrats in Roman (18)   *Republicans in Italic (22)*

1 Holmes, Washington and *parts of* Bay, Escambia, Okaloosa, Santa Rosa, Walton
   Wyon D. "W. D." Childers, Pensacola
2 Parts of Alachua, Clay, Duval, Putnam, St. Johns
   Betty S. Holzendorf, Jacksonville
3 Calhoun, Franklin, Gadsden, Gulf, Jackson, Liberty, Wakulla and *parts of* Bay, Jefferson, Leon, Madison
   Pat Thomas, Quincy
4 Baker, Dixie, Gilchrist, Hamilton, Lafayette, Nassau, Taylor and *parts of* Alachua, Bradford, Citrus, Columbia, Jefferson, Leon, Levy, Madison, Marion, Suwannee, Union
   Charles Williams, Tallahassee
5 Parts of Alachua, Bradford, Clay, Columbia, Levy, Marion, Putnam, Suwannee, Union
   George Grier Kirkpatrick, Jr., Gainesville
6 Parts of Clay, Duval, St. Johns
   Jim Horne, Jacksonville
7 Parts of Bay, Escambia, Oklaloosa, Santa Rosa, Walton
   Robert T. Harden, Fort Walton Beach
8 Flagler and *parts of* Duval, Marion, St.Johns, Volusia
   William G. "Bill" Bankhead, Ponte Vedra Beach
9 Parts of Orange, Seminole
   Toni Jennings, Orlando
10 Hernando and *parts of* Pasco, Polk, Sumter
   Ginny Brown-Waite, Spring Hill
11 Lake and *part of* Citrus, Marion, Seminole, Sumter
   Karen Johnson, Inverness

12 *Parts of* **Orange, Osceola, Seminole, Volusia**
   John Ostalkiewicz, Orlando
13 *Parts of* **Hillsborough, Pasco**
   John A. Grant, Jr., Tampa
14 *Parts of* **Orange, Seminole**
   John H. "Buddy" Dyer, Jr., Orlando
15 *Parts of* **Brevard, Indian River, St.Lucie**
   Patsy Ann Kurth, Malabar
16 *Parts of* **Volusia**
   Wallace Lockwood "Locke" Burt, Ormond Beach
17 *Parts of* **Highlands, Hillsborough, Okeechobee, Polk**
   Rick Dantzler, Winter Haven
18 *Parts of* **Brevard, Osceola**
   Charles H. "Charlie" Bronson, Satellite Beach
19 *Parts of* **Pasco, Pinellas**
   Jack Latvala, Palm Harbor
20 *Parts of* **Hillsborough, Pinellas**
   Charlie Crist, St. Petersburg
21 *Parts of* **Hillsborough, Manatee, Pinellas, Polk**
   James T. "Jim" Hargrett, Jr., Tampa
22 *Part of* **Pinellas**
   Donald C. "Don" Sullivan, St. Petersburg
23 *Part of* **Hillsborough**
   Malcolm E. Beard, Seffner
24 *Parts of* **Charlotte, Lee, Sarasota**
   Katherine Harris, Sarasota
25 *Parts of* **Collier, Lee**
   Fred R. Dudley, Cape Coral
26 **DeSoto, Hardee** and *parts of* **Highlands, Hillsborough, Manatee, Sarasota**
   John M. McKay, Bradenton
27 *Parts of* **Indian River, Martin, Palm Beach, St. Lucie**
   William G. "Doc" Myers, Stuart

28 Parts of **Broward, Palm Beach**
   Robert Wexler, Boca Raton
29 **Hendry** and parts of **Broward, Collier, Palm Beach**
   Kenneth C. "Ken" Jenne II, Fort Lauderdale
30 Parts of **Broward, Palm Beach**
   Matthew Meadows, Fort Lauderdale
31 Parts of **Broward, Palm Beach**
   James A. "Jim" Scott, Fort Lauderdale
32 Parts of **Broward, Dade**
   Howard C. Forman, Pembroke Pines
33 Part of **Broward**
   Peter M. Weinstein, Coral Springs
34 Parts of **Dade**
   Alberto "Al" Gutman, Miami
35 **Glades** and parts of **Charlotte, Lee, Martin, Okeechobee, Palm Beach**
   Tom Rossin, West Palm Beach
36 Part of **Dade**
   William H. "Bill" Turner, Hialeah
37 Part of **Dade**
   Mario Diaz-Balart, Miami
38 Part of **Dade**
   Ronald A. "Ron" Silver, North Miami Beach
39 Part of **Dade**
   Roberto Casas, Hialeah
40 **Monroe** and part of **Dade**
   Daryl L. Jones, Miami

Florida House of Representatives
1995–1996

Peter Rudy Wallace
Democrat, District 52
St. Petersburg

Attorney **Born** April 13, 1954, St. Petersburg. **Education** Harvard College, B.A. 1976; Harvard Law School, J.D., 1979. **Married** Helen Pruitt of St. Petersburg. **Children** Daniel McSwain and Hannah Rudy. **Affiliations** St. Petersburg Kiwanis Club; Suncoast Tiger Bay Club; Bayfront Life Services Board of Trustees. **Legislative Service** Elected to the House in 1982, reelected subsequently. **Other Public Service** Law Clerk to Judge Paul Roney, U.S. 5th Circuit Court of Appeals 1979–1980. **Religious Affiliation** Episcopal **Recreation** basketball, tennis and fishing. **Historical** Henry A. Wallace, great-uncle, Vice President of the United States 1941–1945. Martha Rudy Wallace, mother, Pinellas County School Board 1972–1980. **Highlights** Presidential Scholar 1972. Harvard National Scholar 1972–1979. Leadership St. Petersburg 1981–1982. Outstanding Young Men of America 1982–1985. FTP-NEA Friend of Education 1987. Sierra Club Legislative Award 1987. Preservation 2000 Leadership Award 1992. 1000 Friends of Florida Bill Sadowski Award 1992. Florida Young Democrats Democrat of the Year 1991.

John B. Phelps
Clerk of the House

Born November 17, 1943, Miami **Education** Florida Presbyterian College (now Eckerd College), B.A., 1965; Florida State University, M.S.W., Administration, 1975 **Married** Dr. Pamela C. of Jacksonville **Children** Joi, Neal, and Rene **Legislative Service** Clerk of the House of Representatives November, 1986–present. House of Representatives Deputy Clerk 1982–1986. Rules & Calendar Committee Staff Director 1980–1982. Executive Assistant to the

Speaker 1978–1980. Legislative Analyst for Health Policy 1975-1978. Revision Commission, *Mason's Manual of Legislative Procedure.*

Counties in District and Representative

Democrats in Roman (63)   *Republicans in Italic (57)*

1. *Parts of* **Escambia, Okaloosa, Santa Rosa**
Jerrold "Jerry" Burroughs, Cantonment
2. *Part of* **Escambia**
Jerry L. Maygarden, Pensacola
3. *Part of* **Escambia**
Buzz Ritchie, Pensacola
4. *Parts of* **Escambia, Okaloosa, Santa Rosa**
Jerry Melvin, Fort Walton Beach
5. **Holmes, Washington** and *parts of* **Okaloosa, Walton**
Durell Peaden, Jr., Crestview
6. *Part of* **Bay**
Scott W. Clemons, Panama City
7. **Calhoun, Gulf, Jackson, Liberty** and *parts of* **Bay, Gadsden, Leon, Walton**
Robert DeWitt "Rob" Trammell, Marianna
8. *Parts of* **Gadsden, Leon**
Alfred J. "Al" Lawson, Jr., Tallahassee
9. *Part of* **Leon**
Marjorie R. Turnbull, Tallahassee
10. **Franklin, Jefferson, Levy, Taylor, Wakulla** and *parts of* **Alachua, Dixie, Gilchrist, Leon, Marion**
F. Allen Boyd, Jr., Monticello
11. **Columbia, Hamilton, Lafayette, Madison, Suwannee** and *parts of* **Dixie, Gilchrist**
Joseph R. "Randy" Mackey, Jr., Lake City
12. **Baker, Bradford, Nassau, Union** and *part of* **Duval**
George A. Crady, Yulee
13. *Parts of* **Clay, Duval**
Stephen R. Wise, Jacksonville
14. *Part of* **Duval**
Anthony C. "Tony" Hill, Sr., Jacksonville
15. *Part of* **Duval**
Willye F. Clayton Dennis, Jacksonville
16. *Part of* **Duval**
James B. "Jim" Fuller, Jacksonville
17. *Part of* **Duval**
James E. "Jim" King, Jr., Jacksonville
18. *Parts of* **Duval, St. Johns**
Joseph "Joe" Arnall, Jacksonville Beach
19. *Parts of* **Clay, Duval, St. Johns**
John Thrasher, Orange Park
20. *Parts of* **Clay, Flagler, St. Johns, Volusia**
Tracy W. Upchurch, St. Augustine
21. **Putnam** and *parts of* **Clay, Marion**
Kelley R. Smith, Palatka
22. *Parts of* **Alachua, Marion**
Robert K. "Bob" Casey, Gainesville
23. *Parts of* **Alachua, Marion**
Cynthia Moore Chestnut, Gainesville
24. *Part of* **Marion**
George Albright, Ocala
25. *Parts of* **Lake, Marion, Seminole, Volusia**
Stan Bainter, Eustis
26. *Parts of* **Flagler, Lake, Volusia**
Earl Ziebarth, DeLand
27. *Part of* **Volusia**
Evelyn Lynn, Ormond Beach
28. *Part of* **Volusia**
Jack Ascherl, New Smyrna Beach
29. *Part of* **Brevard**
Randy Ball, Mims
30. *Part of* **Brevard**
Howard E. Futch, Melbourne Beach
31. *Part of* **Brevard**
Harry C. Goode, Jr., Melbourne
32. *Parts of* **Brevard, Indian River, Orange**
Bill Posey, Rockledge
33. *Parts of* **Orange, Seminole, Volusia**
Marvin Couch, Oviedo
34. *Parts of* **Orange, Seminole**
Robert J. "Bob" Starks, Casselberry
35. *Parts of* **Orange, Seminole**
Bob Brooks, Winter Park
36. *Part of* **Orange**
Allen Trovillion, Winter Park
37. *Parts of* **Orange, Seminole**
D. Lee Constantine, Altamonte Springs
38. *Parts of* **Lake, Orange**
Robert B. "Bob" Sindler, Apoka
39. *Part of* **Orange**
Alzo J. Reddick, Orlando
40. *Part of* **Orange**
William E. "Bill" Sublette, Orlando
41. *Parts of* **Lake, Orange, Osceola**
Daniel Webster, Orlando
42. Parts of **Lake, Marion, Sumter**
Everett A. Kelly, Tavares
43. **Citrus** and *parts of* **Hernando, Marion**
Helen L. Spivey, Crystal River
44. *Parts of* **Hernando, Lake, Pasco, Polk, Sumter**
Jeff "Stabe" Stabins, Spring Hill
45. *Parts of* **Hernando, Pasco**
Mike Fasano, New Port Richey
46. *Part of* **Pasco**
Debra A. Prewitt, New Port Richey

47 *Parts of* **Hillsborough, Pinellas**
   Rob Wallace, Tampa
48 *Parts of* **Hillsborough, Pinellas**
   R. Z. Safley, Clearwater
49 *Part of* **Pinellas**
   Larry Crow, Palm Harbor
50 *Part of* **Pinellas**
   John Morroni, Clearwater
51 *Part of* **Pinellas**
   Mary Brennan, Pinellas Park
52 *Part of* **Pinellas**
   Peter Rudy Wallace, St. Petersburg
53 *Part of* **Pinellas**
   Lars A. Hafner, St. Petersburg
54 *Part of* **Pinellas**
   Dennis L. Jones, Treasure Island
55 *Parts of* **Manatee, Pinellas**
   Rudolph Bradley, St. Petersburg
56 *Part of* **Hillsborough**
   Jim Davis, Tampa
57 *Part of* **Hillsborough**
   Faye B. Culp, Tampa
58 *Part of* **Hillsborough**
   Elvin L. Martinez, Tampa
59 *Part of* **Hillsborough**
   Lesley "Les" Miller, Jr., Tampa
60 *Part of* **Hillsborough**
   Victor D. Crist, Temple Terrace
61 *Parts of* **Hillsborough, Pasco**
   Carl D. Littlefield, Dade City
62 *Part of* **Hillsborough**
   Buddy Johnson, Plant City
63 *Part of* **Polk**
   Dean P. Saunders, Lakeland
64 *Part of* **Polk**
   Joseph G. "Joe" Tedder, Lakeland
65 *Part of* **Polk**
   Lori Edwards, Auburndale
66 *Parts of* **Hillsborough, Polk**
   John Laurent, Bartow
67 *Parts of* **Hillsborough, Manatee, Sarasota**
   Mark R. Ogles, Bradenton
68 *Part of* **Manatee**
   Mark G. Flanagan, Bradenton
69 *Part of* **Sarasota**
   Shirley Brown, Sarasota
70 *Part of* **Sarasota**
   Lisa Carlton, Osprey
71 *Parts of* **Charlotte, Sarasota**
   David I. "Dave" Bitner, Port Charlotte
72 **DeSoto, Hardee** and *parts of* **Charlotte, Lee**
   Vernon Peeples, Punta Gorda
73 *Part of* **Lee**
   J. Keith Arnold, Fort Myers
74 *Parts of* **Charlotte, Lee, Sarasota**
   Greg Gay, Cape Coral
75 *Parts of* **Collier, Lee**
   Ralph L. Livingston, Fort Myers
76 *Part of* **Collier**
   Burt L. Saunders, Naples
77 **Glades, Hendry** and *parts of* **Collier, Highlands**
   Bert J. Harris, Jr., Lake Placid
78 *Parts of* **Highlands, Martin, Okeechobee, Palm Beach, St. Lucie**
   O. R. "Rick" Minton, Jr., Fort Pierce
79 *Parts of* **Okeechobee, Osceola**
   Irlo "Bud" Bronson, Kissimmee
80 *Parts of* **Indian River, St. Lucie**
   Charles W. "Charlie" Sembler II, Sebastian
81 *Parts of* **Martin, St. Lucie**
   Kenneth P. "Ken" Pruitt, Port St. Lucie
82 *Parts of* **Martin, Palm Beach**
   Tom Warner, Stuart
83 *Part of* **Palm Beach**
   Sharon J. Merchant, Palm Beach Gardens
84 *Part of* **Palm Beach**
   Addie L. Greene, Mangonia Park
85 *Part of* **Palm Beach**
   Lois Frankel, West Palm Beach
86 *Part of* **Palm Beach**
   Edward J. "Ed" Healey, West Palm Beach
87 *Part of* **Palm Beach**
   William F. Andrews, Delray Beach
88 *Part of* **Palm Beach**
   Suzanne Jacobs, Delray Beach
89 *Part of* **Palm Beach**
   Ron Klein, Boca Raton
90 *Part of* **Broward**
   John C. Rayson, Pompano Beach
91 *Parts of* **Broward, Palm Beach**
   Debby P. Sanderson, Fort Lauderdale
92 *Part of* **Broward**
   Tracy Stafford, Wilton Manors
93 *Part of* **Broward**
   Muriel "Mandy" Dawson, Fort Lauderdale
94 *Part of* **Broward**
   Josephus Eggelletion, Jr., Lauderdale Lakes
95 *Part of* **Broward**
   Jack N. Tobin, Margate
96 *Part of* **Broward**
   Ben Graber, Coral Springs
97 *Part of* **Broward**
   Debbie Wasserman Schultz, Davie
98 *Part of* **Broward**
   Steven B. "Steve" Feren, Sunrise
99 *Part of* **Broward**
   Anne Mackenzie, Fort Lauderdale
100 *Part of* **Broward**
   Frederick "Fred" Lippman, Hollywood
101 *Parts of* **Broward, Dade**
   Steven A. Geller, Hallandale

102 *Parts of* **Collier, Dade**
    Luis E. Rojas, Hialeah
103 *Part of* **Dade**
    Willie Logan, Jr., Opa-locka
104 *Part of* **Dade**
    Kendrick B. Meek, Miami
105 *Part of* **Dade**
    Sally A. Heyman, North Miami Beach
106 *Part of* **Dade**
    Elaine Bloom, Miami Beach
107 *Part of* **Dade**
    Bruno A. Barreiro, Jr., Miami Beach
108 *Part of* **Dade**
    Beryl D. Roberts-Burke, Miami
109 *Part of* **Dade**
    James Bush III, Miami
110 *Part of* **Dade**
    Rodolfo "Rudy" Garcia, Jr., Hialeah
111 *Part of* **Dade**
    Carlos L. Valdes, Miami
112 *Part of* **Dade**
    J. Alex Villalobos, Miami
113 *Part of* **Dade**
    Luis C. Morse, Miami
114 *Part of* **Dade**
    Jorge Rodriguez-Chomat, Miami
115 *Part of* **Dade**
    Alex Diaz de la Portilla, Westchester
116 *Part of* **Dade**
    Annie Betancourt, Miami
117 *Part of* **Dade**
    Carlos Lacasa, Miami
118 *Part of* **Dade**
    Larcenia J. Bullard, Miami
119 *Part of* **Dade**
    John F. Cosgrove, Miami
120 **Monroe** and *part of* **Dade**
    Deborah James "Debbie" Horan, Key West

Legislative Longevity

The typical Member of the Florida House of Representatives serves two terms or four years. The typical Member of the Florida Senate also serves two terms or, since Senate terms are four years, eight years.

Selected Legislative Publications

Persons with a general interest in the Legislature may find one or more of these publications helpful. The publications were selected, by permission, from the *Guide to Legislative Publications* compiled by Florida Information Associates, 2007 West Indianhead Drive, Tallahassee 32301.

Most of these publications are available at no charge from the office listed in parentheses after the title. The Clerk of the House of Representatives may be addressed at 427 Capitol, Tallahassee 32399-1300 or (904) 488-1157. The Secretary of the Senate may be addressed at 404 Capitol, Tallahassee 32399-1100 or (904) 487-5270.

Clerk's Manual. Biennial. (Clerk of the House of Representatives, House Documents, Rm. 513, The Capitol, Tallahassee, FL 32399-1300. (904) 488-7475). ($6)

Biographies and photos of current Representatives, Senators, and legislative officers. Most complete legislative biographical source available. Also includes district and seniority lists, Capitol Press Corps, committees. Published since 1966. Pocket size.

The Florida Senate. Biennial. (Secretary of the Senate).

General public oriented guidebook to the Senate. Includes same photos and biographical data that are in the *Clerk's Manual*, seating chart, diagram on how a bill becomes a law, map of Senate districts, and a brief description of the legislative process. Not indexed.

Welcome To Your House of Representatives. Biennial. (Clerk of the House).
General public oriented guidebook to the House of Representatives. Includes brief biographical data and photos of House members, description of the legislative process, diagram showing how a bill becomes a law, seating chart, statistics on House members, and historical information on the legislature. Indexed.

Journals of the Senate and House. Daily & Annual. (Secretary, Clerk).
Published each day Senate or House meet in formal session. Cumulated and edited into a final bound volume at end of session. Bound volume is considered to be the only official record. The *Journal* is not a verbatim transcript of proceedings, but only records what official actions (i.e., bill titles, amendments, committee referrals, and votes) that have taken place. Indexed by bill number, sponsor, and subject. No charge for daily *Journal*.

Lobbying in Florida, Registrations Under 11.045 Through 11.062 F. S. Annual (periodic updates during year). (Clerk of the House). (Limited Distribution)
Alphabetical listing of all registered lobbyists. Indexed by organization or interest and by subject. List, with no index also published in annual volume of the Senate *Journal*.

Guide To Florida Government, Executive, Legislative, Judicial, Congressional (includes Capitol Press). Annual. (Clerk of the House). (Limited Distribution)
Organizational charts with names and addresses of executive branch officials. Also lists legislators, judges, members of congressional delegation, and members of Capitol Press Corps. Indexed by personal and agency name.

Senate and House Bills. (Secretary of the Senate, Bill Room, Rm. 303, The Capitol, Tallahassee, FL 32399-1100. (904) 487-5285. Clerk of the House, House Documents, Rm. 513, The Capitol, Tallahassee, FL 32399-1300. (904) 488-7475).
Published in "slip-law" format (reduced size) for current sessions. FS revisers' bills and general appropriations bills not published. Senate does not publish local bills and nonconstitutional amendment resolutions. Nonpublished bills, engrossed bills, and enrolled acts are available upon special request. No charge or limits for House bills. Senate charges $25 per session/per set walk-in pickup and $100 mailed. Single copies of Senate bills are free (limit 2 copies of 5 bills, additional copies $1 each).

Final Legislative Bill Information, Annual. (Legislative Information Division, Jt. Legislative Management Committee, Rm. 826, The Capitol, Tallahassee, FL 32399-1400. (904) 488-4371. In Florida, toll free, (800) 342-1827).
Published since 1965. Also known as the "History of Legislation" or the "Citator." This is the most comprehensive legislative research tool available. Contains chronological actions of all bills and resolutions filed in regular and special sessions, sponsor reports and statistics. Indexed by subject, sponsor, and Constitution/statute citation. This is the final product of the Legislative automated bill history system, which includes an on-line ser-

vice during the session, a daily bill history publication and other specialized reports.

The People of Lawmaking in Florida, 1822– Biennial (cumulative). (Clerk of the House).
Alphabetical listing of Florida legislators from territorial period to present. Each listing gives in which house served, session(s) served, district or county, and party affiliation. No charge.

The Language of Lawmaking in Florida, by Allen Morris. (Clerk-Emeritus of the House).
Defines terms and jargon unique to the Florida Legislature. Historical origin, where known, is also given. Revised irregularly. (Limited distribution)

Practical Protocol for Floridians, compiled by Allen Morris. (Clerk-Emeritus of the House).
Covers all aspects of Florida governmental protocol, such as forms of address, greeting line order, seating at head tables, official mourning, investiture of justices, inaugural ceremonies, etc. Indexed. (Limited distribution)

The State's Revenue Estimates

Florida's official revenue estimates are made jointly by economic analysts from the Legislature and Governor's Office. The analysts that participate in this exercise are referred to as the Revenue Estimating Conference. Although the Revenue Estimating Conference began during the 1970s by informal agreement between the Legislature and the Governor, the arrangement has become increasingly formal and was given statutory authority in 1985. Authority for the Conference is found in sections 216.133-137, *Fla. Stat.*

The Revenue Estimating Conference has four principals: one representative from each of the staffs of the Senate and House Finance and Taxation Committees, a representative from the Economic and Demographic Research Division of the Joint Legislative Management Committee, and a representative of the Revenue and Economic Analysis Unit of the Governor's Office of Planning and Budgeting. Decisions are made by consensus; all four principals must agree before a decision is reached. Hence there are no votes in the estimating process, only vetoes.

The consensus revenue estimates provide the budget constraint for both the Governor's budget recommendations and the Legislature's appropriations.

The Revenue Estimating Conference is responsible for forecasting revenues to the General Fund as well as lottery revenues, gross receipts tax revenues (which fund the Public Education Capital Outlay program), and transportation tax revenues. The revenues of the remaining trust funds are not forecast by the Conference.

Although the Revenue Estimating Conference is the best known, there are actually several other consensus estimating conferences authorized by statute that provide forecasts that are used in Florida's budgetary process.

176 / The Legislature

The Social Services conference forecasts Medicaid and AFDC (Aid to Families with Dependent Children) enrollments and expenditures as well as the number and costs of AIDS cases in Florida. The Criminal Justice Estimating Conference forecasts prison, probation, and parole populations. The Education Estimating Conference forecasts school enrollments. Each of these conferences has slightly different membership which is defined in Chapter 216 *Fla. Stat.*

The forecasts of the various consensus estimating conferences on which the Legislature bases its annual appropriations are published each year after the close of the Session by the Economic and Demographic Research Division of the Joint Legislative Management Committee. These reports are available to the public, upon request, at no charge.

—Ed Montanaro, Director
Division of Economic and Demographic Research.
Also, appreciation is due Tom Clemons.

When roads permitted, Sidney J. Catts used an automobile in his campaign for Governor in 1916. Ultimately the victor as the candidate of the Prohibition Party, Catts publicized his novel approach by this banner across his car in his inaugural parade proudly placarding the claim that "this is the Ford that got me there." Florida State Archives

Florida's Budget Process

Article VII, Section 1, of the State Constitution vests in the Legislature the responsibility for determining the fiscal policies of state government. "No money shall be drawn from the treasury except in pursuance of appropriation made by law." Because of this provision, the legislative Appropriations Act is the embodiment of Florida's budget.

The budget process starts with the steps necessary to develop and prepare the budget. The Legislature passes the Appropriations Act during its annual legislative session. Finally, the executive branch carries out the spending plans as set forth in the budget. The Governor and the Cabinet may adjust the budget throughout the fiscal year which runs from July through June.

The state's budget cycle begins in early June each year when the Governor and the Legislature send agencies instructions for developing their budget requests. Agencies must submit their budget requests by September 1st.

The next stage in the cycle focuses mainly on the Governor's role in the budget process. During October, November and December the governor's office prepares a recommended balanced budget. The Governor must submit his recommendation to the Legislature 45 days before the regular session.

The Legislature begins developing a new spending plan as soon as state agencies submit their budget requests. Through its fiscal policy-making, it sets the direction for state government. Using the agency budget requests and the Governor's recommendations, each house prepares its own appropriations bill.

Florida deposits its revenue into various funds or accounts. The most important account is the General Revenue Fund, and the rest are called trust funds. Unlike trust funds, the General Revenue Fund offers legislators great budgetary discretion since the law does not earmark it for specific programs. New and improved state programs are often funded using the natural growth in General Revenue tax collections. Alternatively, the Legislature can enact new or increased taxes. The charts that follow highlight the relative importance of the major taxes which make up the state's General Revenue Fund.

Trust Funds have grown in importance in recent years. Trust funds are spent for specific purposes. For example, with the start of the Lottery in 1987, the state created the Educational Enhancement Trust Fund. Thirty-eight percent of all lottery sales are deposited into this trust fund. It can only be spent

---

The compiler is indebted to Alan W. Johansen, of the House Committee on Finance and Taxation, and Peter Mitchell and a special thanks to Michael Peters of the Committee on Appropriations.

Recurring General Revenue Sources
For Fiscal Year 1994-95

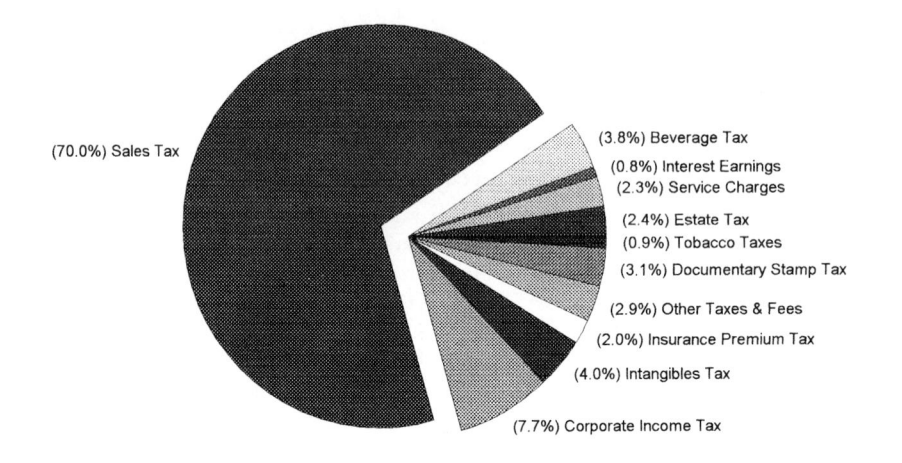

- (70.0%) Sales Tax
- (3.8%) Beverage Tax
- (0.8%) Interest Earnings
- (2.3%) Service Charges
- (2.4%) Estate Tax
- (0.9%) Tobacco Taxes
- (3.1%) Documentary Stamp Tax
- (2.9%) Other Taxes & Fees
- (2.0%) Insurance Premium Tax
- (4.0%) Intangibles Tax
- (7.7%) Corporate Income Tax

Recurring Estimated General Revenue Collections
(millions of dollars)

Source	Final FY 1994–95 Estimate	Percent of Total Collections
Sales Tax	$9,819.7	70.0%
Beverage Tax	$526.2	3.8%
Corporate Income Tax	$1,081.4	7.7%
Documentary Stamp Tax	$429.6	3.1%
Tobacco Taxes	$132.4	0.9%
Insurance Premium Tax	$276.4	2.0%
Intangibles Tax	$567.8	4.0%
Estate Tax	$340.0	2.4%
Interest Earnings	$115.9	0.8%
Service Charges	$328.1	2.3%
Other Taxes & Fees	$402.3	2.9%
Total Recurring Revenues	$14,019.8	100.0%

on public education. The 1994 budget spent $948.8 million in lottery dollars on education.

Similarly, in 1987, the Legislature created the State Infrastructure Fund. $350 million is annually available from the Infrastructure Fund. It can only be spent on state infrastructure such as state office buildings, prisons, roads

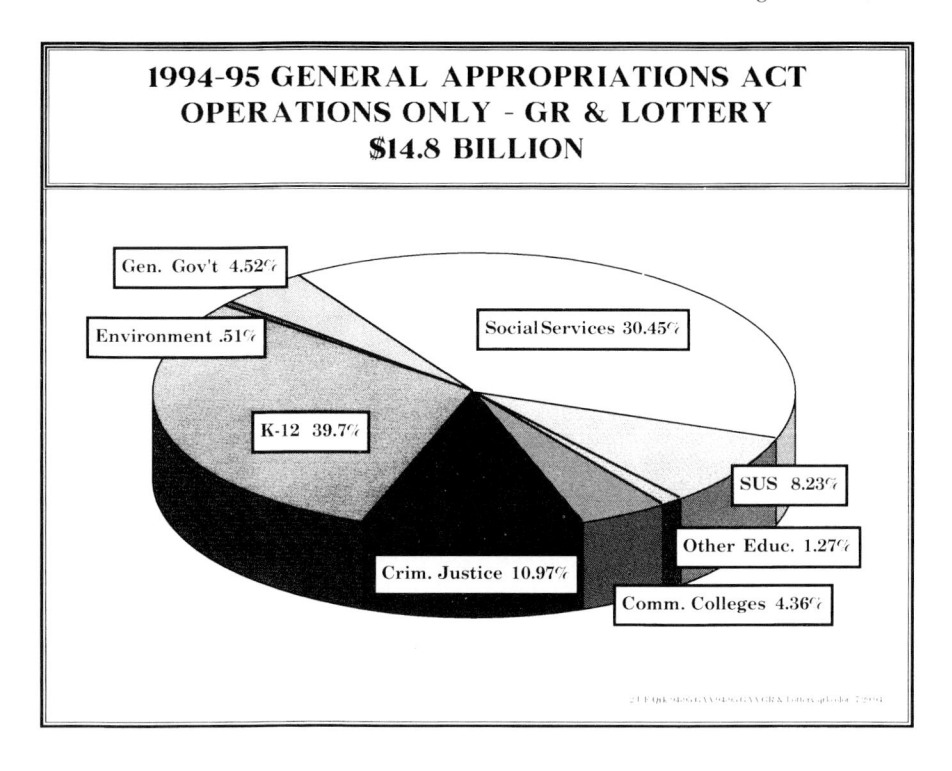

1994-95 GENERAL APPROPRIATIONS ACT
OPERATIONS ONLY - GR & LOTTERY
$14.8 BILLION

- Gen. Gov't 4.52%
- Environment .51%
- K-12 39.7%
- Crim. Justice 10.97%
- Social Services 30.45%
- SUS 8.23%
- Other Educ. 1.27%
- Comm. Colleges 4.36%

and schools. In 1990, the Legislature added operation of prisons to the list of allowable purchases.

The competition for limited fiscal resources generates involvement from industry, local officials, and special interest organizations. These include diverse groups such as environmentalists, teacher unions, and state agencies.

Each house passes its own budget bill reflecting its priorities. Because the two bills will differ, the Speaker and the President typically appoint a conference committee to resolve the spending differences. Once the conference committee reaches a compromise, it sends the bill back to each house for a vote. Neither house can amend a conference committee report. It must be either accepted or rejected.

After the legislative session the Speaker and the President present the General Appropriations Act to the Governor. Article III, Section 8, of the Florida Constitution grants the Governor line-item veto power of the General Appropriations Act. In effect, he can cut any specific issue that the legislature has chosen to fund. Only by a two-thirds vote can the Legislature overturn the Governor's veto.

Florida's six Cabinet officers along with the Governor may amend the budget. Sharing this responsibility with the Cabinet limits the Governor's ability to make changes. Not only must he share this responsibility, he must also consult with the Legislature before carrying out any changes. If the Chairmen of the Appropriations Committees or the Speaker and President believe that a proposed budget adjustment violates legislative intent, they can object in writing. If objected to, the Governor and Cabinet can carry out an adjustment only if approved by a two-thirds vote.

Unlike the federal government's ability to deficit spend, Article VII of Florida's Constitution requires a balanced budget. "Provision shall be made by law for raising sufficient revenue to defray the expenses of the state for each fiscal period."

It is not unusual for revenue collections to vary from the estimate on which the Legislature based the Appropriations bill. The Comptroller deposits all revenues above those needed for the budget into a reserve account known as the Working Capital Fund. When deposits into the General Revenue Fund are below the estimate, the Governor or the Comptroller may certify a deficit. After consulting with the Legislature, the Governor and the Cabinet may then reduce agency budgets enough to prevent the deficit. Alternatively, they can transfer funds from the Working Capital Fund.

Although the law requires the Governor to recommend a biennial budget, the Legislature only enacts a one-year budget. In the second year of each cycle, the Governor develops a supplemental recommendation. The Governor adjusts his recommendation for legislative fiscal policies enacted in the first year. He may also suggest additional revenues or policy changes.

State appropriations are $38.6 billion for the fiscal year which began July 1, 1994 and ends June 30, 1995. Of this amount, $14.3 billion comes from General Revenue Fund sources, and the remaining $24.3 billion from trust funds.

In recent years, fiscal policy makers have come to recognize three distinct budgets within our state budget. These include a "Federal Budget," a

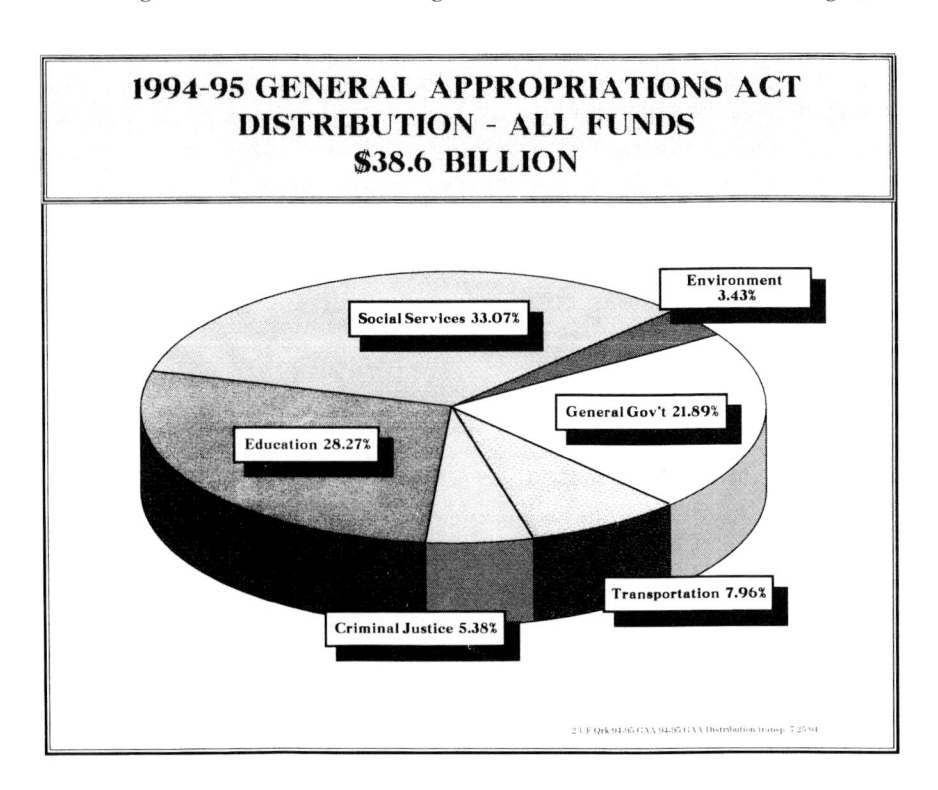

1994-95 GENERAL APPROPRIATIONS ACT DISTRIBUTION - ALL FUNDS $38.6 BILLION

- Social Services 33.07%
- Education 28.27%
- General Gov't 21.89%
- Transportation 7.96%
- Criminal Justice 5.38%
- Environment 3.43%

"Local Budget," and a "State Budget." In part, the state transfers money directly to local governments through various revenue sharing programs. Additionally, Florida spends money on programs and projects which are clearly local in nature. These include grants to libraries, funding of our public schools, recreational facility grants, and water and sewer projects.

Similarly, Aid to Families with Dependent Children, Medicaid and a host of other programs within HRS are directly attributable to federal programs. Although the state participates in these programs, spending levels are mandated based on the number of eligible persons. Along with Unemployment Compensation and portions of the Transportation budget, these program areas are outside of the direct control of the Legislature. Instead, federal government actions strongly influence the level of funding in these areas.

State Budget Director Harry G. Smith and his budget examiner Joe Cresse look over the 1963 budget which totaled a little over one-billion dollars. Then Governor Farris Bryant insisted that three-hundred million dollars be cut out so the state could stay within the anticipated tax income. Associated Press

The Sunshine Amendment

Lawrence A. Gonzalez

Climaxing the first successful initiative campaign in Florida, the electorate overwhelmingly approved passage of the "Sunshine Amendment" in a November 1976 general election referendum. Spearheaded by then Governor Reubin O'D. Askew, this amendment established a comprehensive ethics statement in the State Constitution (Article II, Section 8). It declares at the outset that "a public office is a public trust" and guarantees "that the people shall have the right to secure and sustain that trust against abuse."

Principal among its provisions is a requirement that elected constitutional officers and candidates for such offices make "full and public disclosure of their financial interests." Unlike the more limited source disclosures required by legislative enactment, the Sunshine Amendment requires the listing of net worth and the actual value of each asset and liability in excess of $1,000. Income must be reported either by filing a copy of one's most recent federal income tax return or a sworn statement identifying each source and amount of income exceeding $1,000, including each secondary source of income, i.e., a source of income from a business entity in which the official owns a material interest and derives over $1,000 in income. Full disclosure statements are due to be filed by incumbent officeholders with the Secretary of State by July 1 of each year. The Florida Supreme Court has held that a candidate for elective constitutional office must make full disclosure at the time he submits his qualifying papers.

In addition to personal financial disclosure, the Sunshine Amendment requires full and public disclosure of campaign finances by all elected public officers and candidates for such offices. While such disclosures were required prior to the adoption of the Sunshine Amendment, inclusion of this provision in the Constitution ensures that campaign finance disclosure will continue to exist.

As a further means of securing the public trust against abuse, the Sunshine Amendment:
- Establishes liability to the state by any public officer or employee who breaches the public trust for private gain.
- Provides for forfeiture of retirement benefits upon conviction of a felony involving breach of public trust.
- Prohibits members of the Legislature and statewide elected officers from personally representing another person or entity for compensation before

---

Lawrence A. Gonzalez was the first Executive Director of the Commission on Ethics upon its founding in 1974.

the government body or agency of which the individual was an officer for two years following vacation of office.
- Prohibits members of the Legislature from personally representing clients for compensation during term of office before any State agency other than a judicial tribunal.

Enforcement of ethics in government initially was the responsibility of state prosecutors and the criminal courts. This responsibility was removed from the criminal justice system in 1974, however, when the Legislature deleted criminal penalties associated with violations of the ethics laws. Simultaneously the Legislature created the Commission on Ethics with responsibilities for administering the Code of Ethics for Public Officers and Employees contained in Chapter 112, Part III, of the Florida Statutes.

With the passage of the Sunshine Amendment, the Commission on Ethics was elevated to constitutional status and given the duty of investigating and making public reports on all complaints concerning "breach of public trust." Rules of the Commission equate complaints concerning "breach of public trust" with alleged unethical conduct, including violations of conflict of interest standards for public officials in the Florida Statutes and Constitution. Examples of such provisions include the disclosure requirements of the Sunshine Amendment and Code of Ethics and the standards of conduct set forth in Section 112.313, Florida Statutes. Any citizen may file a sworn complaint with the Commission. Forms for this purpose are available from the Commission and from the Supervisors of Elections in each county.

The Commission on Ethics also prescribes forms for financial disclosure and renders advisory opinions upon the written request of any public official or employee.

Legislative Agencies

Advisory Council on Intergovernmental Relations

Administrative Assistant Sandra Brooks
Suite 4, Holland Building, Tallahassee 32399-1300
(904) 488-9627

Legal basis: Part IV of Chapter 163, F.S. *Created:* 1977. 17 members as follows: four members of the Senate, appointed by the President; four members of the House of Representatives, appointed by the Speaker, and nine members appointed by the Governor. *Duties:* To serve as a forum. To evaluate on a continuing basis the interrelationships among local, regional, state, interstate, and federal agencies in the providing of public services. To analyze the structure and fiscal policies of the State and its political subdivisions. To conduct studies of tax and revenue matters. To examine proposed and existing Federal and State programs for their impact. To encourage and, where appropriate, coordinate studies relating to intergovernmental relations. To review recommendations of national commissions studying intergovernmental relationships. To issue annual reports of its findings and recommendations. To apply for, contract for, receive and expend for its purposes any appropriations or grants from the federal government or any other source, public or private.

Commission on Ethics

Executive Director Bonnie J. Williams
2822 Remington Green Circle, Ste 101, Tallahassee 32308
Mailing Address P.O. Drawer 15709, Tallahassee 32317-5709
(904) 488-7864   Fax (904) 488-3077

Legal basis: Article II, Section 8(f) of the Constitution and Chapter 112.320 F.S. *Created:* 1974. *Method of selection:* Nine members; five appointed by the Governor, one of whom must be a former city or county official and no more than three of whom may be of the same political party; two appointed by the President of the Senate, no more than one of whom shall be from the same political party; two appointed by the Speaker of the House, no more than one of whom shall be from the same political party. No member may be a public officer or employee. *Term:* Two years. *Compensation:* None; reimbursement of travel expense at State rate.
NOTE: The Attorney General in 1976 (AGO 076-54) advised that the Commission on Ethics was in the Legislative branch. The Sunshine Amendment was adopted in 1976 (Article II, Section 8(f), Florida Constitution), elevating the Commission to constitutional status and describing it as an "independent commission." Chapter 88-29, Laws of Florida, exempted Commission employees from Career Service and placed them within the personnel, job classification, and pay plan of the Florida Legislature.

Public Service Commission

Executive Director William D. Talbott
101 East Gaines Street, Tallahassee 32399-0850
(904) 488-7181   Fax (904) 487-0509

Member	Telephone	Term Ends
J. Terry Deason	904-488-2986	Jan. 1, 1999
Diane K. Kiesling	904-488-6943	Jan. 6, 1998
Susan F. Clark	904-488-5573	Jan. 1, 1999
Joe Garcia	904-488-7001	Jan. 6, 1998
Julia L. Johnson	904-488-2445	Jan. 7, 1997

Chairman: Rotates every two years by majority vote of commission for term beginning on first Tuesday after first Monday in odd-numbered years. No member may serve two consecutive terms as Chairman.

Legal basis: Section 350.001, F.S., (as restated in Chapter 78-426, Laws of Florida) declares the Public Service Commission "has been and shall continue to be an arm of the legislative branch." However, the Legislature delegates to the Governor a limited authority so he may participate in the selection of members of the Commission only from the Florida Public Service Nominating Council as provided in s. 350.031. Chapters 350, 351, 364, 365, 366, 367, 368, F.S. *Created:* 1887. *Membership:* Five commissioners appointed pursuant to s. 350.031. *Compensation:* $92,727 a year. *Qualifications:* Commissioners must be competent and knowledgeable in one or more fields, which include, but are not limited to public affairs, law, economics, accounting, engineering, finance, natural resource conservation, energy, or another field substantially related to the duties and functions of the commission. *Term:* Four years. *Method of removal:* By the Governor for cause by and with the consent of the Senate. *Method of financing:* Entirely from fees and assessments from the utilities regulated by the Commission placed in a Regulatory Trust Fund. *Duties:* To regulate telephone company rates and services. To regulate the rates and service of privately-owned electric and gas companies. To regulate rates of privately-owned water and sewer companies. *Purposes:* This regulatory agency was established by the Florida Legislature in 1897. At one time the Chief Justice of the Supreme Court of Florida, George G. McWhorter, resigned his position as Chief Justice to become Chairman of the Florida Railroad Commission. For the first sixty years of its existence, this agency was known as the Florida Railroad Commission; however, in 1947 its name was changed by the Legislature to The Florida Railroad and Public Utilities Commission; in 1963 to Florida Public Utilities Commission, and in 1965 to Florida Public Service Commission. This new name more accurately reflects its purpose and jurisdiction. Originally it had supervision over railroads only, but successive Legislatures have added to its powers and duties. Until 1978 members of the Commission were elected on the statewide ballot. The 1978 Legislature changed the basis for selection. *Powers:* The Commission has the power to summon and require the attendance of witnesses, to require the production of books and records and to levy fines up to $5,000 a day for continuous offenses. In fixing rates to be charged by various utilities, it acts as an agent of the Legislature. Its functions, therefore, are legislative, executive and judicial, combining in one single agency the three primary functions of government.

Public Counsel

Public Counsel Jack Shreve
812 Claude Pepper Building, 111 West Madison Street, Tallahassee
(904) 488-9330

Legal basis: Sections 350.061-0614 (public utilities), 408.40 (health care) 112.3187-112.31895 (whistle-blowers), F.S. *Created:* 1974. *Method of selection:* Appointed by majority vote of the Joint Legislative Auditing Committee. Attorney admitted to practice before Florida Supreme Court. *Tenure:* Serves at pleasure of Auditing Committee. *Duties and powers:* Independent state officer representing the Citizens of the State before the Florida Public Service Commission, the Agency for Health Care Administration, the Legislature, and state and federal courts. In performing these duties (utilities and health care) the Public Counsel participates as a public advocate and presents public and expert witnesses. In the "Whistle-blower's Act" the Public Counsel acts as an ombudsman for state employees who have alleged retaliation because of whistle-blowing.

Public Service Commission Nominating Council

Legal basis: Section 350.031, F.S. *Created:* 1978. *Membership:* Nine. *Method of selection:* Three members, including one member of the House of Representatives, appointed by the Speaker of the House; three members, including one member of the Senate, appointed by the President of the Senate; and three members selected and appointed by a majority vote of the other six members. *Term:* Four years except that those members of the House and Senate shall serve two-year terms concurrent with two-year elected terms of House members. *Qualifications:* No member or spouse shall be an agent, officer, employee, or be any type of partner or shareholder in any industry regulated by the commission, or be in a position to be substantially influenced or affected by the management or managerial policies of any such industry. A member may be removed by the Speaker and President upon a finding that the council member has violated these prohibitions or for any other good cause. *Compensation:* None. *Duty:* Council shall recommend to the Governor not fewer than three persons for each vacancy occurring on the Public Service Commission. If Governor neglects to act, Commission appoints. This occurred in 1991.

Auditor General

Auditor General Charles L Lester
P.O. Box 1735, Claude Denson Pepper Bldg., Tallahassee 32302
(904) 488-5534   Fax (904) 488-6975

Legal basis: Article III, Section 2, Florida Constitution and Sections 11.40–11.48 and 11.50, F.S. *Created:* 1969. *Method of selection:* Auditor General appointed to office by the Legislative Auditing Committee by a majority vote of the members subject to confirmation by both houses of the Legislature. *Qualifications:* Certified under Florida public accountancy law for a period of at least 10 years, with not less than 10 years experience in a governmental agency or 10 years experience in the private sector or a combination of 10 years in government and the private sector. *Term of appointment:* Until terminated by a majority vote of both houses of the Legislature. *Duties:* To make financial audits and performance audits of all State agencies. To make financial audits of all district school boards and district boards of trustees of community colleges. To investigate public assistance made under the provisions of Chapter 409, F.S. and make inquiry of all persons who may have knowledge as to any irregularity incidental to the disbursement of public moneys, food stamps, or other items to recipients. To develop and promulgate an overall plan for management accounting and reporting. To establish, in consultation with the Board of Accountancy, rules for the form and conduct of all governmental entity audits. To review, in consultation with the Board of Accountancy, all audits completed for local units of government by an independent certified public accountant. "Financial Audit" means an examination of financial statements in order to express an opinion on the fairness with which they present financial position, results of operations and changes in financial position in conformity with generally accepted governmental accounting principles and an examination to determine whether operations are properly conducted in accordance with legal and regulatory requirements. "Performance Audit" means an examination of the effectiveness of administration and the efficiency and adequacy of the program of the State agency authorized by law to be performed.

Joint Administrative Procedures Committee

Executive Director Carroll Webb
120 Holland Building, Tallahassee 32399-1300
(904) 488-9110

Legal basis: 11.60, F.S. *Created:* 1974. *Membership:* Six members, three Representatives appointed by Speaker, one of whom shall be from the minority party, and three Senators appointed by the President, one of whom shall be from the minority party. *Chairman:* President shall appoint the chairman in even years and the Speaker in odd years. *Powers and duties:* To maintain continuous review of the statutory authority on which each administrative rule is based. To review administrative rules pursuant to the Administrative Procedures Act, and to advise appropriate agencies and parties of its findings and objections. To advise the appropriate executive agency whenever a rule's statutory authority is amended, repealed, or significantly affected by court decision. To advise the Legislature annually of needed legislation or action. Where rules are not modified, repealed or withdrawn to meet such objections, the committee may seek, after consulting with the affected agency and the Governor, judicial review of the rules' validity. [See: The Phantom Government]

Joint Legislative Management Committee

Executive Director Fred Breeze
712 Pepper Building, Tallahassee 32399
(904) 488-2194   Fax (904) 488-1368

Division Directors: J.C. Pete Ratowski, *Administrative Services;* Ed Montanaro, *Economic & Demographic Research;* Mildred Bunton, *Legislative Information;* Janet Lanigan, *Library Services;* Linda Jessen, *Statutory Revision;* and Richard Langley, *Systems & Data Processing.*

Legal Basis: Section 11.147, F.S. *Membership:* Three members of the House, appointed by the Speaker and three members of the Senate appointed by the President. One member from each house shall be from the minority party. *Term:* Two years, from Organization Session of Legislature. *Chairman:* Rotated between the houses, with the President and Speaker designating the member. Chairmen serve one year. *Purpose:* To serve the House and Senate in those joint functions, including payroll, purchasing, fiscal, personnel, medical clinic, statutory revision, economic and demographic research, library and computer services.

Land Acquisition Selection Committee

Administrator Dr. O. Greg Brock
Bureau of Land Acquisition, 3900 Commonwealth Blvd.
Mail Station 140, Tallahassee 32399-3000
(904) 487-1750   Fax (904) 922-4250

Chairman: George W. Percy. *Members:* Virginia B. Wetherell, Linda Loomis Shelley, Kirby Green and Terry Rhodes.

Legal basis: Section 259.039, F.S. *Purpose:* Land selection process for Conservation and Recreation Lands (CARL), Recreation and parks land acquisition including Save Our Coast (SOC), and Land Acquisition Trust Fund (LATF).

Joint Committee on Information Technology Resources

Staff Director Karen Stolting
Rm 876 Pepper Bldg, 111 West Madison Street, Tallahassee, 32399-1400
(904) 488-4646

Legal basis: Section 11.39 FS. Created: 1983. Membership: Three members each appointed by Senate President and House Speaker. Term: Two years. Purpose: To recommend to the Legislature, at least annually, needed legislation in the area of information technology.

Constitutional Commissions

Constitution Revision Commission

Legal basis: Section 2, Article XXXI. Commission required to be established each twentieth year after adoption of the Constitution in 1968. The Governor appoints fifteen members, the Senate President and House Speaker appoint nine each, the Chief Justice of the Florida Supreme Court appoints three, and the Attorney General also serves. The Governor appoints two alternates, the President and Speaker appoint one alternate each. The Governor designates one of the members as chairman.

Reapportionment in Florida

Neil Skene

A score of young, progressive legislators from Florida's cities swept into office between 1963 and 1967 and took control of Florida. Over the next eight years, they successfully rewrote the Florida Constitution for the first time in 83 years, reorganized state government, imposed a corporate income tax and raised the sales tax, expanded social services, passed legislation to protect the environment and to regulate growth, provided more state support for local schools and distributed it more fairly, and passed no-fault insurance and no-fault divorce. Along the way, they provided themselves year-round staffs, which helped make the Florida Legislature one of the most respected legislatures in the country, and raised their own salaries from $1,200 to $12,000.

All these changes happened because the federal courts forced the Legislature to take seriously the idea of basing legislative districts on population.

Before the federal courts got involved in the apportionment process, 18 percent of Florida's voters could elect a majority of both houses of the Legislature. The principal reason was the tradition for apportioning representation: Each county had no more than one senator and three representatives, and every county could have at least one representative. As a result, Jefferson County in north Florida with 10,000 people had one senator and one representative; Dade County, with 50 times as many people, had one senator and three representatives.

The Early Legislature

Apportionment was not a big problem in the early years of the Florida territory. There were no legislative districts in 1822, when the new territory's first legislative council met in Pensacola. The representatives were required by federal law to be "the most fit and discreet persons of the territory," and they were appointed by the U.S. President. In 1826, Congress decided to let the people in the territory elect their representatives and ordered the state divided into 13 districts, one for each member of the existing legislative council. Each district was to have, "as near as may be, an equal number of free white inhabitants."[1]

The early legislature was unicameral. Not until 1838, after persistent petitioning from the Florida legislators, did Congress create a two-house Gen-

---

Neil Skene is editor and publisher of Congressional Quarterly in Washington, D.C. He was Tallahassee bureau chief for the *St. Petersburg Times* from 1980 to 1984 and editor of the *Evening Independent* in St. Petersburg from 1984 until it was closed in 1986. Skene is also a member of the Florida Bar.

eral Assembly. Twenty-nine members of the House would be elected from the same 13 districts used by the old council, and the number could be increased as the population grew. The Senate would have 11 members initially—three from the area west of the Apalachicola River, three from the area east of the Suwannee River, four from the area in between, and one from the peninsula.

The elections that autumn also produced delegates to a constitutional convention. The constitution drawn up by the convention led to statehood on March 3, 1845. The new state had a 41-member House of Representatives, with representatives from each of the 20 counties. Leon County, the seat of government, got six representatives. Nine counties, including Dade County and a county called Mosquito, got one representative apiece. The formula for the Senate was more complex: There would be not less than one-fourth or more than one-half the number of representatives, and Senate districts were to be as nearly equal in population as possible. Sixteen districts were established. Leon, a district by itself, got two senators. Three districts had more than one county but only one senator. Every other county got one senator apiece.

The constitution specifically provided for reapportionment. A census was to be taken in 1845 and every ten years after that, and representation was to be apportioned equally among the counties. Each county however, was guaranteed at least one representative. The House could have no more than 60 members.

The constitutions of 1861 and 1865 did not change the House formula, but the state was growing. There were 39 counties by 1865, and the House consequently grew to 59 members. The Senate grew to 29. In 1868, another new constitution brought a different formula for the House. Each county would have one representative, plus an additional one for each 1,000 registered voters. The maximum number for any county was four.[2]

Growth and Reapportionment

The young state's first enduring constitution was written at the end of Reconstruction. This Constitution of 1885 lasted through the first six decades of the twentieth century, and it too had provisions for reapportionment.[3] There could be as many as 68 representatives and 32 senators. But fair apportionment was still restricted by the formula. Each county would have at least one and not more than three representatives. Reapportionment actually occurred only twice—in 1925 and 1945.

The famous Florida boom had begun by 1925. Investors, speculators and migrants were pouring into South Florida, and the Legislature took notice by proposing a constitutional amendment on reapportionment. The Constitution would still have the provision that had proven largely ineffective—the requirement of reapportionment every 10 years. But now reapportionment was "mandatorily required." The House formula reflected the growing variations in population by awarding three representatives to each of the five most populous counties, two to the next 18 counties, and one to the remaining counties, with a maximum membership of 95. The Senate would have 38 members, from districts "as nearly equal in population as practicable."

The apportionment did not change in 1935. In 1945, Gov. Millard F. Caldwell called a special reapportionment session of the Legislature, and in such sessions, under the Constitution, no other business could be done. The session lasted 53 days, and the result was hardly drastic: Two Senate seats and three House seats were shifted from North to South Florida.

Still, apportionment was determined primarily by county boundaries, as it had been since the beginning of the state.

The Fight of '55

The Legislature in the middle 1950s still reflected the conservatism of the rural counties of northern Florida. The urban areas, with their political moderates, wanted their share of representation. They fought hard for it in 1955, but they lost.

Gov. LeRoy Collins supported the idea of "fairer distribution of representation" in his 1954 campaign for governor. When he took office in 1955, reapportionment was one of his first undertakings. He wanted the Legislature to draft a new constitution, and reapportionment would be part of it. "The apportionment of representation in the Legislature is grossly unsound and unfair," he said in his first legislative address, "and brings about a situation whereby hundreds of thousands of our citizens are relegated to an inferior class."[4]

Urban newspapers joined the crusade. Editor James Clendinen of the *Tampa Tribune* came up with a pejorative name for the rural conservatives who were running things in the Legislature: "the Pork Chop Gang." They were "fighting for pork, rather than principle," Clendinen said. It appears, however, that the urban newspapers were not opposed to the pork barrel, but merely the use of it for counties other than their own. The cities, moreover, benefited from some "pork chop" programs. One good example is the scattering of new colleges and universities around the state; they served not only the rural areas but the urban ones.

Governor LeRoy Collins
Wanted "fairer Distribution of representation"
Florida State Archives

The Legislature, however, did not pass a reapportionment plan in its regular session of 1955. So Gov. Collins called the legislators back for a special reapportionment session. "For a long time now ," he told them in an address on June 30, "you have been laboring over this matter with great cost to the taxpayers and little constructive results to show for your efforts." He said reapportionment "requires discretion, unselfishness and political courage."

It would turn out to be the longest and least productive legislative session in state history. The Legislature produced a reapportionment plan that summer, but Governor Collins said it was inadequate and vetoed it. The same plan was passed again, and again Governor Collins vetoed it. Columbia County, he observed, had 18,000 people and a senator of its own, while 10 counties, each with larger populations, shared a senator with some other county.

As a sort of compromise, the Legislature proposed a constitutional amendment giving each county one senator and setting the number of representatives at 135. Governor Collins originally opposed that idea, which obviously was a variation of the federal system of giving each state two senators while using population to determine representation in the House. He recalled years later, though, that he acquiesced when the proposal was sent to the voters. Some of the newspapers that had joined Collins in the crusade parted company with him and objected to the compromise. The amendment was defeated at the polls.

It was just as well. A decade later, the U.S. Supreme Court would rule, in a case from Alabama called *Reynolds vs. Sims*,[5] that such plans violated the U.S. Constitution's guarantee of equal protection. Both houses, not just one, had to reflect the principle of "one person, one vote." Alabama had argued that a state ought to be able to allow equal representation from political subdivisions, just as the Senate of the United States had two members from each state. But the Supreme Court said the federal system was a unique compromise with a specific provision in the U.S. Constitution. States, the court said, were bound by the requirement of "equal protection."

No more plans came out of the 1955 Legislature. Since technically it could not adjourn until a plan was approved, it was in session until the members' terms ran out on November 6, 1956.

Gov. Collins tried again in 1957. The legislators were considering the new constitution drafted during the previous two years, and the constitution, as it was put to the voters, raised the Senate membership from 38 to 45 and the House membership from 95 to 114. But the voters never got a chance to pass judgment. The Florida Supreme Court threw the new constitution off the ballot because it violated a provision in the existing Constitution that no amendment consist of more than one article. The Legislature had created, by contrast, a "daisy chain," in which all articles passed or all failed.

Change in the Courts

For a long time, the courts had refused to get involved in reapportionment. In 1946, the U.S. Supreme Court had suggested that reapportionment was a "political thicket" outside the federal courts' jurisdiction.[6] But in 1960, six years after its famous desegregation ruling in 1954, the Supreme Court said it was unconstitutional for a state to gerrymander legislative districts to exclude blacks.[7] Then in 1962 came the case that would change Florida's future: *Baker vs. Carr*.[8] The Supreme Court said federal courts could consider challenges to state apportionment plans.

Almost immediately a three-judge panel of the U.S. District Court in Tallahassee declared Florida's apportionment "prospectively null, void and in-

All Out of Shape

Front page, April 27, 1955 — The Tampa Tribune

Under Florida's 1885 Constitution, equitable legislative apportionment was not possible. That Constitution said there would be 38 Senatorial districts but no county could have more than one Senator and no county could be divided. In 1955, Dade County had 329,960 persons registered to vote, while Jefferson County had 3,227. Yet each had a Senator. In the House of Representatives, with 95 members, Dade County had three Representatives and Jefferson, one. The Constitution placed a ceiling of three Representatives for each of the five most populous counties, two for each of the next 18 more populous counties, and one each for the remaining 44 counties. Thus, in 1955, 18 per cent of the voters could elect a majority in the Senate and 17.6 per cent a majority in the House. Until a three-judge Federal Court struck down in 1962 that inflexible State Constitution formula, it was not possible to provide for legislative districts, in the language of the 1885 Constitution, "as nearly equal in population as practicable"

operative" and ordered reapportionment. Governor Farris Bryant called a special session on August 1, 1962, and by August 11 the Legislature had produced a plan for submission to the voters. The Senate was increased from 38 to 46 members; the House, from 95 to 135. The voters rejected the idea, in what was largely a philosophical vote on federal-court interference.

On November 9, Governor Bryant called a second special session, but it ended in a stalemate after 20 days. On January 29, 1963, Governor Bryant tried again, and this time the Legislature produced a plan within four days. Florida would have 43 senators and 112 representatives. For the first time in more than a century, one county—Dade, the most populous—was allowed more than one senator. The House formula was still based on county boundaries, but it provided for "equal proportions." The 11 most populous counties would elect half of the House.

The new provisions grandfathered in legislators whose terms had not expired, so in the 1963 session there were actually 45 senators and 125 representatives. In the 1965 session, there was still one holdover in the Senate. The new size was actually achieved in the 1967 Legislature, elected in the fall of 1966.

Richard A. Pettigrew   Murray H. Dubbin
"Urban progressives"

Florida State Archives

The three-judge federal court approved the 1963 plan. "The present plan gives some more weight to the population factor than did the rejected plan," the court wrote, referring back to the plan rejected by the voters in 1962. "But if it be required that both branches of the legislature, or either branch, must be apportioned on a strict population basis, then, admittedly, neither the rejected amendment nor [the 1963 plan] would pass the test. On the other hand, if rejected constitutional amendment set up a rational plan, free from invidious discrimination, and by our earlier opinion we have so held, it would follow that the plan now under consideration is likewise rational and free from invidious discrimination."

The first election under that plan brought in such urban progressives as Louis de la Parte and Terrell Sessums of Tampa and Richard Pettigrew and Murray Dubbin of Miami. It also brought in Republicans from Broward and Pinellas counties. But the plan lasted only for the 1963 session. The next year, the U.S. Supreme Court overturned the plan because of its failure to reflect the principle of "one person, one vote." The voters also rejected the plan at the polls by voting down the constitutional change to a 43-member Senate and a 112-member House.

On January 8, 1965, the three-judge court ordered a new reapportionment by July 1. On June 29, the Legislature produced what was said to be a temporary plan with 109 representatives and 58 senators, plus nine legislators who would be grandfathered for the rest of their terms. Again the three-judge panel approved the plan, and again the U.S. Supreme Court rejected it. The Supreme Court said the plan still discriminated against urban citizens, and there was "no warrant for perpetuating what all conceded to be an unconstitutional apportionment for another three years."

So the Legislature went at it again. On March 9, 1966, the Legislature approved a plan with a 117-member House and a 48-member Senate. But to the apparent amazement of Gov. Haydon Burns and other state officials, the U. S. Supreme Court announced on October 10, just a few weeks before the November elections, that it would review the plan. The governor predicted "political and probably economic chaos."

The November election, however, went on as planned, and it brought to Tallahassee another batch of urban progressives. Among them were Bob Graham, who later became Governor, and three members of a later state Cabinet: Secretary of State George Firestone and Comptroller Gerald Lewis of Miami and Treasurer Bill Gunter of Orlando. A host of other reform-minded people came, including Talbot (Sandy) D'Alemberte, who later chaired the 1978 Constitutional Revision Commission, and Maxine Baker, a housewife whose work on behalf of mental health led to the famous Baker Act of 1971.

The extent of the change in the Legislature is measured by the choice of new leaders for the next two years. Ralph Turlington, a moderate college professor from Gainesville, was elected Speaker of the House. Verle A. Pope, a moderate from St. Augustine, was elected President of the Senate. "We were bridges," recalled Turlington, who later became Education Commissioner. "I could never have been elected speaker under the old apportionment. I had been there 16 years. I never had a chance." But to the remnants of the "Pork Chop Gang," he said, "I was the most comfortable option they had."[9]

In January 1967 shortly after the new legislators took office, the Supreme Court acted again. For the third time, it rejected a Florida apportionment plan, which still had population deviations among districts of as much as 30 percent in the Senate and 40 percent in the House. Minor deviations could be tolerated, the court said, but only if the state could prove a special justification.[10]

The three-judge panel of the District Court responded by writing its own apportionment plan. The court set aside the requirements in the state constitution that each county have at least one representative and that no county have more than one senator. Four, five, even six counties were grouped together so that representatives from each district would at last represent nearly the same number of people. The largest county, Dade, had 19 representatives of its own and shared three others with Monroe County. Many Senate districts had previously encompassed more than one county, but some of the new districts had more counties than ever before.

All the incumbents were thrown out of office, and new elections were held. Many older legislators did not return, and younger legislators, such as Bob Graham, found themselves not mere freshmen but leaders. Bob Graham, for example, returned to Tallahassee to discover that all the other members of the House appropriations subcommittee on higher education were gone. "To be immodest about it," Graham recalled 16 years later, "I was the senior member and became chairman of the subcommittee. It was not a case of having to put in four or six years. It was instant involvement."

They forged an odd alliance with the new Republican governor, Claude Kirk, himself a reformist. The Republicans—20 of them in the Senate and 39 in the House—and the urban Democrats created a working majority. These reformers rewrote the state constitution, and it was approved by the voters. State government was reorganized. A Sunshine Law opened government meetings, and more public records were available to the public than ever before. A little-known senator from Pensacola named Reubin Askew took up the reform theme in 1970, and it carried him to the Governor's Mansion. Laws on public ethics and environmental regulation and an income tax for corporations were approved. Governor Askew was followed by another moderate, Bob Graham. People long shut out of government by malapportionment had a "common agenda," Graham recalled as he sat in the Governor's Mansion. "Not to say everybody agreed what the solutions were, but everybody agreed what the questions ought to be."

The Later Years

The new Constitution approved in 1968 required a reapportionment in 1972 that would reflect the 1970 census. There would have to be a reapportionment every 10 years after that, and the courts by now had made it clear that reapportionment had to be *real* reapportionment, reflecting the principle of "one person, one vote." There was a provision for review of the plan by the Florida Supreme Court, and if the Legislature could not agree on a plan, the Florida Supreme Court would write one. The federal courts were not wanted in this process.

The Legislature did the job on its own, without court intervention, in 1972. Both houses would have their maximum membership under the new Constitution—120 representatives and 40 senators. A computer, programmed with the populations of 14,000 census tracts, was used to draw district boundaries. For the first time, counties were divided into separate districts, though many of these districts still had more than one senator or representative.

Republicans and blacks sought smaller, single-member districts, so that

Verle A. Pope   Ralph D. Turlington
              "We were bridges"
                                       Florida State Archives

pockets of Republican or black voters could elect a legislator rather than be outvoted by whites from a larger geographic area, but the effort failed both in the Legislature and in the Florida Supreme Court.

Black and Republican representation grew, nevertheless. The Republicans held a larger percentage in both houses after the 1972 elections, and more blacks joined the two representatives who were elected under the 1967 apportionment. Although the Florida Supreme Court expressed concern about the possible dilution of minority votes through multi-member districts, the justices gave the necessary approval, 4–3.

Ten years later, in 1982, leaders of both houses agreed near the beginning of the reapportionment debate that both houses would have single-member districts. One fundamental dispute, however, finally had to be resolved by the Florida Supreme Court: What was to happen to senators elected in 1980? Were they grandfathered for full four-year terms, in much the same way the legislators in the 1960s were, or were their terms cut short? The problem was one the authors of the Constitution apparently never thought about in 1968. They had provided for two-year Senate terms *after* reapportionment so that half of the Senate would continue to be elected every two years, but there was no provision for two-year terms *before* reapportionment. On a 5–2 vote, the court said all senators' terms expired in 1982.

As had been the case in every reapportionment, individual legislators worked furiously to preserve the safest possible districts for themselves. Extra sessions were required before the Legislature agreed on a new plan. But when it was, the Supreme Court gave its approval.

Republicans, who had supported single-member districts, actually lost a few seats after the 1982 elections. But blacks arrived at the Legislature in greater numbers than ever before. In Miami and Jacksonville, voters elected the first black senators since Reconstruction.

In 1984, as part of the Governor's Oral History Project, LeRoy Collins recalled attending a dinner party in Washington some months after the 1967 reapportionment. He was asked by Justice Hugo Black of the U.S. Supreme Court to talk about his accomplishments as governor a decade earlier. Then, Collins recalled, Black asked about his greatest failure. Reapportionment, Collins replied.

"That was not a failure," said Black, who had been a dissenter in 1946 when the court refused to consider malapportionment and part of the majority in *Baker vs. Carr* in 1962. "It took what you and the *St. Petersburg Times* and the *Miami Herald* and all those who were helping you down there did in your fight to show us that there was a violation of the equal protection of the laws guaranteed by the Constitution. We made the change, but Florida's situation had a big part in helping us see the necessity for it. We needed your step to stand on."

---

[1]IV *U.S. Statutes at Large*, 164–67, sec. 10.
[2]In the constitutions of 1861 and 1865, the apportionment provisions were in Article IX. In the Constitution of 1868, the provisions were in Article XIII.
[3]The apportionment provisions were in Article VII, sec. 3.
[4]Gov. Collins' speeches are reprinted in *Florida Across the Threshold,* a compilation by Allen Morris of documents from the Collins administration.
[5]377 U.S. 533 (1964).
[6]*Colegrove vs. Green,* 328 U.S. 549 (1946).
[7]*Gomillion vs. Lightfoot,* 364 U.S. 339 (1960).
[8]369 U.S. 186 (1962). Apportionment plans in 49 states—every one but Oregon, which already had a population-based plan—were eventually changed because of this ruling. The Supreme Court itself had gotten involved in reviewing plans from 21 states by mid-1966.
[9]Interview by the author with Education Commissioner Ralph Turlington, April 1983.
[10]*Swann v. Adams,* 385 U.S. 440 (1967).

The 1963 House leadership reviewing plans for the House chamber after court-ordered enlargement of the Membership. L-R: E.C. Rowell, Speaker Mallory E. Horne and H.E. Lancaster. Frank Noel/A.P.

The Apportionment of 1992
George Meier

The 1992 cycle of redistricting was marked by partisan hardball, allegations of extreme self interest, charges of racial and partisan bias, three months of legislative gridlock, and extensive court involvement. Unlike the previous two redistrictings under the provisions of the Constitution of 1968, which were comparatively calm and agreeable affairs, redistricting in 1992 saw the Legislature fail to adopt a plan for congressional redistricting and come within one vote of not adopting a joint resolution of legislative apportionment.

The stage was set even before the Legislature convened in regular session, when Miguel De Grandy, a Cuban-American State Representative from Dade County, along with other Hispanics and members of the Republican Party of Florida, filed suit in federal district court alleging that the then current districts were malapportioned and should not be used for the 1992 elections. The suit asked the court to set a deadline by which the Legislature must complete drawing state legislative and congressional lines or, in the event the Legislature failed to act in a timely way, asked the court to undertake the job in order to insure that minority citizens in Florida had a fair chance to participate in the electoral process.

Ultimately the federal district court drew the state's congressional map, creating 23 districts with no deviation among the districts. The ideal population was 562,519 persons; there are 13 districts with 562,519 persons and 11 districts with 562,518 persons (required by the arithmetic of deviation calculations).

The Legislature adopted a joint resolution of apportionment creating 40 single-member Senate districts and 120 single-member House districts. The state Supreme Court conducted an examination of the plans under the provisions of the state constitution and declared them valid. The state then submitted the plans to the U.S. Department of Justice for review under section 5 of the federal Voting Rights Act. The department precleared the plan for the House of Representatives, but interposed an objection to the plan for the Senate, declaring that African-Americans in the Tampa and St. Petersburg areas were unnecessarily divided in order to protect the election chances of incumbents.

The Legislature stated that it did not intend to convene to address the violation and the state Supreme Court adopted a plan which it felt met the objections of the department. The Supreme Court's Senate plan was never subjected to preclearance review as it was adopted by the federal district court as its own in order to hastily proceed to trial on allegations of section 2 violations made by the De Grandy plaintiffs in their third amended complaint and by the United States.

The court found that the state House plan violated section 2 with regard to Hispanic voters in Dade County and ordered the use of a plan which changed 31 districts from the joint resolution adopted by the Legislature. The court also stated, from the bench, that the Senate plan violated section 2 with regard to Hispanic voters in Dade County, but that there was no possible remedy since increasing the number of Hispanic districts would have a retrogressive effect on African-Americans. In other words, the court found that the plan that violated section 2 was, at the same time, the only plan that balanced the competing interests of the two protected classes. A subsequent order issued by the court stated that the Senate plan did not violate section 2.

The state took an immediate appeal, and immediately applied for a stay of the district court's order, which was granted by the Supreme Court.

On appeal the United States Supreme Court upheld Florida's 1992 reapportionment plan (SJR 2-G). The court held that Florida's reapportionment plan did not violate § 2 of the Voting Rights Act of 1965 (42 U.S.C. § 1973). This holding was based on the court's conclusion that "the totality of circumstances" did not support a finding of dilution of minority voters. In essence, the court found that under the plan minority voters had an equal opportunity to participate in the political process and to elect representatives of their choice. Consequently, as a result of the Supreme court decision, future elections for the Florida Legislature will proceed under the plan (SJR 2-G). [Johnson v. DeGrandy 114 S. Ct 2647 (1994).]

Under SJR 2-G, (as amended by the Florida Supreme Court), the most populous House district has 109,810 people (District 2) which is 1,994 (+1.85%) more than the ideal population of 107,816 per district. The least populous district has 104,431 people (District 3) which is 3,385 (−3.14%) less than the ideal population. The absolute overall range of the 120 House single member districts is 5,379 people with a relative overall range of 4.99%. In 13 districts Blacks constitute more than 50% of the total population and in 3 districts Blacks are more than 30% of the total population. There are 9 districts where Hispanics constitute more than 65% of the total population and 4 districts in which Hispanics are more than 30% of the total population.

In the 40 single-member Senate districts, the ideal population is 323,448 people with the most populous district having 324,815 people (District 31) (+1,367, +0.42%), and the least populous district having 322,018 people (District 1) (−1,430, −0.44%). This gives an absolute overall range of 2,797 people with a relative overall range of 0.86%. In 3 districts Blacks constitute more than 50% of the total population and in 3 districts Blacks are more than 30% of the total population. There are 3 districts where Hispanics constitute more than 60% of the total population and 2 districts in which Hispanics are more than 30% of the total population.

The Judicial System
B.K. Roberts

"The judicial power shall be vested in a supreme court, district courts of appeal, circuit courts and county courts. No other courts may be established by the state, any political subdivision or any municipality."
Florida Constitution, Article V, Section 1.

On March 14, 1972, the electors of Florida approved a revision of the judicial article of the State Constitution to give Florida one of the most modern court systems in the nation. Section 1 of Article V provides that "The judicial power shall be vested in a Supreme Court, District Courts of Appeal, circuit courts and county courts. No other courts may be established by the state, any political subdivision or any municipality." The revision eliminated 14 different types of courts which had been created pursuant to the 1885 Constitution. Substituted for these trial courts is a uniform, two appellate and two trial court structure composed of The Supreme Court, District Court of Appeal, circuit courts and county courts. There cannot be any other courts.

B.K. Roberts

You may wish to ask the question, what is meant by the "judicial powers" of a state? The judicial power is, essentially, the authority of a judge to decide, according to law, controversies of which the law takes notice, and to secure the enforcement of the decision rendered. We commonly say that the judicial power is the power to administer justice; and that "equal justice under law" is the supreme object of all courts which perform their proper function.

In those cases where the Legislature may decide that, for matters of convenience or for quicker or more efficient administration or a particular law,

---

Florida Supreme Court Justice B.K. Roberts retired on November 30, 1976, after 27 years of judicial service including six years as its chief justice. He holds a Doctor of Jurisprudence degree, University of Florida, Honorary LLD, University of Miami and Doctor of Humane letters, Florida State University. Justice Roberts served 14 years as Chairman of the Judicial Council taking the leadership in the creation of Florida's Judicial Qualifications Commission, the Public Defender System, and the establishment of the College of Law at Florida State University, a building there having been named in his honor by the Legislature. He was a member of the 1968 Florida Constitutional Revision Commission and provided the leadership in the revision of the judicial article of the Florida Constitution in 1972 giving Florida one of the most modern court systems in the nation. He provided the leadership for the nonpartisan election of judges. Since retiring from the court he has practiced law in Tallahassee.

the determination of controversies arising under such law should be exercised, in the first instance, by a commission or board, the judicial power of a state may also be exercised to a limited degree through public officers or bodies such as a commission or a board, or civil traffic divisions. Such commissions or boards are said to have "quasi-judicial" powers, since they exercise powers in some ways comparable to those exercised by the courts. Article V provides "Commissions established by law, or administrative officers or bodies may be granted quasi-judicial power in matters connected with the function of their offices." The power of the judiciary to review their action on proper procedure is inherent.

The courts do not initiate cases. Our judges serve as arbiters, not advocates. Furthermore, they cannot decide abstract questions of legal philosophy but may exercise their judicial power only when a party seeks their aid in an actual controversy—for example, when one seeks to recover damages for an injury caused by the wrongful act of another. The trial courts also exercise their judicial powers in trying persons who are accused of a criminal offense and if guilty imposing sentence. As exceptions the Supreme Court may render advisory opinion to the Governor and subject to law, may enter declaratory judgments advising litigants of their rights.

Advisory Opinion to the Governor

An exception to the general rule that the judicial power may be exercised only in the hearing and adjudication of actual controversies is found in Section 1(c) of Article 4 of our Constitution. This section provides that "The Governor may, at any time, require the opinion of the Justices of the Supreme Court, as to the interpretation of any portion of this Constitution upon any question affecting his executive powers and duties, and the justices shall render such opinion in writing." It will be noted that the opinion of the justices can be required by the Governor only "as to the interpretation of any portion of this Constitution upon any question affecting his executive powers and duties, . . ." This is not strictly a judicial power, in that there is no actual controversy between parties, but is an additional duty which the Constitution confers upon the justices of the Supreme Court.

Declaratory Judgments or Decrees

An apparent exception to the rule requiring an actual controversy before the judicial power may be exercised appears in Chapter 87, Florida Statutes, as amended. This particular portion of our laws authorizes the courts to enter declaratory judgments and decrees, that is, to determine the rights of a party under some instrument such as a deed, or a will, or a contract, prior to the time that the matter has reached the stage where one party is suing the other. Yet these cases are essentially "actual controversies," since all parties having an interest in the judgment or decree are necessary parties to the suit if they are to be bound by it, and the jurisdiction of the court can be invoked only by a party who has an interest in the subject involved. It is simply an effort on the part of the law to enable parties to learn their rights in a court proceeding before dispute arises which will provoke controversy and perhaps lead to expensive and delayed litigation.

Constitutionality of Executive or Legislative Acts

We have all heard that the three branches of government—the legislative, executive and judicial—are equal, and we may then wonder why it is that the courts may be said to have a greater power than the other two branches of government, in that they may, in a proper case, strike down some acts of the legislative or the executive branches. The reason for this goes back to the fact that the courts are the tribunals where legal controversies are settled; and when any person, through appropriate legal procedure, claims that the provisions of the Constitution are being violated by acts of the legislative or executive branches, to the injury of the complaining party, then the courts may determine the controversy.

Suppose, for example, that the state Legislature passed an act providing for a personal income tax. Any natural person liable to pay the tax could contend that the act violated the constitutional prohibition against a state personal income tax. It would then be the duty of the judiciary, provided the citizen had used an appropriate procedure, to decide whether the act violated the state Constitution. Since our Constitution provides that the state may not levy a personal income tax, and since the acts of all departments are subject and subordinate to the provisions of the Constitution, it would be the duty of the court, in our example, to find that the Legislature, in passing the personal income tax bill had acted without lawful authority and, therefore, the act passed by the Legislature had no validity and the citizen would not have to pay the tax. It must be remembered, however, that it is only when a party, in an appropriate legal proceeding, is contending that the legislative act has violated his constitutional rights, to his injury, that the courts will determine such question. In order to avoid encroachment upon the Legislature, the courts will not in any case, consider the wisdom, or expediency of legislation.

Appellate Courts

Supreme Court
7 Justices
sits in Tallahassee
6 year terms

5 District Courts of Appeal
61 judges
sit in panels of 3
1st District—Tallahassee (15 judges)
2nd District—Lakeland (7 judges)
Tampa (7 judges)
3rd District—Miami (11 judges)
4th District—West Palm Beach (12 judges)
5th District—Daytona Beach (9 judges)
6 year terms

Trial Courts

> **20 Circuit Courts**
> 442 judges—different number in each of the 20 judicial circuits
> preside individually
> 6 year terms

> **67 County Courts**
> 254 judges—at least 1 in each county
> preside individually
> 4 year terms

The Courts

Supreme Court

The highest court in this state is the Supreme Court which is composed of seven justices to be appointed by the Governor from a list of qualified persons submitted by the Judicial Nominating Commission for a term ending on the first Tuesday after the first Monday in January of the year following the next general election occurring at least one year after the date of appointment. (See discussion on the Judicial Nominating Commission.) "In the general election preceding the end of the appointed term, the justice may submit his record to the electors of the state for a merit retention vote to determine whether or not he will be continued in office for a full term. The justice does not have an opponent, but his or her name shall be on the ballot followed by the question, "Shall Justice __(name)__ be retained in office?" If the incumbent fails this test, a vacancy is created and the process starts over. Of these seven justices, each appellate district shall have at least one justice appointed from such district to the Supreme Court. The justices must submit themselves for retention or rejection by the electors in a general election every six years, and failure to submit to such a vote will result in a vacancy in the office upon expiration of the current term.

One of the justices is chosen chief justice by a majority of the members of the Supreme Court. By rule, the Court has established a policy of rotating the chief justiceship in two-year cycles. The chief justice is the chief administrative officer of the judicial system and has the power to assign judges for temporary duty in any court to insure full utilization of judicial manpower and may recall with their consent retired justices or judges who are not engaged in the practice of law. The chief justice has delegated to the chief judge of each judicial circuit, the power to assign circuit or county court judges within the circuit.

Five justices of the court constitute a quorum and it is necessary that four of the justices agree to render a decision. In the event of inability to organize a quorum of five justices, the chief justice may assign for temporary duty another judge, or retired justice who is not engaged in the practice of law and who is willing to serve.

Jurisdiction

The Supreme Court *shall* hear appeals from judgments of the trial courts imposing the death penalty or from decisions of District Courts of Appeal declaring invalid a state statute or a provision of the state Constitution. As provided by general law, the Supreme Court shall hear appeals from final judgments and proceedings for the validation of bonds or certificates of indebtedness and shall review action of statewide agencies relating to rates or service of utilities providing electric, gas or telephone service. In its *discretion,* the Court *may* review any decision of a District Court of Appeal that expressly declares valid a state statute or that expressly construes a provision of the state or federal Constitution or that expressly and directly conflicts with a decision of another District Court of Appeal or of the Supreme Court on the same question of law. Also, the Court may review any decision of a District Court of Appeal that passes upon a question, certified by it to be of great public importance or that is certified by it to be in direct conflict with another District Court of Appeal. The Court may review any order or judgment of a trial court certified by the District Court of Appeal in which an appeal is pending, to be of great public importance or to have great effect on the proper administration of justice throughout the state and certified to require immediate resolution by the Supreme Court. Also, the Court may issue writs of mandamus and quo warranto to state officers and agencies and any justice may issue a writ of habeas corpus before the Supreme Court or any justice, a District Court of Appeal or any circuit judge thereof, also a writ of prohibition to courts and all writs necessary to the exercise of its jurisdiction. These ancient and extraordinary writs will be discussed later.

The Court may promulgate rules governing the practice and procedure in Florida courts, such rules subject to the power of the Legislature to repeal any of them by two-thirds vote of its membership and the Court has authority to review and repeal, with the concurrence of five justices, any rule adopted by the Judicial Qualifications Commission which Commission has been created for the general supervision of judicial conduct. Upon their recommendation, the Supreme Court may discipline by public or private reprimand, or removal from office. The Supreme Court controls the admission and discipline of attorneys and has adopted a code of judicial conduct for judges and also attorneys. The Court may review a question of law certified by the Supreme Court of the United States or a United States Court of Appeals which is determinative of the cause and for which there is no controlling precedent of the Supreme Court of Florida.

District Courts of Appeal

Most trial court decisions which are appealed are reviewed by three-judge panels of the District Court of Appeal in which controversy the concurrence of two judges is necessary for a decision. However, in certain cases in the discretion of the Court, the case may be heard by a district court of appeal en banc, with all eligible judges of the District participating.

The Florida Constitution directs the Legislature to divide the state into appellate court districts. Presently, there are five district courts, headquartered in Tallahassee, Lakeland, Miami, West Palm Beach and Daytona Beach. The judges are appointed and retained in office as are justices of the Supreme Court, and with the same qualifications. They are subject to the jurisdiction of the Judicial Qualification Commission. A chief judge is selected by his or her colleagues to be responsible for the administrative duties of the Court.

The jurisdiction of the District Court of Appeal includes appeals from final judgments or orders of trial courts in cases that either are not directly appealable to the Supreme Court or are not taken from a county court to a circuit court, orders or judgments of a county court which are certified by the county court to be of great public importance, and certain non-final orders specifically defined by the Supreme Court rule. By general law, district courts are granted review power of most actions taken by state agencies. District courts are also granted constitutional authority to issue the extraordinary writs of certiorari, prohibition, mandamus, quo warranto, and habeas corpus, as well as all other writs necessary to the complete exercise of their jurisdiction.

As a general rule, decisions of the district courts of appeal represent the final appellate review of litigated cases although a person dissatisfied with a district court's decision may request review by certiorari in the Supreme Court of Florida, or the Supreme Court of the United States. The overwhelming majority of such requests are denied.

Circuit Courts

The courts of the most general jurisdiction in this state are the circuit courts, each of which is presided over by a circuit judge, now elected every six years by the qualified electors of their respective judicial circuits. They are subject to the jurisdiction of the Judicial Qualifications Commission.

The Constitution provides that a circuit court shall be established to serve each judicial circuit established by the Legislature. Twenty circuits currently exist. Because the number of judges in a circuit depends upon the population and case load of the particular area, there is a varying number of judges in each circuit. Eligibility for office of circuit judge requires Florida and circuit resident electorate status and admission to the practice of law in the state for the preceding five years.

Circuit courts have jurisdiction of appeals from county courts except those appeals of county court orders or judgments declaring invalid a state statute or a provision of the state Constitution and except those orders or judgments of a county court certified by the county court to the district court of appeal to be of great public importance and which are accepted by the district court of appeal for review. Circuit courts also have appellate jurisdiction of final administrative orders of local government code enforcement boards.

Circuit courts have exclusive original jurisdictions in all actions of law not cognizable by the county courts; of proceedings relating to the settlement of the estates of decedents and minors, the granting of letters testamentary, guardianship, involuntary hospitalization, the determination of incompetency, and other jurisdiction usually pertaining to courts of probate; in all cases in equity including all cases relating to juveniles except traffic offenses. (See Chapter 39 and 316, Florida Statutes .) Also, of felonies and all misdemeanors arising out of the same circumstances as a felony which is also charged; in all cases involving legality of any tax assessment or roll, except as provided in Florida Statute 72.011 which provides for challenge through Chapter 120 administrative proceedings; in actions of ejectment; and in all actions involving the title and boundaries of real property.

Circuit judges also have the power to issue the "extraordinary writs" such as the writs of mandamus, quo warranto, certiorari, prohibition, and habeas corpus, to which we have above referred in the discussion of Supreme Court, and all other writs proper and necessary to complete exercise of their jurisdiction. The judges of each judicial circuit shall select a chief judge from among them for a fixed term during which he or she will perform the administrative duties of his circuit and county courts located therein.

The chief judge of a circuit court may authorize a county court judge to order emergency hospitalizations in the absence from the county of the circuit judges in charge of such cases; and the county court judge shall have the power to issue all temporary orders and temporary injunctions necessary or proper to the complete exercise of such jurisdiction.

Effective October 1, 1990, the exclusive jurisdiction of the circuit court was changed. The Legislature, with the passage of Chapter 90-269, gave county courts jurisdiction of additional matters which formerly were solely within the jurisdiction of circuit courts. On that date, the minimal jurisdictional amount for cases brought in circuit court was increased to over $10,000, and after July 1, 1991, $15,000. Also since October 1, 1990, equity jurisdiction will no longer be the exclusive prerogative of circuit courts. For further discussion see "County Courts."

The executive officer of the circuit court and county court is the sheriff of the county where the court is operating.

Not always solemn, as this photograph of the Supreme Court shows. Left to right: Justices Leander J. Shaw, Parker Lee McDonald, James C. Adkins, Joseph A. Boyd, Jr., Ben E. Overton, Raymond Ehrlich and Rosemary Barkett. This photograph was taken during the 1986 term of the court.

Florida's first black justice of the State Supreme Court, Joseph W. Hatchett, takes the oath of office from Sid J. White, Clerk of the Court, on September 2, 1975. He has since left the Court to become a judge of the United States Court of Appeals (Eleventh Circuit). Mark Foley

County Courts

The Florida Constitution provides that there shall be a county court in each county and that there shall be one or more judges for each county. The jurisdiction of the court is prescribed by the Legislature by general law.

Their jurisdiction presently extends to civil cases involving not more than $15,000. The county court also has original jurisdiction in all misdemeanor cases not cognizable by the circuit courts and of all violations of municipal and county ordinances.

County courts have equity jurisdiction in certain limited matters including simple divorces, and jurisdiction in certain statutorily defined declaratory judgment actions within its constitutional jurisdictional amount.

County judges shall be committing magistrates and coroners except where otherwise provided by law.

County judges are elected by the electors of their county for a term of four years. They are subject to the same disciplinary process and to the jurisdiction of the constitutionally created Judicial Qualifications Commission as are the other justices and judges of Florida's judicial system. When a vacancy occurs it will be filled by appointment by the Governor from a list of three or more nominees submitted by the Judicial Nominating Commission.

Specialized Divisions of Courts

Specialized divisions of any court, except the Supreme Court, may be established. Article V gives the Legislature the power to create such division and the Legislature, in turn, has said that such divisions shall be established by the local rule of each circuit as approved by the Supreme Court. Such divisions could include, for example, probate, domestic relations, juvenile, civil and criminal divisions.

Number of Judges

Judges in all courts, except the Supreme Court, shall be created on the basis of need. Article V eliminates any arbitrary population limitation on the number of judges. It provides that if the Supreme Court finds that a need exists for increasing or decreasing the number of judges, it shall, prior to the next regular session, certify to the Legislature its findings and recommendations concerning such needs. The first certification of the Supreme Court under the new article was made in a historic session of the 1972 regular session in the first address by a Chief Justice of the state to a joint session of the Legislature and the Governor and Cabinet. The Legislature may by a majority vote accept in whole or in part the Supreme Court's certification and create additional judges or it may refuse to create any new judicial positions. The Legislature may go beyond the limits of the Supreme Court certification only by a two-thirds vote of the membership of both houses of the Legislature.

Qualifications and Requirements for Judges

All judges are required to devote full time to their judicial duties. Supreme Court judges and judges of the District Courts of Appeal must have been members of the Bar of Florida for ten years and circuit judges must have been members of the Bar of Florida for five years. County court judges must be members of the Bar of Florida unless otherwise provided by general law and be a resident of the county and state. Because of the fact that there are few lawyers in small counties, the Legislature provided that County Court judges in counties under 40,000 need not be lawyers, and even in counties over 40,000 population, non-lawyers who held elective judicial office before the new system was adopted may seek election as county judges. The mandatory retirement age for all justices and judges is seventy. All judges' salaries are paid by the state.

Non-Partisan Election of Judges

Article V provides that judges shall be elected by vote of the qualified electors within the territorial jurisdiction of their respective courts. As previously stated, after appointment by the Governor to a vacancy, the election of Supreme Court justices and District Court judges consists of having their name submitted to the voters for retention or rejection rather than in an election for which other aspirants may qualify. Party labels can no longer be used by candidates for judicial office and the non-partisan election law prohibits judicial candidates from engaging in partisan political activities.

Discipline, Retirement and Removal of Judges

Article V provides for a Judicial Qualifications Commission with power to recommend to the Supreme Court that any justice or judge be disciplined, removed or retired from office. The Supreme Court then acts on that recommendation. As provided in the Constitution, the Judicial Qualifications Commission is composed of two judges of District Courts of Appeal; two circuit judges; two county court judges; two members of The Florida Bar selected by the Board of Governors of The Florida Bar; and five laymen who are electors and who are appointed by the Governor. The judges of each of the courts select their representatives. The members serve staggered terms not to exceed six years as fixed by the Legislature. The Legislature retains the power of impeachment of judges down to the circuit court level and the Governor, his power of suspension and removal of all county court judges.

Judicial Nominating Commission and Vacancies

The Governor is required to fill vacancies in judicial office from nominations made by judicial nominating commissions. Article V provides that there shall be a separate judicial nominating commission for the Supreme Court; each District Court of Appeal and each judicial circuit for all trial courts within that circuit. The composition of such commissions is determined by the Legislature.

The Legislature has provided that each such commission shall be composed of three members of The Florida Bar selected by the Bar's Board of Governors; three electors appointed by the Governor; three laymen who are electors and who are selected by the other six members of the commission. The members serve staggered terms of four years.

Other Judicial Officers

The Supreme Court and each District Court of Appeal is authorized to select a clerk and a marshall. In each county there is elected by the qualified

Chief Justice B.K. Roberts delivers the "State of the Courts" address to the 1972 Legislature in joint session. Seated behind the Chief Justice, left to right, are House Speaker Richard Pettigrew, Governor Reubin O'D. Askew and Senate President Jerry Thomas. Florida State Archives

electors a clerk of the circuit court, who also serves as the clerk of the county court, unless otherwise provided by law.

The State Courts Administrator

To assist the chief justice and the court in the management of the judicial system there has been created the office of state courts administrator, operating under the direction of the chief justice and located in the Supreme Court Building in Tallahassee.

Other Officers of Court

The State Attorney is the prosecuting officer of all trial courts in the circuit in which he or she is elected (except that municipalities may use their own prosecutors to prosecute their ordinances). The State Attorney is elected for a four-year term and must devote full time to the duties. There shall be a Public Defender in each judicial circuit as well, who is elected for a four year term and has the duty of representing indigent persons accused of having committed a non-capital felony. (Legal assistance in cases in which the death penalty could be imposed is provided by the appointment of special counsel by the trial court.) The executive officer of the circuit court and county court is the sheriff of the county where the court is operating. The clerk of the circuit court shall be clerk of the county court unless otherwise provided by law. Under Article V, the duties of the clerk of the circuit court may be divided between a clerk of the court and a clerk of the county commission.

Extraordinary Writs

The Supreme Court also has power to issue writs of mandamus, quo warranto, and prohibition and *conflict* certiorari in a limited class of cases, as well as the writ of habeas corpus. These so-called extraordinary writs are of ancient origin and became a part of the jurisprudence of this state when we adopted the English common law and statutes then in effect on July 4, 1776. The purpose of each of these writs is briefly stated below.

The writ of prohibition is commonly used to prevent a tribunal possessing judicial or quasi-judicial powers from exercising jurisdiction over matters not within its cognizance (that is, which it has no authority to hear and determine) or exceeding its jurisdiction in matters of which it has cognizance. The writ of mandamus, on the other hand, is used to compel the performance of any and all official duties where the official charged by law with the performance of such duty refuses to or fails to perform the same. It proceeds in every case upon the assumption that the applicant for the writ has an immediate and complete legal right to the thing demanded, and that a corresponding duty of an imperative nature rests upon the person to whom the writ is sent. Prohibition and mandamus are, in the general sense, counterparts of each other, in that prohibition arrests proceedings, while mandamus compels performance.

The office of the common law writ of certiorari is to bring before the court for inspection the record of the proceedings of a junior tribunal in order that the superior court may determine from the face of the record whether the court under review has exceeded its jurisdiction, or has not proceeded according to the essential requirements of the law. A writ of certiorari differs from mandamus in that mandamus compels an unperformed duty; certiorari review a performed official act.

The ancient writ of quo warranto was a high prerogative writ of right issued on behalf of the Crown by which one was required to show by what right he exercised any office or franchise. Thus, in the case of public office, while mandamus may be used to compel the performance by public officers of ministerial or nondiscretionary duties, the writ of quo warranto is designed to try the right or title to the office and to oust the intruder.

One of the most important of the ancient common law writs is the writ of habeas corpus, the vital purpose of which is to obtain immediate relief from illegal confinement, to liberate those who may be imprisoned without sufficient cause, and to deliver them from unlawful custody. It is essentially a writ of inquiry, and is granted to test the right under which a person is detained. The writ may not be used to determine the guilt or innocence of a prisoner, however, but only to ascertain whether he is restrained of his liberty by due process of law.

The right of a person to secure their release from illegal restraint is zealously guarded by the Supreme Court of this state. No petition, no matter how poorly or ineptly drawn is turned aside without careful consideration; and a petition written in longhand on a scrap of paper receives the same close attention as one carefully prepared by an able attorney. In fact, a large portion of the petitions which the court receives are written in longhand by the prisoners themselves. An early example of such a case occurred in 1891, when a prisoner dropped a note written on a piece of wrapping paper out of the window of the county jail where he was confined. His "petition" was brought to the attention of this court and, ten days later, he was freed.

Industrial Relations Commission

The Industrial Relations Commission was initially organized from the old Industrial Commission in 1971 by then Governor Reubin Askew so as to provide a quasi-judicial review of compensation claims. This method continued until 1979 when the plan of review was repealed and appeal provided directly to the First District Court of Appeal. This continued until 1990 when a form of the Askew plan was reenacted by the legislature and then in extraordinary session, 1991, the reconstruction of the Askew plan as reenacted in 1990 was repealed leaving some uncertainty as to the review method. In March, 1991, legislation was introduced in the regular session of the Florida Legislature to review the appeal process from orders of the compensation claims judge.

> "Equal justice under law is the keystone
> in the arch of freedom."
> B.K. Roberts

The Supreme Court: L–R Charles T. Wells, Gerald Kogan, Ben F. Overton, Stephen H. Grimes, Leander J. Shaw, Jr, Major B. Harding, Harry Lee Anstead.

Robert M. Overton

The Supreme Court

The Supreme Court Building, Tallahassee 32399-1925
Chief Justice (June 30, 1996—Stephen H. Grimes)
(904) 488-8421
Clerk Sid J. White 488-0125
Marshal Wilson E. Barnes 488-8845
Librarian Joan D. Cannon 488-8919
State Courts Administrator Kenneth R. Palmer 922-5081

The Justices	Place of Residence when first appointed or elected	Date when service began	Present term expires
Ben F. Overton	St. Petersburg	March 27, 1974	January 5, 1999
Leander J. Shaw, Jr.	Tallahassee	January 10, 1983	January 7, 1997
Stephen Grimes	Bartow	January 30, 1987	January 2, 2001
Gerald Kogan	Miami	January 30, 1987	January 2, 2001
Major B. Harding	Jacksonville	January 28, 1991	January 5, 1999
Charles T. Wells	Orlando	June 9, 1994	January 7, 1997
Harry Lee Anstead	Palm Beach County	August 29, 1994	January 7, 1997

Legal basis: Constitutional. Article V, Constitution. *Created:* with statehood in 1845, but present powers derived from revision of Article V adopted by electorate in 1972. *Method of selection:* Vacancies filled by Governor from three nominees selected by nominating commission. Justices may qualify for retention at election limited to question: "Shall Justice _____ be retained in office?" *Qualifications:* A citizen of Florida and a member for 10 years of the Florida bar. *Term:* Six years. *Compensation:* $109,664 a year. *Duties:* To act as the final forum of justice for the state. *Method of financing:* Legislative appropriation from general revenue fund. *Selection of Chief Justice:* Generally, rotated by seniority for two-year term beginning on the second Tuesday in July of odd-numbered years.

Justices

[By Length of Service: Alphabetical Where Service Equal]

Ben F. Overton

Born December 15, 1926, Green Bay, Wisconsin. Florida, 1945. **Education** University of Florida, B.S, 1951, J.D., 1952, Pi Kappa Phi. Alpha Kappa Psi. Phi Alpha Delta. Basketball. Executive Council. President's Cabinet. **Married** Marilyn L. Smith of St. Petersburg. **Children** William Hunter, Robert Murray, and Catherine Louise. **Public service** City Attorney, City of St. Petersburg Beach, 1954–1957. Circuit Judge, Sixth Judicial Circuit, Pinellas County, 1964–1974, Chief Judge, 1968–1971. Appointed to the Supreme Court March 27, 1974, and elected November 1974. **Religious Affiliation** Episcopal, lay reader and vestryman. **Military service** United States Army, Judge Advocate General, Reserve Officer.

Overton

Leander J. "Lee" Shaw, Jr.

Born September 6, 1930, Salem, Virginia. Florida, 1957. **Education** West Virginia State College, B.A., 1952; Brooklyn Law School; Howard University, J.D., 1957; Alpha Phi Alpha. **Married** Vidya B. Lye. **Children** Leander J., III, Sherri Lee, Dione Renee, Dawn Marie, and Sean M. **Public service** Mayor's Police Advisory Committee, Jacksonville. Jacksonville JetPort Authority. Opportunities Industrialization Center, Inc., Jacksonville, Board Chairman. Jacksonville Community Council, Inc., Advisory Committee. Florida Bar Judicial Nominating Commission Committee. Duval County Assistant Public Defender and Assistant State Attorney. Industrial Relations Commission, Judge. First District Court of Appeal Judge. Supreme Court, January 10, 1983. **Religious Affiliation** Baptist. **Military service** United States Army Artillery, Korea. **Recreation** Fishing and boating.

Stephen H. Grimes

Born November 17, 1927, Peoria, Illinois. **Education** Florida Southern College 1946–1947. University of Florida 1947–1951, B.S.B.A., 1950. University of Florida 1953–1954, J.D., 1954. Editor-in-Chief, University of Florida Law Review. Alpha Tau Omega, President. Phi Delta Phi. Florida Blue Key. **Married** Mary Fay Fulqhum of Lakeland. **Children** Gay Diane Jacobs, Mary Jane Maddox, Sue Anne Grimes, and Sheri Lynn Grimes. **Judicial Service** Justice, Supreme Court, from January 30, 1987. Judge, Second District Court of Appeal, 1973–1987, Chief Judge, 1978–1980. Chairman, Florida Conference of District Court of Appeal Judges, 1978–1980. Judicial Qualifications Commission, 1982–1987, Vice Chairman, 1985–1987. Board of Trustees, Polk Community College, 1968–1970. Chairman, 1970. **Religious affiliation** Episcopal. **Military service** U.S. Navy, 1951–1953.

Gerald Kogan

Born May 23, 1933, Brooklyn, New York. Moved to Florida at age 14. **Education** University of Miami, B.B.A. and J.D., President Student Senate. Vice President Student Body. National Intercollegiate Debate Champion. Southern Law School Moot Court Champion. National Moot Court Finalist. **Military service** Active duty, November 1955–1957. **Married** Irene Volgan. **Children** (adult) Robert, Debra, Karen. **Professional career** Private practice, 1955–1960. Assistant State Attorney, Dade County 1960–1967. Private practice, specializing in criminal defense 1967–1980. Circuit Judge, Eleventh Circuit, Criminal Division 1980–1987. Appointed Supreme Court January 8, 1987.

Major B. Harding

Born October 13, 1935, Charlotte, North Carolina. **Education** Wake Forest University, B.S. 1957, LL.B 1959. U.S. Army Infantry School and U.S. Army Judge Advocate General School, 1960. Attended Juvenile Court Judges' College, 1969, and Trial Judges' College, 1971. Admitted North Carolina Bar 1959, and Florida Bar 1960. **Professional** Assistant County Solicitor, Duval County, 1962–1963. Private practice, 1964. Juvenile Court Judge. Appointed Judge of Circuit court, June, 1968. Appointed member of Matrimonial Law Commission and Gender Bias Study Commission, by Chief Justice Supreme Court. Served as First Dean of the New Judges College, held for newly elected and appointed judges at University of Florida Law School. Supreme Court, January 28, 1991. **Religious Afflliation** St. John's Presbyterian Church, Deacon and Elder, Lay preacher. **Family** Married Jane Lewis, December, 1958. Three adult children and three grandchildren. **Civic Affiliations** Board member for Daniel Memorial Home, a psychiatric treatment center for disturbed youth. Legal Aid Association. Past President Rotary Club of Riverside, Jacksonville.

Charles T. Wells

Born March 4, 1939 in Orlando. **Education** University of Florida B.A. 1961, University of Florida J.D. 1964. **Married** Linda Fischer, formerly an attorney partner with the law firm of Carlton, Fields, Ward, Emmanuel, Smith and Cutler, P.A. in its Orlando office. **Children** Charles Talley Wells, Jr.; Shelley Blythe Wells and Ashley Dawn Wells. **Public Service** United States Department of Justice, Washington D.C. 1969. Appointed to the Supreme Court June 1994. **Professional Career** Maguire, Voorhis and Wells, P.A., Orlando 1965–68, 1970–75; Wells, Gattis, Hallowes and Carpenter, P.A., Orlando 1976–1994. **Religious Affiliation** First United Methodist Church of Orlando. **Military Service** United States Army Reserves Ret.

Harry Lee Anstead

Born November 4, 1937, Jacksonville. **Education** Jacksonville University, University of Florida B.A. 1960. American University 1960–61, University of Florida J.D. 1963. University of Virginia L.L.M., 1981. **Married** Susann Fischer, a 1990 law school graduate and Legal Aid Society advocate. **Children** Christopher, James, Laura, Amy and Michael. **Public Service** Fourth District Court of Appeal 1976–1994. Supreme Court's Commission on the Structure of Florida Courts and Committee on Civil Jury Instructions. Appointed Supreme Court August 29, 1994. **Professional Career** Private practice, 1963–77. **Religious Affiliation** Holy Name of Jesus Catholic Church, West Palm Beach.

The Supreme Court and Its Justices

The Constitution written at St. Joseph in 1838, in anticipation of the statehood which came in 1845, provided for a Supreme Court. Its members, however, were the Circuit Court Judges elected by the Legislature. Thus, the Circuit Judges sat as a body to review the decisions of the individual members.

Beginning in 1851, the Supreme Court was established as an independent tribunal. Its Chief Justice and two Associate Justices were still selected by the Legislature. Two years later, however, the people were given the right to elect the members of the Supreme Court. This amendment to the 1838 Constitution fixed the term of the Justices at six years.

The three-judge court was retained in each of the Constitutions which Florida had during the period of the Civil War and its Reconstruction aftermath. The 1861 Constitution provided for the appointment of the Justices by the Governor with the advice and consent of the Senate. The 1865 Constitution carried forward this arrangement. The 1868 Constitution kept the provision for appointment and confirmation but changed tenure from six years to "life or during good behavior." The 1885 Constitution returned the six-year term.

Article V of the 1885 Constitution was revised in 1972. Two of its basic provisions relating to the Supreme Court were not changed. These provided for election of Justices by the people and for regular terms of six years. By subsequent amendment in 1976, the Constitution provided for initial appointment of all justices by the Governor from a list prepared by the Judicial Nominating Commission. Upon completion of this initial term, the name of a justice is submitted to the electorate with the question of whether the justice should be retained.

Initially, the 1885 Constitution provided for the election of three Justices. In 1902, an amendment temporarily increased the court's membership to six but allowed the Legislature, beginning with the session of 1905, to determine the number needed from three to six. In 1911, the Legislature reduced the number to five. In 1923, the Legislature put the number back to six. And, finally, the Constitution was amended in 1940 to fix the number at seven.

Court Commissioners—Commissioners served the Supreme Court during two periods of stress. Three commissioners were appointed by the Court in 1901 to serve until the qualification of the three additional Justices proposed in the amendment to the Constitution submitted by the 1901 Legislature. Again, in 1929, the Legislature helped the Court by allowing the temporary appointment of three commissioners. Serving from September 16, 1929, until November 8, 1932, these commissioners assisted the Justices in coping with the flood of litigation resulting from the great land boom of the 1920s.

Selection of Chief Justice—The 1885 Constitution provided originally for the Chief Justice to be selected by lot and serve as such during the remainder of his current term.

Choosing by Lot—A new law book or a Bible was used in determining the Chief Justice during the years when the choice was made by lot. When William H. Ellis joined the court in 1915, his father-in-law R. Fenwick Taylor was also a senior Justice. The Chief Justice then was selected by "cutting the Bible." Each Justice opened the Bible and taking the last digit on the odd-numbered page, the Justice with the highest number became the Chief Justice.

Justice Ellis once told of an experience with that system. "I was pleased when I cut a '7.' This was the high number. Taylor was the last one to cut. He took the Bible, opened it, and said, 'I have 9.' Then he shut the book quickly, before anyone could check it. I know he didn't have a 9!" "Why didn't you check it or make him cut again?" Justice Ellis was questioned by James C. Adkins, then the court's lone law clerk but afterwards the Dean of the court. Ellis replied: "I couldn't question the honesty of my father-in-law and the Dean of the court."

The Constitution was amended in 1926 to provide that the Justices were to select the Chief Justice for a term of two years. There have been exceptions, but basically the formula has been rotation by seniority.

As an incident to general revision of the appellate provisions of the judicial article in 1956, the Constitution also provided that if the Chief Justice is unable to act for any reason, the Justice longest in service and able to act shall perform the duties of the Chief Justice. The 1972 revision of the judicial article deleted these provisions, but the traditions remain today.

The Retention Elections—The Constitution was amended in 1974 to provide for retention elections for Justices of the Supreme Court and Judges of the District Court of Appeals. In these elections, the question on the ballot is: "Shall _____ of the _____ be retained in office?" The first retention election was in 1978 when certain judges of the district courts were up for review and in 1980 when six justices of the Supreme Court were on a retention ballot. With the instituting of the retention system by Constitutional amendment in 1976, the popular election of judges of the appellate courts ended.

Results of the 1986 Retention Election—The vote on retention of three justices in 1986 were: Rosemary Barkett, for retention 2,088,573, against 630,370; Parker Lee McDonald, for retention 2,033,830, against 629,407; Ben F. Overton, for retention 1,896,848, against 617,536.

The similarity of votes in 1986 against the three justices suggests the votes were cast against the judicial system rather than disapproval of the justices. If a majority of the voters ballot not to retain a judge, the Governor would make a new appointment.

Vacancies in Judgeships—The Governor appoints from three nominees of a commission to fill vacancies on the Supreme Court or District Courts. The appointment would be until the next general election occurring at least one year after the date of appointment. At that election, and thereafter for terms of six years, the name of the Governor's appointee would be submitted to the voters at a retention election. If the appointee failed of election, a vacancy would exist.

Justices of the Supreme Court and Period of Service

Douglas, Thomas 1846–1855
Baltzell, Thomas 1846–1859
Hawkins, George S. 1846–1853
Macrae, George W. 1847–1847
Lancaster, Joseph B. 1847–1853
Anderson, Walker .... January 1, 1851–May 24, 1853
Thompson, Leslie A. .... January 1, 1851–1853
Semmes, Albert G. .... January 1, 1851–1853
Wright, Benjamin D. .... May 24, 1853–1853
DuPont, Charles H. 1854–1868
Pearson, Bird M. 1856–1859
Forward, William A. 1860–1865
Walker, David Shelby 1860–1865
Maxwell, Augustus E. 1865–1866
 (2nd term) .... July 1, 1887–1890
Baker, James McNair 1865–1868
Douglas, Samuel J. 1866–1868
Randall, Edwin M. 1868–January 7, 1885
Hart, Ossian B. 1868–1873
Westcott, James D., Jr. 1868–January 7, 1885
Fraser, Franklin D. .... January 16, 1873–May 1874
Van Valkenburgh, Robert Bruce .... May 20, 1874–August 1, 1888
Raney, George P. .... January 13, 1885–May 31, 1894
McWhorter, George G. .... January 13, 1885–July 1, 1887
Mitchell, Henry Lawrence .... August 7, 1888–January 1, 1891
Taylor, R. Fenwick .... January 1, 1891–February 28, 1925
Mabry, Milton Harvey .... January 1891–1903
Liddon, Benjamin S. .... June 1, 1894–January 1897
Carter, Francis B. .... January 11, 1897–May 25, 1905
Shackleford, Thomas M. .... December 1, 1902–September 1, 1917
Cockrell, Robert S. .... December 1, 1902–January 2, 1917
Maxwell, Evelyn C. .... December 1, 1902–February 15, 1904
Hocker, William A. .... January 6, 1903–January 5, 1915
Whitfield, James B. .... February 15, 1904–January 4, 1943
Parkhill, Charles B. .... May 25, 1905–January 1912
Ellis, William H. .... January 5, 1915–1938
Browne, Jefferson B. .... January 2, 1917–May 20, 1925
West, Thomas F. .... September 1, 1917–December 3, 1925
Terrell, Glenn .... May 15, 1923–January 12, 1964
Brown, Armstead .... July 1, 1925–December 1, 1946
Strum, Louie W. .... March 2, 1925–March 5, 1931
Buford, Rivers .... December 4, 1925–April 3, 1948
Davis, Fred Henry .... March 9, 1931–June 20, 1937
Chapman, Roy H. .... June 23, 1937–August 9, 1952
Thomas, Elwyn .... November 1, 1938–January 7, 1969
Adams, Alto .... November 25, 1940–October 22, 1951
 (2nd term) .... November 13, 1967–August 1, 1968
Sebring, Harold L. .... January 5, 1943–September 15, 1955
Barns, Paul D. .... December 3, 1947–September 1, 1949
Hobson, T. Frank .... April 6, 1948–February 13, 1962
Roberts, B. K. .... September 1, 1949–December 1, 1976
Mathews, John E. .... October 23, 1951–April 30, 1955

Justices of the Supreme Court and Period of Service
(*continued*)

Drew, E. Harris .... August 18, 1952–January 5, 1971
Thornal, Campbell .... May 9, 1955–November 4, 1970
O'Connell, Stephen C. .... October 21, 1955–October 15, 1967
Caldwell, Millard F. .... February 14, 1962–January 7, 1969
Ervin, Richard W. .... January 17, 1964–January 6, 1975
Hopping, Wade L. .... August 1, 1968–January 7, 1969
Carlton, Vassar B. .... January 7, 1969–February 28, 1974
Adkins, James C. .... January 7, 1969–January 6, 1987
Boyd, Joseph A., Jr. .... January 7, 1969–January 6, 1987
McCain, David L. .... December 14, 1970–August 31, 1975
Dekle, Hal P. .... January 5, 1971–April 30, 1975
Overton, Ben F. .... March 27, 1974–
England, Arthur J., Jr. .... January 8, 1975–August 9, 1981
Sundberg, Alan C. .... June 2, 1975–September 15, 1982
Hatchett, Joseph W. .... September 2, 1975–July 18, 1979
Karl, Frederick B. .... January 4, 1977–April 5, 1978
Alderman, James E. .... April 11, 1978–August 31, 1985
McDonald, Parker Lee .... October 26, 1979–May 31, 1994
Ehrlich, Raymond .... December 3, 1981–January 7, 1991
Shaw, Leander J., Jr. .... January 10, 1983–
Barkett, Rosemary .... November 15, 1985–April 21, 1994
Grimes, Stephen H. .... January 30, 1987–
Kogan, Gerald .... January 30, 1987–
Harding, Major Best .... January 28, 1991–
Wells, Charles T. .... June 9, 1994–
Anstead, Harry Lee .... August 29, 1994–

District Courts of Appeal

Legal basis: Article V, Constitution. *Created:* 1957. *Method of selection:* Governor fills vacancies by appointment from three nominees selected by a judicial nominating commission. Judges may qualify for retention at election limited to question: "Shall Judge _____ be retained in office?" *Qualifications:* A citizen of Florida and a member for 10 years of the Florida bar. *Term:* Six years. *Compensation:* $104,181 a year. *Duties:* To serve as the final forum of justice in specified cases. *Selection of Chief Judge:* By a majority of the Judges of the Court.

First Appellate District
[1st, 2nd, 3rd, 4th, 8th, and 14th Judicial Circuits]

First District Court Building, Tallahassee 32399-1185
Martin Luther King Boulevard
(904) 488-8136

Second Appellate District
[6th, 10th, 12th, 13th, and 20th Judicial Circuits]

P.O. Box 327, Lakeland 33802
(813) 686-8171
6th Floor, 801 E. Twiggs Street, Tampa 33602
(813) 272-3430

Third Appellate District
[11th and 16th Judicial Circuits]

P.O. Box 650307, Miami 33165
(407) 554-2900

Fourth Appellate District
[15th, 17th, and 19th Judicial Circuits]

P.O. Box A, West Palm Beach 33402
(407) 686-1903

Fifth Appellate District
[5th, 7th, 9th, and 18th Judicial Circuits]

P.O. Drawer CA, 300 South Beach Street, Daytona Beach 32015
(904) 255-8600

Judicial Circuits

First: Escambia, Okaloosa, Santa Rosa and Walton counties.
Second: Franklin, Gadsden, Jefferson, Leon, Liberty and Wakulla counties.
Third: Columbia, Dixie, Hamilton, Lafayette, Madison, Suwannee and Taylor counties.
Fourth: Clay, Duval and Nassau counties.
Fifth: Citrus, Hernando, Lake, Marion and Sumter counties.
Sixth: Pasco and Pinellas counties.
Seventh: Flagler, Putnam, St. Johns and Volusia counties.
Eighth: Alachua, Baker, Bradford, Gilchrist, Levy and Union counties.
Ninth: Orange and Osceola counties.
Tenth: Hardee, Highlands and Polk counties.
Eleventh: Dade County.
Twelfth: DeSoto, Manatee and Sarasota counties.
Thirteenth: Hillsborough County.
Fourteenth: Bay, Calhoun, Gulf, Holmes, Jackson and Washington counties.
Fifteenth: Palm Beach County.
Sixteenth: Monroe County.
Seventeenth: Broward County.
Eighteenth: Brevard and Seminole counties.
Nineteenth: Indian River, Martin, Okeechobee and St. Lucie counties.
Twentieth: Charlotte, Collier, Glades, Hendry and Lee counties.

Circuit Judges

Legal basis: Article V, Constitution. *Created:* With statehood in 1845, but present powers derived from revision of Article V adopted by the electorate in 1972 which became effective January 1, 1973. *Method of selection:* By election in Circuit (although laws may specify county of residence within Circuits having more than one county) for terms commencing the following January. Vacancies filled by Governor by appointment from three nominees selected by nominating commission. *Qualifications:* A citizen of Florida and for five years a member of the Florida Bar. *Term:* Six years. (Judges retire at age 70 unless they were holding office when Constitution was amended in 1956 to provide for automatic retirement or if he attains 70th birthday after serving half of present term.) *Compensation:* $98,698. *Duties:* To serve as the State courts with the most general jurisdiction. (See detailed description in foregoing articles on the Judicial System.) *Number of Circuit Judges:* The Supreme Court shall establish by rule uniform criteria for determination of need for additional circuit judges. If the Supreme Court finds need for increasing or decreasing number, it will certify such need to the legislature which will consider and act upon the certificate at next regular session.

County Judges

Legal basis: Article V, Constitution. *Created:* With statehood but not specifically named. Present powers derived from revision of Article V ratified by electorate in 1972 to become effective January 1, 1973. *Method of selection:* By election in county. Governor fills vacancies by appointment from three nominees selected by a judicial nominating commission. *Qualifications:* An elector of the state and resident of the county. General law exempts county judges in counties of less than 40,000 population from requirement that county judges be members of The Florida Bar. *Term:* Four years. *Compensation:* $87,731. *Duties:* To exercise original jurisdiction in all misdemeanor cases not reserved to the circuit courts; all violations of municipal and county ordinances, and all actions at law in which the matter at controversy does not exceed the sum of $15,000, exclusive of interest and costs, except those within the exclusive jurisdiction of the circuit courts. Also, to serve as committing magistrates and, unless provided otherwise by law or rule of Supreme Court, as coroners. To have concurrent jurisdiction with circuit courts in landlord and tenant cases involving claims within jurisdictional limit. *Number of County Judges:* At least one in each county, plus additional as determined by the Supreme Court and the Legislature.

Judicial Qualifications Commission

Executive Director Mrs. Brooke Kennerly
Rm. 102, Historic Capitol, Tallahassee 32399-6000
(904) 488-1581

Legal basis: Article V, Section 12, Constitution of Florida, Adopted at the General Election held on November 7, 1974. *Method of selection:* Two Judges of the District Court of Appeal, two Circuit Judges, and two County Judges selected by the membership of the respective appointing groups. Two members of the Florida Bar selected by a majority of its Board of Governors. Five electors who reside in the State appointed by the Governor who have never held judicial office or been members of the Florida Bar. *Term:* Six years. *Duties:* To investigate and by concurrence of two-thirds of its members, to recommend to the Supreme Court the removal from office of any Justice or Judge whose conduct, during his term of office or otherwise occurring on or after November 1, 1966, demonstrates a present unfitness to hold office, or the reprimand of the Justice or Judge whose conduct, during his term of office or otherwise occurring on or after November 1, 1966, warrants such a reprimand. By concurrence of two-thirds of its members, the Commission may recommend to the Supreme Court that any Justice of the Supreme Court or Judge of the District Courts of Appeal, Circuit Courts, or County Courts, be reprimanded or removed from office, for willful or persistent failure to perform his duties or conduct unbecoming a member of the judiciary. By concurrence of two-thirds of its members, the Commission may recommend to the Supreme Court an involuntary retirement of any Justice or Judge for any permanent disability seriously interfering with the performance of his duties.

Justice Administrative Commission

Executive Director Fred T. Reeves
117 West College Ave., Tallahassee 32301
(904) 488-2415   Fax (904) 488-8944

Legal basis: Section 43.16, F.S. *Created:* 1965. Revised/reorganized 1985. *Method of selection:* Two State Attorneys appointed by the President of the Florida Prosecuting Attorneys Association, and two Public Defenders appointed by the President of the Conference of Public Defenders. *Term:* Two years. *Compensation:* None. *Executiue Director:* Employed by and serves at the pleasure of the Commission. *Purpose:* Maintain a central office to administratively serve the Judicial Qualifications Commission, the Capital Collateral Representative, the State Attorneys and Public Defenders; including process of payroll, consultation regarding personnel and automation, and preparation of budgets and accounting for all state expenditures. Acts in a liaison capacity between other state agencies and the legislature.

State Courts Administrator's Office

State Courts Administrator Kenneth R. Palmer
Supreme Court Building, Tallahassee 32399-1900
(904) 922-5081   Fax (904) 488-0156

Legal basis: Article V, Section 2, Florida Constitution; Rule 2.030(e), Florida Rules of Judicial Administration. *Created:* 1973. *Appointment:* The Supreme Court appoints a State Courts Administrator who serves at the pleasure of the Court and performs such duties as the Court directs. *Duties:* Supervises the administrative office of the Florida courts, and employs other personnel as deemed necessary by the Court to aid in the administration of the state courts system. Represents the state courts system before the Legislature and other bodies with respect to matters affecting the state courts system and functions relating to and serving the system. Supervises the preparations and submission to the Supreme Court, for review and approval, a tentative budget request for the state courts system, and appears before the Legislature in support of the final budget request.

Board of Bar Examiners

Executive Director Kathryn Ressel
1891 Elder Court, Tallahassee 32399-1750
(904) 487-1292

Legal basis: Article V, Section 15, Constitution. *Created:* 1955. (Replaced Statutory Board, abolished October 31, 1955, appointed by Governor.) *Method of selection:* Within discretion of Supreme Court. Court has usually appointed from list of names submitted by Board of Governors of The Florida Bar. *Term:* Five years. *Duties:* Through investigation and examination determine the moral and technical qualifications of applicants for admission to the practice of law, as specified in the Rules of the Supreme Court of Florida Relating to Admissions to The Bar.

Youngest Judge

David Elmer Ward, then of Fort Myers, was 20 years old when nominated and elected County Judge (combined with Judge of the County Court and Juvenile Judge) of Lee County in 1932. He defeated the incumbent and three other former judges. Ward attained the legal age of 21 before taking office.

The disabilities of non-age had been removed by the Circuit Court when he was 18 so he could take the examinations and be admitted to practice in Florida, Tennessee and Federal courts.

"Believe It or Not" Ripley, the widely syndicated New York columnist O. O. McIntyre, and Wide World Photos were among the sources crediting Ward with being the youngest judge in the world at that time.

Judge Ward's efforts to rehabilitate juveniles and other offenders resulted in what then were novel approaches, including parole and probation, Big Sisters and Big Brothers. At a convention of County Judges, it was stated there was no lawful authority for Judge Ward to use these measures so he decided to run for the State Senate from the four-county district of Lee, Monroe, Hendry and Collier counties and seek the passage of specific constitutional and statutory basis for what he had been doing.

When elected in 1938, he was said to have been the youngest Senator then. As Senator, he drew the Constitutional amendment authorizing parole and probation together with the accompanying statutory legislation. After his Senate service, he practiced law in Tampa.

Fathers and Sons as Judges

The T. Frank Hobsons, father and son, served concurrently as judges in the 1960s.

T. Frank Hobson, Sr., of St. Petersburg, was a Justice of the Supreme Court when T. Frank Hobson, Jr., also of St. Petersburg, was appointed Circuit Judge in December, 1960. The junior Hobson subsequently, in 1964, became a judge of the Second District Court of Appeal.

In 1961, the Hobsons sat together as Justice and Associate Justice of the Supreme Court. After the senior Hobson's retirement in 1962 and before his death in 1966, the father and son sat together as Judges of the Second District Court.

Thomas E. Kirkland and his son, Thomas R. Kirkland, served concurrently as judges in Orange County. Thomas E. Kirkland was appointed Circuit Judge of the Orange-Osceola Circuit (the 9th) on March 28, 1972. He had served as Orlando Municipal Judge from January 1, 1952, to January 1, 1967. Thomas R. Kirkland was elected County Judge for Orange County and commenced service in January, 1977. He had been Associate Orlando Municipal Judge from 1972 through 1976.

Judicial Authorship

Records indicate that Justice Rivers H. Buford, who served from December 4, 1925, until March 1, 1948, wrote more opinions than any other judge—2,657 under his name and perhaps 300 or 400 more in the anonymity of *per curiam* or "by the court." Lightest impress was that of Judge Benjamin D. Wright, who wrote only three opinions during his five months of service in 1853—the shortest tenure of any Justice. The Justice longest in tenure was Justice Glenn Terrell, who served from May 15, 1923, to his death on January 12, 1964. Justice Terrell wrote some 2,500 opinions.

The First Woman Justice

Judge Rhea Grossman, of Miami, was the first woman to sit on the Supreme Court. In November 1972 she sat in for Justice James C. Adkins who was working on Judicial Reform.

Judge Rosemary Barkett, of West Palm Beach, became the first woman Supreme Court Justice when she was appointed by Governor Bob Graham, on October 14, 1985, to succeed Justice James E. Alderman.

Miami Judge Rhea Grossman, first woman to sit on the Florida Supreme Court, replaced Justice James C. Adkins, who was working on Judicial reform, November 1972
L–R: Justices B.K. Roberts, Vassar Carlton, David McCain and Judge Grossman
Florida State Archives

Husband and Wife as Judges

The first Florida husband and wife to serve concurrently as judges were Circuit Judge Henry F. Atkinson and Juvenile Judge Edith M. Atkinson.

Edith M. Atkinson received an LL.B. degree from John B. Stetson Law School at DeLand in 1922, and thereafter practiced law in Miami. The first woman lawyer there to seek political office, she was nominated Judge of the Juvenile Court for Dade County and took office in January, 1925.

Henry F. Atkinson was Judge of the Circuit Court for the Eleventh Judicial Circuit (Dade and Monroe Counties) at the time of election of his wife. In 1929, both stood for renomination, each with opposition in that primary. Judge Edith Atkinson received the highest number of votes of any candidate on the ballot. Both Atkinsons were renominated and reappointed by the Governor.

First Black Judge

When Lawson E. Thomas, a lawyer, was appointed judge of Miami's new Police Court in May, 1950, he was described as the first black to serve as a judge "in the South since reconstruction days." The court was created to serve a black area. Fifty-seven persons faced Judge Thomas during his first session.

First Black Circuit Judge

Dade County Judge Melvia Green was promoted to the Circuit Court by Governor Martinez on September 15, 1989, the first black woman to be named to a Circuit bench in Florida. A Miami native, Green was Dade's only black woman judge when appointed to a county judgeship in 1987. She was a prosecutor in the U.S. Attorney's office at Miami for three years.

First Cuban Exile Judge

Mario P. Goderich, an exile from his native Cuba who began life in the United States as a Miami Beach hotel employee, was appointed Circuit Judge by Governor Reubin O'D. Askew on December 12, 1978. Goderich was the first Cuban political exile to achieve a place on the Dade Circuit bench. He worked for the hotel because his law degree from the University of Havana did not qualify him to practice in Florida after he came here in 1961. In 1963, he enrolled in the University of Miami Law School and in 1966 earned a *Juris Doctor* degree. Lacking American citizenship, he still could not practice until 1969, when he became a citizen. Governor Askew previously had appointed him as a Workmen's Compensation Deputy Commissioner.

First Hispanic Woman Claims Jurist

Margarita Esquiroz, a 17-year-old refugee, arrived in Miami from Havana in April 1962. She worked as a legal and medical secretary and student until 1974 when she received her *Juris Doctor* degree from the University of Miami. On June 4, 1979, she was appointed by Governor Bob Graham as an Industrial Claims Deputy Commissioner, the first female Hispanic jurist. She was promoted to the Circuit bench in February, 1984.

First Black Woman Judge

The first black woman to hold a judgeship in Florida, so far as could be ascertained, was Leah Aleice Simms, named County Judge of Dade County by Governor Bob Graham on December 17, 1981. Judge Simms had been a student at Howard University in Washington, D.C., at the law school of Willamette University of Salem, Oregon, and served in Detroit with the U.S. Department of Justice organized crime strike force. In 1986 Judge Simms unsuccessfully sought election as Circuit Judge.

First Woman Circuit Judge

Mrs. Rhea Pincus Grossman was appointed a judge of the Eleventh Circuit (Dade County) by Governor Claude R. Kirk, Jr., on December 29, 1970. Inquiries by the Florida Bar and others indicate Mrs. Grossman was the first woman to become a Circuit Judge in Florida. She was 29 years old at the time of appointment.

Then the wife of Dr. Leo Grossman, a Miami Beach physician, Mrs. Grossman had served for a year as a State Industrial Claims Deputy Commissioner when Governor Kirk promoted her to a Circuit judgeship created by Dade's population growth.

A native Miamian, Mrs. Grossman had attended the University of Miami and graduated in 1964 from its law school. She was in private practice for three years prior to the industrial claims judgeship.

First Woman County Judge

Mrs. Bessie Bellinger, of Pensacola, was described as the first woman in Florida ever to serve as a county judge after she was appointed by Governor Cary A. Hardee in February, 1922. Mrs. Bellinger was appointed to complete the term of her late husband, Judge Henry Bellinger, for Escambia County.

First Woman Hispanic Circuit Judge

Maria Marinello Korvick, a 35-year-old Cuban, stepped up from County Judge to Circuit Judge in Miami on August 1, 1981, the first Hispanic woman to become a Circuit Judge.

Judge Korvick had a vivid remembrance of the lawlessness that destined her to become a judge. When she was a 21-year-old student in Miami, she received news that her father had been executed, without trial, by a Castro firing squad.

"His death," she said, "made me think of the value of life and the importance of receiving due process."

She had earned her education, from high school through law college, by working days and attending classes at night.

Judge Korvick, then 33, became a County Judge for Dade County on December 12, 1979, by appointment of Governor Bob Graham. She had come to the United States from Cuba as a refugee in 1961, and prior to being appointed County Judge, had served as an Assistant State Attorney.

First Woman Appellate Judge

Mrs. Anne Cawthon Booth, then 43, was appointed Judge of the First District Court of Appeal (Tallahassee) by Governor Reubin O'D. Askew on

January 1, 1978. She was the first woman in Florida to become the judge of an appellate court. The investiture ceremony was conducted January 3.

A native of Gainesville, Mrs. Booth is a granddaughter of the late W.S. Cawthon, State Superintendent of Public Instruction (Commissioner of Education), 1922–37, and a daughter of Rainey Cawthon, Tallahassee businessman and former member of the Florida House of Representatives.

Mrs. Booth became the second working judge in her family, for her uncle, Victor M. Cawthon, now is a retired Circuit Judge at Tallahassee. Another uncle, the late Stanmore Cawthon, was a political editor for the *St. Petersburg Times* and subsequently speech writer for four Florida governors.

First Woman State Attorney

Miss Janet Reno, then 39, became Florida's first woman State Attorney by appointment of Governor Reubin O'D. Askew on January 4, 1978, upon the resignation of Richard Gerstein as State Attorney for the Eleventh Judicial Circuit (Miami). Her appointment became effective January 20.

Miss Reno served as Administrative Assistant to Gerstein from 1972 to 1976 before becoming a trial partner in a Miami law firm. As Administrative Assistant, she supervised the work of 80 prosecutors, served as legal counsel to the Dade County grand jury, and conducted special investigations. In 1993 Miss Reno was appointed Attorney General of the United States by President Clinton and confirmed by the Senate.

A native of Miami, she received her law degree from Harvard Law School.

The working space of the Supreme Court was doubled in 1990. Auxiliary agencies, some formerly outside, were brought into the building. Offices of the Justices were enlarged, and the offices of the two aides for each Justice were brought into adjoining quarters.

Local Government
John Wesley White

Local governmental services in Florida are provided through either a county, a municipality, or a special district. There are presently 67 counties in Florida of which eleven are chartered, approximately 396 municipalities, and well over 1,000 special districts.

Traditionally, counties have been administrative subdivisions of the state, created by the state to perform essentially state-related functions on a decentralized basis. Cities, on the other hand, are created to provide a variety of local services which the citizens of the municipality desire. Likewise, special districts have been formed to provide usually just single functions, with the costs incurred being paid only by those residing within the district. Special districts may fall entirely within one county or may embrace all or parts of several counties.

These traditional distinctions have become blurred as Florida has become more urbanized, principally because counties have taken on more of the local service functions while surrendering a number of the state functions back to state government. As counties gained authority to provide services, the need for special districts has been somewhat relieved, although their numbers continue to increase. Undoubtedly, there would be far more special districts today had counties not assumed greater responsibility for local services.

The history of local governments in Florida predates possession of the Florida territory by the United States. In an ordinance signed July 21, 1821, four days after having received possession of Florida from Spain, Provisional Governor Andrew Jackson specifically recognized the cities of Pensacola and St. Augustine as existing government entities. The same ordinance also established two counties—Escambia and St. Johns.

Municipal Government

The other form of general purpose local government—municipal—is authorized by Section 2 of Article VIII of the State Constitution, which provides, in part, that "Municipalities may be established or abolished and their charters amended pursuant to general or special law." In fact, most municipalities exist as a result of a charter having been granted by a special act of the Legislature, although a lesser number exist by virtue of procedures previously contained in general laws, whereby a group of citizens could incorporate a municipality locally without specific legislative authorization.

Note: This is an abridgement of an article in *The Florida Handbook 1979–1980*.
John Wesley White, County Administrator of Sarasota County, formerly was Staff Director for the Committee on Community Affairs of the Florida House of Representatives.

Floridians in Federal Office

The Federal Court System

The Constitution provides for the establishment of a Supreme Court of the United States and leaves to the Congress the establishment of inferior courts. The Congress has divided the nation into 12 Judicial Circuits, each embracing specified contiguous States. The Eleventh Circuit, created in 1980, embraces Florida, Georgia and Alabama.

The United States Court of Appeals for the Eleventh Circuit has its headquarters and the office of its Clerk in Atlanta.

Florida is divided into three federal court Districts; they are designated as the Northern, Middle and Southern Districts of Florida, respectively. The Northern District has four judges, the Middle District, fourteen, and the Southern District, twenty.

First Woman Admitted by U.S. Supreme Court

It is believed that Herberta Leonardy of Coral Gables was the first Florida woman admitted to practice before the Supreme Court of the United States. Mrs. Leonardy was admitted on April 17, 1930.

First Woman Federal Judge

State Circuit Judge Susan Black of Jacksonville was appointed by President Carter and confirmed by the Senate in 1979 as the first woman to serve as a U.S. District Judge in Florida. Thirty-five years old at the time of appointment, Judge Black was a native of Valdosta, Georgia. She had received her undergraduate degree from Florida State University and her law degree from the University of Florida. She had served as County Court judge and for six years as a Circuit judge.

Judge Black was not, however, the first Florida woman appointed to a Federal judgeship. Pinellas County Circuit Judge Elizabeth A. Kovachevich was appointed by President Gerald R. Ford in 1976 but, lacking the support of Florida's two U.S. Senators, she never was confirmed by the Senate. Judge Kovachevich had a second chance with the election of President Ronald Reagan. She was again appointed in March, 1982, and was confirmed by the Senate.

First Black District Judge

Alcee L. Hastings of Fort Lauderdale, at 43, was appointed by President Carter, upon the recommendation of U.S. Senators Lawton M. Chiles and Richard (Dick) Stone, a Federal District Judge on November 14, 1979. He was

Floridians in Federal Office / 229

This famous equestrian statue of Andrew Jackson in Lafayette Park across from the White House in Washington was cast from bronze cannon captured at Pensacola during Jackson's last campaign against the Spanish in 1818. The statue is remarkable for its perfect balance, with the center of gravity based in the charger's hindfeet. The statue was the first by Clark Mills. It was erected by the Federal government at a cost of $28,500 plus contribution of $12,000 from the Jackson Democratic Association of Washington, D.C.

"Florida House" serves as a place where Floridians may be at home in Washington. Individuals and groups are offered information about the District of Columbia, a place of rest for tourists, and conference rooms for business visitors. (No sleeping accommodations.) "Florida House" was the idea of U.S. Senator and Mrs. Lawton Chiles, and is administered on a nonpartisan basis by a board of trustees. Situated at 200 East Capitol Street, "Florida House" is a block from the Capitol. This view, from a lounge area, shows the Capitol on the left and the United States Supreme Court building to the right. "Florida House" is a three-story townhouse built in 1887.

This statue honoring Florida's Mary McLeod Bethune stands in Washington's Lincoln Park. For more about Mrs. Bethune, see the chapter on "Names to Remember." The Washington Post Guide describes this as the "only one happy statue in the city." It shows Mrs. Bethune raising two children from ignorance and "the three of them seem to be having a pretty good time of it."

National Park Service

230 / Floridians in Federal Office

the first black to serve as a Federal District Court Judge, in Florida. He was impeached, convicted by the Senate, and removed on August 3, 1988. He was restored to office in 1992 by a federal district judge voiding the removal, subsequently he was elected to Congress.

Judge Hastings had been appointed a Circuit Court Judge by Governor Reubin O'D. Askew on May 2, 1977. He was not the first black to serve in that capacity. Judge Hastings had been an unsuccessful candidate for the Democratic nomination for the United States Senate in 1974 and for the Public Service Commission in 1974. [See: Impeachments in this chapter.]

Presidents in Florida

Florida was a second home to President John F. Kennedy. He long had enjoyed the sun, sand and surf of Palm Beach. Although Florida denied him its electoral votes in 1960, some of the big decisions of the New Frontier were made at Palm Beach during the President-elect's conferences there. In November, 1963, President Kennedy flew from Florida to Texas and assassination at Dallas.

Richard M. Nixon was a Florida landowner and frequent visitor before, as chief executive, he established a winter White House at Key Biscayne. During the off-year campaign of 1970, President Nixon touched down for a political address at Tallahassee's airport on October 28.

Mr. Nixon was one of four Presidents to make formal appearances at the capital, Presidents William McKinley, Jimmy Carter and Bill Clinton being the others, although President Dwight D. Eisenhower used the Tallahassee airport at least once during a trip to the nearby Georgia hunting plantation of his Secretary of the Treasury George M. Humphrey.

General Andrew Jackson went on to the Presidency after having accepted the sovereignty of Florida for the United States from Spain in 1821. And General Zachary Taylor, afterwards President, won a Pyrrhic victory

President-elect Franklin D. Roosevelt rides with Governor Dave Sholtz in a Jacksonville parade in 1933.
Florida TImes-Union from Florida State Archives

President Harry Truman's "Little White House" at Key West in 1949. Built in 1890 as the commandant's residence at the Navy base, Quarters A overlooked the Gulf of Mexico and was situated among palms, banyan, avocado and mango trees.
Florida State Archives

over Seminoles under Billy Bowlegs in the vicinity of the present city of Okeechobee on Christmas Day of 1837.

President Harry S. Truman maintained his "Little White House" on the grounds of the Naval base at Key West. He also dedicated the Everglades National Park to the public's use in 1947.

Other Presidents who knew something of Florida at first hand were U. S. Grant, Chester A. Arthur, Grover Cleveland, Theodore Roosevelt, William Howard Taft, Warren G. Harding, Calvin Coolidge, Herbert Hoover, Franklin D. Roosevelt, and Lyndon B. Johnson. President Eisenhower spoke at Jacksonville and Miami during the 1952 campaign which shook Florida loose from the Solid South of the Democratic party for a second time since Reconstruction, Mr. Hoover having also accomplished this in 1928. Mr. Eisenhower returned to Florida as President in 1957, boarding the carrier Saratoga at Jacksonville for a demonstration cruise.

A torchlight procession greeted former President Ulysses S. Grant at Key West in January, 1880.
Harper's Weekly from Florida State Archives

Former President Grant turned the first spadeful of dirt, in 1880, for the Sanford-Orlando railroad. President Arthur, here in 1883 for an inspection of the Disston company's drainage system in South Florida, spiced newspaper copy by presenting a cigar to a Seminole subchief, Tom Tigertail. President Cleveland was another who visited Florida in the 1880s, relaxing at Magnolia Springs, 24 miles south of Jacksonville. President McKinley's special train traveled from Thomasville, Ga. to Tallahassee, by way of Monticello, on

Former President Theodore Roosevelt visited Punta Gorda for a week in March, 1917, for the purpose of harpooning devilfish. This photograph shows how successful he was with one of the captures measuring 12 feet across. Roosevelt, on the right, was accompanied by a Virginia friend, Russell J. Coles. Not all their visit was spent fishing, for one day was given to inspecting the bird rookeries in the vicinity of Matalacha.
Vernon Peeples, Punta Gorda and the Charlotte Harbor Area.

President William H. Taft (center) visited Key West in December 1912, while traveling to inspect the Panama Canal. On Taft's left is Mayor J. N. Fogarty of Key West.
Wright Langley

March 24, 1899. Cannon, whistles and a cheering populace greeted him at the Capitol.

Theodore Roosevelt led his Rough Riders aboard ship at Tampa in 1898 during the Spanish-American War to gallop another league along the glory road to the White House in 1901. When Governor William D. Bloxham learned the train with Colonel Roosevelt would stop for a few hours in Tallahassee, he appointed a committee to invite the Colonel to meet with members of the Cabinet and Supreme Court and with other dignitaries of Tallahassee at a reception in the Governor's office. When champagne was passed to Colonel Roosevelt, he not only refused to take any but criticized the Governor for having champagne in the Capitol. A hush fell over the gathering, which soon dispersed.

President Taft boarded a battleship at Key West in 1911 for a voyage to Panama. President Harding liked Florida's golf courses. President Coolidge dedicated the Bok Tower in 1929. President Hoover was lured again and again by Florida fishing. And his personal energies to prevent a repetition of the deadly flood caused by a hurricane in 1927 are remembered in the Hoover Dike which retains Lake Okeechobee now.

President Jimmy Carter spent the night of October 9, 1980, as the guest of Governor Bob Graham at the Mansion. The President is seen here in the kitchen. Lois Griffin

President Franklin Roosevelt based at Miami for a number of forays into semi-tropical waters. It was in that city's Bayfront park that an assassin sought his life, as President-elect, and fatally felled the Mayor of Chicago, Anton Cermak. FDR also dedicated the Overseas Highway.

Jimmy Carter was the first President in this century to visit the Capitol. Arriving in Tallahassee in the evening of October 9, 1980, he spent the night at the Mansion. The next morning, he came to the Chamber of the House of Representatives and, in the presence of Governor Bob Graham, U.S. Senator Lawton M. Chiles, Jr., and other political dignitaries, signed into law the Congressional Act appropriating $100,000,000 for refugee relief. The President occupied the guest bedroom at the Mansion. Shortly after daylight he exercised by running the track of Leon High School. From Tallahassee, Air Force One winged him along the campaign trail which ended with his defeat for reelection on November 4, 1980.

President George Bush visited Tallahassee for four hours on September 6, 1990, to lend a hand in the unsuccessful reelection campaign of Congressman Bill Grant, who had earned Republican gratitude by switching parties after having been elected in 1986 as a Democrat. Nevertheless, Grant was defeated. The President addressed two groups, an out-door assembly and a dinner. Admission to each was by payment for the Grant fund.

President Clinton, who had twice visited Tallahassee as a candidate in

1992, was greeted by 4,000 flag-waving supporters on March 29, 1995. After an overnight stay, at the Governor's mansion with Governor and Mrs. Chiles, the President made Florida history when he spoke to a joint session of the legislature.

Impeachments, Federal

Of the 14 impeachments voted by the U.S. House of Representatives during this country's existence, three affected Federal offices in Florida.

The first Florida impeachment was of Charles Swayne of Pensacola, Judge of the U.S. Court for the Northern District of Florida. Swayne, who had moved to Florida from Philadelphia in 1885, was appointed Judge in 1899. In 1903, the House of Representatives impeached Judge Swayne for padding expense accounts, using railroad property in receivership for personal benefit, and misusing contempt power. The Senate acquitted him on 12 articles by votes of fewer than the two-thirds required for conviction.

The next Florida impeachment was of Halsted L. Ritter of Miami, Judge of the U.S. Court for the Southern District of Florida. Ritter, who had moved to Florida from Colorado shortly before his appointment to the bench, was impeached on March 2, 1936. He was accused of a variety of judicial improprieties. He went to trial before the Senate on seven articles. He was acquitted on six but was convicted by a vote of 56 guilty (the precise number necessary) to 28 of the seventh article, a catch-all charging Ritter with bringing the court into disrepute.

After brief but solemn debate, the U. S. House of Representatives voted 413–3 on August 3, 1988, to impeach U.S. District Judge Alcee Hastings of Fort Lauderdale on charges ranging from conspiracy to solicit a $150,000 bribe to perjury. Hastings, a charismatic black political figure in South Florida for more than 20 years, had been acquitted in criminal court on charges which later became the basis of the impeachment. The proceedings then went to the Senate which convicted Hastings. Shortly thereafter he was an unsuccessful candidate for Secretary of State. Hastings had been nominated in 1979 to the court by President Jimmy Carter.

In 1992 a Federal court voided Hastings' conviction. In the election that followed, Hastings was elected to the United States Congress facing as colleagues some of the Congressmen who voted to impeach him.

Floridians as Cabinet Under Secretaries

At least four Floridians have served as Under Secretaries in Cabinet Departments of the Federal Government.

Francis P. Whitehair of Deland was Under Secretary of the Navy under President Harry S. Truman in 1951–53 and for a period of about 10 days under President Dwight D. Eisenhower. Previously, Whitehair had been the first General Counsel in the U.S. Office of Economic Stabilization.

LeRoy Collins of Tallahassee was Under Secretary of Commerce under President Lyndon B. Johnson from July 7, 1965, to October 1, 1966. Collins previously had served as first Director of the U.S. Community Relations Service under the Civil Rights Act of 1964. (See: Collins biography.)

234 / Floridians in Federal Office

Jerry Thomas of Jupiter Island was appointed Under Secretary of the Treasury under President Gerald R. Ford in March, 1976. J. H. Williams of Ocala was appointed Deputy Secretary of Agriculture by President Jimmy Carter on January 15, 1979.

Interestingly, Whitehair, Collins, Thomas, and Williams had been candidates for Governor of Florida prior to their Federal service. Whitehair ran unsuccessfully in 1940 and Thomas unsuccessfully in 1974. Collins was twice elected Governor, in 1954 and 1956. Williams lost in the Democratic first primary of 1978.

Floridians in Cabinet

Florida had its first member of the Cabinet of a President of the United States with the appointment of Alan S. Boyd by President Lyndon B. Johnson as first Secretary of Transportation on January 16, 1967. Boyd served until the Johnson administration ended on January 20, 1969.

Boyd was born in Jacksonville on July 20, 1922, to a Macclenny family. He had attended the University of Florida and received a law degree from the University of Virginia. He was in the European theater with the Army Air Corps during World War II, and returned to duty with the Air Force in 1951–52. He earned the Air Medal, with three Oak Leaf clusters, and two Presidential Unit citations.

As a lawyer in Miami, he entered public service as general counsel for the Florida Turnpike Authority and subsequently was appointed a member of the Florida Railroad and Public Utilities Commission by Governor LeRoy Collins. Boyd later was elected to the Commission and served as its Chairman. He resigned to accept appointment to the U.S. Civil Aeronautics Board by President Eisenhower. He later was appointed Under Secretary of Commerce for Transportation by President Johnson, and stepped up to Secretary of Transportation when the cabinet post was created.

Former Governor Reubin O'D. Askew served in the Cabinet of President Carter as Trade Representative, with the rank of Ambassador Extraordinary and Plenipotentiary from October 1, 1979, until the end of the Carter administration. Robert H. Spiro, Jr., of Jacksonville served, by appointment of President Carter, as Under Secretary of the Army in 1979–1980.

President Bill Clinton drafted two Floridians for his cabinet in 1993. (Miss) Janet Reno as Attorney General and (Mrs.) Carol M.

Ms. Reno was appointed Attorney General by President Clinton on March 12, 1993. From 1978 to the time of her appointment, Ms. Reno served as the State Attorney in Miami, Florida. She was initially appointed to that position by the Governor of Florida and was subsequently elected to that office five times.

Browner as Administrator of the Environment Protection Agency. Janet Reno a career prosecutor, was appointed State Attorney at Miami by Governor Reubin O'D. Askew in 1978 and developed a sterling reputation for integrity in a criminal justice system. Carol Browner stepped into one of the Federal Government's most important posts for setting environmental policy.

Floridian in Confederate Cabinet

Stephen R. Mallory of Pensacola withdrew as a United States Senator from Florida when the state seceded from the Union in January, 1861. Mallory then became Secretary of the Navy in the Cabinet of President Jefferson Davis of the Confederate States.

Territorial Representation

Prior to the admission of Florida as a State on March 3, 1845, the last day of the 29th Congress, the Territory was represented in Congress by a Delegate. David Levy Yulee was the last Delegate, having served in the 27th, 28th and 29th Congresses.

The first Delegate was Joseph M. Hernandez of St. Augustine, who was seated on January 3, 1823, Hernandez was succeeded on March 4, 1823, by Richard K. Call, then of Pensacola and afterwards Territorial Governor.

Florida's First in Congress

The first United States Senators from Florida were David Levy Yulee of St. Augustine and James D. Westcott, Jr., of Tallahassee. Yulee and Westcott took their seats at Washington on December 1, 1845. Yulee won, by lot, the long term, running to March 3, 1851, while Westcott's term expired on March 3, 1849.

Yulee presented credentials as "David Levy," but on January 12, 1846, in conformity with an act of the Florida Legislature, the Senate ordered the surname "Yulee" added to his name in the official records. "Yulee" was the family name in Gibraltar. (*See* Levy County.)

U.S. Senator David Levy Yulee   National Archives

The first Congressman from Florida was Edward C. Cabell of Tallahassee, whose election was successfully contested by William H. Brockenbrough, also of Tallahassee, who took his seat in the House of Representatives on January 24, 1846.

Civil War and Reconstruction

With the secession of Florida from the Union, U.S. Senators Stephen R. Mallory of Pensacola and David Levy Yulee, then a resident of Homosassa, and Representative George S. Hawkins of Pensacola withdrew from Congress on January 21, 1861.

The Last String Tie

A black string tie was for many years the favorite of rural members of the United States House of Representatives. William "Fishbait" Miller, longtime doorkeeper for the House, wrote in 1977 that Congressional observers "seemed to agree that the last man to hang on to the politician's string tie was Robert Alexis Green of Bradford County, Florida, who came to the Hill in 1925 and served until 1944." Better known in Florida as "Lex", the Starke Congressman left Washington to run for Governor in 1944, finishing second in the Democratic runoff primary to a former colleague, Millard F. Caldwell.

Florida's Black Congressman

Josiah T. Walls, a black born of free parents in Winchester, Virginia, has the distinction of having been three times elected to the U.S. Congress from Florida and twice unseated in the election turbulence of Reconstruction. He also served in both the Confederate and Union armies: in the Confederate as an impressed servant with an artillery battery and in the Union as first a private and ultimately at Jacksonville as a sergeant major and instructor of artillery. He was mustered out in Florida and settled in Alachua county as a farmer.

He was elected to the Florida House of Representatives in 1868 and to the Senate in 1869. Joe M. Richardson, in *The Negro in the Reconstruction of Florida 1865–1877*, wrote that "by 1870 Walls was known and respected throughout the state." Walls first was elected to Congress in 1870 and served from March 4, 1871, to January 29, 1873, before being unseated by his white opponent in an election contest. He was reelected and served throughout the next Congress. The third Congress saw Walls presenting Florida's election credentials and serving from March 4, 1875 to April 19, 1876, before he was unseated by another white opponent.

Josiah Thomas Walls   Florida State Archives

After the last unseating Walls returned to Alachua county and, although he was a member of a Gainesville law firm, he resumed farming. He was ruined financially by a freeze which killed his orange trees. He was placed in charge of the farm at Florida Agricultural College at Tallahassee and died there May 5, 1905. He had, as a Congressman, introduced a bill to grant 1,000,000 acres of public lands to the trustees of the college and prevailed to the extent of 90,000 acres.

(See: Richardson's *The Negro in the Reconstruction of Florida 1865–1877*.)

Attendance Record

Representative Charles E. Bennett, served 44 years in the U.S. House of Representatives—longer than any other Floridian in history. Before his retirement in 1992, he set records by never missing a legislative vote in more than 41 years, and by casting more than 18,000 votes on proposed legislation—more than any other congressman in history. Bennett wrote and passed legislation designed to conserve the environment, assist the handicapped, and improve education. He authored the Code of Ethics for Government Service and twice served as chairman of the House Ethics Committee.

Claude Pepper's Service

Claude D. Pepper served in both houses of Congress but in reverse of the usual order. He was a U.S. Senator for 14 years from 1936 until his defeat in 1950, then the second longest term to Thomas Hart Benton's 30 years service. His 26 years of service in the U.S. House of Representatives after service in the U.S. Senate, 1963–1989, is a record. Earlier, in 1929, he served one term in the Florida House from Taylor county. It was there that he displayed his first concern for the aging. He introduced a bill to permit people 65 and older to fish without a licence. During his service in Congress, from a district encompassing part of Dade County, he earned a national reputation as the advocate of the elderly and the ailing.

Replicas of Claude Pepper's offices as United States Senator and Representative have been created at Florida State University in Tallahassee as centerpieces of the Mildred and Claude Pepper Library. The Library is a collection of Pepper's papers and memorabilia for use by graduate students. Florida State University

Floridians in Congress since 1821

Territory of Florida[1]

Seventeenth Congress—March 4, 1821, to March 3, 1823
  Delegate: Joseph M. Hernandez,[2] St. Augustine

---

[1]Formed March 30, 1822, from lands ceded by Spain to the United States by treaty of Washington of February 22, 1819, and theretofore known as "East and West Florida," and granted a Delegate in Congress.
[2]Took his seat January 3, 1823.

238 / Floridians in Federal Office

This photograph was inscribed and sent to George Smathers after his 1950 defeat of Claude Pepper for the United States Senate.
P.K. Yonge Library of Florida History

Eighteenth Congress—March 4, 1823, to March 3, 1825
  Delegate: Richard K. Call, Pensacola
Nineteenth Congress—March 4, 1825, to March 3, 1827
  Delegate: Joseph M. White, Pensacola
Twentieth Congress—March 4, 1827, to March 3, 1829
  Delegate: Joseph M. White, Pensacola
Twenty-First Congress—March 4, 1829, to March 3, 1831
  Delegate: Joseph M. White, Monticello
Twenty-Second Congress—March 4, 1831, to March 3, 1833
  Delegate: Joseph M. White, Monticello
Twenty-Third Congress—March 4, 1833, to March 3, 1835
  Delegate: Joseph M. White, Monticello
Twenty-Fourth Congress—March 4, 1835, to March 3, 1837
  Delegate: Joseph M. White, Monticello
Twenty-Fifth Congress—March 4, 1837, to March 3, 1839
  Delegate: Charles Downing, St. Augustine
Twenty-Sixth Congress—March 4, 1839, to March 3, 1841
  Delegate: Charles Downing, St. Augustine
Twenty-Seventh Congress—March 4, 1841, to March 3, 1843
  Delegate: David Levy (Yulee), St. Augustine

Twenty-Eighth Congress—March 4, 1843, to March 3, 1845[3]
Delegate: David Levy (Yulee), St. Augustine

State of Florida[4]

Twenty-Ninth Congress—March 4, 1845, to March 3, 1847
Senators: David Levy Yulee,[5] St. Augustine; James D. Westcott, Jr.,[6] Tallahassee.
Representative: Edward C. Cabell,[7] Tallahassee; William H. Brockenbrough,[8] Tallahassee.

Thirtieth Congress—March 4, 1847, to March 3, 1849
Senators: David Levy Yulee, St. Augustine; James D. Westcott, Jr., Tallahassee.
Representative: Edward C. Cabell, Tallahassee.

Thirty-First Congress—March 4, 1849, to March 3, 1851
Senators: David Levy Yulee, St. Augustine; Jackson Morton, Pensacola.
Representative: Edward C. Cabell, Tallahassee.

Thirty-Second Congress—March 4, 1851, to March 3, 1853
Senators: Jackson Morton, Pensacola; Stephen R. Mallory,[9] Jacksonville.
Representative: Edward C. Cabell, Tallahassee.

Thirty-Third Congress—March 4, 1853, to March 3, 1855
Senators: Jackson Morton, Pensacola; Stephen R. Mallory, Jacksonville.
Representative: Augustus E. Maxwell, Tallahassee.

Thirty-Fourth Congress—March 4, 1855, to March 3, 1857
Senators: Stephen R. Mallory, Key West; David Levy Yulee, Homasassa.
Representative: Augustus E. Maxwell, Tallahassee.

Thirty-Fifth Congress—March 4, 1857, to March 3, 1859
Senators: Stephen R. Mallory, Key West; David Levy Yulee, Homasassa.
Representative: George S. Hawkins, Pensacola.

Thirty-Sixth Congress—March 4, 1859, to March 3, 1861[10]
Senators: Stephen R. Mallory,[11] Pensacola; David Levy Yulee,[11] Homasassa.
Representative: George S. Hawkins,[11] Pensacola.

Thirty-Seventh Congress—March 4, 1861, to March 3, 1863
Senators: Stephen R. Mallory,[12] Pensacola; Vacant.
Representative: Vacant.

Thirty-Eighth Congress—March 4, 1863, to March 3, 1865
Senators: Vacant.
Representative: Vacant.

---

[3]Granted statehood by act of March 3, 1845.
[4]Admitted as a State into the Union March 3, 1845, the last day of the preceding Congress.
[5]Took his seat December 1, 1845; term to expire, as determined by lot, March 3, 1851. Presented credentials as "David Levy," but on January 12, 1846, in conformity with an act of the Florida Legislature, the Senate ordered the surname "Yulee" added to his name on the official records.
[6]Took his seat December 1, 1845; term to expire, as determined by lot, March 3, 1849.
[7]Served until January 24, 1846; succeeded by William H. Brockenbrough, who contested his election.
[8]Successfully contested the election of Edward C. Cabell, and took his seat January 24, 1846.
[9]Election unsuccessfully contested by David Levy Yulee.
[10]Seceded from the Union January 11, 1861.
[11]Withdrew January 21, 1861.
[12]Seat declared vacant by resolution of March 14, 1861.

240 / Floridians in Federal Office

Thirty-Ninth Congress—March 4, 1865, to March 3, 1867
  Senators: Vacant;[13] Vacant.[14]
  Representative: Vacant.
Fortieth Congress—March 4, 1867, to March 3, 1869[15]
  Senators: Thomas W. Osborn,[16] Pensacola; Adonijah S. Welch,[17] Jacksonville.
  Representative: At Large—Charles M. Hamilton,[18] Marianna.
Forty-First Congress—March 4, 1869, to March 3, 1871
  Senators: Thomas W. Osborn, Pensacola; Abijah Gilbert, St. Augustine.
  Representative: At Large—Charles M. Hamilton, Jacksonville.
Forty-Second Congress—March 4, 1871, to March 3, 1873
  Senators: Thomas W. Osborn, Pensacola; Abijah Gilbert, St. Augustine.
  Representative at Large: Josiah T. Walls,[19] Gainesville; Silas L. Niblack,[20] Gainesville.
Forty-Third Congress—March 4, 1873, to March 3, 1875
  Senators: Abijah Gilbert, St. Augustine; Simon B. Conover, Tallahassee.
  Representatives at Large: Josiah T. Walls, Gainesville; William J. Purman,[21] Tallahassee.
Forty-Fourth Congress—March 4, 1875, to March 3, 1877
  Senators: Simon B. Conover, Tallahassee; Charles W. Jones, Pensacola.
  Representatives: William J. Purman, Tallahassee; Josiah T. Walls,[22] Gainesville; Jesse J. Finley,[23] Jacksonville.
Forty-Fifth Congress—March 4, 1877, to March 3, 1879
  Senators: Simon B. Conover, Tallahassee; Charles W. Jones, Pensacola.
  Representatives: Horatio Bisbee, Jr.,[24] Jacksonville; Jesse J. Finley,[25] Jacksonville; Robert H. M. Davidson, Quincy.
Forty-Sixth Congress—March 4, 1879, to March 3, 1881
  Senators: Charles W. Jones, Pensacola; Wilkinson Call, Jacksonville.
  Representatives: Robert H. M. Davidson, Quincy; Noble A. Hull,[26] Sanford; Horatio Bisbee, Jr.,[27] Jacksonville.
Forty-Seventh Congress—March 4, 1881, to March 3, 1883
  Senators: Charles W. Jones, Pensacola; Wilkinson Call, Jacksonville.
  Representatives: Robert H. M. Davidson, Quincy; Jesse J. Finley,[28] Jacksonville; Horatio Bisbee, Jr.,[29] Jacksonville.

---

[13]On January 19, 1866, William Marvin presented credentials as a Senator-elect for the term ending March 3, 1867, which were ordered to lie on the table and no further action taken thereon.
[14]On June 6, 1866, Wilkinson Call presented credentials as a Senator-elect for the term ending March 3, 1869, which were ordered to lie on the table and no further action taken thereon.
[15]Readmitted to representation June 25, 1868.
[16]Took his seat June 30, 1868; term to expire March 3, 1873; on the same day William Marvin presented credentials dated November 28, 1866, which were read and no further action taken thereon because Mr. Osborn was seated.
[17]Took his seat July 2, 1868; term to expire March 3, 1869.
[18]Took his seat July 1, 1868.
[19]Served until January 29, 1873; succeeded by Silas L. Niblack, who contested his election.
[20]Successfully contested the election of Josiah T. Walls, and took his seat January 29, 1873.
[21]Resigned January 25, 1875.
[22]Served until April 19, 1876; succeeded by Jesse J. Finley, who contested his election.
[23]Successfully contested the election of Josiah T. Walls, and took his seat April 19, 1876.
[24]Served until February 20, 1879; succeeded by Jesse J. Finley, who contested his election.
[25]Successfully contested the election of Horatio Bisbee, Jr., and took his seat February 20, 1879.
[26]Served until January 22, 1881; succeeded by Horatio Bisbee, Jr., who contested his election.
[27]Successfully contested the election of Noble A. Hull, and took his seat January 22, 1881.
[28]Served until June 1, 1882; succeeded by Horatio Bisbee, Jr., who contested his election.
[29]Successfully contested the election of Jesse J. Finley, and took his seat June 1, 1882.

Forty-Eighth Congress—March 4, 1883, to March 3, 1885
  Senators: Charles W. Jones, Pensacola; Wilkinson Call, Jacksonville.
  Representatives: Robert H. M. Davidson, Quincy; Horatio Bisbee, Jr., Jacksonville.
Forty-Ninth Congress—March 4, 1885, to March 3, 1887
  Senators: Charles W. Jones, Pensacola; Wilkinson Call, Jacksonville.
  Representatives: Robert H. M. Davidson, Quincy; Charles Dougherty, Port Orange.
Fiftieth Congress—March 4, 1887, to March 3, 1889
  Senators: Wilkinson Call, Jacksonville; Samuel Pasco, Monticello.
  Representatives: Robert H. M. Davidson, Quincy; Charles Dougherty, Port Orange.
Fifty-First Congress—March 4, 1889, to March 3, 1891
  Senators: Wilkinson Call, Jacksonville; Samuel Pasco, Monticello.
  Representatives: Robert H. M. Davidson, Quincy; Robert Bullock, Ocala.
Fifty-Second Congress—March 4, 1891, to March 3, 1893
  Senators: Wilkinson Call,[31] Jacksonville; Samuel Pasco, Monticello.
  Representatives: Stephen R. Mallory, Pensacola; Robert Bullock, Ocala.
Fifty-Third Congress—March 4, 1893, to March 3, 1895
  Senators: Wilkinson Call, Jacksonville; Samuel Pasco,[32] Monticello.
  Representatives: Stephen R. Mallory, Pensacola; Charles M. Cooper, Jacksonville.
Fifty-Fourth Congress—March 4, 1895, to March 3, 1897
  Senators: Wilkinson Call, Jacksonville; Samuel Pasco, Monticello.
  Representatives: Stephen M. Sparkman, Tampa; Charles M. Cooper, Jacksonville.
Fifty-Fifth Congress—March 4, 1897, to March 1899
  Senators: Samuel Pasco, Monticello; Stephen R. Mallory,[33] Pensacola.
  Representatives: Stephen M. Sparkman, Tampa; Robert W. Davis, Palatka.
Fifty-Sixth Congress—March 4, 1899, to March 3, 1901
  Senators: Samuel Pasco,[34] Monticello; James P. Taliaferro,[35] Jacksonville; Stephen R. Mallory, Pensacola.
  Representatives: Stephen M. Sparkman, Tampa; Robert W. Davis, Palatka.
Fifty-Seventh Congress—March 4, 1901, to March 3, 1903
  Senators: Stephen R. Mallory, Pensacola; James P. Taliaferro, Jacksonville.
  Representatives: Stephen M. Sparkman, Tampa; Robert W. Davis, Palatka.
Fifty-Eighth Congress—March 4, 1903, to March 3, 1905
  Senators: Stephen R. Mallory,[36] Pensacola; James P. Taliaferro, Jacksonville.

---

[30]Elected May 19, 1887, and took his seat December 5, 1887; Jesse J. Finley was appointed by the Governor on February 28, 1887, to fill the vacancy existing after March 4, 1887, until the next meeting of the legislature, but never qualified. Upon the request of the financial clerk of the Senate for an opinion as to his authority to pay Mr. Finley the salary due him as a Senator-designate, President pro tempore Ingalls held that it should not be done, as the appointment "was in anticipation of a vacancy, and not to fill a vacancy that existed, as contemplated by article 3 of the Constitution"; subsequently the Senate adopted a resolution to pay Mr. Finley for services rendered from March 4 to May 19, 1887.

[31]Election unsuccessfully contested by Robert H. M. Davidson.

[32]Reappointed to fill vacancy in the term beginning March 4, 1893, and subsequently reelected.

[33]Elected to fill vacancy in the term beginning March 4, 1807, and took his seat May 25, 1897; John A. Henderson presented credentials as a Senator-designate on March 16, 1897, which were referred to the Committee.

[34]Reappointed to fill vacancy in the term beginning March 4, 1899, to serve until the next meeting of the legislature.

[35]Elected to fill vacancy in the term beginning March 4, 1899, and took his seat December 4, 1899.

[36]Reappointed to fill vacancy in the term beginning March 4, 1903, to serve until the next meeting of the legislature; subsequently reelected.

Representatives: Stephen M. Sparkman, Tampa; Robert W. Davis, Palatka; William B. Lamar, Monticello.

Fifty-Ninth Congress—March 4, 1905, to March 3, 1907
Senators: Stephen R. Mallory, Pensacola; James P. Taliaferro,[37] Jacksonville.
Representatives: Stephen M. Sparkman, Tampa; Frank Clark, Lake City; William B. Lamar, Monticello.

Sixtieth Congress—March 4, 1907, to March 3, 1909
Senators: Stephen R. Mallory,[38] Pensacola; William J. Bryan,[39] Jacksonville; William H. Milton,[40] Marianna; James P. Taliaferro, Jacksonville.
Representatives: Stephen M. Sparkman, Tampa; Frank Clark, Gainesville; William B. Lamar, Monticello.

Sixty-First Congress—March 4, 1909, to March 3, 1911
Senators: James P. Taliaferro, Jacksonville; Duncan U. Fletcher,[41] Jacksonville.
Representatives: Stephen M. Sparkman, Tampa; Frank Clark, Gainesville; Dannitte H. Mays, Monticello.

Sixty-Second Congress—March 4, 1911, to March 3, 1913
Senators: Duncan U. Fletcher, Jacksonville; Nathan P. Bryan,[42] Jacksonville. Dannitte H. Mays, Monticello.

Sixty-Third Congress—March 4, 1913, to March 3, 1915
Senators: Duncan U. Fletcher, Jacksonville; Nathan P. Bryan, Jacksonville.
Representatives: Stephen M. Sparkman, Tampa; Frank Clark, Gainesville; Emmett Wilson, Pensacola; At Large—Claude L'Engle, Jacksonville.

Sixty-Fourth Congress—March 4, 1915, to March 3, 1917
Senators: Duncan U. Fletcher, Jacksonville; Nathan P. Bryan, Jacksonville.
Representatives: Stephen M. Sparkman, Tampa; Frank Clark, Gainesville; Emmett Wilson, Pensacola; William J. Sears, Kissimmee.

Sixty-Fifth Congress—March 4, 1917, to March 3, 1919
Senators: Duncan U. Fletcher, Jacksonville; Park Trammell, Lakeland.
Representatives: Herbert J. Drane, Lakeland; Frank Clark, Gainesville; J. Walter Kehoe, Pensacola; William J. Sears, Kissimmee.

Sixty-Sixth Congress—March 4, 1919, to March 3, 1921
Senators: Duncan U. Fletcher, Jacksonville; Park Trammell, Lakeland.
Representatives: Herbert J. Drane, Lakeland; Frank Clark, Gainesville; John H. Smithwick, Pensacola; William J. Sears, Kissimmee.

Sixty-Seventh Congress—March 4, 1921, to March 3, 1923
Senators: Duncan U. Fletcher, Jacksonville; Park Trammell, Lakeland.
Representatives: Herbert J. Drane, Lakeland; Frank Clark, Gainesville; John H. Smithwick, Pensacola; William J. Sears, Kissimmee.

Sixty-Eighth Congress—March 4, 1923, to March 3, 1925
Senators: Duncan U. Fletcher, Jacksonville; Park Trammell, Lakeland.

---

[37]Reappointed to fill vacancy in the term beginning March 4, 1905, to serve until the next meeting of the legislature, subsequently reelected.

[38]Died December 23, 1907.

[39]Appointed to fill vacancy caused by death of Stephen R. Mallory, and took his seat January 9, 1908; died March 22, 1908.

[40]Appointed to fill vacancy caused by deaths of Stephen R. Mallory and William J. Bryan, and took his seat April 6, 1908.

[41]Appointed to fill vacancy in the term beginning March 4, 1909, and took his seat March 4, 1909; subsequendy elected.

[42]Appointed to fill vacancy in the term beginning March 4, 1911, to serve until the next meeting of the legislature, and took his seat April 4, 1911; subsequently elected.

Representatives: Herbert J. Drane, Lakeland; Frank Clark, Gainesville; John H. Smithwick, Pensacola; William J. Sears, Kissimmee.

Sixty-Ninth Congress—March 4, 1925, to March 3, 1927
Senators: Duncan U. Fletcher, Jacksonville; Park Trammell, Lakeland.
Representatives: Herbert J. Drane, Lakeland; Robert A. Green,[43] Starke; John H. Smithwick, Pensacola; William J. Sears, Kissimmee.

Seventieth Congress—March 4, 1927, to March 3, 1929
Senators: Duncan U. Fletcher, Jacksonville; Park Trammell, Lakeland.
Representatives: Herbert J. Drane, Lakeland; Robert A. Green, Starke; Thomas A. Yon, Tallahassee; William J. Sears, Kissimmee.

Seventy-First Congress—March 4, 1929, to March 3, 1931
Senators: Duncan U. Fletcher, Jacksonville; Park Trammell, Lakeland.
Representatives: Herbert J. Drane, Lakeland; Robert A. Green, Starke; Thomas A. Yon, Tallahassee; Mrs. Ruth Bryan Owen,[44] Miami.

Seventy-Second Congress—March 4, 1931, to March 3, 1933
Senators: Duncan U. Fletcher, Jacksonville; Park Trammell, Lakeland.
Representatives: Herbert J. Drane, Lakeland; Robert A. Green, Starke; Thomas A. Yon, Tallahassee; Mrs. Ruth Bryan Owen, Miami.

Seventy-Third Congress—March 4, 1933, to January 3, 1935
Senators: Duncan U. Fletcher, Jacksonville; Park Trammell, Lakeland.
Representatives: J. Hardin Peterson, Lakeland; Robert A. Green, Starke; Millard F. Caldwell, Milton; J. Mark Wilcox, West Palm Beach; At Large—William J. Sears, Jacksonville.

Seventy-Fourth Congress—January 3, 1935, to January 3, 1937
Senators: Duncan U. Fletcher,[45] Jacksonville; William L. Hill,[46] Gainesville; Claude Pepper,[47] Tallahassee; Park Trammell,[48] Lakeland; Scott M. Loftin,[49] Jacksonville; Charles O. Andrews,[50] Orlando.
Representatives: J. Hardin Peterson, Lakeland; Robert A. Green, Starke; Millard F. Caldwell, Milton; J. Mark Wilcox, West Palm Beach; At Large—William J. Sears, Jacksonville.

Seventy-Fifth Congress—January 3,[51] 1937, to January 3, 1939
Senators: Charles O. Andrews, Orlando; Claude Pepper, Tallahassee.
Representatives: J. Hardin Peterson, Lakeland; Robert A. Green, Starke; Millard F. Caldwell, Milton; J. Mark Wilcox, West Palm Beach; Joe Hendricks, De Land.

Seventy-Sixth Congress—January 3, 1939, to January 3, 1941
Senators: Charles O. Andrews, Orlando; Claude Pepper, Tallahassee.
Representatives: J. Hardin Peterson, Lakeland; Robert A. Green, Starke; Millard F. Caldwell, Milton; Arthur P. Cannon, Miami; Joe Hendricks, De Land.

---

[43]Election unsuccessfully contested by H. O. Brown.
[44]Election unsuccessfully contested by William C. Lawson.
[45]Died June 17, 1936.
[46]Appointed to fill vacancy caused by death of Duncan U. Fletcher, and served from July 1, 1936, to November 3, 1936, but was unable to be sworn in as Congress was not in session.
[47]Elected to fill vacancy caused by death of Duncan U. Fletcher, and took his seat January 5, 1937.
[48]Died May 8, 1936.
[49]Appointed to fill vacancy caused by death of Park Trammell, and took his seat May 27th, 1936.
[50]Elected to fill vacancy caused by death of Park Trammell.
[51]By joint resolution (Pub. Law No. 120, 74th Cong.) the date of assembling the first session of the Seventy-fifth Congress was fixed for January, 1937.

244 / Floridians in Federal Office

Seventy-Seventh Congress—January 3, 1941, to January 3, 1943
  Senators: Charles O. Andrews, Orlando; Claude Pepper, Tallahassee.
  Representatives: J. Hardin Peterson, Lakeland; Robert A. Green, Starke; Robert L. F. Sikes, Crestview; Arthur P. Cannon, Miami; Joe Hendricks, De Land.

Seventy-Eighth Congress—January 3, 1943, to January 3, 1945
  Senators: Charles O. Andrews, Orlando; Claude Pepper, Tallahassee.
  Representatives: J. Hardin Peterson, Lakeland; Emory H. Price, Jacksonville; Robert L. F. Sikes,[52] Crestview; Arthur P. Cannon, Miami; Joe Hendricks. De Land; At Large—Robert A. Green,[53] Starke.

Seventy-Ninth Congress—January 3, 1945, to January 3, 1947
  Senators; Charles O. Andrews,[54] Orlando; Spessard L. Holland,[55] Bartow; Claude Pepper, Tallahassee.
  Representatives: J. Hardin Peterson, Lakeland; Emory H. Price, Jacksonville; Robert L. F. Sikes, Crestview; Arthur P. Cannon, Miami; Joe Hendricks, De Land; Dwight L. Rogers, Fort Lauderdale.

Eightieth Congress—January 3, 1947, to January 3, 1949
  Senators: Claude D. Pepper, Tallahassee; Spessard L. Holland, Bartow.
  Representatives: J. Hardin Peterson, Lakeland; Emory H. Price, Jacksonville; Robert L. F. Sikes, Crestview; George A. Smathers, Miami; Joe Hendricks, De Land; Dwight L. Rogers, Fort Lauderdale.

Eighty-First Congress—January 3, 1949, to January 3, 1951
  Senators: Claude D. Pepper, Tallahassee; Spessard L. Holland, Bartow.
  Representatives: J. Hardin Peterson, Lakeland; Charles E. Bennett, Jacksonville; Robert L. F. Sikes, Crestview; George A. Smathers, Miami; Albert S. Herlong, Jr., Leesburg; Dwight L. Rogers, Fort Lauderdale.

Eighty-Second Congress—January 3, 1951, to January 3, 1953
  Senators: Spessard L. Holland, Bartow; George A. Smathers, Miami.
  Representatives: Chester B. McMullen, Clearwater; Charles E. Bennett, Jacksonville; Robert L. F. Sikes, Crestview; William C. Lantaff, Miami Springs; Albert S. Herlong, Jr., Leesburg; Dwight L. Rogers, Fort Lauderdale.

Eighty-Third Congress—January 3, 1953, to January 3, 1955
  Senators: Spessard L. Holland, Bartow; George A. Smathers, Miami.
  Representatives: Courtney W. Campbell, Clearwater; Charles E. Bennett, Jacksonville; Robert L. F. Sikes, Crestview; William C. Lantaff, Miami Springs; Albert S. Herlong, Jr., Leesburg; Dwight L. Rogers,[56] Fort Lauderdale; James A. Haley, Sarasota; Donald R. Matthews, Gainesville.

Eighty-Fourth Congress—January 3, 1955 to January 3, 1957
  Senators: Spessard L. Holland (D); George A. Smathers (D).
  Representatives: William C. Cramer (R);[57] Charles E. Bennett (D); Robert L. F. Sikes (D); Dante B. Fascell (D); Albert S. Herlong, Jr. (D); Paul G. Rogers (D)[58]; James A. Haley (D); Donald R. Matthews (D). [Democrats 7; Republicans 1]

---

[52]Resigned October 19, 1944; vacancy throughout remainder of the Congress.
[53]Resigned November 25, 1944; vacancy throughout remainder of the Congress.
[54]Died September 18, 1946.
[55]Appointed September 25, 1946, to fill vacancy caused by death of Charles O. Andrews, but was unable to be sworn in as Congress was not in session.
[56]Died December 1, 1954, before the commencement of the Eighty-fourth Congress to which he had been reelected. Vacancy in the Eighty-third Congress not filled.
[57]First Republican elected to Congress since 1875.
[58]Elected to fill vacancy caused by death of his father, Representative-elect Dwight L. Rogers, in the preceding Congress, and took his seat January 13, 1955.

Floridians in Federal Office / 245

Eighty-Fifth Congress—January 3, 1957, to January 3, 1959
  Senators: Spessard L. Holland (D); George A. Smathers (D).
  Representatives: William C. Cramer (R); Charles E. Bennett (D); Robert L. F. Sikes (D); Dante B. Fascell (D); Albert S. Herlong, Jr. (D); Paul G. Rogers (D); James A. Haley (D); Donald R. Matthews (D). [Democrats 7; Republicans 1]

Eighty-Sixth Congress—January 3, 1959, to January 3, 1961
  Senators: Spessard L. Holland (D); George A. Smathers (D).
  Representatives: William C. Cramer (R); Charles E. Bennett (D); Robert L. F. Sikes (D); Dante B. Fascell (D); Albert S. Herlong, Jr. (D); Paul G. Rogers (D); James A. Haley (D); Donald R. Matthews (D). [Democrats 7; Republicans 1]

Eighty-Seventh Congress—January 3, 1961, to January 3, 1963
  Senators: Spessard L. Holland (D); George A. Smathers (D).
  Representatives: 1. William C. Cramer (R). 2. Charles E. Bennett (D). 3. Robert L. F. Sikes (D). 4. Dante B. Fascell (D). 5. Albert S. Herlong, Jr. (D). 6. Paul G. Rogers (D). 7. James A. Haley (D). 8. Donald R. Matthews (D). [Democrats 7; Republicans 1]

Eighty-Eighth Congress—January 3, 1963, to January 3, 1965
  Senators: Spessard L. Holland (D); George A. Smathers (D).
  Representatives: 1. William C. Cramer (R). 2. Charles E. Bennett (D). 3. Claude Pepper (D). 4. Dante B. Fascell (D). 5. Albert S. Herlong, Jr. (D). 6. Paul G. Rogers (D). 7. James A. Haley (D). 8. Donald R. Matthews (D). 9. Don Fuqua (D). 10. Sam M. Gibbons (D). 11. Edward J. Gurney (R). 12. William C. Cramer (R). [Democrats 10; Republicans 2]

Eighty-Ninth Congress—January 3, 1965, to January 3, 1967
  Senators: Spessard L. Holland (D); George A. Smathers (D).
  Representatives: 1. Robert L. F. Sikes (D). 2. Charles E. Bennett (D). 3. Claude D. Pepper (D). 4. Dante B. Fascell (D). 5. Albert S. Herlong, Jr. (D). 6. Paul G. Rogers (D). 7. James A. Haley (D). 8. Donald R. Matthews (D). 9. Don Fuqua (D). 10. Sam M. Gibbons (D). 11. Edward J. Gurney (R). 12. William C. Cramer (R). [Democrats 10; Republicans 2]

Ninetieth Congress—January 3, 1967, to January 3, 1969
  Senators: Spessard L. Holland (D); George A. Smathers (D).
  Representatives: 1. Robert L. F. Sikes (D). 2. Don Fuqua (D). 3. Charles E. Bennett (D). 4. Albert S. Herlong, Jr. (D). 5. Edward J. Gurney (R). 6. Sam M. Gibbons (D). 7. James A. Haley (D). 8. William C. Cramer (R). 9. Paul G. Rogers (D). 10. J. Herbert Burke (R). 11. Claude D. Pepper (D). 12. Dante B. Fascell (D). [Democrats 9; Republicans 3]

Ninety-First Congress—January 3, 1969, to January 3, 1971
  Senators: Spessard L. Holland (D); Edward J. Gurney (R).
  Representatives: 1. Robert L. F. Sikes (D). 2. Don Fuqua (D). 3. Charles E. Bennett (D). 4. William V. Chappell, Jr. (D). 5. Louis Frey, Jr. (R). 6. Sam M. Gibbons (D). 7. James A. Haley (D). 8. William C. Cramer (R). 9. Paul G. Rogers (D). 10. J. Herbert Burke (R). 11. Claude D. Pepper (D). 12. Dante B. Fascell (D). [Democrats 9; Republicans 3]

Ninety-Second Congress—January 3, 1971, to January 3, 1973
  Senators: Edward J. Gurney (R); Lawton Chiles (D).
  Representatives: 1. Robert L. F. Sikes (D). 2. Don Fuqua (D). 3. Charles E. Bennett (D). 4. William V. Chappell, Jr. (D). 5. Louis Frey, Jr. (R). 6. Sam M. Gibbons (D). 7. James A. Haley (D). 8. C. W. (Bill) Young (R). 9. Paul G. Rogers (D). 10. J. Herbert Burke (R). 11. Claude Pepper (D). 12. Dante B. Fascell (D). [Democrats 9; Republicans 3]

Ninety-Third Congress—January 3, 1973, to January 3, 1975
  Senators: Edward J. Gurney (R); Lawton Chiles (D).
  Representatives: 1. Robert L. F. Sikes (D). 2. Don Fuqua (D). 3. Charles E. Bennett (D). 4. William V. Chappell, Jr. (D). 5. Bill Gunter (D). 6. C. W. (Bill) Young (R). 7.

Sam M. Gibbons (D). 8. James A. Haley (D). 9. Louis Frey, Jr. (R). 10. L. A. (Skip) Bafalis (R). 11. Paul G. Rogers (D). 12. J. Herbert Burke (R). 13. William Lehman (D). 14. Claude D. Pepper (D). 15. Dante B. Fascell (D). [Democrats 11; Republicans 4]

Ninety-Fourth Congress—January 3, 1975, to January 3, 1977
  Senators: Lawton Chiles (D); Richard (Dick) Stone (D),
  Representatives: 1. Robert L. F. Sikes (D). 2. Don Fuqua (D). 3. Charles E. Bennett (D). 4. William V. Chappell, Jr. (D). 5. Richard Kelly (R). 6. C. W. (Bill) Young (R). 7. Sam M. Gibbons (D). 8. James A. Haley (D). 9. Louis Frey, Jr. (R). 10. L. A. (Skip) Bafalis (R). 11. Paul G. Rogers. (D). 12. J. Herbert Burke (R). 13. William Lehman (D). 14. Claude D. Pepper (D). 15. Dante B. Fascell (D). [Democrats 10; Republicans 5]

Ninety-Fifth Congress—January 3, 1977, to January 3, 1979
  Senators: Lawton Chiles (D); Richard (Dick) Stone (D).
  Representatives: 1. Robert L. F. Sikes (D). 2. Don Fuqua (D). 3. Charles E. Bennett (D). 4. William V. Chappell, Jr (D). 5. Richard Kelly (R). 6. C. W. (Bill) Young (R). 7. Sam M. Gibbons (D). 8. Andrew Ireland (D). 9. Louis Frey, Jr. (R) 10. L. A. (Skip) Bafalis (R). 11. Paul B. Rogers (D). 12. J. Herbert Burke (R). 13. William Lehman (D). 14. Claude D. Pepper (D). 15. Dante B. Fascell (D). [Democrats 10; Republicans 5]

Ninety-Sixth Congress—January 3, 1979, to January 3, 1981
  Senators: Lawton Chiles (D); Richard (Dick) Stone (D).
  Representatives: 1. Earl Hutto (D). 2. Don Fuqua (D). 3. Charles E. Bennett (D). 4. William V. Chappell, Jr (D). 5. Richard Kelly (R). 6. C. W. (Bill) Young (R). 7. Sam M. Gibbons (D). 8. Andrew Ireland (D). 9. C. William Nelson (D). 10. L. A. (Skip) Bafalis (R). 11. Dan Mica (D). 12. Edward J. Stack (D). 13. William Lehman (D). 14. Claude D. Pepper (D). 15. Dante B. Fascell (D). [Democrats 12; Republicans 3]

Ninety-Seventh Congress—January 3, 1981, to January 3, 1983
  Senators: Lawton Chiles (D); Paula F. Hawkins (R).
  Representatives: 1. Earl Hutto (D). 2. Don Fuqua (D). 3. Charles E. Bennett (D). 4. William V. Chappell, Jr. (D) 5. Bill McCollum (R). 6. C. W. (Bill) Young (R). 7. Sam M. Gibbons (D). 8. Andrew Ireland (D). 9. C. William Nelson (D). 10. L. A. (Skip) Bafalis (R). 11. Dan Mica (D). 12. Clay Shaw (R). 13. William Lehman (D). 14. Claude D. Pepper (D). 15. Dante B. Fascell (D). [Democrats 11; Republicans 4]

Ninety-Eighth Congress—January 3, 1983, to January 3, 1985
  Senators: Lawton Chiles (D); Paula F. Hawkins (R).
  Representatives: 1. Earl Hutto (D). 2. Don Fuqua (D). 3. Charles E. Bennett (D). 4. William V. Chappell, Jr. (D). 5. Bill McCollum (R). 6. Kenneth H. MacKay, Jr. (D) 7. Sam M. Gibbons (D). 8. C. W. (Bill) Young (R). 9. Michael Bilirakis (R). 10. Andrew Ireland (R). 11. C. William Nelson (D). 12. Thomas F. Lewis (R). 13. Connie Mack (R). 14. Dan Mica (D). 15. E. Clay Shaw, Jr. (R) 16. Lawrence J. Smith (D). 17. William Lehman (D). 18. Claude D. Pepper (D). 19. Dante B. Fascell (D). [Democrats, 13; Republicans 6]

Ninety-Ninth Congress—January 3, 1985, to January 3, 1987
  Senators: Lawton Chiles (D); Paula F. Hawkins (R).
  Representatives: 1. Earl Hutto (D). 2. Don Fuqua (D). 3. Charles E. Bennett (D). 4. William V. Chappell, Jr. (D) 5. Bill McCollum (R). 6. Kenneth H. MacKay, Jr. (D). 7. Sam M. Gibbons (D). 8. C. W. (Bill) Young (R). 9. Michael Bilirakis (R). 10. Andrew Ireland (R). 11. C. William Nelson (D). 12. Thomas F. Lewis (R). 13. Connie Mack (R). 14. Dan Mica (D). 15. E. Clay Shaw, Jr. (R) 16. Lawrence J. Smith (D). 17. William Lehman (D). 18. Claude D. Pepper (D). 19. Dante B. Fascell (D). [Democrats 12; Republicans 7]

One Hundredth Congress—January 3, 1987, to January 3, 1989
  Senators: Lawton Chiles (D); D. Robert Graham (D).
  Representatives: 1. Earl Hutto (D). 2. Bill Grant (D). 3. Charles E. Bennett (D). 4. William V. Chappell, Jr. (D) 5. Bill McCollum (R). 6. Kenneth H. MacKay, Jr. (D) 7.

Sam M. Gibbons (D). 8. C. W. (Bill) Young (R). 9. Michael Bilirakis (R). 10. Andrew Ireland (R). 11. C. William Nelson (D). 12. Thomas F. Lewis (R). 13. Connie Mack (R). 14. Dan Mica (D). 15. E. Clay Shaw, Jr. (R). 16. Lawrence J. Smith (D). 17. William Lehman (D). 18. Claude D. Pepper (D). 19. Dante B. Fascell (D). [Democrats 12; Republicans 7]

One Hundred and First Congress—January 3, 1989, to January 3, 1991
  Senators: D. Robert Graham (D), Connie Mack (R).
  Representatives: 1. Earl Hutto (D). 2. Bill Grant (R). 3. Charles E. Bennett (D). 4. Craig James (D). 5. Bill McCollum (R). 6. Clifford Stearns (D). 7. Sam M. Gibbons (D). 8. C. W. (Bill) Young (R). 9. Michael Bilirakis (R). 10. Andrew Ireland (R). 11. C. William Nelson (D). 12. Thomas F. Lewis (R). 13. Porter J. Goss (R). 14. Harry A. Johnston (D). 15. E. Clay Shaw, Jr. (R). 16. Lawrence J. Smith (D). 17. William Lehman (D). 18. Claude D. Pepper[59] (D) Ileana Ros-Lehtinen[60] (R). 19. Dante B. Fascell (D). [Democrats 11; Republicans 9]

One Hundred and Second Congress—January 3, 1991, to January 3, 1993
  Senators: D. Robert Graham (D); Connie Mack (R)
  Representatives: 1. Earl Hutto (D). 2. Douglas (Pete) Peterson (D). 3. Charles E. Bennett (D). 4. Craig James (R). 5. Bill McCollum (R). 6. Clifford Stearns (R). 7. Sam M. Gibbons (D). 8. C. W. (Bill) Young (R). 9. Michael Bilirakis (R). 10. Andrew Ireland (R). 11. Jim Bacchus (D). 12. Thomas F. Lewis (R). 13. Porter J. Goss (R). 14. Harry A. Johnston (D). 15. E. Clay Shaw, Jr. (R). 16. Lawrence J. Smith (D). 17. William Lehman (D). 18. Ileana Ros-Lehtinen (R). 19. Dante B. Fascell (D). [Democrats 9; Republicans 10]

One Hundred and Third Congress—January 3, 1993, to January 3, 1995
  Senators: D. Robert Graham (D); Connie Mack (R).
  Representatives: 1. Earl Hutto (D). 2. Douglas (Pete) Peterson (D). 3. Corrine Brown (D). 4. Tillie Fowler (D). 5. Karen L. Thurman (D). 6. Clifford B. Stearns (R). 7. John L. Mica (R). 8. Bill McCollum (R). 9. Michael Bilirakis (R). 10. C. W. (Bill) Young (R). 11. Sam M. Gibbons (D). 12. Charles T. Canaday (D). 13. Dan Miller (R). 14. Porter J. Goss (R). 15. Jim Bacchus (D). 16. Thomas F. Lewis (R). 17. Carrie Meek (D). 18. Ileana Ros-Lehtinen (R). 19. Harry A. Johnston (D). 20. Peter Deutsch (D). 21. Lincoln Diaz-Balart (R). 22. E. Clay Shaw (R). 23. Alcee L. Hastings (D). [Democrats 11; Republicans 12]

Floridians in the United States Senate

Connie Mack, Cape Coral, Republican, elected 1994
*Bob Graham, Miami Lakes, Democrat, elected 1992

Floridians in the United States House of Representatives

(Elected November 1994)

Congressional District and Representative:
  1st   Joe Scarborough, Pensacola, Republican
  2nd   Pete Peterson, Marianna, Democrat
* 3rd   Corrine Brown, Jacksonville, Democrat
  4th   Tillie Fowler, Jacksonville, Democrat

---

[59]Died May 30, 1989.
[60]Elected 1989.
*Served in the Florida Legislature.

* 5th	Karen L. Thurman, Dunnellon, Democrat	
6th	Clifford B. Stearns, Ocala, Republican	
* 7th	John L. Mica, Winter Park, Republican	
8th	Bill McCollum, Longwood, Republican	
9th	Michael Bilirakis, Palm Harbor, Republican	
*10th	C. W. (Bill) Young, Indian Rocks Beach, Republican	
*11th	Sam Gibbons, Tampa, Democrat	
*12th	Charles T. Canady, Lakeland, Republican	
13th	Dan Miller, Bradenton, Republican	
14th	Porter J. Gross, Sanibel, Republican	
15th	Dave Weldon, Palm Bay, Republican	
*16th	Mark Foley, West Palm Beach, Republican	
*17th	Carrie Meek, Miami, Democrat	
*18th	Ileana Ros-Lehtinen, Miami, Republican	
*19th	Harry Johnston, West Palm Beach, Democrat	
*20th	Peter Deutsch, Lauderhill, Democrat	
*21st	Lincoln Diaz-Balart, Miami, Republican	
22nd	E. Clay Shaw, Fort Lauderdale, Republican	
23rd	Alcee L. Hastings, Fort Lauderdale, Democrat	

*Served in the Florida Legislature

The place is the Democratic National Convention of 1960 at Los Angeles. In a few moments Florida's Governor LeRoy Collins introduced Senator Lyndon B. Johnson of Texas as the party's nominee for Vice President who, in turn, introduces Senator John F. Kennedy of Massachusetts, the nominee for President. Senator Kennedy then delivers his "New Frontiers" speech. In the photograph are, left to right: Governor Collins, Senator Kennedy, Senator Johnson, former Congressman James Roosevelt, son of President Roosevelt, former Governor Adlai Stevenson of Illinois, and Senator Stuart Symington of Missouri.

LeRoy Collins

Women in Government

The woman's suffrage (19th) amendment was declared by the U.S. Secretary of State on August 26, 1920, to have been ratified by 38 states and therefore a part of the Constitution. The amendment had been approved by the states in remarkably short time, having been proposed to the legislatures by Congress on June 5, 1915.

(Florida was not among those states. Ratification in Florida came in 1969 as a symbolic gesture in recognition of the 50th anniversary of the League of Women Voters in Florida.)

In Florida, the Democratic primaries having already been conducted in June, and these then being the equivalent of election, it does not seem likely that any woman's name appeared on the November general election ballots.

Search of newspapers in the microfilm collection of Florida State University's Strozier Library indicates two women were candidates for the State House of Representatives in the Democratic primary of 1922. (Electors then voted their first and second choices for an office, thus combining two elections in one.)

Those two were Mrs. Katherine B. Tippetts of St. Petersburg, who was prominent in the Florida Federation of Women's Clubs, and Miss Myrtice McCaskill of Perry, who had been elected reading clerk of the House for three sessions and of the Senate for one session. Neither was elected although Mrs. Tippetts finished second in a four-candidate contest. Miss McCaskill was defeated in a two-candidate race.

The 1922 newspapers also reported a sprinkling of female candidates for county school boards and supervisor of registration. If any were successful, their nominations went unreported.

In 1928, the first woman was elected to statewide office and the first woman was elected from a Congressional district.

Mrs. Mamie Eaton Greene of Monticello was elected to the Railroad Commission. Mrs. Ruth Bryan Owen of Miami won the first of two terms as a member of Congress from the Fourth District, which then stretched along the East Coast from Jacksonville to Key West and inland to Orlando. Mrs.

Greene　　1927 　　　*McCaskill*　　1922 　　　*Thompson*　　1953 　　　*McDonnell*　　1979

Greene had been appointed to the Railroad Commission by Governor John W. Martin on March 23, 1927, upon the death of her first husband, R. L. (Bob) Eaton.

The next woman after Mrs. Greene to be elected to statewide public office also was to serve on the Railroad Commission's successor agency, the Public Service Commission. She was Paula Hawkins, wife of a Maitland (Orange County) electronics engineer and businessman. She was no novice in politics, serving at the time of her election as a member of the Republican National Committee. She had campaigned unsuccessfully in 1970 for the Republican nomination for a seat in the Florida House of Representatives.

Mrs. Hawkins was elected to the Public Service Committee in 1972 after an incumbent had been turned out in the Democratic primary. In turn, Mrs. Hawkins defeated the Democratic nominee. Mrs. Hawkins was re-elected in 1976. Under the resign-to-run law, she resigned from the Commission to serve as the running-mate of Jack Eckerd, the Republican nominee for Governor. Eckerd had defeated Mrs. Hawkins in 1974 when each was a candidate for the Republican nomination for the U.S. Senate. In 1980, Mrs. Hawkins was elected to the United States Senate. She was defeated for reelection in 1986.

Florida's first Congresswoman, Ruth Bryan Owen of Miami, is shown in this 1929 photograph with her secretary and driver and campaign automobile, "The Spirit of Florida." Mrs. Owen represented Florida's Fourth District, which then stretched from Key West to Jacksonville and mid-state to Orlando. Florida State Archives

Mrs. Ruth Bryan Owen represented the Fourth Congressional District for the four years beginning March 4, 1929. Mrs. Owen was defeated in 1932 when she sought election to a third term. Her attitude against legalizing the sale of beer is said to have contributed to her loss.

Mrs. Owen, afterwards Mrs. Borge Rohde, was the daughter of William Jennings Bryan, "the great Commoner." Before moving to Miami, Bryan had been three times the Democratic nominee for President and had served for a time as Secretary of State during the administration of President Woodrow Wilson. After her Congressional service, Mrs. Owen was American Minister to Denmark, 1933–1936, and an alternate United States representative to the Fourth General Assembly of the United Nations in 1949. She was residing in New York when she died on July 27, 1954.

Cuban-born Ileana Ros-Lehtinen succeeded to the Miami district in Congress seat vacated by the death of Claude Pepper, who died May 30, 1989. Ros-Lehtinen, then a State Senator, received 49,298 votes as the Republican nominee, to 43,274 for Gerald F. Richman as the Democratic nomi-

Women in Government/ 251

Paula Hawkins was Florida's first woman to serve as an United States Senator.

Ileana Ros-Lehtinen, second woman to serve in United States House of Representatives from Florida.

nee. With parents, she emigrated from Havana to Miami in 1960 at the age of eight. She was elected to the State House of Representatives in 1982 and to the State Senate in 1986. While in the House, she met and married Dexter W. Lehtinen, a fellow Representative. He, too, was elected to the State Senate.

In December 1994 she became the first Cuban-American and first Hispanic woman to head a congressional subcommittee when she was named chairwoman of the subcommittee on Africa.

Orange County gave Florida its first feminine members of both the Senate and House of Representatives. Mrs. Edna Giles Fuller of Orlando served in the five regular and special sessions of the 1929 and 1931 House of Representatives. Mrs. Beth (George W.) Johnson of Orlando was elected to the Senate in 1962, serving first in an extraordinary session of that year. Mrs. Johnson previously had been elected three times to the House. (See Legislative chapter for pictures.)

The first black woman ever to serve in the Florida Legislature, Mrs. Gwen Sawyer Cherry, was elected to the House from Dade County in 1970. She was born in Miami in 1923. A lawyer, teacher and author, she received her law degree, *Cum laude,* from Florida A&M University in 1965.

The first woman to serve as member of the Cabinet was Mrs. Dorothy W. Glisson, who was appointed Secretary of State by Governor Reubin O'D. Askew on July 8, 1974. Mrs. Glisson, a careerist in the Department of State, completed the term, to January 7, 1975, of Secretary of State Richard (Dick) Stone, who had resigned to run for the U.S. Senate. She was not a candidate for election.

Mrs. Ina S. Thompson of DeFuniak Springs was Motor Vehicle Commissioner during the six years of the administration of Governor LeRoy

Collins. She was the first woman to be a member of the group of gubernatorial appointees known as the "little cabinet." Mrs. Thompson was an aunt of Senator Bob Graham.

Mrs. M. Athalie Range of Miami was the first black woman to serve as a member of the little cabinet, being appointed Secretary of the Department of Community Affairs by Governor Reubin O'D. Askew on January 14, 1971.

Women have served through the years on executive agencies. Typical was Mrs. Ellen (John) Knight McDonnell of Miami, who was appointed by Governor Spessard L. Holland in 1941 to the State Welfare Board, by Governor Millard F. Caldwell in 1947 to the State Children's Commission, and by Governor Don McCarty in 1953 to the Governor's Committee on Mental Health.

Woman's Suffrage

The 1915 Florida Legislature came within two votes of allowing women to serve by election or appointment to certain public offices.

The bill originated in the Senate, where it was introduced by Senator John P. Jones of Pensacola, and passed by a vote of 15 yeas to eight nays. In the House the bill was moved by Representative Robert H. Anderson of Pensacola but failed by a vote of 30 yeas and 32 nays.

The narrowness of the failure in 1915 of this bill, however limited its scope, evidently encouraged advocates of woman's suffrage to try for the right to vote at the next legislative session in 1917.

Mrs. Marjory Stoneman Douglas of Miami, later to earn recognition as an author (*The Everglades: River of Grass* and *Florida: The Long Frontier* being among her books) and conservationist, joined with Mrs. Frank Stranahan of Fort Lauderdale, Mrs. William S. Jennings and Mrs. Napoleon B. Broward of Jacksonville to address a House committee.

They spoke on behalf of House Bill 274, introduced by Representative W. H. Marshall of Fort Lauderdale. HB 274 would grant "equal suffrage in primary elections to women of Florida . . ."

Mrs. Jennings had been promised the Woman Suffrage bill would be passed by the Senate, explained Mrs. Douglas, "so that we should not have to speak before the Senate committee. We understood the Senate's gallant gesture, since they were sure it would not pass the House." And the Senate was right, the House committee on Constitutional Amendments recommended that it "do not pass." The vote was seven to one. The lone vote for the bill was cast by Representative William D. DeGrove of St. Johns County.

The 19th Amendment was voted in 1919 by Congress and ratified by the last necessary state, Tennessee, on August 18, 1920. Florida was not among the 38 ratifying states. (See: Above)

Equal Rights Amendment

Florida's Legislature was one of the first and one of the last states to consider the Equal Rights Amendment but never to ratify the amendment.

ERA passed Congress on March 22, 1972. The ratifying resolution was adopted by the Florida House on March 24, 1972, by a vote of 84 yeas to 3 nays. It was not considered in the Senate because of a provision of the Florida Constitution, afterwards voided by a Federal court, which prohibited the consideration of amendments to the United States Constitution without an intervening general election.

The history at subsequent sessions: 1973, failed to pass House, 54 yeas, 64 nays, killed in Senate committee. 1974, failed to pass Senate, 19 yeas, 21 nays, died in House committee. 1975, passed House 61 yeas, 58 nays, failed in Senate, 17 yeas, 21 nays. 1976, died in Senate and House committees. 1977, failed to pass Senate, 19 yeas, 21 nays, died on House calendar. 1978, died in House committee, died in Senate committee. 1979, died on House calendar, died in Senate committee. 1980, died in House committee, not introduced in Senate. 1981, died in House committee, not introduced in Senate. 1982, died in Senate and House committees. 1982, passed House, 60 yeas, 58 nays, killed in Senate, 16 yeas, 22 nays.

In a number of the years when the concurrent resolution died on the House calendar or in committee, it was by agreement that the resolution would not be called up for House floor consideration unless the Senate had passed the resolution.

Women's Hall of Fame

The Florida Women's Hall of Fame was initiated in 1982 by Governor Bob Graham. Inductees are:

1982:
- Mary McLeod Bethune, educator, civil-rights leader.
- Helene Coleman, volunteer.
- Elaine Gordon, former legislator, women's advocate.
- Wilhelmina Harvey, educator, civic leader.
- Paula Mae Milton, poet, dramatist, filmmaker.
- Barbard Palmer, pioneer in development of women's athletic programs.

1984:
- Roxcy Bolton, women's advocate.
- Barbara Landstreet Frye, journalist.
- Lena Smithers Hughes, horticulturist, developed Valencia orange.
- Zora Neale Hurston, anthropologist, writer.
- Sybil Mobley, dean of FAMU's School of Business and Industry.
- Helen Muir, writer.
- Gladys P. Soler, medical doctor, devoted practice to poor children.
- Julia DeForest Sturdevant Tuttle, founded Miami, known as "Mother of Miami."

1986:
- Annie Ackerman, political leader, environomentalist.
- Rosemary Barkett, first woman chief justice of Florida Supreme Court.
- Gwendolyn Cherry, first black female attorney in Dade County, state legislator.
- Dorothy Dodd, state's first archivist.
- Marjory Stoneman Douglas, environmentalist, author.
- Elsie Jones Hare, educator.
- Elizabeth McCullough Johnson, first woman in Florida Senate.
- Francis Bartlett Kinne, first woman president of a Florida university (Jacksonville University).
- Arva Moore Parks, writer, filmmaker.
- Marjorie Kinnan Rawlings, author.
- Florence Barbara Seibert, biochemist, developed tuberculosis skin test.
- Marilyn K. Smith, volunteer.
- Eartha Mary Madgalene White, educator, founder of mission for poor.

1992:
- Jacqueline Cochran, aviator, commanded women's air corps in World War II.

254 / Women in Government

- Carrie P. Meek, first black woman elected to Congress from Florida.
- Ruth Bryan Owen, first woman elected to Congress from the South.

1993:
- Betty Skelton Frankman, race-car driver, aviator.
- Paulina Pedroso, fought for Cuban independence from Spain.
- Janet Reno, first female attorney general of the United States.

1994:
- Nikki Beare, advocate for women's issues and mentor to women in Florida government.
- Betty Mae Jumper, first woman elected as head of the Seminole Tribe of Florida.
- Gladys D. Milton, a North Florida midwife for 35 years who represented black women on health-care issues.

Source: Florida Commission on the Status of Women

In August 1994 plaques bearing engraved likenesses and short biographies of 33 inductees were mounted on the Hall of Fame wall outside the office of the Commissioner of Education in the Capitol rotunda. Plaques will be added annually for new inductees.

"Kill this bill dead—black fly dead!" pleaded Senator Carrie Meek, then a Representative, waving her battle flag. Session after session in the years after first heard, Senator Meek's cry is renewed. Donn Dughi

Here are the five women representing Florida in Congress:

CORRINE BROWN
■ **Political affiliation:** Democrat ■ **Hometown:** Jacksonville ■ **Date, place of birth:** November 11, 1946; Jacksonville ■ **Term:** Second ■ **Education:** Bachelor's Degree in Sociology and Criminology Florida A&M University; Master's Degree in Guidance and Counseling, FAMU; specialist in higher education, University of Florida.

TILLIE K. FOWLER
■ **Political affiliation:** Republican ■ **Hometown:** Jacksonville ■ **Date, place of birth:** December 23, 1942; Milledgeville, Ga. ■ **Term:** Second ■ **Education:** Emory University, Bachelor's Degree in Political Science, 1964; Emory University Law Degree, 1967.

CARRIE MEEK
■ **Political affiliation:** Democrat ■ **Hometown:** Miami ■ **Date, place of birth:** April 29, 1926; Tallahassee ■ **Term:** Second ■ **Education:** Bachelor's Degree in Biology and Physical Education from Florida A&M University and Master's Degree in Public Health and Physical Education from the University of Michigan.

ILEANA ROS-LEHTINEN
■ **Political affiliation:** Republican ■ **Hometown:** Miami ■ **Date, place of birth:** July 12, 1952; Havana, Cuba ■ **Term:** Third ■ **Education:** Bachelor's Degree in English and a Master's in Educational Leadership from Florida International University.

KAREN THURMAN
■ **Political affiliation:** Democrat ■ **Hometown:** Dunnellon ■ **Date, place of birth:** January 12, 1951; Rapid City, S.D. ■ **Term:** Second ■ **Education:** Bachelor's Degree in Education, University of Florida.

The Seat of Government

The site of Tallahassee was chosen in 1823 as the seat of government of the recently formed Territory of Florida. In that year, John Lee Williams, of Pensacola, and Dr. W. H. Simmons, of St. Augustine, were named commissioners to select a permanent seat of government at some point between the Ochlockonee and Suwannee Rivers. They met late in October on the Ochlockonee River, near St. Marks. Dr. Simmons, who had made the trip from St. Augustine overland, had already noted that the high lands south of Lake Miccosukee "would form an eligible situation for a town," a view in which Williams readily concurred." "A more beautiful country can scarcely be imagined," wrote the latter; "it is high, rolling, and well watered."

Commissioner Simmons wrote in his journal for October 27, 1823, that the commissioners had encountered the Indian Chief Neamathla near his settlement a few miles north of the present city of Tallahassee.

"Neamathla and his people appeared much disturbed by our visit, and were inquisitive as to what object we had in view. We told him that we came to search out a spot where the Governor and his Council could conveniently meet, and that we should not in any way interfere with the Indians. He seemed, however, much dissatisfied. He invited us to spend the night and in the meantime sent off for an interpreter."

The Commissioners bedded down under a shed of the Indian's Council House but their sleep was broken by the sounds of the Indians dancing, a ritual which always preceded the annual hunting expedition. Commissioner Simmons noted:

"I felt a melancholy interest in watching these exhibitions of the amusement of these poor people, who, by their treaty, were soon to quit the country. In one of their dances, called the 'mad dance,' most of their gestures and movements were highly martial and graceful and served to illustrate the natural elevation and fire of their character."

On the next day, Neamathla again questioned Commissioners Simmons and Williams about the purpose of their visit. Dr. Simmons recorded the conversation:

"... on our reassuring him that we had no design to interfere with the rights of the Indians, he told us we might pro-

This is Neamathla, chief of the Indians at a settlement near the old fields of Tallahassee. The Commissioners seeking a place for Florida's new Capital found Neamathla to be a "shrewd, penetrating man."
Library of Congress

ceed, but not to tell any of the Indians that he had sent us. We passed to the old Tallahassee town, where Chifixico, chief of the settlement, evinced equal opposition to our proceedings.

"He angrily caught up a handful of dirt, and presenting it, asked if that was not his land. . . ."

The exact location seems to have been determined by the proximity of a beautiful stream and waterfall directly east of the "old fields" of the Seminole Indians then living at Neamathla's town on Lake Lafayette. This stream, wrote Williams, "after running about a mile south pitches about 20 or 30 feet into an immense chasm, in which it runs 60 or 70 rods to the base of a high hill which it enters. . . ." The capital site was west and north of the stream.

The St. Augustine Branch, as it was later called, has degenerated into the drainage ditch that is visible on Franklin Boulevard and along Canal Street. The waterfall, known as the Cascade, has long since disappeared. The basin into which it used to fall is now that area between the Seaboard Air Line Railroad track and Oakland Avenue. The "old fields" from which Tallahassee took its name probably extended along the high ground from the pond near Magnolia Drive to the vicinity of the Jacksonville Highway.

The first settlers, headed by John McIver, of North Carolina, arrived at the new town site on April 9, 1824. It has been said that the party, which consisted of two white men, two women, two children, and a mulatto man, pitched camp on a southern slope within sound of the Cascade. If that was so, they probably camped on the hillside near Gaines Street between Adams and Calhoun.

First Capitol

Two days later, Jonathan Robinson and Sherod McCall, planters on Little River in the Forbes Purchase in Gadsden County, brought their hands and erected three log cabins for the accommodation of the Legislative Council, which was to meet at the new capital in the fall. There is a marker on the grounds of the present Capitol building commemorating the log cabin Capitol, but John C. Galbraith, writing in 1853, said that the log cabin Capitol was several hundred yards south of the present Capitol Square. [*This would have been in the vicinity of the present Caldwell building.*]

Soon after the location was made, Congress granted the Territory a quarter section of land at the new capital site, to be sold in order to raise money for the erection of public buildings. The Legislative Council that met in Tallahassee in November, 1824, directed that this quarter section (the southeast quarter of Section 36, Township 1 North, Range 1 West) should be laid off into a town to be called Tallahassee.

The same Council established Leon county, which it named for Ponce de Leon, and made Tallahassee the county seat.

Name Taken from Indian

Tradition credits Octavia Walton, young daughter of George Walton, Secretary of the Territory, with suggesting that the new capital be called "Tallahassee." The name is taken either from the Tallahassee Seminoles, who occupied the area, or from one of their villages. The word "Tallahassee" is of

An 1838 Tallahassee scene, thought to be Jefferson Street, as drawn by a French artist, Francis, Conte de Castelnau.
Library of Congress

Creek derivation, meaning literally "old town." It is frequently translated "old fields."

The town was laid out symmetrically with Capitol Square at the center, four other public squares, and broad streets. It was bounded by the present Park Avenue and Meridian, Bloxham and Boulevard streets on the north, east, south, and west, respectively. The squares were Washington Square, now occupied by the County Courthouse; Wayne Square, on which the City Hall stands; Jackson Square, site of the now demolished Whitfield Building; and Green Square, which is part of the site of the Holland Building. The original town plat, which was required to be filed with the Secretary of the Territory, has disappeared. Consequently, no one knows if the squares were dedicated to the public as public parks or if they were the property of the Territory and later, of the State. In recent years the State has acted on the latter assumption.

The first sale of town lots took place in April, 1825. If we may credit Prince Achille Murat, "elegant houses made of boards and timberwork, painted in all sorts of colors" began to replace log cabins. "Trees are cut down on all sides," he wrote; "their burning stumps and roots indicate the spots destined for streets and public places." By September, Tallahassee could boast of fifty houses, a church, a schoolhouse, "two very commodious hotels," seven stores, an apothecary's shop, a printing office, two shoemakers, two blacksmiths, three carpenters, a tailor, and three brickyards. Most of the establishments were clustered about Capitol Square, as in any small courthouse town.

The LaFayette Grant

A township at Florida's new seat of government was among the gifts of the United States as the Nation sought to balance its Revolutionary War debt to the Marquis de LaFayette after his ruin in France's Reign of Terror.

Congress in 1824 voted the needy Marquis $200,000 and a township located on any unsold public domain. The Marquis was inclined toward Florida because the territory then was experiencing a land boom and be-

Florida's Capitol in 1838, as depicted by a French artist, Francis, Conte de Castelnau, in Vues et Souvenirs de l'Amerique do Nord.

Library of Congress

cause, as Kathryn Abbey Hanna wrote, in Washington "he had come under the magnetic spell of Richard Keith Call, Florida's representative and her most ardent champion."

Florida's climate also was a lure, for LaFayette wished to test his theory that free labor could prove more productive than slave labor. He caused some fifty to sixty Norman peasants to settle near Tallahassee in 1831 to attempt the cultivation of vineyards, olive groves, mulberry trees and silk worms.

The colony failed, LaFayette's land ultimately was sold for approximately $103,000, but Florida has a county called Lafayette as tangible reminder of the Revolutionary hero. The Marquis never saw his Florida land but grandsons did in 1850.

The LaFayette township, formally Township 1 North, Range 1 East, is bounded in today's Tallahassee by Meridian Road on the west, approximately Gaines Street on the south, and extends six miles to the east and six miles to the north, an area of 23,028½ acres.

Second Capitol

Plans for a two-story Capitol building had been approved in 1825 and construction of one wing, forty by twenty-six feet, was completed the following year. The Commissioners of the Tallahassee Fund, who were entrusted with the sale of lots and construction of the building, had offered a prize of $100 for the best plans. Colonel Robert Butler, Surveyor General for Florida, won the competition. The cornerstone was laid with Masonic ceremonies on January 7, 1826.

The well-known Castelnau drawing of this Capitol looks like a frame building, but the *Sentinel* commented in 1843, "The old Capitol was built with mortar made from lime burned in our immediate vicinity at the place known as the 'Cascades.' When it became necessary to demolish the building... the bricks were more readily broken than the mortar which separated and adhered to them. Small portions of the walls for the building are still standing...."

Controversy, later to be recognized as a continuing complication of every change in the Capitol, disrupted construction of the first permanent statehouse. The difficulties caused the Legislative Council to reduce the number of commissioners to one, to enlarge the boundaries of Tallahassee so more land within the community could be sold to provide additional funds for the Capitol, and to limit construction to the single wing, whose cost already had been restricted to not more than $12,000.

Governor William P. DuVal, the first Territorial Governor, urged enlargement of the Capitol and in 1828 his brother, John P. DuVal, then the Commissioner, contracted with Benjamin G. Thornton for construction of a Capitol which would make use of the wing. The foundation and walls were to be of brick, the roof of slate, and the joists and floors of heart pine.

Thornton set up a sawmill at the approximate site of the present Leon County Courthouse, a block from today's Capitol, to process the timbers he hauled there. He also fashioned a kiln to produce lime for mortar from rock he quarried; Thornton, however, ran into money problems through the Territory's inability to pay as the work progressed, and the contractor lost his home, land, slaves, sawmill, kiln, and other belongings. The Territory sued Thornton for non-performance. While a jury decided in Thornton's favor, he could not obtain reimbursement until 1842 when the Legislative Council agreed to pay him $2,500 of the $8,000 claimed.

With the work stopped, the Legislative Council appropriated $1,200 in 1832 for preserving what had been done, including the painting of a fence about Capitol Square. By 1836, the need for space had become sufficiently acute that the Auditor and Comptroller were authorized to rent quarters at a cost of not more than $200 a year. A new fence also was authorized for Capitol Square. Again in 1839, the Legislative Council provided $300 for further attention to the fence, for the installation of a well and pump, and for the planting of ornamental trees.

The Third Capitol

Agitation for a new start resulted in the appropriation by Congress on March 3, 1839, of $20,000 for erection of a "suitable state house or public building for the use of the Territorial Legislature" and for the office of the Secretary of the Territory and preservation of records. The Legislative Council promptly ordered a new building, with demolition of the work commenced in 1826.

It is not known whether the second permanent Capitol was erected on the same spot on the Capitol Square as the original wing but this may be presumed from the centering of the structure on the Square.

Again attended by contention and litigation, mainly among the contractor, the Capitol Commissioner, and a supplier, construction proceeded until February, 1841, when money again ran out. By then, about two-thirds

This is the earliest known photograph of the Capitol. It shows the building as it looked between 1845 and 1891. On the day of the convening of the first Legislature and of the inaugural of the first Governor under statehood, the Capitol may have been painted white, for the Florida Sentinel *speaks of this color.*

Allen Morris

of the building had been roughed in and temporary quarters could be furnished the Legislative Council and the Secretary of the Territory.

Congress was asked for more money, but the national government, mindful that Florida was pressing to become a state and as such would be responsible for its debts, at first ignored the plea.

Concerned by deterioration caused by the weathering of the unfinished and exposed second floor, the Legislative Council in March, 1843, directed the Capitol Commissioner to use whatever means available to have the uncovered rooms roofed over.

The three-story building, as originally constructed, was one hundred and fifty-one feet long and fifty-three feet wide, with both interior and exterior walls of solid brick. The front and rear entrances were through porticos each having six Doric columns thirteen feet in circumference and thirty-four feet in height.

In order to supplement the congressional appropriation for the capitol, the northwest quarter was platted and placed on sale in 1840. This sale did not, however, provide sufficient funds for completion of the Capitol, and Congress in 1844 relented and granted another $20,000 for the purpose. The building was finally completed in 1845, just prior to the organization of the government of the state of Florida.

This second permanent and third Capitol at Tallahassee remained in use until 1978 as the nucleus of the statehouse. The Legislature, despite recurring pleas of State officers for additional space, allowed the 1845 Capitol to remain without noticeable change until 1891, when a small cupola was placed atop the structure. The first major expansion occurred in 1901–1902.

The Changing City

While the statehouse was evolving, the surrounding community also was changing. Ralph Waldo Emerson, visiting in 1827, entered in his notebook: "Tallahassee, a grotesque place, selected three years since as a suitable spot for the capitol of the territory, and since that day rapidly settled by public officers, land speculators and desperadoes... Governor DuVal is the button on which all things are hung."

An 1838 visitor found Tallahassee had about 300 houses, "almost all built of wood and on the Italian model. They rarely have more than one story; two or three only are of brick painted a bright red with green shutters." This lack of imposing residences caused a New Englander in 1841 to remark to a correspondent "Why Benny, your father's Barn is handsomer than any house in Tallahassee."

The appearance of the town was altered for the better by a catastrophe that occurred in 1843. On the evening of May 25 a sweeping fire wiped out practically every business establishment in town, inflicting a half million dollar loss in merchandise and buildings. Before the smoke had cleared away, plans were made for building a better town. The City Council adopted an ordinance permitting only fireproof buildings to be constructed in the devastated area. On the first anniversary of the fire, one of the local newspapers could boast, "Instead of the tumbled down wooden shanties, which formerly disfigured the business part of the town, we now find well arranged and commodious fire proof brick stores." The fire marked the transition of Tallahassee from a frontier community to a pleasant Southern town.

As Capitol appeared between 1891, when cupola was added, and 1901–1902 when the Capitol was enlarged. Florida State Archives

Improved transportation was afforded by the re-building of the St. Marks Railroad and the construction of the Pensacola and Georgia Railroad, which was completed from Lake City to Tallahassee in 1860. The former had been in operation since 1837 but had been mule-drawn for more than a decade because its locomotive had a habit of jumping the track into the bushes. The latter is the present Seaboard Coast Line serving Tallahassee. The "Deep Cut" which is crossed by the overpass at Magnolia Heights and on Magnolia Drive was excavated by slave labor. By 1860 Tallahassee could boast of such other modern facilities as illuminating gas and telegraphic communication with other parts of the country.

Scene of Four Conventions

As the capital of the State, Tallahassee has been the scene of four Constitutional Conventions, all of which were motivated, either directly or indirectly, by the causes and results of the Civil War. On January 11, 1861, the Convention of that year signed the Ordinance of Secession in a ceremony held in the east portico of the Capitol. The Convention of 1865 nullified the Ordinance and reorganized the State government under Andrew Johnson's plan of Reconstruction. The Constitution of 1865 was superseded in 1868 by the carpetbag constitution, which provided a highly centralized government that was acceptable to white Democrats from the end of Reconstruction until they wrote a Constitution in 1885.

Tallahassee was far from the main battle lines of the Confederacy and never felt the direct impact of the war. It was threatened in March, 1865, when Federal troops landed at St. Marks and advanced toward the capital but they were met and defeated at the Natural Bridge by a few regular troops and hastily armed citizens and Seminary cadets. Tallahassee has the distinction of being the only uncaptured Southern state capital east of the Mississippi. It did not escape military occupancy, however, for Federal troops marched into the town on May 20, 1865, and supervised its government until the Constitution of 1868 was adopted.

Florida's turbulent politics of the Reconstruction period naturally centered in the capital. The town attracted freedmen, who took an active part in both local and state politics, and by 1870 1,203 of its 2,023 inhabitants were blacks. National attention was focused on it for a short time in 1876 during the Hayes-Tilden election contest. Tallahassee was so thronged with politicians and reporters from all over the country that the City Hotel employed forty-five waiters to serve them. In due course the Florida Canvassing Board counted in the Hayes electors, the visitors departed, and Tallahassee dropped back into its former obscurity.

This is how the Capitol appeared after the addition of north and south wings and the dome in 1901–1902. Florida State Archives

Vote on Capital Removal

By the 1890s, the business of the State necessitated additional office space. This condition reopened the question of capital removal, which had been unsuccessfully agitated in 1881. The Legislature of 1899 refusing to take action toward either providing more space or removing the capital from Tallahassee, the State Democratic Committee in 1900 called for a referendum on removal. In the primary election of that year, Tallahassee received an absolute majority over its rivals—Jacksonville, Ocala, and St. Augustine.

The Legislature of 1901 accepted the results of this election as a mandate to provide additional accommodations for the conduct of the State's business. Erection of a separate office building was considered, but the final decision was to enlarge the Capitol. An appropriation of $75,000 permitted the construction in 1901–02, of additions to the north and south ends of the building and the erection of a dome, which replaced a small cupola built in 1891.

The additions of the north and south ends of the original building were then used for chambers of the Senate and House of Representatives and of the Supreme Court and to give more space to the Governor and Cabinet officers.

Remodeling of the Capitol had hardly been completed before the need for still more space was apparent. In 1905 Governor Broward recommended a second addition to the Capitol. Nothing was done, however, until 1911, when Governor Gilchrist's proposal to construct a Supreme Court and Railroad Commission Building on Jackson Square was acceded to by the Legislature. This building, named for Chief Justice James B. Whitfield, was occupied entirely by the Public Service Commission (successor to the Railroad Commission) after the Supreme Court moved to its new building in 1949. The Whitfield building was demolished in 1979.

The Capitol was enlarged for a second time in 1921–22 with the addition of east and west wings at a cost of $250,000. The new east portico carried forward the general design of the old east front with its columns. However, the west portico was omitted to allow sufficient space on the second floor for the chamber of the House of Representatives. The Senate was accommodated in the new east wing.

Along with the addition of the wings, there was a refurbishing of the Capitol, including installation of marble stairways at the rotunda and marble wainscoting throughout the building.

Another betterment of the period was a system of electric lights to illuminate Capitol Square, a gift of Tallahassee citizenry acknowledged by resolution of the 1923 Legislature.

In 1925, the $300,000 Martin (after former Governor John W. Martin) Building was erected on Wayne Square. In 1963, the City traded the State land in the Capitol Center for the Martin Building to use as its City Hall. In the 1930s the Mayo (for Commissioner of Agriculture Nathan Mayo) Building was erected at a cost of $350,000, and the north wing of the Capitol was added with federal assistance. In 1940, Tallahassee constructed a $300,000 City Administration Building (now known as the Knott Building, for the former State Treasurer W. V. Knott), for the use of the state. The south wing of the Capitol was completed in 1947 at a cost of $600,000 after being delayed by the war.

The Capitol Center

The end of the war years, a general growth in state government, and a plan conceived by Governor Spessard L. Holland (1941–45) added a new tone to expansion of the capitol complex. Theretofore, the location of state buildings largely was controlled by the free sites laid down on the Old Plan of Tallahassee.

Governor Millard F. Caldwell (1945–49) gave his full support to the new concept of a "Capitol Center" as designed by Albert D. Taylor, landscape architect and town planner. Taylor's original plan called for the ultimate inclusion of 32 city blocks and the erection of ten new buildings.

The State's needs outgrew the Taylor plan and in 1966 the boundaries of the Capitol Center were expanded to include some 50 city blocks. Similarly, a number of State agencies outgrew their original homes, requiring expanded structures or new buildings.

By 1981 there were 18 major State buildings in the Capitol Center. In addition to the old and new Capitols, the adjacent legislative buildings, the Supreme Court Building, the Knott Building and the Mayo Building, there are now these structures clustered in the Center:

The Holland Building, named for Governor and U.S. Senator Spessard L. Holland.

The Caldwell Building, named for Governor and State Supreme Court Justice Millard F. Caldwell.

The Carlton Building, named for Governor Doyle E. Carlton.

The Elliot Building, named for Fred C. Elliot, longtime chief engineer for the Trustees of the Internal Improvement Fund.

The Collins Building, named for Governor LeRoy Collins.

The Johns Building, named for Acting Governor Charley E. Johns.

The Bryant Building, named for Governor Farris Bryant.

The Burns Building, named for Governor Haydon Burns.

The Larson Building, named for State Treasurer J. Edwin Larson.

The Fletcher Building, named for U.S. Senator Duncan U. Fletcher.

The Gray Building, named for Secretary of State R. A. Gray.

The Bloxham Building, named for Governor William D. Bloxham. (The Bloxham Building was erected and long occupied as a public elementary school.)

The District Court of Appeal Building, at Pensacola and Martin Luther King, Jr., Boulevard.

The Legislature's Auditor General Building, named for Florida Congressman Claude Pepper.

The Department of Education Building, named for Commissioner of Education Ralph D. Turlington.

State Mourning at Capitol

Governor William D. Bloxham lay in state in the Governor's suite in 1911.

The rotunda of the old Capitol served for the public farewells to a number of State officials.

Secretary of Agriculture B.E. McLin was mourned there in 1912, as was Justice Fred H. Davis in 1937.

The open casket of Governor Dan McCarty was placed there on September 29, 1953, for officers and employees of the State government and citizens generally to pay their last respects.

The rotunda similarly served the late Comptroller J. M. Lee on October 8, 1946, and the late Treasurer J. Edwin Larson on January 26, 1965.

Non-Governmental Use of the Capitol

Entries in their Journals evidence the fact that the chambers of the Legislature offered space for non-governmental gatherings of many kinds: among these, lectures by visiting professors, a funeral, a wedding, church services, and a college commencement.

266 / Seat of Government

This is the West front of Florida's Capitol. The domed wings house the chambers of the Legislature and offices of the Legislature and of the Executive Department. The House chamber is at the North end, or left hand side of the photograph, and the Senate chamber is at the South end. The adjacent buildings are the office structures of the House and Senate, housing some of the committee meeting rooms and office suites for members and staff. This photograph was taken from the roof of the Supreme Court Building, across Duval Street from the Capitol.

Department of Commerce
Photo by Tom McLendon

There were a number of temperance lectures delivered in the chamber of The House of Representatives but the Journal of 1885 reports in these words the failure of an effort to obtain the use of the chamber for that purpose:

"Mr. Solomon moved that Mr. Forrest be tendered the use of Assembly Hall for the purpose of delivering a temperance lecture on Sunday morning at 10 o'clock.

"Mr. Herndon moved to amend by inserting, that each member failing to attend said lecture shall pay a fine of $5.

"Mr. Wilkerson of Marion moved to lay the whole matter on the table; which was agreed to."

In the years just before and after the Civil War, "The Tournament"—sometimes referred to as "The Tournament of Love"—was a yearly Tallahassee diversion. In these, costumed galloping riders sought to pierce with lances rings suspended from three arches erected at intervals of about fifty yards. The horsemen were known by such names as the Knight of the Red Cross, the Knight of the Golden Horse Shoe, and even as the Unknown Knight. The winner would have the reward of designating the Queen of Love and Beauty.

The tournaments were followed by what was described in the Tallahassee *Floridian* as "the Grand Fancy Ball."

"The Assembly (House) very kindly permitted their hall to be used for the ball-room," continued the *Floridian,* "and the desks, railing and carpet were removed and every thing arranged for the dance. . . . Seldom, if ever, have we seen such a magnificent display of beauty and fashion. The Queen and her Maids of Honor were elegantly attired and promenaded the hall with a graceful dignity. . . . The Knights appeared in the costumes worn in the Tournament, while a great portion of the ladies were in costume, admired by all who surrounded them. . . .

"The Senate Chamber was laid out as a supper room, where a number of tables groaned beneath a liberal and elegant display of the choicest and richest viands, and as the band pealed forth a stately march the gay assemblage filed gracefully in to the festive board, where in place of dry and uninteresting debates, loud and joyous laughter, capital jokes, toasts and sentiments became the order of the evening."

Rental of Offices in Capitol

Private rental of offices in the Capitol is evidenced by advertisements in *The Floridian* during 1845–1848.

Simon Towle, the State Comptroller, placed this advertisement, appearing in *The Floridian* of January 15, 1848: "The offices in the Basement of the Capitol are for rent."

This notice appeared on November 29, 1845: "M. D. Papy, Attorney at Law, will practice in all the Courts in the Middle Circuit. Office on the first floor of the Capitol, South Wing, room formerly occupied by the Secretary of the Territory."

A portrait painter, Willis McK. Russell, advised the public on March 18, 1848: "Removal. I have removed my study to the room on the North East corner of the Capitol, adjoining the office of the Hon. Mr. Brockenbrough, where I propose remaining during my stay in Florida."

The Never Captured Capital

Tallahassee was the only Southern state capital east of the Mississippi to escape capture by Federal troops during the Civil War. The only threats were blunted at the battles of Natural Bridge and Olustee (see index).

After the collapse of the Confederacy, Brigadier General E. M. McCook was assigned to receive the surrender of Southern forces in Florida. On May 20, 1865, General McCook took formal possession of Tallahassee and raised the United States flag over the capitol. It last had been displayed on January 11, 1861, when Florida declared itself an independent nation.

Sources: The basic chapter was written by Dr. Dorothy Dodd, former State Librarian. Other material was drawn from: *Journals* of Dr. W. H. Simmons and John Lee Williams; John Kilgore, "Florida's Capitol," Tallahassee Historical Society *Annual;* Kathryn T. Abbey (Hanna), "The Story of the Lafayette Lands in Florida," Florida Historical *Quarterly;* Sallie E. Blake, *Tallahassee of Yesterday, Journals,* House of Representatives, and *Tallahassee: Downtown Transitions,* Lee H. Warner and Mary B. Eastland.

The Stone Plan

A plan for systematic development of the heart of the Capitol Center, including restoration of the Capitol as it appeared in 1845 when Florida became a state, was approved by the Cabinet on September 16, 1969.

This complex was prepared by Edward Durell Stone & Associates of New York in cooperation with Reynolds, Smith and Hills of Jacksonville. These architects-engineers-designers had been commissioned earlier in the year to develop a comprehensive plan for development of the Capitol and its surrounding area.

Florida's Capitol, with its adjacent legislative office buildings, was one of the last of Stone's design. One of the nation's most eminent and controversial architects, Stone, who died August 6, 1978, changed styles of architecture in mid-life. Of the second period are such structures as the John F. Kennedy Center in Washington, the General Motors building in New York, and the United States Embassy at New Delhi.

Like Florida's Capitol, the second phase buildings designed by Stone bore his trademark, an ornate concrete grill enclosing a white-columned box. The grill was so ubiquitous, reported *The New York Times,* that Stone even used it on a gasoline service station at New York's Kennedy airport.

Stone and his associates envisioned for Florida a four-phase complex which could move along just as fast as the State desired, with existing structures being used until the new facilities were provided.

Site preparation for the first phase was commenced in June, 1970, for construction of two five-story buildings linked to the Capitol on its north and south sides. These buildings were designed to provide legislative committee rooms and offices. Money for this purpose was provided by a $10,000,000 bond issue.

The building for the House of Representatives was placed on a city block which the State had bought and cleared in 1966 for a Legislative Building, housing both the Senate and the House. Construction never was started because of indecision over both the design of the building and the need for renovation of the old, center portion of the Capitol.

The Restored Old Capitol

Representative Herbert Morgan of Tallahassee and Senator Pat Thomas of Quincy wanted to preserve the Capitol as it existed in 1902. The significance of 1902 was primarily in the addition that year of the dome. To many Floridians the dome symbolized the State government.

The decision to preserve and restore the first domed version, supported by an appropriation of $7,039,440, was reached after several years of controversy.

Each version had its proponents. Governor Reubin O'D. Askew and House Speaker Donald L. Tucker strove for outright demolition. They argued that little remained of the 1845 Capitol and preservation of any of the building blocked the view of the east front of the Capitol. There were those who deplored the wrecking of the newest and most serviceable wings, to the north and south, particularly in view of the State's continuing need for office space.

Meanwhile, Secretary of State Bruce Smathers continued to conduct the public's business from the old Capitol for two months after the Governor and other Cabinet members moved. Those two months gave Smathers and others opposed to demolishing the old Capitol time to mobilize support among legislators and the public. The 1978 Legislature opted for the 1902 version.

The decision having been made, the work of restoration proceeded rapidly with Herschel E. Shepard of Jacksonville as the architect and representatives of the Department of General Services and the Department of State as the overseers.

Restored were the light gray wainscoting, powder blue walls, and terra cotta ceilings. Red-and-white awnings were added after researchers turned up a 1903 postcard which showed these. The builders said the awnings would save one-third of the cost of air-conditioning.

Air-conditioning and heating were among the concessions to modern life. These were installed in such a way as not to be readily discernible. Today's safety codes dictated ceiling sprinklers, fire hoses and two new stairwells. Hidden in walls are 2½-inch sliding steel doors which can close off the rotunda when triggered by a heat-activated alarm. To accommodate the handicapped, a new elevator has been installed in the shaft where the Old Capitol's first elevator was placed in 1923.

The restored base of the dome has been painted off-white with gray trim and red windows, a color scheme evoking the Confederate tragedy of which Florida was a part. Atop this base is a dome whose dark copper cover gradually has gained a soft green patina from oxidation.

What came as a surprise to many was the fact that the Old Capitol had two identical fronts, each with Doric columns, on the east and west sides. The west front had been lost since 1923 when a House Chamber pushed out from the existing Capitol. Bas-relief State seals grace the pediments of the two facades. The seals are white, as they were originally, over the objection then of the Governor and Cabinet. The architect had his way until he signed off with completion of the building in 1903 and the next year officialdom had its way with colors added to the seals.

By the fall of 1982 the Old Capitol again was open as a museum of Florida's government. The Department of State's Museum of Florida History had developed exhibits in the restored areas to recall momentous events in the life of Florida and its State government.

Thus, Florida has two Capitols, the Old and the New.

Phase four would embrace two office buildings adjacent to the legislative buildings. These buildings would, however, be for the use of executive department agencies.

The Fourth Capitol

Construction of Florida's fourth, and present, Capitol was commenced November 8, 1973, and declared completed on August 19, 1977.

The building was opened officially on March 31, 1978, when Governor Reubin O'D. Askew, in a service on the unfinished west plaza, said: "We are gathered here then to dedicate this building to the service of the people, ever mindful that in this state and in this nation government exists to serve the people and not the people to serve the government."

The building cost $43,070,741. An additional $1,957,338 was committed to landscaping and to the plaza, fountains, and steps on the west front, an area known formerly as Waller Park, for Curtis L. Waller of Tallahassee, Judge of the United States Circuit Court of Appeals. While the Capitol generally is spoken of as having 22 stories, there is an additional floor below the street level, plus two levels of parking.

Some statistics:

3,700 tons of structural steel. 2,800 tons of reinforcing steel. 25,000 cubic yards of concrete (the equivalent of 16 football fields, each one foot thick), 12,000 square feet of walnut paneling. 12,000 gallons of paint. 62,000 square feet of marble. 60,000 square feet of carpet. 92,000 square feet of terrazzo. 30 miles of telephone cable. 250 miles of electrical wire. 2,000 doors. 66 public and 11 private restrooms. 40 sets of stairs. 14 elevators. 360 parking spaces.

Honor guard stands by bier of former Governor William D. Bloxham in Board Room of old Governor's suite in the Capitol. Bloxham died March 15, 1911. The second of his two full terms as Governor ended January 8, 1901. (For other instances of Capitol used for officials lying in state, see page 265.)
Florida State Archives

Some 3,000 persons work in the Capitol during normal days. When the Legislature is in session, an estimated 4,500 persons occupy the building.

The five-story base structure houses the Capitol offices of the Governor and members of the Cabinet. Four floors of this structure also are used for the chambers of the Senate and House of Representatives, the offices of the Senate President, Secretary and Sergeant at Arms and the House Speaker, Clerk, and Sergeant at Arms, some legislative committee offices and meeting rooms, and Member offices.

(For a description of the legislative chambers, see the chapter entitled The Legislature. Consult the index.)

From a public observation floor on the 22nd level, there may be seen, depending upon the clarity of the day, not only the city of Tallahassee and its environs but many miles of trees.

The architects and engineers charged with responsibility for the Capitol estimated its working life at a century. The Capitol rises 514 feet above sea level.

In his dedicatory remarks, Governor Askew described the new Capitol as "magnificent" but "just a building until we dedicate it, not only here today, but every day as we work for the people who really own it. For those of us who work here are only tenants. We do not own the building.

"So I think we should dedicate this building to the owners."

Capitol Center Cornerstones

The capitol and the two legislative office buildings are among the structures in the Capitol Center with ceremonial cornerstones.

These are polished rectangular stones, placed at eye level on the northeast corner, and dedicated under the auspices of the Grand Lodge of the Free and Accepted Masons of Florida. Each cornerstone also bears the year of the dedication in both the regular and Masonic calendars, plus the square and compass of Masonry.

Usually, cornerstones are hollow and contain items which it is believed will be interesting to those who, in the distant future, have reason to open the cornerstone. The cornerstone for the Capitol, placed in 1976, contains a box including guides to the Florida House of Representatives, the State Senate, and the State Supreme Court; letters from the Governor, Lieutenant Governor, Supreme Court Justices, the Senate President, and the House Speaker, addressed to their successors at the time of opening the box, and Masonic publications.

The stone once served as the first of foundation stones and offered support to a structure. Nowadays the cornerstone has no structural significance and may be in neither the foundation nor outside wall. As the *Encyclopedia Britannica* says, the word has become a figure of speech in many languages. Reference is made to the cornerstones or foundation stones of character, faith, liberty or other excellences.

Ancient customs related cornerstones to the study of the stars and their religious significance, states the *Britannica*. However, Coil's *Masonic Encyclopedia* concludes much is simply legend, and "it is especially to be noted that there is no hint of a cornerstone in Solomon's Temple."

Monuments in the Capitol Center

On the north end of the east front of the old Capitol is a marble shaft with this legend: "To rescue from oblivion and perpetuate in the memory of succeeding generations the heroic patriotism of the men of Leon County who perished in the Civil War of 1861–1865, this monument is raised by their country women."

This monument bears on its faces the names of battles in which Florida soldiers of the Confederate forces participated, including "Gettisburgh." The shaft also shows the name and address of its fabricator: "T. Delahunty, Laurel Hill, Philada."

On the south end is the monument to Capt. John Parkhill of the Leon Volunteers, "erected by his fellow citizens of Leon County, Florida, as a testimonial of their high esteem for his character and public services."

This monument states that Captain Parkhill was born July 10, 1823, and was killed at Palm Hammock, in South Florida, while leading his company in a chase against the Seminole Indians, November 28, AD 1857. The shaft also reminds that "the memory of the hero, is the treasure of his country."

Rehabilitation of the old Capitol caused the removal of a number of commemorative markers from its grounds. These included a gilded miniature of the Statue of Liberty, presented in 1950 as a symbol of the 40th Anniversary of the Boy Scouts' crusade "to strengthen the arm of liberty" and a marker placed by the Florida Federation of Garden Clubs in remembrance of the signing into law by Governor Dan McCarty of a legislative act designating the sabal palmetto as the State Tree. The Governor acted on June 11, 1953, and the marker was placed on February 22, 1954.

Centennial Observance

At the southeast corner of the east side of the old Capitol was a block of granite which symbolized the 100th anniversary of the first session of the Florida Legislative Council. The marker placed the event "on this spot," in November, 1824, although the log cabin is believed to have been about a city block away, perhaps on the site of the present Caldwell building.

The dedication of this marker was a phase of the centennial of the Founding of Tallahassee. This observance included the erection of a replica of the log Capitol. Among the articles placed in a box in the foundation of the granite marker were a list of subscribers to the Centennial Fund, newspapers, and reports of the Governor, administrative officers, and the Tallahassee city government.

John Hays Hammond, an internationally recognized mining engineer, brought greetings from President Calvin Coolidge. Hammond said Tallahassee "has the climate, the soil, beauty of environments and favorable location for growth that make it the most promising capital city in the United States."

Sesquicentennial Celebration

The 150th anniversary of the founding of Tallahassee as the Capital was observed on November 19, 1974, with a ceremony conducted by Governor Reubin O'D. Askew on the steps of the Capitol. There were flags, music, and brief speeches. The ceremony centered upon the placing of documents descriptive of Florida in 1974 in a copper box afterwards sealed in the granite marker of the 1924 centennial. Among the documents intended to tell future Floridians of their past was a copy of *The Florida Handbook 1973–1974.* As in 1924, a replica of the log Capitol was placed on the grounds for the sesquicentennial ceremony.

Liberty Bell Replica

A replica of the Liberty Bell stands now in front of the House Office Building. A marker explains:

"Dedicated to you, a free citizen in a free land."

"This reproduction of the Liberty Bell was presented to the people of Florida by direction of the Honorable John W. Snyder, Secretary of the Treasury."

"As the inspirational symbol of the United States Savings Bonds Independence Drive from May 15 to July 4, 1950, it was displayed in every part of this state."

"The dimensions and tone are identical with those of the original Liberty Bell when it rang out our independence in 1776."

"In standing before this symbol, you have the opportunity to dedicate yourself, as did our founding fathers, to the principles of the individual freedom for which our nation stands."

A Mystery Plaque

Visitors to the Capitol likely will be puzzled by a bronze plaque affixed to the wall of the rotunda. To the knowledgeable it is a reminder of the struggle both to save the Old Capitol and to build the new.

The plaque reads: "This plaque is dedicated to Senator Lee Weissenborn whose valiant effort to move the Capitol to Orlando was the prime motivation for the construction of this building."

The plaque resulted from a tussle of wills between the Senate and the House of Representatives in 1978 over preservation of the Old Capitol. The Senate, through Senator Jack Gordon, made the amendment authorizing the placement of the plaque a condition of passing the bill to save the Old Capitol. The House leadership believed Gordon and the Senate had acted in a moment of whimsy, expecting the House to strike the amendment for the plaque. But this would have necessitated the return of the bill to the Senate for concurrence. The House sponsors were reluctant to risk loss of the controversial bill and took the amendment. There was the unstated belief that the plaque, if ever placed, would be hidden, perhaps in a closet.

Four years later, no plaque having been placed, Senator Gordon asked former Senator Kenneth A. Plante if he would supply the plaque. He did at a cost of several hundred dollars. Excuses gone, the Department of General Services affixed the plaque to the main floor wall, where it serves now as a puzzle to passersby.

Lee Weissenborn, from Miami, served in the House from 1963 to 1965 and in the Senate from 1965 to 1972. Senator Gordon served from Miami Beach between 1972 and 1990. Kenneth A. Plante, then from Winter Park but now a Tallahassee lobbyist, was a Senator from 1967 until 1978. Plante was the Republican leader of the Senate.

Inaugurations

Day of Inaugurations

Governors assuming office by virtue of election are inaugurated on the first Tuesday after the first Monday in January following the General Election in November.

Oath of Office

A new Governor is required by the Constitution to take the following oath of office:

"I do solemnly swear (or affirm) that I will support, protect, and defend the Constitution and Government of the United States and of the State of Florida; that I am duly qualified to hold office under the Constitution of the State, and that I will well and faithfully perform the duties of Governor on which I am now about to enter. So help me God."

Except for substituting the name of the office, every officer of the State, including members of the Legislature, takes exactly the same oath before entering upon the performance of his official duties. The requirement plus the language of the oath is stated in Article II, Section 5(b) of the Constitution.

Hour of Inaugurations

Noon has been the traditional hour for administering the oath to an incoming Governor but as a matter of law he could assume the duties by taking this oath prior to midnight on the first Tuesday after the first Monday in the January following election in November. The inaugural proceedings are ceremonial in nature rather than required by Constitution or law.

Because of ill-will between their supporters, Governor-elect LeRoy Collins agonized over whether he should take the oath in advance of the noon ceremony so Acting Governor Charley E. Johns would be prevented from exercising the powers of Governor after the inaugural day commenced at midnight.

Collins felt the midnight oath could make the later ceremony on the Capitol steps something of a sham. A Collins representative secured Johns' promise—which he kept—to refrain. Collins went to bed as did Justice Glenn Terrell, who was prepared to administer the early oath.

Governor-elect Reubin O'D. Askew signed an oath and filed this with the Secretary of State on December 30, 1970, for the term beginning on January 5, 1971. Thus, Askew automatically became Governor at midnight although he was inaugurated ceremonially just before noon 12 hours later. By so doing, Governor Askew prevented the incumbent, Governor Claude R. Kirk, Jr., from performing any official actions between midnight and the formal inaugural ceremony.

There have been exceptions to the noon hour. Governor William D. Bloxham was, for example, inaugurated in 1881 at a 2 p. m. ceremony.

Governor Bob Graham set a record for advance taking of the oath. He signed on November 22, 1982 the oath which he ceremonially took on January 4, 1983. Since he was succeeding himself, there was no political reason for taking the first oath that far in advance.

When Cabinet Officers Are Installed

The regular terms of members of the Executive Department, the Cabinet officers, begin on the first Tuesday after the first Monday in January following the General Election in November.

For many years, the Cabinet officers were installed either by separately taking the oath of office or as a group in the Board room of the Capitol.

In 1956, however, the swearing in of the Cabinet members was made a part of the ceremonies at the inauguration of Governor LeRoy Collins for his second term.

Inaugural Scenes and Sidelights

The scene of the inauguration of Florida's Governors has moved from place to place about the Capitol since 1845, when William D. Moseley became the first chief executive under statehood.

Mosely took the oath of office on the East steps of the old Capitol, thereby setting a precedent for location of the inaugural ceremonies that lasted, with few exceptions, until 1955.

In 1955, because of highway construction on the East side, the inaugural was shifted to the West side of the Capitol with a platform extending across Adams Street and onto the lip of Waller Park. This remained the scene until 1975 when construction of the new Capitol dictated the return to the East Front. (This gave Reubin O'D. Askew the distinction of being the only Governor to be inaugurated on both fronts, the West in 1971 and the East in 1975.)

In 1979, the site again was changed, this time to the West front of the new Capitol.

The oathtaking at the new scene by Governor Bob Graham was note-

Campaign foes but now all smiles, as is the Florida political tradition, top-hatted Acting Governor Charley E. Johns, at left, and incoming Governor LeRoy Collins ride together from the Mansion to the Capitol for the Collins inauguration on January 4, 1955. Florida State Archives

The tulle butterfly was part of the ensemble handmade by Mrs. William S. Jennings on the occasion of the inauguration of her husband as Florida's 18th Governor on January 8, 1901. Florida State Archives

worthy for two reasons. Both incoming Governor Graham and outgoing Governor Askew wore every-day suits instead of the frock coats and top hats of their predecessors. With a temperature of 42 degrees, wind of 13 knots, and an estimated chill factor of 25 degrees, at 11 a.m., when former Governor LeRoy Collins, as master of ceremonies, convened the ceremony, the throng dwindled rapidly. The *Florida Times-Union* estimated "no more than 500" persons remained for the conclusion of Graham's address. The chill gave grim meaning to a long-standing Florida political witticism that "it'll be a cold day in Tallahassee when a candidate from Dade County becomes Governor."

The second inauguration for Graham was conducted in a new location, on a platform built out from the west steps of the old Capitol so that the ceremony faced the east front of the new Capitol.

Governor Bob Martinez was also inaugurated there, but Governor Lawton Chiles' ceremonies were both held on platforms on the east side of the old Capitol.

Indoor Ceremonies

William D. Bloxham took the oath of faithful performance as Governor in 1881 in the presence of a joint session of the Legislature in the House chamber at the North end of the Capitol. The oath was administered by a Circuit Judge, David S. Walker, instead of the usual Justice of the Supreme Court.

Another exception to the portico ceremonies was that of Albert W. Gilchrist who received the oath in 1909 in the House chamber because heavy rain forced the ceremony indoors. In 1967, a contingency plan was prepared to move the inauguration of Governor Claude R. Kirk, Jr., into the House chamber because of threatening rain. However, although the throng was dampened, it was not necessary to move the ceremony indoors.

Becoming Acting Governor upon the death of Governor Dan McCarty in September, 1953, Senate President Charley E. Johns took the oath in the Senate chamber.

Shortest Notice

George F. Drew, the Democrat whose election in 1876 ended eight years of Republican administration during Reconstruction, had the shortest notice that he would, in fact, become Governor. The election having been contested, the Supreme Court's mandate declaring Drew the winner by 195 votes was filed at 10 o'clock on the morning of the inaugural.

Upon being officially notified that his election had been certified, the Governor-elect walked across the street from the City Hotel, which stood at the southwest corner of Adams and Pensacola Streets, and was administered the oath by Chief Justice E. M. Randall at Noon on the East portico.

The late chief Justice James B. Whitfield related how Democrats feared the outgoing Acting Governor and Republican nominee, M. L. Stearns, might refuse to surrender the office. Judge Whitfield said groups of Democrats, armed with rifles, shotguns and pistols, concealed themselves in buildings near the Capitol, ready to spring into action if followers of Stearns sought to block Drew's inauguration. Stearns, however, accepted the mandate of the Supreme Court and the inauguration occurred without incident.

Triumph and tragedy . . . Governor and Mrs. Dan McCarty are seen here (left) in the inaugural receiving line at the Capitol on January 6, 1953, and, the same place on September 28, when the body of McCarty was on public view. Florida State Archives

Catts, a Different Governor

Sidney J. Catts, the Baptist minister who had been elected as the nominee of the Prohibition party after a prolonged and bitter Democratic primary contest saw W. V. Knott declared the nominee, also had questions as to whether his inauguration would pass without incident. Catts was said to have armed himself with a revolver for the ceremony in 1917. Catts likely excelled every other Governor in quoting Scripture and drawing historical allusions. Catts likened his victory to the triumph of Cromwell over the English royalists or the French Revolution over the nobility or the American colonies over Great Britain. He enumerated the forces he said had opposed him, concluding:

The common people of Florida, the everyday masses of the cracker people have triumphed and the day of your apotheosis has arrived, and you can say, as said the ancient Hebrew devotee, "Lift up your gates, and be ye lifted up, ye everlasting doors, and let the Lord of Glory in."[1]

An Inaugural Sidelight

Even Florida's first inaugural in 1845 had its sidelight. *The Florida Sentinel,* a Whig Tallahassee newspaper critic of Democrat Moseley, printed this aside, prefaced with a disclaimer as to vouching for the truth:

One of the dignitaries of the day, as the Governor was about to take the oath of office, handed him what was supposed to be a written copy of the oath to be taken; but a mistake had been made, and the paper proved to be a petition to His Excellency, by the dignitary aforesaid, to be made Adjutant General.

Moseley was inaugurated to the booming of 28 cannon and the lively jump of Yankee Doodle Dandy.

---

[1]As quoted by Wayne Flint's Cracker Messiah. Psalms, 27, differs from Calls' usage.

Inaugural Parades

With some exceptions, having a parade has been a fixture of inaugural ceremonies since Moseley.

The Star of Florida, a Tallahassee newspaper, set the scene for the Moseley inauguration by reporting, in part:

> The chief marshal of the day, will, upon the firing of a cannon at 12 o'clock, meridian, form the civic procession in front of the courthouse (now the site of the Park Avenue Federal building), when the military will form as an escort, and proceed down Monroe Street to the eastern front of the state house.

Conspicuous among the paraders were the Quincy Lancers, with a gay red pennon fluttering from each horseman's lance. Another smart military outfit, the Tallahassee Guards, made—in the words of *The Sentinel*—"a gallant appearance."

Ceremonies opened with "Hail Columbia" and a prayer. The Governor's address followed presentation of his credentials and, by a committee of its drafters, the Constitution put together at St. Joseph six years earlier, in anticipation of statehood.

"The seal of the Territory was then transferred to the Governor by the late Governor of Florida, John Branch, with a neat address," said *The Sentinel,* "and proclamation was made by the chief marshal of the establishment and organization of the government of the State of Florida, and that William D. Moseley, was duly qualified, as Governor and commander in chief of the Army and Navy of the State."

The fervor of Moseley's inauguration was dampened by news of the death of Andrew Jackson, the man most responsible for the acquisition of Florida by the United States from Spain. Many of the inaugural participants wore black arm bands in Jackson's memory.

Tail coats and top hats were the order of the day as Governor-elect Fuller Warren and Governor Millard F. Caldwell march to the inaugural platform on the east steps of the Capitol on January 4, 1949.
Florida State Archives

Inaugural Firsts

Carriages first were used for the procession at the inauguration of Governor William S. Jennings in 1901; automobiles for Governor Sidney J. Catts in 1917. Catts was the first to use an automobile extensively in campaigning Florida, and his inaugural vehicle carried a sign, "This is the Ford that Got Me There." Catts' inaugural also was the first filmed in Florida with a motion picture camera.

Loud speakers first were used at the inaugural of Governor Doyle E. Carlton in 1929, and the radio broadcast of Governor Dave Sholtz's inauguration in 1933 also was a first. Estimates of the crowd before the

Capitol for the inauguration of Governor Fuller Warren in 1949 varied from 10,000 (by the *Florida Times-Union*) to 40,000 (by Governor Warren) but 28,000 plates of barbecue were served on the Capitol grounds. Governor LeRoy Collins was the first at his inaugural in 1955, to use ministers of the three major religious faiths, Protestant, Roman Catholic, and Jewish. For many years, along with the traditional ball at the gymnasium of Florida State University, a separate ball was held on the campus of Florida A&M University but this was discontinued in 1971 with the inauguration of Governor Reubin O'D. Askew. Governor Haydon Burns sponsored five inaugural balls throughout the state, with a fee charged and the proceeds pledged to university scholarships.

A tradition was created in 1957 when, because Governor LeRoy Collins was succeeding himself and there was no outgoing chief executive with a farewell address, there was a gap in the customary timing of the program. This was filled by Governor Collins inviting members of the Cabinet to take their oath on his platform. This now has become routine.

In 1955, outgoing Acting Governor Charley E. Johns ignored the unwritten custom that departing chief executive leaves the limelight to his successor, staying through the evening to dance at Governor Collins' inaugural balls.

First to be televised was the second inauguration of Governor Collins in 1957. A mobile unit of WTVT-Ch. 13, Tampa, used the microwave facility of WCTV-Ch. 6, Tallahassee, to beam signals to the microwave receiver at the Thomasville, Georgia, station of the American Telephone & Telegraph Company, which relayed the sound and picture to Florida stations.

The first Republican inaugural of this century, in 1967, was memorable for two reasons not on the program.

The new GOP Governor, Claude R. Kirk, Jr., was accompanied by "Madame X," whom Kirk would not introduce to the press. Reporters later discovered "Madame X" was Erika Mattfeld, a native of Germany whom Kirk had met in Brazil. They were wed a month after the inauguration. Kirk had been married before and divorced.

The other surprise, particularly to legislators present, was Kirk's announcement in his inaugural address that he was calling a special session of the Legislature for the following Monday. "It's unbelievable," declared House Speaker Ralph Turlington. "I cannot see the emergency," echoed Senate President Verle A. Pope.

An Evening to be Remembered

Republicans celebrated their party's return to the Governor's office in 1987, after a 20-year absence, with a Tallahassee Civic Center gala for 6,000 invited guests.

The new Governor and Mrs. Martinez led off the ball by dancing to Bruce Springsteen's "My Hometown," a song rather unexpected but somehow appropriate.

Florida Jubilee 1991

The Florida Jubilee 1991 commemorated the inauguration of Governor Lawton Chiles and Lieutenant Governor Buddy MacKay as well as Cabinet officers. The theme of the Inaugural was "A Celebration of Florida and Its

People." The Jubilee was structured to celebrate both the vitality of the people and richness of the history of the state. To capture the spirit of the Chiles/MacKay campaign, all inaugural activities were free and open to the public. A Florida Jubilee was again the theme for Chiles' 1995 inaugural.

Amid Tears, Florida Became American

Finally July 17th was the date set for the ceremonies at Government House and also at Fort Barrancas. At seven-thirty of that cloudy July morning, Colonel George Brooke, with the band in front and colors flying, led the American troops into the Plaza.

The General (Andrew Jackson), walking just a trifle stiffly, called for his horse. The entire American party galloped up the street and into the Plaza. They halted before the saluting soldiers. Jackson, in full dress, every one of the nine bands of glittering gold braid topped by a large gold button, his heavy golden epaulets gleaming, raised his low, cockaded hat to Rachel. She and her party were on the upper gallery of the house.

Almost at once Jackson and his party left the house again and walked briskly across the Plaza between the Spanish and the American soldiers. At the gateway the Spanish sentries presented arms and the big door opened. The few formalities were quickly over. The Spanish guard in front of the Governor's house was called to attention, and marched away. American soldiers took their places. The big doors of the Government House again opened and Jackson, accompanied by Cavalla, walked back across the Plaza to Jackson's house when the brief official visit was over. As Cavalla reappeared, the Spanish flag came slowly down; the American flag went up, "full one hundred feet." The Spanish troops followed with the departing Governor. The band broke into "The Star-Spangled Banner" and the guns on the Hornet boomed.

The citizens of Pensacola, most of whom were Spanish, watched the scene in silence.

Rachel Jackson saw it all from the upper gallery. "Many burst into tears," she wrote. "I have never seen so many pale faces."

THE MANGROVE COAST, Karl A. Bickel
Coward-McCann, 1943. Used by permission

Diorama of the change of flags, from Spain to the U.S., 1821. Florida State Archives

Florida Becomes a State

"Saturday morning's mail brought intelligence of the (Senate) passage of the bill for the admission of Iowa and Florida. The vote was 36 to 9."

Thus soberly, under a single column heading, "The State of Florida" on page 2, did *The Sentinel* at Tallahassee on Tuesday, March 11, 1845, inform its readers of the advent of statehood for Florida's 66,000 inhabitants (including slaves).

By that date actually, President John Tyler had signed the congressional act into law, putting into motion the governmental machinery assembled at St. Joseph in 1839 as the "Constitution of Florida."

The House of Representatives passed the Iowa-Florida bill, 144 to 48, on Feb. 13, and the Senate on March 1, with the President adding his approving signature on March 3, the last day of his term.

So culminated the years of movement toward statehood since Florida became a territory in 1821 with Gen. Andrew Jackson as first Governor under the United States. These had been years of controversy. Floridians debated whether there should be a state at all or if Florida ought to be split into two states. Elsewhere in the country, attention focused upon what the admission of Florida, with two senators, would mean to the delicate balance between pro- and anti-slavery members of the Senate of the United States.

This last was settled by coupling Iowa, a free state, with Florida, a slave state.

Florida had prepared for statehood by the writing of a Constitution which a majority of the electors may or may not have ratified—officially, it was accepted by fewer than 200 votes amid claims of irregularity.

The St. Joseph Constitution limited the franchise to white males more than 21 years old who were enrolled in the state militia, and while it provided the Legislature would be elected by popular vote, only one of the executive officers—the Governor—was elected. Appointed by the Legislature were the State Treasurer, Comptroller, Attorney General, Justices of the Supreme Court and chancellors and judges of the Circuit Courts. One Representative to Congress was elected from the state at large by popular vote, but the two Senators were elected by the Legislature.

When the Iowa-Florida bill first was reported to the House of Representatives, it contained provision for division of Florida when East Florida should possess as many as 35,000 inhabitants (slaves counted as three-fifths) but this was struck out by a floor vote.

John Branch, the last Territorial Governor, acted promptly upon receiving formal notice of Florida's admission, proclaiming an election for May 26, 1845. William Dunn Moseley, the Democratic nominee for governor, triumphed over the Whig candidate, Richard Keith Call, twice territorial governor, by 3,115 votes to 2,602. Both Moseley and Call had their family roots in Princess Anne county, Virginia, where Call was born in 1791. His youth, however, was spent in Kentucky, where he joined Andrew Jackson to fight the Indians and British. He came to Florida with Jackson.

Moseley was born at Moseley Hall in Lenoir County, North Carolina, in 1795. With earnings from teaching school, he attended the University of North Carolina, having James K. Polk, future President, among his classmates. He moved to Florida in 1835 after having been defeated by three votes for governor of North Carolina. He resided on a plantation in Jefferson County until 1851 (except during his official stay in Tallahassee) when he moved to Palatka, where he died in 1863.

Elected with Governor Moseley were members of the state Legislature (41 Representatives and 17 Senators) and Florida's first Congressman, David Levy, later known as David Yulee, also a Democrat. United States Senators then were selected by state Legislatures and Levy was chosen with James D. Westcott, Jr., another Democrat, to take Florida's seats in the upper house.

Levy, therefore, resigned as Congressman before he actually served. To replace him, E. Carrington Cabell, a Whig, and William H. Brockenbrough, a Democrat, offered themselves to the electorate. Cabell was declared the winner in Florida but Brockenbrough successfully contested his seating at Washington, however.

Four Governors in a Year

The year 1865 saw Florida with a succession of four Governors as a consequence of the ending of the Civil War: John Milton, A. K. Allison, William Marvin, and David S. Walker.

Florida: A State in a Federal Republic
Glenn Terrell

Our country is a Federal Republic, a government in which policies are made and laws are enacted by representatives elected by the people. Thus it is not a pure democracy. A pure democracy is one in which all the citizens participate in law making. The City States of Greece, the Mayflower Colony and the New England Town Meeting were typical examples of pure democracies. Federal democracy in this country is defined and administered by a written constitution. Each State is governed by such a constitution patterned on the general plan of the Federal Constitution but some of them antedate the latter. The State Constitution is a limitation of power while the Federal Constitution is a delegation of power. The State Legislature, in other words, is free to legislate in any field not in terms prohibited by the State Constitution, while Congress can legislate only in such fields and on such subjects as are in terms specified in the Federal Constitution.

Glenn Terrell was a Justice of the Florida Supreme Court from May 15, 1923, until January 12, 1964. This is an excerpt from an article in the Fourth Edition of *The Florida Handbook*.

Symbols of the State

The Flags over Florida

At least sixteen flags have flown over Florida or parts of Florida. There have been flags of five countries: Spain, France, Great Britain, the United States, and the Confederacy. There have been State flags, one as the symbol of Florida as a sovereign nation. And there have been flags of such acceptance as people were willing to accord them. Of one, no description is known to exist.

National Flags

Spain

Research indicates Spain had no truly national flag in 1513, when Juan Ponce de León landed on Florida shores, but the Castle and Lion flag of the King was recognized as the flag of the country.

The Burgundian Saltire

The Castillo de San Marcos at St. Augustine and San Marcos de Apalache at St. Marks fly a white flag with the red Cross of Burgundy because that was among the Spanish flags used during the years of construction of the Castillo and its outpost. The white field is for Burgundy a French state; for the French nobility of Philip (Felipe I), and for the traditional color of French royalty. The knobby saltire, or X-shaped red cross, signifies the rough branches of the tree on which Saint Andrew, patron saint of Burgundy, was crucified. As with Spanish flags generally, the Burgundian

Art by Ed Gordon

Art by W. Richard Bivins

cross appeared in a number of designs and colors. On religious occasions, the field was blue with images of the Virgin Mary in the quarters formed by the cross. On other occasions the Spanish coat of arms was added at the ends of the arms of the cross. In 1785, King Charles III decreed the national flag would henceforth be the red and gold-striped ensign which flew when the United States acquired Florida from Spain.

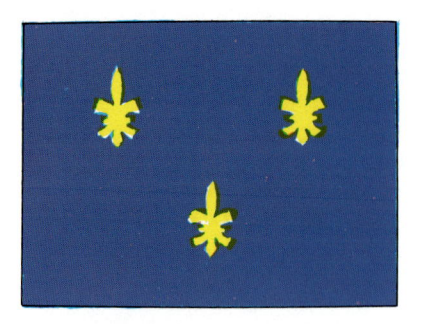

284 / Symbols of the State

Art by Ed Gordon

France
The flags of France of the 1500s had lilies both on white and blue backgrounds but the flag flown in Florida almost surely was the gold lily on blue.

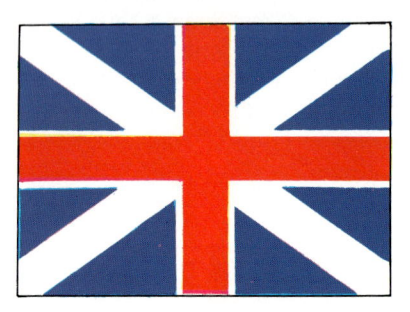

Art by Ed Gordon

Great Britain
By the English period in Florida, the mother county's flag was the Union flag of Great Britain, reflecting the merger of England and Scotland.

Art by Ed Gordon

United States
The flag of the United States had twenty-three stars when the Treaty with Spain, ceding Florida, was ratified and proclaimed on February 22, 1821.

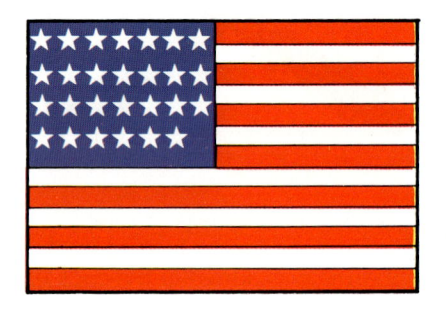

Department of State

Florida's Star
By 1845, when Florida was admitted to statehood, the custom was rooted of adding a star on the following Fourth of July for each new state. Thus, the United States flag gained a twenty-seventh star when Florida became a state on March 3, 1845. The star for Florida was added on July 4, 1845.

Symbols of the State / 285

The Confederacy

The Confederacy had a number of officially adopted national flags. The square-shaped one shown here was known variously as the "battle flag" and the "Southern Cross" flag of the Army and used between September, 1861, and April, 1865. The rectangular flag commonly regarded today as the Confederate standard was in fact the jack of the Confederate Navy.

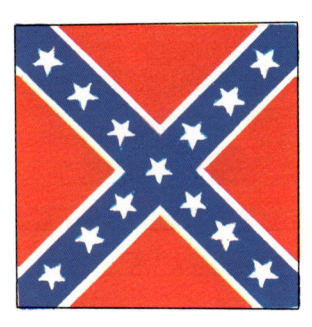

Art by Ed Gordon

The National Flag of the Confederacy

The first official national flag of the Confederacy was approved by Congress at Richmond on March 4, 1865. Since the Civil War ended with the surrender of General Robert E. Lee at Appomattox Courthouse on April 9, it is unlikely that the national flag ever was flown in Florida. By popular acceptance, the Stars and Bars, either in the square or rectangular shape, has been recognized as the flag of the Confederacy.

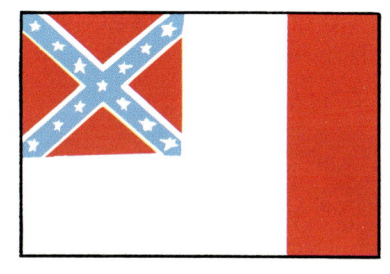

Art by W. Richard Bivins

State Flags

State Flag—1845

This flag was unfurled at the inauguration of William D. Moseley as first Governor of the State of Florida on June 25, 1845. The Florida House of Representatives agreed to a joint resolution on inauguration day adopting the flag as "the Colors of the State of Florida, till changed by law." The Senate, however, objected to the motto "Let Us Alone," and it was not until December 27, during the adjourned session that year, that a Senate resolution "consented to and adopted" the flag and its motto "as the Flag of the State of Florida." Because one house acted through a joint resolution and the other through a simple resolution, it would seem that this flag was never officially adopted although it received the approval of both houses of the General Assembly (Legislature).

Department of State

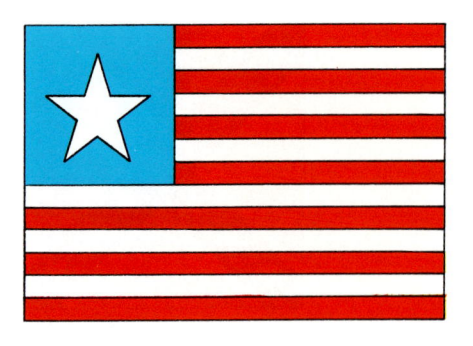

The Lone Star Flag—1861

After the flag of the United States was hauled down at the Pensacola Navy Yard on January 12, 1861, Colonel William H. Chase, commanding the Florida troops, prescribed a secession flag to serve until another could be decreed by the lawmakers at Tallahassee. This flag had thirteen stripes; alternate red and white, and a blue field with a single large star in the center. This flag served for eight months, from January 13, 1861, to September 13, 1861. Interestingly Colonel Chase's lone star flag was the same design as the flag used by the Republic of Texas navy in 1836–1845.

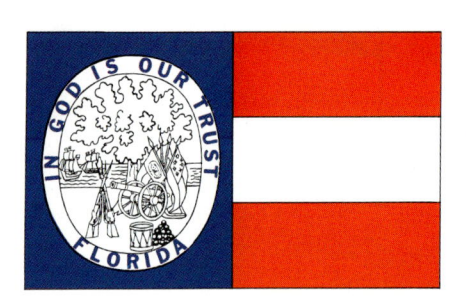

State Flag—1861

After Florida left the Union on January 11, 1861, a number of unofficial flags flew until the General Assembly (Legislature) completed action on February 1 on an act to provide a State uniform and flag. The act directed the Governor, "by and with the consent of his staff," to adopt "an appropriate device for a State flag, which shall be distinctive in character." Six months later, Governor Madison S. Perry had the Secretary of State record the description of the flag adopted in compliance with this act. Governor Perry added, "The flag has been deposited in the Executive Chamber." Whether it ever was raised over the Capitol or elsewhere does not appear from available records.

(An approximation)

Secession Flag—1861

"The Ladies of Broward's Neck," a community in Duval County, presented Governor Madison S. Perry with a flag of their design symbolizing Florida's withdrawal from the Union. The flag, never officially adopted, thus was proffered as an emblem of Florida as a sovereign nation. Governor-elect John Milton presented the flag to the Florida Secession Convention at Tallahassee in 1861 after the signing of the Ordinance of Secession. The stars represent South Carolina, Mississippi, and Florida, the first three states to leave the Union. Mrs. G. E. Ginder, great-niece of one of the ladies of Broward's Neck, in an interview in the *Florida Times-Union* in 1961, said the flag was displayed on the rostrum of the House of Representatives at the Capitol in Tallahassee during the Civil War. Afterwards, it was displayed at the Confederate Museum in Richmond, Virginia, until it was returned to Florida in 1961 and deposited in the State Archives.

State Flag—1868

The Constitutional Convention of 1868 was the first to make constitutional provision for a State flag. The Constitution adopted by that convention provided that the Legislature should, as soon as convenient, "adopt a State Emblem having the design of the Great Seal of the State impressed upon a white ground of six feet six inches fly and six feet deep." The Constitution further directed the Legislature, at its first session, to adopt the seal. This was done on August 6, 1868, and completed the design prescribed for the flag.

Art by William P. Thompson

State Flag—1900

Because the flag when furled lacked color, the Legislature in 1899 submitted to the electorate for ratification in 1900 an amendment to the Constitution adding diagonal red bars.

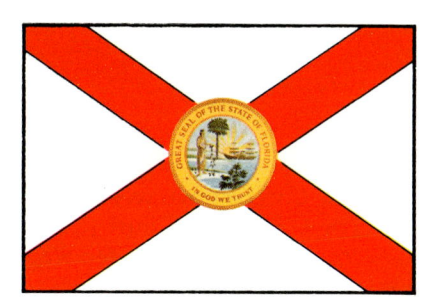

Department of State

State Flag—1966

The voters ratified an amendment to the Constitution in 1966 which caused the dimensions of the State Flag to conform to the shape of flags generally. The former size of the Florida flag had presented a problem to flagmakers, who were being called upon to furnish Florida flags in ever increasing number because of legislative requirements for its display at school and other public buildings. In the rewriting of the Constitution in 1968, the dimensions of the flag were dropped and became statutory language. The flag is described in these words: "The Seal of the state, of diameter one-half of the hoist, in the center of a white ground. Red bars in width one-fifth the hoist, in the center of a white ground. Red bars in width one-fifth the hoist extending from each corner toward the center, to the outer rim of the seal."

Flags During Mourning

The Governor and Cabinet, sitting as the Executive Board of the Department of General Services, on November 23, 1971, reaffirmed this policy for the flying of United States and State flags upon the death of ranking public officials and former officials.

Department of Commerce

For the Governor, a United States Senator from Florida, or a member of the State Cabinet: two weeks from the day of death.

For a Supreme Court Justice, a Congressman from Florida, a former Governor, or a former United States Senator from Florida: one week from the day of death.

For a State Senator, a member of the State House of Representatives, a former member of the State Cabinet, a former member of the Supreme Court, or a former Congressman: from the day of death until interment.

For an unspecified National or State official: at the discretion of the governor but not to exceed a period from the day of death until interment.

Flying the Flag of Canada

After the spiriting of six Americans from Tehran by the Canadian Ambassador to Iran in February, 1980, Governor Bob Graham ordered the flying of the flag of Canada from four poles at the Capitol until the hostages then held at the American Embassy in Tehran were freed. The six rescued were those who had escaped when militants took over the Embassy. The Canadian flags were lowered for the last time at noon on January 26, 1981, as bands played and in the presence of dignitaries headed by Governor Graham and of the public.

Display of P.O.W.-M.I.A. Flag

The 1990 Legislature decreed a P.O.W.-M.I.A. (Prisoner of War, Missing in Action) flag shall be displayed at each State-owned building which displays the Flag of the United States if the P.O.W.-M.I.A. flag is available free of charge to the agency which occupies the building.

Other Flags

State of Muskogee

The English adventurer William Augustus Bowles, elected "Director General of the State of Muskogee" by a congress of Creeks and Seminoles in 1799, designed a flag to raise over the state's capital, a Seminole village near the later site of Tallahassee. An agent of the United States government seized Bowles and delivered him to Spanish authorities in 1803. He died in prison in Havana, and so did the "State of Muskogee."

Department of State

Spanish-American Border Flags

Border friction in the declining days of Spanish rule in Florida saw three flags raised over Amelia Island between 1812 and 1817. The first of these, the so-called Patriots Flag, bore the Latin legend, "Salus populi lex suprema," or "Safety, the supreme law of the people." This handsome flag was hoisted by a force of seventy Georgians and nine Floridians who crossed the St. Marys River on March 13, 1812, to establish the independent "Territory of East Florida." The movement failed with its repudiation by President James Monroe. Next, on June 20, 1817, an expedition headed by Gregor MacGregor pushed onto Amelia Island and raised a white flag with a green cross. MacGregor, a veteran of several Latin American revolutions, was forced to flee from Amelia Island four months later. Luis Aury a reputed general of the Mexican independence movement, raised what has been described as the Mexican flag over Amelia Island on October 4, 1817. Aury surrendered the island to American forces on December 23, 1817. What his flag was no one can say. It may have been green, white and red. But it could not be the official flag of the Republic of Mexico for that country did not gain its independence until 1821.

SALUS POPULI LEX SUPREMA

Department of State

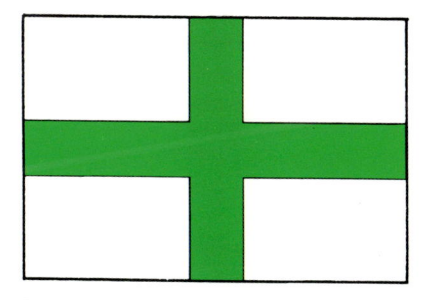

Department of State

290 / Symbols of the State

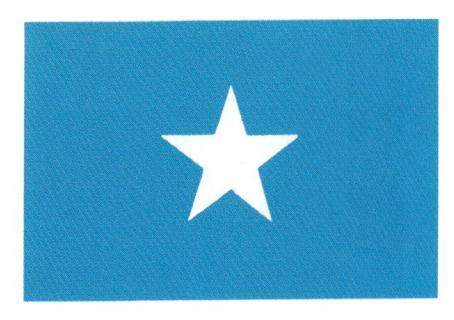

Art by W. Richard Bivins

The Republic of West Florida

The "Bonnie Blue" flag was flown in the "Free and Independent State of West Florida" which existed from September 23, 1810, until December 6, 1810, in the territory between the Pearl and Mississippi Rivers wrested from Spain by American revolters. While "West Florida" was the name given the area, it should be remembered that its easternmost boundary was 140 miles west of the present Florida. Hence, the single-starred flag never flew over any of today's Florida. The memory of the short-lived State of West Florida is preserved today in every allusion to the "Florida Parishes" of Louisiana. Long afterwards, during the Civil War, the Bonnie Blue flag was used unofficially throughout the South. A comedian, Harry McCarthy, inspired by the lone star flag raised in Mississippi after its succession, composed a song, "The Bonnie Blue Flag," which achieved the status of a Confederate anthem. The Bonnie Blue flag also was the banner of the Independence Party of Texas in 1835–1836.

The Miccosukee Tribe

The Miccosukees are said to believe that life spins in a circle, beginning in the east, then north, west and south. The bands of color in the Miccosukee flag symbolize those points of the compass: yellow for east, red for north, black for west, and white for south. The flag was adopted in 1962.

Art by W. Richard Bivins

The Seminole Tribe

Florida's Seminoles have adopted a flag which resembles Florida's State flag. The figures in the center, or seal, represent Seminole life. The dugout canoe long was a way of transportation for the Seminoles. The chickee or palm-thatched open house represents the home, and the council fire symbolizes the council aspect. The palm tree provided the fronds and wood for handicrafts. The Seminole nation was incorporated in 1966.

Art by W. Richard Bivins

Flying of Flags Required

The Legislature has, by law, required the flying of both the United States and the State flags on the grounds of every public school and other educational institution, the weather permitting, on each school day.

Use Prohibited for Advertising Purposes

The Legislature has forbidden the use of the American, Confederate, and State flags for advertising purposes. No person may "publicly mutilate, deface, defile, defy, trample upon, or by word or act cast contempt upon any such flag, standard, color, ensign or shield."

It is, however, lawful to apply the flags to stationery, ornaments, jewelry, and the like, for decorative or patriotic purposes, so long as no design or words encroach upon the flags.

Florida's Seal

The present State Seal was adopted by Governor Bob Graham and the Cabinet on May 21, 1985, upon its presentation by Secretary of State George Firestone.

Firestone had commissioned a revision of the Seal by, Museum of Florida History artist, John Locastro to remove inconsistencies, some of which had survived since 1868. The Secretary of State is the legal custodian of the Seal.

Among the anomalies of the old Seal: a bag of coffee, never a prime crop in Florida; a cocoa palm instead of the state's Sabal (Palmetto) palm; an Indian maiden dressed as a Plains Indian, mountains in a state where the highest elevation is 345 feet, and questionable seaworthiness of the side-wheel steamer.

The Firestone seal was minted from droplets of silver unearthed at the site near the Capitol of the Spanish mission of San Juan de Aspalaga, which was burned in 1704. Since 1868, the official Seal has been the size of a silver dollar.

As custodian of the seal, first by Constitutional authority and since 1968 by statute, the Secretaries of State have caused changes to be made from time to time in the seal within the language of the Constitution and statute. Secretary of State R.A. Gray (1930–1961), for example, altered the length of the skirt of the Indian.

Territorial Seal

The Territory of Florida had a seal which may be described as follows: An American eagle with outspread wings resting on a bed of clouds occupies the center of a circular field. In the right talon of the eagle are three arrows, in the left an olive branch. Above the eagle is a semi-circle of thirteen stars. Around the outer circle is the legend, "The Territory of Florida." The diameter of the seal is two inches.

This seal was used as the seal of the state for more than a year after Florida's admission to the Union in 1845. The Constitution of 1838, under which Florida was admitted, provided (*Art.* III, *sec.* 21), "There shall be a seal of the State which shall be kept by the Governor, and used by him officially,

Territory *First State*

with such device as the Governor first elected may direct, and the present seal of the Territory, shall be the seal of State, until otherwise directed by the General Assembly."

The only action in regard to the seal taken by the General Assembly in 1845, or by any subsequent legislature until 1868, was to give the Secretary of State custody of the "great seal" and to make it the seal of his office (*Acts* 1845, ch. 1, secs. 2, 4). The Secretary of State retained custody of the seal under this act until 1861. While there seems little doubt the Secretary of State had physical possession between 1861 and 1868, the Governor was responsible constitutionally for the seal during those years. The Secretary of State was once again designated as "custodian of the Great Seal of the State" by the Constitution of 1868. Deleted from the Constitution in the revision of 1968, his responsibility was carried over as statutory law.

First State Seal

Governor William D. Moseley evidently exercised his constitutional prerogative as the Governor first elected and ordered a new seal made, for late in December, 1846, the first Great Seal of the State of Florida was delivered to the Secretary of State. The actual designer of the seal, whether Moseley or some person appointed by him, is not known, nor is a contemporary description of it available. The following description is from impressions on official documents.

An outline map of Florida occupies the top and right of a circular field. On an island in the lower left are one large and three small palm trees and an oak tree, under which sits a female figure with one hand outstretched to the Gulf of Mexico and the other holding a pike upon which rests a liberty cap. About her are casks and boxes and a variety of flowering shrubs. On the water are four ships—a three-masted square rigger under full sail, another under jibs and topsails, a schooner, and a fishing smack. The legend around the outer rim is, "State of Florida—In God is Our Trust." The diameter of the seal is two and three-fourths inches.

This seal was in use as late as 1861 and probably until supplanted in 1868. The Constitution of 1861 simply stated (*Art.* III, *sec.* 12), "There shall be a seal of State, which shall be kept by the Governor, and used by him officially," while the Constitution of 1865 provided (*Art.* III, *sec.* 13), "The State

Second State (First Design)   *The Seal in use in years just prior to 1985.*

Seal last heretofore used (until altered by the General Assembly), shall continue to be the Great Seal of the State, and shall be kept by the Governor for the time being, and used by him officially." It does not appear that the General Assembly took any action on the subject.

The Second State Seal

The Constitution of 1868 (*Art.* XVI, *sec.* 20) gave the following directive: "The Legislature shall, at the first session, adopt a seal for the State, and such seal shall be the size of the American silver dollar, but said seal shall not again be changed after its adoption by the Legislature." In compliance with this mandate, the Legislature of 1868 adopted a joint resolution, approved by Governor Harrison Reed on August 6, which provided: "That a Seal of the size of the American silver dollar having in the centre thereof a view of the sun's rays over a highland in the distance, a cocoa tree, a steamboat on water, and an Indian female scattering flowers in the foreground, encircled by the words, 'Great Seal of the State of Florida: In God We Trust,' be and the same is hereby adopted as the Great Seal of the State of Florida."

Someone Else's Seal

The unknown designer of the first seal under the 1868 language hardly could have known Florida. Florida has no mountains. Florida's Indians did not wear the head-dress shown. As T. Frederick Davis pointed out, the headdress was characteristic of tribes farther north and those of the West, and it was an insignia of distinction of the headmen and warriors exclusively. Davis concluded:

"When the 1868 artist put the crown of eagle's feathers on his Indian female he presented Florida with an unclassified savage having the head of a warrior and the body of a squaw."

There is an unconfirmed story that a Northern designer modified for Florida a seal previously prepared for use by a government in the West.

The Constitution of 1885 retained the seal of 1868 in the following words (*Art.* XVI, *sec.* 12), "The present Seal of the State shall be and remain the Seal of the State of Florida." The Constitutional Revision of 1968 permitted the design to be prescribed by law.

Today's seal
[See preceding page for description of changes in prior seal.]

This seal of the State was hand-painted on silk in the early 1900s to be sewn on a Florida flag. The painting was signed by the artist,. T.B. Morris, but nothing else is known of the seal despite intensive research by Bob McNeil, Historian of the Museum of Florida History in the Department of State.
Museum of Florida History

The 1970 Legislature defined the tree in the seal as a Sabal palmetto palm, rather than a "cocoa" tree. This change established the official State Tree as the tree of the State Seal.

Reproduction Limited

Only upon approval of the Department of State, can any facsimile or reproduction of the great seal be manufactured, used, displayed, or otherwise employed by anyone.

Colors in the Seal

The Seal, as used by the Secretary of State to authenticate commissions and other documents, has no color since it leaves impressions on gold wafers or paper. Reproductions use the colors envisioned by the artist since these are not prescribed by law.

State Motto

"In God We Trust," from inscription on Great Seal, as directed by 1868 Legislature.

State Nickname

"Sunshine State" was adopted as the State Nickname by the 1970 Legislature. Previously, official sanction for this nickname could be inferred from the law requiring use of "Sunshine State" on motor vehicle licenses.

The State Song

Stephen Collins Foster's moving composition, *Old Folks at Home,* was adopted by the 1935 Legislature as Florida's official song.

Florida's Suwannee river, which Foster called "Swannee" and spelled "Swanee," has become a world symbol of love for home and family.

Wonderfully contrived dioramas provide a third dimension for songs of Foster at the memorial which the people of Florida have dedicated to the nation's troubadour on the Suwannee at White Springs. The State Folk Culture Center annually attracts thousands of visitors by its museum, bell tower, picnic grounds and special events like the Memorial Day weekend Florida Folk Festival.

Way down upon de Swanee Ribber,
   Far, far away,
Dere's wha my heart is turning ebber,
   Dere's wha de old folks stay.
All up and down de whole creation
   Sadly I roam,
Still longing for de old plantation,
   And for de old folks at home.

Chorus
All de world am sad and dreary,
   Eb-rywhere I roam;
Oh, darkeys, * *how my heart grows*
   weary,
Far from de old folks at home!

2nd verse
All round de little farm I wandered
   When I was young,
Den many happy days I squandered,
   Many de songs I sung.
When I was playing wid my brudder
   Happy was I;
Oh, take me to my kind old mudder!
   Dere let me live and die.

3rd verse
One little hut among de bushes,
   One dat I love
Still sadly to my memory rushes,
   No matter where I rove.
When will I see de bees a-humming
   All round de comb?
When will I hear de banjo strumming,
   Down in my good old home?

*As printed in the program for the dedication of the New Capitol on March 31, 1978, "brothers" was substituted for "darkeys" in the chorus of *Old Folks at Home.* Leon and Lynn Dallin, in *Heritage Songster,* used "dear ones." The Dallins also eliminated all attempts at reproducing dialect.

As an Anthem

When *Old Folks at Home* is played in Florida on a ceremonial occasion as the State Song, the audience should stand, just as would be done with the playing of the official anthem of a university during an event on its campus.

An Earlier State Song

Before *Old Folks at Home,* there was another State Song, *Florida, My Florida,* adopted by the 1913 Legislature. Written in 1894 by the Rev. Dr. C. V. Waugh, a professor of languages at the Florida Agricultural College at Lake City, the song was said by the Legislature to have "both metric and patriotic merit of the kind calculated to inspire love for home and native State."

Sung to the music of *Maryland, My Maryland*, the opening verses were:

Land of my birth, bright sunkissed land,
　Florida, my Florida,
Laved by the Gulf and Ocean grand,
　Florida, my Florida.

Of all the States in East or West,
Unto my heart thou art the best;
Here may I live, here may I rest,
　Florida, my Florida.

The golden fruit the world outshines
　Florida, my Florida,
Thy gardens and thy phosphate mines,
　Florida, my Florida,

In country, town, or hills and dells,
　Florida, my Florida,
The rhythmic chimes of the school bells,
　Florida, my Florida,

Will call thy children day by day
To learn to walk the patriot's way,
Firmly to stand for thee for aye,
　Florida, my Florida.

Yield their rich store of good supply,
To still the voice of hunger's cry—
For thee we'll live, for thee we'll die,
　Florida, my Florida.

A Florida Limerick

Limericks, after a century and a quarter, remain the most popular verse form in the English language and a Florida limerick is regarded as the most popular of all.

The late John P. McKnight of Naples, retired foreign service officer, had surveyed several thousand in four decades of limerick collecting. Of the Florida verses, McKnight said none rivals the one about a well-beloved Florida bird. Authored by the Tennessee newspaperman and humorist Dixon Merritt, the limerick goes:

> "A wonderful bird is the pelican;
> His mouth will hold more than his belican.
> He can take in his beak
> Food enough for a week;
> But damn if I see how the helican."

The limerick was written in April, 1911, for the *Nashville Tennessean*. Slightly different versions are quoted.

State Welcome Song

The 1985 Legislature, by House Concurrent Resolution 1143, designated *Florida*, by Lawrence Hurwit and Israel Abrams, as "an official state welcome song."

The lyric reads:

Florida is sunshine, waterways and sand
Florida's a special kind of promised land
Magic kingdom, the Sunshine State, all these words are fine,
but words can never quite describe nature's own design
Little drops of water, little grains of sand
made the mighty ocean and made this lovely tropic land;
So dream your dreams in Florida and they will all come true,
then when you get sand in your shoes,
Florida will be home to you.

State Symphony and Opera

The 1963 Legislature created a "Florida State Symphony and Florida State Opera" to be administered by the Florida State University School of Music.

State Play

The 1973 Legislature designated "the historical pageant by Paul Green known as the 'Cross and Sword,' presented annually by the citizens of the City of St. Augustine," as "the official play of the state."

State Theaters

The 1965 Legislature established the Asolo Theater Festival as "the State Theater of Florida," with its major season each year at the Asolo Theater of the Ringling Museums at Sarasota.

Administration of the State Theater was vested by the 1970 Legislature in the Department of State with an advisory board of trustees.

Time magazine has described Asolo as "a theater unique in all of North America." The Asolo (pronounced *Ash*-olo) was said by *Time* to be "intimate, enchanting, with a triple tier of embossed balconies." The Asolo was the great Eleonora Duse's home theater, and playgoers of a bygone day included Chopin, George Sand and Robert Browning.

Subsequently, the Coconut Grove Playhouse at Miami and the Hippodrome Theatre at Gainesville were designated State Theaters. The 1986 Legislature appropriated $100,000 to bring the Caldwell Theatre Company at Boca Raton under the State Theater Program.

The Asolo Theater is the only 18th century Italian theater in America. This architectural jewel once occupied the great hall of the castle of Queen Catherine Cornaro in the hill town of Asolo, twenty-odd miles from Venice.
Department of Commerce

State Bird

Florida's State Bird is the Mockingbird, designated by the 1927 Legislature.

Florida shares its designation of the mockingbird with four other states: Arkansas, Mississippi, Tennessee and Texas.

As an editorialist for the *Miami Herald* wrote on August 4, 1972, these states are a part of the region where a country fiddler inserts arpeggios of birdsong between the words:

A mockingbird in pyracantha   Samuel A. Grimes

I'm dreaming now of Hally, sweet Hally, sweet Hally,
I'm dreaming now of Hally,
For the tho't of her is one that never dies

She's sleeping in the valley,
The valley, the valley,
She's sleeping in the valley,
And the mocking bird is singing where she lies.

Listen to the mocking bird,
Listen to the mocking bird,
The mocking bird still singing o'er her grave,

Listen to the mocking bird,
Listen to the mocking bird,
Still singing where the weeping willows wave.

Poet Laureate

Dr. Edmund Skellings of Dania was named Poet Laureate by Governor Bob Graham on April 16, 1980, after an out-of-state committee screened some 400 nominations to narrow the field to Skellings and five others.

An instructor at Florida International University at the time of his designation, Skellings was a nominee for the 1979 Nobel Prize in Literature and two volumes of his trilogy, "Nearing the Millennium," were nominated for a Pulitzer Prize.

The Poet Laureate serves without term and without compensation. Skellings became the third Poet Laureate. The first was Franklin N. Wood, appointed by Governor John W. Martin in 1929. The second was Mrs. Vivian Laramore Rader of Miami, served from 1931 until her death in 1973 at age 83.

Skellings' Florida

We are South looking North.
Or vice versa.
We are international
And exceptionally local.

From here you could go to the moon.
And we can prove it.

Even the natives are transients.
Arriving and departing,
We are of two minds.

Coast to coast here means
One hour through our cotton mountains.
The sun rises and sets under salt waters.

Knowing in the bones that space is time,
We are wise as any peninsula.
We mine the dried beds of forgotten seas.
Fresh mango and orange bloom from the silt.

Outside Gainesville once, I reached down
Into time and touched the sabre tooth of a tiger.
No atlas prepared me for the moist
Sweet smell of his old life.

Suddenly a flock of flamingos
Posed a thousand questions,
Blushing like innocence.

But the moon, perfectly above Miami
Like some great town clock, whispers,
"Now . . . yesterdays . . . tomorrows. . ."

And standing tropically and hugely still
At this port of meditation,
Reduced to neither coming nor going,
We are together on the way to somewhere.

In good time.

—Edmund Skellings
 GEO Journal
 The Magazine of Florida Natural Resources
 reprinted by permission of the author

This is one of the two panels of the mural (described below) in the lobby of the Capitol.

Department of Commerce

Chronicler Laureate

The 1927 Legislature authorized the Governor to appoint a Chronicler Laureate, to serve without compensation.

Governor John W. Martin designated Franklin N. Wood in 1927. Governor Wayne Mixson appointed Allen Morris in 1987, in recognition of Morris having chronicled Florida life in *The Florida Handbook* and other publications for a half century.

Art in the Capitol

A mural in two 8-by-11 foot sections on the plaza level (or main floor) attracts attention and often comments from Capitol visitors.

The mural was painted by James Rosenquist, then 45 years old and a resident of Aripeka on Florida's Gulf coast north of Tarpon Springs. He was born in Grand Forks, North Dakota in 1933, reared in Minneapolis, attended the University of Minnesota's art school, and studied at the New York Art Students' League, where his work was influenced by sculptor Claes Oldenburg and painter Robert Indiana.

The $60,000 mural (financed by public and private funds) uses animals and objects Rosenquist felt were symbolic of Florida. These include the snout of an alligator, an orange blossom, a butterfly, a cow's head, a scuba diver, and a woman swimming. All the images are surrounded by water. There is a State seal slipping into the sea on one panel and a fiberglass cast of a rock tied by an actual rope to a shanty painted in the center of the other section. The rock attracts much visitor attention. Rosenquist describes this as his way of creating "a ballast" for a fragile state.

Florida Artists Hall of Fame

Established by the Legislature in 1986, the Florida Artists Hall of Fame recognizes persons who have made a significant contribution to the arts in Florida as a performer, a practicing artist, of as a benefactor of the arts. The individual may be a native of the state or one who adopted Florida as home. Recipients of this award demonstrate the diversity of artistic accomplishment that comprises the cultural tapestry which is "FLORIDA-State of the Arts."

Inductees receive a commemorative bronze sculpture commissioned by the Florida Arts Council. The sculpture, La Florida, was created by Enzo Torcoletti. Information on the Florida Artists Hall of Fame is located in the 22nd floor gallery of the Capitol.

Inducted have been: 1987, Ernest Hemingway, Marjorie Kinnan Rawlings, John N. Ringling; 1988, George Firestone; 1989, Tennessee Williams; 1990 Zora Neale Hurston; 1991, John D. MacDonald, Robert Rauschenberg; 1992, Ray Charles, Duane Hanson; 1993, George Abbott, A. E. "Bean" Backus, Marjory Stoneman Douglas, Burt Reynolds; 1994, Ralph H. Norton, Jerry Uelsmann, Hiram D. Williams, Ellen Taaffe Zwilich.

State Museum

The 1980 Legislature designated the John and Mable Ringling Museum of Art at Sarasota as the "official art museum of the state." The museum was bequeathed to the State by John Ringling, of circus fame, and has been operated since 1946 by a Board of Trustees appointed by the Governor. The trustees are authorized to loan paintings and other objects of art to the Governor's Mansion and to schools, libraries and other public buildings where such loans are in the interest of the public.

State Fish

The 1975 Legislature designated the Florida Largemouth Bass (*Micropterus salmoides floridanus*) as the official state freshwater fish and the Atlantic Sailfish (*Istiophorus platyperus*) as the official state saltwater fish.

The 1927 Senate designated the mullet as the state fish but rescinded the action. The concurrent resolution had been amended to read, "Said mullet shall wear a tail-light whenever he goes up the Aucilla River."

State Reptile

The 1987 Legislature, through Senate Bill 565, now Section 15.0385, Florida Statutes, designated the American alligator as the "official Florida State reptile."

State Insect

The 1972 Senate passed a bill to designate the praying mantis as the State Insect but the measure failed of passage in the House.

Department of Commerce

State Mammals

The 1975 Legislature designated the manatee, also commonly known as the sea cow, as the "Florida state marine mammal," and the porpoise, also commonly known as the dolphin, as the "Florida state salt water mammal." Florida's own, the manatee, with fewer than 2,000 remaining, may be dying faster than they're being born. Manatees are perishing largely because of motorboat propellers, pneumonia, and pollution.

Writing in the *National Geographic* for September, 1984, Jesse R. White quoted Christopher

Department of Commerce

Columbus as believing manatees, or sea cows, to be mermaids, but "not as beautiful as they are painted, although to some extent they have a human appearance in the face."

Scientists believe manatees are distant cousins of the elephant, who forsook land for water millions of years ago, reported White. They can weigh more than 2,000 pounds and range from eight to 14 feet in length.

Browsing takes up a fourth of their time. Herbivores, they may daily ingest as much as a pound of aquatic grasses for every ten pounds of body weight, adds White.

State Animal

The Florida panther (*Felis concolor coryi*) was designated Florida's State Animal by the 1982 Legislature. In school elections throughout the state, the panther had defeated the manatee, alligator and Key deer.

The Florida panther, a subspecies of the panther which once ranged the Western Hemisphere, was teetering on the brink of extinction when the Legislature acted. In 1994 it was estimated that only 30 to 50 Florida panthers were left in South Florida and they are weak from inbreeding.

The Florida panther usually is a uniform rusty or tawny cinnamon-buff color (deer-colored) on the back and whitish underneath. The tip of the tail, back of the ears, and sides of the nose are dark brown or blackish. Contrary to some belief, the Game Commission says there never has been any conclusive evidence to prove there ever had been a black panther in Florida.

The Florida Panther, along with the Manatee, is a symbol of the state's endangered creatures.
Dept. of Environmental Protection

State Flower

Florida's State Flower is the Orange Blossom, designated by the 1909 Legislature.

State Gem

On the occasion of the appearance at a joint meeting of the 1970 Legislature of two astronauts from the second team to leap from Cape Canaveral to the moon, the "moonstone" was designated Florida's state gem.

The moonstone was described in the law as "a transparent or translucent feldspar of pearly or opaline luster."

State Stone

Agatized coral was designated as the Florida State Stone by the 1979 Legislature. Agatized coral is described as a "chalcedony pseudomorph after coral, appearing as limestone geodes lined with botrydoidal agate or quartz crystal, and drusy quartz fingers, indigenous to" Florida.

Litter Control Symbol

The 1978 Legislature, by passage of SB 1119, designated "Glenn Glitter," the litter control trademark of the Florida Federation of Garden Clubs, Inc., as the "Florida State Litter control symbol."

State Shell

The horse conch was designated by the 1969 Legislature as the State Shell. Its scientific name is *Pleuroploca gigantea*. *Pleuroploca* refers to the ribbed spiral shell, and *gigantea* means giant.

The Department of Natural Resources says the horse conch is among the largest marine snails in the world. Some specimens attain two feet in length, and have a life of perhaps 12 or 14 years.

When very young, horse conch shells are greyish white to salmon. The DNR reports the horse conch has been described as "the toughest guy on the block," feeding mainly on other mollusks but known to consume stone crabs and other relatively large animals. In South Florida, the horse conch can be a pest, sometimes damaging crab and lobster traps with its powerful foot.

Horse conchs are said to have little commercial value. The larger shells have been used as trumpets. The orange flesh is edible, but with a peppery taste. From that taste, the horse conch once was known as the pepper conch. Collectors regard the larger shells highly.

The State Tree

The Sabal palm (*Sabal palmetto*) was designated the State Tree by the 1953 Legislature, concluding some years of controversy.

The 1949 House of Representatives had endorsed the Royal Palm but the Senate did not join in this. There also was strong legislative support in that and other sessions for the slash and longleaf pines.

The argument was resolved in 1953, however, after the Federation of Garden Clubs pressed its contention that palms are characteristics of Florida, and of the palms the Sabal was the most widely distributed over the state. The Sabal long had appeared on the State Seal. It also had been recognized as the State Tree by the U.S. Department of Agriculture.

Particularly in the early days, the Sabal furnished food and shelter. The bud was used as a vegetable. The fibrous trunk served as a wall for fort or cabin, affording good protection against weather and assault. The leaves provided thatching material.

The name "palmetto" can cause considerable confusion in Florida because it is often applied to at least

Reaching skyward as though to drink from the clouds, the slender Sabal palm possesses a majesty which sets it apart from other trees.
Department of Commerce

two distinct varieties of palms. Paul Wills, then Chief, Forest Education, Florida Department of Agriculture and Consumer Services, explained: "The Florida State Tree is properly named the Sabal Palmetto, and is called that throughout its range up into the Carolinas. In Florida, at least, the name 'palmetto' also is applied to the ground-hugging dwarf palm identified by taxonomists as *Serenoa Repens,* and commonly called the saw palmetto. It is the second member of the 'pine and palmetto' flatlands so common over Florida. Its trunk lies along the ground and rarely rears up to form a normal treelike stem, though occasionally it can be found standing erect in heavily shaded locations."

The sabal palm also is the State Tree of South Carolina, whose nickname is The Palmetto State.

State Beverage

The 1967 Legislature declared "the juice obtained from mature oranges of the species *citrus sinensus* and hybrids is hereby adopted as the official beverage of the State of Florida."

State Soil

The 1988 House passed a bill to designate Myakka fine sand (sandy, siliceous, hyperthermic Aeric Haplaquods) as the official Florida state soil but the bill died in the Senate. The bill declared the Myakka fine sand had more acreage (800,000) mapped than any other soil in the state. Sponsors said "by officially designating a state soil, Floridians are saying that they have a valuable heritage to protect and conserve."

Key Lime Pie

The 1988 House designated Key lime pie as the "official pie of Florida." The bill died in the Senate. The pie is distinguished by the use of limes grown in the chain of keys, or islands, dropping from the Florida mainland to Key West.

Florida Toasts

Today's television viewers of the visits of heads of state to the White House are familiar with the custom of the President and the nation's guest exchanging toasts.

In early America, the custom of offering toasts at official dinners was more common than today. "Toasts for Independence Day" in pre-Civil War Florida is a collection gathered by Dr. William Warren Rogers for the Florida State University Bicentennial Celebration Committee.

Here is a sampler from that collection:

To the Fair Daughters of Florida—*All that can be wished, and more than can be expressed.* (1838)

To the Fourth of July—*May it be celebrated by our descendants until time cannot enumerate.* (1838)

To Washington and Lafayette—*Give us such men forever.* (1837)

To the Territory of Florida—*Lovely as her own woodbine bowers, but bleeding under the tomahawks of the cruel savage—Where shall she cry for help? For, alas! her sons are worn out, or have perished in the struggle.* (1837)

To Governor Richard Keith Call—*He has done more to put an end to this disgraceful savage war than all the generals in the regular army. We would be glad to see him again in the chief command.* (1837)

To Women—*The mother of love! The home of endearment! and the heaven of our earthy joys!* (1840)

State Wildflower

The Coreopsis was designated by the 1991 Legislature as the official state wildflower, "as species of this genus are found throughout the state and are used extensively in roadside plantings and highway beautification."

Florida Festival

The 1980 Legislature designated Miami's annual Calle Ocho-Open House 8 as "a festival of Florida," an "original and authentic festival celebrating the cultural heritage of women and men who migrated to this great nation from Hispanic countries."

State Pageant

"Indian River," presented annually in Brevard County, was designated by the 1979 Legislature as "an official state pageant."

State Air Fair

The Central Florida Air Fair was designated by the 1976 Legislature as the official Florida State Air Fair.

The State Day, "Pascua Florida Week"

April 2 was designated by the 1953 Legislature as State Day because Ponce de León first sighted Florida about that date in 1513. The designation by the lawmakers was at the suggestion of Mary A. Harrell, a teacher of social studies in the John Gorrie Junior High School of Jacksonville.

The Legislature also authorized the Governor to annually proclaim March 27–April 2 as "Pascua Florida Week" and to call upon schools and the citizenry for observance of this period as a patriotic occasion. Whenever April 2 falls on Saturday or Sunday, the Governor may declare either the preceding Friday or the following Monday as State Day.

Poetry Day

The 1947 Legislature decreed the 25th day of May of each year to be "Poetry Day in all of the public schools" of Florida.

House Concurrent Resolution No. 2 declared "a knowledge and enjoyment of poetry should be a part of the education of every person."

Emancipation Day

Emancipation Day, June 19, is observed in black communities of Florida on the anniversary of the occupation of Tallahassee by Federal troops, thus freeing the slaves. The Emancipation proclamation was issued by President Abraham Lincoln on September 22, 1862. The proclamation declared slaves in states in rebellion on January 1, 1863, would be free. "Juneteenth Day" was proclaimed Emancipation Day by the 1991 legislation.

Ceremonial Days

These are ceremonial days (Chapter 683, Florida Statutes):
Arbor Day, third Friday in January
[The 1988 House of Representatives, by resolution, declared April to be Arbor Month.]
Pascua Florida Week, March 27–April 2
Pascua Florida (or **State**) **Day,** April 2—(if this be Saturday or Sunday, Governor may declare preceding Friday or following Monday as State Day)
Pan-American Day, April 14 (if this not be a school day, local school authorities may designate preceding Friday or following Monday as State Day)
Patriot's Day, April 19 (first blood shed in Revolution at Lexington and Concord, April 19, 1775)
Law Enforcement Appreciation Month, May, **and Day,** May 15
Memorial Day, May 15
Teacher's Day, third Friday in May
Possum Day, first Saturday in August, if Governor proclaims
Grandmother's Day, second Sunday in October
Retired Teachers' Day, Sunday beginning third week in November
Save the Florida Panthers Day, third Saturday in March

Legal Holidays

These are legal holidays:
New Year's Day, January 1.
Martin Lather King, Jr., Birthday, Observance on third Monday in January.
Robert E. Lee's Birthday, January 19.
Susan B. Anthony's Birthday, February 15.
Presidents' Day, third Monday in February.
Shrove Tuesday, also known as "Mardi Gras," in certain counties.
Good Friday.
Pascua Florida Day, April 2.
Children's Day, second Tuesday in April.
Confederate Memorial Day, April 26.
Memorial Day, last Monday in May.
Jefferson Davis's Birthday, June 3.
Flag Day, June 14.

Independence Day, July 4.
Labor Day, first Monday in September.
Constitution (U.S.) Day, September 17.
Columbus Day and **Farmers' Day,** second Monday in October.
Veterans' Day, November 11.
General Election Day, first Tuesday after first Monday in November of even-numbered years.
Thanksgiving Day, fourth Thursday in November.
Christmas Day, December 25.
All Sundays.

(Whenever a legal holiday, except Sundays, shall fall upon a Sunday, the Monday following is observed.)
In Hillsborough County, the "day known and designated as Gasparilla Day," is a legal holiday.
In Manatee County, the last Friday of DeSoto week is a legal holiday known as DeSoto Day.
In Hillsborough County, the "day known and designated as Parade Day of the Hillsborough County Fair and Plant City Strawberry Festival" is a legal holiday.

The term "legal holiday" appears to have lost much of its meaning. There remains a definition in the Florida Statutes relating to contracts and perhaps to filing dates for legal documents, but nothing speaking to observance by businesses and the public except for the holidays for State employees. Observance otherwise is left to the discretion of individuals.

State Office Holidays

These are holidays observed by the closing of State offices with employees paid (section 683.03, Florida Statutes):

New Year's Day, Martin Luther King, Jr., Birthday, Memorial Day, Independence Day, Labor Day, Veterans' Day, Thanksgiving Day, Friday after Thanksgiving, Christmas Day. If any of these holidays fall on Saturday, the preceding Friday shall be observed as a holiday. If any fall on Sunday, the following Monday shall be observed.

The Department of Management Service may designate when appropriate a "State Day of Mourning" in observance of the death of "a statesman in recognition of services rendered to the state or the nation." The 1988 Legislature designated the birthday of Dr. Martin Luther King, Jr., as a paid state holiday, and provided for observance on the third Monday in January.

"Floridian" or "Floridan"?

Is a citizen of this state a "Floridian" or a "Floridan"? Either is correct but "Floridian" has become more general since the 1920s.

William Roberts, in 1763, wrote of the "longevity of the Floridian Indians." William Bartram, in 1791, said "the Creeks subdued the remnant tribes of the ancient Floridians." During this same period, Jonathan Carver, in 1778, reported that "I must exclude the stories he has introduced of the Huron and Floridian women." The *Oxford English Dictionary* says of "-ian" (meaning "of" or "belonging to") that the suffix forms both the adjective and substantive in "modern formations from proper names, the number of which is without limit."

The 1925 House of Representatives adopted a resolution, which the Senate rejected, resolving that citizens of Florida by birth and adoption "shall henceforth be known as Floridians."

The resolution declared there was need for uniform pronunciation and spelling. "The word Floridian is musical, poetical, euphonious, and easily rolling off the tongue," the House found, while "the word Floridan is harsh, unmusical and unjustified by precedent."

Representative Victor of St. Johns County, sponsor of the resolution, declared the "word Floridian is in keeping with the romance and traditions and beauty of this state." He pointed out that "the 'i' is used in Georgians, Mississippians, Kentuckians, etc."

The Senate Journal shows the Senate summarily disposed of the House resolution upon its first reading there without even the usual reference to a committee.

Crackers and Conchs: Florida Nicknames

Floridians are known as "crackers," but Allen Morris and Ann Waldron in their book *Your Florida Government* suggest the nickname should be used with care. Its acceptance by Floridians depends upon the person and, in some measure, upon the section of the state.

A historian illustrated this shading by saying that if, while out of the state, someone hailed her as a cracker she would respond affirmatively. If, however, someone in Florida described her as a cracker, she would want to think it over. A number of origins are suggested. Francis R. Goulding, in *Marooner's Island* (1869), thought the name was derived from Scotch settlers in whose dialect a "cracker" was a person who talked boastingly. John Lambert, in *Travels Through Lower Canada, and the United States of North America* (1810), wrote: "The waggoners are familiarly called *crackers* (from the smacking of their whip, I suppose)." Emily P. Burke, in *Reminiscences of Georgia* (1850), said crackers were called that "from the circumstance that they formerly pounded all their corn, which is their principle article of diet." Two modern historians, A. J. and Kathryn Abbey Hanna, writing in their *Lake Okeechobee* (1948), said: "The name 'cracker' frequently applied to countrymen of Georgia and Florida is supposed to have originated as a cattle term." Florida cowboys popped whips of braided buckskin, twelve to eighteen feet long. The "crack" sounded like a rifle shot and at times could be heard for several miles. The writer of the newspaper column "Cracker Politics" suggested it might be prudent to accompany the nickname with a smile.

Angus M. Laird, Tallahassee scholar, has traced the word cracker back to Barclay's "Shyp of Folys," a play published in 1509 which made reference to "Crakers and Bosters," apparently meaning traveling troubadours. Shakespeare in his "Life and Death of King John," written about 1590, has the Duke of Austria saying "What cracker is this that deafs our ears/ With this abundance of superfluous breath?" From these early usages, reported Laird, "the word has come to mean many things in the English language through the world."

Today's Conchs are the direct descendants of the Bahamians who settled at Key West with the turn of the century in the 1800s. Many were Empire Loyalists displaced by the American Revolution and the transfer of Florida from Britain to the United States.

Others were descendants of the Eleutheran Adventurers, a group of English political and religious dissenters who immigrated to Bermuda in 1647 and shortly afterward moved to the Bahamas.

Nowadays, "Conch" is applied generally to residents of Key West and adjacent keys. Classic examples of Bahamian homes, built by ship carpenters, remain in Key West. The original Conchs derived their nickname from the shellfish *strombus gigas,* or conch, which early mariners regarded as a delicacy.

Florida's Square Dance

The square dance, as symbolic of "our state character and pride," was designated the "American folk dance of the State of Florida" by the 1986 Legislature's adoption of House Concurrent Resolution 740.

Square dancing was described by the Legislature as "called, cued, or prompted to the dancers, and includes squares, rounds, clogging, contra, line and heritage." The Legislature declared the square dance has been associated with the American people since 1651.

First Theatrical Performance

Research by David D. Mays of the University of Central Florida leads to the reasonable assumption that a performance of *The Beaux' Stratagem* at British St. Augustine on March 3, 1783, was the first play presented in Florida between 1513 and 1783. "In fact," wrote Mays in *Eighteenth-Century Florida: Life on the Frontier,* "the choice of this particular play was a happy one," as *The Beaux' Stratagem* was one of the most popular and best-known plays on the North American continent. By the Late Restoration Playwright George Farquhar, the play was, continued Mays, "a skillful amalgam of lusty double entendre, exciting plots and counterplots, tender romance, and broad comic characterizations."

Florida in Music and Song

A two-year stay in Florida, first at an orange grove on the St. Johns River and then in Jacksonville, by the English composer Frederick Delius (1863–1934) is evident in his work. Delius's *Appalachia* recalls two Negro melodies, "No Trouble in that Land Where I'm Bound" and "Oh, Honey, I am Going Down the River in the Morning."

Delius, who was 21 when he came to Florida, returned to England in 1886 and visited Florida only once again but memories of his youth also inspired his opera *Koanga* and an orchestral suite, *Florida.*

"In Florida," once wrote Delius, "through sitting and gazing at Nature, I gradually learnt the way in which I should eventually find myself."

Also on the classical side is the "Tallahassee Suite" of the British composer Cyril Scott. A recording by violinist Jascha Heifetz, made in 1937, appears to have been issued for the first time in 1975. It was included in RCA Victor's six volume "Heifetz Collection." It is not known why Scott gave the name Tallahassee to the suite. The suite is divided into three descriptive movements, Bygone Memories, After Sundown, and Danse Negre, and has been characterized as a "lightweight work which makes most pleasant listening."

The boom of the 1920s also spawned other topical songs. Among these were: "I'm Never Going to Leave Miami, Where the Sun Shines all the Time," "Miami" as sung by Al Jolson in *Big Boy*, "Mi-a-mi You Owe a Lot to Me," "I'd Rather Be in Miami" "In Old Miami " and the still heard "On Miami Shores Waltz (On the Golden Sands of Miami)."

Stephen Foster's "Old Folks at Home" gave world fame to Florida's Suwannee River. The great land boom of the 1920s had "Moon over Miami" as its theme (although in Coral Gables the Jan Garber orchestra played "When the Moon Shines in Coral Gables"). In mid-century, Bing Crosby and the Andrews Sisters joined in singing Frank Loesser's "Tallahassee" from the Paramount movie, *Variety Girl*.

To their astonishment and utter delight, in 1947 the citizens of Apalachicola, Florida suddenly found themselves squarely in the national spotlight when Bob Hope and Bing Crosby crooned a Johnny Burke ditty in their latest road picture.

It mattered not a whit, of course, whether the country's top comics had ever set foot in the seaside community. All that mattered was that millions of people were hearing the town's name for the first time, and in a highly flattering light. Their day in the sun had finally arrived, and if it would be brief, the people of Apalachicola would relish every minute of it. . . . *Florida State University Research in Review, Frank Stephenson, Editor*

*We're on our way
To AP-A-LA-CHI-CO-LA, F, L, A.
Magnolia trees in blossom and a
pretty southern gal,
It's better than the orange groves in
Cucamonga, Cal.
We're gonna stay*

*Along the Apalachicola Bay.
We may stop at Ochlackonee
for some hominy grits
Or pass through Tallahassee if the
weather permits
But we're on our way
to AP-A-LA-CHI-CO-LA, F, L, A.!*
—from "Road to Rio" (Paramount Pictures)

Florida in Early English Ballad

Research at Florida State University has turned up a good possibility of the earliest poem/song about Florida in an Elizabethan ballad called "Have Over the Water to Florida." It was popular in the streets of London about the time that Shakespeare was born in 1564.

The song was written by a would-be emigrant who lost his fortune supporting an expedition to Florida. He envisioned it as a paradise far to the west where savage people bartered gold for trifles; there were turkeys and tall cedar trees; and pearls grew in oysters along the waterside.

The voyage to Florida was organized by a courtier named Thomas Stukeley. Queen Elizabeth gave him a ship and the enterprising explorer came up with five others on his own. However, it turned out that Stukeley's

Symbols of the State / 311

This is a sampling from Dr. Danny O. Crew's collection of more than 500 different pieces of Florida-related music. Dr. Crew, by profession a public administrator, commenced collecting Florida music "for fun" as he always had been interested in Florida history.

312 / Symbols of the State

real plan was to pursue a course of piracy. As a result, his passengers never reached Florida. They spent the next two years plundering French, Spanish and Portuguese ships instead.

Someone who heard the song copied it down by hand. This copy is now at the Bodleian Library at Oxford University, England.

As converted from old English by Dr. John Mackay Shaw of Strozier Library at Florida State University, "Have Over the Water to Florida" commences:

Have over the water to Florida!
  Farewell gay London now.

Through long delays, by land seas,
  I have come, I know not how,

To Plymouth town in a threadbare gown,
  And not enough money to tell.

*With hy! a tryksy trym go tryksy.**
  Wouldn't a wallet do well?

*Regarded by translator as a meaningless refrain.

First Music

Dean-emeritus Wiley Housewright of the Florida State University School of Music says the "earliest European music heard in Florida was that of the Catholic church, sung by priests who accompanied such Spanish explorers as Ponce de León (1512), Pánfilo de Narváez (1520), Cabeza de Vaca (1528) and Hernando de Soto (1539).

"The soldiers of these explorers probably sang secular Spanish songs of the period. The first music teachers were the priests with the Tristán de Luna y Arelláno company who came to Ochuse (Pensacola) in 1559."

Dean Housewright has documented other early musicians in his 1991 book, *A History of Music and Dance in Florida, 1565–1865.*

Florida on Postage Stamps

1924
Tommon Tinney, Tallahassee

1965

Symbols of the State / 313

1945

1976

1947

1969

1982

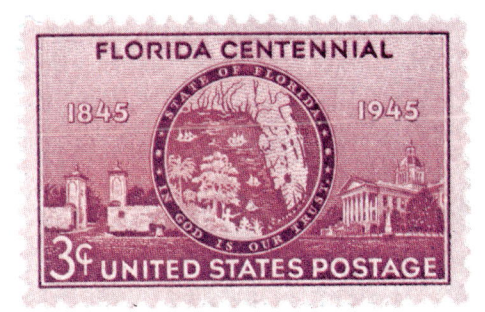

Coral Reefs USA 15c
Elkhorn Coral: Florida

1980

1982

1995 sesquicentennial stamp

1985

Note: The U.S. Treasury Department allows unused stamps to be reproduced in color if 150 percent or more of actual size. The stamps here are slightly larger than 150 percent of actual size.

Beginnings of Religion in Florida

An ecumenical chapel, on the main floor of the Capitol, was dedicated September 4, 1980, to serve as a place of meditation and of Florida's spiritual history.

The chapel occupies a room 13 feet by 22. It was designed and furnished entirely from private funds raised by the Religious Heritage Council, a group established in 1976 by then Secretary of State Bruce Smathers. An effort was made to cause the Council to be broadly representative of all religious groups in Florida.

The stone in the chapel symbolizes the strength and permanence of the earth. The water implies regeneration. The fire symbolizes illumination, renewal, and change as well, the Council declared, "as the hope for man's redemption through his own creative knowledge of his God." The bronze within the chapel symbolizes "those elements of earth forged by human hand, through fire, to the glory of God." Finally the painting "Creation" symbolizes the "mystery of the ordering of ourselves, through God, out of the chaos of a natural world."

Chapel Materials: QUARRY KEYSTONE for the table and the font was quarried in Florida City at the southern most tip of the State. The stones were fashioned by the Georgia Marble Company with the cooperation of The Jim Walter Corporation. The TIDEWATER CYPRESS was originally cut 50–100 years ago and was raised from the Apalachicola river. Its aromatic scent will continue to enhance the space for years to come. The CRYSTALLIZED CORAL FLAME HOLDER was found off Ballast point in Tampa and subsequently fashioned for the Chapel. The COQUINA SHELL WALLS were cast with shells originating on the Atlantic beaches between St. Augustine and Jacksonville. They were cast by Mr. Frank Pedroni of Jacksonville.

There is a font, a flame holder, and a processional candle. On two sides are plaques tracing the development of religion in Florida. Wording for the plaques was composed by two University of Florida historians, Dr. Samuel Proctor, Distinguished Service Professor of History, and Dr. Michael V. Gannon, Professor of History.

Panel One: Prehistoric Indians lived in Florida for thousands of years before the coming of Europeans. Their beliefs helped explain the World and the Cosmos. They found special meaning in natural and supernatural phenomena—the changing seasons. Sun, moon, and stars—and these were things to be worshipped, some revered animals like birds, cats, and snakes, and the higher chiefs were considered gods. In their well ordered lives all things and people had their places.

Panel Two: "Thanks be to thee, O Lord, who has permitted me to see something new." So prayed the Spaniard Juan Ponce de León who discovered this land in Easter Time of 1513 and named it Pascua Florida—"Flowery Easter."

Priests of his Roman Catholic faith accompanied Ponce on a later but unsuccessful expedition to Charlotte Harbor on Florida's lower Gulf coast in 1521.

Panel Three: Pensacola, founded in 1559 by Catholic colonists led by Tristan de Luna, was the first Christian settlement in Florida. The colony lasted three years.

French Calvinists, or Huguenots, under Réne de Goulaine de Laudonniere, founded the first Protestant Christian colony in Florida near the mouth of the St. Johns River in 1564, called Fort Caroline; this settlement was also shortlived.

Panel Four: Divine services in English using the Anglican (Episcopal) book of common prayer took place aboard the English Naval Squadron of Sir John Hawkins while anchored in the Saint Johns River from July 24 to 28, 1565. It was the first Anglican service in Florida and the first in what is now the continental United States.

The Anglican church would return to Florida for a twenty-one year period from 1763 to 1784.

Panel Five: St. Augustine, founded on September 8, 1565, by Spaniards under Don Pedro Menéndez de Aviles, was the first permanent Christian settlement in Florida and North America.

Founding pastor was Father Francisco Lopez de Mendoza. He and other Catholic priests established Florida's first parish, first Indian mission—Nombre de Dins (Name of God)—the first seminary and the first hospital.

Panel Six: In the seventeenth century Franciscan missionary friars founded a chain of missions that stretched from St. Augustine to Tallahassee.

In the mission compounds some 30,000 Timucua and Apalache Indians learned not only the doctrines of Christianity but also the rudiments of European arts and crafts.

Panel Seven: Blacks came to Florida with the Conquistadors as free persons. In 1580–1581 the first slaves arrived, and to one of these families living in St. Augustine a son was born and baptized a Christian in 1606, the first documented baptism of a black in what is now the United States. Blacks and whites worshipped together at the time. Blacks retained few vestiges of their own African religious heritage.

Panel Eight: Records note that Jews had settled in Pensacola by the 1760s, and that a Jewish fur trader was living in St. Augustine in 1785. Other Jews arrived in the early decades of the nineteenth century; they were planters, farmers, and merchants.

Panel Nine: Great Britain ruled Florida in the period 1763–1784, the era of the American Revolution. In occupying the Floridas, King George III declared freedom of worship.

Anglican worshippers with their spiritual leader John Forbes converted the old Spanish Parish Church of La Soledad (at St. Augustine) to their use. Renamed Saint Peter's and given a new belltower, it became the first Protestant Episcopal Church in Florida.

Panel Ten: The first Greek Orthodox Christian in Florida probably was Doroteo Teodoar, who accompanied the expedition of the Spaniard Pánfilo de Narváez in 1528.

The first Greek Orthodox community was established at New Smyrna in 1768. Pioneer Greeks had no priests with them, however, and met to worship there, and later in St. Augustine, with Roman Catholics from Minorca.

Panel Eleven: Pigeon Creek Baptist Church, in what is now Nassau County, was Florida's only known Protestant Church when the territory became part of the United States in 1821. The Baptists were eventually to become the largest Christian group in Florida.

Methodist circuit riders carried their faith into the rural areas, preaching in civic buildings, under the trees, and in open fields if there were not churches available.

Panel Twelve: Presbyterians organized their first church at St. Augustine in 1824 with thirteen people in the congregation. At Tallahassee, before there was a church building, they held services in the Capitol.

The Episcopal church drew planters and merchants. St. Augustine's Trinity Church is the oldest church of that faith in Florida. Christ Church in the city of Pensacola is the second oldest.

Panel Thirteen: Blacks founded their own churches after the Civil War. Spirituals and preaching gave a special vibrancy to their services.

Ministers were not only religious leaders, they were also advisors to their people in troubled times.

Panel Fourteen: Jewish families settled in the small communities of northern Florida after the Civil War.

In 1874 Temple Bethel was established in Pensacola. Ahavath Chesed was founded in Jacksonville in 1882.

Religion / 317

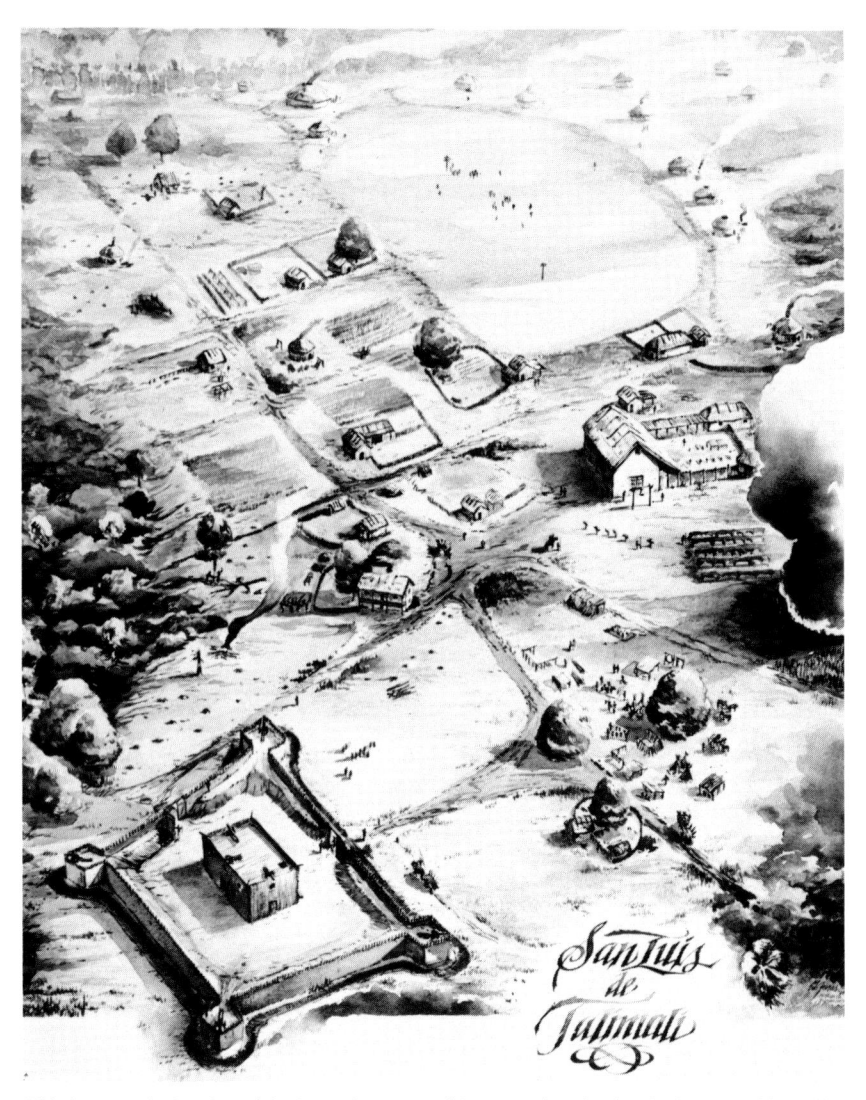

This is a speculative view of the Spanish mission of San Luis de Talmali, which was established between 1633 and 1656 by Franciscan missionaries. The mission occupied a Tallahassee hilltop, and by 1702 had become the provincial capital for more than 40 nearby Apalachee villages. Life there ended abruptly in 1704 when the frightened inhabitants burned their settlement and fled in advance of an attack by the British and their Creek allies. Today San Luis has been rediscovered as a State archaeological and historic site, having been purchased by the state in 1983.

Dept. of State. Division of Archaeological Research

Floridians at War

Source: Department of Military Affairs

Floridians have fought in this country's wars ever since volunteers formed five companies to fight in the War with Mexico in 1846–1848, the year after Florida became a state. Fifty-five of the Mexican War warriors died of disease and one was killed in action.

One Florida Army National Guard unit, with 86 personnel, was called to active duty during the Vietnam Conflict of 1965–1973. Additionally, 40,352 men were inducted through Selective Service and 146,028 personnel voluntarily enlisted. Died in service during the Vietnam Conflict were 1,897 Florida troops.

More than a quarter-million Floridians—a fifth of the population—left their homes to become warriors for World War II and its immediate aftermath. In the vanguard were 3,941 officers and men of the Florida National Guard. Then, from 1940 to 1947, Florida added 254,358 men and women to the armed forces of the United States. One hundred fifty-eight National Guardsmen and 4,516 other Floridians made the supreme sacrifice in World War II.

Incident to the Korean War, units of the Florida National Guard with 972 men were called to active duty. In addition to these, 27,823 Floridians were inducted through the Selective Service System and 84,257 voluntarily enlisted. More than 500 died or were killed in action.

Florida's monument to Vietnam veterans at Tallahassee consists of two black marble pylons tethering a 15 by 28-foot American flag. On the pylons are inscribed the names of 1,942 veterans who either died or were missing in action when the memorial was dedicated November 11, 1985.
Bob O'Lary

In the first World War, when Florida had fewer than a million people, 42,030 Floridians marched in the Army, Navy, Marine Corps, or Coast Guard, and of these 1,287 gave their lives. Just before that, Florida sent a regiment of infantry—1,149 men—to Texas for the punitive expedition into Mexico.

For the Spanish-American War, the state's organized militia was called to Tampa to form the First Florida Volunteer Infantry, of 48 officers and 956 enlisted men. The First Florida sat out the War at Fernandina and Huntsville, Alabama, although some individuals were detached and a few reached Cuba. Of the Florida naval militia, six officers and 93 enlisted men saw active duty with the Navy. Company "C" of the Third United States Volunteer Company, made up of five officers and 98 enlisted men, all from Florida, served in Cuba. Other Floridians served as individuals in regular Army units.

Approximately 16,000 Floridians served in the Confederate forces and 1,290 in the Union Army and Navy during the Civil War. Among those Floridians on the Southern side, more than 3,000 died.

Medal of Honor

Federal records indicate 18 sons of Florida, native or adopted, have won the nation's highest military award for bravery "beyond the call of duty"—the Medal of Honor presented "in the name of the Congress of the United States." For their names, see the Florida Handbook 1987–1988 edition.

The Florida Legislature in 1986 honored the 11 Medal of Honor recipients then resident in Florida. Seven were present when the House and Senate adopted resolutions commending them.

Armed Forces Members and Retirees in Florida

According to Statistical Abstracts, in 1992 Florida was the home of 157,887 members of the armed forces and 74,800 retirees. The total of 232,687 did not include dependents, National Guard or Reverves.

Floridas in the Navy

Six ships of the United States Navy have been named for Florida.

Until recently, it was thought there were five *Floridas,* but a sixth has been found by the Navy's Ship History Section. The first *Florida,* a sloop, was engaged almost constantly in survey work on the southern coast between 1824 and 1831.

The second was a sidewheel steamer, of 1,261 tons displacement, purchased in 1861 and mounting nine guns. The *Florida* served with blockading squadrons during the Civil War. The ship passed out of Navy possession in 1868.

The next *Florida* was a 15-gun steam frigate, of 3,281 tons, built at the New York Navy Yard in 1864 and first known as the *Wampanoog*. The *Wampanoog* was the fastest ship of the time, achieving 16.7 geographic miles an hour. However, she saw little active service since structural defects prevented efficient use of her guns. The name was changed to *Florida* in 1869, and the frigate was stricken from the Navy register in 1885.

The fourth *Florida* was a single turreted coast monitor, of 3,255 tons, authorized by Congress in 1898. Built by Lewis Nixon at Elizabethport, New Jersey, the monitor was placed in service in 1903 and sold in 1922, her name having been changed to *Tallahassee* in 1908 so a new battleship could be named for the state. Her principal service was a submarine tender in the Panama Canal Zone.

Best known thus far of the *Floridas* was the battleship commissioned in 1911. She was launched May 12, 1910, under the sponsorship of Miss Elizabeth Legere Fleming (Mrs. Frank Percival Hamilton) of Jacksonville, daughter of former Governor Francis P. Fleming. Displacing 21,825 tons, with a speed of 22 knots, the *Florida* was 510 feet long and cost $6,400,000.

The *Florida* was dispatched in 1914 to protect American lives and property at Vera Cruz, Mexico. During World War I, the *Florida* first was stationed in the Chesapeake Bay area and then attached to the Atlantic fleet for convoy service, operating with the British Grand Fleet from Scapa Flow and the Fifth of Forth, Scotland. Several submarine attacks were encountered and on one occasion, while in company with the Grand Fleet, contact was made by ships of the advance screen with a German cruiser squadron but no action resulted. In April–May, the *Florida* participated in weather observation for the Trans-Atlantic flight of Seaplanes NC-1, NC-3, and NC-4 and in the search for the NC-3.

Punch bowl from Florida *at Governor's Mansion.*

The *Florida* was modernized in 1926 at the Boston Navy Yard at a cost of $3,852,000, and subsequently was assigned to the training of naval reservists. The *Florida* was stricken from the Navy register on April 6, 1931, and scrapped under the terms of the London Naval Treaty.

Of particular interest is the ornate silver service returned to the State for the Governor's Mansion when the *Florida* was decommissioned. This service had been purchased with $10,000 donated by Floridians, including children who gave pennies, nickels and dimes in school collections.

Latest of the *Floridas,* the sixth, is a Trident-class nuclear submarine. The 500-foot submarine carries a crew of 154 and is armed with 24 Trident missiles. It has a range of 4,000 miles. The SSNB 728, its construction designation, was named the *USS Florida* by President Carter on the day before he left office in 1981. A Melbourne high school student, Doug Heminger, designed the insignia for the *Florida,* winning a contest among junior high and high school and college students.

"Some Corner of a Foreign Field . . ."

Rupert Brooke, in "The Soldier," spoke of "a corner of a foreign field that is forever England." In Florida, there are two such "corners," where are buried Royal Air Force cadets who died in this state during World War II.

There are 23 graves, in the Oak Ridge cemetery at Arcadia, of cadets who

With its birdcage masts of the era, the USS Florida *is shown here during a naval review on October 12, 1912.* Library of Congress

died in training at nearby Dorr and Carlstrom Fields. Another 13 Commonwealth air cadets are buried in Woodlawn cemetery at Miami.

At Arcadia, each grave is marked by a granite headstone furnished by the British government and inscribed with the RAF emblem and with an epitaph supplied by the family. On the United States Memorial day, the flag of Great Britain flies over the graves and a memorial service is attended by representatives of British and American organizations. Maintenance of the graves has been undertaken by the Rotary Club of Arcadia.

In Miami, an annual ceremony honoring the Commonwealth dead of World War I and II is conducted at Woodlawn on the British Veterans' day, in mid-November. There is a parade from the gates of Woodlawn to the Commonwealth plot, where the British Consul delivers an address and places a wreath. The ceremony ends with the firing of a salute by the military escort.

The Last Battle

A year and a half after the surrender of Cornwallis at Yorktown and three months following the signing of the provisional Treaty of Peace at Paris, guns of American and British warships exchanged volleys off the coast of today's Brevard County.

The Continental frigate Alliance and its French consort, the Duc de Lauzun, were en route to Newport, Rhode Island, with gold being loaned to the Continental government by France, when encountered on March 10, 1783, by three British men-of-war, including the Sybil.

In the exchange with the Sybil, the Alliance damaged the British warship sufficiently for the Alliance and the Duc de Lauzun to complete their mission. Sybil's log gave the scene of the post-war engagement as 30 leagues off Cape Canaveral.

The "Battle Off Florida" was recognized in House Concurrent Resolution 620 of the 1986 Legislature.

The American Governors of Florida

United States Commissioner and Governor of the Territories of East and West Florida

General Andrew Jackson was named by President Monroe on March 10, 1821, as "Commissioner of the United States with full power and authority to him to take possession of and to occupy the territories ceded by Spain to the United States . . ."

On the same day, he was also appointed by President Monroe to use in the territories of East and West Florida "all the powers and authorities heretofore exercised by the Governor and Captain General and Intendant of Cuba, and by the Governors of East and West Florida."

The ceremonies of transfer from Spain to the United States took place at Pensacola on July 17, 1821. Jackson's resignation, sent from his home near Nashville, Tennessee, on November 13, 1821, was accepted by the President on December 31. In a letter sent from Pensacola on October 6, Jackson had announced his intention of leaving Florida, and he likely did so on October 8.

Jackson had intended that his Florida stay would be short. He had been offered the Florida appointment in 1819, at a time when it was believed early ratification of the treaty of cession would be made by Spain. He declined the appointment then. President Monroe renewed his offer in a letter on January 24, 1821, and Jackson,

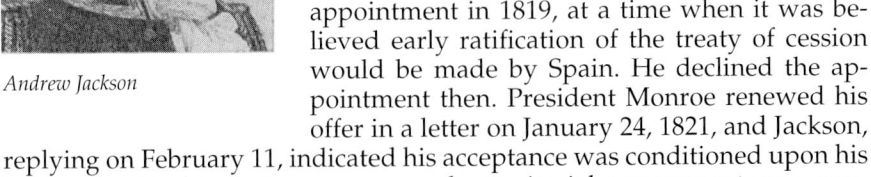

Andrew Jackson

replying on February 11, indicated his acceptance was conditioned upon his being permitted to resign as soon as the territorial government was organized. He accepted Florida from Spain on July 17, 1821, and left Pensacola for good in October.

After Jackson left, William G. D. Worthington of Maryland served as Acting Governor of East Florida and Colonel George Walton of Georgia as Acting Governor of West Florida. Worthington, based at St. Augustine, was Secretary of the Territory of East Florida, and Walton, at Pensacola, was Secretary of West Florida. Walton was the namesake son of a Georgia signer of the Declaration of Independence.

Jackson was born in such obscurity on March 15, 1767, that two States have claimed his birthplace, though he himself stated that he had been told it was in the Waxhaw settlement in South Carolina. He attended the "old field" school and the academy of Doctor Humphries; during the Revolution was captured by the British and confined in the stockade at Camden, S.C.; left an orphan at fourteen years of age; worked for a time in a saddler's shop and afterward taught school. He studied law in Salisbury, N.C.; was admitted to the bar in 1787 and commenced practice in McLeanville, Guilford County, N.C. He was appointed Solicitor of the Western district of North Carolina, comprising what is now the State of Tennessee, in 1788, and located in Nashville, Tenn., in October 1788. He was a delegate to the convention to frame a Constitution for the new State, held in Knoxville in January 1796; upon the admission of Tennessee as a State into the Union he was elected as a Democrat to the Fourth Congress and served from December 5, 1796, to March 3, 1797. He was elected to the United States Senate for the term commencing March 4, 1797, and served from September 26, 1797, until his resignation in April 1798; elected judge of the State Supreme Court of Tennessee and served from 1798 to July 24, 1804. He moved to the "Hermitage," near Nashville, and engaged in planting and in mercantile pursuits; served in the Creek War of 1813; Major General of Volunteers 1812–1814; commissioned Brigadier General in the United States Army April 19, 1814, and Major General May 1, 1814. He led his army to New Orleans, where he defeated the British January 8, 1815, and received the thanks of Congress and a gold medal by resolution of February 27, 1815. He commanded an expedition which captured Florida in 1818. He was Governor of Florida from March 10 to October 8, 1821 (his commission ran until December 31, 1821, but he left Florida on October 8); declined the position of Minister to Mexico; again elected to the United States Senate and served from March 4, 1823, to October 14, 1825, when he resigned. He was the unsuccessful Democratic candidate for President in 1824; elected President of the United States in 1828; reelected in 1832 and served from March 4, 1829, to March 3, 1837. He retired to the "Hermitage," where he died June 8, 1845, and was buried in the garden on his estate.—Adapted from the *Biographical Dictionary of the American Congress.*

For more about Jackson, read

James, Marquis, *Andrew Jackson: Border Captain* (New York, Grossett and Dunlap, 1959)

James, Marquis, *Andrew Jackson: Portrait of a President* (New York, Grossett and Dunlap, 1961)

Schlesinger, Arthur M., Jr. *The Age of Jackson* (Boston, Little, Brown and Company, 1945)

Van Deusen, Glydon G. *The Jacksonian Era, 1828–1848* (New York, Harper and Row, 1959)

Remini, Robert V. *Andrew Jackson and the Course of American Freedom, 1822–1832* (New York, Harper and Row, 1981)

Some 227 books, 353 articles, and innumerable doctoral dissertations had been written by 1980 about Jackson and his influence upon American life.

William Pope DuVal

William P. DuVal

First territorial Governor (April 17, 1822) was born at Mount Comfort, near Richmond, Virginia, in 1784, the son of William and Ann (Pope) DuVal. DuVal was of French Huguenot forbears. His father was associated, as a lawyer, with Patrick Henry in the British debt cases and, as a major of riflemen, captured a British vessel becalmed in the James River during the Revolution. Young DuVal left home at the age of 14 for the Kentucky frontier, settling in Bardstown to study law. He was admitted to the bar at 19. He served as a captain in the mounted rangers in 1812, and as Kentucky representative in the 13th Congress (1813–15). He came to Florida as a Territorial Judge, having been appointed by President Monroe upon the recommendation of DuVal's friend, John C. Calhoun, then Secretary of War. He served about a month at St. Augustine. He was appointed Governor of Florida territory in 1822 by President Monroe, was reappointed by Presidents Adams and Jackson. His administration was notable for the confidence which he enjoyed with the Indians. The capital was established at Tallahassee during his tenure. He was a friend of Washington Irving, who wrote of him in "Ralph Ringwood." James K. Paulding also wrote of him as "Nimrod Wildlife." Duval county perpetuates his name. DuVal uniformly signed himself as "DuVal" though the name usually appears in print as "Duval." DuVal moved to Texas in 1848, and Texas was his home when he died on March 18, 1854, in Washington, D.C.

John Henry Eaton

Second territorial Governor (April 24, 1834), was born near Scotland Neck, in Halifax County, North Carolina, on June 18, 1790, the son of John and Elizabeth Eaton. He had been a lawyer at Nashville and a member for eight years of the United States Senate when his fellow Tennessean, Andrew Jackson, appointed him Secretary of War, an office he relinquished in the cabinet turmoil over his wife, the famous Peggy O'Neale. The short Eaton administration was not a happy one. He arrived in Florida some seven months after his appointment. The Indians were restless in the leaderless Territory.

John H. Eaton
  National Cyclopaedia, American Biography

Richard K. Call

From Florida, Eaton went to Spain as American Minister, remaining until 1840. He wrote a biography of Jackson. He died in Washington, D.C., on November 17, 1856.

Richard Keith Call

Third (March 16, 1836) and fifth territorial Governor (March 19, 1841), was born at Pittsfield, Prince George County, Virginia, on October 24, 1792, the son of Captain William and Helen Meade (Walker) Call and the namesake nephew of Major Richard Keith Call, a Revolutionary War hero. Young Call left Mount Pleasant Academy, near Clarksville, Tenn., in 1813 for the Creek War, in which his conduct endeared him to General Andrew Jackson, whose personal aide he was thereafter. He first came to Florida in 1814 with Jackson as a soldier and returned with him to Pensacola in 1821 to set up the American government for the new Territory. In 1822, he decided to make Florida his civilian home, first as a lawyer at Pensacola. Successively, he was a member of the Legislative Council, delegate to Congress, receiver of the West Florida land office, brigadier general of the West Florida militia and territorial Governor. Commanding the troops in the Seminole war while Governor, he routed the Indians in the second and third battles of Wahoo swamp. He was removed as Governor because of controversy with Federal authorities over help for Florida in the Indian conflict. Although a Democrat, he canvassed in the North for the Whig candidate, William Henry Harrison, who subsequently appointed him to his old place of Governor. When Florida became a State in 1845, he was a candidate for Governor but was defeated, largely because of his part in the election of Harrison. He was married in

General Jackson's home, the "Hermitage," in 1824 to Mary Letitia Kirkman of Nashville. Call's home in Tallahassee, "The Grove," begun in the 1820s, remains today a place of architectural and historic distinction, owned by Mrs. LeRoy Collins, the former Mary Call Darby, a great granddaughter of Governor Call. He died at "The Grove" on September 14, 1862.

Read: *Richard Keith Call, Southern Unionist,* by Herbert J. Doherty, Jr.

Robert Raymond Reid

Fourth territorial Governor (December 2, 1839), was born in Prince William Parish, South Carolina, on September 8, 1789. He was educated in Augusta, Georgia, and practiced law there. He possessed exceptional talent as a public speaker. He began public service at 27 as judge of the Burke County Superior Court, and afterwards served Georgia in Congress and as judge of various courts. In May, 1832, he was appointed United States Judge of East Florida by President Jackson, for whom he had voted as a presidential elector in 1828. He continued in this office until December, 1839, when he was appointed Governor by President Van Buren. He presided at the convention which drafted Florida's Constitution. He advocated as vigorous a prosecution of the Indian War as his predecessor but his relations with the Federal authorities were more amicable. He died in Leon County, near Tallahassee, on July 1, 1841.

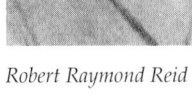

Robert Raymond Reid *John Branch*

John Branch

Sixth territorial Governor (August 11, 1844), was born in Halifax County, North Carolina on November 4, 1782, the son of Colonel John and Rebecca

(Bradford) Branch. After graduating from the University of North Carolina in 1801, he studied law but never practiced, preferring the greater activity of politics. His first public service came with election in 1811 as Senator from Halifax County, an office to which he was chosen annually until 1817, when he was elected Governor of North Carolina. Completing his term as Governor, he was reelected State Senator and subsequently United States Senator. He was appointed Secretary of the Navy by President Jackson, resigning in the hubbub over Peggy O'Neale, wife of his Army colleague and predecessor as Florida Governor, John H. Eaton. Returning to North Carolina, he served in various public offices and in 1844 he was appointed Governor of Florida by President John Tyler. He died at Enfield, North Carolina, on January 3, 1863.

William D. Moseley   *Thomas Brown*

William Dunn Moseley

First Governor under Statehood (June 25, 1845–October 1, 1849), was born at Moseley Hall, Lenoir County, North Carolina, on February 1, 1795, the son of Matthew and Elizabeth (Herring) Moseley. He taught school to earn the money to enter the University of North Carolina, where he topped in educational achievement such classmates as James K. Polk, afterwards President of the United States. He practiced law at Wilmington, North Carolina. After serving as a State Senator, he was defeated in 1834, as the Democratic nominee, by three votes for Governor of North Carolina. He bought a plantation on Lake Miccosukee in Jefferson County, Florida, in 1835, and resided there until 1851. He served in the territorial Legislature and defeated

Richard Keith Call for Governor in the first election under Statehood. He moved in 1851 to Palatka, where he was a planter and fruit grower. He appears to have served from Putnam County in the 1855 extraordinary session of the House of Representatives. He died on January 4, 1863.

Thomas Brown

Second Governor (October 1, 1849-October 3, 1853), was born in Westmoreland County, Virginia, on October 24, 1785, the son of William and Margaret (Templeton) Brown. He served in the War of 1812, entered a mercantile business with a brother at Alexandria, Virginia, and subsequently became chief clerk of the post office at Richmond. While chief clerk, he invented the post office letter box. He was elected in 1817 to the Virginia Legislature. In 1828, he moved with his family to Florida, settling on a plantation near Lake Jackson in Leon County. After a freeze killed his crop, he leased and operated the Planters Hotel in Tallahassee. Later, he bought the square west of the capitol and built the City Hotel. He was Auditor of the Territory in 1834, President of the Legislative Council in 1838, member of the Constitutional Convention in 1839, and member from Leon County of the first (1845) House of Representatives under statehood. As Governor, he was concerned with internal improvements and agriculture, including efforts to determine the cost and feasibility of draining the Everglades. He was an active Mason for more than 60 years, serving as secretary in the Tallahassee lodge for a long time and compiling a book on Masonry. He died in Tallahassee on August 24, 1867.

James Emilius Broome

Third Governor (October 3, 1853–October 5, 1857) was born in Hamburg, Aiken County, South Carolina, on December 15, 1808, the son of John and Jeanette (Witherspoon) Broome. He came to Tallahassee in 1837, engaging in a mercantile business until his retirement in 1841. He was appointed Probate Judge of Leon County in 1843 by Governor Call, a member of the opposing political party, and served until his retirement in 1848. As Probate Judge, he administered the oath of office to the first Governor under statehood. He was elected Governor in 1852 as the Democratic nominee although Whig candidates otherwise prevailed, a tribute to his ability as a speaker. He was an early States-Righter, and also was known as the "veto-Governor," vetoing more Acts than any of his predecessors. He was a member of the 1861 Senate from Nassau County. He had one of the largest plantations in the state. He was married five times. He moved in 1865 to New York City, but died in DeLand on November 23, 1883, while visiting a son.

Madison Starke Perry

Fourth Governor (October 5, 1857–October 7, 1861), was born in South Carolina in 1814. He came to Florida and became a leading planter in Alachua County. He represented Alachua County in the 1850 Senate. Elected Governor as a Democrat, he helped bring about settlement of a long-standing boundary dispute with Georgia. His administration also saw consider-

James E. Broome   *Madison S. Perry*

able extensions of railroads, encouraging development of the state. He foresaw the possibility of Florida's secession from the Union, and in 1858 urged reestablishment of the State's militia. He told the 1860 Legislature that the election of Abraham Lincoln as President made secession inevitable. Florida withdrew, on January 11, 1861, during his administration. After his term ended, he was Colonel of the 7th Florida Regiment until illness forced his retirement. He died at his Alachua County plantation in March, 1865.

John Milton

Fifth Governor (October 7, 1861–April 1, 1865), was born near Louisville, Jefferson County Georgia, on April 20, 1807, the son of General Homer Virgil and Elizabeth (Robinson) Milton. He was a descendant of the poet, John Milton. He was a lawyer who practiced in a number of Georgia and Alabama communities and in New Orleans; served in Florida during the Seminole War as captain of a volunteer company, and in 1846 moved to Jackson County as a farmer. Before coming to Florida, he reputedly killed an adversary in a duel. Entering politics, he became a statewide force in the Democratic party, serving himself as a presidential elector in 1848 and as a member from Jackson County of 1850 House of Representatives. A vigorous States-Righter, he encouraged the seizure by Florida forces of Federal military establishments and also was instrumental in the early secession of Florida from the Union. As Governor, he stressed Florida's ability to serve as an important source of food and salt for the Confederate forces. Collapse of the Southern cause was followed by his death by gun shot at "Sylvania," his home near Marianna, on April 1, 1865. In his last message to the Legislature, he had said "death would be preferable to reunion."

330 / The Governors

John Milton   *A. K. Allison*

Abraham Kurkindolle Allison*

Sixth (acting) Governor (April 1, 1865–May 19, 1865), was born in Jones County, Georgia, on December 10, 1810, the son of Captain James and Sarah (Fannin) Allison. After schooling, he engaged in mercantile trade at Columbus, Georgia, and in Henry County, Alabama, before settling at Apalachicola, where he served as first Mayor, first County Judge of Franklin County, Clerk of the United States Court and a member of the territorial Legislature. He was captain of the Franklin Rifles in the Seminole War. He moved to Quincy in 1839 and commenced the practice of law. He served again in the territorial Legislature and, with statehood, represented Gadsden County in the 1845, 1847 and 1852 House of Representatives and in the 1862, 1863 and 1864 Senate. He was also a member of the Constitutional Convention of 1861. He served with Confederate forces in battles at Macon, Georgia, and Natural Bridge, Florida. Allison was twice Acting Governor. As Speaker of the House, he proclaimed himself Governor on September 16, 1853, because of the absence from Florida of both Governor Thomas Brown and Senate President R. J. Floyd, serving until October 3, when James E. Broome was inaugurated. Allison seems to have regarded himself as being available on a stand-by basis and apparently did not exercise executive powers. For that reason, there has been a disposition not to count Allison's tenure then in the numerical listing of governors. Allison next was Acting Governor when Governor John Milton died on April 1, 1865, and Allison, as Senate President, succeeded to the office. His last official act recorded in the letter book of the Governor's office was dated May 19, 1865, the day before Union troops formally

*Allison's names also appear as "Abram" and "Kyrkendal."

occupied Tallahassee. Allison was taken into custody by Federal authorities and received at Fort Pulaski, Georgia, on June 19, 1865, being imprisoned there with other Confederate officials. He was held about six months. He returned to Quincy and in 1872 was convicted there on a charge of intimidating Negroes, being jailed in Tallahassee for six months and fined. He died at Quincy on July 8, 1893.

William Marvin

Seventh (provisional) Governor (July 13, 1865–December 20, 1865), was born at Fairfield, Herkimer County, New York, on April 14, 1808, the son of Selden and Charlotte (Pratt) Marvin. He was practicing law at Phelps, New York, when appointed by President Jackson as United States District Attorney at Key West. He twice was appointed Federal District Judge and from his experience wrote the nationally recognized textbook *Law of Wreck and Salvage*. He twice was elected a member of the territorial Legislative Council and was a delegate to the first constitutional convention. He was appointed provisional Governor by President Johnson for the purpose of reestablishing State Government. He subsequently was elected as a Democrat to the United States Senate, which declined to seat him. When Congress enacted laws for reconstruction of government in the seceded States, he refused to be a candidate for any office and, in 1867, moved to Skaneateles, New York, where he died July 9, 1902.

David Shelby Walker

Eighth Governor (December 20, 1865–July 4, 1868), was born near Russelville, Logan County, Kentucky on May 2, 1815, the son of David and May

William Marvin   *David S. Walker*

Harrison Reed   Wisconsin Historical Society   *William H. Gleason*   Jeanne Bellamy

(Barbour) Walker. After attending private schools in Kentucky and Tennessee and studying law, he settled in Leon County in 1837. He served in Florida's first Legislature under statehood in 1845 as Senator from Leon and Wakulla Counties and in the House of Representatives from Leon County in 1848. He was from 1849 to 1854 the Register of Public Lands and, by reason of this, State Superintendent of Public Instruction. As such, he did as much as any other person prior to 1861 to create interest in public schools. His energies caused the establishment in Tallahassee of a free school supported by city taxes. He was Mayor of Tallahassee and, in 1860, became a Justice of the Supreme Court, an office he relinquished for the Governorship. A former Whig and a Constitutional Unionist, he had opposed secession but supported his State after it left the Union. His administration had the difficult task of restoring civil government during military occupation. He returned to the practice of law in 1868, and in 1876 was appointed Circuit Court Judge, a position he held until his death at Tallahassee on July 20, 1891.

Harrison Reed

Ninth Governor (took oath June 8, Military recognized July 4, 1868–January 7, 1873), was born at Littleton, Middlesex County, Massachusetts, on August 26, 1813, the son of Serb Harrison and Rhoda (Finney) Reed. He was apprenticed at 16 to the printing trade and was forced to quit after three years' service because of failing health. He went into the mercantile business and, in 1836, moved to Milwaukee, Wisconsin, where he opened the first general store and organized the first Sunday School. He failed in the 1837 depression and, after a brief interval as a farmer, took charge of the new *Milwaukee Sentinel* as printer, editor and publisher. He subsequently was associated with a number of political party newspapers and with the development of a manufacturing community on the Fox River in Wisconsin. He moved to Washington in 1861 as an employee of the Treasury Department and subsequently was sent to Fernandina by President Lincoln in 1863 as one of three tax commissioners with responsibility for Confederate property. His reputation for honesty in this office was said to have brought appointment by President Johnson in 1865 as postal agent for Florida. He held this position until he was elected Governor under the 1868 Constitution. His administration was a stormy one, for he had to cope with factions within his own Republican party. Two serious attempts to impeach him originated with leaders of his party. At the end of his term, he went to his farm on the St. Johns River; in 1875, became editor of the *Semi-Tropical,* a monthly magazine devoted to Southern development, served from Duval County in the 1899 House of Representatives, and from 1889 to 1893 was Postmaster at Tallahassee. He died at Jacksonville on May 25, 1899.

William H. Gleason

William H. Gleason claimed the office of Governor in November, 1868, during efforts by a faction of his own Republican party to oust Governor Harrison Reed. Gleason had been elected Lieutenant Governor. Gleason proclaimed himself Governor after the Legislature, on November 7, 1868, adjourned until January while the Senate was considering the question of trying Governor Reed.

Loyal to Reed, the State's Adjutant General and the county's Sheriff organized volunteers who, by 'round-the-clock sentry duty, guarded the Capitol against entry by Gleason and his adherents. Gleason established headquarters in a nearby hotel and issued documents signed by him as Governor.

Reed asked the Supreme Court for its opinion. The Justices, on November 24, 1868, fully supported him, declaring he had not been impeached because the Senate at the time the charges were preferred was without a lawful quorum.

Governor Reed then took the offensive. He challenged Gleason's right to be Lieutenant Governor since he had not been a citizen of Florida for three years prior to his election, as the law required. Gleason, a former Wisconsin lumberman, actually had come to Florida in 1866. So the Governor won, and Gleason was ousted on December 14. Gleason served from Dade County in the House of Representatives from 1871 to 1874.

Gleason was born in New York State around 1830 and died at Eau Gallie on November 9, 1902.

Samuel T. Day

(No portrait of Day known. Anyone with information, please write Allen Morris at Tallahassee.)

Samuel T. Day claimed to be Acting Governor from February 10 to May 4, 1872, during the pendency in the Senate of impeachment charges against Governor Harrison Reed. Day was Lieutenant Governor in the Reed administration, a Republican physician and from Virginia.

As William Watson Davis tells the story in his *The Civil War and Reconstruction in Florida*, Governor Reed quit the executive offices in Tallahassee soon after his impeachment by the House of Representatives on February 10. Reed considered himself suspended from office because he was constitutionally disqualified from performing any of the duties. He went to his farm near Jacksonville.

When, however, the Legislature adjourned *sine die* shortly afterwards without bringing him to trial, Reed construed its action as equivalent to acquittal. He watched for a chance to emphasize this conclusion. This chance soon came when Day, on April 10, went to Jacksonville for a party caucus.

Reed thereupon went to Tallahassee, entered the executive offices, issued a proclamation declaring himself to be Governor of Florida, appointed a new Attorney General and a Circuit Judge, and then returned quietly to his home in Jacksonville to await results. Reed's proclamation was approved by the Secretary of State with the affixing of the Great Seal of the State.

The Reed document stated Day was "making removals from office and appointments thereto without authority."

Reed proposed to Day that they ask the Supreme Court who was Governor, and when Day paid no attention to this, Reed requested the opinion. The Supreme Court responded on April 29 that Day was "neither *de jure* nor *de facto* Governor of Florida. He is in no sense Governor. He is Lieutenant Governor exercising the functions of the office of Governor. You are still *de jure* Governor."

Meantime, on April 22, Day called a special session of the Legislature, probably expecting to finally drive Reed out of office through the trial of the impeachment charges. The Democrats who sought to benefit politically saw the Republican factions close ranks temporarily. The trial did not materialize. On May 4, the Senate, by a vote of 10 to 7, agreed to dismiss the charges against Reed.

Ossian Bingley Hart

Tenth Governor (January 7, 1873–March 18, 1874), was born in Jacksonville on January 17, 1821, the son of Isaiah David and Nancy (Nelson) Hart. His father was a founder of Jacksonville and the present Ocean Street originally was named for Ossian. He practiced law in Jacksonville, moved in 1843 to farm near Fort Pierce and represented St. Lucie County in the 1845 House of Representatives. He moved in 1846 to Key West, resuming law practice, and in 1856 to Tampa. Although raised amid slaves on his father's St. Johns River plantation, he openly opposed secession and suffered hardship during the War Between the States. He took an active part in the reconstruction of Jacksonville and of the State government and in 1868 was appointed an Associate Justice of the Supreme Court. He was defeated for

Ossian P. Hart *Marcellus L. Stearns*
Green, *School History of Florida*

Congress in a contested election in 1870, but was elected Republican Governor two years later. He was the first Florida-born Governor. He suffered from pneumonia as a consequence of campaign exertions and this resulted finally in his death at Jacksonville on March 18, 1874.

Marcellus Lovejoy Stearns

Eleventh (acting) Governor (March 18, 1874–January 2, 1877), was born at Lovell, Oxford County, Maine, on April 29, 1839, the son of Caleb and Eliza W. (Russell) Stearns. He left Waterville College (now Colby) during his junior year to join the Union Army in 1861, lost an arm at the battle of Winchester and achieved the rank of first lieutenant. He studied law while in the Army and was transferred to the Freedmen's Bureau and eventually sent to Quincy, where he remained after being mustered out of service. He served both in the 1868 constitutional convention and from Gadsden County in the House of Representatives for the annual sessions from 1868 through 1872, being Speaker of the sessions beginning in 1869. He was appointed United States Surveyor-General for Florida by President Grant in 1869, holding this position until 1873. He was elected Lieutenant Governor in 1872 and succeeded to the Governorship upon the death of Governor Hart. He was then 34 years old. He was defeated for a regular term. In January, 1877, he was appointed United States Commissioner at Hot Springs, Arkansas, serving until 1880. He died at Palatine Bridge, New York, on December 8, 1891, and was buried at Lovell, Maine.

George F. Drew

William D. Bloxham

George Franklin Drew

Twelfth Governor (January 2, 1877–January 4, 1881), was born at Alton, New Hampshire, on August 6, 1827, the son of John and Charlotte (Davis) Drew. Learning the machinist's trade, he opened a shop in 1847 at Columbus, Georgia, and subsequently engaged in lumbering in other Georgia counties. In 1865, he built Florida's largest saw mill at Ellaville, on the Madison county side of the Suwannee River. Drew's election as Governor marked the end of the Reconstruction era in Florida. He had much to do with restoring the State's financial and political stability. He afterwards returned to the lumber business, having at one time eleven mills in operation. He was prominent in the mercantile affairs of Jacksonville, and served as first president of its Board of Trade. He died September 26, 1900, in Jacksonville.

William Dunnington Bloxham

Thirteenth (January 4, 1881–January 6, 1885) and seventeenth Governor (January 5, 1897–January 8, 1901), was born in Leon County on July 9, 1835, the son of William and Martha (Williams) Bloxham. He graduated from William and Mary College with a law degree in 1855 but, because of health, chose to be a planter. He was elected from Leon County to the 1861 House of Representatives. He organized an infantry company in Leon County in 1862 and commanded this through the War Between the States. He was in the forefront of Democratic leaders during Reconstruction. He was counted out by the State Canvassing Board of what appeared to be election as Lieutenant Governor in 1870, defeated for Governor in 1872, and appointed Secretary of State in 1877. Then he was elected Governor. His first administration as Gov-

Edward A. Perry   *Francis P. Fleming*

ernor was marked by sale to the Disston interests of 4,000,000 acres in the Everglades for $1,000,000—the money restoring the solvency of the State's Internal Improvement Fund and giving impetus to development in South Florida. He declined appointment in 1885 as Minister to Bolivia but accepted the place of United States Surveyor-General for Florida. He was appointed Comptroller in 1890 and subsequently was elected to this place. He was re-elected Comptroller in 1892, and four years later was returned to the office of Governor. His second gubernatorial administration was occupied with money problems, for freezes in 1894–95 and a hurricane in 1896 had destroyed citrus trees and other tax-producing property. He died at Tallahassee on March 15, 1911.

Edward Aylsworth Perry

Fourteenth Governor (January 6, 1885–January 8, 1889), was born in Richmond, Massachusetts, on March 15, 1831, the son of Asa and Philura (Aylsworth) Perry. He attended Yale, taught briefly in Alabama, and took up residence in Pensacola, where he was admitted to the practice of law in 1853. He fought with distinction in the Civil War. He was twice wounded, and rose in rank from private to Brigadier General. During his gubernatorial administration, Florida adopted a new Constitution and established a State Board of Education to advance public schools. He returned to Pensacola, and died there on October 15, 1889.

Francis Philip Fleming

Fifteenth Governor (January 8, 1889–January 3, 1893), was born at Panama Park, in Duval County, on September 28, 1841, the son of Lewis and Margaret (Seton) Fleming. His father farmed a St. Johns River plantation, and

Henry L. Mitchell   *William S. Jennings*

the son was educated at home by tutors. Prior to Florida's secession from the Union, Fleming engaged in business. With the War, he enlisted as a private in a company of volunteers which was incorporated into the famous 2nd Florida Regiment. He earned a Virginia battlefield promotion to First Lieutenant. While home on sick leave, he commanded a company of volunteers at the Battle of Natural Bridge. After the war, he studied law and achieved a statewide reputation. An outstanding achievement of Governor Fleming's administration was his call for a special session of the Legislature to establish a State Board of Health with the suppression of Yellow Fever as its immediate responsibility. He died in Jacksonville on December 20, 1908.

Henry Laurens Mitchell

Sixteenth Governor (January 3, 1893–January 5, 1897), was born in Jefferson County, Alabama, on September 3, 1831, the son of Thomas and Elizabeth (Starns) Mitchell. At 15, he went to Tampa, where he studied law and was admitted to practice in 1849. He resigned as State Attorney to enlist in the Confederate Army when the Civil War began. He served as Lieutenant and Captain, and, at the close of the Vicksburg campaign, resigned to become a member from Hillsborough County of the 1864 House of Representatives, to which he had been elected in his absence. He served again in the 1873 and 1875 sessions. He was appointed to the Supreme Court in 1888 and served until 1891, when he resigned to become a candidate for Governor. He told his first Legislature the state was "in a prosperous condition" although the government's own finances did not present "a healthy showing " After his term as Governor, Mitchell was elected Clerk of the Circuit Court and then County Treasurer of Hillsborough County. He died at Tampa on October 14, 1903.

Napoleon B. Broward *Albert W. Gilchrist*

Read: *The Life of Henry Laurens Mitchell, Florida's 16th Governor,* by George B. Church, Jr.

William Sherman Jennings

Eighteenth Governor (January 8, 1901–January 3, 1905), was born near Walnut Hill, Illinois, on March 24, 1863, the son of Joseph W. and Amanda (Couch) Jennings and a cousin of William Jennings Bryan, a relationship regarded as an important political asset at the time. He came to Florida in 1885 to complete his legal studies and began practice at Brooksville. He was appointed Circuit Court Commissioner in 1887, and became County Judge of Hernando County the following year. He resigned as Judge in 1893 to serve from Hernando County in the House of Representatives, where he was Speaker in 1895. As Governor, Jennings brought into being the primary election system which displaced the convention method of nominating candidates for public office. The first statewide primary, in 1902, was held during his administration. By his energies, Governor Jennings saved some 3,000,000 acres of public lands for the people. He was an ally of his successor, Governor Broward, in the reclamation of the Everglades, carrying this crusade forward as general counsel for the State's Internal Improvement Fund during the Broward administration. He died in St. Augustine on February 27, 1920.

Read: *May Mann Jennings, Florida's Genteel Activist,* by Linda D. Vance.

Napoleon Bonaparte Broward

Nineteenth Governor (January 3, 1905–January 5, 1909), was born on a farm in Duval County on April 19, 1857, the son of Napoleon B. and Mary

Dorcas (Parsons) Broward. He lost both parents when he was 12 years old; worked at 14 in a log camp and later as a farm hand, steamboat roustabout, cod fisherman on the Grand Banks of Newfoundland, seaman on steam and sail boats, pilot on the St. Johns River, joint owner of a river steamboat, operator of a woodyard, phosphate developer, and owner of steam tug. He commanded this tug, "The Three Friends," on eight voyages through Spanish blockade with war material for Cuban revolutionists. He was twice elected Sheriff of Duval County (having been removed by the Governor and then defeating the Governor's appointee), Jacksonville City Councilman, member of the 1901 House of Representatives, and member of the State Board of Health 1901–04. The Broward gubernatorial administration was a stormy one, for he espoused bold, controversial programs. His energies were successful in unifying the State's institutions of higher learning under a Board of Control, and in the drainage and reclamation of the Everglades. Broward was an unsuccessful candidate for the U.S. Senate in 1908 while Governor, but won the nomination two years later. He died at Jacksonville on October 1, 1910, before becoming Senator.

Read: *Napoleon Bonaparte Broward, Florida's Fighting Democrat,* by Samuel Proctor.

Albert Waller Gilchrist

Twentieth Governor (January 5, 1909–January 7, 1913), was born (during the temporary absence of his mother from Florida) at Greenwood, South Carolina, on January 15, 1858, the son of General William E. and Rhoda Elizabeth (Waller) Gilchrist. He was a descendant of the grandfathers both of George Washington and James Madison. He was a graduate of Carolina Military Institute and a member of the class of 1882 of the United States Military Academy. He was a civil engineer, real estate dealer, and orange grower at Punta Gorda. He resigned as brigadier general of the Florida militia in 1898 to enlist as a private in Company C, 3rd United States Volunteer Infantry, and served in Cuba during the Spanish-American War, being mustered out as a captain in 1899. He was a member of the House of Representatives from DeSoto County for the sessions of 1893–95 and 1903–05, being its Speaker in 1905. As Governor, he sponsored the enactment of much legislation to safeguard the health of both people and livestock. He died in New York on May 15, 1926.

Park Trammell

Twenty-first Governor (January 7, 1913–January 2, 1917), was born in Macon County, Alabama, on April 9, 1876, the son of John W. and Ida E. (Park) Trammell. The family moved to Florida during his infancy. He attended grade school in Polk County, and worked on the farm and in a newspaper office. During the Spanish-American War, he was in the quartermaster service at Tampa. He studied law at Vanderbilt University and at Cumberland University, where he received the LL.B. degree in 1899. He practiced law in Lakeland, where he also was a citrus grower and a newspaper owner-editor. He served two terms as Mayor of Lakeland, was elected to the 1903 House of Representatives from Polk County and was President of

Park Trammell *Sidney J. Catts*

the 1905 Senate. He was elected Attorney General in 1908 and Governor in 1912. As Governor, he successfully urged the passage of a law to control the amount and manner of money spent in election campaigns. He also caused to be created a State tax commission for the purpose of equalizing property assessments among counties. He was elected to the United States Senate in 1916 and served there from March 4, 1917, until his death in Washington on May 8, 1936. He is buried at Roselawn Cemetery, Lakeland.

Sidney Johnston Catts

Twenty-second Governor (January 2, 1917–January 4, 1921), was born near Pleasant Hill, Alabama on July 31, 1863, the son of Capt. S.W. and Adeline R. (Smyly) Catts. He attended the Agricultural and Mechanical College of Alabama, Howard College and Alabama Polytechnic Institute, receiving a LL.B. degree from Cumberland University in 1882. He was ordained a Baptist minister in 1886, and filled pulpits in Alabama until 1904. Catts shot to death a black man in an Alabama country store disturbance. He was freed upon the testimony of several black witnesses. He was a candidate for Congress in the Fifth Alabama district in 1904. He moved to Florida and was elected Governor in 1916, after a campaign which saw him edged out as the Democratic nominee only to win the general election as the nominee of the Prohibition party. His administration was a turbulent one since many of the State's political leaders were in opposition to him. He was defeated in 1920 for the Democratic nomination for the U.S. Senate and in 1924 and in 1928 for nomination for Governor. A Federal grand jury indicted Catts on April 9, 1929, accusing him of counterfeiting. Catts denied all charges. There was a

Cary A. Hardee

John W. Martin

mistrial. On the second trial Catts was acquitted, but revelations tarnished his reputation. He died at DeFuniak Springs on March 9, 1936.

Read: *Cracker Messiah, Governor Sidney J. Catts of Florida,* by Wayne Flynt.

Cary Augustus Hardee

Twenty-third Governor (January 4, 1921–January 6, 1925), was born in Taylor County on November 13, 1876, the son of James B. and Amanda Catherine (Johnson) Hardee. Educated in the public schools, he taught school until 1900, when he was admitted to the bar and began practice at Live Oak. He was State's Attorney 1905–13; member from Suwannee County and Speaker of the House of Representatives for the sessions of 1915 and 1917, and Governor. His administration saw adoption of constitutional amendments reapportioning the Legislature and prohibiting the levying of State income and inheritance taxes. Leasing of convicts to private interests was outlawed. Although a lawyer, he was better known in later years as a banker at Live Oak. He was defeated in 1932 for the Democratic nomination for Governor. He died at Live Oak on November 21, 1957.

John Wellborn Martin

Twenty-fourth Governor (January 6, 1925–January 8, 1929), was born at Plainfield in Marion County on June 21, 1884, the son of John M. and Willie (Owens) Martin. He attended school for four years, then continued his education by study at night. Admitted to the bar in 1914, he began law practice in Jacksonville. He was Mayor of Jacksonville for three terms 1917–24, re-

Doyle E. Carlton   *David Sholtz*

turning to that city after serving as Governor. As Governor during a land boom attracting national attention, he gave leadership to progressive endeavors which outlasted the speculation. These included the building of highways on a statewide basis, the financing of public schools by direct State appropriations, and the furnishing of free textbooks to all pupils in the beginning six grades. He was defeated in 1928 for the Democratic nomination for the U.S. Senate and in 1932 for nomination for Governor. Beginning in the 1940s he was co-receiver and subsequently trustee of the Florida East Coast railroad. He died in Jacksonville on February 22, 1958.

Doyle Elam Carlton

Twenty-fifth Governor (January 8, 1929–January 3, 1933), was born at Wauchula on July 6, 1887, the son of Albert and Martha (McEwen) Carlton. He graduated from Stetson University, and received an A.B. degree from the University of Chicago in 1910 and an LL.B. degree from Columbia in 1912. He began law practice at Tampa in 1912. He represented the District of Hillsborough and Pinellas counties as Senator in 1917–19. He served as Governor during one of the most critical peacetime periods in Florida's history, with four major disasters: collapse of the state's own land boom, a violent hurricane, the Mediterranean fruit fly pest, and the national depression. After his term, he returned to Tampa and the practice of law. He was defeated in 1936 for the Democratic nomination for the U. S. Senate. He was special attorney for the State in the 1947 settlement which brought the State ownership of the Ringling Museums at Sarasota. He was president of the Florida State Chamber of Commerce in 1951–52. He died in Tampa on October 25, 1972.

David Sholtz

Twenty-sixth Governor (January 3, 1933–January 5, 1937), was born in Brooklyn, New York, on October 6, 1891, the son of Michael and Anne (Bloon) Sholtz. He received an A.B. degree from Yale in 1914 and an LL.B. degree from Stetson in 1915. He served in the Navy as an ensign in World War I, afterwards holding the rank in the reserves of lieutenant commander. Living at Daytona Beach, he was a member from Volusia County of the House of Representatives 1917, State's Attorney 1919–21, and City Judge 1921. Becoming Governor in 1933 during the national depression, Sholtz took quick advantage of the social welfare and public works programs instituted by President Franklin D. Roosevelt's New Deal: unemployment compensation, old age assistance, and temporary relief being among these. He served as National Grand Exalted Ruler of the Elks, Commander-in-Chief of the Military Order of the World Wars and Vice Chairman of the Laymen's National Committee. He was defeated in 1938 for the Democratic nomination for the U.S. Senate. While maintaining legal residence in Florida, he spent in New York much of the years after leaving the Governor's office. He died in the Florida Keys on March 21, 1953.

Frederick Preston Cone

Twenty-seventh Governor (January 5, 1937–January 7, 1941), was born at Benton in Columbia County on September 28, 1871, the son of William H. and Sarah Emily (Branch) Cone. He attended Florida Agricultural College and Jasper Normal College, and was admitted to the bar in 1892, practicing at Lake City. He served in the State Senate 1907–13, and was President in 1911. He also was a banker. During the Cone administration, Florida had an outstanding State-sponsored exhibit at the 1939 New York World's Fair, and the licensing of drivers was commenced to finance a highway patrol. He was defeated in 1940 for the Democratic nomination for the U.S. Senate. After serving as Governor, he returned to Lake City, where he died July 28, 1948. "Old Swanee," as Cone was known during his gubernatorial term, possessed the dubious distinction of having in 1888, as a youngster visiting in Hamilton County, shot and wounded, in the words of historian Jerrell H. Shofner, "a stubborn belligerent Republican, a former Union soldier, and an avid member of the Grand Army of the Republic" who was about to take up appointment as postmaster at White Springs.

Spessard Lindsey Holland

Twenty-eighth Governor (January 7, 1941–January 2, 1945), was born at Bartow on July 10, 1892, the son of Benjamin F. and Virginia (Spessard) Holland. He graduated from Emory College (now University) in 1912 and the University of Florida in 1916. Volunteering with the outbreak of World War I, he afterwards was commissioned as a second lieutenant in the coast artillery, but was transferred, at his request in France, to the air force and saw action with the 24th flying squadron on the Meuse-Argonne, Champaign, St. Michel and Lineville fronts. He was awarded the Distinguished Service Cross for valor. Leaving the Army in July 1919, he resumed law practice in

Fred P. Cone *Spessard L. Holland*

Bartow. He served as County Prosecuting Attorney and, in 1920, he was elected County Judge, serving for eight years. He was elected to the State Senate in 1932 from Polk County and served for eight years, until his election as Governor. As Florida's World War II Governor, he assisted the armed forces in their many activities here. Among the Constitutional amendments whose adoption he had recommended were those pledging gasoline tax revenue for highway betterments and establishing the Game and Fresh Water Fish Commission as an independent agency. The Holland administration also was active in strengthening the ad valorem tax structure, establishing the Everglades National Park, adjusting the bond debt of the Everglades Drainage District, and initiating the committee study which brought about the Minimum Foundation Program for financing public schools. In 1946, after U.S. Senator Charles O. Andrews announced his intention not to seek reelection, Holland was nominated to succeed him and, with the death of Senator Andrews, he was appointed to the Senate on September 25, 1946. He was subsequently elected to four six-year terms, voluntarily relinquishing the office in January, 1971. He died at Bartow on November 6, 1971.

Millard Fillmore Caldwell

Twenty-ninth Governor (January 2, 1945–January 4, 1949), was born at the rural home of his parents at Beverly, near Knoxville, Tennessee, on February 6, 1897, the son of Millard F. and Martha Jane (Clapp) Caldwell. He attended Carson Newman College, the University of Mississippi and, after serving in the Army during World War I, the University of Virginia. He came to Florida in 1924, entering practice of law at Milton. He represented Santa

Millard F. Caldwell

Fuller Warren

Rosa County in the 1929 and 1931 Florida House of Representatives and the Third District in the U.S. House of Representatives from 1933 to 1941. He retired from Congress to live on Harwood Plantation, near Tallahassee, and to practice law there. During his congressional service, he represented this country at interparliamentary conferences at The Hague, 1938, and Oslo, 1939. He was elected Governor in 1944. His administration saw enactment of the Minimum Foundation Program for public schools, development of the Capitol Center, and expansion of institutions. Governor Caldwell was Chairman of the National Governors' Conference, 1946–47, and President of the Council of State Governments, 1947–48. He was Chairman of the Board of Control for Southern Regional Education, 1948–51, and Administrator, Federal Civil Defense, 1950–52. He was appointed Justice, Supreme Court of Florida, February 14, 1962, and elected that year without opposition. Elected Chief Justice, 1967. Retired, 1969. He died at his antebellum home in Tallahassee on October 23, 1984.

Fuller Warren

Thirtieth Governor (January 4, 1949–January 6, 1953), was born in Blountstown on October 3, 1905, the son of Charles R. and Grace (Fuller) Warren. He attended elementary schools in Calhoun and Walton counties and the University of Florida and received his law degree from Cumberland University. While a student at the University of Florida, he was elected to the House of Representatives from Calhoun County serving in the 1927 session at the age of 21. He moved to Jacksonville in 1929, engaging there in the practice of law. He served three terms in the City Council 1931–37, and was elected to the 1939 House of Representatives. He was a Navy gunnery officer in World War II, crossing the Atlantic twenty times. He wrote three books, *Eruptions of Eloquence,* 1932, *Speaking of Speaking,* 1944, and *How to Win in Politics,* 1949, with Allen Morris, and also the weekly newspaper column, "Facts and Figures," 1940–48. Governor Warren's active sponsorship resulted in cattle being outlawed from Florida's highways, the passing of the "taste-test" citrus code, a model reforestation program, and preliminary planning for the Florida Turnpike. He also got the Jacksonville Expressway system under way and arranged the financing and construction of the Sunshine Skyway at St. Petersburg. He made speaking tours of the United States and Latin American nations to recruit tourists for Florida and invite new industries to locate in Florida. After serving as Governor, he established residence in Miami and practiced law there. He was defeated in 1956 for the Democratic nomination for Governor. He died at Miami on September 23, 1973.

Daniel Thomas McCarty

Thirty-first Governor (January 6–September 28, 1953), was born in Fort Pierce on January 18, 1912, the eldest son of Daniel Thomas and Frances (Moore) McCarty. He attended the public schools of his native St. Lucie County, and then the University of Florida, where he graduated in 1934 from the College of Agriculture. A citrus grower and beef cattleman at Fort Pierce, he served as St. Lucie's representative in the 1937, 1939 and 1941 sessions of the House of Representatives and as the Speaker of the 1941 House. He distinguished himself in World War II, being among those who landed on D-Day with the Seventh Army in the South of France and came home as a colonel with the Legion of Merit, Bronze Star, Purple Heart and the French Croix de Guerre. He was runnerup for the Democratic nomination for Governor in 1948 and was elected in 1952. He was inaugurated on January 6, 1953, he suffered a disabling heart attack on February 25, 1953, and died September 20, 1953, at Tallahassee.

Charley Eugene Johns

Thirty-second (acting) Governor (September 28, 1953–January 4, 1955), was born in Starke on February 27, 1905, the son of Everett E. and Annie (Markley) Johns. His father, once Sheriff of Bradford County, was killed in line of duty as a Deputy Sheriff in Nassau County. Markley Johns, the Acting Governor's brother, died while President designate of the 1933 Senate and it had been Charley Johns' ambition to complete this service—an aspiration realized when he became President of the 1953 Senate. Upon the death of Governor Dan McCarty on September 28, 1953, he became chief executive and served until LeRoy Collins, elected for the blance of the unexpired term, took office on January 4, 1955. The Johns Administration spurred highway construction and freed the Overseas Highway from tolls. Johns, who had been an unsuccessful candidate for the unfinished McCarty term, resumed his place as Senator from the district of Bradford and Union Counties serving through 1966. Governor Johns was a strong advocate of prison reform during his entire legislative career. He was a railroad conductor who retained his seniority, but was in the general insurance business for forty years

Dan McCarty   *Charley E. Johns*

and served as President of the Community State Bank of Starke. He died at Starke on January 23, 1990.

[Thomas] LeRoy Collins

Thirty-third Governor (January 4, 1955–January 3, 1961), was born in Tallahassee on March 10, 1909, one of four sons and two daughters of a grocer, Marvin Collins, and his wife, the former Mattie Brandon. LeRoy Collins was graduated from Tallahassee's Leon High School, attended the Eastman School of Business at Poughkeepsie, N.Y., and received a law degree from Cumberland University. He was married in 1932 to Mary Call Darby, a great-granddaughter of Richard Keith Call, twice Territorial Governor of Florida. Governor and Mrs. Collins raised their four children in the Call family home, "The Grove," which was acquired by them in 1941, and is located across the street north of the official Governor's Mansion in Tallahassee.

He was elected at 25 in 1934 as Leon County Representative in the Legislature, and reelected in 1936 and 1938. He was elected to the Senate in 1940 to complete an unexpired term, reelected in 1942, resigned to serve in the Navy during World War II, reelected in 1946 and again in 1950. He was the first Governor to be elected for consecutive terms. He was first elected in 1954 to complete the two remaining years of the term of the late Governor Dan McCarty and reelected in 1956 for a regular four-year term. He also made political history in 1956 by being the first Florida Governor to win a first primary victory, defeating five opponents. Governor Collins was the first American Governor to serve simultaneously as chairman of the Southern Governors' Conference and the National Governors' Conference. As

LeRoy Collins *Farris Bryant*

chairman of the latter, he led the first delegation of Governors on a foreign visit, to the Soviet Union in 1959 to compare its republic-level governments with the states. He was the first Governor since the Civil War to serve as permanent chairman of a Democratic National Convention, in Los Angeles in 1960.

He led efforts to establish a strong, diversified state based economy supported by industry, agriculture and tourism through creation of the State Development Commission and assisted in its promotion program. His prime interest was education, and he worked to strengthen and modernize Florida's school system from the grade schools through the universities. He sponsored educational television, nuclear science, a broad community college program and university expansion and improvement. In the racial unrest of his time he took a moderate course, counselling progress under law, and the State experienced only minimal disorder. He served two terms as chairman of the Southern Regional Education Board.

Upon completion of six years as Governor, he became president of the National Association of Broadcasters. He resigned this at the request of President Lyndon B. Johnson to become the first Director of the Community Relations Service under the 1964 Civil Rights Act. Also by Presidential appointment, he became Undersecretary of Commerce on July 7, 1965. He resigned this position effective October 1, 1966, to return to Florida and become a partner in a Tampa law firm. He was successful in obtaining the Democratic nomination for the U.S. Senate in the primary elections of 1968 but was defeated in the general election. In early 1969 he resigned from the Tampa firm and after business associations for one year which required his residence in Miami, continued to live at "The Grove" where he died March

12, 1991. He had practiced law as counsel to the firm of Ervin, Yarn, Jacobs, Odom and Ervin in Tallahassee.

Read: *Governor LeRoy Collins of Florida, Spokesman of the New South,* by Thomas R. Wagy.

[Cecil] Farris Bryant

Thirty-fourth Governor (January 3, 1961–January 5, 1965), was born on July 26, 1914, near the family's Marion County farm. He was one of the three children of Cecil and Lela (Farris) Bryant. While the father farmed, his profession was that of an accountant, and he was one of the early members of the State Board of Accountancy. An uncle of the Governor, Ion Farris, twice served as Speaker of the Florida House of Representatives, and this perhaps influenced Farris Bryant to seek a public career through legislative service. After graduation from the University of Florida and Harvard Law School, he was elected in 1946 to the first of five legislative terms, the last four without opposition, and served as Speaker of the 1953 House.

Education was recognized by Governor Bryant as the critical factor of Florida's future. For the first 12 grades, the Bryant program was an implementing of past trends; in higher education, the Governor said, "We have pioneered—the fight to raise professors' salaries, FICUS (Florida Institute for Continuing University Studies), a degree program for off-campus students, GENESYS (Graduate Engineering Education System), a graduate study program conducted by television, the trimester, the bond issue—I would like for them to be remembered." By the "bond issue," the Governor meant the public's acceptance of a Constitutional amendment authorizing the sale of bonds for construction at institutions of higher learning by which more than $1 billion of construction has been provided. The Bryant administration also saw coordination of state-federal energies for expanded water control projects, including the start of construction of the Cross-Florida Barge Canal. Leadership was given to adoption of another Constitutional amendment authorizing bonds to acquire land for conservation and recreation purposes. The Bryant years brought the Sunshine State Parkway from Fort Pierce to Wildwood, Alligator Alley from Fort Lauderdale to Naples, and a special program for constructing multi-lane highways without regard for road board districts or county boundaries.

After service as Governor, Bryant went to Jacksonville to resume the practice of law as a member of the firm of Bryant, Freeman, Richardson and Watson. He also became Chairman of the Boards of National Life of Florida Corporation and Voyager Life Insurance Company, Atlantic Warranty Company, T.V. Station WTLV, Worth Avenue National Bank and other enterprises. On March 23, 1966, he became director of the Office of Emergency Planning and a member of the National Security Council by appointment of President Lyndon B. Johnson and terminated his service on October 10, 1967. He returned to the practice of law in Jacksonville as a member of the firm of Bryant, Dickens, Franson and Miller. On February 20, 1967, he was appointed by President Johnson as a member of the United States Advisory Commission on Intergovernmental Relations and was appointed Chairman on October 10, 1967, serving for two years. He was defeated in 1970 in the

Haydon Burns   *Claude R. Kirk, Jr.*

runoff for the Democratic nomination for the U.S. Senate. He is married to the former Julia Burnett of Madison and they have three children, Julie Lovett Felter, Cecelia Ann Bryant and Allison Adair Simon. Address: P.O. Box 2918, Jacksonville, Florida 32203.

[William] Haydon Burns

Thirty-fifth Governor (January 5, 1965–January 3, 1967), was born in Chicago, Illinois, on March 17, 1912, the son of Harry Haydon and Ethel (Burnett) Burns. The family home was in Louisville, Kentucky, and Governor Burns regarded himself as a native of Louisville. The family moved to Jacksonville in 1922. Haydon Burns attended Jacksonville public schools and Babson College (Massachusetts). He was a Lieutenant (jg), USNR, during World War II, serving as an aeronautical salvage specialist assigned to the Office of the Secretary of the Navy. Prior to the war he held a pilot's license and operated a flying school. He also owned an appliance business, and after the war he was a business and public relations consultant.

He became a candidate for public office for the first time in 1949, winning election as Mayor-Commissioner of Jacksonville. He was elected again in 1951, 1955, 1959, and 1963, and these elections gave him the longest tenure of any Jacksonville chief executive. He was a candidate for the Democratic nomination for Governor in 1960, finishing third. He tried again in 1964, and was the high man in both the first and second primaries. The cycle of gubernatorial elections having been changed from Presidential election years, he was able constitutionally to run for a successive four-year term and was defeated in the runoff for the Democratic nomination.

The two-year Burns term saw progress on constitutional revision, outdoor recreation, industrial development and tax reform. He had the opportunity of appointing three members of the Cabinet, a Treasurer, a Comptroller, and a Superintendent of Public Instruction. After completing his term, Burns returned to Jacksonville and resumed his practice as a business consultant. He was defeated in 1971 for election as Mayor of Jacksonville. He died in Jacksonville on November 22, 1987.

Claude Roy Kirk, Jr.

Thirty-sixth Governor (January 3, 1967–January 5, 1971), was born on January 7, 1926, in San Bernardino, California, the son of Claude Roy and Myrtle (McLure) Kirk. During his youth, the Kirk family lived also in Chicago and its suburbs of River Forest and Oak Park, Illinois, and Montgomery Alabama. He graduated at 17 from high school in Montgomery and enlisted in the Marine Corps. After officer training at Quantico, he was commissioned a second lieutenant at 19. He ended three years of service in 1946, then returned to duty in Korea, serving both in combat forces and as a fire control spotter. He received a law degree from the University of Alabama in 1949. He began selling insurance and eventually, with two other men, founded the American Heritage Life Insurance Company of Jacksonville. He was president of American Heritage for five years. Later, he became Vice Chairman of the Board and a partner of the national investment house of Harden, Stone & Company. He also established the Kirk Investments Company.

A former Democrat, he led the Floridians for Nixon campaign in 1960. As the Republican nominee in 1964, he unsuccessfully ran for the U.S. Senate. In 1966, he was the Republican nominee for Governor and was elected, being the first GOP chief executive elected since 1872. He was renominated by Republican voters in 1970 but failed of election. He was often at odds with the Cabinet and even with Republicans in the Legislature whose membership was largely Democratic. During the Kirk tenure, there was a substantial revision of the 1885 Constitution and a Democratic-Republican coalition reorganized the Executive Department to lodge greater responsibility with the Governor.

As Governor, he and Miss Erika Mattfeld were wed. He had been married previously, as had she. With the end of his term, the Governor and Mrs. Kirk returned to their home in Palm Beach. He resumed the presidency of Kirk and Company, merchant bankers. He ran unsuccessfully as a Democrat in seeking the nomination for Governor in 1978 and again in 1988 as a Democratic candidate for United States Senate. In 1990 he was an unsuccessful Republican candidate for Commissioner of Education. Address: Kirk, McNabb & Associates, Inc., 2999 NE 191st Street Suite 1001, North Miami Beach 33180.

Read: *Claude Kirk, the Man and the Myth,* by Ralph deToledano and Philip V. Brennan, Jr.

Claude R. Kirk, Jr. *a man and his words,* edited by Arthur H. Simons. *Claude Kirk and the Policies of Confrontation,* by Edmund F. Kallina, Jr.

Reubin O'D. Askew *Bob Graham*

Reubin O'Donovan Askew

Thirty-seventh Governor (January 5, 1971–January 7, 1975, January 7, 1975–January 2, 1979), was born in Muskogee, Oklahoma, on September 11, 1928, one of six children of Leon G. and Alberta Askew. With his mother, he moved to Pensacola in 1937. He married the former Donna Lou Harper of Sanford. The Askews have two children, Angela and Kevin. The Governor received a B.S. from Florida State University and an LL.B. from the University of Florida. At Florida State, he was student body president. There, he also was a distinguished military graduate and a member of Omicron Delta Kappa, Gold Key, Delta Tau Delta, and Alpha Phi Omega. At the University of Florida, he was class president, chairman of the Board of Masters of the Honor Court, executive editor of the Law Review, and justice of the Phi Alpha Delta law fraternity. Graduating from high school at 17, he enlisted in the United States Army paratroopers in 1946–1948 as a private and was discharged as a sergeant. He served in the Air Force in 1951–1953 as a second lieutenant. He began his public career as Assistant County Solicitor for Escambia County in 1956–1958. He was elected to the House of Representatives in 1958 and to the Senate in 1962. He served as President pro tempore in 1969–1970. He was elected Governor in 1970 and reelected in 1974, the first governor to be elected for a second, successive 4-year term.

On Inauguration Day in January, 1971, he began to carry out an uphill fight for the tax reform he had promised the voters. He won legislative approval of a referendum on levying a corporate income tax and campaigned statewide for approval of this constitutional change. This victory was followed by repeal of consumer taxes on household utilities and apartment rentals. Additional State revenues were shared with schools and other units of local government to ease the burden of local property taxes on homeowners. Upon the Governor's urging, the Legislature increased the homestead exemption from $5,000 to $10,000 for persons of 65 years and older and for the disabled. He also supported the rolling back of local school taxes by two mills and the exemption of the first $20,000 in intangibles from State taxes. If tax reform was the top priority of his first administration, Governor Askew saw his reelection as a mandate for full and public financial disclosure by candidates and public officials.

When the Legislature failed to act in what he regarded as a meaningful way, the Governor took the issue to the people, obtaining some 220,000 signatures to place the "Sunshine Amendment" on the ballot with ratification by 80% of the voters. He devoted several of the final months of his administration to aggressively, and successfully, oppose the ratification of a proposed constitutional amendment which would have legalized casino gambling in an oceanfront area of Dade and Broward counties.

He named the first black Justice of the Supreme Court, the first woman to the State Cabinet, and the first black in a hundred years as a member of the Cabinet. He delivered the keynote address at the 1972 Democratic National Convention. He was chairman in 1977 of the National Governor's Conference. He was named by President Carter as chairman of the President's Advisory Committee on Ambassadorial Appointments to recommend names for foreign posts on the basis of merit.

Upon retiring as Governor, Askew joined the Miami law firm of Greenberg, Traurig, Askew, Hoffman, Lipoff, Rosen and Quentel. On October 1, 1979, Askew was sworn in as United States Trade Representative with the rank of Ambassador Extraordinary and Plenipotentiary, serving as a member of President Jimmy Carter's Cabinet. With the end of the Carter Administration, Askew returned to the Miami law firm until in March 1981, he commenced "testing the waters" as a prelude to seeking the Democratic nomination for President of the United States. That campaign ended as he finished last in the New Hampshire primary in February 1984. Harvard professors named Askew one of the 10 greatest governors of the 20th century, a list that included Theodore Roosevelt and Woodrow Wilson. He announced his candidacy for the United States Senate on December 21, 1987, but withdrew on May 7, 1988, citing the rigors of fund-raising.

Askew is teaching Florida Government and Florida Public Administration and Public Policy in Florida universities. He began teaching at Florida International University in 1989, and taught there and at Florida Atlantic University where he became a tenured professor in 1991. His tenure will be moved to Florida State University in September 1995. He is a Senior Fellow of the Florida Institute of Government, and Chair of the Board of Trustees of the LeRoy Collins Center for Public Policy. In 1994 the University of Florida created the Askew Institute of Politics and Society and Florida State University renamed its school of Public Administration and Policy in his honor. He is "Of Counsel" to Akerman, Senterfitt & Eidson, PA. Address: P.O. Box 231, Orlando 32802-0231.

Bob (D. Robert) Graham

Thirty-eighth Governor (January 2, 1979–January 4, 1983, January 4, 1983–January 3, 1987). He was first elected to public office as a member of the Florida House of Representatives in 1966 and then as a state senator in 1970. Graham was born in Coral Gables on November 9, 1936. He grew up in a coral rock house that still stands in Pennsuco, Dade County. His father, Ernest Graham, first went to Dade County in 1919 as a mining engineer. There he founded a dairy and cattle business that is now one of Florida's largest. Later he became a major land developer and a state senator. The Governor's mother, Hilda Simmons Graham, grew up in Walton County the daughter of a country doctor, and worked as a school teacher in DeFuniak Springs. The Governor served in executive positions with the family-owned Sengra Corporation (now The Graham Companies), developer of Miami Lakes and The Graham Company (now Graham Farms), which has extensive cattle holdings in Florida and Georgia. Graham was the youngest of three brothers. The eldest, Phillip, now deceased, was publisher of the *Washington Post* and *Newsweek*. William A. Graham was chairman of the board and chief executive of The Graham Companies.

In February 1959, Bob Graham married Adele Khoury of Miami Springs. They have four daughters: Gwendolyn Patricia; Glynn Adele, Arva Suzanne, and Kendall Elizabeth.

He received a bachelor's degree in 1959 from the University of Florida, where he was Phi Beta Kappa, a member of the Florida Blue Key and president of the Honor Court. Graham received a doctor of law degree from Harvard Law School in 1962.

As Governor, Graham showed leadership in times of unprecedented crises such as the massive Cuban-Haitian influx of 1980 and the civil disturbances in Miami in that same year. In 1979, a strike by truckers threatened to paralyze the state. Graham averted the shutdown by ordering private trucks, under National Guard protection, to transport gasoline. In 1979, two hurricanes threatened Florida back-to-back within two weeks of each other. Graham oversaw the huge evacuation programs that saved lives and prevented injuries. He advocated a strong federal role in fighting crime in Florida because of the state's unique vulnerability to illegal drug smuggling and immigration. Believing that capital punishment is a deterrent, Graham signed more than 120 death warrants.

In 1982, the Florida Legislature approved one of the Governor's environmental priorities, the Save Our Rivers Act. This provided approximately $300 million over a decade for the acquisition of river floodplains and water management land. Also in 1982, Graham pushed through authorization of the sale of $200 million in bonds for the Save Our Coasts program. This provides the state with funds to acquire beaches and barrier islands threatened by development. Graham launched the Save Our Everglades program in 1983 to restore and protect Florida's water supply, vast wetlands, endangered species and their habitats, and to re-establish the natural flow of the Kissimmee River. The Governor supported and approved the 1984 Wetlands Protection Act which placed the responsibility for the regulation of Florida's wetlands with the Department of Environmental Regulation and the state's five water management districts.

Governor Graham believed in a personal style of governing. He carried over into his term as Governor the campaign practice of doing "workdays" through the state. His more than 180 jobs include policeman, railroad engineer, construction worker, sponge fisherman, factory worker, social worker, busboy, teacher and newsman. He was elected United States Senator in November, 1986. Address: 524 Hart Senate Office Bldg., Washington, D.C., 20510.

[John] Wayne Mixson

Thirty-ninth Governor (January 3, 1987–January 6, 1987) served three days in succession to Bob Graham, who resigned as Governor to take the oath of United States Senator. Under the terms of Article IV, Section 3 (a) of the Florida Constitution, the Lieutenant Governor becomes "Governor," not "acting Governor," upon a vacancy in the office of Governor.

Wayne Mixson was born June 16, 1922, at his family's farm near New Brockton, Alabama, the son of Cecil and Mineola Moseley Mixson.

The day after he graduated from high school in Alabama, Wayne Mixson moved to Panama City, Florida, and went to work at a paper mill. He enlisted in the Navy on October 2, 1942, serving in a lighter-than-air unit on anti-submarine duty. He attended Columbia University in New York under a Navy V-12 program, and later the Wharton School of Finance at the University of Pennsylvania. In 1947, he graduated with honors from the University of Florida, with a bachelor's degree in business administration. His college affiliations included the Phi Gamma Delta social fraternity and Phi Kappa Phi honorary fraternity.

On December 27, 1947 he married Margie Grace, the grand-daughter of the founder of her hometown, Graceville, Florida. Mrs. Mixson, who earned a bachelor's degree from Florida State University and a master's degree from the University of Florida, taught English in high school and community college for thirty years.

Wayne Mixson

Governor and Mrs. Mixson owned a 2,000-acre cattle and feed grain farm in Jackson County near Marianna, their former home.

Governor Mixson began his public service career in March, 1967, by election to the Florida House of Representatives. He served six consecutive terms, representing districts including Jackson, Gadsden, Liberty, Washington, Holmes and Walton Counties. Address: 2219 Demeron Road, Tallahassee, 32312.

Robert (Bob) Martinez

Fortieth Governor (January 6, 1987–January 8, 1991) may be remembered by a string of initials: SWIM (Surface Water Management and Improvement Act), SWDA (Solid Waste Disposal Act), CARL (Conservation and Recreational Lands), and Preservation 2000 were among the landsaving undertakings best known by their code names. To the credit of Republican Martinez was his carrying forward environmental programs of his Democratic predecessor, Governor Bob Graham. Among those programs was the dechannelization of the Kissimmee River.

Florida's first American Governor of Hispanic descent, only the second Republican elected chief executive since Reconstruction, and first Governor from the Tampa Bay area in half a century, Bob Martinez brought to the leadership of government a perspective developed during seven eventful years as Tampa's Mayor.

Bob Martinez was born in Tampa on Christmas Day, December 25, 1934, the son of Serafin and Iva Martinez and the grandson of Spanish immigrants who moved to Tampa at the turn of the century. He grew up in Tampa's West Tampa section, an area that still retains the deep ethnic heritage of the Hispanics who operated the city's famed cigar factories through most of the century.

Bob Martinez earned a bachelor of science degree from his hometown University of Tampa. Later he attended the University of Illinois where he received a master's degree in labor and industrial relations.

Bob Martinez

The first significant public initiative to save an environmental asset was begun by Governor Graham with the "Save the Everglades" campaign. Again, Governor Martinez carried forward a program of his predecessor.

Governor Martinez won bipartisan legislative support for SWIM, creating for the first time uniform policies for the management and protection of Florida's surface waters. Water bodies benefiting from SWIM included Lake Okeechobee, Tampa Bay, Lake Jackson, the Winter Haven Chain of Lakes, the St. Johns River, and the Kissimmee River.

A comprehensive program to cope with the disposal of solid waste was saluted by the *Wall Street Journal* as "the most comprehensive of its kind in the nation."

The Governor also gave attention to the interlocking of the state's water resources in newly developing growth management: for agriculture, recreation, and human use.

The Governor's dealings with the members of the Legislature brought aggravation to both sides as Martinez sought, on an individual basis, to weed out "turkeys," and on a general basis, to organize the budgetary process and spending program on a more rational approach. During his four years, the Governor vetoed items totaling $420 million from the appropriations bills enacted by the Legislature. When the Governor was unsuccessful in a cooperative, negotiated approach, he used his veto power. For example, the Governor vetoed 136 items in the 1988 General Appropriations Act. This approach resulted ultimately in budget-making reforms.

The Governor was active in numerous other fields. These included: offshore oil drilling, drug-free work place, and prison construction.

Outgoing national drug czar William Bennett issued a report card on all state drug control programs which gave Florida "very strong grades." Florida, he said, has implemented 14 of 18 federally recommended antidrug measures. Bennett said Florida had "pretty well covered the landscape."

A lasting political embarrassment for the Governor was the Legislature's enactment, at his urging, of a tax on services. Included were first-time levies such as television advertising and services of physicians and professionals. A fire-storm of protest, largely agitated by the media and most particularly the television industry, brought the retreat of the Governor and the Legislature from the tax which was repealed.

As had the first Republican Governor in this century been elected through disruption in the Democratic party, so had Bob Martinez been elected as the second Republican Governor. The Governor strove to build the Republican party through, among other means, insisting that his appointees to political office be Republicans. But the Republican party still was numerically the minority party. On the other side, the Democrats went into the 1990 General Election politically unified. And so, as had Republican Governor Claude R. Kirk in 1970, Bob Martinez was defeated. President Bush appointed Martinez Director in 1991 of the National Campaign Against Use of Drugs.

Martinez presently has an international consulting firm in Tampa, with his son Alan. Bob Martinez and Associates specializes in environmental equipment and services for Central and South America. Address: 4647 San Jose St., Tampa 33627.

Acting Governors

Florida has had a number of Acting Governors although only three succeeded to the governorship by reason of the death of the chief executive.

Two Acting Governors took over when Andrew Jackson returned to Tennessee in October, 1821, after serving briefly as United States Commissioner and Governor of the Territories of East and West Florida. George Walton served as Acting Governor for West Florida, with headquarters at

Pensacola, and William G. D. Worthington was Acting Governor for East Florida, with his base at St. Augustine. Walton had been Secretary of the Territory of West Florida, and Worthington had been Secretary of the Territory of East Florida.

In 1822 the government of the two old Spanish provinces was consolidated. Thereafter, the Secretary of the Territory was Acting Governor if the Governor was away from the capital. Among the Secretaries who functioned as Acting Governor were William M. McCarty, James D. Westcott Jr., and John P. DuVal.

From 1845 to 1865 and from 1885 to 1969 (see Lieutenant Governors), the gubernatorial succession was vested in the presiding officer of the Senate and, in case of his inability to serve, in the Speaker of the House. Only once, however, was a Speaker of the House called upon to act as Governor.

The State's first three Constitutions provided that the succession should become operative in the event of the absence of the Governor from the state. With Governor Thomas Brown in Boston to attend what was described by the Boston Herald as a "convention of governors to promote American industry," and with Senate President R. J. Floyd also out of the state, House Speaker A. K. Allison proclaimed himself Acting Governor on September 16, 1853. He served until October 3 of the same year, when James E. Broome was regularly inaugurated as Governor.

By a quirk of fate, Allison was Senate President and again became Acting Governor when Governor John Milton died on April 1, 1865. Allison served until the later part of May, his last official act recorded in the letter book of the Governor's office being dated May 19. Arrested by U.S. military authorities, Allison was received at Fort Pulaski, Georgia, on June 19, 1865, for imprisonment with other Confederate officials.

Lieutenant Governor Marcellus L. Stearns succeeded to the governorship upon the death of Ossian B. Hart on March 18, 1874. Although Hart died before the mid-term election of 1874, the Constitution then in force permitted Stearns to serve out the full unexpired term and he was Governor until January, 1877.

Prior to Hart's death, Stearns served as Acting Governor for three months while the Governor was out of the state. Philip Dell, President of the 1856 Senate, also functioned as Acting Governor for a brief period, presumably while Governor James E. Broome was away.

Charley E. Johns of Starke, President of the 1953 Senate, succeeded to the governorship with the death of Governor Dan T. McCarty on September 28, 1953. Johns served as Acting Governor until January 4, 1955. The Supreme Court declared Johns' title to be "Acting Governor. " The court also ruled Johns eligible to become a candidate for the McCarty unexpired term. The Constitution then prohibited a four-year Governor from serving a successive term. Johns ran but was defeated.

In territorial days, absence of the Governor from the capital—just the city—sufficed for an Acting Governor to take over. By the time of statehood, in 1845, absence from the state was required. Now, absence of itself is no reason. Governors have traveled to Europe, South America and Japan without any question to their legal ability to function.

Succession to Governorship

Lieutenant Governor Wayne Mixson succeeded to the Governorship on January 3, 1987 for a three-day term ending on January 6. Under the terms of the 1968 Constitution, Mixson was "Governor" rather than "Acting Governor" as prior successors had been. Mixson became Governor upon the resignation of Governor Bob Graham on July 9, 1986, (effective January 3, 1987) as a candidate for the United States Senate.

Drane's Governors

The Compiler commends to anyone interested in Florida's Governors, and particularly those from Jacksonville, a series of profiles by Hank Drane for *The Florida Times-Union* that commenced on March 9, 1981, and appeared on successive Mondays.

Inauguration of Wayne Mixson in the House chamber on January 3, 1987   Tallahassee Democrat

The Governor's Mansion

Florida provides its first family with a residence known generally as "The Mansion" but also designated during one gubernatorial administration as "The Executive Residence." Officially, its name remains "Florida Governor's Mansion."

With an address of 700 North Adams Street, the Mansion is situated at the center of a city block. The Mansion is bordered on two sides, Adams and Brevard Streets, by landscaped buffer areas; on the third by the spacious grounds of "The Grove," and on the remaining side by Duval Street.

"The Grove" is the imposing territorial home of Governor Richard K. Call (see biography) and in recent years the residence of Governor and Mrs. LeRoy Collins (also see biography).

From the portico of "The Grove," the viewer may look south along Adams Street. It was from this portico that Call, a slaveholder but a Unionist, warned Secessionists celebrating Florida's leaving the Union: "Well, gentlemen, all I wish to say to you is that you have just opened the gates of hell."

Thus, the Governor's residence occupies a place of historic significance apart from its own meaning.

The gubernatorial home resembles the mansion of Florida's first American chief executive: Andrew Jackson's "Hermitage," near Nashville, Tennessee. Like the Hermitage, it has a two-story central portion faced with tall columns. Unlike the Hermitage, whose brick has been painted white to give a monolithic appearance, the Florida Mansion has red brick in a range of shades.

The executive residence, designed by noted Palm Beach architect Marion Sims Wyeth, was completed in 1957 at a cost to build and initially furnish of approximately $350,000. It was erected on the site of a predecessor Mansion which had been occupied by first families from that of Governor Napoleon B. Broward in 1907 to that of Governor Charley E. Johns in 1955. This structure, of Georgian-Colonial style designed by Henry J. Klutho, was de-

The family Governor Napoleon B. Broward (1905–1909) brought to the new Mansion in 1907 was substantial, as this photograph evidences. Left to right: Annie Dorcas, Enid Lyle, Mrs. Annie Broward holding Elizabeth Hutchison, Agnes Caroline (back), Elsie (front), Florida Douglas, Governor Broward, Ellen Jeannette, and Josephine. Florida State Archives

The Mansion

molished after an engineering study disclosed structural faults beyond reasonable repair.

Dual Purposes of Mansion

The Mansion was constructed to serve two purposes. It is first the home for the First Family, with rooms tailored for their personal use. But it is also the official residence, with rooms intended for the entertainment and accomodation of guests.

The Mansion's main floor contains the official state rooms used for formal occasions—the large Entrance Hall, Reception Room, Dining Room, Guest Bedroom, and Florida Room plus the main kitchen and pantry. The south wing contains some private living quarters—the family's kitchen, dining room and sitting room. There are also a guest bedroom, powder room and hat and coat room on the first floor.

The basement has offices for the Governor's Mansion staff and headquarters for the agents of the Florida Department of Law Enforcement who are stationed at the Mansion around the clock, laundry rooms and a fallout shelter.

Many authentic antiques, including Sheraton and Chippendale pieces, circa 1775–1830, have been used to furnish the formal rooms. The dining room chandelier, which has been converted from candles to electricity, is of ornate cut glass. Notes about the Mansion's history and furnishings say it dates from a French castle of 1760.

James L. Cogar, a decorator who was previously curator at the colonial restoration project in Williamsburg, Va., was commissioned to furnish the Mansion in its elegant style. And at the suggestion of LeRoy Collins, first Governor to live in the new Mansion, an eight-member Governor's Mansion Commission was established by the 1957 Legislature. Specifically the commission is "charged with preserving the style and character of the original plan of construction and furnishing."

As in any home, the warmth and flavor of the private quarters come mainly from the wife's personality. The Governor's family usually brings along a few favorite furnishings, lounge chairs or a bedroom suite. The family rooms are painted to the family's tastes.

Each wife has added something to the Mansion. Mrs. Collins worked closely with decorator Cogar and had a complete set of pictures taken for the history of the famed Mansion silver. The ornate service was taken from the decommissioned battleship *Florida*, which was scrapped in 1931. The service was purchased for the *Florida* with donations from Florida's school children and adults. It was placed in the old Mansion during Doyle Carlton's administration.

During the Bryant term, the heated swimming pool and cabana were added, along with the four car garage and apartment for full time Mansion guests. A tennis court was built across Brevard street from the Mansion during the Askew Administration.

Mrs. Haydon Burns, with the commission's approval, selected a scenic print wallpaper to decorate the large entrance hall.

A security fence was placed around the Mansion in 1975 during the occupancy of Governor Askew. The metal fence, picket on the north, south and east property lines and chain link on the west, cost $100,806. The Legislature appropriated the money after secret service agents vetoed an overnight stay at the Mansion by Vice President Spiro T. Agnew when he visited Tallahassee in 1971.

The fencing was accompanied by the installation of high intensity lights and the closing of a block of city street between Adams and Duval streets separating the Mansion property from that of The Grove.

The 1975 fence was not the first, for the predecessor Mansion was partially surrounded by a wrought iron fence. The present fence has gates electrically operated by security officers within the Mansion.

Under the auspices of Mrs. Bob Graham, a Florida Governor's Mansion Foundation, Inc., was established in 1980 for the purpose of refurbishing the public rooms of the Mansion. The first fund-raiser, a dinner dance at the Mansion on October 10, 1980, grossed $100,000 from members paying $500 each. The Foundation's first addition to the Mansion was a portrait of Andrew Jackson in formal attire instead of the military regalia. Jackson was painted from life by Asher Durand. The original hangs in the New York Historical Society Museum. The Mansion's copy was painted by Gregory Stapko of McLean, Virginia. This copy is two inches larger in each dimension than the original, a requirement of the New York Historical Society. The Foundation also was responsible for providing the foyer with a Martha Washington chair, and a 1910 Persian rug in the Heriz pattern. (This rug is now in State Dining Room).

The Heriz is an exceptionally large example (14½ feet × 23½ feet). The predominant colors are cobalt blue and brick red. These rugs are not woven;

they are made up of hundreds of thousands of handtied knots. The slight change of color in the light blue background is the *abrash*. The yarn has to be dyed in small batches of vegetable dye and it is hard to match one batch to another. This accounts for the above mentioned irregularity of color. The *abrash* does not affect the quality of the carpet. Heriz carpets are extremely durable. They were made to withstand the rigors of the nomadic life. The rug has a cotton foundation and a wool nap.

Reception Room

This is the largest room in the Mansion. Here guests gather during parties or receptions.

The paintings in the reception room are on loan from the John & Mable Ringling Museum of Art in Sarasota, the state museum. The paintings have been changed in recent years.

All the lamps here and in the other rooms are antiques, and all are electrified. The candlesticks are all antiques and date from the mid-18th to the mid-19th century.

A Persian Heriz rug, 15' $\times$ 25', adds warmth and elegance to this room. This hand-knotted rug, made around 1900, has an intricate diamond medallion in the center with palmettes on each end.

The upholstered sofas and wing chairs are reproductions in the style of the late 18th century.

A handcrafted crystal bowl made in Norway and presented to the Grahams by King Olav V of Norway during his visit to Florida in 1982. The bowl is decorated with a Viking ship on one side. King Olav's royal crest and the state seal of Florida are etched on the opposite side.

Guest Bedroom

VIP visitors have spent the night here. President Jimmy Carter, slept here in October 1980. The next morning he made up his own bed. Mrs. George Bush spent the night here during the Martinez administration, and President Bill Clinton slept here March 29, 1995.

Florida Room

This light informal room has two largely glass paned walls overlooking the northwest corner garden. There is an Empire display cabinet that houses a collection of nine minature portraits, by two Florida artists, of the First Ladies who have lived in the present Governor's Mansion.

Other art in the room includes an Edward Marshall Boehm porcelain of the State Bird. It depicts a male mockingbird bringing a berry to two of his offspring.

The room also houses the Mansion Library, a growing collection of books about Florida and/or by Florida authors.

Children in the Mansion

Children often have been among the families in the old and new Mansions but so far only three have been born to an incumbent Governor.

The first was Elizabeth Hutchinson Broward, daughter of Napoleon Bonaparte Broward, Governor from 1905 to 1909. She was born August 31,

1906, eighth of the nine children of the Governor and his second wife, Annie Rice. (The ninth was born after Broward completed his term as Governor.)

Elizabeth Broward was born in the family's residence on North Monroe Street in Tallahassee for the first State-owned gubernatorial mansion was not occupied until September or October 1907. A section of the attic was arranged as a playroom for the Broward children.

Interestingly, the furniture selected by Mrs. Broward for the Mansion, not including kitchen equipment, cost $4,444.75.

Fifty-two years later, Claudia Kirk was born, on August 14, 1968, to Governor Claude Kirk and his second wife, Erika. Claudia was delivered at Good Samaritan Hospital in West Palm Beach, close to "Duck's Nest," the Kirk family's Palm Beach home. Claudia was Erika's second, and the Governor's fifth child. A second child, Erik Henry, was born to Governor and Mrs. Kirk in Tallahassee on April 9, 1970.

Governor and Mrs. Claude R. Kirk, Jr., on the occasion of the christening of Claudia.
Florida State Archives

The three children of Governor Doyle E. Carlton (1929–33), Martha, Mary and Doyle Jr., were among the youngsters to occupy the Mansion in the years after the Browards. The Carlton family kept a horse and pony stabled at the Mansion, and the Governor occasionally would ride with his children.

Doyle, Jr., had a brief career selling newspapers. At that time, the now defunct *Florida State News* was publishing criticisms of Governor Carlton as biting as any ever printed about a Florida chief executive. A friend persuaded Doyle, Jr., that it would be good business for him to sell copies of the *State News* and net two cents for each one sold. The idea was especially appealing since Doyle, Jr., felt he could sell a dozen or more to members of his father's staff.

"The first person I saw was my father's secretary," recalled Doyle, Jr., years afterward. "He took one look at what I was peddling, bought all the copies and threw them in the wastebasket, and told me to never, never be caught with a copy of that paper again."

There were four young people in the Mansion during the administration (1941–45) of Governor (afterwards U.S. Senator) and Mrs. Spessard L. Holland: Spessard Lindsey Jr., Mary Groover, William Benjamin and Ivanhoe.

First to occupy the present Mansion was the family of Governor (1955–61) and Mrs. LeRoy Collins. They had four children, and the neighborhood was not new to them for they had been raised across the street in "The Grove," ancestral home of Mrs. Collins. There were LeRoy Jr., an Annapolis graduate; Jane, Mary Call and Darby.

Two recollections of Mansion life remain quite vividly in the mind of Mrs. Mary Call Proctor. There was the fun the Collins youngsters had in riding the dumb waiter between floors until their parents put a stop to this.

"I can remember very clearly one of my sister's dates," Mary Call Proctor once said. "I was waiting up for her—we always waited up for each other in our family—when I heard Jane and her friend at the door. I came running down to open the door—it was locked—and fell down the stairs. Daddy heard the commotion and came running to see what had happened and he fell down the stairs, too."

There were children in the present Mansion during the tenure of Governors LeRoy Collins, Farris Bryant, Claude R. Kirk, Jr., Reubin O'D. Askew, Bob Graham and Bob Martinez.

Marriages by Governors

Three Governors married during their terms. Governor Harrison Reed was wed to Miss Chloe Merrick of Syracuse, N.Y. at Wilmington, N.C., on August 10, 1869. Governor Fuller Warren was married to Miss Barbara Manning in Los Angeles, Calif., on June 27, 1949. Governor Claude R. Kirk, Jr., was wed to Miss Erika Mattfeld at West Palm Beach on February 18, 1967.

Mansion Marriages

Daughters of three Governors have been married during their occupancy of the present Mansion. In no case was the ceremony performed at the Mansion.

Miss Jane Brevard Collins, daughter of Governor and Mrs. LeRoy Collins, was wed on October 1, 1960, in St. John's Episcopal Church in Tallahassee to John Karl Aurell, son of Mr. and Mrs. George E. Aurell of Washington, D.C. Following the church ceremony, a reception was given by the bride's parents at the Mansion.

Governor Fuller Warren and his bride, the former Barbara Manning, join hands to cut the wedding cake during the reception which followed their wedding at Los Angeles on June 27, 1949.

Miss Katherine Gilmer Kirk, daughter of Governor Claude R. Kirk, Jr., and of Mrs. Edmund Richardson McDavid of New York City, was married on June 13, 1970, in St. John's (Episcopal) Cathedral of Jacksonville to Alexander Mann (Ander) Crenshaw, son of Mr. and Mrs. McCarthy Crenshaw of Jacksonville.

Gwendolyn Patricia, a daughter of Governor and Mrs. Bob Graham, was wed to Mark Logan of Belleair, on June 1, 1985, at St. John's Episcopal Church of Tallahassee. Mark was the son of Mr. and Mrs. Frank Logan of Clearwater.

Cutler's history of Florida reports Miss Elizabeth Moseley, daughter of William D. Moseley, Florida's first Governor under statehood, was married during his term. Miss Moseley was wed to Judge T. S. Haughton on December 21, 1848, at Moseley Hall, the family's plantation home in Jefferson County.

Mansion Draws a Candidate

Governor Warren also was responsible for making a written record of an anecdote involving the original Mansion. In a tribute to R. A. (Cap'n Bob) Gray, for 30 years Florida's Secretary of State, Governor Warren said Cap'n Bob Gray witnessed what was believed to be the birth of the candidacy of the man who succeeded Governor Park Trammell as chief executive. Mr. Gray was Executive Secretary to Governor Trammell, and he and Mrs. Gray had been invited by Governor Trammell to reside at the Mansion.

In the fall of 1915, related Governor Warren, West Florida Baptists held their annual convention in Tallahassee. Local Baptists agreed to have as guests in their homes the delegates, or messengers as they were called, to the convention.

A wedding kiss is bestowed by Governor Graham upon a daughter, Gwendolyn Patricia.
Tallahassee Democrat

A messenger named Sidney J. Catts, from DeFuniak Springs, was assigned by the convention committee to be the guest of Governor and Mrs. Trammell. Mr. Gray recalled that the Reverend Catts, during dinner the first night there, asked many questions about the Mansion and inspected the entire premises, including the attic and stables. At the last meal before leaving, the Reverend Catts asked Governor Trammell, "Governor, how much rent does this place cost you?" Governor Trammell replied, "Reverend, it is provided rent-free by the taxpayers of Florida."

A few weeks after, the Reverend Catts announced his candidacy for Governor and was elected. Governor Warren said Mr. Gray was inclined to believe the fact that the Mansion was rent-free might have had something to do with the Reverend Catts' decision to run.

When Catts moved into the Mansion in January 1917, he brought with him a milk cow, pastured on the lawn; laying hens, housed in a tool shed; and pigs, fed the slops from the Mansion kitchen.

The First Mansion

Florida's first gubernatorial mansion was occupied in September or October, 1907 after Governor Broward persuaded the Legislature of the need for furnishing the chief executives with a state-owned residence. The architect was H.J. Klutho of Jacksonville and the builder was O.C. Parker of Tallahassee. The original contract was $23,462 but the actual cost was $21,242 for the building and $4,444.75 for furnishings. The mansion and grounds covered eight city lots, four of which were donated by George W. Saxon, Tallahassee banker and developer.

368 / The Governor's Mansion

A George III mahogany butler's secretary topped by a china cabinet holds one of the sets of official china, and the remaining Battleship FLORIDA punch cups. Department of Commerce

"Manatee Dance," this bronze sculpture by Hugh Nicholson of Tallahassee, was installed in 1989 in the fountain in the patio of the Governor's Mansion.

This was Florida's first State-owned Mansion, the Governors having previously lived in private residences they owned or rented. Built in 1906, this Mansion was demolished in 1955 and replaced by the present Mansion. Florida State Archives

Through Some Eventful Years

9000 B.C. Florida may first have been seen by wanderers from the Indians who crossed a land bridge from Siberia to Alaska during the late Pleistocene or Ice Age. Their presence in Florida may be surmised from stone points of javelins and spears found in conjunction with bones of large animals long extinct. A sinkhole at Warm Mineral Springs in Sarasota County contains well preserved botanical, faunal, and human remains deposited 10,000 or more years ago.

5000 B.C. First semi-permanent settlements appeared in Florida as the Indians depended in a large degree upon snails, mollusks, and freshwater shellfish.

1498–1528 Europeans saw Florida coast for the first time. John Cabot of England viewed in 1498 or 1499 a great bay which may have been Miami's Biscayne Bay. Giovanni da Verrazano, a Florentine explorer in the service of France, likely raised the coast of Florida during a voyage in 1528. The Can-

Bold face name indicates expanded entry elsewhere in this book. See index.

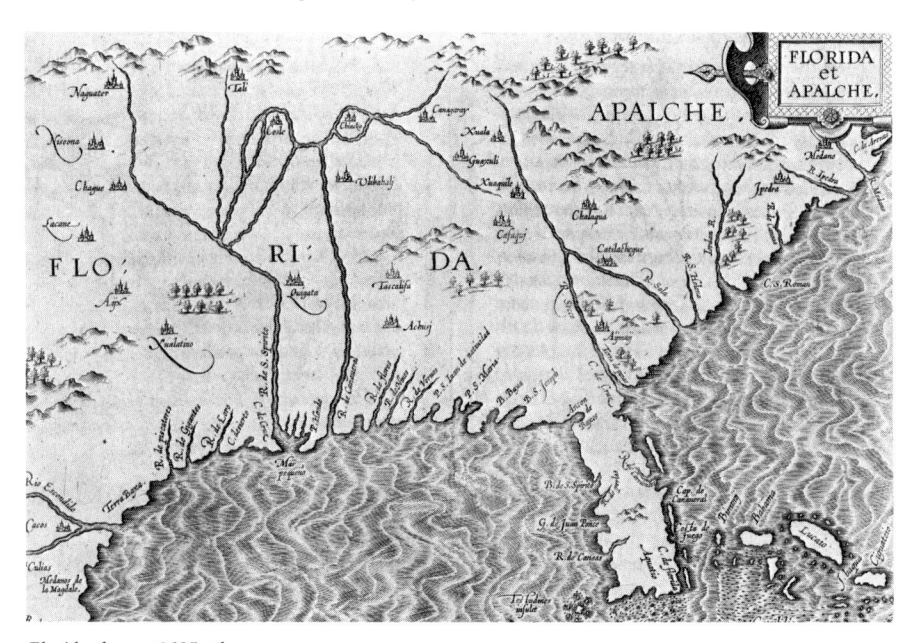

Florida, from a 1605 atlas   Library of Congress

tino map of 1502 shows a New World peninsula not unlike Florida. The Council of the Indies in 1565 claimed Spanish ships since 1510 had "gone to occupy Florida."

1500–1820 Periodic hurricanes along Florida's lower east coast and Keys battered Spanish treasure fleets. Authoritative *Treasure Diver's Guide* calculates some $12 billion in treasure (1970 bullion value) crossed the Atlantic from the Caribbean. Five percent was aboard lost ships and two percent, or $240 million, was never salvaged. A notable loss in 1715 was that of 10 ships driven onto reefs of the forty miles of coast between the Sebastian and St. Lucie Inlets. Some $30 million in gold, silver and jewelry was lost, of which $6 million was recovered by Spanish salvage crews and $1 million by pirates. In 1985 divers found the richest trove of all, the scattered wreckage of the Spanish galleon Nuestra Senora de Atocha. The Atocha sailed from Cuba in 1622 with a manifest of 161 gold bars, 901 silver ingots, and 250,827 silver coins. During a hurricane the Atocha swamped off Alligator Reef, some 50 miles southwest of Key West.

1513 Juan Ponce de León, who first had come to the New World on the second voyage of Columbus, sighted Florida on March 27. Going ashore between April 2 and 8 in the vicinity of St. Augustine, he named the land "Pascua Florida" because of its discovery "in the time of the Feast of Flowers."

1516–1561 Florida explored by Spaniards, including Ponce de León, who was wounded fatally in landing near Charlotte Harbor; Pánfilo de Narváez, **Hernando De Soto,** and Tristan de Luna. De Luna established a colony on the shores of Pensacola Bay in 1559. This settlement, abandoned two years later after a storm wrecked de Luna's fleet, antedated by six years the founding of St. Augustine and was the first attempt at permanent colonization. Fray Luis Cancer de Barbastro, a priest of the Dominican order, was killed by Indians near Tampa Bay in 1549, the first churchman to die for his faith in this country. Spanish Florida embraced most of today's southeastern United States.

1562 A three-ship French expedition under the command of Jean Ribaut or Ribault (see below), searching for a site for a Huguenot colony, entered the St. Johns River on April 30. Sailing inland for about five miles, the ships anchored at a bluff on the south bank. Ribaut, enchanted, described what he saw as "the fairest, frutefullest and pleasantest of all the worlds. The sight of the

---

Note: The spelling of Ribaut's name varies. Jeannette Connor, who edited the volume that Ribaut wrote while in England, used Ribaut. The Jacksonville Historical Society's *Papers,* Vol. IV, (1960), gave the various authors the right of choice. Thus, both spellings were used. In order to agree upon a spelling for general use during Jacksonville's 1962 quadricentennial, Dr. Raymond H. King, the Society's president, was asked to investigate the various forms of the name. His decision, Ribault, was based on a photostat of a letter obtained from the Library of Congress bearing a signature spelled that way. In the facsimile of the Frenchman's own book, as shown in Mrs. Conner's volume, *Jean Ribaut, The Whole and True Discovery of Terra Florida,* five spellings appear: Ribaut, Rybaut, Ribauld, Ribaulde and Ribault. Congressman Charles E. Bennett uses Ribault in his historical writing, and bases that usage on the signature from the Library of Congress.

Bold face indicates expanded entry elsewhere in this book. See index.

Pensacola, the Spanish settlement on Santa Rosa Island, in the mid-1700s.

faire-meadows is a pleasure not able to be expressed with tongue." In honor of the date, May 1, they called the river *Rivière de Mai* or the River of May.

1564 Admiral Ribaut's second in command, René de Goulaine de Laudonnière, returned to the River of May with 300 men and four women, nearly all Huguenots. They built a triangular fort of earth and timbers, and named it Fort Caroline in honor of the French King Charles IX. The colonists did not share Ribaut's idyll, for food was in short supply, there was little opportunity to search for gold, and Laudonnière imposed strict moral curbs. Two mutinies resulted and the mutineers, in stolen ships, sought to plunder Spanish treasure fleets sailing up the Florida coast. These activities by the French alarmed the Spanish authorities to plan protective measures.

1565 The English slave trader John Hawkins (later a hero of the defeat of the Spanish Armada) anchored off Fort Caroline and offered to take the remaining colonists to France. Laudonnière refused but purchased one of Hawkins' four ships. Meanwhile, two fleets were racing across the Atlantic to reach Fort Caroline: Ribaut in command of a French fleet and Admiral Pedro Menéndez de Avilés in command of a Spanish expedition. Menéndez ran into storms and Ribaut reached Florida first. On August 28, Menéndez entered a natural harbor and, celebrating the feast day of Saint Augustine with a High Mass, gave the place the name of San Augustin (afterwards St. Augustine). He sailed north to the St. Johns, had an inconclusive skirmish with four French ships, and returned to St. Augustine, going ashore on September 8, the date which marked the first permanent settlement by Europeans in Florida. Guessing correctly that Ribaut would attack St. Augustine, thereby depleting the garrison at Fort Caroline, Menéndez made a surprise march overland and captured Fort Caroline. Those soldiers not killed in the battle were hanged beneath a placard that read, "I do this, not as to Frenchmen, but as to Lutherans (Huguenots)." Hurrying back, Menéndez intercepted at an inlet 15 miles south of St. Augustine some 200 of Ribaut's men, shipwrecked by a hurricane. Menéndez slaughtered all but a few of the French, giving the place its name Matanzas, the Spanish word for slaughter.

372 / Some Eventful Years

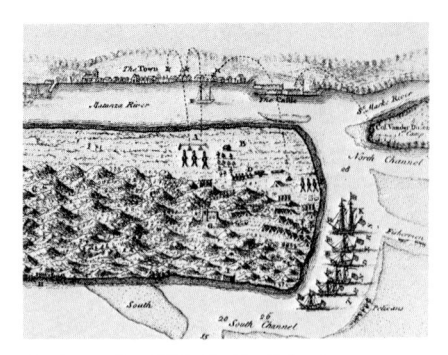

St. Augustine, 1740, the English seige.

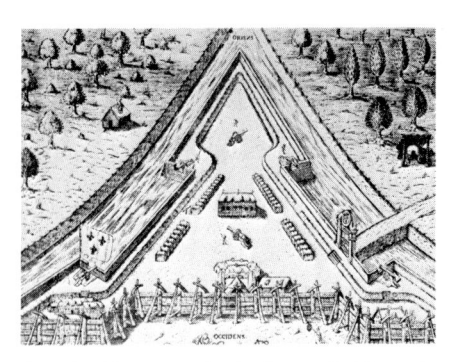

Fort Caroline, engraving by Jacques Le Moyne de Morgues, published 1591.

1566 Intensive, continuing efforts were begun by Jesuit and Franciscan friars to convert the Indians to the Christian faith. Spanish interest in Florida flagged because of the absence of gold and other precious minerals and the infertility of the soil. However, occupation was deemed vital to protect ships sailing along the Gulf Stream to Spain from its Western Hemisphere possessions.

1568 The events in Florida caused an uproar between France and Spain but nothing officially was done. Dominique de Gourgues, in his 30s and a distinguished French Catholic, privately assembled a force said to be for the slave trade, and sailed for Fort Caroline known now as San Mateo. Catching the garrison by surprise, De Gourgues burned the fort and hanged the survivors beneath the legend, "Not as to Spaniards, but as to Traitors, Robbers and Murderers." The reprisal complete, De Gourgues offered up thanks to God and departed for home on May 3. De Gourgues' revenge was, however, the end of French energies in East Florida.

1586 Sir Francis Drake, British seafarer, sacked and burned St. Augustine.

1600 Marked by sporadic Indian outbreaks, the 17th century saw Spanish colonization spread through Florida. San Marcos de Apalache (St. Marks of today) was a fort and a settlement of consequence by the 1680s. Possession of Pensacola was reestablished in 1698 with 300 soldiers and settlers and the building of a wooden fort. In following years five flags would fly over Pensacola.

1605 Franciscan friars were the first Florida schoolmasters. As early as 1605 they were conducting a primary school in the Convent of the Immaculate Conception, where a *"maestro de gramatica"* instructed the children of St. Augustine in elementary subjects and religion.

1672–1698 Pressed by the English, with Indian allies, from the north and by the French from the west, Spain decided to establish a more substantial

---

Bold face indicates expanded entry elsewhere in this book. See index.

Trial of Ambrister, from Frost's Life of Jackson, *1848.*

base at St. Augustine than the wooden forts which had been destroyed in English forays. Thirty years in building, the *Castillo de San Marcos* finally was finished. This fort of coquina, a rock formed of sand and shell, provided a bastion for the Spanish in East Florida.

1702–1703 British raids upon Spanish settlements, including a two-month siege of St. Augustine during which the town was captured but not the fort.

1719 The French captured Pensacola but soon returned the colony in an alliance of French and Spanish to stave off inroads by the English. France occupied the Gulf Coast west of Pensacola.

1740 British General James Oglethorpe invaded Florida from Georgia. Seizing outlying forts, he besieged St. Augustine for 27 days until lack of water and provisions plus the July sun and hordes of insects caused him to turn away, freeing the 1,500 soldiers and 1,000 townspeople crowded into the *Castillo de San Marcos.*

1763 Treaty of Paris, ending the Seven Years War between the English and French (and late-entering Spanish) saw England take Canada from French. Havana, captured by the English, was returned to Spain in exchange for Florida. British East Florida, with St. Augustine and its 900 buildings as capital stretched from the Atlantic to the Apalachicola River. British West Florida, with Pensacola as capital, reached from the Apalachicola to the Mississippi. In the area of present-day Florida, however, there yet was little beyond St. Augustine and Pensacola except *San Marcos de Apalache,* the fort and settlement at the head of the Gulf of Mexico. All the rest was wilderness. The English endeavored to attract investors and settlers.

1776–1778 The English colonies of East and West Florida remained faithful to the Crown during the American Revolution. Tory refugees crowded St. Augustine. Border fighting occurred between American and British forces.

1781 On May 10 at Pensacola, Major General John Campbell surrendered the British flags and arms to the Spanish forces of General Bernando de Galvez. British West Florida ceased to exist.

1783 Florida was returned to Spain by the British for the Bahamas. Nearly 10,000 persons, many of whom had fled the 13 American Colonies during the Revolution, left Florida, going for the most part to the Bahamas and the West Indies. Florida's first newspaper, the *East Florida Gazette*, was published at St. Augustine by William Charles Wells, a Tory. He rushed out an "extra" to proclaim the British defeat in the Revolutionary War.

1785–1821 Spanish-American border disputes. Encouraged by American authorities, a republic was proclaimed in northeastern Florida in 1812 by "patriots" who ran up their flag over Fernandina but were balked at St. Augustine.

1814 Andrew Jackson captured and abandoned Pensacola, which had been garrisoned by the British during War of 1812, over the protest of Spain, as a base of Gulf operations against the Americans.

1816 A red-hot cannon ball, exploding the magazine of an abandoned British fort occupied by free and runaway slaves on the Apalachicola River, killed 300 as Americans sought to stop forays in Spanish territory upon boats supplying American troops and settlers.

1817–1819 Gregor MacGregor, Scotch soldier of fortune, captured Fernandina, menaced St. Augustine, then withdrew personally to leave lieutenants to beat off an attack on Amelia Island by Spanish and volunteer American forces. MacGregor was supplanted as leader by Luis Aury, who declared himself to be a Mexican, annexed Amelia Island to Mexico and flew a Mexican symbol of some kind, there being no national Mexican flag. American forces evicted him in December, 1817, without bloodshed, and held the place until yellow fever caused their withdrawal in 1819.

1818 Andrew Jackson campaigned against Indians and outlaw blacks from Pensacola to the Suwannee in Spanish Florida, executing at St. Marks two British citizens, Alexander Arbuthnot and Robert Ambrister, he accused of inciting the Indians against the United States. Protests were voiced by Great Britain and Spain.

1819 American Secretary of State John Quincy Adams and Spanish Minister Luis de Onís reached an agreement, finally ratified by both nations in 1821, by which Spain gave the United States title to East and West Florida. The Adams-Onís Treaty dealt with other territorial disputes and with the

---

Bold face indicates expanded entry elsewhere in this book. See index.

Hunting Indians with bloodhounds in Florida, lithograph published by J. Baillie, New York, 1848.
Library of Congress

counter property claims of citizens of both countries. The United States gave up its claim to Texas, and Spain assigned its rights in the Pacific northwest to the United States, leaving ownership of the Oregon territory to be settled among the United States, Russia, and Great Britain. The United States paid about $4,100,000 to Americans who proved claims against Spain. But, as Dr. Rembert W. Patrick concluded in *The Colonial Eras of Florida* in the 1961–1962 edition of *The Florida Handbook,* "the Spanish kingdom never received a penny from the American republic for the valuable territory" of Florida.

1821 Andrew Jackson received the Floridas from Spanish authorities at Pensacola on July 17. He left Florida in October, likely on the 8th, and resigned as United States Commissioner and Governor of the Territories of East and West Florida from his Tennessee home in November.

1822 The unified government of Florida was established March 30, 1822, when President Monroe signed into law the Congressional act providing for a Governor and a Legislative Council of 13 citizens, appointed by the President and confirmed by the Senate. **William P. DuVal,** a Virginian who grew to manhood in Kentucky, became the first Territorial Governor.

1824 Governor DuVal, on March 4, proclaimed the site of today's Tallahassee as the seat of the new Territory, with the Legislative Council meeting there in November at a log house erected in the vicinity of today's Capitol. Settlers poured into Florida with southward movement bringing friction with Indians. The Territorial Council, with Congressional appropriation of $20,000, authorized John Bellamy, late of South Carolina, to build a road from the St. Johns River to the Ochlockonee River. Bellamy, who settled a plantation at Monticello, accepted land when money for the road ran out. The Bellamy Road, as it was called, was used until the Civil War.

1825 The **Marquis de Lafayette** was granted $200,000 and a township of land anywhere in the unsold public domain in recognition by Congress of his Revolutionary War services. He accepted a township adjacent to land set aside by the Federal government for establishment at Tallahassee of the new capital of the Territory of Florida. Lafayette never saw his Florida land, much now within the present city of Tallahassee, but caused the settlement there in 1831 of a short-lived colony of 50 to 60 Norman peasants to cultivate vineyards, olive groves, and mulberry trees for feeding silkworms.

1830 Population 34,730 (white 18,395, nonwhite 16,335).

1834–1837 Florida's first railroads began operation. The Tallahassee-St. Marks road was first incorporated (February 10, 1834) of those which actually materialized but the St. Joseph-Lake Wimico line was the first to get into service (early March, 1836). St. Joseph put in service the state's first steam locomotive (September 5, 1836).

1835 Beginning of the Seminole War. Major **Francis L. Dade** and two companies of U.S. Army troops were ambushed and massacred. **Osceola,** Indian leader, was imprisoned in 1837 after entering an American camp under a flag of truce.

1837–1840 General **Zachary Taylor,** afterwards President of the United States, commanded forces combatting the Seminoles. His battle on the eastern shore of Lake Okeechobee on Christmas Day, 1837, has been described as the last organized encounter of any size with the Seminoles.

1838–1839 Fifty-six commissioners elected from Florida's 20 counties gathered at Saint Joseph to draft a constitution in anticipation of statehood. The Convention lasted from December 3, 1838, until January 11, 1839. The Constitution prohibited bank officers, clergymen and duelists from being elected as Governor, U.S. Senator, or member of the General Assembly (Legislature).

1840 Population 54,477 (white 27,961, nonwhite 26,516).

1842 Seminole War ended with 3,824 Indians and blacks relocated in Arkansas. The cost of the war to Federal government, beyond expense of regular army, placed at $20,000,000, while 1,500 soldiers died of wounds or disease. No estimate of civilian dead.

1845 President John Tyler on March 3, last day of his administration, signed into law the act granting statehood to Florida (and Iowa) with its 57,921 people. First State Governor was **William D. Moseley,** Jefferson County planter who had lived in Florida but six years. He was a North Carolinian. Elected to Congress as first Representative was **David Yulee,** of Portuguese and Jewish blood, who had been born in St. Thomas, the West Indies. Before going to Washington as Representative, however, Yulee (then

Bold face indicates expanded entry elsewhere in this book. See index.

Reinforcement of Fort Pickens, Harper's Weekly, *1861.*

Battle of Olustee, published 1894 by Kurz and Allison.

Levy) was elected U.S. Senator by the General Assembly and, with but a four-year interruption, continued in the Senate until Secession.

1850 Population 87,445 (white 47,203, nonwhite 40,242).

1851 Dr. **John Gorrie** of Apalachicola patented the process of making ice artificially, a process he had developed in 1845 to cool the rooms of feverish patients. He died in 1855 without having gained recognition, but today Dr. Gorrie is one of two Florida men honored with a statue at the Capitol in Washington.*

1855 General Assembly passed the first Internal Improvement Act, which used swamp, overflowed and other land ceded State by Federal government to furnish impetus for an all-state system of railroad and canal transportation.

1857 Army Captain Abner Doubleday, remembered a century later as the "father of baseball" in discredited legend, surveyed South Florida and built a wagon trail linking Fort Dallas (Miami) and New River (Fort Lauderdale). It is said that a trace of Doubleday's old road may be seen in Arch Creek Park in north Dade County. Charged with subduing the Seminoles, Doubleday candidly reported: "We had no success in the Indian question whatever. How could we have? They kept out of our way and let us wander around."

1860 The Legislature, meeting after Abraham Lincoln's election as President, rushed through an Act for a constitutional convention to meet at Tallahassee, and appropriated $100,000 for state troops. The Florida Railroad, first cross-state line, linked Fernandina, on the east coast, with Cedar Key on the west. Population 140,424 (white 77,747, nonwhite 62,677).

1861 Florida withdrew from the Union on January 10. Florida was admitted to the Confederacy on February 4, but remained an independent na-

---

*In the Hall of Columns adjoining the crypt under the Great Rotunda of the Capitol is the statue of General Edmund Kirby Smith (1824–93), the other Floridian. Charles Adrian Pillars was the sculptor of both Gorrie and Kirby Smith. Efforts commenced in 1993 to replace Kirby Smith's statue with another of General James A. Van Fleet of Bartow, World War II leader.

Excursion trains played an important role in the development of Florida, as cheap fares enticed prospective settlers to see what opportunities might exist for them. Here, a train being run in the 1880s by the Jacksonville, St. Augustine and Halifax Railway.   Florida East Coast Railway

tion until April 22, when the Secession Convention ratified the Constitution of the Confederate States of America. That day the Confederate flag was raised over the Capitol. State troops occupied the Chattahoochee arsenal, Fort Clinch on Amelia Island and Fort Marion (*Castillo de San Marcos*) at St. Augustine, but Federal authorities held Fort Taylor at Key West, Fort Jefferson in the Dry Tortugas and Fort Pickens at Pensacola.

1861–1865 Florida furnished salt, beef and bacon to the armies of the Confederacy. The voting population of Florida was 14,374 in 1860. This figure gives significance to the fact that more than 16,000 Floridians served in the Civil War: 15,000 in the Confederate army and 1,290 in the Union army. Of those in the Confederate forces, 6,700 served for the entire war or until disabled or killed. Florida troops served in all of the greater battles, and more than 1,000 were killed outright on the field of battle. As a result of campaigning, at least 5,000 Florida soldiers were dead by the spring of 1865.

1864 The defeat of the Union army by Confederates at Olustee in the largest Florida clash of the Civil War saved interior lines of supply from Florida into Georgia and other eastern states of the Confederacy and confined Federal troops to the coast. Raiding parties, instead of Federal troops in force, roved Florida.

1865 Home Guards and Cadets from West Florida Seminary saved Tallahassee from capture by turning back invading Federal forces at the Battle of Natural Bridge. The war ended with Tallahassee the only Confederate state capital east of Mississippi to escape occupation. Federal troops entered Tallahassee on May 10, and the American flag again flew over the Capitol on May 20. A Constitutional convention, convened on October 25, annulled the Ordi-

Bold face indicates expanded entry elsewhere in this book. See index.

These troops, possibly Colonel Theodore Roosevelt and Rough Riders, awaiting embarkation for Cuba at Tampa during the Spanish-American War. Florida State Archives

nance of Secession and decreed slavery no longer existed. The right to vote was restricted to "free white male persons of 21 years or more, and none others."

1868 The faction-torn convention submitted a new Constitution, given voter-approval in May, which granted equal suffrage to male persons of "whatever race, color, nationality, or previous condition. . . ." Military rule ended, with civil government formally resumed on July 4. The State's political destinies were for the time being in the hands of those either new to Florida or new to the right of vote. Claude G. Bowers, whose *The Tragic Era* is a history of Reconstruction after Lincoln, described how it was in Florida. He characterized the legislators as "swindlers, stealing on mileage" and selling public offices and property. "The hotels and boarding houses (in Tallahassee) are filled with shabby strangers, the meanest of carpetbaggers drinking champagne, and the poorest in possession of the finest of beaver hats." In a word, wrote Bowers, "Florida was putrid." Florida's first carpetbag Governor, **Harrison Reed,** was described by Bowers as "something of a hypocrite and everything of a scamp," and by his friends as a "high-minded, honest, and honorable man." William Watson Davis, another Reconstruction historian, found Reed to be "shrewd, combative, and intriguing in dealing with men, but not smooth." Reed was frustrated by a Legislature opposed for reasons of party and personal gain to the Governor's efforts to administer an efficient State government. He was harassed by repeated attempts to oust him as Governor and distracted by murders, whippings, and other acts of terrorism in many of the counties.

1870 Population 187,748 (white 96,057, nonwhite 91,691).

1881 Hamilton Disston, Philadelphia saw industrialist, bought four million acres of Central Florida at 25 cents an acre to free the Internal Improvement Fund of debt and open the way for development of much of peninsular Florida.

First passenger train crossing Long Key Viaduct, of Flagler's Overseas Extension from the mainland to Key West. Library of Congress

A nervous amateur snapped this photograph of people fleeing the advancing Jacksonville fire of 1901. Jacksonville Sesquicentennial

1884 The first train of the new Plant System, created of many short-lines in the south by **Henry B. Plant,** rumbled into Tampa to produce the agricultural and industrial awakening of the West Coast.

1885 A Constitutional convention of 56 days broadened people's share in their government. Cabinet posts were made elective, as were those of Justices of the Supreme Court and all county offices except county commissioner. The State Board of Education was created. The establishment of normal schools was authorized.

1886 Requiring a railroad adequate to serve a great hotel he had built at St. Augustine, **Henry M. Flagler** bought the first transportation link in the chain of railroad and hotel properties he constructed down the East Coast to Key West. People and industry followed his penetration. Flagler's steel bridge across the St. Johns River at Jacksonville, opened for traffic on January 20, 1890, eliminated a ferry and for the first time permitted through trains from New York to St. Augustine and thereafter down the East Coast.

1888 The first commercial shipment of phosphate from the Peace River Valley, in the southwestern peninsular, where the mineral had been discovered in 1881.

1889 A yellow fever epidemic brought creation of the State Board of Health.

1890 A national convention of Farmers' Alliance, a predecessor of the Populist Party, held in Ocala. Population 391,422 (white 224,949, nonwhite 166,473).

1894–1899 Repeated frosts killed much citrus and sent the industry southward.

1897 The State Railroad Commission was established with authority to promulgate "reasonable and just" passenger and freight rates, and to correct

Bold face indicates expanded entry elsewhere in this book. See index.

Movie-making, Coral Gables, 1925.   Florida State Archives

transportation abuses. Floridians gave aid and comfort to the Cubans rebelling against Spain.

1898 The Spanish-American War saw embarkation camps at Tampa, Miami and Jacksonville, with thousands of soldiers and others who visited the state then returning afterwards either as tourists or residents.

1900 Population 528,542 (white 297,333, nonwhite 231,209).

1901 On May 3, flames raced for eight hours across the heart of Jacksonville, covering 146 city blocks and destroying 2,368 buildings, including 23 churches and 10 hotels. An election law was enacted to regulate primaries conducted by, and paid for, by political parties. Primaries were not mandatory.

1905 Construction commenced on "Flagler's Folly," the railroad across the Keys to Key West. Built by Flagler's own civil engineers and crews because the magnitude deterred contractors, the Overseas Extension spanned 127.84 miles from Homestead to Key West. Seventy-five miles over water or marsh. The longest viaduct, between Knights Key and Bahia Honda Key, covered seven miles of almost unbroken open water. The task required seven years and a work force of 3,000 to 4,000 men. The extension was completed January 22, 1912, in time for the 82-year-old Flagler to ride the first train. The extension, intended to carry freight between the United States and Cuba and the West Indies, never was profitable. Its trackage was badly battered by the Labor Day hurricane of 1935 and the railroad was abandoned, but the bridges and viaducts withstood the storm and subsequently were used as the foundation for "the highway that goes to sea."

The Buckman Act consolidated state institutions of higher learning into three: the University of Florida at Gainesville, Florida State College for Women at Tallahassee, and the Florida Agricultural and Mechanical College for Negroes at Tallahassee. The Legislature also created the Everglades Drain-

382 / Some Eventful Years

Carl G. Fisher, developer of Miami Beach, led the Dixie Highway Pathfinders, a fifteen-car cavalcade from Chicago through Indianapolis, Louisville, Nashville and Chattanooga to Miami, arriving on October 25, 1915.
Historical Association of Southern Florida

During World War I, Miamians lined up in front of the Halcyon Hotel, at East Flagler Street and Second Avenue, in support of a war bond campaign.
Historical Association of Southern Florida

age District, of 7,500 square miles, to reclaim water-burdened land for agriculture and cattle raising. Enactment of an automobile registration law with 296 registered in first two years.

1906 Hundreds of workers on the Florida East Coast Railway's Overseas Extension were lost when a hurricane swept the Keys on October 18. Miami battered.

1908 With $400 capital, the Kalem Company, organized in 1907, made in 1908 at Jacksonville what is regarded as the first dramatic motion picture in Florida. It was entitled *A Florida Feud*. Kalem was followed in Jacksonville filming by such pioneer studios as Lubin Selig, Thanhouser, Vitagraph, Essanay, Biograph and Gaumont. In a thesis, "Florida: The Forgotten Film Capital," Richard Alan Nelson says Jacksonville and Hollywood (Cal.) were by 1915 the nation's two leading winter production centers. Among the Florida stars: Clara Kimball Young, Wallace Reid, Owen Moore, and Oliver Hardy. In 1917, the first Technicolor film, *The Gulf Between*, was produced in Florida.

1910 Population 752,619 (white 443,634, nonwhite 308,985).

1911 In March, Lincoln Beachey, at Tampa, made the first night flight in history. He also set a new world's altitude record of 11,500 feet over Tampa during this year.

1912 R.C. Fowler, in January, started the second transcontinental flight at Jacksonville, flying to San Francisco, a distance of 2,232 miles in 151 days.

Two blocks in the business district of Fort Lauderdale were devastated by fire on June 2.

1913 Governor **Park Trammell** sponsored the first Corrupt Practices Law, to reduce the legal cost of seeking public office. The law allowed the ex-

Bold face indicates expanded entry elsewhere in this book. See index.

Tick quarantine station, North Florida, 1920s.   Florida Times-Union

penditure of $4,000 by the candidates for the U.S. Senate and for governor; $3,500 for cabinet positions. The Legislature also enacted a law for State-conducted primary elections. On May 17, Domingo Rosillo flew across the Straits of Florida from Key West to Havana in two hours and 30 minutes, winning the prize offered by the Cuban city for the first flight. On October 9, the Secretary of the Navy appointed a board to select a site for naval aviation training purposes. Pensacola was chosen, with equipment and personnel transferred from Annapolis, Maryland.

Henry M. Flagler, developer of Florida's east coast, died on May 20, after a fall on the marble stairs of Whitehall, the palace at Palm Beach he caused to be built for his third wife. Divorce from his insane second wife was a Florida Legislative scandal in 1901, when a law was enacted to make this possible. The law was repealed after the divorce was obtained.

1914 On January 1, the first regularly scheduled commercial airline between two United States cities was established at St. Petersburg as Antony Jannus flew St. Petersburg's Mayor A.C. Pheil and freight to Tampa. Pheil paid $500 for the privilege of making the first flight. Two daily round trips were flown for 28 consecutive days. On January 8, Mrs. L.A. Whitney flew, the first woman ever to fly on a scheduled airline.

1915 The first legal steps were taken toward establishment of a state constructed and maintained system of highways, a governmental function left previously to local agencies but requiring emergency measures because of rapid development of automobiles and tourist traffic. November 6, Lt. Commander C.H. Mustin made the first catapult launching of an airplane from a moving vessel, the *USS North Carolina,* off Pensacola.

1917 Senator Oscar Eaton of Polk County introduced a bill to appropriate $300,000 for citrus canker eradication.

384 / Some Eventful Years

In 1921, as the great land boom was developing, oceanfront lots at Miami Beach sold for $745 "and up." Knickers were the hallmark of salesmen.
Florida State Archives

Edwin C. Musick, Pan American World Airways' first pilot (right) stands with S. J. Whalton, mechanic, in front of tri-motored Fokker used in 1927 as Pan American inaugurated passenger service between Key West and Havana. From this 90-mile airline, Pan American grew until the airline circled the world.
Pan American

1917–1918 Florida was the scene of training for World War I fighting men, particularly aviators, as weather permitted year-around activity. On October 27, 1918, air passenger service between Key West and Havana was inaugurated by Aeromarine Company.

1919 The first guided missiles were tested at Carlstrom Field, Arcadia, in September.

1920 A campaign to eradicate the Texas cattle tick saw Georgia erect along the boundary a double barbed wire fence, policed by riders, to keep infested Florida cattle from straying into Georgia. Within Florida, for the same purpose, counties were quarantined against other counties. Dipping vats were used to kill the ticks. The higher value of tick-free cattle ultimately brought general cooperation from cattlemen after early resistance. Population 968,470 (white 638,153, nonwhite 330,985).

1921 The flogging death of 21-year-old Martin Tabert of Munich, North Dakota, in a lumber company camp provoked a national outcry which brought an end to Florida's leasing of convicts. Accused of vagrancy after his money ran out as he sought to "see the world" and find employment, Tabert was sentenced at Tallahassee to three months' imprisonment and turned over by the sheriff to the lumber company which paid $20 a month for county convicts.

1922 The U.S. Department of Commerce issued its first Florida radio broadcasting license on May 15, 1922, to WDAE, Tampa. WFAW, afterwards WQAM, Miami, had commenced broadcasting in 1920 with a 50-watt trans-

Bold face indicates expanded entry elsewhere in this book. See index.

The assassin and a victim. Guiseppi Zangara scans Miami newspapers telling of his unsuccessful attempt upon the life of President-elect Franklin D. Roosevelt. Bystanders support the mortally wounded Mayor Anton J. Cermak of Chicago.
Historical Association of Southern Florida

mitter assembled by Frederick William Borton from materials in a shop specializing in electrical repairs to automobiles and fixtures.

1923 Leasing of state convicts to lumber companies and other interests was abolished as a result of the death of a prisoner in a private camp. *(See 1921.)*

1925 Mark Sullivan, in his book *Our Times,* said of Florida's land boom: "All of America's gold rushes, all her oil booms, and all her free-land stampedes dwindled by comparison with the torrent of migration pouring into Florida during the early fall of 1925."

Miami's William Jennings Bryan, three-time Democratic nominee for President, died at Dayton, Tennessee on the afternoon of July 26. Bryan had appeared there as protagonist in the widely publicized Scopes trial.

1926 Florida Airways Corporation on April 1 became the nation's second airline to commence domestic airmail service. (Predecessor was Ford Motor Company which began flying airmail between Detroit, Chicago, and Cleveland on February 15, 1926.) The Federal award called for service between Atlanta and Miami by way of Jacksonville, Tampa and Fort Myers but Florida Airways first flew only among the four Florida cities. Florida's land bubble collapsed in the spring. The Miami area was dealt a second devastating blow by a hurricane on September 17–18. Estimates vary on casualties but Helen Muir's *MIAMI, U.S.A.* states that in Dade County there were 113 deaths, 854 persons required hospitalization and hundreds more were treated at home. Among the victim of collapse of boom was Florida Airways, with the Post Office cancelling the airmail contract on December 31.

Row after row of frame barracks, some shown here, housed trainees at Camp Blanding, the World War II reception center near Starke. Florida Times-Union

World War II trainees at Miami Beach. Florida State Archives

1927 On October 28, a chartered Fokker trimotor airplane rumbled along the dirt runway of Key West's Meacham Field to inaugurate both Pan American Airways and airmail service to Havana. The Pan American plane carried 28 sacks of mail over the 90 miles of water. Service for paying passengers began three months later. Because of Prohibition, the champagne christening of the maiden flight that day had to take place in Havana rather than in Key West. Large scale growing and milling of sugar began in the Everglades at Clewiston.

1928 Hurricane winds and water on September 16 brought death to 1,850–2,000 persons on the southeastern shores of Lake Okeechobee, perhaps the third after the Galveston Hurricane and Johnstown flood among America's natural catastrophes. The exact number of deaths was never determined as many were migrants. The loss of life was so great that funeral pyres were required.

1929 An infestation of Mediterranean fruit fly required tons of citrus fruit to be destroyed in 20 mid-state counties.
Banking historian Raymond B. Vickers reports 117 banks in Florida and Georgia collapsed in ten days of July, 1926.

1930 Eastern Air Transport, Inc. (formerly Pitcairn Aviation, Inc.) in April inaugurated service between New York and Miami, changing pilots at Jacksonville. Population 1,468,211 (white 1,035,390, nonwhite 432,821).

1931 The Legislature, applying part of the proceeds of a gasoline tax, secured bonds issued by counties for roads and bridges during the expansion period of the 1920s. Pari mutuel wagering at horse and dog tracks was legalized.

1933 An assassin seeking to kill President-elect **Franklin D. Roosevelt** in Miami's Bayfront Park on February 15 missed Roosevelt but fatally

---

Bold face indicates expanded entry elsewhere in this book. See index.

wounded Mayor Anton J. Cermak of Chicago. The assassin, Guiseppi Zangara, was put to death in the electric chair at Raiford Prison.

1934 The Depression-exhausted Key West City Council and the Monroe County Commission signed over their powers to the Federal Emergency Relief Administration. FERA's administrator initiated a program to make Key West the American winter resort of the tropics. Citizens volunteered two million manhours of labor in refurbishing the community. Pageants and other cultural events attracted forty thousand visitors that winter.

1935 A storm sweeping the mid-section of the Florida Keys brought death to upwards of 400 persons, including some 200 veterans of World War I. A remnant of the Bonus Army which had marched on Washington, the veterans were employed on highway construction as a federal work relief project.

1937 On June 1, Amelia Earhart took off from Miami on the first overwater leg of a round-the-world flight. She was flying a new Lockheed Pegasus underwritten by friends at Purdue University. She was accompanied by Fred Noonan, veteran aerial navigator. They disappeared over the Pacific on July 2 in an aura of mystery. She left behind this message: 'Please know I am quite aware of the hazards . . . women must try to do things as men have tried. When they fail, their failure must be but a challenge to others."

1939 The Highway Patrol, financed from the sale of driver licenses, was established.

1940 The ad valorem tax for state purposes was abolished. A Constitutional amendment authorized the Legislature to create a parole commission for the supervised release of worthy prisoners. Population 1,897,414 (white 1,381,986, nonwhite 515,428.)

1941 FBI agents, with the declaration of war with Germany, Japan, and Italy, began rounding up aliens in Florida. In Miami, the detainees were housed temporarily beneath the Orange Bowl stadium.

1941–1945 Florida hummed with World War II industry, as training grounds for tens of thousands of men and women of the armed forces at great camps like Camp Blanding and Camp Gordon Johnston and in the forging of vessels and tools for the conflict. Tourist hotels and restaurants at Miami Beach, Daytona Beach, St. Petersburg and other resort centers afforded quick means for accommodating hordes of trainees.

1942 Four Germans on a World War II sabotage mission landed by rubber raft from a submarine at Ponte Vedra during the night of June 17. With four who landed four days earlier on Long Island, the eight were captured by June 28 and six, including all of the Florida party, were put to death in an electric chair on August 8, 1942.

1943 A cigarette tax was levied to replace the war-lost revenue from horse and dog racing.

1945 The cigarette tax was increased from three cents to four and taxes on beer and other alcoholic beverage was raised to finance a multi-million dollar improvement program at state institutions and to provide more money for schools. A state advertising program of $500,000 a year was instituted.

Fire spawned by hurricane winds swept the great blimp base at Richmond Naval Air Station south of Miami on September 15, destroying three of world's largest hangars, 25 blimps, 366 airplanes, and 150 automobiles.

1946 The war's end allowed the start of public institutional improvements, and a statewide building boom. Veterans crowded the colleges. The U.S. Supreme Court, in a 7–0 action, quashed a contempt conviction of *The Miami Herald* and its Associate Editor, John D. Pennekamp, and wrote four opinions upholding a newspaper's right to criticize a court.

1947 The legislature enacted a Minimum Foundation Program to put a floor under educational opportunity for children in elementary schools of all counties and to encourage teachers to improve their qualifications by offering better pay for better training. Florida State College for Women transformed into coeducational Florida State University. The University of Florida was opened to female students.

1949 The legislature banned livestock from highways, enacted an omnibus citrus law designed to raise marketing standards for fresh and canned fruit, and overhauled election laws. The Legislature, in a special revenue-raising session, enacted three percent limited retail sales tax, shared the proceeds of an increased cigarette tax with cities, and earmarked money from the seventh cent of gasoline tax (previously used for schools and general government) for roads. WTVJ, Miami, began operations as Florida's first broadcast television station, with special temporary authorization given by the Federal Communications Commission on January 27, 1949, to WTVJ, Inc.

1950 Frozen concentrates of citrus juices became a major industry. Florida ranked 12th in the nation for beef cattle. On July 24, Bumper 8, a German V-2 rocket carrying an Army WAC Corporal missile from Cape Canaveral was the first American launch from what became the Free World's largest testing ground for space exploration. Population 2,771,305 (white 2,166,051, nonwhite 605,254.)

1952 Voters amended the Constitution to allow the pledge of motor vehicle tax revenue for school construction.

1953 An institutional building program was authorized, particularly to catch up the lag in mental hospitals. Governor **Dan McCarty** died in September after having been disabled by a heart attack suffered in February, some seven weeks after inauguration.

1954 The first Republican since 1885 was elected to Congress. Six Republicans were elected to State House of Representatives. The Sunshine Skyway, stretching 15.2 miles across Lower Tampa Bay, opened to toll traffic.

Bold face indicates expanded entry elsewhere in this book. See index.

The December 1960 boycott and picketing of downtown Tallahassee stores because of the lack of progress in desegrating the lunch counters.
Tallahassee Democrat

1954–1960 The school desegregation decision of the United States Supreme Court in *Brown v. Board of Education* of Topeka had its Florida ramifications. The Florida Supreme Court refused to admit black applicant Virgil Hawkins to the University of Florida Law School, despite an order from the U.S. Supreme Court that it do so promptly, because the Florida Court found that desegregation of the University of Florida would cause great harm to the institution and "great public mischief." Governor **LeRoy Collins** and Attorney General Richard W. Ervin appointed a committee, popularly known as the Fabisinski Committee after its Chairman, to study "legally sound" proposals which would maintain the public schools. The 1957 Legislature adopted an "interposition" resolution denying the Supreme Court had the right to "enact" law, as the legislators defined the Brown decision, and pronounced the Brown decision as null and void. Governor Collins labelled the resolution as a hoax and fraud. Following adoption of a pupil assignment law in 1956, the Governor and members of the Fabisinski committee warned that some voluntary and limited desegregation would have to take place in Florida to avert Federal court decisions invalidating the pupil assignment law. However, the official defiance and public turmoil which resulted in Federal troops being sent to Little Rock, Arkansas, in the fall of 1958 increased racial tensions throughout the South and made local school officials reluctant to act. Nevertheless, in February, 1959, the Dade County School Board voted unanimously to assign four black children to the Orchard Villa Elementary School in Miami when the next school year began in September. When only 14 white students enrolled at Orchard Villa in September, the Dade school board admitted several hundred black children living in that rapidly changing neighborhood and installed an all black faculty. In September, 1960, the Dade board tried again, assigning two black girls to two previously all-white schools. Twenty-two black students also were attending classes with some 750 white students at the Air Base Elementary School operated by the Dade board for children of Air Force personnel at the Homestead base. Governor Collins vetoed a proposal to appropriate $500,000 for an advertising campaign in the North on merits of segregation. "Sit-in" demonstrations at a segregated dime store lunch counter in Tallahassee triggered a riotous situation. Governor Collins, in statewide radio and television broadcasts, declared, "We are going to have law and order in this state." Collins went on to state, "We are foolish if we just think about resolving this thing on a legal basis." He said boycotts could be extremely damaging. "I don't mind saying that I think that if a man has a department store and he invites the public generally to come into his department store and trade, I think then it is unfair and morally wrong for him to single out one department though and say he does not want or will not allow Negroes to patronize that one department. Now he has a legal right to do that, but I still don't think that he can square that right with moral, simple justice." In later days, often through inter-racial committees, segregated lunch counter policies were ended in some 20 Florida communities.

1955 The Legislature authorized a state-long turnpike. Lawmakers were deadlocked for months in a special session over reapportionment of the State Senate.

1956 LeRoy Collins achieved two political "firsts." Elected in 1954 to complete the term of the late Governor McCarty, Collins was the first chief executive reelected to a successive term. Collins also was the first candidate for governor to win a first-primary victory, defeating five opponents for the Democratic nomination. A worm-eaten grapefruit in a Miami Shores backyard brought first aerial spraying to combat the Mediterranean fruit fly. More than a half million acres were sprayed before the battle ended nearly a year later.

1957 The Legislature authorized statewide educational television. Funds were appropriated for the University of South Florida and for expansion of the network of community colleges.

1958 The free world's first earth satellite, Explorer I, was sent aloft from Cape Canaveral.

1960 The Federal census ranked Florida 10th in nation. Population 4,951,560 (white 4,063,881, nonwhite 887,679).

1961 On May 5, the first American astronaut, Alan Shepard, climbed into space from Cape Canaveral. President Kennedy announced that the United States would undertake to fly men to the moon and back during the decade of the 60s, and the National Aeronautics and Space Administration selected Florida for its Spaceport, acquiring 87,763 acres by purchase. The State granted use rights to an additional 53,553 acres. The flight of Cubans from their homeland brought upwards of 50,000 into Florida. The skyjacking of a twin-engined National Airlines plane, flying to Key West from Marathon on May 1, set off a

---

Bold face indicates expanded entry elsewhere in this book. See index.

nationwide wave of air piracy. The skyjacker, a Castro sympathizer, was imprisoned first in Cuba and here upon returning to the United States in 1975.

1962 Space Age ramifications, spreading out from Cape Canaveral's launching base, influenced the state in many ways, higher education and industry being among the most important of these. Florida was the build-up area for the nation's armed forces during a crisis with Russia over missile bases and offensive weapons in Cuba. The first Black students were admitted to undergraduate classes at the University of Florida and Florida State University.

History repeated itself when the Mediterranean fruit fly returned to Dade County. A quarantine was quickly established and spraying commenced, to be continued for a year. Commissioner of Agriculture Doyle Conner said infestation was "mild" when compared with 1929 and 1956.

1963–1964 In May, 1963, blacks demonstrated against discrimination in Daytona and Tallahassee. Governor **Farris Bryant** defended the right to demonstrate but declared he would not tolerate violence or destruction of property. A black woman was killed and a number of other blacks were injured at Jacksonville in efforts to desegregate bars, restaurants and hotels. St. Augustine became the center of disturbances in 1964, with wide coverage by media. Between March 30 and July 1, the chaplain of Yale University, the 72-year-old mother of the Governor of Massachusetts, and The Reverend Martin Luther King, Jr. faced charges resulting from their efforts to desegregate public facilities including an Atlantic Ocean beach. King called off demonstrations when an inter-racial council began efforts to work out the problems.

1963 The Constitution was amended to authorize the sale of State bonds to construct buildings at universities, colleges and vocational schools. Voters also approved the issuance of bonds to purchase land for conservation purposes. The election of Governor and Cabinet was shifted to off-year from Presidential selection. Cape Canaveral was renamed Cape Kennedy after President John F. Kennedy's assassination (reverted to original name in 1973). The U.S. Supreme Court decided, in *Gideon v. Wainwright,* that Clarence Gideon, a Florida prison inmate, was entitled to a new trial because he had not been represented by an attorney when convicted of burglary at Panama City. Upon retrial with a lawyer, Gideon was acquitted. This landmark ruling changed the administration of justice in American courts.

1964 The first classes were held at Florida Atlantic University, Boca Baton. The University of West Florida was the name given to the institution being established at Pensacola. Hurricane Cleo caused property damage estimated at $115,320,000, but no life was lost.

1965 The Board of Regents, of nine members with ultimate nine-year terms, took over policymaking for the State's institutions of higher learning from the Board of Control.

1966 The first Republican since 1872 (**Claude R. Kirk, Jr.**) was elected Governor. GOP nominees also won three of Florida's 12 seats in the U.S. House of Representatives. Voters approved an early-start Legislature, with the Senate and House organizing on the Tuesday following the November general election. Previously, the Legislature organized in April.

1967 Repeated efforts by the Legislature to devise an acceptable plan of apportionment ended when a three-judge Federal court drew the boundaries of Senate and House districts and ordered new elections. Republicans captured 20 of 48 Senate seats and 39 of 119 House seats.

1968 The Legislature submitted and voters ratified three amendments which combined to give the state an almost new Constitution. Republicans held their convention at Miami Beach, the first national gathering of a major political party ever convened in Florida. The first Republican (Edward J. Gurney) ever elected by popular ballot was sent to U.S. Senate. There was a statewide teacher walkout.

1969 With the office reestablished by the revised Constitution, the first Lieutenant Governor (Ray C. Osborne) since 1889 was appointed. On July 16, at 9:32 a.m. (Eastern Daylight Time), Apollo II, with Astronauts Neil Armstrong, Edwin Aldrin and Michael Collins, lifted off Pad A at Cape Kennedy on the journey to the moon. Four days later, at 4:15 p.m. (EDT) on July 20, Armstrong advised the Earth: "The Eagle has landed."

1970 The first Legislature to meet in annual session under the new Constitution enacted a significant package of conservation laws that included protection of alligators, stiffer penalties for air and water pollution, and reduced use of persistent pesticides. Democrats recaptured the Governorship. Population 6,789,443 (white 5,719,343, nonwhite 1,070,100.)

1971 The Legislature submitted and the voters ratified an amendment to the State Constitution permitting the levy of a tax on the income of corporations. Two successful Moon landings by Apollo spacecraft blasted off from Cape Kennedy.

1972 The voters ratified a constitutional amendment reorganizing the sixteen kinds of trial courts into a uniform state system. The new Judicial Article eliminated all Justice of the Peace courts and provided for the phasing out of Municipal Courts by 1977. All judges to be elected without party label. Democratic and Republican national conventions met at Miami Beach.

1973 After seven and a half years and nearly 261,000 refugees, the "freedom flights" from Cuba came to an end on April 7. Premier Fidel Castro opened the doors for the airlift on September 28, 1965. The airlift, bringing refugees into Miami at the rate of 48,000 a year, helped transform the ethnic makeup of Dade County by adding at least 100,000 Cubans to the 150,000 already there. Other refugees resettled elsewhere. Cuban refugee operations since 1961 were estimated by the program's director to have cost more than $800 million by airlift's end but 80 percent of the refugees were believed to be self-sustaining in a matter of weeks. The State commenced defining areas of critical concern to the well-being of the public, first being the 858,000 acres

---

Bold face indicates expanded entry elsewhere in this book. See index.

Miami greets first Cuban air lift arrivals.   Miami Herald

of the Big Cypress in Southwest Florida brought under control by purchase or regulation.

1974 Reubin O'D. Askew became the first Governor to be elected to successive four-year terms. The Legislature enacted legislation for collective bargaining by public employees, and created an ethics commission to oversee public officers and employees. State Commissioner of Education **Floyd T. Christian** resigned after indictment on official misconduct charges was followed by a House committee preparing to vote impeachment articles.

1975 State Treasurer **Thomas D. O'Malley** resigned after being impeached by the House of Representatives. Justices Hal P. Dekle and David L. McCain of the Florida Supreme Court resigned during House impeachment committee inquiries into their official conduct. Governor Askew appointed **Joseph W. Hatchett** to the Supreme Court, the first black Justice in the court's history.

1976 Former Georgia Governor **Jimmy Carter** topped Alabama Governor George C. Wallace and 10 other Democrats in Florida's March Presidential Preference Primary, giving Carter campaign impetus which led to the party's nomination of him for President. In the same primary, Florida Republicans preferred President Gerald R. Ford over former California Governor Ronald Reagan. Carter carried 51.93 percent of Florida's General Election vote.

1977 January 20 saw snow as far south as Cutler Ridge in Dade County. A numbing wind brought death, power failure, agricultural ruin, and hundreds of traffic accidents around Florida.

U.S. Corps of Engineers recommended against resumption of construction on Cross Florida Barge Canal. Work was halted by President Richard M. Nixon in 1971 after construction of about one-third of the project, including 25 miles of canal, with locks and dams. (See index.)

Cinderella's Castle, a symbol of the Magic Kingdom. © Walt Disney Productions

Refusal of the Senate to ratify the Equal Rights Amendment on June 21, 1982, brought angry reaction from ERA supporters. "We will remember in November!" was the cry. This was a reference to the general election. Ray Fairall

Virgil D. Hawkins, who commenced his efforts in 1949, finally gained admission to practice law in Florida. The Florida Supreme Court, which had previously denied his admission as a black applicant to the University of Florida Law School, ordered his admission to The Florida Bar. Hawkins, who meantime had been suspended from practice, died February 11, 1988. The Supreme Court, in a symbolic gesture, reinstated Hawkins posthumously in recognition of his long struggle to be a member of the Bar.

1978 Jesse J. McCrary, Jr. was appointed Secretary of State by Governor **Reubin O'D Askew** on July 19, the second black to serve as Secretary of State and as a member of the Cabinet.

Swayed more by potential damages than the promised windfall, Florida voters rejected casino gambling by a 2–1 marjority. The casinos would have been located inside a 16-mile strip on the Gold Coast.

1980 The "Mariel Boatlift" of myriad small boats risked the Straits of Florida to bring 120,000 Cubans to Key West. Some 30,000 Haitian and 15,000 Nicaraguan refugees added to the monumental resettlement problems of Federal, state and local authorities.

A phosphate carrier, in stormy weather, toppled a main span of the Sunshine Skyway across Tampa Bay on May 9, causing thirty-five persons to plunge to death.

Population 9,746,342 (white 8,178,387, nonwhite 1,342,478, other 225,477.)

1981 The Space Shuttle Columbia rose from Pad 39A at the Kennedy Space Center a few seconds past 7 a.m. on April 12; the dawn of a new age in spaceflight. Successfully completing its series of experiments aloft, Astronauts John Young and Bob Crippen brought the Columbia to a landing at Edwards Air Force Base, California.

Bold face indicates expanded entry elsewhere in this book. See index.

Some Eventful Years / 395

A boat of the 1980 sealift from Cuba arrives at Key West, the gateway to the United States.
Miami Herald

This automobile stopped on the very brink of a 150-foot plunge after a freighter toppled a main span of the Sunshine Skyway. Department of Transportation

A sinkhole, the largest in Central Florida memory, unexpectedly appeared on May 9 in Winter Park, taking a house, part of a municipal swimming pool, trees and other objects into a 350-foot-wide, 150-foot-deep crater. On October 1, Florida's Walt Disney World observed its tenth anniversary. During the decade, the Central Florida theme park spun its magic over more than 125 million visitors and became the world's biggest privately owned tourist attraction.

1982 The Legislature established single-member districts for the House and Senate, thus placing Florida Legislature for the first time on a completely one-man, one-vote basis. The Florida Senate refused by a 22–16 vote June 21 to ratify the Equal Rights Amendment, dashing any remaining hope that the ERA could pass nationwide since the deadline was June 30. Angered ERA supporters in the Capitol chanted: "Vote them out!" A grand jury in 1982 declared there were signs that the nature of life in Dade County had changed. In 1979, the jury found, three quarters of the cocaine and marijuana entering the United States did so by way of South Florida. The rate of violent crime in Dade County nearly doubled. New terms, such as "Cocaine Cowboys" entered the vocabulary. Mrs. **Carrie P. Meek** of Miami was nominated without opposition to be the first black State Senator since 1887 and the first black woman Senator ever.

1983 A devastating Christmas freeze ruined grove after grove in Central Florida with damage to fruit and trees totaling well more than $1 billion.

1985 Nature was unkind to Florida. Citrus and vegetables were frozen in all but one of the 67 counties. A total of 8,949 forest fires charred a record 345,643 acres. The State Forest Division regarded May 12 as "Black Friday" for fires destroyed 200 structures statewide including 130 homes at Palm Coast in Flagler County. Three hurricanes brushed the seacoasts. Disaster stunned the owners of citrus groves and nurseries, with more than 10 million trees uprooted and burned to eradicate citrus canker.

396 / Some Eventful Years

The Orlando International Airport was developed to maximize passenger convenience while minimizing operational and maintenance costs. The airport utilizes a landside/airside concept, linked by a peoplemover. Lakes and waterways have been interspersed. The airport is situated on 7,000 acres.
Greater Orlando Airport Authority

Rosemary Barkett became the first woman Supreme Court Justice on October 14th, when she was appointed to succeed Justice James E. Alderman.

1986 Easy conversion of cocaine into "crack" for greater distribution added to the woes of the South Florida Task Force, established by Vice President George Bush as the nation's most ambitious and expensive drug enforcement operation. After four and a half years, The Task Force members felt they had barely dented the drug traffic.

Devastating citrus canker forced quarantine of groves.
Tampa Tribune

The Space Shuttle Columbia rises off Pad 39A at Florida's Kennedy Space Center a few seconds past 7 a.m. on April 12, 1981, the dawn of a new age in American spaceflight. Onboard, Astronauts John Young and Bob Crippen rise toward orbit following the successful liftoff of the first Space Shuttle mission.
NASA

Bold face indicates expanded entry elsewhere in this book. See index.

The space shuttle Challenger exploded upon take-off from Cape Canaveral on January 28, killing six astronauts and its citizen-passenger, Christa McAuliffe, an elementary school teacher from Concord, New Hampshire.

Floridians split their general election ballots, electing Florida's second Republican Governor of the 20th century and unseating the state's second Republican United States Senator, and the first woman, of the same period. Republican **Bob Martinez,** former Tampa Mayor, was elected Governor, and Democrat **Bob Graham,** retiring Governor, was chosen Senator, displacing one-term Senator **Paula Hawkins.**

1988 Thundering atop a blinding plume of flame, the shuttle Discovery catapulted five astronauts aloft from Florida's Cape Canaveral on September 29. It was 32 months after the Challenger catastrophe suspended American manned space flight. Also in September, a diminutive Winter Springs resident, Sheelah Ryan, won the Florida lottery's $55.1 million jackpot, the largest prize awarded in a North American lottery to that time.

Florida commenced executions by electric chair at Raiford State Prison in 1924. By January, 1989, Florida had taken the lives of 216, with 294 on death row. Theodore Bundy, one of the most notorious killers in the nation's history, died in Florida's electric chair on January 23, 1989. He had confessed to 31 killings in nine states.

1989 Death robbed the country of an outstanding Floridian. U.S. Representative **Claude Denson Pepper,** a self-described Alabama plowboy who became a tireless champion of the poor and the elderly, died May 30, 1989. In his place was elected Florida's first Cuban-born woman member of Congress, **Ileana Ros-Lehtinen.**

1990 The biography of the community, *Miami U.S.A.,* by Helen Muir reported in 1990 that streams of refugees had poured into Miami since Cubans arrived: Nicaraguans, Colombians, Jamaicans, Salvadorans, Guatemalans, Venezuelans, Peruvians, Ethiopians, Cambodians, Lebanese, and Ukrainians, "to name a few." Germans, Japanese, Mexicans, Chinese and citizens of the Arab countries have joined the march to South Florida.

Gwen Margolis, Senator from North Miami Beach, was elected by Democratic colleagues as the first woman President of the State Senate. Republican **Bob Martinez,** defeated for re-election as Governor by Democrat **Lawton M. Chiles,** 1,988,341 (56.5 percent) to 1,526,738 (43.4). Martinez, Florida's second Republican Governor of this century, repeated the pattern of the first GOP governor, **Claude R. Kirk, Jr.,** who similarly was defeated for re-election in 1970.

Federal census ranked Florida fourth in the nation with population of 13,003,362.

1992 Homestead and adjacent South Florida was devastated on August 24 by the costliest natural disaster in American history, with hurricane Andrew wreaking damage demanding billions in aid. There were 58 deaths directly or indirectly related to Andrew. The hurricane destroyed 25,000 homes and damaged 10,000 others. Twenty-two thousand Federal troops were deployed. Shelters housed 80,000 persons.

The first elections since Florida gained four additional seats in the United States House of Representatives saw Cubans and Afro-Americans seated. **Lincoln Diaz-Balart,** Cuban-born, joined **Ileana Ros-Lehtinen.** Among the Afro-Americans elected to Congress were **Carrie Meek** of Miami and **Corrine Brown** of Jacksonville.

1993 Janet Reno, for 15 years State Attorney for Dade County (Miami), was named Attorney General of the United States by President Clinton, the first woman to so serve in U.S. history.

The Florida State University Seminoles defeated Nebraska in the Orange Bowl to become National football champions, and player Charlie Ward won the Heisman Trophy. The slayings of nine foreign tourists within a year sent a chill through the state's tourist industry. Two cases highlighted the growing legal debate over children's rights: The baby-swap case of Kimberly Mays and parental divorce of Shawn Russ. Miami added professional baseball and hockey teams and Jacksonville added an NFL franchise. Federal cutbacks curtailed operations at Florida military bases including Orlando Naval Training Center, Cecil Field and several Navy operations in Pensacola. Abortion doctor David Gunn was murdered in Pensacola by Michael Griffin, an anti-abortion protester.

1994 Violent protests in Havana and political turmoil in Haiti sent more than 35,000 rafters across the Florida Straits toward Key West. Because of Governor Chiles insistence of Federal intervention most were intercepted and detained at Guantanamo Bay and in Panama. In July, tropical storm Alberto caused the worst flooding in 65 years and did at least 40 million dollars in damage to crops, livestock and equipment in the counties west of the Apalachicola River. In August tropical storm Beryl flooded much of panhandle Florida again and in November tropical storm Gordon killed eight in Florida and did $336 million in damage to south Florida winter crops. Voters sent a Republican majority to the State Senate for the first time in this century, and Connie Mack became the first Republican U.S. Senator from Florida to win reelection. Pensacola became the nation's capital of abortion violence when a second abortion doctor, John Britton, and a volunteer escort, James Barrett, were killed in front of a Pensacola clinic by former minister Paul Hill.

Bold face indicates expanded entry elsewhere in this book. See index.

Some Eventful Years / 399

Carmen Rivera of Homestead looks over what remains of her home after the passage of Andrew.
John Luke Miami Herald

Angel Valentine surveys what hurricane Andrew has left to him. The storm has taken the roof and left household belongings as rubble.
Miami Herald

The Discovery and Exploration of Florida
Rembert W. Patrick

Christopher Columbus received a hero's welcome on his return to Spain after the landing on Watling Island of October 12, 1492, and men eagerly asked permission to join him on a return trip. Numbered among the courageous men of the second voyage was Juan Ponce de León, a member of the minor nobility of his land and fighter against Moors. For two decades, Ponce de León was active in the Caribbean Islands: he helped conquer the eastern part of Hispaniola (present Dominican Republic) and was rewarded with the governorship of the province; after discovering gold on Puerto Rico, he conquered and governed the island; and he made a fortune from gold, land, and Indian slaves.

Ruthless Ponce de León was not a lovable character. His despotic rule brought investigation, and this together with overweening ambition for gold, silver, pearls, and slaves motivated his desire to discover and explore the fabulous island of Bimini, located somewhere to the northward. Many years after the explorer's death the legend that he sought a magic fountain of youth was added as a reason for his leaving comfort and position to sail into the hardships of unknown, hostile harbors.

Like the great Columbus, Ponce de León commanded an expedition of three small ships which sailed from Puerto Rico on March 3, 1513, rounded the northwest coast of Cuba, and moved into the Bahama Channel. On Easter Sunday, March 27, his men gave the welcome cry of "Land to port!" but rather than the wonderfully rich Bimini, it was only another island in the Bahama group similar to those sighted in previous days. Sailing northwestward through choppy seas under overcast skies the conquistador landed on April 2, somewhere near Ponte Vedra Beach and named the land *La Florida*.

This colorful land gave no indication of gold or pearls and the explorer sailed southward, hugging the coast and searching for indications of wealth. At Biscayne Bay he met hostile Indians and moved on by the Florida Keys and the Tortugas and up the west coast of the peninsula to Charlotte Harbor. After six months of exploring, the commander returned to Puerto Rico without gold or silver, pearls or slaves.

It is doubtful that Ponce de León was the first white man to touch the wide beaches of Florida, but his was the first recorded visit. To his enterprise goes the credit for discovering a vast land and attaching to it the beautiful

---

Rembert W. Patrick, late Julien C. Yonge Research Professor of History at the University of Florida wrote *The Colonial Eras of Florida* for the 1961–1962 edition of *The Florida Handbook*.

name of Florida. One of his ships did find Bimini off the southeast coast of Florida but the Island contained none of the fabled riches talked about by the primitive Carib Indians of the Caribbean Islands. Similar to Columbus, who probably never realized the magnitude of his discovery, Ponce de León thought he had discovered an island rather than a part of the North American Continent. Spain, however, based her claim to all the area north of the Gulf of Mexico and the Rio Grande to his exploring venture and applied his name of Florida to it.

Death of Ponce de León

Still hopeful of finding hidden riches in Florida, Ponce de León wanted to form a second expedition, but his services were needed to subdue the Carib Indians. His royal patent, giving him title of *adelantado* of the "island" of Florida did not prevent other explorers from searching the land for gold or capturing Indians for slave markets. In 1519 Francisco de Garay sailed along the Gulf coasts looking for a water passage to the Orient and one year later Francisco Gordillo explored the Atlantic Coast as far north as the Cape Fear River. In February, 1521, Ponce de León returned to Charlotte Harbor with soldiers, settlers, domestic animals, and farming equipment to found a settlement. But after being wounded by an Indian arrow, he ordered his two ships back to Cuba where he succumbed to his injury.

The March of Narváez

For a time the discovery of gold and silver in Mexico by Hernando Cortés diverted Spanish attention from Florida. In the end, however, the proven wealth of the New World checked expeditions from seeking passage to India and encouraged conquistadors to explore Florida in the hopes of finding precious metals equal in quantity to those discovered by Cortés. Tall, redhaired Pánfilo de Narváez promised the King of Spain to establish two colonies, build three forts and protect Spanish sailors who were shipwrecked on the Florida coasts. Narváez sailed from Spain with six hundred people and all the animals and supplies requisite for settlement. He probably landed at Tampa Bay but rather than stopping to build houses and clear land, he was

Juan Ponce de León

Hernando de Soto

enticed to march inland by Indian tales of gold. Ordering his ship to meet him later on the northern coast of the Gulf of Mexico, Narváez and three hundred men cut their way through forests and crossed rivers as they proceeded north through the Florida peninsula. Nowhere did they find stores of gold or silver and almost every tribe of Indians fought the Spanish invaders. On turning back to the Gulf near St. Marks, the discouraged men sighted none of the ships which were supposed to meet them. Rather than attempting the difficult overland journey, they built forges and used the iron of their armor to make saws, hammers and nails. With these they fashioned five wooden boats, overloaded them with men and meager supplies, and with sails made of clothing, moved west toward Mexico. One after another the boats capsized and all but four men lost their lives. Cabeza de Vaca, the treasurer and historian of the expedition, and three other men wandered for seven years before they reached Mexico City. The ill-fated Narváez expedition did prove that Florida was part of North America rather than an island in the Caribbean Sea.

The Ordeal of Juan Ortiz

In Havana, Cuba, the wife of Narváez believed her husband alive and in response to her tears, twenty-five men sailed in one ship to hunt for the missing man. Finding the spot where Narváez had landed, brave Juan Ortiz and one sailor went ashore but their seizure by Indians sent the other frightened Spaniards scurrying back to Cuba. After killing the sailor, the Indians danced with glee as the bound Ortiz wriggled in agony from the heat of the burning pile of wood upon which he was tied. But suddenly the Indians scattered the blazing faggots and lifted the blistered Spaniard from his intended funeral pyre. The pleas of the chief's wife and daughter saved Ortiz from immediate death. Yet after the healing of his burns, he was assigned to the menial tasks of women and made sport of by Indian warriors. Even a brave act of Ortiz did not give him security from the angry chief whose nose had been cut off by Narváez, and the Spaniard was again saved from death

Ulelah's rescue of Juan Ortiz.

by the Indian princess who showed him the way to escape to a friendly neighboring tribe with whom he lived until De Soto found him and used him as an interpreter.

De Soto's Wanderings

Meanwhile Cabeza de Vaca had arrived in Spain to request a grant of Florida from the king. No Spaniard knew more of the vast land, but the Spanish monarch had already made famous Hernando de Soto governor of Cuba and *adelantado* of Florida. Immensely wealthy from his share of the spoils gathered in Peru by Francisco Pizzaro, De Soto wanted the honor of commanding a successful expedition. Because of his fame, nobles and knights flocked to his standard and in 1539 more than six hundred men landed near Tampa Bay. For years the explorers wandered all over Spanish Florida—into the present day Southeastern American states and across the muddy Mississippi—to search unsuccessfully for precious metals and to fight battle after battle with the Indians. De Soto died near the Mississippi, his body went to a watery grave in the Father of Waters, and only half of his original company eventually reached Mexico.

The expedition gave Spain valuable information about Florida. This immense land area of rivers and swamps, valleys and mountains, with sandy and fertile soil, was peopled by hostile Indians who would be difficult to subdue. Furthermore, the clearing of land for agriculture and building of houses for settlers would require time and large expenditures. Since other areas of the Spanish empire in the New World offered more profit for less work, the Spaniards decided to concentrate their efforts on locales other than Florida.

Father Cancer's Plan

There were, however, thousands of Indians populating the land and Spain always considered the bringing of the Christian religion to the heathen a national duty. Thus the king gave ear to Father Luis Cancer de Barbastro's

The killing of missionaries by Native Americans previously mistreated by gold hungry explorers.
Florida State Archives

unusual plan of founding a settlement to convert the Indians rather than seeking economic return. The dedicated monk listened to a pilot who promised to place him and other priests on some hitherto untouched Florida shore where the Indians had experienced no mistreatment from gold-hungry Spaniards. The pilot doomed the peaceful expedilion by landing in 1549 at Tampa Bay where the ruthlessness of conquistadors had repeatedly shed Indian blood. Devout Father Cancer went ashore and surrounded by Indians, kneeled in prayer, but they clubbed his life away before he had uttered a word. The martyrdom of the priest determined King Charles to allow no further exploration of a land without gold and silver and populated by hostile Indians.

First Christmas in Florida

R.P. Engle

While many of us spend the holidays visiting with friends, reminiscing around the fireplace with relatives, exchanging gifts or enjoying the tradi-

State Archaeologist Calvin Jones at the site, within one-half mile of the Capitol, where he uncovered pottery pieces that proved to be from Hernando DeSoto's 1539 winter encampment.
Tallahassee Democrat photo by Mike Ewen

tional holiday feast, it is easy to forget how brutal life was for Florida's early inhabitants and colonizers.

On a small hill, within one-half mile of the present day state capitol in Tallahassee, Spanish explorer Hernando De Soto and his army spent the winter of 1539.

While many of the later Spanish explorers' landing and mission sites have been well documented, many of the early explorers were not. Accurate map making was a skill yet to be perfected and journal entries were either vague or nonexistent for much of the trip. It is known that after landing in Florida in or near Tampa, De Soto and his army of more than 600 men started northward.

After finding no gold and being forced to fend off almost daily Indian attacks, De Soto and his men soon ran short of food. It appears that corn was a staple of their diets for little mention is made of sending out hunting parties, but there are many references made to scouts being sent out in search of maize.

De Soto exact route through the wilderness has been open to debate for years. In 1985, The Smithsonian Institution Press published *Final Report Of The United States De Soto Expedition Commission*. This book was a culmination of work originally started in 1939 by the Smithsonian. Though the book admitted that no exact route would ever be known, they were able to make an educated estimation of his route. In the 1980's then governor Bob Graham had markers erected along U.S. 90 and U.S. 319 purportedly retracing De Soto's route.

In March 1987, almost 342 years to the day from when De Soto left Florida, state archeologist Calvin Jones made a discovery at what he thought was an abandoned Spanish mission site. Discarded pieces of broken pottery led him to believe he had found De Soto's 1539 winter camp in downtown Tallahassee. The pottery's style predated any known to exist when the mission were established. More evidence was forthcoming after further excavation work at the encampment. A coin was unearthed which was minted between 1506 and 1517, firmly placing the Tallahassee site as the only substantiated camp of the explorer.

"The only explanation to the pottery pieces was De Soto," noted Jones. "But we didn't feel totally positive until we found the coin. It's the next best thing to a signature."

It was known from diary records that De Soto's camp was in an area of North Florida controlled by the Apalachee Indians. Responding to the Spanish intrusion, the Apalachee conducted a guerilla war against the interlopers. De Soto, known for his brutality, retaliated by hacking off hands and noses of any natives he captured.

It was later in this winter that Catholic priests in the expedition celebrated the first Christmas Mass held on the new continent.

After 147 days of Apalachee attacks and with the weather turning warmer, the conquistador led his depleted army north into Georgia. Eventually the unsuccessful pursuit of gold led De Soto on a curious 10-state trek. The journey cost De Soto his life. In 1542, he fell ill trying to lead his now desperate band to Mexico or back to the Gulf. His men buried him somewhere along the Mississippi River in a hollowed out log.

A Toehold on the Florida Wilderness

Source: National Park Service

Four centuries ago a 50-mile stretch of Florida's east coast witnessed the first conflict between Europeans in North America. In the years that followed, three nations shaped the area's history: Spain, who claimed it on the basis of discovery; France, who challenged that claim, also alleging early exploration; and England, a latecomer in colonial expansion, who stood by waiting to develop the strength to take what she wanted. But the United States—a nation then unborn—won the land.

The French were the first to seize a toehold in the Florida wilderness that Spain believed to be economically worthless. In 1564, France, making a determined effort to control this region, sent troops to the St. Johns River, where they built the sod-and-timber Fort Caroline. Hunger, mutiny and Indian troubles plagued the settlement.

Fort Caroline

Despite these internal problems, Fort Caroline's very existence mocked Spain's claim to Florida and threatened the passage of the Spanish treasure fleets that followed the Gulf Stream and swung close inshore. Spain responded by sending out an expedition both to settle Florida and to drive out the French. When the Spaniards arrived at the mouth of the St. Johns River in 1565, they found the French, tried unsuccessfully to board their ships, and then sailed to a harbor farther south, where they established St. Augustine as a base for further operations.

Almost immediately the French sailed south to attack. Their fleet, however, arriving within view of St. Augustine, was driven off by a violent storm. The Spaniards, realizing that Fort Caroline would be lightly guarded, marched north and attacked the fort, captured it, and executed most of the garrison. The French fleet fared no better. Driven ashore many miles below St. Augustine, the survivors began an overland march to Fort Caroline. The Spanish, learning from the Indians that the French were ashore, moved from St. Augustine to intercept them. At an inlet 14 miles south, the two forces met. While some Frenchmen escaped, most surrendered and were put to death—a measure, Spanish soldiers pointed out, dictated by cold military necessity. The episode gave a name to the area: Mantanzas, Spanish for "slaughters."

Although Spain had ended one threat, she was not to enjoy untrammeled possession of Florida. Other annoyances were to come. In 1568 an expedition of vengeful French freebooters descended upon Fort San Mateo, the

The Castillo de San Marcos in St. Augustine is Florida's dominant Spanish Colonial landmark. Construction of the fortress, which took a quarter century, was completed in 1696. With walls 16 feet thick at the base and protected by a moat, the Castillo was never taken by force. The principal material is coquina, a sedimentary rock formed from billions of tiny seashells and quarried nearby. Most of the labor of quarrying and building was performed by Indians under the supervision of Spanish artisans.
Department of Commerce

former Fort Caroline, burned it, and hanged the survivors. They took revenge on the crews of captured Spanish vessels by throwing them into the sea. In 1586 England's Sir Francis Drake attacked and destroyed St. Augustine.

Castillo de San Marcos

Now Britain entered the scene in earnest, bent upon seizing Spanish-claimed territory. In 1607 Englishmen settled at Jamestown; by 1653 they had pushed south to settle in the Carolinas. The British again sacked St. Augustine in 1668, and this hit-and-run attack, followed by the English settlement of Charleston in 1670, caused Spain to build a defensive stone fort at St. Augustine-Castillo de San Marcos. Construction began in 1672 and continued until 1696.

In the meantime, a watchtower had been built at the mouth of the Matanzas River to warn the city of unfriendly vessels entering the estuary. But despite this precaution, pirates surprised the Matanzas garrison in 1683 and marched toward St. Augustine and the unfinished Castillo. A Spanish soldier, escaping from the corsairs, warned the garrison, which ambushed the pirates and turned them back.

Castillo de San Marcos received its baptism of fire in 1702 during Queen Anne's War, when the English seized St. Augustine and unsuccessfully besieged the fort. As disputes with England continued, and as English settlers and soldiers moved into Georgia, Spain began to modernize the Castillo. Matanzas, however, was still unfortified when the English struck again in 1740. They laid siege to the Castillo but failed to capture it.

An 1874 drawing of Fort Matanzas — Florida State Archives

Fort Matanzas

This abortive attack proved to the Spanish that their fortifications needed strengthening. In 1742 they completed the present stone tower at Matanzas, and continued work on Castillo de San Marcos until 1763. Then, as a result of the French and Indian War, Spain ceded Florida to Great Britain in return for British-occupied Havana. The British garrisoned Matanzas and strengthened the Castillo, holding the two forts through the American Revolution. By the provisions of the Treaty of Paris of 1783, which ended the war, Great Britain returned Florida to Spain, who in turn ceded it to the United States in 1821.

Following the American Revolution, the Spanish abandoned Matanzas, but continued to use Castillo de San Marcos. Later the post became the American Fort Marion, and during the Seminole War of the 1830s it housed Indian prisoners. Confederate troops occupied it briefly during the Civil War. It was last used during the Spanish-American War as a military prison.

About Your Visit

Fort Caroline National Memorial, 10 miles east of Jacksonville, can be reached by Fla. 10, St. Johns Bluff Road, and Fort Caroline Road. The original site washed away in the 1880s when the river channel was deepened, but the fort walls have been reconstructed nearby to help you visualize the scene.

Castillo de San Marcos National Monument, in St. Augustine, can be reached by U.S. 1 and Fla. A1A.

Fort Matanzas National Monument, 14 miles south of St. Augustine, is on Fla. A1A.

This is Fort Jefferson, the largest of the massive brick fortifications built during the 19th century for the defense of the American coast. Located in the Dry Tortugas, 68 miles west of Key West, Fort Jefferson became obsolete before it was completed. This resulted from the development of rifled cannon. Fort Jefferson received international notoriety as the prison of Dr. Samuel A. Mudd, convicted of being one of the "Lincoln conspirators."

Department of Commerce

Key to the Gulf

Fort Jefferson

Fort Jefferson, largest of the massive brick fortifications built during the 19th century for the defense of the American coast, is today principally of interest as an impressive ruin in the tropical Dry Tortugas, where bird and marine life abound.

The Dry Tortugas Islands form the southwestern tip of the Florida reef. Tortugas, Spanish for "turtles," was the name given the group in 1513 by the discoverer Juan Ponce de León, who found hundreds of turtles there.

Known as the "key to the Gulf of Mexico," Fort Jefferson is a six-sided structure about a half mile in perimeter, with walls eight feet thick and 45 feet high. The fort was designed for a garrison of 1,500 men and an armament of 450 cannon in three tiers.

Construction of the fort on Garden Key, most of whose 16 acres it covers, was started in 1846 and continued for 30 years. It never was completed, for invention of rifled cannon made the fortress obsolete before its walls were finished.

Fort Jefferson's strategic position at the inlet and outlet of the Gulf of Mexico hampered Confederate blockade runners in the War Between the States. Dr. Samuel A. Mudd, the Maryland physician who unwittingly set the broken leg of President Lincoln's assassin, John Wilkes Booth, was confined at Fort Jefferson for almost four years and became the hero of a yellow fever outbreak.

Fort Jefferson is 68 miles west of Key West and 180 air miles from Miami. There is a large and well-protected anchorage, with a landing wharf. A National Park Service representative acts as a guide.

Forts Pickens and Barrancas

Fort Barrancas, on a mainland bluff, and Fort Pickens, on Santa Rosa Island, are areas in the vicinity of Pensacola which are parts of the National Park Service's Gulf Islands National Seashore in Florida and Mississippi.

The Florida section consists of Johnson Beach on Perdido Key, Fort Barrancas and other fort ruins, Fort Pickens, Naval Live Oaks on Santa Rosa Sound, and Santa Rosa Beach.

Fort Pickens

Fort Pickens, a massive, five-sided fortification on Santa Rosa Island, was built (1829–1934) soon after Florida was ceded to the United States by Spain in 1821. The fort protected an important naval shipyard on Pensacola Bay.

Fort Pickens came under fire only once, when Confederates tried without success to capture the fort early in the Civil War. (*See* Florida in the Confederacy in this book.) Later, the fort was used as a military prison. Geronimo, leader of the Chiricahua Apaches, was imprisoned here.

Long-range coastal guns were mounted at Fort Pickens during the Spanish-American War. The ordnance was modernized again during World Wars I and II when artillery and anti-aircraft units were trained on the island.

Live Oak Preserve

The live oaks here were first placed under protective management in 1828 as a source of timbers highly prized in the building of sailing ships. Visitors today can see these majestic trees, their branches draped in Spanish moss, on a hike through the deeply forested plantation. This early experiment in the management of valuable forest lands was a pet project of President John Quincy Adams, an amateur botanist.

Fort Barrancas

Inside the Pensacola Naval Air Station are a group of historic fortifications, built by several nations to defend the channel entrance to the harbor. Fort Barrancas, Battery San Antonio and the Advanced Redoubt are open for tours.

A Half Century before Plymouth Rock

Source: An address by U.S. Representative Claude Pepper

We often consider the Spanish Empire as a caravan of miners, gauchos, and adventurers, and forget its solid and permanent everyday life, generation after generation. The quick blooming of modern Florida has obscured the old plantation that flourished much longer than the time since our Government took over in 1821. From Menéndez to Andrew Jackson—men who might have appreciated each other—was a stretch of over two centuries! St. Augustine had flourished over 50 years when the *Mayflower* anchored inside Cape Cod! It is our oldest city, the oldest to be made the see of a Catholic bishop. The parish of St. Augustine has a full record of parochial acts from 1594! That long period dotted the map of Florida with names suggesting Spain's veneration of the saints, and established the traditional architecture. In a distant and incredible future, a successor of Philip II, perhaps a trifle wistfully, would decorate the founder of Coral Gables, for adopting Spanish architecture for his dream city hewn from the same coral rock that went into the ramparts of St. Augustine!

Fort Mose: Free Black Fort

Fort Mose is described by Dr. Kathleen Deagan, of the University of Florida's Florida Museum of Natural History, as the first free black fort and settlement in North America. Fort Mose was established by Spaniards and African former slaves in 1736 about two miles north of the Castillo de San Marcos in St. Augustine.

The site was known to the Spanish as Gracia Real de Santa Teresa de Mose. Fort Mose was manned in part by refugees drifting into Florida from the English colony of Charleston. The 1986 Legislature, at the urging of Representative Bill Clark of Lauderdale Lakes, appropriated $100,000 so that archeologists and historians may endeavor to learn the extent to which Indian and African cultural elements may have been adopted at Fort Mose. Additional funds permitted the construction of a major traveling museum exhibit on Ft. Mose and the events leading to its establishment, and archaeological rediscovery. Ft. Mose was named as a Natural Heritage Landmark by the National Park Service in 1994, and a National Historic Landmark in 1995.

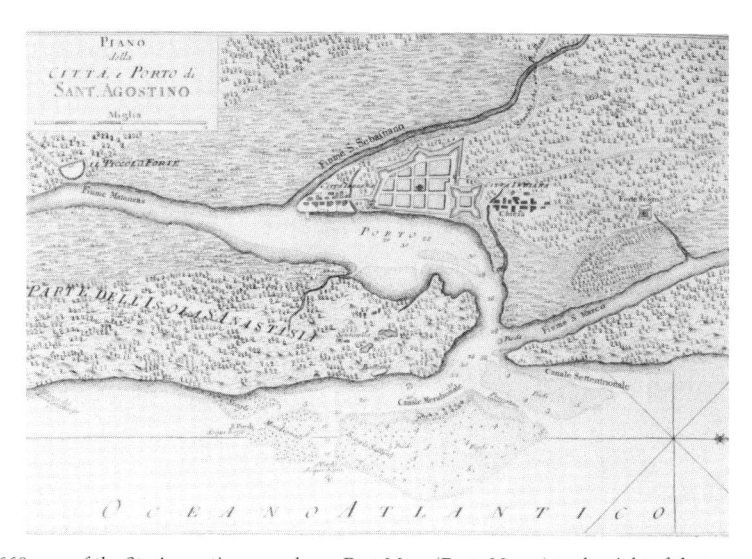

This 1660 map of the St. Augustine area shows Fort Mose (Forte Negro) to the right of the town.
National Archives

The Indian People of Florida

The 1990 Census showed Florida's American Indian population to number 36,335 individuals from 34 different tribes.

The Seminole Tribe and the Miccosukee Tribe are the only two federally recognized tribes in Florida. The Seminole Tribe has four reservations: Hollywood, Big Cypress, Brighton, and Immokalee with a total population of approximately 2,610. The Miccosukee reservation is located on the Tamiami Trail and has a population of about 195.

The Florida Governor's Council on Indian Affairs was created by Executive Order 74-23, signed by Governor Reubin O'D. Askew on April 10, 1974. The council's board consists of 15 persons appointed by the Governor upon the advice of the two co-chairmen, who represent the Seminole and Miccosukee Tribes.

Early Indians in Florida

At some unknown time, estimated to be eight to ten thousand years ago, the first Indians came into Florida from the north and northwest. Through time they increased in number, and by 2,000 B.C. large groups were settled along the St. Johns River and elsewhere in Florida. They lived on the country, gathering wild plant foods, hunting, and fishing. From this nucleus, groups spread, others entered the state, and by the year 1 A.D. most parts of Florida were well populated.

By the time of European settlement the Indians could be divided into two major groups. The Ais, Tekesta, Calusa, and others—those in south Florida below Charlotte Harbor and Cape Canaveral—were nomadic hunters and fishers, moving from place to place with nature's cycle. In the northern part of the state a near-civilization was reached among the Apalachee and Timucua. They lived in large houses, grouped in permanent towns often surrounded by palisade walls for protection. Extensive corn fields surrounded the villages. Town chiefs often became so powerful that they controlled surrounding villages, waging war on enemies many miles away.

Such were the Indians the Spanish first met in 1513. Within the next fifty or so years the Spanish had explored much of the state, endeavoring to establish friendly relations with the natives in order to protect their colonies and to promote the spread of Christianity.

The south Florida Indians were so difficult to deal with that the only missions and forts established there by the Spanish were abandoned in 1569. Thereafter no permanent settlement was ever made by the Spanish in that area.

Condensed from an article by John M. Goggin, Associate Professor of Anthropology, University of Florida, in the 1955–57 edition of *The Florida Handbook*.

In north Florida initial relations between the Europeans and Indians were friendlier. After the founding of St. Augustine in 1565 missionary efforts were made among the local Indians with success. A chain of Spanish missions spread northward along the coast eventually to the present South Carolina region. Another extended westward to the St. Johns, reaching Alachua County in 1606, and by 1633 was established in the present Tallahassee district.

The settlement of the English in the Carolinas in 1670 extended to Florida the centuries-old struggle between Spain and England, and north Florida became a European battleground for the next ninety years. In this struggle the Indians were innocent bystanders or hopeless pawns and, as is so often the case, they bore the brunt of the blows. By 1706 the once flourishing mission chains northward and westward of the St. Johns River had disappeared and a population of 15,000 Indians dwindled to a few hundred in less than a century.

The south Florida Indians for many years continued their old ways of life, little influenced by the newcomers except by obtaining many Spanish goods from wrecked ships. During the 17th century European-introduced diseases made severe inroads on the population, but their real decline came after 1700 with the disappearance of the north Florida missions. This gap allowed the Creeks to raid as far south as Cape Florida where the local tribes armed only with bows and arrows fell easy prey to Creeks supplied with English guns.

In 1763 Spain turned Florida over to the English. With the Spaniards on their departure went the remaining north Florida Indians and many of the south Floridians. The former settled in Cuba and Veracruz, Mexico and never appeared again in Florida.

Seminole History and Culture

The people who came to be known as "Seminole" (the name means "runaways") were Yamasee, driven from the Carolinas in 1717; Hitchiti-speaking Oconee from the Apalachicola River; and Creeks fleeing Georgia after the Creek War. All were fugitives from the whites. Their ranks were swelled by fugitive slaves who found refuge and freedom among the Indians. Attempts by owners to recover these slaves led to Andrew Jackson's campaigns in 1814 and 1818. The Seminole were united by the hostility and fear they felt toward the young United States. In 1821, Florida was annexed by the United States, and pressure by white settlers for Indian lands and farms led to an attempt in 1832 to move the Seminoles west of the Mississippi by force. The wife of their leader, Osceola, was seized as a fugitive, and bloody warfare followed as the Seminole fought bitterly. When Osceola was captured under a flag of truce, some of his warriors fled into the Everglades. Later, a portion of the tribe was transported to Oklahoma where they formed one of the Five Civilized Tribes. A truce with the United States was finally signed in 1934. Another treaty was concluded in 1937.

With the withdrawal of troops, the Seminole continued to live in scattered locations and pursue a nomadic existence, mostly by hunting and fishing. They lived in small houses built with cypress poles and thatched with palmetto leaves. Their clothing is colorful and elaborate; deerskin leggings

Seminoles on a trading expedition to town. About 1909. Fort Lauderdale Historical Society

have been replaced by cloth pants. The tunics and overblouses are laboriously fashioned from small strips of different colored material all sewed into long rows and then stitched together. Seminole folks arts, including dollmaking, are still followed. The turban, once the headdress of every Seminole brave, has been replaced by the 10-gallon hat. Seasonal Green Corn and Hunting Dances are still performed during festivities.

Miccosukee History and Culture

The Miccosukee led a nomadic life hiding out from United States troops for long periods in their history. They survived by hunting and fishing, building small shelters with wooden frames and palmetto leaf roofs. Their homes today are being replaced with more modern units. Their dress is both colorful and difficult to make, being constructed from many strips of different colored material. Folk arts still exist, and the seasonal Green Corn and Hunting Dances are performed. Most of the Miccosukee have retained their Indian religion, whereas the Seminole are largely Christians.

Creek Indian History and Culture

Source: Andrew Boggs Ramsey

Politically, the Seminole people and the Creek people are today a distinct and separate group though culturally in their earlier histories, the Florida Creeks and Seminoles shared a merged history. However, following the signing of the Treaty of Moultrie Creek, 1823, they have become a separate people.

Today, the Florida Creeks reside in Northwest Florida from the Apalachicola River to the Alabama line west of Pensacola. Escambia County is one of the three centers of Creek Indian activity and has the third largest Indian population of Florida counties according to the 1990 U.S. Census Report. The other two centers are Blountstown, Calhoun County, and Bruce, Walton County.

Florida's Creek Indians of today are descendents of the Poarch Band of Creeks in Alabama, the Apalachicola River Creeks in Calhoun County, and others fleeing removal from Alabama and Georgia. Most of these Creeks survived in very small groups by living in isolated conditions apart from white settlers under very poor conditions.

The state of Florida recognized the existence of Creek Indians by the establishment of the Northwest Florida Creek Indian Council appointed by the Governor. The Creek Tribes served by the Northwest Florida Creek Indian Council are The Florida Tribe of Eastern Creek Indians, a state recognized tribe, and the Poarch Band of Creeks, a recently federalized tribe in Alabama with members in Escambia County, Florida.

The Florida Creeks' traditional Square Grounds are located in the Blountstown area where the Berry, Green Corn, Little Green Corn, and Harvest Busks are observed each year. One of the better Creek Museums is located in the Calhoun County Courthouse. The Florida Tribe operates Creek schools in Blountstown, Panama City, Bruce and Pensacola to keep the Creek Language and History alive and used.

Patsy West, photo-historian of the Seminole and Miccosukee tribes, writes that the Seminole photographic record begins in 1852 with Billy Bowlegs, shown here. Regarded by Federal authorities as the most influential leader among the Seminoles in Florida, Bowlegs was shown Washington and New York so he might be convinced of the power of the government. The Third Seminole War began three years later and ended with Bowlegs transported, with other Seminoles, to Oklahoma Indian territory.

Florida in the American Revolution

The American of today often forgets that Great Britain in 1776 had seventeen rather than thirteen colonies on the mainland of North America. The Continental Congress invited the four most northern and most southern colonies to join the other colonies, but Upper and Lower Canada, and East and West Florida remained faithful to England. The reasons for refusal by the Floridas were obvious: the colonies were young and tied to the Mother Country; they needed her protection against the Indians and England's economic aid; and their people were satisfied and had few connections with the colonies to the north. Furthermore, the non-British residents of the Floridas—Minorcans, French, Greek, Italians, and Spaniards—had no desire to be associated with the Protestant peoples of the other English southern colonies.

Neither France nor Spain had accepted the verdict of the Seven Years War as final and for more than a decade they impatiently awaited opportunity to strike at Great Britain. Rebellion of the thirteen American colonies gave them their chance and before 1780 the American Revolution broadened into a world war. From bases at Havana and New Orleans, Spanish armies moved into West Florida to capture Mobile in 1780 and Pensacola the following year. The fall of river settlements along the eastern side of the Mississippi River gave Spain control of West Florida by right of conquest.

The peace settlement following the war accomplished that which military might had not done in the east. To the amazement and anger of East Floridians, many of whom had already been forced from their Georgia and Carolina homes, Great Britain ceded East Florida to Spain. Where twenty years before England had desired the Floridas to round out her geographical possessions east of the Mississippi River, the independence of the United States left Florida isolated and relatively unimportant to Great Britain. The English government had never realized its fond hopes of profits from the Floridas and readily agreed to their surrender to appease Spain, who was demanding Gibraltar.

Considerate England did not leave her loyal subjects stranded and at the mercy of Spain. To compensate them for their losses, they were offered transportation to other parts of the British Empire, land, and money. Thousands of English colonials left Florida for the Bahamas, Jamaica, Nova Scotia, England, or other places, and did receive some payment in money for the loss of their Florida holdings. The Minorcan and other non-English residents of the Floridas remained to become subjects of Spain.

Excerpted from "The Colonial Era of Florida," by Dr. Rembert W. Patrick, then Julien C. Yonge Graduate Professor at the University of Florida, written for the 1961–1962 edition of *The Florida Handbook*.

Florida in the Confederacy
Dorothy Dodd

When the election of Abraham Lincoln precipitated the secession of the Southern states, Florida was the third state to withdraw from the Union. The Ordinance of Secession was signed at Tallahassee on January 11, 1861. Until it joined the provisional government of the Confederate States of America on January 28, Florida was an "independent nation."

Occupation of Forts

Even before the Ordinance of Secession was adopted, Florida moved to seize the federal forts. Fort Marion and Fort Clinch were taken without difficulty. Of the three forts at Pensacola, only Barrancas was garrisoned. Knowing that he could not hold out against attack, its commander hurriedly moved the garrison to Fort Pickens on Santa Rosa Island. The Confederates seized the Navy Yard on January 12 and occupied Forts Barrancas and McRee, but the garrison of Fort Pickens refused to surrender.

Actual hostilities had not commenced and both sides were reluctant to start fighting. Consequently, there was an informal truce until April 12, when Fort Pickens was reinforced by sea. Although the Confederates landed a force on Santa Rosa Island and twice bombarded the fort from the mainland, they were unable to capture it.

Fort Taylor and Fort Jefferson also remained in Union hands throughout the war. The latter, at the western end of the Keys, was too remote to be seized by land forces. Fort Taylor's garrison stood firm against Southern sympathizers in Key West until that port became headquarters for the Gulf Blockading Squadron.

Coastal Blockade

The blockade of the Florida coasts began in June, 1861. Some blockading vessels had regular stations, while others patrolled sections of the coastal waters. They captured many blockade runners, but they could not prevent oth-

---

Dr. Dorothy Dodd was the Florida State Librarian from 1951 until 1965. A native of Cadiz, Kentucky, she received degrees of bachelor of arts and master of arts from Florida State College for Women (now Florida State University), a bachelor of literature from Columbia University's Pulitzer School of Journalism, and a doctor of philosophy from the University of Chicago. She was a reporter for the *Tampa Times*, a teacher at Pensacola, and engaged in historical and archival pursuits. This article is excerpted from a history of the Civil War in Florida written in 1961 for *The Florida Handbook*.

418 / Civil War

A Federal officer sketched this destruction of a Confederate salt works on the coast of Florida by the crew of the U.S.S. Kingfisher.   Harper's Weekly, 1862

ers from slipping in and out of Florida's bays and rivers with arms and scarce goods, such as coffee, tea, and medicines, and outgoing cargoes of cotton, tobacco, and turpentine.

Occasionally, the federal ships would land a party to raid a town. In January 1862, sailors and marines burned the railroad terminus and a number of small vessels docked at Cedar Key. In May 1864, Tampa was pillaged, and its rude defense works burned. The blockading ships also took off contrabands, as runaway slaves were called.

Salt for the Confederacy

Crews of blockading ships raided the coastal salt works. Seawater was almost the only source for the salt that was so badly needed for domestic use and to cure beef for the armies. On the shallow bays and lagoons of the west coast from Tampa to Choctawhatchee Bay, men boiled seawater in large kettles and sheet-iron boilers to make salt for the Confederacy. When the blockaders learned the location of a salt works, they would go ashore, burn the store houses and shanties in which the saltmakers lived, and break up the kettles, boilers, and furnaces with sledge hammers.

A Taylor County salt works raided in September, 1863, had a capacity of 1,500 bushels a day, for which the government paid $12.50 a bushel. The salt-making equipment consisted of 390 large kettles, 52 sheet-iron boilers, 170 brick furnaces, and numerous pumps, wells, and aqueducts. There were 182 storehouses, shanties, and sheds, including a carpenter shop and a fishing house, five large wagons, 18 mules and about 1,000 head of cattle. The to-

This is one of the rarest of Florida photographs, published for the first time in an earlier edition of the Florida Handbook. It catches a moment in the life of a Confederate encampment, probably on Big Bayou near Pensacola. Very possibly it is Company A, First Volunteer Company, of the Orleans Cadets, mustered into service on April 11, 1861. The photograph probably was taken shortly thereafter. The photographer was J. D. Edwards of New Orleans. This photograph and another of similar nature are two original prints donated to the Florida State Archives by R. Bruce Duncan of the Duncan Galleries, Northfield, Illinois. This photograph well may be one of the first of the news type, or documentary, pictures made in Florida.
Florida State Archives

tal value of property destroyed or captured in this single raid was estimated at $2,000,000.

Cattle: Another Contribution

Another important Florida contribution to the Confederacy was cattle, which provided beef for army rations, tallow for candles, and hides for leather. Cattle from South Florida prairies were driven to the railhead at Baldwin for shipment to the armies, each drive taking forty days. By 1864, Florida cattle were almost the only source of beef for the Confederate armies in the east.

Florida hogs, sugar, syrup, and fish, though less important, also helped to feed the soldiers. To conserve food products, the state Legislature forbade the use of grain, sugar, and syrup in distilling liquor. It also instituted a quota system for cotton and tobacco acreage to force the growing of food crops.

Although food was Florida's most effective contribution to the Southern cause, the state's great sacrifice was in the men it gave to the Confederate armies. There were only 14,373 men of voting age in 1860, but at least 15,000 Floridians saw military service. Of these, more than 1,000 were killed in action, some 5,000 were wounded, and another 5,000 died of hardship and disease. A native Floridian, General Edmund Kirby Smith, became one of the seven full generals of the Confederacy. His statue stands today in the Capitol at Washington, with that of Dr. John Gorrie, the inventor.

Florida troops served in all the greater battles of the war, but the state was never the scene of important military operations. In the spring of 1862, most of the soldiers in Florida were withdrawn to bolster the hard-pressed Army of Tennessee. Pensacola was abandoned to the federal troops at Fort Pickens. Union forces occupied Apalachicola, and a naval expedition from Port Royal, South Carolina, took Fernandina, Jacksonville, and St. Augustine. Jacksonville was occupied and evacuated three times in 1862 and 1863. Its fourth occupation in February, 1864, was a preliminary to the Olustee Campaign.

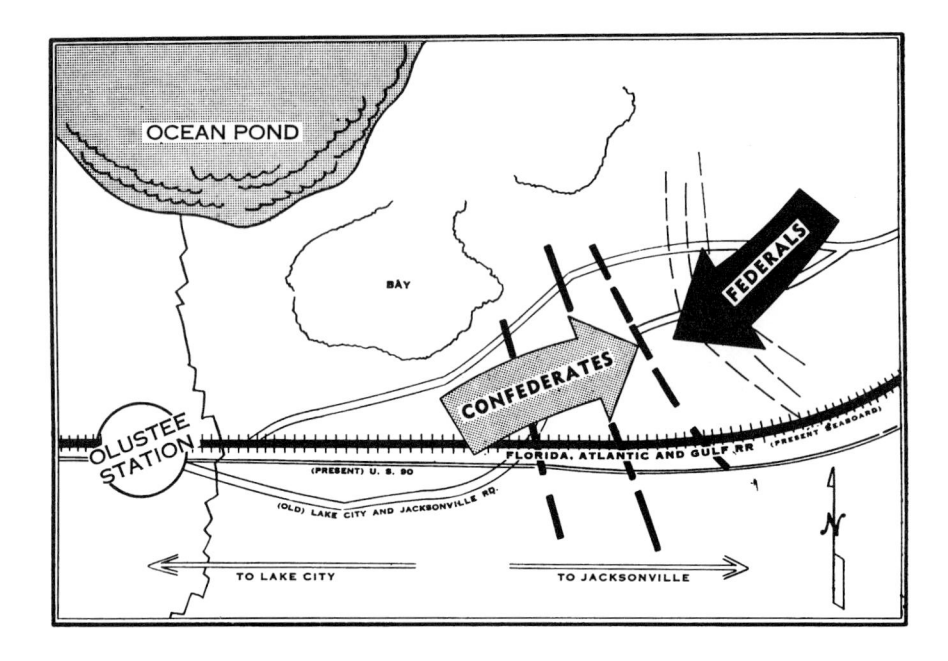

Olustee: Bloody Battle Ground

The Battle of Olustee (Ocean Pond), February 20, 1864, was the major engagement of the Civil War in Florida. The campaign that culminated in the battle began when General Q.A. Gillmore sent a Federal expedition from Hilton Head, South Carolina, to occupy Jacksonville for a fourth time. The general objectives were to break up communications between East and West Florida, thus depriving the Confederacy of large quantities of food supplies drawn from East and South Florida; to procure for Northern use Florida cotton, turpentine and timber; to obtain recruits for black regiments; and to induce Unionists in East Florida to organize a loyal state government.

The expedition landed on February 7 under the command of General Truman A. Seymour. The next day Federal raiders fanned out from Jacksonville, meeting little opposition. On February 9 they took Baldwin, the junction of the railroads from Fernandina to Cedar Keys and from Jacksonville to Tallahassee. There they seized supplies worth half a million dollars. By February 11 their calvary had penetrated to within three miles of

Lake City but, after a sharp skirmish with hastily entrenched Confederates, withdrew to Sanderson.

Confederate Strength

The Confederates encountered near Lake City were under the command of General Joseph Finegan. At the time of the invasion, his forces numbered scarcely 1,200 men widely scattered over East Florida. Upon learning of Seymour's landing, he called for reinforcements, which were sent from Middle Florida and Georgia and concentrated near Lake City. The only natural defensive features of the country, which was flat and covered by open pine forest, were numerous lakes and streams. On February 13, General Finegan selected a position near Olustee Station that offered a maximum natural protection and began defensive works along a line from Ocean Pond on the left to a small pond south of the railroad on the right. The position was strong if attacked directly from the front, but could be readily turned.

The Federals, meanwhile, hesitated as to the course they should take. General Gillmore had given instructions that Union troops should not advance in force beyond Barbers at the Little St. Marys River. Somewhat inexplicably therefore, General Seymour decided on February 17 that he would move against Lake City, meet the enemy there, and push his calvary westward to destroy the railroad bridge over the Suwannee River. With this end in view, on February 19 he concentrated the main body of his troops at the Little St. Marys and at Sanderson.

Union Force

The Federal force consisted of one cavalry and three infantry brigades and three batteries of artillery. Its effective strength was 5,500 officers and men and sixteen guns. About one-third were black troops, the white soldiers being mainly from New York, Connecticut, New Hampshire and Massachusetts. The Confederate force, two-thirds of whom were Georgians, consisted of one cavalry and two infantry brigades and three batteries, with an effective strength of 5,200 officers and men and twelve guns. The opposing forces, therefore, were about equal in number, except that the Federal had an advantage in artillery of four guns.

Early on the morning of February 20, the Federals set out in two columns. One advanced down the sandy road, the other along the railroad. The day was clear, and warm with the sunlight that poured through the pines. Dust from the feet of marching men formed a haze of gleaming motes between the tall trees. As the columns neared Olustee, a regiment was sent ahead to throw out skirmishers.

About an hour before noon, General Finegan sent forward his cavalry and supporting infantry with orders to skirmish with the enemy and draw them to the prepared Confederate position. Deciding, however, that General Seymour would be too cautious to attack directly a position that could be turned, he soon abandoned the idea of enticing the Federals to his line. About 12:30 P.M. he sent forward three regiments under General A. H. Colquitt with instructions to attack whatever force was met and to ask for assistance if needed. The result of this decision was that the battle was fought on an open field with no advantage of ground to either side.

The Battle Commences

The Confederate cavalry made contact with the advance Union elements about 12:30 P.M. For an hour and a half the Federal skirmish line advanced steadily, keeping up a running fire with the cavalry. The latter fell back to the crossing of the road and railroad, two and a quarter miles east of Olustee, where General Colquitt's troops were encountered. The main body of Federal troops followed slowly and advanced on the field in columns of brigades. Soon the sharp crack of rifles and the dull thud of cannon as they sent their balls crashing through the pine trees indicated that the battle had fairly begun.

The Confederate line was formed with cavalry on each flank and infantry in the center. Seymour's plan was to place his three artillery batteries in the center, with attacking infantry on each side. While attempting to deploy into position, the Federal infantry became confused and prevented effective use of their own artillery. Under tremendous fire from the Confederates, the batteries lost so many men and animals that they were forced to abandon their position, leaving six of their guns which were captured by the advancing Confederates. These events were critical, and though the Federal infantry rallied and fought gallantly they were not able to stem the Confederate advance.

Late in the afternoon the Confederates ran out of ammunition. The regiments were halted and the few who had cartridges returned a slow fire to the brisk bombardment from the other side. Staff officers, couriers, and orderlies rode at utmost speed between the front and an ammunition car on the railroad in the rear, bringing cartridges in haversacks, pockets, and caps to the men in the line. Ammunition and the last troops held back near Olustee arrived about the same time, and a general advance caused the Federals to withdraw, leaving their dead and wounded behind.

A Bloody Field

Olustee was a bloody field. Confederate casualties were 93 killed, 847 wounded, and 6 missing. The Union losses were so great—203 killed, 1,152 wounded, and 506 missing—that in Federal camps the battle was spoken of as a second Dade Massacre.

The Confederates failed to gather the full fruits of their victory by pressing the pursuit of the retreating Federals. Following slowly, within six days they pushed their lines to within a dozen miles of Jacksonville. For the remainder of the war, Union forces were confined to Jacksonville, Fernandina, and St. Augustine, from which places an occasional raiding party slipped out to harass the country.

Battle of Natural Bridge: How the Capital Was Saved

The joint military and naval operation that culminated in the Battle of Natural Bridge, March 6, 1865, was primarily a Union expedition against St. Marks and Newport. Had it been successful, the Federals might easily have captured Tallahassee, the capital, against which there had been no other serious military threat during the civil war.

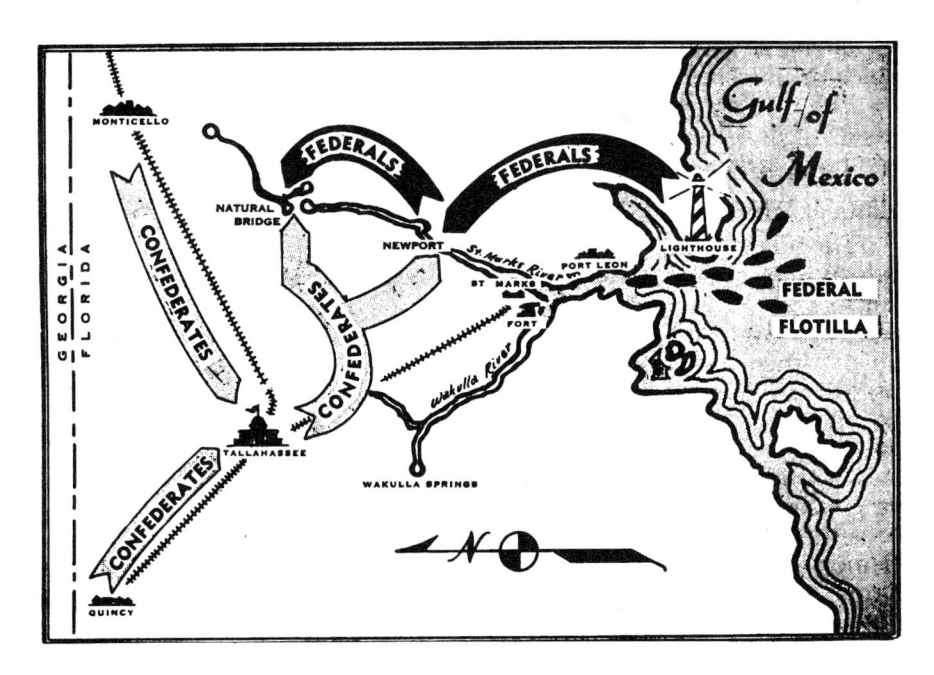

The port of St. Marks, the principal commercial outlet of Middle Florida, had been under blockade since June 22, 1861. Its business was carried on both at the town of St. Marks, situated on the west bank of the river of the same name about a mile above its confluence with the Wakulla River, and at Newport, five miles by river above St. Marks. The importance of Newport was enhanced by the existence there of a mill and iron foundry which had been converted for war use as a Confederate machine shop.

The blockade was not as effective as the Federals might have desired because the bar at the mouth of the river and the shallow waters of Apalachee Bay forced their vessels to stand off four or five miles from shore. It had been conducted with few incidents beyond the routine chasing of blockade runners and raids on Confederate salt works. Only once, in July, 1863, had there been an effort to take St. Marks, and this was on the initiative of a blockading officer who acted without orders and without preparation.

Attack on St. Marks

It was not until February 1865, that responsible Federal officers decided to attack St. Marks. Their decision was based on the belief that the enemy's effective military forces in the state were so dispersed that a raid on the town would be successful. General John Newton commanded the expedition, with which blockading ships cruising between St. George Sound and Tampa were ordered to cooperate. He sailed from Key West on February 23 and arrived with three transports off St. Marks bar on February 28. A dense fog protected the expedition from Confederate observation during the next two days, while nine blockading vessels joined the transports.

While the fleet was assembling a plan of action was devised. The objectives were St. Marks and Newport. Ships were to ascend the river and silence the battery of the fort at St. Marks. Troops were to land at St. Marks lighthouse and march to Newport, destroy the public establishments there, cross the river and take St. Marks from the rear. Preliminary to the main operations, a special detachment was to capture the East River bridge, over which the road ran from the lighthouse to Newport.

The landing of the troops had been planned for the night of Friday, March 3, but debarkation was delayed by difficulties in crossing the bar and by a heavy gale.

Alarm at Tallahassee

The affair at the bridge twenty-four hours before the main body of Federal troops could move destroyed the surprise element of the attack. News of the invasion reached Tallahassee at 9 o'clock Saturday night. The alarm was given and every man and boy capable of bearing arms answered the call. Their response was so prompt that a small body of militia and a company of West Florida Seminary cadets under General William Miller, commander of the Florida reserve forces reached Newport Saturday morning.

The Federal fleet, augmented by four more gunboats, was encountering greater difficulties than the land forces. It was unable to navigate the tortuous river channel, although seven of the lighter draft vessels made the attempt. Three of them got aground and the others, in spite of strenuous efforts, were several miles below St. Marks when word was received on Monday, March 6, that the land force was retreating.

General Newton's column, when it approached Newport Sunday morning saw smoke rising from the town. The Confederates had set afire the east end of the bridge and the iron foundry and workshops. After failing to drive out sharpshooters entrenched in rifle pits on the west bank of the river, General Newton decided to attempt a crossing at the Natural Bridge seven or eight miles above the town. Following an old and unfrequented road his main force arrived there at daybreak, Monday, March 6.

General Newton had hoped that he would not be expected at the Natural Bridge, but he found Confederates in position awaiting his arrival. Anticipating the Federal movement, General Miller had dispatched cavalry to the Natural Bridge, and General Sam Jones, commanding the military district of Florida, who arrived at Newport Sunday night, ordered the reserves, militia, two sections of artillery, and the force of militia and cadets under General Miller at Newport to the same point.

General Jones hastily entrenched his men some fifty paces north of the Natural Bridge, where his artillery commanded the passage. The position was naturally protected in front and on the flanks by sloughs, ponds, marshes, and thickets. General Newton disposed his troops on an open pine barren about three hundred yards from the bridge.

Engagement at Daylight

The engagement began at daylight when two companies of Federal troops drove the Confederate outposts over the bridge. The Federals then attempted a combined frontal and flanking attack, only to find that the enemy's position was impregnable. General Newton therefore withdrew his assault troops to the pine barren, leaving the initiative to his enemy. Early in the afternoon, the Confederates, reinforced by about 1,000 men of the 2nd Florida Cavalry, made two charges under an artillery barrage, but were unable to dislodge the Federals. The latter waited on the field for about an hour and then retreated, harassed by Confederate cavalry to the lighthouse.

The Federal forces actually engaged in the action consisted of 893 black soldiers and their white officers. Confederate forces were estimated at about 2,000. General Newton gave his losses as eight killed, 105 wounded, and 35 missing. The Confederates had three men killed and at least thirty wounded.

The Weary Banners Furled

Toward the end of the War, several Florida regiments sent their battle flags to Governor Milton for safekeeping. The Governor, in acknowledging receipt of two regimental standards, lauded the "patriotism and invincible courage" of Florida troops in the "contest for the maintenance of their right to self government—patriotism and courage which have exhibited their fixed determination to secure at all hazards, to themselves and their offspring, the enjoyment of civil liberty, unrestrained save by a constitution of their own choice, and by laws imposed in accordance with the spirit and provisions of that Constitution."

In these words John Milton expressed the motives which had actuated his own conduct during the War. Although he was a firm believer in states' rights, he recognized that the preservation of those rights in the South depended upon the success of the Confederacy. Consequently, while most other Southern governors were bickering with the Confederate government over measures that infringed the rights of the states, Milton's fixed aim was to assure the success of the common cause. When that cause was lost, he took his own life.

This 1868 drawing from Frank Leslies' Illustrated Newspaper shows "a view of the picturesque city of Tallahassee, the capital of Florida, showing the State House, and the camp of the United States troops."
Florida State Archives

426 / Civil War

Postscript: the Surrender

Brigadier General E.M. McCook was assigned to receive the surrender of the Confederate forces in Florida. The surrender began at Tallahassee on May 10, 1865. During the next month, small bodies of troops surrendered and were paroled at other places in the state. On May 20, General McCook took formal possession of Tallahassee and raised the United States flag over the capitol.

Monument at Natural Bridge State Park. Department of Commerce

The Counties

Counties in Florida date from July 21, 1821, when General Andrew Jackson, as Military Governor, divided East and West Florida into counties by this ordinance:

"All the country lying between the Perdido and Suwaney rivers, with all the islands therein, shall form one county to be called Escambia.

"All the country lying east of the river Suwaney and every part of the ceded territories, not designated as belonging to the former county, shall form a county to be called St. Johns."

A year later, on August 12, 1822, the Territorial Council provided for four counties, adding Jackson and Duval to Escambia and St. Johns, with these boundaries set forth in the act:

"... in West Florida, all that part of the Territory west of the Choctohacha river, shall constitute the County of Escambia—all that part of the Territory east of the said river to the Suwaney river shall constitute another county, to be called Jackson—and that part of East Florida lying north of the river St. Johns, and north of a line; commencing at a place called Cowford, on said river, and terminating at the mouth of the Suwaney river, shall constitute a county by the name of Duval, and all the remaining portion of East Florida shall be constituted a county by the name of St. Johns."

The "place called the Cowford" now is known as Jacksonville.

Other counties were created through the years until the last of the present 67, Gilchrist, was established on December 4, 1925. Counties may be formed at the will of the Legislature.

County Seat Location and Removal

The first seat of county government, or location of the courthouse, is usually specified in the law creating a new county. Counties generally retain the original seat but there have been removals.

The investment of tax dollars in a courthouse, jail, and similar physical properties tends to anchor the seat of county government. In some counties, pressure for change has been eased by the establishment of branches offering some or all of the courthouse services to the public.

A county seat may be changed by that county's voters at an election called by the county commission upon the petition of one-third of the qualified voters who are also taxpayers on real or personal property in the county.

Names of places for the county seat then may be placed in nomination,

---

County names taken from *Florida Place Names,* University of Miami Press, 1974, an accounting of the origin of the names of cities and other geographic features.

428 / Counties

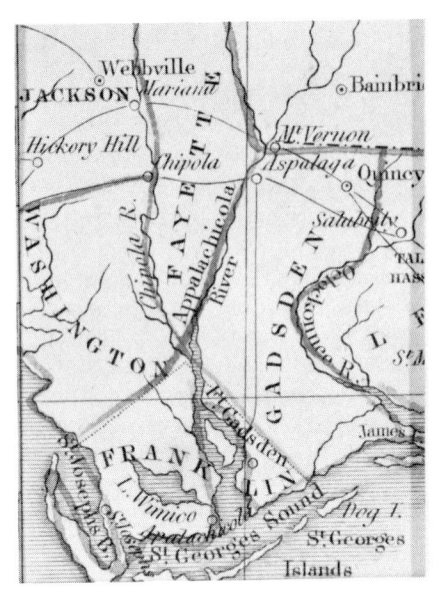

This detail of an 1838 map shows Fayette County, nestled in the "V" of the Apalachicola and Chipola Rivers. Created in 1832 and abolished in 1834, Fayette has the distinction of being the only county to pass completely out of existence. Allen Morris

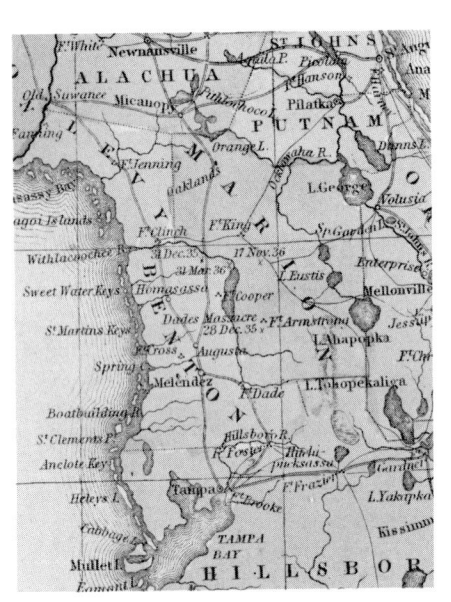

Hernando County was known for six years as Benton County, as this detail from an 1850 map shows. Allen Morris

each by 25 electors. These names are listed alphabetically on the ballot, with space provided for write-in choice. The place receiving a majority of all the votes cast, in two elections if necessary, becomes the county seat for the next ten years—twenty if a new, masonry courthouse is built.

Gulf County voted on May 26, 1964, to change its seat of government from Wewahitchka to Port St. Joe. The referendum saw 2,410 votes cast for Port St. Joe; 1,849 for Wewahitchka.

Collier County moved into a new courthouse at East Naples on September 30, 1962, completing a transfer from Everglades which began with elections in 1959. East Naples had been the choice of Collier's voters in a runoff election with Everglades. Immokalee and Naples were eliminated in the first balloting.

Two other removals:

Washington County shifted its governmental center from Vernon to Chipley in 1927. (Vernon generally is believed to have derived its name from George Washington's Mount Vernon but there are those who say the name was transferred from a place in France.) This was not, however, the first removal for Washington's seat of government. The original courthouse was located at Moss Hill, the next at Arcadia, and then Vernon.

Dade County's first seat of government was at Indian Key, being legally established there on February 4, 1836. It was moved to Miami on March 9, 1844, transferred to Juno on February 19, 1889, and reclaimed by Miami at the first legal opportunity ten years later.

The Lost Counties

Fayette confounds those who say that counties, once born, never die in Florida. Fayette was born in 1832 and died in 1834, the only county to pass completely out of existence.

Presumably named for the Marquis de Lafayette, who died in the same year as the county, Fayette filled the big "V" of the converging Chipola and Apalachicola rivers with Alabama's boundary as the cross bar. Fayette was reincorporated in Jackson County.

New River, Benton and Mosquito have disappeared from the roster of Florida counties, but only through change of name. Unlike Fayette, they live today through their direct descendants. New River has become Baker and Bradford; Benton returned to its original designation of Hernando, and Mosquito is now Orange after almost having been named Leigh Read.

Bloxham existed as a county on paper only, the voters refusing to approve its establishment. There might have been a Call County but for a gubernatorial veto. St. Lucie gave way to Brevard but the name was revived a half century later for a new county.

Origin of County Names

Notes on County Names: The date and numerical order of founding of counties were determined by Judge J. B. Whitfield, late Chief Justice of the State Supreme Court, after a study of statutes and other records.

Alachua—The ninth county, established December 29, 1824. The name can be traced to 1680 when a Spanish ranch of the name was hereabouts. There are two versions of the derivation, each with the same meaning. *La* (Spanish for "the") and *Chua* (Tlmucuan for "sink") is one and *luchuwa* (Seminole-Creek for "jug") is the other. The "sink" or the "jug" was a large chasm in the earth about two and a half miles southeast of the present site of Gainesville. *Seat: Gainesville.*

Baker—The thirty-eighth county, established February 8, 1861. Named for James McNair Baker (1822–92), Confederate States Senator and Judge of the Fourth Judicial District in Florida. *Seat: Macclenny.*

Bay—The forty-ninth county, established April 24, 1913. Named for St. Andrews Bay, on which the county borders. *Seat: Panama City.*

Bradford—The thirty-sixth county, established December 21, 1858, as New River County. Named for Capt. Richard Bradford, the first Florida officer killed in the Civil War. He died in the Battle of Santa Rosa Island, October 9, 1861, and the county was given his name on December 6, 1861. *Seat: Starke.*

Brevard—The twenty-fifth county, established March 14, 1844. Named for Theodore Washington Brevard (1804–77), a North Carolinian who came to Florida in 1847 and later became State Comptroller (1853–61). The county was originally named St. Lucie, but the name was changed to Brevard on January 6, 1855. St. Lucie was restored to the map in 1905 when another county was created and given the name. *Seat: Titusville.*

430 / Counties

Broward—The fifty-first county, established April 30, 1915. Named for Napoleon B. Broward, who, as Governor of Florida from 1905 to 1909, played a leading part in the draining of the Everglades. Earlier, he was the owner of a steam tug, *The Three Friends,* which he commanded in eluding both U.S. and Spanish authorities to supply war materials to Cuban revolutionists. He had a stormy political career. *Seat: Fort Lauderdale.*

Calhoun—The twentieth county, established January 26, 1838. Named for John C. Calhoun, the South Carolina Senator who was the foremost proponent of the doctrine of states' rights. *Seat: Blountstown.*

The twentieth county was named for John Caldwell Calhoun, shown here in an oil on canvas painted about 1823 by Charles Bird King.
National Portrait Gallery
Smithsonian Institution
Washington, D.C.

Charlotte—The fifty-seventh county, established April 23, 1921. Named from the body of water, Charlotte Harbor. Some authorities say Charlotte is a corruption of Carlos of Calos, in turn a corruption of Calusa, the name of the Indian tribe. Calos appears on Le Moyne's map of 1565 (T. De Bry, 1591), with the name applied to the southern part of the Florida peninsula. In the free-handed way of mapmakers, the English surveyors who followed the Spanish appropriated and anglicized the name as a tribute to their queen, Charlotte Sophia, wife of King George III. The Jeffreys map of 1775 shows Charlotte Harbour, formerly Carlos Bay. *Seat: Punta Gorda.*

Citrus—The forty-fourth county, established June 2, 1887. Named as a tribute to Florida's main agricultural product. *Seat Inverness.*

Clay—The thirty-seventh county, established December 31, 1858. Named for Kentucky's Henry Clay Secretary of State under John Quincy Adams and author of the saying "I would rather be right than be president." *Seat: Green Cove Springs.*

Collier—The sixty-second county, established May 8, 1923. Named for Barron G. Collier, one of the leading developers of the southern part of the state and the owner of extensive land holdings in this area. Born in Memphis, Tenn., March 23, 1873, he was graduated from Oglethorpe University. He entered the advertising business in 1890 and became one of the first great advertising tycoons, particularly in "car cards" on New York streetcars, subways, and elevated trains. *Seat East Naples.*

Columbia—The sixteenth county, established February 4, 1832. Named for the poetical name of the United States, the name that was formed from Columbus, the discoverer of America. *Seat: Lake City.*

Dade—The nineteenth county, established February 4, 1836. Named for Maj. Francis Langhorne Dade, U.S. Army, the Virginian commanding a detachment of 110 men ambushed and slaughtered near the present site of Bushnell by Seminoles, December 28, 1835. The column from Fort Brooke (Tampa) was on its way to relieve Fort King (Ocala). Only three soldiers survived. When news reached Tallahassee of the Dade Massacre, the territory's Legislative Council inserted Dade's name in a bill that was pending to create a new county. (Otherwise, Dade would be known today as Pinkney County, for William Pinkney, lawyer, statesman, diplomat, soldier. As a U.S. senator from Maryland, Pinkney gained national recognition as a champion of the slave-holding states during the debates on the Missouri Compromise.) Today this county is the most populous in Florida, the site of Metropolitan Miami. A curiosity among Florida maps is one from 1838 which shows Dade County between Alachua and Hillsborough counties. Apparently a northern cartographer assumed that the lawmakers would recognize the area of the massacre in creating a new county. *Seat: Miami.*

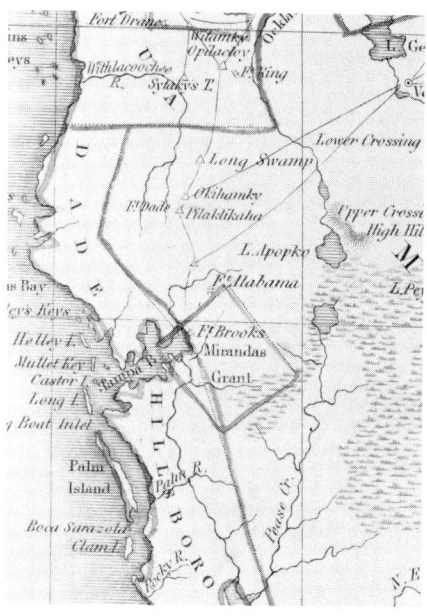

When the Legislative Council memorialized Major Francis L. Dade, the cartographer assumed the new county would be in the vicinity of the scene of the Dade Massacre. Hence, he placed Dade County between Alachua and "Hillsboro" on the west coast, as shown in this detail of an 1838 map.
Allen Morris

De Soto—The forty-second county, established May 19, 1887. This is one of two counties in Florida bearing parts of the name of the Spanish explorer Hernando De Soto with Hernando being the other, an interesting circumstance. *Seat: Arcadia.*

Dixie—The fifty-ninth county, established April 25, 1921. Named from the lyric name for the South. *Seat: Cross City.*

Duval—The fourth county, established August 12, 1822. Named for William Pope DuVal, first Territorial Governor of Florida. DuVal was born at Mount Comfort, near Richmond, Va., in 1784, the son of William and Ann (Pope) DuVal. DuVal was of French Huguenot forebears. His father was associated, as a lawyer, with Patrick Henry in the British debt cases and, as a major of riflemen, with the capture of a British vessel becalmed in the James River during the Revolution. Young DuVal left home at the age of fourteen for the Kentucky frontier, settling in Bardstown to study law. He was admitted to the bar at nineteen. He served as a captain in the mounted rangers in 1812 and as Kentucky Representative in the Thirteenth Congress (1813–15). He came to Florida as a Territorial Judge, having been appointed by

President Monroe upon the recommendation of DuVal's friend John C. Calhoun, then Secretary of War. He served about a month at St. Augustine. He was appointed governor of the Florida territory in 1822 by President Monroe; he was reappointed by Presidents Adams and Jackson. His administration was notable for the confidence that he enjoyed with the Indians. The capital was established at Tallahassee during his tenure. He was a friend of Washington Irving, who wrote of him in "Ralph Ringwood." James K. Paulding also wrote of him as "Nimrod Wildlife." DuVal uniformly signed himself as DuVal, though the name usually appears in print as Duval. DuVal moved to Texas in 1848, and Texas was his home when he died on March 18, 1854, in Washington, D.C. He was buried in the Congressional Cemetery. *Seat: Jacksonville.*

Escambia—Escambia shares with St. Johns the distinction of being one of the first two counties, each having been established July 21, 1821. The Escambia River divides Escambia and Santa Rosa counties. Simpson (1956) reports the river was shown on a 1693 map as the Río de Jovenazo, apparently honoring the Duke of Jovenazo. It also was referred to at the same time as the Pensacola River. Simpson goes on to say that while the word Escambia might be derived from the Spanish *cambiar* "to exchange or barter," "it more likely has an Indian origin, even though the derivation is unknown." Justification for this belief, he continues, "is afforded by the existence in Apalachee during the mission period of an Indian village called San Cosmo y San Damian de Escambé (or Scambé). It is possible that the prefixed 'E' represents the Spanish pronunciation of the letter 'S' when before a consonant." *Seat: Pensacola.*

Flagler—The fifty-third county, established April 28, 1917. Named for Henry Morrison Flagler, one of the two Henrys—the other being Henry B. Plant—who raced to open the east and west coasts of Florida by building railroads and hotels and operating steamships and land development companies. Flagler (1830–1913) lived two lives, the first as a Northern businessman and the associate of John D. Rockefeller in the Standard Oil Company, and the second as a promoter of Florida's east coast. The *Dictionary of American Biography* (1964) says that Flagler "brought up in poverty and trained in the stern Rockefeller school" was a grim, shrewd, rather ruthless man until he was fifty-five. Thereafter, in Florida, he continued to work, but with a new attitude toward humanity "He thoroughly enjoyed his role of builder of a state, and seemed to feel a sense of personal responsibility for every settler on his railroads, and for every one of his many employees," reports the dictionary. "They, in turn, repaid him with admiration and loyalty." Flagler first visited Florida in 1883. Good businessman that he was, even on a holiday, he believed full advantage was not being taken of Florida's natural assets. He thought the state needed better transportation and hotel facilities, and he set about providing these for the east coast. His first project was building the Ponce de León Hotel in St. Augustine, formally opened January 10, 1888. He bought the rickety, narrow-gauge Jacksonville, St. Augustine and Halifax River Railroad on December 31, 1885. Flagler's Florida East Coast Railway paced the building of a chain of hotels down the coast until Key West was officially reached on January 22, 1912. The Overseas Highway still goes to Key

West over some of the bridges and viaducts constructed for Flagler's railroad. Building of the railroad brought Flagler more than a million and one-half acres of state land, and he vigorously sought settlers, making concessions including free seed and reduced freight rates to encourage colonizing, which in turn would produce revenue for the railroad. Flagler died May 20, 1913. *Seat: Bunnell.*

Franklin—The seventeenth county, established February 8, 1832. Named for Benjamin Franklin. *Seat: Apalachicola.*

Gadsden—The fifth county, established June 24, 1823. Named for James Gadsden (1788–1858), a native of Charleston, S.C., and a diplomat who served as aide-de-camp to Gen. Andrew Jackson during the 1818 campaign in Florida. Why the Territorial Council named the county for Gadsden is not known. He had been an associate of Jackson, however, and he had been commissioned to negotiate with the Indians for their removal either to then-remote peninsular Florida or completely out of the territory. Gadsden distinguished himself nationally for what is known now as the Gadsden Purchase, which occurred long after the naming of the Florida county. As an emissary from President Franklin Pierce in 1853, Gadsden negotiated a boundary dispute with Mexico that resulted in American acquisition of 27,640 square miles, now parts of New Mexico and Arizona, for $10 million. For a short time, until the creation of Leon County, Gadsden was the seat of territorial government. *Seat: Quincy.*

Gilchrist—The sixty-seventh county, established December 4, 1925. Named for Albert Waller Gilchrist, the twentieth governor (January 5, 1909–January 7, 1913). The legislature was about to create a new county to be known as Melon when news came that former Governor Gilchrist was dying in a New York hospital. By amendment in floor consideration, Gilchrist was substituted for Melon. Gilchrist was a descendant of the grandfathers of both George Washington and James Madison. A civil engineer, land developer, and orange grower at Punta Gorda, he was a member of the House of Representatives from DeSoto County for the sessions of 1893–95 and 1903–05 and the Speaker in 1905. A bachelor, he provided money in his will to supply Halloween treats for the children of Punta Gorda. This thoughtfulness was but one of Gilchrist's beneficences; his entire estate of a half-million dollars went to charities. *Seat: Trenton.*

Glades—The fifty-eighth county, established April 23, 1921. Named for the Everglades, of which the county forms a part. *Seat: Moore Haven.*

Gulf—The sixty-sixth county, established June 6, 1925. Named for the Gulf of Mexico, which washes the southern shore of the county. *Seat: Port St. Joe.*

Hamilton—The fifteenth county, established December 26, 1827. Named for Alexander Hamilton, embattled conservative and first U.S. Secretary of the Treasury. *Seat: Jasper.*

Hardee—The fifty-fifth county, established April 23, 1921. One of four counties—Highlands, Charlotte, and Glades being the others—created in a massive division of DeSoto County. Named for Cary Augustus Hardee, who was in his first year as Governor when DeSoto was divided. Plowden (1929) reports those supporting a new county had first proposed calling it Seminole, but this name went to another new county. Later, Cherokee was suggested, along with Goolsby and Wauchula. When the bill was introduced, however, it bore the name of Hardee. Perhaps the promoters of county division wanted to make the idea more palatable to a Governor who possessed veto power. Born in Taylor County, Cary Hardee taught school and studied for admission to the bar. Upon becoming a lawyer, he began practice in Live Oak. He served as State Attorney and then was elected to the House of Representatives. His political genius may be evidenced by his selection as Speaker before he took the oath as a member of the House. He served two consecutive terms as Speaker, another rare happening, in 1915 and 1917. He was better known in later years as a banker at Live Oak than as a lawyer. He was defeated for the Democratic nomination for Governor in 1932. He died at Live Oak on November 21, 1957. *Seat: Wauchula.*

Hendry—The sixty-third county, established May 11, 1923. Name honors Capt. Francis Asbury Hendry, whose fascinating history is recited in *Hendry County's Golden Anniversary Issue of the Clewiston News,* July 12, 1973. Hendry married at nineteen and settled near Fort Meade to raise cattle. With the outbreak of the Second Seminole War, he became a dispatch bearer; riding to Fort Harvie (afterward Fort Myers), he became enchanted with the lands along the Caloosahatchee River. During the Civil War, he served the Confederacy as captain of a calvary troop he recruited in Polk County. His admiration for Gen. Robert E. Lee caused him later to give Lee's name to a new county he was instrumental in creating in 1887. After the war he moved the family home to the Caloosahatchee Valley, where cattle easily could be moved to Punta Rassa for shipment to Cuba. He platted the townsite he called LaBelle after his daughters Laura and Belle. He was elected State Senator from Monroe County, which then encompassed all of the present Lee, Hendry, and Collier counties. He promoted the incorporation of Fort Myers and served as one of its first city councilmen. Similarly, he promoted the creation of Lee County, and served as a member of its first county commission and then six terms as State Representative. He pioneered the upgrading of Florida cattle. He bought purebreds and imported grass to improve herds and pastures. With his herd containing as many as 50,000 head at one time, he was known as the "Cattle King of South Florida." He died February 12, 1917, his life having spanned a monumental epoch in Florida's history. *Seat: LaBelle.*

Hernando—The twenty-second county, established February 24, 1843. Named for the Spanish explorer Hernando De Soto. Why his first name was chosen for the county must be a historical curiosity inasmuch as his last name was selected for the county seat. De Soto's last name finally achieved county status in 1887, thus giving Florida two counties named for the same person. The name of the county seat was changed from De Soto to Brooksville. Even the name of the county was briefly lost; it was changed to Benton on March 6, 1844, to honor Thomas Hart Benton of Missouri, U.S. Senator, whose sponsorship of the Armed Occupation Act of 1842 won favor among Floridians eager to evict the Indians. Benton's moderation during the Missouri Compromise caused extremists in the Legislature to switch the name back on December 24, 1850. *Seat: Brooksville.*

Highlands—The fifty-sixth county, established April 23, 1921. The name suggests the pleasant hilliness of the area. *Seat: Sebring.*

Hillsborough—The eighteenth county, established January 25, 1834. Named for Wills Hills, the Earl of Hillsborough (1718–93), an Irish peer who in 1768 became Secretary of State for the colonies. Lord Hillsborough's office was responsible for amassing knowledge about England's possessions overseas. Those agents dispatched in Lord Hillsborough's name in turn affixed that name to places in Florida and elsewhere. Hillsborough was especially curious about Florida since he had received a large grant of land here, so he sent Bernard Romans, a surveyor and naturalist, to examine the east and west coasts of Florida. Romans regarded the Bay of Tampa exceptionally well suited to harbor a large fleet of heavy ships, with the surrounding countryside capable of furnishing timber and water. James Grant Forbes, who navigated the waters of the west coast of 1803, confirmed Romans' opinion, writing (Forbes, 1821; reprint 1964) that "Espiritu Santo, Tampa or Hillsborough Bay is the most spacious bay on the west coast of the peninsula . . . it may be justly considered the key to navigation of the British and Spanish islands to the leeward. . . ." Hillsborough appeared on some maps of the period, and later, as Hillsboro, and the shortened version may be regarded as a contraction. Lord Hillsborough, by then the first Marquis of Downshire, never saw his Florida domain. In 1956, however, a direct descendant, Arthur Wills Percy Wellington Blundell Trumbell Sandys Hills, Marquis of Downshire and Earl of Hillsborough, and his Marchioness, Maureen, were Tampa's distinguished guests during the Gasparilla festival. *Seat: Tampa.*

Hernando De Soto is remembered by the names of two counties. Florida State Archives

Holmes—The twenty-seventh county, established January 8, 1848. Named for Holmes Creek, the eastern boundary of the county (Utley, 1908). The creek was named for Holmes Valley, which received its name "either from an Indian chieftain who had been given the English name of Holmes or else from one Thomas J. Holmes, who settled in that vicinity from North Carolina about 1830 or 1834." Simpson (1956) says the belief the name derived from that of an early white settler cannot be substantiated. After Andrew Jackson occupied Spanish Pensacola in 1818, he sent a raiding party on a sweep along the Choctawhatchee River. During this raid, the troops came upon and killed the halfbreed Indian known as Holmes. Holmes was one of the so-called "Red Sticks," the disaffected Muskogee or Creeks who fled to Florida from Alabama after the Creek War of 1813–14 (American State Papers, Military Affairs, Vol. 1, 1789–1819). The first seat of Holmes County was at Hewett's Bluff, known later as Bear Pen. Cerro Gordon and Westville also served as the courthouse site before Bonifay finally was selected in 1905. *Seat: Bonifay.*

Indian River—The sixty-fifth county, established May 30, 1925. Named for the Indian River, which flows through it. *Seat: Vero Beach.*

Jackson—The third county, established August 12, 1822. Named for Andrew Jackson, who had been U.S. Commissioner and Governor of the Territories of East and West Florida and who later became the seventh President of the United States and the symbol of an emergent democracy. *Seat: Marianna.*

Jefferson—The thirteenth county, established January 20, 1827. Named for Thomas Jefferson, President of the United States, who had died on July 4th of the preceding year. *Seat: Monticello.*

Lafayette—The thirty-third county, established December 23, 1856. Named for the Marquis de Lafayette, 1757–1834. Lafayette pleaded the cause of American independence in France, lent both his prestige and military knowledge to the American Revolutionary Army by serving as a major general, and spent about $200,000 of his private fortune on behalf of the colonies. After his imprisonment and the confiscation of his estates during the French Reign of Terror, Lafayette looked to the United States to save his family from poverty. After other gifts of money and land, Congress in December 1824 appropriated $200,000 and a grant of a township of land anywhere in the unsold public domain. President Monroe was hopeful that Lafayette, then in the United States, would become a resident of Florida. "The General himself was keenly interested in the proposition, for while in Washington, he had come under the magnetic spell of Richard Keith Call, Florida's representative and her most ardent champion. A strong friendship grew up between the two men and before they separated, Lafayette halfway promised to visit Florida" (Hanna, 1932). Although Lafayette did choose a township in Florida at Tallahassee, the visit never was to be. Only once was a Lafayette in Florida; in 1850 Edmond de Lafayette and Ferdinand de Lasteyrie, grandsons of the marquis, visited the United States and conferred with their American land agent. The last of the Lafayette land was sold in

The Marquis de Lafayette chose a township in Florida, at Tallahassee, as part of his reward voted by Congress in recognition of his serives to the colonies during the Revolution. National Archives

1855, although this sale could have been accomplished years earlier if the marquis had not wished to experiment with cultivating (by free labor) vineyards, olive groves, mulberry trees, and silkworms. Some fifty to sixty Normans unsuccessfully tried to reproduce the agriculture of the Old World on a bluff overlooking Lake Lafayette. The Lafayette Grant, as the township is known, is formally Township 1 North, Range 1 East, bounded in today's Tallahassee by Meridian Road on the west, approximately Gaines Street on the south, and extends six miles to the east and six miles to the north. The popularity of Lafayette in the United States was such that forty places were named for him. *Seat: Mayo.*

Lake—The forty-third county, established May 27, 1887, being taken from Orange and Sumter counties. Named for the large number of lakes within its boundaries. When lakes were counted by the state in 1969, Lake County had 505 lakes, either named or unnamed, of 10 acres or more. *Seat: Tavares.*

Lee—The forty-first county established May 13, 1887. Named for Gen. Robert E. Lee. *See* Hendry. *Seat: Fort Myers.*

Leon—The seventh county, established December 29, 1824. Named for Juan Ponce de León, the Spanish explorer who gave Florida its name. *Seat: Tallahassee.*

Levy—The twenty-sixth county, established March 10, 1845. Named for David Levy Yulee, whose career and background are as Nixon Smiley once said in the *Miami Herald,* "almost too improbable for fiction." Yulee's father, Moses, was born in a Moroccan harem. Moses' mother, Rachel Levy, was the beautiful daughter of a Jewish physician living in England. She was on an English ship bound for the West Indies when captured by Barbary pirates. As a young virgin, Rachel was a prize for the slave market in Fez, where she was bought for Jacoub ben Youli, grand vizier to the sultan of Morocco. A revolution enabled Rachel and her small son Moses to escape to Gibraltar. In time Moses took his mother and a sister to St. Thomas in the Virgin Islands. Moses married Hannah Abendanone; in 1811 she gave birth to a son named David. When David was nine he was sent to school in Virginia and his parents moved to Florida, settling near Micanopy. Nixon Smiley observes that David was as sharp and personable as his father, and he progressed rapidly. He became a member of Florida's first constitutional convention in 1838–39, and in 1841 he was

Juan Ponce de León, who gave Florida its name, is remembered by the state's capital county, Leon.
Florida State Archives

elected territorial delegate to the U.S. Congress. After Florida was admitted to statehood in 1845, he became the first U.S. senator. He persuaded the legislature to change his name from David Levy to David Levy Yulee. A short time afterward, he married the daughter of Gov. Charles Wickliffe of Kentucky. Yulee developed a 5,000-acre plantation called Margarita, Spanish for "pearl," on the Homosassa River. His mansion there was burned by Union troops, but his sugar mill escaped. He headed a group that developed railroads, and he fought off, almost to the end of the Civil War, the efforts of the Confederate government to take up some of his rails to make connections more useful to the war effort. Yulee was imprisoned at Fort Pulaski, Ga., after the Civil War and was accused of aiding the flight of President Jefferson Davis and the Confederate cabinet. After release by order of President Grant, Yulee lived in Washington with a married daughter and died in New York in 1886. The name of the county was not changed when he changed his name, so Yulee had a county—Levy—and a community—Yulee, in Nassau County—which bore his name. *Seat: Bronson.*

Liberty—The thirty-second county, established December 15, 1855. Named for the great objective of the people who founded and built the United States. *Seat: Bristol.*

Madison—The fourteenth county, established December 26, 1827. Named for President James Madison. This county drew many of its settlers from Virginia. Carved from Jefferson County, Madison originally included the present counties of Taylor, Lafayette, and Dixie. San Pedro, on the Bellamy Road about 10 miles south of the present city of Madison, was the first county seat. The first courthouse consisted of a one-room log building with a big open fireplace in the south end. The county had perhaps 250 inhabitants, white and black. Carlton Smith, the Madison County historian, wrote that if Christopher Edwards, the first sheriff, found it necessary to travel to Oldtown, in the southeastern part of the county, he would have to go on horseback 15 miles to Charles' Ferry, then by riverboat to Fort Fanning, then on horseback or foot for the remaining 6 or 8 miles to Oldtown. Justice in those days relied upon the people of the community whenever immediate action was required. *Seat: Madison.*

Manatee—The thirty-first county, established January 9, 1855. Named for Florida's manatees, or sea cows, an endangered species. Manatees were once found as far north as the Carolinas and all around the Gulf of Mexico. Now they survive only in isolated pockets of Florida, with man their only natural enemy. When Columbus thought he saw mermaids in 1492, he likely had sighted manatees. Science has preserved a vestige of the mermaid legend—a nineteenth-century taxonomist gave the order the scientific name of Sirenia, from the Spanish *sirenas* or "mermaids." The common name manatee came from the Spanish *manati*. Manatee eat submerged aquatic plants. They usually stay submerged about five minutes but will surface once a minute when swimming because of their need for oxygen. The typical manatee is 10 feet long and weighs 1,000 pounds. They are both friendly and harmless. The reproduction rate of one calf for each adult female every three years explains the reason why the manatee has been unable to cope with man through loss of feeding areas, by hunting, and through injury resulting from the propellers of powerboats. *Seat: Bradenton.*

Marion—The twenty-fourth county, established March 14, 1844. Named for Gen. Francis Marion, the Swamp Fox of the Revolutionary War. This county drew many of its early settlers from South Carolina, the hero's native state. *Seat: Ocala.*

Martin—The sixty-fourth county, established May 30, 1925. Named for John W. Martin, Governor at the time. The belief is that the promoters insured themselves against a gubernatorial veto by giving the proposed new county the name of the chief executive. Martin was three times Mayor of Jacksonville and the Governor in 1925–29. *Seat: Stuart.*

Monroe—The sixth county, established July 3, 1823. Named for James Monroe, fifth President of the United States. His administration has become known as the Era of Good Feeling. Among other achievements of his eight years as president was obtaining the Floridas from Spain. *Seat: Key West.*

Nassau—The tenth county, established December 29, 1824. Named for the Nassau River and the Nassau Sound which, in part, separate Nassau and Duval counties. The river and the sound here and elsewhere in the United States and the capital of the Bahamas were named for the Duchy of Nassau, a former state in the western part of Germany whose seat was Wiesbaden. The line of William the Silent and his descendants, the princes of Orange-Nassau, became extinct when King William III of England died in 1702. The name was brought to Florida during the English occupation of 1763–83. *Seat: Fernandina Beach.*

Okaloosa—The fifty-second county, established June 13, 1915. The word in Choctaw *oka,* "water," and *lusa,* "black" (Read, 1934). Thus, the name probably referred to the Blackwater River in the same county. The county was taken from Santa Rosa and Walton counties. *Seat: Crestview.*

Okeechobee—The fifty-fourth county, established May 8, 1917. The name means "big water," and is derived from two Hitchiti Indian words, *oki,* "water" and *chobi* "big." The word Miami is thought to have the same meaning in another Indian dialect and to apply to the same body of water. *Seat: Okeechobee.*

Monroe County was named for James Monroe, the fifth President, who declared in his second inaugural address, in 1821, ". . . to the acquisition of Florida too much importance cannot be attached."
National Portrait Gallery
Smithsonian Institution
Washington, D.C.

Orange—The eleventh county, established December 29, 1824, under the name Mosquito. Renamed on January 30, 1845, for the many orange groves in the vicinity. *Seat: Orlando.*

Osceola—The fortieth county, established May 12, 1887. Named for the famous leader of the Seminoles, Osceola, who was imprisoned by Gen. Thomas S. Jesup after having been captured under a flag of truce. Osceola was first locked up at Fort Marion (Castillo de San Marcos) in St. Augustine; but, when some Indians escaped from there, he and other prisoners were transferred to Fort Moultrie at Charleston, S.C. Osceola died there on January 30, 1838. Weakened by chronic malaria and quinsy, he lost the will to live in captivity. "Had he not been captured under a flag of truce and sent away to die in prison, he might have died as ignominiously as many of his brethren. As it is his place as the most romantic if not the most heroic figure in the annals of the war seems secure" (Tebeau, 1971). Twenty years after the incident the criticism still was so great that Jesup found himself trying to explain his actions. Osceola was born on the Tallapoosa River, in Creek country, about 1803. Osceola is derived from the Creek *asi-yahola,* "black drink cry." The Creeks and later the Seminoles prepared a ceremonial black drink from the leaves of the yaupon. Research indicates Osceola was a half-breed: part Creek Indian, part Scottish. A Seminole leader of present days was quoted as saying that for the Seminoles, Osceola is a George Washington or an Abraham Lincoln, because of his unquenchable determination to keep the Seminoles free and to retain possession of the Indian lands (Hartley, 1974). Credit for naming the county belongs to State Senator J. Milton Bryan, who represented Orange County when Osceola was split away (Moore-Willson, 1935). The senator lived near Kissimmee, seat of Osceola. His daughter, Mrs. C. A. Carson, said: "When my father came home from Tallahassee there was a great celebration; every one in town (Kissimmee) turned out to meet him at the train and they carried him on their shoulders in celebration of the new county." *Seat: Kissimmee.*

Palm Beach—The forty-seventh county, established April 30, 1909. Named, quite logically, for the profusion of coconut palm trees on the Atlantic Ocean beach. *Seat: West Palm Beach.*

Pasco—The forty-fifth county, established June 2, 1887. Named for Samuel Pasco of Monticello, Speaker of the Florida House of Representatives at the time the county was created. Pasco was elected by the Legislature on May 19, 1887, as U.S. Senator and served until December 4, 1889. *Seat: Dade City.*

Pinellas—The forty-eighth county, established May 23, 1911, being separated from Hillsborough County across Old Tampa Bay. The peninsula that forms the larger part of the county was known to the Spaniards as Punta Pinal, said to mean "point of pines," and the present name was fashioned from that. *Seat: Clearwater.*

Polk—The thirty-ninth county, established February 8, 1861. Named for James Knox Polk, eleventh President of the United States (1845–49). Polk had the political distinction of twice being rejected for reelection as Governor of Tennessee, the last time in 1843, a year before his election as President as the first dark horse nominee of the Democratic party. He was chosen over Henry Clay and Martin Van Buren because he demanded control of the Oregon Territory from Great Britain (the historic "54-40 or fight!") and favored annexation of Texas. *Seat: Bartow.*

Putnam—The twenty-eighth county, established January 13, 1849. Named for Benjamin Alexander Putnam (1801–69), lawyer, soldier, member of the Florida legislature, judge, and first president of the Florida Historical Society. Born on the Putnam plantation near Savannah, Ga., he attended Harvard, studied law privately at St. Augustine, and practiced there. In the Seminole Indian War, 1835–42, he served as major, colonel, and adjutant general. He served in both houses of the Florida Legislature and as Speaker of the House in 1848. By appointment of President Zachary Taylor, he was surveyor-general of Florida from May 1849 to 1854. He died at his home in Palatka on January 25, 1869. *Seat: Palatka.*

St. Johns—Paired with Escambia as one of Florida's first two counties, established July 21, 1821. Named for the St. Johns River. Five names have been applied to the river in its entirety and several others to portions of the river (Snodgrass, 1967). From Miss Snodgrass we learn that the Indians give the river its first name, Welaka or Ylacco, two spellings with much the same pronunciation. A Spanish explorer called it Río de Corrientes, "River of Currents," in recognition of the spectacular way the currents at the river's mouth clashed with the surf. Jean Ribaut, a French explorer, entered the St. Johns on the first day of May, hence the name Riviere de Mai "River of May." A Spaniard, Pedro Menéndez, captured France's Fort Caroline and renamed both fort and river San Mateo. About 1590 the Spanish mission San Juan del Puerto, "St. John of the Harbor," was established and ultimately gave its name, in shortened form, to the river. For a time in the mid-1700s both San Mateo and San Juan were shown on some Florida maps as two names for the one river. During the 20-year period of British ownership of Florida, 1763 to 1783, San Juan finally became St. John's and since has remained except for the dropping of the apostrophe. *Seat: St. Augustine.*

St. Lucie—First established as the twenty-fifth county on March 14, 1844, and recreated as the forty-sixth county on May 24, 1905. Named for St. Lucie of Syracuse. According to legend, she was born in Sicily of noble parents, made a vow of virginity, and was executed in 304 A.D. for being a Christian after having been reported to the Roman authorities by a rejected suitor. More commonly spelled Lucy, the name derives from "lux" or "light," the saint has become associated with festivals of light and with prayers against blindness (Coulson, 1958). The original St. Lucie County was named Brevard County on January 6, 1855. The name of St. Lucie was first given in the area to a fort built by the Spanish near Cape Canaveral in 1565. *Seat: Fort Pierce.*

Santa Rosa—The twenty-first county, established February 18, 1842. Named for Santa Rosa Island, which in turn was named for St. Rosa de Viterbo, a Catholic saint. During Frederick II's campaign against Pope Gregory IX, Rose, then 12 years old, preached against submission to the emperor, resulting in the banishment of her family (Coulson, 1958). *Seat: Milton.*

Sarasota—The sixtieth county established May 14, 1921. The origin of the name is shrouded in dispute and legend. The Spaniards are said by one version to have so named it to designate "a place for dancing," referring to the celebrations held by the Indians on or near the shore of the bay here, but no words in modern Spanish give this meaning to the name. A legend, more colorful but more obviously fabricated, ascribes the name to a beautiful daughter of De Soto, the great Spanish explorer—Sara Sota. An Indian prince is said to have allowed himself to be taken prisoner by the Spaniards so that he could be near her; when he felt sick she nursed him back to health, only to fall sick herself and die. The Indian prince and a hundred of his braves buried her beneath the waters of the bay, then chopped their canoes with their tomahawks, and sank to death themselves. Eighteenth-century maps show the name variously as Sarasote, Sarazota, and Sara Zota. *Seat: Sarasota.*

Seminole—The fiftieth county, established April 25, 1913. Named for the Indian tribe. There is a tendency among non-Indians to think of Florida's Indians as Seminoles. Actually, there are two groups, the Seminoles and the Miccosukee. They are separated by language. The Miccosukees speak a dialect of the Hitchiti, once the most powerful Indian group in south Georgia. The Seminoles speak a dialect of the Creek, originating in Alabama. Simpson (1956) in tracing the development of the most recent aboriginal inhabitants of Florida says the name Seminole was applied by the Creeks to the emigrant Muskogean Indians who settled in Florida during the eighteenth and early nineteenth centuries. The Indians began to realize the completeness of the human vacuum in Florida subsequent to the extermination of the original aboriginal population in the early part of the eighteenth century. Simpson continues that as a consequence of the deserted condition of Florida, the names given to its natural features by the Timucuans, the Apalachians, and the Calusas were forgotten, unless preserved in the literature of European languages, and became supplanted by names derived from the languages of the immigrant Indians, from Creek and from Hitchiti. The derivation of the word Seminole is uncertain. Authorities assume that the name is a corruption of the Creek *ishti semoli*, "wild men," an epithet applied by the Creeks to these separatists, or of the Spanish *cimarrones*, "wild ones." *Seat: Sanford.*

Sumter—The twenty-ninth county, established January 8, 1853. Named for Gen. Thomas Sumter (1736–1832), a native of South Carolina who was prominent in the southern campaigns of the Revolutionary War. Many South Carolinians were early settlers in this area. *Seat: Bushnell.*

Suwannee—The thirty-fifth county, established December 21, 1858. One of the few counties in the United States whose name has been immortalized in song: Stephen Collins Foster wrote in "Old Folks at Home" about "Way down upon the Swanee River." The river that Foster spelled Swanee has become a world symbol of love for family and home. Etymologists disagree on the origin of Suwannee. Utley (1908) says the name comes from a Cherokee Indian word *sawani*, "echo river." Gannett (1947) agrees. Brinton (1859) suggests it may have been a corruption of the Spanish *San Juan*. He mentions a Shawnee tradition that their tribe originated on this river and claims that the name may be a corruption of Shawanese. Simpson (1956) says Suwannee seems to be identical with the name of a village in Gwinnett County, Ga., that stands on the site of a former Cherokee town called Suwani. According to Read (1934) the Cherokees claim their village is from Creek origin. If this is true, the derivation of the name is probably from the Creek *suwani*, "echo." Simpson mentions that good echoes are a feature of this stream. He continues, saying that the stream is probably the one called River of the Deer by De Soto. During the seventeenth century, a Franciscan mission called San Juan de Guacara was located somewhere along the left bank. This name for the river persisted despite the destruction of the mission and the change of flags; an English surveyor named Romans in 1774 called the river the River St. Juan de Guacara vulge Little Sequana. Sequana appears to be an Indian attempt to pronounce San Juan. *Seat: Live Oak.*

Taylor—The thirty-fourth county, established December 23, 1856. Named for Zachary Taylor, twelfth President of the United States and commander of the U.S. Army forces in Florida during a part of the Second Seminole War. *Seat: Perry.*

Union—The sixty-first county, established May 20, 1921. Originally, the name of the county was to have been New River, thereby reestablishing a county name that had existed from December 21, 1858, until December 6, 1861, when New River was changed to Bradford to honor a fallen soldier (*see also* Bradford). The sponsor of the bill to change the name in 1921 amended the bill to replace New River with Union. Union County was separating from Bradford, and a reason for the name the new county chose may be found in the sponsor's statement, quoted in the *Florida Times-Union* for May 6, 1921, that the counties "were united this time in asking for the divorce though the two parts of the [Bradford] county have never before been able to get together on this proposition." This explanation for the use of "Union" seems more logical than the lofty reasons used through the years, one of which has been for the "Union of the United States." *Seat: Lake Butler.*

Volusia—The thirtieth county, established December 29, 1854. Named for a landing called Volusia on the St. Johns River near Lake George. How the landing was named is uncertain. Tradition says the name is of Indian origin, but Simpson (1956) does not include Volusia. Another story attributes the name to a Frenchman or Belgian named Veluché, pronounced Va-loo-SHAY, who owned a trading post at the landing during the English period. Veiuché was then anglicized into Volusia. Gold (1927) says "there is no record either in the Spanish, Territorial or County titles of any land being owned at any time in that vicinity or in the county for that matter, under the name 'Veluche' or any name that resembles it. If such a man held title to the land under the English regime, there would be no way of ascertaining the fact, as all English titles were denied." *Seat: DeLand.*

Wakulla—The twenty-third county established March 11, 1843; name also of the famous Wakulla Springs, of a river that unites with the St. Marks River and falls into Apalachee Bay and of a community. Although the word is interpreted to mean "mystery" by some, Simpson (1956) says there is no factual basis for this meaning. "Since Wakulla was probably a Timucuan word, it is unlikely that its meaning will ever be known. It may contain the word

444 / Counties

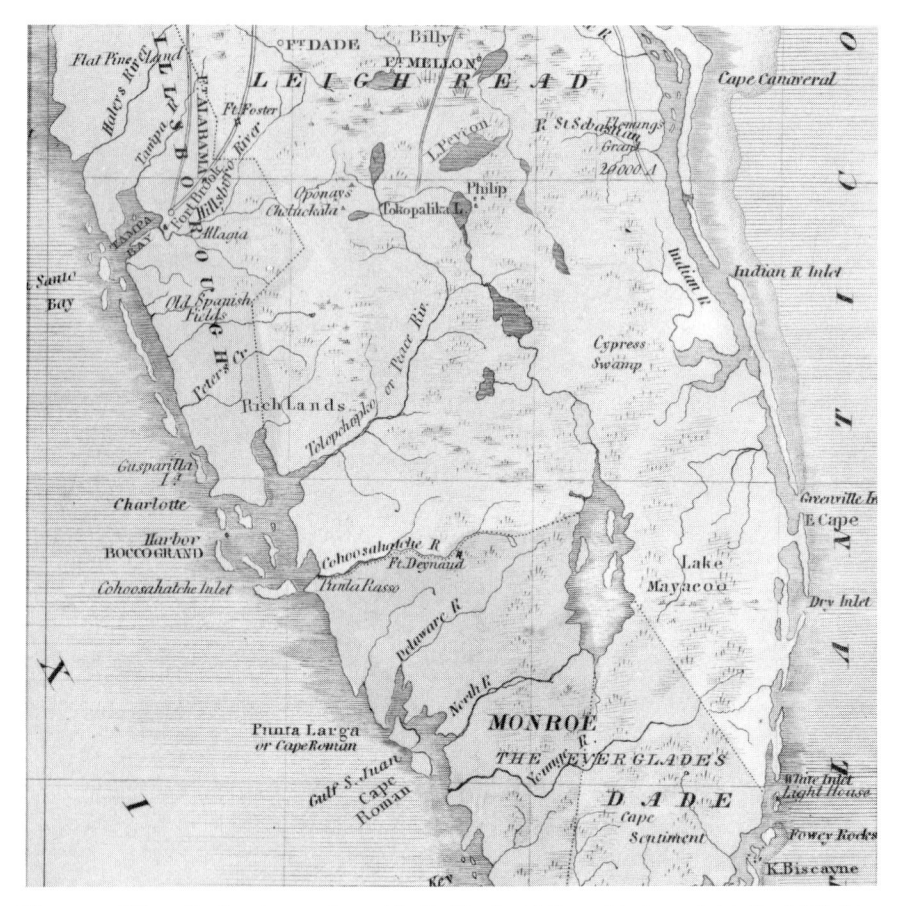

The name of Mosquito County was changed by the Territorial Council to honor Leigh Read, killed in a political duel. However, the act was not presented to the governor within the period allowed for a gubernatorial veto after the Council's sine die adjournment. The next Council did not reenact the flawed law and the county continued to be known as Mosquito. The maker of this 1842 map assumed the change had become effective, as shown by this detail. Notice also that Lake Okeechobee was called Lake Mayacoo.
Allen Morris

Kala which signified a 'spring of water' in some Indian dialects." Read (1934) suggests Wakulla comes from the Creek *wahkola,* "loon," two species of which winter in Florida. *Seat: Crawfordville.*

Walton—The eighth county, established December 29, 1824. Named for Col. George Walton, secretary of the Territory of West Florida during the governorship of Andrew Jackson, 1821–22, and of the combined territory, 1822–26. The colonel was the son of George Walton, governor of Georgia and signer of the Declaration of Independence. Colonel Walton's daughter, Octavia, suggested the name Tallahassee for the new capital. *Seat: DeFuniak Springs.*

Washington—The twelfth county, established December 9, 1825. Named for George Washington. *Seat: Chipley.*

Sources Cited

Brinton, Daniel Garrison. *Notes on the Floridian Peninsula: Its Literary History, Indian Tribes and Antiquities.* Philadelphia: Joseph Sabin, 1859.

Coulson, John, Ed. *The Saints.* New York: Hawthorn Books, 1958.

Forbes, James Grant. *Sketches Historical and Topographical of the Floridas; More Particularly of East Florida.* 1821. Reprint. Gainesville: University of Florida Press, 1964.

Gannett, Henry. *American Names.* Washington, D.C.: Public Affairs Press, 1947.

Gold, Pleasant Daniel. *History of Volusia County Florida.* DeLand Florida: The E.O. Painter Printing Company, 1927.

[Hanna], Kathryn Abbey. "The Story of the Lafayette Lands in Florida." *Florida Historical Quarterly* 10(3), January, 1932.

Hartley, William, and Hartley Ellen. *Osceola, The Unconquered Indian.* New York: Hawthorn Books, 1974.

Moore-Willson, Minnie. *History of Osceola County: Florida Frontier Life.* Orlando: The Inland Press, 1935.

Plowden, Jean. *History of Hardee County.* Wauchula: *The Florida Advocate,* 1929.

Read, William A. *Florida Place-Nanes of Indian Origin and Seminole Personal Names.* Baton Rouge: Louisiana State University Press, 1934.

Simpson, J. Clarence. *Florida Place-Names of Indian Derivation.* Edited by Mark F. Boyd, Florida State Board of Conservation Special Publication No. 1. Tallahassee, 1956.

Snodgrass, Dena. "The St. Johns: River of Five Names." In *The Florida Handbook, 1967–1968,* compiled by Allen Morris. Tallahassee: Peninsular Publishing Company, 1967.

Tebeau, Charlton W. *Florida's Last Frontier: The History of Collier County.* Coral Gables, Florida: University of Miami Press, 1966.

Tebeau, Charlton W. *A History of Florida.* Coral Gables, Florida: University of Miami Press, 1971.

Tebeau, Charlton W. *The Story of the Chokoloskee Bay Country.* Coral Gables, Florida: University of Miami Press, 1955.

Tebeau, Charlton W. *They Lived in the Park.* Coral Gables, Florida: University of Miami Press, 1963.

George Walton

George Washington

Florida Literature: Where Does It Begin and End?

Helen Muir

What exactly *is* a Florida writer? A native son or daughter who publishes, a longtime resident writing in the fields of history or nature, an entrenched scholar? Is it a winter visitor or occasional drop-in who picks up pen to describe the scene? Or is it a non-resident, who writes fiction about the long peninsula, making frequent trips to the library in search of background materials?

Could it even be a 13-year-old boy from Cartagena, carrying $25,000 in gold to see him through his education in Spain and being shipwrecked off the Florida Keys in 1545?

The answer is: any or all of the above. Florida writers present a bulky package of work. In the case of the boy from Cartagena, because Chief Carlos of the Calusas saw fit to spare his life, he spent 17 years among the Indians before being rescued by a Spanish expedition. This provided him with material for the first piece of literature about Florida. His name was Domingo Escalante de Fontaneda and his 15th Century work is known as *Fontaneda's Memoir*.

It gave Florida a headstart in accumulating its literature. Each succeeding century has provided dramatic additions, none more than the 20th Century.

On the contemporary scene, whether it is E. B. White, writing an essay called *What Do Our Hearts Treasure?* during a Christmas spent in Florida, or

---

Helen Muir is the author of *MIAMI USA*, a history of the area published by Henry Holt in 1953, reissued in paperback in 1963 by Hurricane House, revised and published by Pickering Press in 1990. She has written for national magazines (*Saturday Evening Post*, *Nation's Business*, *Woman's Day*) and her article in *This Week Magazine*, "Death of a Child," following the death of her second daughter, Melissa, is said by safety officials to have been instrumental in forcing automobile manufacturers to redesign windshields without the bar down the center. Mrs. Muir came to Miami in 1934 from the *New York Journal* to direct publicity at the Roney Plaza Hotel and since then has written columns for both the *Miami Herald* and the *Miami News*, served as children's book editor of the *Herald* and drama critic of the *News*. For three years she wrote a syndicated column from Miami. She plays an active role in the field of libraries. In 1984 Mrs. Muir, in the presence of 12,000 persons at Dallas, received the Trustee Citation of the American Library Association for, among other reasons, "her eagerness to spotlight the library at every opportunity." That year she was elected to the Florida Women's Hall of Fame at ceremonies at the Governor's Mansion. Her book, *The Biltmore; Beacon For Miami*, was published in 1987 by Pickering Press and updated in 1993. *Frost in Florida: a Memoir*, her latest work was published by Valiant Press in 1995.

the highly professional and popular John D. MacDonald producing a bestselling novel like *Condominium* from his permanent home on Siesta Key off Sarasota, it is, more often than not, the Florida touch caught in the work that encourages Florida to claim it.

The fact that Marjorie Kinnan Rawlings wrote *South Moon Under* and *The Yearling*, which won her the 1939 Pulitzer prize, transcends where she was born or lived. Yet we understand that nobody could have written those books without having been close to north central Florida and the scrub country, with its clear call to the writer in the name of love. The fact that her house stands as a museum today is fitting homage to this writer who, arriving in 1928, caught the region at a particular time, held it, then gave it to the world.

Marjorie Kinnan Rawlings — Erich Hartman

In *Cross Creek* (1942) Mrs. Rawlings wrapped the knuckles of a fellow writer who ended a poem like this: "There is no Spring in Florida." Rising to the defense of her adopted land, she wrote: "A very clever poet, Wallace Stevens . . . did not know Florida. He came as a stranger, a traveler . . . and could not differentiate."

The chastised poet would himself win a Pulitzer prize for his *Collected Poems* in 1954.

Often, there has been interplay between writers and the same Wallace Stevens had an encounter of a different sort when he had his nose bloodied in a fist fight with Ernest Hemingway.

The same year that brought Mrs. Rawlings to Florida saw Hemingway's arrival in Key West.

The Hemingway stamp is on Key West forevermore although the only novel he wrote with that setting was *To Have and Have Not*.

When he arrived that April day in 1928, he was a quarter of a century away from the Nobel prize. He and his second wife, Pauline, arrived by boat from Havana after an 18-day crossing from France on the mail packet *Orita*. He was carrying the beginning of a novel that had started out in March as a short story. When it was finished he would call it *A Farewell To Arms*.

The Hemingways came because Pauline wanted the baby she was carrying born in the United States and Ernest was eager to come home again after writing *The Sun Also Rises*. John dos Passos, who had hitchhiked through the region, praised Key West highly, calling his ride on the train "dreamlike."

Hemingway found the island city perfectly suited to his taste: writing in the morning early and fishing-swimming-wandering about the wharf the rest of the day. They stayed six weeks and returned after the birth of their son Patrick to stay for a dozen years. Hemingway called it one of his favorite

Ernest Hemingway — Helen Breaker, Paris

places to work and moved only at the breakup of his marriage. He even met his third wife, Martha Gelhorn, in Key West. Hemingway was seated on a stool in his favorite bar, *Sloppy Joe's*, that day when she and her mother poked their heads in as tourists.

When Hemingway left, another literary giant appeared in Key West.

Tennessee Williams, whose official name was Thomas Lanier Williams, burst on the scene as a dramatist with *The Glass Menagerie* (1945), then moved on steadily and surely to create *A Streetcar Named Desire*, which brought him the 1947 Pulitzer prize. The brilliant dialogue of his plays, the eloquence of his poetry, marked him as an extraordinary talent from the first. He created his own geography of the universe but Key West claimed him as one of its citizens. He died in 1983.

Florida's first bid for international literary attention occurred way back in the 17th Century with a book called *Jonathan Dickinson's Journal or God's Protecting Providence*.

It describes another shipwreck, this one off Hobe Sound, in which a young Quaker merchant, his wife and infant son, as well as a small number of Quakers, slaves and sailors returning to Philadelphia from Jamaica in 1696, were captured by Indians.

The Indians treated this small band sadistically, tearing the clothes from their backs, then taunting them with torn pages of the *Bible* with which to cover their nakedness. Beaten and starved, the party was eventually freed to walk barefoot the 230 miles to St. Augustine. Five members died.

Yale University has brought out two modern editions of this work, which was widely translated in the 17th Century.

Understandably, much of Florida's literature has been built on its natural beauty. When King George III named John Bartram "Botanist For The Floridas," it caused him to make a trip to the St. Johns River to survey his domain. That was in the winter of 1765–66 and he brought along his son, William.

Portions of that trip were published but it remained for William Bartram's *Travels* (1791), to capture the world's attention as the 18th Century waned.

This book reached out across the broad Atlantic to catch the senses of Coleridge and Wordsworth, as well as the French romantic Chauteaubrind. Each seized on it to create descriptions and figures of speech highly recognized as stemming from Bartram.

In the 19th Century writers poured into Florida.

John James Audubon came in 1831 to investigate bird life and his writings speak as eloquently as the gorgeous paintings. He was followed by naturalists of the quality of John Muir, who made his march from Fernandina to Cedar Key as a young man, notebook swinging from his belt, jotting down observations to be later published in *A Thousand Mile Walk to the Gulf*. He tramped through cypress swamps to see a palm forest and found "tall palms which told me grander things than I ever got from a human priest." The naturalists would keep coming, well into the 20th Century: Charles Torrey Simpson, David Fairchild, John C. Gifford, and Thomas Barbour among others. They would write the books to leave behind when they were gone and "no more seen."

Helen Muir
In Miami, USA, *Helen Muir wrote the definitive history of her home town.*

So would the fiction writers.

Henry James, novelist and critic, never married and travel and literature were his two vital interests. He waited for the railroad to transport him but he too looked on the palm tree and reported: "I found myself loving quite fraternally the palms which had struck me at first for all their humanheaded gravity as merely dry and taciturn but which became finally as sympathetic as so many rows of puzzled philosophers."

Stephen Crane was shipwrecked on the *Commodore* on January 1, 1897 off New Smyrna but made it to Daytona Beach in a dinghy which broke up coming ashore. The author of *The Red Badge of Courage* wrote a short story for *Scribner's Magazine*, *The Open Boat*, turning the experience into a lasting piece of literature.

William Cullen Bryant wrote *A Tour of the Old South*. Georgia poet Sidney Lanier created *Song of the Chattahoochee*. Even Ralph Waldo Emerson enthused about Florida.

Magazine fiction flourished. As early as August, 1821, *Blackwood's Edinburgh Magazine* published *The Florida Pirate* by M. M. Ely in Scotland. Next in time of publication came four stories by the great American writer Washington Irving which included *The Early Experiences of Ralph Ringwood* and *The Conspiracy of Neamathla*, in *Knickerbocker Magazine*.

James Fenimore Cooper's *Jack Tier, or, The Florida Reef* appeared first in *Graham's Magazine*. All the stories mentioned were later published in book form as were the stories Constance Fenimore Woolson sold steadily to *Lippincott's, Appleton's Journal* and *The Atlantic Monthly*.

Travelling writers left a trail of record. Some settled in.

Harriet Beecher Stowe, *Uncle Tom's Cabin* behind her, wrote *Palmetto Leaves* and helped stir the tourist boom along the St. Johns. And, when tourists came to gape at her Mandarin farm, they found a visit would cost them twenty-five cents.

Kirk Munroe, an editor of *Harper's Magazine,* became so enamoured of the region he wrote boy's adventure stories continuously during this period, then settled in South Florida permanently. His wife, Mary Barr, was the daughter of Amelia Barr, who wrote *Remember The Alamo.* The Kirk Munroes put a literary stamp on early Coconut Grove that exists to this day.

This is where Marjory Stoneman Douglas lives, where she wrote *Everglades: River of Grass,* now in its 12th printing, the classic which begins: "There is no other Everglades in the world." Hodding Carter compared it to William Bartram's *Travels.*

There is scarcely a Florida road that this intrepid writer has missed in the intervening years while piling up a literary reputation and establishing herself as a formidable opponent in an environmental fight. She won an O. Henry Award for one of her *Saturday Evening Post* short stories, *He-Man,* another prize for a play, *Gallows Gate.* A juvenile, *Freedom River* and a boom-time novel, *Road To The Sun* are among her published works. On her 96th birthday on April 7, 1986, Mrs. Douglas attended a dinner in Washington, D.C. where the National Parks and Conservation Association named an award for her. The week before she was in Seattle receiving the National Wildlife Award. Shortly before that she was elected to the Florida Women's Hall of Fame.

Another measure of the way she is viewed in Florida was indicated when the State named its Department of Natural Resources Building for her. A series of celebrations marked her 100th birthday, but on her 102nd birthday in 1992 the State of Florida outdid itself by purchasing her home for $140,000 to establish an environmental study center following her death and giving her a life estate. And when she was 103 she travelled to the White House to receive the Presidential Medal of Freedom from President Clinton.

In the Fall of 1994, when she was 104, Valiant Press brought back "Freedom River," a 1953 youth book by Mrs. Douglas, to loud applause.

It was Hervey Allen who persuaded Mrs. Douglas to write *Everglades,* her first and most lasting book. He was the author of *Carolina Chansons,* a volume of verse written with DuBose Heyward and also wrote an acclaimed biography of Poe, *Israfel,* before the bestseller, *Anthony Adverse.*

He proved a catalyst among South Florida writers and served as friend and encourager to Charles H. Baker, Jr. who dedicated his naturalistic novel *Blood Of The Lamb,* which is laid in Central Florida, to Hervey. He talked his friend Robert Frost into purchasing five acres of land close by his own home, *The Glades.* Frost, a four times Pulitzer prizewinner for his poetry, followed his friend's idea of placing pre-fabricated houses on his place, calling it *Pencil Pines* and settled in for a couple of decades until his death. He arrived punctually each late January after lecturing at the University of Florida at Gainesville and became a familiar figure in Coconut Grove and South Miami, tending his fruit trees, shopping around, once arriving at his favorite fishmonger's by taxi, dressed in a bathrobe, after having been put to bed by his physician.

Hervey Allen even had a hand in *Generation of Vipers,* the Philip Wylie book which the American Library Association in 1950 declared one of the major non-fiction works of the first half century.

Allen, who had emerged from World War I as a poet, saw in the 1940s a Mother's Day Army formation of soldiers spelling out the word "Mom." He sputtered in the presence of Wylie, a highly successful fiction writer, with a devoted following for his Crunch and Des deepsea fishing stories in the *Saturday Evening Post*. He had just begun to write *Vipers*. Next day Wylie included the chapter on "Mom."

Wylie was deeply involved in the environment and used the word ecology when many were just beginning to look it up in the dictionary.

It was 1925 when Philip Wylie landed a job on *The New Yorker*. That was the year Zora Neale Hurston landed at Barnard College as a Franz Boas anthropology student. By the 1930s both were on their way to building literary reputations.

Florida native Zora Hurston was born around the turn of the century in Eatonville, an all-black community. Zora's mother died when she was nine years old and, in her teens, she escaped from Eatonville as a lady's maid with a Gilbert and Sullivan touring company.

It is fascinating that during the Harlem Renaissance period of the 1930s she wrote three novels, plays, essays, stories and two social anthropology works. Her writing was electric with vitality and joy.

Blacks had made their mark in literature before Hurston wrote *Jonah's Gourd Vine, Mules and Men* and the lyrical *Their Eyes Were Watching God*, which is set around Lake Okeechobee migrant camps.

Zora Neale Hurston Florida State Archives

There was poet and novelist Paul Lawrence Dunbar, whose parents had been slaves and who contributed highly popular work before his death in 1906. Then there was James Weldon Johnson of Jacksonville, a remarkable man who taught school, became the first black man admitted to the Florida Bar and was very much on the New York scene as collaborator with his brother, J. Rosamund Johnson, of popular songs and light opera.

He wrote *Autobiography of an Ex-Colored Man*, a piece of fiction published anonymously, served as U.S. Consul in Venezuela and became the first executive secretary of the NAACP.

James Weldon Johnson National Portrait Gallery

Frank S. Slaughter Marsh-Kornegay

Hurston took a counter position to the NAACP and her onetime collaborator Langston Hughes. She insisted on "not being tragically colored" and, impishly, took to calling fellow writers "Negrotarians" and "nigerati." The differences went deep.

To the end, Hurston bridled at the idea of "race" as an issue. In 1950 she turned up as a maid in a Miami Beach home. When one of her stories was published in the *Saturday Evening Post*, she was fired. It made her employers uncomfortable to learn of her literary standing. When she died in 1960 she was out of fashion and penniless.

Happily, a new generation is discovering her with publication of *I Love Myself When I Am Laughing . . . and Then Again When I Am Looking Mean and Impressive: A Zora Neale Hurston Reader,* edited by Alice Walker, who won a Pulitzer for *The Color Purple.*

In this skeleton of literary movement in Florida, certain books and writers cry out for mention: Stephen Vincent Benet's *Spanish Bayonet*, Theodore Pratt's *The Barefoot Mailman* and Cecile Hulse Matschat's *Suwannee River;* later works such as Patrick D. Smith's *Forever Island*, the Zachary Ball *Joe Panther* series, Robert Wilder's writings—and so many more. Historians like Rembert Patrick, Kathryn Abbey Hanna and Alfred Jackson Hanna, Charlton Tebeau and writer James Branch Cabell, who combined with Dr. Alfred Hanna to write *The St. Johns,* leap to mind. So does Nixon Smiley who wandered the state gathering stories and photographic studies for his books. Nor can we forget Dr. Frank G. Slaughter of Jacksonville whose French publisher called him "The American Balzac." The death of Gloria Jahoda removed a vibrant voice from the Florida scene.

In 1981, Howard Kleinberg, the editor of the now defunct *Miami News* began to delve back in the files of the newspaper, originally called *The Metropolis*, to reprint a series of stories as a regular feature. When compiled in book form, they launched him on a new career as an historian. His book *Miami Beach: A History* was published in 1994.

Still, it is nice to know that attention is paid and in Florida attention has been paid to a large number of writers beginning with Michael Shaara of Tallahassee, an inspired teacher whose haunting re-creation of the Battle of Gettysburg, *The Killer Angels,* won him the Pulitzer Prize and after his death was turned into a smashing motion picture *Gettysburg.* Dr. Richard Granberry was tapped for the O. Henry Collection with *A Trip to Czardis.*

In the field of children's literature winners abound. Jean Lee Latham of Coral Gables won the Newbery Medal for *Carry On, Mr. Bowditch (1955).* The same medal went to Elaine Konigsburg of Jacksonville for *From The Mixed-Up Files of Mrs. Basil E. Frankweiler* (1968). Other Newbery winners are Irene Hunt of St. Petersburg (1966) for *Up A Road Slowly* and Lois Lenski for *Straw-*

berry Girl (1945). Evaline Ness of Palm Beach, a picture book illustrator, has won several honors, including the Caldecott Medal for *Sam, Bang and Moonshine* (1967).

One feels that when a young writer like Madeleine Blais is awarded a Pulitzer prize for her *Miami Herald* interviews, including one with Tennessee Williams, and Joy Williams of Sarasota is singled out for a National Magazine Award, all in the same period of time, the end of Florida's involvement with literature is not in sight.

Joy Williams, whose first novel *State of Grace* established her as a serious writer, has had stories in numerous anthologies including the O. Henry Prize Story Collection (1966).

Florida today is alive with writers: from Donn Pearce of *Cool Hand Luke* fame to Harry Crews, whose literary reputation advances with each book, beginning in 1968 with *The Gospel Singer*.

In Key West, where Thornton Wilder wrote *The Matchmaker* and the likes of Archibald MacLeish, S. J. Perelman and Hart Crane held forth, writers like James Leo Herlihy, who wrote *Midnight Cowboy,* Thomas McGuane, whose 92 *In The Shade* caused a *New York Times* reviewer to speak of his "brave play of language at the brink of inexpressible horror, " and Philip Caputo, whose *Rumor of War* was awarded the Pulitzer, took their place. Novelist Evan Rhodes chose Key West in which to write *An Army of Children.* More Pulitzer prizewinners answering the call of the island city include Joseph P. Lash, Richard Wilbur and John Hersey. It has become the site of the annual Key West Literary Seminar and Festival with the well known writers and critics appearing in midwinter to call attention to Hemingway, Tennessee Williams and others. In the Spring of 1994 the first annual Robert Frost Poetry Celebration was launched.

Douglas Fairbairn, Coconut Grove novelist, arrived there as a boy, attended public schools, studied painting, went to Harvard. His books, *Shoot* and *Street 8,* sold to the movies. Two delightful volumes deal with taking a pet squirrel into his home. They are *A Squirrel of One's Own* and *A Squirrel Forever.* His last book, *Down and Out in Cambridge,* received critical acclaim and contains rich episodes of Florida during the depression.

The 1980's provided an outpouring of books on Florida with Miami the hot spot. Into the seething scene writers like John Rothchild (*Up For Grabs*) and David A. Kaufelt (*American Tropic*) were followed by a series of books dissecting events in the Magic City. They included Joan Didion's (*Miami*), David Reiff's (*Going to Miami*) and T.D. Allman's (*Miami: City of the Future*). The latter did so well it was decided to issue it in Spanish.

The *Miami Herald's* Edna Buchanan won a Pulitzer for her work as a crime reporter and became the subject for a profile by Calvin Trillin in the *New Yorker* magazine. Following that she wrote a book about crime in Miami, calling it *The Corpse Had a Familiar Face.* It is finding its way into translations for foreign export, a measure of the international interest in Miami. Other books followed.

Another *Herald* writer, Carl Hiaasen, a native-born Floridian schooled in investigative reporting, is on his way to fame and fortune while in his early thirties. His biting wit and fine sense of irony is exhibited in the fast-moving *Tourist Season* and *Double Whammy,* both of which have been received warmly by critics, as have later works.

The 1990's ushered in a much acclaimed first novel, *The Perez Family*, by Christine Bell about Cubans in Miami. In 1994 Evelyn Wilde Mayerson, a University of Miami professor, who had helped usher in the '90's with *Well and Truly*, received the nod from the Literary Guild for *Miami: A Saga*, her sixth novel. She has also written three works of non-fiction and two children's books. She is a Miami native.

Literature, like life, goes on. As Florida grows, so grows its literature. Writers, like everyone else, are continually drawn to Florida by climate.

Today in downtown Miami the Miami International Book Fair attracts distinguished authors, droves of avid readers and book purchasers. It has become the leading such event in the nation.

A gifted young poet, Susan Mitchell, a bona fide Florida resident from Boca Raton, read her work at the 1992 Fair. Even more importantly, the volume *Rapture* was nominated for a National Book Award.

One remembers the lad from Cartagena, being sent to Spain to be educated and carrying $25,000 in pure gold but ending up in South Florida with Indians and then providing Florida with its first piece of literature.

Today there are writers living in Florida, refugees from Castro's Cuba and elsewhere. They come without gold mostly but with glittering literary reputations. We call the names of only a few: Enrique Labrador Ruiz, Lydia Cabrera and Carlos Montenegro.

It makes a nice dramatic twist, doesn't it?

An illustration from Lois Lenski's Strawberry Girl.

Florida Names to Remember

Marjory Stoneman Douglas— (April 7, 1890–). Her mailbox in Coconut Grove carries the initials MSD but the world knows her as Marjory Stoneman Douglas, a fierce foe in any environmental battle, saviour of the Everglades and writer about South Florida for seven and a half decades.

On April 7, 1990 she celebrated her 100th birthday anniversary at a mammoth picnic at Crandon Park with the public invited to come and bring their own basket of food. Every Dade County Library served free birthday cake to patrons that day as a bow to her contributions to literature and to Florida.

Marjory Stoneman Douglas   c-Ray Fisher

The honors for this Minnesota native, who was raised in Massachusetts and educated at Wellesley College, have been too numerous to mention but she takes it all in stride, turning out to speak in flowing phrases for her causes.

And when the public birthday party was ended she turned to close friends for a private party with cake and champagne and the required pre-dinner scotch whiskey.

On that occasion she pointed out that "age is all very comparative. Keeping busy is the answer. I don't see and I don't hear but those things can happen at any age."

Florida named its Department of Natural Resources headquarters for her and her book, *The Everglades: River of Grass*, a monument to the fact that Marjory was here and stayed, actively concerned, and earned a place in the sun. And in 1993 she was awarded the Presidential Medal of Freedom in the White House.

For More about Mrs. Douglas, read—

Alligator Crossing: a Novel. New York: J. Day Co., 1959.
Everglades: River of Grass. New York: Rinehart, 1947; rev. ed. Atlanta: Mock-

---

The original basis for selecting the Floridians to be remembered is detailed in the 1965–1966 edition of *The Florida Handbook.*

ingbird, 1974; rev. ed. Miami: Banyan Books, 1974; rev. ed. Englewood, Florida: Pineapple Press, 1988.
Florida: the Long Frontier. New York: Harper & Row, 1967.
Florida's Calamity Calendar 1984. Winter Park, Florida: Florida Conservation Foundation, 1983.
Freedom River: Florida, 1845. New York: Scribner, 1953.
Gallows Gate, a Play in One Act. Boston: Walter Baker, 1931.
Hurricane. New York: Rinehart, 1958; Atlanta: Mockingbird Books, 1976.
The Joys of Bird Watching in Florida. Miami: Hurricane House, 1969.
Road to the Sun. New York: Rinehart, 1951.

Napoleon Bonaparte Broward—(April 19, 1857–October 1, 1910) is a former Governor of Florida remembered primarily for commanding the small steamer *Three Friends* on several filibustering expeditions to Cuba in 1896. He landed men and munitions on the coast of that Spanish colony, eluding both Spanish and American warships.

Broward had been active in Duval county governmental affairs and the fame of his eight voyages through the Spanish blockade with war material for Cuban revolutionists earned him statewide recognition which was helpful in bringing about his election as Governor in 1904. Broward gave energetic leadership to drainage of the Everglades, a project which had been agitated for a half century.

During the Broward gubernatorial administration (1905–09), 13 miles of canal were dredged and the State committed to doing the job of drainage.

Broward also provided the impetus for unifying the State system of institutions of higher learning under a Board of Control. He helped obtain greater State aid for public schools, reform of primary elections, and supervision of public transportation.

[For other information, see chapter on Governors.]

For More about Broward, read—

Dictionary of American Biography, vol. 3, p. 96.
National Cyclopaedia of American Biography, vol. 14, p. 59.
Broward, Napoleon Bonaparte. *Autobiography, Letter and Short Story of the Steamer "Three Friends," and a Filibustering Trip to Cuba.* n. p. (1904) 40 p.
Buford, Rivers H. "Napoleon B. Broward" in *Apalachee,* 1946, p. 1–4.
Proctor, Samuel. *Napoleon Bonaparte Broward, Florida's Fighting Democrat* (Gainesville, University of Florida Press, 1950) 400 p.
Proctor, Samuel. "The Years of the Governorship" in *Florida Historical Quarterly,* vol. 26, pp. 117–134.
Makers of America, Florida Edition, vol. 4, p. 17–22.

Osceola—(around 1800–January 30, 1838) is certainly the best known now of the Indians who resisted efforts of the United States government to clear Florida of the Seminoles by transporting them across the Mississippi.

As Marjory Stoneman Douglas says, Osceola is "not just a legend, but very real and very great."

There was so much dramatic about the life of Osceola, and even beyond life in death, that it is easy to understand why he has been used as a central character in works of fiction by a number of the bestselling authors of today.

When other Indian leaders simply refused to acknowledge a treaty of submission, Osceola is said to have emphasized his defiance by plunging a dagger into the document put before him for signature. He fought the United States with ruthless daring, and was captured only after coming into camp under a flag of truce.

While General Thomas S. Jesup, the American commander, never lived down the public revulsion which followed this violation of the truce, Osceola remained in prison, first at the Castillo de San Marcos in St. Augustine and later at Fort Moultrie, South Carolina. Osceola died there, and his head was removed from the body before burial.

Osceola was likely born on the Tallapoosa River among the Creek Indians in what is now Georgia. He may have fought against Andrew Jackson. Osceola earned his place of leadership among the Seminoles by the force of his personality and ability, for he was neither born nor selected as a chief.

For More about Osceola, read—

Dictionary of American Biography, vol. 14, p. 76.
National Cyclopaedia of American Biography, vol. 9, p. 211.
Bland, Ceclia, *Osceola, Seminole Rebel,* New York: Chelsea House, Pub., 1994.
Goggin, John M. "Osceola: Portraits, Features, and Dress" in *Florida Historical Quarterly,* vol. 33, p. 161–192.
Hartley, William, and Hartley Ellen, *Osceola, the Unconquered Indian,* New York: Hawthorn Books, 1974.
McCarthy, Joseph Edward. "Portraits of Osceola and the Artists who Painted Them" in *Papers, Jacksonville Historical Society,* vol. 2 (1949), pp. 23–44.
McKinney, Thomas L. and Hall, James. *The Indian Tribes of North America,* vol. 2 (Edinburgh: John Grant, 1934) "Osceola (Asseola) A Seminole Leader," pp. 360–392.
Ward, May NcNeer. "The Disappearance of the Head of Osceola" in *Florida Historical Quarterly,* vol. 33, p. 193–201.
Wickman, Patricia R. *Osceola's Legacy.* (Tuscaloosa: Univ. of Alabama Press, 1991).

Osceola has figured prominently in fiction. Some of the novels in which he is a central character are the following:
Pope, Edith (Taylor). *River in the Wind* (New York: Scribner, 1954).
Pratt, Theodore. *Seminole* (New York: Fawcett, 1954).
Slaughter, Frank Gill. *The Warrior* (New York: Doubleday, 1956).
Wilder, Robert. *Bright Feather* (New York: G.P. Putnam's 1948).

John Gorrie—(October 3, 1802–June 29, 1855) had in mind the salvation of fever sufferers when he conceived the idea of artificially cooling the air. From Dr. Gorrie's humanitarian experiments at Apalachicola have grown the commercial manufacture of ice and today's general usage of air conditioning.

Public acceptance of Dr. Gorrie's invention was the traditional course of rejection and neglect. He was unable to obtain financing for a plant to prove the worth of what he had demonstrated experimentally. This failure brought on nervous collapse and he died at 52.

In 1900, the Southern Ice Exchange recognized the industry's debt by erecting a monument to Dr. Gorrie's memory at Apalachicola, and in 1914 the State of Florida caused a statue of Dr. Gorrie to be placed in the Capitol at Washington as one of the two allowed each state.

John Gorrie was born in Charleston, South Carolina. He continued his medical education in Fairfield, New York, being graduated there in 1827 from the College of Physicians and Surgeons. He came in 1833 to Apalachicola, then an important cotton port, from Abbeville, South Carolina, where he first practiced medicine.

He achieved immediate acceptance as a physician and as a civic leader in Apalachicola. He became Postmaster in 1834, and served for four years. He was a City Councilman, City Treasurer, and Mayor until in 1839 he renounced public office to devote full time to his profession and related research. Ultimately, in 1845, he narrowed his energies to seeking a feasible way of artificial refrigeration to ease the fevers of malaria and other sufferers.

By 1850, Dr. Gorrie had learned how to make ice experimentally. Gorrie's patent, No. 8080, granted May 6, 1851, is said to be the first United States patent on mechanical refrigeration.

For More about Dr. Gorrie, read—

Dictionary of American Biography, vol. 7, p. 436–437.
National Cyclopaedia of American Biography, vol. 15, p. 345.
Becker, Raymond B. *John Gorrie, M.D. Father of Air Conditioning and Mechanical Refrigeration.* (New York: Carlton Press, 1972), 206 p.

Howe, George D. "The Father of Modern Refrigeration" in *Florida Historical Quarterly*, vol. 1, no. 4 (Jan. 1909), pp. 19–23. Reprinted from *Uncle Remus Magazine*, Nov. 1908.

Jelks, Edward. "Dr. John Gorrie, Inventor of the First Artificial Ice Machine," in *Annals of Medical History*, vol. 3, no. 4, pp. 387–390. Also in *Jacksonville Historical Society Annual*, 1933–1934, pp. 76–80.

Mier, Ruth E. "More About Dr. John Gorrie and Refrigeration" in *Florida Historical Quarterly*, vol. 26, no. 2 (Oct. 1947), pp. 167–173.

Rand, Clayton. *Sons of the South* (New York: Holt Rinehart, and Winston, 1961), p. 70, "John Gorrie."

Taylor, H. Marshall. "John Gorrie: Physician Scientist, Inventor" in *The Southern Medical Journal*, vol. 28, no. 12, pp. 1075–1082.

Whiteside, George H. "Sketch of the Career of the Original Inventor of the Ice Machine or the Mechanical Production of Ice and Refrigeration" in *Ice and Refrigeration*, May 1897. Additional articles in the issues of June 1900, August 1901, and June 1914.

Henry Bradley Plant—(October 27, 1819–June 23, 1899) first came to Florida in 1853 so his first wife could cope with a lung congestion in the sunshine at the home of friends near Jacksonville.

His wife's health also caused Plant, a Connecticut Yankee, to become the Southern manager for the Adams Express Company. With the outbreak of the Civil War, Plant converted the Adams properties within the Confederate States to the Southern Express Company. So valuable were his services to the Confederacy that Plant was excused from the prohibition against Northerners remaining in the South without becoming Confederate citizens.

In New York at the end of the Civil War, Plant returned South with money and promises of more to invest in railroads. Plant put together what was known as the "Plant System" with rails fanning out in Florida from Jacksonville to Palatka, Sanford and Tampa. He added steamships to his interests. By 1895, he controlled 1,484 miles of railroad lines and 1,288 miles of coastal steamer lines, each largely in Florida.

Plant has been called the "father of Tampa," for he erected there a Moorish palace known as the Tampa Bay Hotel, developed a deepwater terminal at Port Tampa, and generally stimulated the growth of the community. There was a lively competition between Plant and his onetime business partner, Henry M. Flagler, and biographer Charles E. Harner reports some historians have it that Flagler responded to Plant's invitation to the opening of the Tampa Bay with a telegram saying, "Where is Tampa Bay?" To which Plant is said to have responded, "Just follow the crowd."

As did Flagler on the east coast, Plant built the Tampa Bay and other luxury hotels to provide business for his railroad.

For More about Plant, read—

Dictionary of American Biography, vol. 7, pp. 646–647.
National Cyclopaedia of American Biography, vol. 18, pp. 286–287.
Covington, James W. "The Tampa Bay Hotel" in *Tequesta,* vol. 26, p. 3–20.
Harner, Charles E. *Florida's Promoters.* (Tampa: Trend House, 1973) p. 18–27, "The Connecticut Yankee Who Helped Revive the South."
Johnson, Dudley S. "Henry Bradley Plant and Florida" in *Florida Historical Quarterly,* vol. 45, pp. 118–131.
Rand, Clayton. *Sons of the South.* (New York: Holt, Rinehart and Winston, 1961) p. 172, "Henry Bradley Plant."
Smyth, G. Hutchinson. *The Life of Henry Plant.* (New York: G. P. Putnam's Sons, 1898).

Hamilton Disston—(August 23, 1844–April 30, 1896) bought 6,250 square miles of Florida, saved the state from bankruptcy and developed rich farm lands in the heart of the peninsula while Flagler and Plant were opening the east and west coasts.

As historian Kathryn Abbey Hanna wrote: "The significance of his influence cannot be overstated. It is difficult to see how the peninsula could have flowered as it did without some initial push of this kind."

Often overlooked nowadays in considering the State's sale of 4,000,000 acres to Disston and associates for $1,000,000 ($200,000 in cash), is the fact that litigants already had appealed to the Federal court to sell all lands belonging to the State's Trustees of the Internal Improvement Fund. The forced sale of 14,000;000 acres would have been a disaster.

The Disston purchase at 25 cents an acre was more of a gamble for Disston than it was to the State for until he came along no one was interested in purchasing the "swamp and overflowed" land conveyed to the State by the Federal government in 1850, with any sale subject to the marshland being drained.

Disston, never a millionaire, was caught short of cash by the Panic of 1893. As biographer Charles E. Harner reports, the dredges stopped working and the steamboats quit running. "The boss was out of money." He attended the theater one evening in his native Philadelphia, went home, filled a tub in his bathroom, sat down in the water and shot himself in the head.

For More about Disston, read—

Davis, T. Frederick. "The Disston Land Purchase" in *Florida Historical Quarterly,* vol. 17, no. 3 (January 1939), pp. 200–210.

Dodson, Pat. "Hamilton Disston's St. Cloud Sugar Plantation, 1887–1901", in *Florida Historical Quarterly*, vol. 49, no. 4 (April 1971), pp. 356–369.

Hanna, Alfred J. and Kathryn A. *Lake Okeechobee, Wellspring of the Everglades* (Indianapolis: Bobbs-Merrill, 1948), pp. 91–104, "Disston's Kingly Domain."

Harner, Charles E. *Florida's Promoters* (Tampa: Trend House, 1972), pp. 12–17, "Disston's Million Dollar I.O.U. Rescued Florida from Bankruptcy".

Mueller, Edward A. "Kissimmee Steamboating" in *Tequesta*, vol. 26 (1966), pp. 53–66.

Henry Morrison Flagler—(January 2, 1830–May 20, 1913) led two lives, the first as a Northern businessman and the associate of John D. Rockefeller in the Standard Oil Company, and the second as a master developer of Florida's east coast.

The Dictionary of American Biography says Flagler, "brought up in poverty and trained in the stern Rockefeller school," was a grim, shrewd, rather ruthless man until he was 55. Thereafter, in Florida, he continued to work but then with a new attitude toward humanity.

"He thoroughly enjoyed his role of builder of a state, and seemed to feel a sense of personal responsibility for every settler on his railroads and for every one of his many employees," reports the Dictionary. "They, in turn, repaid him with admiration and loyalty."

Flagler first visited Florida in 1883. Good businessman that he was, even on a holiday he believed that full advantage was not being taken of Florida's natural assets. He thought the state needed better transportation and hotel facilities, and he set about providing these for the east coast.

Flagler combined the Jacksonville, St. Augustine & Halifax River Railroad with some other short lines, and extended his Florida East Coast Railway the full length of the Atlantic shore to Key West. The FEC's Overseas Extension, from the mainland to Key West, was an engineering achievement of the first magnitude. Although the railroad is gone, some of Flagler's great bridges, viaducts and other structural works are still used by the overseas highway across the chain of islands.

As the railroad moved down the east coast, so did Flagler's string of resort hotels. At the same time, he encouraged the settlement of people who would farm, grow fruit, or otherwise develop Florida.

For More about Flagler, read—

Dictionary of American Biography, vol. 6, p. 451–452.
National Cyclopaedia of American Biography, vol. 15, p. 10–11.

Corlis, Carlton J. "Henry M. Flagler—Railroad Builder" in *Florida Historical Quarterly*, vol. 38, pp. 195–205.
Sammons, Sandra Wallus. Henry Flagler, Builder of Florida. (Lake Buena Vista: Tailored Tours Publications, Inc, 1993).
In Memoriam: Henry Morrison Flagler; Born January 2nd, 1830, Died May 20th, 1913. (Buffalo, Cleveland, etc: The Matthews. Northrup Works, 1914?) 53 p.
Lee, Walter Howard. *The Flagler Story and Memorial Church.* (St. Augustine: Presbyterian Church Society, 1949) 32 p.
Martin, John Wellborn. *Henry M. Flagler, 1830–1913; Florida's East Coast is His Monument!* (New York: Newcomen Society in North America, 1956) 24 p.
Martin, Sidney Walter. *Florida's Flagler.* (Athens: University of Georgia Press, 1949), 280 p.
Martin, Sidney Walter. "Flagler Before Florida" in *Tequesta*, 1945, pp. 3–15.

Edmund Kirby Smith—(May 16, 1824–March 28, 1893) was the native of St. Augustine who, at Galveston on June 2, 1865, surrendered the last Confederate force. When he died, Smith was the last surviving full general of the Confederate and Union armies of the Civil War.

A West Point graduate of 1845, Smith was a soldier of considerable versatility. Before resigning to enter the Confederate service in 1861, he had fought in eight battles of the Mexican War, taught mathematics at West Point, been wounded in Indian fighting, and had his botany observations published by the Smithsonian Institution.

His first Civil War duty was in organizing the Army of the Shenandoah. He was severely wounded at First Bull Run. Later, he fought in Tennessee and Kentucky and then was given command of the Trans-Mississippi Department, consisting of Texas, Louisiana, Arkansas and Indian Territory.

With the Federal capture of Vicksburg, the Department was remote from the control of the Richmond authorities and Smith, by then a full General, ran the area so independently that it was known popularly as "Kirby Smithdom."

He signed Civil War reports as E. Kirby Smith to distinguish himself from the war's other General Smiths (there were 37). The family hyphenated the name after his death. For 18 years after the war he taught mathematics at the University of the South. Florida caused his statue to be placed in the Capitol at Washington.

For More about General Smith, read—

Dictionary of American Biography, vol. 10, p. 424–426.
National Cyclopaedia of American Biography, vol. 8, p. 132–133.

Boatner, Mark M. III. *The Civil War Dictionary*. (New York: David McKay Company, 1959), pp. 769–771.
James, Joseph B. "Edmund Kirby Smith's Boyhood in Florida", in *Florida Historical Quarterly,* vol. 14, pp. 244–254.
Noll, Arthur Howard. *General Kirby-Smith*. (Sewannee, Tenn.: University of the South Press (1907)) 293 p.
Parks, Joseph Howard. *General Edmund Kirby Smith, C.S.A.* (Baton Rouge: Louisiana State University Press (1954)) 537 p.
Rand, Clayton. *Sons of the South* (New York: Holt, Rinehart and Winston, 1961), p. 133, "Edmund Kirby-Smith."

Julia De Forest Tuttle—(January 2, 1848–September 14, 1898) is said to have lured developer Henry Flagler to Miami with a winter bouquet of flowers and a promise of land, thus opening a wilderness for conversion into one of the nation's largest metropolitan areas.

Mrs. Tuttle first came from Cleveland to the mouth of the Miami River in 1872 with her husband, Frederick L. Tuttle, to reside with her father, Ephraim T. Sturdevant. She was delighted with the area and returned as a visitor and then, after the death of her husband, in 1891 as a resident. She had purchased 640 acres on the River's north bank, in what later became the heart of Miami.

Her dream, she said in a letter to a friend, was to see the tangle of vines and brush transformed into a place of modern homes surrounded by beautiful lawns. A clever businesswoman, Mrs. Tuttle reasoned that the area would bloom if she could convince Flagler to extend his railroad and proper investments from West Palm Beach to Miami.

It is recorded her persistent pleas to Flagler fell on deaf ears until the winter of 1894–95, when the hardest freeze in a century devastated Florida groves and crops as far south as Palm Beach. As evidence the cold had not tampered with the foliage of Miami, Mrs. Tuttle picked a few flowers (some say orange blossoms), wrapped them in damp cotton, and sent them to Flagler in St. Augustine.

The millionaire was amazed and sent his aides to Miami to make plans for the 66-mile extension of his tracks and for the building of the Royal Palm Hotel on land given him by Mrs. Tuttle.

Flagler, for all his omniscience otherwise, did not share Mrs. Tuttle's faith in the future of the village beside the Miami River. Vetoing the wide streets urged by Mrs. Tuttle in the platting of the town, Flagler was quoted as saying: "It would be silly. This place will never be anything more than a fishing village for my hotel guests!"

For More about Mrs. Tuttle, read—

Blackman, E. V. *Miami and Dade County, Florida, Its Settlement, Progress and Achievement.* Washington, D.C.: Victor Rainbolt, 1921. pp. 58–60.

Blackman, Lacy Worthington. *The Women of Florida.* [Jacksonville, Florida] The Southern Historical Publishing Associates, 1940. Vol. 2, pp. 162–163.

Chapin, George M. *Florida, 1513–1913, Past, Present and Future.* Chicago, Illinois: The S. J. Clarke Publishing Company, 1914. Vol. 2, pp. 122–125.

Martin, Sidney Walter, *Florida's Flagler.* Athens: The University of Georgia Press, 1949. pp. 152–164.

Muir, Helen. *Miami, U.S.A.* New York: Henry Holt and Company, 1953. pp. 46–63.

Ririck, Rowland H. *Memoirs of Florida.* Atlanta: The Southern Historical Association, 1902. Vol. 2, pp. 735–736.

Mary McLeod Bethune—(July 10, 1875–May 18, 1955) had for her first ambition that of missionary service in Africa but this gave way to the dedication of her life to the education of her own people in this country. She became a noted black educator and advisor to the United States Presidents from Coolidge through Truman.

In 1924 Mrs. Bethune was elected president of the National Association of Colored Women's Clubs, one of the first national organizations for black women. In 1935 she founded and became first president of the National Council of Negro Women. During the administration of President Franklin D. Roosevelt, she was a member of the "Black Cabinet," an advisory group on minority affairs. She served as a consultant to the founding conference of the United Nations.

She was the daughter of slave parents of Mayesville, South Carolina, and the first of their seventeen children born in freedom. A white dressmaker in Denver, Colorado, furnished the scholarship which enabled Mary McLeod to attend Scotia Seminary in North Carolina and another scholarship made it possible for her to attend Moody Bible Institute in Chicago.

Mrs. Bethune taught for eight years in Augusta, Georgia, and Palatka, Florida. On October 3, 1904, with capital of $1.50, she opened her own school at Daytona, Florida. Of the school she wrote: "We burned logs and used the charred splinters as pencils, and mashed elderberries for ink. I begged strangers for a broom, a lamp, a bit of cretonne to put around the packing case that served as my desk. I haunted the city dump and the trash piles behind hotels, retrieving discarded linen and kitchenware, cracked dishes, broken chairs, pieces of old lumber. Everything was scoured and mended."

Despite great financial difficulties, the school grew and in 1923 became Bethune-Cookman College.

For More about Mrs. Bethune, read—

Current Biography, 1942, p. 79–81.
The National Cyclopaedia of American Biography, vol. 49, p. 118.
Embree, Edwin R. *13 Against the Odds.* (New York: The Viking Press, 1944) pp. 9–24, "Amazon of God."
Holt, Rackman. *Mary McLeod Bethune, a Biography.* (Garden City, NY: Doubleday and Company, 1964) p. 306.
Peare, Catherine Owens. *Mary McLeod Bethune.* (New York: the Vanguard Press, (1951) p. 219.
Richardson, Ben. *Great American Negroes.* (New York: Thomas Y. Crowell Company (1956), pp. 177–199. "Mary McLeod Bethune."
Sterne, Emma Gelders. *Mary McLeod Bethune.* (New York: Alfred A. Knopf, 1957). p. 268.
Poole, Bernice A. *Mary McLeod Bethune* (Los Angeles: Melrose Square Pub. Co., 1994.)

Daniel (Chappie) James, Jr.— (February 11, 1920–February 25, 1978) was the first black American four-star general. He entered the Army as a member of a segregated unit in Alabama. Once he was barred from leaving the base in uniform so white enlisted men would not have to salute a black flight officer.

Raised in a family of seventeen children, "Chappie," as he was known, left home in Pensacola to attend Tuskegee Institute in Alabama. Following graduation in 1942, he continued his education in civilian flight training until he received appointment as a cadet in the Army Air Corps in January, 1943.

He trained pilots for the all-black 99th Pursuit Squadron. He flew 101 missions in fighter planes in Korea and 78 in Vietnam. Meanwhile, he earned rank: as Colonel, Brigadier General, Major General and Lieutenant General. The pinnacle was reached in December, 1975, when he was promoted to full General and appointed commander of the North American Air Defense Command.

He suffered from heart problems which forced his retirement from the Air Force in 1977. He died the next year and was buried at Arlington National Cemetery. A building in the Governmental Center at Pensacola was named for him.

The Everglades
Jeanne Bellamy

At last, action is underway to repair what's left of the Everglades. Half of the historic area of the once-vast marsh has been drained and "developed." The remnant is drying up because of man's works.

Three levels of government built those works over the past half-century. They are the federal government, the state government and a regional government body. Finally, all three are agreed that they must do their parts to restore a measure of natural conditions to the Everglades.

At stake is not just irreplaceable wildlife and tropical greenery but also drinking water for 6,000,000 people, with more arriving daily.

The Everglades, unique on this planet, will never be the same as it was 50 years ago. Originally, it was the delta of a single watershed comprised of the Kissimmee River, Lake Okeechobee and the Everglades.

Jeanne Bellamy

Floods and drought were perennial. All the water in the region came from plentiful rain averaging about 60 inches a year. It still does; and over the period of record (1891–1994), with minor fluctuations, has remained about the same. The summer rainy season is flood time. The dry winter brings drought. Or that's the way it was until men decided to "reclaim" the Everglades.

The shallow water in the Everglades covered a layer of rich muck formed over the past 5,000 years by rotted vegetation. Canals were dug from Lake Okeechobee to the coast. They proved too small and too few to handle the big floods but by continuously draining the coastal ridge through which they cut, they lowered levels of fresh water in the ground more than five feet and caused salt water encroachment.

A hurricane in 1926 and another in 1928 sloshed waves out of the big

---

Jeanne Bellamy has lived in Florida since 1917. She was graduated from Rollins College in 1933, and moved to Miami in 1934. She was a staff writer of the *Miami Herald* from December, 1937, to December, 1973. She retired to become chairman of the board of the Sun Bank of Midtown, Miami, where she had been a director since 1968. This role led to a directorship of the parent Sun Bank of Miami from 1977 to 1982. In 1948–49, Miss Bellamy was a member of the Citizens Committee on Water Control which wrote recommendations accepted by the Legislature for implementing the $208,000,000 Central and Southern Florida Flood Control project. She also helped marshal public opinion for the creation of the Everglades National Park. In 1984, the Fairchild Tropical Garden awarded her its Thomas Barbour Medal for Conservation. On the occasion of the award, she was cited as having been among the first "to recognize that the wise management of Florida's fresh water resources was the key to the orderly development of the State." Away from her writing desk, Miss Bellamy is Mrs. John T. Bills.

lake that drowned more than 2,000 people. That's when dikes were built around the south shore of the lake to stop overflow. Growers of sugar cane and winter vegetables moved into the deepest muck just south of the lake. Since drainage, the muck has been subsiding at the rate of one inch per year.

People, plants and animals put up with drought. It's almost imperceptible. But they object to floods; people don't like water up to their window sills. Yet more and more people spread from the coastal ridge down into the edges of the Everglades. Two hurricanes after a wet summer in 1947 flooded 15,000 square miles of southeast Florida; you could have paddled a canoe from Miami to Orlando.

Clamor arose to halt floods. Florida's state government called in the United States Corps of Engineers. The corps devised a plan to stop floods and equalize the supply of water the year around. Old canals were widened and deepened. New ones were dug. The Kissimmee River's 98-mile-long meanderings were turned into a straight ditch. Giant pumps were built to suck water off the cane fields and pump it into the lake or into the Glades. The old trough of the Everglades was walled in to form three shallow reservoirs called "water conservation areas" which serve as evaporation dishes like the lake.

The great flood of 1947 was subsiding in December of that year when President Harry Truman dedicated the Everglades National Park. He said: "We have permanently safeguarded an irreplaceable primitive area." He didn't know that the 1,500,000-acre expanse of land and water was dependent largely on water from upstream.

Dredges created canals and roads at the same time in Florida's Everglades. The rock dredged up to make the canal was thrown up on the bank to serve as the foundation for the road. Florida State Archives

A sea of grass, The Everglades. National Park Service

People didn't realize then that life in the Everglades is tuned to the seasonal shift from too much water to too little. Nor did most people understand that water in the Glades fills the natural underground reservoirs that feed wells along the coast. Those stone reservoirs are called aquifers.

Thanks to drainage, sugar cane and winter vegetables spread over most of the 700,000 acres of the protected deep muck. These and other farmlands use 75 per cent of the region's water for irrigation. The rest of the muck will be gone in 20 years or so, and with it farming. Chances of muck reforming appear nil.

Is 20 years enough to decide what use should be made of the barren bedrock when all the muck and farming are gone? This should be a concern now.

Nearly half a century of experience and studies have shown the needs of the Everglades, its plants and creatures, including people. A lot of money is being spent to cure mistakes.

A 1989 Act of Congress added 107,600 acres to the national park. A related report in 1990 from the Corps of Engineers suggests restoring the main watercourse into the park.

Meantime, troubles in the Everglades get worse. A mere 10,000 to 20,000 egrets, ibises and other wading birds remain of the 250,000 to 300,000 which whitened the skies 50 to 60 years ago.

Melaleuca trees cover about 1,500,000 acres. A well-meaning forester, Dr. John C. Gifford, brought the first melaleuca seeds from Australia early in this century. He reasoned that the trees would help dry up the Everglades without need for ditching. One acre of melaleucas can consume 2,100 gallons of water an hour. That's four to five times more water than is drunk by native plants like sawgrass.

Besides, the melaleuca is almost unkillable. It survives fire or lethal injection. Indeed, any wound causes it to cast off millions of seeds. The seeds take root, forming an impenetrable thicket so dense that sunlight can't pierce it.

> **Toward A 'New' Everglades**
>
> Dr. Garald G. Parker, Sr., the Number One authority on water in Southeast Florida, has penned a formula for "restoring" the Everglades:
>
> "If the free-flowing canals are dammed, and the Glades area is set aside and protected from further development, and if by damming the canals the land surface of the Glades once more would be seasonally flooded, a start will be made to the establishment of a new water-dominated ecosystem.
>
> "The seasonal growth of plants (algae-dominated in the early years) with shoreline plants gradually encroaching inward into the Glades, the area slowly would start recovering. Water birds once again would find conditions favorable for nesting. 'Gators, 'coons, possums, rabbits, foxes and maybe even panthers would be able to live and produce, first along the shorelines of the Glades, then on the tree-islands that would be able to make a recovery.
>
> "Such changes I probably will not live to see, but maybe my grandchildren will."

In Florida, the melaleuca has no natural foes. Scientists are testing some 200 insects in Australia which prey on melaleucas as the best hope of stopping their deadly spread in the Glades.

Australian pines (not pine at all but a variety of ironwood) and Brazilian peppers (miscalled Florida holly) also have invaded the Everglades. They, too, choke out native plants and destroy habitat for wildlife.

But pollution may be the worst threat. Vast mats of algae have sprung up in Lake Okeechobee. They reduce oxygen in the water, killing fish. The fault belongs to inflows of phosphorus and nitrogen. These nutrients come from cow manure and urine discharged from dairies and fields north of the lake, and from fertilizers and the muck soil in cane fields.

Water from the cane fields used to be pumped into the lake. Its bad effects on the lake caused a turnaround. The water now is pumped east and south into the Water Conservation Areas. Dense stands of cat tails have appeared where the pumpage enters, displacing native greenery.

Controversy has arisen over what to do with the dirty water. The state and the regional South Florida Water Management District are requiring "best management practices" at dairies, and are buying those which can't afford the changes.

Along the coastline, demand for fresh water is going up while the supply is going down.

Managers of waterworks are testing ways to desalt water from the large Floridan Aquifer buried from about 800 to 1,200 feet deep. The water there is less salty than the sea, flows by artesian pressure and thus is cheaper to develop and refine. It still costs more than water from wells. One estimate was that water bills around Miami would go up by $10 a month if desalting be-

470 / The Everglades

came necessary. So the 6,000,000-plus residents can see a price tag on the health of the Everglades.

In Florida Bay, southernmost tip of the national park, the artificial wet-dry cycle has hurt fish life. The mix of salt and fresh water needs restoring so that fish and shrimps will flourish amid sea grasses forming their nursery.

The number of visitors to Everglades National Park has exceeded the level of 1,000,000 a year. Nearly all, especially Europeans, want to see an alligator. There are few alligators in Europe.

The main entrance to the park is about 10 miles southwest of Florida City on State Road 9336. Newcomers should stop at the Main Visitors Center near the entrance. Entrance fee: $5 per car.

Closer to Miami is the Chekika Center, part of the acreage added to the national park since 1989. Its entrance is on SW 168th St. off SW 177th Ave (Route 997). Entrance fee: $4 per car, $2 per person by bicycle or afoot. The Chekika area offers swimming in a fresh-water pool and camping. There also are campsites for recreational vehicles and tents accessible from the main entrance.

The park also offers a 15-mile, two-hour tram tour into the heart of the Glades from Shark Valley, which is 30 miles west of Miami off the Tamiami Trail (SR 41). This includes a view from a 65-foot observation tower.

For information, write park headquarters, P.O. Box 40001, SR 9336, Homestead FL 33034-6733, or telephone (305) 242-7700.

Construction of the Lake Okeechobee levee, 1935. Estimated to cost nine million dollars, the project called for 66 miles of levees: 51 miles along the south shore and 15 miles along a part of the north shore. The work required over 43 million cubic yards of rock and marl. Florida State Archives

See: "The Lesson of the Everglades: Humility in Dealing with Nature," by Jeanne Bellamy, in the 1983–84 edition of *The Florida Handbook.* Illustrations show how drainage leads to the diminishing of fresh water in porous rock and the creeping in of salt water.

Florida's River in the Ocean

Within sight of lower Florida's southeastern beaches flows a river within the Atlantic Ocean, the Gulf Stream. This stream has influenced the destiny of nations. It was because the Gulf Stream passed so close to the east coast of Florida that St. Augustine's great fort was built to guard the homeward-bound Spanish treasure fleets.

Benjamin Franklin helped put the Gulf Stream on mariners' charts when, as Colonial Postmaster-General, he collected information to solve the puzzle of why the mail packets, following one route, took two weeks longer to cross the Atlantic than did merchant ships following another route.

The Gulf Stream rushes through the Straits of Florida, 43 miles wide at the narrowest point, between the Florida Keys and Cuba, at the speed of 3.048 feet per second. A ship in the Straits of Bimini would be moved forward by 124 miles a day without any effort of its own.

In the year 1952–1953, the average quantity of water passing through the Straits of Florida was measured at 20,655 million cubic yards per second.

The Gulf Stream was the villain during World War II in causing the loss of numerous Allied merchant vessels from German submarines. The Gulf Stream was responsible because it funneled shipping into a relatively narrow path which, coupled with the muffled glow of lights of lower east coast Florida cities, made easy nighttime targets of the silhouetted vessels.

In all, Nazi submarines torpedoed 111 ships in the Gulf Stream, Gulf of Mexico and the Caribbean, with merchant seamen suffering 882 casualties. Nixon Smiley in *Knights of the Fourth Estate,* said the Navy organized an elaborate system of hunting submarines with destroyers, airplanes and blimps. Despite these efforts, however, the Navy was able to claim only one positive and one probable kill.

One of the 111 ships lost to German Submarines in the Gulf Stream, Gulf of Mexico and Caribbean.
National Archives

Climate/Weather
The Natural
Resource

Topographic features—Florida, situated between latitudes 24° to 30′ and 31°N. and longitudes 80° and 87° 30′W., is largely a lowland peninsula comprising about 54,100 square miles of land area and is surrounded on three sides by the waters of the Atlantic Ocean and the Gulf of Mexico. Countless shallow lakes, which exist particularly on the peninsula and range in size from small cypress ponds to that of Lake Okeechobee, account for approximately 4,400 square miles of additional water area.

No point in the State is more than 70 miles from salt water, and the highest natural land in the Northwest Division is only 345 feet above sea level. Coastal areas are low and flat and are indented by many small bays or inlets. Many small islands dot the shorelines. The elevation of most of the interior ranges from 50 to 100 feet above sea level, though gentle hills in the interior of the peninsula and across the northern and western portions of the State rise above 200 feet.

A large portion of the southern one-third of the peninsula is the swampland known as the Everglades. An ill-defined divide of low, rolling hills, extending north-to-south near the middle of the peninsula and terminating north of Lake Okeechobee, gives rise to most peninsula streams, chains of lakes, and many springs. Stream gradients are slight and often insufficient to handle the runoff following heavy rainfall. Consequently, there are sizable areas of swamp and marshland near these streams.

Soils are generally sandy and low in natural fertility, the main exception being a large area of peat and muck soils in the Everglades. About one-third of Florida's soils can be classified as uplands or ridge soils that are generally well- to excessively well-drained. Soils in the remaining two-thirds of the

---

Adapted from "Climate of Florida," a survey by the National Oceanic and Atmospheric Service, June, 1982.

State, including the muck soils, generally have imperfect to very poor natural drainage. Large areas of Florida are underlain by compact subsoils that intensify the effects of both wet and dry weather.

The climate is probably Florida's greatest natural resource. General climatic conditions range from a zone of transition between temperate and subtropical conditions in the extreme northern interior to the tropical conditions found on the Florida Keys. The chief factors of climatic control are: (1) latitude, (2) proximity to the Atlantic Ocean and Gulf of Mexico, and (3) numerous inland lakes. Summers throughout the state are long, warm, and relatively humid; winters, although punctuated with periodic invasions of cool or occasionally cold air from the north, are mild due to the southerly latitude and relatively warm adjacent sea waters. The Gulf Stream, which flows around the western tip of Cuba through the Florida Straits and northward around the lower east coast, exerts a warming influence to the southern east coast largely because the predominate wind direction is easterly. Coastal areas in all sections of the state average slightly warmer in winter and cooler in summer than do inland points at the same latitude.

Rainfall

Florida enjoys abundant rainfall. Except for the northwestern sections, the average year can be divided into two seasons—the so-called "rainy season" and a long, relatively dry season. On the peninsula, generally more than half the rainfall for an average year can be expected to fall during the 4-month period, June through September. In northwest Florida, there is a secondary rainfall maximum in late winter and early spring.

Some Climatic Extremes

Some notable climatic extremes are: Highest recorded temperature, 109° at Monticello on June 29, 1931; lowest recorded temperature, 2° below zero at Tallahassee on February 13, 1899; and the greatest 24-hour rainfall, 38.7 inches at Yankeetown on September 5–6, 1950, a record for the nation.

Temperature

Mean annual temperatures range from the upper 60's in the northern sections to the middle 70's on the southern mainland, and reach nearly 78° at Key West. Summertime mean temperatures are about the same throughout the State, 81° to 82°; during the coolest months, temperatures average about 13° lower in the north than in the south. July and August average the warmest in all areas and December and January average the coolest in the northern and central areas. January and February, on the average, are the coolest months in the extreme south and on the Keys.

Wintertime minimum temperatures are deceptive. While stations in northern Florida record 10 to 20 days in a year with minimum temperatures of 32° or below, there have been only five days in the past 72 years at Jacksonville where the maximum temperature for the day has failed to climb above freezing. This means the coat you might wear at 7 a.m. will become heavy by 10 a.m., and, if you are driving, that you may well be in your shirt sleeves by noon.

Maximum temperatures during the warmest months average near 90°

along the coast and slightly above 90° in the interior; minima average in the low 70's but are slightly higher along the immediate coast and on the Keys than inland. During June, July, and August, maximum temperatures exceed 90° on about 2 days in 3 in all interior areas; in May and September, 90° or higher can be expected about 1 day in 3 in the northern interior, and about 1 day in 2 in the southern interior. Extreme heat waves, characteristic of continental districts, are felt occasionally—but in a modified form—over the northern interior. Temperatures of 100° or higher are infrequent in the northern sections, rare in the central portion, and practically unknown in the southern areas. The summer heat is tempered by sea breezes along the coast and by frequent afternoon or early evening thunderstorms in all areas. During the warm season, sea breezes are felt almost daily within several miles of the coast and occasionally 20 to 30 miles inland. Thundershowers, which on the average occur on about half the summer days, frequently are accompanied by a rapid 10° to 20° drop in temperature, resulting in comfortable weather for the remainder of the day. Gentle breezes occur almost daily in all areas and serve to further mitigate the oppressiveness that otherwise would accompany the prevailing summer temperature and humidity conditions. Since most of the large scale wind patterns affecting Florida have passed over water surfaces, hot drying winds seldom occur.

Frost and Freezing

Although average minimum temperatures during the coolest months range from the middle 40s in the north to the middle 50s in the south, no place on the mainland is entirely safe from frost or freezing. An occasional cold wave of the more severe type brings minima ranging from 15° to 20° over the northern areas to freezing or below to the southern limits of the peninsula. These cold waves, except in rare instances, seldom last more than 2 or 3 days at a time. It is extremely rare for temperatures to remain below freezing throughout the day at any place. On the first night of a cold wave, there usually is considerable wind which, because of the continual mixing of the air, prevents marked temperature differences between high and low ground. By the second night, winds usually have subsided and radiational cooling under clear skies accelerates the temperature fall after sundown. On such occasions, marked differences in temperature are noticeable at places not far apart, depending upon such factors as topography and proximity to bodies of water. These facts are of primary concern in selecting sites for growing plants not tolerant of cold.

Some winters—occasionally several in succession—pass without widespread freezing in the southern areas; others may bring several severe cold waves. Winters with more than one severe cold wave, interspersed with periods of relative warmth, are especially distressing to the agriculture industry because the later freeze almost always finds vegetation in a tender stage of growth and highly susceptible to additional cold damage.

Annual and Seasonal Rainfall

Rainfall in Florida is quite varied both in annual amount and in seasonal distribution. Individual station annual averages range from about 50 to 65 inches. On the Florida Keys, annual averages are only about 40 inches. The main areas of high annual rainfall are in the extreme northwestern counties and at the southern end of the peninsula. Rainfall varies greatly from year to year, with wet years sometimes doubling that received during a dry year. Many localities have received more than 80 inches in a calendar year and a few places more than 100 inches. In contrast, most all localities have received less than 40 inches in a calendar year.

The distribution of rainfall within the year is quite uneven. In the summer "rainy season", there is close to a 50-50 chance some rain will fall on any given day. During the remainder of the year, the chances are much less, some rain being likely on 1 or 2 days per week. The seasonal distribution changes somewhat from north to south. In the northwestern areas there are two high points—late winter or early spring and again during summer—and one pronounced low point October; a secondary low point occurs in April and May. On the peninsula, the most striking features of the seasonal distribution are the dominance of summer rainfall (generally more than half the average annual total falls in the 4-month period, June through September) and the rather abrupt start and end of the summer "rainy season" (June average rainfall tends to be nearly double that of May and, in fall, the average for the last month of the wet season tends to be about double that of the following month). October averages the driest month in northwest Florida but in general is among the wettest on the southeast coast and Keys. The start and end of the "rainy season" varies considerably from year to year. According to past records, it has begun as soon as early May and has been as delayed as late June. Late September or early October usually marks the end of the wet season except for a narrow strip along the entire east coast where relatively large October rainfalls are frequently noted. The tendency for relatively large October rainfall diminishes quite rapidly westward.

Summer Rainfall

Most of the summer rainfall is derived from "local" showers or thundershowers. Many places average more than 80 thundershowers per year and some average more than 100. Showers are often heavy, usually lasting only an hour or two, and generally occur near the hottest part of the day. The more severe thundershowers are occasionally attended by hail or locally strong winds which may inflict serious local damage to crops and property. Day long summer rains are usually associated with tropical disturbances and, hence, infrequent. Even in the wet season, the duration of rainfall is generally less than 10 percent of the time. Because most summer rains are local in character, large differences in monthly and annual totals at nearby points are common but these differences disappear when comparison is made on the basis of long period averages. However, large differences in the long period averages do exist within short distances. For example, the normal annual rainfalls for Miami Beach, and the Miami Airport are 46.26, and 59.76 inches, respectively, yet it is less than 10 airline miles from the Beach to the Airport. Similar conditions undoubtedly exist elsewhere among the immediate coast.

Most localities have, at one time or another, experienced 2-hour rainfalls in excess of 3 inches, and 24-hour amounts of near or greater than 10 inches. Nearly all localities have had, within a single month, from one-third to one-half as much rain as falls during the entire average year. Tropical storms, on occasion, produce copious rainfall over relatively large areas. A detailed survey of the September 1950 hurricane, conducted by the U.S. Corps of Engineers, Jacksonville, Florida District, indicated an amount near 34 inches fell in a 24-hour period in the Cedar Keys area. The 38.70 inches of rainfall that fell during the 24-hour period at Yankeetown on September 5–6, 1950, during this hurricane, is the record 24-hour rainfall for the nation. Because of water disposal problems, heavy rains can be just as serious as droughts.

Droughts

Florida is not immune from drought, even though annual rainfall amounts are relatively large. Prolonged periods of deficient rainfall are occasionally experienced even during the time of the expected "rainy season". Several such dry periods in the course of a year or two can lead to significantly lowered water tables and lake levels which, in turn, may cause serious water shortages for those who depend upon lakes and shallow wells for water supply. Because a large part of the agricultural produce is planted, grown, and marketed during fall, winter, and spring (normally the driest part of the year), growers of high per-acre value crops have long since concluded it is almost mandatory to provide supplemental irrigation for success.

Worst Drought

The worst drought in more than 40 years along the lower east coast occurred in 1971. In that area, the lowest 12-month rainfall of record, 34.59 inches, was set during the period from July, 1970, to June, 1971. The level of Lake Okeechobee dropped to 10.3 feet, only 0.16 of a foot above the record minimum of 10.14 feet.

Snow fell in Tallahassee on February 13, 1899, in sufficient quantity for this snowball contest on the steps of the Capitol. Florida State Archives

Snowfall

Snowfall in Florida is unusual, although measurable amounts have fallen in the northern areas at irregular intervals, and a trace of snow has been recorded as far south as Fort Myers. The greatest recorded snowfalls in Florida occurred on February 13, both in 1899 and 1958. In 1899, 4.0 inches were measured at Lake Butler in Union County and one-half inch at Bartow in Polk County. On the night of February 12–13, 1958, most all of Florida west of the Suwannee River received 2 to 3 inches of snow; areas east of the Suwannee River and north of about latitude 30° received 1 to 2 inches of snow on this same night. The 3 inches measured at Tallahassee on this date is the greatest ever measured there since records began in 1886, and the 1.5 inches measured at Jacksonville approxi-

Climate / 477

Train swept off tracks in Keys by Labor Day hurricane, 1935 U.S. Department of Commerce

mates the only other recorded measurable amount, 1.9 inches on February 13, 1899.

Notable Florida Snowfalls

1774—date unknown. There was a snow storm that extended over parts of Florida. Inhabitants long afterwards remembered the extraordinary "white rain".

January 10, 1800—Surveying party measured 5 inches at Point Peter near the mouth of the St. Mary's River. This is the highest recorded total in Florida history.

January 13, 1852—½" measured at Jacksonville. Press report of 2" at Tallahassee.

December 5, 1886—½" reported at Pensacola.

January 5, 1887—An inch of snow fell at Pensacola.

January 14, 1892—Pensacola again report 0.4 inch.

February 14–15, 1895—3" at Pensacola, 2" at Tallahassee and 1" at Lake City. A trace was reported as far south as Leesburg.

February 12–13, 1899—Greatest snowfall on record and farthest southward extend. 4" at Lake Butler, 3.5" at Marianna, 3.0" at Lake City, Trace amounts were reported as far south as Fort Myers, Avon Park and Titusville.

November 27-28, 1912—1/2" at Mt. Pleasant in Gadsden County.
December 29-31, 1917—1/2" reported at many stations in Panhandle and North Florida as far south as Crescent City.
January 22-23, 1935—1" at Panama City and 0.2" at Apalachicola.
February 2-3,1951—2" at Crescent City and St. Augustine. Trace amounts as far south as Lakeland.
March 6, 1954—4" at Milton, 3" at Niceville and 2" at Pensacola. Trace amounts reported by many stations in Northern Florida.
March 28, 1955—1" at Marianna and 0.4" at Tallahassee. Trace amounts reported as far south as Palatka.
February 12-13, 1958—Second only to snowfall of 1899. 3" reported at many stations from Niceville to Jasper. Measurable amounts at almost all stations north at 30° N.
February 9-10, 1973—First measurable snow since 1958. 3.3" at Milton and 2" at Pensacola, De Funiak Springs and Quincy. Trace amounts reported as far south as Clermont. Unofficial reports of 6 to 8" vicinity of Jay.
Mid-January, 1977—State shivered in week-long cold, with traces of snow observed as far south as Miami.

Prevailing Winds

Prevailing winds over the southern peninsula are southeast and east. Over the remainder of the State, wind directions are influenced locally by convectional forces inland and the "land and sea breeze" effect near the coast. Consequently, prevailing directions are somewhat erratic but, in general, follow a pattern of northerly in winter and southerly in summer. March and April average the windiest months. High local winds of short duration occur occasionally in connection with thunderstorms in summer and with cold fronts moving across the State in other seasons.

Tornadoes

Tornadoes, funnel clouds, and waterspouts also occur, averaging 10 to 15 per year. Tornadoes have occurred in all seasons but are most frequent in spring. Tornadoes also occur in connection with tropical storms. Generally, tornado paths in Florida are short and damages have not been extensive. Occasionally waterspouts come inland, but they usually dissipate soon after reaching land and affect only very small areas.

Hurricanes and Tropical Storms

Hurricanes and tropical storms produce the principal high winds and flooding and frequently are quite destructive. Florida, jutting out into the seas between the subtropical Atlantic and the Gulf of Mexico, is the most exposed of all states to these tropical cyclones since they approach from the Atlantic to the east, the Caribbean to the south, and the Gulf of Mexico to the west.

Since the beginning of records in 1886, the state has never gone more than three years without a tropical storm nor longer than five years without a hurricane. The longest period without a major hurricane is twelve years, 1897-1908. Hurricane Donna, which crossed the Florida Keys and then moved northeastward across the state from about Fort Myers to near Day-

WHAT MOST PEOPLE DON'T KNOW ABOUT STORM TIDES:

This is why a hurricane warning of tides three to six feet above normal doesn't tell the whole story, why the Suncoast didn't know what it was in for, despite National Hurricane Center warnings of higher than normal tides.

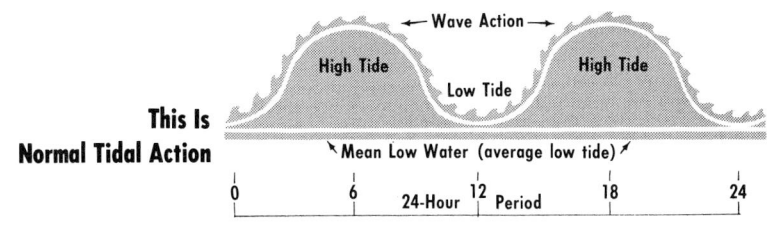

This Is Normal Tidal Action

The line drawing above shows how the tidal function works under normal conditions, which means under the influence of the moon and the sun. In the Tampa Bay area at this time of year, those two bodies produce a tidal cycle that varies about two and one-half feet between high and low tides. That normal, symmetrical cycling — from high to low about six hours later, and back to high in about another six hours — is what meteorologists refer to as the astronomical tide. It is what can be expected of any large body of water on any given date, given the known influence of the sun and moon, and it is represented in this drawing by the curving line on top. The bottom line on which that curve rides represents mean low water, which is the average of all low tides.

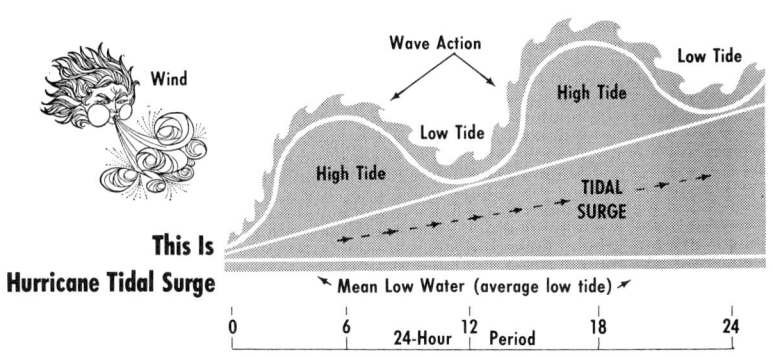

This Is Hurricane Tidal Surge

But when Hurricane Agnes passed offshore in the Gulf on her way north, there was more to worry about than just higher than normal tides. There was Storm Surge, and the simplest way to describe that is as a great wedge of water driven before the radial, counter clockwise swing of the hurricane winds. Agnes slammed that wedge against the face of the Suncoast. Then the high tide, which proved to be nearly six feet, rode in on the back of the Storm Surge, and the winds whipped the top of the tide into waves that at times were 10 feet high, or more. What Agnes did, then, was to mount a three-tiered attack by water. It's all shown in the drawing above, and it all adds up to a lot more than just three to six feet of additional tide.

Source: St. Petersburg Times; artist: Frank Peters

tona Beach on September 9–10, 1960, was the most financially destructive hurricane experienced in Florida to that time. This hurricane caused an estimated $305 million (about $1.4 billion when adjusted to 1990 dollars) damage in Florida. The total of only 13 fatalities during this very intense hurricane indicates the great value of the modern hurricane warning service now available in hurricane threatened areas. Three hurricanes—Cleo, Dora, and

Isabel—in 1964, caused the greatest damage in any one year, $362,000,000. Andrew in 1992 established new records with about $25 billion lost.

The vulnerability of the State varies with the progress of the hurricane season. Early and late in the season (June and October) the region of maximum hurricane activity is in the Gulf of Mexico and the western Caribbean. Most of those systems that move into Florida approach the State from the south or southwest, entering the keys or along the west coast. Mid-season (August and most of September) the tropical cyclones normally approach the State from the east or southeast.

One of the most intense hurricanes of modern times affected the State on Labor Day, 1935. The second lowest sea-level pressure ever recorded in the Western Hemisphere, 26.35 inches, was recorded at that time. The maximum winds in that hurricane were not recorded since the wind measuring equipment was blown down before the peak of the hurricane was reached. However, engineers have calculated that winds of 200 to 250 m.p.h. would have been required to account for some of the damage that occurred during the severe hurricane. During the hurricane of August 1949, winds at West Palm Beach reached 110 m.p.h. with gusts to 125 m.p.h. before the anemometer was blown away. The highest sustained speed was estimated at 120 m.p.h. with gusts to 130. A privately owned anemometer, the accuracy of which is unknown, recorded gusts to 155 m.p.h.

The highest winds in a hurricane are seldom measured since these usually occur at isolated points where no anemometers are installed. It seems likely that winds of 150 m.p.h. occasionally accompany major hurricanes, which (since 1900) have occurred in Florida on the average of once every four years. However, from 1966 through 1993 only three major hurricanes have struck the state: Eloise (1975) Elena (1985) and Andrew (1992).

Newsweek, in words and pictures, perhaps conveyed the scene left in August, 1992, by Hurricane Andrew as well or better than anyone else.

"Like Hiroshima," said *Newsweek*, "they said and it was the Hurricane Andrew, the most costly storm in U.S. history, that turned south Dade County (around Homestead) into a zone of ruination that stretched for miles and miles."

"Find the neighborhood and you couldn't find the street. Find the street and you couldn't find the house. Find the house and all you saw was debris. There was no water, no electricity no phone—only the stench of rotting garbage and here and there spray-painted signs that showed at least some homeowners were hanging on. 'Manned and armed,' these graffiti said. "You loot, we shoot.' "

Newsweek continued: "Into this value of desolation last week marched one of the more remarkable relief forces of modern times—a composite corps of Army, Navy, Air Force, and Marine personnel, not to mention the Red Cross, the National Guard, hundreds of federal bureaucrats and thousands of well-meaning civilian volunteers from all over the United States."

"There was, finally, a joint federal, state, and local response—and it was for the most part, reasonably well coordinated."

On thumbnail, Andrew's toll was listed by the Federal Emergency Management Agency, American Insurance Services Group, Dade County Planning Office, other county officials, and the National Hurricane Center: residents left homeless—160,000; houses damaged—85,000, more than half of them severely or beyond repair; apartments damaged—38,000, two-thirds of them severely or beyond repair; businesses destroyed or damaged—82,000; jobs lost—85,000; deaths—44 in Florida (65 including Bahamas and Louisiana); estimate of insured losses—$10.7 billion; total estimated losses in all areas—$27 billion; insurance claims—610,000; debris—8.3 million cubic yards; travel trailers or temporary mobile homes set up for victims-1,388; meals served—4.7 million; water distributed—192 million gallons; emergency housing grants—$84.1 million; individual and family assistance grants—$120.6 million; loans for repairing homes and replacing property—$178.3 million approved, $29.6 million disbursed; business loans—$31.1 million approved, $2.7 million disbursed; cleanup costs—$225 million for debris removal, $21 million for plastic tarpaulins, $10 million for portable showers, $10 million for pumps and generators, $6 million for portable toilets. One third of a million people in Dade county left their homes, of which only two thirds had returned by late 1994.

Harold Wilkins, 69, of Florida City walks through the rubble of what was once his trailer-home with only the clothes on his back and what he is carrying.   C. M. Gluerrero *El Nuevo Herald*

Rainfall during Storms

Some of the world's heaviest rainfalls have occurred within tropical cyclones. Over 20 inches in 24 hours is not uncommon. The intensity of the rainfall, however, does not seem to bear any relation to the intensity of the wind circulation. For example, a storm entered the west coast of Florida in October, 1941. It was never of hurricane intensity, yet over a 3-day period, it produced a total of 35 inches at Trenton, Fla. The 24-hour total for this same storm was about 30 inches. Another Florida hurricane of 1947 caused a rainfall of about 6 inches in 1 hour at Hialeah. Such extremes, however, are relatively rare; the average hurricane rainfall in Florida usually does not exceed 6 to 8 inches in a 24-hour period.

Humidity and Fogs

The climate of Florida is humid. Inland areas with greater temperature extremes enjoy slightly lower relative humidity, especially during hot weather. On the average, variations in relative humidity from one place to another are small; humidities range from about 85 to 95 percent during the night and early morning hours to about 50 to 65 percent during the afternoons. Heavy fogs are usually confined to the night and early morning hours in the late fall, winter, and early spring months. They occur on about 35 to 40 days per year, on the average, over the extreme northern portion; 25 to 30 days per year in the central portion; and downward to less than 10 days per year in the extreme southern areas. These fogs usually dissipate or thin soon after sunrise, and heavy daytime fog is seldom observed in Florida.

Sunshine

Florida has been called the "Sunshine State". Sunshine measurements made at widely separated points in the State indicate the sun shines about two-thirds of the time sunlight is possible during the year and ranges from more than 70 percent of possible in April and May to slightly more than 60 percent of possible in December and January. In general, southern Florida enjoys a higher percentage of possible sunshine than does north Florida. The length of day operates to Florida's advantage. In winter when sunshine is highly valued, the sun can shine longer in Florida than in the more northern latitudes. In summer, when a little goes a long way, the picture reverses itself with the longer days returning to the north.

While sunshine hours in Miami are 66 percent of possible in December as compared to 51 percent in New York City, greater difference is reflected in the amount of solar radiation that leads to temperature contrasts. New York City receives only an average 116 langleys (a unit of solar radiation) on a horizontal surface each day during December. In contrast, Miami receives an average of 317 langleys, almost three times as much solar radiation.

Air Pollution

Meteorological conditions that aggravate air pollution do not often occur at any place and are probably the least frequent in the southeastern areas. The air over the State is usually sufficiently unstable—a condition conducive to the development of cumulus clouds and thunderstorms—to disperse pollutants to higher levels. This fact, plus the relative constancy of the easterly trade winds in the southeastern areas, greatly reduces the general pollution problem in Florida.

Tropical Climate

Visitors can experience a tropical climate in Florida. A tropical climate is defined as one in which the average temperature of the coldest month is 64.4° or above. The climate found in Florida along the east coast from Vero Beach southward and along the west coast from Punta Gorda southward fits that definition.

Earthquakes in Florida

Most of Florida lies in two zones whose chance of an earthquake is regarded as nil by the National Oceanic and Atmospheric Administration. These zones are Florida south of a line drawn straight west across the peninsula from approximately Daytona Beach and Florida west of the Apalachicola river.

The Administration's *Earthquake History of the United States* records three shocks originating in Florida.

Two of these occurred near St. Augustine at 11:45 p.m. and 11:55 p.m. on January 12, 1879. They were felt in an area of 25,000 square miles, from a line joining Tallahassee and Savannah, Ga., on the north, to a line joining Punta Rassa and Daytona Beach on the South.

These shocks were listed as being of intensity VI on the Mercalli Scale. At St. Augustine and, to a lesser degree, at Daytona Beach, doors and windows were rattled, articles thrown from shelves, and some plaster fell.

Devastating Florida Hurricanes
National Oceanic and Atmospheric Administration

DATES OF HURRICANE	AREAS MOST AFFECTED	LAND STATION WITH HIGHEST WIND SPEED*	DEATHS (U.S. ONLY)	DAMAGE BY CATEGORY #	DAMAGE
1916, June 29–July 10	Mississippi to northern Florida	Mobile, Ala. 99 mph	7	6	Very destructive along the coast from Mobile to Pensacola.
1919, September 2–15	Florida, Louisiana and Texas	Sand Key, Fla. 72 mph†	287	7	Hurricane was severe both in Florida and in Texas. Over 500 casualties in ships lost at sea.
1926, September 11–22	Florida and Alabama	Miami, Fla. 96 mph, Miami Beach, Fla. gust, 132 mph	243	8	Very severe in the Miami area and from Pensacola into southern Alabama.
1928, September 6–20	Southern Florida	Lake Okeechobee, Fla. 75 mph	1,836	7	Wind-driven waters of Lake Okeechobee overflowed into populated areas, causing most of the casualties.
1933, August 31–September 7	Florida	Jupiter Inlet 125 mph	2	6	Much property damage on the coast from Vero Beach; property damage inland was minor; citrus loss nearly complete near the coast.
1934, Ju 21–25	Florida and Texas	Corpus Christi, Tex. 52 mph	11	6	Heavy rains severely damaged the Texas cotton crop.
1935, August 29–September 10	Southern Florida	Tampa, Fla. 86 mph	408	7	"Labor Day Storm"—barometer reading of 26.35 inches on Long Key is lowest of record in the Western Hemisphere. Peak winds were estimated 150–200 mph on some Keys.
1935, October 30–November 8	Southern Florida	Miami, Fla. 94 mph	5	7	"Yankee Storm"—so-called because it moved into the Miami area from the northeast. It was quite small—destructive winds covered only a narrow path.
1944, October 12–23	Florida	Dry Tortugas, Fla. 120 mph	18	8	Warnings and evacuation prevented heavier casualties.

484 / Climate

DATES OF HURRICANE	AREAS MOST AFFECTED	LAND STATION WITH HIGHEST WIND SPEED*	DEATHS (U.S. ONLY)	DAMAGE BY CATEGORY #	DAMAGE
1945, September 11–20	Florida, Georgia, and South Carolina	Carysfort Reef Light, 138 mph	4	8	Damage very heavy in Dade County (Miami), Fla. Evacuation of exposed locations prevented heavy loss of life.
1947, September 4–21	Florida and Middle Gulf Coast	Hillsboro, Light, Fla. 121 mph[1] gust, 155 mph	51	8	Very large and intense storm. Wind and water damage heavy on Florida east coast and in Louisiana and Mississippi.
1947, October 9–16	Southern Florida; Georgia and South Carolina	Hillsboro Light, Fla. 92 mph	1	6	Heavy to excessive rains in Florida climaxed a very wet season. Heavy damage also occurred in the Savannah, Ga. area from wind and along the South Carolina-Georgia coast from high tides.
1948, September 18–25	Southern Florida	Key West, A.P., Fla. 78 mph[†]	3	7	Many lulls and calms reported from widely separated points simultaneously; two lulls at some places near Okeechobee several hours apart.
1948, October 3–15	Southern Florida	Sombrero Key, Fla. E 100 mph[1]	0	7	Damage not as great as could be expected, since much of area had been hit by September storm.
1949, August 23–31	Florida to the Carolinas	West Palm Beach, Fla. 110 mph[5†] Juniper, Fla. gust 153 mph	2	8	Storm center passed over Lake Okeechobee. Levees built since 1928 prevented overflow and casualties.
1950, September 1–9	Florida	Cedar Keys, Fla. gust, 125 mph	2	6	Unusual double loop in storm track in the Cedar Keys area. Coast from Sarasota northward suffered extensive wind and tide damage.
1950, October 13–19 KING	Florida	Miami, WBO, Fla. 120 mph[1]	4	7	A small violent storm which passed directly over Miami, then up the entire Florida peninsula.
1956, September 21–30 FLOSSY	Louisiana to northern Florida	Burrwood, La. 88 mph[5] gust, 110 mph	15	7	Damage over area from New Orleans and mouth of Mississippi eastward to western Florida.
1960, August 29–September 13 DONNA	Florida to New England	Block Island, R.I. 95 mph gust, 130 mph. Ft. Myers, Fla. 92 mph, Cape Henry, Va. 80 mph	50	8	Record amount of damage in Florida. First storm with hurricane force winds in Florida, Middle Atlantic States, and New England in 75-year record. Winds estimated near 140 mph, with gusts 175–180 mph on central Florida Keys.

DATES OF HURRICANE	AREAS MOST AFFECTED	LAND STATION WITH HIGHEST WIND SPEED*	DEATHS (U.S. ONLY)	DAMAGE BY CATEGORY #	DAMAGE
1964, August 20–September 5, CLEO	Southern Florida, Eastern Virginia	Miami, Fla., E 110 mph	0	8	First hurricane in Miami area since 1950. Moderate wind damage extensive along Florida lower east coast. Record rainfall and wide-spread flooding from Hampton Roads area southward in Virginia. Tornadoes in southeast Florida and the Carolinas.
1964, August 28–September 16, DORA	Northeastern Florida, Southern Georgia	St. Augustine, Fla., E 125 mph	5	8	First storm of full hurricane force on record to move inland from the east over Northeastern Florida.
1965, August 27–September 12, BETSY	Southern Florida, Louisiana	Port Sulphur, La. 136 mph	75	9	Much of the damage was caused by flooding, particularly in Louisiana.
1972, June 14–23, AGNES	Florida to New York	Key West, Fla. 43 mph; Jacksonville, Fla. gusts 56 mph. Storm tide 6.4ft. above normal Apalachicola, Fla.	122	9	One of the costliest natural disasters in U.S. history—$2.0 billion. Devastating floods from North Carolina to New York with many recordbreaking river crests. Tornadoes—15 in Florida and 2 in Georgia.
1975, September 13–24 ELOISE	Florida Panhandle and eastern Alabama	5 miles northwest of Ozark, Ala., 104 mph	4	8	Major (almost total) storm surge and wind damage to structures along beach strip from Fort Walton Beach to Panama City, Fla. High winds destroyed property and crops over eastern Alabama. Flooding and miscellaneous damage from heavy rains over northeastern U.S.
1992, August 22–26 ANDREW	Bahamas South Fla. Louisiana	164 Miami, Fla.	38	10	Most costly storm in U.S. History. $20 billion in damages.

#1The figures published are merely approximations of fact. Since errors in dollar estimates vary in proportion to the total damage, storms are placed in categories varying from 1 to 9 as follows:

1 Less than $50
2 $50 to $500
3 $500 to $5,000
4 $5,000 to $50,000
5 $50,000 to $500,000
6 $500,000 to $5,000,000
7 $5,000,000 to $50,000,000
8 $50,000,000 to $500,000,000
9 $500,000,000 to $5,000,000,000

* Fastest one mile unless otherwise noted.
† Wind measuring equipment disabled at speed indicated. Highest winds probably higher.
1 One-minute maximum speed.
5 Five-minute maximum speed.
E Estimated

Importance of the Trade Winds

Source: Department of Natural Resources

Few people realize that the peninsula of Florida, jutting out to the southeastward from the American continent, is almost the only well watered area on the earth's surface between latitudes 24° and 31° north. Following this belt of latitude around the world, all the rest of the land between those parallels is dry, sandy or mountainous waste—only coastal China between Shanghai and Canton, and coastal Texas are exceptions, with Florida, to the desert rule. Our rains in Florida are the result of the Trade Winds sweeping westward out of the warm Atlantic ocean. These winds pick up a tremendous amount of water in their passage across the ocean. When they strike the Florida peninsula, convection currents raise these moisture-laden breezes further aloft where they are suddenly cooled and release rain.

Geographic Facts

Never more than 95 miles wide, the Florida peninsula does not end its meanderings until its last land formation is some 600 miles south of the southern boundary of the state of California.

Yet, Florida is not quite in the tropics (if we are to be technical), lacking a hundred miles. The state lies between the 31st and 24th parallels, North latitude. The southern tip of Florida is 1,700 miles north of the equator, but is nearer the equator than any other part of continental United States.

Now let us fix the location of South America in relation to Florida. Simply draw a line from Miami directly south. *East* of that line is South America, whereas many persons believe South America to be directly south of Florida.

Now draw a line from the northeastern shore of Maine southward. Jacksonville is 837 miles *west* of that line.

We have often pointed out because of these facts that Florida came near being a mid-western state, longitudinally. Jacksonville is directly beneath Cleveland, Ohio, Pensacola is directly beneath Chicago, Illinois.

Thunderstorm Capital

The Florida peninsula is the "thunderstorm capital" of the northern hemisphere. Werner A. Baum, writing in *The Florida Handbook 1957,* said "only in limited portions of the southern hemisphere, particularly in the heart of South Africa, are thunderstorms more frequent than over the Florida peninsula."

Fred Power, of the U.S. Weather Service at Tallahassee, says the " 'whys' and 'wherefores' that bring about this great incidence of thunderstorm activity for Florida fill many books, but to express it simply it is because we have the 'heat and ample moisture' plus other air-mass dynamics that induce thunderstorms."

Sports

Golf
It is not established which golf course was the first in Florida, but an early layout, initially of four holes, was that built by Colonel J. Hamilton Gillespie at Sarasota around 1886.

Jai-Alai
Jai-alai first was played professionally as a pari-mutuel sport in Florida at Miami in 1935.

Heavyweight Championship Bouts
Champion James J. Corbett defeated Charley Mitchell in three rounds at Jacksonville on Jan. 25, 1894.

Champion Primo Carnera defeated Tommy Loughran in 15 rounds at Miami on March 1, 1934.

The bout between heavyweight championship contenders Jack Sharkey and W. L. (Young) Stribling at Miami Beach on Feb. 27, 1929, had a gate among boxing's largest, of the time, drawing 40,000 fans who paid $405,000. Sharkey defeated Stribling.

Muhammad Ali (Cassius Clay) became world heavyweight champion at Miami Beach when he defeated Charles "Sonny" Liston on February 25, 1964

Spring Baseball Training
Although the journey of the Boston National League team to New Orleans in 1884 was the first foray from home grounds for seasoning, spring training for baseball teams got its real foothold in 1901 when the American League became a major.

It was in that same year that Connie Mack started the parade to Florida, herding his Philadelphia Athletics to Jacksonville. Brooklyn trained two years later at St. Augustine.

Daytona Beach—Symbol of Speed
Daytona Beach long has been the world's symbol for speed on wheels, its fame stretching back to 1903, when Alexander Winton broke the kilometer record with his "Bullet" on February 26. His miles per hour speed was 68.198.

During this epochal period in the perfection of the combustion engine, up to Sir Malcolm Campbell's record 276.8 miles per hour with "Bluebird" on March 7, 1935, the wave-packed sand drew such men of renown as Ransom E. Olds, Barney Oldfield, Glenn H. Curtiss, William K. Vanderbilt, Jr., Henry Ford, Louis Chevrolet, Ralph DePalma, Fred Dusenberg, Tommy Milton, Frank Lockhart, Lee Bible, and the steel-nerved Britishers—Major H.O.D. Segrave, Kaye Don and Sir Malcolm.

Early Football
Early collegiate football games in Florida were: 1901, Stetson 6, Florida Agricultural College 0; 1906, University of Florida 16, Gainesville Athletic

Teeing off at the Royal Palm Hotel at Miami in 1899. The Royal Palm, on the Miami River at Biscayne Bay, was one in the string of luxury hotels built by Henry M. Flagler in opening the East Coast of Florida to wealthy winter visitors. Florida State Archives

Club 6; 1926 (freshmen) University of Miami 7, Rollins 0; Florida A&M College 6, Edward Waters 0; 1933, University of Tampa 28, Bowden 0; 1947, Florida State University 6, Stetson 14.

Greyhound Racing

Florida has made important contributions to American greyhound racing. The late O. P. Smith used an electrical rabbit and a circular track for greyhounds at Hialeah in 1923. The St. Petersburg Kennel Club, opened in 1924, is the oldest greyhound track still in operation on this continent.—Everett A. Clay.

Horse Racing

History books record that Hernando De Soto and his party raced in Cuba the winter of 1538–39 prior to the expedition's departure for Florida, and history books further record that the expedition included a goodly number of the Royal Spanish stock among the 225 to 250 horses brought aboard ship.

It is natural to suppose that casual horse racing was the chief diversion after De Soto's party landed on the West Coast. There is also reason to believe that horse racing existed on the peninsula in the early days of Spanish, French and English colonization, as it did in other parts of the South.

The date and location of Florida's first formal track are matters of conjecture, but newspaper files in the State Library at Tallahassee report there were at least three different courses operating major winter racing in Florida in the 1840's: the Calhoun Course in the now non-existent metropolis of St. Joseph, the Marion Course near Tallahassee, and the Franklin track at Apalachicola.

The Daily Picayune of New Orleans for March 16, 1841, quoted the St. Joseph Times as saying of the Calhoun course: "The track is decidedly one of the finest in the Union, and the buildings, such as the judges' stand, ladies' stand, and others, for the accommodation of the members of the club and visitors, are well located and comfortably arranged. The stables, situated within 100 yards of the track, are better adapted to the purpose for which they are intended than any we have ever seen—we make no exceptions, and we have seen a great many."

The five-day annual meeting at the St. Joseph track that winter was reported by the Apalachicola Commercial Advertiser to offer prizes to owners of "any horse, mare or gelding in the United States: First day, one mile heats, purse $200; Second day, two mile heats, purse $400; Third day, three mile heats, purse $600; Fourth day, four-mile heats, purse $1,000. Fifth day, proprietor's purse, mile heats, three best in five, $300".

Similar purses were offered at the Apalachicola track, whose meeting was scheduled two weeks after St. Joseph's closing, so horses could be raced at both.

The Florida Journal for December 10, 1842, informed the public that races near Tallahassee would begin for five days on January 10, 1843.

"A Jockey Club ball will be given by members of the club," announced the Journal. "Columbus, Milledgeville and Macon papers please copy."

The first famous race horse to come to Florida was Rienzi, owned by General Thomas Brown, later to become the state's only Whig governor. Rienzi, sired by the Imported Autocrat, out of Fanny Kemble, was brought here in the Fall of 1838 and a March 16, 1841 story in the New Orleans Daily Picayune reported that the horse won mile heats at St. Joseph in 2:03, 2:05 and 2:06.—Everett A. Clay

Baseball greats Lou Gehrig, Connie Mack, Sr., and Babe Ruth at Spring Training in St. Petersburg, about 1925
St. Petersburg Historical Museum

The Florida Forests

The forests of Florida are one of our great natural resources, ranking with water and sunshine in meeting highly diverse demands placed on them by millions of individual residents and visitors.

Florida, with about 35 million acres of land, has 14.9 million acres classed as commercial forestland, which is that land most capable of growing the best timber in the shortest time. An estimated 14.9 billion cubic feet of wood grow on this land and the gross volume is increasing, though not always in usable form.

U.S. Forest Service surveys indicate that 4.9 million acres of commercial forestland are not sufficiently stocked to have a manageable stand.

About 51 percent of the commercial timberland in Florida is held by thousands of private owners. Their individual decisions as to whether to produce more wood on their land largely will determine Florida's future production. Proper management of their forests can generate many additional benefits for the owners, both in income and intangibles.

The pulpwood and timber-growing industries own about 32 percent of the commercial timberland, and governmental agencies own the remaining 17 percent.

Reforestation

Organized reforestation has been underway in Florida since 1928. It began with the establishment of the Florida Forestry Service which later merged with the Department of Agriculture and Consumer Services as the Division of Forestry. It took nearly 30 years to plant the first one billion seedlings. But since then, about one billion have been planted each ten years, and now the total has passed four billion.

Florida's industrial and private landowners plant more than 125 million seedlings each year. Last season, the total was 137 million on about 190,000 acres of land. Florida is among the leading states in reforestation.

The bulk of the planting was pines, primarily the slash pine which remains Florida's principal commercial tree.

The slash pine is adaptable to a variety of soils and growth conditions, can be started easily from seed and transplanted to the forest with a high survival rate, and grows rapidly to valuable sizes. The plantations established in North Florida since the 1930s are based primarily on slash pines, and the annual cut of pulpwood is the most valuable production from the state's forests.

In 1992, Florida produced 4,354,577 cords of pulpwood.

There is increasing use of other pines, especially longleaf to re-establish

Source: Division of Forestry, Florida Department of Agriculture and Consumer Affairs.

Turpentining in northeast Florida early in this century. The work was lonely, and hard, and the living conditions were primitive, in the early turpentine operations. Gum collected off freshly scarred pines was collected in barrels, hauled by wagon to a distillery and turned into a variety of useful products. Florida turpentining peaked in the first quarter of the present century and now has virtually vanished from the forestry scene.
Division of Forestry

Cut out and get out was the policy of many early loggers in Florida. But so vast were the virgin forests that their decimation took about 50 years. More than one billion board feet were sawed each year between 1889 and 1933; the decline after that was sharp. Here a tram road snaked through a north Florida forest over which pine timbers were brought out to market. The old tram road grades from 50 years ago still can be found in regrown forests of the state.
Division of Forestry

the longleaf pine—wiregrass ecosystem that at one time occupied most of the pine sites in Florida.

The Division of Forestry produces about 18 percent of the 137 million plus seedlings that are planted each year in Florida. In addition, the Division nursery is stepping up production of genetically improved slash pines which can produce mature trees in a substantially shorter time than regular seedlings. The seedlings are grown in special orchards from cuttings taken from "super pines" found growing naturally.

Economics of Forestry

In 1992, the forest and wood-using industries annually generated approximately $6.1 billion in economic wealth at all levels of trade.

Stumpage value of harvest	$ 263 million
Logging	$ 182 million
Manufacture value	$4,328 million
Transportation and marketing	$1,372 million
TOTAL	$6,145 million

More than 120,000 persons in Florida are directly employed by industries based on forest production. The annual payroll that they receive totals more than $1.2 billion.

About 17,000 persons are employed in the pulp and allied industries. An additional 27,000 are employed in the manufacture of lumber and wood products. More than 15,000 people work with industries making wood furniture and fixtures, and more than 60,000 people are employed in housing construction.

Nine pulpmills are in operation in Florida. These utilize most of the pulpwood harvested annually in Florida. In 1992, Florida produced 4,354,577 cords of pulpwood.

492 / Forests

The state also has 80 sawmills, 5 mills producing veneer, and 20 mills that can be classed as miscellaneous. All these add up to 105 primary wood using mills.

In addition to pulpwood and timber, these mills produce charcoal, particleboard, industrial fuel (used mostly by the plants themselves), and wood shavings for packing, agricultural and other purposes.

Also, there are hundreds of plants using wood to produce such items as cabinets, prefabricated and mobile homes, containers, packing crates, furniture, and fixtures, and many others.

The Florida Division of Forestry

This agency provides statewide fire protection for woodlands and rural structures, and assistance with firefighting to municipal and volunteer fire departments. It assists and advises landowners in a wide variety of forestry matters, and aids urban populations and governments in establishing, maintaining and expanding the urban forests that provide invaluable benefits to city environments. The agency operates throughout the state and is administered by the Director, Division of Forestry, 3125 Conner Boulevard, Tallahassee, FL 32399-1650. There are 13 administrative districts under District managers, and two forestry centers under center managers, one at Withlacoochee State Forest near Tampa and another at Blackwater State Forest near Pensacola.

Outdoor recreation is the long suit of Florida's four state forests and three national forests. This scene of a typical outing could be occurring at any of dozens of locations. These publicly owned forests are operated for a variety of benefits, including outdoor recreation, timber production, maintenance of ground water and control of erosion, and for other purposes. In addition, many private landowning companies and individuals allow recreational use of their lands. Through such agreements, the outdoors is never very far from anyone in Florida. Division of Forestry

State and National Forests

The Division of Forestry operates 32 state forests that total 513,468 acres and cooperates with other agencies, in managing 429,197 acres of other state and public lands throughout the state.

Many recreational opportunities are provided in the state forests, particularly at Withlacoochee State Forest near Brooksville and Blackwater River State Forest in West Florida. The forests are used for hiking, camping, boating, fishing and hunting. The Division also manages the sale of about $4 million worth of timber annually. The cut is purposely kept well below the growth rate so that the inventory of valuable trees is constantly increasing.

Endangered wildlife and rare plants find protection in all state forests. An environmental education center open to public school students between 6th and 11th grades is operated in one-week sessions each summer at Withlacoochee State Forest. Annual attendance is more than 700 pupils.

The U.S. Forest Service operates three national forests in Florida, which like the state forests are operated to supply multiple benefits to varied interests. The Apalachicola, Osceola and Ocala National Forests total 1,140,730 acres among them. All offer extensive opportunities for outdoor recreation, with improved facilities as well as natural places suitable for almost every kind of forest-oriented recreation.

Management goals for the national forests include sustained yields of wood, forage, wildlife and water quality. The three forests are administered by the Forest Supervisor, National Forest in Florida, P.O. Box 1050, Tallahassee, FL 32302.

State of Champion Trees

Florida's great trees continue to be the source of woodland legends about which tree is the "biggest" or the "oldest" of the forest monarchs. In 1980 the Division of Forestry of the Florida Department of Agriculture and Consumer Services established the Florida Champion Tree Register to promote awareness of these grand trees and the need for conservation of the forest's bountiful resources.

The Florida Champion Tree Register is linked to the American Forestry Association's National Register of Big Trees, and many of Florida's Champion trees also bear the honored title of National Champion.

In 1994, more than 350 Florida Champion Trees included 106 National Champions. The largest National Champion Tree in Florida is the grand Camphor Tree near Wauchula. This tree is 368 inches (30 feet, 8 inches) in circumference, 72 feet tall and carries an average crown spread of 102 feet.

The biggest tree on the Florida

"The Senator," a huge cypress in Seminole County, is believed to be more than 3,500 years old. Department of Commerce

Champion Tree Register is a great Cluster Fig located in Broward County. This giant is 586 inches (48 feet, 10 inches) in circumference, 108 feet tall and bears an average crown spread of 105 feet. The Florida Champion Baldcypress is another huge tree, measuring 586 inches in circumference. This tree is overshadowed by the National Champion Baldcypress at Cat Island, Louisiana, which is almost 100 inches larger in circumference.

Baldcypresses grow very slowly as they mature so the Florida Champion Baldcypress is estimated to be at least 1,000 years old and experts speculate that as many as 2,000 years may have passed since it sprouted in the Suwannee River's flood plain.

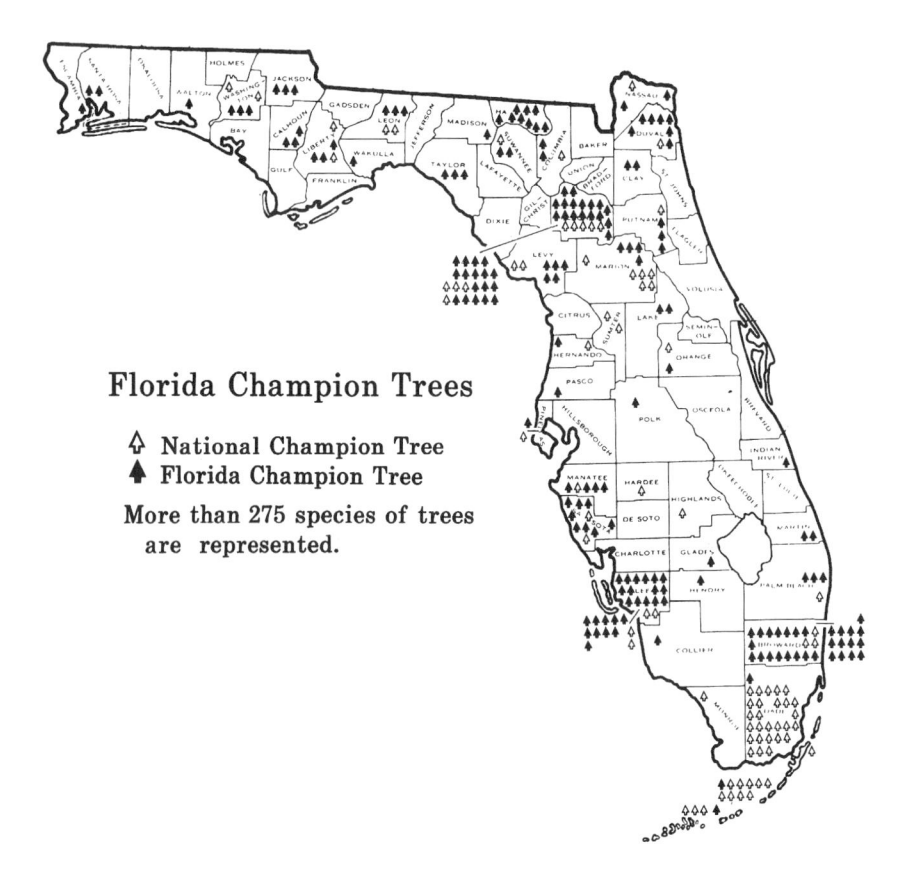

Florida Champion Trees

△ National Champion Tree
▲ Florida Champion Tree

More than 275 species of trees are represented.

Roseate spoonbills are clustered in this Florida water-edge picture.   Department of Commerce

Birds in Florida

The abundance and the variety of bird life in Florida have occasioned exclamation since Spanish, French and English explorers first were impressed. Writings of the day about the journeys of Ribaut, de Soto, Hawkins and others who were among the first to see Florida, testify to the wonderment at the great flights of birds, the brilliance of plumage, and the numerousness of the kinds.

The first important contribution to the study of Florida's birds was made by a forerunner of the great Audubon, Mark Catesby, whose *Natural History of Carolina, Florida, and the Bahama islands* was published in parts during 1731–48.

John Bartram, King George Ill's botanist for the Floridas, made a trip with his son William up the St. Johns River to its headwaters in the winter of 1765–66, and the journal of the elder Bartram contained comment upon the birds observed.

The son received a subsequent commission from a Quaker naturalist to return to Florida and obtain further information on the plant life. *The Travels of William Bartram,* whose excellence may be judged from the fact that it remains in print today although first published in 1791, included a list of 215 species of birds seen in Florida, together with speculation upon the migratory nature of many of these.

John James Audubon, America's foremost ornithologist of the nineteenth century, spent seven months in Florida during 1831–32, observing bird life from St. Augustine to Key West. Knowledge of the birds of the state was fairly well rounded out with the completion in 1939 of publication of Audubon's majestic *Ornithological Biography.*

Florida enjoys more than its share of birds for the state serves as a flyway for migrants—mostly those winging south for the winter. Many of these spend the cold months in Florida; others continue on to the West Indies and Central and South America.

State Parks

Of Florida's state parks, Jay Clarke, *The Miami Herald's* Travel Editor, wrote:

"I've camped under moss-draped oaks and listened to the armadillos scuttling through the brush. I've clambered on the ramparts of a seaside fortress and chatted with a Civil War private.

"I've explored the ruins of an old sugar mill, splashed on a beautiful but uncrowded ocean beach, ridden a miniature train on a barrier island and climbed up on the temple mounds of pre-Columbian Indians.

"I've done all these things in Florida state parks, a great resource that is more extensive than most people realize. For vacationers looking for interesting places not too far away, the park system offers an amazing variety of experience at minimal cost."

For up-to-date information, write: Office of Education and Information, Department of Environmental Protection, Marjory Stoneman Douglas Building, 3900 Commonwealth Boulevard, Tallahassee 32399-3000, or telephone (904) 488-7326.

The beautiful beach at Hugh Taylor Birch State Park, Fort Lauderdale.
Department of Commerce, Division of Tourism

The Wakulla River just below the spring at Edward Ball-Wakulla Spring State Park.

Florida State Archives

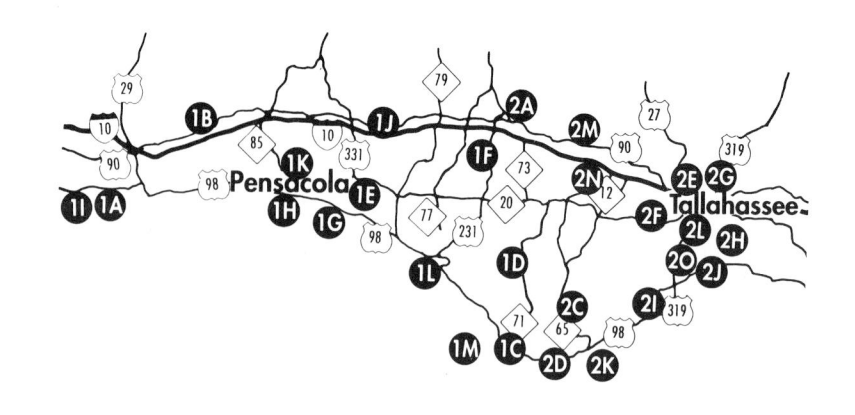

ID	Name	Phone	Recreation Area/Preserve/Park	State Garden	Archeological/Botanical Site	Geological Site	Historical Site	Interpretive Visitor Center	Full Facility Camping	Primitive Camping	Group/Youth Camping	Cabins	Picnic	Swimming	Fishing	Nature Trail	Guided Tours	Canoeing	Boat Ramp	Concession
1A	BIG LAGOON; p. 10	(904) 492-1595			•					•			•	•	•	•			•	•
1B	BLACKWATER RIVER; p. 10	(904) 623-2363	•						•				•	•	•	•		•	•	
1C	CONSTITUTION CONVENTION MUSEUM; p. 10	(904) 229-8029				•				•										
1D	DEAD LAKES; p. 10	(904) 639-2702							•				•		•	•			•	
1E	EDEN GARDENS; p. 11	(904) 231-4214			•		•						•				•			
1F	FALLING WATERS; p. 11	(904) 638-6130			•				•			•	•	•	•	•				
1G	GRAYTON BEACH; p. 11	(904) 231-4210			•				•				•	•	•	•			•	
1H	HENDERSON BEACH; p. 11	(904) 837-7550			•								•	•	•	•				
1I	PERDIDO KEY; p. 11	(904) 492-1595			•								•	•	•					
1J	PONCE DE LEON SPRINGS; p. 12	(904) 836-4281			•								•	•	•	•				
1K	ROCKY BAYOU; p. 12	(904) 833-9144			•				•				•		•	•			•	
1L	ST. ANDREWS; p. 12	(904) 233-5140			•				•				•	•	•	•			•	•
1M	ST. JOSEPH PENINSULA; p. 12	(904) 227-1327	•						•	•	•	•	•	•	•	•			•	
2P	ECONFINA RIVER; p. 13	(904) 584-2135	•						•				•		•	•			•	
2A	FLORIDA CAVERNS; p. 13	(904) 482-9598	•						•	•		•	•	•	•	•	•		•	
2B	FOREST CAPITAL MUSEUM; p. 13	(904) 584-3227				•			•				•							
2D	JOHN GORRIE MUSEUM; p. 13	(904) 653-9347				•														
2E	LAKE JACKSON MOUNDS; p. 14	(904) 922-6007					•						•			•				
2F	LAKE TALQUIN; p. 14	(904) 922-6007											•		•					
2G	MACLAY GARDENS; p. 14	(904) 487-4556				•			•				•	•	•	•	•		•	
2H	NATURAL BRIDGE BATTLEFIELD; p. 14	(904) 922-6007					•						•							
2I	OCHLOCKONEE RIVER; p. 15	(904) 962-2771	•						•			•	•		•	•			•	
2J	SAN MARCOS DE APALACHE; p. 15	(904) 922-6007					•	•					•			•				
2K	ST. GEORGE ISLAND; p. 15	(904) 927-2111							•	•	•		•	•	•	•			•	
2L	TALLAHASSEE-ST. MARKS TRAIL; p. 15	(904) 922-6007											•		•					•
2M	THREE RIVERS; p. 15	(904) 482-9006				•			•				•		•	•			•	
2N	TORREYA; p. 15	(904) 643-2674	•						•	•	•	•	•		•	•				
2O	WAKULLA SPRINGS; p. 16	(904) 922-3633	•										•	•	•	•	•			•
3A	CEDAR KEY MUSEUM; p. 17	(904) 543-5350			•		•						•							
3B	CEDAR KEY SCRUB; p. 20	(904) 543-5567		•												•				
3C	DEVIL'S MILLHOPPER; p. 17	(904) 336-2008				•		•					•			•	•			
3D	GOLD HEAD BRANCH; p. 17	(904) 473-4701	•						•	•	•	•	•	•	•	•	•			
3Q	HAWTHORNE STATE TRAIL; p. 17	(904) 336-2135											•							
3E	ICHETUCKNEE SPRINGS; p. 17	(904) 497-2511											•	•	•	•		•		
3F	MANATEE SPRINGS; p. 17	(904) 493-6072							•			•	•	•	•	•		•	•	
3G	MARJORIE KINNAN RAWLINGS; p. 18	(904) 466-3672					•	•								•	•			
3H	O'LENO; p. 18	(904) 454-1853	•						•	•	•	•	•	•	•	•	•			
3I	OLUSTEE BATTLEFIELD; p. 18	(904) 752-3866					•	•					•			•				
3J	PAYNES PRAIRIE; p. 18	(904) 466-3397		•					•				•		•	•			•	
3K	PEACOCK SPRINGS; p. 19	(904) 497-2511				•								•		•				
3L	SAN FELASCO HAMMOCK; p. 19	(904) 336-2008		•												•				
3M	SILVER RIVER; p. 19	(904) 489-8503	•						•				•			•				
3N	STEPHEN FOSTER; p. 19	(904) 397-2733					•						•			•				
3O	SUWANNEE RIVER; p. 19	(904) 362-2746							•	•	•		•		•	•		•	•	
3P	WACCASASSA BAY; p. 20	(904) 543-5567											•		•					
4A	AMELIA ISLAND; p. 20	(904) 251-2320			•								•	•	•	•			•	
4B	ANASTASIA; p. 20	(904) 461-2033			•				•		•		•	•	•	•			•	
4C	BIG TALBOT; p. 21	(904) 251-2320					•						•		•	•			•	
4D	BULOW CREEK; p. 21	(904) 677-4645											•							
4E	BULOW PLANTATION RUINS; p. 21	(904) 439-2219					•	•					•			•	•			
4F	FAVER-DYKES; p. 21	(904) 794-0997	•						•		•		•		•	•		•	•	
4G	GAMBLE ROGERS (FLAGLER BEACH); p. 21	(904) 439-2474			•				•				•	•	•	•			•	
4H	FORT CLINCH; p. 21	(904) 277-7274					•	•	•				•	•	•	•	•		•	
4I	FORT GEORGE; p. 22	(904) 251-2320	•				•	•					•						•	
4J	GUANA RIVER; p. 22	(904) 825-5071		•									•			•				
4K	LITTLE TALBOT ISLAND; p. 22	(904) 251-2320			•				•				•	•	•	•			•	
4M	RAVINE GARDENS; p. 22	(904) 329-3721				•							•			•				
4N	TOMOKA; p. 23	(904) 676-4050	•						•			•	•		•	•		•	•	
4O	WASHINGTON OAKS GARDENS; p. 23	(904) 445-3161				•							•		•	•	•			

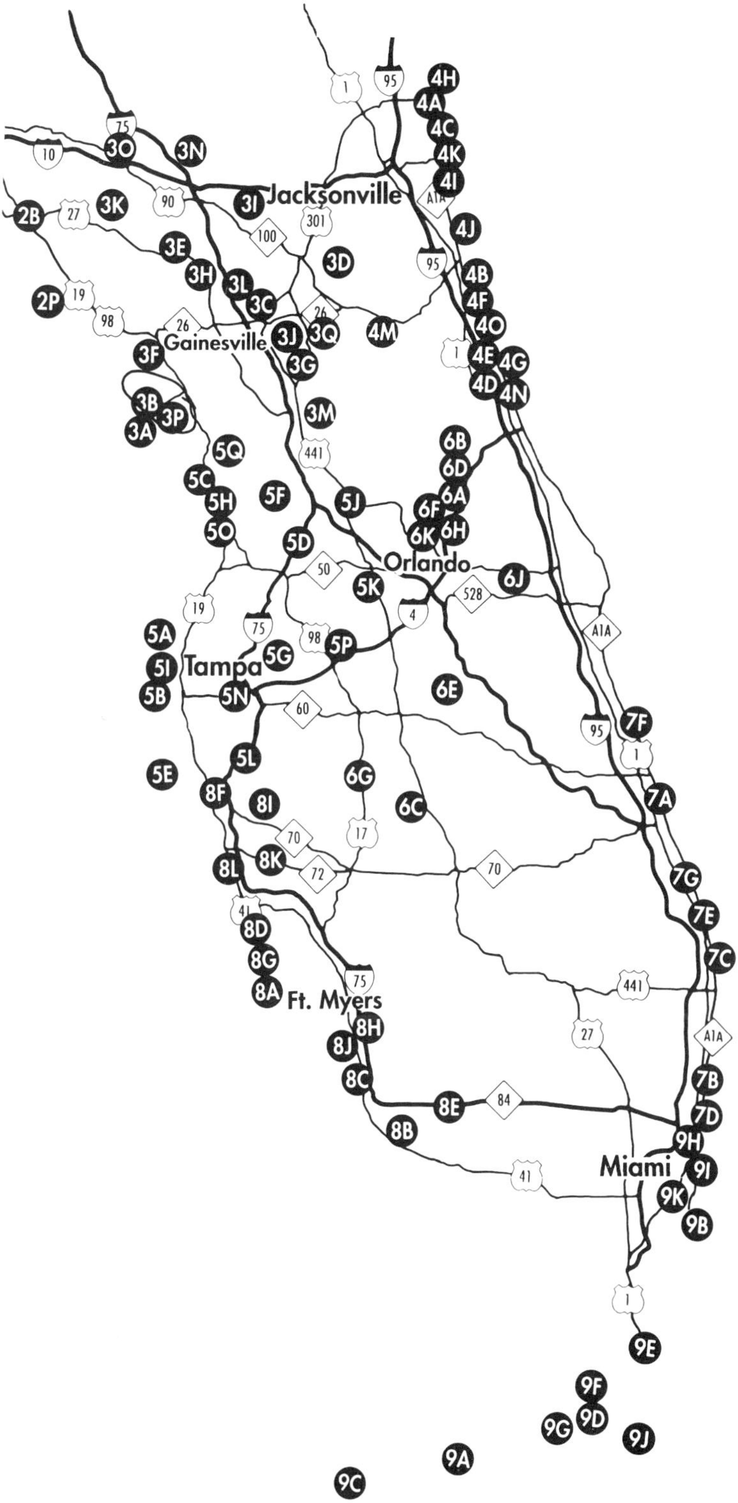

Jacksonville
Gainesville
Orlando
Tampa
Ft. Myers
Miami
95
1
75
10
90
27
19
98
26
100
301
A1A
441
50
528
4
60
17
70
72
41
84
2B 2P
3A 3B 3C 3D 3E 3F 3G 3H 3I 3J 3K 3L 3M 3N 3O 3P 3Q
4A 4B 4C 4D 4E 4F 4G 4H 4I 4J 4K 4M 4N 4O
5A 5B 5C 5D 5E 5F 5G 5H 5I 5J 5K 5L 5N 5O 5P 5Q
6A 6B 6C 6D 6E 6F 6G 6H 6J 6K
7A 7B 7C 7D 7E 7F 7G
8A 8B 8C 8D 8E 8F 8G 8H 8I 8J 8K 8L
9A 9B 9C 9D 9E 9F 9G 9H 9I 9J 9K

500 / State Parks

Code	Park	Phone
5A	ANCLOTE KEY; p. 23	(813) 469-5918
5B	CALADESI ISLAND; p. 23	(813) 469-5918
5C	CRYSTAL RIVER; p. 26	(904) 795-3817
5D	DADE BATTLEFIELD; p. 26	(904) 793-4781
5E	EGMONT KEY; p. 26	(813) 893-2627
5F	FORT COOPER; p. 26	(904) 726-0315
5P	GENERAL JAMES A. VAN FLEET TRAIL; p. 26	(904) 394-2280
5G	HILLSBOROUGH RIVER; p. 26	(813) 987-6771
5H	HOMOSASSA SPRINGS; p. 27	(904) 628-2311
5I	HONEYMOON ISLAND; p. 27	(813) 469-5942
5J	LAKE GRIFFIN; p. 27	(904) 787-7402
5K	LAKE LOUISA; p. 27	(904) 394-3969
5L	LITTLE MANATEE RIVER; p. 27	(813) 671-5005
5Q	RAINBOW SPRINGS STATE PARK; p. 27	(813) 489-8503
5R	WITHLACOOCHEE STATE TRAIL; p. 28	(904) 394-2280
5N	YBOR CITY; p. 28	(813) 247-6323
5O	YULEE SUGAR MILL RUINS; p. 28	(904) 795-3817
6A	BLUE SPRING; p. 29	(904) 775-3663
6B	DE LEON SPRINGS; p. 29	(904) 985-4212
6C	HIGHLANDS HAMMOCK; p. 29	(813) 385-0011
6D	HONTOON ISLAND; p. 29	(904) 736-5309
6E	LAKE KISSIMMEE; p. 30	(813) 696-1112
6F	LOWER WEKIVA RIVER; p. 30	(407) 330-6725
6G	PAYNES CREEK; p. 30	(813) 375-4717
6H	ROCK SPRINGS RUN; p. 30	(407) 884-2009
6J	TOSOHATCHEE; p. 30	(407) 568-5893
6K	WEKIWA SPRINGS; p. 31	(407) 884-2009
7A	FORT PIERCE INLET; p. 31	(407) 468-3985
7B	HUGH TAYLOR BIRCH; p. 31	(305) 564-4521
7C	JOHN D. MACARTHUR BEACH; p. 32	(407) 624-6950
7D	JOHN U. LLOYD BEACH; p. 32	(305) 923-2833
7E	JONATHAN DICKINSON; p. 32	(407) 546-2771
7F	SEBASTIAN INLET; p. 33	(407) 984-4852
7G	ST. LUCIE INLET; p. 33	(407) 744-7603
8A	CAYO COSTA; p. 33	(813) 964-0375
8B	COLLIER-SEMINOLE; p. 33	(813) 394-3397
8C	DELNOR-WIGGINS PASS; p. 34	(813) 597-6196
8D	DON PEDRO ISLAND; p. 34	(813) 964-0375
8E	FAKAHATCHEE STRAND; p. 34	(813) 695-4593
8F	GAMBLE PLANTATION; p. 34	(813) 723-4536
8G	GASPARILLA ISLAND; p. 35	(813) 964-0375
8H	KORESHAN; p. 35	(813) 992-0311
8I	LAKE MANATEE; p. 35	(813) 741-3028
8J	LOVERS KEY; p. 35	(813) 597-6196
8K	MYAKKA RIVER; p. 35	(813) 361-6511
8L	OSCAR SCHERER; p. 36	(813) 483-5956
9A	BAHIA HONDA; p. 36	(305) 872-2353
9B	CAPE FLORIDA; p. 37	(305) 361-5811
9C	FORT ZACHARY TAYLOR; p. 37	(305) 292-6713
9D	INDIAN KEY; p. 37	(305) 664-4815
9E	JOHN PENNEKAMP CORAL REEF; p. 38	(305) 451-1202
9F	LIGNUMVITAE KEY; p. 38	(305) 664-4815
9G	LONG KEY; p. 38	(305) 664-4815
9H	NORTH SHORE; p. 38	(305) 940-7439
9I	OLETA RIVER; p. 39	(305) 947-6357
9J	SAN PEDRO; p. 39	(305) 664-4815
9K	THE BARNACLE; p. 39	(305) 448-9445

Citrus Production and Processing

Although citrus is one of the major fruit crops in the United States, it is not native to Florida. Citrus originated in Asia and was not known in the New World until after Columbus reached the new continent. In fact, citrus was not known even in Europe until around 1400 A.D. Once introduced in Europe, sweet oranges were considered a novelty and growing them was limited to royalty and other wealthy people.

Records indicate that Columbus brought the first citrus to the New World. By the time the first citrus groves were planted in St. Augustine around 1570, however, cirtus could be found growing wild along the rivers in the interior of Florida. The first commercial groves were not established until the 1800s and were planted along the east and west coasts as well as along the St. Johns River to make transporting the fruit to northern markets easier. Grapefruit was not introduced until the 1820s when Odet Phillipe first planted a grove at Safety Harbor.

Commercial production of citrus had reached about five million boxes by 1893–94, but a series of tree-killing freezes in the ensuing years reduced production dramatically. It was not until after the turn of the century that production expanded again. In 1979–80, Florida grew its largest citrus crop in history. That season, growers produced 206.7 million boxes of oranges, 54.8 million boxes of grapefruit and just over 22 million boxes of tangerines, tangelos and other specialty citrus. But another series of devastating freezes struck the industry during the decade of the eighties with the last major freeze in 1989. By the 1984–85 season, production of oranges was cut in half to 103.9 million boxes. Grapefruit production dropped to a low of 39.4 million boxes by the 1982–83 season and specialty fruit production had dropped to less than 10 million boxes by the end of the decade.

As was true in the last century, Florida citrus growers remained resilient through the freeze years and replanted as quickly as possible. With advances in technology, trees were planted more densely on each acre, freeze protection methods were developed and a number of growers moved their groves further south. By 1993–94, the industry had recovered and produced 172.3 million boxes of oranges and slightly more than 51 million boxes of grapefruit. In fact, grapefruit production reached a record of 55.1 million boxes in 1992–93. Production of tangerines, tangelos and other specialty climbed to almost 9.8 million boxes that same year.

Today, there are a record 103 million citrus trees planted on 853,742 acres of land in Florida. Citrus is commercially grown in about 30 of Florida's

Source: Florida Department of Citrus.

67 counties. Putnam and Marion counties have the farthest north commercial groves, while the newest and more densely planted groves are found south of Lake Okeechobee. It is estimated that the industry will exceed record production with these trees before the turn of the twenty-first century.

Today, Florida is the leading producer of grapefruit in the world and ranks second in the world of orange production behind Brazil. The State continues to provide the vast majority of orange juice consumed in the United States. The Florida Department of Citrus, a state agency funded through a grower assessment, conducts an aggressive marketing effort to enhance the sales of Florida-produced and -packed citrus products in the United States and throughout the world.

Great strides have been made in the last five decades both in growing and processing citrus fruit. Prior to the 1940s, Florida citrus was sold primarily as fresh fruit with only a small portion of the fruit made into juice that was then canned. In 1945 the development of frozen concentrated orange juice changed the industry forever. By the decade of the sixties, more oranges grown in Florida were sent to the processing plants than were sold fresh, and today citrus processing is big business. As much as 95 percent of the orange crop is processed while about half of the grapefruit crop is processed. During a recent season, there were nearly 60 processing plants licensed to operate in the state. At least three new processing plants were opened in the southern part of the state during the decade of the nineties to handle the increasing amount of citrus grown in that part of the state.

Frozen Concentrated Orange Juice. The production of frozen concentrated orange juice experienced phenomenal growth following its development. From a beginning of 226,000 gallons produced in 1945–46, the production of this "Cinderella" product had grown to more than 231 million gallons in the 1979–80 season. Due to the freezes during the decade of the eighties production dropped to a low of 90.2 million gallons by the 1989–90 season. But with the replanting of citrus and increasing fruit yield each year, the production of FCOJ has more than doubled. In the 1993–94 season, production had reached 182.2 million gallons and it is expected that production will exceed record levels before the end of this century.

Only the finest oranges are used in frozen concentrate and a large proportion of them move directly from the grove to the concentrate plant. At the processing plants, the oranges are carefully washed, sorted, sterilized and analyzed for uniformity. Every processing plant in Florida is required to have a State inspector at hand whenever the plants are running citrus to insure that the fruit meets Florida's high standards. Any un-

This is an example of an art which largely has disappeared. Packers once vied to produce a label which would attract buyers. This artistry faded when corrugated crates replaced those of wood.
Museum of Florida History

wholesome fruit is removed in the grading process. Once the fruit passes inspection, juice is removed from the fruit automatically by giant extractors. Then the juice is sent to an evaporator where some of the natural water found in the juice is evaporated in a vacuum at temperatures ranging from 60° F to 80° F. Usually the juice is concentrated to 65° Brix or until it reaches about 65 percent soluble solids. During the concentration process, essences are recaptured and added back to the concentrated juice before it is stored in large tanks. Some manufacturers take a portion of that juice and add enough water back to make a 42° Brix product which is then flash frozen in 12-ounce cans and stored at $-10°F$. When consumers add three parts of water to one can of this 42° Brix concentrate, they have a full-bodied, delicious orange juice. In the concentrated form, the product can be stored for up to a year in a freezer.

The same process also is used with grapefruit juice. However, in addition to concentrating grapefruit juice, scientists have developed a way to debitter the juice to make it more palatable for consumers accustomed to sweet juice.

Frozen concentrated orange and grapefruit juice, as well as the manufacture of other types of citrus juice, are strictly regulated by laws established by the State of Florida and several federal government agencies.

Ready-To-Serve Juice. The sales of ready-to-serve, chilled citrus juice have surpassed frozen concentrated juice in recent years and now account for more than half of all the orange juice sold in the United States.

As with the fruit used to make concentrate, oranges and grapefruit are washed, graded and thoroughly inspected before they are sent to extractors. Seeds and large pieces of pulp are screened out of the juice, which is then pasteurized in a flash heating process similar to that used to pasteurize milk. The juice is then chilled rapidly to 30° F and put into waxed cartons, plastic or glass containers. This product is kept very cold until it is consumed.

Another form of ready-to-serve chilled citrus juice is made from reconstituted frozen concentrate. Concentrate that usually is stored at bulk tank farms is shipped to a location near its final destination and has water added back to make a ready-to-drink juice. This product also is pasteurized before it is packed in waxed cartons, plastic or glass containers and chilled. The State of Florida and the U.S. Food and Drug Administration require that reconstituted frozen concentrated orange or grapefruit juice be clearly labeled as reconstituted.

Prior to the widespread use of refrigerated cases at grocery stores, canned citrus juice was the primary form of juice sold. Canned citrus juice still is manufactured in Florida, but not in large quantities. It is made much the same way as pasteurized chilled juice, but it is packed in tin cans and de-aerated to insure maximum preservation. This is a shelf-stable product and can be stored at room temperature until it is opened. In addition, to this product, a new shelf-stable juice has emerged in recent years. This citrus juice product is made much the same way as other forms of ready-to-serve juice, but it is packed in aseptic packages, which gives the product a longer shelf-life.

Citrus Salads and canned sections. Although canned citrus sections and salads are still made in Florida, consumer demand for that product has fallen in recent years. Fruit used for canned segments or salad is washed, graded and inspected. Then the fruit is immersed in hot water for a few minutes, which plumps and loosens the peel without heating the fruit inside. The fruit is hand-peeled and placed in baskets that are immersed in an alkaline bath to remove any excess albedo (the white material under the peel) or loose fibers still adhering to the fruit. The alkali solution is washed off with fresh water and the sections are pulled apart by hand or with the aid of a mechanical knife. The sections are placed in glass jars, covered with a sugar syrup, sealed and sterilized. These fruit sections must be kept cold and generally are found in the refrigerated dairy case at the grocery store. A citrus salad is usually a mix of grapefruit and orange sections packed in the same manner.

In recent years, a new method of peeling fruit has been developed. After washing, grading and inspecting the fruit, it is injected with a natural pectin enzyme to loosen the fruit peel. Then the peel is vacuum suctioned off the fruit. Most often, the whole fruit is then placed on styrofoam trays and wrapped in plastic. This product must be stored at fairly cold temperatures. It currently is popular with restaurants and other institutions, although consumers may begin to see it in grocery stores in the near future.

Production of Oranges and Grapefruit in Florida

Source: USDA, Florida Crop and Livestock Reporting Service, Orlando Florida

Season	Oranges Production 1,000 boxes	% of U.S.	Grapefruit Production 1,000 boxes	% of U.S.
1930–31	16,800	37.5	15,800	86.5
1940–41	28,600	40.6	24,600	59.0
1950–51	67,300	61.4	33,200	74.1
1960–61	82,700	76.6	31,600	75.6
1970–71	142,300	75.1	42,900	70.8
1971–72	137,000	71.6	47,000	73.4
1972–73	169,700	75.5	45,400	69.2
1973–74	165,800	76.7	48,100	73.4
1974–75	173,300	72.8	44,600	72.4
1975–76	181,200	74.8	49,100	70.1
1976–77	186,800	76.4	51,500	69.1
1977–78	167,800	76.2	51,400	68.8
1978–79	164,000	77.9	50,000	74.2
1979–80	206,700	75.5	54,800	74.9
1980–81	172,400	70.4	50,300	74.1
1981–82	129,000	72.5	48,100	67.7
1982–83	144,200	64.1	39,400	65.0
1983–84	116,700	69.0	40,900	76.0
1984–85	108,900	65.0	44,000	79.0
1985–86	119,000	67.0	46,750	81.0
1986–87	119,700	66.0	50,000	80.0
1987–88	139,000	70.0	53,950	79.0
1988–89	146,600	74.3	54,750	81.3
1989–90	110,200	64.0	35,700	76.6

	Oranges		Grapefruit	
	Production		Production	
Season	1,000 boxes	% of U.S.	1,000 boxes	% of U.S.
1990–91	151,600	86.4	45,100	84.9
1991–92	139,800	70.6	42,400	81.0
1992–93	186,500	75.8	55,150	83.1
1993–94	174,200	not available	51,050	not available
1994–95 estimated	196,000	not available	55,500	not available

By-Products

Although juice is the primary product produced by the Florida citrus processing companies, nothing is wasted. The excess pulp and seeds strained from the juice as well as the peel are used to make a variety of by-products.

Stock Feed. Today, more than 20 citrus juice processors also make animal feed from left over citrus peel. Annual production of this stock feed is approximately one million tons a year.

The left over pulp and peel are ground into tiny pieces and a small amount of lime is added. After a preliminary pressing to remove a part of the moisture present in the material, it is dried in giant rotating kilns until the moisture content is between 5 to 10 percent. The driers may be either direct fired or steam heated. Then the material is formed into nutritious pellets and used as a stock feed, particularly to fatten and condition beef and dairy cattle.

Citrus Molasses. The liquid pressed from the stock feed contains about eight percent soluble solids. When the liquor is concentrated under vacuum, it yields a heavy syrup of golden to orange-brown color very similar to black strap molasses. This citrus molasses often is added back to the dried pulp when the pellets are made or it is used in the production of alcohol.

Citrus Seed Oil. Citrus seed oil is pressed from dried orange and grapefruit seeds. The raw oil has a number of uses. The material left over after the oil is removed also is a high source of protein and is added back to the stock feed.

Peel oil. Oil also can be extracted from the peel before it is dried for stock feed. One component of peel oil is d-limonene. Among its other uses, d-limonene is used as a natural, non-toxic solvent used for cleaning.

Both citrus peel and seed oil are used as flavorings in a variety of foods, beverages and perfumes. Citrus by-products are used to make alcohol, dyes, gum drops and other candy, wine, bakery goods, soap, air fresheners, furniture polish, cosmetics, and pesticides. Other processing waste may be used to make methane gas, yeast and dextran gum. Even the waste water from citrus processing plants is recycled and used to irrigate citrus groves.
Source: Florida Department of Citrus

Source: Florida Department of Citrus

Florida's Mineral Industry

Steven M. Spencer and Jacqueline Lloyd
Florida Geological Survey
Tallahassee, Florida

Florida is not generally thought of as a mining state however, reserves of various resources contribute significantly to the economy. The estimated nonfuel production in 1993 was valued by the U.S. Bureau of Mines (USBM) at $1.3 billion dollars. The State dropped from fifth nationally in U.S. non fuel mineral production in 1992, to ninth in 1993 (USBM, 1994). This is due in part to the drop in demand for Florida Phosphate. The State's fuel and non fuel industry generate large revenues to the state and numerous employment opportunities for its residents.

Natural resources fall into two broad categories, renewable and non-renewable. Our forests, animal, soil, and water resources are considered renewable because through proper management, they can be utilized and renewed within time limits. Our mineral resources, however, are an entirely different matter because once they are used they are gone forever.

The Florida mineral industry is largely dependent upon its non-metallic mineral resources: phosphate, heavy minerals, limestone and dolomite, clays, sand and gravel, and peat. The petroleum industry in Florida continues in a declining trend, however, it still ranks 20th in the U.S. in production. Since its discovery in Florida in 1943 to the present more than 541 million barrels of oil and greater than 561 million cubic feet (MCF) of gas have been produced.

The following is a compilation of data which briefly discusses those commodities listed above.

Phosphate Rock

Phosphate was discovered in central Florida in 1881. Early mining was characterized by crude methods, high costs, and poor recovery. Over the years the pick, shovel, and wheelbarrow gave way to the steam shovel and later the more efficient electric dragline.

Although the 2nd half of 1992 and 1st half of 1993 were particularly difficult for the phosphate industry, phosphate remains the leading mineral commodity, in terms of value, mined in Florida. Florida leads the country in the production of phosphate with approximately 80 percent of the total domestic and about 20 to 25 percent of the world market. Production areas in Florida include Hamilton, Hillsborough, Manatee, Hardee, and Polk Counties.

The phosphate deposits in Florida are divided into three types: land pebble, hard rock, and soft rock. The economic land pebble phosphate deposits occur in two widely separated areas, one centered in Hamilton County in northern Florida and the other in Polk, Hillsborough, Manatee, and Hardee counties. These deposits account for over 98 percent of Florida's total phosphate production.

Hard rock phosphate deposits occur in a narrow north-south trend about one hundred miles long located in the northwestern part of the Florida peninsula. In this region the phosphate has been deposited by the downward percolation of waters and deposition of phosphate or replacement of the limestone by phosphate. The hard rock phosphate deposits are not presently mined due to economic limitations.

Soft rock phosphate production is from the tailings of former hard rock mining operations. This commodity constitutes only a very minor fraction of the total production of phosphate mined in Florida.

The principal use of phosphate rock is in the manufacture of fertilizer products. Other products include phosphorous, phosphoric acid, and ferrophosphate. Compounds made from elementary phosphorous include those used in the manufacture of baking powder, water softeners, household detergents, rustproofing compounds, glass, pottery, dental cements, photographic supplies, fireproofing compounds and sugar. Fluorine, a by-product of the phosphate industry, is used in water fluoridation and in aluminum metal production.

Limestone

Limestone of very high grade, analyzing about 95 percent or greater calcium carbonate ($CaCo_3$), occurs at or near the ground surface in several Florida counties including Jackson, Citrus, Alachua, Sumter, and Marion. The uses of high-grade limestone are numerous and varied; the Florida rock is used primarily in road construction and soil conditioning. That used on roads is as a road base upon which concrete or asphalt surfacing is applied. The very pure limestones of Florida lend themselves readily to the manufacture of lime, an essential ingredient of cement, and in the construction industry as plaster and mortar. Lime is produced by calcining limestone at temperatures of 1000 to 1300 degrees centigrade.

Limestone with a high quartz content and other impurities is utilized for road base materials in Dade, Broward, and adjacent counties. This limestone analyzes about 80 percent calcium carbonate. The harder limestone seams are separated, crushed, sized, and sold for aggregate. In Hernando County, indurated, slightly sandy limestone is crushed, sized, and used for aggregate, a much needed and scarce commodity in Florida.

Coquina, a type of limestone composed of broken and whole shells and quartz sand, is present along Atlantic coastal ridges and beaches, and also on the Gulf beaches between Tampa and Venice. In some parts of Florida the hardened coquina rock is used as a road base and as building material. Coquina was used in constructing Castillo de San Marcos at St. Augustine in the 16th Century and in the Bok Singing Tower near Lake Wales. Oyster shell, similar to coquina, is dredged from the old oyster bars and is calcined for lime which is then used in the extraction of magnesium from sea water. Additional uses include road basecourse, concrete aggregate, and screening for chicken feed.

Giant draglines such as this one are symbols of Florida's phosphate mining. Phosphate is an essential fertilizer ingredient. An idea of the size of this four-million pound dragline, with its bucket scooping up some 70 to 100 tons at a bite, may be gained from comparison with the vehicle in the foreground.
International Minerals and Chemical Corporation

Dolomite

Dolomite, $CaMg(CO_3)_2$, is similar to limestone but contains more magnesium and has a slightly greater density. Dolomite, utilizing both wet and dry mining methods, is extracted in Jackson, Taylor, Levy, and Citrus counties.

Mining of dolomite and limestone is by dragline after blasting with explosives where required. In Florida, it is often crushed into fines and used for agricultural purposes as a soil conditioner, or, to a lesser extent, is crushed, sized, and sold as aggregate.

Heavy Minerals

Heavy minerals, so named because their specific gravity is greater than that of quartz, are associated with ancient beach deposits. Minerals comprising a characteristic assemblage may include ilmenite, rutile, leucoxene, monazite, staurolite, kyanite, and garnet.

Quartz sand deposits containing four percent or more heavy mineral sands are mined in Clay County. The mining process utilizes suction dredges to remove the heavy mineral sands. The heavy minerals are then separated from the quartz sands using Humphreys Spiral Concentrators. They are further separated by using their varied electrical and magnetic properties. Titanium dioxide pigment, known for its whiteness, spreading quality and chemical stability, is the primary use for Florida's titanium-rich minerals rutile, ilmenite, and leucoxene.

Staurolite is an iron-aluminum silicate mineral. It is used most often as a source of iron and alumina in the manufacture of portland cement and as an abrasive.

Zircon, a zirconium silicate, is found, although in rather small amounts, in practically all of Florida's beach and stream quartz sand deposits. Its uses include foundry sands, refractories, ceramics, abrasives, and in making zirconium metal and alloys, and in chemical manufacturing.

Monazite makes up but a very small portion of Florida's heavy mineral concentrates. It contains the group of elements known as the rare-earths, the compounds and alloys of which have significant commercial application. The rare-earth elements (cerium, yttrium, lanthanum and thorium) may be combined with various other materials to produce such items as flints for lighters and miners lamps, jet engine parts, and gas turbines. The rare-earth elements have been and continue to be intensively studied by the scientific community.

Clays

Clays are a mixture of aluminum, magnesium, and silica, as well as varying amounts of other impurities such as quartz sand, silt, mica, and other iron-bearing material. In Florida there are three types of clays presently mined, kaolin, fuller's earth, and common clays.

Kaolin is mined in Putnam County where it occurs as a matrix material of the Cypresshead Formation. The clay is removed from the quartz sand by washing and screening, then classified over settling vats before thickening and filtering. The clay may be pulverized and further classified by air winnowing. Kaolin is relatively plastic and has low shrinkage. It is used as a filler material, in the manufacturing of paints, paper products, refractories, and whitewares.

In 1991, Florida ranked second behind Georgia in the production of fuller's earth. This highly absorptive clay material is primarily mined from the Gadsden County region in the Florida panhandle. The clay from this region is a hydrous magnesium silicate. The names floridin (from the Floridin Company, Quincy), and attapulgite (from Attapulgus, Georgia) have been applied locally although the scientific name is actually palygorskite.

Fuller's earth is mined from the Hawthorn Group by dragline, crushed, plasticized in a pug mill, extruded, dried and pulverized during the beneficiation process. This improves the absorptive properties and increases its porosity. The clay is used as a cat litter, an oil well drilling mud, as a filler, an absorber, a filtering medium, and as a carrier for fungicides and other purposes.

Fuller's earth is also mined in Marion County near Lowell. Primary uses for this clay are cat litter, an insecticide carrier, and an intercaking agent for fertilizers.

Clay aggregate is produced from a clay deposit in Clay County. When this clay is heated it expands or bloats and becomes quite hard. Where weight is a critical factor, the lightness of this material combined with its strength make it an ideal ingredient in the production of concrete.

Sand and Gravel

Sand is the name applied to an unconsolidated aggregate of minerals or rock particles that range in size from 2 to 0.062 millimeters (0.078 to 0.002 inches). Similarly, gravel is the name applied when the particles range from 76 to 4.76 mm (2.99 to 0.19 inches). According to these definitions, sand

and gravel are size characterisitcs and do not imply mineralogic composition.

In Florida, sand is predominantly composed of the mineral quartz. The term "high silica" sand is used to distinguish those sands composed of 98 percent or more silica from those that are less pure because of either inclusions or iron content. Much of the State's production of sand is from Dade, Lake, Polk and Putnam counties with lesser amounts from numerous other counties.

The only appreciable source of gravel in the state is the fluvial sediments of the Citronelle Formation in Northwest Florida. Here, gravel is mined by dredge in northeast Escambia County and in the Apalachicola River in Gadsden County. This commodity is then washed and screened and classified for marketing.

Florida's sand and gravel is used primarily in concrete, mortar, concrete blocks, and as asphaltic sand for road surfacing. Lesser amounts of sand are used as blast sand, engine sand, railroad ballast, and for industrial purposes such as manufacturing glass.

Peat

Florida ranked first in the nation in 1992 in production of peat. Peat was produced from several Florida counties including Hillsborough, Orange, Polk, Putnam, Pasco, Lake, Madison, Palm Beach, Dade, Clay, Highlands, and Sumter. It accumulates in low lying, wet areas where the rate of decomposition of organic material is slower than its accumulation.

All of Florida's peat is marketed for agricultural and horticultural purposes. The principal use is as a soil conditioner, to improve the physical characteristics and to retain moisture. Additional uses of peat include as a filler in mixed fertilizer, and acting as a carrier for the primary plant nutrients nitrogen, phosphorus, and potash.

Magnesium

Magnesium is extracted commercially from sea water at only one location in Florida. The oxide of magnesium is produced at Port St. Joe in Gulf County, by recovery from sea water as it passes through lime. The oxide, which is of high-purity chemical and refractory grade, is used in refractory products, rubber, textiles, insulation, ceramics, catalysts, as well as in many chemical processes.

Cement and Lime

Portland cement is manufactured by calcining a finely ground mixture of limestone and quartz with oxides of aluminum and iron to produce a clinker that is pulverized. The properties of the product can be controlled by proportioning the ingredients of the mixture.

There are four cement plants in Florida, two near Miami and two near Brooksville, presently producing cement from locally obtained limestone. There are a number of locations, such as Tampa, Port Manatee, and Fort Pierce where cement is imported into the U.S. from abroad.

Sulfur

Sulfur is a by-product of oil and gas production from the Jay, Florida area. Crude oil and gas from producing wells contain a significant amount of hydrogen sulfide. After the gas is separated from the crude oil, the gas is sweetened by removing sulfur. The by-product sulfur, is then transported to market in a liquid state.

NONFUEL MINERAL PRODUCTION IN FLORIDA[1]

Mineral			1991 Quantity	1991 Value (thousands)	1992 Quantity	1992 Value (thousands)	1993* Quantity	1993* Value (thousands)
Cement:								
	Masonry	thousand short tons	*214	*$13,482	342	$22,424	334	$21,887
	Portland	do.	*3,023	*142,081	3,195	161,969	3,720	188,591
Clays:								
	Fuller's earth	thousand metric tons	332	35,598	332	33,767	341	34,599
	Kaolin	do.	31	3,552	35	3,434	34	3,471
Gemstones			NA	6	NA	1	—	—
Peat		thousand short tons	244	3,991	211	3,158	203	3,192
Sand and gravel:								
	Construction	do.	*16,000	*51,400	23,266	66,141	25,200	73,100
	Industrial	do.	551	5,989	477	5,167	W	W
Stone (crushed)[2]		do.	59,132	260,901	*59,300	*266,900	69,500	323,200
Combined value of clays (common), magnesium compounds, phosphate rock, rare-earth metal concentrates, staurolite (1991–92), stone (crushed marl), titanium concentrates (ilmenite and rutile), zircon concentrates, and value indicated by symbol W			XX	879,164	XX	876,799	XX	649,265
Total			XX	1,396,164	XX	1,439,760	XX	1,297,305

*Estimated. NA Not available. W Withheld to avoid disclosing company proprietary data; value included with "Combined value" data. XX Not applicable.
[1] Production as measured by mine shipments, sales, or marketable production (including consumption by producers).
[2] Excludes certain stones; kind and value included with "Combined value" data.

Petroleum

In 1993, Florida ranked 20th in the country in oil production. Total oil production for 1993 was 5,604,126 barrels. Approximately 71 percent of this oil was from Jay field in northwestern Florida. Florida produces oil from two areas. One is the western panhandle and includes Jay field and four other active fields in Escambia and Santa Rosa counties. The other producing area is a northwest–southeast trend through Lee, Hendry, Collier, and Dade counties in south Florida. The south Florida producing area contains seven active oil fields.

Only one exploratory well was drilled in Florida during 1993. This was a shallow well (3,500 ft.) drilled in Escambia County, which tested the Tuskahama Sand unit of the Eoceen Wilcox Group. The well was plugged and abandoned as a dry hole.

Geophysical exploration during 1993 was within the area of current and historic production in northwest (Escambia, Santa Rosa, and Okaloosa counties) Florida and covered a total of 41.4 miles of seismic line.

1943–1993 Florida Petroleum Production Totals

Field	County	Oil (Barrels)	Gas (1000 CF)	Discovery
Sunniland	Collier	18,445,245	1,824,628	9-26-43
Forty Mile Bend	Dade	32,888	1,656	2-01-54
Sunoco Felda	Hendry	11,598,196	981,828	7-22-64
West Felda	Hendry	42,589,868	3,326,619	8-02-66
Lake Trafford	Collier	278,241	0	3-30-69
Jay (Florida only)	Santa Rosa	379,845,282	491,592,981	6-15-70
Mt. Carmel	Santa Rosa	4,747,283	4,797,292	12-19-71
Blackjack Creek	Santa Rosa	56,148,537	55,772,639	2-14-72
Bear Island	Collier	11,104,989	893,560	12-05-72
Seminole	Hendry	84,755	0	11-14-73
Lehigh Park	Lee	5,368,652	545,525	7-30-74
Sweetwater Creek	Santa Rosa	13,695	14,655	4-22-77
Baxter Island	Collier	1,859	0	8-11-77
Mid-Felda	Hendry	1,457,621	10,094	10-13-77
Raccoon Point	Collier	6,705,411	825,512	6-20-78
Pepper Hammock	Collier	323	0	9-28-78
Townsend Canal	Hendry	519,014	0	6-27-82
Bluff Springs	Escambia	241,871	128,565	3-25-84
Corkscrew	Collier	857,900	0	11-10-85
McLellan	Santa Rosa	309,537	131,046	2-19-86
Coldwater Creek	Santa Rosa	43,965	14,012	6-04-88
McDavid	Escambia	150,323	61,859	7-14-88
TOTAL		540,545,455	560,922,470	

Wildlife and Freshwater Fish
Allan L. Egbert, Ph.D.

Many of nature's greatest wonders belong to Florida. Aside from the sun worshipers that find their niche on Florida's beaches, sportsmen too have a home in the land the ancient explorers called "Festival of Flowers."

The climate and the abundance of water have opened Florida to a wealth of wildlife and freshwater fish that no other place can match. Game abounds for the hunter just as nongame wildlife thrives in a magnificent inter-related system far too complex for any master but nature. Some of the creatures found here occur nowhere else in the world.

Duck hunting, a long standing tradition in Florida, draws sportsman and dog on chilly fall and winter mornings.
Game and Fresh Water Fish Commission

Outdoor Florida Afield

Hunting opportunities are year-round pleasures in Florida. There is no closed season on such species as rabbits, raccoons, opossums, beavers, coyotes and others. Wing-shooters find multi-phase hunting seasons for doves, ducks and coots. Other migratory game birds include snipe, rail, common moorhen and woodcocks.

The most sought-after game animal in Florida is the white-tailed deer that occurs throughout the peninsula and panhandle. Also, Florida's Osceola turkeys occur in no other state, and they are highly prized by turkey hunters. The eastern turkey is another game bird that Floridians and visiting sportsmen alike prize for table fare.

Other resident game animals include bobwhite quail, gray squirrels, fox squirrels and wild hogs (in some areas). Furbearers such as bobcats, mink, otters, skunks and nutria may be taken state-wide. Everglades mink may not be taken.

The Florida Game and Fresh Water Fish Commission publishes hunting

---

Dr. Egbert is Executive Director of the Game and Fresh Water Fish Commission regulations annually in its *Florida Hunting Handbook and Regulations Summary.*

Finding a place to hunt is no problem in Florida. In fact, Florida offers the largest system of public hunting areas in the country. The Commission administers hunting opportunities on more than 5.5 million acres of public and private land, spanning the state from South Everglades to the pine and oak woodlands in the northern reaches of the state. Some public lands are under the type I wildlife management area system and require a $25 management area stamp for hunters. Others are under the type II system, and the landowners may sell permits to sportsmen who use their property to pursue game.

During the first nine days of general gun hunting season and during certain other periods the Commission may limit the number of hunters on type I wildlife management areas by requiring sportsmen to carry free quota hunt permits, which they obtain through random computer selection of applicants.

More than 185,000 persons bought licenses to hunt in Florida during 1993-94. Many other sportsmen are exempt from license requirements because of age, disability or other factors. The dollars these individuals spend pursuing their sport and the taxes they pay on hunting equipment have enabled Florida to maintain excellent harvests and hunting opportunities despite this state's staggering increase in human population. These sportsmen also provide much of the funding for wildlife research, endangered species protection and habitat improvements that benefit all wildlife—not just game.

Outdoor Florida Afloat

Florida's largemouth bass are unmatched by any other sport fish in the world. Nothing else fights like they do, and nothing else compares to the thrill of catching them.

Opportunities to catch "bucketmouths" and other freshwater fish abound in Florida. This state boasts 3 million acres of freshwater lakes and 12,000 miles of rivers and streams. The Game and Fresh Water Fish Commission manages these freshwater fisheries for Florida's resident anglers and the 130,000 non-resident anglers who buy freshwater fishing licenses each year—not to mention the youngsters and others who are free to fish without a license in this state.

No place in Florida is more than a few minutes drive from a fishing spot, and the size restrictions and bag limits are among the most generous in the country for bream, crappie, catfish and many others. Still, anglers continue to catch world record fish here, and state records are impressive too.

Managing fisheries in a state as varied as Florida is a continuous process, so fishermen should keep up with regulation changes. The Commission publishes them annually in a booklet titled *Florida Freshwater Sport Fishing Guide & Regulations Summary.* The publication is free and available from Commission offices, county tax collectors and fishing equipment retailers.

Generally the current bag limits are:

5 Black bass (largemouth, Suwannee, redeye, spotted and shoal basses individually or in total), of which only one may be 22 inches or longer in to-

Florida boasts 3 million acres of freshwater lakes and 120,000 miles of rivers and streams.
Game and Fresh Water Fish Commission

tal length. Minimum size limit is 12 inches for black bass in the Suwannee River and points north and west of the river; elsewhere, the minimum size limit is 14 inches.

20 Striped bass, white bass and sunshine bass (individually or in total), of which no more than six may exceed 24 inches in total length.

15 Chain pickerel

50 Panfish (for example, bluegill, black crappie, redear sunfish, spotted sunfish, warmouth and redfin pickerel, individually or in total).

2 Butterfly peacock bass, only one of which may be longer than 17 inches in total length. All speckled peacock bass must be released unharmed immediately.

Regulations may be more restrictive in certain waters and less restrictive in others, so anglers should take the time to study the fishing handbook in advance.

Resident fishing licenses cost residents $12 per year, and they cost non-residents $30 per year. Non-residents can purchase a seven-day fishing license for $15. Residents age 65 or older can obtain exemption certificates for licenses. Also exempt from license requirements are disabled persons with exemption certificates, children under age 16, military personnel who are home on leave in Florida for 30 days or less and Floridians fishing in their county of resident with poles that have no mechanical reel. Again, some exemptions may not apply in certain waters, so it's best to become familiar with local regulations before the fishing trip.

Also, long-term and lifetime hunting and fishing licenses are available for Florida residents.

516 / Wildlife

Saltwater fishing is not covered by a freshwater fishing license, and any saltwater fish an angler catches incidentally in fresh water must be returned to the water unharmed unless the angler has a saltwater license.

During 1993–94, a total of 631,000 persons obtained licenses or exemption certificates to fish in Florida's fresh waters—not to mention the countless thousands who aren't required to have a license. In Florida, where people can fish all day and all night all year—the average fisherman spends 21 days a year fishing, so the economic impact is enormous. The Commission estimates that freshwater fishermen spend more than $1.4 billion per year in pursuit of their sport, not including big ticket items like bass boats.

Bodies of fresh water, marshes and estuaries comprise roughly 17 per cent of Florida's surface acreage so it's easy to understand how water dominates the typical Floridian's recreational endeavors. It's traditional in Florida to take to leisure activities as seriously as you take to your work. That's a tradition that visitors learn quickly. It's one of the reasons so many visitors become residents.

Outdoor Florida Wildlife

Florida's most famous—and certainly the most beautiful—big game animal is the white-tailed deer, found throughout the state. Even with the ever-increasing hunting pressure and vanishing wildlife habitat acreage, the overall deer population has responded to sound management and environmental factors. In fact, the white-tailed deer population in Florida probably totals 700,000–800,000 animals. That's more than ever before—more than it was before the first European explorers reached Florida's shores.

Given certain habitat and scientifically sound management, deer are prolific reproducers. The deer population stays near or even above the carrying capacity of the habitat in most areas, and that enables hunters to take approximately 80,000 deer annually without causing the deer population to decline during the following year.

The wild turkey favors mature forests, but it is found in all the counties in Florida. Wild turkeys are particularly abundant in the mixed pasture hammock-swamp cattle country of south Florida and the coastal hammock areas along the Gulf Coast.

Wildlife scientists are learning more about the nature and needs of wild turkeys in Florida, and current management practices limit turkey hunting to bearded turkeys or gobblers. Turkeys are vulnerable to nat-

Alto Adams, Jr, writes in his A Cattleman's Backcountry Florida: *"This doe is a perfect animal. Her legs are exactly strong enough to support her well-muscled body and fine enough to give maximum speed. Any heavier or finer and they would not be as effective. Good eyes and ears are sensors that work as well at night as by day."*
Alto Adams, Jr.

The bobwhite quail may be found in every county. It is the states second most popular game bird, after the mourning dove. Game and Fresh Water Fish Commission

ural and man-made setbacks. Management of these birds presents many challenges.

Turkey hunters now must carry a $5 wild turkey stamp affixed to their hunting licenses. Revenue from the sale of the stamps helps fund turkey management and research projects.

Bobwhite quail are found throughout Florida. Two of the best quail hunting areas include the farming country of northwest Florida and the open flatwoods in the southern part of the state. The south Florida quail are smaller and darker than their cousins in the northern reaches of the state, but they maintain the same sporting qualities that make quail the leading game birds of the South.

By nature, quail are birds of the fields and open pinewoods. However, they do occur in other types of habitat as long as there is ample food and cover for them and the vegetation is open enough to allow them to move freely. With quail, as with all wildlife, habitat is all important.

Two squirrel species are game animals in Florida. The smaller gray squirrel, a prime game animal, is found chiefly in hardwood forests and swamps. The less common fox squirrel is an open mature pinewoods animal. The gray squirrel is swift and generally is found among the branches and limbs of trees, while the larger fox squirrel is more slow and awkward in its movements and frequently is encountered on the ground.

Both species build nests from twigs and leaves in the branches of trees or may use tree cavities or deserted woodpecker holes for the rearing of two litters of three or four young each year.

The cottontail rabbit is abundant throughout Florida except in marshy areas where swamp rabbits occur. There is no closed season on rabbits in Florida, and licensed hunters may take a daily bag limit of 12. Even with the continuous open season, there is little hunting pressure on rabbits.

Raccoons and opossums also may be hunted throughout the year in Florida. Hunters pursue these critters at night with dogs and lights, but the hunters may use only single-shot 410 gauge shotguns or .22 caliber rimfire (other than .22-magnum) firearms. The essence of this type of hunting is the chase, and the firearms may not be loaded until the animal is treed or bayed. These animals, particularly raccoons, can be adaptable and are quite at home in all types of habitat. Many farmers consider them to be nuisances because of the damage these animals cause to corn, citrus and truck crops.

Wood ducks and Florida ducks are year-round residents in this state, but during fall, winter and spring other species of wild ducks are common in portions of Florida. Major duck shooting areas can be found in the Gulf and Atlantic coast marshes and delta systems of northern Florida. The Lake Okeechobee-Kissimmee Valley area provides prime wintering habitat for migratory ducks and coots.

Migratory ducks include the mallard, black duck, redhead, canvasback, ring-necked, gadwall, bald pate, blue-winged and green-winged teal, merganser, ruddy duck, bufflehead, goldeneye, pintail, scaup, shoveler and sea ducks.

Mourning doves and white-winged doves also are popular migratory game birds. Mourning doves are found throughout the state during the entire year, but they are most abundant in the fall due to the arrival of migrants from the north. Flocks of doves are attracted to harvested fields of corn, millet or peanuts. Hunting success varies from year to year.

Generally doves travel in flocks, sometimes numbering several hundred birds. However, when they are paired for breeding, they remain alone and shun the company of other doves. They build flimsy nests in trees and the male and female doves alternate in incubating the eggs and caring for the young. Doves produce an average of two young per brood. They may raise three or four broods per year.

Wild hogs are classified as game animals in some counties and within certain wildlife management areas. In those areas, hog hunting season coincides with deer hunting season. On the other hand, Florida's wild or feral hogs are descendants of the hogs that were introduced to Florida by explorers and pioneers. They are not native wild animals. In areas where wild hogs are not classified as game animals, they are classified as livestock even though they are wild.

In most of the state, wild hogs may be taken year-round with no size restriction or bag limit. In areas where they are classified as game, however, the daily bag limit is one, and the minimum shoulder height is 15 inches.

Foxes are relatively abundant in Florida, but their population fluctuates from year to year. Fox hunters may pursue foxes with dogs throughout the year, but foxes may not be shot or killed by hunters. Foxes are extremely clever and swift animals, and gray foxes are capable of climbing trees.

The Florida panther is the last of the big cats east of the Mississippi River, and it is among the most critically endangered species in North America. The remaining Florida panther population is concentrated in the remote Everglades and Big Cypress and Fakahatchee Strand regions of south Florida. At times panthers have roamed far from their usual territories, a practice that has resulted in panther sightings as far north as Flagler County. State and federal wildlife authorities have pooled their resources and expertise in the Florida Panther Interagency Committee in a massive effort to save these great animals from the threat of extinction. Recent scientific breakthroughs are encouraging, but probably fewer than 50 Florida panthers still roam in the wild.

The Game and Fresh Water Fish Commission classifies 40 species of animals as endangered, including the Florida panther. Others on the endangered list include manatees, key deer, American crocodiles, various beach mice and others.

Outdoor Florida Freshwater Fish

Largemouth bass, America's number one game fish is found in every state except Alaska. However, they do not occur naturally west of the Rockies. Because of the more suitable water and climate, the number of largemouth bass is much greater in the South—especially in Florida where there is no more-sought-after freshwater fish, and where the genetically distinct subspecies of Florida bass rules.

The uncertified state record for largemouth bass, established in 1923, is 20 pounds—two pounds shy of the world record. Many anglers believe a new world record bass is swimming in Florida at this moment. More trophy size bass, eight pounds or more, are bagged in Florida than in any other state.

Largemouth bass are green in color although this characteristic varies somewhat depending on the

While most fishermen seek the largemouth bass, there are many other species of fish that are abundant in Florida.
Game and Fresh Water Fish Commission

color of the water where they live. They are easy to recognize due to the large mouth and the dark horizontal band from head to tail. "Bigmouths" are greedy fish that will attack a wide variety of foods, such as minnows, crawfish, frogs, small snakes and insects. The bigger they get, the smarter and harder to catch they get. Still, wherever there is ample water in Florida, there are largemouth bass there to challenge fishermen.

Probably more fisherman's dollars are expended in pursuit of largemouth bass than on any other species of game fish. In Florida alone, this species probably generates nearly $1 billion per year in expenditures for the state's economy.

A wide variety of scrappy pint-sized game fish are found throughout

Florida and are available anytime an angler wants to wet a hook. Panfish in Florida carry a general classification of bream and may include the bluegill, shellcracker, redbreast, warmouth, redfin pickerel and stumpknocker. Fishermen are allowed a generous bag limit of 50 panfish per day which includes the tasty speckled perch (also known as black crappie) for which Lake Okeechobee is world renowned.

The bag limit for chain pickerel is 15 per day.

Panfish are in virtually every body of fresh water in Florida—even in ditches. They are fun to catch on cane poles with worms, crickets and such, but they will also take artificial lures.

Striped bass, are at the southern extreme of their range in Florida and are classified as freshwater game fish here. Efforts are underway to restore the historic population of native Gulf Coast stripers, which is distinctly different from the Atlantic stock and handles Florida's warm temperatures better. Most of the striped bass caught in Florida come from the major rivers in the northern part of the state, and were stocked by Commission biologists. The record 44.25 pound striper caught in the Apalichicola River by Alphonso Barnes, of Quincy, in December 1993 was thought to have been from one of the three million put into the river system in the mid-1980s.

Sunshine bass, a product of hybridization of white bass and striped bass, are becoming more and more popular as game fish. Fisheries biologists produce and rear the hybrids in hatcheries and stock them into freshwater lakes and rivers.

Sunshine bass are not capable of breeding, so the supply must be replenished from time to time. These fish grow rapidly. They may reach a weight of several pounds during their first year. Usually, waters with an abundance of gizzard and threadfin shad, are the best locations for sunshine bass stocking projects since they are the preferred food source for these hybrids.

Two types of peacock bass, introduced to south Florida waters from their native range in South America are furnishing fishing challenges to anglers. Speckled peacock bass must be released unharmed, but anglers can keep up to two butterfly peacock bass per day. Only one of them can be longer than 17 inches, however.

Florida has an abundance of nongame fish, ranging from the huge alligator gar, which may exceed 100 pounds, to minute minnows and darters. Perhaps the most popular of the nongame species are catfish, which provide excellent table fare and are sought by recreational and commercial fishermen. Channel, white, blue and flathead catfish, along with several species of bullheads are here in Florida to challenge anglers.

Other Wildlife

Alligators are found throughout the state, wherever swamps, rivers or lakes provide suitable habitat. From a low level of abundance during the late 1960s, the alligator has made a strong recovery even to the point of constituting a nuisance from time to time. The alligator is being managed as a renewable natural resource in that a tightly controlled commercial alligator harvest occurs annually during September in selected waters.

These reptiles grow about one foot per year in the wild. Females rarely exceed a length of nine feet, whereas males may grow much larger—14 feet or more. Old timers tell stories of 20-foot alligators, and some of these stories may be true. Females lay an average of 35 eggs in late spring in a nest of rotting vegetation piled to a height of two or three feet. Incubation requires nine weeks and is aided by heat generated by the decomposing vegetation. Whether the hatchlings will turn out to be males or females depends on the temperature of eggs during incubation.

During the incubation period, the female protects the nest from marauding animals that might destroy the eggs.

Baby alligators face many perils such as herons, otters, snakes, raccoons and other predators, including larger members of their own species. After the first couple of years, alligators have few effective enemies other than humans and other alligators.

The American crocodile is much less abundant than the alligator and is limited to the southern tip of Florida. It is distinguished from the alligator by its much more pointed snout and lighter color. These reptiles normally are found in salt water or brackish water. They lay their eggs in a hole dug in the sand, much like sea turtles do. Crocodiles are more agile, and are considered more vicious than alligators.

The American crocodile is an endangered species and is completely protected by state and federal law. Males may reach a length of 15 feet.

"Gator" hunter about to bag a big one, ca 1880s.

Florida State Archives

A Look at Florida Exotics

Beautiful as it is, Florida even offers favorable habitats for undesirable species of exotic (non-native) wildlife and fish to live and breed in the wild.

Foreign species of plants and animals which accidentally become established in a new environment constitute a form of pollution. Once these species set up breeding populations in the wild, they effectively displace—and even prey on—native wildlife, seriously disrupting the delicate natural balance that sustains life in Florida and elsewhere. Exotic pets and plants, once introduced and unrestrained, may reproduce at an incredible rate, especially when no natural enemies are around to control them.

Florida is particularly vulnerable to exotics because of the climate and water resources in this state. Virtually any type of wildlife which inhabits regions of subtropical climate is capable of adoption to Florida's mild habitat and lush vegetation.

Florida is the major port of entry for foreign animals and fish. Each year, approximately 35,000,000 foreign animals and fish are imported into Florida through Miami and Orlando. This tremendous volume of exotic specimens is then distributed to nearly every state in the country through the pet trade. Florida also is an ideal site for much of the tropical fish industry in the United States because of its subtropical climate and suitable water.

Unfortunately, careless handling of exotic animals, tropical fishes and aquatic vegetation by persons involved in the wildlife trade and purposeful releases by well-meaning but misinformed hobbyists have resulted in liberation and establishment of between 80 and 100 exotic animal species. Hurricane Andrew, in August 1992, further complicated the problem by destroying zoos, laboratories and exotic pet operations and freeing thousands of animals.

Since one of the primary duties of the Game and Fresh Water Fish Commission is to protect the ecological balance of this state, the agency is extremely concerned about the problem of exotics in the wild. Unlike other forms of pollution, which can be remedied if the pollution is stopped, biological pollution is self-sustaining and generally irreversible.

Catfish of the Southeast Asia Clariidae *family are able to breathe air and to slither across land. "Walking catfish" can stay out of water for hours. This photograph was taken by Paul Shafland, biologist at the Boca Raton laboratory of the Game and Fresh Water Fish Commission. Shafland says the "walking catfish" does not present as serious a threat to Florida fish as was first thought but does alter the native ecosystem.*

Florida's Marine Resources

Kenneth D. Haddad

The beauty, diversity, and abundance of Florida's marine resources are major lures for visitors and new residents to the State. Consequently 80% of Florida's population lives near the coast. From sunning on the beach and watching dolphins frolic in the nearshore waters, to catching the fish of your life, the pleasures are many. Along with these pleasures come associated industries and jobs.

The rich diversity of Florida's marine environment has evolved as a result of its unique geography. There are over 8,000 coastline miles of marine waters (1,300 linear miles) extending 3 miles offshore into the Atlantic Ocean on the east coast and 9 miles into the Gulf of Mexico on the west coast and covering more than 9,800 square miles. Jutting south into a Caribbean-like environment, the coastline from Cape Canaveral on the east coast and Tampa Bay on the west coast is considered tropical to sub-tropical and a wide range of marine fauna and flora exist, in abundance, that cannot be found anywhere else in the United States. A major influence on the stability of the tropical marine resources of the area is the warm ocean currents that flow from the Caribbean and bathe the coastline. The northern half of the state is considered warm-temperate and the marine flora and fauna are more typical of those found in the remainder of the eastern U.S.

Plants, Animals, and the Environment

Thousands of species of plants and animals comprise the marine environment in Florida. They range from marine mammals, such as manatees and dolphins, to coral reefs and their associated fishes. All of the marine plants and animals we see in Florida are the result of the numerous and complex habitats in which they live.

Reefs

Living coral reefs and rocky limestone outcroppings are the two major types of natural reefs found in Florida. The coral reefs off the Florida Keys are spectacular and rival the Caribbean areas to the south. Rocky outcroppings are found all along the Florida coastline and are important to the productivity of our offshore waters. Both types of reefs are complex habitats for fishes and other plants and animals providing food and cover in an otherwise inhospitable environment.

Kenneth D. Haddad is Chief of the Department of Environmental Protection's Florida Marine Research Institute

These shrimp boats are clustered at Tarpon Springs. Department of Natural Resources

Artificial reefs, constructed of rubble and other man-made materials and structures, are becoming important habitats and fish attractors in the marine environment. Programs at the state, county, and local government level encourage artificial reef development in a coordinated and environmentally sound manner.

Estuaries

The estuarine environment is the most productive marine ecosystem in Florida and one of the most productive environments on Earth. Estuaries occur where freshwater meets and mixes with salty ocean waters and include bays, lagoons and shallow, low energy areas such as the Big Bend portion of the west coast. Important wetland habitats in the estuaries are mangroves, saltmarshes, and seagrasses. Mangroves are sub-tropical trees that have adapted to grow in saltwater and cover over 500,000 acres of southern Florida. Saltmarshes are coastal wetlands rich in marine life that grow in low energy areas in the zone between low and high tide. They are found throughout Florida, often mixed with mangroves, and cover over 450,000 acres. Seagrasses are saltwater-adapted, flowering plants that grow below the tidal zone and cover between 600,000 and 900,000 acres of submerged bottom. Seagrasses are probably the single most important marine habitat in Florida and one undergoing serious stress from man's development of the coastline.

The estuary is the sink for the majority of man's activities in Florida, including sewage waste, stormwater runoff and the myriad of associated pollutants. The vegetated portions of the estuary serve to filter and clean the waters in the estuary and their loss through various types of development can lead to serious and compounding problems for our marine resources.

Natural Events

When man alters the natural marine environment it is often permanent and a loss to the marine system is incurred. Natural events can have the same type of impact but often the resources recover or, in some manner, remain a functioning part of the marine ecosystem. Hurricanes and storms can destroy mangroves, saltmarshes, seagrasses, coral reefs, and oyster reefs through uprooting or burial but recolonization is rapid. Winter freezes can kill thousands of acres of sub-tropical mangroves, but new plants germinate as soon as the weather warms. Sea level rise has been occurring and is projected to increase due to the greenhouse effect. This could impact the distribution of many of our marine resources that are tidally and water depth dependent, and consequently impact entire ecosystems.

Florida's red tide is a natural phenomenon resulting from dense concentrations, called blooms, of a microscopic, plant-like organism. The toxins produced by these tiny cells can kill fish, that may wash ashore, and also can cause human illness if ingested through clams, oysters and other bivalves that concentrate the toxins. A local shellfish harvesting ban is announced whenever red tide is imminent inshore.

The Marine Fisheries

Fishing and seafood immediately come to mind when the State of Florida is mentioned in any conversation. The State has large and viable commercial and recreational industries and both are growing. Florida ranks third in the nation in resident anglers (greater than 2,100,000) while over 1,200,000 tourist anglers annually fish in Florida waters. Many of these are saltwater anglers with an economic impact of more than $2 billion. The commercial industry is also significant with the dockside value of landing reaching $186,000,000 in 1992. Florida ranks 2nd nationally in processed fish products. If the commercial fisheries values are economically scaled to retail and combined with the recreational values it is apparent that the industries are worth billions to the state's economy.

It is important to realize that these industries depend on the abundance and health of the species sought. To this end, the estuaries are major producers of fisheries products and serve as the nursery grounds for many of our fishery species. In fact, over 70% of the commercially and recreationally caught species in Florida utilize the estuaries during some portion of their life cycle. Estuaries provide juvenile fish with an abundant food supply and, just as importantly, protective cover in the various mangrove, seagrass, saltmarsh, and other structural habitats found in the estuaries. Many of these fish grow up in the estuary but spend their adult life in our coastal oceans. Shrimp, baitfish, red drum, mullet, and grouper are examples. Others, such as spotted seatrout, spend their entire life in the estuary. Those species which do not directly use the estuary, such as sailfish and swordfish, depend on the estuaries for producing their food.

In 1988 the Florida Legislature instituted a saltwater fishing license. The revenues generated from the licenses are being used for recreational fisheries research, stock and habitat enhancement, and enforcement of Florida fishing regulations.

Commercial Florida Landings of Major Species for 1992

Species	Catch (lbs.)	Value ($)
Groupers	9,606,942	16,688,334
Mullet, Striped	20,614,516	12,821,302
Swordfish	1,991,744	6,469,202
Tuna, Yellowfin	1,471,293	2,596,338
Shark	6,014,821	6,446,439
Snapper, Yellowtail	1,851,549	3,687,706
Menhaden	11,477,445	1,081,591
Snapper, Red	708,579	1,522,944
Mackerel, Spanish	5,625,498	1,872,356
Mackerel, King	2,541,445	3,014,441
Pompano	625,374	1,885,828
Amberjack	2,893,471	2,147,658
Snapper, Vermilion	1,545,040	2,372,539
Seatrout, Spotted	923,338	1,110,912
Snapper, Gray (Mangrove)	474,220	767,077
Dolphin	602,926	725,808
Total Fish (all species)	112,943,251	80,526,643
Shrimp	22,490,526	51,095,100
Lobster, Spiny	5,337,098	20,667,270
Crabs, Stone	6,796,194	16,574,817
Crabs, Blue	15,101,899	6,792,177
Oysters	2,635,062	4,030,219
Clams, Hard	1,114,798	4,289,089
Total Shellfish (all species)	54,760,307	105,504,062
Total Landings (all species)	167,703,558	186,030,705

Fisheries Management

Marine fishery resources are renewable, yet finite. When finite resources are shared among increasingly larger user groups, each individual must settle for a smaller share. Accordingly, many questions arise regarding government's ability to adequately protect and manage this common property resource. Currently, effective management techniques are based on open and closed seasons, minimum and maximum size limits, bag limits, and other regulations that restrict the users access to the resource and cap allowable harvest. Maintaining the information base to regulate in this manner is especially difficult in Florida because of the number of species sought and the fact that open marine systems have so many factors that influence a population; unlike that in freshwater systems.

Florida's fisheries are managed by the Marine Fisheries Commission. Established in 1983, the seven member Commission evaluates the need and effectiveness of marine resource regulations and proposes new rules. Any new rules or changes to existing laws must be approved by the Governor and Cabinet. Since regulations change and there are special local regulations in some areas, it is advisable to contact the Marine Patrol District Office nearest the location where harvest activities are planned.

Ecosystem Management

With such a diverse richness of our marine resources and a resultant diverse group of users, management of the resources is not an easy task. This is compounded by the rapid growth occurring in the State and its unquantifiable impact on our marine resources. Realizing that preservation and protection of the resources are paramount to a healthy ecosystem, the State has developed numerous programs within different agencies to purchase and manage resources, protect them through regulations, and manage growth that is seriously impinging on the health of the natural resources. Currently the state has designated 42 Aquatic Preserves, 37 that are marine or estuarine, covering 3.1 million acres. The Florida Aquatic Preserve Act of 1975 has as its goal the protection of these sensitive areas from over-use by man. Florida also has two National Estuarine Research Reserves—Rookery Bay and Apalachicola River and Bay. Key Largo Coral Reef and Long Key are designated as protected National Marine Sanctuaries. In 1990 Congress designated all waters of the Florida Keys, over 2,600 square miles, as the Florida Keys National Sanctuary, the second largest marine sanctuary in the nation. Other areas within the marine environment are currently being considered for special management.

If the state's Constitutional policy requiring the conservation and protection of its natural resource is to be followed, much work must be accomplished to retain or restore elements of Florida's natural system and preserve our marine resources. The signs are evident that we are seriously stressing our marine resources. We have lost much of the natural habitat and we are using the resources more than ever before. Our marine resources are part of our State's heritage and it is up to us to ensure them a place in Florida's future.

All the waters of the Florida Keys are included in the Florida Keys National Sanctuary.
Department of Commerce. Division of Tourism

General Farming and Truck Crops

Donald L. Brooke

General farming in Florida is confined to the northern and western parts of the state. Those farms produce such crops as tobacco, corn for grain, peanuts, soybeans, wheat, oats, cotton, legumes and grasses for grazing and hay for livestock.

Of the field crops and vegetables commercially important in Florida at the present time only corn was being produced when the Spanish landed on our shores. The "Indians were growing maize, eating game, fish, 'palm berries', 'coco-plumbs', seaside grapes and other wild products".[1] Wild rye and rice were available but were not cultivated. The colony at St. Augustine was dependent upon the mother country and Cuba for almost everything. They did, however, introduce many vegetables, cattle, hogs, garlic and oranges from Spain and sugar cane from the West Indies. These were grown inside or closely adjacent to the stockade from fear of Indian attacks.

Some eighty Spanish missions were established in Florida and up the East Coast to the Carolinas. The priests instructed the Indians in religion and the rudiments of agriculture and gradually helped establish a more settled agriculture.

There was little commercial agriculture until Florida was ceded to England in 1763.[1] Rice and wheat were cultivated in West Florida by that time and indigo was a money crop. Sea Island cotton was introduced in the early 1800s, Cuban tobacco seed for cigar wrappers was introduced in 1828–29.[2] Florida's commercial agriculture has been almost wholly dependent upon introduction and adaptation of plants from other states and other lands.

Field corn grown in Florida finds a ready market as feed for livestock on general and livestock specialty farms. The use of hybrid varieties of corn and the application of fertilizers are increasing the state average yield per acre.

Cotton production, once a mainstay of plantation economy, had been

---

[1] Gray, "History of Agriculture in Southern United States to 1860", Vol. I, pp. 108–9.
[2] Ibid, Vol. II. p. 756.

Donald L. Brooke, Professor-Emeritus, Institute of Food and Agricultural Sciences, received his training at the University of Florida and the University of Illinois. He was employed by IFAS from 1946, specializing in the economics of production and marketing of vegetable crops, citrus, tropical fruits and floriculture. He retired in 1980.

declining in Florida for many years. However, acreage harvested more than quadrupled from 1980 to 1989, and doubled again from 1989 to 1993.

The introduction of improved grasses and legumes adapted to Florida soils has made profitable hay production possible. Florida imports hay from other states each year because it does not produce enough to provide roughage for livestock on farms.

"Peanuts may be grown alone and harvested for hay and nuts or interplanted with corn to provide a high-nutrient grazing crop for livestock. For the latter use they are second only to field corn in Florida. Peanuts harvested for nuts are an important source of income on many general farms.

Soybeans became an established crop for Florida growers after World War II for use as a summer cover crop from which the mature beans could be harvested for cash income. Mechanization of production and favorable prices resulted in rapidly expanding production.

McCarty Hall on the campus of the University of Florida is the headquarters of IFAS, the Institute of Food and Agricultural Sciences. IFAS is responsible for land grant college education, research for agriculture, and the delivery of applied agricultural knowledge through its extension services offices in the 67 counties.

Sugar cane for sugar, although classified as a field crop, is not produced in the general farming area of Florida. It is grown on the rich muckland soils of the Everglades around Lake Okeechobee. Large corporations grow and process sugar cane in that area. With the cessation in purchases of sugar from Cuba its production increased significantly in Florida. Sugar cane used for syrup is grown on a few farms in the northern and western parts of the state.

Florida produces type 14 (flue-cured) tobacco. It is grown on many large and small general farms as a cash crop. It is the only field crop of importance whose production is controlled by government quota.

Crops whose acreage and value are not recorded include lupines, velvet beans, millet, sorghum, field peas, sweet potatoes, and oats.

Truck Crops

Vegetables, or truck crops as a group, are third in value of production among Florida's agricultural products. Citrus and livestock and livestock products are first and second in value, respectively. Vegetables for commercial use are grown in the fall, winter and spring months. While small amounts of some Florida vegetables (snap beans, celery, tomatoes, Irish potatoes and spinach) are processed, the bulk of the production is grown for fresh consumption. Vegetables are shipped under refrigeration by rail and truck to the northern and southern markets. Some even find their way by air and boat to foreign markets. Although the areas of production in Florida are scattered from Dade to Escambia counties, the majority are in the central and southern portion of the state.

Packaging strawberries from a field in Hillsborough County.

The largest and most important truck crop area is found in the Everglades around Lake Okeechobee. Sweet corn, celery, escarole, lettuce and radishes are among the many crops of this area. Dangers of frost and torrential rains add greatly to the problems of production.

The introduction of a successful mechanical harvester has moved snap bean production from the muck soils of the Everglades to the sandy soils of the Pompano area and the marl and rock soils of Dade County. Snap beans require 50 to 60 days from seed planting to harvest and, weather permitting, two to three successive crops can be grown in the Pompano and Dade areas during Florida's season. Pole beans, requiring 80 days to maturity are an important late fall, winter and spring crop in Dade County.

Celery is produced on the mucklands of the Everglades, Oviedo, and Zellwood areas. The production and harvesting of celery require a large amount of costly hand labor. Celery growers are vitally interested and have had considerable success in developing mechanical equipment to offset the growing shortage and increasing cost of labor. Florida celery is marketed from November through June.

Sweet corn, a relatively unimportant crop in Florida until after World War II, is now a most important source of income. The principal areas of sweet corn production are the Everglades and Zellwood. The Dade and East Palm Beach areas produce some winter corn. Florida's major advantage in sweet corn production is a weather factor. It can be grown here during the late fall, winter and early spring months when few other areas are able to compete. The introduction of varieties better adapted to Florida conditions and improvement in quality control measures have contributed greatly to our production possibilities.

The majority of Florida's pepper production is in the Pompano and Immokalee-Lee areas for harvest from November through May. Some May and June production is marketed from Central and North Central Florida areas.

Tomatoes have long been Florida's most important vegetable crop in value of production. Dade and Palm Beach counties, Fort Pierce, Immokalee-Naples and Manatee-Hillsborough and Gadsden County are the principal areas of tomato production. Southeast and southwest production areas market from November until early May. Fort Pierce and Manatee-Hillsborough produce fall and spring crops for November-December and April-June marketing. Imports from Mexico compete continuously with Florida's production.

Watermelons are grown in nearly all of Florida's 67 counties and by a greater number of farmers than any other of our truck crops. A few icebox melons are produced during the late winter in the Dade and Immokalee areas. Major shipments begin in late March and continue into July. This is one of our few truck crops shipped to market without refrigeration in transit.

Among the vegetables not included in the accompanying table but grown in substantial quantity in Florida are carrots, greens, parsley, watercress, okra, cauliflower and radishes. Radishes are the most important of those with more than 27,000 acres being harvested each year. Radishes mature from seed in 21 to 32 days and their production, harvesting and preparation for market are highly mechanized.

Leading Florida Field and Vegetable Crops Harvested and Value of Production 1993

Item	Harvested Acres (000)	Value (thous. dol.)
Principal Field Crops:		
Corn for Grain	100.0	16,575
Cotton	53.5	21,231
Hay, all	220.0	56,760
Peanuts	84.0	57,295
Soybeans	50.0	7,938
Sugarcane	444.0	NA
Tobacco, Flue-Cured	7.1	30,586
Total	958.6	NA
Vegetable Crops:		
Snap Beans	30.4	83,217
Cabbage	9.8	37,539
Celery	7.7	62,955
Sweet Corn	42.1	67,566
Cucumbers	15.2	65,689
Eggplant	2.1	13,568
Escarole	2.5	8,453
Lettuce	7.8	26,042
Green Peppers	19.9	179,383
Potatoes, Irish	41.9	128,472
Squash	12.3	31,209
Strawberries	1.0	102,724
Tomatoes	48.4	626,048
Watermelons	37.0	66,600
Other Vegetables	56.6	166,785
Total	370.9	1,719,847

Source: Florida Crop and Livestock Reporting Service, Orlando, Florida

Livestock

Robert L. Degner

Several classes of livestock are produced commercially in Florida. Beef and dairy cattle, horses, swine, poultry, rabbits and other small animals, bees, and sheep are all raised in the state. Modern livestock production has grown from animals brought by European explorers and settlers, beginning over four centuries ago.

Spanish explorers brought horses as early as 1527, and the DeSoto expedition (1538–41) distributed hogs through Florida and other Southern states. Later, colonists brought cattle, sheep, goats and poultry. By the late 17th century and early 18th centuries, large numbers of cattle, horses and swine were ranging over north and central Florida.

Alto Adams, Jr, writes in his A Cattleman's Backcountry Florida: *"Braford cows are good mothers. They breed naturally at fifteen months of age and calve unassisted. All cattle on the Adams ranches (in Osceola, Okeechobee and St. Lucie Counties) calve without veterinary assistance, just as the deer and other wild animals do. This practice allows natural selection to form the cattle herd."* Alto Adams, Jr.

Robert L. Degner is Director of the Florida Agricultural Market Research Center and Professor, Food and Resource Economics, at the University of Florida.

Horses were the primary means of travel until the 1850s, and horse racing and hunting from horseback were popular sports from Spanish times until the 19th century. Florida cattlemen drove animals from the interior to port cities, where cattle were slaughtered, and tallow and hides exported. One origin of the term "Florida cracker" was from the long whips used by cattle drivers in the late 1700s.

In the late 19th century, Florida beef cattle were still similar to those of 200 years earlier. Improved breeds of cattle were then introduced to replace or upgrade the native or "cracker" cattle. As a result, Florida beef herds improved markedly during the first third of this century. Brahman cattle added size, hardiness and resistance to heat and insects. Crossing with Angus, Hereford, Shorthorn and establishing other improved breeds, such as Santa Gertrudis and Charloais, upgraded Florida beef cattle quality greatly.

Number and values of Florida livestock and products
Sources: Florida Agricultural Statistics Service
and Agricultural Statistical Board, NASS, USDA

Livestock and Products	Number on Farms Number	Rank Among States	Production, and Value, 1993 Production	Rank Among States	Value	Rank Among States
	(1,000)		(Million lbs.)		(Million Dollars)	
All Cattle and Calves[1]	1,980	15	439.3	29	353.2	26
Hogs and Pigs[2]	100	31	35.6	30	14.6	30
Milk Cows[3]	178	15	2,558	14	385.5	12
Layers (eggs)[3]	9,592	12	2,475[4]	12	106.8	11
Broilers[5]	128,400	14	552.1	13	187.7	13
Bees[6]	200	3	22.6	3	11.5	3

[1]Number as of January 1, 1994, production and value statistics are for 1993.
[2]Number as of December 1, 1993; production and value statistics are for 1993.
[3]Average number during 1993.
[4]Million eggs.
[5]Total number produced in 1993.
[6]Thousands of honey producing colonies.

At the same time, eliminating insects like ticks and screwworms, plus identification and correction of nutritional problems peculiar to Florida's sandy soils, paved the way for many other advances. Research and education in using improved grasses, better grazing management, selective breeding and modern health care have helped Florida to become a leading state in beef cattle production. In 1994, Florida ranked ninth in the U.S. in number of beef cows, and fifteenth in total cattle numbers.

The state's beef producers raise their herds on pasture, and market primarily weaned calves that go to feedlots for additional feeding before slaughter. Nearly all beef cattle in central and south Florida are on medium- and large-sized ranches. Beef herds in north and west Florida are generally smaller, and are part of farming operations. Some cattle are fed to slaughter weights in Florida feedlots, but most calves destined for slaughter are shipped to feedlots in other states.

Frederic Remington is best known worldwide for his portrayal of the American West in sculpture, drawings, and paintings. But he also sketched the cattle range in Florida for Harper's Monthly *in the 1890s. This Remington depicts a shootout between two groups of South Florida cowmen, likely over either range rights or unbranded cattle.* Florida State Archives

Florida also has a large and progressive dairy industry standing fifteenth in the U.S. in milk cow numbers in 1993. Dairy cow numbers have increased by about 4 percent during the past decade and milk production per cow has increased by 30 percent, resulting in an increase in total milk production of about 35 percent. Florida dairies produced nearly 2.6 billion pounds of milk in 1993, and nearly all of it was consumed as fluid milk within Florida. Florida also has some of the largest dairies in the U.S. with many having several thousand milking cows. Most dairies are located near the major cities in the state. Dairymen must purchase large quantities of feed, including grain from other states, and molasses and roughage in Florida.

Florida's swine production, while not as important as beef production or dairying, is a far cry from the bands of "piney woods rooters" roaming the state during its first 300 years. Hog farms, concentrated in north and west Florida, are not large by Corn Belt standards. However, high quality hogs are produced under modern conditions. Florida ranked thirty-first in hog numbers in the U.S. in 1993.

Horses, important in Florida since the earliest explorations, are a major livestock enterprise today. The United States Equine Marketing Association (USEMA) estimated Florida's horse population at slightly over 335,000 in 1993, of which approximately 175,000 were registered. According to USEMA, the capital investment in Florida's horse industry amounts to nearly $7.7 billion, which generates a cash flow of over $644 million annually. Thoroughbreds are the predominant breed, followed by Quarterhorses, Appaloosas, Arabians, Standardbreds, Tennessee Walkers, Paso Finos, and Paints. Significant numbers of most recognized breeds are found in the state. Most breeding farms are in and around Marion County. Florida's fine winter weather has attracted breeders from many other states to take advantage of the racing and training opportunities.

Sheep and lambs were imported in large numbers by the Spanish as early as 1565. However, sheep numbers in Florida have been low for many years and are of relatively minor importance. Several other types of animals are raised in certain areas of the state. In recent years, there has been a great deal of interest in goat production for milk and meat. The 1992 Census of Agriculture found that 1,111 Florida farms had nearly 17,000 head of goats. Rabbits are produced for meat and for laboratory animals and mink and chinchilla for furs. Greyhound raising and training for racing is important in several counties. Alligators are also being grown commercially under controlled conditions for their hides and meat. Many consider the meat to be a delicacy. In 1977, there were only four commercial alligator farms in Florida. By 1987 that number had grown to 40 and in 1993 there were 55 licensed alligator farms.

Florida's horse farms are a source of breeders' pride and tourist attraction.   Jernigan

Public Education
Source: Florida Department of Education

Public education in Florida dates back a century and a half, to 1822, when Florida became a territory.

At that time, every sixteenth section of land in each township was reserved for the maintenance of primary schools. However, for ten years there were no schools in Florida except a few private elementary schools.

In 1823, a year after Florida became a territory, Congress enacted legislation reserving townships of land—called "seminary lands"—for two higher education institutions. These early seminaries were the "ancestors" of today's University of Florida and Florida State University.

Early Efforts

In 1831 the Florida Education Society was formed in Tallahassee and branch societies were organized throughout the state. The FES attempted in its first year to operate a free public school in St. Augustine and a manual-labor school in Tallahassee. Both schools were dependent on public subscription, which was unsteady, and the projects were abandoned.

But these early groups were pioneers in the concept of free public education and they met strong opposition from people of wealth and influence who regarded public schools and pauper schools as one and the same.

In 1839 the territorial government attempted to establish a public school system. Three trustees in each township were named to oversee and lease school lands, using proceeds to support public schools. A new law set aside two percent of the territorial tax and auction duties "for the education of orphan children of the county to which the funds belong." But there is no record of the law being implemented.

Another attempt was made in 1844, with county sheriffs being given the authority and duties of the trustees. This did not work, and trustees were restored with provisions made for their election by the people. A year later, judges of probate were appointed as superintendents of common schools.

In a search for sources of revenue, the territorial assembly authorized the use of lotteries to raise funds for Quincy Academy and a school in St. Augustine, but not much is known of the results.

Until 1845, the only true public schools in Florida were in Franklin and Monroe counties. In 1845, when Florida became a state, interest in a state public school system gained impetus. Control of school lands was taken from the counties and reverted to the State Register of Public Lands and in 1848 the state was authorized to sell school lands, using the proceeds to set up a permanent state school fund.

First System in 1849

In 1849 the first real state school system was authorized. The State Register of Lands was designated as State Superintendent, judges of probate were to be county superintendents, local boards of trustees were to be elected by the taxpayers. In 1851, counties were authorized to levy taxes for schools, up to $4 per child, but only Franklin and Monroe Counties are on record as taking advantage of the law.

In 1853 county commissioners were delegated to act as county school boards.

The Constitution of 1868 provided for the same state school officials we have today: a State Superintendent (now Commissioner) and a State Board of Education, composed of the Governor and Cabinet.

The Constitution also set up a state school tax of one mill, with counties required to raise locally an amount equal to one-half of the state's contribution. It also provided that children could not be counted, for state fund distribution purposes, unless they attended school at least three months of each year. This was the first time a minimum school term was established, and the first time the state offered an incentive for raising local funds for schools.

In 1885, the drafters of the Constitution wrote:

"The Legislature shall provide for a uniform system of public free schools, and shall provide for the liberal maintenance of the same."

A special state school tax, of one mill, was included in that Constitution, along with the following provision:

"Each county shall be required to assess and collect annually for the support of public free schools therein, a tax of not less than three mills, not more than five mills on the dollar of all taxable property in the same."

Maximum county millage was raised to seven mills in 1904 and ten mills in 1918. The Constitution of 1968 placed a ten mills ceiling on Board levied millage. In 1994–95, school board levies were as follows: (1) a levy required for participation in the state finance program—6.725 mills (average of all districts), (2) a discretionary local millage of .510 mills, (3) a supplemental levey up to .25 mills provided that no more than $50 per full-time equivalent student is raised, and (4) an optional capital outlay and maintenance levy—up to 2.0 mills.

The options for voted millage continued essentially unchanged under the 1968 Constitution. District electors may vote to levy additional millage for the payment of bonds which are generally paid serially over a twenty year period. Taxes may also be voted for periods not longer than two years, only for the purpose or purposes stated on the ballot.

The "New Law," the School Law of 1889, spelled out in detail the powers and duties of school officials, providing uniformity among county school systems.

Higher Education

Eight public institutions in Florida offered education beyond high school until the late 1800s. In 1905, the Florida Legislature passed the Buckman Act (after Senator Henry Holland Buckman) which abolished the state's miscellaneous colleges, seminaries, normal schools and institutes and replaced them with a three-institution system of higher learning: a state university (University of Florida), a college (now Florida State University) and a normal school (now Florida A&M University).

These three institutions were placed under a Board of Control, forerunner of the present Florida Board of Regents, which directs operation of the present nine state universities.

Conference for Education

Between 1892 and 1920 many changes occurred in education and much of this progress was sparked by the Conference for Education in Florida, an organization of laymen and teachers whose aim was the improvement of all schools in Florida.

The first state compulsory attendance law was enacted in 1919, and in the same session the Legislature passed a uniform public curriculum law, setting minimum requirements. Florida's program of vocational education expanded with passage of the federal Smith-Hughes Act of 1917 and in 1927 the state's program of vocational rehabilitation began.

In the early 30's, Florida schools, like those in most states of the nation, suffered financially during the Depression years. Increased state aid could not offset the losses from local sources and many school systems were unable to meet their current operating costs, with some counties defaulting on school building bonds when local revenue declined.

The 1937 Legislature authorized preparation of the School Code of 1939 which removed old conflicts in school laws and also approved other laws relating to education which reorganized and improved the school program.

Following World War II, Florida schools faced a multitude of accumulated crises. Salaries were too low, buildings were in need of repair, additional classrooms were desperately needed. Enrollments were expanding rapidly and a breakdown in the state's school system threatened unless speedy action was taken.

MFP in 1947

A Florida Citizens Committee on Education was given the task of figuring out a solution. Appointed by the Governor and approved by the 1945 Legislature, the committee made an intensive, two-year, study. Their study and leadership resulted, in 1947, in enactment of a comprehensive school financing plan—the Minimum Foundation Program—which operated with changes and improvements through 1972–73.

In 1955 the Junior College Advisory Board was created and charged by the Legislature with recommending a long-range plan for establishment and coordination of a system of two-year post-high school institutions.

In 1957 the State embarked on a statewide, planned program to bring junior college educational opportunities to every area in the state. Funds were provided for four existing junior colleges and for establishment of six new ones. Today there are 28 community colleges in the state.

In early 1968 a special session was called for the improvement of education, following a "crash" study by the Governor's Commission for Quality Education. Immediately following the end of that session, the Florida Education Association called for a statewide teacher walkout, based on FEA complaints about the legislative program. The walkout lasted about three weeks, and by the end of a month, most of the state's teachers were back in their classrooms.

Unified System

The 1969 Legislature, in its general reorganization of state government, placed all of Florida's tax supported schools—from kindergartens through universities—in a single, unified system of public education.

The State Board of Education, under this reorganization, is responsible for the entire education system in the State. The Commissioner of Education, a member of the Board of Education, is the chief education officer of the State.

The new Constitution, approved by the voters in 1968, provided that the Board of Education would consist of the Cabinet and the Governor (seven members, instead of the previous five members, adding the Comptroller and the Commissioner of Agriculture). The Constitution also eliminated the title of the Superintendent of Public Instruction and created the title of the Commissioner of Education in a broader role.

For administrative purposes, the Department of Education presently is organized into seven divisions: Division of Public Schools; Division of Community Colleges; Division of Applied Technology and Adult Education; Division of Universities; Division of Blind Services; Division of Human Resource Development; and Division of Administration. Each of these is headed by a Director, except for Universities and Community Colleges which are directed by the Board of Regents and the State Board of Community Colleges. [See entries elsewhere in this book for Commissioner of Education and Department of Education.]

Efforts Towards Reform

Standards for student performance, pupil progression and graduation from high school were established and a statewide program of student assessment testing began in 1977. A test to measure high school students' ability to apply basic communications and computations knowledge to practical life requirements was instituted and after successfully withstanding legal challenges, passage of the test was applied in 1983 as a criterion for the award of a standard high school diploma.

Incentives programs were established to stimulate and provide recognition for achievement through academic competition, and to encourage outstanding students to remain in Florida by providing scholarships to students for Florida colleges and universities.

College sophomores were required to pass the College Level Academic Skills Test in order to earn an Associate of Arts degree or be fully admitted to the upper division of a state university. Passage of the Florida Teacher Certification Examination became a requirement for certification of new teachers.

Concurrently, more stringent entry requirements to colleges of education, strengthened requirements for state approval of teacher preparation programs and higher standards for graduation from colleges of education were established. An intensified beginning teacher internship program was implemented to further guarantee adequacy of preparation of teachers for Florida classrooms.

Extension of the education reforms of the 1970's and significant new initiatives marked sessions of the Legislature in the 1980's. The Florida Primary Education program to expand services for kindergarten through grade three students was funded through a decade. The Florida Progress in Middle Childhood Education Program and preschool projects received significant funding. Dropout prevention has been given emphasis by funding through the basic finance formula and by special projects. Stringent high school graduation requirements and teacher certification requirements were set. Scholarship programs were enhanced. Instruction in the prevention of AIDS was made a curriculum requirement for all students.

As the last decade of the 20th century dawned, the focus of education reform shifted to preparing the workforce for the next century. To do so would require Florida to tackle a growing dropout problem. The best longterm solution to the dropout dilemma, ensuring that all students come to school ready to learn, was addressed with the implementation of Prekindergarten Early Intervention for disadvantaged preschoolers, the funding for which has steadily increased. In 1986, 650 children were served in this program. During 1994-95, 26,000 children are expected to be served.

To fight the dropout problem for the short term, the 1989 Legislature passed the "Students Drive, Dropouts Don't" law, which withholds drivers licenses from students who drop out of school.

A new curriculum integrating academic and vocational skills was implemented in pilot schools. The curriculum is based on the *Blueprint for Career Preparation,* an action plan that prescribes how to close the gap between emerging job requirements and the ability of Florida's students to meet them.

Teacher training, recruitment, compensation and recognition became a major emphasis. From 1986 to 1989, teacher salaries improved in national ranking from 32nd to 28th. A major review of teacher-education programs at Florida's public universities was initiated. Minority-teacher recruitment was stressed, and a Distinguished Black Educator Award program was begun. A partnership to retrain separated and retiring military officers for teaching careers was implemented.

As of 1993, Florida had more than 228,000 classroom microcomputers in use and was considered a national leader in instructional technology. Five Model Technology Schools were designated to serve as research and development sites for instructional technology.

Magnet schools and rigorous programs for the best and brightest students were expanded, including the Academic Scholars and International Baccalaureate programs.

Standardized testing was reformed, eliminating minimum competency testing. A writing component was added to statewide testing.

The Gross Receipts Utilities Tax was increased to provide an additional $3.6 billion in funding for educational construction over the 1990s.

Private sector support of education through business partnerships increased significantly. Increased emphasis was placed on family involvement in education.

With the establishment of student assessment, early childhood education and educational accountability programs in the mid 1970's, the stage was set for a reform movement which would thrust Florida education into the national forefront.

Blueprint 2000

A move to restructure education to emphasize school-based management and a greater role for teachers in decision-making was a hallmark of this period. With the passage of the landmark legislation, Blueprint 2000, in 1991, Florida has become a national leader in the restructuring movement. The legislation seeks to raise educational standards and give those closest to the students—schools, teachers and parents—control over school decision-making. The plan has identified seven goals for education in the state in the areas of: readiness to start school, graduation rate and readiness for post-secondary education and employment, student performance, learning environment, school safety and environment, teachers and staff and adult literacy.

Blueprint 2000 also: established The Florida Commission on Education Reform and Accountability to design and oversee the new education system; directed schools to set up School Advisory Councils made up of parents, business leaders and educators selected by their peers; instructed SACs to draft individual school improvement plans to guide their efforts towards reform, and acknowledged their role in school decision-making; established standards of performance for schools and students; requires schools to report their progress toward the state goals, and provides incentives for schools that show improvement towards the goals, and intervention/assistance for those schools not showing adequate progress.

The Department of Education is in the midst of an extensive restructuring effort to better meet the needs of Florida's school districts under Blueprint 2000. Instead of regulating school districts as in the past, the primary role of the department has become one of providing technical assistance to districts and schools as they implement school improvement plans. By 1995, the department is expected to be nearly 60 percent smaller than it was in early 1994.

Financing Public School Education

At the school district level, the sources of funds for operations are primarily from ad valorem (property) taxes and from adult student fees. At the state level, the major sources of money for operations are the General Revenue Fund (the sales tax, corporate income tax, beverage tax, documentary stamp tax, cigarette tax, insurance premium tax, intangible tax, estate tax, service charges, pari-mutuels tax and other taxes) and the Educational Enhancement Trust Fund (Lottery).

Public School Education

During the 1947–48 school year, public elementary and secondary schools received 45.0 percent of their revenue from local sources, 52.3 percent from the State, and 2.7 percent from the federal government. By 1992–93, this had changed to 42.2 percent from the local sources, 49.6 percent from the State and 8.2 percent from the federal government.

From 1947–48 through 1972–73 the core of financial support for the instructional program was provided through the Minimum Foundation Program (MFP): salaries, materials, facilities, and student transportation. As needs changed, legislation was passed which amended the MFP to provide the legal and financial bases for additional programs and services. In 1973–74 state support of public school education was provided through the Florida Education Finance Program (FEFP) and the MFP was abolished.

Florida Education Finance Program (FEFP) in 1973

Like the MFP, more than a quarter century earlier, FEFP was the product of various studies and recommendations by a citizen's committee. Formally known as the Governor's Citizen's Committee on Education, the 22-member group representing individuals from all walks of life met each month for two years. With the aid of professional staff to prepare materials and conduct research, much of the final committee report was incorporated into the "Florida Education Finance Act of 1973" which established the Florida Education Finance Program.

The Florida Education Finance Program (FEFP) changed the focus for funding public school education in the State. Traditionally, State agencies have distributed dollars to school districts by formulas based upon instruction units. The key feature of the FEFP is to base financial support for education upon the individual student participating in a particular program. FEFP funds are generated by multiplying the number of full-time equivalent students (FTE's) by weight factors (program cost factors) to obtain weighted FTE's which are then multiplied by a base student allocation fixed annually by the Legislature.

FEFP

The 1994 Legislature sustained the evolution of policy established to provide operation funds for school districts through the FEFP. The base financial support continues to be the means by which more than 80 percent of the operating funds for school districts are distributed. The 1994–95 Base Student Allocation (BSA) was established at $2,558.17.

Program Cost Factors

Educators have recognized that certain grade levels and special programs require more money to operate than others. The FEFP provides for this through use of program cost factors. These factors are modified each year based on actual expenditure experience. Funded programs are grouped in five categories: Basic Education, Exceptional Student Education, At-Risk Student Education, Vocational Education, and Adult General Education. A cost factor is set for each program within these groups. For the 1994–95 school year there were 53 program cost factors included in the appropriations act: Basic, 6 programs (3 major graded programs of kindergarten through grade 3, grades 4–8, and grades 9–12 plus 3 programs for mainstreaming exceptional students); Exceptional, 15 programs; At-Risk, 4 programs; Vocational, 25 programs (adult and secondary students); and Adult General, 3 programs. Cost factors are indexed on the per pupil cost of the Basic, grades 4–8 program. With that program set as 1.000, examples of 1994–95 factors included kindergarten and grades 1–3, 1.029; grades 9–12, 1.210; physically handicapped, 3.285; gifted, 1.785; and high school agriculture, 1.676. Factors ranged from a high of 16.168 for part-time participation in the visually handicapped program to .718 for the adult basic literacy program.

Basic Amount for Current Operations

The basic amount for current school district operations under the FEFP is determined as follows:
1. the full-time equivalent membership (FTE) in each program; multiplied by
2. the cost factor of each program equals the weighted full-time equivalent membership (WFTE); multiplied by
3. the base student allocation (BSA); multiplied by
4. the district cost differential (DCD) equals the Base Funding.

District Cost Differential (DCD)

The FEFP recognizes that the purchasing power of the dollar is not the same throughout the State. The district cost differentials, which were fixed by the Legislature each year from 1973 through 1976, are now determined based upon the average of the last three Florida Price Level Index Studies. In computing the differential index, this average is factored to apply to 80 percent of each district's FEFP. The rationale is that approximately 80 percent of costs relate to employment of staff. Application of the differential tends to neutralize the effects of high and low cost areas in the employment of educational personnel.

Required Local Effort

After each district's total FEFP entitlement has been determined, the required local effort is deducted. A dollar amount for statewide required local effort is specified in the Appropriations Act each year. The Department of Revenue provides the Department of Education with an estimate of each district's property tax roll. The Department of Education then computes the millage rate which when applied to 95% of the tax roll yields the local effort for each district. This millage varies by district due to application of assessment ratios which reflect the Department of Revenue's most recent determination of the assessment level for each district. Assessment ratios were first applied in 1984–85. In 1994–95, the resultant required local effort millages ranged from a high of 7.054 mills to a low of 5.024 mills.

In addition to the required local effort from ad valorem property taxes, fees are charged to adult students enrolled in vocational and adult education programs. The fees are added to and become a part of the required local effort.

Florida Public School Statistics
for the Twentieth Century

School Year	Number of Schools	Enrollment/Membership[†]	High School Graduates[‡]
1901–1902	2,336	112,384*	136**
1921–1922	2,597	237,770*	1,206**
1931–1932	2,583	367,758*	6,140**
1941–1942	2,589	402,009*	14,171
1951–1952	2,034	556,936*	17,888
1961–1962	1,940	1,136,937*	43,717
1971–1972	1,921	1,473,728	78,296
1973–1974	1,983	1,529,958	83,822
1974–1975	1,955	1,546,392	85,651
1975–1976	2,043	1,551,538	88,932
1976–1977	2,462	1,536,360	89,116
1977–1978	2,251	1,534,040	90,252
1978–1979	2,243	1,513,886	88,203
1979–1980	2,302	1,506,215	87,826
1980–1981	2,228	1,510,517	88,755
1981–1982	2,284	1,488,073	89,199
1982–1983	2,350	1,484,917	86,871
1983–1984	2,347	1,495,593	85,908
1984–1985	2,304	1,524,107	81,140
1985–1986	2,393	1,562,283	83,029
1986–1987	2,478	1,607,320	83,692
1987–1988	2,505	1,664,563	90,813
1988–1989	2,552	1,720,930	92,449
1989–1990	2,676	1,789,925	90,790
1990–1991	2,817	1,861,592	89,494
1991–1992	2,908	1,932,131	93,312
1992–1993	2,912	1,979,933	91,373
1993–1994	2,895	2,039,884	N/A

*Enrollment
**Estimated

[†]Prior to 1960, separate schools existed for black and white students. The decrease in the number of schools in the 1970's was due to desegregation.
[‡]Includes standard diplomas and special diplomas.

Miss Eva Wooten's elementary school class at Cocoa, 1912. Florida State Archives

Highways: Trails to Turnpikes
Source: Department of Transportation

Many of Florida's modern highways have as their origin ancient Indian trails. Here and there, an old terminus has been deleted or a detour made to shorten distance, but in the main, today's complex network of roads, highways and bridges has followed remarkably the older trails.

The first Europeans to come to Florida, the Spanish explorers, often were compelled to rely upon the Indians to guide them overland. These Indian trails served as the major overland routes used by the Spanish in their colonization of Florida.

The Kings Road, built by the British in segments during the 1760's and 1770's, was the first in Florida graded and wide enough to accommodate wheeled vehicles for any appreciable distance. Miss Dena Snodgrass, the Jacksonville historian, reports the Kings Road, when completed, ran from the Georgia line (the St. Marys River) to New Smyrna, via St. Augustine. The road exists today in Duval and Nassau Counties in considerable sections and is still called the Kings Road. It also exists in small segments in Flagler, St. Johns, and Volusia Counties. In Volusia the Interstate passes over it and the overpass is emblazoned "Old Kings Road" at the crossing.

After Florida became a territory in 1822, the United States government appropriated $20,000 for construction of a road from Pensacola to St. Augustine. That leg from St. Augustine westward to the vicinity of Tallahassee came to be known as the Bellamy Road after its contractor. The road was completed in 1826, although settlers complained that it was only 16 feet wide, that tree stumps were left high above the ground, and that causeways and bridges were inadequate.

A portion of present U.S. 27 generally follows a segment of the original road east of Tallahassee, while U.S. 90 generally follows the route west of Tallahassee.

Although these roads across North Florida follow routes similar to the Indian, Spanish and English trails, there is of course little resemblance in the specifications and construction plans used by the early roadbuilders. Only a few paragraphs of specifications were laid down in building the Pensacola-St. Augustine Road. Today, the Department of Transportation has a 600-page book of detailed specifications relating to every phase of highway construction. The $20,000 appropriated by Congress to construct the entire route would not finance even a mile of one of our less expensive secondary roads.

(See also: Department of Transportation, page 85.)

Sunshine Skyway Bridge — Department of Transportation

The critic on architecture of *The New York Times*, Paul Goldberger, described Florida's Sunshine Skyway as startlingly beautiful, almost a religious experience.

The 1,260 foot main span of the 8.1 mile causeway across Tampa Bay, which opened to traffic in 1987, soars "over the water with a lyrical and tensile strength."

The Sunshine Skyway Bridge was designed by Figg & Muller of Tallahassee, an engineering firm which specializes in concrete bridge design. The bridge replaces a pair of steel-truss bridges, one of which collapsed in 1980 when it was rammed by a freighter on a foggy night, killing 35 people.

The State and the Federal government considered repairing the bridge, which was only nine years old at the time. A companion span was 26 years old. But it was decided to replace both spans with a larger and safer bridge instead.

"For roughly $220 million they got not only a bridge that is both large and safe—they also got a structure that from an esthetic standpoint may rank as the most impressive piece of large-scale bridge design in this country in half a century," wrote critic Goldberger. "Not since the George Washington, Bronx-Whitestone and Golden Gate Bridges, the high points of suspension bridge design in the 1930s, has a major bridge been as compelling a visual presence as this one."

Size and Structure of Florida
C. Wythe Cooke

Florida is bounded by two nearly straight imaginary lines, by three rivers, and by a long shore line. The northeastern boundary is formed by St. Marys River from its mouth to Ellicotts Mound near the head of the North Prong. From Ellicotts Mound the line runs N. 87° 17' 22" W. (average direction) to the junction of the Flint and Chattahoochee Rivers at the head of Apalachicola River, whence it continues up the Chattahoochee to the thirty-first parallel of north latitude. These boundaries separate Florida from Georgia. The thirty-first parallel and Perdido River separate it from Alabama. The Gulf of Mexico and Straits of Florida, and the Atlantic Ocean complete the circuit. These boundaries enclose an area of 54,153 square miles[1] of land and 4,424 square miles of water—a total area of 58,677 square miles.

Floridian Plateau

The State of Florida occupies only a part of a much larger geographic unit, the Floridian plateau. The deep water of the Gulf of Mexico is separated from the deep water of the Atlantic Ocean by a partially submerged platform nearly 500 miles long and about 250 to 400 miles wide. This platform, the Floridian Plateau, is attached to the continent of North America and forms part of it. It consists of a core of metamorphic rocks, presumably the continuation of the rocks of the Piedmont region of Georgia, buried under more than 4,000 feet of sedimentary rocks, chiefly limestone, which represent the seaward extension of the rocks making up the Coastal Plain of Georgia and Alabama.

The Floridian Plateau has been in existence for many millions of years, during which it has been alternately dry land or covered by shallow seas. During most of this long time the plateau appears to have been a very stable region, not subject to violent crustal movements, and therefore free from earthquakes of local origin. The principal deformation that it has undergone is a very gentle doming that has made the rocks in the north-central part a little higher than the corresponding beds in other parts of the plateau. Dislocations of the rocks (faults), along which takes place the slipping that causes earthquakes, are completely unknown. The Floridian Plateau is one of the most stable parts of the earth's crust.

The plateau is broad and nearly level. The highest part projects a little

---

Dr. C. Wythe Cooke was senior geologist of the U.S. Geological Survey. The foregoing is a digest, by permission, from Bulletin No. 17 of the Florida Geological Survey.

[1] Land area from U.S. Bureau of Census, revised 1980.

more than 325 feet above sea level and forms the State of Florida. An equally great or greater area is submerged beneath the Gulf of Mexico, and a smaller area beneath the Atlantic Ocean north of Palm Beach. Both of these submerged parts (the Continental Shelf) slope gently away from the land at a rate generally less than 3 feet to the mile. The slope at most places near shore is steeper in the Atlantic than in the Gulf. Beyond a depth approximately 300 feet, the slope of the sea bottom steepens rapidly.

Coastline of Florida

Source: U.S. Coast and Geodetic Survey

	General Coastline	Length in Statute Miles Tidal Shoreline General	Tidal Shoreline Detailed
Atlantic Coast	399	618	3,035
Gulf Coast	798	1,658	5,391
Total for Florida	1,197	2,276	8,426

Explanation: "General" coastline is the measurement of the general outline of the seacoast. "Tidal" shoreline includes measurement of bays, sounds and other waterbodies where these narrow to a width of three statute miles. "Tidal shoreline, detailed" takes bays, sounds and other bodies either to the head of tidewater or to a point where such waters narrow to 100 feet.

The Sands of Florida

Source: State Bureau of Geology

There are several substances that color the sands on the beaches of Florida. For the most part, the browns and tans are broken pieces of shell, and these represent the color of the shell itself, which was formed as a precipitant about the living animal. Some iron is included, which causes the tan color. Sometimes the shells are dark grey and lend some color to local beaches.

Florida's beautiful, white beaches are composed of essentially 100 per cent quartz sand that is kept scrubbed by the scrubbing action on the beach. Quartz is normally colorless to white. It makes an exceptionally beautiful beach, such as those found along the Mediterranean Sea and along the Gulf area of Panama City. If allowed to come to rest for long periods of time, such as in the quiet dunes behind the beaches and in the sands inland from the beach areas of the Panhandle, quartz becomes coated with iron and appears tan to cream-colored.

The black color, found in the sands of beaches, is a result of the occurrence of heavy minerals in the ocean, such as rutile and ilmenite, which may be concentrated from about 5 to 20 per cent along rills on the beaches. The ilmenite, rutile, and other minerals can be mined and separated from the beach sands; thus used for man's benefit. Some beaches, such as those at Venice, Florida, contain large quantities of black, phosphatic material, which consists of fragmented and rounded manatee rib bones, phosphate precipitated from the ocean and as animal excretions, and some phosphatized shells.

Land and Water Area: Area of the State and Counties of Florida April 1, 1990
(square miles)

County	Total 1/	Land area	Water area 1/	County	Total 1/	Land area	Water area 1/
Florida	65,758.3	53,937.2	11,821.1	Lafayette	547.96	542.8	5.1
Alachua	969.2	874.3	94.9	Lake	1,156.51	953.1	203.4
Baker	588.9	585.3	3.7	Lee	1,212	803.6	408.4
Bay	1,033.4	763.7	269.6	Leon	701.83	666.8	35.0
Bradford	300.1	293.2	6.9	Levy	1,412.41	1,118.4	294.0
Brevard	1,557.3	1,018.5	538.8	Liberty	843.22	835.9	7.3
Broward	1,319.7	1,208.9	110.9	Madison	715.89	692.0	23.9
Calhoun	574.4	567.4	7.0	Manatee	892.84	741.2	151.6
Charlotte	859.3	693.7	165.6	Marion	1,663.1	1,579.0	84.1
Citrus	773.2	583.6	189.6	Martin	752.86	555.7	197.2
Clay	643.7	601.1	42.6	Monroe	3,737.42	997.3	2,740.2
Collier	2,305.1	2,025.5	279.6	Nassau	725.9	651.6	74.3
Columbia	801.1	797.2	4.0	Okaloosa	1,082.09	935.8	146.3
Dade	2,429.6	1,944.5	485.1	Okeechobee	891.98	774.3	117.7
De Soto	639.6	637.3	2.2	Orange	1,004.31	907.6	96.7
Dixie	863.7	704.1	159.7	Osceola	1,506.49	1,322.0	184.5
Duval	918.3	773.9	144.4	Palm Beach	2,386.5	1,974.2	412.3
Escambia	893.9	663.6	230.3	Pasco	868.02	745.0	123.0
Flagler	570.8	485.0	85.8	Pinellas	607.75	280.2	327.6
Franklin	1,026.5	534.0	492.5	Polk	2,010.19	1,874.9	135.3
Gadsden	528.5	516.2	12.4	Putnam	827.22	722.2	105.1
Gilchrist	355.5	348.9	6.6	St. Johns	821.47	609.0	212.4
Glades	986.2	773.5	212.7	St. Lucie	688.13	572.5	115.6
Gulf	755.8	565.1	190.7	Santa Rosa	1,155.31	1,015.8	139.5
Hamilton	519.4	514.9	4.5	Sarasota	725.27	571.8	153.5
Hardee	638.4	637.4	1.0	Seminole	344.9	308.2	36.7
Hendry	1,189.9	1,152.7	37.2	Sumter	580.35	545.7	34.7
Hernando	589.1	478.3	110.8	Suwannee	691.94	687.7	4.3
Highlands	1,106.4	1,028.5	77.9	Taylor	1,232.05	1,042.0	190.1
Hillsborough	1,266.4	1,051.0	215.3	Union	249.72	240.3	9.4
Holmes	488.8	482.6	6.2	Volusia	1,432.51	1,105.9	326.6
Indian River	617.0	503.3	113.7	Wakulla	735.78	606.7	129.1
Jackson	954.7	915.8	38.9	Walton	1,238.13	1,057.7	180.5
Jefferson	636.7	597.8	38.9	Washington	615.84	579.9	36.0

1/ Water area measurement figures in the 1990 census data reflect all water, including inland, coastal, territorial, new reservoirs, and other man-made lakes. Measurement figures reported in previous censuses were only for inland water; the total water area of the state has increased substantially.

Source: U.S. Department of Commerce, Bureau of the Census, Geography Division, unpublished data. Florida Statistical Abstract

"No-Man's Lands"

That there are areas in Florida never visited by man, Robert O. Vernon, late Chief of the State Bureau of Geology, was "fairly certain," although "I have no actual knowledge that such a premise would be true."

"Many of our areas such as the Gulf Hammock section, the California swamps (in Dixie County) and the swamps along the Jefferson and Wakulla coasts are highly inaccessible. Yet sportsmen will traverse difficult terrain under acute hardships in order to get into virgin territory.

"Many sections of the Everglades would likewise qualify, and I think it would be very probable that there are some areas that have never been visited by man, perhaps other than Indians. There are some substantial areas which have never been surveyed in the Everglades."

Fossils
Source: Florida Trail, U.S. Department of the Interior

Florida's fossil record is unusually interesting. Particularly impressive is the record of the Late Pleistocene Age, a geologic period extending 20,000 to 200,000 years ago. Fossils of lions, sabertooth tigers, mammoths, horses, camels and giant armadillos are in many limestone deposits.

How Florida's Lakes Are Formed
Source: State Bureau of Geology

Limestone and dolostone are sedimentary rocks that are composed of calcium- and magnesium-carbonates. These make up the large part of the subsurface of Florida. These rocks are soluble in pure water, with the lapse of long periods of time, under conditions where the structure and composition of the rock favor solution in moving water. In the waters of Florida this limestone is readily dissolved, because the humid climate and prolific vegetation contribute organic and mineral acids to water and make it a highly potent solvent that is capable of dissolving large amounts of the rock.

The ultimate source of all of Florida's ground water is from the rain and moisture from the air. As this moisture is mixed or absorbed in the air it becomes charged with carbon dioxide gas to form carbonic acid. On the ground humic acids from rotting vegetation is added. These are the common natural solvents of limestone. A good portion of this acid charged water soaks into the ground, and as it moves through limerock small portions of the rock are disssolved. However, relatively little solution occurs until sufficient water enters the rock to fill completely all the available pores. In this portion of the rock, saturated with water and bathed with weak acids, solution is most active.

Limestone is as a rule jointed vertically and bedded horizontally. Openings along these joints and beds provide easy avenues of travel for water. Because of the pressure of water entering the rock, ground water tends to move horizontally along bedding planes which offer the easiest exit. Thus, cave systems generally are developed horizontally and one system may lie over another and they may be connected by vertical tubes and rooms.

Many Florida lakes are simple sinks affected directly by rainfall. In times of drought, a lake may become grassy ponds or completely dry. The water may run out through chimney-like tubes dropping to the zone of saturation. Shown here is a "disappearing" lake, with its sink hole, and in the background, a pier that gives an idea of the usual water level. Florida State Archives

Any rain water entering the rock from the surface makes its way downward to fill completely all the pores of the rock at some depth. As it moves downward and then into the saturated rock through pores and open spaces it acts as a slow solvent to increase the size of the openings and to connect them to form a continuous system of channels through which streams may run.

As large caverns are formed, solution cavities of irregular shape are gradually cut out and enlarged. Some of these may be expanded to a point near the surface where surface deposits (largely sand in Florida) will deform into the cavern and a sink is formed. The larger part of Florida's natural lakes, sinks, depressions and ponds are the result of the solution of the underlying limestone. These features range from small pits a few feet in diameter to large depressions several miles broad. Many are pefectly round, others are highly irregular. Some are cone-shaped with rocky bottoms, some have broadly developed flat bottoms and are known as prairies. Still others are vertical tubes, only a few inches in diameter in some cases, that extend as much as one hundred feet down into the limestone. These are "natural wells." Many sinks are dry, but many more are filled with water. The lake water may represent the exposure of the shallow water-table which continues into the lake basin walls to form ground water. Other lakes are composed of artesian water, that rises to fill the basin.

Other lake basins are formed by the sea as low places upon a platform of a former sea-bottom. Irregularities in sand dunes blown up from the beaches may cut below the ground-water table and form a lake.

Along some of the Panhandle streams, the association of a stream carrying a heavy sedimentary load with a stream that is clear and spring fed has resulted in the more rapid fill of some valleys and the drowning of the mouths of others to create large lakes. Dead Lake, on the Chipola, is a good example of this lake.

Area of Lakes
Source: U.S. Geological Survey

Lake Okeechobee is a remnant of a shallow sea, known as the Pamlico Sea, which once occupied what is now the Everglades-Lake Okeechobee basin. This basin was formed when the Florida plateau emerged from the ocean as a result of movement of the earth's crust. Lake Okeechobee, although large in surface area, is shallow, and probably contains less than two cubic miles of water.

Lake Okeechobee is the second largest freshwater lake entirely within one state. Alaska has the largest, of 1,033 square miles. Utah's Great Salt Lake covers 1,500 square miles. Lake Okeechobee is the fourth largest natural lake entirely within the United States, Lake Michigan, which touches Wisconsin, Illinois, Indiana and Michigan, being the largest, with 22,400 square miles.

Conservation area No. 1, of the Central and Southern Florida Flood Control District, in the Everglades, has a surface area of 216 square miles. It is the largest artificial reservoir in the state.

Natural Fresh-Water Lakes of 10 Square Miles or More in Florida

	County	Area (sq. miles)
Okeechobee	Hendry, Glades, Okeechobee, Martin, Palm Beach	700
George	Putnam, Marion, Volusia, Lake	70
Kissimmee	Osceola, Polk	55
Apopka	Orange	48
Istokpoga	Highlands	43
Tsala Apopka	Citrus	30
Tohopekaliga	Osceola	29
Harris	Lake	27
Orange	Alachua, Marion	26
E. Tohopekaliga	Osceola	19
Griffin	Lake	14
Monroe	Seminole, Volusia	14
Jessup	Seminole	13
Weohyakapka	Polk	12
Talquin	Gadsden, Leon	11
Eustis	Lake	11
Blue Cypress	Osceola, Indian River	10
Hatchineha	Polk, Osceola	10
Lochloosa	Alachua	10

The Tallahassee Meridian

A small marker near the Capitol in Tallahassee symbolizes the point of beginning for nearly all land descriptions in Florida. The Tallahassee meridian is the zero point from which surveyors identify land.

Highest Known Point

The State Bureau of Geology says the highest known surveyed elevation in Florida is located in the northeastern part of Walton County. That elevation has been fixed at 345 feet and is just south of the community of Lakewood, in the southeastern quarter of the southeastern quarter of section 30, Township 6 North, Range 20 West.

The late Bureau Chief Robert O. Vernon cautioned, however, that undoubtedly there are other elevations in Florida, probably in the Panhandle part, which will exceed this elevation, but are as yet undiscovered.

Iron Mountain, site of Bok Tower near Lake Wales in Polk County, was regarded for years as the state's highest known point. This was based upon a private topographic survey which fixed the elevation at 324.3 feet. An official survey indicated Iron Mountain to be slightly higher than 290 feet but less than 300 feet.

Semiprecious Stones

Chalcedony of rare beauty and structure is found along the valleys of the Suwannee, Santa Fe, Hillsboro, and other rivers that have eroded the sediments of the Tampa and Hawthorn formations. In former years, before the expansion of the City of Tampa, excellent collections could be had at numerous places along the shores of Hillsboro Bay. Today rare and sometimes excellent specimens are still recovered there from dredge tailings, and at Davis Island and Ballast Point, classic collection areas, heavy seas may mine and roll out good examples of these stones.

These lovely stones are coral heads, the calcite of which have been replaced by chalcedony. The heads range from complete, cherty replacements with solid interiors to heads with large cavities that are lined with alternating layers of black onyx, carnelian, sard, sardonyx and agate of radiant and varying color combinations. The cavity-type heads, called geodes, are the most sought after for gem purposes.

The original material of the coral, formed as a case about itself by the animal, has been replaced with all of the structure and shape of the coral having been preserved. These pseudomorphs were formed by water dissolving the coral head and simultaneously depositing an equal volume of silica from solution.

Springs

Source: State Bureau of Geology

The total number of springs in Florida is not known, but there are more than 200.

Florida's springs represent natural overflow from the State's vast groundwater storage and circulation system. Their combined flow is about 11,000 cubic feet per second (ft^3/s) or about 7 billion gallons a day. As a comparison, in 1971, public-water systems delivered 800 mgd (million gallons per day) which is equivalent to only about one-ninth of the water discharged each day from springs in Florida.

Springs vary in flow daily, seasonally, and from year to year. Basically the flow is related to variations in rainfall, although man's use of ground water affects the flow of some springs. During periods of little rainfall, spring flow, streamflow, and ground-water levels all decline, just as they increase during wet periods.

The springs of Florida are used to a limited degree as a source of water supply by agriculture and industry; however, their primary use is recreational. For this they are well suited because of the natural beauty of their surroundings, their normal clarity and consistently moderate temperature, and the seemingly subtle mystery of water upwelling from the earth.

First Magnitude Springs

Florida has 27 first-magnitude springs, those having an average flow of more than 100 ft^3/s.

Nationwise, Florida has more first-magnitude springs than any other state. Their total average flow is 8,700 ft^3/s, or 79 percent of the average flow of all springs in Florida. Silver Springs, with an average flow of 823 ft^3/s, is the largest noncoastal spring although Wakulla Springs has the greatest instantaneous measured flow (1,870 ft^3/s) and also the greatest range of flow. Coastal springs at Crystal River and Spring Creek have higher average flows than the non-coastal springs.

Springs may be classified by the average quantity of water they discharge. First magintude, 100 ft^3/s or more; second magnitude, 10 to 100 ft^3/s; and third magnitude, less than 10 ft^3/s.

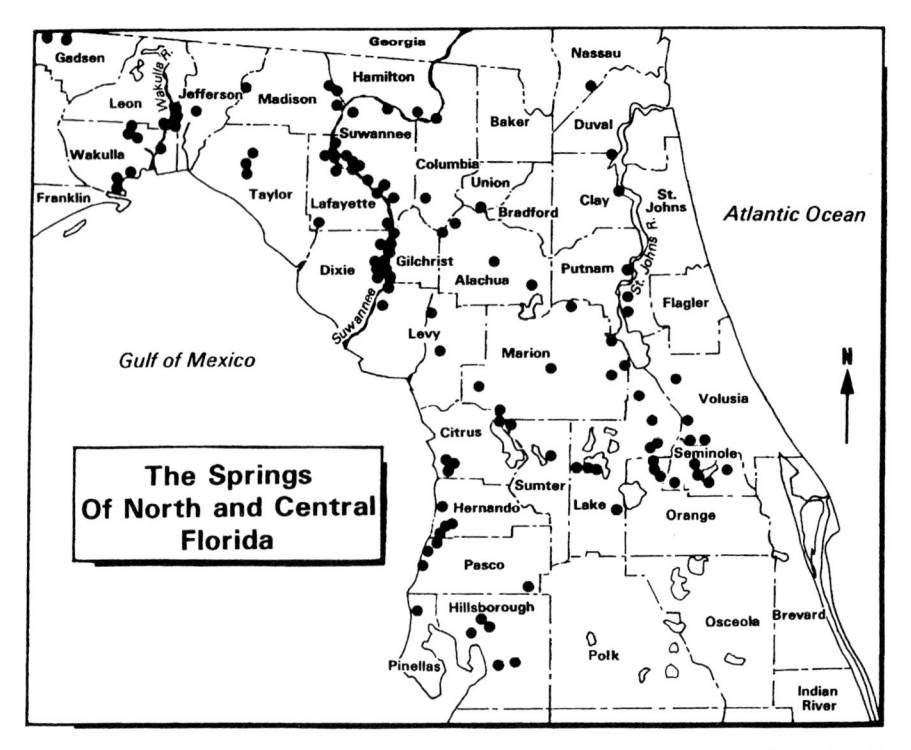

The Springs Of North and Central Florida

The Miami Herald

Why Springs?

Florida is underlain by a thick sequence of limestone and dolomite. These sedimentary rocks were deposited in shallow seas that, at various times in the geologic past, inundated the State. In many places these rocks contain numerous small and large interconnected cavities or caverns that have resulted from solution and removal of limestone by circulating fresh ground water. The fresh water derived from rainfall infiltrated the rocks after the sea level declined and left the surface of Florida above sea level. The majority of Florida's springs emerge from cavities where the rocks open at the land surface. A few springs seep from permeable sands or shell beds that have been deposited over the limestone. These springs are generally small compared with the ones that flow from limestone, and they also are more likely to go dry during long periods of little or no rainfall.

A spring is overflow or leakage from an underground reservoir (aquifer). The source of Florida ground water is rainfall that seeps into the ground and recharges aquifers in northern and central Florida and southern Alabama and Georgia, where rocks of the aquifers are at or near land surface. Most springs in Florida are permanent, that is they flow the year round.

The water of most Florida springs is of excellent quality. It is low in salinity and of moderate hardness depending, at least in part, on how long the water has been in storage in the aquifer. Dissolved solids are generally less than 250 milligrams per liter (mg/l). Spring temperatures range between 68° and 77° Fahrenheit (20° to 25° Celsius). Springs located in the southern part of the State tend to be the warmest.

Spring Names

Spring names used are consistent with previously published reports and maps; local names were used for springs not so identified. Whether "spring" or "springs" appears in the spring-name, bears no relation to whether the spring has a single or a multiple orifice.

NOTE: A listing of first magnitude springs appears in the 1983–1984 and prior editions of *The Florida Handbook*.

Jim Woodruff Lock and Dam
Source: U.S. Army Corps of Engineers

The Jim Woodruff Lock and Dam is located on the Apalachicola River about 1,000 feet below the point where the Chattahoochee and Flint Rivers unite to form the Apalachicola. It lies across the Georgia-Florida state line, about one and a half miles northwest of Chattahoochee, Florida.

The principal purposes are: (1) the provision of navigation channels, nine feet deep by 100 feet wide, in the Chattahoochee River to Columbia, Alabama, and in the Flint River to Bainbridge, Georgia, and (2) the production of hydroelectric power, with an average annual energy output of 220 million kilowatt hours. The dam has created a large lake for recreational activities.

The lock and dam was designed by the U.S. Army Corps of Engineers and built by private contractors. Construction was started in the fall of 1947 and completed in the spring of 1957 at a cost of $46,500,000. The project was named for Jim Woodruff, Sr., of Columbus, Georgia, who had, for more than 40 years, advocated development of the rivers for navigation.

Natural Bridges
Source: U.S. Geological Survey

Most natural bridges in limestone regions were formed by one of two methods—either by the undermining of neighboring sinks along a subterranean stream, or by the gradual diversion of part of a surface stream through a cavern dissolved by seepage through bedrock above a fall or rapid.

Bridges along a subterranean stream are not ordinarily recognized as bridges until they have reached an advanced stage of development. The existence of a bridge made by the diversion of a surface stream might not be suspected were it not that the stream is seen to sink in one place and to rise in another. The archway of most such bridges in Florida is completely filled with water.

Caverns
Source: U.S. Geological Survey

Although the limestones of Florida are honeycombed with caverns, the water table is generally so high that most of the passages are submerged. Important exceptions are those in the Florida Caverns State Park in Jackson County 2 miles north of Marianna. These caverns include twelve or more connected rooms, which are closely hung with myriads of small stalactites, and which rival in beauty, though on a much smaller scale, the justly famous caverns of the Shenandoah Valley of Virginia.

Harbors
Source: U.S. Geological Survey

The harbors of all the world occupy basins that have been deepened by the rising sea level that attended the melting of the last great continental ice sheets. The harbors of Florida are no exception. They differ from those of some other regions, however, because of differences in the topography of the land before the advance of the sea upon it.

Many great harbors occur in regions that were hilly or mountainous or which were trenched by deep valleys. But there were no mountains or deep valleys in Florida. The surface of the Floridian Plateau laid bare by the retreat of the sea during the last Ice Age and submerged again at its close was a very gently sloping plain across which the streams flowed in very shallow valleys. If the shore line during the last Ice Age lay on the steeper slope at the edge of the Plateau, the streams may have cut trenches at its outer margin, but, if so, the trenches did not extend inland as far as the present coast. It thus happens that there are no very deep harbors in Florida. Their depth is no greater than the normal depth of large rivers flowing over soft bottoms.

Size and Structure / 557

A barge in the lock at Jim Woodruff Dam. Florida State Archives

A 1920s view of the Natural Bridge that once spanned Arch Creek near Miami. Florida State Archives

Ports and Inland Waterways

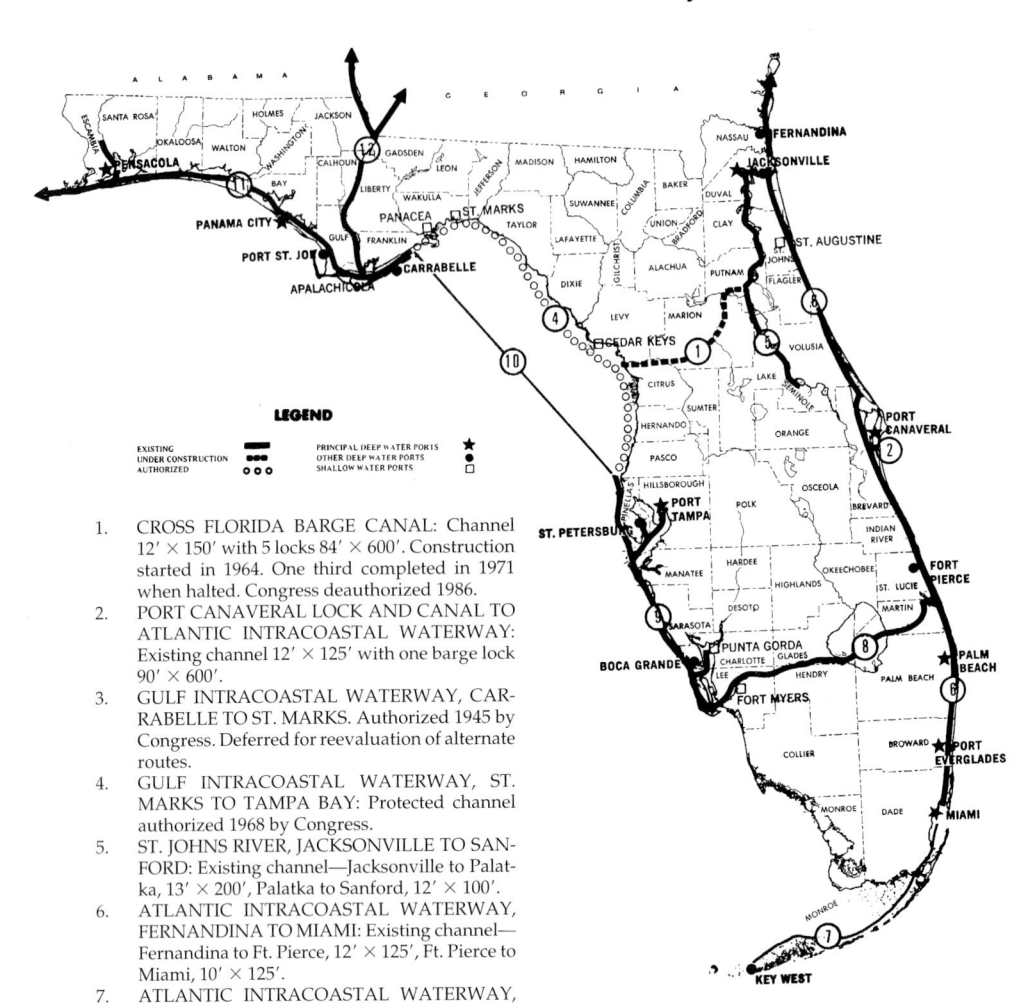

1. CROSS FLORIDA BARGE CANAL: Channel 12' × 150' with 5 locks 84' × 600'. Construction started in 1964. One third completed in 1971 when halted. Congress deauthorized 1986.
2. PORT CANAVERAL LOCK AND CANAL TO ATLANTIC INTRACOASTAL WATERWAY: Existing channel 12' × 125' with one barge lock 90' × 600'.
3. GULF INTRACOASTAL WATERWAY, CARRABELLE TO ST. MARKS. Authorized 1945 by Congress. Deferred for reevaluation of alternate routes.
4. GULF INTRACOASTAL WATERWAY, ST. MARKS TO TAMPA BAY: Protected channel authorized 1968 by Congress.
5. ST. JOHNS RIVER, JACKSONVILLE TO SANFORD: Existing channel—Jacksonville to Palatka, 13' × 200', Palatka to Sanford, 12' × 100'.
6. ATLANTIC INTRACOASTAL WATERWAY, FERNANDINA TO MIAMI: Existing channel—Fernandina to Ft. Pierce, 12' × 125', Ft. Pierce to Miami, 10' × 125'.
7. ATLANTIC INTRACOASTAL WATERWAY, MIAMI TO KEY WEST: Existing channel—Miami to Cross Bank, 7' × 75', Cross Bank to Key West, open bay (Atlantic Ocean).
8. OKEECHOBEE WATERWAY, STUART TO FT. MYERS: Existing channel with controlling depth of 8' × 80', 4 locks of controlling dimensions 50' × 250' × 11' depth.
9. GULF INTRACOASTAL WATERWAY, ANCLOTE TO FT. MYERS: Existing channel 9' × 100'.
10. CARRABELLE TO ANCLOTE OPEN BAY SECTION: Using Gulf of Mexico.
11. GULF INTRACOASTAL WATERWAY, CARRABELLE TO PERDIDO BAY: Existing channel 12' × 125'.
12. APALACHICOLA CHATTAHOOCHEE AND FLINT RIVERS, FLA. AND GA.: Apalachicola-Chattahoochee Rivers—existing channel 9' × 100' from Apalachicola to Columbus, Ga. with 3 locks and dams in Fla. and Ga. (Jim Woodruf, Columbia, and Walter George) each 82' × 450'. Flint River—existing channel 9' × 100' from Jim Woodruff Dam to Bainbridge, Ga.

The Keys
Source: U.S. Geological Survey

The limestone floor of the Everglades continues southward beneath the shallow waters of Florida Bay and emerges again in the Florida Keys. These islands are of two types. The eastern keys, which terminate at Loggerhead Key, are long, narrow islands composed of limestone (Key Largo limestone) containing large heads of corals in place, just as they grew. They evidently were formed as a coral reef that grew at the edge of deep water in the Pamlico sea, to whose surface they did not quite reach. The western keys, which lie behind the eastern keys and extend beyond them to Key West, were merely a shoal in the Pamlico sea. They are similar in origin to the rim of the Everglades and are composed of the same kind of oolitic limestone. This shoal extended, with a few breaks, westward to the Dry Tortugas. Its continuation beyond Key West is marked by the Marquesas Keys, and a few smaller islands.

Number of Keys
Source: Florida Geological Survey

There are 882 islands, or "keys," in the Florida Keys which are large enough to be shown in hydrographic maps of the U.S. Coast and Geodetic Survey.

Here are the map descriptions, the areas covered, and the number of islands:

Map #1248—Virginia Key and Biscayne Key, 11. Map #1249—Fowey Rock to Alligator Reef, 164. Map #1250—Alligator Reef to Sombrero Key, 242. Map #1251—Sombrero Key to Rebecca Shoal, 43.

Lagoons
Source: U.S. Geological Survey

The entire East Coast of Florida is bordered by a once-continuous series of lagoons, which is followed by the Intracoastal Waterway. North of Jacksonville the lagoons have the form of broad salt marshes, through which wander crooked tidal rivers. This northern part of the coast is a continuation of the Sea Island region, which extends northward to Charleston, S.C. South of Jacksonville the lagoons run parallel to the coast, and many of them are broad and open.

Indian River is the longest and one of the straightest lagoons in Florida. It extends from a point about 13 miles north of Titusville to St. Lucie Inlet near Stuart, a length of nearly 120 miles. It is widest (about 5½ miles) near the northern end, where a short passage connects it with Mosquito Lagoon, and a longer, crooked channel passes around the northern end of Merritt Island to Banana River. Its average width is about 2 miles. It is narrower and much obstructed by marshy islands between Sebastian and Vero Beach. Indian River is deepest between Cocoa and Melbourne, where a depth of 10 feet is common, and depths of 15 feet are rarely attained. Tidal currents have scoured the narrow channel connecting it with the south end of Banana River to a maximum depth of 27 feet.

Facts about Streams
Source: Department of Natural Resources

Sunday Rollaway, Botheration, Fiddlestring Bay and Fodderstack Slough. Whiskey George, Brandy Branch and Rudy Slough. Chassahowitzka, Alapaha, Alaqua, Attapulgas and Loxahatchee.

These imagination-ticklers are the names of a few of the 1,711 streams, rivers and creeks in Florida. The Department of Natural Resources has catalogued all of the particulars in a publication called the "Gazetteer of Florida Streams."

Other noteworthy facts:

Total length of all streams is about 10,550 miles.

Some 277 streams are named after people, 200 after animals, 49 after trees, 44 after colors, seven after towns and three after states—including the improbable California Creek. Okaloosa's Brandy Branch shares its spirituous name with Gin Branch in Liberty County.

The Indian names in many cases have unusual derivations. Chassahowitzka means "hanging pumpkin." And California first may have been Califonee, which has been translated as "home camp."

The names are suggestive of historical events, too. Starvation Branch in Liberty County is thought to refer to a famine in this area at one time. Burnt Grocery Creek in Santa Rosa County suggests an outpost was destroyed by fire in the War Between the States.

Long Branch and Mill Creek tie as the most popular name with 15 each. The second most popular name is Alligator Creek with 13, followed by third-place Sweetwater Creek with 12. Next is Juniper Creek and Turkey Creek with 11 each.

Ten creeks are named Boggy Branch while Bear Creek and Camp Branch show nine.

The longest is the St. Johns River with a length variously calculated from 273 miles (U.S. Geological Survey) to 318 (State Board of Conservation), that river's headwaters being so illy defined because of the swampy nature. Rudy Slough in Northwest Florida is the shortest at four-tenths of a mile.

NOTE: A listing of rivers appears in the 1983–1984 and prior editions of *The Florida Handbook*.

The Cross-Florida Barge Canal
Source: U.S. Army Corps of Engineers

Construction of the Cross-Florida Barge Canal, a 185-mile-long waterway across the upper neck of the Florida peninsula, was started February 27, 1964, when President Lyndon B. Johnson detonated an explosive charge near Palatka to ceremonially begin construction.

But on January 19, 1971, President Richard M. Nixon detonated what was to canal advocates another explosive charge by suspending work on the waterway on which some $50 million had been invested. The President said it was time to "prevent a past mistake from causing permanent damage" to the uniquely beautiful Oklawaha valley.

Mr. Nixon said he had made his decision on the recommendation of his Council on Environmental Quality. He said the Council told him that "the project could endanger the unique wildlife of the area and destroy this region of unusual and unique natural beauty".

Congress deauthorized in 1986, providing repayment of $32,004,000 to the State and six counties for money advanced.

As early as 1928 Congress directed an inquiry into the usefulness of a North Florida waterway to reduce by some 600 miles the voyage of ships rounding the peninsula. Among the first reasons for the waterway were these: To provide an escape route from Caribbean pirates, to protect coastal shipping in time of war, to speed the mail between Washington and New Orleans, and to stimulate the development of Florida's interior.

When construction was halted, the estimated cost of the waterway was $169,000,000 to the Federal government and $16,000,000 to Florida, a total of $185,000,000. The 12-foot-deep and 150-foot wide barge canal, stretching 107 miles from Palatka on the St. Johns River to Yankeetown on the Gulf of Mexico, was to be a high-level ribbon of water with five navigation locks intended to assure the safety of the natural groundwater level. Completion had been scheduled for 1977.

Army Engineers had completed three of the locks, three highway bridges, and 25 miles of canal excavation. Rodman Reservoir, covering about 13,000 acres, was filled in 1968 and attracts thousands of boaters, fishermen, and campers.

Canals

	Length in miles
Caloosahatchee River (Lake Okeechobee to Gulf)	69
Hillsboro Canal	52
Miami Canal	81
North New River Canal	65
St. Lucie Canal (Lake Okeechobee to Atlantic Ocean)	40
West Palm Beach Canal	42

Section 9 of the Cross Florida Barge Canal   Florida State Archives

Florida's Islands

Florida has 4,510 islands 10 acres or larger in size, the second highest total in the U.S. (behind Alaska). She is third (behind Alaska and Louisiana) in total island acreage, with 840,727 acres.

By size class they number:

10–99 A.	100–499 A.	500–999 A.	1,000 A. and over
2,444	837	1,112	117

By ownership they fall this way:

Total acreage	Federal	State	Other public	Private
793,042	251,078	54,550	842	486,572

Ownership data is fragmentary; total acreage figure here is less than actual total acreage.

Source: Islands of America, a special report published by the U.S. Department of the Interior, Bureau of Outdoor Recreation, August 1970

Value and Proportion of Land by Use, 1991

Type	Value (million dollars)	Percentage of total value
Residential	288,766.29	68.7
Commerical	86,905.63	20.7
Industrial	21,007.84	5.0
Agricultural	9,491.79	2.3
Institutional	3,732.50	0.9
Miscellaneous	10,741.87	2.6

Florida Statistical Abstract 1994

Land in Farms by Use, 1992

Total Cropland	3,841,505
Harvested Cropland	2,400,704
Woodland	1,922,035
Pastureland	4,456,686
Irrigated land	1,782,680
Other	545,851
Total land in farms	10,766,077
Total acres	10,766,077

Foreign Ownership of Land

Foreign ownership of land in Florida on December 31, 1993, totaled 620,935 acres. Of this 214,132 acres was regarded as crop land, 159,794 pasture land, 123,121 forest, 88,468 other agriculture, and 35,320 other non-agriculture.

Germany headed the countries of foreign ownership, with 50,539 acres. Canada was next with 45,546; then France 40,950, next United Kingdom 36,006 and Switzerland 14,811. All others totaled 432,983.

Value was calculated at $1,150,294,000. The largest holding was in Palm Beach County with 139,755 acres.

Source: Univesity of Florida, Institute of Food and Agricultural Sciences. Dr. Robert L. Degner.

Florida Regional Names

The Suncoast, Gold Coast, Big Bend, Florida's First Coast—these are some of the regional place names used around the state.

In 1952, Mayor Samuel G. Johnson of St. Petersburg organized the Suncoast League of Municipalities and invited cities in counties from Citrus to Collier to become members. Two years later, as the area was preparing to celebrate the opening of the Sunshine Skyway on Labor Day, the *St. Petersburg Times* started referring to the 10-county area from Citrus south to Collier as the Suncoast. This was primarily done to popularize a colorful name to compete with the Gold Coast designation of the Palm Beach-Miami area.

Malcolm B. Johnson, then Editor of the *Tallahassee Democrat,* coined Big Bend to designate its dominant circulation area between the Aucilla-Wacissa and the Chipola-Apalachicola river systems. Johnson afterwards said it was a spur-of-the-moment designation "before sober reflection could produce something like 'Gulf Bend' or 'Apalachee Bend,' which I would much prefer."

Florida Crown, embracing 15 counties fanning out from Jacksonville, was selected in 1964 in a contest sponsored by the Northeast Florida Council of Chambers of Commerce. The name was separately proposed by two Jacksonville men, Kenneth H. Smith and William A. Heard. The judges said Florida Crown made clear the location of the area in relation to the rest of the state; that it suggested solidity, influence, and historical background. By 1984, however, Florida Crown had given way to Florida's First Coast, embracing Baker, Clay, Duval, Nassau and St. Johns counties.

A roving newsman, Claude Jenkins, first used the name, "Miracle Strip," in the Defuniak Springs weekly, *The Breeze,* after having been struck by the beauty of the coast after topping a hill in Walton county where U.S. 98 runs along the Gulf of Mexico. The Miracle Strip is regarded as being the area of coast between Panama City Beach and Fort Walton Beach. It also has been called the "Emerald Coast," but the very informal tag of "Redneck Riviera" has persisted among those who delight in its atmosphere.

The Cocoa newspaper *Today* refers to Brevard and Indian River Counties as the "Space Coast." Eric Lassiter of *Today* reports Indian River County also is sometimes referred to as part of the "Treasure Coast," which includes Martin, St. Lucie, and Palm Beach counties.

In addition to these regional names, there are such local designations as Imperial Polk (county), The Magic City (Miami), America's Riviera (Coral Gables), City Beautiful (Orlando), Cigar City (Tampa), City of Azaleas (Palatka), and City of Five Flags (Pensacola).

Panama City Beach's amusement area, part of the Panhandle's Miracle Strip in 1970.
Department of Commerce, Division of Tourism

A Sense of Rootlessness
Tom Fiedler

It is a place of immigrants, of people who believe in freedom, in self-reliance, in opportunity. It is built on change, yet thinks of itself as conservative. It is a place of many cultures and dialects, a place of big cities, pleasant suburbs, rich farms and vast open spaces.

If this sounds like the United States, it is. But these traits also describe Florida, demonstrating the truth of an old joke that Florida is just like the rest of the country—only more so.

In many ways, Florida indeed is a national microcosm, mimicking national statistics on racial composition, on its percentage of city dwellers, suburbanites and farmers. Only in median age (37.2 years) is Florida unusual, four years older than the national median.

It is also a mirror of elsewhere. In Florida can be found pockets of Brooklyn, Grosse Pointe and Hattisburg, Cape Cod, San Juan and Havana. And just as with California, Florida is an incubator of national trends, the good and the bad.

Douglas Bailey, publisher of the Political Hotline and a keen political analyst, calls Florida "a cutting-edge state. If it is happening in Florida now, it will be happening elsewhere soon."

As a composite, Floridians—like Americans in general—consider themselves moderate to conservative. They distrust government, hate taxes and generally disdain politicians, traits that would seem to pull them toward Republicans. Yet they can be surprisingly liberal on issues such as religious tolerance, abortion rights and in protecting the environment, which might tilt them toward Democrats.

All live in a state fractured by geography, by cultural barriers, by economics and by lingering loyalty to former homestates. They are so fractured, in fact, that Floridians lack a sense of shared destiny—the feeling that "we're all in this together"—common to older states. This, some say, leaves them much more selfish in their approach to politics and voting.

Republican political consultant John M. "Mac" Stipanovich puts it: "Remember that old saying that whatever's good for General Motors is good for America? Here the feeling is, What's good for me is good for Florida."

Tom Fiedler

Even the appearance of political cohesion can be misleading.

Tom Fiedler is the *Miami Herald's* political editor and columnist.

Since 1980, the Republican Party has made staggering gains in registering new members, pulling to within 14 points of the historically dominant Democrats, who make up 54 percent of the vote. But when they enter the voting booth, especially for local or state elections, Floridians—particularly white Democrats—pay little heed to party labels.

"Partisan politics, as they are understood in Massachusetts, New York or Illinois, are not important here," says University of Florida political scientist Richard Scher. "In those states you can tell from the outset of an election that these voters are with me and those voters are with me and those voters are with my opponent just from the way they register. But not here."

Thus, trends that appear to favor one party over the other can be evanescent and talk of Florida as an emerging Republican state could be premature. Indeed, the GOP tide today appears to have slacked, said Florida State University Professor Suzanne Parker, director of the Florida Annual Policy Survey.

More important, Parker's surveys show voters are becoming less conservative—not more—in their attitudes toward issues generally considered to be linked to Democrats, such as the environment, aid to the poor and concern for civil rights. The result: parity between the parties and up-for-grabs elections.

The results of the 1990 gubernatorial race, in which Democrat Lawton Chiles ousted incumbent Republican Bob Martinez, and the 1992 presidential race, in which Democrat Bill Clinton barely lost to Republican incumbent George Bush, underscore Florida's nature as a non-aligned state.

Why all this confusion over where Floridians stand?

There is no single answer, but one comes close: Change, constant and unremitting.

"Politically, we're like a gangly teen-ager who can be very awkward, very clumsy, very immature," says Scher, who has written extensively on state politics. "Of course, we can be very charming at times, but we are also apt to throw a temper tantrum with little provocation."

Much, if not most, of this clumsiness can be attributed to Florida's rapid growth (about 900 people move in daily) and the ramifications it holds for the people involved. When American Demographics magazine listed the nation's 50 "hottest counties"—a measure of both population and income growth—eight were in Florida. It is now the nation's fourth largest state and could be third within two decades.

That is staggering when you consider that in 1940 it was 27th. Since 1980 alone, Florida has passed Ohio and Illinois. It now trails just California, New York and Texas.

As a result, nearly three of every four Floridians were born somewhere else, imparting a sense of rootlessness and restlessness to Florida politics.

"When I think of Florida voters, I think of all the geographic and demographic fragmentation," says pollster Robert Joffee, vice president of Mason-Dixon Political Media Research.

Florida's diversity is duplicated in few other states. Pensacola in the western Panhandle is closer to Chicago than it is to Miami; Miami is closer to Cuba than it is to Orlando—in more ways than one.

To understand Florida politics, the adage once held that the farther north you go from Miami, the farther South you get.

That remains generally true, although it doesn't begin to convey the cleavages within each region. Some argue there are as many as five Floridas, each region having its own political history and culture.

Despite swelling pockets of growth around Panhandle military installations, the counties that lie between Pensacola and Jacksonville—with the exception of Leon, home of the capital city of Tallahassee—draw their political traditions from Dixie, replete with culture of the Bible Belt and the Black Belt. Change and growth come slowly there, where one in five voters lives. Split-ticket voting has long been a Panhandle custom as voters backed conservative Democrats for local offices and Republicans for state and federal ones.

Some of that is changing. In such counties as Okaloosa and Clay, the Republican Party has become the majority (thanks largely to the military) and is in control of virtually every office. The common thread, however, remains voting for the conservative.

At the other end of the Florida funnel lies the Miami-Fort Lauderdale-Palm Beach megalopolis, with its babel of cultures, its urban imperatives and Yankee (read New Yorkish) ways. Surveys of newcomers show that more than one in five comes from New York and New Jersey, and many of them gravitate to the Gold Coast where the hustle and bustle is not unlike back home, just warmer. Their politics tends strongly Democratic, and liberal at that.

Broward, especially, has become the center of gravity of Florida's Democratic Party. It gave President Clinton his biggest surplus of votes of any county in the Southeastern United States. Palm Beach too, despite its toney image, has voted Democratic for several years. Dade, meanwhile, remains a Democrat-leaning swing county, with its conservative-Republican Cuban community almost equally balanced by its liberal-Democrat condominium and Miami Beach vote.

On the lower Gulf Coast, Midwestern Republicanism took root long ago among the Rotary meetings, walled suburban developments and manicured golf courses. Even local governments are dominated by the GOP. Politics seems cleanly transplanted from the outskirts of Cleveland and Minneapolis, with its penchant for non-partisanship and professional managers.

In recent years, growth has planted a similar political face on several Atlantic Coast counties. St. Johns, just below Jacksonville, is rapidly trending Republican and, with the completion of some massive golf-course communities, almost surely will become so soon. And in East-Central Florida, Brevard, Indian River, St. Lucie and Martin Counties are now regarded as making up the right half of the Republican horseshoe of coastal counties arcing from Naples to Stuart.

But even here there are bubbles of change. These good-government voters leaned toward Chiles in his gubernatorial bid. And, while these counties favored Bush in 1992, they gave him far fewer votes than there were registered Republicans, apparently finding much to dislike in his positions on abortion rights and the environment.

Still in flux politically is the even faster-growing midsection, dubbed the I-4 corridor after the stretch of interstate that links Tampa-St. Petersburg to Orlando and Daytona Beach. This is ground zero for the Disney boom, a region where oldtimers are those who arrived B.D. (Before Disney) and where political history is what happened last month. Orlando and its bedroom communities have leaned Republican, but not by much.

Meanwhile, Tampa and St. Petersburg have leaned Democratic by similarly precarious margins. As a result, most political consultants believe that statewide campaigns are won and lost in this corridor, where voters seem more malleable—that is, less rooted—than in other regions.

Some might identify a fifth region, once called "forgotten Florida," which encompasses those counties in the Central Florida interior lying mostly west or north of Lake Okeechobee. These counties have, by and large, been bypassed by the state's rapid growth, which hews closely to both coasts. And what growth there has been tends to be middle-class at best, people apt to live in a mobile home while resisting attempts to collect growth-related taxes. Farming, ranching and mining remain the economic bases there. And conservative Democrats remain in charge at the courthouse.

These divisions are reinforced in other ways.

Unlike many northern states where one or two cities dominate life throughout the state—for example, a Des Moines, St. Louis, Chicago or Philadelphia—Florida is splintered into several urban areas, each looking inward on itself. A South Florida voter likely reads only a South Florida newspaper and watches only Miami-Fort Lauderdale television. The situation is comparable in Orlando, Tampa, Jacksonville and Pensacola.

"Florida has 11 definable media markets," says Joffee, "and every smart politician organizes a campaign that treats each of them separately."

All this regional diversity creates a situation in which candidates for statewide office must wage several different campaigns at once in an effort to stitch together a majority coalition. A message aimed at one region may not register elsewhere.

As David Hill, a nationally active Republican pollster who has worked for the state party once put it: "What does somebody in the Panhandle care about what happens in Miami? And people in Miami hardly care about what happens north of the county line."

For all of this diversity, however, there is that single, common bond: Most Floridians came from somewhere else. That factor alone imparts a view of life that is roughly shared by all such Floridians—and which separates them from many other Americans.

It is this: non-native Floridians are usually risk-takers. They have shown a willingness to leave behind the familiarity of a hometown for the unfamiliarity of a new town, whether that is in Port Charlotte or Pompano Beach or Palatka.

"A question I ask myself is, if I had lived in the 1800s, would I join a wagon train going west?" asks Hill, the GOP pollster. "The people who were willing to pull up stakes and risk what they did were clearly different people.

"The same applies today. The person who leaves Ohio to come to Florida is obviously very different from the one who chooses to stay," he said.

In many ways, that willingness to take a risk has built Florida. People come seeking fortunes, freedoms or the good life and they appreciate those traits in others. That accounts for former President Reagan's popularity in the state as well as the GOP's rise, many believe. It also accounts for George Bush's near-defeat in 1992 as the good life people came to find appeared to be eluding them. They were dreamers who found themselves in an economic nightmare.

Social scientists contend that Floridians have much more in common with residents of the western frontier states than nearby southern states because Florida, like the west, is being built by new "settlers." This shouldn't be a surprise. Until this century, Florida was very much a frontier state in every sense of that word, complete with bloody Indian wars and a forbidding environment that only the heartiest pioneers could tolerate.

There are no more wagon trains, to be sure. But packing up and moving to a new state still reveals something different about a newcomer's character and his or her beliefs. Among those beliefs, say such obsevers as Stipanovich, are "entrepreneurship, self-reliance, individualism, and even cantankerousness." Floridians don't want their government to be overly active; people can take care of themselves, they believe.

But these "frontier" values also have a dark side. To believe in self-reliance can also mean to care little for the needs of others. When those traits combine with the newly arrived Floridian's inability (or unwillingness) to identify with the concerns of the larger community, the result can be "a certain amount of selfishness," Stipanovich admits.

Fact: Florida ranks 47th nationally on social welfare spending. It is second from last on per capita spending for higher education; in the bottom third in per capita spending for elementary schools. Those who argue that improving schools benefits the entire community rarely sway voters without school-aged children. And anyone who contends that homelessness hurts everyone in a community is wasting breath to ask for new tax dollars.

"For most Floridians, there is no reason to sublimate their personal interests to the interests of the whole, because they have no sense of what the whole is," says Stipanovich.

Age differences, which are wider in Florida than anywhere else, also contribute to this politics of selfishness, analysts say. Voters over age 65 make up 18 percent of the state's electorate, although they are just 11 percent of the nation's. They are also twice as likely to vote as Floridians below age 30.

If a politician threatens them with higher taxes to pay for programs they won't use—or even for roads they may not drive—the elderly may rise as one in angry revolt.

"They provide a brake on public policy," Scher said. "There are a lot of things we can't do here in Florida because of them."

In fact, the elderly are generally suspicious of candidates who promise any change that could affect their lives. Change brings instability and uncertainty, and that isn't what they came to Florida for.

"They've already been uprooted once, so it is very important that there be stability in their new life," says Hill. "That leads to a drawbridge mentality, that once they've come here, they don't want anybody else to come along and spoil it."

Florida politicians routinely prey on voters' resentment of government growth (especially to provide social-assistance programs) and taxes, particularly the constitutionally-barred income tax. And they often find it surprisingly easy to manipulate Florida voters through the mass media. The reason: most Florida voters lack that set of political anchors that might make it more difficult to swing them.

In the nation's older communities, voters take their cues from such diverse and trusted sources as the church, labor unions, family members, lifelong friendships, a shared culture and value system.

But most Floridians severed such ties when they left home. And they found little here to compensate.

"If you just arrived from Paducah and settled in West Broward, you wouldn't have a clue about what's going on," says Scher of the University of Florida. And there isn't much available to help you."

Even political parties are of little help in providing solid guidance because they themselves are diverse. A Republican who moves from Pennsylvania is no more likely to fit easily with a Republican who came from Havana than an ex-Alabama Democrat will relate to an ex-Manhattan one.

The result: Many Floridians must take their political cues from the mass media, primarily their newspapers and television. In campaigns, they are unusually receptive to televised, negative commercials because they often have no countervailing information.

A 1990 poll taken during the Democratic gubernatorial race between Chiles, who avioded television in the primary, and challenger Bill Nelson, who used it heavily, demonstrated the medium's power on newcomers.

Among those Democrats who came to Florida after 1980, Nelson led Chiles by 62–26 percent. But among those who had lived in the state for more than 10 years—and who, presumably relied on information other than campaign commercials for their views—favored Chiles by 59–34 percent.

A blemished portrait of the state's electorate? Certainly.

But, like that gangly teen-ager, few doubt the state will survive its growing pains.

"People tend to forget that from a political standpoint, Florida is still a baby, " says Scher. "Its political institutions need time to mature."

Brushstrokes in a political portrait of Floridians: Four out of five are newcomers whose "hometowns" are someplace else. In outlook, they are the American everyman, but older.

Floridians are political conservative. There are nearly twice as many registered Democrats as Republicans—although nearly half the Democrats say they identify with the GOP.

They worry about jobs and taxes, crime and crowds, water and beaches. The elderly worry about being taxed for the young; the young often resent the political clout of the elderly.

Mostly however, Floridians are politically rootless. They cut the bonds that provided stability and predictability in the communities many left up north and drift without loyalty from candidate to candidate.

A Sense of Rootlessness / 571

Gubernatorial campaign posters from the 1940's, 1950's and 1960's.   Florida State Archives

People

Source: U.S. Bureau of the Census
Florida Consensus Estimating Conference 1994

Florida passed Pennsylvania to become the fourth most populous State in 1987, ranking behind California, New York and Texas. Florida passed Ohio in 1984 and Illinois in 1986.

California gained more then 3 million persons, Florida gained more than 2½ million persons, and Texas over 1.5 million persons through net migration between 1985 and 1990.

During the 1980's the number of people in the state rose by 3.2 million, second only to California. This represents nearly a 33% increase in population over that decade. (In 1950 Florida ranked twentieth in size.) Florida has been in the top four States in percentage increase in population every decade beginning with the 1920's.

The Nation's median age continues to climb upward, increasing from 30.0 years in 1980 to 33.7 years in 1992. The median age for States in 1992 ranged from Utah's 26.3 years to Florida's 37.2 years.

The preponderance of growth continues to be in the South and West. Seven of the 10 most rapidly growing States are in these two regions which have gained just over 15 million of the Nation's 28.5 million increase since 1980. Nevada, Arizona, and Florida have been the top three states in number of persons added since 1980, accounting for 43.3 percent of the Nation's growth.

Childbearing by Florida's Baby Boom generation helped swell the ranks of the under 5 age group to 19.2 million in 1991, its highest level since July 1967. Between 1987 and 1991 the age group under 5 grew by nearly 2.8 million.

A major concern will be the slow growth among those in the prime labor force age group (ages 25–54). While this group increased by 1.8 million persons during the 1980's to reach a level of over 5 million in 1990, projected growth for the 1990's is 20 percent and for the following decade the growth rate will decline to 6.8 percent.

From 1980 to 1990, the older population in the United States (65 years and over) expanded by nearly 5.5 million persons. Every State registered increases in the age group. California added the largest number of persons in this age group, followed by Florida (668,353). The elderly constitute 12.5 percent of America's total population; in Florida they constitute 18.2 percent of the population—the largest proportion in any State.

Florida is the State with the highest median age (37.2 years in 1992). The next highest was West Virginia (36.2 years), while Utah's high birth rate has made it the state with the lowest median age (26.3 years).

Where Floridians Live

Florida Environmental Issues 1986 reported "almost 80 percent of Florida's residents now live in the coastal zone and another 80 percent of the state's growth to 1990 will occur there." (A rule-of-thumb on the coastal zone is 10 miles back from the sea.)

Issues continued: "When this is combined with the fact that Florida is experiencing a net gain of 764 people a day (15 more Miamis by the year 2000), the need for extraordinary controls on coastal land use becomes evident.

"The coast varies from sandy beaches backed by protective dunes to low, flat mangrove or saltwater swamps that are flushed regularly by tides. Offshore barrier islands, the Keys, inlets, and great rivers add to the diversity."

On the Move

There has been a dramatic growth in Florida's population during recent years.

Less well known has been outward migration. For example, between 1975 and 1980 nearly seven million people left Florida.

In sum, almost one person leaves Florida for every two who arrive. Unless Florida maintains the qualities of life that draw people here and keep them here, the ratio of out-migrants to in-migrants will change as the population growth slows.

The Internal Revenue Service's migration data for 1990 reports the following rankings:

State	To Florida	From Florida	Net Change
New York	76,820	21,141	55,679
New Jersey	35,213	9,668	25,545
Georgia	28,611	31,879	−3,268
Ohio	25,871	16,534	9,337
California	25,592	19,572	6,020
Pennsylvania	23,240	12,234	11,006
Foreign	26,531	21,312	5,219
Texas	25,995	22,916	3,079
Virginia	22,625	16,446	6,179
Illinois	21,383	11,535	9,848
Massachusetts	20,457	6,987	13,470
Michigan	19,992	11,298	8,694
North Carolina	15,769	19,391	−3,622
Connecticut	15,751	5,196	10,555
Indiana	13,629	8,686	4,943
Maryland	13,482	7,622	5,860
Alabama	12,666	12,985	−319
Tennessee	11,327	11,718	−391
South Carolina	9,606	10,213	−607
Louisiana	9,093	5,248	3,845
Kentucky	7,755	6,728	1,027
Missouri	6,420	4,832	1,588
Wisconsin	6,040	3,743	2,297
Colorado	5,781	4,862	919
New Hampshire	5,435	2,063	3,372
Mississippi	5,242	3,864	1,378

Hispanics in Florida

The 1990 Federal census reported 1,574,143 persons of Hispanic origin residing in Florida. That included 674,052 Cubans, 247,010 Puerto Ricans, and 161,499 Mexicans.

Hialeah, with 70.4 percent, had the highest percentage of foreign-born in Florida cities, according to the 1990 Federal census.

Hialeah was trailed by Miami, with 59.7 percent. Dade County, with 45.1 percent, was highest of the country's counties with more than 50,000 foreign-born residents. The listing of cities included those with more than 25,000 foreign-born residents.

Miami Beach was sixth among the cities with 51.3 percent and Kendall was 23 percent.

The census report included an "other Hispanic" category of 491,582.

In the Florida Supreme Court consideration of legislative apportionment litigation, Justice Parker Lee McDonald inquired:

"How long does it take a Cuban to be an American. That he's no longer considered a Hispanic?"

A few responses reported by *The Miami Herald*:

"Never," said Jorge Sosa, a Cuban-American lawyer in Miami Beach.

"He never loses where he comes from," said Clara Ins Gutierrez, president of the Colombian Volunteer Ladies of Tampa Bay.

"Even if he's here several generations, he's still Hispanic," said Tirso Moreno, a Mexican-American farm worker advocate in Apopka.

The Census Bureau felt it necessary to issue an explanation of how it defined Spanish-American:

Spanish/Hispanic origin—The data on Spanish/Hispanic origin were derived from answers to census questionnaire item 7, which was asked of all persons. Persons of Spanish/Hispanic origin or descent are those who classify themselves in one of the specific Hispanic origin categories listed in the question for example, Mexican, Puerto Rican, or Cuban as well as those who indicated that they were of other Spanish/Hispanic origin. Persons reporting "Other Spanish/Hispanic" are those whose origins are from other Spanish-speaking countries of the Caribbean, Central or South America, or from Spain, or persons identifying themselves generally as Spanish, Spanish-American, Hispano, Hispanic, Latino, etc.

Sex and Race Composition of the Population
Florida: 1950—1990
(Percent of all Persons)

				White			Non-White		
Year	Male	Female	Number	Native Born	Foreign Born	All White	Black	Other	All Non-White
1950	49.1	50.9	2,762,865	73.7	4.4	78.1	21.8	0.1	21.9
1960	49.2	50.8	4,952,788	76.9	5.2	82.0	17.8	0.2	18.0
1970	48.2	51.8	6,789,383	76.7	7.7	84.3	15.3	0.3	15.6
1980	47.9	52.0	9,746,324	N/A	N/A	84.0	13.8	2.2	16.0
1990	48.2	51.8	10,971,995	87.1	12.9	84.8	13.7	1.5	15.2

Sources: U.S. Department of Commerce, Bureau of the Census, *Census of Population, Detailed Characteristics, Florida.*

States Ranked by Median Age: 1992

Rank	State	Median Age	Rank	State	Median Age
1	Florida	37.2	26	Kansas	33.8
2	West Virginia	36.2	27	Nebraska	33.8
3	Pennsylvania	36.0	28	Oklahoma	33.8
4	Connecticut	35.6	29	Washington	33.8
5	New Jersey	35.4	30	Hawaii	33.7
6	Maine	35.1	31	Illinois	33.7
7	Oregon	35.1	32	Nevada	33.7
8	Rhode Island	34.9	33	Virginia	33.7
9	Iowa	34.8	34	Michigan	33.6
10	Montana	34.7	35	North Dakota	33.6
11	Arkansas	34.6	36	Colorado	33.5
12	Massachusetts	34.6	37	Minnesota	33.5
13	New York	34.5	38	South Dakota	33.2
14	Missouri	34.4	39	Arizona	33.1
15	Ohio	34.4	40	South Carolina	33.0
16	Tennessee	34.4	41	Georgia	32.5
17	Vermont	34.2	42	Wyoming	32.5
18	Maryland	34.1	43	Idaho	32.2
19	New Hampshire	34.1	44	New Mexico	32.2
20	North Carolina	34.0	45	California	32.0
21	Alabama	33.9	46	Mississippi	31.9
22	Indiana	33.9	47	Louisiana	31.8
23	Kentucky	33.9	48	Texas	31.5
24	Wisconsin	33.9	49	Alaska	30.5
25	Delaware	33.8	50	Utah	26.3
				Nat'l Avg	33.7

Source: State Policy Reference Book

States Ranked by Largest Number and Increase in Households: 1980 to 1990
(Numbers in thousands)

Rank	State	Number of households, 1990	State	Numerical increase in households, 1980–90	State	Percent increase in households, 1980–90
1	California	10,381	California	1,751	Nevada	53.2
2	New York	6,639	Florida	1,391	Alaska	43.7
3	Texas	6,071	Texas	1,142	Arizona	43.0
4	Florida	5,135	Georgia	495	Florida	37.1
5	Pennsylvania	4,496	North Carolina	474	New Hampshire	27.1
6	Illinois	4,202	Virginia	429	Georgia	26.4
7	Ohio	4,088	Arizona	412	Texas	23.2
8	Michigan	3,419	New York	299	Virginia	23.0
9	New Jersey	2,795	Pennsylvania	276	New Mexico	22.9
10	North Carolina	2,517	New Jersey	247	So. Carolina	22.1

Source: U.S. Bureau of the Census.

576 / People

A household consists of all the persons who occupy a housing unit. A house, an apartment or other group of rooms, or a single room, is regarded as a housing unit when it is occupied or intended for occupancy as separate living quarters; that is, when the occupants do not live and eat with any other persons in the structure and there is direct access from the outside or through a common hall.

Florida has more people than Norway, Sweden, Switzerland or Austria. Florida has about the same population as Cuba, Greece and Belgium.

The *World Almanac* provides these comparative projections for 1990–2025:

Norway, 4,200,000; Sweden, 8,200,000; Switzerland, 6,200,000; Austria, 7,500,000; Cuba, 10,000,000; Greece, 10,200,000, and Belgium, 9,900,000.

Florida's phenomenal population growth is evidenced by the rapid climb up the ranking of the states. Florida was twentieth in 1950; tenth in 1960, and ninth in 1970. The rank was fourth in 1990.

The estimates of resident population for the top 10 states on July 1, 1993 were:

California	31,211,000	Illinois	11,697,000
New York	18,197,000	Ohio	11,091,000
Texas	18,031,000	Michigan	9,478,000
Florida	13,679,000	New Jersey	7,879,000
Pennsylvania	12,048,000	North Carolina	6,945,000

The Florida Consensus Estimating Conference of Spring 1994 estimated that in 2010 Florida's population would be well over 18 million people.

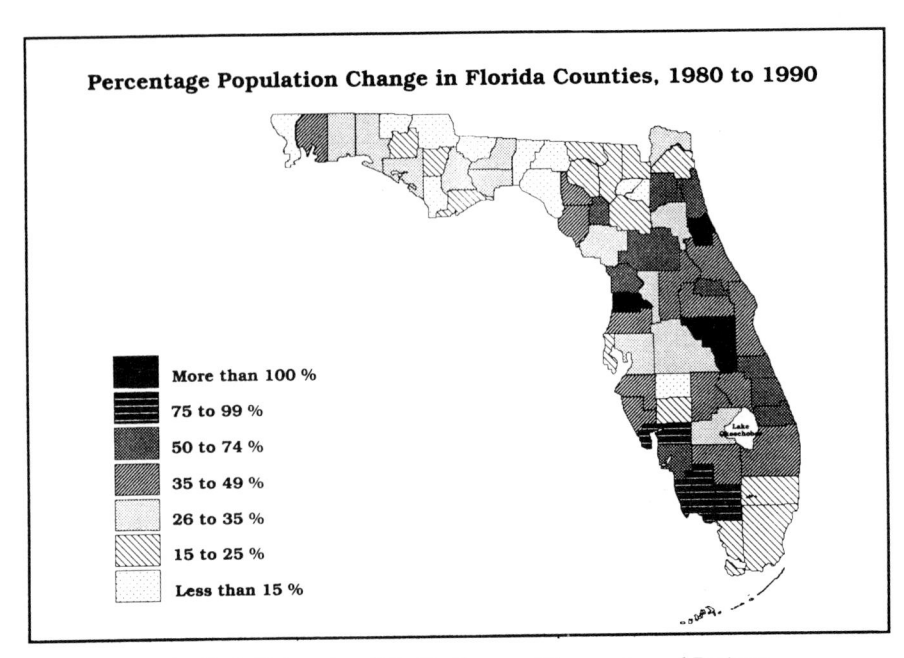

Percentage Population Change in Florida Counties, 1980 to 1990

- More than 100 %
- 75 to 99 %
- 50 to 74 %
- 35 to 49 %
- 26 to 35 %
- 15 to 25 %
- Less than 15 %

Source: *Census Handbook* University of Florida Bureau of Economics and Business

STATE POPULATION BY AGE GROUP, RACE, AND SEX
APRIL 1 ESTIMATES
Thousands of Persons

AGE GROUP	1995 TOTAL	NON-WHITE	WHITE	MALE TOTAL	MALE NON-WHITE	MALE WHITE	FEMALE TOTAL	FEMALE NON-WHITE	FEMALE WHITE
0-4	974.9	256.5	718.4	496.8	130.7	366.1	478.1	125.8	352.3
5-9	912.4	208.1	704.3	466.4	105.9	360.4	446.0	102.1	343.9
10-14	861.7	198.0	663.7	441.4	100.5	340.9	420.4	97.6	322.8
15-19	795.9	176.8	619.0	405.9	88.3	317.6	389.9	88.5	301.4
15-17	451.1	103.6	347.5	230.3	52.3	178.0	220.8	51.3	169.5
18-19	344.8	73.2	271.5	175.6	36.0	139.7	169.1	37.3	131.9
20-24	845.3	176.2	669.1	435.5	87.3	348.1	409.8	88.9	321.0
25-29	904.5	167.6	736.9	458.5	81.5	377.0	445.9	86.0	359.9
30-34	1,088.4	189.1	899.3	547.0	90.9	456.0	541.4	98.2	443.2
35-39	1,111.3	183.3	928.0	549.2	85.3	463.9	562.1	98.0	464.1
40-44	1,012.3	159.3	853.0	479.9	73.8	424.1	514.4	85.5	428.9
45-49	911.8	124.0	787.8	444.3	57.6	386.7	467.6	66.4	401.1
50-54	738.6	91.2	647.4	352.1	41.6	310.5	386.5	49.5	336.9
55-59	645.5	75.0	570.5	299.5	34.0	265.5	346.1	41.1	305.0
60-64	661.2	60.4	600.9	302.8	26.5	276.3	358.4	33.9	324.5
65-69	745.5	51.5	694.0	340.8	21.6	319.2	404.7	29.9	374.8
70-74	713.2	40.9	672.3	318.5	16.4	302.2	394.7	24.5	370.2
75-79	549.1	28.5	520.6	237.5	10.6	227.0	311.6	17.9	293.7
80-84	368.5	18.9	349.6	148.1	6.6	141.5	220.4	12.3	208.1
over 85	269.5	14.4	255.1	92.0	4.5	87.5	177.5	9.9	167.6
ALL AGES	14,109.7	2,219.8	11,889.8	6,834.2	1,063.7	5,770.5	7,275.5	1,156.1	6,119.3

Source: Florida Consensus Estimating Conference v.10, 1994

Florida's Rank by Population 1900–1993

Rank	1900	1910	1920	1930	1940	1950	1960	1970	1980	1993
1	New York	New York	New York	New York	New York	New York	New York	California	California	California
2	Penn.	Penn.	Penn.	Penn.	Penn.	California	California	New York	New York	New York
3	Illinois	Illinois	Illinois	Illinois	Illinois	Penn.	Penn.	Penn.	Texas	Texas
4	Ohio	Ohio	Ohio	Ohio	Ohio	Illinois	Illinois	Texas	Penn.	Florida
5	Missouri	Texas	Texas	Texas	California	Ohio	Ohio	Illinois	Illinois	Pennsylvania
6	Texas	Mass.	Mass.	California	Texas	Texas	Texas	Ohio	Ohio	Illinois
7	Mass.	Missouri	Michigan	Michigan	Michigan	Michigan	Michigan	Michigan	Florida	Ohio
8	Indiana	Michigan	California	Mass.	Mass.	New Jersey	New Jersey	New Jersey	Michigan	Michigan
9	Michigan	Indiana	Missouri	New Jersey	New Jersey	Mass.	Mass.	Florida	New Jersey	New Jersey
10	Iowa	Georgia	New Jersey	Missouri	Missouri	N. Carolina	Florida	Mass.	N. Carolina	N. Carolina
11	Georgia	New Jersey	Indiana	Indiana	N. Carolina	Missouri	Indiana	Indiana	Mass.	Georgia
12	Kentucky	California	Georgia	N. Carolina	Indiana	Indiana	Missouri	N. Carolina	Indiana	Virginia
13	Wisconsin	Wisconsin	Wisconsin	Wisconsin	Wisconsin	Georgia	Virginia	Missouri	Georgia	Massachusetts
14	Tennessee	Kentucky	N. Carolina	Georgia	Georgia	Wisconsin	Wisconsin	Virginia	Virginia	Indiana
15	N. Carolina	Iowa	Kentucky	Alabama	Tennessee	Virginia	Georgia	Georgia	Missouri	Washington
16	New Jersey	N. Carolina	Iowa	Tennessee	Kentucky	Tennessee	Tennessee	Wisconsin	Wisconsin	Missouri
17	Virginia	Tennessee	Minnesota	Kentucky	Alabama	Alabama	Maryland	Tennessee	Tennessee	Tennessee
18	Alabama	Alabama	Alabama	Minnesota	Minnesota	Minnesota	Minnesota	Maryland	Maryland	Wisconsin
19	Minnesota	Minnesota	Tennessee	Tennessee	Virginia	Kentucky	Alabama	Minnesota	Louisiana	Maryland
20	Mississippi	Virginia	Virginia	Virginia	Iowa	Florida	Louisiana	Louisiana	Washington	Minnesota
21	California	Mississippi	Oklahoma	Oklahoma	Louisiana	Louisiana	Maryland	Alabama	Minnesota	Louisiana
22	Kansas	Kansas	Louisiana	Louisiana	Oklahoma	Iowa	Kentucky	Washington	Alabama	Alabama
23	Louisiana	Oklahoma	Mississippi	Mississippi	Mississippi	Washington	Washington	Kentucky	Kentucky	Arizona
24	S. Carolina	Louisiana	Kansas	Kansas	Arkansas	Maryland	Iowa	Connecticut	S. Carolina	Kentucky
25	Arkansas	Arkansas	Arkansas	Arkansas	W. Virginia	Oklahoma	Connecticut	Iowa	Connecticut	S. Carolina
26	Maryland	S. Carolina	S. Carolina	S. Carolina	S. Carolina	Mississippi	S. Carolina	S. Carolina	Oklahoma	Colorado
27	Nebraska	Maryland	W. Virginia	W. Virginia	Florida	S. Carolina	Oklahoma	Oklahoma	Iowa	Connecticut
28	W. Virginia	W. Virginia	Maryland	Maryland	Maryland	Connecticut	Kansas	Kansas	Colorado	Oklahoma
29	Connecticut	Nebraska	Connecticut	Connecticut	Kansas	W. Virginia	Mississippi	Mississippi	Arizona	Oregon
30	Oklahoma	Washington	Washington	Washington	Washington	Arkansas	W. Virginia	Colorado	Oregon	Iowa
31	Maine	Connecticut	Nebraska	Florida	Connecticut	Kansas	Arkansas	Oregon	Mississippi	Mississippi
32	Colorado	Colorado	Florida	Nebraska	Nebraska	Oregon	Oregon	Arkansas	Kansas	Kansas
33	Florida	Florida	Colorado	Colorado	Colorado	Nebraska	Colorado	Arizona	Arkansas	Arkansas

Source: Statistical Abstract of the United States, 78th Annual Edition (1957) and U.S. Bureau of Census

Fastest Growing Metro Areas

Florida had eight of the nation's 10 fastest growing metropolitan areas in 1980–1990, according to the U.S. Department of Commerce's Census Bureau.

Here are the fastest growing metro areas, regardless of size:

Naples	152,099	76.9%
Fort Pierce	251,071	66.1%
Fort Myers-Cape Coral	335,113	63.3%
Las Vegas, NV	741,459	60.1%
Ocala	194,833	59.1%
Orlando	1,072,748	53.3%
West Palm Bch.-Boca Raton-Delray Bch.	863,518	49.7%
Melbourne-Titusville-Palm Bch.	389,978	46.2%
Bakersfield, CA	543,477	45.6%
Daytona	370,712	43.3%

Florida State Archives

580 / People

Distribution of Population

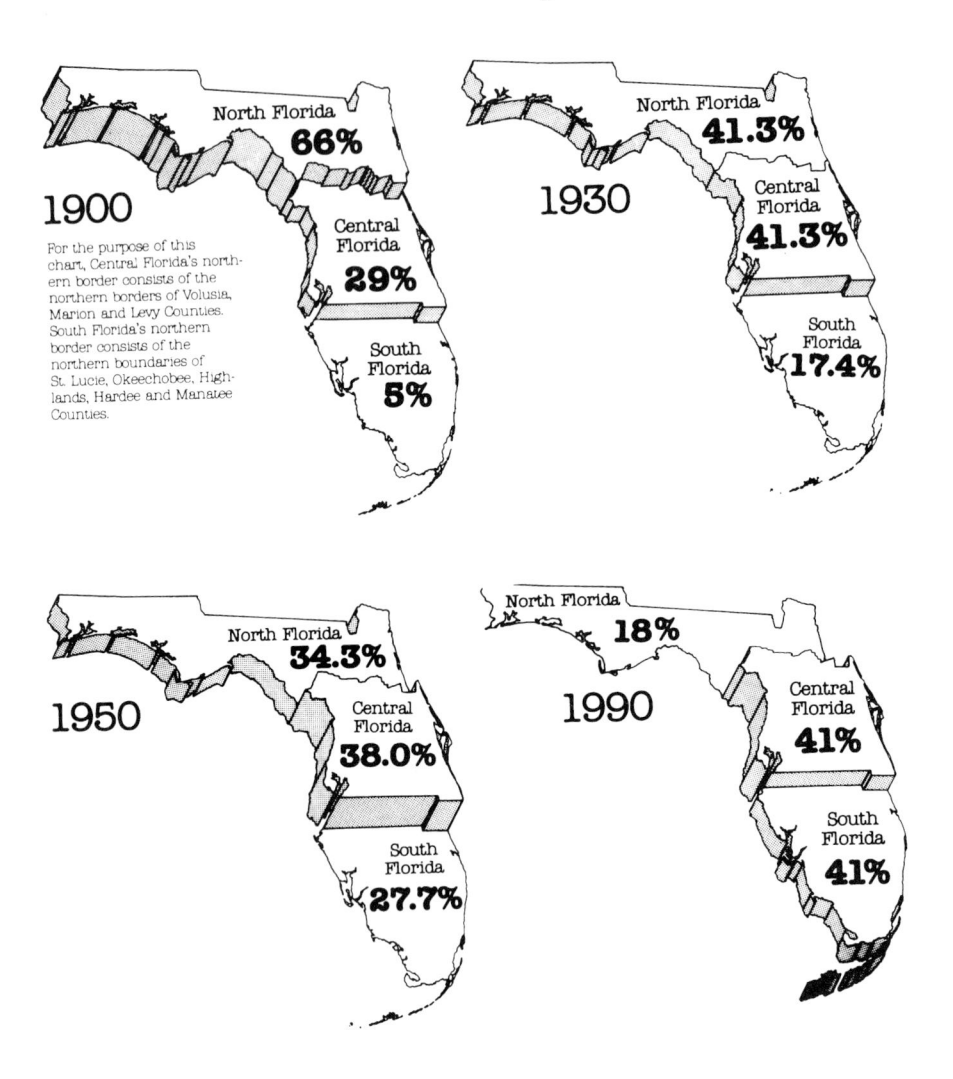

1900

North Florida **66%**
Central Florida **29%**
South Florida **5%**

For the purpose of this chart, Central Florida's northern border consists of the northern borders of Volusia, Marion and Levy Counties. South Florida's northern border consists of the northern boundaries of St. Lucie, Okeechobee, Highlands, Hardee and Manatee Counties.

1930

North Florida **41.3%**
Central Florida **41.3%**
South Florida **17.4%**

1950

North Florida **34.3%**
Central Florida **38.0%**
South Florida **27.7%**

1990

North Florida **18%**
Central Florida **41%**
South Florida **41%**

Source: Governor's Office of Planning and Budgeting

Urban and Rural: Population of the State: Earliest Census to 1990

	The State			Urban					Rural				Percent of total population	
	Total population	Change from preceding census		Places of 2,500 or more	Population	Change from preceding census		Population	Change from preceding census				Urban	Rural
		Number	Percent			Number	Percent		Number	Percent				
Current urban definition:														
1990 (Apr. 1)	12 937 926	3 191 602	32.8	430	10 970 445	2 667 834	48.1	1 967 481	289 047	23.2			84.8	15.2
1980 (Apr. 1)	9 746 324	2 954 906	43.5	285	8 212 385	1 883 168	51.4	1 533 939	-45 285	-3.5			84.3	15.7
1970 (Apr. 1)	6 791 418	1 839 858	37.2	179	5 544 551	1 847 493	101.9	1 244 892	332 762	34.8			81.7	18.3
1960 (Apr. 1)	4 951 560	2 180 255	78.7	98	3 661 383	...	...	1 290 177	...	...			73.9	26.1
1950 (Apr. 1)	2 771 305	873 891	46.1		1 813 890			957 415					65.5	34.5
Previous urban definition:														
1960 (Apr. 1)	4 951 560	2 180 255	78.7	160	3 077 989	1 511 201	96.5	1 873 571	669 054	55.5			62.2	37.8
1950 (Apr. 1)	2 771 305	873 891	46.1	94	1 566 788	520 997	49.8	1 204 517	352 894	41.4			56.5	43.5
1940 (Apr. 1)	1 897 414	429 203	29.2	70	1 045 791	286 013	37.6	851 623	143 190	20.2			55.1	44.9
1930 (Apr. 1)	1 468 211	499 741	51.6	58	759 778	406 263	114.9	708 433	93 478	15.2			51.7	48.3
1920 (Jan. 1)	968 470	215 851	28.7	30	353 515	134 435	61.4	614 955	81 416	15.3			36.5	63.5
1910 (Apr. 15)	752 619	224 077	42.4	23	219 080	112 049	104.7	533 539	112 028	26.6			29.1	70.9
1900 (June 1)	528 542	137 120	35.0	12	107 031	29 673	38.4	421 511	107 447	34.2			20.3	79.7
1890 (June 1)	391 422	121 929	45.2	12	77 358	50 411	187.1	314 064	71 518	29.5			19.8	80.2
1880 (June 1)	269 493	81 745	43.5	4	26 947	11 672	76.4	242 546	70 073	40.6			10.0	90.0
1870 (June 1)	187 748	47 324	33.7	3	15 275	9 567	167.6	172 473	37 757	28.0			8.1	91.9
1860 (June 1)	140 424	52 979	60.6	2	5 708	5 708	...	134 716	47 271	54.1			4.1	95.9
1850 (June 1)	87 445	32 968	60.5	-	-	-	-	87 445	32 968	60.5			-	100.0
1840 (June 1)	54 477	19 747	56.9	-	-	-	-	54 477	19 747	56.9			-	100.0
1830 (June 1)	34 730	...	...	-	-	-	-	34 730	...	...			-	100.0

Source: U.S. Bureau of the Census

Table 1.—Estimates of Population by County and Municipality in Florida: April 1, 1993
(Note: Explanation of terms at end of table)

COUNTY and City	April 1 1993 (Est.)	Total change	April 1 1990 (Census)
ALACHUA	190,655	9,059	181,596
Alachua	5,030	483	4,547
Archer	1,406	34	1,372
Gainesville	93,091	8,016	85,075
Hawthorne	1,387	82	1,305
High Springs	3,398	254	3,144
LaCrosse	117	−5	122
Micanopy	634	8	626
Newberry	1,920	276	1,644
Waldo	1,021	4	1,017
UNINCORPORATED	82,651	−93	82,744
BAKER	19,527	1,041	18,486
Glen Saint Mary	479	−1	480
Macclenny	4,050	84	3,966
UNINCORPORATED	14,998	958	14,040
BAY	134,059	7,065	126,994
Callaway	13,504	1,251	12,253
Cedar Grove	1,501	22	1,479
Lynn Haven	10,050	752	9,298
Mexico Beach	1,013	21	992
Panama City	35,914	1,518	34,396
Panama City Beach	4,341	290	4,051
Parker	4,834	236	4,598
Springfield	9,051	332	8,719
UNINCORPORATED	53,851	2,643	51,208
BRADFORD	23,312	797	22,515
Brooker	312	0	312
Hampton	303	7	296
Lawtey	679	3	676
Starke	5,097	−129	5,226
UNINCORPORATED	16,921	916	16,005
BREVARD	427,035	28,057	398,978
Cape Canaveral	8,177	163	8,014
Cocoa	17,795	73	17,722
Cocoa Beach	12,533	410	12,123
Indialantic	2,863	19	2,844
Indian Harbour Beach	7,325	392	6,933
Malabar	2,187	210	1,977
Melbourne	64,191	4,157	60,034
Melbourne Beach	3,105	27	3,078
Melbourne Village	600	9	591

Table 1.—Estimates of Population by County and Municipality in Florida: April 1, 1993
(*Continued*)

COUNTY and City	April 1 1993 (Est.)	Total change	April 1 1990 (Census)
Palm Bay	69,197	6,654	62,543
Palm Shores	504	294	210
Rockledge	17,182	1,159	16,023
Satellite Beach	9,954	65	9,889
Titusville	40,679	1,285	39,394
West Melbourne	8,635	236	8,399
UNINCORPORATED	162,108	12,904	149,204
BROWARD	1,317,512	61,981	1,255,531
Coconut Creek	31,626	4,357	27,269
Cooper City	25,539	4,204	21,335
Coral Springs	88,944	10,080	78,864
Dania	16,905	3,722	13,183
Davie	52,332	5,189	47,143
Deerfield Beach	47,639	642	46,997
Ft. Lauderdale	148,743	−495	149,238
Hallandale	31,217	220	30,997
Hillsboro Beach	1,747	−1	1,748
Hollywood	123,956	2,236	121,720
Lauderdale-by-the-Sea	2,983	−7	2,990
Lauderdale Lakes	27,691	350	27,341
Lauderhill	49,436	421	49,015
Lazy Lake Village	40	7	33
Lighthouse Point	10,386	8	10,378
Margate	45,274	2,289	42,985
Miramar	42,282	1,619	40,663
North Lauderdale	26,664	191	26,473
Oakland Park	27,969	1,643	26,326
Parkland	7,383	3,610	3,773
Pembroke Park	4,967	34	4,933
Pembroke Pines	75,014	9,448	65,566
Plantation	72,655	5,841	66,814
Pompano Beach	73,219	808	72,411
Sea Ranch Lakes	616	−3	619
Sunrise	71,542	5,859	65,683
Tamarac	46,711	1,889	44,822
Wilton Manors	11,757	−47	11,804
UNINCORPORATED	152,275	−2,133	154,408
CALHOUN	11,479	468	11,011
Altha	536	39	497
Blountstown	2,388	−16	2,404
UNINCORPORATED	8,555	445	8,110

Table 1.—Estimates of Population by County and Municipality in Florida: April 1, 1993
(*Continued*)

COUNTY and City	April 1 1993 (Est.)	Total change	April 1 1990 (Census)
CHARLOTTE	121,695	10,720	110,975
Punta Gorda	11,769	1,132	10,637
UNINCORPORATED	109,926	9,588	100,338
CITRUS	100,829	7,316	93,513
Crystal River	4,076	26	4,050
Inverness	6,462	665	5,797
UNINCORPORATED	90,291	6,625	83,666
CLAY	114,918	8,932	105,986
Green Cove Springs	4,688	191	4,497
Keystone Heights	1,320	5	1,315
Orange Park	9,456	−32	9,488
Penney Farms	651	42	609
UNINCORPORATED	98,803	8,726	90,077
COLLIER	174,664	22,565	152,099
Everglades	342	21	321
Naples	19,881	376	19,505
UNINCORPORATED	154,441	22,168	132,273
COLUMBIA	46,430	3,817	42,613
Ft. White	502	34	468
Lake City	9,764	138	9,626
UNINCORPORATED	36,164	3,645	32,519
DADE	1,951,116	13,922	1,937,194
Bal Harbour	3,053	8	3,045
Bay Harbor Islands	4,738	35	4,703
Biscayne Park	3,062	−6	3,068
Coral Gables	41,055	964	40,091
El Portal	2,453	−4	2,457
Florida City	4,089	−1,889	5,978
Golden Beach	806	32	774
Hialeah	199,923	11,915	188,008
Hialeah Gardens	9,828	2,101	7,727
Homestead	18,732	−7,962	26,694
Indian Creek Village	44	0	44
Islandia	13	0	13
Key Biscayne*	8,881	8,881	0
Medley	862	199	663
Miami	364,679	6,031	358,648
Miami Beach	95,160	2,521	92,639
Miami Shores	10,125	41	10,084

Table 1.—Estimates of Population by County and Municipality in Florida: April 1, 1993
(*Continued*)

COUNTY and City	April 1 1993 (Est.)	Total change	April 1 1990 (Census)
Miami Springs	13,299	31	13,268
North Bay	5,650	267	5,383
North Miami	50,243	242	50,001
North Miami Beach	35,689	328	35,361
Opa-locka	15,216	−67	15,283
South Miami	10,407	3	10,404
Surfside	4,263	155	4,108
Sweetwater	14,081	172	13,909
Virginia Gardens	2,206	−6	2,212
West Miami	5,743	16	5,727
UNINCORPORATED	1,026,816	−10,086	1,036,902
DE SOTO	25,461	1,596	23,865
Arcadia	6,543	55	6,488
UNINCORPORATED	18,918	1,541	17,377
DIXIE	11,810	1,225	10,585
Cross City	2,037	−4	2,041
Horseshoe Beach	245	−7	252
UNINCORPORATED	9,528	1,236	8,292
DUVAL	701,608	28,637	672,971
Atlantic Beach	12,383	747	11,636
Baldwin	1,513	63	1,450
Jacksonville Beach	19,234	1,395	17,839
Neptune Beach	7,235	419	6,816
Jacksonville (Duval)	661,243	26,013	635,230
ESCAMBIA	272,083	9,285	262,798
Century	1,994	5	1,989
Pensacola	59,858	660	59,198
UNINCORPORATED	210,231	8,620	201,611
FLAGLER	33,544	4,843	28,701
Beverly Beach	322	8	314
Bunnell	1,977	104	1,873
Flagler Beach	4,031	213	3,818
Marineland (part)	12	−9	21
UNINCORPORATED	27,202	4,527	22,675
FRANKLIN	9,775	808	8,967
Apalachicola	2,701	99	2,602
Carrabelle	1,258	58	1,200
UNINCORPORATED	5,816	651	5,165

Table 1.—Estimates of Population by County and Municipality in Florida: April 1, 1993
(*Continued*)

COUNTY and City	April 1 1993 (Est.)	Total change	April 1 1990 (Census)
GADSDEN	43,239	2,123	41,116
Chattahoochee	4,380	−2	4,382
Greensboro	599	13	586
Gretna	2,064	83	1,981
Havana	1,784	67	1,717
Midway	1,112	136	976
Quincy	7,551	99	7,452
UNINCORPORATED	25,749	1,727	24,022
GILCHRIST	10,722	1,055	9,667
Bell	282	15	267
Fanning Springs (part)	246	16	230
Trenton	1,310	23	1,287
UNINCORPORATED	8,884	1,001	7,883
GLADES	8,269	678	7,591
Moore Haven	1,538	106	1,432
UNINCORPORATED	6,731	572	6,159
GULF	12,393	889	11,504
Port St. Joe	4,071	27	4,044
Wewahitchka	1,806	27	1,779
UNINCORPORATED	6,516	835	5,681
HAMILTON	11,604	674	10,930
Jasper	2,084	−15	2,099
Jennings	721	9	712
White Springs	726	22	704
UNINCORPORATED	8,073	658	7,415
HARDEE	22,035	2,536	19,499
Bowling Green	1,861	25	1,836
Wauchula	3,496	253	3,243
Zolfo Springs	1,249	30	1,219
UNINCORPORATED	15,429	2,228	13,201
HENDRY	28,061	2,288	25,773
Clewiston	6,144	59	6,085
La Belle	2,897	194	2,703
UNINCORPORATED	19,020	2,035	16,985
HERNANDO	111,695	10,580	101,115
Brooksville	7,659	70	7,589
Weeki Wachee	11	0	11
UNINCORPORATED	104,025	10,510	93,515

Table 1.—Estimates of Population by County and Municipality in Florida: April 1, 1993
(*Continued*)

COUNTY and City	April 1 1993 (Est.)	Total change	April 1 1990 (Census)
HIGHLANDS	73,203	4,771	68,432
Avon Park	8,169	91	8,078
Lake Placid	1,282	124	1,158
Sebring	8,959	118	8,841
UNINCORPORATED	54,793	4,438	50,355
HILLSBOROUGH	866,134	32,080	834,054
Plant City	24,283	1,529	22,754
Tampa	282,848	2,833	280,015
Temple Terrace	17,167	723	16,444
UNINCORPORATED	541,836	26,995	514,841
HOLMES	16,331	553	15,778
Bonifay	2,677	65	2,612
Esto	294	41	253
Noma	211	4	207
Ponce de Leon	433	27	406
Westville	263	6	257
UNINCORPORATED	12,453	410	12,043
INDIAN RIVER	95,641	5,433	90,208
Fellsmere	2,260	81	2,179
Indian River Shores	2,468	190	2,278
Orchid	21	11	10
Sebastian	12,154	1,906	10,248
Vero Beach	17,404	54	17,350
UNINCORPORATED	61,334	3,191	58,143
JACKSON	44,386	3,011	41,375
Alford	489	7	482
Bascom	90	0	90
Campbellton	232	30	202
Cottondale	927	27	900
Graceville	2,675	0	2,675
Grand Ridge	591	55	536
Greenwood	507	33	474
Jacob City	293	32	261
Malone	1,583	818	765
Marianna	6,249	−43	6,292
Sneads	1,854	108	1,746
UNINCORPORATED	28,896	1,944	26,952
JEFFERSON	12,988	1,692	11,296
Monticello	2,733	130	2,603
UNINCORPORATED	10,255	1,562	8,693

Table 1.—Estimates of Population by County and Municipality in Florida: April 1, 1993
(*Continued*)

COUNTY and City	April 1 1993 (Est.)	Total change	April 1 1990 (Census)
LAFAYETTE	5,603	25	5,578
Mayo	925	8	917
UNINCORPORATED	4,678	17	4,661
LAKE	167,167	15,063	152,104
Astatula	1,056	75	981
Clermont	7,013	103	6,910
Eustis	13,711	855	12,856
Fruitland Park	2,810	95	2,715
Groveland	2,373	73	2,300
Howey-in-the-Hills	735	11	724
Lady Lake	11,117	3,046	8,071
Leesburg	14,963	180	14,783
Mascotte	1,997	236	1,761
Minneola	1,783	268	1,515
Montverde	1,051	161	890
Mount Dora	7,606	290	7,316
Tavares	7,766	383	7,383
Umatilla	2,376	26	2,350
UNINCORPORATED	90,810	9,261	81,549
LEE	357,550	22,437	335,113
Cape Coral	81,339	6,348	74,991
Ft. Myers	45,069	−137	45,206
Sanibel	5,616	148	5,468
UNINCORPORATED	225,526	16,078	209,448
LEON	206,302	13,809	192,493
Tallahassee	131,683	6,910	124,773
UNINCORPORATED	74,619	6,899	67,720
LEVY	28,236	2,324	25,912
Bronson	852	−23	875
Cedar Key	694	26	668
Chiefland	1,997	80	1,917
Fanning Springs (part)	291	28	263
Inglis	1,290	49	1,241
Otter Creek	119	−17	136
Williston	2,227	59	2,168
Yankeetown	631	−4	635
UNINCORPORATED	20,135	2,126	18,009
LIBERTY	5,720	151	5,569
Bristol	959	22	937
UNINCORPORATED	4,761	129	4,632

Table 1.—Estimates of Population by County and Municipality in Florida: April 1, 1993
(*Continued*)

COUNTY and City	April 1 1993 (Est.)	Total change	April 1 1990 (Census)
MADISON	17,316	747	16,569
Greenville	948	−2	950
Lee	315	9	306
Madison	3,417	72	3,345
UNINCORPORATED	12,636	668	11,968
MANATEE	223,508	11,801	211,707
Anna Maria	1,808	64	1,744
Bradenton	46,626	2,857	43,769
Bradenton Beach	1,650	−7	1,657
Holmes Beach	4,925	115	4,810
Longboat Key (part)	2,621	77	2,544
Palmetto	9,385	117	9,268
UNINCORPORATED	156,493	8,578	147,915
MARION	212,025	17,190	194,835
Belleview	3,106	428	2,678
Dunnellon	1,705	66	1,639
McIntosh	410	−1	411
Ocala	42,400	355	42,045
Reddick	570	16	554
UNINCORPORATED	163,834	16,326	147,508
MARTIN	106,780	5,880	100,900
Jupiter Island	562	13	549
Ocean Breeze Park	519	0	519
Sewalls Point	1,651	63	1,588
Stuart	12,479	543	11,936
UNINCORPORATED	91,569	5,261	86,308
MONROE	81,766	3,742	78,024
Key Colony Beach	1,017	40	977
Key West	26,122	1,290	24,832
Layton	189	6	183
UNINCORPORATED	54,438	2,406	52,032
NASSAU	46,450	2,509	43,941
Callahan	950	4	946
Fernandina Beach	9,177	412	8,765
Hilliard	1,911	160	1,751
UNINCORPORATED	34,412	1,933	32,479
OKALOOSA	154,512	10,735	143,777
Cinco Bayou	388	2	386

Table 1.—Estimates of Population by County and Municipality in Florida: April 1, 1993
(Continued)

COUNTY and City	April 1 1993 (Est.)	Total change	April 1 1990 (Census)
Crestview	11,567	1,681	9,886
Destin	8,644	554	8,090
Ft. Walton Beach	21,921	514	21,407
Laurel Hill	587	44	543
Mary Esther	4,194	55	4,139
Niceville	11,150	641	10,509
Shalimar	350	9	341
Valparaiso	6,413	97	6,316
UNINCORPORATED	89,298	7,138	82,160
OKEECHOBEE	31,758	2,131	29,627
Okeechobee	4,979	36	4,943
UNINCORPORATED	26,779	2,095	24,684
ORANGE	727,780	50,289	677,491
Apopka	16,307	2,696	13,611
Bay Lake	24	5	19
Belle Isle	5,575	303	5,272
Eatonville	2,470	−35	2,505
Edgewood	1,111	49	1,062
Lake Buena Vista	22	−1,753	1,776
Maitland	9,096	164	8,932
Oakland	746	46	700
Ocoee	16,418	3,640	12,778
Orlando	172,019	7,345	164,674
Windermere	1,667	296	1,371
Winter Garden	11,685	1,822	9,863
Winter Park	24,197	1,574	22,623
UNINCORPORATED	466,442	34,137	432,305
OSCEOLA	125,675	17,947	107,728
Kissimmee	32,759	2,422	30,337
St. Cloud	14,779	2,127	12,652
UNINCORPORATED	78,137	13,398	64,739
PALM BEACH	918,223	54,720	863,503
Atlantis	1,674	21	1,653
Belle Glade	17,249	1,072	16,177
Boca Raton	64,818	3,332	61,486
Boynton Beach	48,428	2,144	46,284
Briny Breeze	394	−6	400
Cloud Lake	121	0	121
Delray Beach	48,644	1,460	47,184
Glen Ridge	215	8	207

Table 1.—Estimates of Population by County and Municipality in Florida: April 1, 1993
(Continued)

COUNTY and City	April 1 1993 (Est.)	Total change	April 1 1990 (Census)
Golf Village	192	8	184
Golfview	150	−3	153
Greenacres City	22,385	3,702	18,683
Gulf Stream	705	15	690
Haverhill	1,170	112	1,058
Highland Beach	3,245	36	3,209
Hypoluxo	1,106	299	807
Juno Beach	2,173	1	2,172
Jupiter	27,291	2,384	24,907
Jupiter Inlet Colony	404	−1	405
Lake Clarke Shores	3,607	243	3,364
Lake Park	6,695	−9	6,704
Lake Worth	28,327	−237	28,564
Lantana	8,316	−76	8,392
Manalapan	318	6	312
Mangonia Park	1,407	−46	1,453
North Palm Beach	11,782	439	11,343
Ocean Ridge	1,600	30	1,570
Pahokee	6,856	34	6,822
Palm Beach	9,814	0	9,814
Palm Beach Gardens	28,635	5,645	22,990
Palm Beach Shores	1,034	−1	1,035
Palm Springs	9,729	−34	9,763
Riviera Beach	27,308	−336	27,644
Royal Palm Beach	16,546	1,014	15,532
South Bay	4,064	506	3,558
South Palm Beach	1,482	2	1,480
Tequesta Village	4,543	44	4,499
West Palm Beach	68,006	242	67,764
UNINCORPORATED	437,790	32,670	405,120
PASCO	293,966	12,835	281,131
Dade City	5,688	55	5,633
New Port Richey	14,352	308	14,044
Port Richey	2,601	80	2,521
Saint Leo	912	−97	1,009
San Antonio	786	10	776
Zephyrhills	8,467	247	8,220
UNINCORPORATED	261,160	12,232	248,928
PINELLAS	864,953	13,294	851,659
Belleair	3,976	13	3,963
Belleair Beach	2,090	20	2,070
Belleair Bluffs	2,213	−21	2,234

Table 1.—Estimates of Population by County and Municipality in Florida: April 1, 1993
(Continued)

COUNTY and City	April 1 1993 (Est.)	Total change	April 1 1990 (Census)
Belleair Shore	60	0	60
Clearwater	100,768	1,984	98,784
Dunedin	34,765	768	33,997
Gulfport	11,812	103	11,709
Indian Rocks Beach	4,019	56	3,963
Indian Shores	1,449	44	1,405
Kenneth City	4,360	9	4,351
Largo	66,369	459	65,910
Madeira Beach	4,222	−3	4,225
North Redington Beach	1,141	6	1,135
Oldsmar	8,498	137	8,361
Pinellas Park	43,762	191	43,571
Redington Beach	1,630	4	1,626
Redington Shores	2,404	38	2,366
Safety Harbor	15,708	588	15,120
St. Petersburg	239,701	−617	240,318
St. Petersburg Beach	9,487	287	9,200
Seminole	9,430	179	9,251
South Pasadena	5,837	193	5,644
Tarpon Springs	18,488	614	17,874
Treasure Island	7,327	61	7,266
UNINCORPORATED	265,437	8,181	257,256
POLK	429,943	24,561	405,382
Auburndale	9,063	205	8,858
Bartow	14,902	186	14,716
Davenport	1,688	159	1,529
Dundee	2,447	112	2,335
Eagle Lake	1,934	176	1,758
Ft. Meade	5,247	254	4,993
Frostproof	2,907	32	2,875
Haines City	12,103	420	11,683
Highland Park	153	−2	155
Hillcrest Heights	220	−1	221
Lake Alfred	3,622	0	3,622
Lake Hamilton	1,113	−15	1,128
Lake Wales	9,759	89	9,670
Lakeland	73,121	2,545	70,576
Mulberry	3,095	107	2,988
Polk City	1,613	174	1,439
Winter Haven	25,006	281	24,725
UNINCORPORATED	261,950	19,839	242,111
PUTNAM	67,625	2,555	65,070
Crescent City	1,846	−13	1,859

Table 1.—Estimates of Population by County and Municipality in Florida: April 1, 1993
(*Continued*)

COUNTY and City	April 1 1993 (Est.)	Total change	April 1 1990 (Census)
Interlachen	1,254	94	1,160
Palatka	10,447	3	10,444
Pomona Park	749	23	726
Welaka	555	22	533
UNINCORPORATED	52,774	2,426	50,348
ST. JOHNS	91,197	7,368	83,829
Hastings	632	37	595
Marineland (part)	0	0	0
St. Augustine	11,747	52	11,695
St. Augustine Beach	3,814	157	3,657
UNINCORPORATED	75,004	7,122	67,882
ST. LUCIE	163,192	13,021	150,171
Ft. Pierce	36,909	79	36,830
Port St. Lucie	65,722	9,961	55,761
St. Lucie Village	627	43	584
UNINCORPORATED	59,934	2,938	56,996
SANTA ROSA	90,259	8,651	81,608
Gulf Breeze	5,802	272	5,530
Jay	669	3	666
Milton	7,451	235	7,216
UNINCORPORATED	76,337	8,141	68,196
SARASOTA	290,612	12,836	277,776
Longboat Key (part)	3,716	323	3,393
North Port	13,591	1,618	11,973
Sarasota	50,820	−77	50,897
Venice	17,768	716	17,052
UNINCORPORATED	204,717	10,256	194,461
SEMINOLE	310,890	23,369	287,521
Altamonte Springs	36,770	1,603	35,167
Casselberry	22,816	3,967	18,849
Lake Mary	6,673	744	5,929
Longwood	13,418	102	13,316
Oviedo	15,722	4,608	11,114
Sanford	34,096	1,709	32,387
Winter Springs	24,008	1,857	22,151
UNINCORPORATED	157,387	8,779	148,608
SUMTER	33,814	2,237	31,577
Bushnell	2,212	214	1,998
Center Hill	762	27	735

Table 1.—Estimates of Population by County and Municipality in Florida: April 1, 1993
(Continued)

COUNTY and City	April 1 1993 (Est.)	Total change	April 1 1990 (Census)
Coleman	854	−3	857
Webster	807	61	746
Wildwood	3,767	207	3,560
UNINCORPORATED	25,412	1,731	23,681
SUWANNEE	28,598	1,818	26,780
Branford	682	12	670
Live Oak	6,479	147	6,332
UNINCORPORATED	21,437	1,659	19,778
TAYLOR	17,374	263	17,111
Perry	7,198	47	7,151
UNINCORPORATED	10,176	216	9,960
UNION	12,031	1,779	10,252
Lake Butler	2,126	10	2,116
Raiford	232	34	198
Worthington Springs	228	50	178
UNINCORPORATED	9,445	1,685	7,760
VOLUSIA	390,066	19,329	370,737
Daytona Beach	62,453	462	61,991
Daytona Beach Shores	2,532	335	2,197
De Land	17,377	755	16,622
Edgewater	16,745	1,394	15,351
Holly Hill	11,258	117	11,141
Lake Helen	2,381	37	2,344
New Smyrna Beach	17,481	932	16,549
Oak Hill	1,015	98	917
Orange City	5,813	466	5,347
Ormond Beach	30,963	1,242	29,721
Pierson	1,222	−1,766	2,988
Ponce Inlet	1,994	290	1,704
Port Orange	38,144	2,837	35,307
South Daytona	12,689	201	12,488
UNINCORPORATED	167,999	11,929	156,070
WAKULLA	15,401	1,199	14,202
St. Marks	303	−4	307
Sopchoppy	398	31	367
UNINCORPORATED	14,700	1,172	13,528

Table 1.—Estimates of Population by County and Municipality in Florida: April 1, 1993
(*Continued*)

COUNTY and City	April 1 1993 (Est.)	Total change	April 1 1990 (Census)
WALTON	30,568	2,809	27,759
De Funiak Springs	5,259	59	5,200
Freeport	867	24	843
Paxton	582	−18	600
UNINCORPORATED	23,860	2,744	21,116
WASHINGTON	17,554	635	16,919
Caryville	615	−16	631
Chipley	3,936	70	3,866
Ebro	264	9	255
Vernon	831	53	778
Wausau	310	−3	313
UNINCORPORATED	11,598	522	11,076
FLORIDA	13,608,627	670,556	12,938,071
Incorporated	6,693,454	278,877	6,414,577
Unincorporated	6,915,173	391,679	6,523,494

*Key Biscayne was not incorporated in 1990.

Explanation of Terms

April 1, 1990 (Census)
The permanent resident population enumerated in the 1990 Census. This includes census revisions through September 30, 1993.

Total change
The total change between the April 1, 1990, U.S. Census figure and the estimate for April 1, 1993, including change due to natural increase (or decrease) and net migration. This figure also includes any population change due to annexation.

April 1, 1993 (Est.)
The estimated permanent resident population for April 1, 1993. This figure is comparable to the Census enumeration and should be used for most purposes of planning and analysis.

Vital Statistics

Source: Department of Health and Rehabilitative Services, Public Health Statistics Section

Marriages and Dissolutions* of Marriage, Rates per 1,000 Population and Dissolutions per 100 Marriages

Year	Marriages	Rate	Diss. of Marr.	Rate	Diss. Per 100 Marr.
1980	108,344	11.0	71,578	7.3	66.1
1981	113,003	11.1	75,490	7.4	66.8
1982	115,830	11.1	71,238	6.8	61.5
1983	118,965	11.2	71,434	6.7	60.0
1984	126,449	11.5	75,535	6.9	59.7
1985	125,516	11.0	77,545	6.8	61.8
1986	129,363	11.0	78,114	6.7	60.4
1987	136,492	11.2	79,467	6.5	58.2
1988	138,072	11.0	78,708	6.3	57.0
1989	137,892	10.7	79,810	6.2	57.9
1990	141,816	10.7	81,121	6.1	57.2

*Source: Florida Department of HRS, Office of Vital Statistics

Resident Deaths for Causes and Rates per 100,000 Population, by Race

Source: Department of Health and Rehabilitative Services, Public Health Statistics Section

Cause of Death	Year	Rank	Total	White	Non-White
Heart Disease	1980	1	38,773	35,560	3,206
	1990	1	45,437	41,702	3,725
Cancer (Malignant Neoplasm)	1980	2	23,762	21,250	2,238
	1990	2	33,541	30,374	3,160
Stroke (Cerebrovascular Disease)	1980	3	9,219	8,125	1,092
	1990	3	8,442	7,448	993
Chronic Obstructive Lung Disease	1980	5	3,320	3,118	202
	1990	4	5,660	5,330	330
Accidents	1980	4	5,149	4,303	842
	1990	5	5,125	4,304	821
Pneumonia & Influenza	1980	6	2,164	1,874	290
	1990	6	3,476	3,135	339
Diabetes Melliitus	1980	8	1,618	1,326	292
	1990	7	2,952	2,434	516
Human Immunodeficiency Virus (HIV)	1980	—	—	—	—
	1990	8	2,239	1,349	890
Suicide	1980	9	1,522	1,457	65
	1990	9	2,073	1,949	124
Chronic Liver Disease & Cirrhosis	1980	7	1,817	1,554	262
	1990	10	1,688	1,531	157
Homicide	1980	10	1,520	858	661
	1990	11	1,594	786	801

Source: Florida Department of HRS, Office of Vital Statistics

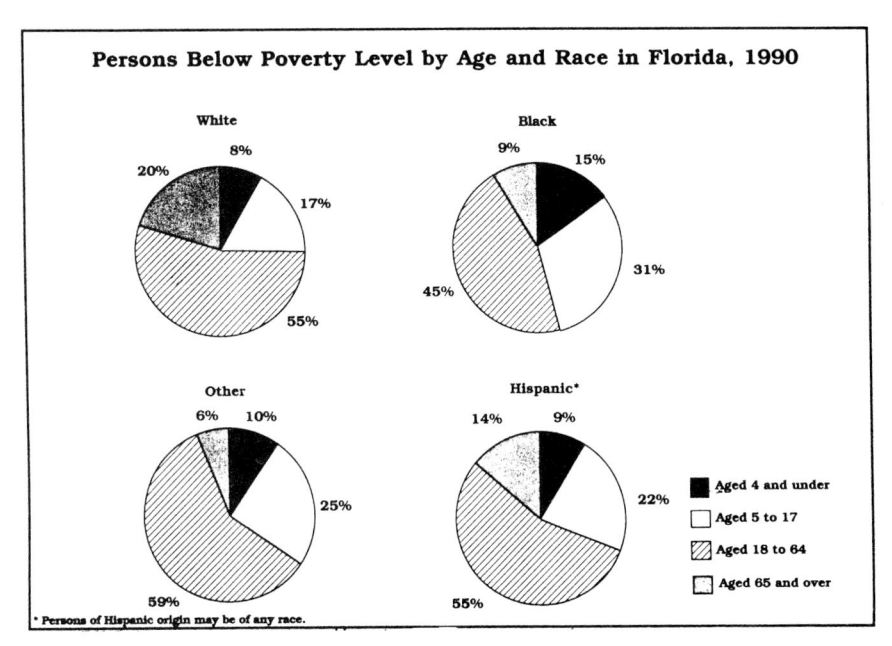

Persons Below Poverty Level by Age and Race in Florida, 1990

White
- 8%
- 20%
- 17%
- 55%

Black
- 9%
- 15%
- 31%
- 45%

Other
- 6%
- 10%
- 25%
- 59%

Hispanic*
- 14%
- 9%
- 22%
- 55%

Legend:
- Aged 4 and under
- Aged 5 to 17
- Aged 18 to 64
- Aged 65 and over

*Persons of Hispanic origin may be of any race.

Census Handbook. University of Florida Bureau of Economics & Business

Acquired Immunodeficiency Syndrome (AIDS): Adult Cases of Aids, 1993 and Cumulative Cases, January 1, 1980 Through December 31, 1993, in the State and Counties of Florida

County	Number of cases Diagnosed	Reported 1/	Cumulative cases 1980–93 Number 2/	Rate per 100,000 population 3/
Florida	5,389	10,559	34,897	256.4
Unknown	0	0	5	(X)
DOC	261	399	810	(X)
Alachua	22	71	215	112.8
Baker	1	1	10	51.2
Bay	13	36	113	84.3
Bradford	3	4	12	51.5
Brevard	98	177	508	119.0
Broward	806	1,290	5,375	408.0
Calhoun	1	3	7	61.0
Charlotte	6	13	83	68.2
Citrus	6	13	46	45.6
Clay	16	36	84	73.1
Collier	57	118	315	180.3
Columbia	6	12	29	62.5
Dade	1,653	2,997	10,669	546.8
De Soto	3	5	21	82.5
Dixie	0	0	5	42.3
Duval	287	799	1,990	283.6
Escambia	66	134	414	152.2
Flagler	7	11	26	77.5

Acquired Immunodeficiency Syndrome (AIDS): (*Continued*)

	Number of cases		Cumulative cases 1980–93	
County	Diagnosed	Reported 1/	Number 2/	Rate per 100,000 population 3/
Franklin	1	2	3	30.7
Gadsden	3	11	40	92.5
Gilchrist	1	1	2	18.7
Glades	0	2	7	84.7
Gulf	1	2	4	32.3
Hamilton	0	0	6	51.7
Hardee	4	6	24	108.9
Hendry	5	13	61	217.4
Hernando	9	20	63	56.4
Highlands	11	26	56	76.5
Hillsborough	367	840	2,157	249.0
Holmes	2	4	10	61.2
Indian River	8	16	80	83.6
Jackson	3	6	20	45.1
Jefferson	2	4	12	92.4
Lafayette	1	1	2	35.7
Lake	14	24	81	48.5
Lee	93	184	732	204.7
Leon	27	52	219	106.2
Levy	3	6	12	42.5
Liberty	1	2	3	52.4
Madison	4	8	15	86.6
Manatee	35	91	258	115.4
Marion	26	63	180	84.9
Martin	7	16	106	99.3
Monroe	64	114	608	743.6
Nassau	5	10	27	58.1
Okaloosa	14	34	90	58.2
Okeechobee	5	7	28	88.2
Orange	283	726	1,846	253.6
Osceola	26	63	144	114.6
Palm Beach	418	807	3,091	336.6
Pasco	29	64	254	86.4
Pinellas	260	484	1,554	179.7
Polk	85	177	494	114.9
Putnam	10	28	52	76.9
St. Johns	19	64	126	138.2
St. Lucie	43	60	430	263.5
Santa Rosa	7	10	31	34.3
Sarasota	50	96	367	126.3
Seminole	46	125	310	99.7
Sumter	7	9	15	44.4
Suwannee	1	6	21	73.4
Taylor	2	5	12	69.1
Union	0	2	13	108.1
Volusia	69	133	459	117.7
Wakulla	3	6	11	71.4
Walton	2	8	18	58.9
Washington	1	2	6	34.2

DOC Department of Corrections.
(X) Not applicable.
1/Includes diagnosed cases from earlier years not previously reported.
2/Excludes 800 diagnosed and reported pediatric (under age 13) cases of AIDS.
3/Based on total population estimates as of April 1, 1993.

Source: State of Florida, Department of Health and Rehabilitative Services, Disease Control and AIDS Prevention, *The Florida HIV/AIDS Monthly Surveillance Report,* January 1994. *Florida Statistical Abstract 1994*

Florida Prison System Inmate Population
on June 30, 1985–1994

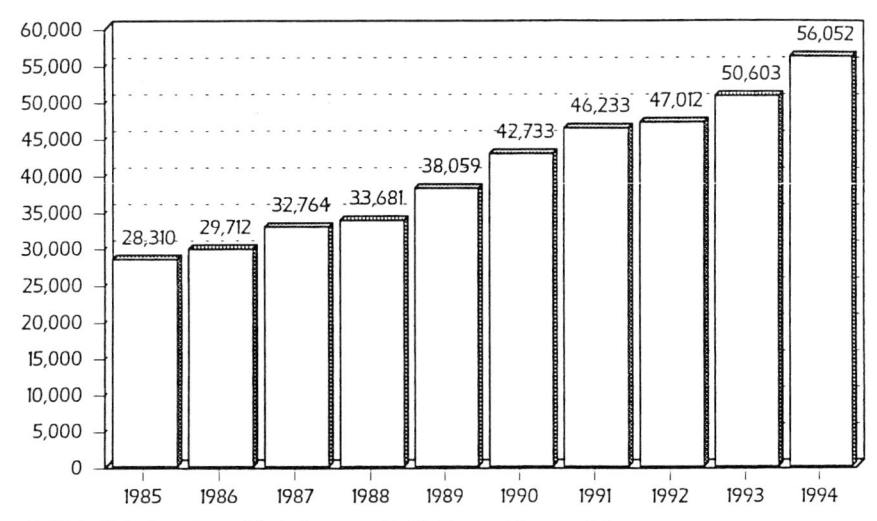

Year	Inmates
1985	28,310
1986	29,712
1987	32,764
1988	33,681
1989	38,059
1990	42,733
1991	46,233
1992	47,012
1993	50,603
1994	56,052

Guide to State Agencies and their Programs, Florida House of Representatives

Juveniles in Jails

Average Daily Population	Number of Juveniles	% of Jail Population
June 1986	333	1.6%
June 1987	445	1.8%
June 1988	579	2.0%
June 1989	667	2.0%
June 1990	796	2.5%
June 1991	790	2.3%
June 1992	917	2.5%
June 1993	989	2.9%

Guide to State Agencies and their Programs, Florida House of Representatives

Resident Deaths

Number of Deaths

Year	Total	White Total	White Male	White Fem	Nonwhite Total	Nonwhite Male	Nonwhite Fem
1978	95,446	84,653	48,286	34,396	10,765	6,241	4,524
1979	98,329	87,052	49,538	37,514	11,254	6,427	4,827
1980	104,479	92,601	52,714	39,877	11,854	6,783	5,068
1981	109,106	96,971	54,346	42,621	12,107	6,838	5,267
1982	108,421	96,958	54,096	42,855	11,447	6,566	4,880
1983	113,038	100,865	56,022	44,835	12,159	6,872	5,285
1984	114,835	102,391	56,688	45,702	12,423	6,969	5,454
1985	120,645	107,742	59,293	48,449	12,877	7,123	5,754
1986	123,540	110,100	60,229	49,867	13,402	7,508	5,893
1987	126,955	112,719	61,439	51,279	14,210	8,047	6,161
1988	131,389	116,662	63,195	53,465	14,700	8,274	6,425
1989	132,037	116,984	63,265	53,716	15,001	8,438	6,562
1990	133,294	118,304	63,814	54,490	14,950	8,383	6,566

Death Rate per 1000 Population / Age-Adjusted Death Rate

Year	Total	White Total	White Male	White Fem	Nonwhite Total	Nonwhite Male	Nonwhite Fem	AA Total	AA White	AA Nonwhite
1978	10.3	10.9	12.9	9.0	7.3	8.9	5.9	5.7	5.4	6.9
1979	10.3	10.9	12.9	9.0	7.3	8.9	5.9	5.6	5.4	6.7
1980	10.6	11.0	12.9	9.0	7.3	8.9	5.9	5.7	5.4	8.5
1981	10.7	11.1	13.0	9.4	8.1	9.7	6.7	5.6	5.3	8.3
1982	10.4	10.9	12.6	9.3	7.5	9.1	7.4	5.4	5.1	7.6
1983	10.6	11.1	12.8	9.5	7.9	9.4	6.5	5.3	5.0	7.9
1984	10.4	10.9	12.5	9.4	7.8	9.2	6.5	5.2	4.9	7.7
1985	10.6	11.1	12.6	9.6	7.8	9.1	6.7	5.2	4.9	7.6
1986	10.5	11.0	12.5	9.6	7.6	9.0	6.4	5.1	4.8	7.6
1987	10.5	10.9	12.3	9.6	7.9	9.3	6.5	5.1	4.8	7.7
1988	10.5	11.0	12.3	9.7	7.8	9.2	6.5	5.2	4.8	7.7
1989	10.3	10.8	12.0	9.6	7.6	8.9	6.4	5.1	4.8	7.6
1990	10.1	10.6	11.8	9.4	7.4	8.6	6.2	5.0	4.7	7.3

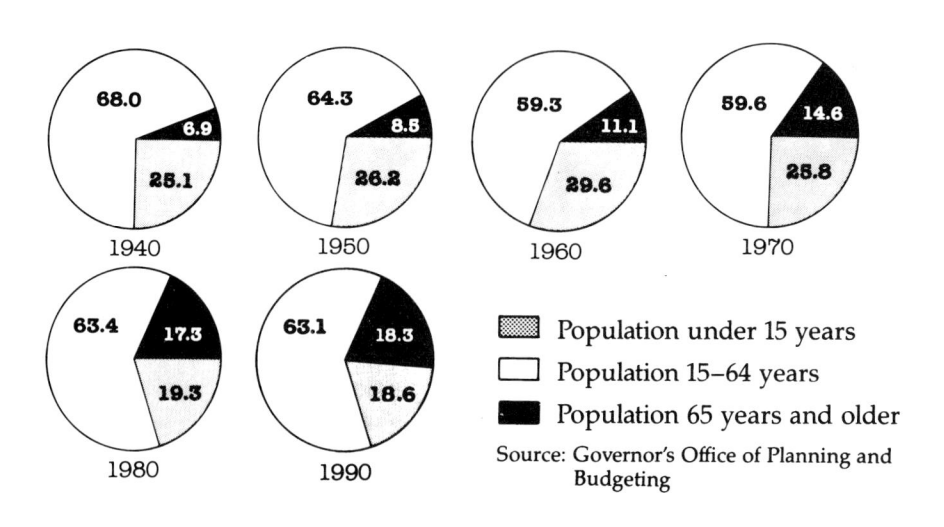

Pie charts showing population age distribution:

- 1940: 68.0 (15–64), 25.1 (under 15), 6.9 (65+)
- 1950: 64.3 (15–64), 26.2 (under 15), 8.5 (65+)
- 1960: 59.3 (15–64), 29.6 (under 15), 11.1 (65+)
- 1970: 59.6 (15–64), 25.8 (under 15), 14.6 (65+)
- 1980: 63.4 (15–64), 19.3 (under 15), 17.3 (65+)
- 1990: 63.1 (15–64), 18.6 (under 15), 18.3 (65+)

▨ Population under 15 years
☐ Population 15–64 years
■ Population 65 years and older

Source: Governor's Office of Planning and Budgeting

Florida Trade, 1992

Port and type of cargo	Short tons	Port and type of cargo	Short tons
Canaveral (fiscal year 1991–92), total	2,975,921	Palm Beach (fiscal year 1991–92), total	3,788,805
Exports	899,625	Exports	2,400,506
Imports	2,076,296	Imports	1,388,299
Everglades (fiscal year 1991–92), total	16,353,376	Panama City (calendar year 1992), total	565,302
Exports	1,317,444	Exports	416,008
Imports	3,434,231	Imports	68,161
Domestic	10,768,580	Domestic	81,133
Bunker	833,121	Pensacola (fiscal year 1991–20, total	1,372,879
Jacksonville[1] (fiscal year 1991–92), total		Exports	1,073,376
JPA terminals	5,001,074	Imports	299,503
General cargo exports	201,132	St. Lucie (calendar year 1992), total	127,659
General cargo imports	671,036	Exports	30,387
Containerized cargo	2,989,211	Imports	97,272
Bulk cargo & petro	1,031,271	Tampa (fiscal year 1991–92), total	49,157,127
Manatee (fiscal year 1991–92), total	5,375,233	Exports	21,511,324
Exports	1,827,062	Imports	20,280,020
Imports	3,548,171	Domestic	7,365,783
Miami (fiscal year 1991–92), total	4,596,481		
Exports	2,332,873		
Imports	2,263,608		

1/ Tonnage passing through facilities owned by the Jacksonville Port Authority only; therefore they differ from movements into and out of the Port of Jacksonville.
Source: Data are reported in annual or cumulative monthly reports of each port authority.

Florida Statistical Abstract 1993

Visitors to Florida 1992

Tourism is a major component of the Florida economy. Visitor estimates are one of several indicators of the importance of the tourism industry which provide many tangible and intangible benefits to Florida residents. Each year millions of people visit the state to enjoy its many natural and man-made attractions. The Florida Department of Commerce provides a measure of visitor activity by generating monthly estimates of air and auto travelers. The following tables contain a state level historical summary, by quarter, of visitors to Florida

1992	Auto	Air	Total
First Quarter	5,895,902	5,333,757	11,229,659
Second Quarter	4,609,263	5,299,421	9,908,684
Third Quarter	4,454,383	5,360,938	9,815,321
Fourth Quarter	4,490,853	5,091,677	9,582,530
Total	19,450,401	21,085,793	40,536,194

Tourist Count 1985–1992
Source: Florida Department of Commerce

1985	28,850,424	1989	38,712,303
1986	31,791,184	1990	40,970,233
1987	34,064,530	1991	39,560,874
1988	36,765,608	1992	40,536,194

Tracking the Florida Tourist
Source: Florida Department of Commerce

Year	Tourists Visiting Florida	Number of Nights in Florida
1981—Air*	10,372,599	8.3
Auto	10,850,132	16.7
1982—Air*	11,023,557	10.0
Auto	11,957,188	14.1
1983—Air*	10,375,151	9.8
Auto	13,307,217	15.5
1984—Air*	12,665,734	10.6
Auto	14,663,772	13.1
1985—Air*	13,049,211	9.5
Auto	15,801,213	12.5
1986—Air*	14,759,939	9.1
Auto	17,031,245	14.6
1987—Air*	16,539,817	8.6
Auto	17,527,713	12.8
1988—Air*	18,032,084	9.8
Auto	18,733,524	16.8
1989—Air*	18,052,968	8.2
Auto	20,659,335	15.7
1990—Air*	20,678,364	7.8
Auto	20,291,869	14.8
1991—Air*	19,139,610	8.7
Auto	20,171,440	13.4
1992—Air*	19,450,401	8.7
Auto	21,085,793	15.1

*Domestic air visitors only

Top Ten Origins of Auto and Domestic Air Visitors Surveyed

1992 Visitors

Auto

ORIGIN	RANK	%
Georgia	1	15.1
Ohio	2	6.8
New York	3	5.3
Alabama	4	5.2
Tennessee	5	4.8
Michigan	6	4.5
North Carolina	7	4.4
Ontario	8	4.3
Illinois	9	4.2
Louisiana	10	4.1
TOTAL TOP 10		58.7

Domestic Air

ORIGIN	RANK	%
New York	1	16.1
New Jersey	2	7.7
California	3	6.4
Pennsylvania	4	5.4
Illinois	5	5.2
Ohio	6	4.9
Texas	7.5	4.7
Massachusetts	7.5	4.7
Georgia	9	4.1
Michigan	10	3.4
TOTAL TOP 10		62.6

Employment by Major Industry in Florida
1960–1990
(Percentages)

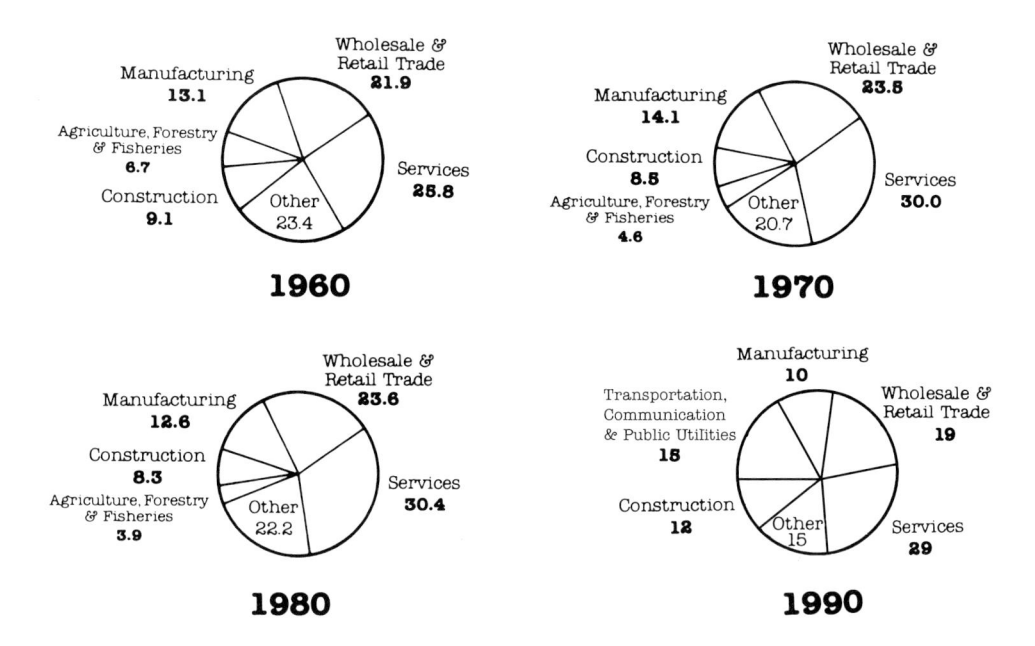

1960
- Manufacturing 13.1
- Agriculture, Forestry & Fisheries 6.7
- Construction 9.1
- Other 23.4
- Wholesale & Retail Trade 21.9
- Services 25.8

1970
- Manufacturing 14.1
- Construction 8.5
- Agriculture, Forestry & Fisheries 4.6
- Other 20.7
- Wholesale & Retail Trade 23.5
- Services 30.0

1980
- Manufacturing 12.6
- Construction 8.3
- Agriculture, Forestry & Fisheries 3.9
- Other 22.2
- Wholesale & Retail Trade 23.6
- Services 30.4

1990
- Manufacturing 10
- Transportation, Communication & Public Utilities 15
- Construction 12
- Other 15
- Wholesale & Retail Trade 19
- Services 29

Source: Governor's Office of Planning and Budgeting and U.S. Bureau of the Census

Personal Income In Millions of Dollars

1980—Florida 96,078
      United States 2,254,076

1990—Florida 241,836
      United States 4,664,057

Per Capita Personal Income In Dollars

1980—Florida 9,764
      United States 9,919
1990—Florida 19,701
      United States 18,696
1992—Florida 19,711
      United States 20,105

Estimated Employment in Florida's Nonagricultural Establishments
(in thousands 1990)

Source: Florida Department of Labor and Employment Security

Published Industry Title	Annual Average
Mining	8940
Oil and Gas Extraction	542
Nonmetallic minerals (except fuels)	7,995
Metal Mining	403
Construction	323,278
General Building Contractors	75,985
Heavy Construction Contractors	45,897
Special Trade Contractors	201,396
Manufacturing	522,133
Durable Goods	307,723
Lumber and Wood Products	22,222
Furniture and Fixtures	13,688
Stone, Clay, and Glass Products	23,027
Primary Metal Industries	5,574
Fabricated Metal Products	32,804
Machinery, Except Electrical	42,616
Electrical and Electronic Equipment	60,986
Transportation Equipment	62,581
Instruments and Related Products	35,245
Miscellaneous Manufacturing Industries	8,980
Nondurable Goods	214,410
Food and Kindred Products	47,378
Tobacco Manufacturers	1,070
Textile Mill Products	4,054
Apparel and Other Textile Products	33,143
Paper and Allied Products	14,096
Printing and Publishing	66,077
Chemicals and Allied Products	23,100
Petroleum and Coal Products	1,556
Rubber and Miscellaneous Plastics Products	21,458
Leather and Leather Products	2,478
Trans and Public Utilities Exc. US Postal Service	278,441
Transportation	170,578
Railroad Transportation	7,787
Local and Interurban Passenger Transit	11,429
Trucking and Warehousing	60,181
Water Transportation	17,843
Transportation by Air	51,760
Communication Exc. US Postal Service	107,863
Electric, Gas, and Sanitary Services	39,532
Wholesale and Retail Trade	1,444,436
Wholesale Trade	293,285
Wholesale Trade Durable Goods	169,863
Wholesale Trade Nondurable Goods	123,422
Retail Trade	1,151,151
Building Materials and Garden Supplies	45,670
General Merchandise Stores	134,766

Estimated Employment in Florida's Nonagricultural Establishments
(in thousands 1990) *(Continued)*

Published Industry Title	Annual Average
Food Stores	206,489
Automotive Dealers and Service Stations	115,386
Apparel and Accessory Stores	64,887
Furniture and Home Furnishings	54,942
Eating and Drinking Places	390,766
Miscellaneous Retail	138,245
Finance, Insurance, and Real Estate	370,700
Banking	116,726
Credit Agencies other than Banks	25,965
Insurance Carriers	62,390
Insurance Agents, Brokers, and Service	39,472
Real Estate	98,402
Services	1,553,466
Hotels and Other Lodging Places	138,782
Personal Services	62,598
Business Services	300,739
Auto Repair, Services, and Garages	55,683
Miscellaneous Repair Services	23,660
Motion Pictures	15,280
Amusement and Recreation Services	107,134
Health Services	411,692
Legal Services	54,434
Educational Services	59,942
Miscellaneous Services	1,641
Total Government	846,565
Total Federal Government	126,303
Total State Government	175,444
Total Local Government	544,818

Public Lodging Establishments
1992–93
Source: Department of Business Regulation

Classification of Business	Number of Licensed Establishments	Number of Rental Units
Apartments	17,194	756,327
Hotels	772	128,265
Motels	3,951	205,220
Rooming Houses	652	8,100
Rental Condominiums	5,860	57,233
Transient Apartments	2,223	20,769
TOTALS	30,652	1,175,914

Public Food Service Establishments

Number of Establishments	Seating Capacity
36,900	2,831,319

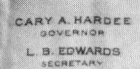

Governor Cary Hardee's early 1920s letter of welcome to Florida tourists. Florida State Archives

Public Employment in Florida
1991

	Florida	
Item	State and local	State only
Total employees, all functions	751,419	184,595
Full-time only	608,793	147,032
Full-time equivalent employees, all functions	657,460	163,450
Education, total	297,648	40,681
Higher education	57,833	38,018
Elementary and secondary schools	237,152	0
Other education	A/	2,663
Libraries	4,132	B/
Public welfare	13,934	8,845
Hospitals	49,817	16,693
Health	18,793	13,126
Social insurance administration	A/	4,641
Highways	23,795	10,217
Air and water transportation	3,301	6
Police protection	45,036	4,225
Police officers only	30,861	2,588
Fire protection	16,649	B/
Correction	40,047	28,623
Natural resources	10,952	6,941
Parks and recreation	15,092	1,041
Housing and community development	3,490	B/
Sewerage	7,195	B/
Solid waste management	7,598	B/
Government administration		
Judicial and legal	18,425	8,980
Financial and other government administration	30,777	8,584
Public utilities		
Water supply	9,558	B/
Gas supply and electric power	5,664	B/
Transit	A/	4,827
Liquor stores	A/	0
All other and unallocable	26,089	10,423
October payroll, total ($1,000)	1,438,591	358,559
Average earnings (dollars)	2,240	2,272

A/ State government only.
B/ Local government only.

Source: U.S. Department of Commerce, Bureau of the Census, *Public Employment in 1991.*
Florida Statistical Abstract 1993

Florida Motion Picture and Television Production
Source: Florida Department of Commerce, Film Bureau

Features

Year	Budget	Employment	Projects
1979	$ 42,868,000	1,967	23
1980	78,512,000	3,184	19
1981	50,375,000	1,431	13
1982	78,195,000	8,789	32
1983	67,980,000	5,365	27
1984	91,210,000	5,896	35
1985	114,000,000	5,328	37
1986	78,333,500	4,882	26
1987	82,190,000	3283	24
1988	98,705,000	10,992	29
1989	49,300,000	7,287	15
1990	154,067,000	3,172	24
1991	152,060,000	4,983	21
1992	98,840,000	4,201	27
1993	136,141,195	5,210	70

Commercials and Music

Year	Budget	Employment	Projects
1979*	$40,000,000	2,000	N/A
1980*	50,000,000	2,000	N/A
1981*	60,000,000	2,500	N/A
1982	63,819,000	5,090	703
1983	79,441,000	6,221	915
1984	96,524,000	7,537	1,121
1985	61,456,000	10,474	1,983
1986	90,520,331	40,553	9,535
1987	61,421,697	19,538	12,125
1988	61,939,812	16,009	16,945
1989	53,917,598	20,478	11,750
1990	67,299,155	17,050	15,572
1991	46,413,158	12,741	10,960
1992	119,665,807	14,233	21,072
1993	240,558,704	25,268	13,085

*Note: The 1979–1982 budgets and 1979–1981 employment for commercials and music are estimates.

Licensed Members of Professions

One out of ten Floridians is licensed by the state. The total was 1,268,579 for 1992–1993.

The Department of Professional Regulation licensed and regulated the following during the fiscal year 1992–93

Cumulative License Totals

Professions	92/93
Accountancy	28,553
Acupuncture	458
Architecture	13,755
Athlete agents	185
Auctioneers	2,708
Barbers	27,464
Cert. social workers	5
Chiropractic	7,269
Clinical lab personnel	15,314
Construction	114,954
Cosmetology	215,516
Csw/mf/mhc	7,174
Dentistry	34,217
Dieticians	2,921
Electrical	14,946
Electrolysis	0
Employee leasing	95
Engineers	34,562
Funeral	4,666
Geologist	1,706
Hearing aid spec.	1,366
Industrial hyg.	69
Interior designers	4,052
Land surveyors	4,430
Landscap arch.	1,499
Massage	15,020
Medical therapies	—
Medicine	57,041
Midwifery	40
Naturopath	56
Nursing	231,247
Nursing home admin.	2,559
Occupational ther.	4,091
Opticianry	4,880
Optometry	3,635
Osteopathic	5,590
Pharmacy	26,621
Physical ther.	10,644
Pilots	112
Podiatry	1,998

Cumulative License Totals (*Continued*)

Professions	92/93
Psychological exam.	2,937
Real estate appraisal	5,531
Real estate commission	321,330
Respiratory ther.	10,145
School psychology	478
Speech-language	4,313
Talent agencies	357
Veterinary medicine	7,431
Waste water mgmt.	14,639
	1,268,579

The Florida Bar lists lawyers qualified to practice in Florida as "members." Total members in good standing February 1, 1995.

Florida	42,130
Out-of-state	9,970
Foreign	109
Total	52,209
Members in selected counties:	
Broward	5,068
Dade	10,353
Hillsborough	3,419
Duval	2,029
Orange	3,051
Pinellas	2,357
Leon	2,366

The Department of Education reported the certification in 1993 of 111,849 teachers, not including Monroe County.

Miss Clare Bowen and the fifth grade of Leon High School, Tallahassee, in 1909. Florida State Archives

Electric Power

Before the turn of the century in Florida, enterprising businessmen installed small electric plants for their own use. They were soon asked by neighbors to sell some of the power produced perhaps as a surplus to, say, the making of ice. Thus, by accident rather than design, small electric utilities came into existence.

The first electric lights in Florida are said to have been installed at Jacksonville's luxurious St. James Hotel in 1883, with eight outlets in the lobby and eight outside. Since Edison invented the incandescent lamp in 1879 and the nation's pioneer central generating plant (New York's Pearl Street) was put in service in 1882, the St. James installation certainly was among the first in the country.

In Miami, Henry M. Flagler built the first plant in 1896 to serve his Royal Palm Hotel, then picked up private users in stringing a pole line to the depot of his Florida East Coast Railway some blocks away.

Florida has a significant place in the history of electricity for it was here, at Fort Myers, that Thomas A. Edison had his winter home and laboratory.

In time the sale of electric power by ice makers, hotels and others grew to the point where it became the preponderant business. Again using Miami as the example, Flagler built in 1904 a plant separate from the Royal Palm installation. The first plant for consumer use in the Miami area was a 200 kilowatt woodburner once the site of the Florida Power & Light steam electric station near the mouth of the Miami River. Its first power customer was the Miami Metropolis (later known as the Miami News) with a 3 horsepower motor to run.

Individual electric systems furnished service by 1900 to Lake City (1891), Palatka (1894), Jacksonville (first municipal, 1895), Monticello (1895), West Palm Beach (1895), Titusville (1895), Miami (1896), Fort Myers (1896), Key West (1899), Tampa (1900) and St. Petersburg (1896). Lake City's rates may serve as an example of those charged. There, in 1905, the rate was 35 cents a month for each 16-candlepower bulb.

By 1910 twenty-four hour service was quite generally available and most of the operations were no longer side lines of other businesses. In the larger cities street railways were electrically operated, as were many of the ice plants. Many of the wood burning plants had been converted to fuel oil and the diesel engine began to be widely used as a prime mover. The following years the utilities branched out and built lines to serve adjoining towns. Even at this time, however, the operations were primarily local in character and each small area was dependent upon its own plant.

The mushroom development of the state in the 1920's was accompanied by a revolutionary change in the development of the electric power industry. During the early years of this decade real estate developers who subdivided large tracts of land frequently found it necessary to put in their own electric and street railway systems. The existing local plants also expanded their facilities but were unable to keep up with the business growth. The generating stations were overloaded, breakdowns were frequent, and even in the major cities the service was frequently off on Sundays so that necessary maintenance and repair work could be done on the equipment.

Beginning about 1925 the first major systems in the state came into existence. The Florida Power Corporation, the Gulf Power Company, The Florida Public Service Company, and the Florida Power & Light Company were organized. Individual electric plants in numerous cities were purchased and long-distance transmission lines were constructed connecting plants in the various cities.

Florida's Electric Power Industry
Source: Florida Electric Power Coordinating Group

Year	Capacity As of Jan.1 in KW	Production in 1000 KWH	Year	Capacity As of Jan.1 in KW	Production in 1000 KWH
1940	499,096	1,769,591	1983	27,883,000	106,651,000
1950	1,029,352	5,610,410	1984	29,715,000	110,969,000
1960	3,846,402	19,710,996	1985	30,391,000	120,149,000
1970	13,482,000	55,469,000	1986	30,732,000	124,923,000
1975	19,059,000	77,047,000	1987	30,863,700	133,027,000
1976	22,170,000	80,957,000	1988	32,597,400	137,970,000
1977	30,757,000	86,803,000	1989	33,054,000	151,337,000
1978	24,581,000	92,024,000	1990	33,437,000	154,519,000
1979	24,583,000	93,995,000	1991	34,454,000	156,506,000
1980	24,583,000	99,761,000	1992	34,930,000	157,008,000
1981	24,879,000	102,757,000	1993	35,697,000	163,443,000
1982	26,798,000	101,305,000	1994	36,920,000	169,267,000

"Capacity" measures the maximum power output of generating units in power plants. "Production" refers to the kilowatt hours generated.

Nuclear Power

Florida's first two nuclear generating units went on line in 1972 and 1973 at Florida Power & Light Company's Turkey Point Plant in Dade County. Both units have capacity ratings of 666,000 kilowatts each.

FPL's third and fourth nuclear power plants went on line in 1976 and 1983; these plants are located mid-way between Ft. Pierce and Stuart on Hutchinson Island. Each unit is capacity rated at approximately 839,000 kilowatts.

Florida Power & Light Company estimates that a total of 295,835,495 barrels of residual oil were not used by reason of the operation of its four nuclear units through the end of 1987. This represents $4.9 billion of avoided costs for FPL customers in its service area since the "start-up" of Turkey Point Unit #1 in 1972.

On the west coast, Florida Power Corporation's 880,000-kilowatt nuclear generating unit at Crystal River became operational in March, 1977. The unit provides energy for Florida Power and 12 other utilities participating in ownership of the plant's output.

Resurgence of Coal/Oil

Jacksonville Electric Authority, together with Florida Power & Light Company, built two coal-fired generating plants in Duval County. Each unit is rated at 620 megawatts.

Florida Power Corporation completed change-over of two oil fired units at Crystal River to coal.

A 320-mile-long interconnection between Florida Power & Light Company and the Southern Companies was completed in 1985. This 500 kv "coal-by-wire" project allows FPL to purchase 2000 megawatts of power and transport it the length of the peninsula. It is a dual line.

The $350 million transmission line allows for a more diverse mix in the fuel used by Florida's largest electric utility and assists in securing additional reliability.

Turkey Point generating plant in Dade County uses both fossil fuels and nuclear reactors to produce electric energy. Department of Commerce, Division of Tourism

Telephone

Florida's first telephone exchange opened in Jacksonville on May 24, 1880. This was just 28 months after the world's first "central office" started functioning in New Haven, Conn. Only four years had elapsed since the first intelligible sentence had been transmitted over Alexander Graham Bell's experimental instrument.

The first telephones in use in Jacksonville antedated the exchange by two years. According to George W. Sparks, the Chronology of the Telephone in Jacksonville said, "It appears the first telephones in Jacksonville (and probably the first in Florida) were on a private line connecting the office of A. M. Beck, corner of Pine and Bay Streets, with the Inland Navigation Co. at foot of Laura Street, constructed in 1878."

A comparative handful of the big wooden telephones was installed and linked through that pioneer exchange at Jacksonville. Development in Florida was quite slow. By 1900, there were only 6,285 telephones in the entire state. Of these, Jacksonville had 822, Pensacola 408, Tampa 375, Gainesville 103, St. Augustine 72, Key West 60, and Fernandina 34.

Miamians first were served in 1898, with 25 subscribers paying $30 a year. The subscribers included Henry M. Flagler, Julia Tuttle, Flagler's Royal Palm Hotel and the *Miami Metropolis*. The first service, from a switchboard at the rear of a drug store, was limited to daytime, with the first operator, Miss Eunice Coons, leaving when the drug store closed. An occasional evening exception was made when John Dewey, the owner, arranged a musical program with all subscribers plugged in to enjoy the program.

"Hello girls" just had replaced young men as telephone operators when this photograph was taken of the Jacksonville central office switchboard. This board was installed in 1891 and removed in 1894.

Southern Bell

The first dial central office in Florida was established in 1913 in Tampa by the Peninsular Telephone Company, now a part of the General Telephone System. The largest company operating in the state, Southern Bell Telephone and Telegraph, converted its last manual office to dial service on June 4, 1961. This exchange was located in Lake City. The goal of 100 per cent dial operation for all telephone in Florida was achieved on August 31, 1961, when the Gulf Telephone Company at Perry converted.

Florida possesses the distinction of being the first state in the South and the fourth in the United States to reach full dial operation. The three preceding states were Connecticut, Rhode Island and Delaware.

Women replaced men as telephone operators for the first time in Florida at the Jacksonville exchange in 1884. (By 1982, the trend had reversed, if only slightly. There were 148 male operators in Greater Miami.) Long distance circuits were extended from Jacksonville to Miami in 1913 and to Key West in 1916.

The first commercial microwave system installed in Florida for long distance telephone transmission was completed in 1953 between Tampa and Bartow by Peninsular. Direct Distance Dialing, which enables a subscriber to dial his own long distance calls, was introduced in Florida in 1955 by the Intercounty Telephone & Telegraph Company (now the United Telephone Company). This made it possible for subscribers in Fort Myers to dial the neighboring exchange of Fort Myers Beach.

Telephone Stations

The Public Service Commission says the figure formerly reported for the number of instruments in use in Florida has become meaningless because subscribers now are able to furnish their own instruments.

The Commission had adopted the term "access line" as the element used in determining the amount of service provided. An "access line" is the line from the telephone company office to the subscriber premises.

In 1985 access lines totaled 5,837,685.

As of September 1992, there were 8,040,485 access lines providing service to Florida customers. There were 13 local telephone companies, but Southern Bell had 58% of the total, or 4,657,735 access lines.

There also were 157 competitive long distance companies and, 593 competitive pay telephone companies, and 46 shared tenant service providers. The number of the coin phone companies changes frequently with businesses getting in or out.

Florida's First Railroads

Florida's first operating railroad was the St. Joseph Railroad, which formally opened with mule-power in March, 1836. The eight-mile railroad linked St. Joseph Bay, on the Gulf of Mexico, with Lake Wimico, a bayou of the Apalachicola River.

The St. Joseph put the state's first steam locomotive into operation on September 5, 1836, when "a train of twelve cars containing upwards of 300 passengers passed over the railroad ... the trip ... was performed in the short space of twenty-five minutes."

The Leon Rail Way Company was chartered by the Legislative Council on February 11, 1831. This charter was repealed and the Leon Rail Road Company was incorporated February 6, 1832. This, too, died. Each charter projected a railroad from Tallahassee to the St. Marks River.

A new company, the Tallahassee Rail Road, was incorporated by legislative act of February 10, 1834. Construction was commenced in January, 1835. Months of haggling over land for the St. Marks River terminus ensued before the first steam locomotive traversed the 22 miles from Tallahassee to Port Leon in December 1837. The locomotive alternated for a time with mules and the locomotive finally was abandoned in favor of the more dependable mule power. The mules took five hours for the one-way trip.

Thus, the St. Joseph Railroad was the first in Florida, a distinction frequently claimed for the Tallahassee Rail Road. Also, neither was the first in the country, as the Baltimore and Ohio, the Chesterfield, the Charleston and Hamburg, the Camden and Amboy, the Mohawk and Hudson, and the Petersburg and Roanoke, all were in operation before the Tallahassee Rail Road Company was even chartered.

Railroad Mileage
Source: Department of Transportation

(These figures computed as of February 17, 1992.)

CSX Transportation	1,778
Florida East Coast	442
Apalachicola Northern	96
Atlanta & St. Andrews Bay	72
Burlington Northern	44
Florida Central	66
Florida Midland	40
Florida West Coast	29
Seminole Gulf	119
Florida Northern	26
Norfolk Southern	245

When the wealthy came to Miami by railroad in the 1920s, they brought trunks for stays of a month or more. Historical Association of Southern Florida

Seaboard System Railroad is now CSX Transportation; Live Oak, Perry & South Georgia, Georgia Southern & Florida, and St. Johns River Terminal Co. now are part of Norfolk Southern.

Alcoholic "Wet-Dry" Counties
Source: Department of Business Regulation

There were seven "dry" counties and 60 "wet" counties in Florida on January 1, 1994. A "dry" county is one in which only beverages not more than 5.0 percent alcohol by weight may be sold; whereas a "wet" county is one in which malt, vinous and spirituous beverages of up to 153 proof may be sold.

The counties classified as "dry" were as follows: Hardee, Lafayette, Liberty, Madison, Santa Rosa, Suwannee and Washington. Calhoun, Jackson, Holmes and Hamilton counties have voted to permit the sales of spirituous beverages by package only. In all other "wet" counties intoxicating beverages may be sold by package and by the drink.

Alcoholic Beverage Licenses

During the license year ending September 30, 1992, the State had issued 38,411 licenses for the sale, distribution, or manufacture of alcoholic beverages. Of that number 13,292 authorized package sale of beer and wine only; 10,957 sale of beer and wine with consumption on premises also allowed; 1,119 sale of beer with consumption on premises allowed; and 7,135 beer, wine and liquor with consumption on premises and by the package. Other licenses accounted for the difference in total licenses issued.

Growth of Condominiums

The Division of Florida Land Sales, Condominiums and Mobile Homes of the Department of Business and Professional Regulation assumed regulatory responsibility for the condominium industry on October 1, 1975. According to a U.S. Department of Housing and Urban Development study approximately 50% of all U.S. condominiums are in Florida. Russell McCaughan is credited with having created Florida's first condominium, a two-story, six-apartment building overlooking the ocean at 1288 Ocean Boulevard in Boca Baton. The first documents were filed in the Palm Beach County Court Clerk's office on November 20, 1962.

As of May 1994, Department of Business and Professional Regulation records reflected a total of 22,010 condominium complexes bringing the total individual units to 997,872. This does not include 784 cooperative complexes with 41,332 units. The condominiums ranged from ground level up to 42 stories.

Motor Vehicle Licenses

The first licenses (not metal plates) were issued in Florida for motor vehicles in 1906. A $2 fee was collected. By the end of 1906, according to the report of the Secretary of State, there were 296 automobiles registered in Florida, of which 11 were owned by non-residents. Interestingly, a fourth of the total number were in the city of Daytona Beach.

Napoleon B. Broward was governor at that time but, unlike today's chief executive, the No. 1 license was not issued to Governor Broward since he had no car. Instead, License No. 1 went to R.E. Brand of Jensen, for a vehicle manufactured by the Locomobile Company of America.

In 1908, the total registration had increased to 437, although automobiles still were regarded as a curiosity. County Tax Collectors began individually issuing metal plates in 1911, and the State in 1918 through the County Tax Collectors. The alpha numeric series was reversed after the issuance of 14,375,000 tags or decals.

During the fiscal year ending June 30, 1993, the Department of Highway Safety and Motor Vehicles licensed 16,257,801 vehicles, including 746,545 for

618 / Licences, Bonds

mobile homes and recreational vehicles. Excluded were temporary licenses and replacement tags.

In 1995 there were more than 60 different plates, tags or decals covering the kinds of vehicles licensed by the state. These included "horseless carriages," vehicles 35 years old, "goats," vehicles used primarily off highways in fields and woods for harvest purposes; "antiques," passenger automobiles manufactured 20 years prior to the current date, and "street rods," modified motor vehicles manufactured before 1949 and used for exhibitions and special functions but not regularly for transportation.

Individual plates are made for members of the Florida Legislature and of Congress, of the National Guard, wheelchair veterans, Paralyzed Veterans of America, Seminole and Miccosukee Indians, former Prisoners of War, Survivors of Pearl Harbor, recipients of the Congressional Medal of Honor, Foreign Honorary Consuls, members of the U.S. Reserve and of volunteer fire departments, the ten state universities, and commemorating the loss of the spaceship Challenger. There are also, plates honoring Veterans, Manatees, Panthers, the Super Bowl, and most recently education, children, sea turtles, professional sports teams and the Indian River Lagoon.

Manatee plates produced the greatest revenue of the specialized plates: $2,725,680 in 1992/93.

State-Supported Bonds

The ability of the State to issue bonds is detailed here by the Executive Director of the State Board of Administration: The Board of Administration has for its members the Governor, as chairman; the State Treasurer, as treasurer, and the State Comptroller, as secretary.

The Board of Administration has the responsibility for approval of legal and fiscal sufficiency prior to the issuance of State bonds.

The State Constitution authorizes the issuance of the three general classifications of bonds:

(1) State bonds pledging the full faith and credit of the State and payable from general revenue tax funds may be issued to finance the cost of State capital projects upon approval by a vote of the electors. Section ll(a), Article VII.

(3) Bonds payable from a constitutionally designated tax source, most of which must or may be additionally secured by the full faith and credit of the State, are authorized. Section 9, Article XII.

The issuance not to exceed $200,000,000 of bonds for environmentally endangered lands and $40,000,000 for outdoor recreation lands were authorized by the legislature and approved by a vote of the electors pursuant to the provisions of subsection 11(a), Article VII.

Revenue bonds that can now be issued under the 1968 Constitution, as amended, include bonds issued to finance toll roads or bridges, university dormitories, student centers, state office buildings, parking areas, etc., and payable solely from the revenue derived from the facility.

Types of revenue bonds authorized pledging a Constitutionally designated tax source are as follows:

(a) Outdoor Recreational bonds, Save Our Coast bonds, and Conservation and Recreation Lands bonds, payable primarily from documentary surtax and severance tax may be issued to acquire lands, water areas and related resources, and to construct, improve, enlarge and extend capital improvements thereon in furtherance of outdoor recreation, natural resources conservation and related purposes. Section 17, Article IX of the Constitution of 1885, and incorporated by reference in Section 9(a), Article XII of the Constitution of 1968.

(b) Higher Education bonds were issued to acquire capital outlay projects for institutions of higher learning, junior colleges, and vocational technical schools, payable solely from the Gross Receipts Taxes, Section 19, Article XII of the Constitution of 1885, and incorporated by reference in Section 9(a), Article XII of the Constitution of 1968.

Beginning July 1, 1975, and for 50 years thereafter, all of the proceeds of the revenues derived from the "Gross Receipts Taxes" (subject to the prior liens on outstanding debt above) are pledged to secure Public Education Bonds, including institutions of higher learning, junior colleges, vocational technical schools, or public schools. These Public Education Bonds are additionally secured by the full faith and credit of the State.

(c) State bonds to finance the acquisition of roads and bridges pledging the full faith and credit of the State may be issued without any election. These bonds are payable primarily from the Constitutional second gasoline tax or a combination of gas tax and tolls and must be additionally secured by the full faith and credit. Section 9(c), Article XII.

(d) State Board of Education capital outlay bonds may be issued to finance education facilities for grades "K" through 12 and junior colleges. These bonds pledge a portion of the State motor vehicle license taxes and are additionally secured under existing law by the full faith and credit of the State. Section 18, Article XII, of the Constitution of 1885, as amended, and incorporated by reference in Section 9(d), Article XII, of the Constitution of 1968.

There are two types of bonds authorized to be issued that do not fit into the three general classifications above:

(1) State bonds pledging the full faith and credit of the State to finance the construction of pollution control and abatement facilities for a local governmental agency, may be issued by the State without an election. The bonds are payable primarily from revenue derived from operation of the facility and any other legally available tax or revenue legally available for such purposes and may be additionally secured by the full faith and credit of the local agency. The bonds must be additionally secured by the full faith and credit of the State. Section 14, Article VII.

(2) The only revenue bonds authorized to be issued to finance anything other than State capital outlay projects are the student loan revenue bonds authorized by Section 15, Article VII of the revised Constitution. These bonds are payable from loan repayments and are additionally secured by certain student fees and they are further secured by a government insurance guarantee, but are not additionally secured by the full faith and credit of the State. Section 15, Article VII.

Florida's Bonded Indebtedness in Thousands
Administered by State Board of Administration
1993

Bond Type	Amount Outstanding	Interest Rates	Annual Maturity To
GENERAL LONG-TERM DEBT ACCOUNT GROUP			
Road and Bridge Bonds	$ 453,575	2.90–10.75	2022
SBE Capital Outlay Bonds	212,790	3.80–10.00	2007
Public Education Bonds	3,844,895	4.00–9.125	2025
Conservation Act Bonds	38,130	5.75–10.90	2012
Environmental Conservation Bonds	22,355	4.50–5.50	1995
Save Our Coast Bonds	260,605	5.25–12.00	2012
Preservation 2000 Bonds	879,300	4.00–6.75	2013
Pollution Control Bonds	653,520	4.50–9.125	2017
	6,365,170		
ENTERPRISE FUNDS			
Toll Facilities Bonds	2,108,143	3.00–10.00	2023
Florida Housing Finance Agency Bonds	2,362,983	3.90–13.40 (Some floating/ variable rates)	2034
Less Payable from Restricted Assets	52,031		
	4,419,095		
INTERNAL SERVICE FUND			
Florida Facility Pool Bonds	212,499	4.80–7.25	2020
STATE UNIVERSITY SYSTEM			
State University System	225,045	2.75–7.70	2023
TOTAL BONDS PAYABLE	$11,221,809		

Source: Comprehensive Annual Financial Report of the Comptroller

Ad Valorem Tax Valuation 1992
Source: Department of Revenue

Taxable Value—Real Property	$501,638,271
Taxable Value—Personal Property	58,586,918
Taxable Value—Centrally Assessed	595,416
Total Taxable Value	560,820,605
Constitutional Homestead Exempt Value	32,962,311
Total Exempt & Immune Value	170,329,831

"Centrally assessed" property means railroad and private car operating equipment. Telegraph property now is assessed as personal and/or real property. Non-exempt value and taxable value are the same. Valuations for county and school purposes are identical.

Total Local Taxes as a Percent of Personal Income Fiscal Year 1990-91

Rank		Percent	Rank		Percent
1	New York	7.87%	25	Pennsylvania	4.14%
2	New Hampshire	6.20%	26	Iowa	4.13%
3	Alaska	5.90%	27	Georgia	4.11%
4	Orgeon	5.58%	28	Minnesota	3.96%
5	Colorado	5.21%	29	California	3.86%
6	Wyoming	5.12%	30	Utah	3.76%
7	Vermont	5.08%	31	Massachusetts	3.71%
8	New Jersy	4.98%	32	Indiana	3.71%
9	Michigan	4.94%	33	Montana	3.57%
10	Texas	4.84%	34	Missouri	3.50%
11	Nebraska	4.77%	35	North Dakota	3.49%
12	Illinois	4.73%	36	Washington	3.31%
13	South Dakota	4.58%	37	Tennessee	3.27%
14	Rhode Island	4.58%	38	Nevada	3.19%
15	Wisconsin	4.52%	39	North Carolina	3.01%
16	Arizona	4.50%	40	South Carolina	2.95%
17	Ohio	4.48%	41	Oklahoma	2.93%
18	Connecticut	4.43%	42	Idaho	2.90%
	U.S. Average	**4.42%**	43	Mississippi	2.65%
19	Maine	4.42%	44	Alabama	2.58%
20	Kansas	4.42%	45	New Mexico	2.56%
21	Maryland	4.36%	46	Hawaii	2.56%
22	Virginia	4.33%	47	Kentucky	2.37%
23	Louisiana	4.26%	48	West Virginia	2.36%
24	**Florida**	**4.18%**	49	Arkansas	2.32%
			50	Delaware	1.76%

- Florida ranks 24th in the percent of personal income used to pay for all local taxes.
- Other local revenue sources—such as federal and state shared revenue or charges for services—are not included in this ranking.
- Local property taxes in Florida make up 83% of local taxes compared to 75% in the U.S.

Source: Overview of State Agencies and their programs. Florida House of Representatives

Elections

The legal basis for Florida's system of elections is provided by Article VI of the State Constitution and Chapters 97–106 of the Florida Statutes, generally referred to as the Election Code.

It is important to note that the Legislature makes frequent changes in the Election Code from session to session and that judicial decisions in this area are having an increasingly strong impact in shaping Florida's election laws. It is therefore prudent to refer to the latest edition of the Florida Statutes and the most recent Laws of Florida for up-to-date information in this area. Inquiries may also be directed to the Division of Elections of the Department of State in Tallahassee.

1996 Election Dates

First primary Election and First Nonpartisan Judicial Election . . . September 3.

Second Primary Election . . . October 8.

General Election . . . November 5.

General elections.—General elections are held on the first Tuesday after the first Monday in November in even-numbered years. All Federal, state, legislative, and county offices are filled at a general election. Proposed amendments to the State Constitution are submitted to the electorate for acceptance or rejection. All registered voters may participate in a general election regardless of party registration.

Primary elections.—Primary elections are held to choose the nominees of a political party to run in the general election. Only those voters registered in a given party may vote in that party's primaries.

First primary.—The first primary election is held on the Tuesday nine weeks before the general election in each year that a general election is to be held. The candidate who receives a majority of the votes cast in his contest in the first primary becomes the nominee of his party at the general election. If no candidate in a given contest receives a majority in the first primary, the nominee for that office is chosen in the second primary (runoff) election.

Second primary.—The second primary election is held on the Tuesday five weeks prior to the general election.

The names of the candidates placing first and second in the first primary are placed on the second primary ballot except under the following circumstances:

This is an excerpt from an article on Florida elections by John French which appeared in prior editions of *The Florida Handbook.* Mr. French was Staff Director for the Committee on Elections of the House of Representatives and Executive Director for The Florida Democratic Party. He presently is a partner in the law firm of Pennington, Haben, Wilkinson, Culpepper, Dunlap, Dunbar, Richmond and French..

1. *Tie for first.*—When there is a tie for first in the first primary, only the names of those tying are placed on the second primary ballot.
2. *Tie for second.*—When the first primary results in a tie for second, the name of the candidate placing first and the names of the candidates tying for second are placed on the second primary ballot.

The person receiving the highest number of votes cast in his contest in the second primary election becomes his party's nominee in the general election for the office sought. If the second primary results in a tie for first, the tying candidates draw lots to determine the nominee.

Unopposed candidates.—When a candidate is unopposed for his party's nomination, he is considered nominated and his name does not appear on the primary ballot. The name of an unopposed candidate does not appear on the general election ballot unless a write-in candidate has qualified pursuant to law.

Judicial elections.—Justices of the Florida Supreme Court and judges of the district courts of appeal are appointed by the Governor as the culmination of a formal selection process. However, the electorate is given the opportunity every six years to vote on whether they retain their judicial offices. In such elections, the issue posed is, "Shall Justice (Judge) _____ be retained in office?" The justice or judge is retained if a majority votes in favor of his retention; if not, the office is deemed vacant and the selection/appointment processes are commenced to fill the vacancy.

Circuit court judges and county judges are elected in nonpartisan judicial elections which coincide with the first primary and the general elections, respectively. As in partisan elections, the names of unopposed candidates do not appear on the judicial ballot unless write-in candidates have qualified pursuant to law. When there are two or more candidates for a judicial post, their names appear on the ballot for the first nonpartisan election, conducted concurrently with the first primary. If no candidate receives a majority of the votes cast, the names of the two candidates receiving the highest number of votes are listed on the second nonpartisan election which is conducted concurrently with the general election. If the second nonpartisan election results in a tie, the winner is determined by lot.

Chapter 105, Florida Statutes, restricts partisan political activities by or on behalf of candidates for judicial office. Judicial candidates report their contributions and expenses on the same basis as other candidates for public office.

Presidential preference primary.—A presidential preference primary is held on the second Tuesday in March of each presidential election year (in 1996, March 12), for the purpose of allowing the voters of a given party to indicate their preference as to who should be their party's nominee for President of the United States. A further explanation of procedures used in this election may be found in a later section relating to political parties.

Vacancies in Office or in Nomination

Vacancies in office.—When an elective office becomes vacant due to the death, resignation, or removal of the officeholder, the vacancy is filled either by a special election or by appointment by the Governor, depending on the office in question.

United States Senate.—When a vacancy occurs in the United States Senate, the Governor may appoint someone to the office until the vacancy has been filled at the next general election.

State Legislature and United States House of Representatives.—When a vacancy occurs in the Florida Legislature or in the United States House of Representatives (vacancies which may not be filled by appointment), the Governor calls a special election to fill the vacated seat. This in turn requires the calling of party primaries for the selection of party nominees.

Other state and county offices.—Article IV, Section (1)(f) of the Florida Constitution states that, when not otherwise provided, the Governor shall fill by appointment any vacancy in state or county office for the remainder of the term of an elective office if less than twenty-eight months, otherwise until the first Tuesday after the first Monday following the next general election. Vacancies in statutory office are generally filled by the Governor for the unexpired term. However, there are a few such offices in which vacancies are filled until the next general election, at which time candidates run for election to the unexpired term.

Special elections to fill vacancies in office or in nomination.—When death, resignation, withdrawal, removal, or any other cause or event creates a vacancy in office or in nomination after the last date for filing for a special or primary election and thus leaves no candidates for nomination or election to a county, district, or state office, the Governor, after conferring with the Secretary of State, calls a special primary election and, if necessary, a second primary election to select nominees of recognized political parties to fill the vacancy in nomination or in office. The Secretary of State fixes the latest practicable filing date and also the dates for candidates to file reports of contributions and expenditures.

In the event the vacancy in nomination or in office occurs later than September 15 of a general election year, special primaries are not called and nominations are made by the appropriate state, congressional district, or county executive committee of the political party losing the candidate or nominee.

Presidential Electors

Nomination by Governor.—The Governor nominates the presidential electors of all political parties who have elected a president of the United States subsequent to January 1, 1900. He nominates the electors from among persons recommended by the state executive committees of the political parties and may nominate only persons who are qualified electors and who have taken an oath that they will vote for the candidate of the party that they are nominated to represent. The Governor certifies to the Secretary of State on or before September 1 in a presidential election year, the names of a number of persons for each political party equal to the number of senators and representatives that Florida has in Congress. These persons are nominated as the electors from this state for President and Vice President of the United States.

A minority political party may devise its own method of selecting its presidential electors.

Number of electors.—Each state is entitled to as many electoral votes as the total of its senators and representatives in Congress. Florida has two United States Senators and 23 Representatives and is thus entitled to 25 electoral votes.

Election of Presidential electors.—The names of a party's candidates for President and Vice President appear on the general election ballot instead of the names of that party's nominees for presidential electors. The nominees for presidential elector of the party whose candidate for President receives the most votes in Florida are elected as Florida's presidential electors.

Oldest Woman Elected

Jessie Alma "Granny" Edge first was elected at 83 in July 1983, as a City Councilman of Niceville. She was then believed to be the oldest elected public officer in Florida and perhaps the United States. She defeated a lawyer and a businessman in polling 52 percent of the vote.

Mrs. Edge once said: "I have sixteen grandchildren and six great-grandchildren. I've spent much of my life working for them. Now, as a Council member, I work for the senior citizens and everyone in Niceville. I don't have time to think about myself. If I did, I might get old."

First under 21 to Vote

The Associated Press reported that Miss Rhonda Spence, a 20-year-old student, stepped into a voting booth at DeFuniak Springs on Tuesday, July 13, 1971, and became the first person under the age of twenty-one to vote in Florida.

The daughter of Mr. and Mrs. C. E. Spence was among sixty-six electors between the ages of eighteen and twenty qualified to participate in the election of three city councilmen.

A 20-year-old sailor, Lennie H. Andrews, turned in an absentee ballot on Friday preceding the election but his ballot was opened after Miss Spence voted.

Woman's Suffrage

Florida was slow to move on statewide woman's suffrage. When the Legislature did ratify the 19th Amendment to the United States Constitution, it was a symbolic gesture occurring a half century after 38 other states had done so meaningfully.

The 19th Amendment was submitted to the states by Congress on June 8, 1919, and ratification by sufficient states had been achieved by August 26, 1920. Florida's action occurred on May 13, 1969, and was taken in recognition of the Florida League of Women Voters, an offshoot nationally of the American Woman Suffrage Association.

Florida women unsuccessfully had urged their legislators since the 1890s to adopt woman's suffrage. In 1917, however, the right to vote in city elections had been granted women at Florence Villa, Moore Haven, Palm Beach and Pass-a-Grille, and in 1918 at DeLand, Aurantia, Daytona, Daytona Beach and Orange City.

First Woman Voter

An election for mayor and constable in Sneads on August 27, 1920, gave Mrs. Fay Bridges the opportunity of being Florida's first woman to vote the day after the U.S. Secretary of State proclaimed ratification of the 19th Amendment. She cast her ballot at a polling station on the porch of the general store where she worked in the Jackson County community.

First Florida Election with Black Participation

Jerrell H. Shofner, in *Nor Is It Over Yet,* wrote that the election of Adolphus Mot as Mayor of Fernandina in 1865 "must have been the first Florida election in which Negroes participated." Chief Justice Salmon P. Chase of the United States, on a political visit to Florida at the time, administered the oath to Mot, a Republican. Shofer wrote that Mot was a "well-educated French immigrant, " formerly on the personal staff of Chase when he was Secretary of the Treasury. Mot had come to Fernandina to grow olives.

First Woman Sheriff

Source: *The Miami Herald*

When Sheriff Claude Simmons of Okeechobee County was felled by pneumonia in 1938, his widow, Eugenia, was left with three teen-age children to support. The townspeople decided she ought to be named Sheriff until an election could be called, and Governor Fred P. Cone agreed. So she became Florida's first woman Sheriff. The Simmons family moved into an apartment at the jail, and Sheriff Simmons fed the prisoners the same fare her family received. She never carried a gun or wore a badge. The workaday duties were performed by her husband's brother, Cossie, who had been his deputy and who succeeded him by election. Mrs. Simmons was not a candidate. She served nine months. In 1975, she was Mrs. Eugenia Simmons Bowden, twice-widowed, with 14 children or grandchildren. She told The Miami Herald's Al Burt, "To tell you the truth, I never did really feel like I was the Sheriff."

First Woman Police Chief

Source: *The Miami Herald*

When Mrs. Sue Wegner was sworn in by Mayor Lucie Black as police chief of Minneola on August 21, 1979, she was regarded as Florida's first. Chief Wegner, married and the mother of two teenagers, headed a force of six in Minneola, a Central Florida community of some 1,000. She was a sergeant and the police department's senior officer when she was appointed by City Manager Richard D. Waters.

Political Convention Votes for Floridians

U.S. Senator George A. Smathers received 30 votes for President at the 1960 Democratic National Convention. Since John F. Kennedy was nominated on the first ballot, Florida's votes for Smathers, as a favorite son holding votes in reserve for Kennedy, meant the state was not in the winner's column. In addition to Florida's 29 votes, Smathers also received a half vote each from Alabama and North Carolina.

Other votes for Floridians were cast in Vice Presidential balloting. Claude Pepper, first U.S. Senator and then Congressman, received three votes each at the 1944 and 1972 Democratic conventions. Governor LeRoy Collins was given 28½ votes at the 1976 Democratic convention. U.S. Senator Duncan U. Fletcher received seven votes at the 1928 Democratic convention. J. Leonard Replogle of Palm Beach, Republican national committeeman, won 23¾ votes at the 1932 Republican convention. Since Florida had 16 votes at that convention, it is obvious that Replogle received votes elsewhere but *Convention Decisions and Voting Records* does not indicate the source of these.

First Primary Election

W.T. Cash, in his *History of the Democratic Party in Florida,* said a Monroe County primary in 1876 "probably was the first held in Florida."

Jeptha V. Harris sought the Democratic nomination for member of the Florida House of Representatives. "Believing that a convention would not pick him," wrote Cash, "he raised such a protest in behalf of leaving nominations up to the people that a primary was called in which he was selected by a majority of the voters as the party's candidate. He won out in the election. Harris should probably be given credit for being the father of primary nominations in Florida."

18-Year-Old Elected to City Council

John Rama was 18 years old and a high school senior when first elected on February 8, 1977, to the City Council of Belleair Beach. He is said to be the first 18-year-old elected to public office in Pinellas County and possibly in Florida.

First Straw Ballot
March 4, 1972

Prohibit forced busing—1,127,631 for; 396,778 against.
Equal education—1,095,879 for; 293,775 against.
Prayer in school—1,171,711 for; 300,745 against.

Registered Voters 1994
Summary by Party and Race

Party	White	Black	Other	Total
Democrat	2,645,910	558,210	41,398	3,245,518
Republican	2,672,062	31,580	43,432	2,747,074
American Taxpayer	161	12	4	177
Florida Socialist Workers	54	13	5	72
Green Party	437	5	11	453
Independent Party of Fla.	417	40	17	474
Independent Party	32,358	1,202	843	34,403
Libertarian	3,472	49	64	3,585
Populist	73	4	4	81
United States Taxpayers	30	4	1	35
Whig	39	6	0	45
Total	5,845,494	614,384	99,720	6,599,598

Compiled by the Department of State, Division of Elections

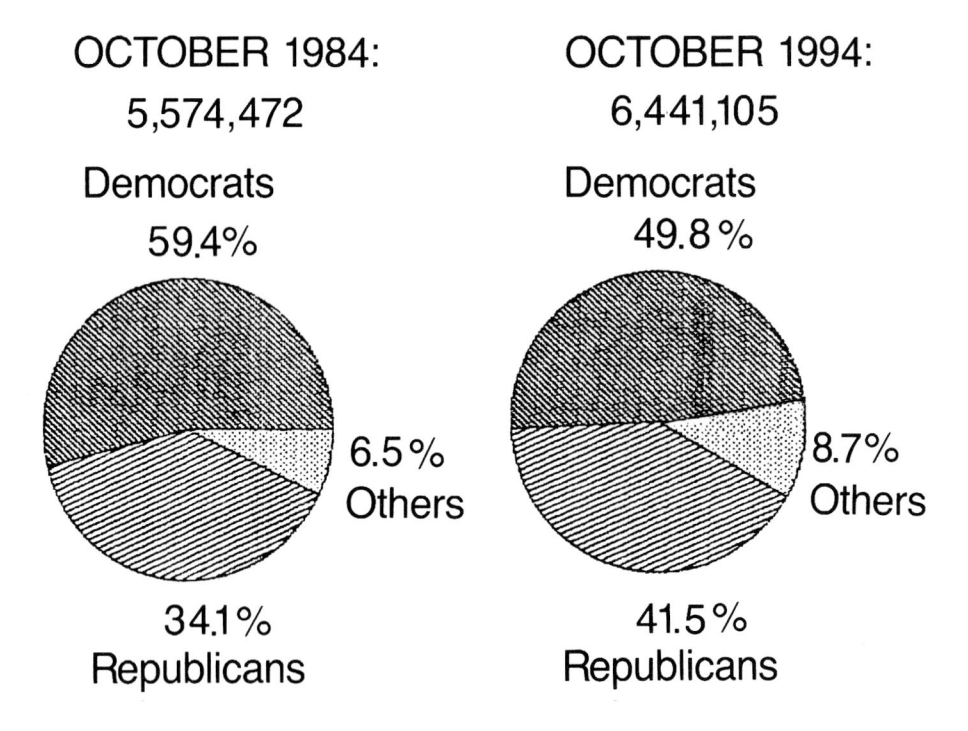

OCTOBER 1984:
5,574,472

Democrats 59.4%
6.5% Others
34.1% Republicans

OCTOBER 1994:
6,441,105

Democrats 49.8%
8.7% Others
41.5% Republicans

1988—Democrats—3,264,105 reg./6,047,347 total reg. = 53.9758
Republicans—2,360,434 reg./6,047,347 total reg. = 39.0325
Others—422,808 reg./6,047,347 total reg. = 6.9916
1992—Democrats—3,318,565 reg./6,541,825 total reg. = 50.7284
Republicans—2,672,968 reg./6,541,825 total reg. = 40.8596
Others—550,292 reg./6,541,825 total reg. = 8.4119

Florida Voter Turnout in Presidential Election Years

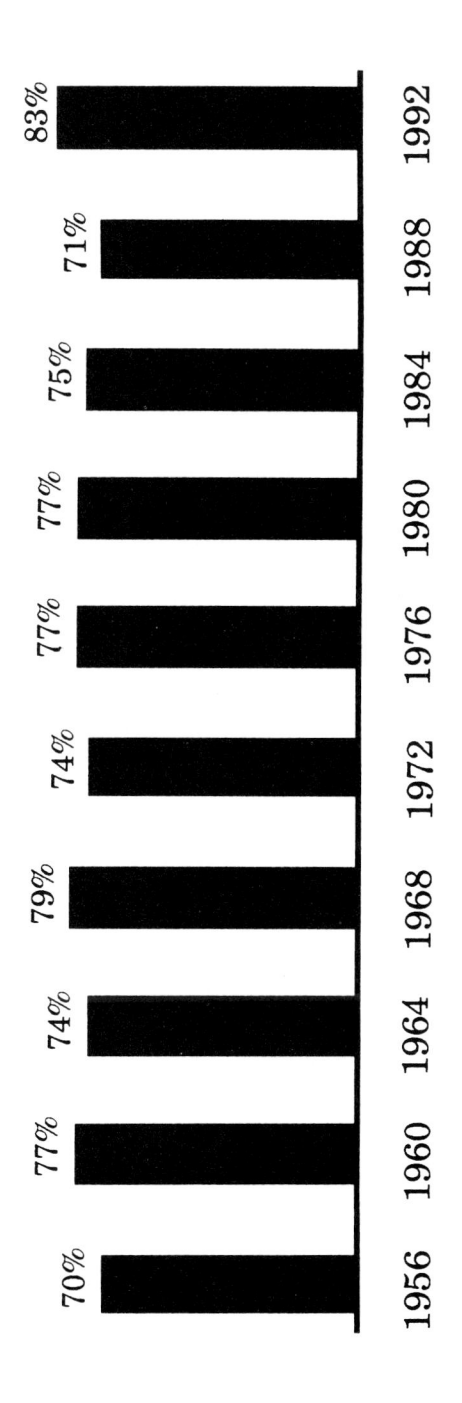

Year	Turnout
1956	70%
1960	77%
1964	74%
1968	79%
1972	74%
1976	77%
1980	77%
1984	75%
1988	71%
1992	83%

Florida Department of State Division of Elections
County Voter Registration
August 8, 1994

County	Democrat	Republican	Minor Parties* INT	LIB	No Party Affiliation	White	Black	Other	Total	Precincts
Alachua	54,677	26,428	119	192	8,282	77,064	11,121	1,613	89,798	48
Baker	9,294	627	9	1	53	8,907	1,076	1	9,984	16
Bay	38,304	19,572	1,923	31	2,041	57,084	4,539	254	61,877	41
Bradford	8,640	1,225	0	3	257	8,855	1,254	17	10,126	19
Brevard	98,374	112,302	184	186	17,193	216,838	11,208	227	228,273	154
Broward	362,042	228,246	3	214	63,275	581,290	63,006	9,546	653,842	597
Calhoun	5,861	284	0	0	26	5,452	694	26	6,172	13
Charlotte	30,674	43,390	16	28	6,167	77,803	1,709	774	80,286	60
Citrus	28,736	23,225	11	8	5,252	56,429	774	34	57,237	30
Clay	19,937	27,634	42	21	5,443	50,381	1,882	816	53,079	45
Collier	21,651	54,066	174	43	6,500	78,961	985	2,494	82,440	83
Columbia	15,592	4,479	52	13	542	17,818	2,869	0	20,687	30
Dade	336,999	255,618	95	163	61,400	510,311	128,034	16,006	654,351	578
Desoto	7,304	2,237	265	1	23	8,701	1,061	68	9,830	15
Dixie	6,904	552	82	4	33	7,128	447	0	7,575	11
Duval	196,053	105,206	751	170	18,430	242,573	74,318	3,764	320,655	235
Escambia	75,610	45,862	77	76	5,858	107,313	18,448	1,747	127,508	97
Flagler	9,242	9,456	35	11	1,904	19,005	1,365	281	20,651	19
Franklin	5,439	443	0	2	54	5,341	587	10	5,938	8
Gadsden	16,673	1,172	0	0	243	8,616	9,410	62	18,088	16
Gilchrist	4,933	702	30	3	84	5,597	147	8	5,752	10
Glades	3,743	839	106	2	15	4,047	428	230	4,705	12
Gulf	7,011	818	0	3	60	6,704	1,175	14	7,893	14
Hamilton	5,784	261	36	0	0	4,122	1,943	16	6,081	8
Hardee	7,149	1,153	2	0	110	7,306	624	490	8,420	11
Hendry	7,684	2,182	10	1	274	8,838	1,217	96	10,151	22
Hernando	32,590	33,531	5	19	6,180	70,295	1,603	445	72,343	46
Highlands	19,129	17,369	5	5	709	35,929	1,883	647	38,459	24
Hillsborough	193,010	138,834	1,240	296	37,145	323,554	38,333	8,405	370,292	277
Holmes	7,570	379	921	0	20	7,824	155	12	7,991	16
Indian River	17,650	31,517	21	13	3,343	50,630	2,122	76	52,828	37
Jackson	16,336	2,113	293	0	233	14,791	3,866	31	18,688	26
Jefferson	5,010	624	5	0	48	3,728	2,024	0	5,752	13
Lafayette	3,216	114	70	0	15	3,154	191	0	3,345	5

Florida Department of State Division of Elections
County Voter Registration
August 8, 1994 (*Continued*)

County	Democrat	Republican	Minor Parties* INT	Minor Parties* LIB	No Party Affiliation	White	Black	Other	Total	Precincts
Lake	32,994	44,239	292	29	5,095	79,255	3,402	0	82,657	74
Lee	73,206	106,009	28	103	17,952	190,255	5,858	1,202	197,315	142
Leon	70,905	27,680	66	77	10,354	84,701	22,160	2,301	109,162	93
Levy	10,882	2,489	374	0	64	12,783	991	35	13,809	21
Liberty	3,105	90	0	0	4	2,859	342	0	3,201	8
Madison	7,029	687	63	0	43	5,337	2,473	13	7,823	11
Manatee	47,892	63,252	78	68	10,392	115,808	5,124	786	121,718	107
Marion	49,551	43,521	74	43	7,683	93,797	7,093	0	100,890	82
Martin	19,312	40,756	1,775	19	3,736	63,815	1,808	0	65,623	34
Monroe	19,306	15,535	219	66	3,508	36,892	1,513	234	38,639	26
Nassau	16,333	6,432	58	8	706	21,702	1,858	11	23,571	17
Okaloosa	30,487	39,111	57	91	5,641	70,037	4,031	1,332	75,400	44
Okeechobee	10,073	3,100	1	0	286	12,477	725	259	13,461	18
Orange	112,586	126,463	1,918	291	18,900	216,166	25,967	18,094	260,227	204
Osceola	25,850	23,565	2,438	20	2,528	46,755	1,847	5,805	54,407	56
Palm Beach	234,231	196,528	365	147	56,699	455,517	32,243	275	488,035	437
Pasco	79,313	74,415	25	68	15,792	166,645	1,702	1,313	169,660	116
Pinellas	197,471	227,724	9,039	334	45,094	449,605	26,401	3,751	479,757	337
Polk	96,309	68,247	20	51	7,559	155,520	15,439	1,237	172,196	150
Putnam	24,772	7,924	1,160	5	422	29,924	3,948	427	34,299	55
Santa Rosa	30,020	21,267	155	22	2,465	51,814	1,603	515	53,932	30
Sarasota	57,948	107,552	0	75	14,429	176,236	3,520	259	180,015	130
Seminole	51,190	74,671	416	123	10,615	124,498	7,465	5,081	137,044	133
St. Johns	24,161	24,043	32	34	3,111	48,365	2,698	339	51,402	45
St. Lucie	42,244	40,260	3,483	37	7,221	83,098	9,646	513	93,257	67
Sumter	10,274	4,461	18	3	523	13,667	1,553	64	15,284	17
Suwannee	12,254	2,381	345	3	6	13,204	1,771	14	14,989	16
Taylor	8,093	753	29	1	22	7,754	1,080	65	8,899	14
Union	4,420	219	4	2	31	4,026	631	19	4,676	11
Volusia	101,414	85,361	810	119	14,732	189,163	12,244	1,069	202,476	178
Wakulla	7,760	1,090	19	5	179	8,097	942	18	9,057	12
Walton	12,717	4,043	18	3	560	16,337	919	85	17,341	33
Washington	8,510	1,110	106	6	53	8,689	1,062	35	9,786	15
TOTAL	3,211,433	2,677,438	30,062	3,362	517,617	5,747,187	600,557	93,361	6,441,105	5,369

Distribution of 1994 Candidate Qualifying Fees

GENERAL REVENUE
Federal Democrats and Republicans	$ 50,874.88	
State Democrats and Republicans	86,401.61	
Nonpartisan (Circuit)	558,996.00	
Nonpartisan (County)	402,248.10	
Total		$1,098,520.59

DEMOCRATIC EXECUTIVE COMMITTEE
Federal Candidates	$123,446.40	
State Candidates	205,726.75	
County Candidates*	282,011.41	
Total		$ 611,184.56

REPUBLICAN EXECUTIVE COMMITTEE
Federal Candidates	$140,280.00	
State Candidates	235,104.33	
County Candidates*	197,873.10	
Total		$ 573,167.43

ELECTIONS COMMISSION TRUST FUND
(1% Election Assessment)
Federal Democrats and Republicans	$ 64,128.00	
State Democrats and Republicans	106,204.67	
Nonpartisan Candidates (Circuit)	186,368.00	
All County Candidates	292,401.37	
Total		$ 649,102.04

CAMPAIGN FINANCING TRUST FUND
(1.5% Election Assessment)
Federal Democrats and Republicans	$ 96,192.00	
State Democrats and Republicans	159,197.34	
Nonpartisan (Circuit)	279,499.00	
All County Candidates	427,662.82	
Total		$ 962,551.16
GRAND TOTAL		$3,894,525.69

*The amount of the qualifying fees from county candidates distributed to the political parties was obtained from a survey of the Supervisors of Elections. Information from eleven counties was not received and is not included in the totals.

Source: Overview of State Agencies and their Programs. Florida House of Representatives

Votes on Significant Amendments
(1885 and 1968 Constitutions)

Right-to-work, 1944—147,860 for; 122,770 against.

Homestead exemption, 1934—123,484 for; 40,842 against.

Approve legislative apportionment with 42 Senate districts (two in most populous county) and 112 Representatives (at least one from each county), 1964—345,637 for; 643,832 against.

Bonds for four or more lane highways, 1965—280,103 for; 429,630 against.

Ratify basic document revising 1885 Constitution, 1968—645,233 for; 518,940 against.

Allow 18-year-olds to vote, 1970—501,764 for; 754,282 against.

Four-year terms for State Representatives, 1970—435,052 for; 675,473 against.

Allow tax on income of corporations, 1971—841,433 for; 355,023 against.

"Sunshine Amendment" to require public officers to file net worth statement (on ballot by petition), 1976—1,765,626 for; 461,940 against.

Supreme Court Justices and District Court of Appeal Judges to be appointed by Governor upon recommendation of Nominating Commissions, with retention vote every six years, 1976—1,600,944 for; 527,056 against.

Legalize casino gambling in certain areas of Dade and Broward counties, on ballot by petition, 1978—687,460 for; 1,720,275 against.

Abolish elective Cabinet, 1978—540,979 for; 1,614,630 against.

Allow counties and cities, with voter approval, to grant tax exemptions to new and expanded businesses, 1980—916,043 for; 541,630 against.

Revision commission's package of eight amendments, 1978—1,058,574 (highest number) for; 1,614,630 (highest number) against, all rejected.

Modify jurisdiction of Supreme Court, 1980—940,420 for; 460,266 against.

Provide a homestead exemption increase up to $25,000 in 1982, 1980—1,251,096 for; 289,620 against.

Allow casino gambling in specified areas after local referendum, 1986—1,056,250 for; 2,237,555 against.

Authorize State-operated lotteries, 1986—2,039,437 for; 1,168,856 against.

Authorize bonds for highways, 1988—2,141,984 for; 1,602,965 against.

Establish English as official language, 1988—3,457,039 for; 664,861 against.

Limit non-economic damages in civil actions, 1988—1,837,041 for; 2,394,932 against.

Establish taxation and budget reform commission, 1988—2,111,320 for; 1,538,470 against.

Commence legislative sessions earlier, 1990—2,605,350 for; 511,970 against.

Handgun waiting period, 1990—2,824,582 for; 530,377 against.

Open government, 1990—2,784,968 for; 380,786 against.

Public access, 1992—3,783,747 for; 769,864 against.

Eight year term limit for Florida's state and federal officers, 1992—3,513,938 for; 1,067,370 against.

Residential property taxes capped at 3-percent or inflation, whichever is less, 1992—2,417,961 for; 2,095,536 against.

Number of Amendments Submitted to Voters

The electors were faced with accepting or rejecting amendments in these selected years:

1956—12	1976—9, 1 by initiative	1990—4
1962—9	1978—9, 1 by initiative	1992—10, two by initiative
1964—13	1984—8	1994—5, four by initiative
1966—13	1988—11, two by initiative	

The Amendments Proposed to Voters in 1994

Amendment 1, proposed by the Legislature, to provide that the annual 60-day regular sessions of the Legislature begin on the first Tuesday after the first Monday in March
——Yes: 2,713,189   No: 955,223

Amendment 2, proposed by a tax reform group, would limit state revenue collections to the prior year's allowed revenue plus an adjustment for growth based on the growth rate of state personal income over the preceding five years, with excess collections deposited in the budget stabilization fund until fully funded and then refunded to taxpayers. Defines "state revenues." Allows the Legislature to increase this limit by 2/3 vote. Requires adjustment of the limitation to reflect transfers of responsibility for funding governmental functions.
——Yes: 2,182,411   No: 1,489,268

Amendment 3, proposed by citizen's initiative would limit the use of nets for catching saltwater finfish, shellfish, or other marine animals by prohibiting the use of gill and other entangling nets in all Florida waters, and prohibiting the use of other nets larger than 500 square feet in mesh area in nearshore and inshore Florida waters. Provides definitions, administrative and criminal penalties, and exceptions for scientific and governmental purposes.
——Yes: 2,876,091   No:1,135,110

Amendment 4, proposed by citizen's initiative would expand the people's rights to initiate constitutional changes limiting the power of government to raise revenue by allowing amendments to cover multiple subjects.
——Yes: 2,167,305   No: 1,560,635

Amendment 8, proposed by citizen's initiative would authorize a limited number of gaming casinos in Broward, Dade, Duval, Escambia, Hills-

LeRoy Collins campaign headquarters on election night.   Red Kerce photo, Florida State Archives

borough, Lee, Orange, Palm Beach and Pinellas Counties, with two in Miami Beach; and limited-size casinos with existing and operating pari-mutuel facilities; and if authorized by the legislature up to five limited-size riverboat casinos in the remaining counties, but only one per county.
——Yes: 1,566,451 No: 2,555,492

Political Party Officers

Democratic

State Headquarters: *Executive Director,* Lynda Russell Stonecipher, 517 N. Calhoun, P.O. Box 1758, Tallahassee 32301. (904) 222-3411.

Officers, State Executive Committee: *Chairman,* Terrie Brady, State Headquarters. *Vice Chairman,* Jon Ausman, State Headquarters. *Secretary,* Juanita Geather, 346 O Street Southwest, Winter Haven 33880. *Treasurer,* George Comerford, 5844 Western Way, Lake Worth 33463.

Republican

State Headquarters: 719 North Calhoun (P.O. Box 311) Tallahassee 32302. (904) 222-7920 *Chief of Staff,* Ellen Darden.

State Executive Committee, *Chairman,* Tom Slade.

Lawton Chiles and "Buddy" MacKay campaign for election in 1991. Phillip Pollock

Popular Vote in Florida for President

Year	Candidate	total votes	percentage of total votes
1848	Zachary Taylor (Whig)	4,177	57.2
	Lewis Cass (Democrat)	3,083	42.8
1852	Franklin Pierce (Democrat)	4,318	60.0
	Winfield Scott (Whig)	2,875	40.0
1856	James Buchanan (Democrat)	6,358	56.8
	Millard Fillmore (American)	4,833	43.2
1860	John C. Breckinridge (Democrat)	8,155	62.2
	John Bell (Constitutional Union)	4,731	36.1
	Stephen A. Douglas (Independent Dem.)	221	1.7
1864	No election		
1868	Republican electors chosen by Legislature		
1872	Ulysses S. Grant (Republican)	17,765	53.5
	Horace Greeley (Democrat, Liberal Republican)	15,428	46.5
1876	Rutherford B. Hayes (Republican)	23,849	51.0
	Samuel J. Tilden (Democrat)	22,923	49.0
1880	Winfield S. Hancock (Democrat)	27,925	54.1
	James A. Garfield (Republican)	23,686	45.9
1884	Grover Cleveland (Democrat)	31,776	53.1
	James G. Blaine (Republican)	28,031	46.9
1888	Grover Cleveland (Democrat)	39,561	58.7
	Benjamin Harrison (Republican)	26,659	39.6
	Alson J. Streeter (Labor)	704	1.0
	Clinton B. Fisk (Prohibition)	417	7
1892	Grover Cleveland (Democrat)	30,143	84.8
	James B. Weaver (People's)	4,843	13.6
	John Bidwell (Prohibition)	570	1.6
1896	William J. Bryan (Democrat)	30,683	66.0
	William McKinley (Republican)	11,288	24.3
	William J. Bryan (People's)	2,053	4.4
	John M. Palmer (National Democrat)	1,778	3.8
	Joshua Levering (Prohibition)	654	1.5
1900	William J. Bryan (Democrat)	28,625	71.8
	William McKinley (Republican)	7,314	18.4
	William J. Bryan (People's)	1,070	2.7
	John G. Woolley (Prohibition)	2,234	5.6
	Eugene V. Debs (Social Democrat)	601	1.5
1904	Alton B. Parker (Democrat)	27,046	68.8
	Theodore Roosevelt (Republican)	8,314	21.2
	Thomas E. Watson (People's)	1,605	4.1
	Eugene V. Debs (Socialist)	2,337	5.9
1908	William J. Bryan(Democrat)	31,104	63.0
	William H. Taft (Republican)	10,654	21.6
	Eugene V. Debs (Socialist)	3,757	7.6
	Thomas L. Hisgen (Independence)	553	1.2
	Thomas E. Watson (People's)	1,946	3.9
	Eugene W. Chafin (Prohibition)	1,356	2.7
1912	Woodrow Wilson (Democrat)	36,417	70.2
	William H. Taft (Republican)	4,279	8.2
	Eugene V. Debs (Socialist)	4,806	9.3
	Eugene W. Chafin (Prohibition)	1,854	3.6
	Theodore Roosevelt (Progressive)	4,535	8.7
1916	Woodrow Wilson (Democrat)	55,984	67.2
	Charles E. Hughes (Republican)	14,611	17.5
	J. Frank Hanly (Prohibition)	4,855	5.8
	A. L. Benson (Socialist)	7,814	9.5

Figures taken from official canvass of returns except in 1876 through 1888.

Popular Vote, President (*Continued*)

		total votes	percentage of total votes
1920	James M. Cox (Democrat)	90,515	58.1
	Warren G. Harding (Republican)	44,853	28.8
	Warren G. Harding (Republican, White)	10,118	6.5
	Eugene V. Debs (Socialist)	5,189	3.3
	Aaron Sherman (Prohibition)	5,124	3.3
1924	John W. Davis (Democrat)	62,083	56.9
	Calvin Coolidge (Republican)	30,633	28.1
	Herman P. Faris (Prohibition)	5,498	5.0
	Robert M. LaFollette (Progressive)	8,625	7.9
	Gilbert O. Nations (American)	2,315	2.1
1928	Herbert C. Hoover (Republican)	144,168	56.8
	Alfred E. Smith (Democrat)	101,768	40.1
	Norman Thomas (Socialist)	4,036	1.6
	William Z. Foster (Communist)	3,704	1.5
1932	Franklin D. Roosevelt (Democrat)	206,307	74.9
	Herbert C. Hoover (Republican)	69,170	25.1
1936	Franklin D. Roosevelt (Democrat)	249,117	76.1
	Alfred M. Landon (Republican)	78,248	23.9
1940	Franklin D. Roosevelt (Democrat)	359,334	74.0
	Wendell L. Willkie (Republican)	126,158	26.0
1944	Franklin D. Roosevelt (Democrat)	339,377	70.3
	Thomas E. Dewey (Republican)	143,215	29.7
1948	Harry S. Truman (Democrat)	282,328	48.8
	Thomas E. Dewey (Republican)	194,347	33.6
	J. Strom Thurmond (States' Rights)	89,880	15.5
	Henry A. Wallace (Progressive)	11,683	2.1
1952	Dwight D. Eisenhower (Republican)	544,036	55.0
	Adlai E. Stevenson (Democrat)	444,950	45.0
1956	Dwight D. Eisenhower (Republican)	643,849	57.3
	Adlai E. Stevenson (Democrat)	480,371	42.7
1960	Richard M. Nixon (Republican)	795,476	51.5
	John F. Kennedy (Democrat)	748,700	48.5
1964	Lyndon B. Johnson (Democrat)	948,540	51.1
	Barry M. Goldwater (Republican)	905,941	48.9
1968	Richard M. Nixon (Republican)	886,804	40.5
	Hubert H. Humphrey (Democrat)	676,794	30.9
	George C. Wallace (George Wallace)	624,207	28.5
1972	Richard M. Nixon (Republican)	1,857,759	71.9
	George McGovern (Democrat)	718,117	27.8
	Scattering	7,407	.3
1976	Jimmy Garter (Democrat)	1,636,000	51.9
	Gerald R. Ford (Republican)	1,469,531	46.6
	Tom Anderson (American)	21,325	.6
	Eugene J. McCarthy (Independent)	23,645	.7
1980	Ronald Reagan (Republican)	2,043,006	55.5
	Jimmy Carter (Democrat)	1,417,687	38.5
	Ed Clark (Libertarian)	30,457	.8
	John B. Anderson (Independent)	189,099	5.1
	Write-in	285	
1984	Ronald Reagan (Republican)	2,728,775	65.3
	Walter Mondale (Democrat)	1,448,344	34.4
	Write-in	865	
1988	George Bush (Republican)	2,616,597	60
	Michael Dukakis (Democrat)	1,655,851	38
	Other	26,701	

Note: Parties other than Republican and Democratic for which votes were cast for President in 1988 were Libertarian, 1,219; Independent Populist, 20,608; New Alliance, 5. Voters professing no party affiliation, 361,463.

Presidential Preference Election
March 10, 1992

Democratic	Total vote	Percentage of total
Jerry Brown	139,590	12.4
Bill Clinton	570,566	50.8
Tom Harkin	13,587	1.2
Bob Kerrey	12,011	1.1
Paul Tsongas	388,124	34.5
Total Democratic votes cast	1,123,867	

Republican		
Patrick Buchanan	235,386	31.9
George Bush	608,077	68.1
Total Republican votes cast	893,463	

How Florida Has Voted in Presidential Elections (General Elections)

Year	Candidate	%	Year	Candidate	%
1992	Bush	40.90%	1980	Reagan	55.52%
	Clinton	39.00%		Carter	38.50%
1988	Bush	60.87%	1976	Ford	46.64%
	Dukakis	38.51%		Carter	51.93%
1984	Reagan	65.32%	1972	Nixon	71.92%
	Mondale	34.66%		McGovern	27.80%

Voter Participation

Votes in Florida
For President of the United States

Year of election	Number of Registered electors	Number of votes cast	Percent of Participation	Republican % of votes	Democrat % of votes	Others % of votes
1944	704,461	482,592	68.5%	29.7%	70.3%	
1948	1,003,503	578,358	57.6%	33.6%	48.8%	17.6%
1952	1,339,538	988,986	73.8%	55.0%	45.0%	
1956	1,606,750	1,124,220	70.0%	57.3%	42.7%	
1960	2,016,586	1,544,180	76.5%	51.5%	48.5%	
1964	2,501,546	1,854,481	74.1%	48.9%	51.1%	
1968	2,765,316	2,187,805	79.1%	40.5%	30.9%	28.5%
1972	3,487,458	2,583,283	74.1%	71.9%	27.8%	.3%
1976	4,094,308	3,150,499	76.9%	46.64%	51.93%	1.43%
1980	4,809,721	3,680,534	76.5%	55.51%	38.52%	5.97%
1984	5,574,472	4,180,051	75.8%	65.28%	34.64%	.08%
1988	5,614,539	4,299,149	76.5%	60.86%	38.52%	.62%
1992	6,541,825	5,310,981	81.1%	40.9%	39.0%	20.1%

President and Vice President
November 3, 1992

County	Clinton and Gore Democrat	Bush and Quayle Republican	Marrou and Lord Libertarian	Perot and Stockdale Independent
Alachua	37,876	22,806	372	15,293
Baker	1,974	3,417	47	1,315
Bay	12,830	22,820	287	9,702
Bradford	3,040	3,671	54	1,572
Brevard	61,070	84,545	664	49,491
Broward	276,309	164,782	905	90,923
Calhoun	1,665	1,721	17	1,176
Charlotte	22,904	24,302	123	14,711
Citrus	15,935	16,402	80	12,310
Clay	10,597	26,313	90	8,414
Collier	18,794	38,447	180	14,514
Columbia	5,526	6,489	28	2,906
Dade	254,444	235,149	911	53,957
Desoto	2,646	3,070	26	1,687
Dixie	1,855	1,401	23	1,094
Duval	92,010	123,480	796	33,335
Escambia	32,018	52,775	382	19,868
Flagler	6,692	6,241	24	3,387
Franklin	1,534	1,660	36	1,143
Gadsden	8,478	3,975	62	1,871
Gilchrist	1,511	1,395	21	1,090
Glades	1,305	1,185	6	878
Gulf	1,938	2,650	20	1,245
Hamilton	1,622	1,402	6	695
Hardee	2,017	2,898	16	1,498
Hendry	2,690	3,279	13	2,032
Hernando	19,171	17,896	161	11,845
Highlands	11,234	14,497	62	6,592
Hillsborough	115,261	130,611	1,503	63,037
Holmes	1,877	3,196	28	1,426
Indian River	12,359	19,137	86	12,375
Jackson	5,481	6,720	19	2,447
Jefferson	2,270	1,506	6	894
Lafayette	866	1,037	7	612
Lake	23,199	30,818	148	15,606
Lee	53,656	73,423	444	38,446
Leon	47,770	31,964	302	17,207
Levy	4,330	3,796	26	2,784
Liberty	820	1,126	13	617
Madison	2,644	2,006	6	1,174
Manatee	33,826	42,708	353	23,282
Marion	30,823	35,438	186	20,524
Martin	14,778	24,768	140	13,433
Monroe	10,435	9,891	125	8,306
Nassau	5,497	9,364	49	3,251
Okaloosa	12,003	32,755	242	16,649
Okeechobee	3,418	3,298	7	2,645
Orange	82,656	108,738	676	44,827
Osceola	15,009	19,139	91	11,021
Palm Beach	187,840	140,317	771	76,223
Pasco	53,125	47,721	440	34,650
Pinellas	160,217	158,733	1,914	101,150

President and Vice President (*Continued*)

County	Clinton and Gore Democrat	Bush and Quayle Republican	Marrou and Lord Libertarian	Perot and Stockdale Independent
Polk	51,442	65,952	276	28,198
Putnam	10,707	8,909	60	5,975
Santa Rosa	6,526	17,229	92	8,735
Sarasota	54,536	66,831	644	34,281
Seminole	35,649	57,085	299	24,477
St. John	12,284	20,173	107	7,397
St. Lucie	23,873	24,397	139	19,813
Sumter	5,027	4,366	34	2,901
Suwannee	3,985	4,571	19	2,790
Taylor	2,568	2,693	23	1,929
Union	1,247	1,543	7	770
Volusia	65,213	59,155	273	30,813
Wakulla	2,319	2,586	18	1,790
Walton	3,886	5,719	48	3,886
Washington	2,544	3,694	35	1,596
Totals	2,071,651	2,171,781	15,068	1,052,481
Percent	39.0	40.9	.3	19.8

Vote for Governor, General Elections

			total vote	percentage of total vote
1845	William D. Moseley (Democrat)		3,292	55.1
	Richard K. Call (Whig)		2,679	44.9
1848	Thomas Brown (Whig)		3,801	53.1
	William Bailey (Democrat)		3,354	46.9
1852	James E. Broome (Democrat)		4,628	51.6
	George T. Ward (Whig)		4,336	48.4
1856	Madison S. Perry (Democrat)		6,214	51.3
	David S. Walker (American)		5,894	48.7
1860	John Milton (Democrat)		6,994	57.1
	Edward Hopkins (Constitutional Union)		5,248	42.9
1865	David S. Walker (Conservative Dem.)		5,873	100.0
1868	Harrison Reed (Republican)		14,421	59.1
	Samuel Walker (Radical Republican)		2,251	9.2
	George W. Scott (Democrat)		7,731	31.7
1872	Ossian B. Hart (Republican)		17,603	52.4
	William D. Bloxham (Democrat)		16,004	47.6
1876	George F. Drew (Democrat)		24,179	50.2
	Marcellus L. Stearns (Republican)		23,984	49.8
1880	William D. Bloxham (Democrat)		28,378	54.9
	Simon B. Conover (Republican)		23,297	45.1

(Note: The Constitution of 1861 gave the governor a two-year term, beginning with an election to be held in October 1865. The defeat of the Confederacy abrogated this Constitution before the election could be held. Walker was elected, without opposition, under the Constitution of 1865.)

Figures taken from official canvass of returns, except in 1845, 1852, 1865, 1868, 1876.

Elections / 641

Vote for Governor, General Elections (*Continued*)

		total vote	percentage of total vote
1884	Edward A. Perry (Democrat)	32,087	53.5
	Frank W. Pope (Republican)	27,845	46.5
1888	Francis P. Fleming (Democrat)	40,255	60.3
	V. J. Shipman (Republican)	26,485	39.7
1892	Henry L. Mitchell (Democrat)	32,064	78.8
	Alonzo P. Baskin (People's)	8,309	20.4
	N. J. Hawley (Prohibition)	297	.8
1896	William D. Bloxham (Democrat)	27,172	66.7
	Edward R. Gunby (Republican)	8,290	20.4
	William A. Weeks (People's)	5,270	12.9
	Arthur C. Jackson (Prohibition)		
1900	William S. Jennings (Democrat)	29,251	81.0
	Matthew B. Macfarlane (Republican)	6,238	17.3
	A. M. Morton (People's)	631	1.7
1904	Napoleon B. Broward (Democrat)	28,971	79.2
	Matthew B. Macfarlane (Republican)	6,357	17.4
	W. R. Healey	1,270	3.4
1908	Albert W. Gilchrist (Democrat)	33,036	78.8
	John M. Cheney (Republican)	6,453	15.4
	A. J. Pettigrew (Socialist)	2,427	5.8
1912	Park Trammell (Democrat)	38,977	80.4
	William R. O'Neal (Republican)	2,646	5.5
	Thomas W. Cox (Socialist)	3,467	7.2
	J. W. Bingham (Prohibition)	1,061	2.2
	William C. Hodges (Progressive)	2,314	4.7
1916	Sidney J. Catts (Democrat/Prohibition)	39,546	47.7
	William V. Knott (Democrat)	30,343	36.6
	George W. Allen (Republican)	10,333	12.5
	C. C. Allen (Socialist)	2,470	3.0
	Noel A. Mitchell	193	.2
1920	Cary A. Hardee (Democrat)	103,407	77.9
	George E. Gay (Republican)	23,788	17.9
	W. L. VanDuzer (Republican)	2,654	2.0
	F. C. Whitaker (Socialist)	2,823	2.2
1924	John W. Martin (Democrat)	84,181	82.8
	William R. O'Neal (Republican)	17,499	17.2
1928	Doyle E. Carlton (Democrat)	148,455	61.0
	W. J. Howey (Republican)	95,018	39.0
1932	Dave Sholtz (Democrat)	186,270	66.6
	W. J. Howey (Republican)	93,323	33.4
1936	Fred P. Cone (Democrat)	253,638	80.9
	E. E. Callaway (Republican)	59,832	19.1
1940	Spessard L. Holland (Democrat) (No Opponent)	334,152	100.0
1944	Millard F. Caldwell (Democrat)	361,007	78.9
	Bert L. Acker (Republican)	96,321	21.1
1948	Fuller Warren (Democrat)	381,459	83.4
	Bert L. Acker (Republican)	76,153	16.6

Vote for Governor, General Elections (*Continued*)

Year	Candidate	total vote	percentage of total vote
1952	Don McCarty (Democrat)	624,463	74.8
	Harry S. Swan (Republican)	210,009	25.2

Note: The election in 1954 was for the two years remaining of the term of the late Governor Dan McCarty.

Year	Candidate	total vote	percentage of total vote
1954	LeRoy Collins (Democrat)	287,769	80.5
	J. Tom Watson (Republican)	69,852	19.5
	(Watson died before election.)		
1956	LeRoy Collins (Democrat)	747,753	73.7
	William A. Washburne, Jr. (Republican)	266,980	26.3
1960	Farris Bryant (Democrat)	849,407	59.8
	George C. Petersen (Republican)	569,936	40.2

Note: The election in 1964 was for a two-year term to shift elections for State offices from Presidential election years.

Year	Candidate	total vote	percentage of total vote
1964	Haydon Burns (Democrat)	933,554	56.1
	Charles R. Holley (Republican)	686,297	41.3
	Write-in votes for others	43,630	2.6
1966	Robert King High (Democrat)	668,223	44.9
	Claude R. Kirk (Republican)	821,190	55.1
1970	Claude R. Kirk, Jr., and Ray C. Osborne (Republican)	746,243	43.1
	Reubin O'D. Askew and Tom Adams (Democrat)	984,305	56.9
1974	Reubin O'D. Askew and J. H. "Jim" Williams (Democrat)	1,118,954	61.2
	Jerry Thomas and Mike Thompson (Republican)	709,438	38.8
1978	Bob Graham and Wayne Mixson (Democrat)	1,406,580	55.6
	Jack Eckerd and Paula Hawkins (Republican)	1,123,888	44.4
1982	Bob Graham and Wayne Mixson (Democrat)	1,739,553	64.7
	Skip Bafalis and Leo Callahan (Republican)	949,023	35.3
1986	Steve Pajcic, and Frank Mann, (Democrat)	1,538,620	45.44
	Bob Martinez, and Bobby Brantley, (Republican)	1,847,525	54.5
1990	Lawton M. Chiles and Kenneth H. "Buddy" MacKay (Democrat)	1,988,341	56.5
	Bob Martinez and Allison Defoor (Republican)	1,526,738	43.4
1994	Lawton M. Chiles and Kenneth H. "Buddy" MacKay (Democrat)	2,135,008	50.8
	Jeb Bush and Tom Feeney (Republican)	2,071,068	49.2

Vote for Governor, Democratic Primaries

Between 1913 and 1931, Florida used a one-primary system intended to serve the same purpose as the present double primary in selecting party nominees. It also was the hope that the elimination of the second primary would reduce the expense of campaigns. Each voter had the opportunity of marking the ballot for both a first and a second choice when there were more than two candidates. The two candidates receiving the most first choice votes were than awarded additionally the second-choice votes marked for them by first-choice supporters of only the eliminated candidates. The total of these first and second choice votes determined the winner. It was not mandatory for the voter to mark two choices and many did not.

		1st choice votes	2nd choice votes
1916	William V. Knott, Tallahassee	24,765	8,674
	Sidney J. Catts, DeFuniak Springs	30,067	3,351
	Ion L. Farris, Jacksonville	13,609	
	F. M. Hudson, Miami	7,418	
	F. A. Wood, St. Petersburg	7,674	
1920	Cary A. Hardee, Live Oak	52,591	1,559
	Lincoln Hulley, DeLand	5,591	
	Van C. Swearingen, Jacksonville	30,240	1,459
1924	John W. Martin, Jacksonville	55,715	17,339
	Sidney J. Catts, DeFuniak Springs	43,230	6,067
	Frank E. Jennings, Jacksonville	37,962	
	Charles H. Spencer, Tampa	1,408	
	Worth W. Trammell, Miami	8,381	
1928	Doyle E. Carlton, Tampa	77,569	28,471
	J. M. Carson, Miami	3,271	
	Sidney J. Catts, DeFuniak Springs	68,984	9,066
	Fons A. Hathaway, Jacksonville	67,849	
	John S. Taylor, Largo	37,304	

		1st primary	2nd primary
1932	David Sholtz, Daytona Beach	55,406	173,540
	Stafford Caldwell, Miami	44,938	
	Charles M. Durrance, Jacksonville	36,291	
	Arthur Gomez, Key West	9,244	
	Cary A. Hardee, Live Oak	50,427	
	Thomas S. Hart, Tampa	9,525	
	John W. Martin, Jacksonville	66,940	102,805
	J. Tom Watson, Tampa	3,949	
1936	Fred P. Cone, Lake City	46,842	184,540
	Grady Burton, Wauchula	24,985	
	Stafford Caldwell, Jasper	19,789	
	Jerry W. Carter, Tallahassee	35,578	
	Dan Chappell, Miami	29,494	
	R. B. Gautier, Miami	1,607	
	William C. Hodges, Tallahassee	46,471	
	Amos Lewis, Marianna	8,068	

Vote for Governor, Democratic Primaries (*Continued*)

		1st primary	2nd primary
	Carl Maples, Wakulla	2,389	
	Mallie Martin, Crestview	4,264	
	B. F. Paty, West Palm Beach	34,153	
	W. Raleigh Petteway, Tampa	51,705	129,150
	Peter Tomasello, Jr., Okeechobee	22,355	
	J. R. Yearwood, Winter Haven	1,049	
1940	Spessard L. Holland, Bartow	118,862	272,718
	James Barbee, Jacksonville	33,699	
	J. H. Clancy, Panama City	2,703	
	Walter B. Fraser, St. Augustine	36,855	
	Carl Maples, Wakulla	2,426	
	B. F. Paty, West Palm Beach	75,608	
	Burton Schoepf, Tampa	8,055	
	Frederick Van Roy, Crystal River	2,716	
	Fuller Warren, Jacksonville	83,316	
	Hans Walker, Ocala	21,666	
	Francis P. Whitehair, DeLand	95,431	206,158
1944	Millard F. Caldwell, Tallahassee	116,111	215,485
	J. Edwin Baker, Umatilla	27,028	
	Ernest R. Graham, Pennsuco	91,174	
	R. A. (Lex) Green, Starke	113,300	174,100
	Raymond Sheldon, Tampa	27,940	
	Frank D. Upchurch, St. Augustine	30,524	
1948	F. D. Akin, Miami	2,792	
	Richard H. Cooper, DeLand	8,152	
	Colin English, Fort Myers	89,158	
	Bernarr Macfadden, Miami Beach	4,540	
	Dan McCarty, Fort Pierce	161,788	276,425
	Basil H. Pollitt, Miami	1,261	
	W. A. Shands, Gainesville	62,358	
	Fuller Warren, Jacksonville	183,326	299,641
	J. Tom Watson, Tampa	51,505	
1952	Alto Adams, Fort Pierce	126,426	
	Bill Hendrix, Oldsmar	11,208	
	Dan McCarty, Fort Pierce	361,427	384,200
	Brailey Odham, Sanford	232,565	336,716
	Dale E. Spencer, Kissimmee	6,871	

Note: The primaries in 1954 were for the two years remaining of the term of the late Governor Dan McCarty.

1954	LeRoy Collins, Tallahassee	222,791	380,323
	Charley E. Johns, Starke	255,787	314,198
	Brailey Odham, Sanford	187,782	
1956	Farris Bryant, Ocala	110,469	
	LeRoy Collins, Tallahassee	434,274	
	Sumter L. Lowry, Tampa	179,019	
	W. B. (Bill) Price, Jacksonville	3,245	

Elections / 645

Vote for Governor, Democratic Primaries (*Continued*)

		1st primary	2nd primary
	Peaslee Streets, Lake Park	5,086	
	Fuller Warren, Miami Beach	107,990	
1960	Harvie J. Belser, Bonifay	30,736	
	Farris Bryant, Ocala	193,507	512,757
	Haydon Burns, Jacksonville	166,352	
	Doyle E. Carlton, Jr., Wauchula	186,228	416,052
	Thomas E. (Ted) David, Hollywood	80,057	
	Fred O. "Bud" Dickinson, West Palm Beach	115,520	
	George Downs, Winter Park	6,320	
	Bill Hendrix, Oldsmar	8,517	
	John M. McCarty, Fort Pierce	144,750	
	Jim McCorvey, Hialeah	5,080	
1964	Haydon Burns, Jacksonville	312,453	648,093
	Fred O. "Bud" Dickinson, West Palm Beach	184,865	
	Robert King High, Miami	207,280	465,547
	Frederick B. Karl, Daytona Beach	85,953	
	Scott Kelly, Lakeland	205,078	
	John E. (Jack) Mathews, Jacksonville	140,210	
1966	Haydon Burns, Jacksonville	372,451	509,271
	Sam Foor, Tallahassee	11,343	
	Robert King High, Miami	338,281	596,471
	Scott Kelly, Lakeland	331,580	

Note: Commencing in 1970, candidates for Governor and Lieutenant Governor ran in tandem. First named is the candidate for Governor.

1970	Reubin O'D. Askew, Pensacola, and Tom Adams, Orange Park	206,333	447,025
	Earl Faircloth, Miami, and George G. Tapper, Port St. Joe	227,413	328,038
	Chuck Hall, Miami, and Pat Thomas, Quincy	139,384	
	John E. Mathews, Jacksonville, and Elton J. Gissendanner, North Miami	186,053	
1974	Tom Adams, Tallahassee and Burl McCormick, Hialeah	85,557	
	Reubin O'D. Askew, Pensacola, and J. H. "Jim" Williams, Ocala	579,137	
	Norman Bie, Clearwater, and Florence S. Keen, Palm Beach	39,758	
	Ben Hill Griffin, Jr., and Eleanor F. Griffin, Frostproof	137,008	
1978	LeRoy Eden, Miami Beach, and Maria Kay, Miami Beach	13,864	
	Bob Graham, Miami Lakes, and Wayne Mixson, Marianna	261,972	482,535

Vote for Governor, Democratic Primaries (*Continued*)

		1st primary	2nd primary
	Claude R. Kirk, Jr., Tallahassee, and Mary L. Singleton, Tallahassee	62,534	
	Robert L. Shevin, Tallahassee, and Jim Glisson, Eustis	364,732	418,636
	Bruce A. Smathers, Tallahassee, and Charles W. Boyd, Hollywood	85,298	
	Hans Tanzler, Jr., Jacksonville, and Manuel Arques, Miami	124,706	
	Jim Williams, Ocala, and Betty Castor, Tampa	124,427	
	Total	1,035,533	
1982	Bob Graham, Tallahassee, and Wayne Mixson, Tallahassee	839,320	
	Fred Kuhn, Homestead, and Jeffrey L. Latham, Davie	93,078	
	Robert P. (Bob) Kunst, Gainesville, and Gary Bryant, Miami	61,136	
	Total	993,534	
1986	Mark Kane Goldstein, Gainesville, and Morris H. Wolff, West Palm Beach	54,077	
	Harry A. Johnston, West Palm Beach, and Mark Gibbons, Tampa	258,038	
	Steve Pajcic, Jacksonville, and Frank Mann, Fort Myers	361,359	429,427
	Jim Smith, Tallahassee, and Marshall S. Harris, Coral Gables	310,479	418,614
	Joan L. Wollin, Tavares, and Sy Simons, Hallandale	22,709	
	Total	1,006,662	848,041
1990	Lawton Chiles, Tallahassee, and Kenneth H. (Buddy) MacKay, Ocala	746,325	
	Bill Nelson, Melbourne, and Tom Gustafson, Fort Lauderdale	327,731	
	Total Votes Cast	1,074,056	
1994	Lawton Chiles, Tallahassee and Kenneth H. (Buddy) MacKay, Ocala	597,412	
	Jack Gargan, Cedar Kay and James King, Naples	230,395	
	Total Votes Cast	827,807	

Vote for Governor, Republican Primaries

		1st primary	2nd primary
1952	Bert Leigh Acker, Miami	9,728	5,995
	Elmore F. Kitzmiller, Dunedin	5,050	
	Harry S. Swan, Miami Shores	11,148	10,217

Vote for Governor, Republican Primaries (*Continued*)
   Note: The primary in 1954 was for the remaining two years of the term of the late Governor Dan McCarty.

1954	Charles E. Compton, Miami	11,552
	J. Tom Watson, Tampa	24,429
1960	George C. Petersen, Fort Lauderdale	65,202
	Emerson H. Rupert, St. Petersburg	24,484
1964	Ken Folks, Orlando	26,815
	H. B. (Bob) Foster, Fort Myers	33,563
	Charles R. Holley, St. Petersburg	70,573
1966	Claude R. Kirk, Jr., Jacksonville	100,838
	Richard B. Muldrew, Melbourne	23,953

Note: Commencing in 1970, candidates for Governor and Lieutenant Governor ran in tandem. First named is the candidate for Governor.

1970	L. A. (Skip) Bafalis, Palm Beach, and Ward Dougherty, Lutz	48,378	
	Jack M. Eckerd, St. Petersburg, and Robert H. Elrod, Windermere	137,731	152,327
	Claude R. Kirk, Jr., Palm Beach, and Ray C. Osborne, St. Petersburg	172,888	199,943
1974	Jerry Thomas, Jupiter, and Mike Thompson, Coral Gables		Unopposed
1978	Jack Eckerd, Clearwater, and Paula Hawkins, Maitland	244,394	
	Lou Frey, Jr., Winter Park, and S. Peter Capua, Miami	138,437	
1982	L. A. (Skip) Bafalis, Fort Myers Beach, and Leo Callahan, Fort Lauderdale ...	325,108	
	Vernon Davids, Winter Garden, and Wendell Davids, Englewood	51,340	
1986	Chester E. Clem, Vero Beach, and Tom Bush, Fort Lauderdale	44,438	
	Lou Frey, Jr., Winter Park, and Marilyn Evans-Jones, Melbourne	138,017	131,652
	Tom Gallagher, Miami, and Betty Easley, Largo	127,709	
	Bob Martinez, Tampa, and Bobby Brantley, Longwood	244,499	259,333
	Total	554,663	390,985
		total vote	*percentage of total vote*
1990	Bob Martinez, Tampa, and Allison Defoor, Key West	460,718	68.9
	Marlene Woodson-Howard, Bradenton, and Eric H. Wieler, St. Petersburg	132,565	19.8
	John Davis, Largo, and Walter Murray, Kenneth City	34,720	5.1

Vote for Governor, Republican Primaries (*Continued*)

		total vote	percentage of total vote
	Warren Folks, Jacksonville, and Charles McDonald, Miami	11,587	1.7
	Anthony Martin, Fort Lauderdale, and Barbara Lindsey, Stuart	28,591	4.2
	Total Votes Cast	668,181	*No runoff*
1994	Jeb Bush, Miami and Tom Feeney, Orlando	408,968	45.7
	Jim Smith, Tallahassee and Barbara Todd, Clearwater	165,045	18.4
	Tom Gallagher, Tallahassee and Curt Kiser, Palm Harbor	116,284	13.0
	Ander Crenshaw, Jacksonville and Chester Clem, Vero Beach	107,692	12.0
	Kenneth L. Conner, Tallahassee and Mel Martinez, Orlando	83,504	9.3
	Josephine A. Arnold, Largo and Robert Brown, Boynton Beach	8,277	.9
	Robert Bell, Miami and George Roller, Miami	5,156	.6
	Total Votes Cast	894,926	

Vote for U.S. Senator General Elections

Note: Prior to the ratification of the seventeenth amendment to the U.S. Constitution in 1913, the Florida Legislature elected the U.S. Senators. With statewide primaries displacing political party conventions in 1902, the Legislature accepted the nominee of the Democratic party as its choice. For example, the 1909 Legislature, meeting in joint session but balloting separately, unanimously elected Duncan U. Fletcher as U.S. Senator. In accepting, Fletcher acknowledged the selection system when he wrote: "In response to the will of the people expressed in the primaries, and in compliance with your pledges, and in obedience to your consciences, you have just conferred upon me, one of your citizens, a very great honor."

		total vote	percentage of total vote
1916	Park Trammell (Democrat)	58,391	82.9
	W. R. O'Neal (Republican)	8,774	12.5
	R. L. Goodwin (Socialist)	3,304	4.6
1920	Duncan U. Fletcher (Democrat)	98,957	69.5
	John M. Cheney (Republican)	37,065	26.0
	G. A. Klock (Republican, White)	2,847	2.0
	M. J. Martin (Socialist)	3,525	2.5
1922	Park Trammell (Democrat)	45,707	88.3
	W. C. Lawson (Independent Republican)	6,074	11.7
1926	Duncan U. Fletcher (Democrat)	51,054	77.9
	W. R. O'Neal (Regular Republican)	6,133	9.4

Vote for U.S. Senator General Elections (Continued)

Year	Candidate	total vote	percentage of total vote
	John M. Lindsay (Republican Del. Convention)	8,381	12.7
1928	Park Trammell (Democrat)	153,816	68.5
	Barclay H. Warburton (Republican)	70,633	31.5
1932	Duncan U. Fletcher (Democrat) (No Opponent)	204,651	100.0
1934	Park Trammell (Democrat) (No Opponent)	131,780	100.0
1936	Claude Pepper (Democrat) (No Opponent)	246,050	100.0
	Charles O. Andrews (Democrat)	241,528	81.0
	H. C. Babcock (Republican)	57,016	19.0
1938	Claude Pepper (Democrat)	145,757	82.4
	Thos. E. Swanson (Republican)	31,035	17.6
1940	Charles O. Andrews (Democrat)	323,216	100.0
	Miles H. Draper (Republican)	Withdrew	
1944	Claude Pepper (Democrat)	335,685	71.3
	Miles H. Draper (Republican)	135,258	28.7
1946	Spessard L. Holland (Democrat)	156,232	78.7
	J. Harry Schad (Republican)	42,408	21.3
1950	George A. Smathers (Democrat)	238,987	76.3
	John P. Booth (Republican)	74,228	23.7
1952	Spessard L. Holland (Democrat) (No Opponent)	616,665	100.0
1956	George A. Smathers (Democrat) (No Opponent)	655,418	100.0
1958	Spessard L. Holland (Democrat)	386,113	71.2
	Leland Hyzer (Republican)	155,956	28.8
1962	George A. Smathers (Democrat)	657,633	66.6
	Emerson Rupert (Republican)	329,381	33.4
1964	Spessard L. Holland (Democrat)	997,585	64.0
	Claude R. Kirk, Jr. (Republican)	562,212	36.0
1968	Edward J. Gurney (Republican)	1,131,499	55.9
	LeRoy Collins (Democrat)	892,637	44.1
1970	Lawton M. Chiles, Jr. (Democrat)	902,438	53.9
	William C. Cramer (Republican)	772,817	46.1
1974	Richard (Dick) Stone, Tallahassee (Dem.)	781,031	43.4
	Jack Eckerd, Belleaire (Rep.)	736,674	40.9
	John Grady, Belle Glade (American)	282,659	15.7
1976	Lawton M. Chiles, Jr., Lakeland (Dem.)	1,810,518	63.1
	John Grady, Belle Glade (Rep.)	1,057,886	36.9
1980	Paula Hawkins, Winter Park (Rep.)	1,819,189	51.6
	Bill Gunter, Tallahassee (Dem.)	1,705,086	48.3
	Write-in	159	
1982	Lawton M. Chiles, Jr., Lakeland (Dem.)	1,636,857	61.7

Vote for U.S. Senator General Elections (*Continued*)

		total vote	percentage of total vote
	Van B. Poole, Fort Lauderdale (Rep.) . . .	1,014,551	38.2
	Write-in	421	
1986	Bob Graham, Miami Lakes (Dem.)	1,877,231	54.74
	Paula Hawkins, Winter Park (Rep.)	1,551,888	45.26
	Write-in	77	
1988	Connie Mack, Cape Coral (Rep.)	2,049,329	50.4
	Buddy MacKay, Ocala (Dem.)	2,015,717	49.6
	Write-in	585	
1992	Bob Graham, Miami Lakes (Dem.)	3,244,299	65.4
	Bill Grant, Tallahassee (Rep.)	1,715,156	34.6
1994	Connie Mack, Cape Coral (Rep.)	2,894,726	70.5
	Hugh Rodham, Coral Gables (Dem.) . . .	1,210,412	29.5
	Write-in	1,038	

Vote for U.S. Senator, Democratic Primaries

		1st primary	2nd primary
1904	James P. Taliaferro	22,222	24,066
	John Stockton	12,771	20,695
	William S. Jennings	9,245	
	Wilkinson Call	1,168	
1908	Duncan U. Fletcher	17,308	29,151
	Napoleon Broward	19,078	25,563
	William B. Lamar	12,572	
	John Beard	4,592	
1910	Napoleon Broward	21,146	25,780
	James P. Taliaferro	21,077	23,193
	Claude L'Engle	4,667	

Senator-elect Broward died before taking office.
A primary election to succeed Broward was held
January 31, 1911.

		1st primary	2nd primary
1911	Nathan P. Bryan	9,749	19,981
	William A. Blount	13,808	19,381
	John Stockton	7,462	

		1st choice votes	2nd choice votes
1916	Park Trammell	37,575	6,014
	Nathan P. Bryan	19,536	3,647
	Albert W. Gilchrist	9,863	
	Perry G. Wall	14,404	
1920	Duncan U. Fletcher	62,304	
	Sidney J. Catts	25,007	
1922	Park Trammell	59,232	
	Albert W. Gilchrist	29,527	
1926	Duncan U. Fletcher	63,760	812
	Jerry W. Carter	39,143	932
	John A. VanValzah	4,226	

Vote for U.S. Senator, Democratic Primaries (*Continued*)

		1st choice votes	2nd choice votes
1928	Park Trammell	138,534	
	John W. Martin	100,454	

		1st Primary	2nd Primary
1932	Duncan U. Fletcher (No Opponent)		
1934	Park Trammell	81,321	103,028
	Charles A. Mitchell	30,455	
	Claude Pepper	79,396	98,978
	James F. Sikes	14,558	
	Hortense K. Wells	8,167	
1936	Claude Pepper (No Opponent)		
	Two seats open for election		
	Charles O. Andrews	67,387	
	Doyle E. Carlton	62,530	
1938	Claude Pepper	242,350	
	T. C. Merchant	4,066	
	Finley Moore	5,417	
	David Sholtz	52,785	
	J. Mark Wilcox	110,675	
1940	Charles O. Andrews	179,195	312,293
	Jerry W. Carter	80,869	137,641
	Charles Francis Coe	33,463	
	Fred P. Cone	68,584	
	O. B. Hazen	4,370	
	Bernarr Macfadden	71,487	
1944	Claude Pepper	194,445	
	Alston Cockrell	9,551	
	Millard B. Conklin	33,317	
	J. Ollie Edmunds	127,158	
	Finley Moore	14,445	
1946	Spessard L. Holland	204,352	
	Polly Rose Balfe	14,553	
	Henry M. Burch	8,600	
	R. A. (Lex) Green	109,040	
1950	Claude Pepper	319,754	
	George A. Smathers	387,215	
1952	William A. Gaston	91,011	
	Spessard L. Holland	485,515	
1956	Erle L. Griffis	87,525	
	George A. Smathers	614,663	
1958	Spessard L. Holland	408,084	
	Claude Pepper	321,377	
1962	Roger L. Davis	74,565	
	George A. Smathers	587,562	
	Douglas Randolph Voorhees	35,832	
1964	Spessard L. Holland, Bartow	676,014	
	Brailey Odham, Orlando	289,454	

Vote for U.S. Senator, Democratic Primaries (*Continued*)

		1st Primary	2nd Primary
1968	LeRoy Collins, Tallahassee	426,096	410,689
	Earl Faircloth, Miami	397,642	407,696
	Sam Foor, Tallahassee	17,725	
	Richard Lafferty, Gainesville	19,100	
1970	Farris Bryant, Jacksonville	240,222	247,211
	Lawton M. Chiles, Jr., Lakeland	188,300	474,420
	Joel T. Daves, III, West Palm Beach	33,939	
	Alcee Hastings, Forth Lauderdale	91,948	
	Frederick H. Schultz, Jacksonville	175,745	
1974	George Balmer, Davie	24,408	
	Robert Brewster, Cape Canaveral	19,913	
	Bill Gunter, Orlando	236,185	311,044
	David B. Higginbottom, Frostproof	17,401	
	Mallory E. Horne, Tallahassee	90,684	
	Neal E. Justin, Boca Raton	14,961	
	Duaine E. Macon, Pensacola	10,525	
	Richard A. Pettigrew, Miami	146,728	
	Richard (Dick) Stone, Tallahassee	157,301	321,683
	Glenn W. Turner, Maitland	51,326	
	Burton Young, North Miami Beach	23,199	
1976	Lawton M. Chiles, Jr., Lakeland (No Opponent)		
1980	John B. Coffey, Moore Haven	17,410	
	Bill Gunter, Tallahassee	335,859	594,676
	Kenneth H. (Buddy) MacKay, Ocala	272,538	
	James L. (Jim) Miller, Lutz	18,118	
	Richard A. Pettigrew, Coral Gables	108,154	
	Richard (Dick) Stone, Tallahassee	355,287	554,268
1982	Lawton M. Chiles, Lakeland (No Opponent)		
1986	Bob Graham, Tallahassee, Miami Lakes	851,586	
	Robert P. (Bob) Kunst, Miami Beach	149,797	
1988	Patricia Frank, Tampa	119,277	
	Bill Gunter, Tallahassee	383,721	340,918
	Claude Kirk, Palm Beach	51,387	
	Kenneth H. (Buddy) MacKay, Ocala	263,946	369,266
	Dan Mica, West Palm Beach	179,524	
	Fred Rader, Homestead	11,820	
1992	Bob Graham, Miami Lakes	968,618	
	Jim Mahorner, Tallahassee	180,405	
1994	Hugh Rodham, Coral Gables	253,079	
	Mike Wiley, Longwood	185,970	
	Ellis Rubin, Miami	159,286	
	Arturo Perez, Winter Haven	148,930	

Vote for U.S. Senator, Republican Primaries

		1st primary	2nd primary
1968	Herman W. Goldner, St. Petersburg ...	42,347	
	Edward J. Gurney, Winter Park	169,805	
1970	George Balmer, Hollywood	10,947	
	G. Harrold Carswell, Tallahassee	121,281	
	William C. Cramer, St. Petersburg	220,553	
1974	Jack Eckerd, Belleair	186,897	
	Paula Hawkins, Maitland	90,049	
1976	Walter Sims, Orlando	74,684	
	John Grady, Belle Glade	164,644	
	Helen S. Hansel, St. Petersburg	62,718	
1980	Ander Crenshaw, Jacksonville	54,767	
	Lewis Dinkins, Ocala	15,174	
	Lou Frey, Jr., Winter Park	119,834	182,911
	Paula Hawkins, Winter Park	209,856	293,600
	Ellis Rubin, Miami	19,900	
	John T. Ware, St. Petersburg	16,341	
1982	David H. Bludworth, West Palm Beach	116,030	95,024
	Van B. Poole, Fort Lauderdale	154,158	131,638
	George Snyder, Sarasota	100,607	
1986	Paula Hawkins, Winter Park	491,953	
	Jon Larsen Shudlick, Ocean Ridge	62,474	
1988	Connie Mack, Cape Coral	405,296	
	Robert W. Merkle, Tampa	250,750	
1992	Hugh Brotherton, Fort Lauderdale	126,878	
	Bill Grant, Tallahassee	413,457	
	Hugh Quartel, Tampa	195,524	
1994	Connie Mack, Cape Coral	Unopposed	

Vote for U.S. Representative, General Election

1964			Total vote
1st District	Robert L. F. Sikes (D)		74,615
2nd District	Charles E. Bennett (D)		99,191
	William T. Stockton, Jr. (R)		37,283
3rd District	Claude Pepper (D)		101,162
	Paul J. O'Neill (R)		52,758
4th District	Dante B. Fascell (D)		94,726
	Jay McGlon (R)		53,468
5th District	A. Sydney Herlong, Jr. (D)		85,851
6th District	Paul G. Rogers (D)		168,573
	John D. Steele (R)		86,657
7th District	James A. Haley (D)		79,504
8th District	D. R. Matthews (R)		49,374
9th District	Don Fuqua (D)		44,917
10th District	Sam Gibbons (D)		69,860
11th District	Thomas S. Kenney (D)		59,746
	Edward J. Gurney (R)		91,731

Vote for U.S. Representative, General Election (*Continued*)

		Total vote
12th District	F. Marion Harrelson (D)	64,378
	William C. Cramer (R)	98,959

1966
1st District	Robert L. F. Sikes (D)	55,547
	scattering	2,862
2nd District	Don Fuqua (D)	71,565
	Harold Hill (R)	22,281
3rd District	Charles E. Bennett (D)	72,038
4th District	A. Sydney Herlong, Jr. (D)	70,155
5th District	Edward J. Gurney (R)	75,875
6th District	Sam M. Gibbons (D)	50,772
7th District	James A. Haley (D)	64,498
	Joe Z. Lovingood (R)	37,586
8th District	William C. Cramer (R)	105,019
	Roy L. Reynolds (D)	43,275
9th District	Paul G. Rogers (D)	76,328
10th District	J. Herbert Burke (R)	80,989
	Joe Varon (D)	51,636
11th District	Claude D. Pepper (D)	62,289
12th District	Dante B. Fascell (D)	62,457
	Mike Thompson (R)	47,226

1968
1st District	Robert L. F. Sikes (D)	116,215
	John Dryazga (R)	21,063
2nd District	Don Fuqua (D)	87,313
3rd District	Charles E. Bennett (D)	131,236
	Bill Parsons (R)	27,696
4th District	Bill Chappell, Jr. (D)	86,251
	William F. Herlong, Jr. (R)	76,974
5th District	Louis Frey (R)	108,620
	James C. Robinson (D)	67,505
6th District	Sam M. Gibbons (D)	84,193
	Paul A. Saad (R)	51,637
7th District	James A. Haley (D)	91,539
	Joe Z. Lovingood (R)	74,896
8th District	William C. Cramer (R)	117,747
9th District	Paul G. Rogers (D)	111,539
	Robert W. Rust (R)	87,074
10th District	J. Herbert Burke (R)	99,844
	Elton J. Gissendanner (D)	82,138
11th District	Claude Pepper (D)	99,154
	Ronald I. Strauss (R)	30,324
12th District	Dante B. Fascell (D)	82,362
	Mike Thompson (R)	62,032

1970
1st District	Robert L. F. Sikes (D)	88,744
	H. D. Shuemake	21,951

Vote for U.S. Representative, General Election (*Continued*)

		Total vote
2nd District	Don Fuqua (D)	not opposed
3rd District	Charles E. Bennett (D)	not opposed
4th District	Bill Chappell, Jr. (D)	75,673
	Leonard V. Wood	55,311
5th District	Louis Frey, Jr. (R)	110,841
	Roy Girod	35,398
6th District	Sam M. Gibbons (D)	78,832
	Robert A. Carter	30,252
7th District	James A. Haley (D)	78,535
	Joe Z. Lovingood	68,646
8th District	C. W. Bill Young (R)	120,466
	Ted A. Bailey	58,904
9th District	Paul G. Rogers (D)	120,565
	Emil F. Danciu	50,146
10th District	J. Herbert Burke (R)	81,170
	James J. Ward, Jr.	68,847
11th District	Claude D. Pepper (D)	not opposed
12th District	Dante B. Fascell (D)	75,895
	Robert A. Zinzell	29,935

1972

1st District	Robert L. F. Sikes (D)	not opposed
2nd District	Don Fuqua (D)	not opposed
3rd District	Charles E. Bennett (D)	101,441
	John F. Bowen	22,219
4th District	Bill Chappell, Jr. (D)	92,541
	P. T. Fleuchaus	72,960
5th District	Bill Gunter (D)	97,902
	Jack P. Insco	78,468
6th District	C. W. Bill Young (R)	156,150
	Michael O. Plunkett	49,399
7th District	Sam M. Gibbons (D)	91,931
	Robert A. Carter	43,343
8th District	James A. Haley (D)	89,068
	Roy Thompson, Jr.	64,920
9th District	Paul G. Rogers (D)	not opposed
10th District	L. A. (Skip) Bafalis (R)	113,461
	Bill Sikes (D)	69,502
11th District	Paul G. Rogers (D)	116,157
	Joe Karl Gustafson	76,739
12th District	J. Herbert Burke (R)	110,750
	James T. Stephanis	65,526
13th District	William Lehman (D)	92,258
	Paul D. Bethel	57,418
14th District	Claude D. Pepper (D)	75,131
	Evelio S. Estrella (R)	35,935
15th District	Dante B. Fascell (D)	89,961
	Ellis S. Rubin	68,320

Vote for U.S. Representative, General Election (*Continued*)

		Total vote
1974		
1st District	Robert L. F. Sikes (D)	not opposed
2nd District	Don Fuqua (D)	not opposed
3rd District	Charles E. Bennett (D)	not opposed
4th District	Bill Chappell, Jr. (D)	74,720
	Warren Hauser	34,867
5th District	Richard Kelly (R)	74,954
	JoAnn Saunders (D)	63,610
	Glenn W. Turner (D)	3,518
6th District	C. W. Bill Young (R)	109,302
	Mickey Monrose	34,886
7th District	Sam M. Gibbons (D)	not opposed
8th District	James A. Haley (D)	63,283
	Joe Z. Lovingood (R)	48,240
9th District	Louis Frey, Jr. (R)	86,226
	William D. Rowland (D)	26,255
10th District	L. A. (Skip) Bafalis (R)	117,368
	Evelyn Tucker	41,925
11th District	Paul G. Rogers (D)	not opposed
12th District	J. Herbert Burke (R)	61,191
	Charles Friedman (D)	58,899
13th District	William Lehman (D)	not opposed
14th District	Claude D. Pepper (D)	45,479
	Mike Carricarte	20,383
15th District	Dante B. Fascell (D)	68,064
	S. Peter Capua	28,444
1976		
1st District	Robert L. F. Sikes (D)	not opposed
2nd District	Don Fuqua (D)	not opposed
3rd District	Charles E. Bennett (D)	not opposed
4th District	Bill Chappell, Jr. (D)	not opposed
5th District	Richard Kelly (R)	138,371
	JoAnn Saunders (D)	96,260
6th District	C. W. Bill Young (R)	151,371
	Gabariel Cazares (D)	80,821
7th District	Sam M. Gibbons (D)	102,739
	Dusty Ownes (R)	53,599
8th District	Andy Ireland (D)	103,360
	Bob Johnson (R)	74,794
9th District	Louis Frey, Jr. (R)	130,509
	Joseph A. Rosier (D)	36,630
10th District	L. A. (Skip) Bafalis (R)	164,273
	Bill Sikes (D)	83,413
11th District	Paul G. Rogers (D)	199,031
	C. Adams (Amer.)	19,406
12th District	J. Herbert Burke (R)	107,268
	Charles Friedman (D)	91,749

Vote for U.S. Representative, General Election (*Continued*)

		Total vote
13th District	William Lehman (D)	127,822
	Lee Arnold Spiegelman (R)	35,357
14th District	Claude D. Pepper (D)	82,665
	E. S. Estrella (R)	30,774
15th District	Dante B. Fascell (D)	121,292
	P. R. Cobb (R)	50,941

1978
1st District	Earl Hutto (D)	85,608
	Warren Briggs (R)	49,715
2nd District	Don Fuqua (D)	112,649
	Peter Brathwaite (R)	25,148
3rd District	Charles E. Bennett (D)	not opposed
4th District	Bill Chappell (D)	113,302
	Tom Boney (R)	41,647
5th District	David Best (D)	101,867
	Richard Kelly (R)	106,319
6th District	Jim Christison (D)	40,654
	C. W. Bill Young (R)	150,694
7th District	Sam M. Gibbons (D)	not opposed
8th District	Andy Ireland (D)	not opposed
9th District	Bill Nelson (D)	89,543
	Edward J. Gurney (R)	56,074
10th District	L. A. "Skip" Bafalis (R)	not opposed
11th District	Dan Mica (D)	123,346
	Bill James (R)	99,757
12th District	Edward J. Stack (D)	107,037
	J. Herbert Burke (R)	66,610
13th District	William Lehman (D)	not opposed
14th District	Claude Pepper (D)	65,202
	Al Cardenas (R)	38,081
15th District	Dante B. Fascell (D)	108,837
	Herbert J. Hoodwin (R)	37,897

1980
1st District	Earl Hutto (D)	119,829
	Warren Briggs (R)	75,939
2nd District	Don Fuqua (D)	138,252
	John R. LaCapra (R)	57,588
3rd District	Charles E. Bennett (D)	104,672
	Harry Radcliffe (R)	31,208
4th District	Bill Chappell, Jr. (D)	147,775
	Barney E. Dillared, Jr. (R)	76,924
5th District	Bill McCollum (R)	177,603
	David Best (D)	140,903
6th District	C. W. Bill Young (R)	not opposed
7th District	Sam M. Gibbons (D)	132,529
	Charles P. Jones (R)	52,138

Vote for U.S. Representative, General Election (*Continued*)

		Total vote
8th District	Andy Ireland (D)	151,613
	Scott Nicholson (R)	61,820
	Rod Rebholz (Ind.)	5,480
9th District	Bill Nelson (D)	139,468
	Stan Dowiat (R)	58,734
10th District	L. A. (Skip) Bafalis (R)	272,393
	Richard D. Sparkman (D)	72,646
11th District	Dan Mica (D)	201,713
	Al Coogler (R)	137,520
12th District	Clay Shaw (R)	128,561
	Alan S. Becker (D)	107,164
13th District	William Lehman	127,828
	Alvin E. Entin (R)	42,830
14th District	Claude D. Pepper (D)	92,820
	Evelio S. Estrella (R)	32,027
15th District	Dante B. Fascell (D)	132,952
	Herbert J. Hoodwin (R)	70,433

1982

1st District	Earl Hutto (D)	82,569
	J. Terryl Bechtol (R)	28,373
2nd District	Don Fuqua (D)	79,143
	Ron McNeil (R)	49,101
3rd District	Charles E. Bennett (D)	73,802
	George Grimsley (R)	13,972
4th District	Bill Chappell (D)	83,895
	Larry Gaudet (R)	41,457
5th District	Dick Batchelor (D)	49,070
	Bill McCollum (R)	69,993
6th District	Buddy MacKay (D)	85,825
	Ed Havill (R)	54,059
7th District	Sam M. Gibbons (D)	85,331
	Ken Ayers (R)	29,632
8th District	C. W. Bill Young (R)	not opposed
9th District	George H. Sheldon (D)	90,697
	Michael Bilirakis (R)	95,009
10th District	Andy Ireland (D)	not opposed
11th District	Bill Nelson (D)	101,746
	Joel Robinson (R)	42,422
12th District	Brad Culverhouse (D)	73,913
	Tom Lewis (R)	81,893
13th District	Dana N. Stevens (D)	71,239
	Connie Mack (R)	132,951
14th District	Dan Mica (D)	128,646
	Steve Mitchell (R)	47,560
15th District	Edward J. Stack (D)	67,083
	E. Clay Shaw, Jr. (R)	89,158

Vote for U.S. Representative, General Election (*Continued*)

		Total vote
16th District	Larry Smith (D)	91,888
	Maurice Berkowitz (R)	43,458
17th District	William Lehman (D)	not opposed
18th District	Claude Pepper (D)	72,183
	Ricardo Nunez (R)	29,196
19th District	Dante B. Fascell (D)	74,312
	Glenn Rinker (R)	51,969
1984		
1st District	Earl Hutto (D)	not opposed
2nd District	Don Fuqua (D)	not opposed
3rd District	Bill McCollum (R)	not opposed
4th District	Bill Chappell (D)	134,694
	Alton H. Starling (R)	73,218
5th District	Bill McCollum (R)	not opposed
6th District	Buddy MacKay (D)	167,409
	Eric Tarnley	1,174
7th District	Sam Gibbons (D)	100,430
	Michael N. Kavouklis (R)	70,280
8th District	Robert Kent (D)	45,393
	C. W. Bill Young (R)	184,553
9th District	Jack Wilson (D)	52,150
	Michael Bilirakis (R)	191,343
10th District	Patricia M. Glass (D)	77,635
	Andy Ireland (R)	126,206
11th District	Bill Nelson (D)	145,764
	Rob Quartel (R)	95,115
12th District	Tom Lewis (R)	not opposed
13th District	Connie Mack (R)	not opposed
14th District	Dan Mica (D)	153,935
	Don Ross (R)	123,926
15th District	Bill Humphrey (D)	66,833
	E. Clay Shaw, Jr. (R)	128,097
16th District	Larry Smith (D)	108,410
	Tom Bush (R)	83,903
17th District	William Lehman (D)	not opposed
18th District	Claude Pepper (D)	76,404
	Ricardo Nunez (R)	49,818
19th District	Dante B. Fascell (D)	115,631
	Bill Flanagan (R)	64,317
1986		
1st District	Earl Hutto (D)	97,532
	Greg Neubeck (R)	55,459
2nd District	Bill Grant (D)	110,141
	Kim O'Connor	625
3rd District	Charles E. Bennett (D)	not opposed
4th District	Bill Chappell (D)	not opposed

Vote for U.S. Representative, General Election (*Continued*)

		Total vote
5th District	Bill McCollum (R)	not opposed
6th District	Buddy MacKay (D)	143,598
	Larry Gallagher (R)	61,069
7th District	Sam Gibbons (D)	not opposed
8th District	C. W. Bill Young (R)	not opposed
9th District	Gabe Cazares (D)	68,578
	Michael Bilirakis (R)	166,540
10th District	David Higginbottom (D)	49,571
	Andy Ireland (R)	122,395
11th District	Bill Nelson (D)	149,109
	Scott Ellis (R)	55,952
12th District	Tom Lewis (D)	150,244
	write ins	936
13th District	Addison S. Gilbert III (D)	62,709
	Connie Mack (R)	187,846
14th District	Dan Mica (D)	171,976
	Rick Martin (R)	61,189
15th District	E. Clay Shaw (R)	not opposed
16th District	Larry Smith (D)	121,219
	Mary Collins (R)	52,809
17th District	William Lehman (D)	not opposed
18th District	Claude Pepper (D)	80,062
	Tom Brodie (R)	28,814
19th District	Dante B. Fascell (D)	99,215
	Bill Flanagan (R)	44,463

1988

1st District	Earl Hutto (D)	142,449
	E. D. Armbruster (R)	70,534
2nd District	Bill Grant (D)	134,269
	Dennis M. Prescott	352
3rd District	Charles E. Bennett (D)	not opposed
4th District	Craig T. James (R)	125,608
	Bill Chappell (D)	124,817
5th District	Bill McCollum (R)	not opposed
6th District	Clifford B. Stearns (R)	136,415
	Jon Mills (D)	118,756
7th District	Sam M. Gibbons (D)	not opposed
8th District	C. W. Bill Young (R)	169,165
	C. Bette Wimbish (D)	62,539
9th District	Michael Bilirakis (R)	223,925
	M. P. Bigenho	242
10th District	Andy Ireland (D)	156,563
	David B. Higginbottom (D)	56,536
11th District	Bill Nelson (D)	168,390
	Billy Tolley (R)	108,373

Vote for U.S. Representative, General Election (*Continued*)

		Total vote
12th District	Thomas F. Lewis (R)	not opposed
13th District	Porter J. Goss (R)	231,170
	Jack Conway (D)	93,700
14th District	Harry A. Johnston (D)	173,292
	Ken Adams (R)	142,635
15th District	E. Clay Shaw (R)	132,090
	Michael A. Kuhle (D)	67,746
16th District	Larry Smith (D)	153,032
	Joseph Smith (R)	67,461
17th District	William Lehman (D)	not opposed
18th District	Claude D. Pepper (D)	not opposed
19th District	Dante B. Fascell (D)	135,355
	Ralph Carlos Rocheteau (R)	51,628

1990

1st District	Earl Hutto (D)	88,416
	Terry Ketchel (R)	80,851
2nd District	Pete Peterson (D)	103,032
	Bill Grant (R)	77,939
3rd District	Charles Bennett (D)	84,280
	Rod Sullivan (R)	31,727
4th District	Reid Hughes (D)	95,320
	Craig T. James (R)	120,895
5th District	Bob Fletcher (D)	63,253
	Bill McCollum (R)	94,453
6th District	Art Johnson (D)	95,421
	Clifford B. Stearns (R)	138,588
7th District	Sam M. Gibbons (D)	99,464
	Charles D. Prout (R)	47,765
8th District	C. W. Bill Young (R)	not opposed
9th District	Cheryl D. Knapp (D)	102,503
	Michael Bilirakis (R)	142,163
10th District	Andy Ireland (R)	not opposed
11th District	Jim Bacchus (D)	120,991
	Bill Tolley (R)	111,970
12th District	Tom Lewis (R)	not opposed
13th District	Porter J. Goss (R)	not opposed
14th District	Harry Johnston (D)	156,055
	Scott Shore (R)	80,249
15th District	Charles Goodmon	2,374
	E. Clay Shaw, Jr. (R)	104,295
16th District	Larry Smith (D)	not opposed
17th District	William Lehman (D)	79,569
	Earl Rodney (R)	22,029
18th District	Bernard Anscher (D)	36,978
	Ileana Ros-Lehtinen (R)	56,364

Vote for U.S. Representative, General Election (*Continued*)

		Total vote
19th District	Dante B. Fascell (D)	87,696
	Bob Allen (R)	53,796

1992
1st District	Earl Hutto (D)	118,941
	Terry Ketchel (R)	100,349
	Barbara Ann Rodgers-Hendricks (G)	9,342
2nd District	Pete Peterson (D)	167,215
	Ray Wagner (R)	60,425
3rd District	Corrine Brown (D)	91,915
	Don Weidner (R)	63,070
4th District	Tillie Fowler (R)	135,883
	Mattox Hair (D)	103,531
5th District	Karen L. Thurman (D)	129,698
	Tom Hogan (R)	114,356
	Cindy Munkittrick (I)	19,462
6th District	Clifford B. Stearns (R)	144,195
	Phil Denton (D)	76,419
7th District	John L. Mica (R)	125,823
	Dan Webster (D)	96,945
8th District	Bill McCollum (R)	141,977
	Chuck Kovaleski (D)	65,145
9th District	Michael Bilirakis (R)	158,028
	Cheryl Davis Knapp (D)	110,135
10th District	C. W. Bill Young (R)	149,606
	Karren Moffitt (D)	114,809
11th District	Sam Gibbons (D)	100,984
	Mark Sharpe (R)	77,640
	Joe DeMinico (I)	12,730
12th District	Charles T. Canady (R)	100,484
	Tom Mims (D)	92,346
13th District	Dan Miller (R)	158,881
	Rand Snell (D)	115,767
14th District	Porter J. Goss (R)	220,351
	James H. King (I)	48,160
15th District	Jim Bacchus (D)	132,412
	Bill Tolley (R)	128,873
16th District	Tom Lewis (R)	157,322
	John P. Comerford (D)	101,237
17th District	Carrie Meek (D)	102,784
18th District	Ileana Ros-Lehtinen (R)	104,755
	Magda Montiel Davis (D)	52,142
19th District	Harry Johnston (D)	177,423
	Larry Metz (R)	103,867
20th District	Peter Deutsch (D)	130,959
	Beverly Kennedy (R)	91,589
	James M. Blackburn (I)	15,341

Vote for U.S. Representative, General Election (*Continued*)

		Total vote
21st District	Lincoln Diaz-Balart (R)	not opposed
22nd District	E. Clay Shaw (R)	128,400
	Gwen Margolis (D)	91,625
	Richard Stephens (I)	15,469
	Michael F. Petrie (I)	6,312
	Bernard Anscher (I)	5,274
23rd District	Alcee L. Hastings (D)	84,249
	Ed Fielding (R)	44,807
	Al Woods (I)	14,879

1994

1st District	Joe Scarboro (R)	112,901
	Vince Whibbs (D)	70,389
2nd District	Pete Peterson (D)	117,404
	Carole Griffin (R)	74,011
3rd District	Corrine Brown (D)	63,845
	Marc Little (R)	46,895
4th District	Tillie K. Fowler (R)	not opposed
5th District	Karen Thurman (D)	125,780
	Don Garlits (R)	94,093
6th District	Clifford Stearns (R)	148,698
	Phil Denton	1,332
7th District	John Mica (R)	131,711
	Edward Goddard (D)	47,747
8th District	Bill McCollum (R)	131,376
	Ron Bedell	439
9th District	Michael Bilirakis (R)	177,253
	Richard Grayson	152
10th District	C. W. Bill Young (R)	not opposed
11th District	Sam Gibbons (D)	76,814
	Mark Sharpe (R)	72,119
12th District	Charles Canady (R)	106,123
	Robert Connors (D)	57,203
13th District	Dan Miller (R)	not opposed
14th District	Porter J. Goss (R)	not opposed
15th District	Dave Weldon (R)	117,027
	Sue Munsey (D)	100,513
16th District	Mark Foley (R)	122,734
	John Comerford (D)	88,646
17th District	Carrie Meek (D)	75,741
	Maureen Coletta	11
18th District	Ileana Ros-Lehtinen (R)	not opposed
19th District	Harry Johnston (D)	147,591
	Peter Tsakanik (R)	75,779
20th District	Peter Deutsch (D)	114,615
	Beverly Kennedy (R)	72,516
21st District	Lincoln Diaz-Balart (R)	not opposed

Vote for U.S. Representative, General Election (*Continued*)

			Total vote
22nd District	E. Clay Shaw (R)		119,690
	Hermine Wiener (D)		69,215
23rd District	Alcee L. Hastings (D)		not opposed

Vote for Other Elective Offices

D—denotes Democratic; R—Republican (If not indicated, Democratic)

Note: The two-year election in 1964 was to shift elections for State office from Presidential election years.

Note: For years prior to 1948, see *The Florida Handbook 1985–1986.*

Secretary of State

		1st primary	2nd primary	General Election
1948	R. A. Gray	Unopposed		282,901
1952	R.A.Gray	Unopposed		588,153
1956	R.A.Gray	476,502		541,751
	Edward G. Hornsby	144,824		
1960	Tom Adams	235,967	437,524	817,927
	E. V. "Gene" Fisher	77,375		
	Thomas S. Fouts	29,981		
	Ed Hornsby	42,472		
	Angus Laird	70,634		
	J. L. (Mac) McMullen	65,727		
	N. D. Wainwright	48,949		
	Jess Yarborough	145,026	306,719	
	Percy W. Thompson (R)	Unopposed		471,770
1964	Tom Adams	Unopposed		868,158
1966	Tom Adams	Unopposed		628,102
1970	Don D. Meiklejohn (R)	Unopposed		662,123
	J. L. (White Acre) McMullen (D)	145,090		
	Richard (Dick) Stone (D)	315,703		863,949
	Stan Tait (D)	92,402		
1974	Beverly F. Dozier, Tallahassee (D)	164,630	280,847	
	J. L. (White Acre) McMullen, Live Oak (D)	100,002		
	Don Pride, Tallahassee (D)	158,588		
	Bruce A. Smathers, Jacksonville (D)	244,953	312,228	902,463
	James A. Sebesta, Temple Terrace (R)	Unopposed		794,177
1978	Beverly F. Dozier, Tallahassee (D)	224,990	342,661	

Secretary of State (*Continued*)

		1st primary	*2nd primary*	*General Election*
	Jim Fair, Tallahassee (D)	81,389		
	George Firestone, Miami (D)	253,395	472,072	1,278,658
	Joe Little, Gainesville (D)	103,275		
	Richard (Dick) Renick, Coral Gables (D)	221,022		
	Ander Crenshaw, Jacksonville (R)	Unopposed		1,045,703
1982	George Firestone, Miami (D)	Unopposed		1,459,084
	Jim (James H., Jr.) Smith, Clearwater (R)	Unopposed		1,129,785
1986	George Firestone, Tallahassee (D)	Unopposed		1,702,659
	Richard R. Renick, Miami (R)	178,475		
	Jim (James H., Jr.) Smith, Clearwater (R)	326,017		1,570,194
1988*	William T. (Bill) Key, Plantation (D)	217,640		
	Tom R. Moore, Tallahassee (D)	366,416	381,347	1,522,663
	Jim Taft, Crystal River (D) ...	228,374		
	Jim Smith, Tallahassee (R) ...	Unopposed		2,617,951
	Write-ins, General Election ..	332		
1990	Alcee L. Hastings, Miami (D)	313,758	146,375	
	Jim Minter, Tallahassee (D) ..	357,340	300,022	1,388,600
	John Rogers, Lake Wales (D) .	275,370		
	Jim Smith, Tallahassee (R) ...	Unopposed		2,030,659
	Jim Fair (write-in)			410
1994	Sandra B. Morthan, Largo (R)	Unopposed		2,075,207
	Ron Saunders, Key West (D)	Unopposed		1,887,688

*To complete term of George Firestone, resigned.

Attorney General

		1st primary	*2nd primary*	*General Election*
1948	L. Grady Burton	132,946	188,531	
	P. Guy Crews	70,134		

Explanation: Where a candidate for party nomination is unopposed, his name does not appear on the primary ballot. Until 1970, the name of a nominee did appear on the general election ballot whether opposed or not because voters then could have the opportunity of writing in the name of another person. This opportunity was eliminated in 1970.

Attorney General (*Continued*)

		1st primary	2nd primary	General Election
	Richard W. Ervin	143,447	275,259	270,451
	Hugh L. McArthur	51,047		
1952	Richard Ervin	Unopposed		577,758
1956	Richard (Dick) Ervin	473,855		529,154
	Prentice P. Pruitt	127,156		
1960	Richard (Dick) Ervin	Unopposed		838,329
	Carl V. Wisner, Jr. (R)	Unopposed		439,208
1964	Earl Faircloth	469,638		826,036
	James W. Kynes	469,039		
1966	Earl Faircloth	Unopposed		717,630
	Ellis S. Rubin (R)	Unopposed		548,504
1970	Elmer Friday (D)	214,192	317,734	
	William A. Meadows, Jr. (D)	157,640		
	Robert L. Shevin (D)	229,389	373,774	943,776
	Thom Rumberger (R)	Unopposed		592,519
1974	Robert L. Shevin, Miami (D)	Unopposed		
1978	Alan Becker, North Miami Beach (D)	232,416	329,455	
	Barry Richard, Tallahassee (D)	231,518		
	Jim Smith, Tallahassee (D)	407,579	497,255	Unopposed
1982	Fred Goldstein, Lauderhill (D)	244,013		
	Jim Smith, Tallahassee (D)	692,575		Unopposed
1986	Robert A. (Bob) Butterworth, Hollywood (D)	301,519	403,413	1,900,890
	Walter T. Dartland, Miami (D)	77,863		
	Edgar M. (Ed) Dunn, Daytona Beach (D)	316,419	402,413	
	Joseph M. (Joe) Gersten, Coral Gables (D)	231,306		
	Lavon Ward, Fort Lauderdale (R)	126,805		
	Jim Watt, Lake Park (R)	346,585		1,341,090
1990	Robert A. Butterworth, Hollywood (D)	Unopposed		
1994	Robert A. Butterworth, Hollywood (D)	Unopposed		2,312,010
	Henry Ferro, Miami Beach (R)	Unopposed		1,709,139

Comptroller

		1st primary	2nd primary	General Election
1948	Edwin G. Fraser	162,358		
	C. M. Gay	242,618		281,356
	H. A. Lee	52,499		
1952	C. M. Gay	Unopposed		588,421
1956	Ray E. Green	Unopposed		526,463

Comptroller (*Continued*)

		1st primary	2nd primary	General Election
1960	Ray E. Green	524,294		718,514
	J. L. Lee	122,753		
1964	Ray Green	Unopposed		851,200
1966	Ronald Brugh	33,986		
	Fred O. (Bud) Dickinson, Jr.	677,598		627,934
	Walter Franzel	29,820		
	Larry Kelley	76,877		
1970	Fred O. (Bud) Dickinson, Jr. (D)	Unopposed		1,013,569
	James R. Sabatino (R)	Unopposed		526,511
1974	Napoleon Bryant, Tallahassee (D)	85,292		
	Fred O. (Bud) Dickinson, Jr. West Palm Beach (D)	274,957	191,138	
	Gerald (Jerry) Lewis, Miami (D)	324,758	415,405	1,098,845
	William Muntzing, Kissimmee (R)	Unopposed		551,703
1978	Don Dansby, Perry (D)	159,238		
	Gerald (Jerry) Lewis, Tallahassee (D)	691,585		Unopposed
1982	Ralph Haben, Palmetto (D)	378,230		
	Gerald (Jerry) Lewis, Tallahassee (D)	589,400		Unopposed
1986	Jerry T. Gates, Wewahitchka (R)	231,794		1,254,288
	S. Craig Kiser, Tallahassee (R)	224,151		
	Gerald Lewis, Tallahassee (D)	Unopposed		1,922,552
1990	Chris Comstrock, St. Petersburg (R)	Unopposed		1,358,069
	Gerald Lewis, Tallahassee (D)	Unopposed		1,999,208
1994	Gerald Lewis, Tallahassee (D)	522,702		1,947,815
	Art Simon Miami (D)	246,082		
	Chris Comstock, St. Petersburg (R)	351,795		
	Bob Milligan, Panama City (R)	364,169		2,026,481

Treasurer

		1st primary	2nd primary	General Election
1948	R. T. Carlisle	81,570		
	J. Edwin Larson	299,337		271,009
1952	J. Edwin Larson	Unopposed		576,082

Treasurer (*Continued*)

		1st primary	2nd primary	General Election
1956	J. Edwin Larson	Unopposed		521,441
1960	Al Cahill	131,027		
	Earnest E. Collins	106,386		
	J. Edwin Larson	417,100		834,638
	William O. Murrell, Jr.	50,046		
	Charles R. Fisher (R)	Unopposed		463,484
1964	J. Edwin Larson	Unopposed		827,534
1966	Ray Gann	53,919		
	Bob Harris	306,398		
	Broward Williams	461,013		748,387
	Joseph S. Yasecko (R)	Unopposed		483,863
1970	Thomas W. Johnston (R)	137,263		
	Thomas D. O'Malley (D)	370,403		869,010
	Tom Slade (R)	181,635		723,755
	Broward Williams (D)	258,340		
1974	Thomas D. O'Malley, Tallahassee (D)	414,052	843,955	
	Fitzhugh Powell, Jacksonville (D)	91,686		
	Jack Shreve, Merritt Island (D)	192,890		
	Jeffrey L. Latham, Davie (R)	124,459		778,550
	Gene Tubbs, Merritt Island (R)	99,460		
1976	Bill Gunter, Orlando (D)	695,591		1,839,830
	Aubyn H. Hodges, Tallahassee (D)	94,316		
	Roosevelt K. Jones, St. Petersburg (D)	71,284		
	Belly Armistead, Rockledge (R)	141,979		848,500
	Jeff Latham, Fort Lauderdale (R)	135,901		

Note: Off-year election by reason of impeachment and resignation of Treasurer Thomas D. O'Malley.

1978	Donald F. Hazelton, West Palm Beach (D)	182,907		
	Bill Gunter, Tallahassee (D)	735,523		1,758,435
	Jeffrey L. Latham, Davie (R)	Unopposed		591,730
1982	Bill Gunter, Tallahassee (D)	Unopposed		
1986	Bill Gunter, Tallahassee (D)	826,205		2,001,936
	Raphael Herman, Miami Beach (D)	129,393		
	Tim Keegan, Vero Beach (R)	186,853		
	Van Poole, Fort Lauderdale (R)	282,878		1,282,707

Treasurer (*Continued*)

		1st primary	2nd primary	General Election
1988*	Walt Dartland, Miami (D) ...	219,727		
	Ken Jenne, Fort Lauderdale (D)	298,624	345,334	1,935,137
	John Vogt, Cocoa Beach (D) .	360,847	310,653	
	Tom Gallagher, Miami (R) ...	459,451		2,223,401
	Raphael Herman, Miami Beach (D)	46,654		
	Jeffrey L. Latham, Davie (D) .	94,608		
1990	Tom Gallagher, Tallahassee (R)	Unopposed		1,965,216
	George Stuart, Orlando (D) ..	688,989		1,469,541
	Jake Crouch, Seminole (D) ...	211,045		
1994	Karen Gievers, Miami (D) ...	294,324		
	Bill Nelson, Melbourne (D) ..	422,724		2,070,604
	Fred Westman, Dade City (D)	58,097		
	R. K. Hunter, Pensacola (D) ..	265,636		
	Tim Ireland, Fort Meyers (R) .	475,204		1,933,570

Superintendent of Public Instruction

		1st primary	2nd primary	General Election
1948	Tom D. Bailey	207,874		267,550
	Robert D. Dolly	105,824		
	Robert C. Marshall	80,947		
1952	Tom D. Bailey	402,838		580,019
	Ray Van Dusen	106,200		
1956	Tom D. Bailey	Unopposed		521,353
1960	Tom D. Bailey	Unopposed		831,829
	Gilbert P. Richardson (R)	Unopposed		457,859
1964	Tom D. Bailey	Unopposed		826,036
1966	Floyd T. Christian	Unopposed		578,624

(Note: In 1968 Constitution, title of office was changed from Superintendent of Public Instruction to Commissioner of Education.)

Commissioner of Education

		1st primary	2nd primary	General Election
1970	Robert L. Froemke (R)	Unopposed		615,259
	Floyd T. Christian (D)	Unopposed		936,184
1974	N.E. (Ed) Fenn, Jr., Tallahassee (D)	57,911		
	Sheila King, Coral Gables (D)	128,097		
	Zollie M. Maynard, Sr., Tallahassee (D)	66,468		

Commissioner of Education (*Continued*)

		1st primary	2nd primary	General Election
	John S. Shipp, Tallahassee (D)	54,574		
	Ralph D. Turlington, Gainesville (D)	342,918		1,046,427
	Carl M. Kuttler, Jr., St. Petersburg (R)	Unopposed		576,947
1978	Ralph D. Turlington, Tallahassee (D)	Unopposed		1,436,240
	Herman B. Williams, Gainesville (R)	Unopposed		811,770
1982	Ralph D. Turlington, Tallahassee (D)	Unopposed		
1986	Betty Castor, Tampa (D)	573,415		1,812,570
	Larry Hawkins, Perrine (D)	276,962		
	Rayma C. Page, Fort Myers (D)	81,231		
	Ron Howard, Boca Raton (R)	147,891	182,970	1,384,762
	Vince Goodman, Riviera Beach (R)	78,367		
	J. Stanley (Stan) Marshall, Tallahassee (R)	141,496	170,900	
	Brian Pappas, Naples (R)	108,118		
1990	Betty Castor, Tallahassee (D)	Unopposed		2,253,809
	Claude R. Kirk, North Palm Beach (R)	316,767		1,167,957
	Amefika Gauka, Tallahassee (R)	52,334		
	Ken Stepp, Inverness (R)	219,153		
	Brian Pappas, Naples (write-in)	3,363		
1994	John Griffin, Ormond Beach (D)	364,440		
	Doug Jamerson, Tallahassee (D)	377,018		1,855,705
	Frank Brogan, Stuart (R)	330,356		2,125,488
	John Kager, Orange Park (R)	134,965		
	Bob Morris, Sarasota (R)	280,943		

Commissioner of Agriculture

		1st primary	2nd primary	General Election
1948	Nathan Mayo	320,712		276,300
	Ammon McClellan	103,621		
1952	Nathan Mayo	Unopposed		586,322
1956	Nathan Mayo	Unopposed		538,142
1960	S. Benson Berger	37,487		
	Loran V. Carlton	93,540		

Commissioner of Agriculture (*Continued*)

		1st primary	2nd primary	General Election
	Doyle Conner	319,944	435,294	712,305
	W. R. (Buster) Hancock	251,122	370,644	
	Charlie Race	15,145		
	Carey Reams	12,960		
1964	Doyle E. Conner	Unopposed		849,593
1966	Doyle E. Conner	Unopposed		599,795
1970	Doyle E. Conner (D)	Unopposed		
1974	Doyle E. Conner, Tallahassee (D)	Unopposed		1,097,452
	Donald W. Webb, Lakeland (American)	Unopposed		302,650
1978	Doyle E. Conner, Tallahassee (D)	Unopposed		
1982	Doyle E. Conner, Tallahassee (D)	Unopposed		1,568,591
	Barbara Lindsey, Stuart (R)	Unopposed		1,010,946
1986	Charles H. Bronson, Jr., Orlando (R)	309,476		1,419,833
	Doyle E. Conner, Tallahassee (D)	Unopposed		1,797,276
	J. Smith, Fort Lauderdale (R)	165,650		
1990	Charles Bronson, Satellite Beach (R)	292,027		1,502,324
	Jack Dodd, Tallahassee (R)	103,702		
	Ron Howard, Boca Raton (R)	207,503		
	Bob Crawford, Winter Haven (D)	Unopposed		1,867,204
	Brett Merkey (write-in)			551
1994	Bob Crawford, Tallahassee (D)	Unopposed		2,044,995
	Frank Darden, Tallahassee (R)	Unopposed		withdrew
	Jim Smith, Tallahassee (R)			1,968,418

Supreme Court

Non-partisan selection of Justices of the Supreme Court and Judges of the District Courts of Appeal began in 1972. In these elections, the second primary serves as the general election. All electors, regardless of political party affiliation, if any, may vote in judicial elections.

In 1976, the Constitution was amended to provide for the Governor to fill each vacancy on the Supreme Court from among three persons deemed eligible by the Judicial Nominating Commission. This appointment would be until the next general election occurring at least one year after the date of appointment. At that election, and thereafter for terms of six years, the Justice's name would be presented to the voters in the language: "Shall Justice

_____ be retained in office?" If a majority of the voters ballot not to retain the Justice, a vacancy would exist and the Governor makes a new appointment.

The first contested elections for incumbents occurred in 1984 when Justices Raymond Ehrlich and Leander J. Shaw, Jr., were confronted by a campaign organized by disgruntled supporters of a proposed revenue-limiting constitutional amendment ruled off the ballot by the Supreme Court.

The results: Ehrlich, for 2,271,158, against 891,942; Shaw, for 2,232,038, against 870,113.

Chief Justice Leander Shaw was the target in 1990 of an organized campaign to oust him because of an opinion he had written upholding the privacy rights of pregnant women. A counter campaign by lawyers and editorial support by media resulting in Shaw prevailing by 1,821,534 or 59.6 percent, to 1,236,853.

Again in 1992, there was a statewide campaign to unseat a Justice, this time the Chief Justice, Rosemary Barkett. She received 2,665,302 votes to be retained, against 1,710,772.

Public Service Commissioner

		1st primary	2nd primary	General Election
1972	Gerald Lewis (D)	394,815		1,091,742
	Jess Yarborough (D)	314,659		
	Paula Hawkins (R)	Unopposed		1,123,801
1974	*Group No. 1*			
	Alcee L. Hastings, Fort Lauderdale (D)	242,122		
	William T. Mayo, Tallahassee (D)	329,555		Unopposed
	Group No. 2			
	William H. Bevis, Tallahassee (D)	Unopposed		926,197
	Noel R. Bacon, Fort Lauderdale (R)	Unopposed		648,056
1976	Phil Brewer, Miami (D)	328,032		
	Katie Nichols, Tallahassee (D)	426,823		1,294,724
	Paula F. Hawkins, Maitland (R)			1,406,014

(Note: The 1978 Legislature changed this office from elective to appointive, with Governor to select from list provided by bipartisan nominating commission.)

Other Parties, Statewide Registrants, 1994

American Taxpayers	163
Florida Socialist Workers	67
Green Party	393
Independent Party of Florida	433

Elections / 673

Independent Party 30,062
Libertarian Party 3,362
Populist 74
United States Taxpayers 27
Whig Party 36

Grand Total Registrants—6,441,105

Total precincts—5,369

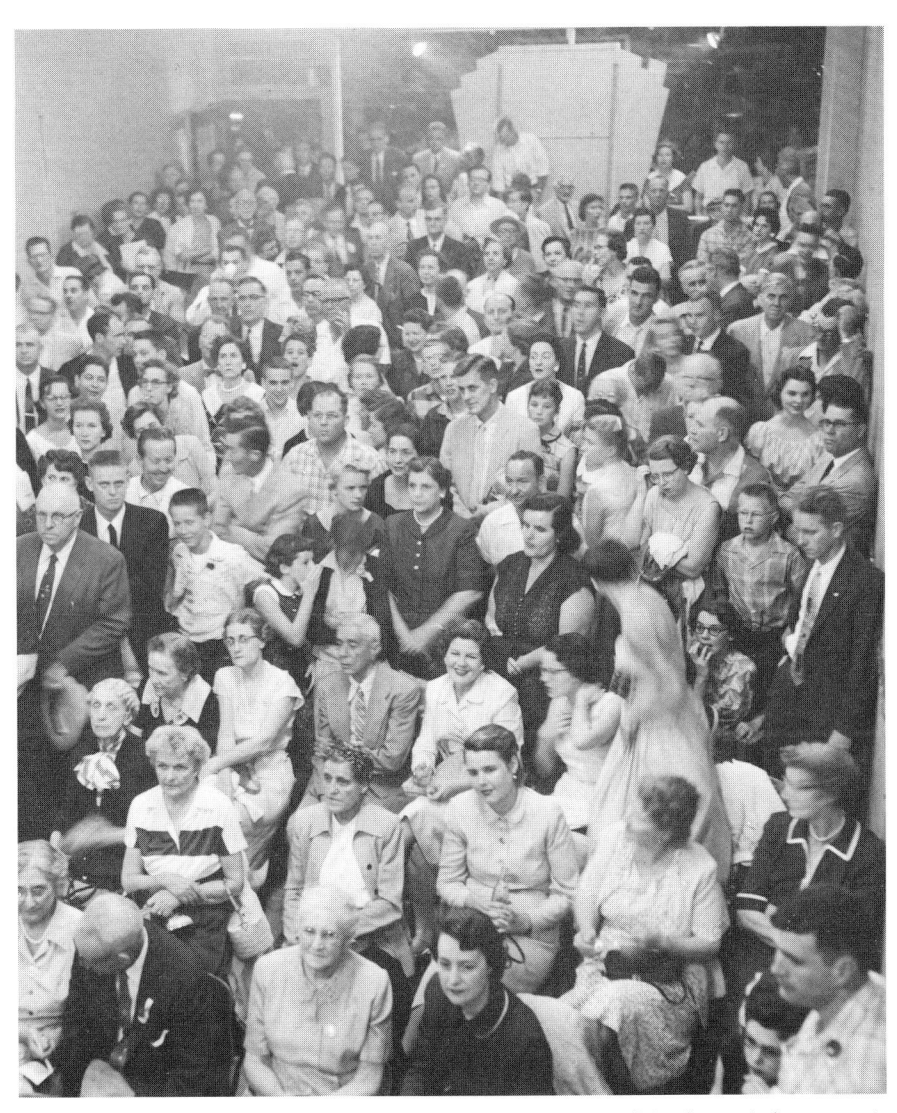

Before the days of exit polls and almost instant election returns, it was traditional to await the returns via the newswires and teletype machines at a candidate's campaign headquarters or the county court house.
Florida State Archives

The State Constitution

"All political power is inherent in the people. The enunciation herein of certain rights shall not be construed to deny or impair others retained by the people."
—Florida Constitution, Declaration of Rights

The foundation for government in Florida is the State Constitution. The Constitution tells officers of Florida's government at all levels—State, county, city, and district—what they can do and what they cannot. These directions are subject to the limitations of the Constitution of the United States.

Florida's present basic Constitution was ratified by the voters at elections in 1968 and 1972.

To obtain this Constitution, the voters first approved on November 5, 1968, three amendments proposed by the Legislature. These amendments revised all of the twenty articles of the Constitution of 1885 except Article V, governing the courts. A revision of Article V was ratified at a special election on March 14, 1972.

Adoption of the four amendments climaxed a quarter century of efforts to revise the Constitution. State commissions, legislative committees, the old Florida Bar Association and the Florida Bar, and individuals had labored to replace the old Constitution.

Amending the Constitution

The Constitution is a living body of basic laws, reflecting the changing needs of the people.

This may be illustrated by the fact that the Legislature and the voters in 1969 amended the revised Constitution despite the years of thought and drafting which had gone into the year-old Constitution.

The Constitution is amended by the Legislature passing a *joint resolution* by a three-fifths vote of the membership elected to each house. The text of a joint resolution is set forth in full in the Journals of the Senate and House of Representatives, together with the names of the Senators and Representatives showing how they voted.

Once the Legislature has proposed the amendment through adoption of the joint resolution, the Secretary of State is required by the Constitution to publish the text of the proposed amendment twice—once in the tenth week prior to the election and once in the sixth week—in a newspaper of general circulation in each county in which a newspaper is published.

Ordinarily, a proposed amendment is submitted to the voters at the next general election held ninety days after the amendment has been filed by the Legislature with the Secretary of State. However, by a law enacted by the Yes votes of three-fourths of the members elected to each house of the Legislature, a special election can be held on a date more than ninety days after the filing.

Since general elections are held regularly in November of each even numbered year, an amendment proposed by a Legislature meeting in an odd-numbered year could not receive voter action for about a year and a half unless the amendment was regarded by the extraordinary majority of the legislators as being sufficient of an emergency to justify the expense of a special election.

In drafting the revised Constitution, the Legislature separated the issues of the amendment and the special election, previously combined. Thus, should the bill for a special election fail of the required three-fourths affirmative votes, the amendment itself would be submitted at the next regular election.

Adoption of an amendment requires the Yes votes of a majority of those voting on the amendment at the general election.

Initiative

The power of the people generally to propose amendments may be invoked by petition.

This petition would set forth the proposed amendment. Signatures for its activation would be required from eight percent of the electors in each of one half of the State's Congressional districts and of the state as a whole. The percentage would be based upon the number of votes cast in both the Congressional districts and the state in the most recent Presidential election.

The Secretary of State would determine whether the petition met the requirements as to signatures and, if so, then advertise the amendment twice in each county and place it on the next general election ballot.

Constitutional Convention

Initiative could be used where an amendment is sought to a single subject of the Constitution. Power to consider revision of the entire Constitution also has been reserved to the people through a provision for calling a constitutional convention.

Again, a petition would be used. This would state the desire for a convention. Signatures would be required of fifteen percent of the electors in each of half of the Congressional districts and of the state at large. This percentage also would be based upon the number of votes cast at the most recent Presidential election.

Should such a petition be certified by the Secretary of State, this question would be placed on the ballot of the next general election held more than ninety days after the filing of the petition:

"Shall a constitutional convention be held?"

If a majority of those voting on that question said Yes, the voters at the next general election would choose one member of the convention from each district of the House of Representatives. Twenty-one days following that election, the convention would meet at Tallahassee to organize.

The work product of that convention, if any, would be filed with the Secretary of State not later than ninety days before the next succeeding general

Revision Commission

The drafters of the 1968 Constitution provided for the convening of a Constitution Revision Commission of 37 members to periodically review the Constitution with a view to initiating changes deemed desirable. (See: Article XI, Section 2.)

The first such commission organized on July 7, 1977, and completed its deliberations on May 5, 1978, the deadline for reporting. Between those dates, the commission had held 33 full membership meetings in Tallahassee and others around the state.

The commission's work product was packaged in eight amendments. All were rejected by the electorate. The 1980 Legislature submitted an amendment to repeal the provision of the Constitution for a revision commission. That, too, was rejected. This left the requirement for another revision commission to be organized in 1997 or 1998.

Votes on Significant Amendments
[See page 632.]

Constitutional Amendments
[Including questions submitted by petition]

Submitted	Ratified	Rejected
Under Constitution of 1885 (1889–1968)		
214	151	63
Under Constitution of 1968 through 1994		
98 (7 invalidated before election)	70	28

Text of Constitutions

Text of the Constitutions of 1838, 1861, 1865 and 1868 may be found in *Florida Statutes 1941, Volume 3,* identified as "Useful and Helpful Matter" and better known as "Whitfield's Notes." Text of the 1885 Constitution, as amended, may be found in many editions of *The Florida Handbook* for years prior to 1965–1966. The 1968 Constitution appears in editions beginning with 1969–1970.

The First Constitution—1838

To prepare for statehood, a convention was convened at St. Joseph at noon on December 3, 1838, to draft a constitution. St. Joseph, a compromise site, was a bustling boom town which in 1841 was devastated by yellow fever and a hurricane and passed out of existence.

A reflection of the newness of American occupation, only three of the 56 delegates were natives of Florida. The others were natives of 13 of the Union's then 26 states and four foreign countries. Lawyers and planters predominated, but there were at least two clergymen, two newspaper editors, three physicians, an innkeeper, a sea captain and fisherman, and a merchant.

Regulation of Banks

Regulation of banks was the overriding question of the convention. The territory's three great banks were secured by bonds of the Territory. Proceeds of the sale of these bonds went to the banks although the Territory was liable for their maturity. The face amount of these bonds was $3,900,000, and their subsequent default damaged Florida's governmental credit for years. The banks had based their substance upon a pyramiding scheme which used cotton and slaves as collateral. Three years after the convention the banks had collapsed.

The convention established a governmental pattern which already prevailed in many of the states: a one-term governor, a bicameral legislature, and departmental administrators selected by the legislature and eligible for reelection. (Florida's governors did not receive the right to run for reelection until 1968.)

Bankers, Clergymen Ineligible

The 1838 Constitution included three unusual provisions. Bank presidents, directors, cashiers and other officers were declared to be ineligible to serve as governor or legislator during their bank service and for a year after ceasing to serve. This was a reflection of the bank/anti-bank turmoil.

Similarly, no clergyman could serve as governor or legislator. The record does not reflect the reason for this prohibition but likely it was an outgrowth of the fierce desire of some to separate church from state. Interestingly, two delegates were clergymen, and each was shown to have voted for the prohibition although one may have been voted by proxy.

The third provision, and this lasted in Florida's Constitutions until ratification of the 1968 Constitution, denied public office to anyone participating in a duel, as the challenger, challenged, or second.

The 1838 Constitution initially provided for the offices of Secretary of State, Treasurer, Comptroller and Attorney General. In 1845, the Legislature created the executive office of Registrar of Public Lands, and in 1851 the appointment of the Board of Agriculture. These two became the basis for the Office of Commissioner of Agriculture created by the Constitution in 1868.

By the morning of January 11, the President put the question, "Shall this be the Constitution of Florida?" The vote was: Ayes, 55, Nays, 1. (The lone "Nay" was cast by Richard Fitzpatrick of Dade, who earlier had sought to repeal the law authorizing the convention.) The President then arose and said: "I solemnly proclaim and declare, this to be the Constitution of the State of Florida."

Then commenced the struggle to persuade the voters to ratify the Constitution. Suffice to say the document was adopted by the narrowest of margins. The official return was 2,070 for the Constitution and 1,975 against, but the actual figures may have been even closer.

First Ex-Officio Board

In 1855, the Legislature took the step described by Florida State University's Doctor Daisy Flory as "singularly prophetic" of a practice to become a distinguishing mark of Florida government: the first ex-officio board was established; the governor and "the departmental officers" of the executive branch were named the Board of Trustees of the Internal Improvement Fund.

The Second Constitution—1861

The onrush of the Civil War brought in Florida the election in 1860 of a convention "for the purpose of taking into consideration the position of this State in the Federal Union."

This convention met in Tallahassee on January 3, 1861, and had produced for adoption on January 10 an Ordinance of Secession and a Constitution which largely altered the existing Constitution by substituting "Confederate States" for "United States." The Ordinance of Secession declared Florida to be "a sovereign and independent Nation."

The terms of the governor and secretary of state were changed from the 1838's four years to two, to become effective in 1865 so the incumbents would not be deprived of a portion of their terms. The treasurer, comptroller and attorney general similarly had terms reduced from four years to two. Because of the collapse of the Confederacy, the 1861 Constitution became void before the 1865 election.

New to the Constitution was the duty imposed upon the General Assembly (Legislature) to "provide for the purchase or erection of a suitable building for the residence of the governor, and the governor shall reside at the seat of government."

This Constitution was not submitted to the electorate for ratification, the law creating the convention having empowered the convention to make necessary changes in the 1838 Constitution.

The Third Constitution—1865

To restore Florida to the Union, President Andrew Johnson on July 13, 1865, appointed William Marvin as Provisional Governor and directed Marvin to convene a convention. Its members having been elected, the convention met in Tallahassee on October 28, 1865. The convention annulled the Ordinance of Secession and adopted a constitution which was to have become effective on November 7, 1865, without being submitted to the people for ratification.

The Constitution never became operative, however, as Congress rejected President Johnson's plan for returning Florida and other states of the Confederacy to their pre-war status. Instead, Congress established five military districts for those states, each under the command of a general. Florida was designated as the third district.

The abortive 1865 Constitution was interesting for several of its provisions. There would have been, for the first time, a lieutenant governor, separately elected with a governor, for four-year terms with no limitation on re-election. Also, the Constitution provided for the election by the people, also for the first time, of a secretary of state, an attorney general, a comptroller, and a treasurer, for four-year terms to coincide with the term of the governor.

The Fourth Constitution—1868

This, the "Reconstruction" or "Carpetbag" Constitution, was born of partisan turmoil, largely resulting from the disenfranchisement of many whites and emancipation of blacks.

By military order, Florida was divided into 19 districts for the election of delegates to a constitutional convention. During the three days beginning November 14, 1867, this election was held under military supervision.

Soon after the delegates met in Tallahassee on January 20, 1868, bitter antagonisms arose among the delegates which divided them into factions, none of which could command the presence of a quorum. One minority faction gathered at Monticello and returned in force at midnight to Tallahassee to occupy the convention hall. Joined by two from the faction which had been engaged in writing the constitution, the new majority ousted the former majority. After much debate, the commanding general for the district of Florida finally made the choice and his selection wrote the constitution, which the people ratified May 4, 1868.

Power of Populous Counties Restricted

Those who wrote the "Carpetbag" Constitution provided for political power to reside in the governor by causing all county offices to be appointive rather than elective. The relative importance of the populous counties was reduced by limiting the number of legislators they could elect. The Constitution established a system of public schools with some state support, and of institutions for the mentally ill, blind and deaf, and a state prison.

This Constitution was the first to use "cabinet" in describing the administrative officers. To the traditional offices of secretary of state, treasurer, comptroller, and attorney general were added a surveyor general, superintendent of public instruction, adjutant general and commissioner of immigration.

Seats for Seminoles

A unique provision was the allocating of a seat in the House and Senate for the Seminole Indians. This representation was limited to Seminoles "and in no case by a white man." So far as records show, only one person sought to serve under this provision and his seating was denied because it was claimed that he was a white.

Two of the political factions of the time were the Carpetbaggers, the name applied to out-of-state adventurers whose belongings were said to be carried in satchels fashioned of carpeting, and Scalawags, who were Floridians.

The Fifth Constitution—1885

To reverse political decisions embedded in the 1868 Constitution, the calling of a new convention was approved by the voters at the general election of 1884. Convened at Tallahassee on June 9, 1885, the convention required an unexpected fifty-six days to produce its draft. The Constitution was ratified at the general election of November, 1886, and became effective January 1, 1887.

The Constitution restored the election of public offices to the people, reduced the salaries of the governor and cabinet officers and judges, made the governor ineligible for reelection, abolished the office of lieutenant governor, provided for a legislature of fixed numbers, a Senate of thirty-two members and a House of sixty-eight, and reduced the pay of legislators.

The Constitution authorized the imposition of a poll tax as a prerequisite for voting, and this became one of the two hotly contested issues, the other being appointive versus elective local offices. The poll tax, designed to reduce black voting, lasted until 1937.

This Constitution remained the basic law of the state until superseded in major part in 1968. By then, however, it was a vastly different document. Two hundred and fourteen amendments had been submitted to the voters and 151 were ratified.

The Sixth Constitution—1968

Technically, the 1968 Constitution is a revision of the 1885 Constitution. How this was accomplished is detailed in the preface to the Constitution which follows in this book.

The 1965 Legislature established a constitutional revision commission consisting of thirty-seven members, the attorney general and representatives of the governor, Supreme Court, Florida Bar, Legislature, and the public.

The commission organized on January 11, 1966, and delivered its recommendations to the Legislature on December 13. The Legislature freely exercised its right to revise the commission's draft in four special sessions, lasting a total of sixty-one days, the last adjourning on July 2, 1968.

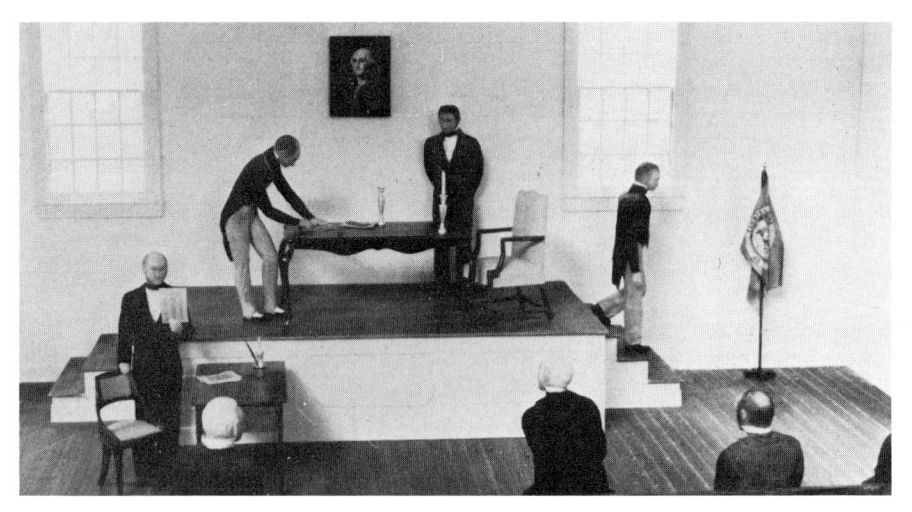

This diorama in the State Constitution Museum at Port St. Joe depicts the signing of Florida's first Constitution by delegates who assembled at old St. Joseph in 1839 to draft the document in anticipation of statehood. Department of Natural Resources

CONSTITUTION

OF THE

STATE OF FLORIDA

AS REVISED IN 1968 AND SUBSEQUENTLY AMENDED

The Constitution of the State of Florida as revised in 1968 consisted of certain revised articles as proposed by three joint resolutions which were adopted during the special session of June 24–July 3, 1968, and ratified by the electorate on November 5, 1968, together with one article carried forward from the Constitution of 1885, as amended. The articles proposed in House Joint Resolution 1-2X constituted the entire revised constitution with the exception of Articles V, VI, and VIII. Senate Joint Resolution 4-2X proposed Article VI, relating to suffrage and elections. Senate Joint Resolution 5-2X proposed a new Article VIII, relating to local government. Article V, relating to the judiciary, was carried forward from the Constitution of 1885, as amended.

Sections composing the 1968 revision have no history notes. Subsequent changes are indicated by notes appended to the affected sections. The indexes appearing at the beginning of each article, notes appearing at the end of various sections, and section and subsection headings are added editorially and are not to be considered as part of the constitution.

PREAMBLE

We, the people of the State of Florida, being grateful to Almighty God for our constitutional liberty, in order to secure its benefits, perfect our government, insure domestic tranquility, maintain public order, and guarantee equal civil and political rights to all, do ordain and establish this constitution.

ARTICLE I
DECLARATION OF RIGHTS

Sec.
1. Political power.
2. Basic rights.
3. Religious freedom.
4. Freedom of speech and press.
5. Right to assemble.
6. Right to work.
7. Military power.
8. Right to bear arms.
9. Due process.
10. Prohibited laws.
11. Imprisonment for debt.
12. Searches and seizures.
13. Habeas corpus.
14. Pretrial release and detention.
15. Prosecution for crime; offenses committed by children.
16. Rights of accused and of victims.
17. Excessive punishments.
18. Administrative penalties.
19. Costs.
20. Treason.
21. Access to courts.
22. Trial by jury.
23. Right of privacy.
24. Access to public records and meetings.
25. Taxpayers' Bill of Rights.

SECTION 1. Political power.—All political power is inherent in the people. The enunciation herein of certain rights shall not be construed to deny or impair others retained by the people.

SECTION 2. Basic rights.—All natural persons are equal before the law and have inalienable rights, among which are the right to enjoy and defend life and liberty, to pursue happiness, to be rewarded for industry, and to acquire, possess and protect property; except that the ownership, inheritance, disposition and possession of real property by aliens ineligible for citizenship may be regulated or prohibited by law. No person shall be deprived of any right because of race, religion or physical handicap.
History.—Am. S.J.R. 917, 1974; adopted 1974.

SECTION 3. Religious freedom.—There shall be no law respecting the establishment of religion or prohibiting or penalizing the free exercise thereof. Religious freedom shall not justify practices inconsistent with public morals, peace or safety. No revenue of the state or any political subdivision or agency thereof shall ever be taken from the public treasury directly or indirectly in aid of any church, sect, or religious denomination or in aid of any sectarian institution.

SECTION 4. Freedom of speech and press.—Every person may speak, write and publish his sentiments on all subjects but shall be responsible for the abuse of that right. No law shall be passed to restrain or abridge the liberty of speech or of the press. In all criminal prosecutions and civil actions for defamation the truth may be given in evidence. If the matter charged as defamatory is true and was published with good motives, the party shall be acquitted or exonerated.

SECTION 5. Right to assemble.—The people shall have the right peaceably to assemble, to instruct their representatives, and to petition for redress of grievances.

SECTION 6. Right to work.—The right of persons to work shall not be denied or abridged on account of membership or non-membership in any labor union or labor organization. The right of employees, by and through a labor organization, to bargain collectively shall not be denied or abridged. Public employees shall not have the right to strike.

SECTION 7. Military power.—The military power shall be subordinate to the civil.

SECTION 8. Right to bear arms.—
(a) The right of the people to keep and bear arms in defense of themselves and of the lawful authority of the state shall not be infringed, except that the manner of bearing arms may be regulated by law.
(b) There shall be a mandatory period of three days, excluding weekends and legal holidays, between the purchase and delivery at retail of any handgun. For the purposes of this section, "purchase" means the transfer of money or other valuable consideration to the retailer, and "handgun" means a firearm capable of being carried and used by one hand, such as a pistol or revolver. Holders of a concealed weapon permit as prescribed in Florida law shall not be subject to the provisions of this paragraph.
(c) The legislature shall enact legislation implementing subsection (b) of this section, effective no later than December 31, 1991, which shall provide that anyone violating the provisions of subsection (b) shall be guilty of a felony.

(d) This restriction shall not apply to a trade in of another handgun.
History.—Am. C.S. for S.J.R. 43, 1989; adopted 1990.

SECTION 9. Due process.—No person shall be deprived of life, liberty or property without due process of law, or be twice put in jeopardy for the same offense, or be compelled in any criminal matter to be a witness against himself.

SECTION 10. Prohibited laws.—No bill of attainder, ex post facto law or law impairing the obligation of contracts shall be passed.

SECTION 11. Imprisonment for debt.—No person shall be imprisoned for debt, except in cases of fraud.

SECTION 12. Searches and seizures.—The right of the people to be secure in their persons, houses, papers and effects against unreasonable searches and seizures, and against the unreasonable interception of private communications by any means, shall not be violated. No warrant shall be issued except upon probable cause, supported by affidavit, particularly describing the place or places to be searched, the person or persons, thing or things to be seized, the communication to be intercepted, and the nature of evidence to be obtained. This right shall be construed in conformity with the 4th Amendment to the United States Constitution, as interpreted by the United States Supreme Court. Articles or information obtained in violation of this right shall not be admissible in evidence if such articles or information would be inadmissible under decisions of the United States Supreme Court construing the 4th Amendment to the United States Constitution.
History.—Am. H.J.R. 31–H, 1982; adopted 1982.

SECTION 13. Habeas corpus.—The writ of habeas corpus shall be grantable of right, freely and without cost. It shall be returnable without delay, and shall never be suspended unless, in case of rebellion or invasion, suspension is essential to the public safety.

SECTION 14. Pretrial release and detention.—Unless charged with a capital offense or an offense punishable by life imprisonment and the proof of guilt is evident or the presumption is great, every person charged with a crime or violation of municipal or county ordinance shall be entitled to pretrial release on reasonable conditions. If no conditions of release can reasonably protect the community from risk of physical harm to persons, assure the presence of the accused at trial, or assure the integrity of the judicial process, the accused may be detained.
History.—Am. H.J.R. 43–H, 1982; adopted 1982.

SECTION 15. Prosecution for crime; offenses committed by children.—
(a) No person shall be tried for capital crime without presentment or indictment by a grand jury, or for another felony without such presentment or indictment or an information under oath filed by the prosecuting officer of the court, except persons on active duty in the militia when tried by courts martial.

(b) When authorized by law, a child as therein defined may be charged with a violation of law as an act of delinquency instead of crime and tried without a jury or other requirements applicable to criminal cases. Any child so charged shall, upon demand made as provided by law before a trial in a juvenile proceeding, be tried in an appropriate court as an adult. A child found delinquent shall be disciplined as provided by law.

SECTION 16. Rights of accused and of victims.—
(a) In all criminal prosecutions the accused shall, upon demand, be informed of the nature and cause of the accusation against him, and shall be furnished a copy of the charges, and shall have the right to have compulsory process for witnesses, to confront at trial adverse witnesses, to be heard in person, by counsel or both, and to have a speedy and public trial by impartial jury in the county where the crime was committed. If the county is not known, the indictment or information may charge venue in two or more counties conjunctively and proof that the crime was committed in that area shall be sufficient; but before pleading the accused may elect in which of those counties he will be tried. Venue for prosecution of crimes committed beyond the boundaries of the state shall be fixed by law.
(b) Victims of crime or their lawful representatives, including the next of kin of homicide victims, are entitled to the right to be informed, to be present, and to be heard when relevant, at all crucial stages of criminal proceedings, to the extent that these rights do not interfere with the constitutional rights of the accused.
History.—Am. S.J.R. 135, 1987; adopted 1988.

SECTION 17. Excessive punishments.—Excessive fines, cruel or unusual punishment, attainder, forfeiture of estate, indefinite imprisonment, and unreasonable detention of witnesses are forbidden.

SECTION 18. Administrative penalties.—No administrative agency shall impose a sentence of imprisonment, nor shall it impose any other penalty except as provided by law.

SECTION 19. Costs.—No person charged with crime shall be compelled to pay costs before a judgment of conviction has become final.

SECTION 20. Treason.—Treason against the state shall consist only in levying war against it, adhering to its enemies, or giving them aid and comfort, and no person shall be convicted of treason except on the testimony of two witnesses to the same overt act or on confession in open court.

SECTION 21. Access to courts.—The courts shall be open to every person for redress of any injury, and justice shall be administered without sale, denial or delay.

SECTION 22. Trial by jury.—The right of trial by jury shall be secure to all and remain inviolate. The qualifications and the number of jurors, not fewer than six, shall be fixed by law.

SECTION 23. Right of privacy.—Every natural person has the right to be let alone and free from governmental intrusion into his private life except as otherwise provided herein. This section shall not be construed to limit the public's right of access to public records and meetings as provided by law.

History.—Added, C.S. for H.J.R. 387, 1980; adopted 1980.

SECTION 24. Access to public records and meetings.—

(a) Every person has the right to inspect or copy any public record made or received in connection with the official business of any public body, officer, or employee of the state, or persons acting on their behalf, except with respect to records exempted pursuant to this section or specifically made confidential by this Constitution. This section specifically includes the legislative, executive, and judicial branches of government and each agency or department created thereunder; counties, municipalities, and districts; and each constitutional officer, board, and commission, or entity created pursuant to law or this Constitution.

(b) All meetings of any collegial public body of the executive branch of state government or of any collegial public body of a county, municipality, school district, or special district, at which official acts are to be taken or at which public business of such body is to be transacted or discussed, shall be open and noticed to the public and meetings of the legislature shall be open and noticed as provided in Article III, Section 4(e), except with respect to meetings exempted pursuant to this section or specifically closed by this Constitution.

(c) This section shall be self-executing. The legislature, however, may provide by general law for the exemption of records from the requirements of subsection (a) and the exemption of meetings from the requirements of subsection (b), provided that such law shall state with specificity the public necessity justifying the exemption and shall be no broader than necessary to accomplish the stated purpose of the law. The legislature shall enact laws governing the enforcement of this section, including the maintenance, control, destruction, disposal, and disposition of records made public by this section, except that each house of the legislature may adopt rules governing the enforcement of this section in relation to records of the legislative branch. Laws enacted pursuant to this subsection shall contain only exemptions from the requirements of subsections (a) or (b) and provisions governing the enforcement of this section, and shall relate to one subject.

(d) All laws that are in effect on July 1, 1993 that limit public access to records or meetings shall remain in force, and such laws apply to records of the legislative and judicial branches, until they are repealed. Rules of court that are in effect on the date of adoption of this section that limit access to records shall remain in effect until they are repealed.

History.—Added, C.S. for C.S. for H.J.R.'s 1727, 863, 2035, 1992; adopted 1992.

[1]**SECTION 25. Taxpayers' Bill of Rights.**—By general law the legislature shall prescribe and adopt a Taxpayers' Bill of Rights that, in clear and concise language, sets forth taxpayers' rights and responsibilities and government's responsibilities to deal fairly with taxpayers under the laws of this state. This section shall be effective July 1, 1993.

History.—Proposed by Taxation and Budget Reform Commission, Revision No. 2, 1992, filed with the Secretary of State May 7, 1992; adopted 1992.

[1]**Note.**—This section, originally designated section 24 by Revision No. 2 of the Taxation and Budget Reform Commission, 1992, was redesignated section 25 by the editors in order to avoid confusion with section 24 as contained in H.J.R.'s 1727, 863, 2035, 1992.

ARTICLE II

GENERAL PROVISIONS

Sec.
1. State boundaries.
2. Seat of government.
3. Branches of government.
4. State seal and flag.
5. Public officers.
6. Enemy attack.
7. Natural resources and scenic beauty.
8. Ethics in government.
9. English is the official language of Florida.

SECTION 1. State boundaries.—

(a) The state boundaries are: Begin at the mouth of the Perdido River, which for the purposes of this description is defined as the point where latitude 30°16'53" north and longitude 87°31'06" west intersect; thence to the point where latitude 30°17'02" north and longitude 87°31'06" west intersect; thence to the point where latitude 30°18'00" north and longitude 87°27'08" west intersect; thence to the point where the center line of the Intracoastal Canal (as the same existed on June 12, 1953) and longitude 87°27'00" west intersect; the same being in the middle of the Perdido River; thence up the middle of the Perdido River to the point where it intersects the south boundary of the State of Alabama, being also the point of intersection of the middle of the Perdido River with latitude 31°00'00" north; thence east, along the south boundary line of the State of Alabama, the same being latitude 31°00'00" north to the middle of the Chattahoochee River; thence down the middle of said river to its confluence with the Flint River; thence in a straight line to the head of the St. Marys River; thence down the middle of said river to the Atlantic Ocean; thence due east to the edge of the Gulf Stream or a distance of three geographic miles whichever is the greater distance; thence in a southerly direction along the edge of the Gulf Stream or along a line three geographic miles from the Atlantic coastline and three leagues distant from the Gulf of Mexico coastline, whichever is greater, to and through the Straits of Florida and westerly, including the Florida reefs, to a point due south of and three leagues from the southernmost point of the Marquesas Keys; thence westerly along a straight line to a point due south of and three leagues from Loggerhead Key, the westernmost of the Dry Tortugas Islands; thence westerly, northerly and easterly along the arc of a curve three leagues distant from Loggerhead Key to a point due north of Loggerhead Key; thence northeast along a straight line to a point three leagues from the coastline of Florida; thence northerly and westerly three leagues distant from the coastline to a point west of the mouth of the Perdido River three leagues from the coastline as measured on a line bearing south 0°01'00" west from the point of beginning; thence northerly along said line to the point of beginning. The State of Florida shall also include any additional territory within the United States adjacent to the Peninsula of Florida lying south of the St. Marys River, east of the Perdido River, and south of the States of Alabama and Georgia.

(b) The coastal boundaries may be extended by statute to the limits permitted by the laws of the United States or international law.

SECTION 2. Seat of government.—The seat of government shall be the City of Tallahassee, in Leon County, where the offices of the governor, lieutenant governor, cabinet members and the supreme court shall be maintained and the sessions of the legislature shall be held; provided that, in time of invasion or grave emergency, the governor by proclamation may for the period of the emergency transfer the seat of government to another place.

SECTION 3. Branches of government.—The powers of the state government shall be divided into legislative, executive and judicial branches. No person belonging to one branch shall exercise any powers appertaining to either of the other branches unless expressly provided herein.

SECTION 4. State seal and flag.—The design of the great seal and flag of the state shall be prescribed by law.

SECTION 5. Public officers.—

(a) No person holding any office of emolument under any foreign government, or civil office of emolument under the United States or any other state, shall hold any office of honor or of emolument under the government of this state. No person shall hold at the same time more than one office under the government of the state and the counties and municipalities therein, except that a notary public or military officer may hold another office, and any officer may be a member of a constitution revision commission, taxation and budget reform commission, constitutional convention, or statutory body having only advisory powers.

(b) Each state and county officer, before entering upon the duties of the office, shall give bond as required by law, and shall swear or affirm:

"I do solemnly swear (or affirm) that I will support, protect, and defend the Constitution and Government of the United States and of the State of Florida; that I am duly qualified to hold office under the Constitution of the state; and that I will well and faithfully perform the duties of _(title of office)_ on which I am now about to enter. So help me God.",

and thereafter shall devote personal attention to the duties of the office, and continue in office until his successor qualifies.

(c) The powers, duties, compensation and method of payment of state and county officers shall be fixed by law.

History.—Am. H.J.R. 1616, 1988; adopted 1988.

SECTION 6. Enemy attack.—In periods of emergency resulting from enemy attack the legislature shall have power to provide for prompt and temporary succession to the powers and duties of all public offices the incumbents of which may become unavailable to execute the functions of their offices, and to adopt such other measures as may be necessary and appropriate to insure the continuity of governmental operations during the emergency. In exercising these powers, the legislature may depart from other requirements of this constitution, but only to the extent necessary to meet the emergency.

SECTION 7. Natural resources and scenic beauty. It shall be the policy of the state to conserve and protect its natural resources and scenic beauty. Adequate provision shall be made by law for the abatement of air and water pollution and of excessive and unnecessary noise.

SECTION 8. Ethics in government.—A public office is a public trust. The people shall have the right to secure and sustain that trust against abuse. To assure this right:

(a) All elected constitutional officers and candidates for such offices and, as may be determined by law, other public officers, candidates, and employees shall file full and public disclosure of their financial interests.

(b) All elected public officers and candidates for such offices shall file full and public disclosure of their campaign finances.

(c) Any public officer or employee who breaches the public trust for private gain and any person or entity inducing such breach shall be liable to the state for all financial benefits obtained by such actions. The manner of recovery and additional damages may be provided by law.

(d) Any public officer or employee who is convicted of a felony involving a breach of public trust shall be subject to forfeiture of rights and privileges under a public retirement system or pension plan in such manner as may be provided by law.

(e) No member of the legislature or statewide elected officer shall personally represent another person or entity for compensation before the government body or agency of which the individual was an officer or member for a period of two years following vacation of office. No member of the legislature shall personally represent another person or entity for compensation during term of office before any state agency other than judicial tribunals. Similar restrictions on other public officers and employees may be established by law.

(f) There shall be an independent commission to conduct investigations and make public reports on all complaints concerning breach of public trust by public officers or employees not within the jurisdiction of the judicial qualifications commission.

(g) This section shall not be construed to limit disclosures and prohibitions which may be established by law to preserve the public trust and avoid conflicts between public duties and private interests.

(h) Schedule—On the effective date of this amendment and until changed by law:

(1) Full and public disclosure of financial interests shall mean filing with the secretary of state by July 1 of each year a sworn statement showing net worth and identifying each asset and liability in excess of $1,000 and its value together with one of the following:
   a. A copy of the person's most recent federal income tax return; or
   b. A sworn statement which identifies each separate source and amount of income which exceeds $1,000. The forms for such source disclosure and the rules under which they are to be filed shall be prescribed by the independent commission established in subsection (f), and such rules shall include disclosure of secondary sources of income.
(2) Persons holding statewide elective offices shall also file disclosure of their financial interests pursuant to subsection (h)(1).
(3) The independent commission provided for in subsection (f) shall mean the Florida Commission on Ethics.
History.—Proposed by Initiative Petition filed with the Secretary of State July 29, 1976; adopted 1976.

SECTION 9. English is the official language of Florida.—
(a) English is the official language of the State of Florida.
(b) The legislature shall have the power to enforce this section by appropriate legislation.
History.—Proposed by Initiative Petition filed with the Secretary of State August 8, 1988; adopted 1988.

ARTICLE III
LEGISLATURE

Sec.
1. Composition.
2. Members; officers.
3. Sessions of the legislature.
4. Quorum and procedure.
5. Investigations; witnesses.
6. Laws.
7. Passage of bills.
8. Executive approval and veto.
9. Effective date of laws.
10. Special laws.
11. Prohibited special laws.
12. Appropriation bills.
13. Term of office.
14. Civil service system.
15. Terms and qualifications of legislators.
16. Legislative apportionment.
17. Impeachment.
18. Conflict of interest.
19. State Budgeting, Planning and Appropriations Processes.

SECTION 1. Composition.—The legislative power of the state shall be vested in a legislature of the State of Florida, consisting of a senate composed of one senator elected from each senatorial district and a house of representatives composed of one member elected from each representative district.

SECTION 2. Members; officers.—Each house shall be the sole judge of the qualifications, elections, and returns of its members, and shall biennially choose its officers, including a permanent presiding officer selected from its membership, who shall be designated in the senate as President of the Senate, and in the house as Speaker of the House of Representatives. The senate shall designate a Secretary to serve at its pleasure, and the house of representatives shall designate a Clerk to serve at its pleasure. The legislature shall appoint an auditor to serve at its pleasure who shall audit public records and perform related duties as prescribed by law or concurrent resolution.

SECTION 3. Sessions of the legislature.—
(a) ORGANIZATION SESSIONS. On the fourteenth day following each general election the legislature shall convene for the exclusive purpose of organization and selection of officers.
(b) REGULAR SESSIONS. A regular session of the legislature shall convene on the first Tuesday after the first Monday in March of each odd-numbered year, and on the first Tuesday after the first Monday in March, or such other date as may be fixed by law, of each even-numbered year.
(c) SPECIAL SESSIONS.
(1) The governor, by proclamation stating the purpose, may convene the legislature in special session during which only such legislative business may be transacted as is within the purview of the proclamation, or of a communication from the governor, or is introduced by consent of two-thirds of the membership of each house.
(2) A special session of the legislature may be convened as provided by law.
(d) LENGTH OF SESSIONS. A regular session of the legislature shall not exceed sixty consecutive days, and a special session shall not exceed twenty consecutive days, unless extended beyond such limit by a three-fifths vote of each house. During such an extension no new business may be taken up in either house without the consent of two-thirds of its membership.
(e) ADJOURNMENT. Neither house shall adjourn for more than seventy-two consecutive hours except pursuant to concurrent resolution.
(f) ADJOURNMENT BY GOVERNOR. If, during any regular or special session, the two houses cannot agree upon a time for adjournment, the governor may adjourn the session sine die or to any date within the period authorized for such session; provided that, at least twenty-four hours before adjourning the session, he shall, while neither house is in recess, give each house formal written notice of his intention to do so, and agreement reached within that period by both houses on a time for adjournment shall prevail.
History.—Am. C.S. for S.J.R. 380, 1989; adopted 1990; Am. S.J.R. 2606, 1994; adopted 1994.

SECTION 4. Quorum and procedure.—
(a) A majority of the membership of each house shall constitute a quorum, but a smaller number may adjourn from day to day and compel the presence of absent members in such manner and under such penalties as

it may prescribe. Each house shall determine its rules of procedure.

(b) Sessions of each house shall be public; except sessions of the senate when considering appointment to or removal from public office may be closed.

(c) Each house shall keep and publish a journal of its proceedings; and upon the request of five members present, the vote of each member voting on any question shall be entered on the journal. In any legislative committee or subcommittee, the vote of each member voting on the final passage of any legislation pending before the committee, and upon the request of any two members of the committee or subcommittee, the vote of each member on any other question, shall be recorded.

(d) Each house may punish a member for contempt or disorderly conduct and, by a two-thirds vote of its membership, may expel a member.

(e) The rules of procedure of each house shall provide that all legislative committee and subcommittee meetings of each house, and joint conference committee meetings, shall be open and noticed to the public. The rules of procedure of each house shall further provide that all prearranged gatherings, between more than two members of the legislature, or between the governor, the president of the senate, or the speaker of the house of representatives, the purpose of which is to agree upon formal legislative action that will be taken at a subsequent time, or at which formal legislative action is taken, regarding pending legislation or amendments, shall be reasonably open to the public. All open meetings shall be subject to order and decorum. This section shall be implemented and defined by the rules of each house, and such rules shall control admission to the floor of each legislative chamber and may, where reasonably necessary for security purposes or to protect a witness appearing before a committee, provide for the closure of committee meetings. Each house shall be the sole judge for the interpretation, implementation, and enforcement of this section.

History.—Am. S.J.R.'s 1990, 2, 1990; adopted 1990.

SECTION 5. **Investigations; witnesses.**—Each house, when in session, may compel attendance of witnesses and production of documents and other evidence upon any matter under investigation before it or any of its committees, and may punish by fine not exceeding one thousand dollars or imprisonment not exceeding ninety days, or both, any person not a member who has been guilty of disorderly or contemptuous conduct in its presence or has refused to obey its lawful summons or to answer lawful questions. Such powers, except the power to punish, may be conferred by law upon committees when the legislature is not in session. Punishment of contempt of an interim legislative committee shall be by judicial proceedings as prescribed by law.

SECTION 6. **Laws.**—Every law shall embrace but one subject and matter properly connected therewith, and the subject shall be briefly expressed in the title. No law shall be revised or amended by reference to its title only. Laws to revise or amend shall set out in full the revised or amended act, section, subsection or paragraph of a subsection. The enacting clause of every law shall read: "Be It Enacted by the Legislature of the State of Florida:".

SECTION 7. **Passage of bills.**—Any bill may originate in either house and after passage in one may be amended in the other. It shall be read in each house on three separate days, unless this rule is waived by two-thirds vote; provided the publication of its title in the journal of a house shall satisfy the requirement for the first reading in that house. On each reading, it shall be read by title only, unless one-third of the members present desire it read in full. On final passage, the vote of each member voting shall be entered on the journal. Passage of a bill shall require a majority vote in each house. Each bill and joint resolution passed in both houses shall be signed by the presiding officers of the respective houses and by the secretary of the senate and the clerk of the house of representatives during the session or as soon as practicable after its adjournment sine die.

History.—Am. S.J.R. 1349, 1980; adopted 1980.

SECTION 8. **Executive approval and veto.**—

(a) Every bill passed by the legislature shall be presented to the governor for his approval and shall become a law if he approves and signs it, or fails to veto it within seven consecutive days after presentation. If during that period or on the seventh day the legislature adjourns sine die or takes a recess of more than thirty days, he shall have fifteen consecutive days from the date of presentation to act on the bill. In all cases except general appropriation bills, the veto shall extend to the entire bill. The governor may veto any specific appropriation in a general appropriation bill, but may not veto any qualification or restriction without also vetoing the appropriation to which it relates.

(b) When a bill or any specific appropriation of a general appropriation bill has been vetoed by the governor, he shall transmit his signed objections thereto to the house in which the bill originated if in session. If that house is not in session, he shall file them with the secretary of state, who shall lay them before that house at its next regular or special session, and they shall be entered on its journal.

(c) If each house shall, by a two-thirds vote, re-enact the bill or reinstate the vetoed specific appropriation of a general appropriation bill, the vote of each member voting shall be entered on the respective journals, and the bill shall become law or the specific appropriation reinstated, the veto notwithstanding.

SECTION 9. **Effective date of laws.**—Each law shall take effect on the sixtieth day after adjournment sine die of the session of the legislature in which enacted or as otherwise provided therein. If the law is passed over the veto of the governor it shall take effect on the sixtieth day after adjournment sine die of the session in which the veto is overridden, on a later date fixed in the law, or on a date fixed by resolution passed by both houses of the legislature.

SECTION 10. **Special laws.**—No special law shall be passed unless notice of intention to seek enactment thereof has been published in the manner provided by general law. Such notice shall not be necessary when the law, except the provision for referendum, is conditioned to become effective only upon approval by vote of the electors of the area affected.

SECTION 11. Prohibited special laws.—
(a) There shall be no special law or general law of local application pertaining to:
(1) election, jurisdiction or duties of officers, except officers of municipalities, chartered counties, special districts or local governmental agencies;
(2) assessment or collection of taxes for state or county purposes, including extension of time therefor, relief of tax officers from due performance of their duties, and relief of their sureties from liability;
(3) rules of evidence in any court;
(4) punishment for crime;
(5) petit juries, including compensation of jurors, except establishment of jury commissions;
(6) change of civil or criminal venue;
(7) conditions precedent to bringing any civil or criminal proceedings, or limitations of time therefor;
(8) refund of money legally paid or remission of fines, penalties or forfeitures;
(9) creation, enforcement, extension or impairment of liens based on private contracts, or fixing of interest rates on private contracts;
(10) disposal of public property, including any interest therein, for private purposes;
(11) vacation of roads;
(12) private incorporation or grant of privilege to a private corporation;
(13) effectuation of invalid deeds, wills or other instruments, or change in the law of descent;
(14) change of name of any person;
(15) divorce;
(16) legitimation or adoption of persons;
(17) relief of minors from legal disabilities;
(18) transfer of any property interest of persons under legal disabilities or of estates of decedents;
(19) hunting or fresh water fishing;
(20) regulation of occupations which are regulated by a state agency; or
[1](21) any subject when prohibited by general law passed by a three-fifths vote of the membership of each house. Such law may be amended or repealed by like vote.
(b) In the enactment of general laws on other subjects, political subdivisions or other governmental entities may be classified only on a basis reasonably related to the subject of the law.

[1]**Note.**—See the following for prohibited subject matters added under the authority of this paragraph:
s. 112.67, F.S. (Pertaining to protection of public employee retirement benefits).
s. 121.191, F.S. (Pertaining to state-administered or supported retirement systems).
s. 145.16, F.S. (Pertaining to compensation of designated county officials).
s. 189.404(2), F.S. (Pertaining to independent special districts).
s. 190.049, F.S. (Pertaining to the creation of independent special districts having the powers enumerated in two or more of the paragraphs of s. 190.012, F.S.).
s. 215.845, F.S. (Pertaining to the maximum rate of interest on bonds).
s. 235.26(10), F.S. (Pertaining to the "State Uniform Building Code for Public Educational Facilities Construction").
s. 236.014, F.S. (Pertaining to taxation for school purposes and the Florida Education Finance Program).
s. 298.76(1), F.S. (Pertaining to the grant of authority, power, rights, or privileges to a water control district formed pursuant to ch. 298, F.S.).
s. 370.083, F.S. (Pertaining to the sale or purchase of speckled sea trout or weakfish).
s. 370.172(4), F.S. (Pertaining to spearfishing in salt waters and saltwater tributaries).
s. 373.503(2)(b), F.S. (Pertaining to allocation of millage for water management purposes).

SECTION 12. Appropriation bills.—Laws making appropriations for salaries of public officers and other current expenses of the state shall contain provisions on no other subject.

SECTION 13. Term of office.—No office shall be created the term of which shall exceed four years except as provided herein.

SECTION 14. Civil service system.—By law there shall be created a civil service system for state employees, except those expressly exempted, and there may be created civil service systems and boards for county, district or municipal employees and for such offices thereof as are not elected or appointed by the governor, and there may be authorized such boards as are necessary to prescribe the qualifications, method of selection and tenure of such employees and officers.

SECTION 15. Terms and qualifications of legislators.—
(a) SENATORS. Senators shall be elected for terms of four years, those from odd-numbered districts in the years the numbers of which are multiples of four and those from even-numbered districts in even-numbered years the numbers of which are not multiples of four; except, at the election next following a reapportionment, some senators shall be elected for terms of two years when necessary to maintain staggered terms.
(b) REPRESENTATIVES. Members of the house of representatives shall be elected for terms of two years in each even-numbered year.
(c) QUALIFICATIONS. Each legislator shall be at least twenty-one years of age, an elector and resident of the district from which elected and shall have resided in the state for a period of two years prior to election.
(d) ASSUMING OFFICE; VACANCIES. Members of the legislature shall take office upon election. Vacancies in legislative office shall be filled only by election as provided by law.

SECTION 16. Legislative apportionment.—
(a) SENATORIAL AND REPRESENTATIVE DISTRICTS. The legislature at its regular session in the second year following each decennial census, by joint resolution, shall apportion the state in accordance with the constitution of the state and of the United States into not less than thirty nor more than forty consecutively numbered senatorial districts of either contiguous, overlapping or identical territory, and into not less than eighty nor more than one hundred twenty consecutively numbered representative districts of either contiguous, overlapping or identical territory. Should that session adjourn without adopting such joint resolution, the governor by proclamation shall reconvene the legislature within thirty days in special apportionment session which shall not exceed thirty consecutive days, during which no other business shall be transacted, and it shall

be the mandatory duty of the legislature to adopt a joint resolution of apportionment.

(b) FAILURE OF LEGISLATURE TO APPORTION; JUDICIAL REAPPORTIONMENT. In the event a special apportionment session of the legislature finally adjourns without adopting a joint resolution of apportionment, the attorney general shall, within five days, petition the supreme court of the state to make such apportionment. No later than the sixtieth day after the filing of such petition, the supreme court shall file with the secretary of state an order making such apportionment.

(c) JUDICIAL REVIEW OF APPORTIONMENT. Within fifteen days after the passage of the joint resolution of apportionment, the attorney general shall petition the supreme court of the state for a declaratory judgment determining the validity of the apportionment. The supreme court, in accordance with its rules, shall permit adversary interests to present their views and, within thirty days from the filing of the petition, shall enter its judgment.

(d) EFFECT OF JUDGMENT IN APPORTIONMENT; EXTRAORDINARY APPORTIONMENT SESSION. A judgment of the supreme court of the state determining the apportionment to be valid shall be binding upon all the citizens of the state. Should the supreme court determine that the apportionment made by the legislature is invalid, the governor by proclamation shall reconvene the legislature within five days thereafter in extraordinary apportionment session which shall not exceed fifteen days, during which the legislature shall adopt a joint resolution of apportionment conforming to the judgment of the supreme court.

(e) EXTRAORDINARY APPORTIONMENT SESSION; REVIEW OF APPORTIONMENT. Within fifteen days after the adjournment of an extraordinary apportionment session, the attorney general shall file a petition in the supreme court of the state setting forth the apportionment resolution adopted by the legislature, or if none has been adopted reporting that fact to the court. Consideration of the validity of a joint resolution of apportionment shall be had as provided for in cases of such joint resolution adopted at a regular or special apportionment session.

(f) JUDICIAL REAPPORTIONMENT. Should an extraordinary apportionment session fail to adopt a resolution of apportionment or should the supreme court determine that the apportionment made is invalid, the court shall, not later than sixty days after receiving the petition of the attorney general, file with the secretary of state an order making such apportionment.

SECTION 17. Impeachment.—

(a) The governor, lieutenant governor, members of the cabinet, justices of the supreme court, judges of district courts of appeal, judges of circuit courts, and judges of county courts shall be liable to impeachment for misdemeanor in office. The house of representatives by two-thirds vote shall have the power to impeach an officer. The speaker of the house of representatives shall have power at any time to appoint a committee to investigate charges against any officer subject to impeachment.

(b) An officer impeached by the house of representatives shall be disqualified from performing any official duties until acquitted by the senate, and unless the governor is impeached he may by appointment fill the office until completion of the trial.

(c) All impeachments by the house of representatives shall be tried by the senate. The chief justice of the supreme court, or another justice designated by him, shall preside at the trial, except in a trial of the chief justice, in which case the governor shall preside. The senate shall determine the time for the trial of any impeachment and may sit for the trial whether the house of representatives be in session or not. The time fixed for trial shall not be more than six months after the impeachment. During an impeachment trial senators shall be upon their oath or affirmation. No officer shall be convicted without the concurrence of two-thirds of the members of the senate present. Judgment of conviction in cases of impeachment shall remove the offender from office and, in the discretion of the senate, may include disqualification to hold any office of honor, trust or profit. Conviction or acquittal shall not affect the civil or criminal responsibility of the officer.

History.—Am. S.J.R. 459, 1987; adopted 1988.

SECTION 18. Conflict of interest.—

A code of ethics for all state employees and nonjudicial officers prohibiting conflict between public duty and private interests shall be prescribed by law.

SECTION 19. State Budgeting, Planning and Appropriations Processes.—

(a) ANNUAL BUDGETING. Effective July 1, 1994, general law shall prescribe the adoption of annual state budgetary and planning processes and require that detail reflecting the annualized costs of the state budget and reflecting the nonrecurring costs of the budget requests shall accompany state department and agency legislative budget requests, the governor's recommended budget, and appropriation bills. For purposes of this subsection, the terms department and agency shall include the judicial branch.

(b) APPROPRIATION BILLS FORMAT. Separate sections within the general appropriation bill shall be used for each major program area of the state budget; major program areas shall include: education enhancement "lottery" trust fund items; education (all other funds); human services; criminal justice and corrections; natural resources, environment, growth management, and transportation; general government; and judicial branch. Each major program area shall include an itemization of expenditures for: state operations; state capital outlay; aid to local governments and nonprofit organizations operations; aid to local governments and nonprofit organizations capital outlay; federal funds and the associated state matching funds; spending authorizations for operations; and spending authorizations for capital outlay. Additionally, appropriation bills passed by the legislature shall include an itemization of specific appropriations that exceed one million dollars ($1,000,000.00) in 1992 dollars. For purposes of this subsection, "specific appropriation," "itemization," and "major program area" shall be defined by law. This itemization threshold shall be adjusted by general law every four years to reflect the rate of inflation or deflation as indicated in the Consumer Price Index for All Urban Consumers, U.S. City Average, All Items, or successor reports as reported by the United States Department of Labor, Bureau of Labor Statistics or its successor. Substantive bills containing appropriations shall also be subject to the itemization requirement mandated under this provision and shall be subject to the governor's specific appropriation veto power described in Article III, Section 8. This subsection shall be effective July 1, 1994.

(c) APPROPRIATIONS REVIEW PROCESS. Effective July 1, 1993, general law shall prescribe requirements for each department and agency of state government to submit a planning document and supporting budget request for review by the appropriations committees of both houses of the legislature. The review shall include a comparison of the major issues in the planning document and budget requests to those major issues included in the governor's recommended budget. For purposes of this subsection, the terms department and agency shall include the judicial branch.

(d) SEVENTY-TWO HOUR PUBLIC REVIEW PERIOD. Effective November 4, 1992, all general appropriation bills shall be furnished to each member of the legislature, each member of the cabinet, the governor, and the chief justice of the supreme court at least seventy-two hours before final passage thereof, by either house of the legislature.

(e) FINAL BUDGET REPORT. Effective November 4, 1992, a final budget report shall be prepared as prescribed by general law. The final budget report shall be produced no later than the 90th day after the beginning of the fiscal year, and copies of the report shall be furnished to each member of the legislature, the head of each department and agency of the state, the auditor general, and the chief justice of the supreme court.

(f) TRUST FUNDS.

(1) No trust fund of the State of Florida or other public body may be created by law without a three-fifths ($^3\!/_5$) vote of the membership of each house of the legislature in a separate bill for that purpose only.

(2) State trust funds in existence before the effective date of this subsection shall terminate not more than four years after the effective date of this subsection. State trust funds created after the effective date of this subsection shall terminate not more than four years after the effective date of the act authorizing the creation of the trust fund. By law the legislature may set a shorter time period for which any trust fund is authorized.

(3) Trust funds required by federal programs or mandates; trust funds established for bond covenants, indentures, or resolutions, whose revenues are legally pledged by the state or public body to meet debt service or other financial requirements of any debt obligations of the state or any public body; the state transportation trust fund; the trust fund containing the net annual proceeds from the Florida Education Lotteries; the Florida retirement trust fund; trust funds for institutions under the management of the Board of Regents, where such trust funds are for auxiliary enterprises and contracts, grants, and donations, as those terms are defined by general law; trust funds that serve as clearing funds or accounts for the comptroller or state agencies; trust funds that account for assets held by the state in a trustee capacity as an agent or fiduciary for individuals, private organizations, or other governmental units; and other trust funds authorized by this Constitution, are not subject to the requirements set forth in paragraph (2) of this subsection.

(4) All cash balances and income of any trust funds abolished under this subsection shall be deposited into the general revenue fund.

(5) The provisions of this subsection shall be effective November 4, 1992.

(g) BUDGET STABILIZATION FUND. Beginning with the 1994–1995 fiscal year, at least 1% of an amount equal to the last completed fiscal year's net revenue collections for the general revenue fund shall be retained in a budget stabilization fund. The budget stabilization fund shall be increased to at least 2% of said amount for the 1995–1996 fiscal year, at least 3% of said amount for the 1996–1997 fiscal year, at least 4% of said amount for the 1997–1998 fiscal year, and at least 5% of said amount for the 1998–1999 fiscal year. Subject to the provisions of this subsection, the budget stabilization fund shall be maintained at an amount equal to at least 5% of the last completed fiscal year's net revenue collections for the general revenue fund. The budget stabilization fund's principal balance shall not exceed an amount equal to 10% of the last completed fiscal year's net revenue collections for the general revenue fund. The legislature shall provide criteria for withdrawing funds from the budget stabilization fund in a separate bill for that purpose only and only for the purpose of covering revenue shortfalls of the general revenue fund or for the purpose of providing funding for an emergency, as defined by general law. General law shall provide for the restoration of this fund. The budget stabilization fund shall be comprised of funds not otherwise obligated or committed for any purpose.

(h) STATE PLANNING DOCUMENT AND DEPARTMENT AND AGENCY PLANNING DOCUMENT PROCESSES. The governor shall recommend to the legislature biennially any revisions to the state planning document, as defined by law. General law shall require a biennial review and revision of the state planning document, shall require the governor to report to the legislature on the progress in achieving the state planning document's goals, and shall require all departments and agencies of state government to develop planning documents consistent with the state planning document. The state planning document and department and agency planning documents shall remain subject to review and revision by the legislature. The department and agency planning documents shall include a prioritized listing of planned expenditures for review and possible reduction in the event of revenue shortfalls, as defined by general law. To ensure productivity and efficiency in the executive, legislative, and judicial branches, a quality management and accountability program shall be implemented by general law. For the purposes of this subsection, the terms department and agency shall include the judicial branch. This subsection shall be effective July 1, 1993.

History.—Proposed by Taxation and Budget Reform Commission, Revision No. 1, 1992, filed with the Secretary of State May 7, 1992; adopted 1992.

ARTICLE IV

EXECUTIVE

Sec.
1. Governor.
2. Lieutenant governor.
3. Succession to office of governor; acting governor.
4. Cabinet.
5. Election of governor, lieutenant governor and cabinet members; qualifications; terms.
6. Executive departments.
7. Suspensions; filling office during suspensions.
8. Clemency.
9. Game and fresh water fish commission.
10. Attorney General.
11. Department of Veterans Affairs.
12. Department of Elderly Affairs.
13. Revenue Shortfalls.

SECTION 1. Governor.—
(a) The supreme executive power shall be vested in a governor. He shall be commander-in-chief of all military forces of the state not in active service of the United States. He shall take care that the laws be faithfully executed, commission all officers of the state and counties, and transact all necessary business with the officers of government. He may require information in writing from all executive or administrative state, county or municipal officers upon any subject relating to the duties of their respective offices. The governor shall be the chief administrative officer of the state responsible for the planning and budgeting for the state.

(b) The governor may initiate judicial proceedings in the name of the state against any executive or administrative state, county or municipal officer to enforce compliance with any duty or restrain any unauthorized act.

(c) The governor may request in writing the opinion of the justices of the supreme court as to the interpretation of any portion of this constitution upon any question affecting his executive powers and duties. The justices shall, subject to their rules of procedure, permit interested persons to be heard on the questions presented and shall render their written opinion not earlier than ten days from the filing and docketing of the request, unless in their judgment the delay would cause public injury.

(d) The governor shall have power to call out the militia to preserve the public peace, execute the laws of the state, suppress insurrection, or repel invasion.

(e) The governor shall by message at least once in each regular session inform the legislature concerning the condition of the state, propose such reorganization of the executive department as will promote efficiency and economy, and recommend measures in the public interest.

(f) When not otherwise provided for in this constitution, the governor shall fill by appointment any vacancy in state or county office for the remainder of the term of an appointive office, and for the remainder of the term of an elective office if less than twenty-eight months, otherwise until the first Tuesday after the first Monday following the next general election.

History.—Am. proposed by Taxation and Budget Reform Commission, Revision No. 1, 1992, filed with the Secretary of State May 7, 1992; adopted 1992.

SECTION 2. Lieutenant governor.—There shall be a lieutenant governor. He shall perform such duties pertaining to the office of governor as shall be assigned to him by the governor, except when otherwise provided by law, and such other duties as may be prescribed by law.

SECTION 3. Succession to office of governor; acting governor.—

(a) Upon vacancy in the office of governor, the lieutenant governor shall become governor. Further succession to the office of governor shall be prescribed by law. A successor shall serve for the remainder of the term.

(b) Upon impeachment of the governor and until completion of trial thereof, or during his physical or mental incapacity, the lieutenant governor shall act as governor. Further succession as acting governor shall be prescribed by law. Incapacity to serve as governor may be determined by the supreme court upon due notice after docketing of a written suggestion thereof by four cabinet members, and in such case restoration of capacity shall be similarly determined after docketing of written suggestion thereof by the governor, the legislature or four cabinet members. Incapacity to serve as governor may also be established by certificate filed with the secretary of state by the governor declaring his incapacity for physical reasons to serve as governor, and in such case restoration of capacity shall be similarly established.

SECTION 4. Cabinet.—
(a) There shall be a cabinet composed of a secretary of state, an attorney general, a comptroller, a treasurer, a commissioner of agriculture and a commissioner of education. In addition to the powers and duties specified herein, they shall exercise such powers and perform such duties as may be prescribed by law.

(b) The secretary of state shall keep the records of the official acts of the legislative and executive departments.

(c) The attorney general shall be the chief state legal officer. There is created in the office of the attorney general the position of statewide prosecutor. The statewide prosecutor shall have concurrent jurisdiction with the state attorneys to prosecute violations of criminal laws occurring or having occurred, in two or more judicial circuits as part of a related transaction, or when any such offense is affecting or has affected two or more judicial circuits as provided by general law. The statewide prosecutor shall be appointed by the attorney general from not less than three persons nominated by the judicial nominating commission for the supreme court, or as otherwise provided by general law.

(d) The comptroller shall serve as the chief fiscal officer of the state, and shall settle and approve accounts against the state.

(e) The treasurer shall keep all state funds and securities. He shall disburse state funds only upon the order of the comptroller. Such order may be in any form and may require the disbursement of state funds by electronic means or by means of a magnetic tape or any other transfer medium.

(f) The commissioner of agriculture shall have supervision of matters pertaining to agriculture except as otherwise provided by law.

(g) The commissioner of education shall supervise the public education system in the manner prescribed by law.

History.—Am. H.J.R. 435, 1983; adopted 1984; Am. H.J.R. 386, 1985; adopted 1986.

SECTION 5. Election of governor, lieutenant governor and cabinet members; qualifications; terms.—

(a) At a state-wide general election in each calendar year the number of which is even but not a multiple of four, the electors shall choose a governor and a lieutenant governor and members of the cabinet each for a term of four years beginning on the first Tuesday after the first Monday in January of the succeeding year. In the general election and in party primaries, if held, all candidates for the offices of governor and lieutenant governor shall form joint candidacies in a manner prescribed by law so that each voter shall cast a single vote for a candidate for governor and a candidate for lieutenant governor running together.

(b) When elected, the governor, lieutenant governor and each cabinet member must be an elector not less than thirty years of age who has resided in the state for the preceding seven years. The attorney general must have been a member of the bar of Florida for the preceding five years. No person who has, or but for resignation would have, served as governor or acting governor for more than six years in two consecutive terms shall be elected governor for the succeeding term.

SECTION 6. Executive departments.—All functions of the executive branch of state government shall be allotted among not more than twenty-five departments, exclusive of those specifically provided for or authorized in this constitution. The administration of each department, unless otherwise provided in this constitution, shall be placed by law under the direct supervision of the governor, the lieutenant governor, the governor and cabinet, a cabinet member, or an officer or board appointed by and serving at the pleasure of the governor, except:

(a) When provided by law, confirmation by the senate or the approval of three members of the cabinet shall be required for appointment to or removal from any designated statutory office.

(b) Boards authorized to grant and revoke licenses to engage in regulated occupations shall be assigned to appropriate departments and their members appointed for fixed terms, subject to removal only for cause.

SECTION 7. Suspensions; filling office during suspensions.—

(a) By executive order stating the grounds and filed with the secretary of state, the governor may suspend from office any state officer not subject to impeachment, any officer of the militia not in the active service of the United States, or any county officer, for malfeasance, misfeasance, neglect of duty, drunkenness, incompetence, permanent inability to perform his official duties, or commission of a felony, and may fill the office by appointment for the period of suspension. The suspended officer may at any time before removal be reinstated by the governor.

(b) The senate may, in proceedings prescribed by law, remove from office or reinstate the suspended official and for such purpose the senate may be convened in special session by its president or by a majority of its membership.

(c) By order of the governor any elected municipal officer indicted for crime may be suspended from office until acquitted and the office filled by appointment for the period of suspension, not to extend beyond the term, unless these powers are vested elsewhere by law or the municipal charter.

SECTION 8. Clemency.—

(a) Except in cases of treason and in cases where impeachment results in conviction, the governor may, by executive order filed with the secretary of state, suspend collection of fines and forfeitures, grant reprieves not exceeding sixty days and, with the approval of three members of the cabinet, grant full or conditional pardons, restore civil rights, commute punishment, and remit fines and forfeitures for offenses.

(b) In cases of treason the governor may grant reprieves until adjournment of the regular session of the legislature convening next after the conviction, at which session the legislature may grant a pardon or further reprieve; otherwise the sentence shall be executed.

(c) There may be created by law a parole and probation commission with power to supervise persons on probation and to grant paroles or conditional releases to persons under sentences for crime. The qualifications, method of selection and terms, not to exceed six years, of members of the commission shall be prescribed by law.

SECTION 9. Game and fresh water fish commission.—There shall be a game and fresh water fish commission, composed of five members appointed by the governor subject to confirmation by the senate for staggered terms of five years. The commission shall exercise the regulatory and executive powers of the state with respect to wild animal life and fresh water aquatic life, except that all license fees for taking wild animal life and fresh water aquatic life and penalties for violating regulations of the commission shall be prescribed by specific statute. The legislature may enact laws in aid of the commission, not inconsistent with this section. The commission's exercise of executive powers in the area of planning, budgeting, personnel management, and purchasing shall be as provided by law. Revenue derived from such license fees shall be appropriated to the commission by the legislature for the purpose of management, protection and conservation of wild animal life and fresh water aquatic life.

History.—Am. C.S. for H.J.R. 637, 1973; adopted 1974.

SECTION 10. Attorney General.—The attorney general shall, as directed by general law, request the opinion of the justices of the supreme court as to the validity of any initiative petition circulated pursuant to Section 3 of Article XI. The justices shall, subject to their rules of procedure, permit interested persons to be heard on the

questions presented and shall render their written opinion expeditiously.
History.—Added, H.J.R. 71, 1986; adopted 1986.

SECTION 11. Department of Veterans Affairs.—The legislature, by general law, may provide for the establishment of the Department of Veterans Affairs.
History.—Added, C.S. for H.J.R. 290, 1988; adopted 1988.

SECTION 12. Department of Elderly Affairs.—The legislature may create a Department of Elderly Affairs and prescribe its duties. The provisions governing the administration of the department must comply with Section 6 of Article IV of the State Constitution.
History.—Added, C.S. for H.J.R. 290, 1988; adopted 1988.

SECTION 13. Revenue Shortfalls.—In the event of revenue shortfalls, as defined by general law, the governor and cabinet may establish all necessary reductions in the state budget in order to comply with the provisions of Article VII, Section 1(d). The governor and cabinet shall implement all necessary reductions for the executive budget, the chief justice of the supreme court shall implement all necessary reductions for the judicial budget, and the speaker of the house of representatives and the president of the senate shall implement all necessary reductions for the legislative budget. Budget reductions pursuant to this section shall be consistent with the provisions of Article III, Section 19(h).
History.—Proposed by Taxation and Budget Reform Commission Revision No. 1, 1992, filed with the Secretary of State May 7, 1992; adopted 1992.

ARTICLE V
JUDICIARY

Sec.
1. Courts.
2. Administration; practice and procedure.
3. Supreme court.
4. District courts of appeal.
5. Circuit courts.
6. County courts.
7. Specialized divisions.
8. Eligibility.
9. Determination of number of judges.
10. Retention; election and terms.
11. Vacancies.
12. Discipline; removal and retirement.
13. Prohibited activities.
14. Judicial salaries.
15. Attorneys; admission and discipline.
16. Clerks of the circuit courts.
17. State attorneys.
18. Public defenders.
19. Judicial officers as conservators of the peace.
20. Schedule to Article V.

SECTION 1. Courts.—The judicial power shall be vested in a supreme court, district courts of appeal, circuit courts and county courts. No other courts may be established by the state, any political subdivision or any municipality. The legislature shall, by general law, divide the state into appellate court districts and judicial circuits following county lines. Commissions established by law, or administrative officers or bodies may be granted quasi-judicial power in matters connected with the functions of their offices. The legislature may establish by general law a civil traffic hearing officer system for the purpose of hearing civil traffic infractions.
History.—S.J.R. 52-D, 1971; adopted 1972; Am. H.J.R. 1608, 1988; adopted 1988.

SECTION 2. Administration; practice and procedure.—
(a) The supreme court shall adopt rules for the practice and procedure in all courts including the time for seeking appellate review, the administrative supervision of all courts, the transfer to the court having jurisdiction of any proceeding when the jurisdiction of another court has been improvidently invoked, and a requirement that no cause shall be dismissed because an improper remedy has been sought. These rules may be repealed by general law enacted by two-thirds vote of the membership of each house of the legislature.
(b) The chief justice of the supreme court shall be chosen by a majority of the members of the court. He shall be the chief administrative officer of the judicial system. He shall have the power to assign justices or judges, including consenting retired justices or judges, to temporary duty in any court for which the judge is qualified and to delegate to a chief judge of a judicial circuit the power to assign judges for duty in his respective circuit.
(c) A chief judge for each district court of appeal shall be chosen by a majority of the judges thereof or, if there is no majority, by the chief justice. The chief judge shall be responsible for the administrative supervision of the court.
(d) A chief judge in each circuit shall be chosen from among the circuit judges as provided by supreme court rule. The chief judge shall be responsible for the administrative supervision of the circuit courts and county courts in his circuit.
History.—S.J.R. 52-D, 1971; adopted 1972.

SECTION 3. Supreme court.—
(a) ORGANIZATION.—The supreme court shall consist of seven justices. Of the seven justices, each appellate district shall have at least one justice elected or appointed from the district to the supreme court who is a resident of the district at the time of his original appointment or election. Five justices shall constitute a quorum. The concurrence of four justices shall be necessary to a decision. When recusals for cause would prohibit the court from convening because of the requirements of this section, judges assigned to temporary duty may be substituted for justices.
(b) JURISDICTION.—The supreme court:
(1) Shall hear appeals from final judgments of trial courts imposing the death penalty and from decisions of district courts of appeal declaring invalid a state statute or a provision of the state constitution.
(2) When provided by general law, shall hear appeals from final judgments entered in proceedings for the validation of bonds or certificates of indebtedness and shall review action of statewide agencies relating to rates or service of utilities providing electric, gas, or telephone service.

(3) May review any decision of a district court of appeal that expressly declares valid a state statute, or that expressly construes a provision of the state or federal constitution, or that expressly affects a class of constitutional or state officers, or that expressly and directly conflicts with a decision of another district court of appeal or of the supreme court on the same question of law.

(4) May review any decision of a district court of appeal that passes upon a question certified by it to be of great public importance, or that is certified by it to be in direct conflict with a decision of another district court of appeal.

(5) May review any order or judgment of a trial court certified by the district court of appeal in which an appeal is pending to be of great public importance, or to have a great effect on the proper administration of justice throughout the state, and certified to require immediate resolution by the supreme court.

(6) May review a question of law certified by the Supreme Court of the United States or a United States Court of Appeals which is determinative of the cause and for which there is no controlling precedent of the supreme court of Florida.

(7) May issue writs of prohibition to courts and all writs necessary to the complete exercise of its jurisdiction.

(8) May issue writs of mandamus and quo warranto to state officers and state agencies.

(9) May, or any justice may, issue writs of habeas corpus returnable before the supreme court or any justice, a district court of appeal or any judge thereof, or any circuit judge.

(10) Shall, when requested by the attorney general pursuant to the provisions of Section 10 of Article IV, render an advisory opinion of the justices, addressing issues as provided by general law.

(c) CLERK AND MARSHAL.—The supreme court shall appoint a clerk and a marshal who shall hold office during the pleasure of the court and perform such duties as the court directs. Their compensation shall be fixed by general law. The marshal shall have the power to execute the process of the court throughout the state, and in any county may deputize the sheriff or a deputy sheriff for such purpose.

History.—S.J.R. 52-D, 1971; adopted 1972; Am. C.S. for S.J.R.'s 49, 81, 1976; adopted 1976; Am. S.J.R. 20-C, 1979; adopted 1980; Am. H.J.R. 71, 1986; adopted 1986.

SECTION 4. District courts of appeal.—

(a) ORGANIZATION.—There shall be a district court of appeal serving each appellate district. Each district court of appeal shall consist of at least three judges. Three judges shall consider each case and the concurrence of two shall be necessary to a decision.

(b) JURISDICTION.—

(1) District courts of appeal shall have jurisdiction to hear appeals, that may be taken as a matter of right, from final judgments or orders of trial courts, including those entered on review of administrative action, not directly appealable to the supreme court or a circuit court. They may review interlocutory orders in such cases to the extent provided by rules adopted by the supreme court.

(2) District courts of appeal shall have the power of direct review of administrative action, as prescribed by general law.

(3) A district court of appeal or any judge thereof may issue writs of habeas corpus returnable before the court or any judge thereof or before any circuit judge within the territorial jurisdiction of the court. A district court of appeal may issue writs of mandamus, certiorari, prohibition, quo warranto, and other writs necessary to the complete exercise of its jurisdiction. To the extent necessary to dispose of all issues in a cause properly before it, a district court of appeal may exercise any of the appellate jurisdiction of the circuit courts.

(c) CLERKS AND MARSHALS.—Each district court of appeal shall appoint a clerk and a marshal who shall hold office during the pleasure of the court and perform such duties as the court directs. Their compensation shall be fixed by general law. The marshal shall have the power to execute the process of the court throughout the territorial jurisdiction of the court, and in any county may deputize the sheriff or a deputy sheriff for such purpose.

History.—S.J.R. 52-D, 1971; adopted 1972.

SECTION 5. Circuit courts.—

(a) ORGANIZATION.—There shall be a circuit court serving each judicial circuit.

(b) JURISDICTION.—The circuit courts shall have original jurisdiction not vested in the county courts, and jurisdiction of appeals when provided by general law. They shall have the power to issue writs of mandamus, quo warranto, certiorari, prohibition and habeas corpus, and all writs necessary or proper to the complete exercise of their jurisdiction. Jurisdiction of the circuit court shall be uniform throughout the state. They shall have the power of direct review of administrative action prescribed by general law.

History.—S.J.R. 52-D, 1971; adopted 1972.

SECTION 6. County courts.—

(a) ORGANIZATION.—There shall be a county court in each county. There shall be one or more judges for each county court as prescribed by general law.

(b) JURISDICTION.—The county courts shall exercise the jurisdiction prescribed by general law. Such jurisdiction shall be uniform throughout the state.

History.—S.J.R. 52-D, 1971; adopted 1972.

SECTION 7. Specialized divisions.—All courts except the supreme court may sit in divisions as may be established by general law. A circuit or county court may hold civil and criminal trials and hearings in any place within the territorial jurisdiction of the court as designated by the chief judge of the circuit.

History.—S.J.R. 52-D, 1971; adopted 1972.

SECTION 8. Eligibility.—No person shall be eligible for office of justice or judge of any court unless he is an elector of the state and resides in the territorial jurisdiction of his court. No justice or judge shall serve after attaining the age of seventy years except upon temporary assignment or to complete a term, one-half of which he has served. No person is eligible for the office of justice of the supreme court or judge of a district court

of appeal unless he is, and has been for the preceding ten years, a member of the bar of Florida. No person is eligible for the office of circuit judge unless he is, and has been for the preceding five years, a member of the bar of Florida. Unless otherwise provided by general law, no person is eligible for the office of county court judge unless he is, and has been for the preceding five years, a member of the bar of Florida. Unless otherwise provided by general law, a person shall be eligible for election or appointment to the office of county court judge in a county having a population of 40,000 or less if he is a member in good standing of the bar of Florida.

History.—S.J.R. 52-D, 1971; adopted 1972; Am. H.J.R. 37, 1984; adopted 1984 (effective July 1, 1985).

SECTION 9. Determination of number of judges.—

The supreme court shall establish by rule uniform criteria for the determination of the need for additional judges except supreme court justices, the necessity for decreasing the number of judges and for increasing, decreasing or redefining appellate districts and judicial circuits. If the supreme court finds that a need exists for increasing or decreasing the number of judges or increasing, decreasing or redefining appellate districts and judicial circuits, it shall, prior to the next regular session of the legislature, certify to the legislature its findings and recommendations concerning such need. Upon receipt of such certificate, the legislature, at the next regular session, shall consider the findings and recommendations and may reject the recommendations or by law implement the recommendations in whole or in part; provided the legislature may create more judicial offices than are recommended by the supreme court or may decrease the number of judicial offices by a greater number than recommended by the court only upon a finding of two-thirds of the membership of both houses of the legislature, that such a need exists. A decrease in the number of judges shall be effective only after the expiration of a term. If the supreme court fails to make findings as provided above when need exists, the legislature may by concurrent resolution request the court to certify its findings and recommendations and upon the failure of the court to certify its findings for nine consecutive months, the legislature may, upon a finding of two-thirds of the membership of both houses of the legislature that a need exists, increase or decrease the number of judges or increase, decrease or redefine appellate districts and judicial circuits.

History.—S.J.R. 52-D, 1971; adopted 1972.

SECTION 10. Retention; election and terms.—

(a) Any justice of the supreme court or any judge of a district court of appeal may qualify for retention by a vote of the electors in the general election next preceding the expiration of his term in the manner prescribed by law. If a justice or judge is ineligible or fails to qualify for retention, a vacancy shall exist in that office upon the expiration of the term being served by the justice or judge. When a justice of the supreme court or a judge of a district court of appeal so qualifies, the ballot shall read substantially as follows: "Shall Justice (or Judge) __(name of justice or judge)__ of the __(name of the court)__ be retained in office?" If a majority of the qualified electors voting within the territorial jurisdiction of the court vote to retain, the justice or judge shall be retained for a term of six years commencing on the first Tuesday after the first Monday in January following the general election. If a majority of the qualified electors voting within the territorial jurisdiction of the court vote to not retain, a vacancy shall exist in that office upon the expiration of the term being served by the justice or judge.

(b) Circuit judges and judges of county courts shall be elected by vote of the qualified electors within the territorial jurisdiction of their respective courts. The terms of circuit judges shall be for six years. The terms of judges of county courts shall be for four years.

History.—S.J.R. 52-D, 1971; adopted 1972; Am. C.S. for S.J.R.'s 49, 81, 1976; adopted 1976.

SECTION 11. Vacancies.—

(a) The governor shall fill each vacancy on the supreme court or on a district court of appeal by appointing for a term ending on the first Tuesday after the first Monday in January of the year following the next general election occurring at least one year after the date of appointment, one of three persons nominated by the appropriate judicial nominating commission.

(b) The governor shall fill each vacancy on a circuit court or on a county court by appointing for a term ending on the first Tuesday after the first Monday in January of the year following the next primary and general election, one of not fewer than three persons nominated by the appropriate judicial nominating commission. An election shall be held to fill that judicial office for the term of the office beginning at the end of the appointed term.

(c) The nominations shall be made within thirty days from the occurrence of a vacancy unless the period is extended by the governor for a time not to exceed thirty days. The governor shall make the appointment within sixty days after the nominations have been certified to him.

(d) There shall be a separate judicial nominating commission as provided by general law for the supreme court, each district court of appeal, and each judicial circuit for all trial courts within the circuit. Uniform rules of procedure shall be established by the judicial nominating commissions at each level of the court system. Such rules, or any part thereof, may be repealed by general law enacted by a majority vote of the membership of each house of the legislature, or by the supreme court, five justices concurring. Except for deliberations of the judicial nominating commissions, the proceedings of the commissions and their records shall be open to the public.

History.—S.J.R. 52-D, 1971; adopted 1972; Am. C.S. for S.J.R.'s 49, 81, 1976; adopted 1976; Am. H.J.R. 1160, 1984; adopted 1984.

SECTION 12. Discipline; removal and retirement.—

(a) There shall be a judicial qualifications commission vested with jurisdiction to investigate and recommend to the Supreme Court of Florida the removal from office of any justice or judge whose conduct, during term of office or otherwise occurring on or after November 1, 1966, (without regard to the effective date of this section) demonstrates a present unfitness to hold office, and to investigate and recommend the reprimand of a justice or judge whose conduct, during term of office or otherwise occurring on or after November 1, 1966 (without regard to the effective date of this section), warrants such a reprimand. The commission shall be composed of:

(1) Two judges of district courts of appeal selected by the judges of those courts, two circuit judges selected by the judges of the circuit courts and two judges of county courts selected by the judges of those courts;

(2) Two electors who reside in the state, who are members of the bar of Florida, and who shall be chosen by the governing body of the bar of Florida; and

(3) Five electors who reside in the state, who have never held judicial office or been members of the bar of Florida, and who shall be appointed by the governor.

(b) The members of the judicial qualifications commission shall serve staggered terms, not to exceed six years, as prescribed by general law. No member of the commission except a justice or judge shall be eligible for state judicial office so long as he is a member of the commission and for a period of two years thereafter. No member of the commission shall hold office in a political party or participate in any campaign for judicial office or hold public office; provided that a judge may participate in his own campaign for judicial office and hold that office. The commission shall elect one of its members as its chairman.

(c) Members of the judicial qualifications commission not subject to impeachment shall be subject to removal from the commission pursuant to the provisions of Article IV, Section 7, Florida Constitution.

(d) The commission shall adopt rules regulating its proceedings, the filling of vacancies by the appointing authorities, the disqualification of members, and the temporary replacement of disqualified or incapacitated members. The commission's rules, or any part thereof, may be repealed by general law enacted by a majority vote of the membership of each house of the legislature, or by the supreme court, five justices concurring. Until formal charges against a justice or judge are filed by the commission with the clerk of the supreme court of Florida all proceedings by or before the commission shall be confidential; provided, however, upon a finding of probable cause and the filing by the commission with said clerk of such formal charges against a justice or judge such charges and all further proceedings before the commission shall be public. The commission may with seven members concurring recommend to the supreme court the temporary suspension of any justice or judge against whom formal charges are pending.

(e) The commission shall have access to all information from all executive, legislative and judicial agencies, including grand juries, subject to the rules of the commission. At any time, on request of the speaker of the house of representatives or the governor, the commission shall make available all information in the possession of the commission for use in consideration of impeachment or suspension, respectively.

(f) Upon recommendation of two-thirds of the members of the judicial qualifications commission, the supreme court may order that the justice or judge be disciplined by appropriate reprimand, or be removed from office with termination of compensation for willful or persistent failure to perform his duties or for other conduct unbecoming a member of the judiciary demonstrating a present unfitness to hold office, or be involuntarily retired for any permanent disability that seriously interferes with the performance of his duties. Malafides, scienter or moral turpitude on the part of a justice or judge shall not be required for removal from office of a justice or judge whose conduct demonstrates a present unfitness to hold office. After the filing of a formal proceeding and upon request of the commission, the supreme court may suspend the justice or judge from office, with or without compensation, pending final determination of the inquiry.

(g) The power of removal conferred by this section shall be both alternative and cumulative to the power of impeachment and to the power of suspension by the governor and removal by the senate.

(h) Notwithstanding any of the foregoing provisions of this section, if the person who is the subject of proceedings by the judicial qualifications commission is a justice of the supreme court of Florida all justices of such court automatically shall be disqualified to sit as justices of such court with respect to all proceedings therein concerning such person and the supreme court for such purposes shall be composed of a panel consisting of the seven chief judges of the judicial circuits of the state of Florida most senior in tenure of judicial office as circuit judge. For purposes of determining seniority of such circuit judges in the event there be judges of equal tenure in judicial office as circuit judge the judge or judges from the lower numbered circuit or circuits shall be deemed senior. In the event any such chief circuit judge is under investigation by the judicial qualifications commission or is otherwise disqualified or unable to serve on the panel, the next most senior chief circuit judge or judges shall serve in place of such disqualified or disabled chief circuit judge.

(i) SCHEDULE TO SECTION 12.—

(1) The terms of office of the present members of the judicial qualifications commission shall expire on January 1, 1975 and new members shall be appointed to serve the following staggered terms:

a. Group I.—The terms of five members, composed of two electors as set forth in s. 12(a)(3) of Article V, one member of the bar of Florida as set forth in s. 12(a)(2) of Article V, one judge from the district courts of appeal and one circuit judge as set forth in s. 12(a)(1) of Article V, shall expire on December 31, 1976.

b. Group II.—The terms of four members, composed of one elector as set forth in s. 12(a)(3) of Article V, one member of the bar of Florida as set forth in s. 12(a)(2) of Article V, one circuit judge and one county judge as set forth in s. 12(a)(1) of Article V shall expire on December 31, 1978.

c. Group III.—The terms of four members, composed of two electors as set forth in s. 12(a)(3) of Article V, one judge from the district courts of appeal and one county judge as set forth in s. 12(a)(1) of Article V, shall expire on December 31, 1980.

(2) The 1976 amendment to section 12 of Article V, if submitted at a special election, shall take effect upon approval by the electors of Florida.

History.—S.J.R. 52-D, 1971; adopted 1972; Am. H.J.R. 3911, 1974; adopted 1974; Am. H.J.R. 1709, 1975; adopted 1976.

SECTION 13. Prohibited activities.—All justices and judges shall devote full time to their judicial duties. They shall not engage in the practice of law or hold office in any political party.
History.—S.J.R. 52-D, 1971; adopted 1972.

SECTION 14. Judicial salaries.—All justices and judges shall be compensated only by state salaries fixed by general law. The judiciary shall have no power to fix appropriations.
History.—S.J.R. 52-D, 1971; adopted 1972.

SECTION 15. Attorneys; admission and discipline.—The supreme court shall have exclusive jurisdiction to regulate the admission of persons to the practice of law and the discipline of persons admitted.
History.—S.J.R. 52-D, 1971; adopted 1972.

SECTION 16. Clerks of the circuit courts.—There shall be in each county a clerk of the circuit court who shall be selected pursuant to the provisions of Article VIII section 1. Notwithstanding any other provision of the constitution, the duties of the clerk of the circuit court may be divided by special or general law between two officers, one serving as clerk of court and one serving as ex officio clerk of the board of county commissioners, auditor, recorder, and custodian of all county funds. There may be a clerk of the county court if authorized by general or special law.
History.—S.J.R. 52-D, 1971; adopted 1972.

SECTION 17. State attorneys.—In each judicial circuit a state attorney shall be elected for a term of four years. Except as otherwise provided in this constitution, he shall be the prosecuting officer of all trial courts in that circuit and shall perform other duties prescribed by general law; provided, however, when authorized by general law, the violations of all municipal ordinances may be prosecuted by municipal prosecutors. A state attorney shall be an elector of the state and reside in the territorial jurisdiction of the circuit. He shall be and have been a member of the bar of Florida for the preceding five years. He shall devote full time to his duties, and he shall not engage in the private practice of law. State attorneys shall appoint such assistant state attorneys as may be authorized by law.
History.—S.J.R. 52-D, 1971; adopted 1972; Am. H.J.R. 386, 1985; adopted 1986.

SECTION 18. Public defenders.—In each judicial circuit a public defender shall be elected for a term of four years. He shall perform duties prescribed by general law. A public defender shall be an elector of the state and reside in the territorial jurisdiction of the circuit. He shall be and have been a member of the Bar of Florida for the preceding five years. Public defenders shall appoint such assistant public defenders as may be authorized by law.
History.—S.J.R. 52-D, 1971; adopted 1972.

SECTION 19. Judicial officers as conservators of the peace.—All judicial officers in this state shall be conservators of the peace.
History.—S.J.R. 52-D, 1971; adopted 1972.

SECTION 20. Schedule to Article V.—
(a) This article shall replace all of Article V of the Constitution of 1885, as amended, which shall then stand repealed.
(b) Except to the extent inconsistent with the provisions of this article, all provisions of law and rules of court in force on the effective date of this article shall continue in effect until superseded in the manner authorized by the constitution.
(c) After this article becomes effective, and until changed by general law consistent with sections 1 through 19 of this article:
(1) The supreme court shall have the jurisdiction immediately theretofore exercised by it, and it shall determine all proceedings pending before it on the effective date of this article.
(2) The appellate districts shall be those in existence on the date of adoption of this article. There shall be a district court of appeal in each district. The district courts of appeal shall have the jurisdiction immediately theretofore exercised by the district courts of appeal and shall determine all proceedings pending before them on the effective date of this article.
(3) Circuit courts shall have jurisdiction of appeals from county courts and municipal courts, except those appeals which may be taken directly to the supreme court; and they shall have exclusive original jurisdiction in all actions at law not cognizable by the county courts; of proceedings relating to the settlement of the estate of decedents and minors, the granting of letters testamentary, guardianship, involuntary hospitalization, the determination of incompetency, and other jurisdiction usually pertaining to courts of probate; in all cases in equity including all cases relating to juveniles; of all felonies and of all misdemeanors arising out of the same circumstances as a felony which is also charged; in all cases involving legality of any tax assessment or toll; in the action of ejectment; and in all actions involving the titles or boundaries or right of possession of real property. The circuit court may issue injunctions. There shall be judicial circuits which shall be the judicial circuits in existence on the date of adoption of this article. The chief judge of a circuit may authorize a county court judge to order emergency hospitalizations pursuant to Chapter 71-131, Laws of Florida, in the absence from the county of the circuit judge and the county court judge shall have the power to issue all temporary orders and temporary injunctions necessary or proper to the complete exercise of such jurisdiction.
(4) County courts shall have original jurisdiction in all criminal misdemeanor cases not cognizable by the circuit courts, of all violations of municipal and county ordinances, and of all actions at law in which the matter in controversy does not exceed the sum of two thousand five hundred dollars ($2,500.00) exclusive of interest and costs, except those within the exclusive jurisdiction of the circuit courts. Judges of county courts shall be committing magistrates. The county courts shall have jurisdiction now exercised by the county judge's courts other than that vested in the circuit court by subsection (c)(3) hereof, the jurisdiction now exercised by the county courts, the claims court, the small claims courts, the small claims magistrates courts, magistrates courts, justice of the peace courts, municipal courts and courts of chartered counties, including but not limited to the

counties referred to in Article VIII, sections 9, 10, 11 and 24 of the Constitution of 1885.

(5) Each judicial nominating commission shall be composed of the following:
    a. Three members appointed by the Board of Governors of The Florida Bar from among The Florida Bar members who are actively engaged in the practice of law with offices within the territorial jurisdiction of the affected court, district or circuit;
    b. Three electors who reside in the territorial jurisdiction of the court or circuit appointed by the governor; and
    c. Three electors who reside in the territorial jurisdiction of the court or circuit and who are not members of the bar of Florida, selected and appointed by a majority vote of the other six members of the commission.

(6) No justice or judge shall be a member of a judicial nominating commission. A member of a judicial nominating commission may hold public office other than judicial office. No member shall be eligible for appointment to state judicial office so long as he is a member of a judicial nominating commission and for a period of two years thereafter. All acts of a judicial nominating commission shall be made with a concurrence of a majority of its members.

(7) The members of a judicial nominating commission shall serve for a term of four years except the terms of the initial members of the judicial nominating commissions shall expire as follows:
    a. The terms of one member of category a. b. and c. in subsection (c)(5) hereof shall expire on July 1, 1974;
    b. The terms of one member of category a. b. and c. in subsection (c)(5) hereof shall expire on July 1, 1975;
    c. The terms of one member of category a. b. and c. in subsection (c)(5) hereof shall expire on July 1, 1976;

(8) All fines and forfeitures arising from offenses tried in the county court shall be collected, and accounted for by clerk of the court, and deposited in a special trust account. All fines and forfeitures received from violations of ordinances or misdemeanors committed within a county or municipal ordinances committed within a municipality within the territorial jurisdiction of the county court shall be paid monthly to the county or municipality respectively. If any costs are assessed and collected in connection with offenses tried in county court, all court costs shall be paid into the general revenue fund of the state of Florida and such other funds as prescribed by general law.

(9) Any municipality or county may apply to the chief judge of the circuit in which that municipality or county is situated for the county court to sit in a location suitable to the municipality or county and convenient in time and place to its citizens and police officers and upon such application said chief judge shall direct the court to sit in the location unless he shall determine the request is not justified. If the chief judge does not authorize the county court to sit in the location requested, the county or municipality may apply to the supreme court for an order directing the county court to sit in the location. Any municipality or county which so applies shall be required to provide the appropriate physical facilities in which the county court may hold court.

(10) All courts except the supreme court may sit in divisions as may be established by local rule approved by the supreme court.

(11) A county court judge in any county having a population of 40,000 or less according to the last decennial census, shall not be required to be a member of the bar of Florida.

(12) Municipal prosecutors may prosecute violations of municipal ordinances.

(13) Justice shall mean a justice elected or appointed to the supreme court and shall not include any judge assigned from any court.

(d) When this article becomes effective:

(1) All courts not herein authorized, except as provided by subsection (d)(4) of this section shall cease to exist and jurisdiction to conclude all pending cases and enforce all prior orders and judgments shall vest in the court that would have jurisdiction of the cause if thereafter instituted. All records of and property held by courts abolished hereby shall be transferred to the proper office of the appropriate court under this article.

(2) Judges of the following courts, if their terms do not expire in 1973 and if they are eligible under subsection (d)(8) hereof, shall become additional judges of the circuit court for each of the counties of their respective circuits, and shall serve as such circuit judges for the remainder of the terms to which they were elected and shall be eligible for election as circuit judges thereafter. These courts are: civil court of record of Dade county, all criminal courts of record, the felony courts of record of Alachua, Leon and Volusia Counties, the courts of record of Broward, Brevard, Escambia, Hillsborough, Lee, Manatee and Sarasota Counties, the civil and criminal court of record of Pinellas County, and county judge's courts and separate juvenile courts in counties having a population in excess of 100,000 according to the 1970 federal census. On the effective date of this article, there shall be an additional number of positions of circuit judges equal to the number of existing circuit judges and the number of judges of the above named courts whose term expires in 1973. Elections to such offices shall take place at the same time and manner as elections to other state judicial offices in 1972 and the terms of such offices shall be for a term of six years. Unless changed pursuant to section nine of this article, the number of circuit judges presently existing and created by this subsection shall not be changed.

(3) In all counties having a population of less than 100,000 according to the 1970 federal census and having more than one county judge on the date of the adoption of this article, there shall be the same number of judges of the county court as there are county judges existing on that date unless changed pursuant to section 9 of this article.

(4) Municipal courts shall continue with their same jurisdiction until amended or terminated in a manner prescribed by special or general law or ordinances, or until January 3, 1977, whichever occurs first. On that date all municipal courts not previously abolished shall cease to exist. Judges of municipal courts shall remain in office and be subject to reappointment or reelection in the manner prescribed by law until said courts are terminated pursuant to the provisions of this subsection.

Upon municipal courts being terminated or abolished in accordance with the provisions of this subsection, the judges thereof who are not members of the bar of Florida, shall be eligible to seek election as judges of county courts of their respective counties.

(5) Judges, holding elective office in all other courts abolished by this article, whose terms do not expire in 1973 including judges established pursuant to Article VIII, sections 9 and 11 of the Constitution of 1885 shall serve as judges of the county court for the remainder of the term to which they were elected. Unless created pursuant to section 9, of this Article V such judicial office shall not continue to exist thereafter.

(6) By March 21, 1972, the supreme court shall certify the need for additional circuit and county judges. The legislature in the 1972 regular session may by general law create additional offices of judge, the terms of which shall begin on the effective date of this article. Elections to such offices shall take place at the same time and manner as election to other state judicial offices in 1972.

(7) County judges of existing county judge's courts and justices of the peace and magistrates' court who are not members of bar of Florida shall be eligible to seek election as county court judges of their respective counties.

(8) No judge of a court abolished by this article shall become or be eligible to become a judge of the circuit court unless he has been a member of bar of Florida for the preceding five years.

(9) The office of judges of all other courts abolished by this article shall be abolished as of the effective date of this article.

(10) The offices of county solicitor and prosecuting attorney shall stand abolished, and all county solicitors and prosecuting attorneys holding such offices upon the effective date of this article shall become and serve as assistant state attorneys for the circuits in which their counties are situate for the remainder of their terms, with compensation not less than that received immediately before the effective date of this article.

(e) LIMITED OPERATION OF SOME PROVISIONS.—

(1) All justices of the supreme court, judges of the district courts of appeal and circuit judges in office upon the effective date of this article shall retain their offices for the remainder of their respective terms. All members of the judicial qualifications commission in office upon the effective date of this article shall retain their offices for the remainder of their respective terms. Each state attorney in office on the effective date of this article shall retain his office for the remainder of his term.

(2) No justice or judge holding office immediately after this article becomes effective who held judicial office on July 1, 1957, shall be subject to retirement from judicial office because of age pursuant to section 8 of this article.

(f) Until otherwise provided by law, the nonjudicial duties required of county judges shall be performed by the judges of the county court.

[1](g) All provisions of Article V of the Constitution of 1885, as amended, not embraced herein which are not inconsistent with this revision shall become statutes subject to modification or repeal as are other statutes.

(h) The requirements of section 14 relative to all county court judges or any judge of a municipal court who continues to hold office pursuant to subsection (d)(4) hereof being compensated by state salaries shall not apply prior to January 3, 1977, unless otherwise provided by general law.

(i) DELETION OF OBSOLETE SCHEDULE ITEMS. The legislature shall have power, by concurrent resolution, to delete from this article any subsection of this section 20 including this subsection, when all events to which the subsection to be deleted is or could become applicable have occurred. A legislative determination of fact made as a basis for application of this subsection shall be subject to judicial review.

(j) EFFECTIVE DATE.—Unless otherwise provided herein, this article shall become effective at 11:59 o'clock P.M., Eastern Standard Time, January 1, 1973.
History.—S.J.R. 52-D, 1971; adopted 1972.

[1]Note.—All provisions of Art. V of the Constitution of 1885, as amended, considered as statutory law, were repealed by ch. 73-303, Laws of Florida.

ARTICLE VI

SUFFRAGE AND ELECTIONS

Sec.
1. Regulation of elections.
2. Electors.
3. Oath.
4. Disqualifications.
5. General and special elections.
6. Municipal and district elections.

SECTION 1. Regulation of elections.—All elections by the people shall be by direct and secret vote. General elections shall be determined by a plurality of votes cast. Registration and elections shall, and political party functions may, be regulated by law.

SECTION 2. Electors.—Every citizen of the United States who is at least twenty-one years of age and who has been a permanent resident for one year in the state and six months in a county, if registered as provided by law, shall be an elector of that county. Provisions may be made by law for other bona fide residents of the state who are at least twenty-one years of age to vote in the election of presidential electors.

SECTION 3. Oath.—Each eligible citizen upon registering shall subscribe the following: "I do solemnly swear (or affirm) that I will protect and defend the Constitution of the United States and the Constitution of the State of Florida, and that I am qualified to register as an elector under the Constitution and laws of the State of Florida."

SECTION 4. Disqualifications.—

(a) No person convicted of a felony, or adjudicated in this or any other state to be mentally incompetent, shall be qualified to vote or hold office until restoration of civil rights or removal of disability.

(b) No person may appear on the ballot for re-election to any of the following offices:
(1) Florida representative,
(2) Florida senator,

(3) Florida Lieutenant governor,
(4) any office of the Florida cabinet,
(5) U.S. Representative from Florida, or
(6) U.S. Senator from Florida

if, by the end of the current term of office, the person will have served (or, but for resignation, would have served) in that office for eight consecutive years.

History.—Am. by Initiative Petition filed with the Secretary of State July 23, 1992; adopted 1992.

SECTION 5. General and special elections.—A general election shall be held in each county on the first Tuesday after the first Monday in November of each even-numbered year to choose a successor to each elective state and county officer whose term will expire before the next general election and, except as provided herein, to fill each vacancy in elective office for the unexpired portion of the term. A general election may be suspended or delayed due to a state of emergency or impending emergency pursuant to general law. Special elections and referenda shall be held as provided by law.

History.—Am. S.J.R. 162, 1992; adopted 1992.

SECTION 6. Municipal and district elections.— Registration and elections in municipalities shall, and in other governmental entities created by statute may, be provided by law.

ARTICLE VII

FINANCE AND TAXATION

Sec.
1. Taxation; appropriations; state expenses; state revenue limitation.
2. Taxes; rate.
3. Taxes; exemptions.
4. Taxation; assessments.
5. Estate, inheritance and income taxes.
6. Homestead exemptions.
7. Allocation of pari-mutuel taxes.
8. Aid to local governments.
9. Local taxes.
10. Pledging credit.
11. State bonds; revenue bonds.
12. Local bonds.
13. Relief from illegal taxes.
14. Bonds for pollution control and abatement and other water facilities.
15. Revenue bonds for scholarship loans.
16. Bonds for housing and related facilities.
17. Bonds for acquiring transportation right-of-way or for constructing bridges.
18. Laws requiring counties or municipalities to spend funds or limiting their ability to raise revenue or receive state tax revenue.

SECTION 1. Taxation; appropriations; state expenses; state revenue limitation.—

(a) No tax shall be levied except in pursuance of law. No state ad valorem taxes shall be levied upon real estate or tangible personal property. All other forms of taxation shall be preempted to the state except as provided by general law.

(b) Motor vehicles, boats, airplanes, trailers, trailer coaches and mobile homes, as defined by law, shall be subject to a license tax for their operation in the amounts and for the purposes prescribed by law, but shall not be subject to ad valorem taxes.

(c) No money shall be drawn from the treasury except in pursuance of appropriation made by law.

(d) Provision shall be made by law for raising sufficient revenue to defray the expenses of the state for each fiscal period.

(e) Except as provided herein, state revenues collected for any fiscal year shall be limited to state revenues allowed under this subsection for the prior fiscal year plus an adjustment for growth. As used in this subsection, "growth" means an amount equal to the average annual rate of growth in Florida personal income over the most recent twenty quarters times the state revenues allowed under this subsection for the prior fiscal year. For the 1995-1996 fiscal year, the state revenues allowed under this subsection for the prior fiscal year shall equal the state revenues collected for the 1994-1995 fiscal year. Florida personal income shall be determined by the legislature, from information available from the United States Department of Commerce or its successor on the first day of February prior to the beginning of the fiscal year. State revenues collected for any fiscal year in excess of this limitation shall be transferred to the budget stabilization fund until the fund reaches the maximum balance specified in Section 19(g) of Article III, and thereafter shall be refunded to taxpayers as provided by general law. State revenues allowed under this subsection for any fiscal year may be increased by a two-thirds vote of the membership of each house of the legislature in a separate bill that contains no other subject and that sets forth the dollar amount by which the state revenues allowed will be increased. The vote may not be taken less than seventy-two hours after the third reading of the bill. For purposes of this subsection, "state revenues" means taxes, fees, licenses, and charges for services imposed by the legislature on individuals, businesses, or agencies outside state government. However, "state revenues" does not include: revenues that are necessary to meet the requirements set forth in documents authorizing the issuance of bonds by the state; revenues that are used to provide matching funds for the federal Medicaid program with the exception of the revenues used to support the Public Medical Assistance Trust Fund or its successor program and with the exception of state matching funds used to fund elective expansions made after July 1, 1994; proceeds from the state lottery returned as prizes; receipts of the Florida Hurricane Catastrophe Fund; balances carried forward from prior fiscal years; taxes, licenses, fees, and charges for services imposed by local, regional, or school district governing bodies; or revenue from taxes, licenses, fees, and charges for services required to be imposed by any amendment or revision to this constitution after July 1, 1994. An adjustment to the revenue limitation shall be made by general law to reflect the fiscal impact of transfers of responsibility for the funding of governmental functions between the state and other levels of govern-

ment. The legislature shall, by general law, prescribe procedures necessary to administer this subsection.
History.—Am. H.J.R. 2053, 1994; adopted 1994.

SECTION 2. Taxes; rate.—All ad valorem taxation shall be at a uniform rate within each taxing unit, except the taxes on intangible personal property may be at different rates but shall never exceed two mills on the dollar of assessed value; provided, as to any obligations secured by mortgage, deed of trust, or other lien on real estate wherever located, an intangible tax of not more than two mills on the dollar may be levied by law to be in lieu of all other intangible assessments on such obligations.

SECTION 3. Taxes; exemptions.—

(a) All property owned by a municipality and used exclusively by it for municipal or public purposes shall be exempt from taxation. A municipality, owning property outside the municipality, may be required by general law to make payment to the taxing unit in which the property is located. Such portions of property as are used predominantly for educational, literary, scientific, religious or charitable purposes may be exempted by general law from taxation.

(b) There shall be exempt from taxation, cumulatively, to every head of a family residing in this state, household goods and personal effects to the value fixed by general law, not less than one thousand dollars, and to every widow or widower or person who is blind or totally and permanently disabled, property to the value fixed by general law not less than five hundred dollars.

(c) Any county or municipality may, for the purpose of its respective tax levy and subject to the provisions of this subsection and general law, grant community and economic development ad valorem tax exemptions to new businesses and expansions of existing businesses, as defined by general law. Such an exemption may be granted only by ordinance of the county or municipality, and only after the electors of the county or municipality voting on such question in a referendum authorize the county or municipality to adopt such ordinances. An exemption so granted shall apply to improvements to real property made by or for the use of a new business and improvements to real property related to the expansion of an existing business and shall also apply to tangible personal property of such new business and tangible personal property related to the expansion of an existing business. The amount or limits of the amount of such exemption shall be specified by general law. The period of time for which such exemption may be granted to a new business or expansion of an existing business shall be determined by general law. The authority to grant such exemption shall expire ten years from the date of approval by the electors of the county or municipality, and may be renewable by referendum as provided by general law.

[1](d) By general law and subject to conditions specified therein, there may be granted an ad valorem tax exemption to a renewable energy source device and to real property on which such device is installed and operated, to the value fixed by general law not to exceed the original cost of the device, and for the period of time fixed by general law not to exceed ten years.

(e) Any county or municipality may, for the purpose of its respective tax levy and subject to the provisions of this subsection and general law, grant historic preservation ad valorem tax exemptions to owners of historic properties engaging in the rehabilitation or renovation of these properties in accordance with approved historic preservation guidelines. This exemption may be granted only by ordinance of the county or municipality. The amount or limits of the amount of this exemption and the requirements for eligible properties must be specified by general law. The period of time for which this exemption may be granted to a property owner shall be determined by general law.
History.—Am. S.J.R.'s 9–E, 15–E, 1980; adopted 1980; Am. C.S. for S.J.R.'s 318, 356, 1988; adopted 1988; Am. S.J.R. 152, 1992; adopted 1992.
[1]**Note.**—This subsection, originally designated (c) by S.J.R. 15–E, 1980, was redesignated (d) by the editors in order to avoid confusion with subsection (c) as contained in S.J.R. 9–E, 1980.
cf.—s. 19, Art. XII Schedule.

SECTION 4. Taxation; assessments.—By general law regulations shall be prescribed which shall secure a just valuation of all property for ad valorem taxation, provided:

(a) Agricultural land, land producing high water recharge to Florida's aquifers or land used exclusively for non–commercial recreational purposes may be classified by general law and assessed solely on the basis of character or use.

(b) Pursuant to general law tangible personal property held for sale as stock in trade and livestock may be valued for taxation at a specified percentage of its value, may be classified for tax pusposes, or may be exempted from taxation.

(c) All persons entitled to a homestead exemption under Section 6 of this Article shall have their homestead assessed at just value as of January 1 of the year following the effective date of this amendment. This assessment shall change only as provided herein.

1. Assessments subject to this provision shall be changed annually on January 1st of each year; but those changes in assessments shall not exceed the lower of the following:

(A) three percent (3%) of the assessment for the prior year.

(B) the percent change in the Consumer Price Index for all urban consumers, U.S. City Average, all items 1967=100, or successor reports for the preceding calendar year as initially reported by the United States Department of Labor, Bureau of Labor Statistics.

2. No assessment shall exceed just value.

3. After any change of ownership, as provided by general law, homestead property shall be assessed at just value as of January 1 of the following year. Thereafter, the homestead shall be assessed as provided herein.

4. New homestead property shall be assessed at just value as of January 1st of the year following the establishment of the homestead. That assessment shall only change as provided herein.

5. Changes, additions, reductions or improvements to homestead property shall be assessed as provided for by general law; provided, however, after the adjustment for any change, addition, reduction or improve-

ment, the property shall be assessed as provided herein.

6. In the event of a termination of homestead status, the property shall be assessed as provided by general law.

7. The provisions of this amendment are severable. If any of the provisions of this amendment shall be held unconstitutional by any court of competent jurisdiction, the decision of such court shall not affect or impair any remaining provisions of this amendment.

History.—Am. S.J.R. 12-E, 1980; adopted 1980; Am. H.J.R. 214, 1987; adopted 1988; Am. by Initiative Petition filed with the Secretary of State August 3, 1992; adopted 1992.

SECTION 5. Estate, inheritance and income taxes.

(a) NATURAL PERSONS. No tax upon estates or inheritances or upon the income of natural persons who are residents or citizens of the state shall be levied by the state, or under its authority, in excess of the aggregate of amounts which may be allowed to be credited upon or deducted from any similar tax levied by the United States or any state.

(b) OTHERS. No tax upon the income of residents and citizens other than natural persons shall be levied by the state, or under its authority, in excess of 5% of net income, as defined by law, or at such greater rate as is authorized by a three-fifths ($3/5$) vote of the membership of each house of the legislature or as will provide for the state the maximum amount which may be allowed to be credited against income taxes levied by the United States and other states. There shall be exempt from taxation not less than five thousand dollars ($5,000) of the excess of net income subject to tax over the maximum amount allowed to be credited against income taxes levied by the United States and other states.

(c) EFFECTIVE DATE. This section shall become effective immediately upon approval by the electors of Florida.

History.—Am. H.J.R. 7-B, 1971; adopted 1971.

SECTION 6. Homestead exemptions.—

(a) Every person who has the legal or equitable title to real estate and maintains thereon the permanent residence of the owner, or another legally or naturally dependent upon the owner, shall be exempt from taxation thereon, except assessments for special benefits, up to the assessed valuation of five thousand dollars, upon establishment of right thereto in the manner prescribed by law. The real estate may be held by legal or equitable title, by the entireties, jointly, in common, as a condominium, or indirectly by stock ownership or membership representing the owner's or member's proprietary interest in a corporation owning a fee or a leasehold initially in excess of ninety-eight years.

(b) Not more than one exemption shall be allowed any individual or family unit or with respect to any residential unit. No exemption shall exceed the value of the real estate assessable to the owner or, in case of ownership through stock or membership in a corporation, the value of the proportion which his interest in the corporation bears to the assessed value of the property.

(c) By general law and subject to conditions specified therein, the exemption shall be increased to a total of twenty-five thousand dollars of the assessed value of the real estate for each school district levy. By general law and subject to conditions specified therein, the exemption for all other levies may be increased up to an amount not exceeding ten thousand dollars of the assessed value of the real estate if the owner has attained age sixty-five or is totally and permanently disabled and if the owner is not entitled to the exemption provided in subsection (d).

(d) By general law and subject to conditions specified therein, the exemption shall be increased to a total of the following amounts of assessed value of real estate for each levy other than those of school districts: fifteen thousand dollars with respect to 1980 assessments; twenty thousand dollars with respect to 1981 assessments; twenty-five thousand dollars with respect to assessments for 1982 and each year thereafter. However, such increase shall not apply with respect to any assessment roll until such roll is first determined to be in compliance with the provisions of section 4 by a state agency designated by general law. This subsection shall stand repealed on the effective date of any amendment to section 4 which provides for the assessment of homestead property at a specified percentage of its just value.

(e) By general law and subject to conditions specified therein, the Legislature may provide to renters, who are permanent residents, ad valorem tax relief on all ad valorem tax levies. Such ad valorem tax relief shall be in the form and amount established by general law.

History.—Am. S.J.R. 1-B, 1979; adopted 1980; Am. S.J.R. 4-E, 1980; adopted 1980.

SECTION 7. Allocation of pari-mutuel taxes.—

Taxes upon the operation of pari-mutuel pools may be preempted to the state or allocated in whole or in part to the counties. When allocated to the counties, the distribution shall be in equal amounts to the several counties.

SECTION 8. Aid to local governments.—

State funds may be appropriated to the several counties, school districts, municipalities or special districts upon such conditions as may be provided by general law. These conditions may include the use of relative ad valorem assessment levels determined by a state agency designated by general law.

History.—Am. S.J.R. 4-E, 1980; adopted 1980.

SECTION 9. Local taxes.—

(a) Counties, school districts, and municipalities shall, and special districts may, be authorized by law to levy ad valorem taxes and may be authorized by general law to levy other taxes, for their respective purposes, except ad valorem taxes on intangible personal property and taxes prohibited by this constitution.

(b) Ad valorem taxes, exclusive of taxes levied for the payment of bonds and taxes levied for periods not longer than two years when authorized by vote of the electors who are the owners of freeholds therein not wholly exempt from taxation, shall not be levied in excess of the following millages upon the assessed value of real estate and tangible personal property: for all county purposes, ten mills; for all municipal purposes, ten mills; for all school purposes, ten mills; for water management purposes for the northwest portion of the state lying west of the line between ranges two and three east, 0.05 mill; for water management purposes for the remaining portions of the state, 1.0 mill; and for all other special districts a millage authorized by law approved by vote of the electors who are owners of freeholds therein not wholly exempt from taxation. A county furnishing municipal services may, to the extent authorized by law, levy additional taxes within the limits fixed for municipal purposes.

History.—Am. S.J.R. 1061, 1975; adopted 1976.

SECTION 10. Pledging credit.—Neither the state nor any county, school district, municipality, special district, or agency of any of them, shall become a joint owner with, or stockholder of, or give, lend or use its taxing power or credit to aid any corporation, association, partnership or person; but this shall not prohibit laws authorizing:

(a) the investment of public trust funds;

(b) the investment of other public funds in obligations of, or insured by, the United States or any of its instrumentalities;

(c) the issuance and sale by any county, municipality, special district or other local governmental body of (1) revenue bonds to finance or refinance the cost of capital projects for airports or port facilities, or (2) revenue bonds to finance or refinance the cost of capital projects for industrial or manufacturing plants to the extent that the interest thereon is exempt from income taxes under the then existing laws of the United States, when, in either case, the revenue bonds are payable solely from revenue derived from the sale, operation or leasing of the projects. If any project so financed, or any part thereof, is occupied or operated by any private corporation, association, partnership or person pursuant to contract or lease with the issuing body, the property interest created by such contract or lease shall be subject to taxation to the same extent as other privately owned property.

(d) a municipality, county, special district, or agency of any of them, being a joint owner of, giving, or lending or using its taxing power or credit for the joint ownership, construction and operation of electrical energy generating or transmission facilities with any corporation, association, partnership or person.

History.—Am. H.J.R. 1424, 1973; adopted 1974.

SECTION 11. State bonds; revenue bonds.—

(a) State bonds pledging the full faith and credit of the state may be issued only to finance or refinance the cost of state fixed capital outlay projects authorized by law, and purposes incidental thereto, upon approval by a vote of the electors; provided state bonds issued pursuant to this subsection may be refunded without a vote of the electors at a lower net average interest cost rate. The total outstanding principal of state bonds issued pursuant to this subsection shall never exceed fifty percent of the total tax revenues of the state for the two preceding fiscal years, excluding any tax revenues held in trust under the provisions of this constitution.

(b) Moneys sufficient to pay debt service on state bonds as the same becomes due shall be appropriated by law.

(c) Any state bonds pledging the full faith and credit of the state issued under this section or any other section of this constitution may be combined for the purposes of sale.

(d) Revenue bonds may be issued by the state or its agencies without a vote of the electors to finance or refinance the cost of state fixed capital outlay projects authorized by law, and purposes incidental thereto, and shall be payable solely from funds derived directly from sources other than state tax revenues.

(e) Each project, building, or facility to be financed or refinanced with revenue bonds issued under this section shall first be approved by the Legislature by an act relating to appropriations or by general law.

History.—Am. C.S. for C.S. for S.J.R. 612, 1984; adopted 1984.

SECTION 12. Local bonds.—Counties, school districts, municipalities, special districts and local governmental bodies with taxing powers may issue bonds, certificates of indebtedness or any form of tax anticipation certificates, payable from ad valorem taxation and maturing more than twelve months after issuance only:

(a) to finance or refinance capital projects authorized by law and only when approved by vote of the electors who are owners of freeholds therein not wholly exempt from taxation; or

(b) to refund outstanding bonds and interest and redemption premium thereon at a lower net average interest cost rate.

SECTION 13. Relief from illegal taxes.—Until payment of all taxes which have been legally assessed upon the property of the same owner, no court shall grant relief from the payment of any tax that may be illegal or illegally assessed.

SECTION 14. Bonds for pollution control and abatement and other water facilities.—

(a) When authorized by law, state bonds pledging the full faith and credit of the state may be issued without an election to finance the construction of air and water pollution control and abatement and solid waste disposal facilities and other water facilities authorized by general law (herein referred to as "facilities") to be operated by any municipality, county, district or authority, or any agency thereof (herein referred to as "local governmental agencies"), or by any agency of the State of Florida. Such bonds shall be secured by a pledge of and shall be payable primarily from all or any part of revenues to be derived from operation of such facilities, special assessments, rentals to be received under lease–purchase agreements herein provided for, any other revenues that may be legally available for such purpose, including revenues from other facilities, or any combination thereof (herein collectively referred to as "pledged revenues"), and shall be additionally secured by the full faith and credit of the State of Florida.

(b) No such bonds shall be issued unless a state fiscal agency, created by law, has made a determination that in no state fiscal year will the debt service requirements of the bonds proposed to be issued and all other bonds secured by the pledged revenues exceed seventy-five per cent of the pledged revenues.

(c) The state may lease any of such facilities to any local governmental agency, under lease-purchase agreements for such periods and under such other terms and conditions as may be mutually agreed upon. The local governmental agencies may pledge the revenues derived from such leased facilities or any other available funds for the payment of rentals thereunder; and, in addition, the full faith and credit and taxing power of such local governmental agencies may be pledged for the payment of such rentals without any election of freeholder electors or qualified electors.

(d) The state may also issue such bonds for the purpose of loaning money to local governmental agencies, for the construction of such facilities to be owned or operated by any of such local governmental agencies. Such loans shall bear interest at not more than one-half of one per cent per annum greater than the last preceding issue of state bonds pursuant to this section, shall be secured by the pledged revenues, and may be additionally secured by the full faith and credit of the local governmental agencies.

(e) The total outstanding principal of state bonds issued pursuant to this section 14 shall never exceed fifty per cent of the total tax revenues of the state for the two preceding fiscal years.

History.—C.S. for H.J.R.'s 3853, 4040, 1970; adopted 1970; Am. H.J.R. 1471, 1980; adopted 1980.

SECTION 15. Revenue bonds for scholarship loans.—

(a) When authorized by law, revenue bonds may be issued to establish a fund to make loans to students determined eligible as prescribed by law and who have been admitted to attend any public or private institutions of higher learning, junior colleges, health related training institutions, or vocational training centers, which are recognized or accredited under terms and conditions prescribed by law. Revenue bonds issued pursuant to this section shall be secured by a pledge of and shall be payable primarily from payments of interest, principal, and handling charges to such fund from the recipients of the loans and, if authorized by law, may be additionally secured by student fees and by any other moneys in such fund. There shall be established from the proceeds of each issue of revenue bonds a reserve account in an amount equal to and sufficient to pay the greatest amount of principal, interest, and handling charges to become due on such issue in any ensuing state fiscal year.

(b) Interest moneys in the fund established pursuant to this section, not required in any fiscal year for payment of debt service on then outstanding revenue bonds or for maintenance of the reserve account, may be used for educational loans to students determined to be eligible therefor in the manner provided by law, or for such other related purposes as may be provided by law.

History.—Added, H.J.R. 46-D, 1971; adopted 1972.

SECTION 16. Bonds for housing and related facilities.—

(a) When authorized by law, revenue bonds may be issued without an election to finance or refinance housing and related facilities in Florida, herein referred to as "facilities."

(b) The bonds shall be secured by a pledge of and shall be payable primarily from all or any part of revenues to be derived from the financing, operation or sale of such facilities, mortgage or loan payments, and any other revenues or assets that may be legally available for such purposes derived from sources other than ad valorem taxation, including revenues from other facilities, or any combination thereof, herein collectively referred to as "pledged revenues," provided that in no event shall the full faith and credit of the state be pledged to secure such revenue bonds.

(c) No bonds shall be issued unless a state fiscal agency, created by law, has made a determination that in no state fiscal year will the debt service requirements of the bonds proposed to be issued and all other bonds secured by the same pledged revenues exceed the pledged revenues available for payment of such debt service requirements, as defined by law.

History.—Added, S.J.R. 6-E, 1980; adopted 1980.
cf.—s. 18, Art. XII Schedule.

SECTION 17. Bonds for acquiring transportation right-of-way or for constructing bridges.—

(a) When authorized by law, state bonds pledging the full faith and credit of the state may be issued, without a vote of the electors, to finance or refinance the cost of acquiring real property or the rights to real property for state roads as defined by law, or to finance or refinance the cost of state bridge construction, and purposes incidental to such property acquisition or state bridge construction.

(b) Bonds issued under this section shall be secured by a pledge of and shall be payable primarily from motor fuel or special fuel taxes, except those defined in Section 9(c) of Article XII, as provided by law, and shall additionally be secured by the full faith and credit of the state.

(c) No bonds shall be issued under this section unless a state fiscal agency, created by law, has made a determination that in no state fiscal year will the debt service requirements of the bonds proposed to be issued and all other bonds secured by the same pledged revenues exceed ninety percent of the pledged revenues available for payment of such debt service requirements, as defined by law. For the purposes of this subsection, the term "pledged revenues" means all revenues pledged to the payment of debt service, excluding any pledge of the full faith and credit of the state.

History.—Added, C.S. for C.S. for S.J.R. 391, 1988; adopted 1988.

SECTION 18. Laws requiring counties or municipalities to spend funds or limiting their ability to raise revenue or receive state tax revenue.—

(a) No county or municipality shall be bound by any general law requiring such county or municipality to spend funds or to take an action requiring the expenditure of funds unless the legislature has determined that such law fulfills an important state interest and unless: funds have been appropriated that have been estimated at the time of enactment to be sufficient to fund such expenditure; the legislature authorizes or has authorized a county or municipality to enact a funding source not available for such county or municipality on February 1, 1989, that can be used to generate the amount of funds estimated to be sufficient to fund such expenditure by a simple majority vote of the governing body of such county or municipality; the law requiring such expenditure is approved by two-thirds of the membership in each house of the legislature; the expenditure is required to comply with a law that applies to all persons similarly situated, including the state and local governments; or the law is either required to comply with a federal requirement or required for eligibility for a federal entitlement, which federal requirement specifically contemplates actions by counties or municipalities for compliance.

(b) Except upon approval of each house of the legislature by two-thirds of the membership, the legislature may not enact, amend, or repeal any general law if the anticipated effect of doing so would be to reduce the authority that municipalities or counties have to raise revenues in the aggregate, as such authority exists on February 1, 1989.

(c) Except upon approval of each house of the legislature by two-thirds of the membership, the legislature may not enact, amend, or repeal any general law if the anticipated effect of doing so would be to reduce the percentage of a state tax shared with counties and municipalities as an aggregate on February 1, 1989. The provisions of this subsection shall not apply to enhancements enacted after February 1, 1989, to state tax sources, or during a fiscal emergency declared in a written joint proclamation issued by the president of the senate and the speaker of the house of representatives, or where the legislature provides additional state-shared revenues which are anticipated to be sufficient to replace the anticipated aggregate loss of state-shared revenues resulting from the reduction of the percentage of the state tax shared with counties and municipalities, which source of replacement revenues shall be subject to the same requirements for repeal or modification as provided herein for a state-shared tax source existing on February 1, 1989.

(d) Laws adopted to require funding of pension benefits existing on the effective date of this section, criminal laws, election laws, the general appropriations act, special appropriations acts, laws reauthorizing but not expanding then-existing statutory authority, laws having insignificant fiscal impact, and laws creating, modifying, or repealing noncriminal infractions, are exempt from the requirements of this section.

(e) The legislature may enact laws to assist in the implementation and enforcement of this section.

History.—Added, C.S. for C.S. for C.S. for H.J.R.'s 139, 40, 1989; adopted 1990.

ARTICLE VIII

LOCAL GOVERNMENT

Sec.
1. Counties.
2. Municipalities.
3. Consolidation.
4. Transfer of powers.
5. Local option.
6. Schedule to Article VIII.

SECTION 1. Counties.—

(a) POLITICAL SUBDIVISIONS. The state shall be divided by law into political subdivisions called counties. Counties may be created, abolished or changed by law, with provision for payment or apportionment of the public debt.

(b) COUNTY FUNDS. The care, custody and method of disbursing county funds shall be provided by general law.

(c) GOVERNMENT. Pursuant to general or special law, a county government may be established by charter which shall be adopted, amended or repealed only upon vote of the electors of the county in a special election called for that purpose.

(d) COUNTY OFFICERS. There shall be elected by the electors of each county, for terms of four years, a sheriff, a tax collector, a property appraiser, a supervisor of elections, and a clerk of the circuit court; except, when provided by county charter or special law approved by vote of the electors of the county, any county officer may be chosen in another manner therein specified, or any county office may be abolished when all the duties of the office prescribed by general law are transferred to another office. When not otherwise provided by county charter or special law approved by vote of the electors, the clerk of the circuit court shall be ex officio clerk of the board of county commissioners, auditor, recorder and custodian of all county funds.

(e) COMMISSIONERS. Except when otherwise provided by county charter, the governing body of each county shall be a board of county commissioners composed of five or seven members serving staggered terms of four years. After each decennial census the board of county commissioners shall divide the county into districts of contiguous territory as nearly equal in population as practicable. One commissioner residing in each district shall be elected as provided by law.

(f) NON-CHARTER GOVERNMENT. Counties not operating under county charters shall have such power of self-government as is provided by general or special law. The board of county commissioners of a county not operating under a charter may enact, in a manner prescribed by general law, county ordinances not inconsistent with general or special law, but an ordinance in conflict with a municipal ordinance shall not be effective within the municipality to the extent of such conflict.

(g) CHARTER GOVERNMENT. Counties operating under county charters shall have all powers of local self-government not inconsistent with general law, or with special law approved by vote of the electors. The governing body of a county operating under a charter may enact county ordinances not inconsistent with general law. The charter shall provide which shall prevail in the event of conflict between county and municipal ordinances.

(h) TAXES; LIMITATION. Property situate within municipalities shall not be subject to taxation for services rendered by the county exclusively for the benefit of the property or residents in unincorporated areas.

(i) COUNTY ORDINANCES. Each county ordinance shall be filed with the secretary of state and shall become effective at such time thereafter as is provided by general law.

(j) VIOLATION OF ORDINANCES. Persons violating county ordinances shall be prosecuted and punished as provided by law.

(k) COUNTY SEAT. In every county there shall be a county seat at which shall be located the principal offices and permanent records of all county officers. The county seat may not be moved except as provided by general law. Branch offices for the conduct of county business may be established elsewhere in the county by resolution of the governing body of the county in the manner prescribed by law. No instrument shall be deemed recorded in the county until filed at the county seat according to law.

History.—Am. H.J.R. 1907, 1973; adopted 1974; Am. H.J.R. 452, 1984; adopted 1984.

SECTION 2. Municipalities.—

(a) ESTABLISHMENT. Municipalities may be established or abolished and their charters amended pursuant to general or special law. When any municipality is abolished, provision shall be made for the protection of its creditors.

(b) POWERS. Municipalities shall have governmental, corporate and proprietary powers to enable them to conduct municipal government, perform municipal functions and render municipal services, and may exercise any power for municipal purposes except as otherwise provided by law. Each municipal legislative body shall be elective.

(c) ANNEXATION. Municipal annexation of unincorporated territory, merger of municipalities, and exercise of extra-territorial powers by municipalities shall be as provided by general or special law.

SECTION 3. Consolidation.—

The government of a county and the government of one or more municipalities located therein may be consolidated into a single government which may exercise any and all powers of the county and the several municipalities. The consolidation plan may be proposed only by special law, which shall become effective if approved by vote of the electors of the county, or of the county and municipalities affected, as may be provided in the plan. Consolidation shall not extend the territorial scope of taxation for the payment of pre-existing debt except to areas whose residents receive a benefit from the facility or service for which the indebtedness was incurred.

SECTION 4. Transfer of powers.—

By law or by resolution of the governing bodies of each of the governments affected, any function or power of a county, municipality or special district may be transferred to or contracted to be performed by another county, municipality or special district, after approval by vote of the electors of the transferor and approval by vote of the electors of the transferee, or as otherwise provided by law.

SECTION 5. Local option.—

Local option on the legality or prohibition of the sale of intoxicating liquors, wines or beers shall be preserved to each county. The status of a county with respect thereto shall be changed only by vote of the electors in a special election called upon the petition of twenty-five per cent of the electors of the county, and not sooner than two years after an earlier election on the same question. Where legal, the sale of intoxicating liquors, wines and beers shall be regulated by law.

SECTION 6. Schedule to Article VIII.—

(a) This article shall replace all of Article VIII of the Constitution of 1885, as amended, except those sections expressly retained and made a part of this article by reference.

(b) COUNTIES; COUNTY SEATS; MUNICIPALITIES; DISTRICTS. The status of the following items as they exist on the date this article becomes effective is recognized and shall be continued until changed in accordance with law: the counties of the state; their status with respect to the legality of the sale of intoxicating liquors, wines and beers; the method of selection of county officers; the performance of municipal functions by county officers; the county seats; and the municipalities and special districts of the state, their powers, jurisdiction and government.

(c) OFFICERS TO CONTINUE IN OFFICE. Every person holding office when this article becomes effective shall continue in office for the remainder of the term if that office is not abolished. If the office is abolished the incumbent shall be paid adequate compensation, to be fixed by law, for the loss of emoluments for the remainder of the term.

(d) ORDINANCES. Local laws relating only to unincorporated areas of a county on the effective date of this article may be amended or repealed by county ordinance.

(e) CONSOLIDATION AND HOME RULE. Article VIII, Sections [1]9, [2]10, [3]11 and [4]24, of the Constitution of 1885, as amended, shall remain in full force and effect as to each county affected, as if this article had not been adopted, until that county shall expressly adopt a charter or home rule plan pursuant to this article. All provisions of the Metropolitan Dade County Home Rule Charter, heretofore or hereafter adopted by the electors of Dade County pursuant to [3]Article VIII, Section 11, of the Constitution of 1885, as amended, shall be valid, and any amendments to such charter shall be valid; provided that the said provisions of such charter and the said amendments thereto are authorized under said [3]Article VIII, Section 11, of the Constitution of 1885, as amended.

(f) DADE COUNTY; POWERS CONFERRED UPON MUNICIPALITIES. To the extent not inconsistent with the powers of existing municipalities or general law, the Metropolitan Government of Dade County may exercise all the powers conferred now or hereafter by general law upon municipalities.

(g) DELETION OF OBSOLETE SCHEDULE ITEMS. The legislature shall have power, by joint resolution, to delete from this article any subsection of this Section 6, including this subsection, when all events to which the subsection to be deleted is or could become applicable have occurred. A legislative determination of fact made as a basis for application of this subsection shall be subject to judicial review.

[1]Note.—Section 9 of Art. VIII of the Constitution of 1885, as amended, reads as follows:

SECTION 9. Legislative power over city of Jacksonville and Duval County.—The Legislature shall have power to establish, alter or abolish, a Municipal corporation to be known as the City of Jacksonville, extending territorially throughout the present limits of Duval County, in the place of any or all county, district, municipal and local governments, boards, bodies and officers, constitutional or statutory, legislative, executive, judicial, or administrative, and shall prescribe the jurisdiction, powers, duties and functions of such municipal corporation, its legislative, executive, judicial and administrative departments and its boards, bodies and officers; to divide the territory included in such municipality into subordinate districts, and to prescribe a just and reasonable system of taxation for such municipality and districts; and to fix the liability of such municipality and districts. Bonded and other indebtedness, existing at the time of the establishment of such municipality, shall be enforceable only against property theretofore taxable therefor. The Legislature shall, from time to time, determine what portion of said municipality is a rural area, and a homestead in such rural area shall not be limited as if in a city or town. Such municipality may exercise all the powers of a municipal corporation and shall also be recognized as one of the legal political divisions of the State with the duties and obligations of a county and shall be entitled to all the powers, rights and privileges, including representation in the State Legislature, which would accrue to it if it were a county. All property of Duval County and of the municipalities in said county shall vest in such municipal corporation when established as herein provided. The offices of Clerk of the Circuit Court and Sheriff shall not be abolished but the Legislature may prescribe the time when, and the method by which, such offices shall be filled and the compensation to be paid to such officers and may vest in them additional powers and duties. No county office shall be abolished or consolidated with another office without making provision for the performance of all State duties now or hereafter prescribed by law to be performed by such county officer. Nothing contained herein shall affect Section 20 of Article III of the Constitution of the State of Florida, except as to such provisions therein as relate to regulating the jurisdiction and duties of any class of officers, to summoning and impanelling grand and petit jurors, to assessing and collecting taxes for county purposes and to regulating the fees and compensation of county officers. No law authorizing the establishing or abolishing of such Municipal corporation pursuant to this Section shall become operative or effective until approved by a majority of the qualified electors participating in an election held in said County, but so long as such Municipal corporation exists under this Section the Legislature may amend or extend the law authorizing the same without referendum to the qualified voters unless the Legislative act providing for such amendment or extension shall provide for such referendum.

History.—Added, S.J.R. 113, 1933; adopted 1934.

[2]Note.—Section 10, Art. VIII of the Constitution of 1885, as amended, reads as follows:

SECTION 10. Legislative power over city of Key West and Monroe county.—The Legislature shall have power to establish, alter or abolish, a Municipal corporation to be known as the City of Key West, extending territorially throughout the present limits of Monroe County, in the place of any or all county, district, municipal and local governments, boards, bodies and officers, constitutional or statutory, legislative, executive, judicial, or administrative, and shall prescribe the jurisdiction, powers, duties and functions of such municipal corporation, its legislative, executive, judicial and administrative departments and its boards, bodies and officers; to divide the territory included in such municipality into subordinate districts, and to prescribe a just and reasonable system of taxation for such municipality and districts; and to fix the liability of such municipality and districts. Bonded and other indebtedness, existing at the time of the establishment of such municipality, shall be enforceable only against property theretofore taxable therefor. The Legislature shall, from time to time, determine what portion of said municipality is a rural area, and a homestead in such rural area shall not be limited as if in a city or town. Such municipality may exercise all the powers of a municipal corporation and shall also be recognized as one of the legal political divisions of the State with the duties and obligations of a county and shall be entitled to all the powers, rights and privileges, including representation in the State Legislature, which would accrue to it if it were a county. All property of Monroe County and of the municipality in said county shall vest in such municipal corporation when established as herein provided. The offices of Clerk of the Circuit Court and Sheriff shall not be abolished but the Legislature may prescribe the time when, and the method by which, such offices shall be filled and the compensation to be paid to such officers and may vest in them additional powers and duties. No county office shall be abolished or consolidated with another office without making provision for the performance of all State duties now or hereafter prescribed by law to be performed by such county officer. Nothing contained herein shall affect Section 20 of Article III of the Constitution of the State of Florida, except as to such provisions therein as relate to regulating the jurisdiction and duties of any class of officers, to summoning and impanelling grand and petit juries, to assessing and collecting taxes for county purposes and to regulating the fees and compensation of county officers. No law authorizing the establishing or abolishing of such Municipal corporation pursuant to this Section shall become operative or effective until approved by a majority of the qualified electors participating in an election held in said County, but so long as such Municipal corporation exists under this Section the Legislature may amend or extend the law authorizing the same without referendum to the qualified voters unless the Legislative Act providing for such amendment or extension shall provide for such referendum.

History.—Added, S.J.R. 429, 1935; adopted 1936.

[3]Note.—Section 11 of Art. VIII of the Constitution of 1885, as amended, reads as follows:

SECTION 11. Dade County, home rule charter.—(1) The electors of Dade County, Florida, are granted power to adopt, revise, and amend from time to time a home rule charter of government for Dade County, Florida, under which the Board of County Commissioners of Dade County shall be the governing body. This charter:

(a) Shall fix the boundaries of each county commission district, provide a method for changing them from time to time, and fix the number, terms and compensation of the commissioners, and their method of election.

(b) May grant full power and authority to the Board of County Commissioners of Dade County to pass ordinances relating to the affairs, property and government of Dade County and provide suitable penalties for the violation thereof; to levy and collect such taxes as may be authorized by general law and no other taxes, and to do everything necessary to carry on a central metropolitan government in Dade County.

(c) May change the boundaries of, merge, consolidate, and abolish and may provide a method for changing the boundaries of, merging, consolidating and abolishing from time to time all municipal corporations, county or district governments, special taxing districts, authorities, boards, or other governmental units whose jurisdiction lies wholly within Dade County, whether such governmental units are created by the Constitution or the Legislature or otherwise, except the Dade County Board of County Commissioners as it may be provided for from time to time by this home rule charter and the Board of Public Instruction of Dade County.

(d) May provide a method by which any and all of the functions or powers of any municipal corporation or other governmental unit in Dade County may be transferred to the Board of County Commissioners of Dade County.

(e) May provide a method for establishing new municipal corporations, special taxing districts, and other governmental units in Dade County from time to time and provide for their government and prescribe their jurisdiction and powers.

(f) May abolish and may provide a method for abolishing from time to time all offices provided for by Article VIII, Section 6, of the Constitution or by the Legislature, except the Superintendent of Public Instruction and may provide for the consolidation and transfer of the functions of such offices, provided, however, that there shall be no power to abolish or impair the jurisdiction of the Circuit Court or to abolish any other court provided for by this Constitution or by general law, or the judges or clerks thereof although such charter may create new courts and judges and clerks thereof with jurisdiction to try all offenses against ordinances passed by the Board of County Commissioners of Dade County and none of the other courts provided for by this Constitution or by general law shall have original jurisdiction to try such offenses, although the charter may confer appellate jurisdiction on such courts, and provided further that if said home rule charter shall abolish any county office or offices as authorized herein, that said charter shall contain adequate provision for the carrying on of all functions of said office or offices as are now or may hereafter be prescribed by general law.

(g) Shall provide a method by which each municipal corporation in Dade County shall have the power to make, amend or repeal its own charter. Upon adoption of this home rule charter by the electors this method shall be exclusive and the Legislature shall have no power to amend or repeal the charter of any municipal corporation in Dade County.

(h) May change the name of Dade County.

(i) Shall provide a method for the recall of any commissioner and a method for initiative and referendum, including the initiation of and referendum on ordinances and the amendment or revision of the home rule charter, provided, however, that the power of the Governor and Senate relating to the suspension and removal of officers provided for in this Constitution shall not be impaired, but shall extend to all officers provided for in said home rule charter.

(2) Provision shall be made for the protection of the creditors of any governmental unit which is merged, consolidated, or abolished or whose boundaries are changed or functions or powers transferred.

(3) This home rule charter shall be prepared by a Metropolitan Charter Board created by the Legislature and shall be presented to the electors of Dade County for ratification or rejection in the manner provided by the Legislature. Until a home rule charter is adopted the Legislature may from time to time create additional Charter Boards to prepare charters to be presented to the electors of Dade County for ratification or rejection in the manner provided by the Legislature. Such Charter, once adopted by the electors, may be amended only by the electors of Dade County and this charter shall provide a method for submitting future charter revisions and amendments to the electors of Dade County.

(4) The County Commission shall continue to receive its pro rata share of all revenues payable by the state from whatever source to the several counties and the state of Florida shall pay to the Commission all revenues which would have been paid to any municipality in Dade County which may be abolished by or in the method provided by this home rule charter; provided, however, the Commission shall reimburse the comptroller of Florida for the expense incurred if any, in the keeping of separate records to determine the amounts of money which would have been payable to any such municipality.

(5) Nothing in this section shall limit or restrict the power of the Legislature to enact general laws which shall relate to Dade County and any other one or more counties in the state of Florida or to any municipality in Dade County and any other one or more municipalities of the State of Florida, and the home rule charter provided for herein shall not conflict with any provision of this Constitution nor of any applicable general laws now applying to Dade County and any other one or more counties of the State of Florida except as expressly authorized in this section nor shall any ordinance enacted in pursuance to said home rule charter conflict with this Constitution or any such applicable general law except as expressly authorized herein, nor shall the charter of any municipality in Dade County conflict with this Constitution or any such applicable general law except as expressly authorized herein, provided however that said charter and said ordinances enacted in pursuance thereof may conflict with, modify or nullify any existing local, special or general law applicable only to Dade County.

(6) Nothing in this section shall be construed to limit or restrict the power of the Legislature to enact general laws which shall relate to Dade County and any other one or more counties of the state of Florida or to any municipality in Dade County and any other one or more municipalities of the State of Florida relating to county or municipal affairs and all such general laws shall apply to Dade County and to all municipalities therein to the same extent as if this section had not been adopted and such general laws shall supersede any part or portion of the home rule charter provided for herein in conflict therewith and shall supersede any provision of any ordinance enacted pursuant to said charter and in conflict therewith, and shall supersede any provision of any charter of any municipality in Dade County in conflict therewith.

(7) Nothing in this section shall be construed to limit or restrict the power and jurisdiction of the Railroad and Public Utilities Commission or of any other state agency, bureau or commission now or hereafter provided for in this Constitution or by general law and said state agencies, bureaus and commissions shall have the same powers in Dade County as shall be conferred upon them in regard to other counties.

(8) If any section, subsection, sentence, clause or provisions of this section is held invalid as violative of the provisions of Section 1 Article XVII of this Constitution the remainder of this section shall not be affected by such invalidity.

(9) It is declared to be the intent of the Legislature and of the electors of the State of Florida to provide by this section home rule for the people of Dade County in local affairs and this section shall be liberally construed to carry out such purpose, and it is further declared to be the intent of the Legislature and of the electors of the State of Florida that the provisions of this Constitution and general laws which shall relate to Dade County and any other one or more counties of the State of Florida or to any municipality in Dade County and any other one or more municipalities of the State of Florida enacted pursuant thereto by the Legislature shall be the supreme law in Dade County, Florida, except as expressly provided herein and this section shall be strictly construed to maintain such supremacy of this Constitution and of the Legislature in the enactment of general laws pursuant to this Constitution.

History.—Added, H.J.R. 858, 1941; adopted 1942; Am. S.J.R. 1046, 1955; adopted 1956.

[4]**Note.**—Section 24 of Art. VIII of the Constitution of 1885, as amended, reads as follows:

SECTION 24. Hillsborough County, home rule charter.—

(1) The electors of Hillsborough county are hereby granted the power to adopt a charter for a government which shall exercise any and all powers for county and municipal purposes which this constitution or the legislature, by general, special or local law, has conferred upon Hillsborough county or any municipality therein. Such government shall exercise these powers by the enactment of ordinances which relate to government of Hillsborough county and provide suitable penalties for the violation thereof. Such government shall have no power to create or abolish any municipality, except as otherwise provided herein.

(2) The method and manner by which the electors of Hillsborough county shall exercise this power shall be set forth in a charter for the government of Hillsborough county which charter shall be presented to said electors by any charter commission established by the legislature. The legislature may provide for the continuing existence of any charter commission or may establish a charter commission or commissions subsequent to any initial commission without regard to any election or elections held upon any charter or charters theretofore presented. A charter shall become effective only upon ratification by a majority of the electors of Hillsborough county voting in a general or special election as provided by law.

(3) The number, qualifications, terms of office and method of filling vacancies in the membership of any charter commission established pursuant to this section and the powers, functions and duties of any such commission shall be provided by law.

(4) A charter prepared by any commission established pursuant to this section shall provide that:

(a) The governments of the city of Tampa and the county of Hillsborough shall be consolidated, and the structure of the new local government shall include:

1. An executive branch, the chief officer of which shall be responsible for the administration of government.
2. An elected legislative branch, the election to membership, powers and duties of which shall be as provided by the charter.
3. A judicial branch, which shall only have jurisdiction in the enforcement of ordinances enacted by the legislative branch created by this section.

(b) Should the electors of the municipalities of Plant City or Temple Terrace wish to consolidate their governments with the government hereinabove created, they may do so by majority vote of the electors of said municipality voting in an election upon said issue.

(c) The creditors of any governmental unit consolidated or abolished under this section shall be protected. Bonded or other indebtedness existing at the effective date of any government established hereunder shall be enforceable only against the real and personal property theretofore taxable for such purposes.

(d) Such other provisions as might be required by law.

(5) The provisions of such charter and ordinances enacted pursuant thereto shall not conflict with any provision of this constitution nor with general, special or local laws now or hereafter applying to Hillsborough county.

(6) The government established hereunder shall be recognized as a county, that is one of the legal political subdivisions of the state with the powers, rights, privileges, duties and obligations of a county, and may also exercise all the powers of a municipality. Said government shall have the right to sue and be sued.

(7) Any government established hereunder shall be entitled to receive from the state of Florida or from the United States or from any other agency, public or private, funds and revenues to which a county is, or may hereafter be entitled, and also all funds and revenues to which an incorporated municipality is or may hereafter be entitled, and to receive the same without diminution or loss by reason of any such government as may be established. Nothing herein contained shall preclude such government as may be established hereunder from receiving all funds and revenues from whatever source now received, or hereinafter received provided by law.

(8) The board of county commissioners of Hillsborough county shall be abolished when the functions, duties, powers and responsibilities of said board shall be transferred in the manner to be provided by the charter to the government established pursuant to this section. No other office provided for by this constitution shall be abolished by or pursuant to this section.

(9) This section shall not restrict or limit the legislature in the enactment of general, special or local laws as otherwise provided in this constitution.

History.—Added, C.S. for H.J.R. 1987, 1965; adopted 1966.

ARTICLE IX
EDUCATION

Sec.
1. System of public education.
2. State board of education.
3. Terms of appointive board members.
4. School districts; school boards.
5. Superintendent of schools.
6. State school fund.

SECTION 1. System of public education.—Adequate provision shall be made by law for a uniform system of free public schools and for the establishment, maintenance and operation of institutions of higher learning and other public education programs that the needs of the people may require.

SECTION 2. State board of education.—The governor and the members of the cabinet shall constitute a state board of education, which shall be a body corporate and have such supervision of the system of public education as is provided by law.

SECTION 3. Terms of appointive board members. Members of any appointive board dealing with education may serve terms in excess of four years as provided by law.

SECTION 4. School districts; school boards.—

(a) Each county shall constitute a school district; provided, two or more contiguous counties, upon vote of the electors of each county pursuant to law, may be combined into one school district. In each school district there shall be a school board composed of five or more members chosen by vote of the electors for appropriately staggered terms of four years, as provided by law.

(b) The school board shall operate, control and supervise all free public schools within the school district and determine the rate of school district taxes within the limits prescribed herein. Two or more school districts may operate and finance joint educational programs.

SECTION 5. Superintendent of schools.—In each school district there shall be a superintendent of schools. He shall be elected at the general election in each year the number of which is a multiple of four for a term of four years; or, when provided by resolution of the district school board, or by special law, approved by vote of the electors, the district school superintendent in any school district shall be employed by the district school board as provided by general law. The resolution or special law may be rescinded or repealed by either procedure after four years.

SECTION 6. State school fund.—The income derived from the state school fund shall, and the principal of the fund may, be appropriated, but only to the support and maintenance of free public schools.

ARTICLE X
MISCELLANEOUS

Sec.
1. Amendments to United States Constitution.
2. Militia.

Sec.
3. Vacancy in office.
4. Homestead; exemptions.
5. Coverture and property.
6. Eminent domain.
7. Lotteries.
8. Census.
9. Repeal of criminal statutes.
10. Felony; definition.
11. Sovereignty lands.
12. Rules of construction.
13. Suits against the state.
14. State retirement systems benefit changes.
15. State operated lotteries.
16. Limiting Marine Net Fishing.

SECTION 1. Amendments to United States Constitution.—The legislature shall not take action on any proposed amendment to the constitution of the United States unless a majority of the members thereof have been elected after the proposed amendment has been submitted for ratification.

SECTION 2. Militia.—

(a) The militia shall be composed of all ablebodied inhabitants of the state who are or have declared their intention to become citizens of the United States; and no person because of religious creed or opinion shall be exempted from military duty except upon conditions provided by law.

(b) The organizing, equipping, housing, maintaining, and disciplining of the militia, and the safekeeping of public arms may be provided for by law.

(c) The governor shall appoint all commissioned officers of the militia, including an adjutant general who shall be chief of staff. The appointment of all general officers shall be subject to confirmation by the senate.

(d) The qualifications of personnel and officers of the federally recognized national guard, including the adjutant general, and the grounds and proceedings for their discipline and removal shall conform to the appropriate United States army or air force regulations and usages.

SECTION 3. Vacancy in office.—Vacancy in office shall occur upon the creation of an office, upon the death of the incumbent or his removal from office, resignation, succession to another office, unexplained absence for sixty consecutive days, or failure to maintain the residence required when elected or appointed, and upon failure of one elected or appointed to office to qualify within thirty days from the commencement of the term.

SECTION 4. Homestead; exemptions.—

(a) There shall be exempt from forced sale under process of any court, and no judgment, decree or execution shall be a lien thereon, except for the payment of taxes and assessments thereon, obligations contracted for the purchase, improvement or repair thereof, or obligations contracted for house, field or other labor performed on the realty, the following property owned by a natural person:

(1) a homestead, if located outside a municipality, to the extent of one hundred sixty acres of contiguous land and improvements thereon, which shall not be reduced without the owner's consent by reason of subsequent inclusion in a municipality; or if located within a municipality, to the extent of one-half acre of contiguous land, upon which the exemption shall be limited to the residence of the owner or his family;

(2) personal property to the value of one thousand dollars.

(b) These exemptions shall inure to the surviving spouse or heirs of the owner.

(c) The homestead shall not be subject to devise if the owner is survived by spouse or minor child, except the homestead may be devised to the owner's spouse if there be no minor child. The owner of homestead real estate, joined by the spouse if married, may alienate the homestead by mortgage, sale or gift and, if married, may by deed transfer the title to an estate by the entirety with the spouse. If the owner or spouse is incompetent, the method of alienation or encumbrance shall be as provided by law.

History.—Am. H.J.R. 4324, 1972; adopted 1972; Am. H.J.R. 40, 1983; adopted 1984.

SECTION 5. Coverture and property.—There shall be no distinction between married women and married men in the holding, control, disposition, or encumbering of their property, both real and personal; except that dower or curtesy may be established and regulated by law.

SECTION 6. Eminent domain.—

(a) No private property shall be taken except for a public purpose and with full compensation therefor paid to each owner or secured by deposit in the registry of the court and available to the owner.

(b) Provision may be made by law for the taking of easements, by like proceedings, for the drainage of the land of one person over or through the land of another.

SECTION 7. Lotteries.—Lotteries, other than the types of pari-mutuel pools authorized by law as of the effective date of this constitution, are hereby prohibited in this state.

SECTION 8. Census.—

(a) Each decennial census of the state taken by the United States shall be an official census of the state.

(b) Each decennial census, for the purpose of classifications based upon population, shall become effective on the thirtieth day after the final adjournment of the regular session of the legislature convened next after certification of the census.

SECTION 9. Repeal of criminal statutes.—Repeal or amendment of a criminal statute shall not affect prosecution or punishment for any crime previously committed.

SECTION 10. Felony; definition.—The term "felony" as used herein and in the laws of this state shall mean any criminal offense that is punishable under the laws of this state, or that would be punishable if committed in this state, by death or by imprisonment in the state penitentiary.

SECTION 11. Sovereignty lands.—The title to lands under navigable waters, within the boundaries of the state, which have not been alienated, including beaches below mean high water lines, is held by the state, by virtue of its sovereignty, in trust for all the people. Sale of such lands may be authorized by law, but only when in the public interest. Private use of portions of such lands may be authorized by law, but only when not contrary to the public interest.

History.—Am. H.J.R. 792, 1970; adopted 1970.

SECTION 12. Rules of construction.—Unless qualified in the text the following rules of construction shall apply to this constitution.

(a) "Herein" refers to the entire constitution.
(b) The singular includes the plural.
(c) The masculine includes the feminine.
(d) "Vote of the electors" means the vote of the majority of those voting on the matter in an election, general or special, in which those participating are limited to the electors of the governmental unit referred to in the text.
(e) Vote or other action of a legislative house or other governmental body means the vote or action of a majority or other specified percentage of those members voting on the matter. "Of the membership" means "of all members thereof."
(f) The terms "judicial office," "justices" and "judges" shall not include judges of courts established solely for the trial of violations of ordinances.
(g) "Special law" means a special or local law.
(h) Titles and subtitles shall not be used in construction.

SECTION 13. Suits against the state.—Provision may be made by general law for bringing suit against the state as to all liabilities now existing or hereafter originating.

SECTION 14. State retirement systems benefit changes.—A governmental unit responsible for any retirement or pension system supported in whole or in part by public funds shall not after January 1, 1977, provide any increase in the benefits to the members or beneficiaries of such system unless such unit has made or concurrently makes provision for the funding of the increase in benefits on a sound actuarial basis.

History.—Added, H.J.R. 291, 1975; adopted 1976.

SECTION 15. State operated lotteries.—
(a) Lotteries may be operated by the state.
(b) If any subsection or subsections of the amendment to the Florida Constitution are held unconstitutional for containing more than one subject, this amendment shall be limited to subsection (a) above.
(c) This amendment shall be implemented as follows:
(1) Schedule—On the effective date of this amendment, the lotteries shall be known as the Florida Education Lotteries. Net proceeds derived from the lotteries shall be deposited to a state trust fund, to be designated The State Education Lotteries Trust Fund, to be appropriated by the Legislature. The schedule may be amended by general law.

History.—Proposed by Initiative Petition filed with the Secretary of State June 10, 1985; adopted 1986.

SECTION 16. Limiting Marine Net Fishing.—
(a) The marine resources of the State of Florida belong to all of the people of the state and should be conserved and managed for the benefit of the state, its people, and future generations. To this end the people hereby enact limitations on marine net fishing in Florida waters to protect saltwater finfish, shellfish, and other marine animals from unnecessary killing, overfishing and waste.

(b) For the purpose of catching or taking any saltwater finfish, shellfish or other marine animals in Florida waters:
(1) No gill nets or other entangling nets shall be used in any Florida waters; and
(2) In addition to the prohibition set forth in (1), no other type of net containing more than 500 square feet of mesh area shall be used in nearshore and inshore Florida waters. Additionally, no more than two such nets, which shall not be connected, shall be used from any vessel, and no person not on a vessel shall use more than one such net in nearshore and inshore Florida waters.

(c) For purposes of this section:
(1) "gill net" means one or more walls of netting which captures saltwater finfish by ensnaring or entangling them in the meshes of the net by the gills, and "entangling net" means a drift net, trammell net, stab net, or any other net which captures saltwater finfish, shellfish, or other marine animals by causing all or part of heads, fins, legs, or other body parts to become entangled or ensnared in the meshes of the net, but a hand thrown cast net is not a gill net or an entangling net;
(2) "mesh area" of a net means the total area of netting with the meshes open to comprise the maximum square footage. The square footage shall be calculated using standard mathematical formulas for geometric shapes. Seines and other rectangular nets shall be calculated using the maximum length and maximum width of the netting. Trawls and other bag type nets shall be calculated as a cone using the maximum circumference of the net mouth to derive the radius, and the maximum length from the net mouth to the tail end of the net to derive the slant height. Calculations for any other nets or combination type nets shall be based on the shapes of the individual components;
(3) "coastline" means the territorial sea base line for the State of Florida established pursuant to the laws of the United States of America;
(4) "Florida waters" means the waters of the Atlantic Ocean, the Gulf of Mexico, the Straits of Florida, and any other bodies of water under the jurisdiction of the State of Florida, whether coastal, intracoastal or inland, and any part thereof; and
(5) "nearshore and inshore Florida waters" means all Florida waters inside a line three miles seaward of the coastline along the Gulf of Mexico and inside a line one mile seaward of the coastline along the Atlantic Ocean.

(d) This section shall not apply to the use of nets for scientific research or governmental purposes.

(e) Persons violating this section shall be prosecuted and punished pursuant to the penalties provided in section 370.021(2)(a),(b),(c)6. and 7., and (e), Florida Statutes (1991), unless and until the legislature enacts more stringent penalties for violations hereof. On and after the effective date of this section, law enforcement officers in the state are authorized to enforce the provisions of this section in the same manner and authority as if a violation of this section constituted a violation of Chapter 370, Florida Statutes (1991).

(f) It is the intent of this section that implementing legislation is not required for enforcing any violations hereof, but nothing in this section prohibits the establishment by law or pursuant to law of more restrictions on the use of nets for the purpose of catching or taking any saltwater finfish, shellfish, or other marine animals.

(g) If any portion of this section is held invalid for any reason, the remaining portion of this section, to the fullest extent possible, shall be severed from the void portion and given the fullest possible force and application.

(h) This section shall take effect on the July 1 next occurring after approval hereof by vote of the electors.

History.—Proposed by Initiative Petition filed with the Secretary of State October 2, 1992; adopted 1994.

ARTICLE XI

AMENDMENTS

Sec.
1. Proposal by legislature.
2. Revision commission.
3. Initiative.
4. Constitutional convention.
5. Amendment or revision election.
6. Taxation and budget reform commission.

SECTION 1. Proposal by legislature.—Amendment of a section or revision of one or more articles, or the whole, of this constitution may be proposed by joint resolution agreed to by three-fifths of the membership of each house of the legislature. The full text of the joint resolution and the vote of each member voting shall be entered on the journal of each house.

SECTION 2. Revision commission.—

(a) Within thirty days after the adjournment of the regular session of the legislature convened in the tenth year following that in which this constitution is adopted, and each twentieth year thereafter, there shall be established a constitution revision commission composed of the following thirty-seven members:

(1) the attorney general of the state;
(2) fifteen members selected by the governor;
(3) nine members selected by the speaker of the house of representatives and nine members selected by the president of the senate; and
(4) three members selected by the chief justice of the supreme court of Florida with the advice of the justices.

(b) The governor shall designate one member of the commission as its chairman. Vacancies in the membership of the commission shall be filled in the same manner as the original appointments.

(c) Each constitution revision commission shall convene at the call of its chairman, adopt its rules of procedure, examine the constitution of the state, except for matters relating directly to taxation or the state budgetary process that are to be reviewed by the taxation and budget reform commission established in section 6, hold public hearings, and, not later than one hundred eighty days prior to the next general election, file with the secretary of state its proposal, if any, of a revision of this constitution or any part of it.

History.—Am. H.J.R. 1616, 1988; adopted 1988.

SECTION 3. Initiative.—The power to propose the revision or amendment of any portion or portions of this constitution by initiative is reserved to the people, provided that, any such revision or amendment, except for those limiting the power of government to raise revenue, shall embrace but one subject and matter directly connected therewith. It may be invoked by filing with the secretary of state a petition containing a copy of the proposed revision or amendment, signed by a number of electors in each of one half of the congressional districts of the state, and of the state as a whole, equal to eight percent of the votes cast in each of such districts respectively and in the state as a whole in the last preceding election in which presidential electors were chosen.

History.—Am. H.J.R. 2835, 1972; adopted 1972; Am. by Initiative Petition filed with the Secretary of State August 3, 1993; adopted 1994.

SECTION 4. Constitutional convention.—

(a) The power to call a convention to consider a revision of the entire constitution is reserved to the people. It may be invoked by filing with the secretary of state a petition, containing a declaration that a constitutional convention is desired, signed by a number of electors in each of one half of the congressional districts of the state, and of the state as a whole, equal to fifteen per cent of the votes cast in each such district respectively and in the state as a whole in the last preceding election of presidential electors.

(b) At the next general election held more than ninety days after the filing of such petition there shall be submitted to the electors of the state the question: "Shall a constitutional convention be held?" If a majority voting on the question votes in the affirmative, at the next succeeding general election there shall be elected from each representative district a member of a constitutional convention. On the twenty-first day following that election, the convention shall sit at the capital, elect officers, adopt rules of procedure, judge the election of its membership, and fix a time and place for its future meetings. Not later than ninety days before the next succeeding general election, the convention shall cause to be filed with the secretary of state any revision of this constitution proposed by it.

SECTION 5. Amendment or revision election.—

(a) A proposed amendment to or revision of this constitution, or any part of it, shall be submitted to the electors at the next general election held more than ninety days after the joint resolution, initiative petition or report of revision commission, constitutional convention or taxation and budget reform commission proposing it is filed with the secretary of state, unless, pursuant to law enacted by the affirmative vote of three-fourths of the membership of each house of the legislature and limited to a single amendment or revision, it is submitted at an earlier special election held more than ninety days after such filing.

(b) Once in the tenth week, and once in the sixth week immediately preceding the week in which the election is held, the proposed amendment or revision, with notice of the date of election at which it will be submitted to the electors, shall be published in one newspaper of general circulation in each county in which a newspaper is published.

(c) If the proposed amendment or revision is approved by vote of the electors, it shall be effective as an amendment to or revision of the constitution of the state on the first Tuesday after the first Monday in January following the election, or on such other date as may be specified in the amendment or revision.

History.—Am. H.J.R. 1616, 1988; adopted 1988.

SECTION 6. Taxation and budget reform commission.—

(a) Beginning in 1990 and each tenth year thereafter, there shall be established a taxation and budget reform commission composed of the following members:

(1) eleven members selected by the governor, none of whom shall be a member of the legislature at the time of appointment.

(2) seven members selected by the speaker of the house of representatives and seven members selected by the president of the senate, none of whom shall be a member of the legislature at the time of appointment.

(3) four non-voting ex officio members, all of whom shall be members of the legislature at the time of appointment. Two of these members, one of whom shall be a member of the minority party in the house of representatives, shall be selected by the speaker of the house of representatives, and two of these members, one of whom shall be a member of the minority party in the senate, shall be selected by the president of the senate.

(b) Vacancies in the membership of the commission shall be filled in the same manner as the original appointments.

(c) At its initial meeting, the members of the commission shall elect a member who is not a member of the legislature to serve as chairman and the commission shall adopt its rules of procedure. Thereafter, the commission shall convene at the call of the chairman. An affirmative vote of two thirds of the full commission and the concurrence of a majority of the members appointed by the governor pursuant to paragraph (a)(1), a concurrence of a majority of the members appointed by the speaker of the house of representatives pursuant to paragraph (a)(2), and a concurrence of a majority of the members appointed by the president of the senate pursuant to paragraph (a)(2) shall be necessary for any revision of this constitution or any part of it to be proposed by the commission.

(d) The commission shall examine the state budgetary process, the revenue needs and expenditure processes of the state, the appropriateness of the tax structure of the state, and governmental productivity and efficiency; review policy as it relates to the ability of state and local government to tax and adequately fund governmental operations and capital facilities required to meet the state's needs during the next ten year period; determine methods favored by the citizens of the state to fund the needs of the state, including alternative methods for raising sufficient revenues for the needs of the state; determine measures that could be instituted to effectively gather funds from existing tax sources; examine constitutional limitations on taxation and expenditures at the state and local level; and review the state's comprehensive planning, budgeting and needs assessment processes to determine whether the resulting information adequately supports a strategic decisionmaking process.

(e) The commission shall hold public hearings as it deems necessary to carry out its responsibilities under this section. The commission shall issue a report of the results of the review carried out, and propose to the legislature any recommended statutory changes related to the taxation or budgetary laws of the state. Not later than one hundred eighty days prior to the general election in the second year following the year in which the commission is established, the commission shall file with the secretary of state its proposal, if any, of a revision of this constitution or any part of it dealing with taxation or the state budgetary process.

History.—Added, H.J.R. 1616, 1988; adopted 1988.

ARTICLE XII

SCHEDULE

Sec.
1. Constitution of 1885 superseded.
2. Property taxes; millages.
3. Officers to continue in office.
4. State commissioner of education.
5. Superintendent of schools.
6. Laws preserved.
7. Rights reserved.
8. Public debts recognized.
9. Bonds.
10. Preservation of existing government.
11. Deletion of obsolete schedule items.
12. Senators.
13. Legislative apportionment.
14. Representatives; terms.
15. Special district taxes.
16. Reorganization.
17. Conflicting provisions.
18. Bonds for housing and related facilities.
19. Renewable energy source property.
20. Access to public records.
21. State revenue limitation.

SECTION 1. Constitution of 1885 superseded.—Articles I through IV, VII, and IX through XX of the Constitution of Florida adopted in 1885, as amended from time to time, are superseded by this revision except those sections expressly retained and made a part of this revision by reference.

SECTION 2. Property taxes; millages.—Tax millages authorized in counties, municipalities and special districts, on the date this revision becomes effective, may be continued until reduced by law.

SECTION 3. Officers to continue in office.—Every person holding office when this revision becomes effective shall continue in office for the remainder of the term if that office is not abolished. If the office is abolished the incumbent shall be paid adequate compensation, to be fixed by law, for the loss of emoluments for the remainder of the term.

SECTION 4. State commissioner of education.—The state superintendent of public instruction in office on the effective date of this revision shall become and, for the remainder of the term being served, shall be the commissioner of education.

SECTION 5. Superintendent of schools.—

(a) On the effective date of this revision the county superintendent of public instruction of each county shall become and, for the remainder of the term being served, shall be the superintendent of schools of that district.

(b) The method of selection of the county superintendent of public instruction of each county, as provided by or under the Constitution of 1885, as amended, shall apply to the selection of the district superintendent of schools until changed as herein provided.

SECTION 6. Laws preserved.—

(a) All laws in effect upon the adoption of this revision, to the extent not inconsistent with it, shall remain in force until they expire by their terms or are repealed.

(b) All statutes which, under the Constitution of 1885, as amended, apply to the state superintendent of public instruction and those which apply to the county superintendent of public instruction shall under this revision apply, respectively, to the state commissioner of education and the district superintendent of schools.

SECTION 7. Rights reserved.—

(a) All actions, rights of action, claims, contracts and obligations of individuals, corporations and public bodies or agencies existing on the date this revision becomes effective shall continue to be valid as if this revision had not been adopted. All taxes, penalties, fines and forfeitures owing to the state under the Constitution of 1885, as amended, shall inure to the state under this revision, and all sentences as punishment for crime shall be executed according to their terms.

(b) This revision shall not be retroactive so as to create any right or liability which did not exist under the Constitution of 1885, as amended, based upon matters occurring prior to the adoption of this revision.

SECTION 8. Public debts recognized.—All bonds, revenue certificates, revenue bonds and tax anticipation certificates issued pursuant to the Constitution of 1885, as amended by the state, any agency, political subdivision or public corporation of the state shall remain in full force and effect and shall be secured by the same sources of revenue as before the adoption of this revision, and, to the extent necessary to effectuate this section, the applicable provisions of the Constitution of 1885, as amended, are retained as a part of this revision until payment in full of these public securities.

SECTION 9. Bonds.—

(a) ADDITIONAL SECURITIES.

(1) [1]Article IX, Section 17, of the Constitution of 1885, as amended, as it existed immediately before this Constitution, as revised in 1968, became effective, is adopted by this reference as a part of this revision as completely as though incorporated herein verbatim, except revenue bonds, revenue certificates or other evidences of indebtedness hereafter issued thereunder may be issued by the agency of the state so authorized by law.

(2) That portion of [2]Article XII, Section 9, Subsection (a) of this Constitution, as amended, which by reference adopted [3]Article XII, Section 19 of the Constitution of 1885, as amended, as the same existed immediately before the effective date of this amendment is adopted by this reference as part of this revision as completely as though incorporated herein verbatim, for the purpose of providing that after the effective date of this amendment all of the proceeds of the revenues derived from the gross receipts taxes, as therein defined, collected in each year shall be applied as provided therein to the extent necessary to comply with all obligations to or for the benefit of holders of bonds or certificates issued before the effective date of this amendment or any refundings thereof which are secured by such gross receipts taxes. No bonds or other obligations may be issued pursuant to the provisions of [3]Article XII, Section 19, of the Constitution of 1885, as amended, but this provision shall not be construed to prevent the refunding of any such outstanding bonds or obligations pursuant to the provisions of this subsection (a)(2).

Subject to the requirements of the first paragraph of this subsection (a)(2), beginning July 1, 1975, all of the proceeds of the revenues derived from the gross receipts taxes collected from every person, including municipalities, as provided and levied pursuant to the provisions of chapter 203, Florida Statutes, as such chapter is amended from time to time, shall, as collected, be placed in a trust fund to be known as the "public education capital outlay and debt service trust fund" in the state treasury (hereinafter referred to as "capital outlay fund"), and used only as provided herein.

The capital outlay fund shall be administered by the state board of education as created and constituted by Section 2 of Article IX of the Constitution of Florida as revised in 1968 (hereinafter referred to as "state board"), or by such other instrumentality of the state which shall hereafter succeed by law to the powers, duties and functions of the state board, including the powers, duties and functions of the state board provided in this subsection (a)(2). The state board shall be a body corporate and shall have all the powers provided herein in addition to all other constitutional and statutory powers related to the purposes of this subsection (a)(2) heretofore or hereafter conferred by law upon the state board, or its predecessor created by the Constitution of 1885, as amended.

State bonds pledging the full faith and credit of the state may be issued, without a vote of the electors, by the state board pursuant to law to finance or refinance capital projects theretofore authorized by the legislature, and any purposes appurtenant or incidental thereto, for the state system of public education provided for in Section 1 of Article IX of this Constitution (hereinafter referred to as "state system"), including but not limited to institutions of higher learning, community colleges, vocational technical schools, or public schools, as now defined or as may hereafter be defined by law. All such bonds shall mature not later than thirty years after the date of issuance thereof. All other details of such bonds shall be as provided by law or by the proceedings authorizing such bonds; provided, however, that no bonds, except refunding bonds, shall be issued, and no proceeds shall be expended for the cost of any capital project, unless such project has been authorized by the legislature.

Bonds issued pursuant to this subsection (a)(2) shall be primarily payable from such revenues derived from gross receipts taxes, and shall be additionally secured by the full faith and credit of the state. No such bonds shall ever be issued in an amount exceeding ninety percent of the amount which the state board determines can be serviced by the revenues derived from the gross receipts taxes accruing thereafter under the provisions of this subsection (a)(2), and such determination shall be conclusive.

The moneys in the capital outlay fund in each fiscal year shall be used only for the following purposes and in the following order of priority:

a. For the payment of the principal of and interest on any bonds due in such fiscal year;

b. For the deposit into any reserve funds provided for in the proceedings authorizing the issuance of bonds of any amounts required to be deposited in such reserve funds in such fiscal year;

c. For direct payment of the cost or any part of the cost of any capital project for the state system theretofore authorized by the legislature, or for the purchase or redemption of outstanding bonds in accordance with the provisions of the proceedings which authorized the issuance of such bonds, or for the purpose of maintaining, restoring, or repairing existing public educational facilities.

(b) REFUNDING BONDS. Revenue bonds to finance the cost of state capital projects issued prior to the date this revision becomes effective, including projects of the Florida state turnpike authority or its successor but excluding all portions of the state highway system, may be refunded as provided by law without vote of the electors at a lower net average interest cost rate by the issuance of bonds maturing not later than the obligations refunded, secured by the same revenues only.

(c) MOTOR VEHICLE FUEL TAXES.

(1) A state tax, designated "second gas tax," of two cents per gallon upon gasoline and other like products of petroleum and an equivalent tax upon other sources of energy used to propel motor vehicles as levied by [4]Article IX, Section 16, of the Constitution of 1885, as amended, is hereby continued. The proceeds of said tax shall be placed monthly in the state roads distribution fund in the state treasury.

(2) [4]Article IX, Section 16, of the Constitution of 1885, as amended, is adopted by this reference as a part of this revision as completely as though incorporated herein verbatim for the purpose of providing that after the effective date of this revision the proceeds of the "second gas tax" as referred to therein shall be allocated among the several counties in accordance with the formula stated therein to the extent necessary to comply with all obligations to or for the benefit of holders of bonds, revenue certificates and tax anticipation certificates or any refundings thereof secured by any portion of the "second gas tax."

(3) No funds anticipated to be allocated under the formula stated in [4]Article IX, Section 16, of the Constitution of 1885, as amended, shall be pledged as security for any obligation hereafter issued or entered into, except that any outstanding obligations previously issued pledging revenues allocated under said [4]Article IX, Section 16, may be refunded at a lower average net interest cost rate by the issuance of refunding bonds, maturing not later than the obligations refunded, secured by the same revenues and any other security authorized in paragraph (5) of this subsection.

(4) Subject to the requirements of paragraph (2) of this subsection and after payment of administrative expenses, the "second gas tax" shall be allocated to the account of each of the several counties in the amounts to be determined as follows: There shall be an initial allocation of one-fourth in the ratio of county area to state area, one-fourth in the ratio of the total county population to the total population of the state in accordance with the latest available federal census, and one-half in the ratio of the total "second gas tax" collected on retail sales or use in each county to the total collected in all counties of the state during the previous fiscal year. If the annual debt service requirements of any obligations issued for any county, including any deficiencies for prior years, secured under paragraph (2) of this subsection, exceeds the amount which would be allocated to that county under the formula set out in this paragraph, the amounts allocated to other counties shall be reduced proportionately.

(5) Funds allocated under paragraphs (2) and (4) of this subsection shall be administered by the state board of administration created under said [4]Article IX, Section 16, of the Constitution of 1885, as amended, and which is continued as a body corporate for the life of this subsection 9(c). The board shall remit the proceeds of the "second gas tax" in each county account for use in said county as follows: eighty per cent to the state agency supervising the state road system and twenty per cent to the governing body of the county. The percentage allocated to the county may be increased by general law. The proceeds of the "second gas tax" subject to

allocation to the several counties under this paragraph (5) shall be used first, for the payment of obligations pledging revenues allocated pursuant to [4]Article IX, Section 16, of the Constitution of 1885, as amended, and any refundings thereof; second, for the payment of debt service on bonds issued as provided by this paragraph (5) to finance the acquisition and construction of roads as defined by law; and third, for the acquisition and construction of roads and for road maintenance as authorized by law. When authorized by law, state bonds pledging the full faith and credit of the state may be issued without any election: (i) to refund obligations secured by any portion of the "second gas tax" allocated to a county under [4]Article IX, Section 16, of the Constitution of 1885, as amended; (ii) to finance the acquisition and construction of roads in a county when approved by the governing body of the county and the state agency supervising the state road system; and (iii) to refund obligations secured by any portion of the "second gas tax" allocated under paragraph 9(c)(4). No such bonds shall be issued unless a state fiscal agency created by law has made a determination that in no state fiscal year will the debt service requirements of the bonds and all other bonds secured by the pledged portion of the "second gas tax" allocated to the county exceed seventy-five per cent of the pledged portion of the "second gas tax" allocated to that county for the preceding state fiscal year, of the pledged net tolls from existing facilities collected in the preceding state fiscal year, and of the annual average net tolls anticipated during the first five state fiscal years of operation of new projects to be financed, and of any other legally available pledged revenues collected in the preceding state fiscal year. Bonds issued pursuant to this subsection shall be payable primarily from the pledged tolls, the pledged portions of the "second gas tax" allocated to that county, and any other pledged revenue, and shall mature not later than forty years from the date of issuance.

(d) SCHOOL BONDS.

(1) [5]Article XII, Section 9, Subsection (d) of this constitution, as amended, (which, by reference, adopted [6]Article XII, Section 18, of the Constitution of 1885, as amended) as the same existed immediately before the effective date of this amendment is adopted by this reference as part of this amendment as completely as though incorporated herein verbatim, for the purpose of providing that after the effective date of this amendment the first proceeds of the revenues derived from the licensing of motor vehicles as referred to therein shall be distributed annually among the several counties in the ratio of the number of instruction units in each county, the same being coterminus with the school district of each county as provided in Article IX, Section 4, Subsection (a) of this constitution, in each year computed as provided therein to the extent necessary to comply with all obligations to or for the benefit of holders of bonds or motor vehicle tax anticipation certificates issued before the effective date of this amendment or any refundings thereof which are secured by any portion of such revenues derived from the licensing of motor vehicles.

(2) No funds anticipated to be distributed annually among the several counties under the formula stated in [5]Article XII, Section 9, Subsection (d) of this constitution, as amended, as the same existed immediately before the effective date of this amendment shall be pledged as security for any obligations hereafter issued or entered into, except that any outstanding obligations previously issued pledging such funds may be refunded by the issuance of refunding bonds.

(3) Subject to the requirements of paragraph (1) of this subsection (d) beginning July 1, 1973, the first proceeds of the revenues derived from the licensing of motor vehicles (hereinafter called "motor vehicle license revenues") to the extent necessary to comply with the provisions of this amendment, shall, as collected, be placed monthly in the school district and community college district capital outlay and debt service fund in the state treasury and used only as provided in this amendment. Such revenue shall be distributed annually among the several school districts and community college districts in the ratio of the number of instruction units in each school district or community college district in each year computed as provided herein. The amount of the first motor vehicle license revenues to be so set aside in each year and distributed as provided herein shall be an amount equal in the aggregate to the product of six hundred dollars ($600) multiplied by the total number of instruction units in all the school districts of Florida for the school fiscal year 1967-68, plus an amount equal in the aggregate to the product of eight hundred dollars ($800) multiplied by the total number of instruction units in all the school districts of Florida for the school fiscal year 1972-73 and for each school fiscal year thereafter which is in excess of the total number of such instruction units in all the school districts of Florida for the school fiscal year 1967-68, such excess units being designated "growth units." The amount of the first motor vehicle license revenues to be so set aside in each year and distributed as provided herein shall additionally be an amount equal in the aggregate to the product of four hundred dollars ($400) multiplied by the total number of instruction units in all community college districts of Florida. The number of instruction units in each school district or community college district in each year for the purposes of this amendment shall be the greater of (1) the number of instruction units in each school district for the school fiscal year 1967-68 or community college district for the school fiscal year 1968-69 computed in the manner heretofore provided by general law, or (2) the number of instruction units in such school district, including growth units, or community college district for the school fiscal year computed in the manner heretofore or hereafter provided by general law and approved by the state board of education (hereinafter called the state board), or (3) the number of instruction units in each school district, including growth units, or community college district on behalf of which the state board has issued bonds or motor vehicle license revenue anticipation certificates under this amendment which will produce sufficient revenues under this amendment to equal one and twelve-hundredths (1.12) times the aggregate amount of principal of and interest on all bonds or motor vehicle license revenue anticipation certificates issued under this amendment which will mature and become due in such year, computed in the manner heretofore or

hereafter provided by general law and approved by the state board.

(4) Such funds so distributed shall be administered by the state board as now created and constituted by Section 2 of Article IX of the State Constitution as revised in 1968, or by such other instrumentality of the state which shall hereafter succeed by law to the powers, duties and functions of the state board, including the powers, duties and functions of the state board provided in this amendment. For the purposes of this amendment, said state board shall be a body corporate and shall have all the powers provided in this amendment in addition to all other constitutional and statutory powers related to the purposes of this amendment heretofore or hereafter conferred upon said state board.

(5) The state board shall, in addition to its other constitutional and statutory powers, have the management, control and supervision of the proceeds of the first motor vehicle license revenues provided for in this subsection (d). The state board shall also have power, for the purpose of obtaining funds for the use of any school board of any school district or board of trustees of any community college district in acquiring, building, constructing, altering, remodeling, improving, enlarging, furnishing, equipping, maintaining, renovating, or repairing of capital outlay projects for school purposes to issue bonds or motor vehicle license revenue anticipation certificates, and also to issue such bonds or motor vehicle license revenue anticipation certificates to pay, fund or refund any bonds or motor vehicle license revenue anticipation certificates theretofore issued by said state board. All such bonds or motor vehicle license revenue anticipation certificates shall bear interest at not exceeding the rate provided by general law and shall mature not later than thirty years after the date of issuance thereof. The state board shall have power to determine all other details of the bonds or motor vehicle license revenue anticipation certificates and to sell in the manner provided by general law, or exchange the bonds or motor vehicle license revenue anticipation certificates, upon such terms and conditions as the state board shall provide.

(6) The state board shall also have power to pledge for the payment of the principal of and interest on such bonds or motor vehicle license revenue anticipation certificates, including refunding bonds or refunding motor vehicle license revenue anticipation certificates, all or any part from the motor vehicle license revenues provided for in this amendment and to enter into any covenants and other agreements with the holders of such bonds or motor vehicle license revenue anticipation certificates at the time of the issuance thereof concerning the security thereof and the rights of the holders thereof, all of which covenants and agreements shall constitute legally binding and irrevocable contracts with such holders and shall be fully enforceable by such holders in any court of competent jurisdiction.

(7) No such bonds or motor vehicle license revenue anticipation certificates shall ever be issued by the state board, except to refund outstanding bonds or motor vehicle license revenue anticipation certificates, until after the adoption of a resolution requesting the issuance thereof by the school board of the school district or board of trustees of the community college district on behalf of which the obligations are to be issued. The state board of education shall limit the amount of such bonds or motor vehicle license revenue anticipation certificates which can be issued on behalf of any school district or community college district to ninety percent (90%) of the amount which it determines can be serviced by the revenue accruing to the school district or community college district under the provisions of this amendment, and shall determine the reasonable allocation of the interest savings from the issuance of refunding bonds or motor vehicle license revenue anticipation certificates, and such determinations shall be conclusive. All such bonds or motor vehicle license revenue anticipation certificates shall be issued in the name of the state board of education but shall be issued for and on behalf of the school board of the school district or board of trustees of the community college district requesting the issuance thereof, and no election or approval of qualified electors shall be required for the issuance thereof.

(8) The state board shall in each year use the funds distributable pursuant to this amendment to the credit of each school district or community college district only in the following manner and in order of priority:

a. To comply with the requirements of paragraph (1) of this subsection (d).

b. To pay all amounts of principal and interest due in such year on any bonds or motor vehicle license revenue anticipation certificates issued under the authority hereof, including refunding bonds or motor vehicle license revenue anticipation certificates, issued on behalf of the school board of such school district or board of trustees of such community college district; subject, however, to any covenants or agreements made by the state board concerning the rights between holders of different issues of such bonds or motor vehicle license revenue anticipation certificates, as herein authorized.

c. To establish and maintain a sinking fund or funds to meet future requirements for debt service or reserves therefor, on bonds or motor vehicle license revenue anticipation certificates issued on behalf of the school board of such school district or board of trustees of such community college district under the authority hereof, whenever the state board shall deem it necessary or advisable, and in such amounts and under such terms and conditions as the state board shall in its discretion determine.

d. To distribute annually to the several school boards of the school districts or the boards of trustees of the community college districts for use in payment of debt service on bonds heretofore or hereafter issued by any such school boards of the school districts or boards of trustees of the community college districts where the proceeds of the bonds were used, or are to be used, in the acquiring, building, constructing, altering, remodeling, improving, enlarging, furnishing, equipping, maintaining, renovating, or repairing of capital outlay projects in such school districts or community college districts and which capital outlay projects have been approved by the school board of the school district or board of trustees of the community college district, pursuant to the most recent survey or surveys conducted under regulations prescribed by the state board to determine the capital outlay needs of the school district or community college district. The state board shall have power at the time of issuance of any bonds by any school board of any school district or board of trustees of any community college district to covenant and agree with such school board or board of trustees as to the rank and priority of payments to be made for different issues of bonds under this subparagraph d., and may further agree that any amounts to be distributed under this subparagraph d. may be pledged for the debt service on bonds issued by any school board of any school district or board of trustees of any community college district and for the rank and priority of such pledge. Any such covenants or agreements of the state board may be enforced by any holders of such bonds in any court of competent jurisdiction.

e. To pay the expenses of the state board in administering this subsection (d), which shall be prorated among the various school districts and community college districts and paid out of the proceeds of the bonds or motor vehicle license revenue anticipation certificates or from the funds distributable to each school district and community college district on the same basis as such motor vehicle license revenues are distributable to the various school districts and community college districts.

f. To distribute annually to the several school boards of the school districts or boards of trustees of the community college districts for the payment of the cost of acquiring, building, constructing, altering, remodeling, improving, enlarging, furnishing, equipping, maintaining, renovating, or repairing of capital outlay projects for school purposes in such school district or community college district as shall be requested by resolution of the school board of the school district or board of trustees of the community college district.

g. When all major capital outlay needs of a school district or community college district have been met as determined by the state board, on the basis of a survey made pursuant to regulations of the state board and approved by the state board, all such funds remaining shall be distributed annually and used for such school purposes in such school district or community college district as the school board of the school district or board of trustees of the community college district shall determine, or as may be provided by general law.

(9) Capital outlay projects of a school district or community college district shall be eligible to participate in the funds accruing under this amendment and derived from the proceeds of bonds and motor vehicle license revenue anticipation certificates and from the motor vehicle license revenues, only in the order of priority of needs, as shown by a survey or surveys conducted in the school district or community college district under regulations prescribed by the state board, to determine the capital outlay needs of the school district or community college district and approved by the state board; provided that the priority of such projects may be changed from time to time upon the request of the school board of the school district or board of trustees of the community college district and with the approval of the state board; and provided, further, that this paragraph (9) shall not in any manner affect any covenant, agreement or pledge made by the state board in the issuance by said state board of any bonds or motor vehicle license revenue anticipation certificates, or in connection with the issuance of any bonds of any school board of any school district or board of trustees of any community college district.

(10) The state board shall have power to make and enforce all rules and regulations necessary to the full exercise of the powers herein granted and no legislation shall be required to render this amendment of full force and operating effect. The legislature shall not reduce the levies of said motor vehicle license revenues during the life of this amendment to any degree which will fail to provide the full amount necessary to comply with the provisions of this amendment and pay the necessary expenses of administering the laws relating to the licensing of motor vehicles, and shall not enact any law having the effect of withdrawing the proceeds of such motor vehicle license revenues from the operation of this amendment and shall not enact any law impairing or materially altering the rights of the holders of any bonds or motor vehicle license revenue anticipation certificates issued pursuant to this amendment or impairing or altering any covenant or agreement of the state board, as provided in such bonds or motor vehicle license revenue anticipation certificates.

(11) Bonds issued by the state board pursuant to this subsection (d) shall be payable primarily from said motor vehicle license revenues as provided herein, and if heretofore or hereafter authorized by law, may be additionally secured by pledging the full faith and credit of the state without an election. When heretofore or hereafter authorized by law, bonds issued pursuant to [6]Article XII, Section 18 of the Constitution of 1885, as amended prior to 1968, and bonds issued pursuant to Article XII, Section 9, subsection (d) of the Constitution as revised in 1968, and bonds issued pursuant to this subsection (d), may be refunded by the issuance of bonds additionally secured by the full faith and credit of the state.

(e) DEBT LIMITATION. Bonds issued pursuant to this Section 9 of Article XII which are payable primarily from revenues pledged pursuant to this section shall not be included in applying the limits upon the amount of state bonds contained in Section 11, Article VII, of this revision.

History.—Am. H.J.R. 1851, 1969; adopted 1969; Am. C.S. for S.J.R. 292, 1972, and Am. C.S. for H.J.R. 3576, 1972; adopted 1972; Am. C.S. for H.J.R.'s 2289, 2984, 1974; adopted 1974; Am. S.J.R. 824, 1980; adopted 1980; Am. S.J.R. 1157, 1984; adopted 1984; Am. proposed by Taxation and Budget Reform Commission, Revision No. 1, 1992, filed with the Secretary of State May 7, 1992; adopted 1992; Am. S.J.R. 2-H, 1992; adopted 1992.

[1]**Note.**—Section 17 of Art. IX of the Constitution of 1885, as amended, reads as follows:

SECTION 17. Bonds; land acquisition for outdoor recreation development.—The outdoor recreational development council, as created by the 1963 legislature, may issue revenue bonds, revenue certificates or other evidences of indebtedness to acquire lands, water areas and related resources and to construct, improve, enlarge and extend capital improvements and facilities thereon in furtherance of outdoor recreation, natural resources conservation and related facilities in this state; provided, however, the legislature with respect to such revenue bonds, revenue certificates or other evidences of indebtedness shall designate the revenue or tax sources to be deposited in or credited to the land acquisition trust fund for their repayment and may impose restrictions on their issuance, including the fixing of maximum interest rates and discounts.

The land acquisition trust fund, created by the 1963 legislature for these multiple public purposes, shall continue from the date of the adoption of this amendment for a period of fifty years.

In the event the outdoor recreational development council shall determine to issue bonds for financing acquisition of sites for multiple purposes the state board of administration shall act as fiscal agent, and the attorney general shall handle the validation proceedings.

All bonds issued under this amendment shall be sold at public sale after public advertisement upon such terms and conditions as the outdoor recreational development council shall provide and as otherwise provided by law and subject to the limitations herein imposed.

History.—S.J.R. 727, 1963; adopted 1963.

[2]**Note.**—Prior to its amendment by C.S. for H.J.R.'s 2289, 2984, 1974, subsection (a) read as follows:

(a) ADDITIONAL SECURITIES. Article IX, Section 17, of the Constitution of 1885, as amended, as it existed immediately before this Constitution, as revised in 1968, became effective, is adopted by this reference as a part of this revision as completely as though incorporated herein verbatim, except revenue bonds, revenue certificates or other evidences of indebtedness hereafter issued thereunder may be issued by the agency of the state so authorized by law.

Article XII, Section 19, of the Constitution of 1885, as amended, as it existed immediately before this revision becomes effective, is adopted by this reference as a part of this revision as completely as though incorporated herein verbatim, except bonds or tax anticipation certificates hereafter issued thereunder may bear interest not in excess of five percent (5%) per annum or such higher interest as may be authorized by statute passed by a three-fifths (3/5) vote of each house of the legislature. No revenue bonds or tax anticipation certificates shall be issued pursuant thereto after June 30, 1975.

[3]**Note.**—Section 19 of Art. XII of the Constitution of 1885, as amended, reads as follows:

SECTION 19. Institutions of higher learning and junior college capital outlay trust fund bonds.—(a) That beginning January 1, 1964, and for fifty years thereafter, all of the proceeds of the revenues derived from the gross receipts taxes collected from every person, including municipalities, receiving payment for electricity for light, heat or power, for natural or manufactured gas for light, heat or power, for use of telephones and for the sending of telegrams and telegraph messages, as now provided and levied as of the time of adoption of this amendment in Chapter 203, Florida Statutes (hereinafter called "Gross Receipts Taxes"), shall, as collected be placed in a trust fund to be known as the "Institutions of Higher Learning and Junior Colleges Capital Outlay and Debt Service Trust Fund" in the State Treasury (hereinafter referred to as "Capital Outlay Fund"), and used only as provided in this Amendment.

Said fund shall be administered by the State Board of Education, as now created and constituted by Section 3 of Article XII [now s. 2, Article IX] of the Constitution of Florida (hereinafter referred to as "State Board"). For the purpose of this Amendment, said State Board, as now constituted, shall continue as a body corporate during the life of this Amendment and shall have all the powers provided in this Amendment in addition to all other constitutional and statutory powers related to the purposes of this Amendment heretofore or hereafter conferred by law upon said State Board.

(b) The State Board shall have power, for the purpose of obtaining funds for acquiring, building, constructing, altering, improving, enlarging, furnishing or equipping capital outlay projects theretofore authorized by the legislature and any purposes appurtenant or incidental thereto, for Institutions of Higher Learning or Junior Colleges, as now defined or as may be hereafter defined by law, and for the purpose of constructing buildings and other permanent facilities for vocational technical schools as provided in chapter 230 Florida Statutes, to issue bonds or certificates, including refunding bonds or certificates to fund or refund any bonds or certificates theretofore issued. All such bonds or certificates shall bear interest at not exceeding four and one-half per centum per annum, and shall mature at such time or times as the State Board shall determine not exceeding, in any event, however, thirty years from the date of issuance thereof. The State Board shall have power to determine all other details of such bonds or certificates and to sell at public sale, after public advertisement, such bonds or certificates, provided, however, that no bonds or certificates shall ever be issued hereunder to finance, or the proceeds thereof expended for, any part of the cost of any capital outlay project unless the construction or acquisition of such capital outlay project has been theretofore authorized by the Legislature of Florida. None of said bonds or certificates shall be sold at less than ninety-eight per centum of the par value thereof, plus accrued interest, and said bonds or certificates shall be awarded at the public sale thereof to the bidder offering the lowest net interest cost for such bonds or certificates in the manner to be determined by the State Board.

The State Board shall also have power to pledge for the payment of the principal of and interest on such bonds or certificates, and reserves therefor, including refunding bonds or certificates, all or any part of the revenue to be derived from the said Gross Receipts Taxes provided for in this Amendment, and to enter into any covenants and other agreements with the holders of such bonds or certificates concerning the security thereof and the rights of the holders thereof, all of which covenants and agreements shall constitute legally binding and irrevocable contracts with such holders and shall be fully enforceable by such holders in any court of competent jurisdiction.

No such bonds or certificates shall ever be issued by the State Board in an amount exceeding seventy-five per centum of the amount which it determines, based upon the average annual amount of the revenues derived from said Gross Receipts Taxes during the immediately preceding two fiscal years, or the amount of the revenues derived from said Gross Receipts Taxes during the immediately preceding fiscal year, as shown in a certificate filed by the State Comptroller with the State Board prior to the issuance of such bonds or certificates, whichever is the lesser, can be serviced by the revenues accruing thereafter under the provisions of this Amendment; nor shall the State Board, during the first year following the ratification of this amendment, issue bonds or certificates in excess of seven times the anticipated revenue from said Gross Receipts Taxes during said year, nor during each succeeding year, more than four times the anticipated revenue from said Gross Receipts Taxes during such year. No election or approval of qualified electors or freeholder electors shall be required for the issuance of bonds or certificates hereunder.

After the initial issuance of any bonds or certificates pursuant to this Amendment, the State Board may thereafter issue additional bonds or certificates which will rank equally and on a parity, as to lien on and source of security for payment from said Gross Receipts Taxes, with any bonds or certificates theretofore issued pursuant to this Amendment, but such additional parity bonds or certificates shall not be issued unless the average annual amount of the revenues derived from said Gross Receipts Taxes during the immediately preceding two fiscal years, or the amount of the revenues derived from said Gross Receipts Taxes during the immediately preceding fiscal year, as shown in a certificate filed by the State Comptroller with the State Board prior to the issuance of such bonds or certificates, whichever is the lesser, shall have been equal to one and one-third times the aggregate amount of principal and interest which will become due in any succeeding fiscal year on all bonds or certificates theretofore issued pursuant to this Amendment and then outstanding, and the additional parity bonds or certificates then proposed to be issued. No bonds, certificates or other obligations whatsoever shall at any time be issued under the provisions of this Amendment, except such bonds or certificates initially issued hereunder, and such additional parity bonds or certificates as provided in this paragraph. Notwithstanding any other provision herein no such bonds or certificates shall be authorized or validated during any biennium in excess of fifty million dollars, except by two-thirds vote of the members elected to each house of the legislature; provided further that during the biennium 1963-1965 seventy-five million dollars may be authorized and validated pursuant hereto.

(c) Capital outlay projects theretofore authorized by the legislature for any Institution of Higher Learning or Junior College shall be eligible to participate in the funds accruing under this Amendment derived from the proceeds of bonds or certificates and said Gross Receipts Taxes under such regulations and in such manner as shall be determined by the State Board, and the State Board shall use or transmit to the State Board of Control or to the Board of Public Instruction of any County authorized by law to construct or acquire such capital outlay projects, the amount of the proceeds of such bonds or certificates or Gross Receipts Taxes to be applied to or used for such capital outlay projects. If for any reason any of the proceeds of any bonds or certificates issued for any capital outlay project shall not be expended for such capital outlay project, the State Board may use such unexpended proceeds for any other capital outlay project for Institutions of Higher Learning or Junior Colleges and vocational technical schools, as defined herein, as now defined or as may be hereafter defined by law, theretofore authorized by the State Legislature. The holders of bonds or certificates issued hereunder shall not have any responsibility whatsoever for the application or use of any of the proceeds derived from the sale of said bonds or certificates, and the rights and remedies of the holders of such bonds or certificates and their right to payment from said Gross Receipts Taxes in the manner provided herein shall not be affected or impaired by the application or use of such proceeds.

The State Board shall use the moneys in said Capital Outlay Fund in each fiscal year only for the following purposes and in the following order of priority:

(1) For the payment of the principal of and interest on any bonds or certificates maturing in such fiscal year.

(2) For the deposit into any reserve funds provided for in the proceedings authorizing the issuance of said bonds or certificates, of any amounts required to be deposited in such reserve funds in such fiscal year.

(3) After all payments required in such fiscal year for the purposes provided for in (1) and (2) above, including any deficiencies for required payments in prior fiscal years, any moneys remaining in said Capital Outlay Fund at the end of such fiscal year may be used by the State Board for direct payment of the cost or any part of the cost of any capital outlay project theretofore authorized by the legislature or for the purchase of any bonds or certificates issued hereunder then outstanding upon such terms and conditions as the State Board shall deem proper, or for the prior redemption of outstanding bonds or certificates in accordance with the provisions of the proceedings which authorized the issuance of such bonds or certificates.

The State Board may invest the moneys in said Capital Outlay Fund or in any sinking fund or other funds created for any issue of bonds or certificates, in direct obligations of the United States of America or in the other securities referred to in Section 344.27, Florida Statutes.

(d) The State Board shall have the power to make and enforce all rules and regulations necessary to the full exercise of the powers herein granted and no legislation shall be required to render this Amendment of full force and operating effect on and after January 1, 1964. The Legislature, during the period this Amendment is in effect, shall not reduce the rate of said Gross Receipts Taxes now provided in said Chapter 203, Florida Statutes, or eliminate, exempt or remove any of the persons, firms or corporations, including municipal corporations, or any of the utilities, businesses or services now or hereafter subject to said Gross Receipts Taxes, from the levy and collection of said Gross Receipts Taxes as now provided in said Chapter 203, Florida Statutes, and shall not enact any law impairing or materially altering the rights of the holders of any bonds or certificates issued pursuant to this Amendment or impairing or altering any covenants or agreements of the State Board made hereunder, or having the effect of withdrawing the proceeds of said Gross Receipts Taxes from the operation of this Amendment.

The State Board of Administration shall be and is hereby constituted as the Fiscal Agent of the State Board to perform such duties and assume such responsibilities under this Amendment as shall be agreed upon between the State Board and such State Board of Administration. The State Board shall also have power to appoint such other persons and fix their compensation for the administration of the provisions of this Amendment as it shall deem necessary, and the expenses of the State Board in administering the provisions of this Amendment shall be paid out of the proceeds of bonds or certificates issued hereunder or from said Gross Receipts Taxes deposited in said Capital Outlay Fund.

(e) No capital outlay project or any part thereof shall be financed hereunder unless the bill authorizing such project shall specify it is financed hereunder and shall be approved by a vote of three-fifths of the elected members of each house.

History.—S.J.R. 264, 1963; adopted 1963.

[4]**Note.**—Section 16 of Art. IX of the Constitution of 1885, as amended, reads as follows:

SECTION 16. Board of administration; gasoline and like taxes, distribution and use; etc.—(a) That beginning January 1st, 1943, and for fifty (50) years thereafter, the proceeds of two (2¢) cents per gallon of the total tax levied by state law upon gasoline and other like products of petroleum, now known as the Second Gas Tax, and upon other fuels used to propel motor vehicles, shall as collected be placed monthly in the 'State Roads Distribution Fund' in the State Treasury and divided into three (3) equal parts which shall be distributed monthly among the several counties as follows: one part according to area, one part according to population, and one part according to the counties' contributions to the cost of state road construction in the ratio of distribution as provided in Chapter 15659, Laws of Florida, Acts of 1931, and for the purposes of the apportionment based on the counties' contributions for the cost of state road construction, the amount of the contributions established by the certificates made in 1931 pursuant to said Chapter 15659, shall be taken and deemed conclusive in computing the monthly amounts distributable according to said contributions. Such funds so distributed shall be administered by the State Board of Administration as hereinafter provided.

(b) The Governor as chairman, the State Treasurer, and the State Comptroller shall constitute a body corporate to be known as the 'State Board of Administration,' which board shall succeed to all the power, control and authority of the statutory Board of Administration. Said Board shall have, in addition to such powers as may be conferred upon it by law, the management, control and supervision of the proceeds of said two (2¢) cents of said taxes and all moneys and other assets which on the effective date of this amendment are applicable or may become applicable to the bonds of the several counties of this state, or any special road and bridge district, or other special taxing district thereof, issued prior to July 1st, 1931, for road and bridge purposes. The word 'bonds' as used herein shall include bonds, time warrants, notes and other forms of indebtedness issued for road and bridge purposes by any county or special road and bridge district or other special taxing district, outstanding on July 1st, 1931, or any refunding issues thereof. Said Board shall have the statutory powers of Boards of County Commissioners and Bond Trustees and of any other authority of special road and bridge districts, and other special taxing districts thereof with regard to said bonds, (except that the power to levy ad valorem taxes is expressly withheld from said Board), and shall take over all papers, documents and records concerning the same. Said Board shall have the power from time to time to issue refunding bonds to mature within the said fifty (50) year period, for any of said outstanding bonds or interest thereon, and to secure them by a pledge of anticipated receipts from such gasoline or other fuel taxes to be distributed to such county as herein provided, but not at a greater rate of interest than said bonds now bear; and to issue, sell or exchange on behalf of any county or unit for the sole purpose of retiring said bonds issued by such county, or special road and bridge district, or other special taxing district thereof, gasoline or other fuel tax anticipation certificates bearing interest at not more than three (3) per cent per annum in such denominations and maturing at such time within the fifty (50) year period as the board may determine. In addition to exercising the powers now provided by statute for the investment of sinking funds, said Board may use the sinking funds created for said bonds of any county or special road and bridge district, or other unit hereunder, to purchase the matured or maturing bonds participating herein of any other county or any other special road and bridge district, or other special taxing district thereof, provided that as to said matured bonds, the value thereof as an investment shall be the price paid therefor, which shall not exceed the par value plus accrued interest, and that said investment shall bear interest at the rate of three (3) per cent per annum.

(c) The said board shall annually use said funds in each county account, first, to pay current principal and interest maturing, if any, of said bonds and gasoline or other fuel tax anticipation certificates of such county or special road and bridge district, or other special taxing district thereof; second, to establish a sinking fund account to meet future requirements of said bonds and gasoline or other fuel tax anticipation certificates where it appears the anticipated income for any year or years will not equal scheduled payments thereon; and third, any remaining balance out of the proceeds of said two (2¢) cents of said taxes shall monthly during the year be remitted by said board as follows: Eighty (80%) per cent to the State Road Department for the construction or reconstruction of state roads and bridges within the county, or for the lease or purchase of bridges connecting state highways within the county, and twenty (20%) per cent to the Board of County Commissioners of such county for use on roads and bridges therein.

(d) Said board shall have the power to make and enforce all rules and regulations necessary to the full exercise of the powers hereby granted and no legislation shall be required to render this amendment of full force and operating effect from and after January 1st, 1943. The Legislature shall continue the levies of said taxes during the life of this Amendment, and shall not enact any law having the effect of withdrawing the proceeds of said two (2¢) cents of said taxes from the operation of this amendment. The board shall pay refunding expenses and other expenses for services rendered specifically for, or which are properly chargeable to, the account of any county from funds distributed to such county; but general expenses of the board for services rendered all the counties alike shall be prorated among them and paid out of said funds on the same basis said tax proceeds are distributed among the several counties; provided, report of said expenses shall be made to each Regular Session of the Legislature, and the Legislature may limit the expenses of the board.

History.—Added, S.J.R. 324, 1941; adopted 1942.

[5]**Note.**—Prior to its amendment by C.S. for H.J.R. 3576, 1972, subsection (d) read as follows:

(d) SCHOOL BONDS. Article XII, Section 18, of the Constitution of 1885, as amended, as it existed immediately before this revision becomes effective is adopted by this reference as part of this revision as completely as though incorporated herein verbatim, except bonds or tax anticipation certificates hereafter issued thereunder may bear interest not in excess of five per cent per annum or such higher interest as may be authorized by statute passed by a three-fifths vote of each house of the legislature. Bonds issued pursuant to this subsection (d) shall be payable primarily from revenues as provided in Article XII, Section 18, of the Constitution of 1885, as amended, and if authorized by law, may be additionally secured by pledging the full faith and credit of the state without an election. When authorized by law, bonds issued pursuant to Article XII, Section 18, of the Constitution of 1885, as amended, and bonds issued pursuant to this subsection (d), may be refunded by the issuance of bonds additionally secured by the full faith and credit of the state only at a lower net average interest cost rate.

[6]**Note.**—Section 18, Art. XII of the Constitution of 1885, as amended, reads as follows:

SECTION 18. School bonds for capital outlay, issuance.—

(a) Beginning January 1, 1965 and for thirty-five years thereafter, the first proceeds of the revenues derived from the licensing of motor vehicles to the extent necessary to comply with the provisions of this amendment, shall, as collected, be placed monthly in the county capital outlay and debt service school fund in the state treasury, and used only as provided in this amendment. Such revenue shall be distributed annually among the several counties in the ratio of the number of instruction units in each county in each year computed as provided herein. The amount of the first revenues derived from the licensing of motor vehicles to be so set aside in each year and distributed as provided herein shall be an amount equal in the aggregate to the product of four hundred dollars multiplied by the total number of instruction units in all the counties of Florida. The number of instruction units in each county in each year for the purposes of this amendment shall be the greater of (1) the number of instruction units in each county for the school fiscal year 1951-52 computed in the manner heretofore provided by general law, or (2) the number of instruction units in such county for the school fiscal year computed in the manner heretofore or hereafter provided by general law and approved by the state board of education (hereinafter called the state board), or (3) the number of instruction units in each county on behalf of which the state board of education has issued bonds or motor vehicle tax anticipation certificates under this amendment which will produce sufficient revenues under this amendment to equal one and one-third times the aggregate amount of principal of and interest on such bonds or motor vehicle tax anticipation certificates which will mature and become due in such year, computed in the manner heretofore or hereafter provided by general law and approved by the state board.

Such funds so distributed shall be administered by the state board as now created and constituted by Section 3 of Article XII [now s. 2, Article IX] of the Constitution of Florida. For the purposes of this amendment, said state board, as now constituted, shall continue as a body corporate during the life of this amendment and shall have all the powers provided in this amendment in addition to all other constitutional and statutory powers related to the purposes of this amendment heretofore or hereafter conferred upon said board.

(b) The state board shall, in addition to its other constitutional and statutory powers, have the management, control and supervision of the proceeds of the first part of the revenues derived from the licensing of motor vehicles provided for in subsection (a). The state board shall also have power, for the purpose of obtaining funds for the use of any county board of public instruction in acquiring, building, constructing, altering, improving, enlarging, furnishing, or equipping capital outlay projects for school purposes, to issue bonds or motor vehicle tax anticipation certificates, and also to issue such bonds or motor vehicle tax anticipation certificates to pay, fund or refund any bonds or motor vehicle tax anticipation certificates theretofore issued by said state board. All such bonds shall bear interest at not exceeding four and one-half per centum per annum and shall mature serially in annual installments commencing not more than three years from the date of issuance thereof and ending not later than thirty years from the date of issuance or January 1, 2000, A.D., whichever is earlier. All such motor vehicle tax anticipation certificates shall bear interest at not exceeding four and one-half per centum per annum and shall mature prior to January 1, 2000, A.D. The state board shall have power to determine all other details of said bonds or motor vehicle tax anticipation certificates and to sell at public sale after public advertisement, or exchange said bonds or motor vehicle tax anticipation certificates, upon such terms and conditions as the state board shall provide.

The state board shall also have power to pledge for the payment of the principal of and interest on such bonds or motor vehicle tax anticipation certificates, including refunding bonds or refunding motor vehicle tax anticipation certificates, all or any part from the anticipated revenues to be derived from the licensing of motor vehicles provided for in this amendment and to enter into any covenants and other agreements with the holders of such bonds or motor vehicle tax anticipation certificates at the time of the issuance thereof concerning the security thereof and the rights of the holders thereof, all of which covenants and agreements shall constitute legally binding and irrevocable contracts with such holders and shall be fully enforceable by such holders in any court of competent jurisdiction.

No such bonds or motor vehicle tax anticipation certificates shall ever be issued by the state board until after the adoption of a resolution requesting the issuance thereof by the county board of public instruction of the county on behalf of which such obligations are to be issued. The state board of education shall limit the amount of such bonds or motor vehicle tax anticipation certificates which can be issued on behalf of any county to seventy-five per cent of the amount which it determines can be serviced by the revenue accruing to the county under the provisions of this amendment, and such determination shall be conclusive. All such bonds or motor vehicle tax anticipation certificates shall be issued in the name of the state board of education but shall be issued for and on behalf of the county board of public instruction requesting the issuance thereof, and no election or approval of qualified electors or freeholders shall be required for the issuance thereof.

(c) The State Board shall in each year use the funds distributable pursuant to this Amendment to the credit of each county only in the following manner and order of priority:

(1) To pay all amounts of principal and interest maturing in such year on any bonds or motor vehicle tax anticipation certificates issued under the authority hereof, including refunding bonds or motor vehicle tax anticipation certificates, issued on behalf of the Board of Public Instruction of such county; subject, however, to any covenants or agreements made by the State Board concerning the rights between holders of different issues of such bonds or motor vehicle tax anticipation certificates, as herein authorized.

(2) To establish and maintain a sinking fund or funds to meet future requirements for debt service, or reserves therefor, on bonds or motor vehicle tax anticipation certificates issued on behalf of the Board of Public Instruction of such county, under the authority hereof, whenever the State Board shall deem it necessary or advisable, and in such amounts and under such terms and conditions as the State Board shall in its discretion determine.

(3) To distribute annually to the several Boards of Public Instruction of the counties for use in payment of debt service on bonds heretofore or hereafter issued by

any such Board where the proceeds of the bonds were used, or are to be used, in the construction, acquisition, improvement, enlargement, furnishing, or equipping of capital outlay projects in such county, and which capital outlay projects have been approved by the Board of Public Instruction of the county, pursuant to a survey or surveys conducted subsequent to July 1, 1947 in the county, under regulations prescribed by the State Board to determine the capital outlay needs of the county.

The State Board shall have power at the time of issuance of any bonds by any Board of Public Instruction to covenant and agree with such Board as to the rank and priority of payments to be made for different issues of bonds under this Subsection (3), and may further agree that any amounts to be distributed under this Subsection (3) may be pledged for the debt service on bonds issued by any Board of Public Instruction and for the rank and priority of such pledge. Any such covenants or agreements of the State Board may be enforced by any holders of such bonds in any court of competent jurisdiction.

(4) To distribute annually to the several Boards of Public Instruction of the counties for the payment of the cost of the construction, acquisition, improvement, enlargement, furnishing, or equipping of capital outlay projects for school purposes in such county as shall be requested by resolution of the County Board of Public Instruction of such county.

(5) When all major capital outlay needs of a county have been met as determined by the State Board, on the basis of a survey made pursuant to regulations of the State Board and approved by the State Board, all such funds remaining shall be distributed annually and used for such school purposes in such county as the Board of Public Instruction of the county shall determine, or as may be provided by general law.

(d) Capital outlay projects of a county shall be eligible to participate in the funds accruing under this Amendment and derived from the proceeds of bonds and motor vehicle tax anticipation certificates and from the motor vehicle license taxes, only in the order of priority of needs, as shown by a survey or surveys conducted in the county under regulations prescribed by the State Board, to determine the capital outlay needs of the county and approved by the State Board; provided, that the priority of such projects may be changed from time to time upon the request of the Board of Public Instruction of the county and with the approval of the State Board; and provided further, that this Subsection (d) shall not in any manner affect any covenant, agreement, or pledge made by the State Board in the issuance by said State Board of any bonds or motor vehicle tax anticipation certificates, or in connection with the issuance of any bonds of any Board of Public Instruction of any county.

(e) The State Board may invest any sinking fund or funds created pursuant to this Amendment in direct obligations of the United States of America or in the bonds or motor vehicle tax anticipation certificates, matured or to mature, issued by the State Board on behalf of the Board of Public Instruction of any county.

(f) The State Board shall have power to make and enforce all rules and regulations necessary to the full exercise of the powers herein granted and no legislation shall be required to render this Amendment of full force and operating effect from and after January 1, 1953. The Legislature shall not reduce the levies of said motor vehicle license taxes during the life of this Amendment to any degree which will fail to provide the full amount necessary to comply with the provisions of this Amendment and pay the necessary expenses of administering the laws relating to the licensing of motor vehicles, and shall not enact any law having the effect of withdrawing the proceeds of such motor vehicle license taxes from the operation of this Amendment and shall not enact any law impairing or materially altering the rights of the holders of any bonds or motor vehicle tax anticipation certificates issued pursuant to this Amendment or impairing or altering any covenant or agreement of the State Board, as provided in such bonds or motor vehicle tax anticipation certificates.

The State Board shall have power to appoint such persons and fix their compensation for the administration of the provisions of this Amendment as it shall deem necessary, and the expenses of the State Board in administering the provisions of this Amendment shall be prorated among the various counties and paid out of the proceeds of the bonds and motor vehicle tax anticipation certificates or from the funds distributable to each county on the same basis as such motor vehicle license taxes are distributable to the various counties under the provisions of this Amendment. Interest or profit on sinking fund investments shall accrue to the counties in proportion to their respective equities in the sinking fund or funds.

History.—Added, S.J.R. 106, 1951; adopted 1952; (a), (b) Am. S.J.R. 218, 1963; adopted 1964.

¹SECTION 10. Preservation of existing government.
All provisions of Articles I through IV, VII and IX through XX of the Constitution of 1885, as amended, not embraced herein which are not inconsistent with this revision shall become statutes subject to modification or repeal as are other statutes.

¹Note.—See table in this volume tracing various provisions of the Constitution of 1885, as amended, into the Florida Statutes.

SECTION 11. Deletion of obsolete schedule items.
The legislature shall have power, by joint resolution, to delete from this revision any section of this Article XII, including this section, when all events to which the section to be deleted is or could become applicable have occurred. A legislative determination of fact made as a basis for application of this section shall be subject to judicial review.

SECTION 12. Senators.
—The requirements of staggered terms of senators in Section 15(a), of Article III of this revision shall apply only to senators elected in November, 1972, and thereafter.

SECTION 13. Legislative apportionment.
—The requirements of legislative apportionment in Section 16 of Article III of this revision shall apply only to the apportionment of the legislature following the decennial census of 1970, and thereafter.

SECTION 14. Representatives; terms.
—The legislature at its first regular session following the ratification of this revision, by joint resolution, shall propose to the electors of the state for ratification or rejection in the general election of 1970 an amendment to Article III, Section 15(b), of the constitution providing staggered terms of four years for members of the house of representatives.

SECTION 15. Special district taxes.
—Ad valorem taxing power vested by law in special districts existing when this revision becomes effective shall not be abrogated by Section 9(b) of Article VII herein, but such powers, except to the extent necessary to pay outstanding debts, may be restricted or withdrawn by law.

SECTION 16. Reorganization.
—The requirement of Section 6, Article IV of this revision shall not apply until July 1, 1969.

SECTION 17. Conflicting provisions.
—This schedule is designed to effect the orderly transition of government from the Constitution of 1885, as amended, to this revision and shall control in all cases of conflict with any part of Article I through IV, VII, and IX through XI herein.

SECTION 18. Bonds for housing and related facilities.
—Section 16 of Article VII, providing for bonds for housing and related facilities, shall take effect upon approval by the electors.

History.—Added, S.J.R. 6–E, 1980; adopted 1980.

¹SECTION 19. Renewable energy source property.
The amendment to Section 3 of Article VII, relating to an exemption for a renewable energy source device and real property on which such device is installed, if adopted at the special election in October 1980, shall take effect January 1, 1981.

History.—Added, S.J.R. 15–E, 1980; adopted 1980.

¹Note.—This section, originally designated section 18 by S.J.R. 15–E, 1980, was redesignated section 19 by the editors in order to avoid confusion with section 18 as contained in S.J.R. 6–E, 1980.

SECTION 20. Access to public records.
—Section 24 of Article I, relating to access to public records, shall take effect July 1, 1993.

History.—Added, C.S. for C.S. for H.J.R.'s 1727, 863, 2035, 1992; adopted 1992.

SECTION 21. State revenue limitation.
—The amendment to Section 1 of Article VII limiting state revenues shall take effect January 1, 1995, and shall first be applicable to state fiscal year 1995–1996.

History.—Added, H.J.R. 2053, 1994; adopted 1994.

INDEX

A=Article, S=Section

A

AD VALOREM TAXES
See TAXATION

ADMINISTRATION, STATE BOARD OF, A12 S9(a), (c)

ADMINISTRATIVE AGENCIES
Judicial review, administrative action, A5 S3(b), A5 S4(b), A5 S5(b)
Penalties, imposition of, A1 S18
Quasi-judicial power, A5 S1
Sentence of imprisonment, A1 S18
Utilities regulation, Supreme Court review, A5 S3(b)

AGRICULTURE, COMMISSIONER OF
(See also CABINET)
Agricultural matters, supervision, A4 S4(f)
Cabinet, member, A4 S4(a)
Education, State Board of; member, A9 S2
Election, A4 S5(a)
Impeachment, A3 S17(a)
Office location, A2 S2
Powers and duties, A4 S4(a), (f)
Qualifications, A4 S5(b)
Term of office, A4 S5(a)

AIR POLLUTION, A2 S7, A7 S14

AIRCRAFT, A7 S1(b)

AIRPORTS, A7 S10(c)

ALCOHOLIC BEVERAGES, A8 S5, A8 S6(b)

ALIENS, A1 S2

AMENDMENT
Constitutional convention, A11 S4, A11 S5(a)
Effective date, A11 S5(c)
Election for approval, A11 S5
House of Representatives, proposed term of office, A12 S14
Initiatives, A11 S3, A11 S5(a)
Legislative joint resolution, A11 S1, A11 S5(a)
Publication, A11 S5(b)
Revision commission, A11 S2, A11 S5(a)
Taxation and budget reform commission, A11 S5(a), A11 S6(e)

APPORTIONMENT OF LEGISLATURE
See LEGISLATURE

APPROPRIATIONS
Bond debt service, A7 S11(b)
Current state expenses, A3 S12
Education lottery funds, A10 S15
Game and Fresh Water Fish Commission, A4 S9

APPROPRIATIONS (Cont.)
General appropriation bills, A3 S8, A3 S12, A3 S19(b), (d)
Itemization requirements, A3 S19(b)
Judiciary, A5 S14
Local government aid, A7 S8
Mandated expenditure of funds by local governments, A7 S18(a)
Money drawn from state treasury, A7 S1(c)
Review process, A3 S19(c), (d)
Salaries for public officers, A3 S12
School district aid, A7 S8
State school fund, A9 S6
Veto, A3 S8, A3 S19(b)

ARMS, RIGHT TO BEAR, A1 S8(a)

ASSEMBLY, RIGHT OF, A1 S5

ATTAINDER, BILLS OF, A1 S10, A1 S17

ATTORNEY GENERAL
(See also CABINET)
Cabinet, member, A4 S4(a)
Chief legal officer of state, A4 S4(c)
Constitution Revision Commission, member, A11 S2(a)
Education, State Board of; member, A9 S2
Election, A4 S5(a)
Impeachment, A3 S17(a)
Initiative petitions, requesting Supreme Court advisory opinion, A4 S10, A5 S3(b)
Legislative apportionment
Judicial reapportionment petition, A3 S16(b), (e)
Judicial review petition, A3 S16(c), (e)
Office location, A2 S2
Powers and duties, A4 S4(a), (c)
Qualifications, A4 S5(b)
Recreation development bond validation proceedings, A12 S9(a)
Statewide prosecutor, appointment, A4 S4(c)
Term of office, A4 S5(a)

ATTORNEYS-AT-LAW
Admission to practice, A5 S15
Bar, See BAR OF FLORIDA
Criminal defendants, right to counsel, A1 S16(a)
Discipline, A5 S15

AUDITOR, A3 S2

B

BAR OF FLORIDA
Attorney General, A4 S5(b)
Attorneys, admission and discipline, A5 S15
County court judges, A5 S8, A5 S20(c), (d)
Judges, A5 S8
Judicial nominating commission members, A5 S20(c)
Judicial Qualifications Commission members, A5 S12(a)

BAR OF FLORIDA (Cont.)
  Public defenders, A5 S18
  State attorneys, A5 S17

BEACHES, A10 S11

BILLS OF ATTAINDER, A1 S10, A1 S17

BLIND PERSONS, A7 S3(b)

BOATS, A7 S1(b)

BOND (PUBLIC OFFICERS), A2 S5(b)

BONDS
  Airports, A7 S10(c)
  Bridges, A7 S17
  Capital projects, A7 S10(c), A7 S11(a), (d), A7 S12(a), A12 S9
  Certificates of indebtedness, A7 S12
  Counties, A7 S10(c), A7 S12
  Debt limitation, A7 S11(a), A7 S14(e), A7 S16(c), A12 S9(e)
  Faith and credit of state, pledging, A7 S11(a), (c), A7 S14(a), A7 S16(b), A7 S17, A12 S9
  Fixed capital outlay projects, A7 S11(a), (d)
  Housing and related facilities, A7 S16, A12 S18
  Industrial or manufacturing plants, A7 S10(c)
  Issued pursuant to 1885 Constitution, A12 S8
  Local bonds, A7 S10(c), A7 S12
  Motor vehicle license revenue anticipation certificates, A12 S9(d)
  Municipalities, A7 S10(c), A7 S12
  Outdoor recreation development, A12 S9(a)
  Pollution control and abatement facilities, A7 S14
  Port facilities, A7 S10(c)
  Public education, A7 S12, A12 S9(a), (d)
  Refunding bonds, A7 S11(a), A7 S12(b), A12 S9
  Revenue bonds
    Airports, A7 S10(c)
    Capital projects, A7 S11(d), A12 S9(b)
    Housing and related facilities, A7 S16, A12 S18
    Industrial or manufacturing plants, A7 S10(c)
    Legislative approval of project, A7 S11(e)
    Outdoor recreation development, A12 S9(a)
    Pollution control and abatement facilities, A7 S14
    Port facilities, A7 S10(c)
    Refunding bonds, A12 S9(b), (c), (d)
    Repayment, source of funds, A7 S11(d)
    Student loans, A7 S15
    Waste disposal facilities, A7 S14
    Water facilities, A7 S14
  Roads and highways, A7 S17, A12 S9(b), (c)
  Sale, combining issues, A7 S11(c)
  School capital outlay projects, A7 S12, A12 S9(a), (d)
  School districts, A7 S12
  Special districts, A7 S10(c), A7 S12
  State bonds, A7 S11, A7 S14, A7 S15, A7 S16, A7 S17, A12 S9
  Student loans, A7 S15
  Tax anticipation certificates, A7 S12
  Tax levies for payment of debt
    Ad valorem taxes, A7 S12
    Gross receipts tax, utility services, A12 S9(a)
    Second gas tax, A12 S9(c)
  Transportation rights-of-way, A7 S17
  Validation, A5 S3(b)
  Voter approval, A7 S11(a), A7 S12(a)
  Waste disposal facilities, A7 S14

BONDS (Cont.)
  Water facilities, A7 S14

BOUNDARIES (STATE), A2 S1

BRANCHES OF GOVERNMENT, A2 S3

BRIDGES, A7 S17

BUDGETING
  Budget stabilization fund, A3 S19(g), A7 S1(e)
  Governor, responsibility, A4 S1(a), A4 S13
  Reductions to meet revenue shortfalls, A3 S19(h), A4 S13
  State budgeting processes, A3 S19, A7 S1(e)

C

CABINET
  Appointment or removal of officers, approval, A4 S6(a)
  Civil rights, restoration, A4 S8(a)
  Clemency, A4 S8(a)
  Composition, A4 S4(a)
  Creation, A4 S4(a)
  Education, State Board of; membership, A9 S2
  Election of members, A4 S5(a)
  Executive departments, supervision, A4 S6
  Impeachment of members, A3 S17(a)
  Incapacity of Governor, A4 S3(b)
  Offices of members, A2 S2
  Pardons, A4 S8(a)
  Qualifications of members, A4 S5(b)
  Revenue shortfalls, budget reductions, A4 S13
  Term limitations on members, A6 S4(b)
  Terms of members, A4 S5(a)

CAPITAL, A2 S2

CAPITAL OFFENSES
  Death penalty, appeal, A5 S3(b)
  Homicide victims, rights of next of kin, A1 S16(b)
  Presentment or indictment, A1 S15
  Pretrial detention, A1 S14

CAPITAL PROJECTS
  Airports, A7 S10(c)
  Bridges, A7 S17
  Fixed capital outlay projects, bond financing, A7 S11(a), (d)
  Housing and related facilities, A7 S16
  Industrial and manufacturing plants, A7 S10(c)
  Legislative approval, A7 S11(e)
  Local governments, bond financing, A7 S10(c), A7 S12(a)
  Outdoor recreation facilities, A12 S9(a)
  Pollution control facilities, A7 S14
  Port facilities, A7 S10(c)
  Public education, A12 S9(a), (d)
  Roads and highways, A7 S17, A12 S9(b), (c)
  Schools, A12 S9(a), (d)
  State, bond financing, A7 S11(a), (d), A7 S14, A7 S16, A7 S17, A12 S9
  Transportation rights-of-way, A7 S17
  Turnpike authority, A12 S9(b)
  Waste disposal facilities, A7 S14
  Water facilities, A7 S14

CENSUS, A3 S16(a), A8 S1(e), A10 S8, A12 S13

CERTIORARI, WRIT OF, A5 S4(b), A5 S5(b)

CHARITIES, A7 S3(a)

CHILDREN
Adoption or legitimation, special laws pertaining to, A3 S11(a)
Juvenile delinquency proceedings, A1 S15(b)
Relief from legal disabilities, special laws pertaining to, A3 S11(a)

CIRCUIT COURTS
(See also COURTS)
Administrative action, review, A5 S5(b)
Administrative supervision, A5 S2(d)
Appeal of judgments and orders, A5 S3(b), A5 S4(b)
Appellate jurisdiction, A5 S4(b), A5 S5(b), A5 S20(c)
Chief judge
  Assignment of judges, A5 S2(b)
  Discipline panel for Supreme Court justice, A5 S12(h)
  Emergency hospitalizations, authority delegation to county court judges, A5 S20(c)
  Location of court proceedings, designation, A5 S7, A5 S20(c)
  Responsibilities, A5 S2(d)
  Selection, A5 S2(d)
Clerk, A5 S16, A8 S1(d)
Death penalty, A5 S3(b)
Divisions, A5 S7, A5 S20(c)
Hearings, A5 S7
Judges, See JUDGES
Judicial circuits, See JUDICIAL CIRCUITS
Judicial power vested in, A5 S1
Jurisdiction, A5 S5(b), A5 S20(c)
Organization, A5 S5(a)
Prosecuting officer, A5 S17
Trials, location, A5 S7
Writs, power to issue, A5 S5(b)

CIVIL ACTIONS
Defamation, A1 S4
Due process of law, A1 S9
Special laws pertaining to, A3 S11(a)
Suits against state, A10 S13
Validity upon adoption of constitutional revision, A12 S7

CIVIL RIGHTS
Declaration of rights, A1
Restoration, A4 S8(a), A6 S4(a)
Voting and elections, See ELECTIONS

CIVIL SERVICE SYSTEM, A3 S14

CIVIL TRAFFIC HEARING OFFICERS, A5 S1

CLEMENCY, A4 S8

CLERKS OF CIRCUIT COURTS, A5 S16, A8 S1(d)

COLLECTIVE BARGAINING, A1 S6

COLLEGES AND UNIVERSITIES
Community colleges, A12 S9(a), (d)
Institutions of higher learning, A7 S15(a), A9 S1, A12 S9(a)
Junior colleges, A7 S15(a)

COMMISSIONER OF AGRICULTURE
See AGRICULTURE, COMMISSIONER OF

COMMISSIONER OF EDUCATION
See EDUCATION, COMMISSIONER OF

COMMISSIONS, A5 S1

COMMUNICATIONS, INTERCEPTION, A1 S12

COMMUNITY COLLEGES, A12 S9(a), (d)

COMMUNITY DEVELOPMENT, A7 S3(c)

COMPTROLLER
(See also CABINET)
Administration, State Board of; member, A12 S9(c)
Cabinet, member, A4 S4(a)
Chief fiscal officer of state, A4 S4(d)
Education, State Board of; member, A9 S2
Election, A4 S5(a)
Impeachment, A3 S17(a)
Office location, A2 S2
Powers and duties, A4 S4(a), (d), (e)
Qualifications, A4 S5(b)
Term of office, A4 S5(a)

CONSTITUTION (UNITED STATES)
See UNITED STATES

CONSTITUTION OF 1885
Bonds
  Institutions of higher learning and junior college capital outlay, A12 S9(a)
  Outdoor recreation development, A12 S9(a)
  Provisions retained until payment in full, A12 S8
  Roads and highways, A12 S9(c)
  School capital outlay, A12 S9(d)
County courts, A5 S20(c)
Criminal sentences, A12 S7(a)
Dade County, home rule charter, A8 S6(e)
Gross receipts taxes, A12 S9(a)
Hillsborough County, home rule charter, A8 S6(e)
Jacksonville and Duval County, consolidation, A8 S6(e)
Judges, A5 S20(d)
Judiciary provisions, repeal, A5 S20(a)
Key West and Monroe County, consolidation, A8 S6(e)
Local government, A8 S6(a), (e)
Motor vehicle fuel taxes, A12 S9(c)
Motor vehicle license revenues, A12 S9(d)
Provisions conflicting with revision, A12 S17
Provisions reverting to statutes, A5 S20(g), A12 S10
Provisions superseded, A12 S1
Superintendents of public instruction, A12 S5(b), A12 S6(b)
Taxes, penalties, fines, and forfeitures owed to state, A12 S7(a)

CONSTITUTION REVISION COMMISSION, A2 S5(a), A11 S2, A11 S5(a)

CONSTITUTIONAL CONVENTION, A2 S5(a), A11 S4, A11 S5(a)

CONSTRUCTION, RULES OF, A10 S12

CONTEMPT, A3 S4(d), A3 S5

CONTRACTS
Laws impairing, A1 S10
Special laws pertaining to, A3 S11(a)
Validity upon adoption of constitutional revision, A12 S7

CORPORATIONS
Income tax, A7 S5(b)

CORPORATIONS (Cont.)
 Public credit or taxing power in aid of, A7 S10
 Rights and obligations, validity upon adoption of constitutional revision, A12 S7
 Special laws pertaining to, A3 S11(a)

COUNTIES
 Abolishment, A8 S1(a)
 Ad valorem taxation, A7 S9, A7 S12, A12 S2
 Alcoholic beverage sales, A8 S5, A8 S6(b)
 Boards of county commissioners
  Composition, A8 S1(e)
  Districts, A8 S1(e)
  Election, A8 S1(e)
  Ex officio clerks, A5 S16, A8 S1(d)
  Terms of office, A8 S1(e)
 Bond financing, A7 S10(c), A7 S12
 Branch offices, A8 S1(k)
 Change of, A8 S1(a)
 Charter, A8 S1(c), (g)
 Civil service system, A3 S14
 Consolidation of local governments, A8 S3, A8 S6(e)
 County courts, See COUNTY COURTS
 County seat, A8 S1(k), A8 S6(b)
 Creation, A8 S1(a)
 Credit, pledging, A7 S10
 Dade County, home rule powers, A8 S6(e), (f)
 Districts, county commissioner, A8 S1(e)
 Duval County, consolidation, A8 S6(e)
 Electors, A6 S2
 Electric generation and transmission facilities, A7 S10(d)
 Funds
  Care, custody, and disbursement, A8 S1(b)
  Custodian, A5 S16, A8 S1(d)
  Investment, A7 S10
 Governing bodies, A8 S1(e)
 Government
  Charter, A8 S1(c), (g)
  Noncharter, A8 S1(f)
 Hillsborough County, home rule charter, A8 S6(e)
 Home rule, A8 S6(e), (f)
 Indebtedness, certificates of, A7 S12
 Joint ownership with private entities, A7 S10
 Local option, alcoholic beverage sales, A8 S5, A8 S6(b)
 Mandated expenditure of funds, funding by Legislature, A7 S18(a)
 Meetings, access to, A1 S24(b)
 Monroe County, consolidation, A8 S6(e)
 Motor vehicle fuel tax, allocation, A12 S9(c)
 Municipal services, taxes for, A7 S9(b)
 Officers
  Abolishment of office, A8 S1(d)
  Auditor, A5 S16, A8 S1(d)
  Bond, A2 S5(b)
  Clerk of circuit court, A5 S16, A8 S1(d)
  Commissioners, See COUNTIES subtitle Boards of county commissioners
  Compensation, A2 S5(c)
  Continuance in office, A8 S6(c)
  Election, A6 S5, A8 S1(d)
  Holding other offices, A2 S5(a)
  Oath of office, A2 S5(b)
  Office and records, location, A8 S1(k)
  Performance of municipal functions, A8 S6(b)
  Powers and duties, A2 S5(b), (c)
  Property appraiser, A8 S1(d)
  Prosecuting attorney, A5 S20(d)
  Recorder, A5 S16, A8 S1(d)

COUNTIES (Cont.)
 Officers (Cont.)
  Selection, A8 S1(d), A8 S6(b)
  Sheriff, A8 S1(d)
  Solicitor, A5 S20(d)
  Superintendent of public instruction, A12 S5, A12 S6(b)
  Supervisor of elections, A8 S1(d)
  Suspension, A4 S7(a), (b)
  Tax collector, A8 S1(d)
  Terms of office, A8 S1(d)
  Vacancy in office, A4 S1(f)
 Ordinances
  Charter government, A8 S1(g)
  Community and economic development tax exemptions, A7 S3(c)
  Conflict with municipal ordinances, A8 S1(f), (g)
  Effective date, A8 S1(i)
  Historic properties tax exemption, A7 S3(e)
  Local laws, amendment or repeal, A8 S6(d)
  Noncharter government, A8 S1(f)
  Violations, A8 S1(j)
 Pari-mutuel tax revenue, A7 S7
 Pollution control facilities, state bond financing, A7 S14
 Recording of documents, A8 S1(k)
 Reduction of authority to raise revenue, legislative approval, A7 S18(b)
 Roads and highways, A12 S9(c)
 Second gas tax, allocation, A12 S9(c)
 Self-government powers, A8 S1(f), (g)
 State aid, A7 S8
 State tax revenues, legislative approval of reduction, A7 S18(c)
 Status, continuation upon adoption of Constitution, A8 S6(b)
 Tax anticipation certificates, A7 S12
 Taxes, A7 S9, A12 S2
 Taxing power, limitation, A7 S10, A8 S1(h)
 Transfer of function or power, A8 S4
 Waste disposal facilities, state bond financing, A7 S14
 Water facilities, state bond financing, A7 S14

COUNTY COURTS
 (See also COURTS)
 Administrative supervision, A5 S2(d)
 Appeal of judgments and orders, A5 S3(b), A5 S4(b)
 Clerks, A5 S16, A5 S20(c)
 Divisions, A5 S7, A5 S20(c)
 Fines and forfeitures, A5 S20(c)
 Hearings, A5 S7
 Judges, See JUDGES
 Judicial power vested in, A5 S1
 Jurisdiction, A5 S6(b), A5 S20(c)
 Location, A5 S7, A5 S20(c)
 Organization, A5 S6(a)
 Trials, location, A5 S7, A5 S20(c)

COURTS
 Access to, A1 S21
 Administrative supervision, A5 S2
 Appeals, A5 S2(a), A5 S3, A5 S4, A5 S5(b)
 Appellate districts, See DISTRICT COURTS OF APPEAL
 Appropriations, power to fix, A5 S14
 Attorneys, admission to practice and discipline, A5 S15
 Bar, See BAR OF FLORIDA
 Budgeting processes, A3 S19(a), (c)
 Chief administrative officers, A5 S2(b)
 Circuit courts, See CIRCUIT COURTS
 County courts, See COUNTY COURTS

724

COURTS (Cont.)
  Dismissal of cause, improper remedy sought, A5 S2(a)
  District courts of appeal, See DISTRICT COURTS OF APPEAL
  Divisions, A5 S7, A5 S20(c)
  Establishment, A5 S1
  Generally, A5
  Hearings, A5 S7
  Judges and justices, See JUDGES
  Judicial circuits, See JUDICIAL CIRCUITS
  Judicial nominating commissions, A5 S11, A5 S20(c)
  Judicial office, justices, and judges; construction of terms, A10 S12(f)
  Judicial power, A2 S3, A5 S1
  Judicial Qualifications Commission, A2 S8(f), A5 S12, A5 S20(e)
  Juries and jurors, See JURIES
  Jurisdiction
    Abolished courts, A5 S20(d)
    Circuit courts, A5 S5(b), A5 S20(c)
    County courts, A5 S6(b), A5 S20(c)
    District courts of appeal, A5 S4(b), A5 S20(c)
    Municipal courts, A5 S20(d)
    Supreme Court, A5 S3(b), A5 S20(c)
    Transfer, jurisdiction of court improvidently invoked, A5 S2(a)
  Justice administration without sale, denial, or delay, A1 S21
  Military courts, A1 S15(a)
  Municipal courts, A5 S20(d)
  Open for redress of injury, A1 S21
  Planning processes and planning documents, A3 S19(a), (c), (h)
  Records of judicial branch, access to, A1 S24
  Rules of practice and procedure, A5 S2(a), A5 S11(d)
  Supreme Court, See SUPREME COURT
  Transition provisions, A5 S20
  Trials, See TRIALS
  Writs, power to issue, A5 S3(b), A5 S4(b), A5 S5(b)

COVERTURE, A10 S5

CREDIT, PLEDGING OF
  Housing bonds, A7 S16(b)
  Joint ownership with private entity, A7 S10
  State bonds, A7 S11(a), (c), A7 S14(a), A7 S17, A12 S9

CRIMINAL OFFENSES
  Accused, rights of, A1 S16(a), A1 S19
  Bills of attainder, A1 S10, A1 S17
  Breach of public trust, A2 S8(d)
  County ordinance violations, A8 S1(j)
  Criminal statutes, effect of repeal or amendment, A10 S9
  Defamation, A1 S4
  Ex post facto laws, A1 S10
  Felony
    Definition, A10 S10
    Disqualification from vote and public office, A6 S4(a)
    Prosecution, A1 S15(a)
    Public officer or employee, forfeiture of retirement rights and privileges, A2 S8(d)
  Fraud, imprisonment for debt, A1 S11
  Handgun purchases, waiting period violations, A1 S8(c)
  Homicide victims, rights of next of kin, A1 S16(b)
  Juvenile offenders, A1 S15(b)
  Marine net fishing violations, A10 S16(e)
  Penalties, See PUNISHMENT
  Prosecution, see CRIMINAL PROSECUTION

CRIMINAL OFFENSES (Cont.)
  Treason, A1 S20, A4 S8(b)
  Victims' rights, A1 S16(b)

CRIMINAL PROSECUTION
  Accused, rights of, A1 S16(a), A1 S19
  Capital crime, A1 S15(a)
  Communications, unreasonable interception of, A1 S12
  Costs, payment by accused, A1 S19
  Counsel, right to, A1 S16(a)
  County ordinance violations, A8 S1(j)
  Criminal statutes, effect of repeal or amendment, A10 S9
  Defamation, A1 S4
  Defendants, rights of, A1 S16(a), A1 S19
  Double jeopardy, A1 S9
  Due process of law, A1 S9
  Evidence, inadmissible, A1 S12
  Felonies, A1 S15(a)
  Grand jury, A1 S15(a)
  Indictment or information, A1 S15(a), A1 S16(a)
  Jurors, A1 S22, A3 S11(a)
  Juvenile offenders, A1 S15(b)
  Penalties, See PUNISHMENT
  Pretrial release and detention, A1 S14
  Search and seizure, unreasonable, A1 S12
  Search warrants, A1 S12
  Self-incrimination, A1 S9
  Special laws pertaining to, A3 S11(a)
  Statewide prosecutor, A4 S4(c)
  Treason, A1 S20
  Trial by jury, A1 S16(a), A1 S22
  Venue, A1 S16(a), A3 S11(a)
  Victims' rights, A1 S16(b)
  Witness against oneself, A1 S9
  Witnesses, A1 S9, A1 S16(a)

CURTESY, A10 S5

D

DADE COUNTY, A8 S6(e), (f)

DEBT
  Homestead property, A10 S4(a)
  Imprisonment for, A1 S11
  Public debt
    Bond financing, See BONDS
    Certificates of indebtedness, A7 S12
    Consolidation of local governments, A8 S3
    Counties, A8 S1(a)
    Incurred under 1885 Constitution, A12 S8
    Municipalities, A8 S2(a)

DECLARATION OF RIGHTS, A1

DEEDS OF TRUST, A7 S2

DISABLED PERSONS
  Discrimination, A1 S2
  Tax exemptions, A7 S3(b), A7 S6(c)

DISTRICT COURTS OF APPEAL
  (See also COURTS)
  Administrative action, direct review, A5 S4(b)
  Administrative supervision, A5 S2(c)
  Appeal of decisions, A5 S3(b)
  Appellate districts
    Court serving, A5 S4(a)

Index   CONSTITUTION OF THE STATE OF FLORIDA   Index

DISTRICT COURTS OF APPEAL (Cont.)
Appellate districts (Cont.)
   Establishment, A5 S1, A5 S20(c)
   Redefining, A5 S9
   Supreme Court justices, residency, A5 S3(a)
Case consideration, number of judges required, A5 S4(a)
Certification of cases for Supreme Court review, A5 S3(b)
Chief judges, A5 S2(c)
Clerks, A5 S4(c)
Decisions, A5 S3(b), A5 S4(a)
Divisions, A5 S7, A5 S20(c)
Final judgments and orders, review, A5 S4(b)
Interlocutory orders, review, A5 S4(b)
Judges, See JUDGES
Judicial nominating commissions, A5 S11(d)
Judicial power vested in, A5 S1
Jurisdiction, A5 S4(b), A5 S20(c)
Marshals, A5 S4(c)
Organization, A5 S4(a)
Process, A5 S4(c)
Rules of procedure, A5 S11(d)
Trial court judgments and orders, review, A5 S4(b)
Writs, power to issue, A5 S4(b)

DISTRICTS
Appellate, See DISTRICT COURTS OF APPEAL
Community college, A12 S9(d)
County commissioner, A8 S1(e)
Legislative, A3 S1, A3 S15(a), (c), A3 S16(a)
School, See SCHOOL DISTRICTS
Special, See SPECIAL DISTRICTS

DIVORCE, A3 S11(a)

DOUBLE JEOPARDY, A1 S9

DOWER, A10 S5

DUE PROCESS OF LAW, A1 S9

DUVAL COUNTY, A8 S6(e)

E

ECONOMIC DEVELOPMENT, A7 S3(c)

EDUCATION
Appointive boards, terms of members, A9 S3
Bond financing
   Capital projects, A7 S12, A12 S9(a), (d)
   Student loans, A7 S15
Capital outlay funds, A12 S9(a), (d)
Commissioner of Education, See EDUCATION, COMMISSIONER OF
Community colleges, A12 S9(a), (d)
Free public schools, A9 S1, A9 S4(b), A9 S6
Health-related training institutions, A7 S15(a)
Institutions of higher learning, A7 S15(a), A9 S1, A12 S9(a)
Joint educational programs, A9 S4(b)
Junior colleges, A7 S15(a)
Lotteries, A10 S15
Property tax exemption, A7 S3(a)
Public education system, A4 S4(g), A9 S1, A9 S2
School boards, A9 S4, A9 S5, A12 S9(d)
School districts, See SCHOOL DISTRICTS
State Board of Education, A9 S2, A12 S9(a), (d)
State school fund, A9 S6

EDUCATION (Cont.)
Student loans, A7 S15
Superintendents of public instruction, A12 S4, A12 S5, A12 S6(b)
Superintendents of schools, A9 S5, A12 S5, A12 S6(b)
Taxes
   Gross receipts tax, utility services, A12 S9(a)
   Property tax exemption, A7 S3(a)
   School district, A7 S9, A9 S4(b)
Vocational training schools, A7 S15(a), A12 S9(a)

EDUCATION, COMMISSIONER OF
(See also CABINET)
Cabinet, member, A4 S4(a)
Education, State Board of; member, A9 S2
Election, A4 S5(a)
Impeachment, A3 S17(a)
Office location, A2 S2
Powers and duties, A4 S4(a), (g)
Public education system, supervision, A4 S4(g)
Qualifications, A4 S5(b)
Statutes under 1885 Constitution, applicability, A12 S6(b)
Superintendent of Public Instruction, transfer of office, A12 S4
Term of office, A4 S5(a)

EDUCATION, STATE BOARD OF, A9 S2, A12 S9(a), (d)

ELDERLY AFFAIRS, DEPARTMENT OF, A4 S12

ELDERLY PERSONS, A7 S6(c)

ELECTIONS
Alcoholic beverage sales, local option, A8 S5
Bond financing approval, A7 S11(a), A7 S12(a)
Cabinet members, A4 S5(a)
Candidates
   Campaign finances, disclosure, A2 S8(b)
   Financial interests, disclosure, A2 S8(a), (g), (h)
   Community and economic development tax exemption ordinances, authorization, A7 S3(c)
Constitutional amendment or revision, A11 S5
Constitutional convention question, A11 S4
County commissioners, A8 S1(e)
County officers, A8 S1(d)
Districts, A6 S6
Electors
   Disqualification, A6 S4(a)
   Freeholders, A7 S9(b), A7 S12(a)
   Oath, A6 S3
   Presidential, A6 S2
   Qualifications, A6 S2, A6 S4(a)
   Registration, A6 S1, A6 S3, A6 S6
   Vote of electors, definition, A10 S12(d)
General elections
   Cabinet members, A4 S5(a)
   Constitutional amendment or revision, A11 S5(a)
   Constitutional convention question, A11 S4(b)
   Date, A6 S5
   Emergency, suspension or delay, A6 S5
   Governor and Lieutenant Governor, A4 S5(a)
   Superintendents of schools, A9 S5
   Winner determination, A6 S1
Governor, A4 S5
Judges, A5 S10, A5 S11(b)
Legislators, A3 S1, A3 S2, A3 S15
Lieutenant Governor, A4 S5(a)
Municipal elections, A6 S6

726

ELECTIONS (Cont.)
Party primaries, A4 S5(a)
Political party functions, A6 S1
President, A6 S2
Referenda, A3 S10, A6 S5, A7 S3(c)
Registration, A6 S1, A6 S3
School boards, A9 S4(a)
Secret vote, A6 S1
Special elections
  Alcoholic beverage sales, A8 S5
  Community and economic development tax exemption ordinances, A7 S3(c)
  Constitutional amendment or revision, A11 S5(a)
  County charter, A8 S1(c)
  Regulation, A6 S5
Superintendents of schools, A9 S5
Supervisors of elections, A8 S1(d)
Tax authorization, A7 S9(b)
Term limitation, certain elective offices, A6 S4(b)
Vote of the electors, definition, A10 S12(d)

ELECTIONS, SUPERVISORS OF, A8 S1(d)

ELECTRICAL ENERGY FACILITIES, A7 S10(d)

EMERGENCIES
Budget stabilization fund, withdrawals, A3 S19(g)
Continuity of government, measures to ensure, A2 S6
Elections, suspension or delay, A6 S5
Habeas corpus, suspension of writ, A1 S13
Seat of government, transfer, A2 S2

EMINENT DOMAIN, A10 S6

ENEMY ATTACK
See INVASION

ENERGY
Electrical energy facilities, public support, A7 S10(d)
Renewable energy source devices, tax exemption, A7 S3(d), A12 S19

ENGLISH, OFFICIAL LANGUAGE, A2 S9

EQUALITY BEFORE THE LAW, A1 S2

ESTATE TAX, A7 S5(a)

ETHICS, COMMISSION ON, A2 S8(f), (h)

ETHICS IN GOVERNMENT, A2 S8, A3 S18

EVIDENCE
Defamation, A1 S4
Inadmissible, A1 S12
Special laws pertaining to, A3 S11(a)
Treason, A1 S20

EX POST FACTO LAWS, A1 S10

EXECUTIVE BRANCH OF GOVERNMENT
Executive power, A2 S3, A4 S1(a)
Generally, A4
Planning processes and planning documents, A3 S19(a), (c), (h)
Public records and meetings, access to, A1 S24

EXECUTIVE DEPARTMENTS, A4 S6, A12 S16

EXECUTIVE POWER, A2 S3, A4 S1(a)

F

FEDERAL GOVERNMENT
See UNITED STATES

FELONIES
See CRIMINAL OFFENSES

FINANCE
Appropriation of state funds, See APPROPRIATIONS
Bonds, See BONDS
Generally, A7
Revenue, See REVENUE
State funds, See STATE FUNDS
Taxation and budget reform commission, A2 S5(a), A11 S2(c), A11 S5(a), A11 S6
Taxes, See TAXATION
Trust funds, See TRUST FUNDS (PUBLIC)

FINES AND FORFEITURES
Administrative penalties, A1 S18
County courts, A5 S20(c)
Excessive, A1 S17
Owing under 1885 Constitution, A12 S7(a)
Remission, A3 S11(a), A4 S8(a)
Suspension, A4 S8(a)

FIREARMS
Handgun purchases, waiting period between purchase and delivery, A1 S8(b), (c), (d)
Right to bear arms, A1 S8(a)

FISHING
Game and Fresh Water Fish Commission, A4 S9
Marine net fishing, limitations, A10 S16
Special laws pertaining to freshwater fishing, A3 S11(a)

FLAG (STATE), A2 S4

FREEDOM OF PRESS, A1 S4

FREEDOM OF RELIGION, A1 S3

FREEDOM OF SPEECH, A1 S4

G

GAMBLING
Lotteries, A10 S7, A10 S15
Pari-mutuel pools, A10 S7
Pari-mutuel taxes, A7 S7

GAME AND FRESH WATER FISH COMMISSION, A4 S9

GENERAL PROVISIONS, A2

GOVERNOR
Acting, A4 S3(b)
Administration, State Board of; member, A12 S9(c)
Advisory opinions from Supreme Court, A4 S1(c)
Appointments
  Constitution Revision Commission members, A11 S2(a), (b)
  Executive officers or boards, A4 S6

GOVERNOR (Cont.)
  Appointments (Cont.)
    Game and Fresh Water Fish Commission, A4 S9
    Judges, A5 S11(a), (b), (c)
    Judicial nominating commission members, A5 S20(c)
    Judicial Qualifications Commission members, A5 S12(a)
    Militia officers, A10 S2(c)
    Taxation and budget reform commission members, A11 S6(a)
    Vacancies in state or local offices, A3 S17(b), A4 S1(f), A4 S7
  Bills
    Executive approval, A3 S8(a)
    Veto, A3 S8, A3 S9, A3 S19(b)
  Budgeting, A4 S1(a), A4 S13
  Capacity, restoration, A4 S3(b)
  Civil rights, restoration, A4 S8(a)
  Clemency, A4 S8(a), (b)
  Commander-in-chief, military forces, A4 S1(a)
  Education, State Board of; member, A9 S2
  Election, A4 S5(a), (b)
  Executive departments, supervision, A4 S6
  Impeachment, A3 S17(a), A4 S3(b)
  Impeachment trial, presiding officer, A3 S17(c)
  Incapacity to serve, A4 S3(b)
  Judicial proceedings, initiation, A4 S1(b)
  Legislature
    Adjournment of session, A3 S3(f)
    Apportionment sessions, convening, A3 S16(a), (d)
    Meetings between Governor and legislative leadership, open to public, A3 S4(e)
    Message on condition of state, A4 S1(e)
    Special session, convening, A3 S3(c)
  Lieutenant Governor, assignment of duties, A4 S2
  Militia, calling out, A4 S1(d)
  Office location, A2 S2
  Pardons, A4 S8(a), (b)
  Planning, A3 S19(h), A4 S1(a)
  Powers, generally, A4 S1
  Proclamations
    Apportionment sessions of Legislature, convening, A3 S16(a), (d)
    Seat of government, transfer, A2 S2
    Special session of Legislature, convening, A3 S3(c)
  Qualifications, A4 S5(b)
  Revenue shortfalls, budget reductions, A4 S13
  Seat of government, emergency transfer, A2 S2
  Supreme executive power, A4 S1(a)
  Suspension of officers, A4 S7, A5 S12(g)
  Term limitations, A4 S5(b)
  Term of office, A4 S5(a), (b)
  Vacancy in office, A4 S3(a)

GRAND JURIES, A1 S15(a)

GRIEVANCES, PETITION FOR REDRESS OF, A1 S5

H

HABEAS CORPUS
  Circuit courts, A5 S5(b)
  District courts of appeal, A5 S4(b)
  Grantable of right, A1 S13
  Supreme Court, A5 S3(b)
  Suspension, A1 S13

HANDICAPPED PERSONS
  Deprivation of rights, A1 S2

HANDICAPPED PERSONS (Cont.)
  Tax exemptions, A7 S3(b), A7 S6(c)

HEAD OF FAMILY, A7 S3(b)

HILLSBOROUGH COUNTY, A8 S6(e)

HOME RULE CHARTERS
  Dade County, A8 S6(e)
  Hillsborough County, A8 S6(e)

HOMESTEAD PROPERTY
  Alienation, A10 S4(c)
  Condominiums, A7 S6(a)
  Contractual obligations, A10 S4(a)
  Devise, A10 S4(c)
  Equitable title, A7 S6(a)
  Estate by the entirety, A7 S6(a), A10 S4(c)
  Exemptions
    Forced sale, A10 S4(a), (b)
    Judgment lien, A10 S4(a), (b)
    Taxation, A7 S6
  Extent of property, A10 S4(a)
  Heirs of owner, A10 S4(b)
  Joint ownership, A7 S6(a)
  Leasehold, A7 S6(a)
  Legal title, A7 S6(a)
  Limitation on assessments, A7 S4(c)
  Renters, A7 S6(e)
  Stock ownership, A7 S6(a)
  Surviving spouse, A10 S4(b)
  Taxes and assessments, A7 S4(c), A7 S6, A10 S4(a), (b)
  Time for assessments, A7 S4(c)

HOUSE OF REPRESENTATIVES
  See LEGISLATURE

HOUSING BONDS, A7 S16, A12 S18

HUNTING, A3 S11(a), A4 S9

I

IMPEACHMENT
  Acquittal, A3 S17(b), (c)
  Cabinet members, A3 S17(a)
  Civil responsibility of impeached officer, A3 S17(c)
  Clemency, A4 S8(a)
  Conviction, A3 S17(c)
  Criminal responsibility of impeached officer, A3 S17(c)
  Disqualification from office, A3 S17(b), (c)
  Governor, A3 S17(a), A4 S3(b)
  House of Representatives, power to impeach, A3 S17
  Justices and judges, A3 S17(a), A5 S12(g)
  Lieutenant Governor, A3 S17(a)
  Misdemeanor in office, A3 S17(a)
  Officers liable to impeachment, A3 S17(a)
  Power, A3 S17(a)
  Presiding officer, impeachment trial, A3 S17(c)
  Senate trial, A3 S17(b), (c)
  Vacancy in office, temporary appointment, A3 S17(b)
  Vote, A3 S17(a), (c)

IMPRISONMENT
  Administrative sentence, A1 S18
  Contempt of Legislature, A3 S5
  Debt, sentence for, A1 S11

IMPRISONMENT (Cont.)
Indefinite, A1 S17
Sentences under 1885 Constitution, A12 S7(a)

INALIENABLE RIGHTS, A1 S2

INCOME TAX, A7 S5

INCOMPETENT PERSONS
Disqualification from vote and public office, A6 S4(a)
Homestead property, alienation, A10 S4(c)

INDICTMENTS, A1 S15(a), A1 S16(a)

INDUSTRIAL PLANTS, A7 S10(c)

INFORMATIONS, A1 S15(a), A1 S16(a)

INHERITANCE
Aliens, A1 S2
Tax, A7 S5(a)

INITIATIVES, A11 S3, A11 S5(a)

INSTITUTIONS OF HIGHER LEARNING, A7 S15(a), A9 S1, A12 S9(a)

INSURRECTION, A1 S13, A4 S1

INVASION
Continuity of government, measures to ensure, A2 S6
Habeas corpus, suspension of writ, A1 S13
Militia, calling out, A4 S1
Seat of government, transfer, A2 S2

J

JACKSONVILLE, CITY OF, A8 S6(e)

JEOPARDY, DOUBLE, A1 S9

JOINT OWNERSHIP
Governmental body with private entities, A7 S10
Homestead property, A7 S6(a)

JUDGES
Age limit, A5 S8, A5 S20(e)
Appointment, A5 S11(a), (b), (c)
Bar membership, A5 S8, A5 S20(c), (d)
Circuit courts
 Election, A5 S10(b), A5 S11(b)
 Impeachment, A3 S17(a)
 Judges of abolished courts, A5 S20(d)
 Number, A5 S20(d)
 Term of office, A5 S10(b), A5 S11(b)
 Vacancy in office, A5 S11(b)
Conservators of the peace, A5 S19
County courts
 Bar membership, A5 S8, A5 S20(c), (d)
 Election, A5 S10(b), A5 S11(b)
 Impeachment, A3 S17(a)
 Judges of abolished courts, A5 S20(d)
 Nonjudicial duties, A5 S20(f)
 Number, A5 S6(a), A5 S20(d)
 Term of office, A5 S10(b), A5 S11(b)
 Vacancy in office, A5 S11(b)
Discipline, A5 S12

JUDGES (Cont.)
District courts of appeal
 Election, A5 S10(a)
 Impeachment, A3 S17(a)
 Number, A5 S4(a)
 Retention, A5 S10(a)
 Term of office, A5 S10(a), A5 S11(a)
 Vacancy in office, A5 S10(a), A5 S11(a)
Election, A5 S10, A5 S11(b)
Eligibility, A5 S8, A5 S20(d)
Impeachment, A3 S17(a), A5 S12(g)
Involuntary retirement, A5 S12(f)
Judicial nominating commissions, A5 S11, A5 S20(c)
Judicial Qualifications Commission, A2 S8(f), A5 S12, A5 S20(e)
Nomination, A5 S11
Number, determination, A5 S9
Political party office, holding, A5 S13
Practice of law, A5 S13
Prohibited activities, A5 S13
Qualifications, A5 S8, A5 S20(c), (d)
Removal from office, A5 S12(a), (f), (g)
Reprimand, A5 S12(a), (f)
Retired judges, temporary duty, A5 S2(b)
Rule of construction, A10 S12
Salaries, A5 S14, A5 S20(h)
Supreme Court justices
 Definition, A5 S20(c), A10 S12
 Discipline proceedings, A5 S12(h)
 Election, A5 S10(a)
 Impeachment, A3 S17(a)
 Judges, temporary assignment, A5 S3(a)
 Number, A5 S3(a)
 Quorum, A5 S3(a)
 Recusal, A5 S3(a)
 Residency requirement, A5 S3(a)
 Retention, A5 S10(a)
 Retired, temporary duty, A5 S2(b)
 Temporary duty with other courts, A5 S2(b)
 Term of office, A5 S10(a), A5 S11(a)
 Vacancy in office, A5 S10(a), A5 S11(a)
Suspension from office, A5 S12(d), (f)
Temporary assignments, A5 S2(b), A5 S3(a)
Terms of office, A5 S10, A5 S11(a), (b)
Transition provisions, A5 S20
Vacancy in office, A5 S10(a), A5 S11

JUDICIAL CIRCUITS
Chief judges, *See* CIRCUIT COURTS
Circuit courts, generally, *See* CIRCUIT COURTS
Court serving, A5 S5(a)
Establishment, A5 S1, A5 S20(c)
Judges, generally, *See* JUDGES
Judicial nominating commissions, A5 S11(d), A5 S20(c)
Public defenders, A5 S18
Redefining, A5 S9
Rules of procedure, A5 S11(d)
State attorneys, A5 S17
Statewide prosecutor, A4 S4(c)

JUDICIAL NOMINATING COMMISSIONS, A4 S4(c), A5 S11, A5 S20(c)

JUDICIAL POWER, A2 S3, A5 S1

JUDICIAL QUALIFICATIONS COMMISSION, A2 S8(f), A5 S12, A5 S20(e)

JUDICIARY, A5

JUNIOR COLLEGES, A7 S15(a)

JURIES
Grand jury, A1 S15(a)
Impartial, right of accused, A1 S16(a)
Jurors, qualifications and number, A1 S22
Special laws pertaining to, A3 S11(a)
Trial by jury, A1 S22

JUVENILE DELINQUENCY, A1 S15(b)

K

KEY WEST, CITY OF, A8 S6(e)

L

LABOR ORGANIZATIONS
Collective bargaining, A1 S6
Right to work, A1 S6

LAWS
Amendment, A3 S6
Appropriations, A3 S8, A3 S12
Bill of attainder, A1 S10, A1 S17
Bills, See LEGISLATURE
Classification of political subdivisions, A3 S11(b)
Constitution of 1885 provisions, continuance as statutes, A5 S20(g), A12 S10
County charters, A8 S1(c)
Criminal statutes, effect of repeal or amendment, A10 S9
Effective date, A3 S9
Enacting clause, A3 S6
Enactment, A3 S7, A3 S8
Ex post facto law, A1 S10
Florida Statutes, chapter 203, A12 S9(a)
General laws of local application, A3 S11(a)
Local laws, A8 S6(d), A10 S12(g)
Ordinances
  County, See COUNTIES
  Municipal, See MUNICIPALITIES
Preservation upon adoption of Constitution, A12 S6
Prohibited laws, A1 S3, A1 S4, A1 S10, A3 S11(a)
Revision, A3 S6
Special laws
  Consolidation of local governments, A8 S3
  County charters, A8 S1(c)
  County self-government powers, A8 S1(f)
  Definition, A10 S12(g)
  Notice, intention to enact, A3 S10
  Prohibited subjects, A3 S11(a)
  Superintendents of schools, A9 S5
Subject matter, A3 S6, A3 S11, A3 S12
Title, A3 S6

LEGISLATIVE POWER, A2 S3, A3 S1

LEGISLATURE
Apportionment
  Applicability of constitutional provisions, A12 S13
  Extraordinary apportionment session, A3 S16(d), (e), (f)
  Failure to apportion, A3 S16(b)
  Joint resolution of apportionment, A3 S16
  Judicial reapportionment, A3 S16(b), (f)
  Judicial review, A3 S16(c), (d), (e), (f)
  Representative districts, A3 S16(a)

LEGISLATURE (Cont.)
Apportionment (Cont.)
  Senatorial districts, A3 S16(a)
  Special apportionment session, A3 S16(a), (b)
  Time for mandated reapportionment, A3 S16(a)
  Validity, A3 S16(c), (d), (e), (f)
Appropriations, See APPROPRIATIONS
Auditor, A3 S2
Bills
  Amendment, A3 S7
  Amendment of laws, A3 S6
  Appropriations, A3 S8, A3 S12, A3 S19(b), (d)
  Classification of political subdivisions, A3 S11(b)
  Effective date, A3 S9
  Enacting clause, A3 S6
  Executive approval, A3 S8
  Item veto, A3 S8, A3 S19(b)
  Origin, A3 S7
  Override of veto, A3 S8(c), A3 S9
  Passage, A3 S7, A3 S8(a), (c), A3 S9
  Presentation to Governor, A3 S8(a)
  Readings, A3 S7
  Revision of laws, A3 S6
  Special laws, A3 S10, A3 S11(a)
  Subject matter, A3 S6, A3 S11, A3 S12
  Title, A3 S6, A3 S7
  Veto, A3 S8, A3 S9, A3 S19(b)
  Vote for passage, A3 S7, A3 S8(c), A7 S1(e), A10 S12(e)
Branch of government, A2 S3
Budgeting processes, A3 S19, A7 S1(e)
Business of, A3 S3(c), (d)
Capital projects, approval, A7 S11(e)
Committees
  Impeachment investigations, A3 S17(a)
  Investigations, A3 S5, A3 S17(a)
  Meetings, open to public, A3 S4(e)
  Planning documents and budget requests, review, A3 S19(c)
  Subpoena power, A3 S5
  Votes, recording, A3 S4(c)
  Witnesses, A3 S4(e), A3 S5
Composition, A3 S1
Concurrent resolutions, A3 S3(e), A5 S9
Constitution
  Amendment, A11 S1, A11 S5(a), A12 S14
  Schedules, deletion of obsolete items, A5 S20(i), A8 S6(g), A12 S11
  United States, proposed amendment, A10 S1
Contempt, A3 S4(d), A3 S5
Courts
  Appellate districts, establishment, A5 S1, A5 S9
  Judges, increasing or decreasing number, A5 S9
  Judicial circuits, establishment, A5 S1
  Judicial Qualifications Commission rules, repeal, A5 S12(d)
  Rules of practice and procedure, repeal, A5 S2(a), A5 S11(d)
  Supreme Court rules, repeal, A5 S2(a)
Emergency powers, A2 S6
Enemy attack, power to ensure continuity of government, A2 S6
General laws requiring local expenditures, limiting ability to raise revenue, or reducing percentage of state tax shared, A7 S18
Generally, A3
Governor
  Adjournment of session, A3 S3(f)
  Apportionment sessions, convening by proclamation, A3 S16(a), (d)

LEGISLATURE (Cont.)
  Governor (Cont.)
    Meetings between Governor and legislative leadership, open to public, A3 S4(e)
    Message on condition of state, A4 S1(e)
    Restoration of capacity, A4 S3(b)
    Special session, convening by proclamation, A3 S3(c)
    Veto of bills, A3 S8, A3 S9, A3 S19(b)
  House of Representatives
    Clerk, A3 S2, A3 S7
    Composition, A3 S1
    Districts, A3 S1, A3 S15(c), A3 S16(a)
    Impeachment of officers, A3 S17
    Members
      Absence, penalties, A3 S4(a)
      Assumption of office, A3 S15(d)
      Contempt, A3 S4(d)
      Disorderly conduct, A3 S4(d)
      Election, A3 S1, A3 S2, A3 S15(b)
      Expulsion, A3 S4(d)
      Qualifications, A3 S2, A3 S15(c)
      Representation of clients before government body, A2 S8(e)
      Term limitations, A6 S4(b)
      Term of office, A3 S15(b), A12 S14
      Vacancy in office, A3 S15(d)
    Officers, A3 S2, A3 S3(a)
    Quorum, A3 S4(a)
    Rules of procedure, A3 S4(a), (e)
    Speaker
      Constitution Revision Commission members, appointment, A11 S2(a)
      Impeachment investigation committee, appointment, A3 S17(a)
      Revenue shortfalls, budget reductions, A4 S13
      Selection, A3 S2
      Signature, bills and joint resolutions, A3 S7
      Taxation and budget reform commission members, appointment, A11 S6(a)
  Income tax rate, increase authorization, A7 S5
  Investigations, A3 S5, A3 S17(a)
  Joint resolutions, A3 S7, A3 S16, A11 S1
  Journals
    Bill titles, publication, A3 S7
    Constitutional amendment resolution, A11 S1
    Governor's vetoes, entry, A3 S8(b)
    Publication, A3 S4(c)
    Requirement, A3 S4(c)
    Votes of members, A3 S4(c), A3 S7, A3 S8(c)
  Legislative power, A2 S3, A3 S1
  Marine net fishing violations, enactment of more stringent penalties, A10 S16(e)
  Meetings, open to the public, A1 S24(b), A3 S4(e)
  Motor vehicle license revenues, legislative restrictions, A12 S9(d)
  Pardon, treason cases, A4 S8(b)
  Planning documents, review, A3 S19(c), (h)
  Public education capital projects, authorization, A12 S9(a)
  Punishment power, A3 S4(d), A3 S5
  Reapportionment, See LEGISLATURE subtitle Apportionment
  Records of legislative branch, access to, A1 S24
  Revenue collection limitation, increase by two-thirds vote, A7 S1(e)
  School capital outlay projects, authorization, A12 S9(a)
  Senate
    Appointment or removal of public officers, A3 S4(b), A4 S6(a), A5 S12(g)

LEGISLATURE (Cont.)
  Senate (Cont.)
    Closed sessions, A3 S4(b)
    Composition, A3 S1
    Confirmation of appointments
      Game and Fresh Water Fish Commission, A4 S9
      Militia general officers, A10 S2(c)
      Requirement, A4 S6(a)
    Districts, A3 S1, A3 S15(a), (c), A3 S16(a)
    Impeachment trial, A3 S17(b), (c)
    Officers, A3 S2, A3 S3(a)
    President
      Constitution Revision Commission members, appointment, A11 S2(a)
      Revenue shortfalls, budget reductions, A4 S13
      Selection, A3 S2
      Signature, bills and joint resolutions, A3 S7
      Special sessions, convening, A4 S7(b)
      Taxation and budget reform commission members, appointment, A11 S6(a)
    Quorum, A3 S4(a)
    Rules of procedure, A3 S4(a), (e)
    Secretary, A3 S2, A3 S7
    Senators
      Absence, penalties, A3 S4(a)
      Assumption of office, A3 S15(d)
      Contempt, A3 S4(d)
      Disorderly conduct, A3 S4(d)
      Election, A3 S1, A3 S2, A3 S15(a)
      Expulsion, A3 S4(d)
      Qualifications, A3 S2, A3 S15(c)
      Representation of clients before government body, A2 S8(e)
      Term limitations, A6 S4(b)
      Term of office, A3 S15(a), A12 S12
      Vacancy in office, A3 S15(d)
    Special sessions, A4 S7(b)
    Suspended officers, removal or reinstatement, A4 S7(b)
  Sessions
    Adjournment, A3 S3(e), (f), A3 S4(a)
    Apportionment sessions
      Extraordinary, A3 S16(d), (e), (f)
      Regular, A3 S16(a)
      Special, A3 S16(a), (b)
    Closed, A3 S4(b)
    Extension, A3 S3(d)
    Length, A3 S3(d)
    Location, A2 S2
    Organization sessions, A3 S3(a)
    Public, A3 S4(b)
    Regular sessions, A3 S3(b), (d), (f)
    Special sessions, A3 S3(c), (d), (f)
  Subpoena power, A3 S5
  United States Constitution, proposed amendment, A10 S1
  Voting, A3 S4(c), A3 S7, A3 S8(c), A10 S12(e)
  Witnesses, A3 S4(e), A3 S5

LEON COUNTY, A2 S2

LICENSING BOARDS, A4 S6(b)

LIENS
  Exempt property, A10 S4(a)
  Intangible personal property tax, obligations secured by lien, A7 S2
  Special laws pertaining to, A3 S11(a)

LIEUTENANT GOVERNOR
  Acting Governor, A4 S3(b)

731

LIEUTENANT GOVERNOR (Cont.)
Creation of office, A4 S2
Duties, A4 S2
Election, A4 S5(a)
Executive departments, supervision, A4 S6
Impeachment, A3 S17(a)
Office location, A2 S2
Qualifications, A4 S5(b)
Succession to office of Governor, A4 S3(a)
Term limitations, A6 S4(b)
Term of office, A4 S5(a)

LIFE AND LIBERTY, RIGHT TO, A1 S2

LOCAL GOVERNMENT
Bond financing, *See* BONDS
Classification in general laws, A3 S11(b)
Consolidation, A8 S3, A8 S6(e)
Counties, *See* COUNTIES
Credit, pledging, A7 S10
Districts, *See* SPECIAL DISTRICTS
Electric generation and transmission facilities, A7 S10(d)
Generally, A8
Home rule, A8 S6(e)
Joint ownership with private entities, A7 S10
Municipalities, *See* MUNICIPALITIES
Public funds, investment, A7 S10
Taxes, A7 S9
Taxing power, limitation, A7 S10
Transfer of powers, A8 S4

LOTTERIES, A10 S7, A10 S15

M

MANDAMUS
Circuit courts, A5 S5(b)
District courts of appeal, A5 S4(b)
Supreme Court, A5 S3(b)

MANUFACTURING PLANTS, A7 S10(c)

MARINE ANIMALS
See FISHING

MILITARY POWER, A1 S7

MILITIA
Adjutant General, A10 S2(c), (d)
Call to duty, A4 S1(d)
Commander-in-chief, A4 S1(a)
Composition, A10 S2(a)
Courts martial, A1 S15(a)
National Guard, A10 S2(d)
Officers
　Appointment, A10 S2(c)
　Holding public office, A2 S5(a)
　Suspension, A4 S7(a), (b)
Organization, maintenance, and discipline, A10 S2(b)
Power subordinate to civil, A1 S7

MINORS
See CHILDREN

MISCELLANEOUS PROVISIONS, A10

MOBILE HOMES, A7 S1(b)

MONROE COUNTY, A8 S6(e)

MORTGAGES, A7 S2

MOTOR VEHICLES
Ad valorem taxes, A7 S1(b)
Fuel taxes, A7 S17(b), A12 S9(c)
License revenues, A12 S9(d)
License tax, A7 S1(b)
Trailers and trailer coaches, A7 S1(b)

MUNICIPALITIES
Abolishment, A8 S2(a)
Ad valorem taxation, A7 S9, A12 S2
Annexation, A8 S2(c)
Bond financing, A7 S10(c), A7 S12
Charter, A4 S7(c), A8 S2(a)
Civil service system, A3 S14
Consolidation of local governments, A8 S3, A8 S6(e)
Courts, A5 S20(d)
Credit, pledging, A7 S10
Dade County, Metropolitan Government of, A8 S6(f)
Elections, A6 S6
Electric generation and transmission facilities, A7 S10(d)
Establishment, A8 S2(a)
Extraterritorial powers, A8 S2(c)
Indebtedness, certificates of, A7 S12
Investment of public funds, A7 S10
Jacksonville, City of, A8 S6(e)
Joint ownership with private entities, A7 S10
Key West, City of, A8 S6(e)
Legislative bodies, A8 S2(b)
Mandated expenditure of funds, funding by Legislature,
　A7 S18(a)
Meetings, access to, A1 S24(b)
Mergers, A8 S2(c)
Officers
　Continuance in office, A8 S6(c)
　Holding other offices, A2 S5(a)
　Prosecutor, A5 S17, A5 S20(c)
　Suspension from office, A4 S7(c)
Ordinances
　Community and economic development tax exemptions,
　　A7 S3(c)
　Conflict with county ordinances, A8 S1(f), (g)
　Historic properties tax exemptions, A7 S3(e)
　Violations, prosecution, A5 S17
Pollution control facilities, state bond financing, A7 S14
Powers, A8 S2(b), (c), A8 S6(b)
Property owned by, taxation, A7 S3(a)
Property within, taxation by county, A8 S1(h)
Reduction of authority to raise revenue, legislative
　approval, A7 S18(b)
State aid, A7 S8
State tax revenues, legislative approval of reduction,
　A7 S18(c)
Status, continuation upon adoption of Constitution,
　A8 S6(b)
Tax anticipation certificates, A7 S12
Taxes, A7 S9, A12 S2
Taxing power, limitation, A7 S10
Transfer of function or power, A8 S4
Utility services gross receipts tax, payment, A12 S9(a)
Waste disposal facilities, state bond financing, A7 S14
Water facilities, state bond financing, A7 S14

N

NATURAL RESOURCES
Conservation and protection, A2 S7, A12 S9(a)
Fish and marine animals, *See* FISHING
Outdoor recreation land acquisition, bond issuance, A12 S9(a)
Pollution and noise abatement, A2 S7
Scenic beauty, conservation and protection, A2 S7

NAVIGABLE WATERS, A10 S11

NET FISHING, A10 S16

NOISE POLLUTION, A2 S7

NOTARIES PUBLIC, A2 S5(a)

O

OATHS
Electors, A6 S3
Public officers, A2 S5(b)

OCCUPATIONAL REGULATION
Licensing boards, A4 S6(b)
Special laws pertaining to, A3 S11(a)

OFFICIAL LANGUAGE, A2 S9

OPEN MEETINGS, A1 S24(b), (c), (d), A3 S4(e), A12 S20

ORDINANCES
County, *See* COUNTIES
Municipal, *See* MUNICIPALITIES

OUTDOOR RECREATION DEVELOPMENT, A12 S9(a)

P

PARDON, A4 S8(a), (b)

PARI-MUTUEL GAMBLING, A7 S7, A10 S7

PAROLE, A4 S8(c)

PAROLE AND PROBATION COMMISSION, A4 S8(c)

PENSION SYSTEMS (PUBLIC), A2 S8(d), A10 S14

PETITION
Constitutional amendment initiative, A11 S3, A11 S5(a)
Constitutional convention call, A11 S4(a)
Redress of grievances, A1 S5

PLANNING
Governor, responsibility, A3 S19(h), A4 S1(a)
State planning processes and planning documents, A3 S19(a), (c), (h)

POLITICAL PARTIES, A5 S13, A6 S1

POLITICAL POWER, A1 S1

POLITICAL SUBDIVISIONS
Classification in general laws, A3 S11(b)

POLITICAL SUBDIVISIONS (Cont.)
Counties, *See* COUNTIES
Municipalities, *See* MUNICIPALITIES
Special districts, *See* SPECIAL DISTRICTS

POLLUTION CONTROL AND ABATEMENT, A2 S7, A7 S14

PORT FACILITIES, A7 S10(c)

POWERS OF GOVERNMENT
Executive power, A2 S3, A4 S1(a)
Judicial power, A2 S3, A5 S1
Legislative power, A2 S3, A3 S1
Military power, A1 S7
Political power, A1 S1
Separation of powers, A2 S3

PRESS, FREEDOM OF, A1 S4

PRETRIAL RELEASE AND DETENTION, A1 S14

PRIVACY, RIGHT OF, A1 S23

PROBATION, A4 S8(c)

PROHIBITION, WRIT OF, A5 S3(b), A5 S4(b), A5 S5(b)

PROPERTY
Acquisition, possession, and protection; rights of, A1 S2
Ad valorem taxes, *See* TAXATION
Aliens, real property ownership and disposition, A1 S2
Curtesy, A10 S5
Deprivation without due process of law, A1 S9
Dower, A10 S5
Drainage easements, A10 S6(b)
Eminent domain, A10 S6
Forced sale, exemptions from, A10 S4
Homestead, *See* HOMESTEAD PROPERTY
Leases, publicly financed facilities, A7 S10(c)
Liens, A3 S11(a), A7 S2, A10 S4
Married women, A10 S5
Municipal property, taxation, A7 S3(a)
Recreation lands, state bond financing, A12 S9(a)
Rights to acquire, possess, and protect, A1 S2
Sovereignty lands, A10 S11
Special laws pertaining to, A3 S11(a)
Submerged lands, A10 S11
Taking for public purposes, A10 S6
Taxation, *See* TAXATION

PROPERTY APPRAISERS, A8 S1(d)

PUBLIC DEFENDERS, A5 S18

PUBLIC EMPLOYEES
Breach of public trust, A2 S8(c), (d), (f)
Civil service system, A3 S14
Conflicts of interest, A3 S18
Ethics, code of, A2 S8, A3 S18
Financial interests, disclosure, A2 S8(a), (g), (h)
Records, access to, A1 S24(a)
Representation of clients before government body, A2 S8(e)
Strike, right to, A1 S6

PUBLIC LANDS, A10 S11, A12 S9(a)

PUBLIC MEETINGS
Access to and notice of, A1 S24(b), (c), (d), A3 S4(e), A12 S20

733

PUBLIC MEETINGS (Cont.)
  Legislature, A3 S4(e)

PUBLIC OFFICERS
  Bond, A2 S5(b)
  Breach of public trust, A2 S8(c), (d), (f)
  Campaign finances, disclosure, A2 S8(b)
  Civil service system, A3 S14
  Compensation, A2 S5(c), A3 S12, A12 S3
  Conflicts of interest, A3 S18
  Continuance in office upon adoption of Constitution, A8 S6(c), A12 S3
  County officers, *See* COUNTIES
  Creation of office, limitation of term of office, A3 S13
  Ethics, code of, A2 S8, A3 S18
  Felons, disqualification from holding office, A6 S4(a)
  Financial interests, disclosure, A2 S8(a), (g), (h)
  Holding other offices, A2 S5(a)
  Impeachment, *See* IMPEACHMENT
  Mentally incompetent persons, disqualification from holding office, A6 S4(a)
  Municipal officers, *See* MUNICIPALITIES
  Oath of office, A2 S5(b)
  Powers and duties, A2 S5(b), (c)
  Quasi-judicial power, A5 S1
  Records, access to, A1 S24(a)
  Representation of clients before government body, A2 S8(e)
  Special laws pertaining to, A3 S11(a)
  Succession, enemy attack emergency, A2 S6
  Suspension from office, A4 S7
  Terms of office, *See* TERMS OF OFFICE
  Vacancies in office, *See* VACANCY IN OFFICE

PUBLIC RECORDS
  Access to, A1 S24(a), (c), (d), A12 S20
  Exemptions from disclosure, A1 S24(a), (c)

PUNISHMENT
  Administrative penalties, A1 S18
  Breach of public trust, A2 S8(c), (d)
  Clemency, A4 S8
  Contempt, A3 S4(d), A3 S5
  Costs, payment by accused, A1 S19
  County ordinance violations, A8 S1(j)
  Criminal statutes, effect of repeal or amendment, A10 S9
  Cruel or unusual, A1 S17
  Death penalty, appeal, A5 S3(b)
  Excessive, A1 S17
  Imprisonment for debt, A1 S11
  Judges, discipline, A5 S12(f)
  Juvenile delinquents, A1 S15(b)
  Legislators, A3 S4(a), (d)
  Pardon, A4 S8(a), (b)
  Parole, A4 S8(c)
  Penalties, fines, and forfeitures under 1885 Constitution, A12 S7(a)
  Probation, A4 S8(c)
  Sentences under 1885 Constitution, A12 S7(a)
  Special laws pertaining to, A3 S11(a)
  Witnesses, legislative investigation, A3 S5

Q

QUALITY MANAGEMENT AND ACCOUNTABILITY PROGRAM, A3 S19(h)

QUASI-JUDICIAL POWER, A5 S1

QUO WARRANTO, WRIT OF, A5 S3(b), A5 S4(b), A5 S5(b)

R

RACIAL DISCRIMINATION, A1 S2

REBELLION, A1 S13, A4 S1

RECREATION LANDS AND FACILITIES, A12 S9(a)

RELIGION
  Discrimination based on, A1 S2
  Establishment and free exercise of, A1 S3
  Military duty, exemption, A10 S2(a)
  Property used for religious purposes, tax exemption, A7 S3(a)
  Public revenue in aid of, A1 S3

RELIGIOUS FREEDOM, A1 S3

RENEWABLE ENERGY SOURCE DEVICES, A7 S3(d), A12 S19

RESIDENCE
  Cabinet members, A4 S5(b)
  County commissioners, A8 S1(e)
  Electors, A6 S2
  Governor, A4 S5(b)
  Homestead, A7 S6(a), A10 S4(a)
  Judges, A5 S3(a), A5 S8
  Legislators, A3 S15(c)
  Lieutenant Governor, A4 S5(b)
  Public defenders, A5 S18
  State attorneys, A5 S17
  Supreme Court justices, A5 S3(a)

RETIREMENT SYSTEMS (PUBLIC), A2 S8(d), A10 S14

REVENUE
  (*See also* STATE FUNDS; TAXATION)
  Aid to church, sect, or religious denomination, A1 S3
  Bond repayment, A7 S11(d)
  Gross receipts tax, application, A12 S9(a)
  License fees, Game and Fresh Water Fish Commission, A4 S9
  Limitation on collection, A7 S1(e), A11 S3, A12 S21
  Local government authority to raise revenue, reduction by Legislature, A7 S18(b)
  Motor vehicle fuel taxes, allocation, A7 S17(b), A12 S9(c)
  Motor vehicle license revenues, A12 S9(d)
  Pari-mutuel taxes, allocation, A7 S7
  Raising to defray state expenses, A7 S1(d)
  Revenue shortfalls, budget reductions, A3 S19(h), A4 S13
  Second gas tax, allocation, A12 S9(c)
  Taxation and budget reform commission, review of revenue needs, A11 S6(d)

REVENUE BONDS
  See BONDS

REVISION
  See AMENDMENT

RIGHT OF PRIVACY, A1 S23

RIGHT TO ASSEMBLE, A1 S5

RIGHT TO BEAR ARMS, A1 S8(a)

RIGHT TO WORK, A1 S6

RIGHTS, DECLARATION OF, A1

RIGHTS OF ACCUSED, A1 S16(a), A1 S19

RIGHTS OF TAXPAYERS, A1 S25

RIGHTS OF VICTIMS OF CRIME, A1 S16(b)

RIGHTS, PROPERTY, A1 S2

ROADS AND HIGHWAYS, A3 S11(a), A7 S17, A12 S9(b), (c)

S

SCENIC BEAUTY, A2 S7

SCHEDULES
Bonds, A12 S9, A12 S18
Conflicting provisions, A12 S17
Consolidation and home rule, A8 S6(e)
Constitution of 1885 superseded, A12 S1
Dade County, A8 S6(f)
Deletion of obsolete items, A5 S20(i), A8 S6(g), A12 S11
Education, Commissioner of, A12 S4, A12 S6(b)
Ethics in government, A2 S8(h)
Existing government, preservation, A12 S10
Judicial Qualifications Commission, A5 S12(i)
Judiciary, A5 S12(i), A5 S20
Laws preserved, A12 S6
Legislative apportionment, A12 S13
Local governments, A8 S6
Officers to continue in office, A8 S6(c), A12 S3
Ordinances, A8 S6(d)
Property taxes, A12 S2, A12 S19
Public debts recognized, A12 S8
Public records and meetings, access to, A12 S20
Reorganization, A12 S16
Representatives, A12 S14
Revenue limitation, A12 S21
Rights reserved, A12 S7
Senators, A12 S12
Special district taxes, A12 S15
Superintendents of schools, A12 S5, A12 S6(b)
Transition from 1885 Constitution, A12

SCHOOL BOARDS, A9 S4, A9 S5, A12 S9(d)

SCHOOL DISTRICTS
Ad valorem taxes, A7 S6(c), A7 S9, A9 S4(b)
Bonds, A7 S12
Boundaries, A9 S4(a)
Capital projects financing, A7 S12, A12 S9(a), (d)
Credit, pledging, A7 S10
Indebtedness, certificates of, A7 S12
Investment of public funds, A7 S10(a), (b)
Joint educational programs, A9 S4(b)
Joint ownership with private entities, A7 S10
Meetings, access to, A1 S24(b)
Motor vehicle licensing revenue, distribution, A12 S9(d)
School boards, A9 S4, A9 S5, A12 S9(d)
State aid, A7 S8
Superintendents of schools, A9 S5, A12 S5, A12 S6(b)
Tax anticipation certificates, A7 S12
Taxes, A7 S6(c), A7 S9, A9 S4(b)
Taxing power, limitation, A7 S10

SCHOOLS
See EDUCATION

SCHOOLS, SUPERINTENDENTS OF, A9 S5, A12 S5, A12 S6(b)

SEAL (STATE), A2 S4

SEARCH WARRANTS, A1 S12

SEARCHES AND SEIZURES, A1 S12

SEAT OF GOVERNMENT, A2 S2

SECRETARY OF STATE
See STATE, SECRETARY OF

SELF-INCRIMINATION, A1 S9

SENATE
See LEGISLATURE

SEPARATION OF POWERS, A2 S3

SHERIFFS, A5 S3(c), A5 S4(c), A8 S1(d)

SOVEREIGN IMMUNITY, A10 S13

SOVEREIGNTY LANDS, A10 S11

SPECIAL DISTRICTS
Ad valorem taxation, A7 S9, A12 S2, A12 S15
Bond financing, A7 S10(c), A7 S12
Civil service system, A3 S14
Credit, pledging, A7 S10
Elections, A6 S6
Electric generation and transmission facilities, A7 S10(d)
Indebtedness, certificates of, A7 S12
Investment of public funds, A7 S10
Joint ownership with private entities, A7 S10
Meetings, access to, A1 S24(b)
Pollution control facilities, state bond financing, A7 S14
State aid, A7 S8
Status, continuation upon adoption of Constitution, A8 S6(b)
Tax anticipation certificates, A7 S12
Taxes, A7 S9, A12 S2, A12 S15
Taxing power, limitation, A7 S10
Transfer of function or power, A8 S4
Waste disposal facilities, state bond financing, A7 S14
Water facilities, state bond financing, A7 S14

SPECIAL LAWS
See LAWS

SPEECH, FREEDOM OF, A1 S4

STATE ATTORNEYS, A5 S17, A5 S20(e)

STATE BOUNDARIES, A2 S1

STATE FLAG, A2 S4

STATE FUNDS
(See also REVENUE)
Aid to local governments, A7 S8
Appropriations, See APPROPRIATIONS
Comptroller, duties, A4 S4(e)

STATE FUNDS (Cont.)
  Disbursement by electronic means or by magnetic tape, A4 S4(e)
  Investment, A7 S10(a), (b)
  Mandated expenditure of funds by local governments, funding by Legislature, A7 S18(a)
  Money drawn from treasury, A7 S1(c)
  School fund, A9 S6
  Treasurer, duties, A4 S4(e)
  Trust funds, See TRUST FUNDS (PUBLIC)

STATE RETIREMENT SYSTEMS, A2 S8(d), A10 S14

STATE SEAL, A2 S4

STATE, SECRETARY OF
  (See also CABINET)
  Cabinet, member, A4 S4(a)
  Documents received and maintained
    Constitution revision proposals, A11 S2(c), A11 S4(b)
    Constitutional amendment initiative petitions, A11 S3
    Constitutional convention petitions, A11 S4(a)
    County ordinances, A8 S1(i)
    Governor's certificates of incapacity or capacity, A4 S3(b)
    Governor's executive orders of clemency, A4 S8(a)
    Governor's objections to vetoed bills, A3 S8(b)
    Governor's orders of suspension of officers, A4 S7(a)
    Judicial apportionment orders, A3 S16(b), (f)
    Official acts, A4 S4(b)
    Taxation and budget reform commission proposals, A11 S6(e)
  Education, State Board of; member, A9 S2
  Election, A4 S5(a)
  Impeachment, A3 S17(a)
  Office location, A2 S2
  Powers and duties, A4 S4(a), (b)
  Qualifications, A4 S5(b)
  Term of office, A4 S5(a)

STATE TREASURY, A7 S1(c)

STATEWIDE PROSECUTOR, A4 S4(c)

STUDENT LOANS, A7 S15

SUBMERGED LANDS, A10 S11

SUFFRAGE AND ELECTIONS
  See ELECTIONS

SUITS AGAINST STATE, A10 S13

SUPERINTENDENTS OF SCHOOLS, A9 S5, A12 S5, A12 S6(b)

SUPERVISORS OF ELECTIONS, A8 S1(d)

SUPREME COURT
  (See also COURTS)
  Advisory opinions, A4 S1(c), A4 S10, A5 S3(b)
  Appellate districts, recommendations for redefining, A5 S9
  Attorneys, admission to practice of law and discipline, A5 S15
  Chief justice
    Appointment, A5 S2(b)
    Assignment of temporary judges, A5 S2(b)
    Constitution Revision Commission members, appointment, A11 S2(a)

SUPREME COURT (Cont.)
  Chief justice (Cont.)
    Impeachment trials, presiding, A3 S17(c)
    Revenue shortfalls, budget reductions, A4 S13
  Clerk, A5 S3(c)
  Death penalty, review, A5 S3(b)
  Decisions, A5 S3(a)
  Direct appeal, A5 S3(b)
  Discipline of justices and judges, A5 S12(f), (h)
  District court of appeal decisions, review, A5 S3(b)
  Final judgments and orders, review, A5 S3(b)
  Governor
    Advisory opinions, A4 S1(c)
    Incapacity determination, A4 S3(b)
  Habeas corpus, writ of, A5 S3(b)
  Initiative petitions, review, A4 S10, A5 S3(b)
  Judges
    Certificates of need, A5 S9
    Discipline, A5 S12(f)
    Temporary assignment to Supreme Court, A5 S3(a)
  Judicial circuits, recommendations for redefining, A5 S9
  Judicial nominating commission, A4 S4(c), A5 S11(d)
  Judicial power vested in, A5 S1
  Judicial Qualifications Commission rules, repeal, A5 S12(d)
  Jurisdiction, A5 S3(b), A5 S20(c)
  Justices, See JUDGES
  Legislative apportionment
    Apportionment orders, A3 S16(b), (f)
    Declaratory judgments of validity, A3 S16(c), (d), (e), (f)
  Location, A2 S2
  Mandamus, writ of, A5 S3(b)
  Marshal, A5 S3(c)
  Organization, A5 S3(a)
  Process, A5 S3(c)
  Prohibition, writ of, A5 S3(b)
  Quo warranto, writ of, A5 S3(b)
  Quorum, A5 S3(a)
  Regulatory agency actions, review, A5 S3(b)
  Rules
    Appellate districts, criteria for redefining, A5 S9
    Appellate review, interlocutory orders, A5 S4(b)
    Chief circuit court judges, selection, A5 S2(d)
    Court practice and procedure, A5 S2(a), A5 S11(d)
    Judges, determination of need, A5 S9
    Judicial circuits, criteria for redefining, A5 S9
  Trial court judgments and orders, review, A5 S3(b)
  United States courts, certified questions of law, A5 S3(b)
  United States Supreme Court, A1 S12, A5 S3(b)
  Writs, power to issue, A5 S3(b)

T

TALLAHASSEE, CITY OF, A2 S2

TAX COLLECTORS, A8 S1(d)

TAXATION
  Ad valorem taxes
    Agricultural land, A7 S4(a)
    Aquifer recharge lands, A7 S4(a)
    Assessment of property, A7 S4, A7 S6(d), A7 S8, A7 S13
    Bonds payable from, A7 S12
    Businesses, new or expanding, A7 S3(c)
    Counties, A7 S9, A8 S1(h), A12 S2
    Educational, literary, scientific, religious, or charitable-use property, A7 S3(a)

736

TAXATION (Cont.)
Ad valorem taxes (Cont.)
Exemptions, A7 S3, A7 S4(b), A7 S6
Historic properties, restoration, A7 S3(e)
Homestead property, A7 S4(c), A7 S6, A10 S4(a), (b)
Household goods, A7 S3(b)
Illegal assessments, relief from, A7 S13
Intangible personal property, A7 S2, A7 S9(a)
Leases, publicly financed facilities, A7 S10(c)
Livestock, A7 S4(b)
Local governments, A7 S9
Millages, A7 S2, A7 S9(b), A12 S2
Mortgages, obligations secured by, A7 S2
Municipal properties, A7 S3(a)
Municipalities, A7 S9, A12 S2
Personal effects, A7 S3(b)
Property appraisers, A8 S1(d)
Property within municipalities, benefit for county unincorporated areas, A8 S1(h)
Rates, A7 S2, A7 S9(b), A12 S2
Real property
Exemptions, A7 S3, A7 S6
Local taxes, A7 S9
Rate, A7 S2, A7 S9(b), A12 S2
State tax, A7 S1(a)
Valuation, A7 S4
Recreational lands, A7 S4(a)
Renters, tax relief, A7 S6(e)
School purposes, A7 S6(c), A7 S9, A9 S4(b)
Special districts, A7 S9, A12 S2, A12 S15
State, A7 S1(a)
Stock-in-trade, A7 S4(b)
Tangible personal property
Exemptions, A7 S1(b), A7 S3
Local taxes, A7 S9
Rate, A7 S2, A7 S9(b), A12 S2
State tax, A7 S1(a)
Valuation, A7 S4
Tax anticipation certificates, A7 S12
Valuation of property, A7 S4
Voter authorization, A7 S9(b)
Water management purposes, A7 S9(b)
Airplanes, A7 S1(b)
Blind persons, exemption, A7 S3(b)
Boats, A7 S1(b)
Community development exemptions, new or expanding businesses, A7 S3(c)
Consolidation of local governments, A8 S3
Corporation income tax, A7 S5(b)
Counties, A7 S9, A8 S1(h), A12 S2
Disabled persons, exemption, A7 S3(b), A7 S6(c)
Economic development exemptions, new or expanding businesses, A7 S3(c)
Elderly persons, exemption, A7 S6(c)
Estate tax, A7 S5(a)
Exemptions, A7 S3, A7 S5(b), A7 S6
Gas tax, A12 S9(c)
Generally, A7
Gross receipts tax, utility services, A12 S9(a)
Heads of families, exemption, A7 S3(b)
Historic properties, restoration; exemption, A7 S3(e)
Homestead property, A7 S4(c), A7 S6, A10 S4(a), (b)
Illegal taxes, relief from, A7 S13
Income tax, A7 S5
Inheritance tax, A7 S5(a)
Leases, publicly financed facilities, A7 S10(c)
License tax, A7 S1(b)
Limitations
Consolidation of county and municipalities, effect, A8 S3

TAXATION (Cont.)
Limitations (Cont.)
Pledging credit of state or political subdivisions, A7 S10
Revenue collection limitations, A7 S1(e), A11 S3, A12 S21
Unincorporated areas, A8 S1(h)
Local taxes, A7 S9
Mobile homes, A7 S1(b)
Motor vehicles
Ad valorem taxes, A7 S1(b)
Fuel taxes, A7 S17(b), A12 S9(c)
License tax, A7 S1(b)
Municipalities, A7 S9, A12 S2
Natural persons, A7 S5(a)
Pari-mutuel tax, A7 S7
Raising sufficient revenue, A7 S1(d)
Renewable energy source devices, exemption, A7 S3(d), A12 S19
Renters, tax relief, A7 S6(e)
Revenue, generally, *See* REVENUE
School districts, A7 S6(c), A7 S9, A9 S4(b)
Second gas tax, A12 S9(c)
Special districts, A7 S9, A12 S2, A12 S15
Special laws, A3 S11(a)
State-preempted taxes, A7 S1(a)
Tax collector, A8 S1(d)
Tax liens, homestead property, A10 S4(a)
Taxation and budget reform commission, A2 S5(a), A11 S2(c), A11 S5(a), A11 S6
Taxes under 1885 Constitution, A12 S7(a)
Taxpayers' Bill of Rights, A1 S25
Widows and widowers, exemption, A7 S3(b)

TAXATION AND BUDGET REFORM COMMISSION, A2 S5(a), A11 S2(c), A11 S5(a), A11 S6

TERMS OF OFFICE
Cabinet members, A4 S5(a)
County commissioners, A8 S1(e)
County officers, A8 S1(d)
Education boards, appointive, A9 S3
Game and Fresh Water Fish Commission, A4 S9
Governor, A4 S5(a), (b)
House of Representatives, A3 S15(b), A12 S14
Judges, A5 S10, A5 S11(a), (b)
Judicial nominating commissions, A5 S20(c)
Judicial Qualifications Commission, A5 S12(b)
Lieutenant Governor, A4 S5(a)
Limitation of term, A3 S13, A4 S5(b), A6 S4(b)
Parole and Probation Commission, A4 S8(c)
Public defenders, A5 S18
School boards, A9 S4(a)
Senate, A3 S15(a), A12 S12
State attorneys, A5 S17
Superintendents of schools, A9 S5

TRAFFIC HEARING OFFICERS, A5 S1

TRANSPORTATION RIGHTS-OF-WAY, A7 S17

TREASON, A1 S20, A4 S8(b)

TREASURER
(*See also* CABINET)
Administration, State Board of; member, A12 S9(c)
Cabinet, member, A4 S4(a)
Education, State Board of; member, A9 S2
Election, A4 S5(a)

TREASURER (Cont.)
  Impeachment, A3 S17(a)
  Office location, A2 S2
  Powers and duties, A4 S4(a), (e)
  Qualifications, A4 S5(b)
  State funds and securities, maintenance, A4 S4(e)
  Term of office, A4 S5(a)

TRIAL BY JURY, A1 S16(a), A1 S22

TRIALS
  Appeals, A5 S3(b), A5 S4(b)
  Criminal, A1 S16(a)
  Evidence, *See* EVIDENCE
  Jury, A1 S16(a), A1 S22, A3 S11(a)
  Juvenile proceedings, A1 S15(b)
  Pretrial release and detention, A1 S14
  Site designation, A5 S7

TRUST FUNDS (PUBLIC)
  Budget stabilization fund, A3 S19(g), A7 S1(e)
  Education lottery funds, A10 S15
  General revenue fund, A3 S19(f), (g), A5 S20(c)
  Institutions of higher learning and junior college capital outlay, A12 S9(a)
  Investment, A7 S10(a)
  Land acquisition, A12 S9(a)
  Legislative approval, A3 S19(f)
  Public education capital outlay and debt service, A12 S9(a)
  School district and community college district capital outlay and debt service, A12 S9(d)
  State roads distribution fund, A12 S9(c)
  State school fund, A9 S6
  Sunset provisions, A3 S19(f)

TURNPIKE AUTHORITY, A12 S9(b)

U

UNITED STATES
  Census, A10 S8
  Congressional members from Florida, term limitations, A6 S4(b)
  Constitution
    Amendment, A10 S1
    Apportionment of Legislature, A3 S16(a)
    Court interpretation, review, A5 S3(b)
    Fourth amendment search and seizure rights, conformity with, A1 S12
    Oath to defend, A2 S5(b), A6 S3
  Courts of Appeals, A5 S3(b)
  Estate tax, A7 S5(a)
  Income tax, A7 S5, A7 S10(c)
  National Guard, A10 S2(d)
  Obligations, investment of public funds in, A7 S10(b)
  Officers, holding state office, A2 S5(a)
  Senators from Florida, term limitations, A6 S4(b)
  Supreme Court, A1 S12, A5 S3(b)

UNIVERSITIES, A7 S15(a), A9 S1, A12 S9(a)

V

VACANCY IN OFFICE
  Circumstances constituting vacancy, A10 S3

VACANCY IN OFFICE (Cont.)
  Constitution Revision Commission, A11 S2(b)
  County offices, A4 S1(f)
  Election to fill vacancy, A6 S5
  Enemy attack emergency, A2 S6
  Governor, A4 S3(a)
  Impeachment, A3 S17(b)
  Judges, A5 S10(a), A5 S11
  Judicial Qualifications Commission, A5 S12(d)
  Legislators, A3 S15(d)
  State offices, A4 S1(f)
  Suspended officers, A4 S7
  Taxation and budget reform commission, A11 S6(b)

VENUE, A1 S16(a), A3 S11(a)

VETERANS AFFAIRS, DEPARTMENT OF, A4 S11

VETO, A3 S8, A3 S9, A3 S19(b)

VICTIMS OF CRIME, RIGHTS OF, A1 S16(b)

VOCATIONAL TRAINING SCHOOLS, A7 S15(a), A12 S9(a)

VOTE
  Electors, A10 S12(d)
  Legislative house or governmental bodies, A10 S12(e)

VOTING
  Elections, *See* ELECTIONS
  Legislature, A3 S4(c), A3 S7, A3 S8(c), A10 S12(e)

W

WASTE DISPOSAL FACILITIES, A7 S14

WATER FACILITIES, A7 S14

WATER POLLUTION, A2 S7, A7 S14

WIDOWS AND WIDOWERS
  Homestead property, A10 S4(b), (c)
  Tax exemption, A7 S3(b)

WILDLIFE
  Fish, *See* FISHING
  Game and Fresh Water Fish Commission, A4 S9

WITNESSES
  Compulsory process, A1 S16(a)
  Confrontation by accused, A1 S16(a)
  Criminal trials, A1 S9, A1 S16(a)
  Legislature, A3 S4(e), A3 S5
  Self-incrimination, A1 S9
  Treason, A1 S20
  Unreasonable detention, A1 S17

WORK, RIGHT TO, A1 S6

WRITS
  Certiorari, A5 S4(b), A5 S5(b)
  Circuit court, A5 S5(b)
  District courts of appeal, A5 S4(b)
  Habeas corpus, *See* HABEAS CORPUS
  Mandamus, *See* MANDAMUS
  Prohibition, A5 S3(b), A5 S4(b), A5 S5(b)
  Quo warranto, A5 S3(b), A5 S4(b), A5 S5(b)

WRITS (Cont.)
  Supreme Court, A5 S3(b)

Index

A

Abbott, George, 300
Abortion rights, 398
Accountancy, Board of, 89
Accounting and Auditing, Division of, 53
Acquired Immunodeficiency Syndrome (AIDS), 176, 596, 597–598
Adams, Tom, 133
  BIOGRAPHY, 1973–74 edition, 118
Adkins, James C., *206*
Administration, Board of, 71
Administration, Department of, 7
  see also Management Services, Department of
Adult Education, Division of Applied Technology and, 66
African-American Affairs Commission, 89
Agency for Health Care Administration, 4
Agriculture
  alligators, 535
  cattle, 532–534
  cattle tick eradication program, *383,* 384
  citrus *see* Citrus
  cotton, 528–529
  early, 528
  Everglades, 530
  grains, 529
  horses, 532–534, *535*
  land used for, 562
  Marquis de LaFayette, 259, 437
  peanuts, 529
  sheep, 535
  soybeans, 529
  sugar cane, 386, 529
  tobacco, 529
  vegetables, 529–531
  watermelon, 531
  see also specific crops or animals
Agriculture and Consumer Services, Commissioner of, 8, 58–60, *58,* 670–671
Agriculture and Consumer Services, Department of, 8, 61–62
Alachua County, 429
Alcoholic beverage licenses, 617
Allen, Hervey, 450–451
Alligators, 520–521, *521,* 535
Allison, Abraham K., 282, 330–331, *330,* 359
Amelia Island, 374
American crocodile, 519, 521
American Revolution, 374, 416
Amos, Ernest, 9
Animal Industry, Division of, 61
Anstead, Harry Lee, 214–215, *214*
Apalachee Indians, 405
Appellate courts, 202
  see also District Courts of Appeal; Supreme Court of Florida
Armory Board, 89
Art, Capitol, *299,* 300, 314–317
Arthur, Chester A., 231
Artificial reefs, 524
Arts
  first theatrical performance, 309
  Florida Artists Hall of Fame, 300
  Ringling Museum of Art, 300
  motion pictures, *381,* 382
Ashler, Philip F.
  BIOGRAPHY 1977–78 ed. 97, *97*
Askew, Reubin O'D., 19, *209,* 353–354, *353*
  governor 1971–79, 7
  inauguration of successor, 276
  inaugurations, 275, 279
  Industrial Relations Commission, 211
  quoted, 6, 14, 270
  reapportionment, 195

NOTE: Entries in capital letters are references to previous editions of *The Florida Handbook.* Numbers in italics refer to illustrations.

742 / Index

Askew, Reubin O'D.—*Continued*
successive terms, 394
U.S. Trade Representative, 234
Asolo Theater, 297
Athletic Commission, 72, 89
Atkinson, Edith M., 223–224
Atkinson, Henry F., 223–224
Attorney General, 2, 8, 45–46, 665–666
see also Legal Affairs, Department of
Auditor General, 101, 186
AUDUBON HOUSE, 1973–74 edition, *344*
AUDUBON IN FLORIDA, 1975–76 edition, 30
Audubon, John James, 448–449, 495
Aury, Luis, 289, 374
Automobile racing, 487
Aviation
ARTICLE ABOUT 1955–56 edition, 71
air mail, 385
aircraft carrier operations, 383
Amelia Earhart, 387
combat training, 384
commercial, 383
night flights, 382
overseas service, 384, *384*, 386
Richmond Naval Air Station, 388
skyjacking, 390–391
transcontinental flights, 382

B

Backus, A. E. "Bean,", 300
Baker, Charles H., Jr., 450
Baker County, 429
Baker, James McNair, 429
Baker, Mary Lou, 150
Baker, Maxine, 194
Banking and Finance, Department of, 8, 52–53
see also Comptroller
Barbour, Thomas, 449
BAREFOOT MAILMAN, excerpt, 1955–56 edition, 61
Barkett, Rosemary, *206,* 216, 223, 396
Barrio Latino Commission, 4
Bartram, John, 448, 495
Bartram, William, 448, 495
BARTRAM, WILLIAM, *TRAVELS,* excerpt, 1955–56 edition, 102

Baseball, 487, *489*
Battle of Natural Bridge, 263, 267, 338, 378, 422–425, *423*
Battle of Olustee, 263, 267, *377,* 378, 420–422, *420*
Bay County, 429
Bell, Christine, 454
BELLAMY, JEANNE, article by,
1955–56 edition, 43
1989–90 edition, 300
Bellamy, Jeanne, article by, 466–470, *466*
Bellamy, John, 375
Bellamy Road, 375, 545
Bellinger, Bessie, 225
Bennett, Charles E., 237
Benton County, 429
Bethune, Mary McLeod, *229,* 464–465, *464*
Big Cypress Swamp, 393
Bills
claim, 112–113
committee reference 140
committee substitute, 125, 141
companion, 113, 140
debate, 127–129
first reading, 140
identification, 123
local, 113
number of, 113, 116
prefiling, 135, 140
reading 140–142
reconsideration, 128
reference to committee, 124–125
roll call votes, 142
Special Order Calendar, 141
sponsor, 140
voting on, 113
veto, 142–143
BIOGRAPHIES: NEWSMAKERS, PEOPLE IN GOVERNMENT, STATE OFFICERS
1947–48 edition, 279–298
1955–56 edition, 360–383
1957–58 edition, 364–387
1959–60 edition, 370–408
1961–62 edition, 158–183
1963–64 edition, 147–176
1965–66 edition, 388–422
Birds, 495, *495,* 513, 516–518, *517*
Black, Susan, 228
Blacks
desegregation *see* Desegregation
first

circuit judge, 224
congressman, 236–237
federal district judge, 228
four star general, 465
judge, 224
justice, *206,* 393
legislators, 152–154, 251, 395
woman
  Florida Senate, 395
  judge, 224
  Legislator, 251
FIRST CABINET MEMBER, 1981–82 edition, 131
Blais, Madeleine, 453
Blind Services, Division of, 66
Bloxham, William D., 232, 265, *270,* 276, 336–337, *336*
Board of Bar Examiners, 222
Board of Regents, 391
Bonds, 618–620
BOOM, FLORIDA, 1981–82 edition, 273–277
Booth, Anne Cawthon, 225–226
BOUNDARY, 1989–90 edition, 300–303
Bowlegs, Billy, 231, *414*
Bowles, William Augustus, 289
Boyd, Alan S., 234
Boyd, Joseph A., Jr., *206*
Bradford, Capt. Richard, 429
Bradford County, 429
BRADLEY, GUY, SLAIN AUDUBON AGENT, 1955–56 edition, 48
Branch, John, 278, 281, 326–327, *326*
Brevard County, 429
Brevard, Theodore Washington, 429
Brockenbrough, William H., 235, 282
Brogan, Frank T., *1,* 63–64, *63*
Brooke, Donald L, Article by 528–531
Broome, James E., 328, *329*
Broward, Annie Douglas, 252
Broward County, 430
Broward, Napoleon B., 339–340, *339, 361,* 429, 456, *456*
Brown, Corrine, 255, *255,* 398
Brown, J. Hyatt, 163
Brown, Joe, 169, *169*
Brown, Thomas, *327,* 328
Browner, Carol M., 234–235
Bryan, William Jennings, 385
Bryant, Cecil Farris, 13, 17, 193, 265, *349,* 350–351, 391
Bryant, William Cullen, 449
Buchanan, Edna, 453

Buckman Act, 381, 538
Budget
  1994–95 expenditures, 179–180
  1994–95 revenue sources, 178
  amendments, 179–180
  balanced, 180
  Cabinet, 177, 179
  federal programs, 181
  General Revenue Fund, 177, 180
  Governor, 5, 177, 179
  Legislature, 175–176, 177, 179–180
  local programs, 181
  revenue, 178
  trust funds, 177–178
  Working Capital Fund, 180
Bundy, Theodore, 397
Bureau of Minority Business Assistance, Department of Commerce, 83
Burke, James C., 153
Burns, William Haydon, 28, 265, 279, 351–352, *351*
Bush, George Herbert Walker, 232
Business and Professional Regulation, Department of, 4, 7, 17, 32, 72–73
Butler, Robert, 259
BUTLER, ROBERT, 1989–90 edition, 301
Butterworth, Robert A., *1,* 9, 45–46, *45*

C

Cabell, Edward Carrington, 235, 282
Cabinet, 1–10, *1, 49*
  aides, 18
  elections, 664–671
  first woman, 251
  impeachment, 15, 132
  inaugurations, 275
  incumbents defeated, 9
  members, qualifications, 14
  pardons, 7
  protocol, 11
  unique, 3
  see also individual officers
Cabinet, Confederate, 235
Cabinet day, 9
Cabinet, federal, 6, 233–235
Cabinet *See also* individual officers
Cabot, John, 369
Caldwell, Millard F., 190, 265, 278, *278,* 345–346, *346*

744 / Index

Caldwell, Millard F.—*Continued*
  ARTICLE BY, 1947–48 edition, 214–216
Caldwell Theater Company, 297
Calhoun County, 430
Calhoun, John C., 430, *430*
Call, Richard K.
  friend of Marquis de LaFayette 259
  territorial governor, 281, 325–326, *325*
  territorial representative to United States Congress, 235
  "The Grove," 361
  toast to, 305
Camp Blanding, *386,* 387
Camp Gordon Johnston, 387
CAMPAIGNS, 1979–80 edition, 466–470
Campbell, John, 374
Canals, *558,* 560–561, *561*
Cancer de Barbastro, Luis, 370, 403–404
Cape Canaveral, 388, 390, 391
  see also Cape Kennedy; Kennedy Space Center
CAPE FLORIDA LIGHT, 1957–58 edition, 41
Cape Kennedy, 391, 392
  see also Cape Canaveral; Kennedy Space Center
Capital
  history of, 256–273
  removal, 263–264
  sesquicentennial, 272
  see also Tallahassee
Capital Collateral Representative, 90
Capitol
  art, *299,* 300, 314–317
  chapel, 314–316
  first, 257, 272
  fourth, *2, 266,* 268, 270–271, 273
  history of, 257–280
  House chamber, 130
  Legislative floor, *131*
  mourning, 264
  non-governmental use, 265–267
  second, 259–260
  Senate chamber, 130–131
  third, 260–261, *261, 263,* 264, 268–269
Capitol Center, 264–265, 268, 272–273
Caputo, Philip, 453
Carlton, Doyle E., 265, 278, 343, *343*
Carter, James Earl (Jimmy), 230, 232, *232,* 234, 364, 393

Castillo de San Marcos, 283, 373, 407, 408, *408*
Castor, Elizabeth B. (BETTY), 161
  BIOGRAPHY 1993–93 edition, 70, *70*
Catesby, Mark, 495
Cattle, production, 388
Catts, Sidney J., 28, *176,* 277–278, 341–342, *341,* 367
Cavalla, Governor Jose, 280
Cawthon, W. S., 9
Ceremonial days, 306
Cermak, Anton J., 232, 386–387
Champion trees, 493–494
Charles, Ray, 300
Charlotte County, 430
Chase, William H., 286
Chemistry, Division of, 61
Cherry, Gwen Sawyer, 153, 251
Child Support Enforcement Program, 4
Chiles, Lawton M., Jr.
  governor, *1,* 28, *29,* 30–31, *30–31, 49,* 233, 397
  inaugurations, 276, 279, 280
  Senator, 232
  "Walkin' Lawton," 30
Chiles, Rhea Grafton, 31, *31, 35*
Christian, Floyd T., 134, 393
  BIOGRAPHY 1973–74 edition, 130
Christmas, first, 404–405
Chronicler Laureate, 300
Circuit courts, 200, 205–206, 219–220
Citizen's Assistance Office, 90
Citrus, 501–505
  byproducts, 505
  citrus canker, 383, 395, *396*
  commercial production, 501–505
  frosts 1894–1899, 380
  frozen concentrate, 388
  Mediterranean fruit fly, 386, 390–391
  peeling, 504
  ready to serve juice, 503
  salad and sections, 503–504
  table of production, 504–505
Citrus County, 430
Citrus, Department of, 7, 17, 32, 73–74
Civil War
  Battle of Natural Bridge, 263, 267, 338, 378, 422–425, *423*
  Battle of Olustee, 263, 267, *377,* 378, 420–422, *420*
  cattle, 419
  coastal blockade, 417–418

Index / 745

Confederate surrender in Florida, 426
encampment, *419*
Florida secession from U.S., 377–378
Floridians killed in, 378
Fort Clinch, 417
Fort Jefferson, 417
Fort Marion, 417
Fort Pickens, 410, 417, 420
Fort Taylor, 417
governors during, 282
Jacksonville, 420
monument, 272
Newport, 422–424, *423*
Ordinance of Secession, 263, 417
Pensacola, 417, *419*, 420
Reconstruction, 263
St. Marks, 422–424, *423*
salt, 418–419
Tallahassee, 263, 267, 422, 424–426, *425*
West Florida Seminary, 378, 424
CIVILIZATION, ANCIENT, IN FLORIDA, 1975–76 edition, 34
Clay County, 430
Clay, Henry, 430
Clays, mining, 509
Cleveland, Grover, 231
Climate
  air pollution, 482
  droughts, 476
  extremes, 473
  fog, 481–482
  frosts and freezing, 474
  humidity, 481–482
  hurricanes and tropical storms, 478–481
  prevailing winds, 478
  rainfall, 473–476, 481
  snow, 393, 476–478
  storm tides, *479*
  sunshine, 482
  temperature, 473–474
  thunderstorms, 486
  tornadoes, 478
  trade winds, 485–486
Clinton, William, *29*, 230, 232–233, 234, 364
Coconut Grove Playhouse, 297
Collier, Barron G., 430
Collier County, 430
Collins, Mary Call, 365
Collins, Thomas LeRoy
  1955 inauguration, 274
  1957 inauguration, 275
  1955 legislative reapportionment, 190–191, *190*
  biography, 348–350, *349*
  Collins Building, 265
  desegregation, 389–390
  "firsts," 390
  governor 1955–61, 2, 18, *248*
  inauguration, 279
  marriage of daughter, 366
  quoted, 3, 14
  reapportionment, 197
  Under Secretary of Commerce, 233
Colquitt, General A. H., 421–422
Columbia County, 430
Columbus, Christopher, 400, 430
Commerce, Department of, 7, 17, 32, 74, 388
Commission on Lay Midwifery, 4
Community Affairs, Department of, 7, 17, 32, 74–75
Community colleges, 390
Community Colleges, Division of, 66
Comptroller, 8, 50–51, *50*, 666–667
  see also Banking and Finance, Department of
Condominiums, 617
Cone, Frederick P., 28, 344, *345*
Conner, Doyle E., 155
  BIOGRAPHY 1989–90 edition, 55, *55*
Conservation laws, 392
Constitution
  1838 version, 39, 46, 51, 55, 281
    drafted, 376, 676–678
    legislative apportionment, 189
  1861 revision, 39, 46, 51
    drafted, 378, 678
  1865 revision, 37, 46, 55
    drafted, 378–379, 678
  1868 revision, 37, 39, 46, 51, 59, 64
    drafted, 679
  1885 revision, 11, 37, 39, 46, 51, 55, 59, 64, 200
    drafted, 679–680
  1940 amendment, 387
  1952 amendment, 388
  1965 revision, 11, 64
  1968 revision, 6, 8, 15, 20, 39, 46, 51, 55, 59, 101, 392
    drafted, 680
  1972 amendment, 200, 392
  amendment of, 111, 632–635, 674–676
  corporate income tax, 392

Constitution—*Continued*
  Declaration of Rights, 674
  history of, 676–680
  legislative apportionment, 189–190
  personal income tax, 202
  public education, 538
  Sunshine Amendment, 134
  Text, 681–740
Constitution Revision Commission, 187
Constitution of the United States, 102, 103, 228
Constitutional Conventions, 263, 675–676
Consumer Services, Division of, 61
Convict leasing, 384, 385
Cooke, C. Wythe, Article by 547–564
Coolidge, Calvin, 231, 232
Cooper, James Fenimore, 449
Corporations, Division of, 41
Correction Privatization Commission, 90
Corrections Commission, 90
Corrections, Department of, 7, 17, 32, 75–76
Counties
  county seat, 427–428
  "dry," 616–617
  lost, 429
  names, 429–445
  subdivision of state 227
COUNTY, THE LOST, 1947–48 edition, 92
County courts, 200, 207, 220
County Solicitor, 15
Courts, 200–226
  clerk of, 209
  divisions, 207
  extraordinary writs, 204, 206, 209–210
  officers, 208–209
  reorganization of, 392
  see also Circuit courts; County courts; District Courts of Appeal; Industrial Relations Commission; judges; Supreme Court of Florida; Supreme Court of the United States
Crane, Stephen, 449
Crawford, Robert B. (Bob), *1*, 58–59, *58*
Creek tribes, 414–415
Crenshaw, Ander, 160
Cresse, Joe, *181*
Crews, Harry, 453

Criminal Justice Standards and Training Commission, 90
Cross Florida Barge Canal, 393, *558*, 560–561, *561*
Cuban exile, first
  Florida Legislator, *143*
  judge, 224
  woman, U.S. House of Representatives, 397
Cuban immigration, 392, *393*, 394, *395*, 574
Cuban Missile Crisis, 391
Cultural Affairs, Division of, 43

D

Dade County, 431
Dade, Maj. Francis Langhorne, 431
Dairy Industry, Division of, 61
D'Alamberte, Talbot, 194
Davis, Fred H., 265
Day, Samuel T., 333–334
de Galvez, Bernando, 374
de Gourgues, Dominique, 372
de Grandy, Miguel, 198
de León, Juan Ponce *see* Ponce de León, Juan
de Luna, Tristan, 315, 370
de Soto, Hernando
  counties named after, 431, 434
  expeditions, 370, *401,* 403, 405, *435*
  horse racing, 488
  winter encampment, *404*
de Vaca, Cabeza, 402–403
Death penalty, 387, 397
Deer, 516, *516*
Defense Conversion and Transition Commission, 91
Degner, Robert L. article by, 532–535
Delius, Frederick, 309
Democratic Party, national convention, 392
Dekle, Hal P., 134, 393
Depression
  bank failures, 386
  Federal Emergency Relief Administration, 387
Desegregation, 389–390, *389,* 391
DeSoto County, 431, 433
Developmental Disabilities Council, 92
Diaz-Balart, Lincoln, 398
Dickinson, Fred O., Jr., 9, 134
  BIOGRAPHY, 1973–74 edition, 124

Dickinson, Jonathan, 448
Disston, Hamilton, 379, 460–461, *460*
District Courts of Appeal, 202, 204–205, 218–219
Division of Forestry, 62, 492
Dixie County, 431
Dolomite, 508
Doubleday, Abner, 377
Douglas, Marjory Stoneman
  author, 450
  biography, 455–456, *455*
  Florida Artists Hall of Fame, 300
  and women's rights, 252
Drake, Sir Francis, 372, 407
Drew, George F., 276, 336, *336*
Drugs, cocaine, 396
Dry Tortugas, 409–410, *409*
Dubbin, Murray H., *193*, 194
Dunbar, Paul Lawrence, 451
Duval County, 431–432
DuVal, William P., 260, 324, *324*, 359, 431–432

E

Earhart, Amelia, 387
Earthquakes, 482–483, 547
Eaton, John H., 324–325, *325*, 327
ECONOMY, AN EXPANDING, 1963–64 edition, 227
EDISON, THOMAS A., 1955–56 edition, 333
Education, Commissioner of, 8, 63–65, *63*, 669–670
Education, Department of, 8, 65–70, *70*, 539
Education, Public, 536–544
Edward Ball State Park, *497*
Egbert, Allan L., article by 513–522
Ehrlich, Raymond, *206*
Eisenhower, Dwight David, 230, 231, 234
Elder Affairs, Department of, 7, 10, 17, 32, 76
Elected offices
  oldest woman, 625
  qualifying fees, 632
  vacancies, 623–624
Elections, 622–627
  Cabinet officers, 664–671
  dates, 622
  first primary, 627
  first straw ballot, 627

gubernatorial, 640–648
presidential, 636–640
U.S. House of Representatives, 653–664
U.S. Senate, 648–653
Elections Canvassing Commission, 91
Elections Commission, 91
Elections, Division of, 40
Elliot, Fred C., 265
Emancipation Day, 306
Employment
  by industry, 603–605, 608–610
  motion picture, 608
  professional, 609–610
  public, 607
Endangered species, 519
Energy Office, 91
Engle, R. P., article by, 404–405
ENGLISH, COLIN, 1947–48 edition, 14, *14*
Environmental Equity and Justice Commission, 92
Environmental Protection, Department of, 7, 17, 32, 76–77
Equal Rights Amendment, 252–253, *394*
ERVIN, RICHARD W., JR., 1963–64 edition, 50
Escambia County, 432
Esquiroz, Margarita, 224
Ethics, Commission on, 134, 184, 393
ETHNIC COLONIES, 1979–80 edition, 305–308
Everglades, 466–470
  agriculture in, 386, 467–468
  counties, 433
  draining, 466–468
  exotic wildlife, 468–469
  pollution of, 469
  sugarcane, 386
Everglades Drainage District, 381–382
Everglades National Park, 467, 470
Ex Officio boards, 8
Executive Clemency, Office of, 92
Executive Department, 1–11, *12*
Executive order, 26–27
EXECUTIVE REORGANIZATION, 1971–72 edition, 167
Executive Reorganization Act, 6–8, 100
Exotic species, 522
EXOTICS IN ECOLOGY, 1977–78 edition, 430–432

F

Fairbairn, Douglas, 453
Fairchild, David, 449
Faircloth, Earl, 9
  BIOGRAPHY, 1969–70 edition, 35
Family Lines Railway System, 4
Farmers' Alliance, 380
Farming *see* Agriculture
Fayette County, 429
Federal Cabinet Under Secretaries, 233–234
Federal courts, 228
Ferre, Maurice, 155
Fiedler, Tom, article by, 565–571
Figueredo, Fernando, *143,* 155
Finance *see* Bonds; Taxes
Finance, Division of, 53
Finegan, General Joseph, 421
Fires
  forest, 395
  Fort Lauderdale, 382
  Jacksonville, *380,* 381
  Richmond Naval Air Station, 388
  Tallahassee, 262
Firestone, George 194, 291, 300
  BIOGRAPHY 1987–88 edition, 137, *137*
First
  black
    circuit judge, 224
    congressman, 236
    federal district judge, 228
    four star general, 465
    judge, 224
    justice, *206,* 393
    woman
      Florida Senator, 395
      judge, 224
      Legislator, 251
  Christmas in Florida, 404–405
  congressional delegate, 235
  Congressman, 235
  Cuban exile
    Florida Legislator, *143*
    judge, 224
    woman, U.S. House of Representatives, 397
  Hispanic
    woman
      circuit judge, 225
      claims jurist, 224
  U.S. Senator, 235
  woman
    admitted to practice before Supreme Court of the United States, 228
    appellate judge, 225
    black
      Florida Senator, 395
      judge, 224
      Legislator, 251
    Cabinet, 251
    circuit judge, 224
    county judge, 225
    Cuban exile, U.S. House of Representatives, 250
    federal judge, 228
    Florida House of Representatives, 251
    Florida Senate, 251
    Florida Senate president, 397
    Hispanic
      circuit judge, 225
      claims jurist, 224
    U.S. House of Representatives, 250–251
    justice, 223, 396
    police chief, 626
    Public Service Commission, 250
    Railroad Commission, 250
    sheriff, 626
    state attorney, 226
    U.S. House of Representatives, 250
    voter, 626
First ladies, list of, 34–35
First theatrical performance, 309
Fish
  freshwater, 514–516, 519–520
  saltwater, 516
  see also Marine resources
Fisher, Carl G., *382*
Flagler County, 432–433
Flagler, Henry M., 432–433, 461–462, *461,* 463
  death of, 383
  Florida East Coast Railroad, 380
  Overseas Extension, *380,* 381
Flags, during periods of mourning, 287
Flags of Florida, 283–291
  Burgundian Saltire, 283
  Canada, 288
  Confederacy, 285
  etiquette, 291
  France, 284
  Great Britain, 284, 321

Index / 749

P.O.W.-M.I.A., 288
Spain, 283
state, 285–287
state seal on, 287
United States, 284
Fleming, Francis P., 337–338, *337*
Fletcher, Duncan, 265
Floods, 398, 467
Florida
  flags, 283–291
  history of
    American Revolution, 321, 375
    ceded by Spain, 280, 374–375
    Civil War see Civil War
    discovery and exploration, 369–370, 400–405
    Huguenot settlement, 315, 370–371
    Pre-Columbian, 369
    Spanish exploration, 400–405
    Spanish-American War, 379
    statehood, 280–282, 376
    World War I, 318, *382*, 384, 410
    World War II see World War II
  Ships named, 319–320
Florida Agricultural College, 237
  see also Florida Agricultural and Mechanical University (FAMU)
Florida Agricultural and Mechanical College for Negroes, 381
  see also Florida Agricultural and Mechanical University (FAMU)
Florida Agricultural and Mechanical University (FAMU), 538
Florida Artists Hall of Fame, 300
Florida Atlantic University, 391
FLORIDA BOOM, 1981–82 edition, 273–277
Florida Caverns State Park, 556
Florida Crime Information Center, 82
Florida Education Center, *70*
Florida Folk Festival, 295
Florida Governor's Mansion Foundation, Inc., 363
Florida High Speed Rail Transportation Act, 86
Florida Highway Patrol, 79, 387
Florida House of Representatives, *100*
  1995–1996 members of, 170–173
  Clerk of, 121, 140, 170–172
  first woman, 150, 251
  governors as former members, 15
  impeachment, 102, 132–135
  qualifications, 118

Speaker of, 121, 159–163, 170
Speakers, list of 166–167
term, 118
youngest member 155
Florida House, Washington, D.C., *229*
Florida Inland Navigation District, 92
Florida Intelligence Center, 82
Florida Keys National Marine Sanctuary, 527
Florida Marine Patrol, 77
Florida National Guard, 318
Florida panther, state animal, 302
Florida Retirement System Trust Fund, 71
Florida Senate
  1982 reapportionment, 119
  1995–1996 members 168–170
  confirmation of appointments, 85
  first black woman, 153, 395
  first woman member, 150, 251
  first woman president, 150, 397
  governors as former members, 15
  impeachment, 102, 132–135
  President of, 121, 159–163, 168
  Presidents, list of 164–165
  qualifications, 118
  Secretary of, 121, 140, 169
  suspension session, 105
  term, 118
  youngest member of 154
Florida State College for Women, 381, 388
  see also Florida State University
Florida State Opera, 297
Florida State Symphony, 297
Florida State University, 297, 388, 391, 398, 538
Florida Transportation Commission, 85, 87
Florida Transportation Plan, 85
Florida Turnpike, 85, 87
Florida Women's Hall of Fame 253–254
FLORIDAS: WHERE DREAMS ARE MADE AND LOST 1989–90 edition, 405–408
FLORIDIAN, FIRST, 1952 edition, 343
Floridians
  income, 603
  nicknames, 308
  political profile, 565–571
  statistics, 572–611
Flory, Dr. Daisy Parker, 6
Fontaneda, Domingo Escalante de, 446

Football, 398, 487–488
Ford, Gerald R., 234
Forestry, Division of, 62
Forests, 490–494
Fort Barrancas, 410
Fort Caroline, 315, 371–372, *372*, 406–407, 408
Fort Jefferson, 409–410, *409*, 417
Fort Lauderdale, fire, 382
Fort Matanzas, 408, *408*
Fort Mose, 411, *411*
Fort Pickens, *377*, 410, 417, 420
Fossils, 550
Foster, Stephen Collins, 295, 442
Fowler, R.C., 382
Fowler, Tillie K., 255, *255*
France
  American Revolution, 416
  expeditions to Florida, 369, 370–371, 372, 373, 406
Franklin, Benjamin, 433
Franklin County, 433
Fruit and Vegetable Inspection, Division of, 61
FRENCH, JOHN, 1979–80 edition, 473
Frosts and freezes, 380, 395, 474
Fuller, Edna Giles, 150, 251
Fuller's earth, 509

G

Gadsden County, 433
Gadsden, James, 433
GALLAGHER, CHARLES THOMAS, III (TOM), 1993–94 edition, 61–62, *61*
Gambling, 386, 394
Game and Fresh Water Fish Commission, 77–78
GASPARILLA, 1953–54 edition, 21
GAY, CLARENCE M., 1953–54 edition, 248, *248*
General Services, Department of, 7
  see also Management Services, Department of
Geography
  coastline, 548
  description, 472, 486
  Floridian Plateau, 547–548
  highest point, 553
  lakes, 552
  Tallahassee Meridian, 552
  waterways, *558*

Geology, 472–473
  caverns, 556
  gems, 553
  harbors, 556
  keys, 559
  lagoons, 559
  lakes, 550–552
  natural bridges, 556, *557*
  sands, 548
  soils 472–473
  springs, 553–555
  streams, 560
GIBBS, JONATHAN C., 1981–82 edition, 131
Gifford, John C., 449
Gilchrist, Albert W., 28, 276, *339*, 340, 433
Gilchrist County, 433
Gilmore, General Q. A., 420–421
Girardeau, Arnette E., 153
Glades County, 433
Gleason, William H., *332*, 333
Glisson, Dorothy W., 251
Goderich, Mario P., 224
Golf, 487, *488*
Gonzalez, Lawrence A., 182
Gordon, Elaine, 161
Gorrie, John, 377, 458–459, *458*
  ARTICLE ABOUT, 1949–50 edition, 144
Government Accountability to the People, Commission on, 93
Governmental Reorganization Act of 1969, 85
Governor
  address to Legislature, 24, 108
  aides, 18
  air travel, 21–22
  appointments, 4, 17, 18–19, 85
  budget, 5
  and Cabinet, 1–3
  commander-in-chief, 26
  compensation, 31
  correspondence, 22
  election, 640–648
  Executive Office of, 32
  executive orders and proclamations, 26–27
  extradition power, 21
  former members of Legislature, 15
  impeachment, 15, 132
  incapacity, 16
  legislative program, 22–24
  legislative special sessions, 25

Little Cabinet, 17–18
 and news media, 27–28
 oath of office, 121, 274
 Office of, 13, 17
 pardons, 7
 power of removal, 20
 powers, 13, 20–21, 118
 qualifications, 14, 31
 removal from office, 15–16, 31
 responsibilities, 13
 succession to office, 16
 term, 15, 31
 veto power, 5, 25–26, 107, 110–111, 116, 136, 142–143
Governors
 acting, 358–359
 age at election, 28
 biographies
  state, 327–360
  territorial, 322–327
 former occupations, 28
 list of, 33–34
 prior public service, 28
 territorial, 33
Governor's Mansion
 children in, 364–366
 first, 361–362, 367, *368*
 Florida Governor's Mansion Foundation, Inc., 363
 Governor's Mansion Commission, 93–94, 363
 second, 316, *362*, 362–364, *368*
Graham, D. Robert
 Canadian flag, 288
 de Soto trail, 405
 governor, 18, 28, 232, *353*, 355–356, 360
 inauguration, 275–276
 marriage of daughter, 366, *367*
 quoted, 101
 reapportionment, 194–195
 and state seal, 291
 U.S. Senator, 397
Grant, Ulysses S., 231, *231*
Grant, William, 232
Gray, Robert A., 9, 265, 291
 BIOGRAPHY, 1959–60 edition, 110
Great Britain
 acquisition of Florida from Spain, 408
 expeditions to Florida, 407–408
 Florida returned to Spain, 408, 416
Green, Melva, 224

GREEN, RAY E., 1963–64 edition, 52, *52*
Green, Robert Alexis, 236
Greene, Mamie Eaton, 249–250, *249*
Greyhound racing, 488, 535
Grimes, Stephen H., 213, *213*
Grizzle, Mary R., 152
Grossman, Rhea Pinkus, 223, *223*, 225
"Grove, The," 361, 363
Gulf County, 433
Gulf of Mexico Regional Fishery Management Council, 93
Gulf States Marine Fisheries Commission, 93
Gulf Stream, 471
Gunter, William D., 194
 BIOGRAPHY 1987–88 edition, 53
Gurney, Edward J., 392

H

Haben, Ralph H. Jr., 149, *149*
Haddad, Kenneth D, Article by, 523–527
Haitian immigration, 398
Hamilton, Alexander, 433
Hamilton County, 433
Hanson, Duane, 300
Hardee, Cary A., 342, *342*, 433–434
Hardee County, 433–434
Harding, Major B., 214, *214*
Harding, Warren G., 231, 232
Hart, Ossian B., 334–335, *335*, 359
Hastings, Alcee L., 228, 230, 233
Hatchett, Joseph W., *206*, 393
Hawkins, George S., 236
Hawkins, John, 315, 371
Hawkins, Paula, 249, *251*, 397
Hawkins, Virgil, 389, 394
Health Care Cost Containment Board, 94
Health and Rehabilitative Services, Department of, 3–4, 7, 17, 32, 78–79
Hemingway, Earnest, 300, 447–448, *448*
Hendry, Capt. Francis Asbury, 434
Hendry County, 434
Herlihy, James Leo, 453
Hermitage, The, 323
Hernandez, Joseph M., 235
Hernando County, 434
Hersey, John, 453

752 / Index

Hiaasen, Carl, 453
Highest point in Florida, 553
Highlands County, 435
Highway Safety and Motor Vehicles, Department of, 7, 32, 79
Highways, 383, 386, 388, 390, 545–546
Hillsborough, Earl of, 435
Hillsborough County, 435
Hippodrome Theater, 297
Hispanic Affairs, Commission on, 94
Hispanics, 155, 250, 574
Historic Resources, Division of, 41
Hobson, T. Frank, Jr., 222–223
Hobson, T. Frank, Sr., 222–223
Holidays, official state, 307
Holland, Spessard L., 265, 344–345, *345*
  ARTICLE BY, 1947–48 edition, 77
Holmes County, 435
Holt, George E., 132
HOMER, WINSLOW, WATER-COLOR, 1975–76 edition, 29
Hoover, Herbert, 231, 232
Horne, Mallory E., *149, 197*
Horse racing, 488–489
House of Representatives *see* Florida House of Representatives; United States House of Representatives;, *see also* Legislature
Housing Finance Agency, 94
Hugh Taylor Birch State Park, *496*
Huguenots, 315, 370–371
Human Relations, Commission on, 95
Human Resource Development, Division of, 66
Human Resource Development Commission, 95
Hunt, Irene, 452
Hunting, 513–514, *513*, 516–519
Hurricanes, 478–481, 483–485
  in 1906, 382
  in 1926, 385
  in 1928, 386
  in 1935, 387, *477*, 480
  in 1949, 480
  in 1964, 479–480
  in 1985, 395
  Andrew (1992), 397–398, *399*, 480–481, *481*
  Cleo (1964), 391
  Donna (1960), 478–479
  Elena (1985), 480
  Eloise (1975), 470
  listing of major, 483–485
Hurston, Zora Neale, 300, 451, *451*, 452

I

ICE, HE FIRST MADE, 1949–50 edition, 144
IMMIGRANTS, 1979–80 edition, 305–308
Immigration, 390, 392, 394, *395*, 397, 398
Impeachment, 15, 102, 132–135, 393
Impeachments, federal, 233
Inaugurations, 274–280
  cabinet, 275
  day, 274
  "firsts," 278
  oath of office, 274
  parades, 278
  site of, 275–276
  time of, 274
Income, 597, 603
Indian River County, 436
Indians, 412–415, *414, 415*, 442
  Apalachee, 405
  conversion to Christianity, 372
  earliest settlers, 412–413
  opposition to European settlement, 372
  opposition to Spanish explorations, 400–405
  SEMINOLES: THROUGH PHOTOGRAPHS, 1985–86 edition, 370–372
  Spanish missions, 413
  see also name of specific tribe
Industrial Relations Commission, 211
Inspection, Division of, 61
Insurance, Commissioner of, 54–57, *54*
Insurance, Department of, 8, 56–57
Intergovernmental Relations, Advisory Council on, 95
Internal Improvement Trust Fund, 7
International Affairs Commission, 96

J

Jackson, Andrew, 104, *229*, 230, 322–323, *322*
  county named after, 436
  death of, 278
  Florida campaign, 374
  Florida ceded by Spain, 280, 375
  military governor, 281, 375, 427
  War of 1812, 374

Jackson County, 436
Jackson, Rachel (Mrs. Andrew), 280
Jacksonville, 381, 382
Jai-alai, 487
James, Daniel, Jr. (Chappie), 465
James, Henry, 449
Jannus, Antony, 383; 1955–56 edition, 69
Jefferson County, 436, 438
Jefferson, Thomas, 436
Jennings, May Mann (Mrs. William S.), 252, *275*
JENNINGS, MAY MANN (MRS. WILLIAM S.) 1985–86 edition, *231*
Jennings, William S., 278, *338*, 339
Jim Woodruff Lock and Dam, 555–556, *557*
Johns, Charley E.
  acting governor (1953–1955), 18, 28, 157, 265, 359
  biography, 347–348, *348*
  inauguration, *10*, 276
  inauguration of successor, *275*, 279
Johns, Charley Jerome, *10*
Johnson, Beth, 150, 251
Johnson, James Weldon, 451, *451*
Johnson, Lyndon Baines, 231, 233, 234, *248*
Joint Administrative Procedures Committee, 186
Joint Committee on Information Technology Resources, 187
Joint Legislative Management Committee, 187
Jones, General Sam, 424
Judges
  county, 220
  discipline, 208
  election, 208
  fathers and sons, 222–223
  firsts, 223–226, 228
  impeachment, 15, 132
  number of, 207
  qualifications, 207
  removal, 208
  retirement, 208
  spouses, 223–224
  youngest, 222
  see also Supreme Court of Florida, justices
Judicial branch, 5, 200–226
Judicial Nominating Commission, 203, 208

Judicial power, 200–202
  advisory opinions, 201
  declaratory judgments, 201
  defined, 200
  quasi-judicial power, 201
Judicial Qualifications Commission, 204, 205, 220–221
JUDICIARY IN A FEDERAL REPUBLIC, 1951–52 edition, 164
Justice Administrative Commission, 221
Juvenile Justice, Department of, 3, 7, 17, 32, 80

K

Kaolin mining, 509
Karl, Frederick B., 15
Kaufelt, David A., 453
Kelly, William W. J., 37
Kennedy, John Fitzgerald, 230, *248*, 391
Kennedy Space Center, 394, *396*
  see also Cape Canaveral; Cape Kennedy
Kershaw, Joe Lang, 152, 153
Keys, 559
King, Martin Luther, Jr., 391
Kirk, Claude R., Jr.
  christening of daughter, 365, *365*
  governor, 15,, 18, 28, *351,* 352, 391, 397
  inauguration, 276, 279
  marriage of daughter, 366
  marriage of, 366
  reapportionment, 195
Kirkland, Thomas E., 223
Kirkland, Thomas R., 223
Kleinberg, Howard, 452
Knott Building, 264
Knott, W. V., 264
Kogan, Gerald, 213, *213*
Konigsburg, Elaine, 452
Korean War, 318
Korvick, Maria Marinello, 225
Kynes, James W., 9

L

Labor and Employment Security, Department of, 7, 17, 32, 80–81
Lafayette County, 436–437

754 / Index

LaFayette Grant, 258–259, 376, 436–437
  MAP, 1965–66 edition, 214
LaFayette, Marquis de, 258–259, *376,* 429, 436–437, *436*
Lake County, 437
Lake Okeechobee, 386, 466, *470,* 472
Land Acquisition Selection Committee, 187
Land boom, *384,* 385
Land use statistics, 562
Land and Water Adjudicatory Commission, 96
Larson, J. Edwin, 265
  BIOGRAPHY, 1963–64 edition, 54, *54*
Lash, Joseph, 453
Latham, Jean Lee, 452
Laudonniere, Réne de Goulaine de, 315, 371
Law Enforcement, Department of, 7, 32, 81–82
Law making, 107–108, 110, *139,* 140–143
Laws
  effective date, 111
  general, 103
  general laws of local application, 104
  number passed, 116
  oldest, 104–105
  population, 104
  recording by Secretary of State, 103
  Resign to run, 137–138
  special, 103–104
  sunset, 123
Lee County, 437
Lee, J. M., 265
Lee, Robert E., 434, 437
  LAST VISIT IN FLORIDA, 1969–70 edition, 345
Legal Affairs, Department of, 8, 47–48
  see also Attorney General
Legal holidays, 306–307
Legislative agencies
  Advisory Council on Intergovernment Relations, 183
  Auditor General, 186
  Commission on Ethics, 184
  Joint Administrative Procedures Committee, 163, 186
  Joint Committee on Information Technology Resources, 187
  Joint Legislative Management Committee, 187
  Land Acquisition Selection Committee, 187
  Public Counsel, 185
  Public Service Commission, 184–185
  Public Service Commission Nominating Council, 185
Legislators
  BIOGRAPHIES
    1955–56 edition, 360–383
    1957–58 edition, 364–387
    1959–60 edition, 370–408
    1961–62 edition, 158–183
    1963–64 edition, 147–176
    1965–66 edition, 388–422
    1967–68 edition, 465–518
    1969–70 edition, 134–151
  black, 152–154
  compensation, 146–147
  discipline, 155–156
  election, 118
  ethics, 150
  Hispanic 155
  motivation, 144–145, 158
  oath of office, 121
  occupations, 145–146
  political parties, 147–148, 150–153, 157–158
  qualifying fee 149
  Republicans, 151–152, 157, 388
  seniority, 120
  single-member districts, 148, 157
  statistics, 146–148
  term, 118, 120, 146, 173
  women, 150
Legislature *See Also Florida House of Representatives and Florida Senate*
  1955 reapportionment, 190–191
  apportionment, 118, 119, 198–199
  apportionment session, 25, 101, 105
  Black Caucus, 154
  blacks in, 152–154
  budget, 175–176
  claims bills, 112
  closed sessions, 131
  committees, 101, 109, 122–126, 140–141
  conference committees, 126–127
  Cuban-American Caucus, 155
  debate, 127–129
  extended session, 105, 107
  filibuster, 129
  first black woman, 251
  first women, 251
  general session, 105

governor's address to, 24
governors as former members, 15
Hispanics in, 155
impeachment, 132
independence of, 135–137
investigating committee, 118
journals, 121–122, 140–141
law making, 103, 107
   general laws, 103
   general laws of local application, 104
   population laws, 103
   special laws, 103
leadership, 146, 159–168
lobbying, 129–130
longest session, 107
memorials, 111
organizational session, 101, 105, 391–392
pairing, 114
pork chop gang, 190
proxies, 114
publications, 173–175
quasi-judicial functions, 102, 113
reapportionment
   of 1955, 190–191
   of 1963, 191–195
   of 1967, 392
   of 1972, 195–196
   of 1982, 196–197
   of 1992, 198–199
Reconstruction, 154
resolutions, 111
rules of procedure, 109
self-starter session, 101, 105
shortest session, 107
single-member districts, 119, 148, 157, 395
Special Order Calendar, 141
special session, 25, 101, 105, 106, 107
Sunshine amendment, 182–183
suspension session, 106
veto override, 110, 143
voting records, 113
voting requirements, 115
women in 150, 152
Legislature, territorial, 188–189
Lenski, Lois, 452, *454*
Leon County, 437
Leonardy, Herberta, 228
Levy County, 437–438
Levy, David *see* Yulee, David Levy
Lewis, Gerald, 9
   BIOGRAPHY, 1993–94 edition, 57

Liberty Bell Replica, 273
Liberty County, 438
Library and Information Services, Division of, 40
Licenses, 617
Licensing, Division of, 42
Lieutenant Governor, 6, 15, 36–37, 132, 392
Limestone mining, 507
Literature, 446–454
"Little Cabinet," 17, 18, 252
Lobbying, 129–130
Logging, 490–493
Lopez de Mendoza, Father Francisco, 315
Lost counties, 429
LOST COUNTY, THE, 1947–48 edition, 92
Lottery, 397, 537, 541
Lottery Commission, 96
Lottery, Department of, 7, 17, 32, 82
Lowe, James, 103

M

McCain, David L., 134, 393
McCarty, Daniel T., 18, 28, 265, 276–277, *277*, 347, *348*, 359, 388
McCaskill, Myrtice, 249, *249*
McCook, Brigadier General E. M., 267, 426
McCrary, Jesse J., Jr., 394
McDermott, John, 132,
   BIOGRAPHY 1981–82 edition, 132, *132*
MacDonald, John D., 300, 447
McDonald, Parker Lee, *206*, 216
McDonnell, Ellen Knight, *249*, 252
MacGregor, Gregor, 289, 374
McGuane, Thomas, 453
Mack, Connie, 398
MacKay, Kenneth H. (Buddy), 36–37, 279
McKinley, William, 230
McLin, B. E., 265
Madison County, 438
Madison, James, 438
Mallory, Stephen R., 235, 236
Management Services, Department of, 17, 32, 82–83
Manatee County, 438–439
Manatees, 301, 438–439
Mansfield, William C., 132

756 / Index

Margolis, Gwen, 150, 161, 397
Mariel boatlift, 394, *395*
Marine Fisheries Commission, 96–97, 526
Marine resources, 523–527
  estuaries, 524
  fishing, 525–526
  management of, 526–527
  reefs, 523–524
  shrimp, *524*
Marion County, 439
Marion, General Francis, 439
Marketing, Division of, 61
Martin Building, 264
Martin County, 439
Martin, John W., 264, 342–343, *342*
Martinez, Robert
  biography, 357–358, *357*
  governor 1987–91, quoted, 18
  governor, 30, 397
  inauguration, 276, 279
Marvin, William, 282, 331, *331*
Mathews, John E., *10,* 129
Mattfeld, Erika (Mrs. Claude R. Kirk, Jr.), 279
Mayerson, Evelyn Wilde, 454
Mayo Building, 264
Mayo, Nathan, 8–9, *62,* 264
  BIOGRAPHY 1959–60 edition, 120, *120*
Means, Dr. Ernest E., 104
Medal of Honor, awarded to Floridians, 319
Medical Examiners Commission, 47, 81, 97
Meek, Carrie P., 153, 154, *254, 255, 255,* 395, 398
Meier, George, article by, 198–199
Menéndez de Aviles, Pedro, 315, 371
Mental Health Institute, 97
MERIDIAN MARKER, 1989–90 edition, 303
Mexican War 1846–1848, 318
Miami International Book Fair, 454
Miccosukee tribe, 290, *290,* 414, 442
Military Affairs, Department of, 83–84
Military fortifications, 406–411
Military service members and retirees, 319
Miller, General William, 424
Milligan, Robert F. (Bob), *1,* 50–51, *50*
Milton, John, 282, 286, 329, *330,* 359, 425
Minerals and mining, 506–512
  cement and lime, 510
  chart of production, 511
  clays, 509
  dolomite, 508
  heavy minerals, 508–509
  limestone, 507
  magnesium, 510
  peat, 510
  petroleum, 511–512
  phosphate, 506–507, *508*
  sand and gravel, 509–510
  sulfur, 511
MINTER, JAMES H., JR., article by, 1989–90 edition, 405
Missiles, 384, 388
Mission, San Luis de Talmali, *317*
Mitchell, Henry L., 338–339, *338*
Mitchell, Susan, 454
Mixson, John Wayne, 18, 28, 356, *356,* 360, *360*
Moffitt, H. Lee, 149
MONEY, FLORIDA, 1987–88 edition, 276
Monroe County, 439
Monroe, James, 439
Monuments, 272, 273, 318
Morgan, Herbert, 268
MORMINO, GARY R., article by 1989–90 edition, 409
Morris, Allen, 300, 308
Mortham, Sandra B., *1,* 38–39, *38,* 162
Moseley, William D., 275, 277–278, 281, 292, 327–328, *327,* 366, 376
Mosquito County, 429, *444*
Motion pictures, *381,* 382, 608
Motor vehicle licenses, 617–618
Mourning, flags, 287
MUELLER, EDWARD A., article by, 1983–84 edition, 303–307
Muir, Helen, article by 446–454, *449*
Muir, John, 449
Municipalities, 227
Munroe, Kirk, 450
Murat, Prince Achille, 258
Music and songs, 309–312

N

NAMES, ORIGIN OF, 1973–74 edition, 377
NAMING THE LAND, 1987–88 edition, 396
Narváez, Pánfilo de, 370, 401–402
Nassau County, 439

National Aeronautics and Space Administration (NASA), 390
National Conference of Commissioners on Uniform State Laws, 97
National Crime Information Center, 82
National forests, 493
National political conventions, 626–627
Native Americans *see* Indians; *see also names of specific tribes*
Neamathla, 256–257, *256*
Nelson, C. William (Bill), *1*, 54–55, *54*
Ness, Evaline, 453
New River County, 429
Newman, Rex, 132
Newton, General John, 423–425
Nixon, Richard Milhous, 230, 393, 560
NOAH'S ARK, 1949–50 edition, 202
Northwest Florida Regional Housing Authority, 94
Norton, Ralph H., 300
Nuestra Senora de Atocha, 370

O

Offender Rehabilitation, Department of, 7; *see also* Corrections, Department of
Office of Executive Clemency, 14
Okaloosa County, 439
Okeechobee County, 439
Oglethorpe, James, 373
O'Malley, Thomas D., 134, 393
  BIOGRAPHY 1975–76 edition, 148, *148*
O'Neale, Peggy (Mrs. John H. Eaton), 324, 327
Orange County, 440
Ordinance of Secession, 263, 417
Orlando International Airport, *396*
Ortiz, Juan, 402–403
Osborne, Ray C., 392
  BIOGRAPHY 1969–70 edition, 30, *30*
Osceola, 413, 440, 457–458, *457*
Osceola County, 440
Overton, Ben F., *206*, 212, *212*, 216
Owen, Ruth Bryan, 249–250, *250*

P

Palm Beach County, 440
Panama City Beach, *564*

Panther, 302, 518–519
Pardons, 7
Parkhill, John, 272
Parks, 496–500
  see also specific state and national parks
Parole Commission, 97–98, 387
Pasco County, 440
Pasco, Samuel, 440
Pascua Florida Week, 305
Pearce, Donn, 453
PENNEKAMP CORAL REEF STATE PARK, 1993–94 edition, 456–457
Pennekamp, John D., 388
Pensacola
  aviation, 383
  British West Florida, 374
  captured by French, 373
  Civil War, 417, *419,* 420
  first colony, 370
  Florida seceded by Spain, 375
  permanent colony established, 372
  War of 1812, 374
Pepper, Claude D., 237, 265, 397
  ARTICLE BY, 1947–48 edition, 85
Perry, Edward A., 337, *337*
Perry, Madison S., 286, 328–329, *329*
Pettigrew, Richard, *193*, 194, *209*
PETTIGREW, RICHARD A.
  1985–85 edition, 136, *136*
  article by, 1971–72 edition, 167
Phantom government, 163–164
Phelps, John, 170, *170*
Phosphate, minerals and mining, 506–507, *508*
PHOTOGRAPHIC BOOKS, 1979–80 edition, 358
Physical Fitness and Amateur Sports, Council on, 98
Pinellas County, 440
PLACE NAMES, ORIGIN OF, 1973–74 edition, 377
Plant, Henry B., 380, 459–460, *459*
Plant Industry, Division of, 62
Plummer, John, 153
Poet Laureate, 298–299
Poetry Day, 305
POLITICAL GIMMICKS, 1989–90 edition, 619
Political parties, 635
  CAMPAIGNS, 1979–80 edition, 466–470
Political profile of Floridians, 565–571
Polk County, 440–441
Polk, James K., 440–441

758 / Index

Ponce de León, Juan
  expediations to Florida, 283, 305, 370, 400–401, *401, 437*
  county named after, 437
  Dry Tortugas, 409
  prayer of, 315
POPE, EDITH, excerpt, 1957–58 edition, 90
Pope, Verle A, 194, *196*
Population
  age, 575, 577
  death rate, 596, 600
  distribution, 573, *580,* 581, 582–595
  divorce rate, 596
  marriage rate, 596
  metropolitan areas, 579, 582–595
  net growth, 573, 578
  prison inmates, 599
  race and sex, 574, 577
  statistics, 572–611
POPULATION OF PLACES: 1960 AND 1970, 1979–80 edition, 510–518
Pork chop gang, 136, 163, 190, 194
Postage stamps, *312–314, 435, 437*
Poston, Ralph, 156
P.O.W.-M.I.A. flag, 288
Power, electricity, 555, 611–613
Presidential election, 624–625, 636–640
Presidents of the United States, 6, *29,* 230–233, *230–232,* 281
Pride, Don, 131
Prison Rehabilitative Industries and Diversified Enterprises (PRIDE), 98
Public Counsel, 185
Public Defender, 15, 209
Public education
  Blueprint 2000, 541
  Buckman Act, 538
  College Level Academic Skills Test, 539
  early efforts, 536–537
  first state system, 537
  Florida Education Finance Program, 542–543
  funding, 537–538, 540, 541–543
  magnet schools, 540
  Minimum Foundation Program, 538
  Prekindergarten early intervention program, 540
  statistics, 544
  teacher certification, 539–540
Public Schools, Division of, 66

Public Service Commission, 184–185, 250, 672
Pulpwood, 490–492
Putnam, Benjamin Alexander, 441
Putnam County, 441

R

Racing
  automobile, 487
  greyhound, 488, 535
  horse, 488–489
Rader, Vivian Laramore, 298
Radio, first station, 384
Railroad Commission, 250, 380–381
Railroads
  excursion trains, *378*
  history, 376, 377, 615–616
  mileage, 616
  Overseas Extension, *380,* 381, 382
Range, M. Athalie, 252
Rauschenberg, Robert, 300
Rawlings, Marjorie Kinnan, 300, 447, *447*
Real Estate Commission, Board of, 98
Reapportionment, 188–199
  Congressional, 1992, 198
  legislative
    1955, 190–191
    1962, 191–195
    1972, 195–196
    1982, 196–197
    1992, 198–199
Red tide, 525
Reed, Harrison, 133, 156, 332–333, *332,* 366, 379
Regional names, 563–564
Reid, Robert R., 326, *326*
Religion in Florida
  Anglican, 315, 316
  Baptists, 316
  blacks, 315–316
  Episcopal, 316
  Greek Orthodox, 316
  Huguenots, 315
  Judaism, 316
  Methodists, 316
  missions, 315, *317*
  Native Americans, 315
  Presbyterians, 316
  Protestant, 315
  Roman Catholic, 315
Reno, Janet, 226, 234, 398

Index / 759

Republican Party, 388, 391–392, 635
Resign to run law, 137–138
Resolutions, Legislative, 111–112
Retirement Commission, State, 98
Revenue, Department of, 3, 32, 84
Revenue Estimating Conference, 175
Revolutionary War, 321, 374–375
Reynolds, Burt, 300
Rhodes, Evan, 453
Ribaut, Jean, 370–371
   DISCOVERY OF FLORIDA, excerpt 1953–54 edition, 135
Richardson, Joe Martin, 154
Riddle, E. Bert, 156
Ringling, John N., 300
Ringling Museum of Art, 300, 364
Ritter, Halsted L., 233
RIVER IN THE WIND, excerpt, 1955–56 edition, 42
Roberts, B. K., *209,* article by 200–226
Rogers, William Warren, 304
ROMANS, BERNARD, 1987–88 edition, 396
Roosevelt, Franklin Delano, *230,* 231–232, *385,* 386–387
Roosevelt, James, *248*
Roosevelt, Theodore, 231, *231,* 232, *379*
Ros-Lehtinen, Ileana, 155, 250–251, *251,* 255, *255,* 397
Rothchild, John, 453
Rowell, F.C., *197*
Ryals, John, 161

S

St. Augustine
  American Revolution, 374
  British siege, 372–373
  founding of, 315, 371
  map of, *410*
St. Johns County, 441
St. Johns, River of Many Names, 1975–76 eidtion, 26
St. Lucie County, 441
St. Lucie of Syracuse, 441
St. Marks, Civil War, 422–424
St. Petersburg-Tampa Airboat Line, 1955–56 edition, 69
St. Rosa de Viterbo, 441
Saltwater fishing *see* Marine resources
San Marcos de Apalache, 283, 372, 373 *see also* St. Marks
Sand and gravel mining, 509–510

Santa Rosa County, 441
Sarasota County, 442
Satellites, 390
Scott, Cyril, 309
Scott, James A., 149, 168, *168*
Seat of Government, 256–273
SECRETS FROM SEAS, 1953–54 edition, 125–134
Securities, Division of, 53
Seminole County, 442
Seminole tribe, 290, *290,* 413–414, *414,* 442
Seminole War, 376
SEMINOLE WAR, BOOKS ABOUT, 1979–80 edition, 361
SEMINOLES: THROUGH PHOTOGRAPHS, 1985–86 edition, 370–372
Senate *see* Florida Senate; United States Senate;, *see also* Legislature
Sentencing Commission, 99
Separation of powers, 102
Seymour, General Truman A., 420–422
Shaara, Michael, 452
Shaw, Leander J., Jr., *206,* 213, *213*
Sheats, William N., 9
Shepard, Alan, 390
Shepard, Herschel E., 269
Shevin, Robert L., 6
  BIOGRAPHY, 1977–78 edition, 82, *82*
Sholtz, David, *230, 278, 343,* 344
Simmons, Dr. W. H., 256
Simms, Leah Aleice, 224–225
Simpson, Charles Torrey, 449
Sinkhole, 395
Skellings, Edmund, 298–299
Skene, Neil, article by, 188–199
Skyjacking, 390–391
Slaughter, Frank G., 452, *452*
Smathers, Bruce, 269
  BIOGRAPHY 1977–78 edition, 79, *79*
Smiley, Nixon, 452, 471
Smith, Edmund Kirby, 377, 419, 462–463, *462*
Smith, Guy H., *117*
Smith, Harry G., *181*
SMITH, JAMES C. (Jim), 1993–94 edition, 46–47, *46*
SMITH, MARY ELLEN, article by, 1987–88 edition, 447
Smith, Samuel S., 134–135

SNODGRASS, DENA, article by, 1975–76 edition, 26
Snow, 393, 476–478
Soil types, 472–473
South Atlantic Regional Fishery Management Council, 93
Southeastern Interstate Forest Fire Protection Compact, Advisory Committee, 94
Space Age, 391
see also specific topics
Space shuttle
  Challenger, 397
  Columbia, 54, 394, *396*
  Discovery, viii, 397
Spaceport, 390
Spaceport Florida Authority, 99
Spain
  American Revolution, 416
  early settlements in Florida, 406–408, *407–408,* 411–412
  expeditions to Florida, 400–405
  missions, *317,* 413
  treasure fleets, 370
Spanish-American War, 319, *379,* 381, 410
Special districts, 227
Spiro, Robert H. Jr., 234
Sports, 487–489
Springs, 553–555
Standards, Division of, 61
State, flags, 283–291
State Attorney, 15, 209
State Courts Administrator, 209, 221
State, Department of, 8, 40–44
  see also State, Secretary of
State Fire Marshall, 55, 57
State Folk Culture Center, 295
State forests, 493
State motto, 285, 294
State office holidays, 307
State officials, oath of office, 274
State parks, listing of, 498–500
State Road Department, 85
State seal, 291–294
State, Secretary of, 38–39, *38*
  compensation, 39
  custodian of state seal, 291
  duties, 40, 103, 112
  elections, 664–665
  list of, 39
  memorials, 112
  qualifications, 39
  recording laws, 103

removal, 39
selection, 39
sunshine amendment, 182
term, 39
see also State, Department of
State symbols
  air fair, 305
  animal, 302
  beverage, 304
  bird, 298
  dance, 309
  fish, 301
  flower, 302
  gem, 302
  insect, 301
  limerick, 296
  litter control symbol, 302
  mammals, 301–302
  motto, 285, 294
  nickname, 294
  pageant, 305
  pie, 304
  play, 297
  reptile, 301
  shell, 303
  soil, 304
  song, 295–296
  stone, 302
  theaters, 297
  tree, 272, 303–304
  welcome song, 296
  wildflower, 305
State Theater Program, 297
STATEHOOD, THE LONG BATTLE
  • FOR, 1953–54 edition, 87–95
Statewide Human Rights Advocacy Committee, 95
Statewide Prosecutor, Office of, 48
Statue of Liberty miniature, 272
STEAMBOAT ERA, 1987–84 edition, 303–307
Stearns, Marcellus L., 276, 335, *335,* 359
Stevens, Wallace, 447
Stevenson, Adlai, 248
STONE, RICHARD, 1973–74 edition, 120, *120*
Stone, Edward Durell, 268
Stowe, Harriet Beecher, 449
Stranahan, Mrs. Frank, 252
Sufferage, women's, 252; *see also* Women's rights
Sulfur mining, 511
Sumter County, 442
Sumter, General Thomas, 442

Index / 761

Sunset law, 122–123
Sunshine amendment, 182–183
Sunshine Skyway, 388, 394, *395*, 546, *546*
Superintendent of Public Instruction, 64, 669
  see also Education, Commissioner of
Supervisors of Elections, 183
Supreme Court of Florida
  1992 legislative reapportionment, 198–199
  advisory opinions, 201
  buildings, 264
  extraordinary writs, 209–210
  history of, 215–218
  impeachment, 15
  independence of Legislature, 135–137
  interpretation of governor's powers, 21
  jurisdiction, 204
  justices, 212–218
    authorship, 223
    first black, 206
    first woman, 223, 396
    impeachment, 132
    list of, 217–218
    resignation, 134
    retention, 216
    vacancies, 208, 216
  protocol, 11
  quorum, 204
  retention, 671–672
  separation of powers, 102
  sunshine amendment, 182
Supreme Court of the United States, 228
  1992 legislative reapportionment, 199
  legislative apportionment, 191
  Miami Herald, 388
SURVEYING, EARLY, 1989–90 edition, 300–303
Suwanee County, 442
SUWANEE RIVER, 1983–84 edition, 299–300
Swayne, Charles, 233
Symington, Stuart, *248*

T

Taft, William Howard, 231, *231*, 232
Tallahassee
  before the Civil War, 262
  capital, 375
  centennial, 272
  desegregation, *389*
  during the Civil War, 263, 267
  founding of, 256–259
  fire 262
  occupation by federal troops, 263
  origin of name, 257–258
  Reconstruction, 154, 263
  sesquicentennial, 272
  snow, 476
Tallahassee Meridian, 552
Taxes
  ad valorem, 387, 620
  alcohol, 388
  corporate income, 392
  funding public education, 541–543
  gasoline, 386, 388
  gross receipts utilities, 540
  percent of personal income, 621
  sales, 388
  tobacco, 387, 388
Taylor County, 443
Taylor, Zachery, 230–231, 376, 443
Telephones, 614–615
Television, 388, 390
Terrell, Glenn, 133, 282
  ARTICLE BY, 1951–52 edition, 164
Territorial representatives, 235
Territorial seal, 291–292
Thomas, Jerry, 19, *209*, 234
Thomas, John, 154
Thomas, Lawson E., 224
Thomas, Pat, 160, 268
Thompson, Ina S., *249*, 251–252
Thoroughbred Racing Advisory Commission, 4
Thurman, Karen, 255, *255*
THURSTON, GEORGE L., III, article by, 1983–84 edition, 295–297
Timber, 490–492
Tippetts, Katherine B., *117*, 249
Topography, 472
Torcoletti, Enzo, 300
Tourism, 601–602, 605, *606*
TOURISM, HISTORY OF, 1989–90 edition, 409–415
Trammell, Park, 28, 340–341, *341*, 382
Transportation, Department of, 7, 17, 32, 85–86
  Florida Transportation Plan, 85
Transportation Disadvantaged Commission, 99

762 / Index

Transportation, Secretary of, 85
Treasurer, 2, 8, 54–57, *54*, 667–669
Treasury, Department of, 56
Treaty of Paris, 373
Trees
 champion, 493–494
 LIST OF, 1973–74 edition, 464–467
Trial courts, *see also* Circuit Courts; County Courts
Truman, Harry S, *230*, 231
Tucker, Donald L., 161, 269
Turkeys, 513, 516–517
Turlington, Ralph D., 194, *196*, 265
 BIOGRAPHY, 1985–86 edition, 64, 138
Tuttle, Julia De Forest, 463–464, *463*
Tyler, John, 281, 376

U

Uelsmann, Jerry, 300
Unemployment Appeals Commission, 99
Uniform State Laws, National Conference of Commissioners on, 97
Union County, 443
United States Congress
 Florida delegates withdraw, 236
 Florida women in, 255, *255*
 list of Florida delegates, 237–248
 territorial representatives, 235
 see also United States House of Representatives; United States Senate
United States House of Representatives
 elections, 653–664
 first Floridian woman, 250
 Florida delegates 237–248
 Republicans from Florida, 388
United States Senate, 135, 237–248, 648–653
Universities, Division of, 68
University of Florida, 381, 388, 391, 538
University of Florida Law School, 389
University of South Florida, 390
University of West Florida, 391
University Press of Florida, 69
U.S.S. Florida, 319–320

V

Verrazano, Giovanni de, 369–370
Veteran and Community Affairs, Department of, 7, *see also* Community Affairs, Department of *and* Veterans' Affairs, Department of
Veterans' Affairs, Department of, 7, 10, 32, 87–88
Veto, 5, 25–26, 107, 110–111, 142–143
 line item, 111, 136, 179
Vietnam Memorial, 318, *318*
Volusia County, 443
VOTE, WHAT MAKES FLORIDIANS, 1989–90 edition, 614
Voters
 first blacks, 626
 first woman, 626
 registration, 628, 630–631, 672–673
 turnout, 629
 under age 21, 625

W

Wakulla County, 443–444
Wakulla Springs, *497*
"WAKULLY, GREAT FOUNTAIN OF," 1957–58 edition, 25
Waldron, Ann, 308
Walker, David S., 282, 331–332, *331*
"Walking catfish," 522
Wallace, Peter Rudy, 170, *170*
Walls, Josiah T., 236–237
Walt Disney World, *394*, 395
Walton County, 444
Walton, Col. George, 322, 358, 444, *445*
Ward, Charlie, 398
Ward, David Elmer, 222
Warren, Fuller, 6, 133, 144–145, 155, *155*, 278–279, 346–347, *346*, 366, *366*
 BIOGRAPHY, 1949–50 edition, 6
Washington County, 444
Washington, George, 444, *445*
WATER: THE LIFEBLOOD OF FLORIDA, 1989–90 edition, 463
Water and Sewer District of Immokalee, 4
Weather, 472–486
Weissenborn, Lee, 273
Wells, Charles T., 214, *214*
Wells, William Charles, 374

WEST, PATSY, article by, 1985–86 edition, 370–372
West Florida Seminary, 378, 424
Westcott, James D., Jr., 235, 281
White, E. B., 446
White, John Wesley, article by, 227
Whitehair, Francis P., 233
Whitfield, James B., 264
Wilbur, Richard, 453
Wilder, Thorton, 453
Wildlife, 513–514
  LOSS OF, 1987–88 edition, 498–507
Williams, Broward, 9
  BIOGRAPHY, 1969–70 edition, 43, *43*
Williams, Frank, 158
Williams, Hiram D., 300
Williams, J. H., 234
Williams, John Lee, 256
Williams, Joy, 453
Williams, Thomas Lanier (Tennessee), 300, 448
Wilson, Lori, 152
Women
  firsts in government, 249–251
  woman
    admitted to practice before Supreme Court of the Unites States, 228
    appellate judge, 225
    black
      Florida Senator, 395
      judge, 224
      Legislator, 153, 251
    Cabinet, 251
    circuit judge, 224
    county judge, 225
    Cuban exile, U.S. House of Representatives, 250
    federal judge, 228
    Florida House of Representatives, 152, 251
    Florida Senate, 251
    Florida Senate president, 397
    Hispanic, 250–251, *251*, 255, *255*, 397

circuit judge, 225
claims jurist, 224
U.S. House of Representatives, 250–251
justice, 223, 396
police chief, 626
Public Service Commissioner, 250
Railroad Commissioner, 250
sheriff, 626
state attorney, 226
U.S. House of Representative, 250
voter, 626
in government, 249–255
oldest elected official, 625
Women's Hall Of Fame, 253–254
Women's rights, 252–253, 394, 625–626
Wood, Franklin N., 298, 300
World War I, 318, *382*, 384, 410
World War II
  British airmen buried in Florida, 320–321
  capture of saboteurs, 387
  combat training in Florida, *386*, 387
  Floridians in 318
  Fort Pickens, 410
  Gulf Stream, 471, *471*
  internment of aliens, 387
WRECKING, 1981–82 edition, 320–325
Wylie, Philip, 450

Y

Yellow fever, 374, 380
Yulee, David Levy, 235, 236, 281, 376–377, 437–438

Z

Zangara, Guiseppe, 387
Zwilich, Ellen Taaffe, 300

About Florida

Because so many Floridians are relatively recent arrivals from other states, they are inquisitive about their new home. *The Miami Herald* seeks to answer their questions through its Action Line. Ann S. Baumgartner, Editor of Action Line, says some 200 letters are received each week. Some of Action Line's most frequently asked questions and answers are among those given here. The *Herald's* answers are footnoted by the initials "AL".

Florida has been described as an old state of new people. How many Floridians are natives?

In 1990, only 3.9 million of the 12.9 million people in Florida (30 percent) were born in Florida.

I just moved to Florida and discovered that restaurants and supermarkets are selling dolphin. Please tell me that these aren't the loving and affectionate creatures I saw at Sea World.

They aren't. The dolphin that's sold for eating is a fish that goes by the Latin name of *Coryphaena hippurus*. The dolphins you saw at Sea World are mammals that are members of the family *Delphinidae*. Somewhere along the line, the mammal and the fish ended up with the same common name and it's been confusing and upsetting people ever since. AL

I was admiring the blossoms on my bush when this little lizard came running up the branch, stopped, looked at me and bulged out its neck until it turned into a bright red balloon. I have the feeling that lizard was trying to tell me something. What was it?

It was either "I love you" or "Get lost." The hanging fold of skin under a lizard's jaws is commonly referred to as the throat fan. Lizards use it to communicate. If a male lizard wants to score a few points with a female lizard, he puffs himself up to impress her with his good looks. But lizards are also territorial critters. If a lizard wants to let another lizard know it's trespassing, the throat fan does the talking. Both male and female lizards have throat fans. AL

Here in Miami we wonder why Tallahassee, "way up there," is Florida's capital?

When Florida was acquired by the United States from Spain in 1821, the provincial capitals were Pensacola, for West Florida, and St. Augustine, for East Florida. The peninsula was wilderness. The site of Tallahassee, approximately midway between Pensacola and St. Augustine, was chosen as the consolidated seat of government.

People are always saying Florida is a newly-settled state and doesn't have much history. When did people first come here?

About 8,000 to 10,000 years ago. That's when the Indians first got here. By 2000 B.C., large groups had settled all over Florida. Some groups founded small empires and others developed elaborate religions. By the time the first Europeans go around to showing up, the Apalachee and Timucua were living in permanent walled towns that enclosed large houses. The first European to see Florida and go home to brag about it was Juan Ponce de Leon in 1513. The Spaniards colonized the Pensacola Bay area in 1559. AL

Leaping lizards! They're everywhere! Anywhere you walk there's another lizard running for cover. Are there more lizards in Florida than in any other state? Are we indeed The Lizard State?

Nobody's ever conducted a lizard census (for obvious reasons) but herpetologists agree that Florida has the largest population of reptiles and amphibians. "Florida is considered to be the herp state," says Bill Zeigler, general curator of Metrozoo. In case you're wondering, herp's short for herpetological. Our subtropical climate and our geography (the Everglades is a herp haven) lends itself to a thriving lizard population. Florida is also a popular port of entry for new varieties of lizards. Many non-native types have come into the area from such spots as Cuba and The Bahamas. AL

What is that big "hole" in maps in peninsular Florida?

That's Lake Okeechobee, 700 square miles in size but shallow in depth. Lake Okeechobee is the second largest freshwater lake entirely within one state: Alaska has the overall largest, of 1,033 square miles. Lake Okeechobee is the fourth largest natural lake entirely within the United States. Lake Michigan, which touches Wisconsin, Illinois, Indiana and Michigan, is the largest, with